D0161577

Vaudeville
Old & New

Vaudeville Old & New

An Encyclopedia of Variety Performers in America

Volume 1

Frank Cullen
with
Florence Hackman
Donald McNeilly

Routledge
Taylor & Francis Group
New York London

Routledge is an imprint of the
Taylor & Francis Group, an informa business

Published in 2007 by
Routledge
Taylor & Francis Group
270 Madison Avenue
New York, NY 10016

Published in Great Britain by
Routledge
Taylor & Francis Group
2 Park Square
Milton Park, Abingdon
Oxon OX14 4RN

Printed in the United States of America on acid-free paper
10 9 8 7 6 5 4 3 2 1

International Standard Book Number-10: 0-415-93853-8 (Hardcover)
International Standard Book Number-13: 978-0-415-93853-2 (Hardcover)
Library of Congress Card Number 2005030588

Library of Congress Cataloging-in-Publication Data

Cullen, Frank, 1936-
Vaudeville, old and new : an encyclopedia of variety performers in America / Frank Cullen with Florence Hackman and Donald McNeilly.
p. cm.
Includes bibliographical references and index.
ISBN 0-415-93853-8 (hb)
1. Vaudeville--United States--Encyclopedias. 2. Entertainers--United States--Biography--Dictionaries. I. Hackman, Florence. II. McNeilly, Donald. III. Title.

PN1968.U5C85 2006
792.7097303--dc22

2005030588

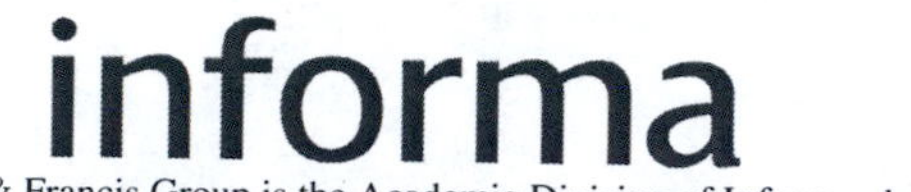

Taylor & Francis Group is the Academic Division of Informa plc.

Visit the Taylor & Francis Web site at
http://www.taylorandfrancis.com

and the Routledge Web site at
http://www.routledge-ny.com

Contents

Dedication

This volume is dedicated to the tens of thousands of performers who were proud to be vaudevillians, especially those who have been forgotten and do not appear within these pages.

The author and editors can make no claim for completeness. There were more than 50,000 performers, and many more thousands offstage, who spent all or some portion of their careers in variety and vaudeville. The great majority have faded from history. It would fill many volumes of great size if we knew all the performers, theatre managers, pit musicians, front and back of the house employees, bookers, agents, song and sketch writers, scenery and prop makers, song pluggers and reviewers who gave life to vaudeville from beginning to end. The true history of vaudeville resides in the sum of all their stories.

Time has destroyed or scattered much of the evidence, especially for those acts that did not cap their careers with sound and sight recordings in electronic media. The primary and secondary sources available, often the product of diligent and earnest inquiry, are sometimes compromised by faulty recollection, blind spots and bias. Much of any history is what is recalled of events and personalities after repetition has ordered them into the stuff of a good story. Invaluable as they are for providing firsthand reports and for revealing feelings, memoirs vary in usefulness. Most can be relied upon to settle old scores and present the case for the defense but little else.

Entertainment reviews and feature articles about people in show business were less ubiquitous in the time of variety and vaudeville, an age before entertainers were considered likely subjects to retain or increase circulation. Some critics such as Robert Benchley and Ashton Stevens respected and enjoyed vaudeville; others disdained it. Many chroniclers were untrained in the performing arts and as susceptible to flattery and slights as their present-day successors. The trade papers were usually factual, cold-eyed and fair when they reviewed an entire bill but teasingly terse about individual acts, especially those on the undercard.

A researcher, consulting primary and secondary sources, often feels like a fourth-century Christian monk tasked to sort apocrypha from that deemed divinely inspired. Faced with conflicting evidence or reports, an arbiter must weight the overall reliability of the sources and exercise informed historical possibilities to decide which version was more likely.

Many talented and skilled performers were dogged by bad luck and unblessed by providential timing. The record of their careers has been reduced to a few yellowed programmes, the paper as fragile as the reputations of those whose names they hold in faded print. So, the performers whose stories appear in this volume were those with acts successful enough to win a place in the contemporary record. Some were vaudevillians who earned success in many other forms of show business and remain too famous to ignore. Others were highly regarded in their time, but their reputations have dissolved in the mist of a receding past, and they merit reconsideration. Some have symbolic importance apart from any prominence or lack of it, because their stories personalize the impact that larger events had upon vaudeville and its people. Still others serve as representative acts from vaudeville—including black vaudeville—and, in a number of instances, from revue and burlesque, for those entertainers had acts, too, and were variety performers.

The number and length of entries in this encyclopedia were determined by the amount of reliable information available to the author about the performers and the specific incidents in their careers and lives that reflected experiences common to many other vaudevillians. More subjective was the author's desire to offer another *call* to many favorites.

Secondary sources vary from invaluable to misleading. A majority of those who have written chronicles of vaudeville or studies of particular skills have done so with honest intentions and produced laudable results; the cumulative result is a sturdy, if limited, body of factual knowledge. Many of these references are listed in the bibliography, and we gratefully acknowledge them and those who researched and wrote them.

Beyond the professional and personal stories of individual players is vaudeville as a business, a branch of show business and a social institution. What really happened in vaudeville, indeed all show business and mass media, can be verified, amplified or disputed by looking to the larger world where political, social and economic history intersects with developments in the technologies that transformed the entertainment industry.

A NOTE ON LANGUAGE

The authors have chosen to employ, along with currently accepted racial designations, the terms of the previous era, but not those that were offensive then and remain so, unless they are part of a quote or title. The sense of an era is best conveyed in the language of the day.

Terms once considered polite, such as *colored* and *Negro,* have been scorned for several generations by many but not all of those whom we now call *African American. Black,* long an epithet among some who preferred to be called *Negro* or *colored*, is now common usage. *Colored* has fallen out of favor, but *people of color* has gained currency.

In the matter of gender identification, *dancer, singer, acrobat, juggler, magician, ventriloquist* and *musician*, among others, do not admit feminized suffixes, so we have opted for *comedian* instead of *comedienne* and *actor* in place of *actress.*

Acknowledgments

Vaudevillians and their families, critics, fans, academics, journalists and historians have contributed over a lifetime to my knowledge and understanding of vaudeville, its performers, and the events and customs that attended it. This book would not have been possible without the many histories, memoirs, interviews and reviews that preceded it.

My particular thanks for their generosity of spirit to performers June Havoc, Larry Weeks, Estelle Rooney, Levent Cimkentli, Rudy Horn, Rose Marie, Nancy Hennings Tomlin, Larry Storch, Mary Simpson Howard, Robin Geoffrion and the late variety performer and historian Valantyne Napier.

This project was proposed by the executive editor for music and dance at Routledge, Richard C. Carlin, whose vision, guidance and kind patience have been my good fortune. Many people graciously shared their meticulous research and advice with us. We thank Chet Dowling for his firsthand knowledge of vaudeville and for material from his extensive archives; the late Mike Gilmore for his experience in the workings of vaudeville backstage; Stan Spence for providing us with his research into theatres and the various circuits with which they were connected. Arthur Dong was generous with his groundbreaking research on Asian American performers; and dancer, choreographer and documentary creator Betsy Baytos shared information from her dance archives.

Levent the Magician collected and passed on the histories of a dozen and more new vaudevillians. Both Armond Fields and Chris Simmons gave us the benefit of their special knowledge of early vaudeville. Archeologist, child vaudevillian and historian David Soren shared his research into American music and theatre.

Tony Barker, author of a celebrated series of *Music Hall* monographs, and Richard Anthony Baker and Max Tyler, both of the British Music Hall Society, were able to resolve difficult inquiries about British music-hall performers. Some searches for information about American vaudeville led me to Australian researchers Frank von Stratton, Bill Egan and, especially, Gary Le Gallant, who generously provided many materials from his archives. Novelist Elizabeth McCracken was generous in her professional assistance and offered golden advice: put joy into this book. Emily Leider, author of superbly researched and written show-business biographies, provided encouragement and support, and playwright Ed Bullins shared some of his research into nearly forgotten African American performers.

Dudley Heer, Barbara Lea, Linda Mihovich, Linda Maranis, G. M. Sanborn, Chatty Collier Eliason, Paul Gerard Smith III and Gail Erwin encouraged us, believed in what we are doing and provided research materials. Thanks also to Charlie Holland; Ron Hutchinson of the Vitaphone Project; Alan Howard, juggler and editor of *Juggler Magazine;* Paul Wesolowski of the *Freedonia Gazette;* Marc Bankert; and new vaudevillians Daniel Rosen, Mickey O'Connor, Travis Stewart, Stephanie Monceu and Keith Nelson.

Acknowledgments

I am grateful for the cordial reception and assistance that met my inquiries to Mark E. Swartz and Maryann Chach of the Shubert Archive, Marty Jacobs of the Museum of the City of New York, Madeline Matz at the Division of Film, Broadcasting & Sound Recording of the Library of Congress, Jean Morrow and Richard Vallone of the New England Conservatory of Music, the New York City Public Library at Lincoln Center, and the venerable Boston Public Library, particularly Roberta Zonghi, keeper of rare books and manuscripts, Eric Frazier, reference librarian for rare books and manuscripts, and their predecessors, William Faucan, former curator of manuscripts, and Eugene Zepp, former reference librarian of the Rare Books and Manuscripts Department, as well as Jan Dovenitz and Kris Springer in the Humanities Reference Department.

Thanks seem insufficient to Susan Roberts and Irene Cruikshank, good friends who have spared me the embarrassment of careless errors. I am indebted to the American Vaudeville Museum for the use of its archives and collections.

I am especially grateful to Donald C. McNeilly and Florence Hackman, two writers who have been involved in this project since its inception many years ago and whose good sense, knowledge and contributions to this book have been so varied and extensive that they must be considered coauthors.

The photographs and other illustrations that appear in this volume were provided by the American Museum of Vaudeville and the authors' collections.

Frank Cullen

Vaudeville History

Vaudeville was more than an assembly of ragtime pantaloons, topical monologists, eccentric dancers, barrelhouse songbirds, ventriloquists, magicians, tumblers and jugglers, more than a coast-to-coast network of once-gilded theatres now shambling into plaster dust. Vaudeville was a people's culture.

For centuries beyond count, motley entertainments have been performed for all manner of celebrations. Variety acts—juggling, tumbling, conjuring, storytelling, singing and dancing—found their first audiences at harvest celebrations around the globe and in the marketplaces of old Timbuktu, Cairo, Istanbul, Bombay, Shanghai, Mexico City, London, Berlin, Prague and Vienna.

Over time, variety arts have been expressions of religion, community ritual, politics and casual entertainment. In America, the United Kingdom and Australia, variety was strictly a matter of entertainment. If it had any political overtone, it was a thumb to the nose at pretension and the people who ruled the roosts of business, government and culture.

Some scholars have focused on France as the birthplace of vaudeville. The word itself is thought to derive from the val-de-Vire (or vau-de-Vire), a river valley in Normandy, home to fifteenth-century poet Oliver Basselin, who was born in the town of Calvados.

Orpheum Theatre, Lincoln, Nebraska

He wrote popular songs, some say drinking songs, which he named *chansons du* vau-de-Vire, after his native valley. At agricultural fairs, around the close of the seventeenth century, these songs, refreshed with topical lyrics, were put together with sketches and called *vaudevilles.* Other academics hold that vaudeville's French origins were more urban, growing out of the medieval entertainments found in Paris: *vaux de ville* ("worth of the city" or, twisted about, worthy of the city and its patronage) or *voix de ville* ("voice of the town/city," more liberally interpreted as voice of the people). In a stricter sense, *voix de ville* refers to collaboration between poets and musicians of the sixteenth century. Described at the time as profane and pagan, poems by writers such as Joachim de Bellay, Clément Marot, Pierre Ronsard and François Rabelais were set to lyrical tunes by musicians of the day such as Pierre Certon, Jean Chardavoine, Clément Janequin and Pierre Sandrin.

In England, the term *vaudeville* was used by Ernest Short and others as a catchall for musical comedy, revue and cabaret as well as music-hall and variety, which were more nearly the English equivalent of American vaudeville. All were dependent upon highly individual turns, or acts, to be successful. Both music-hall and variety offered a series of unrelated acts grouped together on a bill for an evening's entertainment. Variety spread from London to all corners of the English-speaking world.

To say that vaudeville originated in Normandy or Paris does little to explain American vaudeville. The connections between the entertainments of sixteenth- or seventeenth-century France and American vaudeville were neither lineal nor logical. *Vaudeville* was a word appropriated to look good on a programme and to sell a product.

Perhaps an American theatre owner traveled to Paris where he noticed *comédie à vaudeville* emblazoned on a theatre, or perhaps a French company, with *vaudeville* in its name, came to the USA. The older term, *variety,* had been debased in America through its associations with unsavory elements, ribald performance and its male-only clientele.

The entrepreneurs who first labeled their entertainments vaudeville, likely had no clear understanding of the word's origins. These men were street-smart promoters, not cultural anthropologists, and they were persuaded to call their offerings vaudeville because it sounded French, and if something were French, it was presumed classy, fancy and lively. In time, vaudeville was defined anew by the people who put their

New Orpheum Theatre, Kansas City, Missouri

Handbill for the Vaudeville Saloon, 1840, the earliest known appearance of a season of American vaudeville. (One of eleven Vaudeville Saloon handbills, July and August, 1840, preserved by the Boston Public Library, Rare Books Department. Reproduction courtesy of the Trustees.)

personalities and talent onstage, the people who ran the theatres and the preferences of their audiences.

Unlike in England, where popular musical entertainments and variety acts had been discouraged through the issuance of charters that conferred legitimacy on some theatres and forced others to mark uneasy time in an extralegal limbo, variety acts in Colonial and post-Revolutionary America often attracted less opposition from the rostrums of power than did plays, especially melodrama. If the blood-and-lust plot could claim Shakespeare as its author, there was likely to be less censure, though not universal acceptance. Because drama depended upon conflict, the deeds depicted therein were likely to vex moralists. Even if virtue triumphed by the final curtain, that did not absolve the experience of being tainted by the sins that led to redemption. Some religious leaders condemned entertainment simply because it failed to promote religiosity.

For some of its critics, the very atmosphere of a theatre was enough to qualify its balconies and pits as descending levels to hell and damnation. In truth, most theatres, with or without the support of managers, had sections in which prostitutes met their customers and sometimes conducted business on the premises. From Colonial times forward into the twentieth century, a certain segment of the American public held fast to the conviction that there was no clear demarcation between show business and harlotry.

If the clergy targeted a theatre, people shied away from patronage, fearing a ruined reputation. So theatres, at the first hint of trouble, would replace an offending play with a variety program. Most actors had polished set pieces that showed them to advantage, so a program could be cobbled together easily and quickly. Certain soliloquies from Shakespeare were above reproach. Orations were deemed morally instructive, whether from ancient Greek philosophers, Roman statesmen or esteemed contemporary American political figures. The actors' young children were judged to be pure and beyond the reach of Satan until puberty, so their simple recitations, songs, dances and playing of musical instruments did not threaten moral well-being. Dancing was acceptable on a variety bill, but only if the dances were familiar forms like hornpipes, clogs and jigs from the

→✻ PLACES ∙ OF ∙ AMUSEMENT ✻←

NEW YORK CITY.

Wallack's Theatre, . . .	Broadway and 30th Street.
Madison Square Theatre, .	24th St. near 5th Ave.
Grand Opera House, . . .	8th Ave. and 23d St.
Fifth Avenue Theatre, .	28th St. near Broadway.
Standard Theatre, ...	6th Ave. near 32d St.
Abbey's Park Theatre, . .	Broadway and 22d St.
Haverly's 14th St. Theatre,	14th St. and Sixth Ave.
Union Square Theatre, ...	Union Square.
Booth's Theatre, ...	6th Ave. and 23d St.
Theatre Comique, . . .	728 and 730 Broadway.
Windsor Theatre, ...	Bowery and Canal St.
Germania Theatre, . . .	Broadway and 13th St.
Thalia Theatre, ...	46 and 48 Bowery.
Tony Pastor's 14th St. Theatre,	14th St. near 3d Ave.
Daly's Theatre, ...	Broadway and 30th St.
Bijou Opera House, . .	Broadway near 30th St.
Niblo's Garden, . . .	Broadway and Prince St.
San Francisco Minstrels, .	Broadway and 30th St.
Chickering Hall, ...	5th Ave. and 18th St.
Steinway Hall, . . .	14th St. near Fourth Ave.
Academy of Music, . .	14th St. and Irving Place.
Bunnell's Museum, . . .	Broadway and 9th St.
American Institute, . . .	3rd Ave. and 63d St.
Belgian Panorama Company,	55th St. and 7th Ave.
Metropolitan Alcazar, . . .	585 Broadway.

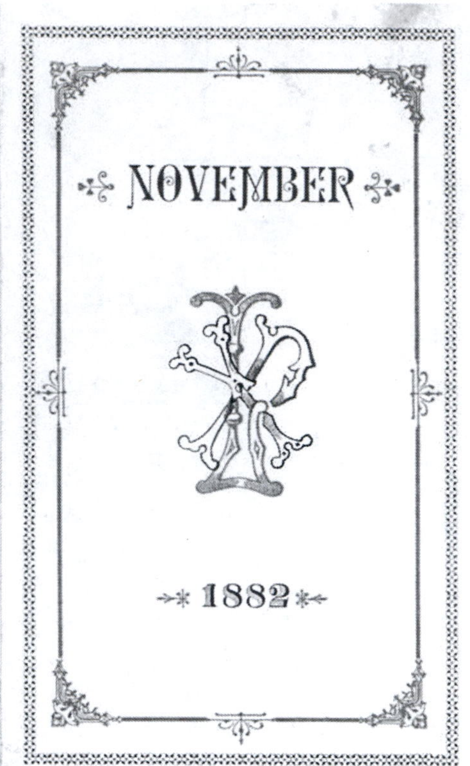

Variety and vaudeville theatre in Manhattan, 1882

mother countries or chastely performed ballets and the dancers were decorously clad. Acrobatics were popular, but the performers had to be careful that their clothing did not accent too much their fine figures.

The reign of the Puritan pulpit did not survive the growing heterogeneity of the United States that accelerated after 1820. Naval wars had led to better-built and faster ships, and the defeat of Napoleon had left the Atlantic Ocean safe for travel. With the cessation of war, European immigration began anew to the New World, and the pace increased by the decade. By the midpoint of the eighteenth century, the great majority of new Americans came from Ireland and Germany, and their concepts of morality did not always jibe with the Puritan codes. In the old country, the immigrants' idea of a good time included beer, ale, liquor, music and dancing.

Many settled in the port cities of New York, Baltimore and Boston because they had no money to travel farther. They lived in squalid, airless flats, a few rooms home to several families, their outhouses stuck along fetid alleyways. Entertaining at home was for more established Americans who had accumulated both space and money. Immigrants, consigned to poorly paid and unsafe labor when they could find work, sought relief in saloons. The saloons were for single and married men; women stayed home tending hearth and raising children, unless they had been disgraced or were willing to risk disrepute.

As the larger saloons prospered, some offered entertainment: the inevitable piano player, perhaps a cornetist and a drummer, waitresses who danced, bartenders who sang harmony, knockabout comics and bare-knuckle boxers whose 30-round battles ended with both victor and vanquished bloody and insensate.

Concert saloons, as they came to be called, did not have the entertainment field to themselves. Dime museums, beer gardens and melodramas competed for the immigrants' coin as did minstrel shows, burlesque, variety and farces with music, such as those presented by Harrigan & Hart.

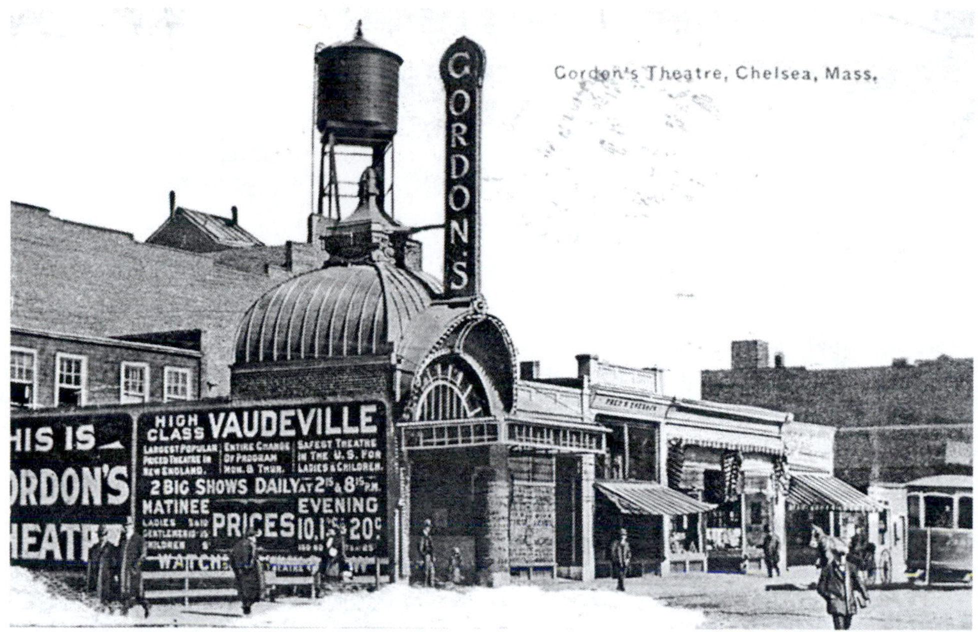

Gordon's Theatre, Chelsea, Massachusetts

Along with immigrant performers intending to stay, itinerant European acts visited America to play on its stages, sometimes en route to South America or Australia. Many came from a circus background rather than the theatre. Accustomed to playing to the audience, they charmed customers with a performance style that disregarded the fourth wall so central to the growing movement toward naturalistic drama in the nineteenth century. The European acts brought a blend of music, comedy, dance and acrobatics that raised the bar for native performers, and the competition gave rise to the beginnings of the star system.

By custom, performers had been listed by their surnames, prefaced simply by Mr., Mrs., Miss, Mme., Mlle., or Master, and their pay was governed by their casting type and their utility to the company. The more valuable and celebrated members of a company were accorded a seasonal benefit, a single performance from which the proceeds were given to the honored actor or performer.

Certain entertainers and actors became audience favorites. Their appearance in a production demonstrably increased box-office income, and they were sought after by various competing managements. The salaries given to the emerging stars changed the system of payment. The new stars negotiated salaries that reflected their special status rather than the going rate for a leading man, character actor or juvenile. The star system arrived to stay, and the later success of most vaudeville bills, dramas, musical comedies and revues was due to the particular abilities of the stars and their appeal to the audience.

In 1840, vaudeville, in what may have been its first appearance under the term, played a summer season in Boston at Boylston Hall, which had been rechristened the Vaudeville Saloon. The bills were a mixture of recitations, ballets and hornpipes, songs from the concert repertoire as well as lighter melodies, and dramatic and comedy sketches. Located on the southwest corner of Boylston and Washington Streets, the Vaudeville Saloon of 1840 established Boston's claim to be the birthplace of American vaudeville.

Variety and vaudeville were unlike plays and operas because they brought together a series of unrelated acts on a single bill. There was no unifying theme or scheme, as was found in classic drama, melodrama, comic opera, operetta and burlettas (burlesque). Eventually, vaudeville would surpass variety in appeal and influence, but until the 1870s, saloons provided the usual venue and set the (low) standard for variety.

In 1862, during the Civil War, the New York State Legislature, responding to innumerable complaints, enacted a series of laws designed to cripple the concert saloons. Although the concert saloons actually did close down, the setback was temporary. Their managements found ways to accommodate the law, corrupt its servants and circumvent its penalties. Because laws were enforced locally by people who also might be customers or beneficiaries of largesse, concert saloons continued to prosper past the turn of the twentieth century.

Many concert-saloon owners, however, sought safer endeavors and produced more acceptable entertainments. They were motivated by the prospect that they could increase their potential audience with shows that were appropriate for women and children. Also, by turning away from the crude diversions and coarse audiences of concert saloons, they hoped to be free of the graft extorted by the local constabulary.

The entrepreneurial pioneers struggled for a quarter century to deflect disapproval and to earn the public's trust and patronage through a series of experiments. There was no guiding standard of presentation, either in terms of quality or format. Most of the owner-managers decided to convert their places into theatres. Some gambled and built new theatres. Many no longer sold liquor, and they offered a greater variety of acts and discouraged gamblers, pickpockets and prostitutes.

In the effort to appeal to a more respectable audience, a few managers reached a bit high when they cobbled together, into an evening's program, a series of dramatic scenes—some taken from Shakespeare, concert music and lectures. Such high-flown fare soon yielded to lighter entertainment. Short, sensational melodramas replaced Shakespeare on the bill, lecturers yielded to storytellers, and popular song and dance set the pace.

A decade after the Vaudeville Saloon's experiment in variety, a French vaudeville company was advertised in 1850 at a *new* Washington Hall, located on Washington Street near Montgomery Street in San Francisco. (The former Washington Hall had been turned into that city's most stylish brothel.)

It was reported, some years after the fact, that, in lower Manhattan, William P. Valentine opened The Bowery (also known as The Bowerie), the first concert saloon, perhaps in 1848 or 1849, but there is little if any extant documentation for this event beyond the claim passed down through lore. It has been established, however, that, in 1859, Mr. Valentine was proprietor of the Vauxhall Garden and advertised its bills both as variety and as vaudeville. Valentine was not alone.

Frank Rivers, a former circus performer, opened the Melodeon Concert Hall in 1859 at 539 Broadway, which was an uptown Manhattan location in those days. Rivers, as had many others, took variety on the road, touring a troupe at least as far as New England during the 1861–62 season. During the early 1860s, Robert Butler promoted wholesome shows, appropriate for women, at the American Music Hall (one of several houses he operated in Manhattan and Philadelphia).

The Civil War had not stopped performers from traveling; indeed, there were increasing numbers of variety troupes touring in competition with minstrel companies. Soldiers away from home patronized concert saloons in many of the larger cities in the USA. Officials looked away during the war. After the hostilities, many concert saloons survived censure by evolving into respectability, either as restaurants and cafés of the late nineteenth and the twentieth centuries or rebuilt to include theatres that would play vaudeville, comic opera and burlesque.

Vaudeville performances in Boston, San Francisco, Louisville and Cincinnati over the previous 30 years predated others, such as those produced by M. L. "Mike" Leavitt, John W. Ransom or Tony Pastor.

Before his emergence as a performer-manager, Tony Pastor had sung in a few melodeons, music-halls and theatres that had catered, whether occasionally or as standard

Klondyke Theatre, Klondyke, Alaska, Pantages' first theatre

policy, to family audiences. Pastor, a graduate of minstrelsy, circus and concert-saloon variety, began his own management career in 1865. There is evidence that he strove toward respectable entertainments from the start, but there was a transition period between his intention and his accomplishment. Unlike other experiments that faded with the seasons, Tony Pastor's management was unique in that it succeeded and endured for a quarter century. Pastor sniffed at the term *vaudeville,* loyally burnishing the older name *variety* through the quality and wholesomeness of his shows.

B. F. Keith's shows, which have been mistakenly credited as the first or among the first appearances of vaudeville, were produced a couple of generations after the first vaudeville shows, such as the Vaudeville Saloon in 1840 and Sargent's Great Vaudeville Company that toured the Midwest as early as 1871. Keith and his partners F. F. Proctor and E. F. Albee, however, were the first to turn vaudeville into an industry.

Keith, whose first showbiz enterprise was a dime museum of oddities, was persuaded in 1885 by his right hand man, Albee, to open a theatre, which they named the Bijou, on Boston's busiest commercial thoroughfare, Washington Street. They introduced a daylong repeating cycle of variety acts that they promoted as vaudeville, geared to the passersby who, spur of the moment, were looking to pass an hour before resuming shopping or returning home. Later, this rotation of acts would be called *continuous vaudeville.*

As Keith and Albee prospered, their ambitions grew. One theatre in Boston was not enough. As they began to acquire and build, Keith and Albee set out to control the industry. F. F. Proctor, based in New York, had the same goal. Proctor partnered with Keith for a time, but Albee saw Proctor as a rival, and the relationship between Keith-Albee and Proctor seesawed until Proctor capitulated in a sense and tied his fortunes to the Albee-dominated United Booking Office.

Unlike Pastor, Keith and Albee made monopoly a hallmark of their operations. Like Pastor, however, Keith and Albee were committed to wholesome entertainment,

Waldemann's Theatre, Newark, New Jersey, 1906

which they called *polite vaudeville,* and stressed its suitability for the entire family. To court family patronage, neutralize censors and encourage favorable press, it was critical to set apart vaudeville from the coarse and common entertainments of the concert saloons, the dime museums and the circus. Various theatre owners adopted the policy—calling it *polite variety, polite vaudeville,* or *refined vaudeville.* The goal was to provide a respectable place and decent entertainment that families could patronize without damage to their reputations.

Vaudeville developed into a big business. Its growing popularity prompted the building of more and ever-larger theatres. Modern American show business had arrived. It was a by-product of a uniform system of railroads, the telegraph and telephones, willing bankers, aggressive lawyers, a popular daily press and a nation expanding in size and opportunity.

As more people with theatrical ambitions turned to vaudeville, they found talent was not enough. They had to have an act, and an act could only be developed through the experience of playing to vaudeville audiences to discover what they liked and what they did not.

To get work, vaudevillians, novices and veterans alike, wrote ahead to theatre owners asking for bookings and asking which dates were open around the time that they would be in that area. Of course, if an act had played a theatre previously and had new material, it could generally count on a booking. Sometimes a manager booked an act because he had heard good things about it. The newcomer took bookings wherever he could. The process, even for the experienced act, was time-consuming, usually frustrating, and it resulted in badly plotted routes.

Enter the booker and the agent. Bookers worked for the theatre owners and managers; agents worked for performers and actors, theoretically, then as now. Usually bookers and agents worked together, and, gradually, an efficient, often dictatorial and unfair system of booking developed. The performer surrendered autonomy (and a hefty percentage of his paycheck) for more bookings and a coherent schedule.

As transportation linked the outlying regions of America and show business prospered, booking agents became booking agencies and theatres were linked into circuits. The larger theatre chains began their own booking agencies. For a successful and compliant act, this was heaven-sent and might mean a full season of 40 weeks of work with a minimum of layoffs and travel jumps. An unsuccessful act, or one that management

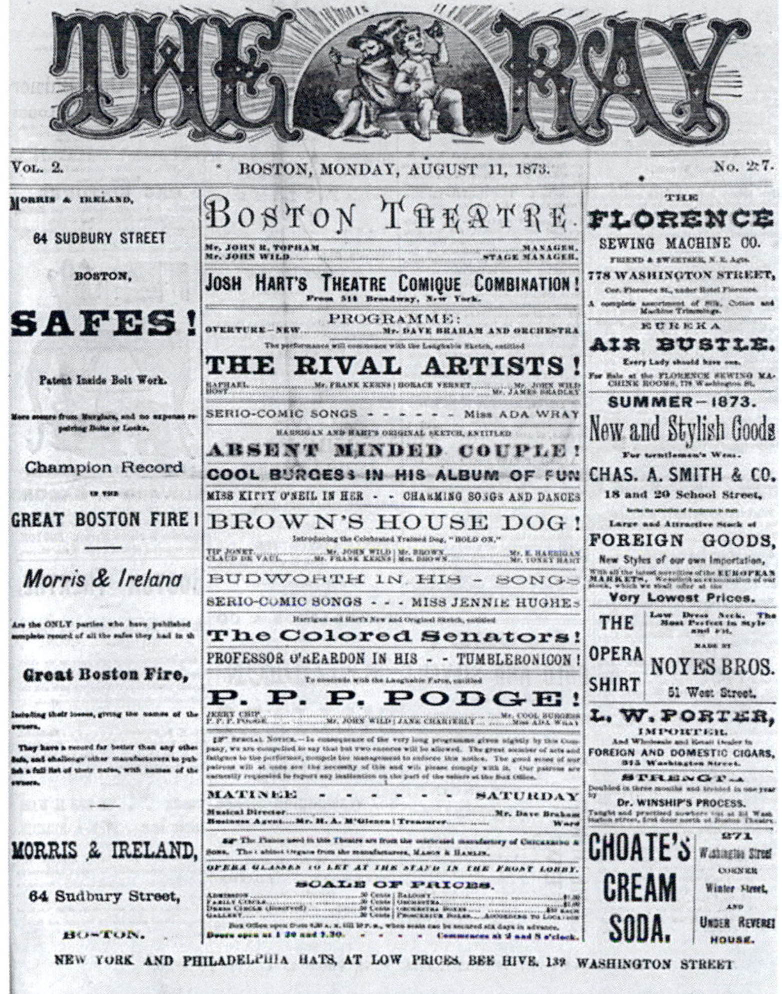

THE RAY

Vol. 2. BOSTON, MONDAY, AUGUST 11, 1873. No. 27.

MORRIS & IRELAND,

64 SUDBURY STREET

BOSTON.

SAFES!

Patent Inside Bolt Work.

More secure from Burglars, and no expense repairing Bolts or Locks.

Champion Record

GREAT BOSTON FIRE!

Morris & Ireland

Are the ONLY parties who have published complete record of all the safes they had in th

Great Boston Fire,

Including their losses, giving the names of the owners.

They have a record far better than any other Safe, and challenge other manufacturers to publish a full list of their sales, with names of the owners.

MORRIS & IRELAND,

64 Sudbury Street,

BOSTON.

BOSTON THEATRE.

Mr. JOHN R. TOPHAM ... MANAGER.
Mr. JOHN WILD ... STAGE MANAGER.

JOSH HART'S THEATRE COMIQUE COMBINATION!

From 514 Broadway, New York.

PROGRAMME:

OVERTURE—NEW ... Mr. DAVE BRAHAM AND ORCHESTRA

THE RIVAL ARTISTS!

RAPHAEL ... Mr. FRANK KERNS | HORACE VERNET ... Mr. JOHN WILD
HOST ... Mr. JAMES BRADLEY

SERIO-COMIC SONGS - - - - - - Miss ADA WRAY

HARRIGAN AND HART'S ORIGINAL SKETCH, ENTITLED

ABSENT MINDED COUPLE!

COOL BURGESS IN HIS ALBUM OF FUN

MISS KITTY O'NEIL IN HER - - CHARMING SONGS AND DANCES

BROWN'S HOUSE DOG!

Introducing the Celebrated Trained Dog, "HOLD ON."

TIP JONES ... Mr. JOHN WILD | Mr. BROWN ... Mr. E. HARRIGAN
CLAUD DE VAUL ... Mr. FRANK KERNS | Mrs. BROWN ... Mr. TONEY HART

BUDWORTH IN HIS - SONGS

SERIO-COMIC SONGS - - - MISS JENNIE HUGHES

Harrigan and Hart's New and Original Sketch, entitled

The Colored Senators!

PROFESSOR O'REARDON IN HIS - - TUMBLERONICON!

To conclude with the Laughable Farce, entitled

P. P. P. PODGE!

JERRY CHIP ... Mr. COOL BURGESS
P. P. P. PODGE ... Mr. JOHN WILD | JANE CHARIVELY ... Miss ADA WRAY

MATINEE - - - - - - SATURDAY

Musical Director ... Mr. Dave Braham

Business Agent....Mr. H. A. M'Glenen | Treasurer ... Ward

OPERA GLASSES TO LET AT THE STAND IN THE FRONT LOBBY.

SCALE OF PRICES.

Doors open at 1.30 and 7.30. - - - - - Commences at 2 and 8 o'clock.

THE FLORENCE SEWING MACHINE CO.

FRIEND & SWEETSER, N. E. Agts.

778 WASHINGTON STREET,

EUREKA

AIR BUSTLE.

Every Lady should have one.

SUMMER—1873.

New and Stylish Goods

CHAS. A. SMITH & CO.

18 and 20 School Street,

Large and Attractive Stock of

FOREIGN GOODS,

New Styles of our own Importation,

Very Lowest Prices.

THE OPERA SHIRT

MADE BY

NOYES BROS.

51 West Street.

L. W. PORTER,

IMPORTER.

FOREIGN AND DOMESTIC CIGARS,

STRENGTH

Dr. WINSHIP'S PROCESS.

CHOATE'S CREAM SODA.

271 Washington Street CORNER Winter Street, AND UNDER REVERE HOUSE.

NEW YORK AND PHILADELPHIA HATS, AT LOW PRICES. BEE HIVE. 139 WASHINGTON STREET

Early vaudeville bill, Boston Theatre, 1873

deemed uncooperative, was punished by less-desirable bookings and billing, and the jumps could take as long as the engagements.

The cities of the Northeast were not alone in evolving from variety to vaudeville. By the 1880s and 1890s, Seattle, San Francisco and Sacramento were fast-growing urban centers fueled by shipping, railroads, mining and lumber industries. The escalating influx of families, churches, schools and a free press began to tame Seattle's Skid Row, San Francisco's Barbary Coast and the mining camps that blossomed into small towns in the Sierra Nevadas.

John Considine was a young man who had followed the advice to "go west, young man" all the way to Seattle and San Francisco. He began managing rough-and-ready box houses for the People's Theatre chain until, with "Big Tim" Sullivan, his Tammany Hall partner in Manhattan, Considine built the first vaudeville circuit that could legitimately lay claim to being (nearly) a coast-to-coast operation capable of offering more than a year's work to acts.

Alexander Pantages became Considine's major rival as Pantages established a somewhat parallel circuit, longer lasting but with a bit less reach. Not far behind them were Martin Beck and Morris Meyerfeld, who took a bankrupt Orpheum Theatre in San Francisco and built it into the largest big-time vaudeville circuit west of the Mississippi River. The Orpheum was anchored in San Francisco and Chicago and, like Pan-

Orpheum Theatre, Allentown, Pennsylvania

Atlantic City Steel Pier Theatre

tages and Sullivan & Considine time, it filled in gaps in its own circuit by hooking up with small-time chains like Interstate or Webster and booking independent theatres in sparsely populated areas along the route.

Orpheum time was Keith-Albee's chief rival, especially when Beck made his move into Manhattan by building the Palace Theatre that opened in 1913. Albee won the contest. Through a combination of muscle, money and maneuvering, the two giants eventually merged into Keith-Albee-Orpheum time, and Albee was in control.

There were dozens of other entrepreneurs who cobbled together circuits large and small, and Albee's way of subjugating rivals, bookers, agents and performers was to

Gaiety Theatre, Galesburg, Illinois

establish the United Booking Office (UBO). Ostensibly, the UBO brought coherence into a chaotic situation. In practice, it brought most important theatres under Albee's cooperative tent, decided which bookers and agents had access to the system and required acts to accept take-it-or-leave-it terms and play only when and where the UBO booked them. Any act who tried to circumvent the terms was threatened with blackballing.

Earlier, in 1907, Abe Erlanger of the Theatrical Trust and the Shuberts had taken a crack at Keith-Albee when they teamed Erlanger's money with Shubert theatres. It is more likely that their joint Advanced Vaudeville venture was a successful effort to extort Albee into buying them out. Because of the competition for top-quality acts, vaudevillian salaries increased significantly across the board after 1907. The third member of the Advanced Vaudeville organization was William Morris, a beloved agent who joined Erlanger and Lee Shubert only to diminish Albee's stranglehold on vaudeville and vaudevillians.

Morris booked the acts for Advanced Vaudeville until his partners sold out. Thereafter, he reverted forever to his independent status and even tried to turn his reputation for ethical dealings into a fair practices circuit. The tide was with monopoly, but Morris' legacy lasted longer; the William Morris Agency grew into one of the biggest and most venerable representation outfits in show business.

Other independents, large and small, were less self-sufficient and more cautious than Morris, hoisting and dipping their colors as events played out. F. F. Proctor, Percy Williams, Sylvester Poli, Gus Sun and the like were like small nations caught in the battle of empires. Whatever they did, in cooperation or occasional defiance, they did to survive. Some were more inclined to bravery and ethics than others.

The growing popularity of motion pictures was hard to miss by the mid-1910s. Some of the more perspicacious vaudeville independents realized that motion pictures had the potential to replace vaudeville as the premier popular entertainment. Among the smarter of those who kept a foot in both camps before they made the transition were Marcus Loew and his lieutenants, Joseph and Nicholas Schenck, Adolph Zukor, William Fox and Louis B. Mayer, who among them created MGM, Paramount and Fox Pictures, whereas Abe Balaban, with his brother Barney, stayed out of movie production and, instead, created a chain of movie palaces coast to coast.

Maryland Theatreland, Baltimore, Maryland

It is difficult to estimate the number of theatres that played vaudeville at any given time between the 1870s and the 1930s because few theatres other than the vaudeville palaces were built as single-purpose houses. The Shuberts were a good example of showbiz entrepreneurs whose theatres played whatever sold. Smaller theatres, the *nabes* (urban neighborhood houses), and those away from the big urban centers needed to be even more flexible.

Depending upon the year, and whether vaudeville, burlesque or traveling musical comedy was in the ascendant, there were approximately 800 to 1,200 big-time vaudeville houses that more or less maintained a two-(shows)-a-day policy between 1910 and 1925. Factoring in quality, small-time operations like Marcus Loew's, Pantages and dozens of independents and quasi independents, the number approached 2,000 theatres.

In addition to the recognized vaudeville chains and theatres, there were 1,000 and more other venues that booked vaudeville, sometimes in concert with silent movies (before they were widely and formally distributed), or hosted packaged shows such as touring vaudeville units, burlesque revues and acting troupes. On most weekend nights, in the hundreds of small towns down South, on the Great Plains and in the Rocky Mountain states, shows were put on in converted churches and grange halls, tents, auditoriums or any space that could accommodate enough folks to make the venture pay.

Even if the amount of vaudeville shows on a given weekend reached a fairly conservative 3,000 (and some estimates go as high as 5,000), that meant, with a conservative average of 10 people, not acts, per bill, there were no less than 30,000 performers who could claim to be vaudevillians. The number of vaudevillians may have approached or exceeded 50,000, if the high estimate of 5,000 theatres of various kinds is accepted. One should also account for turnover; although some performers logged a lifetime in vaudeville, some lasted little more than a few seasons.

Add to this total the number of people in all the pit bands, those working in the front of the house and back stage, plus agents and bookers, trade-paper personnel and those who provided costumes, wigs and makeup, or built and painted scenery, and it is clear that vaudeville was a major branch of a major industry.

Imperial Theatre, Providence, Rhode Island

Vaudeville had become a commodity, one quarter of a winning show-business combination. The other parts were just as critical to its commercial success. Without a network of railroads stimulating settlements that grew into prosperous towns along their routes, there would have been no chains of theatres crossing the nation. Without communication through telegraph and telephone, bookers could not have devised an efficient and profitable way to keep the theatres supplied with acts. Without a popular press, promoters would have been hard-pressed to let the public know about the delights that awaited them at their local theatres.

Vaudeville put the four pillars of show business in place: product (the performers), distribution (a booking system to get performers to the right places at the right time), marketplaces (the theatres), and communications (electric telegraphic and telephone and the lithographic and printing operations that manufactured handbills, posters and

Air Dome, Wilkinsburg, Pennsylvania

Colonial Theatre, Onset, Cape Cod, Massachusetts

programmes efficiently and inexpensively and produced the new daily and weekly newspapers more timely and affordably to a wide readership).

The movie business became the primary beneficiary of vaudeville's business foundation. Vaudeville had thrived from the 1880s through the early 1900s despite bank failures, economic depressions and the growing urban and rural poverty of the late nineteenth century. During the first decade of the twentieth century, it looked as though vaudeville was king and would last forever. By 1914, when the First World War erupted in Europe, its future seemed less sure as motion pictures began to tell stories artisti-

Temple Theatre, Rochester, New York

cally and stole some of vaudeville's audience. By 1921, one out of five vaudeville houses had switched to silent films or split their bills between movies and vaudeville. Yet classic, big-time vaudeville managed to survive for another decade, and salaries for the big-name performers continued to grow, due largely to competition for stars. The rise, dominance and decline of an institution are a progression, with spikes and slumps in the flow, and it was difficult for those in the midst of it to know when an accumulation of incidents presaged a trend. In vaudeville's case, there were four major factors in play, but not one offered a certain portent.

First was Hollywood. Silent films, already jostling vaudeville for popularity, added sound in 1926. It had taken more than a decade to convince movie producers and exhibitors that sound was worth the investment. Thomas Edison had made sound films in 1913, but his Kinetophone process was not well received. Many other inventors,

Vanity Fair, Providence, Rhode Island

including Lee De Forest, had experimented with various technologies to marry sound and sight recording. None of these attempts solved all the technical problems of amplification, clarity and synchronization, and most were not financially or technically feasible for either the studios or the exhibitors.

Vitaphone used a process that recorded the sound on a wax disk and synchronized the record with the reel of film through the use of a single motor that powered both mechanisms. In 1926, Warner Brothers, which had invested in the Vitaphone process, released the first in a series of short films and then a feature, *Don Juan,* with an electronically recorded, totally synchronized music score. On 6 October 1927, Warner Brothers followed up with *The Jazz Singer,* a motion picture in which audiences heard Al Jolson sing. Talkies offered sight and sound for the lowest ticket price around, although it took a couple of years as two sound systems competed for dominance and for theatre owners to commit to the financial investment needed to convert their theatres for talkies.

The success of sound pictures should not have been a shock to people in show business. It was. The question of when sound would pass from a novelty into the standard should have been the only uncertainty, but it took two years before all the major studios—Paramount, Warner Brothers, MGM, Fox and Universal—fully committed to sound. The exhibitors were no faster. Converting to sound on their end of the business was a gamble. Which system would prevail: Warner Brothers' Vitaphone or Fox's Movietone? Was the rate of return on investment sufficient to quickly amortize conversion costs? How many seats did a theatre need to make the conversion financially feasible? What about color, which was on the technology horizon?

A second factor affecting Vaudeville's viability was radio. An enthusiasm shared by amateurs who communicated with each other quietly turned into a commercial endeavor as independent stations popped up. Each had a limited broadcasting range. It is doubtful that anyone not professionally involved with the broadcast industry at the time fully understood the future impact of a radio network. There had been sporadic broadcasts since 1906. Ten years later, inventor Lee De Forest reported the 1916 presidential election returns over the air. In 1922, nearly a third of a million people clustered around radio receivers to listen to a play-by-play account of Jack Dempsey knocking out Georges Carpentier.

Star Theatre, Monessen, Pennsylvania

Big radio began when the federal government convened an assembly of broadcasters to standardize the use of radio frequencies and eliminate the overlap of signals. On 15 November 1926, the National Broadcasting Company, a small network of local radio stations linked by cable, broadcast its first day of centralized programming from the Grand Ballroom of the Waldorf Astoria Hotel in Manhattan. The event probably held less significance for the average vaudevillian than it did for the average citizen. After the purchase of a radio set, radio entertainment was free, but it took a couple of years for broadcasters to be able to hook up enough stations, attract the sponsors that paid the bills and entice into the studio the big names in show business that could draw the large audiences that sponsors sought. By the early 1930s, people were staying home to listen to Rudy Vallee, Amos 'n' Andy and Kate Smith.

A third event was set in play on 24 October 1929 when, after a month of shakiness, the stock market heaved as 13 million shares were traded. Five days later, 29 October

Keith's Theatre, Philadelphia, Pennsylvania

turned into Black Thursday as 16 million shares were traded on Wall Street. Panic ensued, and the value of once-reliable blue-chip stocks crashed to one third, even one half, of their values a day earlier. It took the better part of a decade and the onset of the Second World War to stimulate a recovery that offered enough jobs and opportunity to millions of Americans to pull out of poverty. In the meantime, what little money families could spend on entertainment went for a new radio or cheap movie tickets. Even the cost of a burlesque show was less expensive than much of vaudeville and all of Broadway. Financial panics had been usual in the USA since the Civil War; they had occurred in 1869, 1873, 1882, 1893 and 1907. There were other periods before and after the First World War when the economy was uncertain. Regulatory controls were largely absent in 1929 while, for more than a month, the stock market was on the brink of collapse.

Unlike previous panics, many ordinary people from the growing middle class had followed financiers into the market, each expecting that a high tide would float rather

World Theatre, Omaha, Nebraska

than submerge all boats, whether dinghies or yachts. Even when it became obvious that the market had crashed, not merely stumbled, few could imagine how events would reverberate and spread. By 1930, the economies of the USA and Europe were depressed. It would take a decade to reverse the slide. That was a long time to wait for vaudeville to come back.

Taken together, these three events constituted a one-two-three-strikes-you're-out defeat for vaudeville. They also provided financiers the chance to turn the movie business into a major industry. The template already had been developed in vaudeville. The product became movies rather than live performances, and the theatres were waiting, underutilized, for the product. The distribution system of getting performers from place to place was retooled for cans of film, and newspapers covered the release of new movies as the studios and exhibitors paid for display ads.

There was another reason for vaudeville's slow eclipse, one that sometimes has been ignored or denied. Vaudeville, once the cheeky upstart of show business, had lost its novelty as it grew more polished with the decades. Critics and customers complained that it had become too homogenized, too predictable, complacent, hackneyed and stale.

As the vaudeville business had grown big, standardized and self-regulated, its captains had grown old and distracted by finance and the struggle to hold onto what they had. They were no longer in show business; they were in investments and real estate, trying to keep their theatres open. A few saw change coming and adapted, however slowly. For too many, the solution was to pack more shows into the day and night, making the vaudeville performance continuous, cheaper, less special and tired. Once, the repetition of four or more shows a day had motivated young performers to reach the big time that required only two shows a day. When there no longer was two-a-day big time to which to aspire, the grind became demoralizing.

Vaudevillians themselves contributed to the public's disenchantment. In the quest to perfect their acts and win audience approval, they became imitative and their acts formulaic. They stuck with what worked until it no longer did. Sometimes, changing the gags, the songs and the costumes just was not enough. A new song, a new gag, a new set of combinations in a dance routine, a new illusion in a magic act, juggling seven balls, or a new finish to an act—they were new about a week, then other acts stole them.

To be fair to the performer, audiences grew blasé with the standard of excellence and no longer were awed by effects that took months or years to perfect. The technological marvels of the big silver screen became the standard by which a live act was judged. Like most historical events in retrospect, the decline and death of vaudeville appear clear, certain and inevitable. For participants, with no such perspective, each day differed little from the last or the next, and the worry whether one was engaged beyond next month's bookings precluded thinking much farther ahead. Speculation about the future was fueled by gossip, guessing and past experience.

When were vaudevillians to know that their way of earning a living was over? When the recessions of the 1890s hit? When motion pictures began offering plots or later matured into an art form? When burlesque offered great comedians, sultry strippers and less-expensive tickets? When radio hookups meant that one singer, one orchestra and one comedian could play 1,000 cities and towns at once? When they understood the promise and threat of films that could talk, sing and dance?

Many vaudevillians realized that the final curtain was descending when network radio emerged and the talkies debuted. The immediate need to survive ruled out reengineering their careers. Hundreds, perhaps thousands, hopped a train to Los Angeles, where a few became stars and many more filled less-featured parts in the industry, often behind the camera or as coaches or in the wardrobe and shop departments or in offices as agents. Those whose skills were primarily verbal or musical hoped against odds that radio would rescue them. Some continued their careers in Broadway revues and musical comedies, but Broadway struggled, too, during the Great Depression. Many performers moved their acts to nightclubs, circuses and carnivals, wherever somebody would book them.

Most drifted away from show business, but the economy did not facilitate a hospitable return to civilian ranks. Just as it was during their years in show business, resilience was the vaudevillians' strength, and in time most of them adapted and succeeded in their new roles as shopkeepers, truck farmers, waiters, agents, ballroom dance instructors, stock brokers, motel owners, restaurateurs, dry cleaners and factory workers. For some, it was the first time they were able to earn a living and live in one place.

Vaudeville did not burst like a bubble. After the early shocks that rocked and reduced it, vaudeville took its time dying. It never regained its previous stature, but it survived, sharing the bill with feature films in presentation houses and on its own, often under another name, in small theatres, resorts, nightclubs, at fairs, carnivals and amusement parks. The United Service Organizations (USO) shows were, in most particulars, vaudeville shows, and they kept old-time acts along with the new acts working from the early 1940s through the early 1970s, with a few years at liberty between hostilities.

Variety shows were a staple of early television, but popular variety was no longer feasible when the singing and musical numbers were amplified to a degree that was in radical imbalance to the monologues and comedy sketches. The comedy clubs of the last decades of the twentieth century were vaudeville without variety. Specialty acts found work in circuses, even ice shows, that showcased acrobats, contortionists, jugglers, wire walkers and clowns. Those institutions, however, were inclining toward extravaganza, scenic dazzle, canned music and large production ensembles.

On those occasions when old-time vaudeville was exhumed for revival, in the main it was as a sugarcoated piece of nostalgia, an amateur event trotted out as a happy-time revue for a wholesome family or a cozy remembrance for senior citizens. Equipped with faux straw boaters, striped blazers, feather boas and canes, the young performers, who had little idea of the spice and bite of real vaudeville, sported wide smiles and mustered a golly-gee-whiz attitude that was sad in its artificiality. Vaudeville was theatrical, but it was not fake. It was corny, sophisticated, sarcastic, sentimental, melodramatic, subtle, sly, raucous, intimate, flamboyant, rude, exotic, hilarious, sad, lovely and, on occasion, boring. Until it faltered, it was real, as real as the people who pulled something out of themselves—their spirit, their talent, their personality, their fear and their courage—and put it onstage.

The institution of vaudeville was peculiar to its time and place, and there will never again be vaudeville as the people of the USA once knew it: a vibrant branch of show business filling theatres coast to coast. In the last four decades of the twentieth century, however, a small-scale revival of the vaudeville spirit and skills began.

After the Second World War and the USA's wholesale rejection of the old for the new, there was a sense among some souls that America's artistic heritage was being bulldozed to make way for modernity. The revival of crafts like pottery, weaving, glassblowing and metalsmithing was a reaction to the deadening monotony of mass production. Urban renewal prompted its opposing reaction: historical preservation. The bicentennial stimulated interest in the history of the United States of America. It prompted re-creations of events and reenactments of battles, and historians rediscovered the arts of Colonial America. Scholars made field recordings of American folk and blues music. Some ethnic groups kept their music alive through religious and cultural events. Societies and coffeehouses devoted to folk music were soon followed by instrumental aggregations and concerts playing the medieval and Renaissance music of Europe.

All of which led to the birth of Renaissance Faires, celebrations that required skills as diverse as pottery, woodworking, horsemanship, blacksmithing, jousting, playing music, dancing, singing, fencing, juggling, tumbling, rope walking, clowning and stilt walking. Renaissance Faires became an alternative to busking, although busking was a more authentic reproduction of olden days.

There had always been street performers in the USA: musicians playing guitar and kids dancing for coppers. To lure tourists, metropolitan areas created large marketplaces that attracted street performers, or buskers. Urban mass transit authorities began to allow street performers, musicians mostly, to play in subway stations.

Busking and various types of fairs produced generations of acrobats, mimes, jugglers, balloon twisters, slapstick comedians, sword swallowers, puppeteers, hoop spinners, trick cyclists, slack-wire walkers, dancers, contortionists, one-person bands, fire-eaters and magicians. All manner of talents contributed to a resurgence of the specialty act. In some big cities, there are small, innovative theatres that reinvent vaudeville, burlesque or circus into shows for a twenty-first-century audience. A few uniquely gifted, inspired, motivated and lucky performers have been able to expand their acts into evening-length performance pieces. Yet, too often, the public and press have regarded magic, puppetry, ventriloquism, juggling and clowning as entertainments for children, and the performers have found kiddie shows and birthday parties the more likely way to earn their keep.

Whether as street entertainers, fairground re-creators or performance artists, the variety arts and new vaudevillian are heirs to thousands of years of traditional skills, and they restore vitality to old arts by adapting them for their own time and place. They have reinvented the circus, revitalized burlesque and reinterpreted the vaudeville act.

Step right up folks!

Vaudevillians

At its peak, from 1905 to 1925, big-time vaudeville usually presented, in well-appointed theatres, eight or nine acts on a bill that played twice a day—a matinee and an evening show. Thus *two-a-day* became synonymous with big time. The reality for most performers, however, was three, four or more shorter shows per day, playing a range of venues from the functional to the wretched. Performers prayed to make it into the big time to escape the meanness and dulling repetition of small-time vaudeville almost more than for the recognition and the higher salaries.

In the late 1910s, estimates of the number of theatres that played nothing but vaudeville were around 2,000. About 1,200 of these were big-time vaudeville houses, and the rest were the better small-time houses. Conservatively, that meant these 2,000 theatres offered six to nine acts, with a low average of 12 to 15 persons per bill, totaling about 25,000 performers working in big-time and small-time vaudeville during any season in the 1910s.

There was another group of theatres, what some called *small, small time* vaudeville houses. These were as various as dime museums, melodeons, opera houses, ramshackle theatres too run down for more established fare, storefront theatres, saloons, tabernacle tents, converted grange halls, nickelodeons, medicine wagons, showboats, seaside piers and beer halls. Because these operations were often independent ventures, reporting to no higher corporate level of administration and leaving next to nothing in the way of ledgers and other records, it is impossible to estimate with much confidence the number of performers who depended upon the small, small time for their livelihoods or even the true number of such venues that booked vaudeville on a fairly consistent basis in any given season. Estimates of their number vary widely among sources, yet it may be reasonable to assume that there were another 2,000 or so venues that hired vaudeville acts or contracted with barnstorming vaudeville units on a fairly regular basis.

Performers playing the small, small time may have worked daily in combination with silent films or only a few shows on weekends, but they considered themselves vaudevillians. If movies shared the bill, the number of live acts was fewer, so a conservative estimate would average three to five acts per bill. Allowing another low average of seven performers in a four- or five-act bill, the number of performers playing small, small time and fringe vaudeville reached 14,000. Adding big time, small time and the small, small time, there were nearly 40,000 performers playing some form of vaudeville on any given weekend.

There was turnover. Some performers played vaudeville for most of their lives; others left after a few years—for marriage or because of disappointment or death. Also, there were growing opportunities in musical comedy and silent movies that enticed performers to leave vaudeville. Factoring in turnover between 1905 and 1925, the number of performers who played vaudeville during its heyday probably topped 50,000.

Performers used letterhead to advertise their act and correspond with bookers, agents and theatre managers

There were always a few college-educated vaudevillians and a handful that came from successful, even prominent, families, but they were exceptions. The same was true of vaudeville audiences; there were intellectuals and professional people who patronized vaudeville. The vast majority of folks onstage and in the audience, however, were from working-class families, struggling to make their ways in life.

Most African Americans had a parent or grandparent who had been enslaved, and when they looked into an audience of fellow African Americans, whether it was in Winston-Salem, Baton Rouge, Oklahoma City, Chicago or Philadelphia, they knew they were playing to other grandsons and granddaughters of people who had been in bondage.

Both African American and European American vaudevillians sought a role in the American dream, but their art and their view of American society were molded in the land of their fathers and mothers.

For rural youth, black or white, vaudeville offered an escape from dreary landscapes, hardscrabble livelihoods and a future that promised nothing less grim than the toil and care that bent the bodies and etched the faces of their parents. Sometimes, there were no parents, just elders who exploited them.

The prospect for city youth was different only in the particulars. The slums bred disease, domestic violence and crime. A career meant sweatshops and domestic service for the women and backbreaking manual labor for men. The white-collar alternatives paid no better and required of their employees greater literacy, specific training, costlier clothes and more genteel comportment.

The trades, once they were unionized and offered living wages, were usually dominated by a particular ethnicity and closed to others. Show business was more open than society at large. An applicant needed only talent, a thick skin, resilience, ego and the determination not to be daunted by the odds against success.

Often, boys and girls left home at an early age to make a living in show business, with or without parental blessings. They left the countryside and the city ghettoes behind them, unaware of the odds against success and the general distrust and contempt held by many civilians toward those in show business. Soon, they were toughened by rejection; they heard "no" a hundred times for every "yes."

Most vaudevillians were brave and resilient. If they were not, they did not last long in vaudeville. They learned to bear up under assaults on their frayed self-respect. They were canceled by theatre managers, skimmed by agents, beset by lost luggage and missed train connections, forced by circumstance to abide in flea-infested hotel rooms and to eat bad food. They survived surly stagehands, musicians who could neither read music nor fake it, filthy theatres without running water, indifferent audiences, loneliness, and performing when ill or despondent. If a budding performer failed in vaudeville, he changed his name and his act, and he tried again.

Vaudevillians learned to weather the larger bumps as well: a spouse running off with an acrobat, children who rebelled and became stock brokers, or the bank's foreclosure on the little turnip farm or boardinghouse that was to see them through their old age. No one rolled with the punches better than the vaudevillian. Every performance held the possibility of defeat. What did send a vaudevillian into a tailspin was another performer purloining his act.

In many ways, the vaudevillian was parochial, seldom looking beyond his own world. In that, he was a typical American, perhaps typically human. He saw more of the nation than others of his day, but what registered were the length of the jump, the condition of the theatre and his lodging, the receptivity of his audiences and how much

Rare group photo of headliners

Venza Noble & Margie Ogden, Sass & Class

he was paid for the gig. He probably did not know how many churches or schools there were in town, but he knew whether it was "wet" or "dry" and what degree of conviviality it offered to troupers and traveling salesmen.

Performers seemed to be intensely patriotic when national safety, health and prosperity were threatened, yet they increasingly took progressive stands when justice was at stake. If they were in advance of the American public on issues, it was only in regard to those issues to which they were exposed through their professions, such as tolerance and inclusion.

People found their way into vaudeville from different routes. Many began their careers in circus, concert saloons, minstrelsy, burlesque and the legitimate theatre. Some went back and forth between vaudeville and other forms of show business. Circuses and carnivals, which traveled under tents, laid off in the winter, and that schedule allowed specialty acts to play vaudeville. Acrobats, animal acts and cyclists from the circus had skills that could not be faked. They either performed the act successfully or failed. An act with a good reputation was a safe bet for vaudeville. Pantomime clowns, aerial acts, tumblers and animal acts leapt from the circus ring onto the vaudeville stage. Sharpshooters and trick ropers arrived from Wild West shows. Marching bands and showboats boasted brass and percussion instrumentalists able to sight-read or improvise, always desired skills for pit band players.

Some of vaudeville's dancers, singers and cross-talk comedy teams developed their acts in minstrelsy, on showboats and in comic opera. Concert saloons yielded male quartets, boxing exhibitions and slapstick clowns. Pitchmen making a transition from medicine wagons to vaudeville replaced commercials for elixirs with funny stories and jokes. The traveling theatrical troupe created the abbreviated playlet or sketch that, dramatic or comical, became another vaudeville fixture.

Although some performers stayed in vaudeville their entire careers, most took the best work that was offered at the time, be it vaudeville, legitimate theatre, comic opera or, eventually, musical comedy, revues, burlesque, speakeasies, radio, motion pictures or, still later, nightclubs, USO shows and television. No matter the medium, or how a routine or style was adapted for different venues or changing audiences, a vaudeville act was a vaudeville act and proud of it.

Because the vaudevillian was betting on the American dream for himself, he tended to be patriotic, but very few engaged in politics. Vaudevillians were late to the labor movement. They saw themselves as artists and professionals, not workers and wage slaves, although they continually groused about theatre owners, managers and booking agents.

Early white vaudevillians were capable of discrimination if not bigotry. Their first organizations, like the White Rats, admitted neither women nor racial minorities. The White Rats were part labor union (although it pained some performers to think of themselves as laborers) and part fraternal organization.

Vaudevillians as a whole, however, were more representative of the diverse population of the USA than most professions, and, in the main, performers appreciated that personal worth and talent were independent of race, ethnicity or gender. Integration on vaudeville's stages occurred two generations before it happened in baseball or the armed forces of the USA.

A few decades later, while American business and political leaders debated the merits of an ascendant Germany and questioned the threat of an aggressive Nazi-led government, vaudevillians of every race and nationality demonstrated that some Americans were aware of Nazi atrocities, and far earlier than most Americans. *Night of Stars* was a one-night benefit at Yankee Stadium in 1934 for the United Jewish Appeal on be-

The Bizarro Brothers

half of German Jews. The acts included Jack Benny, Milton Berle, Burns & Allen, Cab Calloway, George M. Cohan, Eddie Dowling, Gus Edwards, Stuart Erwin, George Gershwin, Phil Harris, Lou Holtz, Bob Hope, J. Rosamond Johnson, Jerome Kern, the Mills Brothers, Mae Murray, Jack Pearl, Jan Pierce, Molly Picon, Harry Richman, Blanche Ring, Bill Robinson, Rose Marie, Jimmy Savo, Vivienne Segal, Kate Smith, Leopold Stokowski, Ed Sullivan, Arthur Tracy, Rudy Vallee, Paul Whiteman, Walter Winchell and Ed Wynn.

Vaudevillians, including those who had moved on to motion pictures and network radio, turned out in great numbers to sell war bonds during both world wars, to publicize and collect money for the March of Dimes and to entertain American troops on various battlefronts. For many, this was another way to earn a living, although the hazardous conditions were worse than those encountered on the Death Trail or at Keith's Colonial Theatre in New York City. Many headliners, however, donated their services to the USO.

In marriage, the success or failure of vaudevillians was not unrepresentative of America, especially those families whose breadwinner was on the road. Family life allowed a few choices. A spouse could be drafted into the act, but wives had to leave the act for the better part of a season when they were along in their pregnancies, gave birth and took care of their infants. If the wife was the star of the act, the family livelihood was jeopardized. Kids could travel with their parents, at least until school age, and maybe take small parts in the act.

Pearl E. Abbott

Maarya & Rene Gunsett

Many vaudevillians took their spouses, even their entire families into the act. This was good business as well, because there was an incremental increase based upon the number of people in an act. Spouses became part of the act as accompanists, straight men and dance partners. Husbands found something to sing or say to the audience while the performer-wife changed costume. Wives became prop assistants to magicians, cyclists and jugglers, learned to feed straight lines, harmonize in song or pick their way through a soft shoe. Those who shunned the spotlight or had not the disposition took on the roles of managers, handling the negotiations, baggage, promotion and press.

Many a vaudevillian's child slept in a wardrobe or trunk drawer until old enough to toddle onstage in an outfit that was a miniature of dad's or mother's. Until they grew past three feet tall, they did not have to do much more than look cute and as young as possible. By the time the audience began to expect something more, the chances were the kids had developed a talent, if they had been born with any, or they had learned how to manage to stay on key, tap a basic time step in unison with the family or stay slender enough to be tossed around in a comedy or acrobatic act. Some children hated being onstage. Most enjoyed it more than the threat of a formal schoolroom. A few carried the family act and became bigger stars on their own.

Not all married vaudevillians chose to have children. Some, on the road year after year, believed they could not rear children properly absent a fixed abode, a school and a neighborhood.

Vaudeville could be either the most or least attractive option for a family, depending upon its members' temperaments and circumstances. If there were children to raise, the parents often longed for the stability of a home where meals could be cooked, laundry washed and offspring sent to school. For others, the road was an honorable tradition, and each new family member found a place in the act and never had to live among *civilians.*

Vaudeville closed down for nearly three months every summer until theatre owners found effective and economical ways to cool their theatres. For those acts that wished or needed to work, there were bookings at summer resorts. Those whose season had been a success could lay off the summer and spend it with their families.

The single man and woman had little responsibility beyond themselves, their luggage, the props, music charts and drop curtain for their act, unless they were sending money home to the old folks. Loneliness was a curse for some. There were then, as ever, the hazards of drink, drugs and sexually transmitted disease. Alcoholism was not rare, even if drug addiction was.

Male performers were no different from other American males except that, when traveling on the road, opportunity could lead to irresponsibility. On the road, they were assumed to be on the prowl, and the families and authorities in the various towns they played were usually on guard against any attempted liaisons with the eligible maidens.

Single women as well as men in vaudeville might couple up on tour to the extent that individual itineraries permitted, whereas some shied away from entanglements

Larry Weeks

Joe Budd

with other performers on tour for the sake of their privacy and possible complications and recriminations in the future. It was not unusual for young women to be chaperoned on the road by mothers who were eager to safeguard virtue and investment.

On tour for up to 40 weeks a year, young and middle-aged men formed hasty and sometimes careless attachments, either within the profession or with women who, through choice or necessity, offered sex for sale yet often escaped the ministrations of the budding public health movement. Performers who contracted socially transmitted diseases were liable to pass them on to spouses. Even among the last two generations of vaudevillians, those who toured in the 1910s, 1920s and 1930s, there was speculation that so many of them adopted children because they were unable to sire them. At least it was a blessing for those children who found families.

Homosexuals were presumed to have been attracted to vaudeville in numbers proportionate to other art forms and greatly in advance of their percentage in the general population. Queer men and women were no less prone to loneliness, temptation, alcoholism and social disease than their straight counterparts, although opportunities outside metropolitan areas were harder to find and apt to be more dangerous. Most preferred the discretion that was expected of them, and a few could incorporate their mates in the act.

Carl Freed's Harmonica Harlequins

There was never unqualified acceptance but most straight entertainers adopted an attitude more tolerant than found outside show business. An anecdote provides perspective: when Joe Frisco and Jay C. Flippen were on the Friars membership committee, someone nominated a vaudevillian known to be homosexual. Flippen jokingly remarked, "We've already got one fag, why do we need another?" Frisco retorted, "Yeah, but what if he dies?"

Where vaudevillians differed mostly among themselves was in their attitude toward vaudeville. Some loved it; others hated it. Most loved and hated it. A good route and a good rate in decent theatres with appreciative audiences raised the spirits and made all other professions seem tedious. Playing to sparse, indifferent audiences in the middle of winter along the Death Trail for the lowest salary because there was no alternative was a measure of how far one could sink in the world.

Dumb acts appreciated vaudeville for the work it offered when circuses and fairs closed for the winter, but the acrobats, aerialists and balancing acts did not enjoy the loss of status accorded the dumb acts, and they missed the camaraderie of the circus.

There were vaudevillians whose commitment was total, and, at lowest ebb, they would not give up trying to make it. They deprecated in-and-outers who turned to vaudeville only when the legitimate stage, musical comedy or the movies failed them. For others, less enthralled, the years of touring palled as they grew older, and they yearned for a long run on Broadway so that they could live in one place amid family and friends for a few months or even an entire season.

Movies promised a stable home life and little or no traveling. When movies began to sing and dance, some vaudevillians were willing to jettison their act along with the sinking ship of vaudeville for a foothold on dry, sunny California shores. They became dance directors, vocal coaches, assistant directors, talent scouts, dialogue writers and bit players. A few became stars.

Stars were not typical in vaudeville. The headliners who got top billing also got a full season's work at a salary that was handsome for the day, and they probably had the option to appear in revue, musical comedy or drama if they wished. Some became stars of radio and movies. The great majority of vaudevillians were journeyman performers, some more successful than others. Their pay was well below the headliners'. If they worked steadily season after season and saved some money for retirement, they came as close to the American dream as most citizens. Others led hand-to-mouth existences, always hopeful that the big break was just over the horizon.

Most vaudevillians, men, women or children, were torn between alternatives that offered incomplete satisfaction. They chose vaudeville as much to escape their parents' drab and mean existence as to have the chance to perform. Many never wished to go back to a truly *civilian* life, yet they also yearned for love, a mate and, sometimes, children. Most looked forward to a day when they could settle down in one place, with their own beds and linens, and have a kitchen in which to cook meals. Sometimes, they called it quits and took *civilian* jobs, working in real estate and restaurants, running a retail shop or boardinghouse, or trying to make a go of the small farm where they fancied spending retirement. Maybe, after they gave up the stage, they stayed close to show business, working for an agency, a box office, a theatrical hotel or selling ads for a show-business trade paper.

At the end of the day or a career, vaudevillians had little to talk about with bank clerks, grocers or insurance underwriters. The retired troupers needed their own community. Some found fellowship in rural vacation colonies that attracted show folk, such as those

Burdell & Burdell

at Lake Hopatcong in New Jersey, Blaisdell Lake in New Hampshire or Lake Muskegon in Wisconsin. Others lived in residency hotels when they retired. Manhattan and Hollywood were entertainment-industry towns where an old vaudevillian was sure to find others of his kind. Film studios from the 1930s through the 1950s offered work as bit players and extras to those old show folk who needed the money or the action. New York offered occasional radio work until the late 1950s, and voice-overs and on-camera work in commercials provided some income thereafter in Gotham.

Those who had not been happy in vaudeville willingly left it behind to marry and live a *civilian* life, one that gave them, unlike their parents, a fair measure of reward and hope for the future of their children. Gradually, the scrapbooks made their way into attics, and photographs of their children and grandchildren decorated the mantles. Some vaudevillians were still famous long after vaudeville because they were successful in films, radio and television. Others, highly regarded in their time, now merit reconsideration as their reputations are in danger of slipping from the pages of theatrical history. Most, however, were never in the right place at the right time for the big break for which every vaudevillian yearned. Yet, year after year, they filled most of the spots on the vaudeville bill, delivered solid performances and were welcomed by their audiences.

Performers were not the only folks drawing salaries in vaudeville. There were layers of management in all the circuits: Keith-Albee, Orpheum and the rest. At individual theatres, there were the managers, pit bands, stage crews, spotlight operators, ticket sellers and cleanup crews, although at many small houses, the manager was also the

Al Hernandez & Carmelita

Weston Duo

ticket taker and janitor. Thousands more made their living from vaudeville: bookers, agents, songwriters, sketch writers, newspaper critics and the folks who made wigs, costumes, makeup, drop curtains, sold the ads and printed the programmes. Conceivably there may have been as many as 100,000 people drawing all or part of their income from vaudeville and believing themselves to be not just in show business but in vaudeville.

All that most vaudevillians shared in common was the poverty and drudgery of their parents' lives and the struggle to make their own lives more independent and meaningful through a career in show business. Beyond that, each person's experience yielded an individual story. A few were saints, a few were sinners, and most were in between, doing the best they could with little opportunity to rise above circumstance.

ABBOTT & COSTELLO

Bud Abbott

b: (William Alexander Abbott) 2 October 1895, Asbury Park, NJ—d: 24 April 1974, Woodland Hills, CA

Lou Costello

b: (Louis Francis Cristello) 6 March 1906, Paterson, NJ—d: 3 March 1959, Los Angeles, CA

No comedians since Charlie Chaplin in 1915 and Amos 'n' Andy in 1929 made such a splash with the American public as Bud Abbott & Lou Costello when they scored with four smash hit movies, all released in 1941: *Buck Privates, Abbott and Costello in the Navy, Keep 'Em Flying* and *Hold That Ghost.* (The previous year Universal had test-marketed the team in *One Night in the Tropics,* in which a couple of Bud's and Lou's routines were added to enliven a routine musical comedy.) The boys proved their worth in gold, and Universal rushed them into ten motion pictures between 1941 and 1943. Just as Mae West had saved Paramount Pictures from bankruptcy a decade earlier, Abbott & Costello rescued Universal Pictures, Hollywood's oldest (1915) and creakiest studio. The duo propelled Universal into the front ranks for the first time since its early-1930s cycle of horror flicks starring Bela Lugosi and Boris Karloff, directed by James Whale and Tod Browning.

Bud and Lou were an overnight success. Both were in burlesque, booked into the Eltinge Theatre, when they teamed in 1936. There are several reports how this happened. Essentially, Abbott was straight man to comic Harry Evanson when he met Costello. Lou, half of Lyons & Costello, was in the market for a more adept straight man. Bud approached Lou. They teamed, played a number of dates, accommodated themselves to each other and found they both liked it fast and furious. Bud could feed lines with the best of them, and that gave Lou the rhythm and bounce he needed to improvise and embellish his reactions.

Abbott & Costello

In 1937, Mayor Fiorello La Guardia managed to ban burlesque from New York City, so Abbott & Costello went on tour with *Life Begins at Minsky's.* Seeing a dim future in burlesque, the team wangled an engagement at Atlantic City's Steel Pier, where they headlined (as Buddy Abbott and Lew Costello) in *Varieties of 1937,* part of the Steel Pier Modern Minstrels DeLuxe Vaudeville and Big Variety Show. They received a great reception, and their gig was extended to ten weeks. They demonstrated their gratefulness to the Steel Pier management by performing a short engagement there each year thereafter until 1946. Their success did not go unnoticed. Topflight vaudeville bookings followed in Washington, D.C., and in Manhattan, where they set box-office records at Loew's State.

Ted Collins, Kate Smith's manager and partner, saw Abbott & Costello perform and hired them for a guest shot on the *Kate Smith Hour* in 1938. For this radio broadcast they nixed the blue stuff and showed they were funny even without the dirty bits. The team's fast cross talk triggered so much mail to the network that the boys were signed on as *Kate Smith Hour* regulars at $1,250 per show for the better part of two seasons.

Broadway beckoned in 1939, so Bud and Lou joined Bobby Clark, Carmen Miranda and Gower Champion in the hit revue *The Streets of Paris* (what were two guys from Jersey and a Brazilian bombshell doing there?), produced by Olsen & Johnson for the Shuberts. The public loved Bud and Lou; so did the critics, who hailed their vitality. Their material was ancient, the time-tested product of a century of burlesque. Writer John Grant tweaked the old routines to make them seem fresher than they were. Bud dressed in the latest style, as did Lou but to less spiffy effect. An often-overlooked element in Abbott & Costello's popularity is that they looked and talked the way their audience did. Fifty years earlier, accents—Italian, Irish, German, Jewish—were commonplace, and the comedians of the day looked and sounded like first- and second-generation Americans. In Abbott & Costello's time, especially during the Second World War and its aftermath, being American was a matter of pride and "acting American" was synonymous with being modern, relevant and triumphant. Slang was peculiarly American, and Lou said *ain't, guys, dames* and *yeah.* Bud was more careful, but the audience knew good grammar was part of his con.

Even Hollywood, not always impressed by Broadway success, quickly discovered Abbott & Costello. As the USA came to realize that the nation's entry into a war in Europe was inevitable, few looked beyond to imagine how the USA would change in ways great and small. Hollywood studios, having enjoyed a banner year of prestige and profits in 1939 with films like *The Wizard of Oz, Gone with the Wind, Stagecoach, Wuthering Heights, The Women, Mr. Smith Goes to Washington, Ninotchka* and *Goodbye, Mr. Chips,* were largely unaware that the next few years would bring nearly as many changes and new stars as sound technology had done a decade earlier. The profitable overseas market, especially, was closed for the duration of the war. Despite the success of a few Tracy-Hepburn films, screwball farce and sentimental Capra-corn comedy had run their course; public taste in comedy was changing.

The studios sensed that classic comedy needed a fresh infusion. Paramount had lost some its irreverent zest: W. C. Fields was ailing and old, Mae West's material had been bowdlerized by the Production Code, and Leon Errol, the oldest, had taken refuge in short films where he was left alone to work as he wished. The Marx Brothers had moved to Metro-Goldwyn-Mayer (MGM), where they were defanged. The rest of MGM's comedy pictures seemed to be expensive and well-produced bumpkin fare that Universal and Fox did nearly as well and cheaper. Other big comics of the talkie era like Eddie Cantor, Jack Benny and Burns & Allen were hardly young comedy finds, and they had become more important in radio than movies. Charlotte Greenwood and Joe E. Brown slid into character roles, whereas Bert Wheeler looked for any kind of work. Chaplin was off in his own world, taking a decade to make three films. Buster Keaton was writing gags for Red Skelton films, and Harold Lloyd had tired of financing his own films for little return. The Ritz Brothers had failed to catch fire at Fox, and Olsen & Johnson, a minor attraction in Hollywood, became sensational stars on Broadway.

Paramount was banking on Martha Raye and Bob Hope, MGM on Red Skelton, and independent Samuel Goldwyn was hoping Danny Kaye would be his next Eddie Cantor, though Mr. Kaye proved a bit outré for middle America. Late to the auction block, Universal was betting across the board in 1940 by contracting with the Ritz Brothers and Olsen & Johnson as well as Abbott & Costello. The studio figured one team might pan out. The studio stuck the Ritzes with scripts inferior to even the second-rate programmers they had made at Fox, so the Ritz Brothers were the first Universal casualties, dropped in 1943. Olsen & Johnson, preoccupied with one Broadway triumph after another throughout the duration of the war, were cut loose in 1945. Abbott & Costello struck the public's funny bone with wartime comedies and became Universal's workhorses. Only Bob Hope challenged their supremacy as comedians at the box office during the 1940s.

Bud and Lou were prepared for the whirlwind as comedians but not as businessmen. Nothing in their lives prepared them for their new circumstances and the pitfalls they encountered. Bud Abbott was born into a small-time showbiz family. His father worked as an advance man for Ringling Bros. and Barnum & Bailey and later for the Hurtig & Seamon burlesque producers. Bud's mother was a bareback rider who joined her husband behind the scenes in burlesque management. Instead of a newspaper route or setting up pins in the bowling alley like many young Americans, Bud worked as a pitchman for Coney Island amusement park games and carnivals and as a shipman on a freighter. He started in burlesque theatre management as a bookkeeper at Casino (burlesque theatre) in Brooklyn, graduated to managing traveling burlesque shows, and, finally, took charge of production at the National Theatre in Washington, D.C. Whether out of desire or necessity (perhaps a straight man went on a toot), it was at the National that Bud Abbott stepped into his finest role, as a straight man. By then he knew all the hoary routines.

Lou Costello was born into an Irish Italian family, all of them civilians except Lou's older brother Pat, who had changed his surname to Costello and become a bandleader. Lou, who at five feet, four inches was initially dismissed as too short, was an all-around athlete, agile and strong, playing basketball and doing some semipro boxing. He and a buddy hopped a freight train to Hollywood with the dream of making it in motion pictures. Lou settled for day jobs as a carpenter's assistant, movie extra and stuntman. Although good as a stuntman, he recognized that he was going nowhere in the movies, so in 1929 he began working his way back East, at one point talking himself into a job as a third banana, or stooge, at the Lyceum Theatre, a burlesque house in St. Joseph, Missouri. His ability to take pratfalls ensured his success as a burlesque comic, and he worked his way up the banana tree over a seven-year period.

Success was slow in coming for both Lou and Bud before they met. When it hit, they did not think ahead to the days when success would desert them. They neither saved for the rainy days nor paid attention to business. Both were faithful family men, but Bud and his wife, Betty, loved the highlife of racetracks and nightclubs, and Lou, a patriarchal parent and more of a homebody, turned his palatial houses into clubhouses for whoever might show up to sample his hospitality.

Bud Abbott and Lou Costello starred in three dozen feature films in the 16 years between 1940 and 1956, made public appearances at major theatres and broadcast a half-hour weekly radio show (1942 through 1949) on NBC (ABC in 1947), switching to television for the *Colgate Comedy Hour* (1951–53, NBC) and a syndicated series of 52 half-hour situation comedies filmed in 1952 and 1953 that reran for decades on various networks and local stations.

Most great comedians made about a dozen films, and not all were top quality. Certain bits that an audience once looked forward to—sharing the joke—became stale without warning. Not only was Bud's and Lou's material getting older, so were the boys. By the early 1950s, Bud Abbott, in his mid-50s, was bald and paunchy, looking more like a failed racetrack tout than the lean, slick and snide sharpie who had paced the team's cross talk into the big time. Slowed down by epilepsy, which was not made public, Bud no longer moved as quickly as needed in physical comedy, and his verbal setups seemed harsh and rote. Toward the end of their association, there were reports of Bud's drinking on the job, but how much of his diminished delivery was due to drink or to illness is not easily divined.

Lou Costello was one of the great physical comedians of the twentieth century, a member of a select community inhabited by Marie Dressler, Leon Errol, Charlie Chaplin, Harold Lloyd, Buster Keaton, Fanny Brice, Charlotte Greenwood, Bobby Clark and Joan Davis. Even by his mid-40s, Lou was still capable of amazing physical stunts, but he looked tired and puffy, especially under his eyes, and his character, older, seemed to be more stupid and forced than the innocent and lovable dupe that had won fans of all ages. A more serious fault was the diminished rapport between the pair by the mid-1940s. Although Bud was regarded as a great straight man or feed—on a par with George Burns and Moe Howard—their success relied upon Lou's ability to be funny and sympathetic.

Offstage troubles between the two tainted their on-camera relationship. In burlesque, the straight man was king and often received 60% of the team's wages. It began that way for Bud Abbott and Lou Costello, yet when their success prompted Lou to insist on parity, Bud acquiesced. Still, Lou grew increasingly resentful over the years and at one time was restrained by saner heads from renaming the team Costello & Abbott. In real life, Lou called the shots for the team and his brother Pat managed their business. Neither Pat nor Lou was an easy man to please or placate. Life was not made easier for anyone, especially Lou's wife, when their baby boy, momentarily unattended, drowned in the family swimming pool.

Both Bud and Lou spent money lavishly, frivolously and fast, gambling away much of their millions of dollars, investing in foolish and ostentatious projects like nightclubs, supporting hangers-on, giving money to old acquaintances down on their luck and being bilked by associates.

At first, Bud fought back when Lou proclaimed for all to hear that he, Costello, was Abbott's meal ticket. As he got older, Bud muted the combative attitude he once had put up against Lou's insults. Bud simply wanted to avoid strife and keep the money train rolling. Gradually, Abbott's parts in their movies and TV shows were reduced to supporting roles. Lou's business partners and the team's employees were his brother and brothers-in-law. Eventually, Abbott ended up more as another employee of Lou Costello productions than as Lou's partner.

Those of the team's business handlers who were not skimming or padding accounts were incompetent, and their errors left Bud and Lou defenseless against IRS audits. Finally, in 1957, amid a storm of tax troubles and impending bankruptcies, the team split and Lou went solo. Abbott, saddled with several afflictions, was too sick to work much, although he essayed a straight role opposite Lee Marvin on *General Electric Theater.* Lou enjoyed his new opportunities. Almost immediately, he became a special guest star (at $7,500 per television show) on *The Steve Allen Show,* with younger comics Louis Nye, Don Knotts, Tom Poston and Bill Dana. Lou also acquitted himself credibly in two dramatic roles for television (*Wagon Train* and *General Electric Theater*). Then he died. He had worked like a demon for 20 years. He was tired, worn out. Lou's health had been suspect since he had been sidelined for six months with rheumatic fever in 1943 (the same year his baby boy died). Two heart attacks within five days killed him early in 1959.

After Lou's death, Bud Abbott played a few nightclub dates with a Lou Costello look-alike, Candy Candido. Much later, in 1967, when the Hanna-Barbera animation studio created a 200-show cartoon series with Bud and Lou characters, Bud got work voicing his own character. He and wife Betty lived in reduced but adequate circumstances until a series of strokes and falls and the onset of cancer led to his death in 1974. Betty, his wife of 55 years, had to sell their house to meet yet another tax bill.

The team's 1941 and 1942 films were consistently good films; at least five of them were among their best: *Buck Privates, In the Navy* (both with the Andrews Sisters), *Hold That Ghost* (with Joan Davis), *Keep 'Em Flying* (with Martha Raye in dual roles) and *Who Done It?* (with Mary Wickes). The rest of the Abbott & Costello movies were hit or miss, the most rewarding among them being, arguably, *The Time of Their Lives* (1946), *Buck Privates Come Home* (1947), *Abbott & Costello Meet Frankenstein* (1948), *Abbott & Costello Meet the Invisible Man* (1951) and *Abbott & Costello Meet the Mummy* (1955). Ten superior feature-film comedies constitute a record few, if any, film comedians surpassed.

ABORN CIRCUIT OF POLITE VAUDEVILLE HOUSES

A tiny chain of Pennsylvania theatres in Scranton, Wilkes-Barre, Harrisburg, Reading and Erie.

ACKERMAN & HARRIS CIRCUIT

The Ackerman & Harris Circuit was known as the Death Trail because their theatres were so widely scattered throughout the Northwest and Mountain States that an act could barely break even because of the long jumps between engagements. Acts were billed for split weeks at the various theatres along the A&H circuit, so they only got half a week's pay. Worse, it could take an act the rest of the week to reach the next theatre.

The list of the theatres attributed to this circuit is a composite of lists culled from several sources, including *Julius Cahn's Official Theatrical Guide* (1910, 1916), *The Clipper Red Book and Date Book* (1910), Jack B. Shea's *Official Vaudeville Guide* (1928) and Herbert Lloyd's *Vaudeville Trails thru the West* (1919). Theatre affiliations with circuits, however, changed over time. A Proctor theatre later may have become a Keith-Albee house; a Pantages' or a Loew's theatre may have been a former Sullivan & Considine theatre; and independent circuits were often taken over by larger enterprises, like Keith-Albee. Theatres were bought and sold, and names were changed entirely or simply altered to reflect their new owners.

Some theatres were specifically designed as opera houses or vaudeville theatres, but generally theatres were able to accommodate several types of show. A theatre could host vaudeville for ten years and then change to exhibiting only motion pictures. A former burlesque house might be converted to vaudeville.

The following list of theatres is not a snapshot in time. It includes theatres that functioned at various times over a period of nearly 20 years, thus there will be duplications with other circuits.

Vancouver	British Columbia	Columbia Theatre
Bakersfield	California	Hippodrome Theatre
Chico	California	Majestic Theatre
Fresno	California	Hippodrome Theatre
Los Angeles	California	Clune Theatre
Los Angeles	California	Hippodrome Theatre
Oakland	California	Hippodrome Theatre
Sacramento	California	Hippodrome Theatre
San Diego	California	Hippodrome Theatre
San Francisco	California	Casino Theatre
San Francisco	California	Hippodrome Theatre
San Francisco	California	Princess Theatre
San Jose	California	Hippodrome Theatre
Stockton	California	Hippodrome Theatre
Denver	Colorado	Tabor Grand
Fort Collins	Colorado	Empress Theatre
Greeley	Colorado	Sterling Theatre
La Junta	Colorado	Rourke Theatre
Pueblo	Colorado	Princess Theatre
Rock Springs	Colorado	Grand Theatre
Trinidad	Colorado	Trinidad Theatre
Wallace	Idaho	Grand Theatre
Anaconda	Montana	Blue Bird Theatre
Anaconda	Montana	Margaret Theatre
Billings	Montana	Babcock Theatre

Butte	Montana	Peoples Hippodrome Theatre
Great Falls	Montana	Palace Theatre
Livingston	Montana	Strand Theatre
Fargo	North Dakota	Grand Theatre
Jamestown	North Dakota	Opera House
Portland	Oregon	Hippodrome Theatre
Aberdeen	South Dakota	Orpheum Theatre
Ogden	Utah	Ogden Theatre
Provo	Utah	Columbia Theatre
Salt Lake City	Utah	Salt Lake City Theatre
Seattle	Washington	Palace Hippodrome
Spokane	Washington	Hippodrome Theatre
Tacoma	Washington	Hippodrome Theatre
Walla Walla	Washington	Liberty Theatre
Yakima	Washington	Empire Theatre
Cheyenne	Wyoming	Princess Theatre

ACROBATS

In vaudeville, bookers, managers, agents and other performers tended to use the term *acrobat* as a catch-all for trapeze acts, balancing acts, tumblers, Risley acts, teeterboard, and wire walkers and ropewalkers. Some tossed in jugglers, contortionists, strong men (and women), along with all types of acts that required physical strength, skill and dexterity. More narrowly, an acrobatic act is one in which the performers leap, tumble or balance—with or without apparatus such as poles, trapezes, and tight or slack ropes.

From firsthand experience, Joe E. Brown understood the old joke in vaudeville: "Good evening, ladies and gentlemen—and acrobats." Although acrobats were among the royalty of the circus, they did not received similar respect in vaudeville. They were classified as *dumb acts*, and consigned to the difficult opening or closing spots on a vaudeville bill.

A surfeit of acrobats in vaudeville did not help their prestige. *Dime a dozen* could have been coined to describe their dilemma. What little cachet attended acrobatics was usually reserved for European, Asian or Latin American acts; like all things imported, it was presumed they were better than the homegrown variety. The domestic acrobatic act had little to recommend it other than talent and skill.

Many acrobats were foreign born; they did not speak English or spoke it poorly and haltingly, and this added to their isolation within the vaudeville fraternity. Often a family act, theirs was a tradition born in Europe, the Near East and Pacific Asia where a single family act might last for generations, the elders teaching their spouses and their youngsters. Acrobats surpassed

Rice & Prevost, "The Greatest of All Acrobatic Acts"

many acting families (the Websters and Barrymores, for instance) in the number of generations they could trace as a family act.

Rope dancers and stilt walkers were frequently among the variety entertainments in Colonial American theatres and were either introduced as *divertissements* between the acts of a play or as part of a variety bill of songs, dancing, comedy sketches and recitations. During the nineteenth century, with the influx of many European acrobatic acts, the overall quality improved as native acts were challenged by acts from Europe. After 1859, thrills more than technique attracted attention. That year in Paris, Jules Léotard invented the first flying trapeze known in the Western world. He also designed the gym tights, subsequently named for him, that have become the ubiquitous wear of the dance class. Léotard built an act around his trapeze and played it for a decade throughout Europe until his death. Also in 1859, Charles Blondin walked a tightrope across Niagara Falls. It caused a sensation, and he repeated the feat on several occasions, adding various novelties such as carrying a man and later a stove on which he cooked an omelet.

Acrobats found another home as circuses moved toward greater variety in their acts and beyond the eques-

Tubby & Spatz, "Excentric Acrobatic" [*sic*]

trian exhibitions that had been the modern circus' *raison d'être* since the late eighteenth century. Rope dancers and tumblers were welcomed by circuses and their audiences. By the third decade of the nineteenth century in the USA, traveling circuses began to use tents for the exhibitions and performances, but it was not until late in the nineteenth century that circus tents grew large and high enough to accommodate aerialists.

In the 1890s, Arabian and Japanese acrobats touring the world appeared for the first time in the USA, where they made a great impression upon their counterparts there as well as winning audiences. In addition to expanding the horizons of American acrobats, the Arab and Japanese acrobats attracted the rapt attention of percussive dancers who were looking to add spatial movement to heel and toe beats, thus creating a style of vernacular dance called acrobatic or eccentric.

The trick with all feats of strength and agility was to make the move appear deft and graceful. It took years of practice not only to perfect the mechanics of an acrobatic feat but to disguise the discomfort with graceful nonchalance. Acrobats had less time to socialize because they, like dancers, jugglers, contortionists and other specialty acts, needed to practice constantly. Of necessity, the acrobatic troupe became self-contained, closed off from other acts.

An Arab Pyramid

An individual could create an act alone, performing a series of back bends, belly rolls, somersaults, rollovers, handsprings, cartwheels, tinsicas (handsprings into cartwheels), and head and hand balancing. Typically, however, there were at least two people, a thrower and a tumbler (or performer), and partners often alternated between roles. In aerial acts, the anchor was known as the catcher and the airborne equivalent of a tumbler was called a flier. When there were three or more acrobats in an act, one (usually the least heavy, least muscular and perhaps the youngest) was the performer and the other three were throwers. The formula varied depending upon the requirements of the act. Acts that teamed between two and six individuals—seldom more—multiplied the options, devising a dazzling array of rapid combinations of moves among the partners—tossing, catching and balancing each other in an overlapping series of tricks.

Acrobatic remains a broad term and covers a variety of performance. Most practitioners disliked being lumped into the broad category of *acrobat* and preferred to be known by their specialty: Risley act, contortionist, equilibrist, barrel jumper, club swinger or tumbler. Beyond these critical distinctions were those of style. Acrobats could surround themselves with a glamorous aura or cavort comically. Some incorporated dance moves, and it was a moot decision whether to peg them as acrobatic dance acts or as dancing acrobats. Others wrapped their gymnastics in tomfoolery, and it was a tossup whether to call them acrobats or clowns.

Whatever the particulars of their acts, acrobats invariably required the full stage in which to work. This meant that any act following them would have to perform in one or two while the full stage was reset for a later large act such as a sketch or a flash act.

THE ACT

One thing above all else was important to the vaudevillian: the act. A vaudevillian's act was his essence, the product of his personality, talent and skill. Any threat to his act was a threat to his livelihood, his sense of self, his reason for living. Take away his spouse and, although he would be gravely hurt, time would ease his sorrow. Deserted by his children, he could have more. Steal his act or forbid him to perform it, you have cut out his heart. A vaudevillian played his act for years, adding, changing and refining—or not. The act represented everything he was and knew, polished into a few minutes of stage time: his magnum opus, his gift back to the gods.

An act was a distillation of a performer's best material into a near-perfect performance piece. Every minute had been purged of dead or extraneous moments. Comic lines were honed into sharp arrows aimed at the audience's funny bone; any change in tone or a reordering of words and the shaft missed its mark. Every musical phrase, note and word of a song was weighed to best evoke the audience's individual memories and harmonize them into shared experience. Each dance step was perfected to marshal the audience's spirit so that it glided, jumped, beat, turned and soared with joy. The smallest tricks were carefully practiced until stage wizardry trumped logic and made each witness believe what they saw. Balls tossed in the air modeled an ordered universe. Creatures of wood, deftly manipulated and invested with the performer's voice, took on life. Human bodies took acrobatic flight because their balance and strength made light of weight and gravity. Clowns had the grace to fall, the wit to stumble and the generosity to make an audience feel good about themselves.

Years of practice and performance were trimmed into a tight act. Whether it was 8 minutes, 22 minutes or in between, the ideal vaudeville act was proof that human performance can be perfect and that we, the audience, shared in its celebration. The essence of the act was the wedding of performance to personality. The material was born of the performers' own gifts and skills, shaped by their particular sound, movement, appearance and traits. The act could have been a duo, trio or quartet but seldom more because the force of personality and individual talent could never be subordinated to an ensemble performance, which is much admired in the stage play, opera, ballet or symphony.

A great act could prompt its audience to deep and exquisite feelings as well as the more usual responses of laughter, longing, gaiety, sentiment or sympathy. Its genius was that it did so without requiring its audience to understand the classical elements of harmony, rhythm, construction or the relation of movement to space.

Vaudeville was primarily the stuff of popular art. The performer was never inferior to the material as sometimes is true with serious music, concert dance, opera, art song, or great stage tragedies or comedies. Sometimes serious artists developed an act. Reaching beyond aficionados to audiences more attuned to entertainment than art, Anna Pavlova, Sarah Bernhardt and Mary Garden, among many serious artists, took bravura moments from their stage triumphs and presented them to enthralled witnesses who would never have sat for the entire artwork.

The concerto, the ballet, the aria, the heroic or tragic role continually comes alive through interpretations by a succession of great musicians, dancers, singers and actors, but the vaudeville act barely existed separate from its performing creator. Except in memory or recording, it did not long endure.

ADAGIO ACT

Equal parts dancing, acrobatic moves, balancing and lifting, this type of act was often performed to music by one man (the lifter or understander) and one woman who assumed graceful postures as she was lifted, tossed, dipped, spread and carried. Adagio acts also combined two male-female couples or formed a trio of two men and one woman. Usually the act was elegantly dressed or done in costume (Harlequin and Columbine or a couple from a Renaissance court ball). Sometimes the act was performed as comedy following either of two formulas: the same balletic moves done in an ungainly fashion or inept attempts at minor acrobatics that left the woman flying across the stage to land in a heap.

One distant variant was the Apache Dance, purported to have originated in the slums of Paris and Marseilles. Short slit skits and blouses sliding off one shoulder were standard issue for the women, and men usually sported a beret and a kerchief knotted around the neck. Both entered with cigarettes dangling from their lips. The relationship was, frankly, one of prostitute and pimp. The man quickly got down to the basics of the act, grabbing the woman by the hair, shaking her and tossing her to the floor. At some point, turnabout was supposed to count as fair play, and the woman slapped her pimp a few times, tripped him and kicked him. Too often the dancers concluded their humiliating battle in a passionate embrace that suggested a sadomasochistic fling was just the thing to restore the zing in lovemaking.

ADELAIDE & HUGHES

ca. 1885–1950

Regarded by many dancers as vaudeville's top class dance act, Adelaide Dickey and John Hughes toured the big time on the Keith and Orpheum circuits. E. F. Albee praised them as "a model act." They were the type he liked, classy and no arguments about billing and salary; they earned everyone's respect.

Adelaide & Hughes performed short dance numbers grounded in ballet and ballroom dance and anointed with blue-chip titles such as "Divertissements," "Classic of an Age," "Birth of the Dance" and "The Garden of the World." They not only pleased Albee, they were one of the most popular dance acts to play the Palace during the 1910s and were among the select few acts of any type to be held over for multiple weeks.

They appeared in revues as well as vaudeville. Among their revues were: *Up and Down Broadway* (1910) with Emma Carus, Eddie Foy Sr., Lenore Ulric, Irving Berlin and Oscar Shaw; *The Passing Show of 1912* with Willie & Eugene Howard, Trixie Friganza, Charlotte Greenwood, Harry Fox and Ernest Hare; *Ned Wayburn's Town Topics* (1915) with Will Rogers, Trixie Friganza, Blossom Seeley, Clifton Webb and Lew Hearn; and a musical comedy, *Monte Cristo, Jr.* (1919).

Adelaide teamed with Hughes in 1911. By 1913, they had choice spots on big-time bills. Ms. Dickey was the more balletically inclined partner, solidly grounded in European technique, and in interviews she spoke seriously, even loftily at times, about dance in America. Adelaide & Hughes, however, were attuned to vaudeville audiences. Their dances were varied, brief and often novel. Adelaide often included a toe dance specialty. The act was finely rehearsed and well dressed, their changes in costumes adding interest and novelty. Each dance suggested a story, and the music varied from semiclassical to waltzes and trots to ragtime. Their dancing led to the kind that surfaced on Broadway after 1943 when Agnes DeMille revolutionized theatre choreography for a generation. Perhaps Mata & Hari later came closest in style to Adelaide & Hughes, offering characterizations and a specific, nonabstract situation.

AD LIB

Adapted from the musical notation, *ad libitum,* that permits a phrase to be played with a degree of interpretation and timing, the term was abbreviated and used to refer to unscripted dialogue by an actor or performer. An ad lib can be an invention by the actors or performers to cover a mishap on stage or an improvisation—primarily verbal—such as a comedian might make to a comment from the audience or to top a prepared gag with a spontaneous one. In practice, an ad lib can also be stretched to cover stage business, as when a comedian does something physically extemporaneous or extends a bit of business with a partner or a prop by inventing new sight gags on the spot.

ADVANCE AGENT

Preparing the way for a show was more a function than a specifically defined job. In the days before booking agents arranged multiple engagements in advance and telephones became the communication medium of choice, bookings were arranged by post. The company manager wrote ahead to various theatre managers and tried to arrange bookings. The touring melodramas and variety show units usually had a few engagements booked in advance that committed the troupe to appear at particular places on prearranged dates. These dates were obtained because the company had performed at the same venue in previous seasons and had not displeased the theatre management. As best they could, company managers arranged dates a season in advance to provide relative security in an otherwise uncertain future of bookings and cancellations. As troupes toured, they tried to fill in their schedule with more hastily arranged dates. If they did not find theatres to play, the actors did not get paid and nobody ate.

The advance agent preceded a traveling troupe or a collection of variety acts, town by town, handling preshow publicity, hotel accommodations and the conveyance of company, costumes, props and scenery to and from theatres. Those were the bare bones of the job. Advance agents needed to be entrepreneurial, audacious and inventive. As often as not, a major portion of their time and energy was given to resolving, or at least patching over, misunderstandings and the failure of others to do their jobs. For this, the agent needed diplomacy, bluff, good humor, resilience, complimentary tickets to the show and, if he could squeeze it out of the company manager, a bit of cash to grease less obliging palms.

With names changed to protect the craven, a humorous report first printed in 1905 encapsulated the advance agent's chores through a series of pithy reports to the company manager. Though they were fictional in their particulars, they shone with the truth of a career spent, like John the Baptist, preparing the way.

> The name of the transfer man here is Shorthaul. He can not move your stuff until afternoon, as he serves a milk route in the morning. He will haul the baggage for 20 cents per piece, round trip, or two dollars per load. His milk wagon only holds two trunks, so you had better pay him by the piece.
>
> Hotels: The Commercial, $1, single or double. The Central, $1 straight, if the whole company occupy one room. Merchants, 80 cents, double if you were downstairs. The American, 75 cents, straight; no heat in rooms but a large stove pipe runs through the hall. You had better stop at the Merchants as the Opera House Manager is the landlord's brother-in-law. The table is fierce, but the dining room girls are very kind. The red-haired one is all right.
>
> Newspapers: The Morning Serpent, The Evening Stinger and the Daily Hiss. I could not do anything with the papers, as they are all sore on the [theatre] manager. You will have to buy the soap boxes you use for Juliet's balcony, as none of the stores will lend the house [theatre] anything.
>
> You can get the Town Band to play here if you give them "comps" for themselves and their families. There are 42 men in the band. The leader works in Underwaites Grocery. You can see him when you go after the soap boxes.
>
> The manager here would not lift the paper [pay for handbills, posters], so I billed the town [put up posters] with "pick-ups" and faked the dates with a marking brush. Your name is spelled wrong on all of them. I will have to leave an order for my hotel bill, also a small bar bill at Finnegan's; the day bar tender is a Prince. I could not take out my washing; it is at the Silver Star Laundry. I wish you would get it and keep it for me. It is 40 cents. Don't try to wear the under clothes. They are too small for you and too tender to take the strain.
>
> I needed an overcoat badly, so I got one at Solomon's Clothing Store, and he agreed to take it out in advertising. He has a large sign painted to hang on Juliet's balcony; it is six feet long and four feet wide. He also wants it hung on the wall in the garden scene of Faust, and if you don't do it you will have to pay for the coat ($6). Work him up strong and I think you can get a pair of shoes out of it.
>
> Pemmerton's Players showed here last week. They are all here yet. They must be up against it for their property man told me that he had to swap pants with the dummy they use in their show. I think they are waiting for you to land and will try to make a touch as I gave them a lot of hot air about turning them away [sold-out performances] all season.
>
> There is no mail here for you except a postcard canceling your week in Puke City, so I will have to dig up another village for that week.
>
> I found a lot of Wild West paper in the bill room here, so if the man in Puckerbush won't lift the C.O.D. I will bill the town with Wild West paper and you can put on "The Boy Scout" to match the lithographs.
>
> The bill trunk went to pieces here. I tried to rope it up but it looked like a bundle of lath. I will take a bunch of pick-ups under my arm to the next town, provided I get out of here. I must have $3.80 or I can't move. The landlord here is a cold mark, so don't bring any trunks to the hotel. I have arranged for you to plant them at Finnegan's. Try to get acquainted with some people on the train and walk up the street with them when you land. It will swell the size of the show. Pick up people with good hand baggage to make a front. If the man here gets that there are only four people with the troupe, he won't let you open. I told him you had 30 people and made a street parade, so you will have to square it somehow.

AERIAL ACTS

Aerial acts include trapeze work, ropes and strap acts, any form of acrobatics that can be performed above the ground in midair. Few vaudeville stages could accommodate aerial acts. Some circus acts tried to scale their presentations to fit the limits of height, width and depth of most stages, but only a few theatres had dimensions that allowed aerialists to perform at their best—the Hippodrome was one. Besides, whether people admitted it to themselves or not, peril was as much an attraction as skill, and the higher a performer was, the more perilous it appeared. The audience cheered what were rightly described as death-defying stunts.

When a proscenium was only 20 feet high, the aerial act was robbed of much of its drama. In truth, that limitation only reduced the amount of damage an aerialist could sustain. A fall from 20 feet might not kill a person as surely as a fall from twice or thrice the height, but limited stage height allowed the performer less time to straighten out after a somersault, and an injury could end a career. Even the safety net, four feet off the ground, could maim a performer. A net would break a fall, but its mesh of rough knots could scrape off one's skin and, if an acrobat landed at the wrong angle, break bones, tear muscles and damage nerves.

Probably no vaudeville or circus act depended upon the reliability and goodwill of stagehands more than aerial acts. Their equipment had to be set up in advance of the show, secured to the grid over the stage and tested for safety. Tipping stagehands was part of any aerial act's budget.

Usually, in the circus, an aerial act gave a matinee and an evening performance. In small-time vaudeville, there was often a schedule of four or more shows each day. Injuries never had time to heal, and simple sprains or chafed wrists and ankles could develop into more serious and chronic problems.

The trapeze was introduced in 1859 by a 20-year-old Frenchman named Jules Léotard when he performed with his father at Cirque Napoleon in Paris. Two trapezes moved back and forth between two high platforms. As Léotard swung from one to the other platform, his father sent the second trapeze toward Léotard, who grabbed it in midair. This established the function of the catcher, a partner or team member who caught the trapeze or the flier. As there were no nets at the time capable of withstanding the impact of a falling body, large mattresses were placed on the ground below. He also designed and introduced the skintight garment that bears his name, the leotard, worn by dancers as well as acrobats. Léotard died a star, age 28, not from a mishap but of smallpox.

Those who followed built upon the fundamentals, adding somersaults, adapting balletic postures, hanging by their teeth by biting onto a spiraling grip, and trying every gyration imaginable. Related to the trapeze were the flying rings from which aerialists spun and twisted like gymnasts. Among old-timers, it was held that aerialists, if they performed long enough, got killed.

Among the aerial acts that successfully adapted to vaudeville were Aerial Buds, Alcide Capitaine, C-H-A-R-M-I-O-N, Dainty Marie, Flying Martins, the Jungman Family, Harry Thriller and the Flying Wallendas. Those who saw them all considered Lillian Leitzel peerless.

AFRICAN AMERICANS IN VAUDEVILLE

After the Civil War ended, Jim Crow law reigned in the South. Reports of greater freedom and better economic prospects in the lawless West and the industrial North stimulated large black migrations from the South. White resentment sprung up in the path of the northern migration, and the Ku Klux Klan (KKK), founded in 1865 at Polaski, Tennessee, took root along the Mississippi and Ohio River valleys into the northern states of Indiana, Illinois, Ohio and Pennsylvania. In Chicago, which became the most important black city in the USA until the rise of Harlem, race riots greeted African Americans. By 1900, new arrivals had nearly doubled the black populations of Chicago and New York.

Vaudeville was never an easy life, despite the rosy remembrances of its top stars decades after they had landed on Broadway or in films, radio and television. For them the struggle turned into success. For many others it was a grueling grind of small-time theatres, cheap boardinghouses and tiring hours of travel. The performers had no security beyond their current contracts, and they dwelled in an isolation that ill prepared them for life after the death of Lady Vaudeville.

The experience of the African American vaudevillian who performed for black audiences paralleled in part that of the European Americans who played for white audiences. Most entertainers were struggling to rise above impoverished and restricted backgrounds. They began their careers in dirty firetraps passing as theatres, where audiences were rough and rude, and the managers frequently more so. The black entertainer also had to

The Payton Trio

work for a lot less money and live within the pervading and pernicious world of racism and second-class rights.

More than a few had the grit and persistence to achieve stardom among their own and then the courage to make the leap into mainstream, white vaudeville. The main appeal that mainstream vaudeville held for African American performers was the benefit of higher salaries and better theatres. Most black entertainers preferred to play for their own people or had developed acts that were too culturally specific to make the transition to white time, so they continued in vaudeville, playing for the Theatre Owners' Booking Association (TOBA or TOBY time) or the northeast circuit of black theatres and filled in with beer-hall gigs and civilian work between vaudeville engagements.

The rise of vaudeville during the first three decades of the twentieth century coincided with the revival of the KKK, which grew particularly strong in the Old South, where most of the black theatres were located. Although the old KKK itself had become moribund by the end of the nineteenth century, other groups, such as the Knights of the White Camellia and the White Caps, took up the KKK message of hate and continued its policy of intimidation, torture and killing. The success of other racist groups and the film *Birth of a Nation* led to a new KKK that was formed in 1915.

Radcliffe & Rogers

A few years and a continent away, the First World War introduced Negro troops to European racial tolerance, and the black soldiers returned home with expectations of economic and political justice from a grateful nation. Instead of equality and gratitude, or even tolerance, violence against Negroes soared. Mob burnings and lynchings made headlines, yet the federal government did little. Persecution drove more Negroes northward and westward.

Newly mechanized industry in the Midwest offered opportunities to some Negroes who had defended a nation that did not defend them. For good and ill, the Far West was part of the USA in little more than name. The administration of law in the West was no less capricious than it had been in the South, but a rugged individualist, black or white, had some measure of opportunity to carve out a life and defend himself.

Once those African Americans who came to the North were segregated in Chicago, Pittsburgh, Philadelphia, Baltimore and New York in sufficient numbers to secure relative safety, they were left to live in a semblance of benign neglect, as long as they stayed on their side of town. Most African Americans, however, continued to live in the South, and most did not own the land they farmed or the businesses that sold them food, clothing or entertainment.

In 1909, TOBA was formed to centralize booking for theatres that played black acts for black audiences. By the early 1920s, there were about 100 theatres—most owned by whites—playing black vaudeville in the South, Southwest and Border States. In general, it was not a pleasant experience for black performers. In most places, the atmosphere was hostile. African Americans were treated routinely as less than full-fledged citizens, and some local theatre owners took advantage of a prevailing attitude among the citizenry and local law enforcement to cheat and demean the Negro acts they hired.

Lodgings for black performers were no better. They were restricted to certain places in certain parts of town, usually those areas where bedbugs and other undesirables thrived. It was take it or leave it, and often as not the theatre owner got a kickback. The audiences were rough and ready. If the audiences liked an act, they loved the act, and their stomping and shouting approval sometimes threatened to bring down the shabby house. When they did not like performers, they showed their contempt by yelling and throwing things at them. In the event the act bored them, they simply opened up their bags and ate sandwiches and fruit or walked up and down the aisles to visit with friends and neighbors.

Even under the best of conditions, nonheadliners received no travel expenses, and the long jumps between bookings required ingenuity and a lid on self-esteem.

Grabbing a week or two with a passing carnival or medicine show paid little, and the performers slept in the hay, but the carnival provided pocket money and was better than dishwashing or sharecropping. A traveling carnival or medicine show brought performers closer to their next gig, and it was certainly safer than roaming by foot or car through a countryside where performers were sometimes ambushed, robbed and killed by the local KKK. Headliners were paid enough that they could afford a new car and fine clothes, but there were numerous stories of Southern white law officers stopping and threatening black headliners because the police refused to believe any black person could pay for fine clothes and cars honestly.

Although TOBA had become synonymous with black vaudeville, there were black vaudevillians and theatres that catered to black audiences long before TOBA, and there were theatres for Negro audiences that remained independent of TOBA. Theatres for African Americans, affiliated with TOBY time or not, were spread out across most of the country, southward from Chicago to St. Louis, New Orleans and Galveston, Texas; eastward to Macon and Atlanta, Georgia, and Norfolk, Virginia; northward to Baltimore, Philadelphia, New York City and Boston; and westward from Philadelphia to Pittsburgh, Cleveland and Chicago.

Within rough perimeters that included a few states west of the Mississippi River and most of those states east of it, there were at least 100 towns and cities of all sizes that had theatres that played black acts for mostly black audiences. All the larger cities and some smaller ones had more than one black theatre. Fewer than a half were allied with TOBA, even at its peak during the late 1920s. Added to those theatres were probably an equal number of night spots, large and small, that booked black talent.

Whether run by whites or blacks, by gangsters, crooked businessmen or upstanding citizens, the prevailing ethic was to keep as much of the profit as possible and pay as little as the performers and stagehands would accept.

This held true for white performers in mainstream vaudeville. For every Eva Tanguay, Elsie Janis, Eddie Foy or Sophie Tucker making a couple of thousand dollars every week they wished to work, there were hundreds of acts collecting $75 to $125 a week and paying for their own transportation, drayage and hotels. And there were thousands who laid off more than they worked and would have thought that ten weeks at $125 each were gifts from the gods.

There were some differences in performance between white and black vaudeville. On white time, acts were almost invariably individual units: a solo performer, a duo, a quartet or even a flash act with a chorus line. Whether a single or a group, each act generally was booked on its own and traveled on its own—at least east of the Mississippi River. The act was hired to perform for, say, 8, 10 or 17 minutes in one spot during each show. In the old days, some theatres insisted on the entire bill participating in an afterpiece at the end of the show, but in other respects, a white act remained an entity unto itself.

While there were tab shows (abbreviated musical revues or musical comedies) that toured white vaudeville and played for 40 to 50 minutes, the custom was much more usual in black vaudeville. Black Patti's Troubadours, the Smart Set, the Whitman Sisters and other similar units engaged dancers, singers, comics and musicians for the season and created self-contained units. A package of acts was able to perform from 30 minutes to two-and-a-half-hour shows, as needed, and the company or unit sported from 6 or 8 to as many as 50–75 people. As the majority of black theatres were located in the South, it was a lot safer and cheaper for vaudeville acts to travel in units or as packaged shows.

Some producers such as the Whitman Sisters were sufficiently financed, smartly organized and so popular that they were able to choose TOBA routes or book their own shows as it suited them. In many instances, when they could not be accommodated on their own terms by large theatres, they played in tents, as did the revival shows and circuses, or they hired a nearby hall and ran their shows in opposition to the established theatre.

When the giants of vaudeville management periodically battled with insurgent unions or with each other, there sometimes occurred a shortage of experienced and talented acts for the white circuits. White bookers then scouted black entertainment venues for acts suitable for mainstream vaudeville. After one of those various crises passed, most of the African American acts went back to black vaudeville and revues, but a few remained draws with white audiences, and some became high-priced stars in constant demand by big-time vaudeville, Broadway revues and musicals.

Broadway's call was a renewed and growing demand. For a decade, beginning in the late 1890s, shows written by African Americans and starring Bob Cole & J. Rosamond Johnson, Ernest Hogan, or Bert Williams & George Walker, among others, had astonished white producers as those early Negro shows won considerable success with white audiences as well as black. The phenomenon faded with the deaths of Cole, Hogan, Walker and other great black stars of the period and as white producers replicated much of the blacks' rhythm, energy, pace and flippancy as they had the wits to copy.

The black musical again came into great favor when, in the early 1920s, Eubie Blake & Noble Sissle partnered with Flournoy Miller & Aubrey Lyles and created *Shuffle Along* (1921). Quickly there were white producers and a few blacks trying to duplicate *Shuffle Along*'s formula and success on Broadway and in nightclub floor shows. For black performers, a run on Broadway or in a Harlem floor show meant living in one place for a few weeks or, if lucky, a few months.

By the early 1930s, all of the USA was in the throes of the Great Depression. Because radio was free, blacks as well as whites listened to it if they could afford to buy a receiver. Gradually, Negroes accepted white radio favorites as their own.

The chief black theatres in the five big cities of New York, Chicago, Baltimore, Philadelphia and Washington, D.C., survived, as did the nightclub hot spots of Harlem and Chicago's South Side, but many others in cities like Boston, Newark and Detroit were converted to second run movie theatres or striptease burlesque houses by their owners.

Vaudeville as an institution, black or white, was officially dead before 1940, despite pockets of survival like the Apollo Theater in Harlem and the USO tours. For more than 30 years, over the course of three wars, vaudevillians toured battle zones in Europe and Asia. During the Second World War, entertainment was still segregated. Black acts entertained black troops. The U.S. armed services were integrated by the time of the Korean War, and by then some of the USO units featured black as well as white performers.

During the Vietnam War, the U.S. armed forces were officially integrated, but many of the draftees were African Americans who lacked the deferments that more affluent young men obtained to go to college. The USO units often included a black act or two, but black performers were not hired for the USO in numbers proportionate to the black soldiers serving in Southeast Asia.

After the Second World War and the Korean Conflict, racial attitudes in the USA began to change markedly, publicly and seemingly in advance of political, religious and business leaders.

Before Rosa Parks, Martin Luther King, James Meredith, Medgar Evers, Thurgood Marshall, Ralph Abernathy and Bayard Rustin spotlighted through acts of civil disobedience and well-reasoned arguments that it was impossible to be at once equal yet separated from mainstream life, a new generation of African American performers, actors and sport stars had won admiration from much of white America.

In 1947, Jackie Robinson became the first Negro to play major league baseball in 50 years (there were several African American players in the early nineteenth century leagues), and other black ball players followed Robinson into big league ball. By the late 1940s and early 1950s, Sammy Davis, Jr., Ella Fitzgerald, Nat "King" Cole, Sarah Vaughan, Ruby Dee, Sidney Poitier, Eartha Kitt, Pearl Bailey and Sam Cooke had entered mainstream show business—the record industry, posh nightclubs, network television and big studio motion pictures—and they, too, had found success with white audiences while resisting stereotypes. If only because whites outnumbered blacks ten to one, a majority of their fans were white.

Not all African American entertainers were part of the expanding diversity in show business, rhythm & blues, gospel music and comedy material were still geared to the Negro audience, although there had always been a segment of the white public that were fans of Negro music from blues to jazz and enjoyed black comedians. At the same time that opportunities were opening in mainstream show business, the Negro drama movement revived, soul music was on the horizon and hip hop and break dancing came along in the 1970s.

It was those niche entertainments that continued to infuse mainstream entertainment with vitality and innovation. As soon as black America riffed on a performing art form, it was adopted, adapted and co-opted into mainstream show business.

AFTERPIECE

At the end of a program, after individual acts had performed, the acts on the bill might participate in a planned, if largely unrehearsed, finale or afterpiece. This could be a musical number, a dramatic sketch or a comedy sketch. The order of the day was to improvise lines, lyrics and movements and keep the whole thing moving at a smart pace.

The afterpiece faded in vaudeville as it matured. It survived in burlesque where every comedian, straight man and talking woman was assumed to know at least the outlines of hundreds of sketches or bits, to be performed at a day's notice. The afterpiece flourished in revue and early musical comedy as ensemble production numbers and was briefly revived at some theatres, especially Keith-Albee operations like the Palace in Manhattan, in the last years of two-a-day of vaudeville to regain audiences.

AGENTS & TALENT AGENCIES

In the beginning there was word of mouth and the U.S. Postal Service. Word of mouth had limited circulation, unless it was scandalous, so actors and performers had to write to theatre owners to get bookings. It was wise to include reviews if the act had any, and only if they were good. It was more effective if the performer got testimonials from other theatre managers confirming how much the audience liked his act and how much business it brought to the box office.

Generally, troupes and individuals tried to line up as much of the season's bookings as they could at the end of one season and the beginning of the next, hoping to receive enough responses and encouragement to plan key segments of a tour. Later, they would try to plug in the holes in their schedules. Before the twentieth century, repertory stock companies or any full-length show on tour would map out a route of cities and towns where they thought they could find audiences. They employed an advance agent or a road agent to precede them into the towns ahead to make arrangements for a theatre, for housing and laundry and, most important, to plaster the town with handbills announcing the imminent arrival of an incomparable company that would amaze and delight. To the degree that their reputation was good and known, the troupers knew they could play certain theatres that they had played in previous tours.

If the company had no contract to perform in a particular town on their route, the road agent tried to find a suitable theatre (or tent, saloon, grange hall or church) and negotiate with the owner or manager. The best deal for the troupe was to have the theatre owner hire the company outright, but often the deal came down to playing for a percentage of the box office or paying the manager rent for the hall.

Few vaudeville acts had the budget to hire advance men. If the act was large enough and there was time between engagements, one member of the act might leave town after the final evening performance so as to line up business in the next town.

By the time vaudeville began to emerge in the late 1870s and early 1880s, there were more than 50 telegraph companies operating in the USA. The telegraph was relatively expensive, however, and an unsubtle form of communication better suited to bulletins than negotiation. At the same time, 85 cities and towns in the USA had some form of local telephone service. By 1895, American Telephone & Telegraph had merged more than 100 local phone systems, yet the telephone had not become the preferred instrument of commerce, nor was long-distance service dependable or universal. A few years made a difference, and the telephone and telegraph became central to the business of booking acts.

Nobody planned to be an agent. They had no prescribed course of study. People drifted into work as an agent from some other corner of show business. Knowing theatre managers and being trusted by them was key. Someone handling advertising for a trade paper got to know many theatre managers. They might ask him if he had heard anything about a certain act. The same was true of a well-regarded former entertainer. Each informal recommendation that ended with good results was another step along the road to becoming an agent.

The agent was paid by the performers, and, ethically, an agent should have represented the person who paid him. The need to put a deal together, however, trumped other considerations. A successful agent had many clients to sell to a particular buyer, and he was motivated to retain that buyer—and all other buyers—as a steady customer. Steady customers kept the agent in business and most of his clients working. Some clients got sold, some got sacrificed. The performer really was the product, not the client. By the time E. F. Albee set up the United Booking Office in 1900, the agents' real clients were no secret.

Behind every great star is a great agent, and great agents may be rarer than great stars. For every William Morris or Abe Lastfogel who nurtured their clients, there were dozens of *ten percenters* who were determined to make money even if the acts they represented did not. The least competent were either ineffective or lazy. The worst were those who used their talents against their clients. Some approached a rising act and offered to get them twice as much money. Once signed, the agent sold the act for three times what the act was getting, and the agent and booker split the difference. The best agents worked tirelessly for their clients, shielded them from demoralizing comments and were savvy enough to make suggestions that improved their clients' acts.

As vaudeville declined in appeal and the pall of the Great Depression spread wider, topflight agents turned to films and network radio, taking their star clients with them. For the rest, the bookings got meaner, and agents had less to offer in vaudeville.

WILL AHERN

b: 9 October 1896, Bridgeport, CT—
d: 16 May 1983, Burbank, CA

A young teen when he began entertaining at amateur nights, Will Ahern recalled that his first professional vaudeville date was in 1913 at the Lyric Theatre in Bridgeport, Connecticut, doing tricks with a lariat. Inspired by Will Rogers, he combined some comedy patter with the rope spinning. Ahern also worked dude ranches and circuses, where he displayed roping tricks. His next stint was in uniform during the First World War, during which he entertained fellow servicemen and performed at war bond rallies. After his discharge in 1918, Will and another demobilized sailor, Blitz Cooper, joined a burlesque unit that toured a full season.

Cooper returned to civilian life in 1919, and Ahern went solo until later that year, when he met Gladys Reese, a dancer. He brought her into his act to add dancing and a bit of glamour. They also married. The act by this time was a mixture of Western-style rope spinning, with Gladys dancing inside the opened lasso, and both dueting in a song-and-dance routine. Many of their bookings were in the central and western USA on Gus Sun, Interstate, Pantages, Western Vaudeville and Orpheum time.

Max Gordon, a man of many interests who represented vaudevillians and produced vaudeville acts and full-length shows, brought Will & Gladys Ahern east. The Aherns got roles in a 1927 musical comedy, *Sidewalks of New York,* which featured a great cast: Ray

Dooley, Eddie Dowling, Smith & Dale, Barney Fagan, Ruby Keeler, Jim Thornton and Bob Hope. Will's brother, Dennis, took Will's place with Gladys in the couple's act when Will went alone into Ed Wynn's 1930 show, *Simple Simon.* Songs were by Rodgers & Hart, the script was co-penned by Guy Bolton and Ed Wynn, and Florenz Ziegfeld was listed as producer. It was a fine show, but even with Ed Wynn, Ruth Etting (singing "Ten Cents a Dance") and Harriet Hoctor, it ran little more than three months. A Gordon show, *Making Mary* (1931), closed before it even made it to Broadway, but the Aherns had faith, and Gordon managed the Aherns for the next quarter of a century. Under his guidance, they played the Palace Theatre several times, toured Europe (the Aherns learned their patter in French, Spanish, Italian and German) and played the Moss Empire circuit in the United Kingdom. All told, they spent seven years abroad.

From the mid-1930s onward, Will traveled to Hollywood for film chores. He appeared in at least one short, *The Whole Show* (1934), and several feature-length movies, including *One Year Later* (1933); *Picture Brides* (1934), for which he prepared the script; *A Torch Tango* (1934); and *Git Along, Little Dogies* (1937).

The USO shows of the Second World War continued the Aherns' careers after the collapse of vaudeville. When they retired from the stage, they opened a dance and performance school in Los Angeles.

E. F. ALBEE

b: (Edward Franklin Albee) 8 October 1857, Machias, ME—d: 11 March 1930, Palm Beach, FL

The most feared man in vaudeville and among the least liked, E. F. Albee is seldom credited with doing any good in vaudeville. He, more than any other, had the power to make decisions that changed the way the business of vaudeville was conducted and, once convinced of a strategy to enhance the dominance and profitability of the vaudeville empire he ruled, did not hesitate to exercise that power. Like most leaders, he made improvements, caused some misery and could not see beyond his own time and experience. Still, he remained extraordinarily successful and powerful for 35 years.

On the plus side, he brought organization to vaudeville by taking an idea voiced by someone else (Pat Shea, a theatre owner from Springfield, Massachusetts)—that of a centralized booking agency—and turning it into actuality in the form of the United Booking Office. Centralized booking did a lot to standardize the process and remove inefficiency, error and confusion. It also limited negotiation by acts and their agents and went a long way toward standardized salaries. In Al-

E. F. Albee, 1923

bee's hands, the United Booking Office also became an instrument of monopoly and retribution.

Albee built glorious entertainment palaces that were as much of an attraction as the acts. He designed a ventilation system and made more efficient the old air-cooling system of blowing air over large blocks of ice into ducts beneath the seats, a system that was widely adopted in private and public buildings elsewhere, including those built for the United States House of Representatives and Senate.

Paintings, statuary and carpets created an aura of luxury for his audiences. Ordinary folks had never seen such splendor, and they appreciated being admitted into a world of polished marble, vaulted ceilings, murals, plush drapery, gold and jewel-like ornamentation, grand staircases, elegant lounges, state-of-the-art plumbing and a high-tea atmosphere presided over by courteous managers, ushers and attendants who made the customers feel privileged. If there was too much ornamentation, gilt and red plush for those with refined tastes, the less sophisticated were awed by the rococo splendor of a big-time Keith Theatre. Though Albee demonstrated contempt for performers, he provided them with unmatched amenities in his two-a-day houses: clean and attractive dressing rooms, private toilets and bathing facilities.

Albee treated performers scornfully and dismissively. He sabotaged their efforts to bargain collectively and secure fair treatment. His strong hand in the creation of the Vaudeville Managers Association and the United Booking Office consolidated the power of the owners and managers and reduced to petitioner status all but the most popular drawing cards or the most demonstrably loyal among vaudevillians. Those acts that crossed him were blacklisted. B. F. Keith was petty. E. F. Albee was vindictive, and there is scant evidence of forgiveness for those acts whose behavior Albee deemed fractious, disloyal or transgressive.

It is noteworthy that a number of the more prominent leaders in the vaudeville industry had begun their careers in circus sideshows: P. T. Barnum, George Batcheller, B. F. Keith and E. F. Albee among them. In his circus days, Albee was known as Ned, and he began as a 19-year-old roustabout, working for Barnum in 1876. A strong and willing worker, Albee won grudging respect but no affection from other roustabouts. He was not cut from the same cloth. Most circus laborers were rough and unlettered men. According to some sources, including Charles and Louise Samuels, Albee's forebears had fought in the American Revolution (and not with the Tories, though the Albees were relatively prosperous), and his father owned a shipyard in Machiasport. In his entire life, Albee neither suffered fools nor concealed his disdain for most of the species.

E. F. Albee, 1894

He lacked the talent to make friends and did not seem to miss it. His intimates were few, and as he grew older they tended to be outside show business.

Gaffers (circus managers) found Albee literate, a good talker, businesslike and shrewd, and he found increasing success as he traveled with several circuses: the Great London, Van Amburgh, Sells Bros. and Doris. He first leased a concession that allowed him to sell tickets outside the fairgrounds at an increased price. There were always some people who could be persuaded to buy tickets early to avoid the supposed rush, and, by arrangement, Ned Albee pocketed the premium. When a gaffer noticed that Albee was a notch above most of his less-sober pitchmen, Ned Albee advanced to the role of a fixer, expert at staving off creditors, sheriffs and cheated customers. The gaffer may have been either John Doris or even George Batcheller, and it was probably under the Batcheller & Doris combined or individual tented shows that Keith met Albee. If Batcheller was Albee's former employer, then he may have agreed readily to bring in Albee to put things right at the Keith and Batcheller dime museum in Boston.

Although Keith was ten years older than Albee, Keith must have respected and trusted the younger man, for when Keith got into difficulties with his Boston dime museums, it was to Albee he turned for advice and some financial backing. The understanding and trust the two men shared were based also on Albee's loyalty to Keith.

Although Keith remained a small-time operator at heart, Albee had the instincts, skills and nerve of an entrepreneur. Abe Erlanger, the power and the money behind the Theatrical Trust, or Syndicate, was Albee's model. What Erlanger did to the legitimate theatre, Albee intended to do to vaudeville: create a monopoly. Erlanger pulled together the leading theatrical powers of the day and formed the Syndicate, got control through leases or contracts of several hundred of the principal playhouses in the major cities across the USA, and then dictated to play producers the terms for renting these theatres—take it or leave it. Erlanger provided Albee with the template.

Keith, for all of his sideshow canniness, was not up to managing an empire, and by the time his organization had expanded into Providence, Philadelphia and Manhattan, Keith had ceded primacy to Albee, who, in 1886, became general manager of the Keith operations and chief administrator of the United Booking Office in 1891. By 1906, Albee was the unquestioned boss and presided over their growing empire from his roosts in Manhattan and Boston. Keith, who remained in Boston, exercised nominal power, but all his decisions had to be ratified by Albee. When there were any disagreements about matters, Albee was able to persuade Keith.

By the mid-1890s, Albee had established Keith theatres in other cities, importantly in Providence, Philadelphia and New York City (the Union Square Theatre), but his power did not reside in real estate. It was in his control of the managers' associations and the central booking office. By the early 1920s, about 1,400 theatres coast to coast booked through the Keith Exchange (the successor to the United Booking Organization).

Keith had become somewhat of a figurehead by 1900. Albee made the decisions, and Keith took the bows. After the death of Keith and his son, there no longer was a figurehead or the fiction of an heir apparent. In 1914, Albee took over the Boston Theatre, a 3,000-seat sometime opera house that first opened on 11 September 1854 at 537–541 Washington Street, and renamed it B. F. Keith's Boston Theatre.

It was closed on 4 October 1925 and demolished the next March, and was eventually replaced by the magnificent B. F. Keith Memorial Theatre, which, according to Boston theatre historian Fred McLennan, was built by Harvard University and owned by them until about 1940. It is a puzzle why Albee needed or sought such financing when his organization already owned the land.

The B. F. Keith Memorial Theatre opened on 29 October 1928 at 537–541 Washington Street, cheek by jowl with the old Bijou and B. F. Keith Theatres, but the Keith Memorial came too late in the waning days of big-time vaudeville to succeed with a straight vaudeville policy, so it quickly became a presentation house, pairing five or so acts of vaudeville or a big swing band concert with a major motion picture.

On 5 October 1925, a few years before erecting the Keith Memorial, Albee had opened B. F. Keith's New Boston Theatre on the opposite side of Washington Street at number 816. It was situated on the corner of Essex Street, diagonally across from Boylston Hall, the site of the former Vaudeville Saloon, where the first known vaudeville season in America had taken place 65 years earlier in 1840. In its last incarnation, Keith's New Boston was converted in 1951–52 to show the short-lived Cinerama phenomenon. Renamed the Keith Boston, it closed in 1970 and then reopened for a period as the Essex I and II. It was demolished to make space for a large office building with street-front shops, but part of the stage and housing still exist in the belly of the new building.

Like Keith, E. F. Albee had his limits. His interest was in the design of theatres and not in the acts of the performers. Although a vision of what was possible to achieve had grown with him as he moved from the sidelines of the circus to the throne of a vaudeville empire, his vision was blunted by a defensive posture and reactionary impulses. Instead of looking to the future, he concentrated on threats to Keith-Albee hegemony and failed to recognize the significance of the development and appeal of sound- and sight-recording technology. Although it was clear to Marcus Loew, Joe Schenck, William Fox, Adolph Zukor, William Morris and many other vaudeville entrepreneurs that big-time vaudeville could not survive the challenges of phonograph recordings, silent pictures, free network radio, inexpensive talking pictures and cheaper-than-vaudeville burlesque, Albee failed to see the writing on the wall. Perhaps he thought he had settled everything in 1927 when Keith-Albee merged with the Orpheum circuit into Keith-Albee-Orpheum (K-A-O).

Albee did not even protect his own interests. He generously rewarded his aide, J. J. Murdock, with an option to purchase Keith-Albee-Orpheum stock. Murdock exercised that option and then quietly sold his shares to Joseph P. Kennedy. Later the same year that Albee opened the B. F. Keith Memorial, the writing was no longer on the wall but emblazoned in flashing electric lights on marquees across the USA: "All Talking, All Singing, All Dancing" motion pictures.

Perhaps Albee, who had turned 70 in 1927, finally perceived that the years ahead were unpromising for vaudeville, or maybe he was feeling old, tired, sick and ready to retire when, in 1928, he sold the 200,000 shares of his Keith-Albee-Orpheum stock. Joseph P. Kennedy, a man every bit as hard as Albee, purchased the stock. Albee probably did not know Kennedy already had a block of stock purchased from Murdock. With a substantial percentage of ownership of K-A-O, Kennedy arranged a partnership with David Sarnoff to make sound motion pictures, to distribute them through the Keith-Albee-Orpheum circuit, and to convert its theatres into RKO movie houses. Once the deal was set, Kennedy, mustering his considerable contempt for those whom he vanquished, marched into Albee's office and told him, "You're through, Ed. Get out." Whether that was true or not, it is what some of Albee's employees gleefully reported. Edward Franklin Albee died within two years of being forced out of the Keith-Albee-Orpheum enterprise, but not before witnessing a final indignity: his name, alone, was removed from the K-A-O successor organization, RKO Corp.

Later, RKO had its problems. Its film studio, redundantly named RKO (Radio-Keith-Orpheum) Radio Pictures, had some success as a movie studio but never made it into the top tier of major studios like Paramount, Warner Brothers or MGM.

Movie exhibitor Ben Sack acquired the RKO Keith Memorial Theatre in the 1950s and dubbed it Sack's Savoy Theatre. Later, the grand old theatre enjoyed a decade or so as an opera house, but, despite an impressive effort, Sarah Caldwell's opera seasons left too many days and nights dark, and there was insufficient income to purchase, repair and maintain the 2,800-seat theatre with its many lobbies and chambers. In 2003, Clear Channel Communications acquired the property to serve as its flagship in Boston and restored the Keith Memorial to its former splendor.

Albee left millions to charity, but not to charities founded to help vaudevillians. He never understood them, believed himself ill-used by them and seldom went to the theatre. It is odd that E. F. Albee rose to the topmost perch of a profession in which he had little interest in its primary product: entertainment.

See B. F. Keith, Keith-Albee Circuit, Keith Vaudeville Exchange, Joseph P. Kennedy, National Vaudeville Artists, United Booking Office, Vaudeville Managers Association, Vaudeville Managers Protective Association, Western Managers' Vaudeville Association and White Rats

HERBERT ALBINI

b: (Abraham Laski) 1859, Poland— d: 1913, Chicago, IL

In 1891, Abraham Laski arrived in the USA by way of England. By the time he was appearing on Sullivan Considine time, he had adopted Herbert Albini as his stage name. Most of his early work was prestidigitation, the manipulation of decks of cards and smaller objects such as coins. Albini was noted for his effectiveness as a close-up performer.

By 1911, he was billing himself as Albini the Great, and had developed an act that filled the second half of a vaudeville bill with daringly flamboyant and expensive grand illusions, including the execution of a military prisoner and the levitation, disappearance and materialization of lovely young ladies as orchestrated by Mephistopheles (Albini). He died on tour two years later at age 53.

CHARLES T. ALDRICH

b: 1869, Cleveland, OH— d: 1955, New Jersey

The man many contemporaries regarded as America's greatest quick-change performer, Charles T. Aldrich, began his career as a tramp comedian who was chased by a dancing red handkerchief all around the stage. He tried to outrun it. Of course it was a magician's trick, and one end of the red cloth was attached to a long black wire that crossed the stage. Assistants hidden behind the wings on both sides of the stage yanked, raised and lowered the wire so that the handkerchief appeared to dance up and down or travel sideways in any direction, chasing Aldrich, who tried to escape his tormentor. Finally, he turned and shot it with a pistol and buried the red handkerchief on stage under a pile of sawdust. As soon as he stepped away, the handkerchief arose from its grave, shook itself free of sawdust and resumed chasing Aldrich, driving him off stage. Stage trickery was always part of his act, and Aldrich developed a quick-change routine and acted out characterizations. His signal contribution to the craft was a bit in which he stood, clad only in tights, atop a pedestal while a cloth cylinder began to descend. The moment the bottom of the cylinder reached the top of the pedestal, a pulley was released and the cloth cylinder crumpled to the stage revealing Aldrich bearded, completely garbed anew in a peddler's costume and holding a tray.

At one point in his early vaudeville career, when Ching Ling Foo was creating a stir with his conjuring act, Aldrich did an impersonation dressed in a Chinese robe and wearing a detachable queue, or pigtail. Ching was famous for producing a huge bowl of water from beneath his gown. Aldrich produced a barrel.

As early as 1901, Aldrich began his acting career. He joined the vaudeville team Dave Montgomery & Fred Stone in *The Girl from Up There* (1901). Aldrich played (and sang) the leading man role. The show transferred to London. Aldrich and Stone became close friends; Aldrich was Stone's best man in 1904.

He married actor Gloria Gordon (1884–1962) around 1904, and their son became the famous character actor of radio and television, Gale Gordon (1905–95), best remembered as Osgood Conklin, the principal of Our Miss Brooks' high school, Lucille Ball's boss and Dennis the Menace's next-door neighbor, Mr. Wilson.

Before the start of the First World War, Aldrich toured Europe. He performed on the bill of the first Royal Command Variety Performance at the Palace Theatre, London, in 1912. When he returned to the United States, Aldrich once more appeared in a Montgomery & Stone show, *Chin Chin* (1914–15) and portrayed a magician, a role that encouraged him to perform a number of tricks. Aldrich played in *Jack O'Lantern* (1917), his third show with Fred Stone; Dave Montgomery had died before the show got under way. *Everything* (1918) was a spectacular extravaganza typical of the Hippodrome. Music was by John Phillips Sousa and Irving Berlin, and the large cast included Houdini, opera singer Belle Story and comedian De Wolf Hopper.

Charles T. Aldrich returned to vaudeville in the closing days of the big time. By then he was at least 60 years old, and two shows a day may have suited him better than a full-length musical comedy every night. He revived his handkerchief dance, but instead of being chased by one red cloth, Aldrich produced a small platoon of dancing beards of varying colors, shapes and sizes. He orchestrated the beards in a dance. This time they not only jumped up and down, they paraded in formation and marched off the stage in time with the music.

Aldrich made one silent movie and one talkie; neither did a thing to advance his career or reputation. His wife, Gloria Gordon, made a few silent pictures and several talkies, but it was not until late in her career that she landed her most important role, Mrs. O'Reilly, the eccentric landlady on *My Friend Irma.* The show starred Marie Wilson as the dumbest of beautiful but dumb blondes and ran on radio from 1947 through 1954 and on television from 1952 through 1954. Two movies were made, *My Friend Irma* (1949) and *My Friend Irma Goes West* (1950). The sequel movie was the only Irma show in which Gloria Gordon did not appear; otherwise, she stayed with the project all through radio, television and the movies. Gloria Gordon Aldrich died in Hollywood. Charles T. Aldrich retired to rural New Jersey where he died at age 86.

HADJI ALI

b: ca. 1892, Egypt—d: 5 November 1937, Wolverhampton, England

Hadji Ali elevated regurgitation from a marketplace and sideshow demonstration into a full-blown vaudeville act, complete with costumed assistants, special effects and an exotic setting. His act was filmed, and present-day audiences can view a segment of his act in the KCTS-produced documentary *Vaudeville,* which has been broadcast many times since its initial airing in November 1997 on PBS' *American Masters* series.

He began his act with small feats, such as swallowing then spitting up quantities of watermelon seeds and nuts, building to a startling finish. A model of a castle was mounted on a pedestal placed about head high. Inside was a small flame. First he drank a gallon of water, then a quart of kerosene. The percussionist in the pit band performed a drumroll, and Hadji Ali emitted a stream of kerosene that ignited the castle. He followed the kerosene with a longer stream of water that doused the conflagration.

A large, barrel-chested and bearded man, Hadji Ali was an imposing figure in his Arab costume. Although he was a hit with many audiences, such as those on the Pantages circuit and at fairs, he was pegged as a freak act and never played the really big time. Because he billed himself as The Egyptian Enigma, an alliteration easy to remember, it is speculated that his birthplace was Egypt. His name was likely one adopted, or at least simplified for the stage, and he may have been born in Syria or any of a dozen Middle Eastern states. That he retired to England suggested that he was relatively comfortable with the English language and customs, and his homeland may have been a British colony. He died while touring his act in British variety houses.

Hadji Ali, 1927

ALLARDT CIRCUIT

The Allardt was a small-time circuit with vaudeville houses in the Midwest and Canada.

FRED ALLEN

b: (John Florence Sullivan) 31 May 1894, Boston, MA—d: 17 March 1956, New York, NY

Curdled-faced comedian Fred Allen had a caustic mind and a nasal delivery and was most at home where he could find cosmopolitan audiences to regale with his stream-of-consciousness monologues. He found his first admiring audiences in big-time, big-city vaudeville and, later, smart revues. Radio brought Fred Allen to a larger, hospitable public. When radio was supplanted by televi-

Fred Allen

sion, book publishers welcomed his work. A fair proportion of Fred's listeners proved to be readers as well.

A cynical Don Quixote whose weapons were words, Fred took on the pompous, the petty and the smug. His particular targets were the bureaucrats who infested the private as well as public sectors; in Fred's view, traffic on the road to ruin was directed by network vice presidents. Allen was a forefather of the acerbic stand-up comics and TV talk-show hosts who, two generations later, continued Allen's habit of biting hands that fed him. His love of learning, which endeared him to critics and commentators more than to the general public, was fostered in the stacks of the Boston Public Library, where he worked in his teens, yet he proved to be more an iconoclast than an intellectual.

He was 18 years old before he started in show business, and it took Allen some time before he found his groove in vaudeville. Thinking he had the makings of an act with a few gags and some rudimentary juggling, Fred matriculated into vaudeville as a so-called professional amateur in the Sunday-evening contests so loved by neighborhood vaudeville managers and their audiences.

Young Fred turned professional in 1914, auditioning several stage names before he settled on Freddy James. At first his gags were off the whiz-bang joke book shelf, but as he rode the ups and downs of small-time vaudeville, his distinctive viewpoint emerged. Irreverent from the start, he billed himself as the World's Worst Juggler and did nothing on stage to refute the claim.

Wearing a too-small suit and hat, he built his act along the lines of a nut comic, but consistency was his problem. Perhaps Emerson anticipated Fred's act when he wrote that "a foolish consistency is the hobgoblin of little minds," for although Fred's flight of lunacy might enchant one audience, it could alienate another. He was guided—sometimes misguided—by the impulse to ad lib.

Fred delighted in poking fun at the conventions of vaudeville (and he would treat radio, movies and television in a like manner). He developed a phony ventriloquist act; his dummy gradually fell apart in front of the audience. Another season, he interrupted his scripted act to sit on the edge of the stage and read aloud his reviews, including the bad ones, much to his audiences' amusement. For a finish to his act, Fred ridiculed those vaudevillians whose acts climaxed in hokey applause-getting devices; Fred ended his low-key turn with a fevered burst of music and the projection on a drop screen of patriotic images of Washington, Lincoln and the flag.

Over the course of six years of apprenticeship, Fred Allen played small-time Northeast circuits like Loews, Proctor and Poli, made it to the West Coast on Pantages time, toured Australia and played the big-time Keith circuit. He tried several partners on stage: Bert Yorke and, later, Portland Hoffa, who became his wife. Both were incidental to the act, for the viewpoint was always Fred's.

By 1919 he won a booking at the Palace that affirmed his headliner status in vaudeville and won the attention of revue producers. His first success in revue was the Shuberts' *The Passing Show of 1919,* in which Fred shared honors with James Barton, Blanche Ring and the Avon Comedy Four. Vaudeville dates alternated with other revues: *Vogues of 1924* with Odette Myrtil and Jimmy Savo, *The Little Show* (1929) with Libby Holman and Clifton Webb, and *Three's a Crowd* (1930) again with Webb and Holman plus ballerina Tamara Geva and Fred's wife, Portland Hoffa. When new technology, the economy and changing public taste undermined vaudeville and closed most Broadway shows before they recouped costs, Fred was not among the sentimental mourners. He did, however, need to find another way to earn his living. He loved living in Manhattan, so broadcasting every week from a Midtown studio presented a very attractive alternative to the constant travel of vaudeville. A period of relative inactivity gave Fred the time to study radio. Fred understood better than Ed Wynn or Eddie Cantor, two early and successful entries in the radio sweepstakes, that radio was an aural medium that depended upon the success of the program's words and sound effects to suggest in the listeners' minds a vivid mental picture of the situation. Fred came to radio with an advantage; with very few exceptions during his long career, Fred Allen wrote his own material. Allen believed he did not need to rely on others to direct his transformation from the stage to the radio studio; however, as the networks and sponsors controlled the formats of his shows, conflict arose.

The Linit Bath Club Revue debuted in 1932 on the CBS network. Although it gave Allen the chance to learn what worked on radio, it did not play to Fred's strength as a storyteller. The next season he switched to NBC, where he stayed for a decade broadcasting under various formats and show titles: *The Salad Bowl Revue* (1933); *The Sal Hepatica Revue* (1933–34), which turned into *The Hour of Smiles* (1934–35); and *Town Hall Tonight* (1935–39), which became the *Fred Allen Show* in 1940. In 1940, Fred switched the *Fred Allen Show* to CBS but returned with the show to NBC in 1945.

His radio shows of the 1940s represent his zenith as a comedian. It was in 1940 that Fred Allen created the Mighty Allen Art Players, memorialized by Johnny Carson a generation later. Fred also launched his fake feud with Jack Benny in 1940: "Jack Benny couldn't ad lib a belch at a Hungarian banquet." Over a period of months, the barbs flew back and forth between the two shows and boosted both Benny's and Allen's radio ratings. Benny once got the upper hand when he retorted, "You wouldn't dare say that if my writers were here!" Fred also had developed a real feud with network censors who tried to blue-line anything they did not understand, which was most of the script, according to Fred.

Inspired by newspaper columnist O. O. McIntyre, in 1942 Fred created a new segment, Allen's Alley, to put some of his vexations into other mouths. Senator Bloat (portrayed by Jack Smart), John Doe (played by John Brown), Socrates Mulligan (enacted by Charles Cantor), Falstaff Openshaw (voiced by Alan Reed) and other transients were among Fred's earliest tenants. Longer leases were given to four diverse favorites whom Fred would visit to seek their opinions on topics of the day.

On government: Southern Senator Beauregard Claghorn (played by Kenny Delmar), a cornpone blowhard ("Stand aside, son! Don't hold me up! Ah'm busier than a flute player's upper lip during a rendition of William Tell") declared that the "Army's throwin' money around like the taxpayers was the enemy." On network programming: taciturn New Englander Titus Moody (portrayed by Parker Fennelly) opined that radio was just "furniture that talks." When Fred complimented Mrs. Pansy Nussbaum (acted by Minerva Pious), a Jewish matron, on her dress, she replied, "It is mine cocktail dress. We are only living once. N'est ce pas? Why not enjoining? Life is a deep breath. You are exhaling, it is gone." Peter Donald as Ajax Cassidy incurred the ire of some Irish listeners when, asked about used car dealers, he claimed that the station wagon was the only vehicle for him, "Every Saturday night when they take me to the station, they send the wagon." The *Fred Allen Show* lasted until 1949, when television proved once again that a picture is worth a thousand words, at least to sponsors. By this time, the burden of both writing and performing a weekly show plus battling the small-minded network executives that he constantly lampooned had sent Fred's blood pressure higher than his ratings.

Fred Allen was not an intellectual comic; few if any comedians who have achieved his level of popularity could be. Yet he had a disciplined mind that enjoyed playing with language and turning images into words. Typical was his remark that a town was so small, a four-way cold tablet had nowhere to go. Less topical and more worthy of him were these observations: "The last time I saw [Frank] Fay he was walking down Lovers' Lane holding his own hand." "Hollywood was started many years ago by a writer who went West with a cliché." "If all the politicians in the world were laid end to end they would still be lying." "Hollywood is a place where a person works all his life to become recognized, then wears dark glasses so nobody will know who he is."

Although Fred was no stranger to sketch comedy, as he proved in revues, he was essentially a humorist whose tools were words and whose act could play nearly as well on the page as on the stage. In his later years, Allen secured his reputation with two memoirs: *Treadmill to Oblivion* (1954) and *Much Ado about Me* (1956), the last of which was published posthumously, as was a volume of *Fred Allen's Letters* (1965).

Fred made six films, three of which remain clever and amusing to present-day audiences: *Thanks a Million* (1935), with Fred as an oppressive agent in a snappy spoof of show business and politics; *Love Thy Neighbor* (1940), built around Fred's mock feud with radio rival Jack Benny; and *It's in the Bag* (1945), which brought the denizens of Allen's Alley to the screen, offered the added bonuses of Binnie Barnes, Jack Benny and Robert Benchley in the cast, and was truly a Fred Allen vehicle. A fourth film, *Sally, Irene and Mary* (1938), was likeable and notable for a cast that included Alice Faye, Joan Davis, Jimmy Durante and Gypsy Rose Lee.

Without any real success, Fred attempted various formats on television, including variety, quiz and panel shows. He slipped from a rotating star host (for a half season in 1950) of NBC's *Colgate Comedy Hour* to an emcee (1951–52) of *Chesterfield Sound Off Time* to quizmaster (1951–53) for NBC's *Judge for Yourself* (1953–54) and, finally, to a panelist (1954–56) on *What's My Line* on CBS.

Some critics held that his humor was too cerebral for TV, but it may be closer to the truth to admit that Allen, looking drawn and dyspeptic—he had a serious heart condition—did not make an attractive appearance. When television production shifted to Los Angeles, the hub of show business, the publishing business was still centered in New York. So Fred Allen remained, in body and spirit, resolutely in Manhattan, writing books and letters until, two-and-a-half months before his 62nd birthday, he suffered a fatal heart attack while strolling the streets of his beloved Manhattan. He remains much admired.

ALLEY-OOP

Humorous slang term *alley-oop* refers to an acrobatic act. Probably first used in European circuses, it translates as "all up" (probably from the French *allez,* the imperative of "to go," and *oop,* a lower-caste English rendition of "up").

ALPHONSE

b: (Alphonse Berg) ca. 1895—d: 1955

The curtains opened upon Alphonse, elegantly dressed in a tuxedo, and two or three slender living mannequins clothed in tights. In a briskly paced act, armed only with various bolts of fabric, Alphonse created a series of high-fashion gowns by artistically wrapping and tucking the yards of fabric around each of his models. Billed simply by his first name in vaudeville and supper clubs, he added Bergé, a variant of his surname, when he performed his specialty act in movies such as *Double or Nothing* (1937), *That's My Baby* (1944) and *Ali Baba and the Forty Thieves* (1944).

His type of act was popular from the 1920s through the 1950s and was played in vaudeville, nightclubs and on television variety shows. It provided inspiration for comedians like Ed Wynn and Danny Kaye. In *Earl Carroll's Vanities* (1930), Jimmy Savo did a burlesque (in every sense) of Alphonse's "Creation" act. In "Modes—A Window at Merl's," Savo, as a store window designer, reversed Alphonse's act. He removed the clothing from each of the five human mannequins in the window. By the time Savo reached for their garter belts, the police were on their way to the New Amsterdam Theatre. Despite the Great Depression, that year's *Vanities* ran more than 200 performances.

In American culture, the name Alphonse symbolized two opposing types, one more dominant than the other. Alphonse was the given name of America's most famous gangster, Al Capone, yet it also served as shorthand for the dandified or effeminate male. From comic strips (Frederick Burr Opper's "After you, my dear Gaston. After you, my dear Alphonse.") to vaudeville, revue and burlesque (most notably, The Marx Brothers in *I'll Say She Is*) to comedy movies, Alphonse became the name of choice for French waiters, couturiers and hairdressers, and for French gentlemen of delicate sensibilities. Alphonse of vaudeville and supper-club fame epitomized the latter.

AMATEUR

Through careless usage, the word *amateur* has been corrupted from its original meaning (from the French *amare,* meaning "to love"). Given its most favorable connotation, an amateur is one who is devoted to a particular form of art, science or pastime and who pursues it for knowledge and pure pleasure rather than as a profession and a means of making money.

On the other hand, an amateur can be regarded as a dilettante or a dabbler, a nonprofessional with insufficient training and experience, lacking commitment, skills, rigor and standards.

AMATEUR NIGHTS

Neighborhood theatre managers often hosted amateur nights, usually on Sundays. Local audiences loved to see their friends and neighbors perform. In some municipalities, local blue laws prohibited Sunday performances, but local politicians relaxed their interpretation of the law rather than annoy potential voters. Also, professional vaudeville acts worked six-day weeks (when they could) and traveled on Sundays. By keeping his house open a seventh day, the vaudeville theatre owner or manager garnered additional income with a minimum of additional expense. Amateur nights did not require display advertising in newspapers, nor were several stagehands needed to change settings. The manager was often the emcee, and he was aided by a spotlight man, an electrician and someone who managed the travelers. Often, music was supplied by a single piano.

Winners were rewarded with small cash prizes or tokens such as silver cups that did not tarnish until the entire roster of relations and friends had had a chance to handle them. Amateur contests engendered community support as families and friends in the neighborhood turned out to cheer their favorites.

A successful amateur sometimes became a *professional amateur,* getting experience by entering and winning as many amateur contests as he was able to reach by streetcar. By listening to the various audiences and practicing, the amateur fashioned an act and then tried to get bookings in small-time vaudeville.

A professional amateur could also earn a pittance of a living by staying bad. It never hurt an amateur contest to include someone who was so untalented and daftly inept that he stimulated the event. Audiences loved to hoot at a bad performer and hoped with shouts of "Get the hook!" to goad the manager into dragging him off. Sometimes, on the sly, the manager offered the same performer a few dollars to return next week or play another of his theatres. Amateur nights were not solely the province of burlesque and vaudeville, and they have endured longer than either. Hilariously bad amateurs earned the gong on *Major Bowes' Original Amateur Hour* on network radio and *The Gong Show* on television.

MOREY AMSTERDAM

b: 14 December 1908, Chicago, IL— d: 27 October 1996, Los Angeles, CA

A member of the last generation to work two-a-day vaudeville, Morey Amsterdam began in 1922 as the 14-year-old partner of his piano-playing comedian brother. Both the antic spirit and musical ability ran in the family. His father was a violinist who played in orchestras for the Chicago Opera and San Francisco Symphony. Morey was an accomplished cellist, but he also had a yen to get laughs. He alternated between vaudeville and speakeasies in his native Chicago, until he was caught in gangster crossfire while working at Al Capone's club. He left Chicago for Hollywood, where he got work as a gag writer, an experience he would mine to great profit in his role of Buddy Sorrell, scriptwriter for the fictitious *Alan Brady Show* on the TV classic *The Dick Van Dyke Show.* Amsterdam is secure in the television pantheon for his part in *The Dick Van Dyke Show,* which ran from 1961 through 1966 and has continued to be broadcast in reruns ever since. His role was tailor-made for Morey's impish personality and his reputation as a human joke machine. Yet *The Dick Van Dyke Show* represents a mere 5 years of a career that lasted for more than 70.

Over the years he wrote original songs. He scored his greatest success with an arrangement of a Trinidadian song into "Rum and Coca-Cola," a hit for the Andrews Sisters. Morey wrote the lyrics, directed and starred (with Nancy Andrews and Sid Stone) in *Hilarities,* a revue that quickly died on Broadway in 1948. He authored a couple of books (*Keep Laughing* and *Morey Amsterdam's Book for Drinkers*) and performed as a comedian in vaudeville and nightclubs.

As vaudeville declined, radio provided a reasonably steady source of work. His gag writing led to appearances on a West Coast radio show, *Al Pearce and His Gang,* a show that hopped around several networks from 1934 to 1942. This led to a number of guest shots on various shows over the course of more than a decade. His best-known radio work came during the 1947–48 season with *Stop Me if You've Heard This One,* which debuted in 1939, one year ahead of *Can You Top This,* its better-known imitator. Its vaudeville-incubated panelists included Amsterdam, Harry Hershfield and Lew Lehr.

Stop Me if You've Heard This One was easily adapted to television in 1948, and Morey came along with it; he also rejoined the show when it revived in syndication for the 1969–70 season. He was one of a dozen competitors in the summer of 1948 to host the *Texaco Star Theater,* but Milton Berle won out. Later that year, Morey opened in his own, self-named TV show, the cast of which included Art Carney before his association with Jackie Gleason. If radio had been good to Amsterdam, television was even better; although few of the series he signed onto lasted much more than a season or two, he continued to get opportunities.

He had been on hand to assist in the birth of network TV. The granddaddy of late-night talk shows was *Broadway Open House,* which carved out the weeknightly spot on the NBC schedule that was later inherited by Steve Allen, Jack Paar, Johnny Carson and Jay Leno. When *Broadway Open House* debuted in 1950, Morey emceed the program Mondays and Wednesdays, but only for the first season (Jerry Lester hosted the Tuesday, Thursday and Friday editions and inherited all five nights the next year). Morey led a talent-search show, *Battle of the Ages,* for a single season in 1952. This was followed by *Guide Right,* a two-season variety show (1952–53), *Who Said That?* (1954) and *Keep Talking* (1958–60), both celebrity-panel shows. Morey often appeared as a guest (sometimes with his cello as a comic prop) on many variety shows, including Ed Sullivan's. Between 1958 and 1980, Amsterdam had featured roles in one drama and three comedy films.

As late as 1985–86, Morey was guesting on *Hollywood Squares,* a syndicated TV series; *Comedy Break* and the soap opera *The Young and the Restless* in 1990; and *Caroline in the City* (1995). He lived to be 87 and was married to his wife, Kay, for a half century. Like other notable insult comics, Milton Berle, Henry Youngman and Don Rickles, Morey Amsterdam could machine-gun his targets with a combination of off-the-cuff insults and long-remembered put-downs. In contrast to the others, his mischievous grin and slight lisp made him seem more playful and less abrasive. It was all in the delivery.

EDDIE "ROCHESTER" ANDERSON

b: 18 September 1905, Oakland, CA— d: 28 February 1977, Los Angeles, CA

Eddie Anderson, who turned a one-shot on Jack Benny's radio show into a new career, was born into a showbiz family. His father, Big Ed, was a minstrel man, and his mother, Ella Mae, was a circus tightrope walker. Later, his dad won notice as a comedian in his act, Anderson & Goines, which played both black and white vaudeville. Eddie's grandparents were slaves until they were smuggled out of the South through the Underground Railway.

Eddie earned his trademark foghorn voice as a youngster hawking newspapers and found it gave him a distinctive sound when he entered show business at 13 or 14. He and his brother Lloyd sang and danced for servicemen stationed at San Francisco's Presidio, and Eddie got work in the chorus of *Struttin' Along,* a West Coast show, and went out as a solo performer in black vaudeville and all-colored revues, including a stint in one of the Whitman Sisters shows, where he developed as a comic.

From 1920 until 1930, Eddie played black vaudeville as a solo song-and-dance man and joined a variety of black revues in burlesque. Eddie clowned, spoke lines, sang and danced when he teamed with another brother, Cornelius, and a third performer in a song-and-dance act. As The Three Black Aces, they were booked eventually into the bigger black vaudeville theatres, such as the Apollo in Harlem, and big-time white vaudeville, playing the Roxy on Broadway by the end of the 1920s.

The Three Black Aces played vaudeville theatres and nightclubs across the country until it was apparent to all but the most myopic that vaudeville's days were numbered. Reaching the end of a tour with the act in Los Angeles, Eddie sought and got a few minor film roles on his own; *What Price Hollywood* (1930) was his first. Still, vaudeville seemed to offer the most promise, and the partners revived The Three Black Aces. They weathered the early years of the Great Depression with a two-and-a-half-year engagement at Harlem's Cotton Club. When it ended, Eddie decided to relocate to Hollywood and fit in some bit parts in movies with theatre, nightclub, and radio work. His best opportunity in those days was a 1932 black revue, *Lucky Day,* directed by Earl Dancer and LeRoy Prinz.

Anderson's first notable films were *Three Men on a Horse* (1935) and *Show Boat* (1936). In 1936, he won a major role in the West Coast stage production of Marc Connolly's *The Green Pastures* that captured the notice of the Hollywood community. Several film roles quickly followed in *Melody for Two* (1937), *One Mile from Heaven* (1937) and *Jezebel* (1937).

Eddie Anderson was a well-established performer in film, radio and on stage when a 1937 appearance on the Jack Benny radio show as Eddie, a Pullman car porter, hit the national radio audience's funny bone and led to a continuing role as Rochester Van Jones, Mr. Benny's valet. Rochester became the most popular personality on *The Jell-O Program* after Jack Benny ("Jello Everybody!"). Although his role was that of a servant, his radio personality was not. The writers, with Jack Benny's enthusiastic support, turned Rochester into the crafty, domineering manservant that has been a beloved stock theatre character for centuries around the world. Every culture has celebrated the crafty, subversive servant who appears in theatre pieces from folk plays to grand opera.

Anderson remained with *The Jack Benny Show* throughout its radio years and into its TV era. He continued to appear in films, as well, with and without Jack Benny. Among Anderson's major film credits are *You Can't Take It with You* (1938), *Gone with the Wind* (1939), *Topper Returns* (1941, in which he plays against type doing Mantan Moreland/Willie Best shtick), *Tales of Manhattan* (1942), *Meanest Man in the World* (1942), *Star-Spangled Rhythm* (1942, which allowed Anderson to strut his song-and-dance stuff with Katherine Dunham), the all-star *Cabin in the Sky* (1943, in which he received star billing), *Broadway Rhythm* (1944), *Brewster's Millions* (1945), *The Sailor Takes a Wife* (1946) and *The Show-Off* (1946).

When the civil rights community took on the entertainment industry for its demeaning portrayals of blacks, one might have thought that Eddie Anderson's sassy and superior character would be exempt from criticism. After all, *The Jack Benny Show* had endured criticism from some in the South who objected to the social parity that Rochester shared with his employer, Jack Benny. Unfortunately, in 1950, when the show's intended script was not ready, the producers revived one from ten years earlier that got some of its laughs from Rochester's gambling and romancing. This broadcast triggered a protest, but, despite some sticky moments, Eddie Anderson and Jack Benny weathered the squall.

Eddie Anderson was as identified with Rochester as Jack Benny was with his stingy, vain character. Despite a substantial film career that encompassed about 60 movies and television success in two different television productions of *The Green Pastures,* Eddie could never completely escape his legendary role, and he remained with the Benny show until Jack's final series show in 1965. Mr. Anderson enjoyed a wealthy retirement.

HARRY ANDERSON

b: 14 October 1952, Newport, RI

Although he chose to step out of the television spotlight around 2000 after 20 years of success on the home screen, Harry "The Hat" Anderson is well remembered as a television personality, comedian and trickster. He played the judge in the long-running situation comedy *Night Court* (1984–92) and writer Dave Barry in the sitcom *Dave's World* (1993–97), based on the humor columnist's supposed real life.

Harry's more devoted fans admire him for his fast-talking-hustler–comedian-magician act that he developed through years on the comedy club circuit and brought to television in several specials, *Saturday Night Live* and Johnny Carson's and Dave Letterman's late-night talk fests.

Like the stage illusionists he grew up admiring, Anderson chose to preserve some mystery about his life. He was not raised by lizards nor kidnapped by Gypsies, the usual answers he gives interviewers to deflect their inquiries. His parents separated during his boyhood. The court granted his father, a traveling salesman, custody of Harry, and his school years were peripatetic. When they landed in Los Angeles, Harry's mother followed, and he went to live with her for a few years, perhaps until he graduated from high school in 1970. In a couple of interviews he claimed to be dyslexic, but fellow actors claimed he could read and memorize a script in an enviably short time.

Harry admired his mother for doing whatever was necessary to support her kids and keep the family together. He struck out on his own, moving into his own apartment sometime between age 16 and finishing high school. Quick-witted and resourceful, he relied upon his ability to con to earn money. He tried to stay one step ahead of the local law as he set up street-corner hustles—shell, card and dice games—to fleece passersby. Harry seldom saw his father. Around 1980, he was notified of his dad's death and was asked to claim the body.

Harry's sidewalk hustles were based on sleight-of-hand skill, the ability to manipulate objects without being detected. Harry told reporters that he was arrested in New Orleans and was punched out by an angry mark he tried to fool and cheat in San Francisco. When he decided to reform for safety's sake, he adapted his spiel and sleight of hand for busking on the streets; he passed the hat instead of picking pockets. He moved on to country fairs, college campuses and comedy clubs. Anderson hit the wave with comedy clubs as they proliferated across the USA. He presented as a comedy magician, keeping the fast-talking palaver and creating a wise-guy comic character. An engagement at the Magic Castle in Hollywood attracted the notice of an agent who saw something new, vital and very salable about Harry's stage persona and his skill. Las Vegas was still a show town that played small acts in lounges, and Harry got booked there and was discovered by scouts for *Saturday Night Live.*

He made an impression on the producers and the audience with his initial performance of 17 October 1981, and he made seven more appearances between 1982 and 1985. By that time, he was in his second year as a star in one of television's most popular series, *Night Court,* which ran until 1992. His agent had arranged the audition, and although the producers had some concern that Harry looked too young for a television audience to accept him as a judge, they were impressed by his audition and chose him. It was a decision they never regretted. Harry also helped write scripts for the show and found places during the filming to work in a few sleight-of-hand tricks. Harry was not the whole show; the producers had assembled a fine cast of contrasting personalities, including the repressed assistant D.A. played by John Laroquette (who won four Emmys for his role), comedy writer Selma Diamond's world-weary character, deadpan zinger Marsha Warfield, Richard Moll and Markie Post. Harry's next series, *Dave's World,* was tamer, suffered for it and was not as well cast; still, it achieved a respectable run of four seasons, 1993–97.

Married three times, Anderson has two children. His first was an early marriage that seems to have disappeared from his chronology. The second lasted more than 20 years. By the early 2000s, Harry Anderson seemed to shun publicity and severely curtailed his professional performances. He makes an occasional movie and television special but mostly follows his interests, all related to toys, technology and tricks. He moved to New Orleans, where he used his considerable collection of stage magic paraphernalia as the core of a specialty business for professionals and collectors, and opened a retail outlet, Sideshow, along the lines of the old magic shops. In a 2003 interview, Harry said that, contrary to his stage persona, he is not at ease among crowds of people and that he is afflicted with stage fright. Harry and his wife opened a club in New Orleans, called Oswald's Speakeasy.

ANIMAL ACTS

All types of animals were trained to amuse and astonish, most often dogs, monkeys and birds, but also horses, lions, elephants, seals, bears, house cats, chickens, goats, rabbits and all manner of rodents. Because any act had to pay their own transport in vaudeville, and because managers were afraid of the liability should a large animal try to escape and terrify their audience, it was less usual in vaudeville to see large animals from the wild than acts using domesticated animals. Still, there were dozens of large-animal acts, most of them taking winter bookings in vaudeville between circus seasons.

Chained and caged between performances, the big animals were prodded up makeshift ramps onto the stage. Some of the larger houses were built with holding pens in the bowels of the theatre, where an elevator lifted them to the stage level. Even in the Keith Memorial in Boston, one of the largest, latest and best-equipped of vaudeville houses, the animal pens were windowless concrete cells. Regularly hosed down, concrete floors in pens were always damp, so they contributed to the arthritis that plagued large captive animals. The lions, leopards and tigers that appeared in acts were often old, and their claws and teeth had been extracted.

Among the best-known animal acts were Coin's Dogs, Swain's Cats and Rats, Fink's Mules, May Wirth & Family, Poodles Hanneford Family and Powers' Elephants. Few vaudevillians relished playing on a bill with animals. Usually, animal acts attracted a large number of children who were charmed by the animals—and only them. Performers, only somewhat more accustomed to large animals than the audience, worried about sharing space with creatures that did not want to be there and sometimes managed to get loose backstage. There was also the chance, if a performer followed an animal act, that the audience would not be attuned to him and that he could step or fall into something left over.

The majority of animal acts were reasonably well cared for, if only because of the investment in purchase and training time. Still, it was an unnatural life for animals from the wild, especially, and for domesticated animals as well. Because they were caged and chained, they had little opportunity of escape, so strange loud noises and unfriendly or angry stagehands could quickly panic an animal. Dogs were the only animals that seemed to enjoy performing.

Some acts, especially those that originated in the circus, were less humane. Chickens and ducks were often trained to dance by heating the surface on which they were confined; bears, chained, were also trained by fire to dance. Whips were used to make large cats like tigers and lions submit, elephants were pulled by metal hooks and hit with two-by-fours, whereas cats and dogs were cajoled with food and intimidated with beatings. To this day, force and terrorization is the preferred method for some of the less savory animal acts. In the 1990s in Las Vegas, the master of an orangutan act was captured on videotape beating his animals before each performance. Even in cases where animals are decently treated, if there is only one of their species in the act, the loneliness and isolation from others of their kind can be devastating.

A number of vaudevillians deplored the cruelty of some animal acts. May Irwin was vocal about it, and Sarah Bernhardt and Elsie Janis had clauses inserted into their contracts that no animal act was allowed on the same bill with them.

There is, however, a lighter and apocryphal side of the issue. Comedians sometimes told of a small-time magician who had not worked in a long time. Each week he would call his agent, asking—begging—for work. Finally the call came: "Can you make Newark by 7 P.M. today? You're replacing a canceled act." "Now you call!" the magician cried, "I just ate my rabbit for dinner!"

ANNUNCIATORS

The backlit, translucent cards, slotted unseen into a window set in either side of the proscenium, that announced the name of the next act were called annunciators. In more mechanically advanced theatres, a chain drive lifted each card into view. Prior to this fancy technology, an easel was set up near the proscenium arch at the side of the stage; the management announced the name of the next act by placing a new lettered card (approximately three feet wide and two feet high) that showed the name of the next act and removed or covered the card for the previous act.

DAVE APOLLON

b: 1898, Kiev, Russia—d: 30 May 1972, Las Vegas, NV

More than a leader of an orchestra or a novelty band, Dave Apollon gave the customers an entertaining show, and they, in turn, supported his career that spanned more than a half century. Upon his arrival in the United States of America from Russia, he entered vaudeville as a mandolin player. Milton Berle recalled when he and his partner, Elizabeth Kennedy, were breaking in their act at Fox's Bay Ridge Theatre in Brooklyn, in 1921, that "a little Russian guy who danced and played the mandolin," Dave Apollon, proved an audience favorite among a bill of impressive acts, including the popular Watson Sisters. Apollon went on to form his Filipino Orchestra and develop a line of comic patter. In the latter days of vaudeville, he occasionally served as an emcee in addition to playing his mandolin and conducting his Filipino Orchestra.

He was one of vaudeville's pallbearers on two momentous occasions. Dave Apollon and his Filipino Orchestra "augmented with a quartet of Albertina Rasch dancers and an octet of black 'rhythmicians,'" closed the last two-a-day bill at the Palace the week of 7 May 1932. Crushing as was the end of two-a-days at the Palace, even the brightest optimist had to face the fact of vaudeville's death when, on 23 December 1947, Loew's State Theatre on Broadway played its last vaudeville bill. Appropriately, Apollon closed the bill again, playing a requiem on his mandolin.

Dave Apollon's career neatly spanned the options of the last generation of vaudevillians. He entered vaudeville around 1920, soon after his arrival in the USA, and worked steadily in the big time and the best of small time. In the 1930s, Dave and his Filipino Orchestra made an appearance in the Bert Lahr, Jimmy Savo and Alice Brady musical comedy feature film, *Merry-Go-Round of 1938* and performed in a few film shorts. In 1940, Dave joined the cast of *Boys and Girls Together,* a revue produced and directed by its star, Ed Wynn. Like many of the more popular vaudeville headliners of his time, Dave found work in Las Vegas during the 1960s. He performed at the Desert Inn for seven years, an engagement cut short only by his death in 1972.

Dave Apollon

APRON

Also known in other nations as the forestage, the apron is the area between the front tabs or the dress velvet curtain and the front edge of the stage bordered by footlights.

ROSCOE "FATTY" ARBUCKLE

b: (Roscoe Conkling Arbuckle) 24 March 1887, Smith Center, KS—d: 29 June 1933, New York, NY

He was blonde, blue-eyed, five feet nine or ten inches tall, and 300 pounds of good-natured grace. Agile and athletic, Roscoe "Fatty" Arbuckle floated through his films like a large, fast-moving balloon. Unlike most other large-size comedians who worked in the silent movie shorts—Mack Swain, Oliver Hardy, Joe Roberts and Ernest Torrence—who were cast either as villains or as intimidating bulls, Roscoe played "Fatty," a big, lovable and mischievous youth. If someone tried to do dirt to Fatty in a film, Arbuckle knew how to handle himself, but he was never an unprovoked aggressor.

Charlie Chaplin, Harold Lloyd, Buster Keaton and Laurel & Hardy had the good fortune to make their films in the sound era as well as the silent era. Only Laurel & Hardy were as well-suited to talkies as they were to silent pictures, perhaps because they were growing as a team at the dawn of sound, whereas Chaplin, Lloyd and Keaton developed in tandem with the silent form. Roscoe Arbuckle came to movie comedy early—around 1908. By 1920, he had signed a contract that gave him sufficient capital and authority to make feature films. One year later, on the threshold of greater promise, he was forced out of the motion picture industry when the Virginia Rappe scandal wrecked his career and ruined his life. When Arbuckle was able to regain a toehold in motion pictures, it was at the low end of the ladder. Keaton joined him there, but Buster's fall had come after making 11 feature-length silent classics and several successful sound films.

As a boy, Roscoe Arbuckle had begun in stock company theatre, burlesque and vaudeville. After the court trials, friends provided some work behind the cameras, and vaudeville once again sustained Arbuckle. It took a decade of undeserved penance to get the opportunity to act again in the movies. When he returned to the screen it was in six two-reel comedies for Vitaphone. He had come full circle, and his style seemed dated. The crackling repartee and musical numbers that enlivened the sound tracks of films made for comedians like Eddie Cantor, W. C. Fields, The Marx Brothers, Mae West, Joan Blondell and Wheeler & Woolsey pro-

Roscoe "Fatty" Arbuckle (R) with friend Buster Keaton (L)

duced a style of Broadway wiseacre comedy that was a world of comedy apart from that of Arbuckle, Chaplin, Lloyd and other silent clowns.

Everyone who knew Roscoe Arbuckle found him to be an open, generous, fun-loving, benevolent human being; he was trusting and loyal to a fault. Most who knew him used words like *gentle* and *shy* to describe him. He must have had a strong core of goodness to turn out that way, because his early life was wretched. His father, William Goodrich Arbuckle, seems to have hated Roscoe from birth. He even named the boy after a man he hated, antislavery Radical Republican Roscoe Conkling. Baby Arbuckle's weight at birth is reported to have been 14 pounds.

According to Arbuckle's biographer, David Yallop, who rescued Roscoe's reputation, one family member mused that Mr. Arbuckle might have doubted fathering the youngest child in his household. As his wife was a devout Baptist, isolated on a rural farm with her brood and plenty of hard work, the suspicion seems groundless. What are beyond doubt are the regular, almost savage beatings the boy had to endure at the hands of his father.

The Arbuckles were part of the mid-nineteenth century westward migration in the USA. Like others, Mr. Arbuckle had dreams of finding wealth and independence, and for a couple of years the family resided and farmed in Smith Center, Kansas. After a year and a half, Arbuckle senior yielded to the lure of California and moved his family to Santa Ana, where they opened a boardinghouse. Soon, William Arbuckle was off to goldfields in northern California, taking his older sons. Yallop reports that Roscoe did chores around the house from the time he could toddle and lift.

Roscoe was eight when he made his stage debut. In 1895, a troupe of players came to Santa Ana, and they were in need of a youngster to play a small part. Always to be found hanging backstage whenever he skipped school (often) or had time away from chores (less often), Roscoe was ready. The troupe blacked up Roscoe, and he appeared nightly, earning 50 cents for his first week's work as an actor. Over the next four years, Roscoe became an unofficial utility player for the various performers who appeared at Santa Ana's Grand Opera House. Roscoe handled props, assisted magicians, jugglers and acrobats, and he played small parts with traveling stock companies like the Frank Bacon's Stock Company and Webster-Brown Stock Company. It was a very different education from the one the local little schoolhouse offered. Instead of readin', 'ritin, and 'rithmatic, young Arbuckle learned singling, juggling, acrobatics and pratfalls. Matriculating through the Grand Opera House was far more agreeable than enduring taunts from schoolchildren who pegged him with the nickname he despised but could never escape: Fatty.

In 1899, when he was 12 and the only child remaining at home with his mother, she died and left her son bereft. A married sister packed his bags and sent him north to live with his father. By the time Roscoe got to Watsonville, his father had sold his small hotel and left town without leaving a forwarding address. Roscoe was stranded. He supported himself by working in the kitchen for the man who had bought his father's hotel.

Watsonville had a theatre called the Victory Theatre. Not surprisingly, Roscoe was drawn to it. Like many theatres, the Victory hosted a weekly amateur contest. Those affairs were money in the bank for the theatre owner. Instead of paying five or six acts, they awarded one or two small cash prizes that amounted to about 10% of what a professional bill cost for a single night. The townsfolk enjoyed amateur nights; they razzed the inept and cheered favorites.

Roscoe's first appearance made him a favorite. He sang a few songs in his lovely soprano and, when the audience encouraged him, announced he would sing a few more. The theatre manager was standing backstage with the hook in hand. The hook was a long-handled device originally used in theatres to untangle ropes and cables in the fly space above the stage. It doubled as a huge shepherd's crook to yank off the stage those who had outstayed their welcome. The manager tried to pull

Roscoe off the stage, but Roscoe danced about, dodging the hook and having a grand time. The audience enjoyed it no less, especially when Roscoe surprised them as he somersaulted off the stage and landed in the orchestra pit for a wow finish. This antic earned Roscoe the $5 first prize and a weekly Friday-night gig. Arbuckle had the makings of an act.

Word came that his father had been located farming in San Jose. Roscoe found his way there. His father put him to work on the farm and the beatings resumed. He had a new stepmother, however, and she was more kindly disposed toward Roscoe. In 1902, Roscoe's father moved the family again; he bought a restaurant in Santa Clara, and Roscoe became the drudge. His father usually refused to pay him, so 15-year-old Roscoe earned pin money at the local theatre and a beer hall during his off hours. Sometimes he got to sing; more often he sold tickets at Sid Grauman Sr.'s Unique Theatre or waited on tables at the beer hall. Soon Grauman hired Roscoe to sing songs as the illustrated slides flickered on the screen.

Two years later, Roscoe's voice landed him his first truly professional engagement as an entertainer: a month-long engagement in San Francisco at a café owned by Alexander Pantages, who was in the process of building a very successful vaudeville circuit. The month stretched into a year and was capped by a tour of Pantages' Pacific Coast vaudeville houses. By 1905, Roscoe was earning $50 a week and playing all the Pantages vaudeville theatres. He returned to San Francisco in time for the legendary earthquake. Also in town were John Barrymore and Joe E. Brown. Arbuckle and Barrymore, along with every other healthy man encountered by the U.S. Army, were drafted to help clean up the wreckage of quake and fire. Brown, then the youngest member of an acrobatic troupe, was exempted from this duty.

Following the San Francisco disaster, Roscoe accepted an invitation from Australian comedian Leon Errol to join him in burlesque in Portland, Oregon. Roscoe had found his first mentor. Errol was only a decade or so Roscoe's senior, but he was experienced in everything from management to performing in Shakespeare, burlesque, variety and circus. He must have recognized in Roscoe a fellow clown, although Roscoe had spent the past few years as a singer. Arbuckle blossomed in the company of Errol and the other comedians in the troupe. His gift for improvisation got them out of a potentially dangerous situation in Butte, Montana's, Last Chance Saloon. When the voluptuous but often drunk prima donna failed to show up, Roscoe saved the day by performing in drag. He nearly got through their week's engagement when the prima donna ended her toot on the fourth day and, breathing fire, came to the saloon. When she saw Roscoe in her wig and finery, she stormed the stage. Roscoe turned the rout into a romp, and the miners thought it great fun as Arbuckle leapt, somersaulted and took trick falls as the inflamed prima donna chased him. However much the merriment, Leon and Roscoe knew it was time to get out of town. Errol took a burlesque troupe on the road and worked his way toward New York (and the *Ziegfeld Follies*). Arbuckle continued to tour in burlesque revues through the Rockies, into Canada and back to the Pacific Coast.

Upon reaching Southern California in 1908, Arbuckle approached the movie business. Still largely based in New York and Chicago, some filmmakers had moved farther west, primarily to escape the patent detectives hired by Thomas Edison who was trying to collect royalties from everyone who used a motion picture camera. Many chose the little town of Los Angeles, where there was enough daily sunshine to keep film production on schedule without adding to expense by shooting indoors with artificial light. When Edison's men picked up the scent, the Mexican border was not too far away.

Although most actors looked down their noses at *the flickers,* the unassuming one-reel films were making inroads within the entertainment industry. Variety performers were indifferent, except for those who realized that once their act was filmed and seen for ten cents, it might not be salable in vaudeville houses for a dollar.

Films were not rented in those days; they were bought, and those who had made them or had purchased copies, toured villages and towns, showing their novelties after normal business hours in grange halls, haberdasheries and drugstores. Short silent films were appearing as the last act on vaudeville bills. The derogatorily named nickelodeons were opening in storefronts along the main streets of American cities, large and small. Like vaudeville, they offered more than one show a day, although the various items on their bill were films rather than live acts. Eventually, they forced vaudeville into a continuous showings policy, but it was easier for films to play six shows a day than it was for performers.

In Long Beach, Roscoe courted Minta Durfee while she was in the dance chorus of a musical for which he was the featured singer. While performing on the stage at night, Arbuckle found daytime employment at Selig Studios. In 1909–10 he made two one-reel and two half-reel shorts for Selig. Three years later, he made another Selig short as well as several for Al Christie. In between, Roscoe formed a vaudeville unit with another versatile comedian, Walter Reed. Minta traveled with the company as a singer. By 1910, Roscoe and Minta were doing a double act in vaudeville. Roscoe sang, clowned acrobatically and tap-danced. They joined the Ferris Hartman Musical Comedy and Opera Company for a West Coast tour, and they rejoined it in 1911 for a tour to Hawaii, Japan, China and the Philippines, boldly performing the Mikado and other musicals.

Back in the USA, there was little demand for Arbuckle & Durfee. One day, Roscoe took the trolley to Mack Sennett's Keystone Studios. The outfit was less than a year old, and the original contract comedians were Mabel Normand, Ford Sterling, Fred Mace and Mack Sennett himself. Arbuckle was in on the ground floor of the most famous movie-making madhouse in the history of American cinema.

Arbuckle made 90 Keystone shorts in two years (1913–15), of which about ten were half-reelers and eight or so were two-reelers. The rest were one reel in length. Early on, he was a Keystone Kop. Later, he paired with Mabel Normand in the Mabel & Fatty series. The hated nickname was now official.

When Keystone was consolidated into Triangle, Roscoe made another dozen two-reelers in less than a year at both the Hollywood and Fort Lee, New Jersey, studios. Joe Schenck sought out Arbuckle and set him up in his own studio, the Comique (which would go to Buster Keaton after Arbuckle signed with Paramount in 1920 to make feature films). At Comique (which released through Paramount Pictures), Roscoe made 20 two-reelers from 1917 until 1920. In those shorts, Arbuckle was joined by his nephew, Al St. John, an athletic if unsubtle comedian, and in 15 of the comedies, Arbuckle and St. John were partnered with Buster Keaton, who was lured by Arbuckle into film and away from certain stardom on Broadway.

Arbuckle's first two features were such successes that to please his Paramount employers, primarily Adolph Zukor, Roscoe made six more within six months, dashing from one role, one picture, one costume and one set to another picture, role, costume and set. He was happy but exhausted. A vacation was in order. He and Lowell Sherman drove up to San Francisco, where they took a three-room suite, which they stocked with plenty of bootleg hooch and food. Various motion-picture people and hangers-on found their way to Sherman's and Arbuckle's suite. Trouble soon followed.

What actually occurred that fatal and fateful Labor Day weekend in 1921 emerged over the course of three trials during a period of six months. The record has since been added to through research by David Yallop, Arbuckle's biographer, for whom these reprehensible trials are the centerpiece of his book *The Day the Laughter Stopped*. Briefly, the facts were that Virginia Rappe, a party girl with the pox, invited herself to the suite, as did Maude Delmont, who made a living as a procurer, extortionist, embezzler and bigamist. After drinking heavily, Rappe went into spasms, probably from an attack of peritonitis and other infections, but Delmont charged that Roscoe had raped Virginia, a charge Virginia denied before she died a week later.

Truth was secondary to the ambitions of the district attorney, who used the trial to propel his campaign for governor. Roscoe's first two trials ended with hung juries. By the third trial, the lies and manufactured evidence were evident to all but the corrupt and bigoted, and Arbuckle was acquitted in five minutes by a jury that did something rare: they wrote him an apology and announced to all who would listen that "acquittal was not enough" and that "a great injustice has been done to him. . . . Roscoe Arbuckle is entirely innocent and free from all blame." Even this extraordinary statement did not persuade those zealots who supposedly knew in their hearts that the big fat man was guilty of ravishing an innocent girl.

During the Arbuckle trials, hell had broken loose in Tinseltown, and fear permeated the studios. Between Roscoe's second and third trials, William Desmond Taylor, a suave, womanizing director, was murdered. After Arbuckle was exonerated and waiting for the ban on his films to be lifted by Will Hays, the small-minded hack who had been entrusted with enforcing the movie industry's code of moral behavior, movie idol Wallace Reid died of a drug overdose. He had been given morphine after an injury on a movie set and had become addicted. The revived panic cost Roscoe. He remained barred from pictures, although he directed a good number over the next decade under his father's name, William Goodrich.

Even when Hays and the movie industry bowed to public support for Arbuckle and decided to allow him to make films again, they quickly bowed in another direction when women's groups across the USA started a campaign that was joined by religious groups. It did not matter to them that Roscoe Arbuckle had been acquitted.

The less reputable newspapers of the day, like those of the Hearst syndicate, portrayed Arbuckle as a fat, gross monster of uncontrollable appetites. According to those who knew him, he ate less than most people and did not become much of a drinker until later, when he tried to escape the torment of the three trials and his great embarrassment of being charged with manslaughter and rape.

Nearly worse than the shame was the nearly $1 million he owed in legal fees. Arbuckle refused to declare bankruptcy. Despite being blackballed, he managed to pay nearly every cent he owed before he died. The studios that had made millions of dollars from Roscoe's films did not help. Instead, they overruled the jury and banned him from appearing in films.

Friends like Buster Keaton and director James Cruze tried to help. They sent him on a trip to the Orient, but scurrilous press stories followed him. *The New York Times* was among the culprits. Roscoe actually made two gag appearances in friends' movies, their way of defying Hays and his puppeteers, the studio bosses. In Cruze's 1923 film *Hollywood,* Roscoe played an actor waiting in vain at the casting office. In Buster's *Go West* (1925), Roscoe appeared as a woman in a department store.

When, after a few years, Hays lifted the ban, hell broke loose again. Mayors pledged they would forbid his films in their cities, and clergymen and women's groups launched vituperative letter-writing campaigns. Once again, Hays and his bosses capitulated to the mob.

Arbuckle's comeback started in nightclubs, where he joked and clowned for his A-list audience by singing, dancing, juggling and taking great acrobatic falls. Newspapers and civic and religious groups would not leave him alone, however. Despite doing good business, clubs were forced to cancel Arbuckle.

In 1924, Alexander Pantages hired Roscoe to play his circuit of theatres. Ironically, Pantages would face a similar scandal five years later when a 17-year-old chorus girl accused Pantages of rape. Rumor has it that Joe Kennedy, having wrested control of the Keith circuit, resorted to setting up Pantages on rape charges when Pantages balked at selling his theatres to Kennedy. Pantages was cleared on appeal, but questions lingered.

Roscoe went to France, where, after a bad start playing his act in English, quickly learned it phonetically in French and wound up with standing-room-only business. When he returned to the USA, it was back to vaudeville. He and Doris Deane divorced amicably. "I hadn't taken on one man for better or worse," she told his biographer, David Yallop. "I'd taken on the American nation, or at least a big part of it. . . . God, it wasn't his [Roscoe's] fault the marriage shattered."

Roscoe kept busy in 1927; he made his Broadway debut in legitimate theatre in *Baby Mine* and played vaudeville dates on Loew's time. In 1928, along with backers, Arbuckle opened the Plantation Club, a Culver City nightclub that became the place for Hollywood to play and to pay guilty homage to Roscoe. The stock market crash on Wall Street reverberated across the continent, however, and shook the foundation of Roscoe's club. Arbuckle sold it in 1930, the year he met and married his third wife.

Addie McPhail was nearly 20 years younger than Roscoe, but it was a love match that saw him through his last three years. Professionally, too, things were looking up. Roscoe's ten-year sentence to a performer's purgatory was lifted when, in 1932, Jack Warner gave the green light to Roscoe Arbuckle to resume performing in films. Will Hays consented to a single short to see if public opinion would support Roscoe's return as a screen comic. A public letter of support was signed by most of Hollywood's star actors, including comedians Stan Laurel and Marie Dressler.

Roscoe made six Vitaphone two-reel talkies for Warner Brothers, all in 11 months. The shorts were successful, and Warner Brothers signed Roscoe to appear in a feature film. Roscoe and Addie joined friends for dinner. His spirits had not been better in years. They got back to their hotel, and Roscoe laid down on his bed. Within minutes, his heart gave out. He was dead at 46.

ARTIC CIRCLE

North of the Broadway theatre district, the few theatres uptown from Columbus Circle were considered second rate and outside the area a Broadway audience would visit. The uptown area was dubbed by wags as the Artic Circle. Consequently, the Theatrical Trust (or Syndicate), headed by Abe Erlanger, had no interest in these theatres. Shows that played the Artic Circle were produced by those who had been shut out by the Syndicate or were unable to meet their terms for theatre rentals (which included a percentage of the box office).

ARTISTE

Specialty acts, especially those from places other than the USA, unabashedly used the term *artiste* to refer to themselves; the tradition extended back to the old circuses. Singers, dancers and musicians from the concert stage sometimes chose the title. Acts that did not require the lifetime of discipline and training needed for opera, ballet or acrobatics tended to define themselves as *pros* or by the type of act they did (singer, hoofer, juggler, illusionist). Only the more pretentious of American acts claimed to be *artistes;* most vaudevillians considered it to be a jumped-up term.

ASCAP

American Society of Composers, Authors and Publishers. To secure royalties for the performance of their music, a group of songwriters formed ASCAP in 1914, a few years after the Copyright Act of 1909 had been enacted. Their concern began with the posh restaurants whose orchestras accompanied diners with popular music of the day. The songwriters reasoned that they deserved a fee when their music was played.

Envisioned as a membership association, members retained their own copyrights and paid dues. In turn, ASCAP leadership devised a system to estimate the distribution and sales of printed sheet music and later included sound recordings in their tabulations. The purpose was to exact royalties, and the composer or writer would receive payment for each copy distributed. ASCAP won its quasi-legal authority through a consent decree granted by the federal court in New York.

ASCAP extended its reach to protect its members as new technologies evolved and new uses were found for musical compositions. From sheet music and live performance, ASCAP's scope widened to sound recordings, movies, radio stations, commercial jingles and television. In the last decades of the twentieth century, the system of tabulation was severely tested as music was used for elevators, phone systems, office music, home computer systems, movie scores and radio broadcasts as well as live music events everywhere from neighborhood bars and coffeehouses to circuses to marching bands to nightclubs and Broadway revues.

In 1940, Broadcast Music, Inc. (BMI) began as a small, rival upstart put together by music people, including some broadcasters, who felt that ASCAP was a near monopoly that ignored country & western and rhythm & blues. By the turn of the twentieth century, BMI had grown into a competitor more than half the size of ASCAP.

Because paying a fee for each individual song every time it is used is impractical, the music user, such as a musical aggregation or a radio or television station, purchases a license from ASCAP or BMI or both. The yearly fee is determined by a formula that weighs the size of the listening audience, the seating of a hall or the estimated number in the home audience, how the music is used and how often (a hit song can be played dozens of times on a single radio station). Like a government regulatory agency, ASCAP and BMI employ field agents to keep tabs on music activities—concerts, nightclubs, retail sales—and report their findings.

Various court battles have ensued, against the small and the mighty—school bands to retail chain stores, community radio stations to hotel chains—and ASCAP and BMI have usually prevailed. In calculating which of their member artists receive royalties and how much, the two organizations have relied mostly on airplay. Critics have maintained that this shortchanges members whose music has been performed in more alternative venues rather than featured on commercial radio's playlists. By the dawn of the twenty-first century, estimates of the total amount of fees collected yearly for distribution ran as high as $1 billion.

ANNIE ASHLEY

b: ca. 1872—d: 1940

Much of the recorded history of the stage, whether vaudeville, burlesque, musical comedy or drama, focuses on theatre in the more prominent cities of America and slights the theatre world of small-town America and the frontier. A reminiscence by Annie Ashley, chronicled by Bernard Sobel, has significance beyond the show and the performer because it provides a detailed eyewitness account of the Wild West of the 1880s and 1890s.

A singer and dancer, Ashley was the principal girl in a touring production of *Adamless Eden* in 1886. The company was managed for Mike Leavitt by Sam T. Jack, not yet on his own. The troupe traveled by train, playing dates in New Mexico, Texas and northern Mexico. Mike Leavitt insisted that his companies travel in Pullman cars, one for the women, who were the great majority of the cast, and another carried the two male performers, Mr. Jack, and the cook and his wife, the latter appointed as chaperone for the young women. There was a freight car for baggage, drops, sets and props. The principals were given staterooms; the others had berths.

Adamless Eden was early burlesque, still an amalgam of its influences: the British Blondes leg show, the format of a minstrel show and a number of variety acts performed in the olio. All the performers joined in the afterpiece, which was probably the naughtiest thing in a rather clean show. The young women played all the parts, some as women, others in trouser roles as men. The two female leads were referred to as principal girl and principal boy, a holdover from English tradition. The two men in the company took comedy parts, and one may have served as interlocutor.

The show opened with a walk-around, and then the company, with the principals, sat ringed in a half circle facing the audience. The two *end-men* were played by young women, and the show proceeded with banter and songs. During the middle portion of the show, the olio, some individual cast members performed their specialties. The entire cast participated in the concluding afterpiece, a sketch in which comedy predominated over the music.

When the company arrived in town, their Pullman and freight cars were diverted from the main track to the siding, where they remained during the engagement. The company dressed ahead of time and then paraded on horseback from the railway station down the main drag to the theatre. A trumpeter and drummer, at the least, served notice to all that the show was in town. Doubtless, the advance man arranged for the hire of horses in each town, as that was far less expensive than the transport and full-time care and feeding of the animals.

The theatres were mostly melodeons or music halls, auditoriums connected to saloons. Usually the audience was armed, and occasionally a patron would upstage the show by shooting a prop out of the hand of one of the two men on stage. Ashley told Sobel that there was a lot of gunplay and feuds in every town they played, and often the cast did not feel safe.

Neither Sam T. Jack nor his employer, Mike Leavitt, wished to lose any of their girls to matrimony or worse, so sometimes local bodyguards were hired, and, along with the cook and his wife, they guarded the young women. The women slept in the train, took their breakfast there and then proceeded to the theatre for their matinee performance. After the matinee, they had one hour to return to their Pullman car for supper and get back to the theatre for the evening performance. After the show, they were permitted a bit of leeway, but they had to return to the train within an hour of the show's end for lockup. A strict curfew was enforced, and women who were caught flouting the rule were dismissed on the spot.

On stage, as was the practice in leg shows, the girls were corseted so tightly that their busts threatened to push out of the low-cut tops of their tunics. Their short skirts allowed full appreciation of their calves and thighs and offered a hint of rounded buttocks, all of which were encased in skintight fleshings.

In 1890, Annie Ashley was a principal with a Harry Montague show, also traveling the Southwest. She and the other girls were billeted in what passed for hotels. Annie saw a man shot at the bar while she was collecting her salary of $17.50, and she and the other girls fled the melodeon back to the adobe dwelling they shared. The show was canceled that night, and none of the women ventured forth from the comparative protection of their rooms.

In the morning, before dawn, the girls were roused by a clamor. There was a group of men outside who insisted that the young women come out immediately or they would break down the door. When they opened the door, they were told to get dressed and get out of town; there was train coming that would take them to Tombstone, Arizona, where they were to be given parts in the show at the box house called the Bird Cage. Later, they found out that the man who was shot in the bar had been a U.S. marshal. The Bird Cage was a combination theatre, saloon and gambling parlor, typical of its time and so named for the row of boxes at the balcony level. The occupants of these boxes had the option of closing them off for privacy in the event they found other entertainment more to their satisfaction than the show.

During the three months that Annie Ashley was employed at the Bird Cage in Tombstone, she and the other girls were well paid, and life was exciting. The audience whooped and hollered when they liked the show, and sometimes they showered the stage with so many gold pieces that the prop man had to broom the money into a pile off to the side, where it would be divided after the show. Other times, feuds took precedence, and the aggrieved parties might start fights or even shoot at each other from opposite sides of the auditorium.

Despite the rowdiness and lawlessness, Annie Ashley claimed that women of every stripe were greeted with a certain level of respect, whether they were upstanding members of the community, show girls or prostitutes. The men treated each woman as she presented herself. The prostitutes were expected to take all customers, provided they paid and did not harm them. Women deemed virtuous were expected to remain so. "All the men give, you take, but never give yourselves, because when you do, you're finished." That was the rule. "As long as they think you're a good girl, they'll take care of you." Annie was in Tombstone when the gun battle between the Earp brothers and outlaws Frank Stillwell and Curly Bill took place. It was nearly ten years after the famous gunfight at the O.K. Corral, but Marshal Wyatt Earp had not curbed all lawlessness. Morgan Earp was killed, and his brothers caught up with Stillwell and Curly Bill outside of town.

Annie Ashley continued in Tombstone after the incident but then moved to Los Angeles, where she danced and sang at the Perry Brothers Theatre. After a year there, she moved north to San Francisco for a season or so and then worked her way back east. She married John Barton. Several members of the Barton family were fixtures in burlesque. His brother James did a husband-and-wife act, and James had a son, also named James Barton, who became a great star in burlesque, vaudeville, revue, musical comedy, dramatic stage, movies and television.

Barton & Ashley performed a comedy sketch with a bit of song and dance. John Ashley was a tramp comic, and Annie Ashley played straight as his foil. They went to England in the 1905–6 season to play the music halls in their most successful vaudeville act, "Canal Boat Sal."

Barton & Ashley were a well-known act into 1930, even as vaudeville was collapsing. Like many performers, Annie Ashley moved between burlesque and vaudeville. She and John Barton played vaudeville before its glory days and into its decline.

ASIANS IN AMERICAN VAUDEVILLE

The Asian experience in American vaudeville has yet to receive the scholarly investigation accorded to African Americans and many European Americans in show business. The research that had been done by the turn of the twentieth-first century more often remained within various Asian communities where it originated, or, if the study was initiated by the American academic community, the Asian experience in vaudeville in the USA was usually a subset of larger studies of immigration, culture, civil rights and sociology.

Anna Chang

The two largest nonwhite racial populations performing in American vaudeville were African Americans and Asians. Although both groups suffered substantially as the larger American society debated morality and inclusion and sorted out its laws, the separate experiences of African Americans and Asian Americans (and Asians) within show business, and their relations with European and European American performers differed markedly.

Black performers were invariably born in the USA, although a fair number migrated from various islands in the Caribbean. They were wrenched from homelands in West Africa but shared as much of a common culture that survived or was reclaimed. Despite hatred, bigotry, unfair laws and denial of opportunities that confronted African Americans throughout the vaudeville era, the English language was their language and did not impose further barriers. Black innovations and contributions to American music, dance, drama and comedy pulled the majority culture in their direction.

The so-called Asian identity, however, embraces half the world's population, and the diversity among Asian Americans is far greater than that among European Americans or African Americans. There is no culture or language common to all, and the experiences among the many people of Asian heritage cannot be synthesized.

Chinese men had come to the USA before the Civil War to work as laborers building railroads or to prospect when gold was discovered in California and Alaska. San Franciscan newspapers reported in 1848 that three Chinese, two men and one woman, had jumped a Chinese frigate moored in the bay and disappeared into the surrounding hills. By 1852, newspapers claimed that 10,000 Chinese had flooded the Bay Area, and the governor's office issued a report that hiked the number to 22,000. The United States of America census of 1870 fixed the number of Chinese immigrants at a bit more than 70,000. Most remained in San Francisco or struck out for gold rush sites, whereas others fanned out across the state. Chinese prospectors, like the Native Americans who also tried to find gold on their own lands and stake claims, were often swindled. The Chinese found it safer and more reliable to set up laundries and cooking shacks to serve the white prospectors who flocked to gold rush camps.

Chinese laborers were encouraged to work in the United States as long as they did not bring their families from China. There were railroads to build in the 1860s, and crews were assembled on the West Coast and east of the Mississippi. The most dangerous and backbreaking work of dynamiting mountainsides and burrowing tunnels through the Rocky Mountains was done by Chinese men for a dollar or two a day. (Irish immigrants, extending rail lines westward, earned the same paltry wage.) After the rail links linked the eastern United States with the western, there was no further use for Chinese laborers. During the 1880s, a widespread hysteria among whites led to the enactment of several exclusionary acts designed to prevent importation of additional Chinese laborers.

The earliest contact with Asians by Americans was through Yankee shipping and trade. From Colonial times into the mid-nineteenth century, American collectors grew to greatly admire the arts and crafts of the Orient. Because Asian art was much admired, Asians, usually typified in the American mind by the Chinese, had to be acknowledged as capable of producing great art, because the alternative debased American critical judgment as well as Asians themselves.

Instead, Asians, and the Chinese in particular, were deemed in racist theory as a once-great culture and people that had degenerated through fecundity, been corrupted by opium and debased by an appetite for cruelty. Hence they constituted a Yellow Peril that would swamp the planet. Their heathen ways called for religious conversion; if there must be so many of them, it was held, at least they should be Christians.

Insularity was the only sane reaction to the constant inhospitable reception the Chinese received in the USA and spasmodic instances of mob violence against them. Together with the barriers of quite different religions, heritage, language and their own wish to preserve their culture and customs, the Chinese in America created semiautonomous communities. When they stepped beyond those borders, they adopted a low profile.

This was also true of most Native Americans, the Chilenos (Chileans who had sailed north for the gold rush), native Mexican residents of California, and the Japanese and Filipinos who began arriving in appreciable numbers a few generations later. Very few of these ethnic populations ventured the gamble of a life upon the American stage. Chinese musicians, singers and acrobats performed almost solely for their own communities.

In the early years of vaudeville during the late nineteenth century, the majority of Asian performers coming to America were Chinese, Japanese and Arab. The Arab and Japanese acts often were acrobats, and they attracted the attention of American (both white and black) dancers and tumblers. In China and Japan, the singing and playing of musical instruments, dancing, acrobatics, contortion, juggling and feats of illusion or conjuring were all part of their native theatrical tradition, whereas in Europe and the USA, the spoken drama was set well apart from musical and physical performances.

Until an American-born generation of Asian entertainers emerged to play vaudeville and nightclubs during the 1930s and 1940s, the great majority of Asian variety performers of the nineteenth and the early twentieth centuries were born overseas. They were isolated by language as well as customs and skin color. Theirs were *dumb acts,* featuring displays of magic, balancing, contortion and acrobatics in which spoken language was unnecessary and even inimical to the exotic illusion that enthralled audiences.

Unfortunately, the barrier of language also made interviews difficult and prevented the general public from learning much about such stars as Ching Ling Foo. Some European Americans (such as William Epsworth Robinson, who performed as Chung Ling Soo), noting the popularity and supposed superiority of Chinese conjurers, tried through makeup and costuming to pass themselves off as genuine Chinese. When interviewed, their rattle of gibberish passed for Chinese to the untutored ears of newsmen. Translators were employed by both real and fake *Orientals,* but being show business types, what they told newspaper reporters was intended to hype the box office receipts rather than contribute to an accurate record.

Long Tack Sam, the Chinese illusionist born in China, was not typical. He had lived in Germany before moving to the USA, and he made an effort to reach out to journalists, other performers and the public by learning the rudiments of several languages.

Like other Old World peoples, most Asians in America did not wish to see their children take to the stage for a career. What made *The Jazz Singer* popular was its universal appeal. It was not just Orthodox Jews who viewed the prospect of their children choosing a life in show business as a betrayal of values

Ishikawa Brothers

Sun Fong-Lin, "Best Chinese Variety Act of the Season," 1927

Keyo, Taki & Yoki, "Versatile Entertainers from Nippon"

and aspirations. Many, perhaps a great majority of African Americans and Asian Americans, shared that fear well into the twentieth century.

The internment of Japanese Americans during the Second World War resulted in the confiscation of their homes and lands as well as their imprisonment for the duration. One act, the dance team Toy & Wing, was split by the war. Toy, an American-born Japanese whose birth name was Dorothy Takahashi, watched helplessly as her parents were rounded up and imprisoned in the internment camps with other Japanese. The authorities assumed she was Chinese, so she was able to continue working. Paul Wing Jew was born in the USA of Chinese parents; he served in the U.S. Army fighting in the Pacific theatre against the Japanese.

The rise in visibility of Asian American entertainers began in the 1930s. Following the repeal of Prohibition in 1933, Chinese drinking establishments could openly advertise, and they attracted white customers, much as Harlem had in the 1920s. The bars developed into nightclubs and restaurants with entertainment. Chinatowns flourished as tourist destinations, particularly in New York and San Francisco and on a smaller scale in other cities, such as Boston, Chicago, Oakland, Portland, Tacoma, Seattle and Honolulu.

Arthur Dong conducted much of the research about Asian American performers in the mid- and late-twentieth-century USA. His studio, Deep Focus, issued a DVD called *Forbidden City U.S.A.* that contained a history of performance in San Francisco and interviews with many of the performers. The title refers to one of the more famous Chinese American nightclubs and serves as a reminder that such places catered to the exotic appetite of tourists and were mainstream to neither the Chinese Americans nor the larger society.

When Dong embarked on his study, focusing on the best-known club, Charlie Low's Forbidden City, he discovered "that recent Asian American history books made no mention of the club. I located only one picture and one reference in all my search!" The post–Second World War generation of performers in the *chop-suey circuit* of variety modeled themselves after the prevailing types in mainstream American vaudeville, burlesque and popular music. There were crooners like Larry Chin and songbirds like Frances Chun. Toy Tat Mar was called the Chinese Sophie Tucker, and Toy and Wing were billed as the Chinese Fred Astaire and Ginger Rogers. There were also stripteasers, dance bands and comedians.

The turn toward mainstream American popular performance was necessary to attract white patronage, and there were likely a number of the younger Asian performers who wished to be judged as singers, dancers and musicians rather than Chinese American singers, dancers and musicians.

Not all were Chinese, a fact that was not apparent to the white clientele. There were Japanese, Filipino and Burmese among the entertainers and musicians. The partial homogenization of Asian American entertainment reached its largest audience with the stage musical *Flower Drum Song*. The production was a mixture of ersatz *Oriental* decor, the type employed by Hollywood, melodies by Richard Rodgers and performances by Chinese, Japanese, African Americans, Hispanics and white Canadians, Texans, and New Yorkers, all passing as Chinese or Chinese Americans.

FRED & ADELE ASTAIRE

b: (Adele Marie Austerlitz) 10 September 1897, Omaha, NE—d: 25 January 1981, Tucson, AZ

b: (Frederick Austerlitz) 10 May 1899, Omaha, NE—d: 22 June 1987, Los Angeles, CA

One name above all others remains prominent in American dance: Astaire. It does not matter that theatrical dancing first attracted attention before the American Revolution, that, from Colonial times onward, dance in various forms has been a staple of the American stage, or that the country's contributions to twentieth-century dance were unsurpassed and, at least in the fields of percussive, interpretive and modern dance, unique.

Despite all the hundreds of good dancers, and dozens of great ones, who graced American stages and films throughout the heyday of vaudeville and musical comedy, one dancer first springs to mind when talk turns to American dancing: Fred Astaire. Being a great dancer and a good musician was not enough to set Astaire apart and above his peers; many of Fred's contemporaries were great dancers and good musicians. Many of them were also black, so in their time they could not expect the opportunities that came Fred's way, but more than a few were white, yet they failed to achieve success equal to Astaire's.

The public, as a whole, did not notice if a dancer had an acute rhythmic sense; tapped clearly, fast and close to the floor; maintained an elegant line; or was inventive in combining steps. Fred Astaire understood that. He also understood that a dance between a man and a woman was not simply an athletic exercise, that the dance had to add to a viewer's understanding of the lovers' characters and their needs, fears, hopes and desires. What he brought to movies was not new to Broadway, but it was new to Hollywood: exhibition ballroom dancing.

Part of Astaire's phenomenal success was earned playing for the critics and the audience. Other dancers did not consider Fred Astaire the best tapper, the best ballroom dancer, or the best eccentric or acrobatic dancer. Many dancers performed for each other. Each recognized and appreciated moves that were beyond the appreciation of a general audience. Fred Astaire's genius lay in his rhythmic sense and the synthesis of many styles. In his Broadway and Hollywood musicals, he performed solos in which he combined acrobatics, a bit of soft shoe, some balletic attitudes and jumps, used a prop or two, and let go with a burst of staccato taps much like John Bubbles. Elsewhere in the show, Astaire turned to a theatrical version of ballroom dancing, embellishing a tango, a waltz or a foxtrot with a bit of soft shoe, an acrobatic lift or some swing dancing. Not only did he offer various types of dancing within each show or movie, he changed style and tempo several times within each dance. Audiences never tired of him.

Fred's eventual dominance of dance in the popular mind, however, was linked to his role as a partner. It was a role that evolved slowly because he began as a five-year-old tot in support of his sister, Adele, and it was many years before his contribution to the act was recognized. When Adele and Fred debuted in 1904, an age of comparative innocence and sexual discretion, the Astaires were wholesome, energetic and playful stand-ins for American youth. Theirs was a brother-and-sister act, and Adele overshadowed Fred for nearly 20 years. It was she who was the darling of the critics and the public, whereas reviewers saw Fred the dancer, largely the way he said he saw himself at the time, growing from perfunctory to uninspired to serviceable.

Fred had developed into an effective and original dancer well before Adele retired from the stage to marry into minor British royalty after the team's final Broadway show, *The Band Wagon,* in 1931. Their mother, who had always shared living quarters with Adele and Fred, moved to the United Kingdom with her daughter and new son-in-law. Fred remained on Broadway to star in *The Gay Divorce* and found he could go it alone on stage.

As the Great Depression worsened, however, few stage musicals made a profit. They were costly shows to mount and run; consequently, tickets were expensive. Tickets to movie musicals were far cheaper. Hollywood had flooded the market, and by 1932, the public had tired of the fizzy musical comedies in the 1920s mold. When the Broadway musical again captured an audience, it was with more worldly books and lyrics and a jazzier sound.

Fred had always been clever at making connections, and he used them to begin making motion pictures. Although he had signed with RKO, his first release was an MGM movie, *Dancing Lady* (1931), in which he had a bit part as himself partnering Joan Crawford. (Interestingly, this picture also provided a prominent audition for Ted Healy and His Stooges—Moe, Curley and Larry—and was only the second movie for Nelson Eddy, whose single solo was part of the finale.)

The twentieth century had reached puberty several years before the movies learned to talk and sing, but there was a lingering if declining suspicion in some parts of America that dancers, especially men, were sensual exhibitionists who did not do honest work for a living.

Although he had greatly improved as a dancer during his partnership with Adele, the Fred Astaire who made *Dancing Lady* and *Flying Down to Rio* was relatively gangly rather than graceful. Probably the experience of seeing himself on screen drove Fred to make his dancing smoother in his first costarring film role with Ginger Rogers.

By the time Fred was paired with his second long-term partner, Ginger, he was in his mid-30s and no longer relegated to brother roles. Fred and Ginger were still young America, but the focus of the Astaire-Rogers films was romance, and their union was enthusiastically welcomed by the public. Fred was no continental lounge lizard, and Ginger was neither vamp nor frivolous flapper. She was quite attractive, yet one would not have been shocked to see her selling fabric in a department store. He was less attractive, but his blend of confidence, cool and seeming diffidence charmed the ladies and reassured the guys in the audience. Apart from each other, Rogers was a 22-year-old utility player in the Hollywood studio system. A hardworking youngster with dancing experience, she had already made about 20 movies. Fred was an industrious, experienced and inventive stage dancer. The result of the Fred and Ginger partnership was very different from his work with Adele. Fred took Ginger in hand in their films, and what the public willingly witnessed on the silver screen was Fred Astaire making love to a woman through the symbols of dance.

That was unusual. Dick Powell sang to Ruby Keeler while she danced; he was pleading his love. Fred Astaire took Ginger and pulled her close to him, guiding her through a series of intimate physical moves. Fred never really kissed Ginger (until late in their partnership), but it was plain through the dancing that he had his way with her: twirling, lifting, bending, exciting her. Fred was the ordinary Joe winning the prettiest girl around and initiating her into lovemaking—this during the era when the puritanical Production Code insisted on twin beds in the matrimonial boudoir.

A decade earlier, Valentino had seduced women with the tango on the silent screen, but he was an exotic creature who had played a sheikh, a raja, a bullfighter, a Russian Cossack, a French courtier and a denizen of the demimonde, and his licentious screen behavior was denounced as frequently as it was envied and enjoyed. Contemporary with Astaire, Clark Gable and his manly brethren of handsome celluloid heroes wrangled at least one smoldering kiss before the final reel faded, but they never got to handle their leading ladies the way Astaire did. If Clark Gable, Gary Cooper or any of the other handsome heroes had gotten as physically intimate onscreen as Fred did dancing with Ginger, women would have been forever disillusioned with their real-life options, men would have become furious and discouraged with their fate, and censors, apoplectic.

Fred was not one of the rugged Romeos, however. He looked like he was kin to the audience, perhaps a haberdashery clerk in the same department store in which Ginger might have worked. Astaire was a Nebraska-bred American. He looked like an ordinary Joe, sounded like one, and behaved like a lucky one, and that ordinariness masked the fact that he became one of early sound films' most sexual performers.

Fred Astaire was not the only dancer around Hollywood during the 1930s. Jimmy Cagney and George Raft were there, but they worked on the Warner Brothers lot, where male stars were cast in gangster films and gritty urban dramas, and dancing was left to Ruby Keeler, blonde chorus girls, and the scenery and props in Busby Berkeley's mechanized dance drills. Fox also had a male-female dance team, but rather than a romantic pairing, the team of Bill Robinson and Shirley Temple was a lesson in sentiment and servility. Little Shirley was a spunky, white and precocious, but limited, partner for Bojangles, who was protective, black, a dance master and very careful not to dance rings around Shirley.

Fred's contemporary and Broadway rival, Hal Leroy, was as ordinary in appearance as Fred, but Hal was an eccentric dancer and a true tapper, not a ballet-influenced ballroom dancer. When Hal partnered Mitzi Mayfair, there was no romantic seduction. They were like pals, high-spirited youths whose dancing was athletic. (This emphasis on exhibiting exuberant fun and not teenage lust held true a few years later for Mickey Rooney's dancing and singing with Judy Garland and in the 1940s when Donald O'Connor partnered Peggy Ryan.) Ray Bolger and Buddy Ebsen showed up on screen in the mid-to-late 1930s, but they also were eccentric dancers, never romantic and usually comic. Black dancers of the day were restricted to specialty spots and, with about three exceptions, never figured in the plots of films.

The male musical stars of the early 1930s movies were singers or comedians like Al Jolson, Maurice Chevalier, Eddie Cantor, Charles King, The Marx Brothers, Bing Crosby, Bert Wheeler, Dick Powell, Jack Oakie, Bob Hope, Nelson Eddy, Allan Jones, the Ritz Brothers, Don Ameche, Kenny Baker and John Payne. Even after Fred Astaire had made dancing in movies safe for the masculine image, men usually did not dance with each other unless expressing their rivalry (like Astaire and George Murphy), were massed together like a cadet formation in support of a female dance star like Eleanor Powell, or demonstrating athleticism like various combinations of the four Condos Brothers. Throughout the 1930s, it seemed as if the only male performers who were excluded from romantic leads in movie musicals were dancers—except Fred Astaire. There was no shortage of white male dancers in Hollywood. Louis DaPron was handsomer than Astaire but less representative of the average American male who paid for the movie tickets. DaPron, Hermes Pan and Jack Cole found greater opportunity behind the camera, devising and directing dances. George Murphy at MGM was a potential rival to Astaire; Murphy was more masculine and conventionally attractive than Astaire, but his studio failed to push him as a rival. Consequently, Murphy made as many dramas as he did musicals, and, except for the musicals that costarred him with Eleanor Powell or Shirley Temple, his body of work is unmemorable. Murphy's strength was tap, whereas Fred's romantic dancing was primarily exhibition ballroom enlivened by tap and eccentric sequences.

It was not until the early 1940s that Fred Astaire got worthy competition in the persons of Gene Kelly, Gene Nelson and Dan Dailey. A decade later, there were male dancers galore in Hollywood. Few boys were brave enough to regularly attend dancing school and endure the taunts of their peers.

Fred Astaire was not yet five years old when he began dance class. His sister and mother took him along when they moved to Manhattan to pursue a career for Adele. Their father stayed in Omaha to run the family business and generate income for his wife and children until Adele's career could sustain them. Fred's attendance at class was perhaps an afterthought, an alternative to finding a babysitter or nursery school. Fred neither objected nor took dance class too seriously. Mrs. Astaire tutored her children; their curriculum included nights at the theatre.

The source for much of the Astaires' early career is Fred's autobiography, *Steps in Time* (1959). It is an annoying book, as full of name-dropping as the worst of Hollywood star memoirs. If one took his story at face value, the Astaire family was on the fringe of society, and Fred was preoccupied with horse racing and being one of the carefree, well-dressed young bloods around town. Fred Astaire had little to say about dance. Between the accounts of shooting parties in the United Kingdom with the duke of this and the laird of that and chumming around with Jock Whitney and other young and privileged sports in New York, Astaire laid out the bones of the team's early career. Mother was their manager. Amateur shows and recitals prepared Adele and Fred for their professional debut, a novelty vaudeville act encumbered by props, settings, costumes and mechanical devices designed to distract the audience from the kids' shortcomings as dancers. They spent about five years in small-time vaudeville, playing mostly in heartland America. As they got better, so did their salary and their place on the bill (they had started as an opening act). Regarded as child prodigies, they got booked on the Orpheum circuit and played some larger cities, including Seattle, San Francisco and Los Angeles.

There were only two problems in their immediate future. One was the Gerry Society, the name given to the Society for the Prevention of Cruelty to Children, whose concern for the moral well-being of child performers far exceeded their concern for the children who tried to make a living selling newspapers or working long hours in factories. The Gerry Society was particularly strong in Manhattan, so the Society kept a lot of kid acts like Elsie Janis, the Three Keatons (Buster), Baby June (Havoc), and Adele & Fred Astaire from working where they could best forge ahead in their careers. Mrs. Astaire somehow convinced Mr. Gerry that her children were well schooled and hardly exploited. The second problem was also universal to kid acts. The youngest needed to be little more than cute and personable; a smidgeon of talent and skill was often enough to please a friendly audience. As kids entered the awkward age, however, they outgrew their cuteness, voices changed, bodies grew long and lanky, and the young teens grew uncertain and self-conscious. They needed talent and skill. Fred and Adele began to fade as an attraction around 1909.

In 1911, Mrs. Astaire bought an act from Ned Wayburn, a theatrical entrepreneur who staged top-notch Broadway shows, including some *Ziegfeld Follies*, and ran a large dancing school that the Astaires attended. The singing and dancing act Wayburn devised for Adele and Fred debuted at Proctor's Fifth Avenue Theatre. They were stuck in the opening slot on the bill, and they flopped and were canceled.

Fred, then 12, had accepted the fact he was a dancer, however. He took lessons, practiced and rehearsed more seriously. The next two seasons were rough. To get work, they had to go back to the small-time theatres of the Midwest. Gradually, they refined their act, cutting out the palaver and sticking to the singing and dancing. They also found an agent and a teacher who believed in them and had time for them. By the time they did their final season in vaudeville (1915–16), the act was back on the big time, with a better spot on the bills, playing New York, earning $350 to $500 per week and working every week. Meanwhile, Fred maneuvered Adele and himself into a Broadway revue.

The movement for Prohibition that was spreading in the USA, especially in the Bible Belt, and the future of Mr. Astaire's *brewmeister* livelihood became uncertain. For years he had supported his family while Fred and Adel found their footing in vaudeville, and he engaged a good dance teacher and a capable agent for Adele and Fred. By 1920, when he joined the family in Manhattan, Adele and Fred were making good in Broadway revues. He lived to see their success continue in London but died before Fred and Adele returned to the USA.

From 1917 until 1931, Adele and Fred Astaire appeared in 11 revues and musical comedies. They started with the Shuberts in *Over the Top* (1917) and ended with *The Band Wagon* (1931). Most were hits, and *Lady Be Good* (1924–25) and *Funny Face* (1927–28) earned particular fame and were performed in London. Adele and Fred were as popular with London audiences as with New Yorkers, but Adele was still copping the lion's share of the notices. She was petite, had a fine sense of comedy and charmed audiences and critics with her fey grace and fine dancing.

Fred worked ever harder, taking the dominant hand in devising their routines and creating solos for himself. His last Broadway show, *The Gay Divorce* (1932–33)—the only one he appeared in without his sister—quieted any doubts that Fred Astaire was an accomplished and personable performer in his own right. He no longer had doubts about himself, and he had decided that he wanted to make motion pictures.

The best-known period of Fred Astaire's career encompassed the nine musicals he made with Ginger Rogers for RKO Pictures. (Their final pairing in *The Barkleys of Broadway* was made for MGM, a decade after their RKO series concluded). By the early 1930s, all the studios knew what kind of pictures they made best, wanted to make and wanted to avoid—except RKO.

As Ethan Mordden pointed out in *Hollywood Studios,* RKO was organized simply to make profitable motion pictures with sound. The studio's agenda was a *tabula rasa.* Without an institutional heritage or philosophy to guide it, RKO was more open to experiment than the old-line studios that, in one form or another, had begun in the silent era. Also, as the inheritor of the Keith Orpheum vaudeville theatres that were situated in all the major cities of the northern United States, from New York to Chicago to San Francisco, RKO could attract large, urban and comparatively sophisticated audiences for its films. Fred Astaire's availability appealed to RKO's producer Pandro Berman, director Mark Sandrich and the studio's team of technicians, most of them refugees, like Astaire, from Broadway. They alone of the idea men in Hollywood knew how to work with Fred.

Adele had taken to the genteel life as though born to it. She became lady of the manor after 1932 when she wed Lord Charles Francis Cavendish, son of the ninth duke of Devonshire, known to family and friends as Charlie. After her marriage, Adele Astaire never again appeared on the stage. A decade into their marriage, Charlie died. Mother Astaire, who had been living with them, moved to the USA and spent most of the remainder of her very long life with Fred and his family. In 1947, Adele married Kingman Douglas and returned to the USA. She remained out of the public eye until her death at age 83.

It was Fred, the somewhat reluctant boy who preferred playing with his friends to lessons and dance class, who became the enduring star of the Astaire family. Despite a cultivated air of insouciance, he grew into a determinedly hard worker. From the time he realized, while supporting his sister in their vaudeville act, that he was a dancer, not simply a boy passing his youth on the vaudeville stage, he made a commitment to do his best. In all, and apart from Adele, he made more than 30 films and numerous television appearances. His discipline enabled him to score 50 years as a top-notch dancer. At 60 he was still able to acquit himself respectably, as his two television dance specials (1958, 1959) demonstrated.

In addition to Adele and Ginger, Fred had excellent partners in almost all of his films. Joan Fontaine was perhaps willing but barely able, and a few others were not top-notch, but Rita Hayworth, Lucille Bremer, Vera-Ellen, Leslie Caron, Cyd Charisse, Jane Powell and Barrie Chase were expert, versatile and hardworking dance partners.

Astaire knew that nobody was interested in how much time, muscle ache, sweat and practice went into his performances. Fred worked hard to make his dancing seem like a breeze. His singing and acting styles were all of a piece with his dancing. Although he danced better than he sang and sang better than he acted, he owed no apologies for any of it. Indeed, in his final decade in movies, he worked as a dramatic actor and light comedian.

Throughout his 75-year career, by seeming to be the most levelheaded and modest of performers, he did not wear out his welcome. He tried as best he could to change his style to match the changes in taste of his audience. In his films for MGM and others in the post–Second World War era, however, Fred's novelty solos sometimes misfired. In his films of the 1930s, his solos were jazzy counterparts to his ballroom duos, but Fred was sophisticated and never hip. Although his sense of what was right for himself had been unfailing, some of his solo work in 1950s films seemed strained and bordered the ridiculous; his attempt to spoof beatniks and hipsters made Astaire seem outdated and a bit foolish.

Fred always understood publicity; he allowed glimpses of his personal life but never intrusion. He was married to Phyllis Livingstone Potter from the time he entered motion pictures to the day in 1954 when she died. It was presented to his fans as happy a marriage as it was private, and doubtless it was. When at 80 he married Robyn Smith, he astounded the press and public, but they had no more success penetrating his personal life in 1980 than in all previous decades. To a remarkable degree, Fred Astaire controlled his life, his career, his movies and what people thought of him. Fred Astaire never betrayed the amount of labor and sweat it took to achieve his stage effects. He said he worried only about getting his work ready. Otherwise, he claimed to be uncomplicated and easy-going. Perhaps that was the true man, or maybe he deflected unwarranted analysis with a studied air of casualness. The result is an enduring persona and a body of exceptional work.

ROSCOE ATES

b: 20 January 1895, Grange MO—d: 1 March 1962, Los Angeles, CA

"Th-th-that's easy f-f-for you to say!" The comedian with a lumpy-featured, worried face and a practiced stutter, Roscoe Ates learned to control his childhood stutter and used it to get laughs in small-time vaudeville. He had begun playing violin in nickelodeons, accompanying the silent films, then parleyed his stutter and a fine sense of comedy into a career that spanned 1920s small-time vaudeville, a flop musical comedy (*Sea Legs,* 1937), supporting roles in more than 100 feature-length films (including *Freaks, Cimarron, Alice in Wonderland, The Champ* and *Gone with the Wind*), a few two-reel movies, a couple of movie serials and some television appearances, including a stint costarring with Russell Hayden in a summer replacement series, *The Marshall of Gunsight Pass* (1950).

Although Roscoe acquitted himself well in the few dramatic films in which he appeared, most of his movies were comedies, and many of them were Westerns, especially in the late 1930s and early 1940s. In Westerns, he had a costarring role as a bumptious sidekick; in comedies his parts were usually smaller, but the bits afforded his character the opportunity to stutter and sputter, and his appearances provided a lift to the movie at the point in the plot when it was needed.

CHOLLY ATKINS

b: (Charles Atkinson) 30 September 1913, Pratt Coty, AL—d: 19 April 2003, Las Vegas, NV

Few black dancers of his generation were as fortunate as Cholly Atkins. He was one of the classic tap dancers whose career was interrupted when America entered the Second World War. After the war, he teamed with Charles "Honi" Coles and, as one of the most polished and accomplished tap acts of their generation, appeared on Broadway, television and in nightclubs, even as audiences began to forsake tap for jazz dance and more balletic theatrical dance forms.

Cholly, however, instead of shuffling off at the tap dance wake, made a second career that rivaled his first. Sometime around 1950, he began to help singing groups develop some moves and stage presence. By 1964, he was choreographer in residence for Motown Records, the upstart Detroit record label that revolutionized the sound of pop music. The Motown acts were all young kids with little stage experience. The sales of their records led to demands for personal appearances. It was Cholly Atkins who made stageworthy and visual such acts as the Cadillacs, Gladys Knight and the Pips, the O'Jays, Martha & the Vandellas, the Temptations, the Supremes, Smoky Robinson and the Miracles, and the Four Tops, among the many.

Cholly grew up in Buffalo, New York, where his mother had moved with her two sons after they were deserted by their father. He enjoyed a typical boyhood for the era, working odd jobs after school and going to youth centers to play basketball and to attend dances. His studies included music classes, and he even learned rudimentary tap. According to Atkins' recollection, Buffalo was quite free of overt racism. There were several vaudeville theatres in town, and all were integrated, with blacks and whites seated anywhere they pleased.

Cholly's first showbiz job was as a singing waiter in a local resort, Alhambra on the Lake (Erie). A dancing waiter, William "Red" Porter, and Cholly began working together during the floor show. Soon Red and Cholly developed an act, Billy and Charles, the Two Rhythm Pals. Cholly was musical but not a trained dancer, yet he picked up steps quickly from Red. Cholly went on the road for six months with the *Sammy Lewis' Revue* in 1930, playing second-tier cities and towns in Ohio, West Virginia and North Carolina. To control expenses, everyone had to do a little of everything: comedy bits, singing and dancing. It was his first truly professional work, but when bookings thinned, Lewis ran off with the take. Cholly and the others were stranded.

Back in Buffalo, Cholly and Red teamed again as the Rhythm Pals and went out with another revue that played New England. The Will Mastin Trio was part of the show, and tiny, seven-year-old Sammy Davis Jr. was beginning to work in the act. Despite the Great Depression, the Rhythm Pals continued to get work. They had become a tight dance act and were featured in shows starring Billy Eckstine, Willie Bryant, Valaida Snow, Leonard Reed and Lil Hardin. It was Lil who, in 1935, brought Cholly and Red along with her band to the Apollo Theater in Harlem. And it was at the Apollo that Cholly met Honi Coles, his future partner.

Valaida Snow brought Cholly to Los Angeles, where there was a lot of nightclub work plus some movie work. Cholly and his friends did extra work in films and dubbed tap sounds for movie musicals. He organized a group of 16 dancers, who laid down the taps for the sound tracks for which the white chorus dancers faked the moves on screen. Cholly and Red joined Ralph Cooper's burlesque and vaudeville show that toured white burlesque houses from Seattle to L.A. Cholly began choreographing the numbers for the chorus line.

The Rhythm Pals returned to the East Coast around 1938, when Red married and quit dancing to help run his wife's business. Cholly's girlfriend danced in the Apollo alongside Honi Coles' girlfriend, and all four lived in the same building. The two men began hanging out, but it took quite a while before they teamed. Cholly had never learned the business end of entertainment, and he did not know how to scare up gigs. Eventually, Honi got Cholly some work and taught him which bookers to see. As work was scarce in New York, Cholly swallowed his pride and joined the chorus of the *Hot Mikado* as a replacement. After its New

York stand, the show toured. Cholly was glad he accepted the gig because Bill Robinson was the show's star, and Cholly got to study the master's rapport with audiences. Cholly also found a new partner, Dottie Saulters, and Cholly & Dottie hit the big time traveling as part of, first, Louis Armstrong's show and, later, Cab Calloway's.

When the USA entered the Second World War, summonses from the draft board put the brakes to many careers, including Cholly's. He was not alone. His friend Honi Coles, then doing a single, had been inducted in 1942; Cholly followed him in 1943. Cholly was the luckier of the two; he was assigned to Army band duties and was able to takes club jobs on weekends.

When Cholly and Honi formed their act after the Second World War, they got top-notch bookings right away: tours with bands headed by Louis Armstrong, Charlie Barnet, Andy Kirk and Count Basie. They played the familiar northern circuit of black theatres (known informally as *round the world*): the Royal in Baltimore (its poorly constructed and maintained floor was ill-suited for dancers), the Howard in Washington, D.C., the Earle in Philadelphia, the Regal in Chicago and, of course, the Apollo in Harlem. They went to England and played variety houses.

Back in the USA in 1949 and on Broadway in *Gentlemen Prefer Blondes,* they stopped the show every night when they performed their specialty dance. Carol Channing was the star. Although they spent three years with a top-notch show, on Broadway and on the road, there was not much work for them after it closed. Television offered a few guest shots on variety shows, which paid poorly, as did the small clubs and the *nabes* (neighborhood theatres) that booked a couple of acts of vaudeville to play between showings of a feature motion picture.

When the 1960s rocked and rolled around, tap was pushed aside. To some, it was a relic of 1920s and 1930s stage shows; to others, it had been superceded by jazz dancing. There was still interest in jazz tap, and Cholly and other rhythm tappers appeared at festivals (Newport Jazz in 1962 and 1963) and conferences and seminars conducted by Marshal and Jean Stearns. The jazz and dance cognoscenti were the audience for these events.

Cholly Atkins' work was as much about the future as the past, and he was kept busy throughout the 1960s and 1970s with vocal choreography, which was what Cholly called his work with the rhythm-and-blues and soul acts. It was devised for performers who were primarily singers, and Atkins arranged the movements in such ways that allowed the acts to handle microphones and breathe properly while adding visual flourishes to their numbers. Cholly understood lighting and sound technology as well, and he prepared cue sheets for his clients. He also helped the younger ones to adjust to the pressure and discipline of show business. Cholly worked for Motown during its innovative years in the late 1960s. When he freelanced, acts clamored for his help, and he sent them, well prepared, on the same road he himself had traveled.

Cholly moved to Las Vegas in the 1970s and began choreographing stage revues for the hotels. It was 1989, and Atkins was 75, when he, Fayard Nicholas, Henry LeTang and Frankie Manning choreographed the Broadway show *Black and Blue.* His career had taken him from Bill Robinson to the New Kids on the Block and Savion Glover.

AT LIBERTY

Out of work in show business.

AUDIENCE LEFT

That side of the theatre auditorium left of the center aisle as the audience faces the stage.

AUDIENCE RIGHT

That side of the theatre auditorium right of the center aisle as the audience faces the stage.

AUDIENCES

The Founding Fathers of the United States of America did not attach great importance to the arts beyond letters and architecture, the arts in which they themselves were skilled. Neither the merchant class nor the clergy was sympathetic. Other than having family portraits painted and ordering fine furniture, the merchant class, as a whole, viewed the arts as frippery. The clergy ranged from suspicious to hostile. There were

B. F. Keith's Theatre Program

Week Commencing Monday, September 25, 1922

1755th Week of B. F. Keith Vaudeville in Philadelphia

NOTICE TO PATRONS!

The last act on our bill is always interesting and often is one of the features of our show, and in justice to this act, the audience is requested to remain seated until it is finished. It is very disconcerting to have part of the audience leave while the artists are doing their best to please those remaining seated who are discommoded by having their attention distracted from the stage by people leaving.

THE MANAGEMENT.

Audience notice

no princely states to foster the arts, and indifference was the most benevolent attitude encountered by most theatres and performers during Colonial times and the early years of the republic.

It was not a land of philistines; there was a healthy percentage of literacy for the times, and many families read books, sketched and played musical instruments in the home. Learning and artistic expression, however, were expected to be pursued modestly, not crassly exhibited on stage to attract attention to one's self.

Repression of the performing arts by local government and denunciation of the evils of the stage from local pulpits flowed and ebbed with the political current. In response, early theatres had to pay attention to which way the wind was blowing. They hoisted their canvas when the air was favorable, trimmed their sails when there was an ill wind. Expectations that theatre should be morally instructive led to melodrama; the audience understood that they could enjoy numerous scenes of sin and sensation before the final act of repentance and retribution. Singing and dancing by adult men and women were licentious displays of the sinful body but charmingly innocent when performed by children who had yet to be contaminated by the lust that must attend puberty. Theatre managers, with a moistened finger in the air, alternately produced classical drama, melodrama, recitations and variety to avoid censure and attract and build audiences.

The theatres of the Colonies and early Republic were run by small resident groups and extended families. Beginning with the advent of the modern industrial era, theatre turned into show business. It had ever been a matter of finding audiences to support performers and theatres, but as society and business became more complex, entrepreneurs were attracted to the growing business of giving shows. Most entrepreneurs had a genuine affection for show business and found ordinary work a dulling bore and trial. They were attracted to the hustle, the gamble, the hoopla, the payoff and the bragging rights that attached to show business.

Princess Wah-letka

In the years between 1780 and 1820, Europe and the United States created the conditions for the modern era. A long stretch of European and North American wars had powered the Industrial Revolution with innovations in mining, smelting and casting, machinery, shipbuilding and land transport.

Political revolutions in the American Colonies and France preached that all men were equal, and the divine right of kings got trumped by those playing the equality card. Increasingly direct elections transferred some power from traditional elites and their electors to emergent paternal organizations that husbanded and exercised the votes of their constituents. The limits of franchise to white males with property were not abolished, simply extended, yet not so far as to include women or non-Caucasians. Not only had the young nations of the Americas proved they were here to stay, but for the first time in 50 years, the Atlantic Ocean was not a battleground. England finally defeated Napoleon after a quarter century of conflict, and, in turn, the young United States completed its effort to throw off English claims when the War of 1812 was called a draw. Within a decade or so, most of the Spanish and Portuguese colonies in Central and South America gained their independence. By 1820, Europeans could come to America in ships made bigger, faster and safer through 40 years of improvements in naval warfare.

From 1820 to 1860, immigrants came by the millions into a federation of commonwealths and states made ever more tenuous by exacerbating differences in heritage, race, station and local economies. The people who populated agrarian America were divided into two groups: those who owned the land and those who worked the land or had lost it. In the agricultural states of the South, the slaves worked the land. As whites moved steadily westward, the Native Americans lost it.

Some new European immigrants became landholding middle-class farmers within a single generation, thanks to hard work. Others, unable or unwilling to chance the ever-farther frontier, took a couple of generations to reach the bottom rung of the lower middle class. Often driven from impoverished European lands, these folks tended to cluster in the port cities in which they landed. Few had money to travel farther. Their skills were in farming, military service or as commercial seamen, so they were ready laborers for any kind of hire: building trades, slaughterhouses, breweries, constabularies and shipping. In time, the luckiest and pluckiest prospered.

All together, rural and urban, the immigrants and their children constituted a new class, one that was expanding between the have-nots and the have-everythings: a middle class.

Not all the well-to-do were educated and cultured, but, as a class, they increasingly turned to the fine arts, well-crafted objects and the performance of classical music and serious drama such as Shakespeare. For some, their patronage of the arts may have been motivated less by appreciation and more for prestige and the appearance of sophistication as epitomized by Europe.

Similarly, not all the poor or the aspiring middle class were without refinement, but, as a whole, their tastes had not been cultivated nor had they the money to become supporters of the arts. Concert halls and museums seemed forbidding to some, emphasizing differences in social and economic class. Many immigrants preferred the entertainments of the marketplace, circus and popular theatre that they had enjoyed in the old country as well as the music and dances they had performed in their homes and at their community celebrations.

Every variety entertainer had once been a member of the audience. The performers shared the same miseries and joys of the general public, although they did not share the public's willingness to be herded into imagination-numbing occupations. It was this nexus between performer and public that made vernacular entertainment, rather than the classical performing arts, the bedrock of show business. Still, there were varying degrees of what was acceptable to family audiences.

As the agrarian society of the early nineteenth century became increasingly isolated by an urbanized and industrialized economy after the Civil War, the gulf grew between urban and rural interests. From Colonial times there had been great plantations, like those of George Washington and Thomas Jefferson. These gentlemen farmers of the South had little in common with their slaves or the tenant farmers who worked land they did not own or the families that scratched a living out of the small, rocky farms in the northeastern states. Yet country people, rich or poor, white or black, shared one thing: much of their art was enjoyed in the home or outdoors in fine weather. Farm folk, North or South or West, learned to play instruments, sing and dance. They made their own music and told their own stories.

The northern elite, like their southern brethren, entertained at home for the most part, and they founded symphony orchestras, art museums and libraries. Today, we remain blessed by the monuments to culture built by masters of commerce in the Victorian era, but their factories set the terms of employment, including low wages and unsafe working conditions. For much of the nineteenth century, the urban poor lived in disease-breeding warrens, several families sharing a few rooms and a common outdoor privy; sanitation and public health were not yet the responsibility of government. Wealth provided not only comfort but safety; the rich could afford to insulate themselves from the poor. The only power the poor had was in organization, either pooling enough of their votes in direct elections or massing in large enough mobs to negotiate with strength backed by the threat of riots and destruction of property. This dynamic between privilege and disenfranchisement, between established families and immigrants, played out on American stages for a century, both as drama and burlesque.

The tenements of the poor were not places for entertainment. As village people had for centuries, families met in church, and the men took refuge in saloons. Women, stuck in cramped flats, tended house, cooked, gave birth to children, raised them and, too often, buried them.

Men who lacked privileged options had to follow their work: the Army, the railroads, mining or shipping. Some took a chance that, in striking out for the West, they could find prosperity through gold, farming or herding and bring their families together again. Some, cowed by adversity or despair, struck out and left their hapless families behind. Frontier towns, shipping ports, railroad centers, mill cities and mining camps were men-only affairs at first, and there were entrepreneurs who, depending upon one's view, catered to their needs or exploited their weaknesses. The most common diversions were boozing, brawling, gambling and whoring. Men did not have to leave home to find such distraction. New York City and every other growing city had a tenderloin that hosted many a *free-and-easy.*

Poor women who did not yet have children to nurture worked outside the home. They were mill workers, domestics and laundry workers. Some took their chances out West, but, in the main, the double standard prevailed, and their choices for employment were limited. Any suspicion or appearance of immoral behavior was grounds for dismissal; asserting oneself or giving rise to gossip also could cost a young woman her job. If she married and became pregnant she was likely to be fired. An unmarried woman who became pregnant was forced into the underworld if she was without means or family. Out of doors, society expected women to be accompanied by husbands or other women; at the end of their workday, they could not repair to the local saloon unless they had no reputation left to lose. Entertainment was for the men and by the women, and a woman who entertained by singing or dancing for strangers was assumed to have no respectable limits to her behavior.

It remained for the more farseeing of showmen to create entertainment suitable for women and children and yet retain male patronage. To increase their potential audience threefold, the entrepreneurs of the late nineteenth century needed to convince the public and the arbiters of public morality that shows were respectable and that spending leisure time at a theatre was also respectable. As law and order came to the frontier and to the hell's kitchens of America's urban areas, it made sense for theatre owners and producers to upgrade from outlaw status and to position their business as a community service like markets, banks, churches and baseball teams.

With the rise of industrial wealth, the "business of America became business." A national ethic emerged that encouraged Christian values and social Darwinism, often hand in hand. The inhabitants of slums, shantytowns and hillbilly hollows were considered beyond fruitful exhortation and of no real economic consequence. The greener pastures held the emerging middle class, urged to respectability and hard work with the lure of a stake in the American promise fulfilled. Individually, the workers and their families had little to spend on luxuries like entertainment. Collectively, they were a growing market. Showmen attracted the new middle class by keeping individual ticket prices low and building theatres with more seats. All manner of tastes could be accommodated; if one act did not appeal to a segment of the audience, the next act might.

A respectable middle-class life in Victorian America meant at least the appearance of stable family life, civic virtue, safer streets and honest government. This was not good news to operators of free-and-easies. The smart ones followed Tony Pastor's lead in New York. Pastor was the quintessential variety performer of his day, but he is remembered as the showman who promoted refined variety for the whole family—women and children invited—and moved his theatre away from the Bowery and farther uptown, where respectable folks were more likely to attend. His success was the starting gun for showmen in many cities, and the rise of vaudeville and burlesque was rapid.

The people's art form was presented in so many different types of venues that it was accessible to all. There were the bare-bones houses of small towns and poorer neighborhoods, and there were ornamented palaces whose appointments and comfort offered a ribbon clerk's vision of paradise. Vaudeville came a long way from the skid-row free-and-easy where a guy could get drunk, cuddle up to a buxom cutie, lose the rest of his money in a crooked toss of the dice, get slipped a Mickey Finn and end up working as crew in a slow freighter to Shanghai. By 1900, the free-and-easies were largely a memory of the bad old good old days.

Hollanders, "Fun in the Land of Dykes"

In turn, the vaudeville audience represented the America of big cities, small towns and frontier settlements. Vaudeville attracted women, men and children. As was true on stage, every nationality was represented in vaudeville's audiences. Although vaudeville did not heal the racial divide, it went further toward integration than any other institution in the USA—churches, government, colleges or business—because its mainstream stages hosted black acts like Miller & Lyles, Ethel Waters, Avery & Hart, Sissle & Blake and Buck & Bubbles along with white acts. Where local laws forbade integration in the audience, custom did the job. Slowly, city by city, and in individual theatres, if not row by row, Americans came together.

Even the class divisions that rose in the mid-nineteenth century were bridged early in the twentieth. Although some critics continued to sniff at vaudeville, the more perspicacious embraced it. Robert Benchley, whose fame as a topical humorist has eclipsed his keen common sense as a theatre critic for *The New Yorker,* wrote as one "who once considered an afternoon at the Palace the richest cultural experience in life." By the early 1910s, the Vanderbilts and the rest of society's 400 attended vaudeville, and they embraced jazz music and high-stepping colored acts. Not content being observers, they hired black dancers to teach them the latest steps and hired black dance bands to come into their mansions to play for their parties. By the onset of the 1920s, the variety performances of vaudeville had breached portions of the lines dividing the classes.

AUDITION

Vaudevillians seldom, if ever, submitted to an audition. Instead, they followed custom and played a show date (*See "Show Date"*) for agents and bookers. Auditions were usual for those performers and actors seeking roles, large or small, in musical comedies and plays.

AUGUSTES AND CLOWNS

Simply put, augustes are madcaps, and clowns are naïfs. Both had been fixtures of European circuses for centuries, but the auguste was the more recent innovation. *Clown* has been used as a term to describe physical comedians who performed in pantomime, vaudeville, music-hall, revue and silent films, but many so-called clowns, American and European, are more carefully considered augustes. An auguste is a physical comedian who is not in the classic, white-faced tradition of Pierrot. *Auguste* translates as "silly fool," and it had long been held that the origin of the auguste began around 1870, when Tom Belling, an American acrobat performing with the Renz Circus, a German outfit, was kidding around in clown alley. Donning various mismatched clothes and a red wig, he began a mocking impersonation of the company manager, who happened into the dressing room. Belling flew out into the ring; he stumbled, fell and scored a hit with the audience, who thought it was an act; they yelled, "Auguste!" Most reliable sources consider this anecdote a fiction, noting that coinage of the word *auguste* came later that century. More likely is that the new characterization was based on a Russian clown that Belling had worked within Eastern Europe.

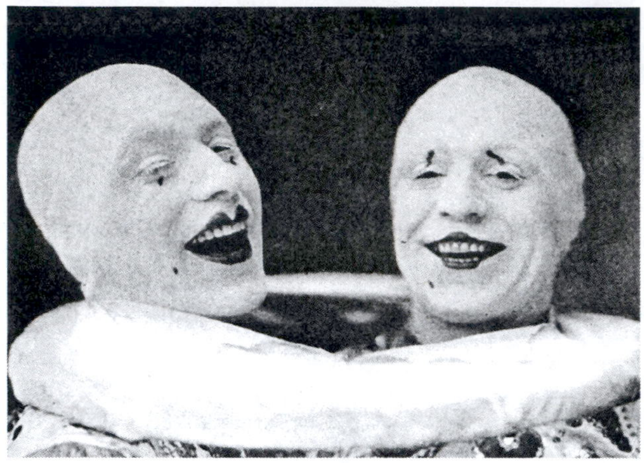

Gaudsmith Brothers

Ferry Corwey, "The Musical Clown"

Arnaut Brothers

Whatever the true circumstances of its origin, the auguste was a marked change in characterization from the Pierrot-like sprites that gleefully ran about in whiteface. They remained popular in European circus longer than on American stages. The augustes eliminated the whiteface but added many vibrant colors to their face: red noses, large black eyebrows, exaggerated red mouths and blue shadowing reduced to abstract shapes around the eyes and on the cheeks. The range of their costumes was unlimited, and the entire effect was intended to be bizarre.

American and British clowns that continued to use whiteface makeup (except for the English Pierrot troupes) shed the traditional pajama-style clown suits with pom-poms for more contemporary characterizations. These so-called character clowns sometimes assumed tramp outfits, and to give an appearance of being unshaven, they added a smear of black makeup to the lower halves of their faces.

The distinction between an auguste and a clown has been used to differentiate between types of circus funnymen, George L. Fox was a nineteenth-century example of the clown on the American stage. Many vaudeville comedians can be divided into clowns and augusts. Harpo Marx, Stan Laurel, Larry Semon, Harry Langdon, Jimmy Savo and Red Skelton were clowns. Weber & Fields, Ed Wynn, Groucho Marx, Bert Lahr and Bobby Clark were augustes.

AUNT JEMIMA

The name and image of Aunt Jemima was appropriated so often and continuously since the 1880s that it is doubtful anyone has clear title. The legend of Aunt Jemima started before the Civil War; the original Jemima was reputed to be a cook on a Louisiana plantation owned by a Colonel Higbee.

Among the earliest appearances of the famed mammy figure is a vaudeville (or minstrel) performance of a song called "Aunt Jemima," sung in a minstrel show by a blackface comedian in drag. One of the owners of Pearl Milling Company attended a performance of the show in 1889 and decided that the image of a stout, jovial colored mammy would help promote his company's new product, a premixed, self-rising pancake mix. There is no record that the performer or the songwriter agreed to the use of Aunt Jemima to sell pancake flour.

The Pearl Milling Company had been in financial trouble, and its owners were forced, a year later, to sell their new pancake formula to the R. T. Davis Milling Company. Davis promoted both product and image; in 1893 the company hired 59-year-old Nancy Green, an African American woman who was a cook for a Chicago judge, to dress in gingham, apron and head bandana to demonstrate their new Aunt Jemima Pancake Mix. The Davis Company risked an expensive promotion and took a booth at Chicago's Columbian Exposition and World's Fair in 1893. They constructed a 16-foot-tall, 12-foot-diameter flour barrel, and over the duration of the event, fed 1 million of Aunt Jemima's ready-mixed, self-rising pancakes to those who visited their display. Ms. Green was possessed of friendly mien and temperament, charming each visitor to the Aunt Jemima booth. The response was nearly overwhelming; a police detail was required, and Davis' gamble paid handsomely.

Over the succeeding decades, until 1967, seven different women have portrayed Aunt Jemima for the pancake manufacturer. The most famous of these was Edith Wilson, a well-known blues singer from the 1920s, who made personal appearances as Aunt Jemima from 1948 until 1967 for the Quaker Oats Company, who then owned the Aunt Jemima brand.

As supermarket demonstrations grew in popularity through the 1940s, there were probably many women who were hired to dress up like Aunt Jemima and demonstrate the product at the local A&P or the competing First National Store.

There was, however, another Aunt Jemima, a character played by Tess Gardella, an Italian American singer who performed in blackface. Gardella played Aunt Jemima from the 1910s through the 1940s, and she had no connection with Aunt Jemima's pancakes and syrup.

See Tess "Aunt Jemima" Gardella and Edith Wilson

LOVIE AUSTIN

b: (Cora Calhoun) 19 September 1887, Chattanooga, TN—d: 10 July 1972, Chicago, IL

Vaudeville provided a means of making a living for many musicians who later earned their reputations as giants of jazz. Looking through catalogs of old blues recordings, it is impossible to miss Lovie Austin and Her Blues Serenaders. They accompanied the top blues singers of the day: Ma Rainey, Ida Cox, Ethel Waters, Hattie McDaniels and Alberta Hunter.

Various sidemen who worked with Lovie included trumpeter Tommy Ladnier (1900–39), clarinetists Jimmy Noone (1895–1944) and Johnny Dodds (1892–1940), trombonist Kid Ory (1886–1973) and drummer W. E. "Buddy" Burton (1890–1976).

Lovie and Bessie Smith came from the same hometown, Chattanooga, Tennessee, and Lovie recalled that she and Bessie both were taken with Gertrude "Ma"

Rainey. When Ma's show came to town to play the Ivory or the Liberty Theatres, the two girls would hang out in the alley outside the stage door. Bessie sang along with Rainey.

Unlike Smith, Austin was formally educated in music at Roger Williams University in Nashville, Tennessee, and at Knoxville College, unusual in that era for a blues and jazz musician, a Negro or a woman. About the same time, she wed a nickelodeon manager, but the marriage soon ended.

Professionally, Lovie Austin played piano in several vaudeville acts, including one with her second husband, before she put together her own act, Lovie Austin & Her Blues Serenaders, and played black vaudeville with considerable success. In the late 1920s, she and her group took up residence at several clubs, most notably Harlem's Club Alabam.

Producers had begun making *race records,* as they were called, in 1921. The success of the recordings by blues singers and instrumentalists proved that Negroes, North and South, had phonograph players and were willing and ready buyers. Paramount Records was the premier label of New York Recording Laboratories, and Lovie Austin became its house musical director and pianist, playing on a number of sides with her own Blues Serenaders.

Austin's playing was noted for a strong two-handed approach. With her left hand, she maintained a steadily rocking bass beat behind the singer, the clarinet and cornet players; with her right, she improvised countermelodies.

In the late 1920s, Lovie Austin decided to make Chicago her home, and she lived and worked there for the rest of her life. She became the leader and arranger of the Monogram Theatre's pit band as well as its pianist. Lovie and the pit band were the only classy things about the Monogram, and they were the only reason so many black vaudevillians affectionately recalled their bookings at that cheesy and rundown theatre.

Mary Lou Williams, herself a piano player with the Whitman Sisters troupe before she won recognition as a great jazz pianist, was greatly impressed by Austin. In liner notes for Stash Records, Mary Lou remembered her attention focused on "this great woman sitting in the pit and conducting a group of five or six men, her legs crossed, a cigarette in her mouth, playing the show with her left hand and writing music [arrangements] for the next act with her right. Wow! She was a fabulous woman and a fabulous musician." Williams wrote that the theatre where she first saw Lovie leading that pit band was in Pittsburgh (though it may have been the Monogram in Chicago).

Lovie Austin was a fancy dresser and a colorful and well-liked character. In Chicago, she tooled around town in her flashy Stutz Bearcat, driving like a demon, as Alberta Hunter recalled. She liked a bit of flash, and she was a professional from the tips of her fingers through every bone in her body, but Lovie did not put on airs. When Hunter came to Lovie with a song she had composed in her head, Austin not only wrote it down for her but showed her how to copyright it.

Lovie Austin devised the sheet music for several of Hunter's songs, including "Downhearted Blues," a big hit for Bessie Smith. Alberta later acknowledged that Austin could have taken advantage of her but did not. Hunter praised Austin's professionalism, generosity and honesty.

The craze for the blues waned along with vaudeville. During the Second World War years, Lovie was reported to be a security guard at a defense plant. She was not the only female vaudeville star to work in a defense plant. Wartime work helped pay the bills for interpretive dancers Ruth St. Denis and Maud Allan and jazz and blues singer Helen Humes.

Austin made a few scattered recordings during the 1940s, 1950s and 1960s—one was a Riverside album that she recorded with her friend Alberta Hunter in 1961—and she played sporadic theatre and club engagements, but her main source of work was playing piano for a dance school. There was a resurgence of interest in the blues during the folk music revival in the late 1950s and 1960s. The surviving blues masters and blues queens were lionized and began earning money again with their music.

There was a bit of bias in the folk music world against what was dismissively termed *vaudeville blues,* and some of the old-timers were judged deficient in blues purity by many of the young, white aficionados. Also, many of the new venues were coffeehouses that lacked a piano, so that favored guitar-based blues as well. The revival pretty much passed by Lovie Austin. Besides, she was in her 70s and home was in Chicago. As the saying has it: Lovie had been there, done that.

AVERY & HART

Dan Avery and Charles Hart were among those African American acts that emerged at the turn of the twentieth century, the first generation to be able to escape working in minstrel shows. Like most black comedy and song-and-dance acts of the time, Avery & Hart played both vaudeville and revues.

According to some sources, Dan Avery was a dancer performing in theatres and saloons when he teamed up with Charles Hart, a bartender who had a yen for the stage. Yet both were working independently on the stage before they teamed. Dan Avery toured with Black Patti's Troubadours in 1899, playing a leading role in one of the show's musical comedy sketches, "A Ragtime Frolic at Ras-Bury Park." And Charles Hart was working in 1901 as part of the replacement cast of *A Lucky Coon,* a Williams & Walker vehicle that the team left in spring 1899 after playing it in New York and on the road for nearly six months.

The comedy pairing of a conniving sharpie with his slower-witted buddy had long been a standard formula for comedy teams, black or white, from Williams & Walker to Abbott & Costello and Martin & Lewis. Dan Avery essayed the flamboyantly dressed ladies man (as did George Walker), and Charles Hart played the clown (as did Bert Williams). Both men sang and danced along with the comedy banter.

Their onstage relationship occasioned comparisons from white chroniclers who likened Avery & Hart to Bert Williams and George Walker, and it may be that Dan Avery and Charles Hart were first put together with the intention of evoking the Williams & Walker magic. Certainly, in at least two shows, they took the Williams and Walker roles for the national tour. Avery & Hart made a fine success touring *The Sons of Ham* (1903–04) in the USA.

Meanwhile, Williams & Walker had made so great a success of their next musical comedy, *In Dahomey,* on Broadway that the show was booked for the 1903–04 season in the United Kingdom, where it was a sensation, playing nine months in London at the Shaftsbury Theatre and another five months touring the English provinces and Scotland.

When Walker wished to return to the USA in late spring 1904, a second company headed by Avery & Hart was sent to London in the same show to start the 1904–5 season in August on the Strand. They scored as big a hit with the critics as had Williams & Walker, and the new team stayed in Britain well into 1905.

Later, when booked into white big time, the management felt impelled to bill Avery & Hart as "a Williams & Walker act," hoping to capitalize on the greater fame of a pair who had become the most well-known African American song-dance-comedy act in the country.

In 1909, Dan Avery and Charles Hart teamed with J. Rosamond Johnson, forming a trio to play white vaudeville. The success led to an engagement in London that, in turn, was expanded into a musical revue, *Come Over Here,* that went over there and became a big London hit. Dan Avery died in 1912, immediately after Avery & Hart completed a show at Proctor's Fifth Avenue Theatre. Charles Hart teamed again with J. Rosamond Johnson who, a year earlier, had lost his partner, Bob Cole, after a long illness.

Avery & Hart are credited with songwriters Cecil Mack and Chris Smith as creators of the song "Down among the Sugar Cane." Another song associated with the team was "I Care Not for the Stars That Shine."

Despite the success of black acts like Williams & Walker, Avery & Hart and Miller & Lyles in white vaudeville and in Broadway revues and musical comedy, they never escaped completely the undercurrent of racial prejudice. On one occasion, when Avery & Hart were playing white vaudeville, they were on the bill with Walter C. Kelly, a monologist who was as mean-spirited and bigoted against blacks as he was witty. The Virginia Judge, as he was known in his bill matter, was always miffed when he had to share a vaudeville bill with an African American act. Kelly stood backstage while Avery & Hart were on stage. As they were taking their calls after closing their act with "I Care Not for the Stars That Shine," Kelly let everyone backstage know how he felt as he picked up the Avery & Hart tune and sang, "I care not for the shines that star."

AVNER THE ECCENTRIC

b: (Avner Eisenberg) 26 August 1948, Atlanta, GA

In an era when comedians swagger on stage spewing deprecation and ridicule, Avner Eisenberg is truly the eccentric, a gentle man who does not regard the audience as an enemy to be tamed. Often during his one-person shows, he brings people on stage from the audience. Instead of making them the butt of a joke, he treats them good-naturedly and makes them part of the act.

Back in the mid-nineteenth century, most clowns had some training in acrobatics, aerial work, juggling or dancing. Their skill was in transforming into a ballet of sorts the seemingly clumsy act of falling, tripping, sliding or fighting. Later audiences thrilled as Charlie Chaplin dodged and ducked around an overbearing bully or Buster Keaton, without flinching, grabbed onto a speeding car without breaking stride or his physical line. Bobby Clark manipulated a cigar with sleight of hand and clambered over stage furniture. Bea Lillie nonchalantly twirled a string of pearls around her neck and stepped out of them after they spiraled to the floor, or she lifted her floor-length evening gown to her knees and roller-skated off into the wings. The Wiere Brothers played stringed instruments, danced and cartwheeled in precision. Each movement by these clowns and comedians was deft, cleanly executed and pure. One marveled at their control and grace.

Avner's approach to physical comedy is different. Against the natural expectation that Avner is going to dazzle with slick, showy moves is a series of bumbles. In a mimed prologue to the Goodman Theatre Company's production of *The Comedy of Errors* when it opened in Manhattan in 1987, Avner shambled on stage wearing a fake, bright red, bulbous nose held in place

Avner the Eccentric

by an elastic cord, a derby, striped shirt, bow tie, overalls and a pair of slightly oversized shoes. He pushed a broom, as though he were a stagehand cleaning up before the curtain rose on that evening's production. He stopped for a break, shook a cigarette from a pack, but the entire contents fell, a few at a time, on the floor, in a cascade he was unable to stop, nor could he catch a single cigarette. When he opened a box of matches, it was upside down, and the match sticks tumbled to the floor. He tried to sweep them up with a push broom that separated itself from the long handle, and soon his bowler hat was missing, only to be found atop the end of the broom handle.

At first, instead of an adroit performance, his movements seemed awkward and poorly integrated. More slowly for some than others in the audience came the realization that every move was carefully calibrated and that Avner took care not to indulge in clever and showy moves at the expense of laughs. Critic Joel Siegel put his finger on it. "My problem with mimes is that most mimes confuse the means with the end." Siegel praised Avner for using his skills to create a show that is "hurt yourself funny."

The same principle applies in his solo shows, such as *Avner the Eccentric: Exceptions to Gravity,* which he began performing shortly after 2000. During his performance, it dawned on the audience that he was skilled in juggling, balancing, sleight of hand, eccentric dancing and ropewalking, yet he put all of it at the service of clowning and making people laugh. Some props were large; others were tiny. He lifted an open 12-foot wooden stepladder onto his chin and balanced it. He celebrated the completion of a trick by executing an acrobat's backflip. He juggled popcorn kernels. He picked up from the floor small scraps of paper and wadded them into a lump that unfolded into a single, large sign. He sat at a table to dine on paper-thin pancakes that turned out to be a stack of paper napkins. One by one, he popped them into his mouth—12, 16, 20. One wondered where in his hollowed cheeks he could have secreted them. A slight hiccup produced a long, multicolored streamer that he pulled from his mouth; as Avner regarded the streamer, a sizeable bouquet in full bloom popped out of his mouth.

Avner approached rope walking with the same innocence; there was no sense of a confident, cat-like mastery. Once he hoisted himself up, he walked a slack rope with a bogus safety rope tied around his waist. He suffered rope burns, got one foot stuck beneath the other and wobbled a bit before he grew confident enough to lie down on the rope and sway gently as if in a hammock. After he traversed the rope's entire length and safely reached the other end, he tugged on the safety rope and pulled onto the stage a wash line of laundry.

His skills stem from a lifetime of training. As a boy in Atlanta, Georgia, his passions were snakes and juggling. Later, he attended four universities, studied chemistry and biology, and ended up with a B.A. in theatre from the University of Washington in 1971. He went to Paris to study mime with Jacques LeCoq, and took a year off in the middle of his two-year course to tour as a puppeteer with Vagabond Marionettes. Once, while street performing in Paris, he was arrested for buffoonery in public, a law one would expect any politician with a sense of self-preservation to have voted down.

After Avner returned to the USA, he taught at Carlo Clementi's Dell'Arte School of Physical Comedy in California. Enigmatically, Avner praises both men: "LeCoq taught me everything I know, and Carlo taught me the rest."

Avner credits the Renaissance Faires with incubating many *new vaudevillians.* He found work with the Minnesota Renaissance Faire and at the Experimental Theatre Company in Minneapolis, then became part of a theatre movement that has taken many of them to Broadway and around the world since the 1970s. Avner laughs that the new vaudeville movement had reached middle age by 2000, but notes that "the great European clowns are born at the age of 50, after 30 years of performance."

His own career has taken him to Europe, Broadway and Hollywood, where he has performed guest shots on both public and commercial television programs. He is still remembered for his endearing turn as The Jewel, a gentle, umbrella-balancing holy man, in *The Jewel of the Nile* (1985), which starred Michael Douglas, Kathleen Turner and Danny DeVito and featured Avner (billed as Avner Eisenberg) and his friends and fellow new vaudevillians, The Flying Karamazov Brothers.

Avner the Eccentric made his Broadway debut in 1984 in a one-man, self-named show. Three years later, he was brought in to provide the prologue to *The Comedy of Errors* at Lincoln Center. Adapted and directed by Greg Mosher, Shakespeare was transformed into a mad romp of juggling, magic and all types of specialty turns. The show did not quite work for audiences until Avner adapted his push-broom routine to open the production. He did his usual bits, but, when sweeping, he pushed all the detritus down a hole in the stage. Up popped Shakespeare, trashed as it were (or, perhaps, rising above the rubbish heaped upon him by experimental directors determined to make the Bard relevant), and the audience was properly introduced to the show.

Avner the Eccentric returned to Broadway in 1989 for a principal role, that of Srulik the ventriloquist in *Ghetto.* The production, staged at Circle in the Square's theatre in Duffy Square, also featured Donal Donnelly, Helen Schneider and George Hearn. In regional theatre, Avner has played both Vladimir and Estragon in *Waiting for Godot,* costarred with his wife, Julie Goell, in the world premier of *Zoo of Tranquility* and played R. Crumb in *Comix.*

Because Avner the Eccentric works wordlessly, he can and does work everywhere in his one-person shows and as a guest star in various festivals the world over: the Edinburgh Festival, the Israel Festival, the Montreal International Comedy Festival, the London International Mime Festival, the Festival of American Mime, the New York Clown Theatre Festival, the Fool's Festival, the New York Magic Symposium, the Hudson Clearwater Revival, the International Movement Theatre Festival and the International Festival du Cirque in Monte Carlo. At a number of these, he was awarded juried honors.

He has appeared on television from Japan to the USA to South America to Europe. In 2005, he completed a four-month run of another of his one-person shows in Paris. When not performing, he lives in coastal Maine, where he and his wife Julie teach Clowning and Eccentric Performing at the Celebration Barn in Maine each summer.

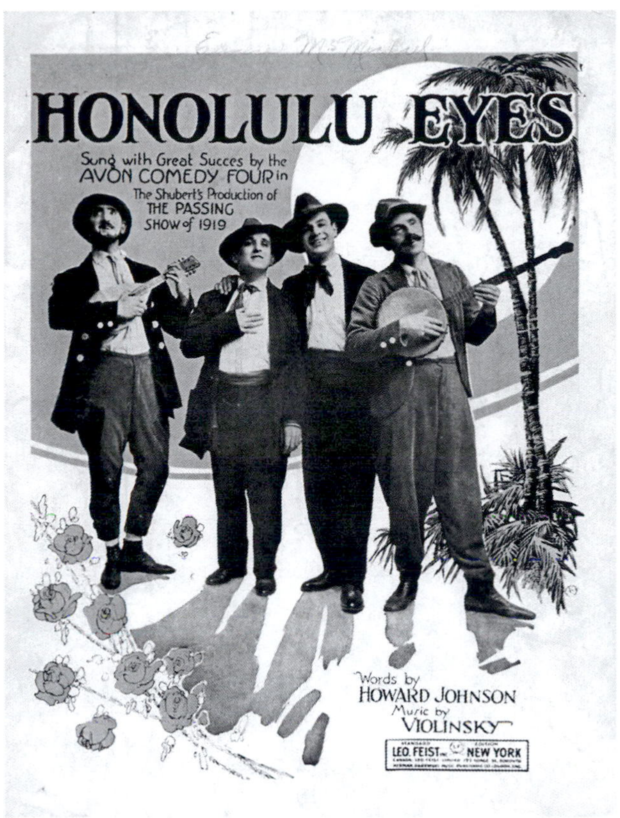

Avon Comedy Four

AVON COMEDY FOUR

The quartet started out as singing waiters at the Avon Café around 1901. Jack Coleman and Will Lester were already working as singing waiters at the saloon when Charlie Dale and Joe Smith were hired. The response to their harmony and occasional jokes was heartening, and the four lads took engagements elsewhere but kept the name.

Over the 20 years of the act's life, the personnel changed, and a dozen or more performers, whose primary qualification was singing, spent some time in the act. Smith and Dale remained with the group from start to finish.

See Smith & Dale

B

BACK OF THE HOUSE

Closely related to the term *backstage*, yet, whereas backstage refers to a physical area, *back of the house* refers to a domain of sorts, where the stage manager is in charge. Similarly, the front of the house is the business area of the theatre governed by the house manager.

BACKSTAGE

In addition to the performance area, backstage included the wing space on either side of the stage, the electrical switchboard, scenery dock, dressing rooms and the fly space over the stage that held the grid, drops and rigging. A stage manager of a large, big-time house would have a crew to help set and clear the stage, change drops and run the lighting board. In a modest, small-time theatre, the stage manager might do it all with minimal assistance. In the meanest of venues, the owner would sell tickets, then, after the house was closed, run backstage to pull the curtain and raise and lower drops.

BELLE BAKER

b: (Bella Becker) 25 December 1893, New York, NY—d: 28 April 1957, Los Angeles, CA

There may be some capricious fourth Fate that governs reputation. When the talented and accomplished of every field are called before her, some are ushered into a Valhalla of remembrance, whereas others are dismissed, without weighing their merit, into some unmarked recess of history.

Sophie Tucker, Al Jolson and Burns & Allen are recalled as symbols of the golden age of vaudeville. Equally fine headliners, famous in their day, like Blossom Seeley, James Barton and Buck & Bubbles, are known only to aficionados. This is true of Belle Baker.

Beginning around 1950, record companies began issuing long-playing vinyl record albums that contained previously recorded songs from early 78-rpm discs made by stars like Ruth Etting, Ethel Waters, Bessie Smith and Sophie Tucker. Belle Baker was not among them, although she was as famous as any singer of her day. Consequently, the nostalgia craze of the 1960s and 1970s did not celebrate her or renew interest in her recordings.

In 1980, Take Two Records released the LP recording *A Pair of Red Hot Mamas: Sophie Tucker & Belle Baker,* one side of the record devoted to each singer. As time thinned further the rank of once-beloved singers and their audiences, only singers who remained marketable were given an extended life. In an era of CDs, the legacy of Belle Baker is reduced to a few songs scattered through several anthologies.

Musically, Belle Baker was as accomplished as the best singers of the vaudeville era and better than most. She possessed a deep, rich contralto that, without straining, could reach every member of the audience, and she had a keen rhythmic lilt somewhere between ragtime and early jazz.

She was plump enough in a matronly way to be called a red-hot mama, and Baker performed a lot of character comedy songs, as did Sophie Tucker, Eva Tanguay, Nora Bayes and most of the singing single

Belle Baker

headliners of vaudeville. A dark-eyed brunette, Belle was also a superb torch singer, putting across the lyrics with a throb in her voice that would have seemed hokey from a less able performer.

Little Bella Becker was sure that the theatre was her destiny from the time of her first visit to the neighborhood Yiddish theatre. Some chroniclers report that she performed small roles in Jacob Adler's company at the Grand Theatre. Earlier, and while still a child, Belle sold newspapers and lemonade on the streets of her neighborhood. More usual and dependable was her work in a garment sweatshop. She quit school when she was nine to make shirtwaists that she could not afford to purchase. The Becker family was poverty-stricken.

Belle decided that vaudeville was her chance to escape drudgery and hopelessness. She performed in some amateur-night contests, and these gave the chubby, but determined, 13-year-old the courage to ask for a vaudeville date in 1906. She persuaded the manager of the Cannon Street Music Hall, a small nickelodeon and vaudeville house next door to the tenement in which she lived, to put her on the bill for a week at no pay. Her voice was a wonder, and she was held over, this time for $3 a week. Buoyed by the acceptance, Belle began the rounds of small-time vaudeville in New York. At first, she sang novelty songs, such as "Becky Ritkowitz, Tell Me Witz is Witz" and "Make up Your Yiddisher Mind," that appealed to her Jewish audiences. As she matured, she moved more toward material with broader appeal.

Around 1912, she met and married her first husband, Lew Leslie, who took command of her career. While playing Baltimore, according to Douglas Gilbert, author of *American Vaudeville: Its Life and Times,* Belle Baker appeared on the bill just before Houdini, who was one of the top draws in vaudeville at the time. Lew Leslie was shilling for her outside the theatre, giving free tickets to people who promised to applaud and stomp their feet for Belle. Lew Leslie's ruse worked so well that the audience demanded encores. An infuriated Houdini marched onto the stage and told the audience that he would defer to their decision: if they preferred to hear more from Miss Baker, then he would leave the stage, but if they chose her above him, he vowed he would never play Baltimore again. The audience chose Houdini, but the stir that Belle had caused in Baltimore reached the notice of important bookers.

Comic songs were not fulfilling for Belle Baker. She was an emotional person, dramatic in everyday life. Her first love had been Yiddish drama, and Sarah Bernhardt was Belle's inspiration. Baker hoped to convey through words and music the tragic themes of love lost and stolen. A two-a-day headliner beginning with the 1913–14 season, 21-year-old Belle was booked at the Palace Theatre in Manhattan in 1915. Her act included two Irving Berlin songs: one a dialect number, "Cohen Owes Me 97 Dollars," and the other a peppy tune called "Michigan." Belle was billed as "The Sarah Bernhardt of Song," billing matter justified by her singing of "Eli, Eli" (the lament written in Yiddish by Jacob K. Sandler in 1896, not the better-known song written at the time of the Second World War by Chanah Szenes).

In 1918, Belle and Lew Leslie divorced. He had helped make her a headliner, but he was looking to be celebrated in his own right, not as Mr. Belle Baker. He reached his peak with a series of inexpensively produced African American revues during the 1920s and early 1930s, with several editions of *Blackbirds* among them. Lew Leslie was show business start to finish, not the love of Belle Baker's life. That role was filled by Maurice Abrams (Maurice Abrahams, born 1883, Russia), a songwriter. They were married in 1919, and their son, writer and songsmith Herbert, was born in 1920. (Herbert chose Baker for his professional name.)

Belle earned as much as $2,500 a week in the big time. In addition to that, she made a small fortune for introducing new songs. Engaging in an early form of payola, big stars like Al Jolson, Sophie Tucker, Nora Bayes, Fanny Brice and Belle Baker were paid to introduce songs. Some like Jolson and Bayes sometimes insisted on credit as a co-lyricist or co-composer in order to receive a slice of the royalties. In fairness, the singers sometimes made suggestions to improve the songs.

In 1919, Pathé Records gave Belle her first chance to record. Although "Eli, Eli" remained in her repertoire, Belle sought a larger audience through upbeat popular songs of the Jazz Age and the torch songs that became the vogue later in the 1920s and the early 1930s. These were collected for the long-playing, 33 rpm anthology album of 1980. "I'm Walking with the Moonbeams," "If I Had a Talking Picture of You" and "You're the One That I Care For" were representative of her upbeat pop songs of the day. Baker set a standard for torch songs with "My Sin," "I'll Always Be in Love with You," "There Must Be Somebody Else" and "The One I Love Just Can't Be Bothered with Me."

She was a popular vaudeville attraction who played the Palace many times. She was not successful in musical comedy, even a Ziegfeld production peppered with songs by Rodgers & Hart. *Betsy* opened on 28 December 1926 and closed a month later. The one hit song in the show was an interpolation by Irving Berlin, "Blue Skies."

Belle remained a vaudeville headliner throughout the 1920s. Indeed, her career was essentially in vaudeville. When vaudeville began to fade in the early 1930s, so did opportunities for Belle Baker. First, however, was an attempt at a film career. *The Song of Love,* released by Columbia in 1929, was a melodrama with songs: "I'll Still Go On Wanting You," "I'm Somebody's Baby Now" and "I'm Walking with the Moonbeams (Talking with the Stars)" among them. Belle played a wife and mother betrayed by roving husband; they were brought back together by a son too good to be true. The temptress Maizie was played by Eunice Quedens, who soon wisely changed her name to Eve Arden. Although Belle was admired for her performance, especially her singing, box-office returns failed to create a demand for further Belle Baker movies.

The Great Depression adversely affected most Americans, but the early 1930s were particularly rough on Belle Baker. Her husband, Maurice, died in 1931 at the age of 48, leaving her with a ten-year-old son. Vaudeville was an anachronism, and the Palace, where she had topped the bill frequently, switched to a continuous-showing policy in 1932. Hollywood did not want her, and the record industry was on its uppers. She had sung on network radio shows, like the *Eveready Hour,* in the 1920s, and after Maurice's death, she sought more broadcast work. The networks were based in New York, and she could remain at home with her son. On the whole, however, work was not as plentiful as it had been in the 1920s.

Variety was faring better in England, and, in 1934, she accepted an offer to headline with Bea Lillie at the London Palladium. While in England, she made an appearance as herself in *Charing Cross Road* (1935), a film starring John Mills. Nightclubs provided some work, but Belle Baker was competing with swing-era singers: *crooners* and *chirpers.* In 1944, she appeared with a host of other vaudeville veterans (Buck & Bubbles, Al Shean, Joe Frisco, Gus Van, Louis Armstrong and Paul Whiteman) in *Atlantic City,* an attempt by the ill-suited Republic Pictures to blend a historical romance with a revue. Her contribution was "Nobody's Sweetheart (Now)," rendered in a voice that had not worn well. It was husky and a trifle harsh like a smoker's voice, and it lacked the richness and tone of her glorious contralto of the 1920s and 1930s.

In 1950, Belle Baker again played the Palace after the fabled theatre reinstituted a mix of vaudeville with its usual fare of films. Her last hurrah was as the subject of a *This Is Your Life* telecast in 1955. It is one of the few episodes that is not available at the Museum of Television and Radio in Manhattan. Belle died two years later at 63 in Los Angeles. Her son returned her body to New York, where it was interred next to Maurice Abrahams' in a large mausoleum at Mt. Judah Cemetery in Queens.

JOSEPHINE BAKER

b: (Frida Josephine McDonald) 3 June 1906, St. Louis, MO—d: 12 April 1975, Paris, France

She was the first African American to become an international sex symbol. Certainly, other black entertainers, both women and men, were admired for their beauty, even furtively lusted after, by people of various races, but Josephine Baker molded herself into a potent and sophisticated sexual icon whose magnetism few denied.

Her road to the Folies Bergère in Paris began, improbably, in a one-room shack in St. Louis, Missouri, and continued through broken-down theatres and flea-ridden boardinghouses in one tank town after another. As a child, Josephine sensed and refused to accept the dreary fate ahead for most black children born into poverty in the early 1900s. She ran off, at age 13, with the Dixie Steppers, a black vaudeville unit masquerading as a revue.

Josephine did not quite fit into the show. She seemed too skinny and small; she had told the show's manager that she was 15. She could not dance well enough for the chorus. She was too light-skinned; the rest of the

Josephine Baker

chorus girls were shades of chocolate. Josephine was part Spanish and looked it. It was her willingness to do any chores in order to stay with the show and her antics and funny faces that made a place for her onstage with the Dixie Steppers.

When the unit disbanded in Philadelphia, Josephine tried out for the chorus in *Shuffle Along,* a show created by two teams, Sissle & Blake and Miller & Lyles. She auditioned for Noble Sissle, who rejected her as too young and (this time) too dark, according to Baker. She followed the show to New York. Baker tried again and was hired as a dresser for the road company. Her goal was to learn all the dance routines and wait for one of the chorus girls to get ill. It happened. She made the most of her opportunity, even as it antagonized the star and the other chorus girls. Stuck on the end of the line, Baker mugged and vamped. The audience loved her. So did the local reviewer, and his opinion saved her from being sacked. (Often thought to have originated with Josephine Baker, the mugging, clowning chorus girl was, as Marshall Stearns outs it, a "perennial gag." Ethel Williams hoked up the "Circle Dance" in *Darktown Follies* of 1913–15.)

In July 1922, she was called into the Broadway cast of *Shuffle Along* that was embarking on a national tour, starting in Boston, where the show ran 15 weeks. On tour, she returned home to St. Louis. Thereafter and for years to come, she sent money home every month to help family members, eventually enabling them to buy a house. They did not see her again, however, for 14 years; St. Louis was a place she wished to leave in the past.

Two years later, *Shuffle Along* folded its tents after a stunning Broadway stand and a successful road trip. Meanwhile, Sissle & Blake had created another show, *In Bamville,* and invited Baker to be in it. Elisabeth Welch also was featured in the cast. Welch became Baker's primary African American rival as an exotic sex symbol. Both were expatriate Americans. Baker became the toast of Paris, and Elisabeth Welch, the darling of London's West End musicals. On the road, *In Bamville* was retitled *Chocolate Dandies.* It lacked the spark and irreverence of *Shuffle Along,* and, despite greater production values, the critics thought it a tepid brew. It closed after three months on Broadway.

Immediately, Josephine Baker was invited to share the stage at the Plantation Club with Ethel Waters. Waters was the star and Baker was again in the chorus, but she repeated her habit of learning the star's songs and dances (and praying for her to get sick). One day, Waters was unable to go on, and Josephine convinced the revue's director that she could perform Ethel's numbers. According to Josephine, her one-night substitution for Ethel was the medicine Waters needed.

Waters had been approached by an American producer to appear in *La Revue Nègre* in Paris. Ethel was unwilling to take a cut in pay and face the prospect of appearing before a white French audience when it had taken her ten years to agree to play before white American audiences. The producers hired Josephine. Another member of the show was the supreme reeds player Sidney Bechet. It was 1925, and it was many years before either Baker or Bechet came back to the USA.

Baker was a great success. The French found her blend of sophistication and naïveté, sleek elegance and comic touch irresistible. They adopted her and she, them. Throughout the 1930s, she starred in one revue after another at the Folies Bergère. Josephine was a sensation whether dressed in Parisian couture or bare breasted with a string of bananas riding low on her hips. At her impish best, she was a good eccentric dancer, rolling and crossing her eyes, wiggling her fingers, prancing barefoot. Adopting another persona and made up like a mannequin, hair pomaded into a sleek helmet with patented spit curls and bedecked like a showgirl on a parade float, Le Baker indulged the French passion for songs of melodramatic romance.

For at least a decade, she remained one of Paris' most beloved stars, living a glamorous fairy tale of romance. She made several French films, including *Zou Zou* (1934) and *Princesse Tam Tam* (1935), both of which were well made and allowed her to shine. In 1936, she returned to the USA to star with Fanny Brice and Bobby Clark in the *Ziegfeld Follies of 1936,* but her presentation was too mannered for swing-era New York audiences, and she failed to impress, left the show and returned to Paris where, in 1937, she became a French citizen.

With the same determination that forged a career, Josephine Baker approached the coming war with the Nazis. She was active in the French Resistance, not merely a symbol. She adopted children from all over the world and called them "her rainbow tribe." Baker and her husband, Jo Bouillon, began with two small boys and agreed to two more. Josephine raised the limit, and then there were seven. Eventually, there were 12. Josephine and Jo installed the children on an estate, Les Milandes. They were joined by an ever-growing staff. As Baker toured a lot to earn income, it fell to others to do the daily work of raising the children and keeping the estate in order. Jo Bouillon was the day-to-day parent, and he ran the estate that they had turned into what they hoped was a tourist attraction, adding hotels, a theatre, a zoo and other features in addition to maintaining a farm. One of her four or five husbands, Jo stayed with her the longest and was devoted to their adopted children, and they, to him.

Baker was fearless in forging ahead in life but lacked the temperament to deal with life's necessary minutia, like taxes and other bills. The 1950s and 1960s were difficult financially. She made good money, but her expenses maintaining Les Milandes and her adopted children grew faster and greater than her income. Often, she was described as heedless, impetuous and difficult—not in theatre, though, only at home. The turnover among the household staff was constant.

Baker remained trim and glamorous and was still a proud reminder to the French of their valor and their humanity, but she was no longer the youthful gamin. Her talent, as a dancer, singer or actor, was never the basis of her popularity. There were times in the 1950s and 1960s when, as in Montreal and Los Angeles, people flocked to see the fabled Le Baker, and she triumphed. She had become celebrated less as a performer than as a legendary institution: a recipient of the Medal of Resistance, a member of the Legion of Honor and the fiercely stubborn defender of her dream to make Les Milandes and her rainbow tribe an example for the world. She worked relentlessly to keep creditors at bay. The whirlwind she created brought her down; she suffered two heart attacks and a stroke in the 1960s.

The new Paris shows she appeared in were less well produced than those people remembered; some were slipshod and pedestrian in inspiration. Critics suggested she was going though the motions to pay bills. By the late 1960s, she was regarded by Parisian youth as a political reactionary who supported the chauvinist regime of Charles De Gaulle. Finances worsened, and her health was jeopardized by a weak heart.

Finally, in summer 1969, she had a fantastic success in Monaco, and offers for other bookings were plentiful. She returned to Monaco the following season and again delighted the celebrity-filled audience. Her finances improved but she had lost Les Milandes. Josephine and the children were ensconced in a villa in Monaco, courtesy of Princess Grace and other rich and influential Monacans. More success followed when she returned to the USA for sold-out events at Carnegie Hall. She also had another heart attack.

Her latest performances were gradually assuming the form of a retrospective: revues and concerts worthy of her reputation and tailored to her talent. Finally, the obvious step was taken, and in *Josephine* the story of her life was put into a revue. She sang, danced, introduced other performers and talked with the audience. After a fortnight of previews, she braved Paris, where she had not appeared for some time. Josephine in *Josephine* was a triumph. She symbolized the indomitable spirit, nostalgia and ageless beauty. To the old, she represented their youth; to the young, she was an engaging discovery and a living example of France's days of glory.

On 8 April 1975, Josephine Baker was honored with a gala to celebrate her 50th year in France and French theatre. Royalty, movie stars and politicians gathered. Over the next two days, the reviews were printed, and they glowed with praise. On 10 April, Josephine did not appear at the theatre. She was discovered in her apartment in a coma. Her heart had quit at last. She died two days later.

There remains no more enduring symbol of glamour than Josephine Baker. The flair she brought to performance and appearance, and the way she wore and moved in clothes set a vogue for models and fashion for decades to come.

PHIL BAKER

b: 26 August 1896, Philadelphia, PA—d: 30 November 1963, Copenhagen, Denmark

Although Phil Baker's most famous moment came during his network radio days, his career spanned small-time and big-time vaudeville, Broadway revues, the legitimate stage, Hollywood movies, network radio and the briefest of careers in television.

Phil Baker began as a contestant in amateur nights at his neighborhood movie theatre in Boston where his family had moved from Philadelphia. He and another young fellow, Ed Janis, formed a musical act for the small time, with Janis out front and Baker playing piano accompaniment. Baker switched to accordion, probably because it was easy to tote and more reliable in tone than the out-of-tune pianos found in the worst of small-time theatres. Around 1915, Baker teamed with Ben Bernie. At first, they really did not have an act. Ben Bernie and Phil Baker simply played their respective instruments: violin and accordion. Gradually, Bernie & Baker worked in some comedy bits. Bernie opened the act playing violin and chatting to the audience. Seemingly unexpectedly, Phil Baker popped up in a box seat with his accordion and turned Bernie's solos into duets.

The USA's entry into the First World War put a few careers on hold, including Phil's. After he was demobilized from the U.S. Navy, he returned to vaudeville, this time as a single. On his own, he began adding some patter, prompted by a few run-ins with hecklers. The accordion yielded pride of place to his monologue and an occasional song. To help in the laughs department, Phil engaged Sid Silvers as his stooge, a planted heckler in the audience. The public personality of Phil Baker, like a number of entertainers then and since, was made up of casual bonhomie, the well-timed quip and a hint of Broadway Romeo. It was not a stretch from his offstage self. Phil, like many vaudevillians, lived to gamble and worked to pay off his losses.

Phil Baker

Although Baker was building his act into headliner status, he absented himself on a couple of occasions to perform in Broadway revues. Irving Berlin signed Phil for the third edition of the *Music Box Revue* (1923). It ran the season with a good cast: Frank Tinney, Joe Santley, Grace Moore, the Brox Sisters, Robert Benchley and Baker. Almost as soon as the Berlin revue closed, Phil costarred with George Jessel in a Shubert revue, *The Passing Show of 1923*. The Passing Shows were running out of verve as they moved into the 1920s, and these editions came up short at the box office and with critics. Phil Baker became a Shubert favorite, however, and was engaged for the 1925 edition of *Artists and Models,* another of Jake Shubert's annual shows. This *Artists and Models* edition proved the most successful entry and played for 50 weeks at the huge Winter Garden. Yet, the 1930 edition of *Artists and Models,* also with Baker, flopped. Between the two editions, however, were other shows.

A Night in Spain (1927) achieved a modest run and starred Ted Healy, Helen Kane, Aileen Stanley and Phil Baker, who brought along vaudeville sidekick Sid Silvers. Baker's fourth Shubert show, *Pleasure Bound* (1929), another revue, did not fare much better. In fact, it closed in plenty of time for Baker to try his hand at coproducing a straight play, *Cafe de Danse,* in time for the second half of the 1929–30 season. Neither Baker nor his coproducer and erstwhile onstage partner, Ben Bernie, were in the cast, so they were free to take other bookings. That was fortunate because *Cafe de Danse* failed to pay the rent. Baker turned back to vaudeville. Again flush, he preferred, as ever, to invest in bookies rather than banks.

Broadway was getting battered at the box office as the Great Depression deepened. *Billy Rose's Crazy Quilt* (1931) starred Fanny Brice, Billy's wife, along with Ted Healy and Phil Baker. It was the third time out for this show, previously titled *Corned Beef and Roses* and *Sweet and Low,* each version undergoing changes in numbers and casts but never meeting expectations.

Phil was still doing well in vaudeville, but the great days of two-a-day big time were over, even at the Palace. In 1932, the first bill booked at the Palace under its continuous-vaudeville policy was headlined by Phil Baker, and Sid Silver was on hand to heckle Baker.

Phil was back in a Broadway revue in 1934, but not for long; *Calling All Stars* lasted a month, despite a stage full of talent, including Martha Raye, Lou Holtz,

Ella Logan, Judy Canova, Mitzi Mayfair, Jack Whiting and Gertrude Niesen. Against the odds, Phil produced *Geraniums in My Window* that same year with predictable results.

Fortunately, *The Fleischmann Hour,* that great gateway to work on network radio, opened to Phil Baker. Host Rudy Vallee introduced Phil Baker to a large network radio audience. On 17 March 1933, Baker debuted in his own show, *The Amour Jester,* on NBC's Blue Network. Two years later, Baker switched the program to CBS, and it was renamed *The Phil Baker Show.* Harry McNaughton and Sid Silvers were along for support as Bottle, his oh-so-English butler, and Beetle, the heckling ghost, respectively. The show enjoyed five successful years, although ratings sagged toward the end. By then, quiz shows were cutting into the audience for comedy programs, and Phil returned to the stage in 1939, when he assumed Alfred Lunt's role for a national tour of Robert E. Sherwood's play *Idiot's Delight.*

In 1941, three popular comedians found themselves without a comedy series. In the spirit if-you-can't-beat-'em-join 'em, Phil Baker, Garry Moore and even Eddie Cantor took turns (along with newcomers Bob Hawk and Jack Paar), in succession, hosting the quiz show, *Take It or Leave It.* Phil hosted the show for more than five years, winter 1942 through spring 1947.

His most famous moment in broadcast history involved Fred Allen, whose show Baker followed. Fred always had difficulty hewing to the tight timelines demanded by radio. Right up to airtime, Fred fiddled with the scripts he wrote, made last minute changes insisted on by network censors and sponsors, and then ad-libbed on air. Allen's shows often ran seconds, even a minute, overtime and bumped into the time slot for *Take It or Leave It.* One night, Phil Baker barged into Allen's program 15 minutes before it was scheduled to end. He reported that he had added up all the stolen seconds, and Fred Allen now owed Baker 15 minutes of airtime, and he, Phil Baker, was going to start *Take It or Leave It* right there and then. Of course, the brouhaha was a setup—like the Fred Allen and Jack Benny feud—but the press actually reported it.

With his renewed popularity, Phil Baker tried Broadway again. *Priorities of 1942* was a vaudeville show weighted with comedians: Phil Baker, Willie Howard, Lou Holtz and Gene Sheldon. Hazel Scott, Joan Merrill and Paul Draper handled the music and dancing. Surprisingly, this inexpensive show ran from the end of the 1941–42 season through most of the 1942–43 season.

The quiz show phenomenon reached its peak in 1947 when *Stop the Music* debuted in the same time slot as *The Fred Allen Show* on CBS and Edgar Bergen's *The Charlie McCarthy Show* on NBC. Allen, with his tongue tucked only partway in his cheek, offered his listeners a guarantee: if the producers of *Stop the Music* chose their phone number and called them while they were tuned into Allen's, then Fred would pay them whatever they lost by not knowing the question. It did not help. Bergen took a year's sabbatical from radio. Fred Allen fought it out. Within the year, Fred Allen's distinguished radio career was sidelined. By the next season, the quiz show had lost its novelty, and Bergen returned to his old time slot almost as popular as ever.

Phil Baker never was a major star in movies, but he made at least seven; several are still amusing. In all of them, he essentially played himself. *In Spain* and *A Bad Boy from a Good Family,* both made in 1929, and *Poor Little Rich Boy* (1932) have disappeared from public notice. *Gift of Gab* was a badly made all-star curiosity of 1934. *Thanks a Million* (1935) was a deftly made romp that is one of Fred Allen's better films. *The Goldwyn Follies* (1938) was a mess made enjoyable by the Ritz Brothers, Vera Zorina, Edgar Bergen & Charlie McCarthy, songs by the Gershwins and Technicolor splendor, Sam Goldwyn style. Fox's *Take It or Leave It* (1944) capitalized on Phil's radio show and used it as a container to recycle sequences from previously made Fox films.

On 25 June 1951, Phil Baker and a panel show, *Who's Whose,* made their debut on television. The object was for four barely known panelists to discover, through questioning, which of three people was really the spouse of the fourth. The CBS show was yanked after its initial broadcast.

Not one to sock it away for a rainy day as long as there were bookies to support, Phil Baker, like most of the horses he backed, finished out of the money. He was living in Denmark when he gave his last major performance: a major role in *Elefanter på loftet* (1960), released in the USA as *The Green-Eyed Elephant.* Phil Baker died in Copenhagen three years later.

BALABAN & KATZ

The careers of the seven Balaban sons permeated Chicago's theatrical life and the larger film industry. A. J. (Abraham Joseph) Balaban was the dominant brother; in 1908, when he was 18, he talked the family into taking a lease on a West Side nickelodeon on Kedzie at 12th Street. A. J. had been singing there and at other local theatres and cafés, accompanied on the piano by his sister Ida. His parents looked favorably at the prospect of a cash business because the custom at the small grocery store required extending credit to customers who did not always settle their weekly accounts promptly, or before they moved to another neighborhood.

Barney Balaban was A. J.'s elder brother and first partner, but Barney needed to hold onto his civilian job until the theatre began to pay, although he continued to have a voice in management and took responsibility for finances.

Almost from the start, A. J., often called Abe, insisted on adding live performance to his slate of films. After all, Abe was a singer and Ida was willing. Instead of always singing from the stage, Abe sometimes roamed the aisles, encouraging his patrons to sing along. The next development was to unify the program with a theme. St. Patrick's Day called for Irish ballads, and Independence Day ushered in a set of patriotic songs. From this modest beginning, Abe's pic-vaude house policy grew.

Five months under Balaban management, the Kedzie Theatre had attracted the notice of competitors, established and potential. Real estate in the neighborhood began to rise as inquiries and offers were made to the Kedzie's commercial neighbors. Abe decided the only way to hold their edge was to build their own theatre, bigger and fancier than their rivals.' Abe and Barney announced through the press that the Balabans were building "the finest $25,000 theatre" at the corner of Sawyer and 12th Street. This blunted the opposition, but the family was nearly done in by nine months of construction delays and unanticipated costs.

They named their new 600-seat theatre, replete with large balcony, the Circle. It opened in September 1909, little more than 18 months after the Balaban brothers had made their debuts as movie exhibitors with the small Kedzie nickelodeon.

A. J. Balaban was the polar opposite of another budding mogul, E. F. Albee, although both men took pride in building palatial theatres. Perhaps their contrasting attitudes toward show business stemmed from their beginnings. Albee apprenticed in sideshows and circus, where the purpose was to lure the suckers into the tent and take their money. Balaban grew up in his parents' grocery and fish shop, where the emphasis was on service and keeping customers. He used to take tickets at the door, where he could smile and greet his clientele. Later in the show, he performed a vocal solo or led the audience in singing along to an illustrated song. Albee wanted to awe, perhaps intimidate, his audiences by the ornate majesty of his theatres; Balaban wanted to show off his theatres but also send his customers home feeling they had had a grand time in a friendly environment.

Abe's presentation policy evolved from his combination of offering movies and a few live acts and directly engaging the audience. The Balabans booked live acts through Western Vaudeville Association (WVA). Sometime around 1910, the song "That Mysterious Rag" was popular. Abe added the number to one of his shows. He staged it so that the pit band violinist played from the balcony, directly in front of the projection booth. The spotlights from the booth cast the violinist's silhouette onto the movie screen as he played. Meanwhile, Abe and three singers from the live acts on the bill ran around the theatre, each man appearing in different corners and aisles and singing a verse of a chorus until the next performer picked it up from a different location. It was not complicated staging, but the surprise of various singers popping up here and there gave a twist to "That Mysterious Rag."

In 1914, Abe Balaban met Sam Katz, who, with his father, owned a few motion-picture theatres. Two years later, the Balabans and the Katzes combined to build the Central Park Theatre; it seated 2,000. Barney Balaban handled finance and real estate for the family. Sam Katz studied law. Abe was the idea man. In 1918, Balaban & Katz opened the Riviera. Then, in succession, nearly one a year, they opened the Tivoli, the Chicago and the Uptown, each seating about 4,000 patrons and playing a mix of vaudeville and motion pictures. More followed throughout the 1920s: the Roosevelt, the Oriental and the Paradise.

Another difference between Abe Balaban and Ed Albee was their attitude toward motion pictures. J. J. Murdock tried to edge his boss Albee toward movies, but Albee preferred to ignore the film industry and thereby became the architect of his own doom. Balaban had always balanced the two, emphasizing one over the other as the times, conditions and venues dictated. When in 1925 Paramount Pictures asked Abe to manage the McVickers Theatre, a competitor of Balaban & Katz's Chicago theatres, a very rewarding relationship began between Paramount/Publix and Balaban & Katz. Both Abe's and Barney's involvement with Paramount/Publix Pictures deepened; in 1926–27, the Balabans sold their theatres to Paramount/Publix for cash and stock. Barney took a position with Paramount Pictures and eventually became chairman of the corporation. Abe took over booking vaudeville acts for the Paramount/Publix operation and oversaw making sound shorts and producing radio programs under the Paramount banner.

In 1929, Abe Balaban retired. He was wealthy, powerful, respected and loved by associates when he decided to devote the rest of his life to broadening himself by seeing the larger world and enjoying his family. He left show business at the top of his game. *Variety*, the so-called showbiz bible, devoted its 27 February 1929 weekly edition to A. J. Balaban—an extraordinary salute.

About the same time, Ed Albee was handed his head by Joe Kennedy, who told Albee that he was an anachronism in show business. There were no special editions of trade papers to wish Albee well. There was no citizens' testimonial dinner, replete with a 200-piece orchestra, to honor Albee as there was in Chicago for Abe Balaban, a dinner that attracted far more friends and admirers than the 1,600 who could be seated.

Among the luminaries who paid tribute to Abe Balaban were Harry Lauder, Sophie Tucker, Jack Dempsey and Eddie Cantor.

Abe announced that he, his wife, children and parents were taking a long tour of Europe and the Middle East. When they embarked in 1930, Abe Balaban was only 40 years old. He lived in Switzerland for a few years, but the Great Depression pushed Paramount Pictures close to bankruptcy, and the brothers' investment in the corporation was in peril. During the 1930s, Abe came back to work at Paramount until they regained stability.

Variety credited A. J. Balaban with establishing the presentation-house policy, the continuous performance of films, the use of a master of ceremonies (in the person of Paul Ash), booking large bands to play onstage, and offering single-price tickets that allowed patrons to sit wherever they pleased. William Morris, the respected booker, agent and theatre manager, wrote to A. J. Balaban to say, "you have done more for its [vaudeville's] proper presentation than any other man ever connected with it."

BALANCE

Balance in vaudeville bills required two considerations. First, the acts that were booked had to contrast and complement the others, not duplicate them. If there were two female singers on a bill, one of them might be refined and sweet-voiced, whereas the other was likely to be a hoydenish shouter of comic songs. If there were two comedians and one was a monologist and the other a physical clown, the balance was not upset. Preferably, a bill sported a juggling act, ventriloquist, a comedy sketch, a tap dancer, an instrumental act and a novelty like paper tearing or handkerchief tossing in addition to a singing act and a comedy team.

Balance was also a matter of a fast-flowing program. Speed in transition was essential to momentum and energy, both for the audience and in the acts. A sketch that required a room-sized set could not immediately follow an act that featured twin grand pianos. There was not time to effect the changeover: moving the pianos offstage while moving furniture onstage. So between the acts requiring a full stage, there had to be acts that worked *in one* (behind the footlights but in front of the dress and fire curtains) or *in two* (on the front half of the stage) so that a following act could be set up behind the acts currently performing onstage.

In a different vein, balance refers to a type of acrobatic act in which an understander supports and guides either a partner or a series of props through a series of maneuvers.

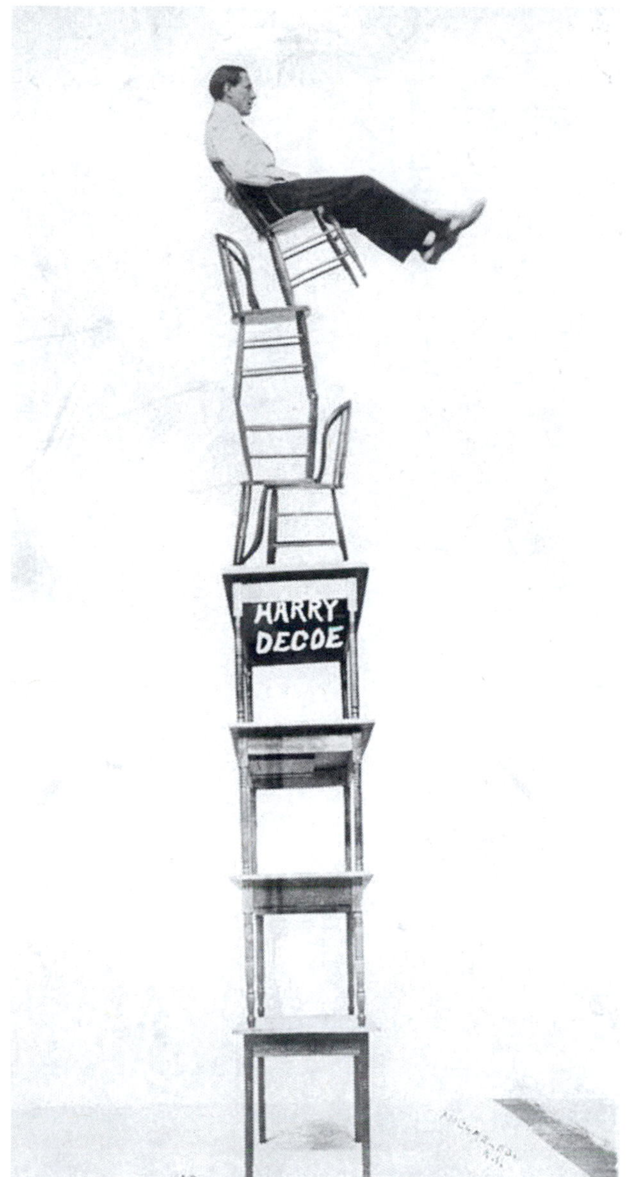

Harry DeCoe

BALANCING ACTS

A balancing act could be a solo or a group act. When there were two or more people in the act, they balanced each other on their feet, hands, their heads or a combination of feet, hands and heads. The feats of balancing were often combined with tumbling and teeterboards, so one tumbler might be sent hurtling across the stage by a second performer to land atop the hands, shoulders or head of a third performer.

Props were also used; a performer might balance the props (chairs, canes, sharp swords or cannonballs) on his head, nose, chin, hands or feet, or he might balance

Kay Farrelli

himself on a prop. Women walked en pointe over a series of open tops of upright bottles; men and women balanced spheres or weights on their heads, or they balanced themselves on canes, swords, rolling balls and other improbable choices of objects.

BALASIC FAMILY

Carl Merkel and Maria Dogmar Merkel—ca. 1850

Victor Balasic Sr.

b: 12 December 1869, Pozega, Croatia—d: 21 August 1931, Chicago, IL

Paula Enders Balasic

b: 6 January 1874, Uj-Szent Anna, Hungary—d: 22 April 1956, Chicago, IL

Alfred Balasic

b: 13 June 1896, Miskolc, Hungary—d: 6 October 1967, Chicago, IL

Victor Balasic Jr.

b: 16 November 1897, Lubeck, Germany—d: 18 August 1943, New York, NY

Maria Holz Balasic

b: 5 August 1896, Vienna, Austria—d: 5 October 1963, Chicago, IL

The Balasic family produced at least four generations of acrobatic performers who played the variety theatres and circuses of Europe. The origin of Balasic (pronounced *ba-la-shich*) family name is Croatian. They altered or changed the family name for performance reasons or to suit political conditions.

The earliest records find Karlu Balasz Balasic, who was born, probably in the late 1840s, in western Croatia. Karlu adopted the stage name Carl Merkel; his wife's name was Maria Dogmar. A son, Victor, was born in Pozega in 1869. Little is known about Carl's and Maria's career except theatre dates in Paris around 1907, when Carl was likely in his late 50s, and an appearance in Berlin in 1921, when he was in his early 70s. He was in poor health in Berlin and died there sometime in the early 1920s.

Karlu's son Victor served in the Austro-Hungarian Empire's Imperial Army until 1893 and married Paula Enders in Hungary in 1894. Paula was a Czech whose parents ran the Circus Enders in Hungary until 1905, when they joined the Sarrasini Circus touring Europe. Her sister, Maria Enders, who had married into the Rieffenach bareback riding act, came to the USA in 1922 to perform with Ringling Bros. and Barnum & Bailey, among other circuses until 1943. She died in 1956.

Victor and Paula had a daughter and two sons: Maria, Alfred Joseph and Victor Balasic Jr. Daughter Maria suffered from cerebral palsy and was placed in a church sanitarium in Budapest, Hungary, where she remained for the rest of her life.

By the late 1890s and early 1900s, the family was managing their own circus, traveling around Europe to Germany, Italy, Poland and Norway. After 1905, they were based in Berlin with the Das Program/Das Organ agency and began performing in European theatres as the Great Merkels.

The family invented some of the gymnastic apparatus that showcased their feats of strength and balance. These devices were as important to the originality of the act as were steps to a dancer. Their devices included a shoulder-supported axle, above which two performers would revolve, and a finger stand of five metal rods. Their most spectacular feat involved a see-

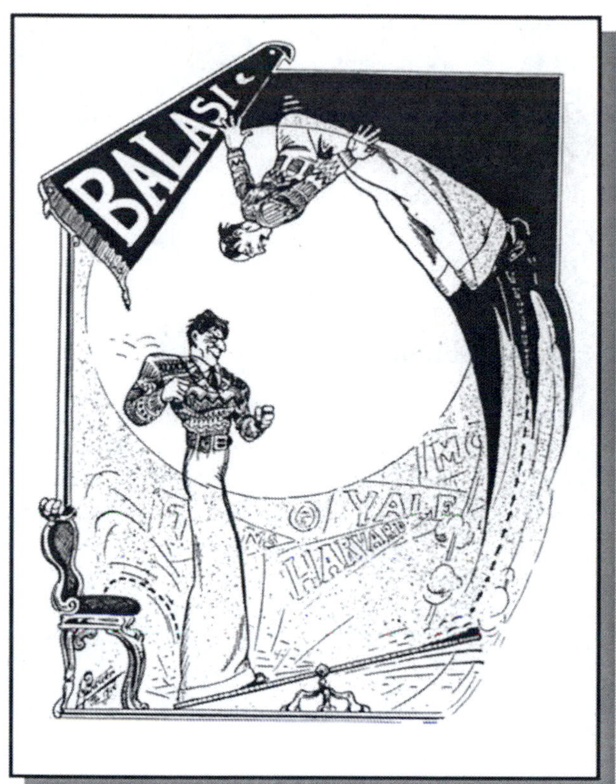

Alfred & Victor Balasic

saw and padded leather helmets. With Victor standing on the lowered end of the seesaw, Alfred would jump onto the raised end, propelling Victor into the air in an arc that ended in a head-to-head balance without the use of hands.

This routine appears to have been developed sometime around 1908, with a blindfold version following in 1912. Variations of this feat included hand-to-head and foot-to-head balanced landings. Other tricks included a variety of person-to-person balance and strength moves, wire walking, and ladder apparatus and tumbling stunts. As he grew older, Victor Sr. adapted his role into a slapstick comedy routine that complemented his sons' thrilling feats.

In 1911, the act traveled to America. They toured as the 5 Merkels on the Pantages circuit, playing Calgary, Edmonton, Seattle, Portland, San Francisco, Sacramento and Los Angeles. Working their way eastward, they played the Empire Theater in New York City before returning to Germany at the end of 1912.

In 1913, they went on a tour of imperial Russia that included visits to St. Petersburg, the Urals and Baku, Azerbaijan. They were in St. Petersburg performing at the Narodi-Dom when the First World War broke out in 1914. They were interned by the czar's government in Siberia, where they spent five months before escaping. Making their way to Denmark, they resumed performing and traveled to Sweden and Norway billed as the Merkels and, briefly, as the Great Enders in an Oriental-themed acrobatic act.

Around 1915, they began performing as The 5 Balasis, but the act was suspended between 1917 and 1918 when Alfred and Victor Jr. served in the Austro-Hungarian army, as did their father. Between 1918 and 1923 The 5 Balasis performed at the Cirque Royal in Brussels, the Corso in Zurich, the Alhambra in Paris, the Winter Garden in Berlin and the Apollo in Vienna, as well as other theatres in Norway, the Netherlands and Czechoslovakia.

In August 1923, with a Keith contract in hand, the troupe sailed from Göteborg, Sweden, to New York. Billed as the "5 Balasis, the Boys with the Steel Heads, World's only Head to Head Jugglers," the act included Victor Sr., Paula, Alfred and Victor Jr. A young lady, not a family member, was the fifth in the act. Maria Holz, an Austrian solo dance performer who had been a member of the Imperial Vienna Ballet, also sailed with the Balasics but was not yet part of the act.

They began their 19-week tour in Chicago, then played St. Louis, Detroit, Cleveland, Buffalo, Rochester, Toronto, Montreal, Boston and the Palace Theater in New York City before continuing to Newark, Washington, D.C., Norfolk, Richmond, Schenectady, Amsterdam, Albany and Binghamton, New York.

The family had originally planned to return to Europe in 1924 to fulfill a January date in Madrid. Instead, they extended their American tour on the Orpheum circuit. Reviews for the Balasics were very good, one describing the act as "a fast 15 minutes of acrobatics and balancing that stamp them professionals of the first order, surprising with one of the most breath-catching feats of the present day vaudeville stage, namely, a free head to head leap with the catcher doubly blind-folded!"

Meanwhile, Alfred and Maria had married. Their son, Alfred Balasic, was born during September 1924 in Portland, Oregon, while the act was playing Pantages time. In October, the young Danish woman who had accompanied them from Europe left the act, and the family finished the season as the Balasi Troupe.

In 1925, Victor Sr. and Paula decided to retire and settled in Chicago, where they purchased several properties, managing them as theatrical boardinghouses. Reorganized as the Balasi Trio, Alfred, Victor Jr. and Maria played across the USA from 1925 to 1927 on Keith, Loew's, Pantages and Gus Sun time. Their act attracted notice in *Variety* and *Vaudeville News*, and the act was again booked at Keith's Palace Theatre in New York City in June 1926.

In 1928, although gymnastics by Alfred and Victor remained important in the act, the focus shifted to Maria dancing, accompanied by Alfred on stringed instruments. They continued to tour on the Keith-Orpheum and Pantages circuits through 1929, but the craze for talking, singing and dancing films was changing show business. Live shows employed fewer specialty acts, and often the second half of the bill was a motion picture.

The Balasi Trio disbanded in 1930. Victor Jr. left the act to pair with his wife as Balasi and Skaren. Alfred and Maria retired to Chicago. Their son Alfred, the great-grandson of Karlu Balasic, did not join the family entertainment business, although, as a young stagehand at the Palmer House in Chicago in 1946, he met his future wife, Betty Biggs, who was performing there at the time with the Merriel Abbott Dancers.

No less than four generations of Balasics devoted themselves to the family act, its constant discipline and training. Like many performing dynasties, they passed on the leading parts in the act to the succeeding generation, responded to changes in the public's fancy, saved and invested wisely for the day when their performing careers would end.

ERNEST R. BALL

b: 21 July 1878, Cleveland, OH—
d: 3 May 1927, Santa Ana, CA

Songwriter and singer Ernie Ball probably made more money from song royalties ($30,000 in 1914 alone) than he earned in vaudeville as a performer. He appeared either as a single, accompanying himself on the piano, or in a double act: with his wife, Maude Lambert, in the 1910s and with George MacFarlane in the 1920s.

Ball was a pleasant entertainer, but the applause was more for the many sentimental, Irish-themed songs he composed, some of which were being sung a century after he wrote them: "Love Me and the World Is Mine," "Mother Machree," "A Little Bit of Heaven," "Will You Love Me in December as You Do in May?" and "When Irish Eyes Are Smiling," the last of which was used as the title of the fictionalized biography of Ball filmed by Fox in 1944.

Ball was classically trained; he had enrolled at the Cleveland Conservatory in preparation for a career as a concert pianist. Work was easier to find in vaudeville pit orchestras and as a staff composer for M. Witmark & Sons, a leading music publisher that signed Ball to a 20-year contract. Ernie Ball had many collaborators, but the most celebrated were Jimmy Walker, who forsook Tin Pan Alley for City Hall, and Chauncey Olcott, whose great popularity was based upon his fine Irish tenor and a style that elevated parlor songs to the concert stage.

Ernie Ball performed in vaudeville between 1911 and his death, in a dressing room, in 1927. He was a couple of months shy of his 50th birthday.

LUCILLE BALL

b: 6 August 1911, Jamestown, NY—
d: 26 April 1989, Los Angeles, CA

Lucille Ball never played vaudeville, but for a number of years, she exhibited the flair and talents of a vaudevillian, appeared in comedy films, comedy series on television, and dancing, clowning and singing on the musical-comedy stage.

When her death made newspaper front pages across the USA, it seemed as though Lucy had been around forever. She had made more than 80 movies, from her screen debut in 1933 onward, but only a handful of them remained memorable. Her period as a productive star lasted little longer than a decade, from the late-1940s through the early 1960s, but in that time she created a television series, one of a half-dozen touchstones for situation comedy.

I Love Lucy began in the twilight of network radio as *My Favorite Husband.* Lucy transferred it to CBS television in 1951. Her husband, Cuban American bandleader Desi Arnaz, was coproducer and replaced Richard Denning, who played Lucy's husband on the radio series. Lucy hoped that giving Desi the costarring role on television might help steady his responsibilities as her offscreen husband. Their divorce in 1960 proved her wrong, but their on-screen chemistry endeared them to the public, and the series was the most talked-about television show from 1951 through 1957. Thirty or so years after it ended, *I Love Lucy* is still in continuous reruns around the world.

Ball was 40 years old when TV stardom at last justified her tenacious resolve to make it big. She began acting (and directing) in high school and community theatre plays and recalled that vaudeville acts made a deep impression. A determined youngster even at 16, she talked her mother into sending her to acting school in Manhattan. The teachers at the John Murray Anderson/Robert Milton Academy were not impressed. Neither were the directors of two shows that had hired her as a chorus girl. Out of school and out of work, she dyed her hair blond and took up modeling, but a long illness interrupted her career. Recovered, she landed bit roles in two 1933 movies, *Broadway thru a Keyhole* and *Roman Scandals,* an Eddie Cantor film, but it was as a poster girl for Chesterfield cigarettes that she caught the attention of a Hollywood agent.

Lucille Ball was one of thousands of girls who flocked to Hollywood during the Great Depression, hoping against ridiculously unfavorable odds that they would be lucky. Few of the small-town beauty queens and department-store models—even those who won a screen test and found an agent—ever achieved more than a walk-on or two and some cheesecake photos printed in tabloids and magazines. The lucky few were commonsensical enough to treat the movies as a business and to develop thick (though Camay soft) skin; they worked with reasonable regularity as clotheshorses in musicals, bit players in dramas and wisecracking working girls in comedies. Ball had a lovely figure, an expressive face with big eyes, a good smile and lots of hair—red, blonde, then bright red.

Off camera, she was the regular working girl as well, better liked by the crews and seasoned veterans (like Buster Keaton, who helped her understand props and timing) than studio and department heads who were put off by her frankness, smart-ass sense of humor and sailor's vocabulary. Lucy made the rounds, working at Columbia, United Artists, RKO, Samuel Goldwyn, MGM and Paramount. She acted with many of the great comedians: Laurel & Hardy, Buster Keaton, the Three Stooges, The Marx Brothers and Bob Hope. As her bit roles increased in size and importance to supporting roles in the 1940s, Lucy joined a casting pool of attractive but snappy second leads like Joan Blondell, Glenda Farrell, Eve Arden and Rosalind Russell, and, like them, she was able to get laughs from her facial expressions, her posture and her funny moves, as well as her wise-cracking dialogue.

In 1943, she was cast opposite Red Skelton in *DuBarry Was a Lady,* her first Technicolor movie. She grabbed opportunity and dyed her hair the brightest orange red she could find. If people had failed to place a name with her face, that would happen no more. Lucille Ball became *the* Redhead. Among the better of her costarring movies were *Stage Door* (1937), *Room Service* (1938), *The Affairs of Annabel* (1938), *Easy to Wed* (1946), *Miss Grant Takes Richmond* (1949), *Sorrowful Jones* (1949), *Fancy Pants* (1950) and *Fuller Brush Girl* (1950).

In the late 1940s, Lucille Ball was hovering between 35 and 40 years old, a bit mature at the time for female romantic leads, even in comedies. So when radio beckoned in 1947, she heeded. The next ten years were her greatest. *I Love Lucy* was her graduate thesis. All she had absorbed about playing comedy, plus her own gifts, made the show a slapstick delight. The show began to slip a bit in its last year or so when Lucy and Ricky Ricardo moved from their modest New York City apartment to a designer homestead in Hollywood, and the use of guest stars heightened the unlikely rise in the show-business world of Ricky Ricardo.

When Lucy and Desi jettisoned their weekly half hour for a series of one-hour shows, what was left of the everyman quality of their work dissipated. The Hollywood shows moved Lucy out of a society she shared with lots of Americans into a rarefied environment of celebrity. The Lucy shows had always been madcap, but they had been rooted in everyday middle-class life. Always dazzled by show business, Lucy's attempts to crash showbiz in Manhattan had been thwarted or turned into disasters. In Hollywood, Desi's new celebrity brought Lucy into contact with superstars like Betty Grable, Tallulah Bankhead, Fred MacMurray, Ann Sothern, Fernando Lamas, Milton Berle and Danny Thomas. Unlike most Americans, Lucy and Desi got to travel to Japan, Sun Valley, Alaska and Mexico.

Lucy never fell out of favor with television audiences, and she had shed the relative anonymity of being one of many B-list stars who turned to television. *I Love Lucy* made her television's most successful female performer and the richest woman in Hollywood. Her sensational divorce from Desi, subsequent marriage to comic Gary Morton, and winning control of Desilu Productions confirmed that she was a smart businesswoman and not a rattle-brained middle-class woman. There were still enough fans to keep her various successor shows popular—all but the last.

Lucy ran a large production company and starred on Broadway in *Wildcat,* a so-so musical that managed 171 performances solely on the strength of her fame. She made a few more movies and was a guest star on whatever TV shows she wished to bless, but she took it easier as the years wore on. Decades after her death, Lucille Ball is still regarded by many as one of America's finest female comedians, for the way she handled physical gags as well as funny dialogue.

CARL BALLANTINE

b: 27 September 1922, Chicago, IL

Dressed in a tux, he strode onto the stage carrying a magician's stand from which he unfurled a small banner proclaiming himself as "The Great Ballantine." Garbed in a tuxedo, he looked like a standard-issue magician (that was the point). His facial expression varied from long-haired music conductor to Broadway mugg.

He doffed his top hat and placed it, open end up, on a pedestal. Holding up a piece of clothesline, he cut it into several foot-long lengths and explained that he, the Great Ballantine, would extract the original rope, all in one piece. When he pulled the rope out, an invisible-to-the-eye thread held all the pieces six inches apart. Pretending to be undaunted, he plopped the rope back into the hat and bluffed, "It's not done yet."

Later, when reaching into the hat to extract a rabbit, a momentary flash of panic in his face yielded to a look of ingratiating false confidence as he vainly searched deeper into the hat. When he was in up to his armpit, it was evident that another bogus trick had gone wrong. His bustling bravado dissipated as trick after trick collapsed in a gag.

Actually, Carl had begun practicing magic as a youngster and was performing at local events while attending high school. Early on, he took a comic approach to magic, and when he went into small-time vaudeville, in 1941, it was with a comedy magic act. Years later, in an interview, Carl Ballantine recalled that when he first performed his comic magic act in vaudeville, less-sophisticated audiences viewed it at face value, assuming him to be both serious and incompetent. It took big-city audiences, like those in his hometown, Chicago, to pick up on his style of humor and goof along with the act. During the 1940s and 1950s, Carl enjoyed a successful career in nightclubs and what was left of vaudeville. His close-up style of comedy magic proved suitable for the small screen, and he was a welcomed guest on early live television variety shows.

Segueing into situation comedy shows, Carl costarred with Ernest Borgnine, Joe Flynn and Tim Conway in *McHale's Navy* (1962–68). In 1969's *The Queen and I*, Carl joined three other fine comedians—Larry Storch, Pat Morita and Billy DeWolfe—on another ocean voyage, but the old liner, *Amsterdam Queen*, was quickly towed into dry dock by CBS.

The *McHale's Navy* television show had been so popular, however, that it led to a feature-length film version, *McHale's Navy* (1964), in which Carl reprised his role as Lester Gruber. Carl acted in movies for more than 40 years. Among his more notable appearances were *The Shakiest Gun in the West* (1968) with Don Knotts; *World's Greatest Lover* (1977) with Gene Wilder; *The North Avenue Irregulars* (1979) with Barbara Harris, Patsy Kelly and Cloris Leachman; *Just You and Me, Kid* (1979) with George Burns and Ray Bolger; *The Best of Times* (1986) with Robin Williams; *Mr. Saturday Night* (1992) with Billy Crystal, Jerry Lewis and Slappy White; *The Million Dollar Kid* (2000) with Kaye Ballard; and *Farewell to Harry* (2002), in which Carl played a dramatic role.

Ballantine guest starred on many of the major television series of the 1960s, 1970s and 1980s: *Car 54, Where Are You?; The Monkees; Mayberry R.F.D; I Dream of Jeanie; The Virginian; The Partridge Family; Laverne and Shirley; Alice; Fantasy Island; Trapper John, M.D.; Night Court* and *The Cosby Show.*

As late as 1978, The Great Ballantine performed his act on a television special, *The Magic of David Copperfield,* and 20 years later, he was one of the vaudevillians interviewed on the documentary *Vaudeville* (1997), which was broadcast by PBS on the *American Masters* series.

BALLOON ACTS

A late bloomer among variety acts, balloon acts, in which performers blew up and twisted balloons into various shapes, became popular and numerous after the Second World War. Television made their work easier to see than in a large theatre. Balloon acts were thick on the ground during the busking revival in the late twentieth and early twenty-first centuries.

The essential elements of this type of act are speed, comic shapes and fast patter. Most children are charmed by the deft manipulation of something regarded as a decoration or a toy into cartoon shapes of familiar animals (rabbits, dogs, giraffes). Consequently, balloon twisters have come to be regarded as an act primarily suited to youngsters, but there are clever monologists who use balloons as comic props in acts that are geared to adults.

BAND CALL

Another name for orchestra rehearsal is band call. The acts for the new week's bill arrived at the theatre mid-morning on the opening day of the bill, generally a Monday. They submitted their music to the pit band leader, who usually took them in the order they arrived; however, deference might be shown to headliners. Certainly, they had first choice of songs. If another act was going to use the same music, the headliner could, and usually did, forbid it. The other important acts were accommodated, as much as possible. The remaining acts, those stuck in number one, two or closing spots, sometimes waited, hoping they would receive more than cursory attention from the pit band leader.

There was not a full rehearsal (unless a headliner insisted). Instead, the performers would review their charts with the leader to ensure the tempos were correct and that the cues (for music or sound effects) were understood. The sooner the band call was over, the quicker the acts could get to their hotels, settle in, find someplace to eat and then get ready for the first show of the day.

BAND PARTS, CHARTS OR SIDES

All vaudeville acts used music except, perhaps, monologists, and even they had to have music to walk them on and off the stage. Using store-bought sheet music for piano or ukulele was acceptable only on amateur nights.

Each act was expected to have sides (band parts or charts, as they were also called) for the various instruments in the pit orchestra. In a small-time house, the piano might be the only accompanist, or there might be a horn, violin and drum as well. In better houses, there might be five, six or eight pieces in the pit band. Often, the pianist was also the conductor or leader. When playing a first-class big-time vaudeville house, the same act would have to have charts prepared for as many as 20 instrumentalists.

In addition to the music and music cues, an act would have cues for sound effects to coincide with a fall or the shooting of a gun in the act or the telling of a joke (rim shot—ba-da-bing!). Musicians could always tell whether an act played the big-time or better small-time by the signs of wear on their charts. Soiled piano, cornet and drum sides yet crisp unmarked sides for the clarinet and flute were a sure sign of a small-time act.

BAR ACT

The acrobatic turn known as a bar act is performed on a series of horizontal bars that were secured into a stable framework rather than suspended from an overhead grid. The performer(s) leapt from one bar to another, under and over, sometimes turning somersaults or reversing direction by crossing arms and hands in mid-flight and twisting around as they landed.

BARBETTE

b: (Vander Clyde) 9 December 1904, Round Rock, TX—d: 5 August 1973, Austin, TX

One way for the public to handle the evidence of an aerialist drag queen soaring through midair was to consign the creature to a netherworld and ignore the obvious. Barbette was not playing Charley's Aunt nor was he one of the female impersonators like Julian Eltinge who winked his way through his roles. He was written of as an elf, a fairy, an angelic creature or a statue of a mythical god come to life only to perform.

In his glory days of the 1920s, he entered the vaudeville stage or circus ring like a Ziegfeld showgirl, swathed in ostrich feathers, stunningly gowned, bejeweled, and bewigged. He then removed his headdress, cape and gown, and, garbed in as little as possible to suggest near nudity but not run afoul of the law, Barbette began the acrobatic part of his act. He walked a tight wire, slack wire, and performed on the rings and the trapeze. He was a master of the dramatic, seeming to fall only to catch himself by a last-second hook of his foot. He kept his audiences aghast and amazed until he left the stage. When he returned to acknowledge the sustained applause, he doffed his wig, revealing his bald head and reminding all that they had marveled at a man playing a woman.

Young Vander saw his first circus as a boy in Texas, and he determined that he would become an aerialist. Without training, he practiced daily in the family yard. He was about 14 when he answered an ad by the Alfaretta Sisters, "World Famous Aerial Queens," one of whom had just died. He passed the audition and got the job, provided he agreed to perform as a sister. He seems to have had no objection, and the act provided a fine apprenticeship for young Mr. Vander Clyde.

He moved on to other acts and shows, some of them circuses, but his aim was to perform as a single. He made his debut as a solo in 1919 at the Harlem Opera House. He got reviewed and became a successful vaudeville act, but Parisian revue and European circuses proved to be far more congenial environments for Barbette's persona and act. In 1923, Barbette appeared at the Casino de Paris, the Folies Bergère and other legendary music halls whose exotic aesthetics provided a near-perfect setting. He came back to New York to appear in *The Passing Show of 1924,* which opened early in September and played until the start of the Christmas season.

Whether in Europe or the USA, revue, circus or vaudeville, Barbette practiced his acrobatics and labored over his presentation. His costumes were cleaned and his wig(s) dressed after each performance. Before he went onstage, he applied a thick cream to his body and then powdered. He was described as a "jazz age Botticelli" and was the greatest acrobatic draw of his day.

Washed clean, his musculature was apparent, his hands were dark and calloused, his skin broken, and his torso and limbs scraped raw in places from the seemingly effortless act on the wire, rings and trapeze. Paris, London, Brussels and Berlin adopted him. Barbette became part of a charmed circle that enveloped Jean Cocteau, Josephine Baker, Anton Dolin, Mistinguette and Serge Diaghilev. Barbette appeared in Cocteau's first film, *Le Sang d'un Poète* (*Blood of the Poet,* 1930).

At one point, he was a starring attraction for the Ringling Bros. and Barnum & Bailey Circus, and a production number was framed around his aerial act. He appeared atop a 30-foot column in a costume with a huge gauzy skirt that fanned out over the length of the column and spread wide on the floor. Barbette began twirling on top of the column. As he did and the skirt gradually gathered momentum and began to lift off the floor, he created an aerial ballet.

One evening, during an engagement at the London Palladium, he and another man were caught in a compromised position in his dressing room. Babette was not the first actor interrupted in flagrante delicto in that hall, but Val Parnell, the theatre's manager, was a man of limited tolerance, and Barbette fell into scandal. It was made clear he would never get another British work permit. According to some sources, Barbette returned to the USA in 1935 to appear in *Billy Rose's Jumbo,* a show that would seem a natural for him. Other sources list him as neither in the original nor replacement casts, however, so there may have been another acrobat imitating Barbette, as there was in the Hitchcock film *Murder.* Or, perhaps Barbette had signed to appear in the show when disaster befell him.

Sometime in the early or mid-1930s, Barbette suffered a severe fall that broke both of his legs. He returned to New York, where he contracted pneumonia, developed a mastoid and contracted infantile paralysis (polio). The most encouraging prognosis was that he would never work again; the worst was that he was crippled, if not paralyzed, for life.

Barbette asked to be allowed to die, but a doctor who had just lost his son to the disease cajoled Barbette into agreeing to experimental therapies and medicine.

When he could again walk, he returned to Texas, where he lived in Austin with a sister who could help care for him. Barbette lived with his pain and put the same energy and determination into regaining control of his body as he once had put into his act. His reputation brought him some work. He coached aerial acts for circuses, choreographed routines and served as a consultant to a few Disneyland shows and the occasional circus movie.

He missed Europe and his old life, and could not adjust to growing old in the Austin of the late 1960s and early 1970s. He took an overdose of medication one evening and left Texas.

MAE BARNES

b: (Edith Mae Stith) 7 January 1907, New York, NY—d: 13 December 1996, Boston, MA

Mae Barnes, the round and wide-eyed black singer with a pretty face, penetrating voice and sassy sense of humor, spanned modern show business from vaudeville to Broadway to the nightclubs of the post–Second World War era. She began as a child singing, playing piano and dancing. When she was 12, she lied her way into the chorus line at Harlem's Plantation Club. Tap dancing and singing, she created an act and played the Theatre Owners' Booking Association (TOBA) circuit for about five years until she made her musical-comedy debut in *Running Wild* as a tap dancer in 1924 during the hit show's second season on Broadway. The producers were billing her as the "Bronze Ann Pennington." After touring with *Running Wild* she went into another show, *Rang Tang.* This one starred Bill Robinson, who publicly attested to her dancing talent.

Unfortunately, in 1938, Barnes was injured in an automobile accident. She concentrated on her singing. At first she played dives with a repertoire of smutty songs, punctuated with a modified hootchy-kootchy, and worked the audience table by table. Gradually, the clubs got better—Cerutti, the Little Casino and the Blue Angel—yet Mae continued to keep her material naughty if nice. Several record albums produced in the 1950s preserved her sound, but Barnes was an act best appreciated in live performance, where she could kid with the customers, kick up her heels in an echo of her former precision tap dancing and feed off the reaction of her enthusiastic audiences.

In the 1950s, Mae was one of the most popular entertainers at the Bon Soir, a fabled cabaret in Greenwich Village. Mae Barnes had come back home, for the Village was where Mae was born. She made all of her songs into *special material.* Some were standards in which she interpolated risqué lyrics, others were songs written for her. She returned to musical comedy when she appeared in the 1950 edition of the *Ziegfeld Follies,* but it closed in Boston. She made it to Broadway in 1954 in the cast of *By the Beautiful Sea,* starring Shirley Booth. Mae Barnes remained active in clubs, both in the USA and Europe, into the 1960s.

P. T. (PHINEAS TAYLOR) BARNUM

b: 5 July 1810, Bethel, CT—d: 7 April 1891, Bridgeport, CT

P. T. Barnum was the best-known showman of his era, and much of his activity involved the so-called dime museums that he operated in New York, Philadelphia and Baltimore. Generally, dime museums included a performance hall for variety acts. Because many first-generation vaudevillians got their start in dime museums, these exhibit halls and the men who ran them are of interest to vaudeville historians.

The eldest of five children, the future "Prince of Humbug" was born to a father, Philo, who fared poorly at several trades—tailor, livery-stable owner, farmer, tavern keeper and country-store proprietor. At grammar school, Phineas showed little promise yet excelled at arithmetic, a subject that partnered well with what Barnum later called his "organ of acquisitiveness." More useful to his career than an elementary education was a natural talent for turning a dollar. At ten, he was selling cherry rum to the soldiers at a local military installation and making more money than his father.

To augment income from the farm, Philo Barnum had bought both a tavern and a small dry-goods shop in town. Finding Phineas useless on the farm, Mr. Barnum set him to work in the shop. Young Phineas was in his element. In a small town, many transactions were barters, and it was he who dealt with the flinty farm women who brought in eggs, butter and beeswax to trade for store-bought supplies. Phineas proved a canny negotiator, extracting the best of the bargain without losing custom. On the side, he sold lottery tickets, which were not only legal but had the blessings of the local churches. The Methodist minister found he was able to extract more support from his congregation through raffles than donations.

Young Barnum fell in with a group of older townsmen who eschewed work, whenever possible, for the fun and profit of chiseling one another and trading tall stories. When business was slow, they gathered at Barnum's store or he joined them at the family's tavern. The long folk tradition of the Connecticut Yankee trying to gain advantage in deals was Barnum's first apprenticeship. In his later years, Barnum liked to tell of a small-town grocer who served the local church as a deacon. Each morning, he called down from his upstairs living quarters:

"John, have you watered the rum?"

"Yessir."

"And sanded the sugar?"

"Yessir."

"And dusted the pepper?"

"Yessir."

"And chicoried the coffee?"

"Yessir."

"Well, then, come up to prayers."

In more sober moments of recollection, Barnum confessed to a less folksy version of daily life. "It was dog eat dog. The customers cheated us, and we cheated them. Each party expected to be cheated if it was possible." Yet these same folks, including Barnum himself, considered themselves upright Christians. This dichotomy was an enduring characteristic of Barnum's career.

His father died when Barnum was 15, and his mother took over the running of the family tavern. The extended family, which included his grandparents, worked the farm and managed the dry-goods shop. Barnum was 17 when he left home and for two years worked in porterhouses (ale and beer halls) in both Brooklyn and Manhattan. It was in New York that he became an avid theatregoer, always with an appraising eye toward theatrical effectiveness and the degree of profitability of various shows.

He returned to Bethel to marry Charity Hallet (1808–73). A short time later, one of the many religious revivals that swept the nineteenth-century America reached Bethel in its course. Barnum took exception to the rise in power of rock-ribbed revivalist ministers who were trying to dictate politics. He inaugurated his own newspaper, *The Herald of Freedom*, and attacked individuals whose presumed hypocrisy lent itself to exposés. He included abolitionists among his targets.

Barnum understood the force of publicity, and his few years of publishing *The Herald of Freedom* proved he knew how to command public notice. Being a gadfly landed him in jail, where he managed to hold court, wrote his news and commentary and publicity fostered the groundswell for his release. Still, advertisers failed to pay their accounts, and *The Herald of Freedom* foundered in a sinkhole of red ink.

Unexpectedly, some of his debtors did pay off, and, in 1835, Phineas, Charity and their young daughter, Caroline, moved to New York City, where P. T. Barnum found his calling. As a stopgap, the Barnums opened a boardinghouse, but 25-year-old Phineas was looking for the big score. He found it in Joice Heth, an ancient Negro woman who was being represented as the 161-year-old slave who raised George Washington. In Manhattan, Barnum met Coley Bartram, who had just sold his financial interest in Miss Heth to a Philadelphia promoter who was exhibiting her. Barnum struck a deal and bought Miss Heth for $1,000, half of which he had to borrow. He brought her back to Manhattan, hired a hall, exhibited her, sold newspaper editors on the story of Joice Heth as George Washington's nurse, papered the town with handbills and grossed a then-phenomenal figure of $1,500 a week.

When business dropped off, he took Miss Heth on a tour of New England. Barnum was quite sophisticated in his understanding of the public, the press and the craft of publicity. When business failed to materialize in Boston, he sent an anonymous letter to the newspapers protesting that Joice Heth was not the blind, toothless old woman with four-inch finger- and toenails who had raised the first president but a compound of India rubber, whalebone and an interior mechanism that was controlled offstage, like a puppet, just as a ventriloquist gave voice to the contraption. The controversy turned the trick, and the Boston engagement proved profitable as suspicious Bostonians flocked to the exhibition hall to see for themselves if the allegations were true. Miss Heth may have been as much a party to the deception as her exploiters. She lived with some measure of comfort and enjoyed more visitors than a blind, aged African American of her day could have expected. Willingly, for audiences and interviewers, she manufactured detailed stories about George Washington's life that passed muster. In February 1836, a few months after Barnum acquired rights to Miss Heth, she died. An autopsy determined she was about 80 years old.

Barnum was not fortunate during the next five years. He had determined to enter the circus business but suffered a few stumbles. Barnum cut a deal with Aaron Turner, with Barnum handling the sideshow activities of the Aaron Turner Traveling Circus. The show began its tour in the South. Among Barnum's attractions was an African American singer. The man, still a slave under the law, escaped once the show reached North Carolina. Barnum refused to forego ticket sales, so he blacked up and performed the black singer's songs. The African Americans who traveled in the South with Barnum were slaves he bought. Those who tried to escape or steal were flogged.

When the Aaron Turner Traveling Circus failed to draw crowds in Rochester, New York, Barnum came up with the idea of a circus parade. Later, after Barnum left Aaron Turner's outfit, he bought a paddle-wheel showboat and steamed up and down the Mississippi River, but this proved no more successful than his other schemes. Next, he launched Barnum's Grand Scientific and Musical Theatre, but income failed to meet expenses. He leased the Vauxhall saloon for a summer and fared poorly. Finally, in 1842, he was reduced to writing advertisements for the Bowery Amphitheater for $4 a week.

At the lowest point in his career, opportunity again visited and wasted no time in bestowing its blessings. The nearby American Museum was for lease. Although Barnum had not a penny to his name, he was heir to a worthless bog upstate; this he used as collateral for a ten-year lease to the premises and an agreement to purchase the museum's collections from its landlord.

In the exhibit hall, there were dioramas of biblical scenes and fabled cities like Paris and Jerusalem, a newly invented knitting machine, a giant, a fat boy, an automaton and various jarred specimens. Barnum's prime exhibit was the "Fejee Mermaid," two dead animals reputedly sewn together: the upper half a mummified monkey and the lower a large, preserved fish. Upstairs, in what Barnum called "the lecture room," visitors saw a variety show. A typical bill included rope dancers, jugglers, living statues (*tableaux vivant*), gypsy musicians, trained dogs and acrobatic fleas (only accidentally on the same bill). Barnum made $28,000 his first year, an impressive sum for the time; he paid off his debts and established the American Museum among New York City's attractions.

In November of that same year of 1842, Barnum was visiting his brother Philo, manager of the Franklin Hotel in Bridgeport, Connecticut, when he was told about the town's most celebrated curiosity, Charles Sherwood Stratton, a five-year-old boy who weighed only 16 pounds. Phineas contracted with the boy's father to allow the boy to make a four-week appearance at Barnum's American Museum. Mrs. Barnum accompanied her son to New York City. Barnum groomed this bright, articulate little person into a sensational attraction he named General Tom Thumb.

Four weeks extended into years, as Barnum and Tom toured America, England, Belgium and France; in each place, the little boy—whom Barnum promoted as a dwarf and to whose age he added six years—charmed all levels of society in person and onstage, where he sang, danced, recited and performed impressions of the celebrities of the day.

From a twenty-first-century vantage, Barnum seems exploitive, which he was. The issue is whether business opportunity was tempered by care for his exhibits. Joice Heth, touring with Barnum, enjoyed the comfort and care he provided during her last year on Earth. Tom Thumb, who was not really wanted by his family, found a friendly adviser in Barnum and attained a measure of financial success, business acumen and respect unknown to other little people and dwarfs of that or any era.

On the other hand, the animals Barnum had captured were kept in horrid conditions, and they were burned to death in the fire that later destroyed Barnum's American Museum. The barbaric conditions for animals at Barnum's were not exceptional at the time. Forty years later, B. F. Keith's menagerie was confined in unclean, unhealthy conditions, and a century-and-a-half later, there were still squalid roadside animal exhibits and disreputable traveling circuses that treat animals shamefully.

By 1846, four years after taking over the American Museum, Barnum was in his mid-30s, a very wealthy man and living like a prince. For the family seat, he built and furnished a fantasy palace, which he named Iranistan, on a 17-acre plot in Bridgeport, Connecticut, on Long Island Sound. It was inspired by the Brighton Pavilion in England and was the first of four mansions he built.

Success stoked ambition in Barnum, and he ventured in various directions at once. He acquired Peal's Museum in Philadelphia, financed an expedition to capture elephants in Ceylon, and won out over all other American impresarios to present Jenny Lind in America. Jenny Lind was the most glittering of European opera stars. In 1849, Barnum signed "The Swedish Nightingale" for a series of 150 appearances in the USA at $1,000 per performance. Although she had earned a great reputation in Europe, Miss Lind was relatively unknown in the USA. Beginning with her American debut, a brilliantly planned and heralded concert at Castle Garden, Barnum's publicity campaign made her the most famous woman in North America. Lind completed 93 concerts from 1850 through 1851 before she broke her contract and quit the tour due to the strain of travel, singing and the constant hoopla. She had earned nearly $100,000, and Barnum made an additional $200,000. Their parting was amicable, they remained friends and always spoke well of each other.

Barnum's interests became increasingly diverse, and many of them did not receive the attention they required. Barnum bought a lot of Bridgeport land and invested in various business enterprises that failed. He was drinking heavily. Bankrupted again, he surrendered Iranistan to creditors, moved his family to New York City and, sober, turned in 1851 to giving temperance lectures.

To recoup his financial position, he undertook a tour of England with members of the Howard family, actors and in-laws of George L. Fox, fast becoming the country's premier comedian. The Howards may have performed *Uncle Tom's Cabin.* Barnum also asked Tom Thumb to join him in England. Although Tom Thumb had been managing his own career and affairs since he and Phineas had ceased touring, the *Little General* came to Barnum's rescue. While the Howards and Tom Thumb played English theatres, Barnum took to the lecture circuit, expounding upon "The Art of Money-Getting," one subject on which he was a master.

Once again successful, Barnum took to the public life, serving as a representative in the Connecticut state legislature, where he announced in support of Negro enfranchisement. During his second term, on 13 July 1865, Barnum received news that the American Museum had been destroyed by fire. Almost all the caged creatures, including a whale, alligators, snakes, pigs, rabbits, rats and monkeys, were burned alive, asphyxiated or crushed in the crumbling building. His museum burned down twice more, after which he turned to the circus business.

By the late 1860s, Barnum was again wealthy. In 1871, the 61-year-old Barnum joined with two smart and well-regarded circus men, Don Costello and W. C. Coup; together the trio eventually produced the largest circus ever seen in the USA. It boasted a gigantic tent and more acts and animals than the American public had ever seen. Barnum's circus underwent various changes over a decade, and several names appeared in its advertising: World's Fair and Hippodrome, Barnum's Great Moral Show (a two-ring circus that became the first to travel by train), and P. T. Barnum's Grand Traveling Museum, Menagerie, Caravan & Circus. It was dutifully reported that the road show required 100 railway carriages and grossed $400,000 in its first year, although press reports may have been no more reliable than P. T. Barnum's inflated prose.

A year later, while Phineas was traveling, his wife died. The marriage had petered out. While Phineas gadded about, Charity, beset with various ailments, some of which were emotional, lived at home. Left behind were four children, all girls (born between 1832 and 1846). Barnum did not return home for his wife's funeral. He was in Europe with his new love, Nancy Fish, a 22-year-old that he married the following year when he was 64. There were no children from the second marriage.

In 1880, Barnum's circus combined with one of its major competitors, James A. Bailey, whose London Circus was part of the Grand International Allied Shows. Barnum had one more coup left in his career: the purchase in 1882 of Jumbo, a magnificently large elephant, from the London Zoo. The sale and loss of Jumbo angered Britons. Jumbo was exhibited in the USA for a year-and-a-half until he was hit and killed by a railway locomotive.

The merged show adopted several names: P. T. Barnum's Greatest Show on Earth, the Great London Circus, Sanger's Royal British Menagerie and the Grand International Allied Shows United. All proved too cumbersome and soon became known as the Barnum & London Circus. Barnum and Bailey split their outfit in 1885 but rejoined in 1888 as Barnum & Bailey Greatest Show on Earth. The combined circus traveled all over the USA, and, in 1888, the huge show even made the difficult sail to England. The circus played for Queen Victoria and her son Edward, Prince of Wales. Three years later, after Barnum's death, Bailey became sole operator. In 1907, it was acquired by the Ringling Brothers.

Barnum had fallen seriously ill in 1890 but lived long enough to enjoy reading a premature obituary. When he died in 1891, he left an estate in excess of $4 million, much of it to his only grandson, C. Barnum Seeley, a member of the stock exchange. His surviving wife, Nancy Fish Barnum, moved to Europe after his death. She married twice more and died in 1927 in Paris.

The Ringling Bros, and Barnum & Bailey Circus, although greatly changed, continues to tour the USA at the turn of twenty-first century, and has kept the

Barnum name alive, a name that has endured longer than that of any other American showman.

THE BARRYMORES

Maurice Barrymore

b: (Herbert Blyth) 21 September 1847, Fort Agra, India—d: 26 March 1905, Amityville, NY

Sidney Drew

b: (Sidney Drew White) 28 August 1863, New York, NY—d: 9 April 1919, New York, NY

Lionel Barrymore

b: 12 April 1878, Philadelphia, PA— d: 16 November 1954, Los Angeles, CA

Ethel Barrymore

b: 15 August 1879, Philadelphia, PA— d: 18 June 1959, Los Angeles, CA

John Barrymore

b: 14 February 1882, Philadelphia, PA— d: 29 May 1942, Los Angeles, CA

Money was the great leveler. All the Barrymores were in continual need of money and remained so throughout their lives, even when their services commanded outstandingly high fees. Vaudeville paid high salaries to entice renowned artists of the legitimate theatre. Movies and radio later did the same.

Ethel Barrymore once had thought of being a concert pianist, but when the time came to grow up—and it came when she was still a girl—she put away dreams and assumed her role as the head of the family and inheritor of its business. If, perhaps, she did so dutifully at first, she grew willingly into her role as the First Lady of the American Theatre.

Both Lionel and John Barrymore had studied fine art and were as accomplished and talented as illustrators as Ethel was as a musician. Yet, without means to support themselves, they bowed to Ethel's insistence that they follow the family craft because it held out the hope of earning sufficient money to pursue personal freedom.

Maurice Barrymore

Ethel Barrymore was the last of her clan to play vaudeville. A few years earlier, in 1910, Ethel became furious when her elder brother, Lionel, had announced that he and his young wife, Doris Rankin, were joining the Barrymores' uncle, Sidney Drew, and his wife, Gladys Rankin, in vaudeville. Her later conversion was possible only, it seems, by the example of the great Sarah Bernhardt and Irene Vanbrugh.

Sidney Drew and Gladys Rankin were longtime vaudeville favorites in short, light plays such as *The Jail Bird, The White Slaver, Stalled, The Still Voice* (the last two written by Gladys) and *Bob Acres* (a distillation of Sheridan's *The Rivals*). Also appearing with Sidney Drew and Gladys Rankin in their vaudeville act was Sidney Rankin Drew, their son and cousin to Lionel, Ethel and John, bringing the number to five when Lionel and Doris joined the troupe.

Doris Rankin was Gladys' younger sister; they were 14 years apart in age. Lionel, who had left the legitimate stage for vaudeville because he dreaded performing before an audience and forgetting his lines, soon left vaudeville for moving pictures, which, together with radio, provided him a long career far away and safe from live audiences.

Sidney Drew seems not to have agonized over playing in motion pictures any more than he did vaudeville. He had a respectable first career on the legitimate stage but found vaudeville and films more congenial. Gladys Rankin died in 1914, and Drew and his second wife, Lucille McVey, made a series of short photoplays between 1915 and 1916 for Metro Studios, then located at One West 61st Street in Manhattan. Sidney's son, by then known as S. Rankin Drew, had a promising career as a film director until his battlefront death in the First World War.

Audiences expected Ethel Barrymore to appear in a new production each season. Uninspired by impresario Charles Froman's choice of a play for her 1913 season on Broadway, and mindful of Sarah Bernhardt's great success in vaudeville, Ethel signed with Martin Beck for her vaudeville debut. She appeared in Richard Harding Davis' one-acter *Miss Civilization* for the week of 8 April 1913 at the Palace Theatre in New York. Her $3,000 salary for the week was far more than she could command on the legitimate stage and far more than the fledgling Palace could afford during its sixth week of operation. Still, Ethel's appearance that week spiked receipts at the box office, so the $3,000 paid her was a reasonable investment in the Palace's prestige and future.

Later that year, Ethel Barrymore made her first appearance in *The Twelve Pound Note,* a one-act play by James M. Barrie. In 1914, she took another sketch, *Drifted Apart,* into vaudeville but with far less success. Whenever she needed money, she returned to the safety of *The Twelve Pound Note,* reviving it for vaudeville tours in 1917, 1921, 1923, 1926 and again in 1933, when, with conditions rather desperate for both Miss Barrymore and vaudeville, she had to perform four times a day. In 1926, *Variety's* reviewer described her act as "Sir James Barrie moralizing and our first actress Barrymorealizing."

Early in his career, even John Barrymore appeared in vaudeville, touring with the short plays *The Honeymoon* and *His Wedding Morn.* John's matinee-idol looks soon threatened to pin him to a career of romantic heroes—first on Broadway, then in Hollywood—until he insisted he was a character actor and proved it. Later, as his life and career began to sadly shadow his father's, he played the clown and played it masterfully.

It was the handsome and tragic Maurice, father of Lionel, Ethel and John, who became the first great actor of the legitimate stage to enter vaudeville. The date was 29 March 1897, and the stage was that of the Union Square Theatre. It was on another vaudeville stage, Harlem's Lion Palace Vaudeville Hall, that Maurice Barrymore suffered his final breakdown in 1901. When, instead of performing his piece, he ranted and cried, he drew laughs from the audience and ran from the theatre. His horrified 19-year-old son John, who had been sitting in the audience, pursued his father in the streets and tried to calm him. It was John who had to commit his father to such refuge as Bellevue Hospital then provided.

EL BARTO

b: (James Barton) 21 April 1859, St. Louis, MO—d: 30 April 1935, Clemington, NJ

Young James Barton was enjoying a baseball game in Philadelphia one day when the large sign for El Bart Dry Gin in center field caught his eye. He played with the name until it yielded El Barto, a Spanish-sounding title that would attract attention and look good on a vaudeville bill. It suggested mystery as well, and that was as much the stock-in-trade of a magician as was his sleight of hand and his props. Henceforward, young Barton would be known as El Barto, the Merry Wizard.

The name Barton meant little to him. It certainly had not brought him stardom during the decade he had been knocking about in the bowels of show business. Born a year before the start of the Civil War, he had been orphaned at six months and adopted by a poor family who abused him. He ran away when he was 11 years old, sold papers and did whatever else he and the thousands of other rootless youngsters who came to New York did to survive. These were the boys who filled the gallery at George L. Fox's and Harrigan & Hart shows.

It was a hard era in America's social history. The waves of destitute immigrants reached a peak in the 1860s. Cities and towns with more commerce than law sprung up along the growing network of railways, and rural American agriculture was transformed into an industrialized farming industry. Smokestacks would soon tower over church steeples in cities where the poor—six out of every seven Americans—worked and lived in dingy, dangerous and disease-festering conditions.

Barton hopped milk and freight trains to escape urban miseries for a day or two. On a day that would change his life, he ended up in Tarrytown, New York, and visited the local theatre, where he became entranced by the magician onstage, Antonio Blitz. He stayed after the show and approached Blitz as the man was stowing his gear. The magician spoke to the young fellow, and, before their meeting had ended, Barton was invited first to supper and then, when Blitz understood that the boy had no home, to become the magician's assistant. For three years, the youngster packed and carried, learning the basics of illusion, even figuring as the center of Blitz's decapitation stunt, when the magician "cut off" Barton's head and paraded it around the stage on a platter.

At 14, Barton was a bit too sure he had learned what he could and thought he was in a position to improve the act. Señor Blitz agreed neither with Barton's estimate of himself nor with his prescription for change, and Barton found himself suddenly at liberty with nowhere to go. He opted for the familiar: the road, where he spent several years in various medicine shows, circuses and carnival sideshows, refining his magic skills, learning to throw his voice, juggle, speak in public, and other basics for a variety performer.

Young James Barton (not to be confused with the rising comic song-and-dance man of the same name) had become El Barto by 1895, the year he began in vaudeville. El Barto played his magic act all over the USA, starting on small-time circuits around New York City, including Loew's and Fox's. As he traveled westward, he hooked up with the W. S. Butterfield circuit, the Interstate Theatres, the Pantages and Sullivan & Considine circuits.

El Barto graduated to the big time when he was booked on the Keith circuit in the East, the Western Vaudeville Association out of Chicago, which controlled all the theatres and fairgrounds in the Midwest, and the Orpheum on the West Coast. The Western Vaudeville Managers' Association (WVMA) and the Orpheum soon merged.

It is reported that the Shubert Brothers engaged El Barto, who resembled Woodrow Wilson, to impersonate the president in their *Passing Show of 1913* in New York City's Winter Garden. It is uncertain whether or not he performed any of his vaudeville act in the revue. *The Passing Show* cast was huge and featured comic actors Charlotte Greenwood, May Boley and Lew Brice; dancer Bessie Clayton; singers John Charles Thomas and Charles King; Carter De Haven; and song, dance and patter act George Whiting & Sadie Burt.

Unlike many magic acts in vaudeville, El Barto worked without assistants and did not employ a lot of props and scenery. He could work in front of the curtain and be slotted anywhere on the bill as needed. His billing advertised him as either "The Merry Wizard" or the "Conversational Trixer," and his specialty, unlike magicians who remained distant and aloof from their audiences, was to work close to his audiences. He charmed them with patter and explained his methods while regaling them with card tricks, torn paper that became whole, and silk handkerchiefs that appeared and vanished with a wave of a wand or a hand.

Reputedly, El Barto knew and could perform hundreds of tricks but, like any good vaudevillian, he opted for those few he had polished into performance gems. One of these was the water-into-wine trick, which caused more than its usual sensation when in 1910 he performed it in Sorel, a small French Canadian town on the St. Lawrence River. Handbills had been floated around town ballyhooing his appearance at the local theatre, which announced "Vaudeville par le fameux EL BARTO, le grand magician du tour" and promised that he would change water into wine. Good, religious folk, naive by current standards and quite innocent of theatrical hyperbole, crammed the theatre. When he left the theatre after the show, a crowd of the curious followed him to his hotel. El Barto did not speak French, and the citizens did not speak English, so both audience and magician were mystified. The bilingual innkeeper explained: although some of the audience doubtless thought El Barto a charlatan, others were certain he had re-created the Gospel miracle of changing water into wine!

El Barto was active in the International Brotherhood of Magicians. In 1934, he announced his retirement; he was 76 years old and had entertained at fairs, parties, society engagements, vaudeville and revue for 65 years. He died the following year.

BARTON & ASHLEY

John Barton, a tramp comic, teamed with Annie Ashley in an act, "Canal Boat Sal," that was a slapstick battle that Ms. Ashley always won. They were popular with variety, burlesque and vaudeville audiences in the late nineteenth and early twentieth centuries. Johnny Barton was the uncle of vaudeville, burlesque and Broadway legend James Barton.

See also Annie Ashley and James Barton

JAMES BARTON

b: (James Barton Jr.) 1 November 1890, Gloucester City, NJ—d: 19 February 1962, Mineola, NY

Variety critic Robert Landry judged that James Barton "was perhaps the most singularly talented of all headliners—[he] sang as sensationally as Jolson, danced like Bill Robinson and was a stand-up comedian like Will Fyffe or whoever else one might name."

Joe Laurie Jr., in his 1953 elegiac valentine, *Vaudeville: From the Honky-Tonks to the Palace,* opined, "that the top all-around artist of today is Jim Barton, who was a burley comic, a skater, a storyteller, a dancer, a singer, a dramatic actor, and a pic, radio and TV star. He can also play an instrument and baseball! There were many single men who could do more things, but Jim was tops in all the things he did."

James Barton

In *Jazz Dance,* Marshall Stearns wrote, "In his day Barton was preferred by critics to Jolson, Cantor, Bojangles [Bill Robinson], Astaire, Bolger—as *Variety* reports—'whoever anybody was inclined to mention as a master.'" Yet, although lesser talents from the same era are remembered, James Barton has been forgotten.

A third-generation entertainer, Jim Barton had eagerly taken up the family business. Show business defined his world from the moment he first came onstage. He was born in New Jersey while his Dad was on the road with the Primrose & West's Minstrels, for which he served as interlocutor. Jim's mother was a toe dancer, and an uncle, John, was a dancer who taught two-year-old James his first steps. Baby James made his debut in 1892, playing an infant in arms when his parents acted in a creaky melodrama, *The Silver King.*

At four years of age, Jim was a member of Barton & Williams, his parents' knockabout act that played both burlesque and vaudeville. At first, he was a novelty. Baby James had a walk-on as a tiny sheriff, handcuffed to his prisoner, played by Barton Sr. The audiences howled at tiny Jim Barton locking up his prisoner and swaggering off the stage. By seven, he was being featured as "The Boy Comedian" in the family act.

Jim stepped into a number of different roles whenever his parents toured in various productions of *Uncle Tom's Cabin.* Barton later claimed to have played every role in the venerable melodrama except Little Eva, and he and his parents worked where they could: stock companies, touring companies, vaudeville and burlesque. At eight, he partnered with his mother, as Clara & James Barton, and played the (old) Howard Athenaeum in Boston, among other dates. This may have been during the time that Barton Sr. was offstage, managing the Front Street Theatre in Baltimore.

James Barton picked up his dance steps from older dancers with whom he shared the bill throughout his youth. Instead of being imitative, however, Barton was versatile and original. He remembered being very impressed with the great black song-dance-comedy team of Bert Williams and George W. Walker: Walker's vital presence and his peerless strut, Williams' eccentric comic steps.

Barton left the family act when he turned 17 and hitched up with the Johnson Repertory Company on tour out of Baltimore. At 19, he was playing in a production of *Uncle Tom's Cabin* with the Academy of Music Repertory Company, which he joined in Newport News. At tour's end, he brought a solo novelty act—song and dance plus roller-skating—into vaudeville but soon joined a repertory company—possibly the Academy of Music again—for a tour of *Peck's Bad Boy.* Management was unable or unwilling to pay regularly, so Barton and another cast member, Johnny Barry, quit the show in Fort Scott, Kansas and worked their way back to Philadelphia with a short series of vaudeville dates in a roller-skating act, Barry & Barton. Jim took the work he could get in show business—stock, minstrelsy, variety, vaudeville and burlesque—and honed his various talents as a comedian, actor, dancer and singer. For a time, he even played semiprofessional baseball.

In 1913, 22-year-old Jim Barton joined the stock burlesque company at Hart's Theatre in Philadelphia. Within a year, he was playing the Progressive wheel as lead comic in Jeanette Dupree's *Her Own Big Show.* A year later, Barton was engaged for George Clark's revue *Hello Paris* on the American wheel. Both the American and Progressive wheels were small-time circuits operating in the shadow of the Columbia wheel.

By 1917, Barton had built a fine reputation in burlesque as an eccentric dancing comedian. It was probably on its stages where Barton developed the drunk and mad-dog comic dance routines that became his signature turns. The biggest burlesque wheel, Columbia, beckoned, and Jim signed for a touring revue, *Twentieth Century Maids.* It provided steady work for a couple of seasons, and it was in this show that J. J. Shubert spotted Barton and signed him for the next edition of the *Passing Show.*

Thus far, Barton's fame had been confined to burlesque. Broadway critics first discovered him while he was among the featured acts in the Shuberts' *The Passing Show of 1919* (which, with 280 performances, extended into 1920). Also in the cast were Blanche Ring, Charles Winninger, Mary Eaton, Reginald Denny and the Avon Comedy Four. Two of the Avon Comedy Four, Joe Smith and Charlie Dale, introduced their soon-to-be-famous "Doctor's Office" sketch, later known as "Dr. Kronkheit," in the *Passing Show of 1919.* Barton was known, if at all, as a burlesque comedian, and his status was on par with another unknown dancer in the show, George Raft.

During the course of the show's run, Barton had been one of the first performers to sign up with Actors Equity, and he was asked to be a standby act for the union's benefit show headlined by Broadway's best, including Ethel Barrymore, W. C. Fields and Ed Wynn. Wynn's producers, the Shuberts, would not let Ed appear onstage, so he sat in the audience until he was introduced, and then Wynn did his act from the aisle. Because Barton had been drafted to fill Wynn's spot on the benefit bill, he also went on. The relatively unknown burlesque comic and eccentric dancer made his reputation that night and stole the show from the stars. As he left the stage, he saluted the audience, "Thanks for the use of the hall." The audience of pros loved it.

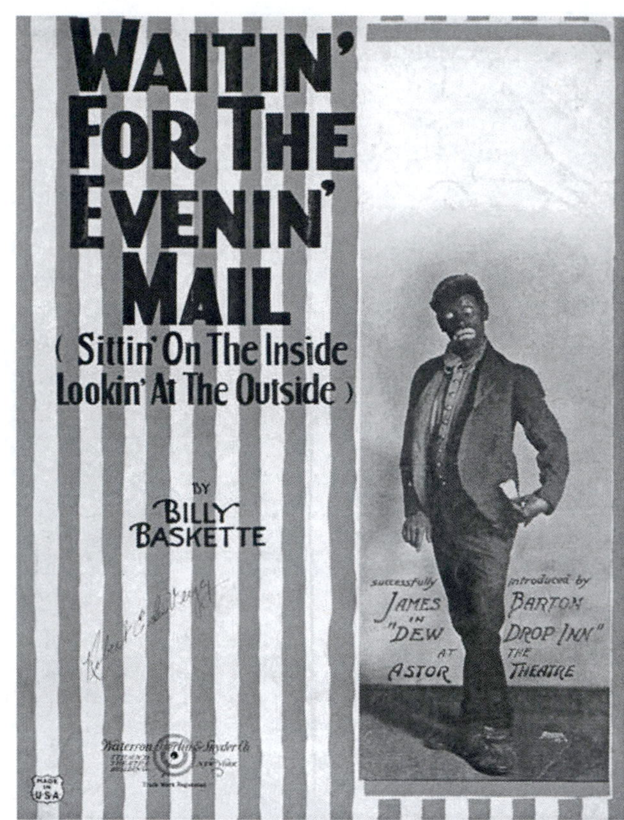

James Barton

Jim Barton appeared on Broadway every year between 1919 and 1926. *The Last Waltz* (1921) scored 185 performances at the Century Theatre. For a month, Barton was doubling after the show; he also performed upstairs on the Century Roof in *The Mimic World,* which featured Mae West. *The Rose of Stamboul* (1922), an operetta, managed 111 performances, but the *Dew Drop Inn* (1923) closed after 52 performances, despite enthusiastic revues for Jim (one of his stunts was to jump over a line of seven chairs in a row; usually, he made it). Originally, the show and the lead role was created as a vehicle for Bert Williams, but the great black comedian died before the show was produced. Barton was hired to take the role created for Williams, and he played it in blackface. The critics dismissed the *Dew Drop Inn* book, but *Variety* reported that Barton "stopped the show ten times." Alexander Woollcott, always effusive in praise of his favorites, placed Barton "in the great company of Nijinsky and Charlie Chaplin."

When Barton went into his second *Passing Show,* he was billed as a star. *The Passing Show of 1924* also starred comedian Lulu McConnell, but their presence was not enough to keep the tired old *Passing Show* formula from failing after 106 performances; the 1924 edition proved the final entry in the Shubert series. *When Summer Comes* (1925) fared even more poorly, and it closed out of town.

A. J. Erlanger, perhaps the most powerful man in live theatre and Florenz Ziegfeld's longtime backer, assumed control of the title *Ziegfeld Follies* to show Ziegfeld who was boss. Instead of mounting the *Ziegfeld Follies of 1926,* Ziegfeld had to choose another title. He assembled a cast headed by Ray Dooley and Moran & Mack and opened his revue in Florida as *Ziegfeld's Palm Beach Girl.* By the time the show reached Broadway, it was *Ziegfeld's American Revue.* The parochial Floridian numbers had been eliminated, and James Barton had been engaged to provide urban box-office pull. When "No Foolin'" proved the hit song of the show, the show was again retitled, this time *No Foolin'.* It only managed 108 performances at the Globe Theatre before it went on the road. By the time the show hit Chicago, Ziegfeld had gotten his name out of hock, and the show continued as the *Ziegfeld Follies of 1926.*

Barton shared top billing with Fanny Brice and George Jessel in Billy Rose's revue *Sweet and Low* (1930). As the stars' names were presented alphabetically, Barton got pride of place. Arthur Treacher was featured in support. The critics sniffed at it, yet the show tallied up 184 performances at the 46th Street Theatre.

Barton was one of the few white dancers—Hal Leroy, Eleanor Powell and the Condos Brothers were others—who was admired by black tappers. Barton came from a family of Irish clog and reel dancers, but his style had been broadened and enlivened by African American dancers, and his torso and leg work showed their influence. Conversely, Barton was such an exceptional eccentric dancer that black dancers were influenced by him. Snakehips—a fairly slow but intensely sinuous grind—was a torso-twisting dance that originated with African Americans. Its most famous exponent was Earl "Snakehips" Tucker. Before Mr. Tucker arrived in Harlem in the late 1920s, however, James Barton was shocking white New York audiences with his version of the dance. He wore a large bejeweled buckle on his belt, and, as his pelvis and hips gyrated, the buckle flashed the spotlight back into the audience.

On several occasions, Bill Robinson said that he owed a lot of his skill and artistry to James Barton, but his compliment is best regarded skeptically, for Robinson once said the same of Jack Donahue, about whom it was even less likely. Jim and Bill got along well, better than Robinson got along with many dancers of his own race. According to Marshall and Jean Stearns, who wrote the definitive book on percussive dance, *Jazz Dance,* there was talk, before Bill Robinson died, of Barton and Robinson performing together in a proposed show called *Two Gentlemen from the South,* during which Barton would play the master and Robinson the servant until the midpoint of the story, when they would reverse roles, wear masks representing each other's face, and dance in their own and each other's style. In retrospect, it sounded as arty a proposal as it was interesting, but more likely a pipe dream than a producer's proposition.

Throughout the 1920s and early 1930s, James Barton worked steadily as a comedian and eccentric dancer in Broadway revues, filling in with big-time vaudeville dates in and around New York City. He played the Palace many times, including a 1930 engagement with a one-act play by Arthur Hopkins titled *Moonshine* (which won a Pulitzer Prize for its author) and other dates such as the Boulevard Theatre in Jackson Heights in 1933.

That same year, James Barton switched to straight drama, playing Jeeter Lester in *Tobacco Road.* He did not originate the role—Henry Hull did—but Barton racked up more than 2,000 performances of the more than 3,100 the show gave during the seven-and-a-half years it remained on Broadway between 1933 and 1941. Given the economic situation at the time, the dominance of sound and motion pictures and the decline of vaudeville, it probably was the wise thing to do. His association with the play and the look of his increasingly mashed and lined face typecast him permanently. For the remainder of his career, Jim Barton rarely escaped character parts as drunken dreamers, telling tall tales and cadging on the sidelines of society.

When he left *Tobacco Road,* Jim was nearing 50 years old, and his attitude toward show business seemed to have changed. He and his wife lived on Long Island, where they owned a roadhouse, to which Mr. and Mrs. Barton repaired each evening after the show and stayed until closing time. Jim also owned or sponsored two baseball teams, one a farm team and the other for kids.

If Barton needed a reminder that the old days had passed, *Bright Lights of 1944* provided one. His old friends from the Shuberts' *Passing Show* 20 years earlier, Joe Smith and Charlie Dale, played two waiters who had ambitions as producers. Barton and Frances Williams pretended to be hopefuls looking for their big chance. After four performances of this revue with a slender premise, the curtain rang down on everyone's hopes. As other vaudeville revues of the 1940s proved—with the notable exceptions of the Olsen & Johnson shows—vaudeville had lost much of its audience.

James Barton had two grand hurrahs left in his career. In 1946, Barton, originally contracted for a featured role, moved up to play the lead role of Hickey in Eugene O'Neill's *The Iceman Cometh* when the Theatre Guild reshuffled the cast before opening. The role of Hickey confirmed Barton's credentials as a serious actor; he played a garrulous drunk who proved to be a murderer. It was his greatest dramatic role.

In 1951, Barton made his final appearance in a musical-comedy role, starring in Lerner & Loewe's *Paint Your Wagon.* The only musical or revue that season that made back its investment was Leonard Sillman's *New Faces of 1952. Paint Your Wagon* drew for 289 performances, and Barton, Olga San Juan and Tony Bavaar were much praised, but some critics found Loewe's music too European to suit a gold rush plot. The show did find an appreciative audience, although one smaller than its producers wished. Barton left the show before it closed; Burl Ives, then Eddie Dowling, took over Barton's role.

In the first years of talking pictures, Barton starred in several two-reelers for Paramount, Vitaphone and Universal. He had made one silent photoplay that did little for his career, and the trio of films he made in the 1930s did no more. He made another three pictures in the 1940s, but Barton appeared more frequently in films during the 1950s, bringing his career total to about 15 features. A few were musical comedies: *Daughter of Rosie O'Grady* (1950), *Wabash Avenue* (1950) with

Betty Grable and Reginald Gardiner, and *The Golden Girl* (1951), the story of Lotta Crabtree. More often, he was a featured dramatic actor, as in William Saroyan's *The Time of Your Life:* the most important film of his career and the one that gave him his best dramatic opportunity. His final screen performance was in a bit role in Arthur Miller's *The Misfits* (1961). It was the last film for Gable and Monroe as well.

During the last decade of his life—and Barton was an active actor until the end—he made more than two dozen television appearances. Jim guest starred in a few variety shows, such as Ed Wynn's, and acted in many of the most prestigious live broadcasts of dramatic anthologies and series of the period: *Kraft Television Theatre* (no less than six times), *Lux Video Theatre, Playhouse 90, Ford Television Theatre, Jane Wyman Show* (an anthology), *The Rifleman, Alcoa Premier, Naked City, Studio One* and *Alfred Hitchcock Presents.*

Barton's costars included several generations of great burlesquers, vaudevillians and dramatic actors: Bobby Clark, Ed Wynn, Thomas Mitchell, Edgar Bergen, Blanche Yurka, Charles Winninger, Art Carney, Patsy Kelly, Frank McHugh, Red Buttons, Jack Carson, Arthur Treacher, Ed Begley and a young James Dean. In 1959, Barton re-created his 1948 role as Kit Carson in a televised version of William Saroyan's play *The Time of Your Life;* Jackie Gleason took the Jimmy Cagney role, and Jack Klugman and Bobby Van were in the cast.

In his delightful chronicle, *Golden Age of Television,* Max Wilk presents eyewitness accounts of the early days of TV when broadcasts were live, not on magnetic tape or film. Ed Wynn was the first major comedian to broadcast his weekly show from Los Angeles. Movie stars were reluctant to appear as guests on television in those days; it was live and perilous, it did not pay much, they were not used to it and they feared it. It did not faze most vaudevillians. Scriptwriter Hal Kanter contributed a delicious anecdote to Wilk's book. Kanter was working on Ed Wynn's weekly show in 1949. For a particular show, Wynn was able to secure James Barton as his guest star.

It had been decided that Barton was to sing "You Made Me Love You." The day of the actual broadcast was a long one. Barton appeared in the afternoon to rehearse while the director, Ralph Levy, figured out camera placement and set the sound levels. The music rehearsal had been run by the concert master. All had gone well. At the dress rehearsal before broadcast, the musical director took over. He was Lud Gluskin, a man whose appearance was nearly as unfortunate as his name.

Levy was calling the show from the control booth. James Barton, in rumpled old clothes—his usual street garb—was standing off to the side as Gluskin reviewed the musical numbers for the evening's broadcast. When he came to the *sides* for "You Made Me Love You," he called out to Levy, asking if Al Jolson was on the show. Levy told him no, that James Barton was going to sing the number. For all to hear, Gluskin yelled, "Who the hell is James Barton?!" Ralph Levy instructed Gluskin to just play the number. Barton said not a word. He walked over to his spot in the stage and sang the entire number, gave it everything he had, which was considerable, and never took his eyes off Gluskin. Barton mesmerized the entire crew, and Gluskin grew increasingly embarrassed, red flushing his bald scalp. When Barton finished, there was the stunned silence of having been in the presence of a master still at the top of his game. Barton, glaring at Gluskin, broke the spell. "That's who James Barton is, you bald-headed son of a bitch!"

BILLY BARTY

b: (William John Bertanzetti) 25 October 1924, Millsboro, PA—d: 23 December 2000, Glendale, CA

Barty stood at three feet, nine inches and weighed about 70 pounds. He believed that if he put his mind to it and worked hard, he could succeed at anything, an attitude fostered by his loving parents. His mother and father, of average size, as were his sisters, left the mining country of Pennsylvania for Los Angeles, looking for opportunity and the clear air Southern California enjoyed in the late 1920s; it was better for Billy's hay fever.

It was the last days of the silent era, when small film companies took advantage of the sunshine and shot their comedies outdoors on Los Angeles' streets and empty lots. Barty often told interviewers that he and his dad had stopped to watch a two-reel comedy being made. Reputedly, the director was attracted by Barty's size and his ability to stand on his head. He was three at the time. His career would span nearly three quarters of a century.

From 1927 to 1931, Billy Barty appeared in short comedy films, including a stint as Mickey Rooney's baby brother in the Mickey McGuire series. By the early 1930s, Billy was appearing in feature films, mostly cameo roles in musicals and comedies, often as a baby, although he was approaching his early teens. Busby Berkeley used him in several musicals for Warner Brothers. One of the movies that Billy Barty was not in was *The Wizard of Oz.* He was passed over because he was not yet 18 and therefore unable, under law, to work the long days the film's director required.

Billy Barty

By 1935, the American people understood that prosperity was not around the corner. Fewer musicals were being filmed, so the Bertanzetti family took to the road in what was left of vaudeville. Billy's two sisters, Evelyn and Dolores, joined him in the act, Billy Barty and Sisters. They played presentation houses and some of the small surviving circuits. Sister Dolores played violin, Evelyn, the accordion and piano, and Billy drummed and did impersonations. Father and mother managed and took care of the troupe of youngsters. Billy claimed he had seen most of the USA and much of Canada by the time he was 12.

Despite his acting ability, Barty was viewed as a novelty act, and the only places that booked novelty acts were vaudeville, nightclubs and circuses. Vaudeville was petering out, the better nightclubs booked sophisticated singers and comedians, and the family felt that the circus was demeaning.

During the Second World War, Barty went to college. He majored in journalism and even played a little football and basketball. Had not show business promised a practical way of earning a very good income, Billy might have become a sports announcer.

After the war, he had to start all over again in show business, playing nightclubs with an act built around comedy, music and impersonations. Spike Jones caught his act in the late 1940s and invited Billy to join his madcap entourage, the City Slickers. Billy appeared with Spike off and on for nearly a decade, including several years on television.

Barty was always an added attraction with the Spike Jones outfit, reserving his right to work in films and television shows as a single. In addition to appearing as a regular in a dozen or more TV series, Barty was a guest star in many types of shows, from comedy to crime to straight drama. Increasingly recognized as a skilled character actor, Barty began to get serious film work, as in *Day of the Locust* (1975) and *Willow* (1988).

There were other equally important aspects of Billy Barty's life. He was a family man who enjoyed a 35-year union with his wife, Shirley. They had two children: a six-foot son, who is a filmmaker, and a small person from Russia, whom they adopted when she was an infant.

Mr. Barty founded several organizations to educate both small and average-size people about small people. The Little People of America, founded in 1957, provided vocational guidance, health information and social services. The Billy Barty Foundation raised money for scholarships and other benefits.

GEORGE H. BATCHELLER

b: ca. 1828—d: 1913

If remembered at all, George H. Batcheller is recalled as one of B. F. Keith's partners. Batcheller started in show business as a 14-year-old singer in minstrel shows, which were all the rage as he was coming of age. According to Mike Leavitt, Batcheller became a musician; later, as a tumbler, he joined a circus run by Isaac Burke. After Burke's circus settled in for a run at the Bowery Amphitheater in Lower Manhattan, Batcheller switched to Howe & Cushing's Great American Circus, which was embarking on a tour of Britain, beginning with a booking at the Alhambra in London. Batcheller claimed to be the first acrobat to appear before British royalty; he was included in a special performance for Queen Victoria and her family in 1858.

Upon his return to the USA, Batcheller bought a farm in North Providence, Rhode Island. A decade later, in 1868, he was back with the circus, first Forepaugh's and then O'Brien's, where he quit performing and leased some concessions.

His last work with the circus was with one of his own, Batcheller & Doris' Circus. In 1882, he sold his share—or was forced—to his partner, John B. Doris, and took on a much younger man, Benny Keith (the future B. F. Keith), to open a dime museum in Boston. The Batcheller-Keith partnership dissolved after a year or so, and Batcheller returned to Providence. In 1886,

Batcheller opened the Westminster Musée, a dime museum and performance hall. Later, he changed its policy to vaudeville, closed the exhibits and renamed it the Westminster Theatre. In 1898, the then-80-year-old Batcheller began booking burlesque revues. He died at age 85.

PEG LEG BATES

b: (Clayton Bates) 11 October 1907, Fountain Inn, SC—d: 6 December 1998, Fountain Inn, SC

Overall, stage dancers have improved so much since the days of vaudeville that yesterday's headliner would have a hard time making the chorus of a twenty-first century show. The continuing debate about who was the greatest tap dancer seldom extends outside the period between 1890 and 1950. The candidates are many, from the well-known like Harland Dixon, Bill Robinson, Eddie Rector, John Bubbles, the Nicholas Brothers, Eleanor Powell, Ann Miller, Sammy Davis Jr. and Savion Glover to the obscure like King Rastus, Ginger Wiggins, Alice Whitman, Willie Covan, Pete Nugent, Pops Whitman, Jeni Le Gon and Steve Condos, a partial list that leaves many contenders unnamed.

Peg Leg Bates' name appears on many lists, but he is without comparison. That he became a dancer was a marvel. That he became a great tapper made him an amazing phenomenon. His family was poor even by South Carolinian standards for sharecroppers in the 1910s. In despair, his father deserted his family when Clayton was three. To support her son and her mother, Clayton's mother continued to work the fields. Clayton, running errands and doing odd jobs, did what he could to earn money. He taught himself to tap by the time he was five years old, and, within a few years, he danced on the town's sidewalks for pennies.

When he was 12, he got a job in the local cotton mill. It was 1918, and with men overseas fighting a war, there were women and children operating the large machinery. He had been working there only a few days, on the midnight to morning shift, when the central event of Clayton Bates' life occurred. The mill's lighting went out, and Clayton slipped in the dark and caught his leg in a large uncovered pulverizing conveyor (safety conditions were nonexistent). His leg was mangled and had to be amputated below the knee. Because white hospitals did not accept Negroes, the operation was performed on his mother's kitchen table. He was given some makeshift crutches; later an uncle whittled him a peg leg. Athletic by nature, Clayton refused to be daunted by his injury, and he continued to dance and play sports.

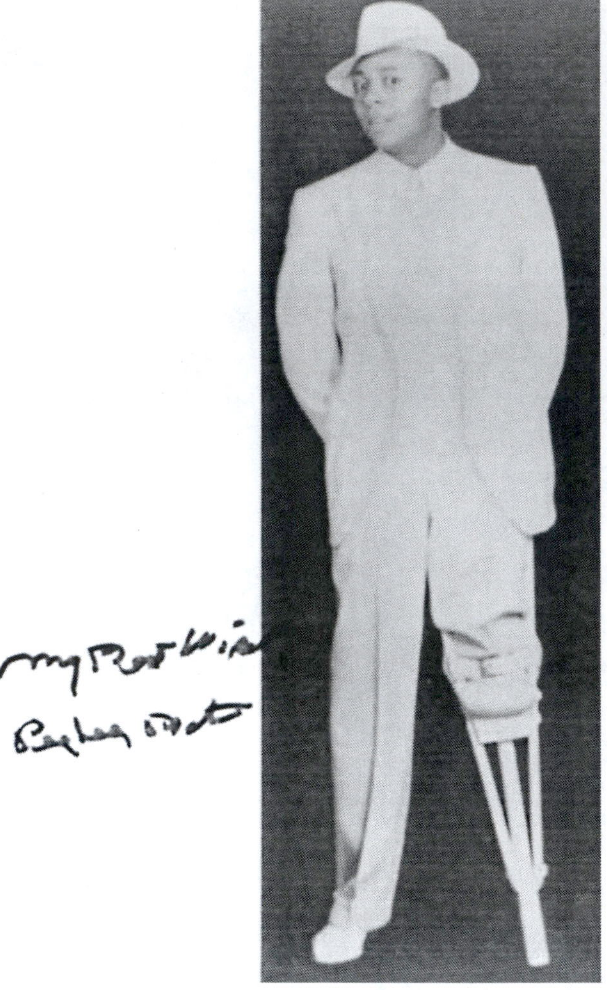

Peg Leg Bates

Bates was 15 when he realized he was good enough to enter and win amateur-night contests. These led to his first job in show business, tap dancing in a small-time minstrel show. He was still 15 in 1922 when he began playing black vaudeville on the Theatre Owners' Booking Association (TOBA) circuit. In between vaudeville dates, or for safety when traveling between one Southern town and another, Peg Leg, as he became known, hooked up with touring carnivals. Four years on Toby time led to bookings in the Northern theatres that served the black audiences of Cleveland, Pittsburg, Philadelphia, Washington, D.C., Baltimore, Newark and New York.

White producer Lew Leslie caught his performance at the Lafayette Theatre in Harlem and signed Peg Leg for the European tour in 1929 of *Blackbirds of 1928,* a Cotton Club show that followed the enormous success in London of the 1926 edition of *Blackbirds* that starred Florence Mills. The later show with Peg Leg closed in Paris, and he came back to the USA and worked vaudeville and the bigger Harlem hot spots: the Savoy Ballroom, Cotton Club, Connie's Inn and Club Zanzibar.

Bates was an inventive dancer. He had to be to adapt steps for two-legged dancers. He was not the only one-legged dancer on the stage, but he used his peg leg like another leg and foot, beating out rhythms, balancing and propelling himself into the air. He became known for a step he called "Imitation American Jet Plane," in which he jumped several feet into the air and landed on his peg leg with his good leg extended straight out behind him.

Bates was more than good enough as a dancer and a stage personality to play the Keith-Albee-Orpheum combined big time, and he did, but two-a-day vaudeville was surrendering to economics, and Bates also took dates on the Loew's circuit, small time but good small time, and the better clubs, and there was also the occasional touring show. Bates, comedian Tim Moore and dancer-singer-trumpeter Valaida Snow were newcomers to the revised edition of *Blackbirds of 1934* that retained Bill Robinson and Edith Wilson.

Larger theatres began to feature first-run major motion pictures with four or five acts of vaudeville or a unified stage presentation. Fanchon & Marco were the team famous for presenting packaged one-act musical revues, and Peg Leg worked in their shows during the early 1930s. Another unit show that proved profitable for Peg Leg was the *Ed Sullivan Revue* (1937–38) that played what remained of big-time vaudeville from New York to San Francisco and then sailed to Australia, where the troupe scored a hit and ten weeks of bookings on Australia's Tivoli circuit. Upon his return to the USA, Bates joined the Four Step Brothers in *Cotton Club Parade* (1938).

During the 1940s and early 1950s, nightclubs offered more work than theatres, but in 1947, Peg Leg performed in *Ken Murray's Blackouts* when it opened in Los Angeles, where it set the record for long-running shows.

During the late 1940s and the 1950s, television variety shows provided work and, especially, name recognition that counted greatly when appearing at nightclubs. Peg Leg Bates appeared 21 times on CBS-TV's Sunday night *Toast of the Town* (*Ed Sullivan Show*), the most by any tap dancer.

Married to Alice Bates, with whom he had a daughter, Melodye Bates (Holden), Peg Leg realized it was time to cease travel and face the fact that the era of variety performance was largely over, and tap dancing had lost popularity. Bates opened the 60-acre Peg Leg Bates Country Club in Kerhonkson, New York, which he owned and ran from 1951 to 1987 and which catered to a family clientele primarily African American. He became the first black resort owner in the predominantly Jewish vacation colony in the Catskill Mountains, which was known as the Borscht Belt.

As an accomplished dancer of legendary reputation, and as one of the last living vaudeville performers, Peg Leg Bates accepted many invitations to talk about his career, his life and his times. In 1998, Bates visited his hometown of Fountain Inn, South Carolina, and attended an event in his honor on a Saturday night. He was 91 years old. The next day, Sunday, 8 December, Bates collapsed and died on his way to church. He was buried in Palentown Cemetery, Ulster County, New York.

An hour-long documentary, *The Dancing Man: Peg Leg Bates*, was released in 1991 and played on PBS television stations. The film covers highlights of Peg Leg Bates' life and career with vintage film footage, still photographs and interviews with contemporaries Honi Coles and Chuck Green (of Chuck & Chuckles), singer Ruth Brown and tapper Gregory Hines.

NORA BAYES

b: (Leonora/Dora Goldberg) 1880—
d: 19 March 1928, Brooklyn, NY

A delightful bundle of contradictions, Nora Bayes was alternately generous and competitive, self-deprecatory and prideful, down-to-earth and a star in the grand and imperious manner. She was also a roundly talented performer with a beguiling stage personality and presence.

Although Nora joked that she had only seven notes to her singing voice, she had a warm contralto, clear diction and good rhythm. Her repertoire was broader than most, ranging from semiclassical and parlor songs to ragtime and comedy and novelty numbers. She did not simply sing the melody, she acted out the song through expression, gesture and movement. She offered anecdotes between songs, and told funny stories. She treated people in the audience as though they had been invited to a party in her home.

Bayes had a hand in writing some of her best-known songs: "Shine on Harvest Moon" and "Turn Off Your Light, Mr. Moon Man," although many claimed that her contribution was a matter of additions and alterations rather than creating whole cloth. Bayes got credit, like Jolson, because, like Jolson, she made hits out of songs other people wrote, like "Has Anyone Here Seen Kelly?" and "Over There," among the more enduring.

Nora did not like to sing patriotic (or lachrymose) songs, but she was an enthusiastic and tireless supporter of American men in uniform. She entertained the troops often and was happy to introduce George M. Cohan's flag-waver "Over There," which became the

Nora Bayes

anthem for war bond rallies during the First World War and was revived during the Second World War.

Nora Bayes won stardom in the early 1900s and kept that status for 20 years. By 1920, she earned $100,000 a year and commanded for a week on tour a figure as high as $5,000, a salary few performers could match. Playing vaudeville dates across the country or touring with a show, Nora Bayes traveled in her own private railway car. She spent profligately, urged gifts on friends and gave generously to charity. In addition to donating money, she sometimes entertained at rescue missions.

Reporters found Nora a rewarding interview except when discussing her life before she entered show business. From what could be gathered and assessed, Dora Goldberg came from a family of strict Orthodox Jews, and, by getting married, she escaped what she felt was a restrictive environment. She also adopted the first of several temporary stage names and put her past behind her. Milwaukee, Wisconsin, was often claimed as her birthplace, but Joliet and Chicago, in Illinois, and Los Angeles were also cited. Throughout her career, Bayes always refused to play Milwaukee, so many chroniclers assume that it was the city of her birth and childhood.

She was 17 when she wed for the first time and got a job singing in the olio between acts of various shows playing the Chicago Opera House. Nora left Chicago and Otto Gressing, husband number one, for San Francisco, where she was accepted into a stock company. She then began appearing in vaudeville. It may have been in San Francisco that she first worked with the Rogers Brothers in one of their yearly tours. Nora left San Francisco for New York where, in 1901, she appeared in *The Rogers Brothers in Washington.* The Rogers Brothers' shows made their money on long tours across the country, and their Broadway stays were brief, a month or two. Nora was not a principal in the show, so she had not much chance to make an impression on New York critics or audiences. What did catch the critics' eyes and ears, as well as the fancy of the vaudeville-going public, was her singing of "Down Where the Wurzburger Flows," which Nora introduced during a 1902 date at the Orpheum Theatre in Brooklyn. Written by Vincent P. Bryan and Harry von Tilzer, it was a Tin Pan Alley version of a drinking song. Nora made the song, it made her, and she became known as the Wurzburger Girl.

From American vaudeville, Nora Bayes turned to British music-hall. She played many dates in the British Isles and more than a few on the Continent between 1904 and 1907. Back in the USA, Bayes, appearing in vaudeville, was invited to join the cast of the *Follies of 1907.* This became the first Florenz Ziegfeld annual show, although at the time it was intended only as a summertime filler on the New York Theatre Roof between the 1906–07 and 1907–08 seasons. The primary performers were opera singer Emma Carus, dancer Mlle Dazie, singer Grace LaRue and the comedy team Harry Watson Jr. & George Bickel. Bayes made a sufficient impression to return the following year with her new husband, Jack Norworth. Teaming first in vaudeville, their double act quickly found favor among audiences, bookers and theatre managers. They introduced "Shine on Harvest Moon" in the *Follies of 1908.* According to some sources, Nora also appeared in *Nearly a Hero,* a musical comedy of the 1907–08 season that supposedly played between the first two *Follies.*

Nora and Jack also appeared in the third edition of the *Follies* in 1909, but not for long. Nora caught Jack kissing a chorus girl, and, as a penalty, she revised their billing matter to read, "Nora Bayes, Assisted and Admired by Jack Norworth." Jack was no pushover, and he walked out of the act and the show. So did Nora, in pursuit. Ziegfeld went to court for an injunction against them appearing elsewhere. It was the first of Nora Bayes' self-made imbroglios.

Nora Bayes and Jack Norworth patched up matters and sailed to England, where they made far more money as a music-hall turn than Ziegfeld could pay them. They returned to America after Ziegfeld withdrew his suit. After all, Ziggy, Bayes and Norworth had received a lot of sensational publicity. Nora and Jack's weekly salary rocketed up to $2,500. Although the press coverage had made more people willing to pay to see them, Bayes and Norworth had a great act and were at the peak of their performing powers.

In 1910, Nora and Jack switched from vaudeville to the musical-comedy stage to perform in Lew Fields' production of *The Jolly Bachelor.* By then, Nora Bayes could sell a song as well as anyone of her era, and few could sell as many different types of songs: ballads, ragtime ditties and comic tunes such as "Has Anybody Here Seen Kelly?," which Nora introduced in *The Jolly Bachelor.* So successful was her rendition of the song that she made a record of it that same year for Victor. Throughout the 1910s, many copies were sold of Nora Bayes' sound recordings, among which were "You Can't Get Away from It," "That Lovin' Rag," "How Ya Gonna Keep 'Em Down on the Farm?," "You Can't Get Lovin' Where There Ain't No Love," "Oh How I Laugh When I Think That I Cried over You," "Broadway Blues," "Why Worry?," "Make Believe," "Cherie," "All over Nothing at All," "Good Mornin'," "Homesick," "Lovin' Sam (the Sheik of Alabam)," "Dearest, You're Nearest My Heart," "Tomorrow I'll Be in My Dixie Home Again," "Freckles," "The Japanese Sandman" and, of course, "Over There," "Turn Off Your Light, Mr. Moon Man" and "Shine on Harvest Moon," the last two recorded with Jack Norworth. Sheet music of Nora's songs also sold well.

In 1910, Nora and Jack returned to the stage for *Little Miss Fix-It,* in which they introduced "Turn Off Your Light, Mr. Moon Man." The show ran about six weeks on Broadway. Joe Weber and Lew Fields were persuaded to reunite in 1912 for a show they called *Roly Poly.* It was their usual two-part formula: first half a musical comedy and the second, a burlesque. Lew and Joe performed along with Nora and Jack, Marie Dressler, Frank Daniels, Bessie Clayton and others. After eight weeks in New York, Fields and Weber agreed to tour the show; tours allowed them to play much larger theatres than Broadway offered, and it was on the road that they recouped their investment and saw a profit. Nora and Jack decided against the tour, however. They also decided against continuing their partnership and marriage, divorcing in 1913. According to many, it was Jack who most wanted to split.

Both Nora and Jack prospered. Nora commanded as much money solo as she had with Jack, and she flaunted her success throughout the rest of the decade with extravagant billing matter such as "The Empress of Vaudeville" and "The Greatest Single Woman Singing Comedienne in the World." She also continued to get married. Only a couple of weeks after her divorce from Jack Norworth, as if in defiance, she wed Harry Clarke, husband number three. Harry Clarke did not last and was not seen with Nora when she sailed to England for some variety dates. Her health reportedly deteriorated, and she went to a Germany spa for treatment. War was near, but Nora may not have been aware of it.

Bayes came back to America for 30 weeks of big-time vaudeville, including a week at the Palace starting 14 September 1914. The booking on Keith-Albee time was marred by conflict between Nora and the booking office, yet all was forgiven when she resumed Keith vaudeville again, until the next contretemps, which occurred because Nora refused to perform an extra show on Thanksgiving 1916.

From the mid-1910s, her behavior grew increasingly temperamental, but she still reigned as one of vaudeville's queens. She lived like a queen, as well, with several full-time servants on hand in her Manhattan brownstone. The same temperament that initiated scrapes with management also prompted her to take up causes fervently. She entertained troops in the First World War, assisted at rescue missions, adopted orphaned children and gave lavishly to charity. As fast as the money came in—and it was big money—it went out.

So did Arthur Gordoni, husband number four and partner number three. Tenor Arthur Gordoni must have been conditioned and fortified for a bumpy relationship because he had come into show business as the junior partner in a vaudeville act with Chico Marx, who, though not given to emotional outbursts, was a wild man whose life was a series of gambles and narrow escapes that involved everyone around him. Arthur Gordoni stayed wed to Nora Bayes until 1922.

During one of her spats with Keith management, Nora returned to Broadway in *Maid in America* (1915). Also in the cast were Mlle Dazie, Lew Brice, the Dolly Sisters, Joe Jackson, Harry Fox and Blossom Seeley. It ran a respectable 108 performances. Although her salary was a bit lower for musical comedy and revues, Nora appeared in several other revues. *The Cohan Revue of 1918* opened on New Year's Eve 1917 and ran for the first three months of 1918. Fred Santley and Charles Winninger shared the spotlight with Nora. *Ladies First,* a musical comedy about a suffragette's daughter (Bayes) running for mayor, opened on 24 October 1918, ran through spring 1919 and then toured into the next season. Nora did not work that steadily again.

By the mid-1920s, Nora Bayes' bouts of illness and her rows with producers began to undermine her career. There were still choice vaudeville dates and a couple of Broadway musicals. In 1920, Nora produced and starred in *Her Family Tree,* a trifle about séances and reincarnation that managed to pull customers for three months on Broadway. Solid pros Julius Tannen and Frank Morgan assisted. *Snapshots of 1921* was a vaudeville revue with Bayes, Lew Fields, De Wolf Hopper, Lulu McConnell and Gilda Gray. It ran six weeks.

Nora Bayes had entered the 1920s commanding $3,500 a week. By 1924, work was scarce, and she tried to repeat her earlier success in London, but she had slipped. The voice was still there, as well as the engaging personality, but she lost discipline. Although she played no character but herself onstage, even in musical-comedy roles, audiences were charmed by this approach. By 1924, however, she went overboard; the number of songs and funny stories in her act diminished, and she began to bore audiences with anecdotes about her adopted children. She also had developed a penchant for dramatic songs performed with dramatic flourishes, a style that did not suit her personality.

By 1926, Nora met and married her fifth and last husband, Benjamin Friedland. He was wealthy, worked outside show business and deferred to Nora's wishes about her career. She seemed happier, and her career revived for a while, but illness and brouhahas persisted to occur. Nora did not cause all the trouble. Joe Frisco, Sophie Tucker and others, equally obstinate and as protective of their careers as Nora, butted heads with her.

After all the years in show business, however, Nora should have learned to yield to the greater good. She had not. She successfully played a route of Keith-Albee-Orpheum dates for good money in an act plus an afterpiece that she performed with Jack Benny and a double-hoofing act, Burns & Lynn. Nora returned with them for an engagement at the Palace Theatre, where she got into a dustup with Sophie Tucker. When Eddie Darling, the Palace booker, tried to intervene, Nora directed him to the nether regions and walked out on Jack Benny and Burns & Lynn. Her tantrum did her no good, and she was once again blackballed on Keith-Albee-Orpheum time.

Midway in March 1928, Nora Bayes unexpectedly contacted Eddie Darling at the Palace Theatre. Darling, several times, had found himself squeezed between Bayes and whomever she was battling. In *American Vaudeville: Its Life and Times,* chronicler Douglas Gilbert related a poignant rapprochement. On March 16, Nora phoned Darling and invited him to her Manhattan home for a midnight party. He arrived to find himself the only guest. She sang him some of her old songs and asked a favor. Would he, tomorrow morning, please put up her photographs in the lobby of the Palace and an announcement that she was playing a week hence? Nora did not ask for an engagement, and she said he could take the photos down in the afternoon; she only wished to drive by and see the photos and signage. Perhaps Eddie Darling had a presentiment, for he did as Nora requested. Two days later, Nora Bayes, age 46, died of cancer. In 1944, Hollywood romanticized the story of Nora Bayes and Jack Norworth, and Ann Sheridan and Dennis Morgan played Nora and Jack. The biopic was called *Shine on Harvest Moon.*

ORSON BEAN

b: (Dallas Frederick Burroughs) 22 July 1928, Burlington, VT

A gift of some basic magic tricks fascinated Orson Bean as a boy. He learned to master them and a few that were more involved. After moving to Cambridge, Massachusetts, Orson graduated from high school just in time to make his debut at the Brattle Theatre in a two-word walk-on before being drafted for the closing act of the Second World War. He spent two years with an artillery outfit in the Pacific theatre of operations, during which time he produced, directed and performed in two revues with armed-service personnel. The shows toured various island bases during the mop-up phase of the war.

Back home, he worked up a comedy magic act that played a variety of dates: dinner events, nightclubs and vaudeville. Bean claims he worked the Harvard Club without getting a single laugh. As he left, however, people walked up and congratulated him. One older fellow said, "You were so funny I could hardly keep from laughing." That's Orson's story, and he stuck with it through several retellings.

Throughout much of his career, he has looked like the conventional Harvard preppie he once was or the Ivy League businessman he never became, but he has played a happy eccentric onstage, and his humor has tended toward bizarre observations. Through the course of his club dates, he shed much of the magic and concentrated on stand-up comedy.

He was booked at the Palace Theatre during its revived vaudeville policy, but more frequent dates for performers like Bean were in the burgeoning small-club movement of the 1950s, and Orson was frequently booked at the Blue Angel in Greenwich Village.

His film career began auspiciously with featured roles in *How to Be Very, Very Popular* (1955), *Showdown at Ulcer Gulch* (1956) and *Anatomy of a Murder* (1959), and television and Broadway competed for his time. Orson Bean had his own brief series, *The Blue Angel* (1954), frequently performed on variety shows (Ed Sullivan's *Toast of the Town*), appeared on talk shows (Johnny Carson's *Tonight Show*), acted in television dramas and had continuing roles in several series (*Mary Hartman, Mary Hartman* and *Dr. Quinn, Medicine Woman*).

Orson's Broadway career included a half-dozen notable musicals, revues and plays: *John Murray Anderson's Almanac* (1953–54), *Will Success Spoil Rock Hunter* (1955–56), *Subways Are for Sleeping* (1961–62), *Never Too Late* (1962–65) and *Illya Darling* (1967–68). In the 1990s and 2000s, he remained very active as a featured actor in films, such as *Being John Malkovich* (1999).

Show business has not been his only interest. In taking control of his life after early, nearly overwhelming unhappiness, including the suicide of his mother, Orson's goal was to forge a happy and useful life. He became involved in Reichian therapy, an alternative approach to children's education, and the Laurel & Hardy fan club, Sons of the Desert, of which he was a cofounder.

BEARER

The *bearer* (or *understander*) supports the top mount in a balancing or *perch* act.

MARTIN BECK

b: (Lipto Zert Mikols) 30 July 1867 (?), Czechoslovakia—d: 16 November 1940, New York, NY

Little is known of Martin Beck's early life other than what he wished to relate or invent. As reliable sources differ about the date, he may have been born as early as 1865, either in Germany or Austria. Beck claimed to be, and likely was, a member of a troupe of actors who came to the Americas in the early 1880s. Their tour began in South America, but the troupe seems to have disbanded without returning to Europe. Beck's activity and whereabouts during the next decade are lost to the record, but, according to Beck himself, he did whatever came his way to stay alive.

By the time the 1893 World's Columbian Exhibition opened in Chicago, Martin Beck was ready and waiting, working at the Royal Music Hall on the South Side and, a bit later, at Engel's beer hall next door, where he rose from barman to waiter to cashier and then to bookkeeper as the world's fair added to business. His employers found very useful Beck's growing business know-how, his showbiz background, energy and intelligence. Beck was promoted next to stage manager, then to beer-garden manager.

Soon Beck was made a partner, and he acquired a second location. Sticky-fingered barmen were an occupational aggravation that he could deal with, but the economic crash of 1897 temporarily destroyed the demand for entertainment along with the local economy. So Beck hit the road once again, heading west as the manager of the Schiller Vaudeville Company, an all-in-one show.

The Schiller show disbanded in San Francisco at the Orpheum Theatre, then owned by Gustave Walters. The company collapsed because Walters decided to book only a few of the acts in the troupe, but he offered Beck a job as manager and assistant booker for his theatre. Walters was typical of the owners of the free and easies whose box-house saloons gradually became vaudeville theatres. They knew a lot about booze, gambling, prostitution and showing the frontier men a good time but less about booking family entertainment and meeting expenses.

Walters owed $50,000 in back booze bills to Morris Meyerfeld and his partner, Dan Mitchell. Failing to pay, Walters' operation was taken over in 1899 by Meyerfeld and Mitchell, who realized that they needed experienced showmen to make the enterprise profitable. First engaged was Martin Lehman, who owned a theatre in Los Angeles. The Orpheum management in San Francisco had persuaded him to fold his theatre into their operation. When Martin Beck took over the day-to-day operation of the budding Orpheum circuit, he reportedly was given a 10 percent share and the title general manager, but Meyerfeld was the overall boss, and he proved to be a savvy shobiz tycoon. Soon the circuit added theatres in Chicago and Kansas City and began promotional arrangements with others.

It was either Lehman's or Beck's idea to base the operation in Chicago because it was very expensive to hire acts to travel to the West Coast unless there were additional dates to play between Chicago and California. A whiz at finding and taking over management of theatres that proved profitable, Beck chose the sites for their new theatres and set up alliances with Kohl & Castle, powerful managers in the Midwest, to establish the Western Vaudeville Managers' Association. With that, Meyerfeld, Beck and their partners controlled many of the significant bookings in the Midwest from their offices at 609 Ashland Block in Chicago. Beck emerged as the front man, but Meyerfeld always held the purse.

They took booking business away from B. F. Keith and Edward F. Albee, who not only controlled the Keith-Albee circuit but the very profitable United Booking Office as well. Beck made a further move that challenged Keith and Albee when, around 1906, Beck set up a booking office in New York. He picked the St. James Building, the same building in which Keith and Albee had their United Booking Office. This bold move could not have failed to nettle Albee.

When, in 1913, Martin Beck built the Palace Theatre in the heart of Manhattan's theatre district, Albee viewed the move for the invasion it was. Albee won the ensuing battle, but victory came neither easily nor inexpensively. When all the cards were on the table, the Keith Albee combine took control of the Palace. Beck retained a 25-percent interest in the Palace and the right to book its acts, but they had to be Keith-Albee acts. Albee had to pay Willie Hammerstein $200,000 cash to buy back the franchise Hammerstein had negotiated for all the vaudeville business between 42nd Street and Columbus Circle. Hammerstein's Victoria Theatre lost business and closed a year after the Palace opened.

Although Martin Beck was acquisitive, street smart and hard-nosed when dealing with competitors, he was also intelligent, and his show-business ambitions included quality as well as cash. It was Beck who, in 1913, enticed the legendary Sarah Bernhardt into three vaudeville tours. Thereafter, no stars of the legitimate drama, opera or ballet could claim that vaudeville was beneath them.

Beck was well-traveled, enamored of art and culture, and claimed he spoke as many as five languages. His detractors insisted double-talk was one of them. Yet he was usually fair, sometimes generous, in his dealings with performers unless he was crossed, and then he could be unforgiving.

He married Meyerfeld's daughter and assumed the presidency of the Orpheum circuit, a position he held for three years until replaced in 1923. When vaudeville began to flag, he branched out into the legitimate theatre, no great stretch for a man who had booked Sarah Bernhardt and Ethel Barrymore in vaudeville. He opened the Martin Beck Theatre in 1924. In the legitimate theatre, Beck could still be his own man.

Changes in show business were coming at a rapid rate. The beginning of the end of big-time vaudeville was heralded in 1926: two radio networks were launched, and the first full-length sound movie, *Don Juan,* demonstrated the feasibility of the Vitaphone system and the public's acceptance of recorded sound. When Jolson sang from the silver screen on 6 October 1927, everyone in show business heard the vibrations. The question of whether motion pictures that talked and sang were here to stay was soon answered.

Live entertainment required relatively high ticket prices. The Great Depression sank vaudeville and nearly swamped the legitimate theatre. Radio was free, and movies cost a few nickels. As the Great Depression deepened, alliances were forged and broken, pieces of empires reassembled and Keith-Albee-Orpheum became Keith-Orpheum, then merged into RKO.

By 1930, Beck was about 65 years old and knew he had made his mark. The Martin Beck Theatre was succeeding as a legitimate theatre. For the next decade, he was content to manage his investments and enterprises and smart enough to realize that show business had become a new game that called for younger players.

After his death in 1940, his wife, Louise, managed the Beck interests and took an active role in theatrical charities, including the Theatre Wing, which would begin, in 1947, to bestow the Tony Awards for distinguished achievement in the theatre.

JEAN BEDINI

b: (Jehan Pefsner) ca. 1880—d: 1955

A substantial name in vaudeville, Jean Bedini was a legend in burlesque. He gave a leg up to Ted Healy, Eddie Cantor, Clark & McCullough and George White, the dancer who went on to produce annual revues called *George White's Scandals.*

A superior juggler, Bedini came to American vaudeville from British music-hall and made a career in both vaudeville and burlesque, producing a number of burlesque revues as well as performing. Like Housini, he knew how to drum up business. Newspapers were happy to help promote his appearances; photographers on hand, they would record in pictures and words his stunt; he caught—with a large fork clenched between his teeth—turnips and beets as they were dropped from the tallest buildings in the cities where he played. Sometimes, just to make a point, he purposely let a hurtling rutabaga smash onto the sidewalk.

In the 1900s, he had formed an act called Bedini & Arthur, although Bedini was the star and Roy Arthur was little more than a blackfaced assistant who comically mishandled the various items that Bedini juggled. Although 20 years or more older than Eddie Cantor, Roy Arthur knew Cantor from their Henry Street neighborhood on the Lower East Side of Manhattan. Arthur convinced Bedini to give the 16-year-old Cantor a chance as a stooge. Cantor constantly expanded his part, began singing in the act, consistently pleased audiences and repeatedly asked for raises and got them, until he jumped ship for more money and joined "Gus Edwards Kid Kabaret."

A few years later, in 1919, another of Bedini's protégés, Joe Cook—comedian, juggler, acrobat and dancer—acceded to Bedini's request to join the cast of *Peek-A-Boo,* a burlesque revue. A vaudeville headliner at the time, Cook took a big cut in pay to play burlesque, simply explaining that Jean Bedini "gave me my first job in show business."

By this time, Jean Bedini's chief occupation was as a prolific burlesque producer on the Columbia wheel, in which he was a theatre franchise holder. In addition to putting shows together, he occasionally performed in his own productions. Eschewing plots for his shows, he understood that his public wanted laughs, song, dancing and chorus cuties to ogle more than a story.

Jean Bedini

The hearty box-offices returns that his revues delivered week after week, year after year, marked him as one of burlesque's most successful producers. His 1921 show, *Puss Puss* (a variation of 1919's *Peek-A-Boo*), introduced the ineffable comedy team Bobby Clark & Paul McCullough and grossed $350,000.

By 1929, almost a decade after the collapse of the Columbia wheel, Bedini directed a much dirtier version of burlesque than he once produced. In 1941, a couple of years after burlesque had been broomed off Broadway and under the Hudson River to New Jersey, the grand old man of burlesque was still producing shows, but these were, in the main, a series of ill-fated attempts to resurrect burlesque.

Among Bedini's last engagements was a 1948 stand at the Hippodrome in Baltimore, where he re-created his old Bedini & Arthur act on a Gay Nineties' bill. Jean Bedini was assisted by Joe Melanio (in Roy Arthur's part) in a comedy juggling act that pleased audiences and critics as much as it had 40 years earlier. Bedini juggled plates and balls while his partner set up the laughs. He had come full circle in a long and varied career.

BEER GARDENS

The name tells much about them. These open air gardens sold food and beer, ales and, usually, liquor. They were very popular in the nineteenth century after the Civil War and endured until the First World War in the twentieth century. Often, there was a stage where a band played and various vaudeville-type acts performed. Beer gardens were common in Manhattan and in German American communities across the American Midwest farm belt.

BELLY DANCERS

See Oriental Dancers

BENDER

Slang; slightly dismissive term for a contortionist.

BENEFIT

The more recent reason for hosting benefits are to aid performers and actors, brought low by prolonged illness, who are unable to pay for their medical care and other bills. In the eighteenth and nineteenth centuries, a benefit did not need the excuse of penury. It was based on the actor's popularity and value to the company. So, during an engagement, the box-office take for one performance was set aside for a particular actor. The evening was publicized as being "for the benefit of," and the actor's fans would turn out to honor him and thereby increase the box office.

These benefits for the principal players in a troupe continued into the early twentieth century, after which a benefit ceased to be a matter of financial reward for specific services and assumed its present-day charitable connotation.

JACK BENNY

b: (Benjamin Kubelsky) 14 February 1894, Chicago, IL—d: 26 December 1974, Los Angeles, CA

There are several observations that can be made about Jack Benny with some certainty. He was the funniest straight man in American show business. He was widely admired and well liked. He was respected, even loved, by comedians of all generations for his performing prowess. He was a capable comedy writer and a superb comedy editor. And he had more common

Jack Benny, 1926

sense about his act than most people who made a living by turning themselves into a performance.

Jack Benny never suffered a slump in popularity. If he were not as popular in movies as he was in radio and television, he was, nevertheless, successful enough to star in 17 feature films between 1930 and 1945, appear in several early short films, and make cameo and gag appearances in a half-dozen later features. He was set to make his first starring film role in 30 years when he died. As Jack would have wished, his dearest friend, George Burns, assumed Benny's role in *The Sunshine Boys,* which earned Burns an Oscar and a new lease on his career.

Jack Benny liked to joke that he was deprived as a comedian. He neither grew up in poverty nor escaped from a sordid environment. His father, Meyer, owned a haberdashery, and the family, middle class and nearly comfortable, lived in Waukegan, Illinois. His mother, Emma, insisted on a Chicago hospital for Jack's birth, but Jack always claimed Waukeegan as his hometown. She also expected Jack to practice the violin and become another child prodigy like Mischa Elman, but Jack had a desultory attitude toward all studies, academic or musical. Asked to leave high school at the end of his first year, Jack went to work for his father and demonstrated even less aptitude and concentration. Of course, that was Jack Benny's recollection, or the story he chose to tell. In truth, as a youngster, he had shown promise as a pianist and a violinist and had played several semiprofessional engagements.

His first job in show business was playing violin in the pit band at the Barrison Theatre in Waukegan. Minnie (Marx) Palmer, mother of The Marx Brothers and agent for that band of obstreperous boys making the transition from a singing act into comedy, came to town to play the Barrison. Impressed with Jack's ability to sight-read and his facility in picking up The Marx Brothers' music cues, she tried to hire him to travel with the act as their orchestra leader and violinist. Benny's family nixed the offer. A year later, in 1912, he became half—the lesser half—of Salisbury & Benny. His parents were still reluctant to have a son in vaudeville—the concert stage would have been an honor—but Jack, then 18 and unemployed (the Barrison Theatre had closed), wanted to accept the invitation of Cora Salisbury to accompany her in a vaudeville act. Ms. Salisbury, 45, recently widowed, thoroughly respectable and known to the family, assured the family that Jack would not be corrupted by stage folk.

Jack's name became a problem. It sounded too much like concert violinist Jan Kubelík, whose management objected. Hastily Jack became Ben Benny. A few years later, he became Jack Benny when Ben Bernie, a monologist who played the violin, objected that Ben Benny (by that time also a monologist who played violin) seemed to be trading on Ben Bernie's greater recognition.

Salisbury & Kubelsky performed semiclassics and dance tunes, mostly playing split weeks on the small time. After two seasons, Cora Salisbury had to return home to care for her ailing mother. Jack hooked up with another pianist, Lyman Woods, who was about Jack's age. Benny & Woods kept some of the parlor-type music but ragged it and added some sight gags to their playing. The act scored well, making as much as $350 a week and getting some big-time bookings (including the Palace, where they failed to go over). When the USA entered the First World War, Jack enlisted in the U.S. Navy.

After basic training, some of the other showbiz pros in the outfit began staging impromptu weekend shows in the dining hall, and Benny participated. A bunch of gobs did not wish to listen to Jack play "The Poet and the Peasant Overture" or the "Flight of the Bumblebee," so Jack was forced to talk onstage. He knew he was capable of being funny when trading jokes and quips with friends, but he had to work to bring his breezy way of talking into his act. The informal shows evolved into a full-blown production that traveled theatres for the Navy Relief Fund. Jack Benny had become a comedy actor and monologist.

Upon demobilization late in 1918, Jack returned to vaudeville, this time as a single. Again he played violin, performing a few funny tricks with his instrument, but he also sang a couple of songs and told jokes. The next few years were critical to forming the first Jack Benny character, and the change in his billing matter tells the story: he went from "Jack Benny, fiddle funologist" to "Jack Benny: Aristocrat of Humor." By that time he had ceased to sing, and the only time he used his violin was to play himself off at the end of his act.

A primary element of Jack's style was his understatement, and that changed little over the decades, although by the time his character was remodeled for radio, Jack could pop his cork: "Now, cut that out!" The Jack Benny who was the Aristocrat of Humor, however, was quite different from Jack Benny of network radio and television. In vaudeville and revue, Jack was nonchalant, a bit of a smart aleck, impeccably dressed and a Broadway Romeo type, an image born of his own personality and way of living at the time. He was relaxed, easy-going, amiable but confident and quite the handsome ladies' man, although he had been quite shy with women and girls in his teens.

Jack Benny, like hundreds of other excellent acts, was successful in vaudeville. He earned $350 to $450 a week as a single—excellent wages in the 1920s, but not a big star's salary. Jack was compared with other smooth monologists of the day, such as Frank Fay, Jules Tannen and Frank Tinney, who worked in an intimate and relaxed style.

By the mid-1920s, Benny was working steadily in good houses on good routes—at one point doubling: he did one routine at the Little Club and another at Loew's State, scoring a nifty double salary. Although Loew's was small time, it was about the best of small time, and Loew sometimes paid top salaries at those of his houses that were situated near big-time vaudeville houses, as was Loew's State in Times Square, which had to compete with the Palace Theatre, the diadem of Keith-Albee big time.

Jack took some offers from the Broadway stage. *The Great Temptations* played the huge Winter Garden for more than six months beginning on 18 May 1926, and Jack headlined along with Hazel Dawn, Flournoy Miller & Aubrey Lyles and Jay C. Flippen. *Earl Carroll's Vanities of 1930* had music by Harold Arlen, lyrics by Ted Koehler and a fine cast headed by Jack Benny, Jimmy Savo, Patsy Kelly, the Condos Brothers, Herb Williams and Thelma White. It also had some smutty skits typical of Earl Carroll that Benny refused to perform. At one point, the show was raided. Between the publicity and the talent, the show lured Broadway customers for much of the season.

In 1932, Jack joined a cast of fellow Friars, including Phil Baker (to whom Jack was often compared), Eddie Foy Jr., Joe Frisco, Bert Lahr, Hal Leroy, Georgie Price, Harry Richman, Pat Rooney, Smith & Dale and Arthur Tracy (no producer could have afforded that lineup) for the club's annual evening at the Met, *The Friars Frolic.*

Bring on the Girls, a 1934 farce by George S. Kaufman and Morrie Ryskin, flopped out of town and marked the end of Jack Benny's Broadway career, except for several major benefits. Jack limped back to New York for the 20 September 1934 *Night of Stars,* a benefit for the United Jewish Appeal held at Yankee Stadium to raise money and call attention to the perilous situation of Jews in Nazi Germany. This benefit was emceed by George M. Cohan and featured Jack Benny, Milton Berle, Burns & Allen, Cab Calloway, Lou Holtz, Bob Hope, the Mills Brothers, Mae Murray, Jack Pearl, Jan Peerce, Molly Picon, Harry Richman, Blanche Ring, Bill Robinson, Rose Marie, Jimmy Savo, Vivienne Segal, Kate Smith, Leopold Stokowski, James Thornton, Arthur Tracy, Rudy Vallee, Paul Whiteman and Ed Wynn among many other show-business stars.

On 5 October 1941, Jack once again joined the cream of Broadway: Tallulah Bankhead, Eddie Cantor, Melvyn Douglas, Morton Downey, Paul Draper, Lynn Fontanne, Betty Grable, Helen Hayes, George Jessel, Ella Logan, Burgess Meredith, Ethel Merman, George Raft, Harry Richman, Bill Robinson and Sophie Tucker. They all performed in the production *Fun to Be Free,* part of the Fight for Freedom Rally to build support among Americans for the USA to enter the Second World War, two months in advance of Pearl Harbor.

Jack's movie career began before he entered radio. Irving Thalberg was looking for someone to emcee MGM's filmed vaudeville show, *The Hollywood Revue of 1929,* which was intended to introduce MGM's new roster of talkie stars along with those stars of its silent stable who were deemed fit to make the transition to sound. Thalberg paired Jack with movie veteran Conrad Nagel, and the two cohosted a series of turns by Buster Keaton, Laurel & Hardy, Marie Dressler, Polly Moran, Bessie Love, Joan Crawford, Gus Edwards, John Gilbert, Norma Shearer (Thalberg's star wife), Marion Davies, William Haines and Cliff "Ukulele Ike" Edwards. Considering that Jack risked comparison with Frank Fay, who emceed *Paramount on Parade* (1930) the following year, Jack did himself credit, whereas Fay seemed overbearing in his stint.

Jack looked forward to his new movie career and moved to Hollywood with his bride, Sadie Marks, soon to become known as Mary Livingstone. His second movie, *Chasing Rainbows* (1929), did not catch fire despite the presence of Marie Dressler and Bessie Love in the cast. (Jack called it "Chasing Audiences," beginning his tradition of trashing his movies.) Jack was getting $1,000 per week but no future film assignments, so he and Thalberg agreed to void their contract. Jack headed to Broadway, where he joined *Earl Carroll's Vanities,* but Benny was back in Hollywood soon enough to make three 1930 releases that, although pleasant for the most part, did little to make him a hot Hollywood commodity. He returned to the studios in 1934 for another minor picture that soon sank, but in 1936, MGM hired Benny to play a Walter Winchell–type gossip columnist in *Broadway Melody of 1936* (1935), which starred Eleanor Powell and Robert Taylor and featured Vilma & Buddy Ebsen. *The Hollywood Revue of 1929* and *Broadway Melody of 1936,* plus a couple of two-reelers, remain available for home viewing and provide the best evidence of Benny's sophisticated stage character.

Jack Benny's stage personality changed quite a bit over the years, but the change was so gradual and logical that it slipped the notice of most chroniclers. Few of his early 1930s films showed up with regularity on television, and, although old-time radio shows were collected by their fans (and still are), they were not played for large audiences, so the early Jack Benny was seldom around to contrast with the Benny who matured on his radio program and his television show. It was on radio, and in the mid- to late 1930s, that Jack Benny shucked his man-about-town persona for the familiar fall guy with foibles.

In the early 1930s, Ed Wynn and Eddie Cantor had very popular shows on network radio, although their studio audiences probably found them funnier than the radio audience that could not see their clowning. Jack Pearl and Joe Penner were two other popular vaudevillians who entered radio but they quickly unloaded their bag of tricks and wore out their welcome with home audiences by overreliance on catch phrases.

After a number of offers, Jack finally decided to enter radio and found that the offers had evaporated. Ed Sullivan was starting a show and asked Jack to stop by and say hello on air, just a few minutes of informal chitchat. Jack prepared for it like a performance at the Palace. He came with five tight minutes of gags that began with "Hello, this is Jack Benny. There will now be a slight pause so everyone can say, 'Who cares.'" This debut landed Jack his network show in 1932 over NBC's Blue Network. His first show costarred Ethel Shutta, a fine all-around comedy and music performer, and her husband, bandleader George Olsen, who was the show's music director.

Jack Benny studied radio. He learned something each season, and he adapted his show each season. He paid to assemble and keep a superior staff of comedy writers. He was determined not to become a nuisance to his fans by hogging all the jokes and airtime. He understood that he was not hosting an audience in his theatre but that the audience was hosting him in their homes. He also knew that it did not pay to act superior to his audience, and Jack began to make fun of himself.

Benny relied upon an accomplished group of character comedians to get laughs at his expense. Phil Harris came on board in 1936 with sass as well as music. Eddie "Rochester" Anderson, the most popular second banana on the show, was hired in 1937 for a single show and stayed with Jack for nearly 20 years. Irish Tener Kenny Baker was succeed by Dennis Day, who followed in 1939, and Verna Felton came along as his mother. Artie Auerbach introduced the Jewish character Mr. Kitzel in 1946. Others included Benny Rubin and Sheldon Leonard, who both played the racetrack touts; Joe Kearns, guardian of Benny's private money vault; Bea Benaderet and Sara Berner, two gossipy and rather tarty telephone operators; and Frank Parker, the supercilious salesman ("Yee-e-e-e-es-s?!). Mel Blanc was probably the most valuable utility player on the show. With sputters, coughs and all manner of odd sounds, he impersonated Benny's ancient Maxwell automobile, portrayed the occasional Mexican, whose various answers were "Si. . . So. . . Sue. . . Sue. . . Sy. . . Soy," Professor Le Blanc, Benny's long-suffering violin teacher, and the train conductor who intoned, "Anaheim, Azusa, and Cuc—amonga!"

No comedy radio show had such a wealth of supporting characters or the breadth of plot possibilities that his cast presented. Add the standard gag bits about Jack's vanity, his cheapness, his lackluster movie career, his blue eyes, his toupee, his perennial insistence that he was only 39, and each show seemed familiar but fresh. Audiences waited for the creaking opening of Jack's vault or the sputter of his Maxwell or the telephone operators or Mr. Kitzel. They did not get them every week or every few weeks, so the familiar bits did not wear out their welcome, yet there were so many familiar routines that those that made it into the script satisfied the audience for decades.

Many chroniclers have told of what may be the longest laugh ever earned on radio. Jack Webb, later Sergeant Friday on TV's long-running *Dragnet,* played a stickup man who cornered Jack Benny and demanded, "Your money or your life." A long silence ensued until, prompted by the gunman, Jack snapped, "I'm thinking, I'm thinking!" More remarkable was the broadcast that featured a Hollywood tour bus making the rounds and pointing out the homes of various stars. When they came to Dennis Day's house, there was a scene between Dennis and his mother. At Phil Harris' home and Don Wilson's home there were other scenes. In each scene they made jokes about Benny. Not until the end of the program, when the driver announced Jack

Benny's house, did Jack have a line. He simply said, "Driver, here's where I get off." It was a nervy thing to absent the star of the show until the end and then give him only one line. Of course, the one line fed into Jack's stinginess myth.

Benny made a clutch of Paramount Pictures in the mid- to late 1930s, most of which, like *Big Broadcast of 1937* (1936), *College Holiday* (1936), *Artists and Models* (1937), *Artists and Models Abroad* (1938), put him into all-star potlucks or cast him as a romantic comedian, as in *It's in the Air* (1935) and *Man About Town* (1939).

By 1940, Jack Benny's radio popularity could not be ignored, even by Hollywood studios that tried to dismiss all free entertainment like radio (later TV). So it was as his radio character that Jack Benny made *Love Thy Neighbor* (1940), an intriguing two-hander with Fred Allen, and *It's in the Bag* (1945), a Fred Allen vehicle in which Jack did a scene as his radio self. Jack did his best to move a bit away from his branded radio character, and he succeeded with *Charley's Aunt* (1941), *To Be or Not To Be* (1942), *George Washington Slept Here* (1942) and *The Horn Blows at Midnight* (1945).

Ed Wynn, Eddie Cantor, Jimmy Durante, Bob Hope, Milton Berle, Olsen & Johnson, Martha Raye and most of the vaudeville-trained comedians who went into television on a regular basis did so in a variety format. When Jack Benny was finally persuaded by CBS to move into television, he did so carefully, entering the medium relatively late, in 1950, and on a limited basis. To Jack, the problem was how to maintain the standard and meet the expectations of listeners turned viewers. The radio show had a great cast of characters, and the TV audience already knew what Rochester, Don Wilson and Dennis Day looked like, so there was no disillusion. The minor characters played by Mel Blanc, Artie Auerbach and Frank Nelson did not disappoint either. Mary Livingstone, never comfortable as an entertainer despite her many years in the business, could not be persuaded by her husband Jack to appear more than a few times. Dennis Day, who was getting a bit old for his juvenile role, was a less frequent character on the TV show than he had been on radio. Phil Harris, who played Jack's hard-drinking, partying, skirt-chasing bandleader, was among the missing.

Jack Benny

There were ten half-hour shows aired during the 1950–51 and 1951–52 seasons. Jack increased the number to one every four weeks for the 1952–53 season and appeared every two weeks beginning in the 1953–54 season and until the 1959–60 season. Thereafter, until 1965, the Jack Benny Show was broadcast weekly. Having turned 70 by then, Jack quit weekly television for the occasional hour-long *special,* as they were then called.

Jack never truly retired. He had a shrewd manager, Irving A. Fein, who made Jack millions of dollars almost as fast as Mary Livingstone Benny could spend it. Jack had a good attitude; he simply avoided things that were unpleasant. He was very close to his daughter, Joan, who wrote a counterpoint to Jack's unfinished memoir and published both their memories as *Sunday Nights at Seven.* Giselle MacKenzie, who appeared a number of times with Jack on TV and in nightclub engagements, was reported to be Jack's last romantic companion. His wife, Mary, who relished her position in Hollywood society and was reputed to behave imperiously toward servants and salespersons, found that after Jack's death few returned her phone calls or showed deference.

In 1963, Benny returned to Broadway with a revue built around himself. Despite a newspaper strike, he managed to play five weeks. Jack Benny spent his last years doing what he wished when he wished until his death in 1974 at 80 from pancreatic cancer. In addition to the many lucrative bookings that Fein arranged, Jack appeared on TV talk shows that featured hosts he liked and admired, such as Johnny Carson and Dick Cavett. For a number of seasons, by threatening to play his violin and actually doing so, he raised $6 million for many charities and 100 symphony orchestras across the USA and Europe. He had resumed lessons at age 61 and could play several numbers in concert well enough not to shame himself, but mostly he played to get laughs. When Jack died the day after Christmas, it became a day of mourning. His death made the front pages. Television networks interrupted their programs to announce his death. Among comedians, Jack Benny was the most respected and beloved.

ROY BENSON

b: (Edward Ford Emerson McQuaid) 17 January 1914—d: 6 December 1977, Courbevoie, France

Roy Benson was the son of two vaudevillians: Eddie Emerson (McQuaid) of the juggling duo, Emerson & Baldwin, and Dora Ford of the Four Dancing Fords and the Ford Sisters.

As a youngster, Roy pursued magic as a hobby. In his teens, he had the good fortune to be befriended and mentored by Nate Leipzig, a masterful sleight-of-hand vaudevillian. Nate's tutelage enabled Roy to become more deft and to develop professionally.

When Roy turned to show business, vaudeville was already in decline, but, like most of his generation of performers, he was able to adapt to the demands of both still lingering vaudeville and the rise of post-Prohibition nightspots. One of Roy's early credits was on a bill of unknowns in a small-scale vaudeville revue, *Belmont Varieties*, that played a single week at the Belmont Theatre, a 500-seat hard luck Broadway house.

Nightclubs offered a more intimate environment that suited Benson's small-scale act, but the more social atmosphere meant that performer did not win easily the rapt attention of an audience. Vaudeville audiences attended to watch the acts, but as theatres had grown larger since vaudeville's heyday, a degree of intimacy was sacrificed along with subtlety.

In 1938, Roy Benson appeared in a bottom-of-the-bill, hour-long quickie flick, *The Lady Objects*. As part of the action took place in a nightclub, it is likely that Benson was more atmosphere than plot in this long forgotten film. He didn't make another movie until the mid-1940s when he was billed in *Sweet and LowDown* (1944) and unbilled in *Diamond Horseshoe* (1945).

Roy Benson combined close-up magic with juggling and *nut comedy*. He executed difficult manipulations with billiard balls or made a shaker full of salt crystals vanish from one hand to reappear in the other. On some occasions, he simply laid down across the footlights and talked to the audience as though he was confiding in his psychiatrist while swatting at imaginary insects and blowing a moose call.

Historian and comedy writer Chet Dowling noted that "Roy Benson's *forte* was clever dialogue and some brilliant juggling moves that aided in his magic presentation."

Benson's act was recalled by Levent the Magician, co-biographer with Todd Karr of Roy Benson by Starlight. "Carrying a small stand that held various magic props, Roy sprightly stepped to center stage and said, 'You know what I've got here on this stand thing? I've got a magician's act. I do all kinds of tricks and everything. So if any of you folks would care to examine any of the paraphernalia that I employ during my repertoire, it's absolutely out of the question!'

"Roy began his act with a spoof magic trick in which a large candle is covered with a scarf and transformed into a bouquet of flowers. That the scarf was actually a dirty, moth-eaten rag and the flowers were made out of a shabby and frayed feather duster, made his trick, which he introduced as 'Oh, See the Pretty Thing,' especially funny. The capper was when the vanished candle (actually a lead pipe painted white) 'accidentally' fell from the folds of the scarf and hit the stage floor with a thud.

"One expected that such an opening would lead into a clownish performance. But each subsequent trick, such as the 'Chinese Sticks,' the manipulation of billiard balls and lit cigarettes and the hand-to-hand transposition of table salt, became increasingly complex and impressive and his comedy became increasingly highbrow and clever.

"Roy Benson was able to open his act by appealing to the lowest common denominator and, in a step-by-step fashion, he transformed himself as well as his audience into a room full of sophisticates."

Among the more prestigious venues in which Roy did his act were the Palace Theatre, Radio City Music Hall, the Blue Angel and the Latin Quarter in Manhattan. Roy Benson also performed on many television variety shows including Ed Sullivan's *Toast of the Town*.

EDGAR BERGEN & CHARLIE MCCARTHY

Edgar Bergen

b: (Edgar John Berggren) 16 February 1903, Chicago, IL—d: 29 April 1978, Las Vegas, NV

Charlie McCarthy

b: (Charlie Mack) 1922, white pine, forest unknown

If one compiled a list of the most popular entertainers of the decade between 1935 and 1945, there would be one among them that was neither a human nor a non-human animal: Charlie McCarthy. Not that any of his listening public would have agreed. To them, Charlie McCarthy was as real as Amos, Andy, Sapphire and the Kingfisher, Kate Smith, Bing Crosby, Bob Hope, Gary Cooper, Clark Gable, Myrna Loy, Betty Grable, Benny Goodman and other great stars of the era.

Charlie McCarthy was one of three child characters who won large audiences on radio. Two of them were similar. Baby Snooks, the on-air persona of Fanny Brice, was an impish, mischief maker. Junior, the Mean Widdle Kid, one of Red Skelton's radio characterizations, was rambunctious and incorrigible.

Charlie McCarthy was different. First, he seemed to be a few years older and much smarter. Snooks and Junior could not even spell puberty; Charlie had aced it. You could hear him pant when gorgeous filmland beauties like Dorothy Lamour, Rita Hayworth or Marilyn Monroe were guests. Likewise, he never indulged in childish temper tantrums. Charlie was insolent toward adults. He cut them down to his size through well-targeted insults, although he might give way to a more juvenile threat, "So help me, Bergen, I'll mow him down." Charlie's most prominent antagonist was W. C. Fields. Aging and ill, Fields found his semiregular status on the Bergen-McCarthy radio show as fortuitous as Bergen did. It gave Fields work that was physically undemanding yet afforded him continued public exposure. In turn, Fields gave Bergen/McCarthy an antagonist who was as easily vexed by Charlie as he had been by Baby Leroy.

> "You'd better come out of the sun, Charles, before you come unglued."
>
> "Do you mind if I stand in the shade of your nose?"
>
> "Silence, you little flophouse for termites."

Charlie was impudent even when dealing with Edgar Bergen, who pulled the strings in their relationship. Charlie belittled his gentle guardian, mocking his sense of propriety, even ridiculing his competence as a ventriloquist.

Edgar Bergen & Charlie McCarthy

> "You can say that again, Charlie."
>
> "Not without you moving your lips."

In a business noted for the success of the bizarre, there was no success more bizarre in American show business than that enjoyed by Edgar Bergen. (In Great Britain, Peter Brough achieved the same sort of fame on BBC radio with his wooden partner, Archie Andrews.) If George S. Kaufman or Moss Hart had wished to ridicule network radio as they had Broadway and Hollywood, their script might have contained the improbable plot of a popular radio show that starred a ventriloquist. As a candidate for radio success, ventriloquism was, logically, on a par with pantomime, juggling, magic, acrobatics, puppetry or Dunninger's mind-reading radio show. Admittedly, dialogue was a component of ventriloquism and most other forms of puppetry, but the prevailing wisdom was that the point of ventriloquism was making the act seem as if the puppet were alive and speaking for itself, something that had to be seen to be appreciated.

Not that Edgar Bergen was unskilled. Although there were a dozen *vents* who could talk without moving their lips more convincingly than Bergen, no one could animate a puppet better than he. Charlie did not simply sit, face forward to the audience, or swivel his neck and head 90 degrees occasionally. Charlie's repertoire of movements was more subtle: an incline of the head to appear querulous, slow sidelong glances, looking an antagonist up and down before skewering him with an insult, or looking up and down at an attractive starlet before proposing a night on the town, an invitation that implied a look at his etchings would follow.

Bergen's skill as a ventriloquist was immaterial on radio although an immeasurable delight to his live audiences in vaudeville and nightclubs. What sold the show to his listening audiences was Bergen's talent as a creator of character, as a writer and editor, and as one of the best comedy teams in show business. Not only was Edgar Bergen as good a feed as the best of straight men, George LeMaire, Margaret Dumont, Moe Howard, George Burns and Bud Abbott included, but Bergen also played Charlie's partner with a fully developed and very popular character. More than most vents, Bergen was a master of timing and vocal modulation. The cross talk between Edgar and Charlie almost seemed to overlap, yet Edgar precisely maintained the difference of vocal patterns as well as tone and pitch between the two voices.

Unfortunately, puppetry, along with juggling, magic and clowning, too often surrendered to market forces that infantilized the performance. Some producers regarded puppeteers, clowns and jugglers as appropriate only for audiences of children. Although children of the day felt a kinship with Charlie McCarthy, identifying with his impatience to assume adult rank and privilege, they often did not understand his witty references or lechery.

The adult level of the Bergen-McCarthy repartee was pitched to an older audience of some education. No, it was not Noël Coward; neither were Fred Allen or Groucho Marx, but Fred, Groucho and Edgar certainly offered shows a cut or two above the level of wit in most other comedy programs on radio. The dialogue on occasion skirted the risqué, as when Mae West invited Charlie to "play in my woodpile" or when a starlet refused his invitation to play post office: "Why, that's a kid's game," and Charlie countered, "Not the way I play it."

Charlie McCarthy may have been Edgar Bergen's suppressed self. As a boy, Edgar seems to have toed the mark at home and in his studies, but his antic self played around with drawing, magic and mind reading until he discovered, through a 35-cent pamphlet, *Herrmann's Wizard's Annual,* how to throw his voice, a skill he used to confound the family at home and teachers and classmates at school.

Bergen's purposeful side guided the antic. While he studied premed at Northwestern University, he earned money on the side entertaining in the semiprofessional world of amateur nights, house parties and small-time vaudeville. Bergen had not yet focused his talents. His performances in his college days were a mix of Swedish dialect jokes, cartooning, mind reading, voice throwing and magic tricks. When Bergen decided to pursue show business instead of medicine, he switched his major and got summer work playing the Chautauqua circuit, a round of genteel vaudeville.

There are at least two stories about Charlie's birth. In one, reported by Valentine Vox, Arthur Frank Wertheim and others, Bergen early on had commissioned a carpenter, Theodore Mack, to carve from white pine a dummy's head based on sketches Edgar had made of an Irish newsboy named Charlie. Bergen created mechanics and the dummy's body. In the second story, Arthur Frank Wertheim related that another Charlie was made with rolling eyes and moving eyelids and mouth out of basswood by Chicago carpenters Frank Marshall and Alex Camero. The mechanicals included levers and cords. Somewhere along the way a third Charlie was created.

When the first dummy was assembled and named Charlie Mack, Edgar took his revised act back on the Chautauqua circuit and into small-time vaudeville. It was the start of a ten-year stint on the road, a road that took Edgar and Charlie through American vaudeville circuits and the variety houses of Europe and South America. By the mid-1930s, the growing unrest in Europe meant Edgar had to concentrate on the USA for bookings, but America was still mired in the Great Depression, and vaudeville was a shadow of its former glory. Wisely, Bergen decided to revamp his act for nightclubs, starting at the Helen Morgan Club. His partner, Charlie Mack, got the Pygmalion treatment: gone were the urchin cap and clothes. Instead, Charlie adopted the attire of the smart supper-club gentleman: white tie, top hat and tails. To this sartorial elegance were added a monocle and a trace of a British accent. The monocle lasted longer than the accent.

The new Charlie was inspired by Esky, the cartoon mascot of Esquire magazine, whose readership was smart but more sophisticated than intellectual. When the magazine stipulated a license fee for the name Esky, Bergen decided to forego the name change. Merely adjusting his dummy's name to Charlie McCarthy was a shrewd choice. Bergen seemed to the clothes and manner born, but Charlie's streetwise character suggested that his status was little different from those in the audience who had worked or muscled their way from humble beginnings into café society. After more than a decade of plodding along as a run-of-the-bill act, it only took a few months for Edgar Bergen & Charlie McCarthy to score with the smart set.

Late that same year, on 17 December 1936, Edgar and Charlie made their first network radio broadcast on the *Royal Gelatin Hour,* headlined by Rudy Vallee. Mr. Vallee, along with his producers, must be considered great talent scouts for network radio, as they introduced Broadway stars like Eddie Cantor, Olsen & Johnson, Ed Wynn, Beatrice Lillie and Milton Berle to national audiences from Trenton to Tallahassee and Topeka to Tucson.

Bergen brought 15 years of professional experience to radio, and it took only 17 weeks on radio to make him and Charlie household names. Their one shot on Vallee's show led to a three-month extension. In May 1937, Edgar and Charlie were back at NBC to headline the *Chase & Sanborn Hour,* a variety show with Don Ameche as the master of ceremonies, Dorothy Lamour, and Ray Noble and his orchestra. Bergen was the head writer. The show had a good budget, and the writing was sharp, so the cast regulars and guests were top-notch. The show soared to the top of the ratings and remained there for three years, besting airwave favorites Jack Benny, Fred Allen, Eddie Cantor and Bing Crosby.

Bergen created Mortimer Snerd and Effie Klinger for several reasons. The new personalities displayed his versatility as an actor and kept the radio show fresh. It may also have signaled Edgar's wish for a greater share of the acclaim, if only for his versatility as an actor, even if the audience could not appreciate his skill as a *feed* for his wooden creation. Snerd's stupidity provided a line of comedy opposite Charlie's, and Mortimer gained a fair amount of fans. But Charlie remained the star and Bergen accepted it, even providing the puppet his own room in the home Edgar shared with his wife, café society singer Frances, his daughter, Candice, who would achieve the television success that eluded her dad, and his son, Kris, who traveled with Edgar as his assistant. Edgar and Charlie remained successful long after other radio headliners either segued to television or retired from the field. Their last radio show, in 1956, was 20 years after their first.

Bergen & McCarthy made several short films even before their broadcast careers, sometimes adapting one of Bergen's vaudeville routines, such as "The Operation," which presented Edgar as a surgeon and Charlie as the patient, or with Edgar and Charlie cast as a headmaster and student. In those cases, the script called for Charlie to lie down on a gurney or sit at a desk while Edgar moved about.

The Bergen & McCarthy feature-film appearances were linked with their radio fame, and one of their best was with W. C. Fields, *You Can't Cheat an Honest Man* (1939). Edgar took dramatic roles independent of his creations, and, over the decades, he appeared in dozens of films. As early as 1948, he played an earnest suitor in the film of *I Remember Mama,* and he acted several times in television dramas.

Edgar Bergen could not replicate his radio success on TV. Ventriloquism on TV directed the audience's attention to the manipulator's lips. Voicing Charlie without moving his lips was not Edgar's strength, and the competition was strong and numerous, from old pros like Señor Wences, who did not have the burden of living up to a top-rated radio show, to newcomers like Paul Winchell, Shari Lewis and Jimmy Nelson, to whom television was a welcoming media of new opportunity.

Edgar Bergen had made a lot of money, and he continued to be able to live well, work when he wished, and command high fees. A score of years after his last radio series, Edgar and Charlie were performing in Las Vegas when the master announced his retirement. A few weeks later, Edgar Bergen, still performing in a Vegas casino theatre, died peacefully in his sleep. His death was not noticed until the following morning.

One Charlie McCarthy rests at the Smithsonian, another is owned by magician David Copperfield, and a third is ensconced at the Museum of Broadcasting Communications in Chicago, Edgar's home town.

BERK & SAUN

Sammy Berk

b: ca. 1894, Russia—d: 5 August 1983

Juanita Saun

As a young man in his homeland, Sammy Berk had performed as an acrobat and dancer. In those days, Russian dance troupes were expected to be acrobatic. After his family arrived in New York and settled on the Lower East Side, he kept up his acrobatics in the local gym and danced in the family act, the Sokoloff Troupe, headed by his uncle.

An amateur contest at Tony Pastor's Theatre gave young Sammy his first opportunity as a solo dancer, and he was encouraged enough to apply and get a job at the Jardin de Danse, a Manhattan cabaret. This led to a job dancing in a musical show, *Lilac Domino,* which ran better than three months at the 44th Street Theatre in autumn 1914. Sammy teamed with another dancer from the show, Lillian Broderick, and the pair decided to do a double act in vaudeville. The act got booked in and around New York City until Sammy Berk joined the navy just as the USA was drawn into the First World War. Lillian, a beautiful young woman, took a job in the chorus in a Ziegfeld show and then married Joe Schenck of Van & Schenck.

Upon his discharge from the navy in 1918, Sammy needed a new partner, whom he found in a young woman called Valda. They performed a few dates in vaudeville, but Sammy was sidelined by an injury and the act broke up.

Sammy laid off while his knee healed. Once able to return to the stage, his agent introduced Sammy to a potential new partner, Juanita Saun; she was dancing at a Broadway nightclub.

Berk & Saun clicked. They showed the new act at the Fox in Jamaica, Long Island, and got booked on both Keith and Orpheum time. They celebrated and sealed their partnership with a wedding in 1920. It was not all cakes and ale or big-time bookings. They played plenty of small-time houses, especially when they were making the jumps between large cities in the South and central USA.

By the late 1920s, Berk & Saun were touring in packaged vaudeville units, usual on the Orpheum circuit. All bills had their headliners, a different one every week in each new theatre, but in unit shows, the same acts stayed together with minor changes. This gave the headliner more power over what material other acts could perform and where on the bill they were placed. The star act not only got top billing, he called the shots for the unit.

Berk & Saun combined ballroom and tap with acrobatic dancing. Because they were a physical act, they could play worldwide. In 1926, they went to Europe; in London, they played high on the bill at the Victoria Palace.

With the decline of vaudeville, Sammy switched to the management end of show business, and he became an agent. Juanita retired.

MILTON BERLE

b: (Milton Berlinger) 12 July 1908, Harlem, New York, NY—d: 27 March 2002, Los Angeles, CA

Milton Berle's life and career spanned a century of modern show business. His legendary mother, Sarah Glantz Berlinger, found work for five-year-old Milton in the silent films being shot in Manhattan, Long Island and New Jersey, where the USA movie industry began. Although it meant little to a young child, Berle, with his sense of showbiz history, later marveled that he had small parts in films starring John Bunny and Flora Finch, Marie Dressler, Charlie Chaplin, Mabel Normand, Mary Pickford, Douglas Fairbanks, Corinne Griffith, Pearl White and Ruth Roland.

Sarah Berlinger's husband, Moses, an amiable man, never succeeded as the breadwinner, and, increasingly, he took the role of a househusband. Perhaps Sarah liked it that way; she had enough ambition for the whole family and was dauntless. She had taken charge of the family's fortunes and launched herself into a career as a store detective and an occasional movie extra when her younger children, Milton and Rosalind, were babies.

Propelled by his mother into a show-business career, Milton, age five or six, won a silver cup in an amateur show. The cup was really tin, but then Milton was not the usual child performer. The Berlingers were not a show-business family. Milton had never been trained in singing or dancing or acting.

Among his first gigs were boy-girl pairings in kiddie shows at temple affairs or social clubs. After school, he modeled for advertisements and plugged songs in five-and-dime emporia. His mother's passion for show business must have been genetic; when at age seven Milton found himself temporarily at liberty, he gave penny-a-seat shows to the neighborhood kids. Already, Milton had learned not to sit and wait for opportunity; in later years he would be, as often as not, his own producer.

When he got a real chance at stage work, the Society for the Prevention of Cruelty to Children (SPCC), informally known as the Gerry Society, was too often there to save him from being exploited. To escape their good intentions, Mother Berle said good-bye to her family, left the other children in Papa's charge, packed up Milton and headed to Philadelphia, where the SPCC was less vigilant.

Milton's first opportunity to play vaudeville came in 1919 from E. W. Wold, a Philadelphia producer who specialized in copying Gus Edwards' better-known kiddie acts that toured big-time vaudeville. Wold's troupe, called Tid Bits, was strictly small time and played theatres in eastern Pennsylvania. The act was three girls and three boys in song and dance. Milton did an imitation of Eddie Cantor, whom he had never seen.

Milton Berle

In 1920, Sarah engineered Milton into one of the revivals of the turn-of-the-twentieth-century musical hit *Floradora.* It gave Milton nearly a year's work (with time out for a summer layoff), but the Shubert Brothers did not give billing to any of the baby Floradora Sextette, so it did little to advance Milton's career. It did provide Milton, however, an opportunity to enjoy the personal charms of one of the grown-up Floradora Girls in the show.

Berle claimed few heartwarming memories of his years as a child performer. He did not doubt that he enjoyed the limelight, but he also missed the chance to grow up normally. Although he worked with other kids, most stage mothers maneuvered their children like chess pieces, each one trying to promote her child's position in the act at the expense of the others. Neighborhood kids, spotting Berle on the way to the theatre in his stage outfits, found him an easy target for taunting until a stagehand gave Milton some boxing lessons. He kept practicing, and a few years later, during the awkward years when his height precluded any more youngster roles, Berle even turned to prizefighting for a very short time when he was "too old for the kiddie stuff. . . and too young for the grownup stuff."

Before he got to that unemployable stage, however, Milton was hired in 1921 to be one half of Kennedy & Berle, the Twinkling Stars, in the act "Broadway Bound." It was put together by Milton Hocky and Howard J. Green, who wrote, produced and owned various acts that they booked on the big-time vaudeville circuits. They shortened Berlinger to Berle. Sarah, who felt she was in show business, too, adopted Berle as her surname as well.

The act was successful for about three years, and they even played the Palace Theatre in New York on 2 May 1921, when Milton was 12 years old. Milton was growing too tall for a juvenile, however, and the act broke up in 1924. Berle put together another act and it was favorably reviewed by the showbiz trade papers. His new act won Berle a berth in the big time until vaudeville began to peter out. Milton segued easily into nightclubs and Broadway revues.

Although Berle became a respected elder statesman among comedians, he was accused in his youth of lifting material from other acts. Later, he did penance by tagging himself as "The Thief of Bad Gags" and acknowledging his cribbing: "Jack Benny is really great. I laughed so hard I dropped my pencil."

Although the Great Depression made a nightmare of many Americans' dreams, it did not touch Milton. He had many options. Although he never became a top radio star, the airwaves provided him with a good paycheck and fairly consistent work for more than 15 years. *Earl Carroll's Vanities of 1932,* a couple of flop musical comedies and numerous vaudeville appearances at presentation houses added to his radio and nightclub income. Soon, movies beckoned, and Berle, usually as a second lead, made nine movies between 1937 and 1943. He later made almost twice as many more.

Berle left Hollywood to star in the *Ziegfeld Follies of 1943*. He was the show's biggest name, and, although there was not one hit song, this show holds the *Follies* record at 553 performances. At the same time, Berle was also producing other stage shows and still another radio series.

The man who was credited (or accused) by critics of bringing back vaudeville through television did it first on 21 September 1948, when he and the *Texaco Star Theater* debuted. Milton Berle is credited with selling more TV sets than anyone else. Joe E. Lewis joked that, once people watched his show, they sold their sets. Milton agreed: "My uncle sold his set, my brother sold his and my sister sold hers."

Berle's television's success was more than the highlight of his career; it was a historic event. Dismissed at first for its eight-inch screen, erratic image and programming dominated by test patterns, fashion parades, quiz shows and hokey wrestling matches, TV quickly built an audience when Berle burst into living rooms with a mishmash of vaudeville, revue and burlesque. Burglaries went down and water consumption up (but only during the commercials) as Tuesdays quickly became family's and friends' night at home, putting a severe dent in competing entertainments like movies and sport events. Berle's success drew other old vaudevillians, former film stars and reluctant radio personalities to the tube.

In 1954, after six years in the lead, Berle's ratings began to slide to the fifth or sixth spot. Panicking, NBC tried to refit Berle into an hour-long situation show, but that did not play to his strengths or his spontaneity. The real problem was the change in public taste. A couple of decades' worth of vaudeville and revue had been crammed into six years, and some shows were done badly. The year 1954 was also the year Sarah Berle died.

NBC made a number of other missteps. By the time Berle left his Tuesday-night series, the same network already had split the team of Sid Caesar and Imogene Coca. The *All Star Revue* went out of business in 1952, and *The Colgate Comedy Hour* closed shop in 1955. Ed Wynn, Jimmy Durante, Abbott & Costello and Danny Thomas were out of variety and into sitcoms. Eddie Cantor and Martha Raye were just out.

One of the first modern comedians, Milton Berle coined a rapid-fire style that remained the hallmark of stand-up comedy for 50 years. Milton's arsenal contained old gags, new jokes and put-downs of hecklers and stooges. He was never at a loss for an ad-lib, whether it was manufactured on the spot or remembered.

> "Listen, Mister, I always remember a face but in your case I'll make an exception."
>
> "Oh, it's novelty night—you're here with your wife."
>
> "You look like you just stepped out of Vogue. And fell flat on your face."
>
> "Poor guy, what does he know? I've got underwear older than him!"

Nothing defeated Berle in his long career. If he did not find work, he made it. He produced stage shows and movies, wrote and promoted his autobiography, acted in straight dramatic roles, and repackaged his TV shows for video sales and rentals. Perhaps the setting most suited to Berle was his beloved Friars Club, where he swapped stories and quips with other masters of the trade.

IRVING BERLIN

b: (Israel Isidore Baline) 11 May 1888, Mohilev, Russia—d: 22 September 1989, New York, NY

When Alexander Woolcott, preparing an essay about Irving Berlin as a man of the theatre, asked Jerome Kern to provide an assessment of Berlin's importance as a songwriter, Kern wrote "that Irving Berlin has *no* place in American music. He *is* American music."

Unlike most of the other white composers of the great American songbook, and a goodly number of the black composers, Irving Berlin had a meager general education, and his musical training was provided by saloon *"perfessers"* at the *"piana."* He chose songwriting as a career because he wished to better himself and make money. In pursuit of a career in show business, Irving Berlin wrote songs that debuted in saloons, burlesque, vaudeville, revues, musical comedies, radio and motion pictures, not just on Broadway for the sophisticated theatre audience.

Of the hundreds of songwriters who found success in the early part of the twentieth century, perhaps 20 or so are the major contributors to the enduring Great American Songbook. Berlin was one. Of his contemporaries, both black and white, composers and lyricists such as George M. Cohan, Cole & Johnson, Jerome Kern, Oscar Hammerstein II, Sissle & Blake, Cole Porter, the Gershwins and Rodgers & Hart wrote mostly for revues and musical comedies.

Berlin was more like songwriters who strove for hit songs and more often wrote for singers instead of shows. No one wrote songs more perfectly suited to the voices and personalities of his singers than Irving Berlin, and no one approached his ability to write duets. Noël Coward came close with his ability to suit his singers, and Coward gained his experience the same way Irving did: by performing for all sorts of audiences.

Consequently, there was no single recognizable style of Irving Berlin's music. He wrote lovely ballads, funny character songs, jazzy syncopation, roundelays, simple patriotic anthems, contrapuntal melodies, songs that ordinary people quickly learned and sang, and songs that only an Ethel Merman or a Harry Richman had the vocal equipment to render properly. His lyrics could be farmhouse plain or the result of tricky wordplay and sophisticated rhyming technique. He wrote for 60 years, so there was enough to suit everyone. Sheet music and phonograph records spread Irving Berlin's music across the USA.

The quintessential American composer grew up as Izzy Baline. Like millions of other immigrants, he reinvented himself and became one of his adopted nation's most spectacular success stories.

Ellis Island in New York Harbor had been open as the new immigration-processing center for less than two years when, in 1891, Moses and Lena Baline debarked with their six children. Israel Baline was the youngest. Seven years before Izzy was born, conditions in Russia worsened under the new czar of Russia, Alexander III, who instituted pogroms. Jewish villages were burned to the ground, and the inhabitants were either slain or driven to hide in the wilds. It took a long time, but Moses managed to collect the $35 per person needed to transport his wife and six children to America. They were crammed into steerage on an old sailing ship.

Arriving in Manhattan, the Balines found shelter on the Lower East Side, the most notorious, squalid, disease-ridden, violent section of New York. One daughter died soon after arriving. Moses, the father, died in 1901 when Izzy was 13. Lena was left with five children to support. Fortunately, the oldest boy, Benjamin, was 20 and the three girls, Sarah, Rebecca and Chasse, were 24, 18 and 16, respectively. They worked in sweatshops. Izzy, the youngest, sold newspapers and junk to add a few pennies to the family purse.

Later, when asked about his childhood, Irving Berlin refused to dredge up sordid memories and tell sad tales. He told interviewers, instead, that he was encircled by a loving family working together to better themselves and that, "There was always bread and butter and hot tea." His resilient nature and optimistic outlook brightened the stories he told in song and lifted the melodies he wrote. Some of his songs were tinged with sadness, but few were anthems of despair.

The truth was slightly at odds with his recollections. Izzy left school and home shortly after his father's death. He felt he was a drain on the family, unable to pay his way, and he joined the thousands of homeless boys who shined shoes, formed gangs, sold newspapers and stole to stay alive. He slept in alleys and flophouses. Part of Izzy's wish to be on his own was that, as the youngest and most Americanized member of the family, he did not share his family's old-world attitudes and customs. There was nothing modest or traditional about his ambition.

He had inherited his father's musical sense but only a thin, raspy variant of his voice. Izzy had a quiet type of nerviness that bolstered his hope that he could earn his bread and bedding by singing and passing the hat in concert saloons along the Bowery. The saloons were frequented by seamen on shore leave, prostitutes, gamblers, muscle for hire, psychotic brawlers and pathetic souls lost to drugs, booze and disease. Like their denizens, the names of the saloons were unabashed and colorful: Morgue, Biggie Donovan's Saranac, Brodie's (the guy who jumped off Brooklyn Bridge on a dare), the Dance Hall and Sailor's Drinking Place, and Nigger Mike's (to which Irving later moved up to a position as a singing waiter).

Saloons provided Izzy's first audiences. They were not musically educated, they were not polite, but they knew what they liked and were willing to listen as long as they were not bored or patronized. They showed their favor when they tossed money into the hat. Encouraged by his reception, Izzy sought and got a chance to tour as a chorus boy in *The Show Girl* (1902), but he was dumped from the cast in upstate New York.

When he returned to Manhattan, he set his sights on becoming a song plugger. He was hired by songwriter Harry Von Tilzer to be a *boomer,* a song plugger who sat in the audience and stimulated applause and encores for his client's songs. Izzy started as a bogus audience member at Tony Pastor's 14th Street Theatre, a vaudeville house. The song for which he was supposed to generate enthusiasm was used by an act called The Three Keatons. Izzy's job ended when Joe, Myra and Buster moved on to their next vaudeville date.

Back to the saloons he went, this time to the Pelham Café, known to initiates as Nigger Mike's. Upstairs was a brothel and opium den run by Chinatown Gertie. The entire venue was a crossroads of culture. Slumming parties from uptown met rival gangs who sometimes did not take it outside. The Eastmans were a Jewish gang, the Five Pointers were Irish and Italian; both were the legatees of a century of clashes over ethnicity and territory.

Like the other waiters, Izzy was most often called upon to sing sentimental songs from the "ould sod" or newer tunes, grabbed royalty-free from George M. Cohan's latest show. When he turned 18, Izzy chided himself that he had been on his own nearly five years and had progressed in show business no further than a job as a *nickel kicker* (singing for throw money and kicking it into a corner where it was safe until the song was finished).

When a singer at a rival saloon wrote a modest hit song, Izzy was challenged. He saw that the sheet-music publishing business needed a constant supply of new songs. Izzy gave it a try, and his first song, "Marie from Sunny Italy," got published. The sheet music credited Izzy as I. Berlin. The publisher got his name wrong, and Israel Baline went along with it.

Most early Berlin songs were risqué parodies suitable only for concert-saloon audiences, but he came to understand that what he wanted was respectability as well as money. Although Berlin never hid his beginnings, he took control of the story and fashioned it to fit the Horatio Alger morality mold. Although Berlin did not drink, was careful about the women with whom he associated and strictly avoided criminal activity, he was a tough-talking Lower East Side youth who lived and earned his keep in a world of vice. He was also ambitious, focused and impatient to rise above the underworld.

From Nigger Mike's, he moved a bit uptown to Jimmy Kelly's. Izzy was still a singing waiter but earned a bit more money. Accepting his limits as a singer and performer, Berlin decided to pursue songwriting and made connections wherever and whenever he could. His parodies were too smutty to publish, so he tried his hand at clean dialect songs. These proved popular. The sales of sheet music for "Sadie Salome, Go Home" earned Berlin a steady job in 1909 as a staff lyricist with its publisher, Waterson & Snyder.

After a half century of dominance by the Irish, show business in New York was increasingly being penetrated by Jews. Irving Berlin was in the right place at the right time. He still could not play piano or read or write music, but Irving had an ear for lyrics. His years as an entertainer in rough-and-ready saloons made keen his sense of what engaged the public. He distilled. Instead of telling the listeners how the person singing his lyrics felt about something, his lyrics began to show them. Berlin's first real hit, "My Wife's Gone to the Country (Hurrah, Hurrah)," made the point. As Berlin explained it, the singer does not tell the audience he is happy, he shouts "hurrah!" This made Berlin's songs ideal material for vaudevillians to perform.

Fanny Brice was the first soon-to-be star to buy a song from Irving Berlin. In 1910, Fanny was a soubrette in burlesque and as anxious as Irving to move up in the world. Ziegfeld was taking a chance on her for the fourth edition of his *Follies.* She needed material, and Irving dragged out a trunk song, "Sadie Salome, Please Go Home," which she liked, so he wrote expressly for Fanny another dialect number, "Goodbye, Becky Cohen."

These were just two songs out of dozens he had been turning out, often with music by Ted Snyder, one of the two partners in Waterson & Snyder. Within two years after he left Nigger Mike's and Jimmy Kelly's, songwriter Irving Berlin made $10,000 to $15,000 in royalties within a year. Although he did not bother to learn to play piano, he was intrigued by all types of music. He first had heard black ragtime and ribald parodies in the saloons where he worked. He then discovered the dialect songs and *coon songs* that were staples of variety and vaudeville. A business trip to England afforded Irving the opportunity to listen to and study English music-hall songs. Later, in the 1920s, he was intrigued by the avant-garde composers, especially Eric Satie. Berlin's genius was in absorbing many influences and putting them together into the most *American* sounds of any major composer, classical or vernacular, in the USA.

His first three years as a songwriter had earned him $100,000 in royalties, a membership in the Friars' Club, the soubriquet the Ragtime King, and the envious and malicious whisperings that one man could not have written so many songs—so many good songs. Among them were "Snookey Ookums," "Everybody's Doin' It," "The Grizzly Bear," "When That Midnite Choo-Choo Leaves for Alabam" and "I Love a Piano."

Rumors abounded that he had hired a colored boy to write some of his hits. His denial was unqualified and unadorned. Accusers tracked down Lukie Johnson, the piano player at Nigger Mike's. Despite the opportunity to cash in big time, Lukie made it clear that he was not Berlin's ghostwriter. Those who knew Irving well insisted the charge was baseless. Later, when someone brought the charge to court, Irving Berlin was vindicated. Yet the rumor persisted a century later, and it fastened to Fats Waller, who, it is said, needed money badly so often that he sold his work to white songwriters for a pittance. That Irving Berlin was assumed to be Waller's client is a compliment to how jazzy and Harlemesque some of Irving's music sounds.

Irving Berlin was becoming rich by the mid-1920s, and he got only richer. Naturally a shy and private man, he disliked any publicity about himself that was not directed toward making his songs or shows a hit. When charges were made, he withdrew even further from the public eye. His retreat into privacy sparked rumors about drug use, and some maintained he had been a hophead since his days playing in Chinatown saloons and opium dens. Wannabe jazz musician and would-be big man on the bandstand Mezz Mezzrow, who retailed drugs on the side, claimed he sold marijuana to Irving, but the boast was as unreliable as the source. It is pretty certain that Berlin did not use illegal drugs; it is also quite certain that, beginning after the Second World War, he became overly dependent on prescription drugs, especially Nebutal, to relax and sleep. Fanning this rumor was Ethel Merman, star of Berlin's *Call Me Madam,* who, for years after every Broadway show, would gather with her coterie at Sardi's and other showbiz haunts and drink themselves silly and gossip at the top of their formidable lungs about anyone and everyone.

If Irving hated publicity and was a private person, he was never a pushover. He was resilient, self-sufficient and complicated. When Willie Hammerstein offered Irving the headliner's spot on the bill at Hammerstein's Victory Theatre, many were surprised that Irving accepted. He threw together the semblance of an act and seemed to enjoy it almost as much as the audiences who demanded encores, but he enjoyed it only as a lark, a very well-paid lark. Then it was back to writing and composing and a retreat to such privacy as could be arranged.

The past was dead for Irving. There is no question that he did not revisit the Chinatown saloons or keep up with his former associates. Irving Berlin's eye was on the future. He was in his early 20s, a very successful songwriter earning $100,000 a year, and a partner in the music publishing firm of Waterson, Berlin & Snyder Co. Successful, in 1913 he bought his mother a home. By 1914, he formed his own firm, Irving Berlin, Inc.

His first marriage, to the spirited Dorothy Goetz, ended five months later with her death from pneumonia or typhoid fever. She was 20 years old. In sadness, he wrote "When I Lost You." He published it, and it became his first ballad to become a hit. Before Dorothy had fallen ill, Irving returned to Hammerstein's Victoria as the headliner of another vaudeville bill. Berlin's song "Everybody's Doin' It" ("Doin' What? Turkey Trot!") was a smash hit, and Irving staged it ingeniously with the stage crew doin' it with their brooms, stage furniture and stage ropes. It was not the first clue that Irving Berlin possessed smart theatre sense and that his eventual goal was to write shows for Broadway.

Charles Dillingham, the producer, brought together Vernon & Irene Castle as his stars, Harry Smith to adapt a musty French play into a snappy musical comedy book, and Irving Berlin to write all the songs. *Watch Your Step* opened in 1914 along with the First World War. Berlin frankly gave credit to Frank Sadler, who orchestrated Irving's songs. As Irving said, he was used to writing for a *piano and ten,* meaning the standard vaudeville orchestra of the day, common in the better small time and all but the grandiose big time. The show was a hit; Izzy Baline had finally cracked his way onto Broadway. He was 26, a young widower who worked very hard and sat in the audience with his mother, sisters and brother.

He was on his way to becoming a national institution. There were many other Broadway shows in his future, including 15 for which he wrote the complete scores. He produced shows, beginning with his four *Music Box Revues* in the early 1920s. The Music Box Theatre was built by Irving Berlin. There was also a second marriage, this time to socialite Ellin Mackay.

When Berlin started to work for Hollywood, it was his old friend, Joe Schenck, to whom he turned. Berlin and Schenck knew each other from their youth on the Lower East Side. Schenck was an apprentice pharmacist at Olliffe's Drugstore. Founded in 1805, the apothecary was precisely that more than a century later; they dispensed everything from the ingredients of a Mickey Finn to opium. Joe became a power at Loew's, the corporation that controlled MGM. A dozen-and-a-half films were centered on songs by Irving Berlin; five of these films were adaptations of Berlin musical comedies. But Irving Berlin is most identified with three of the better Fred Astaire & Ginger Rogers movies: *Top Hat* (1935), *Follow the Fleet* (1936) and *Carefree* (1938).

It was after his vaudeville years that Irving Berlin became a giant in American show business. Irving's stage hits included a list of his hit songs ran more than 100. "God Bless America," "White Christmas," "Alexander's Ragtime Band," "Blue Skies," "Always," "Easter Parade" and "There's No Business Like Show Business" remain songs that are familiar to most Americans four generations after they were first sung. The royalties those songs continued to earn reaffirmed their worth and Irving Berlin's position as America's premier songwriter.

Irving and Ellin Berlin were wed 42 years when she died at 85 in 1988. Irving died the following year at 101. Irving Berlin, Inc., the music corporation, lives on, as do his songs.

SAM BERNARD

b: (Samuel Barnett) 3 or 5 June 1863, Birmingham, England—d: 16 May 1927, Atlantic Ocean

When he was four years old, Sam and his family immigrated to the USA. He and his brother, Dick, were both stagestruck; as children they put on shows in their father's woodshed. The Bernard Brothers jettisoned the family name of Barnett for something more ethnic, surely a first! They had their first semiprofessional engagement in 1876 at the old Grand Duke Theatre at Baxter and Worth Streets in Manhattan's notorious Five Points section. Far from its grand-sounding name, the Grand Duke was a backyard, basement theatre, crowded and sweaty, with a nickel admission and operated by a teenage gang of thugs who called themselves the Baxter Street Dudes.

Sam and Dick performed after school, doing a song-and-dance act with a knockabout finish, a standard routine of the day. As the years progressed, their act became more polished and kept them working in vaudeville and variety houses like the New York Museum until 1884, when Sam Bernard went single. He joined a troupe at B. F. Keith's theatre in Providence, Rhode Island, and played comedy roles.

In 1885, Bernard went to England, touring a comedy sketch in music-halls and variety houses. A year later, he was back in the USA, where for the next couple of seasons he was a comedian with a company called the Night Owls, a troupe that hovered between vaudeville and burlesque. Sam then became part owner of the French Folly Company in which he played the leading comic roles and perfected his German dialect characterization in burlesks of popular shows.

Sam Bernard had known both Joe Weber and Lew Fields since they were boys starting in show business. All three friends began in show business the same year. Because of Sam Bernard's experience in managing his own burlesk troupe and their long friendship with him, Lew and Joe asked Sam to manage the Russell Brothers Comedians that Weber and Fields sent out on the road in 1890. The next year, they chose Sam to manage and star in the third of their three touring companies, the Vaudeville Club.

Five years later, when Lew and Joe created the Weber & Fields Music Hall, Sam Bernard was one of the first performers Joe and Lew signed up. As one of the three Dutch comics in the show (the other two being Weber & Fields), Sam was a Weberfields principal in their first two seasons, 1896 through 1898. A typical sketch would have them portraying swindlers trying to outfox each other with a contract. This scene presaged several scenes 40 years later between Groucho and Chico Marx in *A Night at the Opera* (1935) and *A Day at the Races* (1937).

Sam Bernard left Weber & Fields Music Hall in 1898 to star with Marie Dressler in *The Man in the Moon* for the 1899–1900 season, but he returned for the 1901–02 season to star along with Joe, Lew, Lillian Russell, Fay Templeton, De Wolf Hopper, David Warfield and John T. Kelly in *Hoity Toity.* That proved to be his final season with his old pals.

Broadway musicals had captured Sam Bernard, and, over the next quarter of a century, he maintained his star status in them. In 1904, under Charles Frohman's prestigious management, Sam appeared with Hattie Williams and future stars Marie Doro and Elsie Ferguson at the Herald Square Theatre in *The Girl from Kay's,* which became one of Sam Bernard's greater successes. He repeated with Miss Williams in *The Rollicking Girl* at the same theatre in 1905.

The next few years brought *The Rich Mr. Hoggenheimer* in 1906, *Nearly a Hero* in 1908 with Ethel Levey and Ada Lewis, *The Girl and the Wizard* with Kitty Gordon in 1909, *He Came from Milwaukee* in 1910, *All for the Ladies* in 1912, and *The Belle of Bond Street* with Gaby Deslys in 1914.

The Keystone Company's payroll for 1916 shows Sam Bernard earning $2,500 a week for making film comedies in their New York studios. Weber & Fields were drawing $3,000 a week jointly on that same payroll, whereas De Wolf Hopper held out for an annual salary of $125,000, whether he worked or not!

Back on the musical stage for 1916's all-star *The Century Girl,* Bernard costarred with Elsie Janis, Hazel Dawn, Leon Errol, Frank Tinney and Van & Schenck. In 1918, he costarred with Louis Mann, another Dutch comic and Weberfields graduate, in the long-running hit *Friendly Enemies.* In 1920, he shared top billing in *As You Were* with Irene Bordoni and Clifton Webb. Sam joined yet another Weberfields alumnus, William Collier, in Irving Berlin's first *Music Box Revue* for 1921. Collier and Bernard shared the stage and top billing again for the revue *Nifties of 1923.* Sam Bernard worked onstage until 1927, when he died onboard ship while crossing the Atlantic Ocean.

SARAH BERNHARDT

b: (Henriette Rosine Bernard) 23 October 1844, Paris, France—d: 26 March 1923, Paris, France

The illegitimate daughter of a Parisian courtesan and a weak, tubercular child, Henriette Rosine was raised in the lonely atmosphere of boarding schools. At 15 years of age, despite her lack of experience in theatre, she won an audition that admitted her to the Conservatoire, the French government-sponsored school of acting. Eccentric, even as a child, often visiting morgues, her unconventional behavior and preoccupation with death extended throughout her adult life. She was eccentric in appearance too: thin, with a small head topped by a mass of frizzy red hair. Even her friend and supporter, Alexander Dumas, said of her that, "She has the head of a virgin and the body of a broomstick."

Sarah Bernhardt in the title role of *La Dame aux Camélias* from a 1912 Palace Theatre souvenir programme.

Three years after her studies with the Conservatoire had begun, Henriette Rosine, age 18, went onstage and reinvented herself as Sarah Bernhardt. She made her professional debut with the Comédie-Française. After nearly ten years of learning her craft by playing melodrama, Sarah hit her stride with the female lead role of Ann Danby in Dumas' *Kean* at the Odéon. She was a quick study. Even in her old age she was able to keep 25 roles word perfect in her mind, including the lead roles in *Ruy Blas, Britannicus, Phèdre, Hernani, Frou-Frou, Adrienne Lecouvreur, La Dame aux Camélias, L'Aiglon, La Tosca, Jeanne d'Arc* and even *Hamlet.*

Sarah was extravagant in all matters. When the Franco-Prussian War broke out, she opened a field hospital that she managed and where she served as head nurse. Her romances were tempestuous, her lovers prominent. She painted and sculpted, and her works were displayed and sold in respected art galleries. She collected wild animals as exotic pets and, somewhat advanced for her time, treated them as well as they could be cared for in captivity. She quarreled with theatrical impresarios, managed her own theatre, traveled like royalty and toured often to pay debts of her profligate spending.

Bernhardt crossed the Channel in 1879 to appear at London's Gaiety Theatre. As in France, and later in the USA, she was feted by both society and bohemia. In 1880, she sailed to America to play Boston, Montreal, Philadelphia, Chicago and New Orleans among the 51 cities in which she totaled 157 performances. The favorite of American audiences was *La Dame aux Camélias.* In 1886, she ventured to South America; she traveled its length and breadth and escaped the yellow fever that felled her maid. In 1891, she toured much of Europe, including Russia, North America, South America and far-off Samoa.

When she arrived in the USA in January 1901 for her sixth American tour, she brought with her 50 trunks, five servants, one secretary, her costar, the great Benoit Constant Coquelin, a troupe of supporting actors and a repertory that included *L'Aiglon, La Dame aux Camélias, Cyrano de Bergerac, La Tosca* and *Hamlet.* Some reviewers were beginning to judge her performances critically, and the tour was not a complete artistic success, although Madame Bernhardt had the consolation of moneybags full of the gold coin that she required as payment. Bernhardt was angry enough at her reception to stay away from America for another five years. In 1906, however, Bernhardt consented to tour the USA again, and she left with more bags of gold.

At the urgings of Martin Beck, Bernhardt first toured American vaudeville from December 1912 through May 1913. She capped her engagements with three weeks at the newly opened Palace Theatre in Manhattan. It was not yet the pinnacle of vaudeville; indeed, critics had panned its bills during its first weeks.

Sarah Bernhardt's appearance turned the corner for the Palace. Appearing with her onstage in *Une Nuit de Noel sous la Terreur,* subtitled *A Christmas Night under the Terror,* was Lou Tellegen, a virile and handsome man, soon to become an American favorite in silent films. Other playlets in their repertoire included adaptations of Sardou's *Théodora,* Hugo's *Lucrezia Borgia,* Racine's *Phèdre* and the final act of *La Dame aux Camélias.*

For the entire company, Bernhardt was paid $1,000 per day at the end of each day she performed; she did not trust anyone to hold onto her wages for seven days. The money went out as soon as it came in because Sarah had incurred a host of financial obligations. In

1914, two years after her first tour of American vaudeville, Bernhardt was made a chevalier of the Légion d'honneur.

Bernhardt returned to the Palace in December 1917, its reputation now solid, and followed that engagement with another tour, part of which included one-night stands. She was 73 years old, desperate for money and in poor health; two years earlier she had a diseased leg amputated at the hip, but performers, who were on the bill with her, recall her ability to rally her energy and stir the Palace audiences with her *tour de force,* the trial scene from *Jeanne d'Arc.*

BEN BERNIE

b: (Benjamin Anselvitz) 30 May 1891, Bayonne, NJ—d: 20 October 1943, Los Angeles, CA

Ben Bernie was an affable and voluble celebrity who won a loyal following that kept him a radio star for decades. By the time he was a radio star, Ben Bernie was selling personality, and there was scant evidence of his interest in music. True, he still fronted a band, although he often did not conduct it and never rehearsed it; those chores were the responsibility of first violinist Mickey Garlock. Actually, he did not even assemble the band; he simply had bought an aggregation put together by bandleader Don Juelle.

As a youth, however, Ben Bernie had his heart set on a career as a concert violinist. He was skilled but was discouraged along the way. Until he entered vaudeville, the best living his violin could provide him was as a part-time teacher and a full-time salesman in a music store. He was nearing 20 when, around 1910, he and a young accordion player, Charlie Klass, entered small-time vaudeville as a musical duo. It had to have been a rough five years because when, in 1915, he teamed with another accordionist, Phil Baker, Bernie was still playing the small time.

Luckily, the two men hit it off, and Bernie & Baker developed a comedy and music act. Bernie played violin, talked a bit to the audience; Baker began stooging from a box seat, dueting his accordion with Bernie's violin, and getting some laughs. The team had several good years, gradually emphasizing the comedy and getting better dates, until Phil Baker joined the U.S. Navy to fight in the First World War.

In 1923, Bernie bought the Don Juelle band, which he renamed Ben Bernie and All the Lads. Instead of the endless trail of vaudeville dates, Bernie managed to get his outfit hired by the Roosevelt Hotel in Manhattan, where he and his dance band became fixtures for six years. From the very first year on the Roosevelt bandstand,

Ben Bernie

Bernie sidelined in radio. He was a pioneer in the medium, broadcasting remote from the hotel's supper club. In 1930, radio became Bernie's primary gig.

A local Friday-night broadcast beginning in January 1930 on WJZ led to his Tuesday-night show on CBS in 1931. Instrumental music had been the easiest entertainment to arrange when radio was in its infancy. It remained popular and easy as radio coalesced into networks.

What distinguished Ben Bernie from most bandleaders was that the others thought their job was to play music for the listeners, whereas Bernie understood that his job was to entertain them. His breezy, relaxed manner was well suited to the intimacy of the microphone and the single listener or family at home. He sang-talked his way through an occasional lyric, and his chatter was a blend of the sophisticate and the neighborhood pal. He archly referred to his musicians as "all the lads" yet addressed his listeners as "youse guys and youse gals." His tag line "Yow-sah, yow-sah, yow-sah" and his closing "Au revoir, pleasant dre-ea-eams" became public catchphrases. In photos, he was shown smiling with the ever-present fat cigar clenched between his teeth.

Most important to his success was the faux feud he and Walter Winchell devised. It fast made Ben Bernie famous. His program, under various sponsorships, enjoyed success all through the 1930s, alternating between CBS and NBC. Shortly after establishing himself on network radio, he and his band toured with Maurice Chevalier in a series of presentation-house engagements.

Ben Bernie, the Old Maestro proved a good showcase for singers. Over the span of the program, audiences heard Jane Pickens, Dick Stabile and Buddy Clark. In 1939, Ben Bernie gave pop singer Dinah Shore her first network radio job.

In Hollywood, Ben played one role in four films: *Shoot the Works* (1934), in which Bernie played a bandleader who devises a mock feud with a fictional gossip columnist (based on Walter Winchell); *Stolen Harmony* (1935), in which Ben Bernie was a bandleader who hired an ex-con saxophonist played by George Raft; *Wake Up and Live* (1937), which costarred Walter Winchell with Ben Bernie and Alice Faye, Joan Davis, Walter Catlett, Patsy Kelly, Ned Sparks and Jack Haley; and *Love and Hisses* (1937), which cast Ben Bernie as a bandleader and Walter Winchell as a columnist. Joan Davis and Bert Lahr did what they could to add zest to the formula.

On radio, Bernie switched to a 15-minute slot heard in early evenings each weekday. He became ill and was only 52 when he died. He left his family well off in Beverly Hills and his friends sad.

BERRY BROTHERS

Ananias (Nyas) Berry

b: 1912, New Orleans, LA—d: 6 October 1951

James Berry

b: 1914, New Orleans, LA—d: 28 January 1969, New York, NY

Warren Berry

b: 25 December 1922, Denver, CO—d: 10 August 1996, Los Angeles, CA

In the 1930s, there were many fine tap-dance acts. The top groups included the Four Step Brothers, the Nicholas Brothers, Tip, Tap & Toe and the Berry Brothers. Their feats remain unmatched. The Berry Brothers were not tap dancers in the usual sense. They tapped, but they never wore taps, so they called their dance style soft-shoe acrobatic. Other people called it the greatest of all flash dance acts.

Ananias and James were only two years apart in age, and both were born in New Orleans. The family moved from New Orleans westward, and, while in Denver, Warren was born ten years after James. When they were children, their mother taught Ananias and James to dance. She helped the two boys to develop a routine like a miniature Bert Williams and George Walker; they tried it in Los Angeles in an amateur contest in 1925. They took lessons from an eccentric dancer, Henri Wessels.

Their father, strict and religious, was not supportive until he saw that his sons were exceptionally talented. He became the boys' agent and business manager and obtained jobs for Nyas and James. They danced and did their Williams & Walker impersonation at movie-star parties. James also appeared in the silent versions of *Our Gang* shorts at Hal Roach's studios. His career took off because he was a natural comedian.

When Tim Moore produced and starred in the *Southland Revue* (1927–28), a show that toured, he signed Dusty Fletcher and the two Berry Brothers for the show. Nyas and James got their first Cotton Club booking in 1929, and they worked there periodically for the next few years. Nyas was 18, already handsome, and James was 16 when they went into their next Broadway show, *Blackbirds of 1930* with Ethel Waters, Buck & Bubbles, Flournoy Miller, and Mantan Moreland and Tim Moore. As soon as the *Blackbirds'* Broadway stand and subsequent tour were over, the Berry Brothers went into *Rhapsody in Black* (1931–32) with Ethel Waters, Valaida Snow, Eddie Rector, Edith Wilson, Ada Ward and Earl "Snakehips" Tucker. Sometime during this show, Ananias began his romance with Valaida Snow. Ananias and James performed at Radio City Music Hall in 1932.

The act supported the entire family, and it was said that Mr. Berry held the reins tightly. When 19-year-old Ananias left the act in 1932 and married Valaida, 27, Mr. Berry drafted Warren, then 11, to take Nyas' place in the Berry Brother's act. Warren, who was studying piano and acrobatics and looking forward to college, had no choice, and James taught Warren the routines.

Mr. Berry, unhappy that his 19-year-old son had become involved with a woman eight years older, investigated Valaida. He discovered that she had been married previously to Knappy Brown, and there was no record of a divorce. Brown was persuaded to start proceedings against Valaida. The ensuing scandal persisted in the black press through 1934 until Valaida produced some documents that quashed the charges in New York State. Ananias spent a few years working with Valaida both in the USA and Europe, but it had been a messy period, and the couple split up while on the West Coast late in 1935. Nyas appeared, uncredited, in the movies *San Francisco* (1936) and *The Music Goes 'Round* (1936).

James and Warren had worked hard to create an act that was earning decent bookings and a good salary. According to Warren's interview with Rusty Frank,

James was happy in the duo with younger brother Warren. When Nyas contacted his father and asked to rejoin the team, James may have been a bit resentful at first. Their father and Nyas prevailed, and the trio was established around 1936.

The trio of Berry Brothers went into the Cotton Club at the new downtown location, where they remained off and on for the rest of the decade. They earned a lot of money although the country was in an economic depression. The Berry Brothers, the Nicholas Brothers and the Four Step Brothers were three of the great tap-dance acts that were regulars at the Cotton Club. Like the bands (Calloway, Ellington, Millinder), they alternated with each other when they went on tour or made movies.

Europe called in 1937, and the bosses packaged the *Cotton Club Revue* to play London and the Continent. Teddy Hill and His Band went over with the Berry Brothers, singer Alberta Hunter (who was already a favorite in London), tapper Bill Bailey and the jitterbugging Whyte's Hopping Maniacs. The show played to enthusiastic audiences at the London Palladium, Dublin's Palace Theatre and Paris's Moulin-Rouge.

In 1938, the Berry Brothers were back in a new Cotton Club floor show, which was heavily weighted to dancing: the Berry Brothers, the Nicholas Brothers, the Dandridge Sisters and the Lindy Hoppers. It was a long show, overbooked with dance acts, and the Berrys were scheduled to close the show. Ananias decided that they needed something spectacular to hold up their end. At the back of the stage floor, behind Cab Calloway's onstage band, there was a 12-foot-high platform where showgirls usually stood. The Berrys did their cane, strut and acrobatic routine, and, for a finish, Warren stayed on the stage dancing while Nyas and James raced up to the platform, jumped off it, over the heads of the musicians—14 or 15 feet in the air—and landed in perfect splits on the stage floor. Warren timed his backflip and body twist to land in a split at the same time that James and Nyas, still in splits, slid into position beside Warren. Their flash finish set the bar so high that few attempted it.

The decade from 1936 to approximately 1946 was the heyday of the Berry Brothers act. Most observers believed that Nyas was the best dancer of the three. Their brief four-minute, 30-second act opened with Ananias. Posture perfect, he did a strut that was unequaled for the straight line of his high kicks over his head, the quicksilver freeze-and-melt changes in rhythm and steps. James entered the stage singing and smartly fit into Ananias' routine of strut, turns and high kicks that built into acrobatics, at which point Warren joined them onstage, and the act increased in power and speed with somersaults, turns and splits as the three brothers engaged and released each other.

The three Berry Brothers made a couple of movies: *Lady Be Good* (1941) with Eleanor Powell, Ann Sothern, Red Skelton and Phil Silvers, in which the Berrys performed their entire act, and *Panama Hattie* (1942) with Ann Sothern, Red Skelton, Ben Blue, Rags Ragland, Lena Horne and Virginia O'Brien.

James left the act after the Second World War. Ananias and Warren performed in two films as a team: *Boardinghouse Blues* (1948) with Moms Mabley and Dusty Fletcher and *You're My Everything* (1949) in support of star Dan Dailey. Years of injuries and wear had begun to slow down Nyas. Warren, who had simply accommodated the family, was sick of doing the same routine every performance, but bookers insisted on it. He had tried to quit or dissolve the act several times, but it was a death and an accident that finished the act in 1951. Warren's hip gave out—he was 29—and Nyas died of a heart attack at 39.

JOE BESSER

b: 12 August 1907, St. Louis, MO—
d: 1 March 1988, Los Angeles, CA

"O-o-o-h, I'll *harm* you!" he hissed, following the threat with a tentative slap, then skittering away, his pudgy body garbed in a Little Lord Fauntleroy outfit. That is the enduring memory of a comedian who did his best work with other comedians. As Joe Besser was seldom on the wrong end of the punishment stick, he may qualify more as a foil than a stooge, but he is best remembered as a stooge par excellence to many acts.

His brother, Manny Besser, older by nearly a decade, was a successful burlesque comic. Manny's example, plus Joe's own addiction to movies, ensured that Joe would try to get into show business somehow.

Only 13 and an errand boy for a hometown song plugger, Joe was thrilled when Howard Thurston, the eminent magician, brought his act to St. Louis around 1920. Joe finagled his way into getting hired as a *plant* in the audience, and, when Thurston moved on to his next booking in Chicago, he found little Joe stowed away among the prop baggage. Besser learned the basics of illusion as Thurston's assistant, but he wanted to move up the showbiz ladder, so Joe left the great magician around 1923. At first, the best he could find was another job as an magician's assistant. Madame Herrmann, who was working her late husband's act, took on Joe. After a two-year stretch, Joe knew it was time to move on.

In 1926, Joe found work stooging for the comedy team of Alexander & Olsen (brother to Ole Olsen of Olsen & Johnson fame). Then, determined to score as a comedian on his own, he formed his own act to play vaudeville. Joe still gravitated toward partners, teaming first with Richy Craig Jr. and then Sam Critcherson. Within a few years Joe Besser had patented his exasperated sissy character, yet big-time success was a decade off. Too often, his routine descended into what was then called a *swish* or a *pansy* act.

In the 1930s, after more than a dozen lean years in show business, Joe began to get work in revue, movies and radio as a character comedian. In fact, he grew more successful at a time when most vaudeville comics were watching their pay scale drop and their bookings thin as the Great Depression made theatregoing an unaffordable luxury for many. Besser's distinctive voice made him a natural for network radio comedy shows, and big-name comics like Eddie Cantor, Fred Allen, Jack Benny and Milton Berle drafted him to work on their radio shows. Besser never became a star, however, nor did he win a permanent berth on radio.

His style was that of a burlesque comic, yet Joe never played burlesque. Most of his success was won working in packaged vaudeville revues that played what was left of the circuits. He seemed a natural for musical comedy or revue, but his appearances in those type of shows were few, and only one was truly successful, and that came a quarter of a century after he started in the business. *The Passing Show of 1932,* a Shubert revue, had closed out of town, but it is worth noting that both Joe Besser and Shemp Howard were in the cast; a generation later, Joe replaced Shemp as one of the Three Stooges. Besser enjoyed his only Broadway success when, beginning on 1 December 1941, he was featured in Olsen & Johnson's *Sons O' Fun,* a vaudeville revue produced by the Shuberts. Others in the cast included Ella Logan and Carmen Miranda. *Sons O' Fun* scored 742 performances at the Winter Garden and then toured nationally for months. Joe came back to Broadway in the 1946–47 season for Leonard Sillman's book musical *If the Shoe Fits,* but Joe and the show barely eked out 20 performances, despite the prestige and talent of Florence Desmond, the esteemed English musical star, and play doctoring by Nat Hiken, who later wrote the Sergeant Bilko show for Phil Silvers.

Meanwhile, films paid the rent. Columbia Pictures put him under a contract that eventually extended for 14 years. Besser had principal roles in a few features such as *Hot Steel* (1940), *Eadie Was a Lady* (1945), *Talk About a Lady* (1946), *Outside the Wall* (1950) and Besser's two favorites, *Hey, Rookie,* a 1944 wartime comedy starring Ann Miller, and *Feudin', Fussin' and a-Fightin',* a comedy Western that starred Donald O'Connor with Universal's latest comedy team, Marjorie Main and Percy Kilbride of Ma & Pa Kettle fame. Each of these films was promoted by personal appearance tours, and, as a one-time vaudevillian, Joe Besser was able to perform during his appearances instead of simply waving to an audience or making a short speech. Joe worked very hard to entertain, to be professional and to win a spot among the first tier of comedians.

Joe Besser is best remembered for putting some life into the last series of shorts that The Three Stooges made for Columbia Pictures. When Shemp, who had replaced Curly a decade earlier, died in 1955, Joe Besser took his place in the act starting in 1956. The number of theatres showing shorts was declining year by year, so Columbia had been cutting their short-subjects budget. The writing was below pedestrian, and the production values were bargain basement. The Three Stooges were in a slump that not even Joe Besser's energy could spark. Moe and Larry were getting old, tired and possibly discouraged. In fairness, Besser did not seem to try too hard to fit the Stooges mold and viewed the assignment as a stopgap until he got better work. Further, whereas Curly or Shemp had always been the dimwitted fall guy of the act, Besser seemed brighter than Moe and Larry and almost as aggressive as Moe, so the formula was skewed. The new team of Larry, Moe and Joe made 16 shorts until Columbia Pictures failed to renew their contract in 1958.

The revival of The Stooges old shorts on TV stimulated personal-appearance tours, but Joe opted to stay put in North Hollywood to care for his ailing wife. Later in his career, Joe had to admit he had underestimated the importance of The Stooges to their loyal legions of fans and to the endurance of his own legend.

Television provided Besser with some of his most lucrative and memorable work. All told, he made nearly 200 appearances on television. In 1946, NBC launched its first major TV show, *Hour Glass,* a 60-minute variety program, and Joe Besser was among the acts recruited for the show's debut. From 1950 to 1951, he was a regular on *The Ken Murray Show* and the *Alan Young Show,* which alternated weekly. When Abbott & Costello left live television to film a syndicated series in 1951, that team, like The Stooges, was in a slump. The series drew good-enough ratings for 52 episodes to be filmed. Those 52 half-hour programs were still airing as reruns 50 years later.

Joe Besser's Little Lord Fauntleroy character was renamed Stinky for the show, and he joined the very capable Hillary Brooke and Sid Fields in support of Bud and Lou. In 1959, Joe got roles in two films, *Say One for Me,* starring Bing Crosby, and *The Rookie,* with Vince Barnet. In 1960, he had a small role in Marilyn Monroe's film *Let's Make Love.* Next, Joe joined a large cast that included Joe Flynn, Marlo Thomas, Bill Bixby and Corbett Monica when Joey Bishop began a self-named situation comedy series that endured for four seasons starting in 1961.

The 1970s and 1980s were the least active period of Besser's career. He found some work as a guest star in television situation comedies and variety programs, including the *Spike Jones Show.* Jerry Lewis used Joe in two films: *The Errand Boy* (1962) and *Which Way to the Front?* (1970). TV cartoon shows were replacing live shows, but they offered a new avenue of work.

Voicing cartoon characters for animated TV series turned out to be a blessing. Joe's wife of 50 years, Erne, suffered a series of illnesses, and Joe's primary career became caregiving. Then Joe had a mild stroke and discovered he had diabetes, so the once-a-week voice-over sessions for cartoons suited Joe's and his wife's needs better than more demanding work. *Not Just a Stooge,* Joe's story, written by Joe Besser along with Jeff and Greg Lenburg, was published in 1985.

In 1983, The Three Stooges were belatedly awarded a sidewalk star on Hollywood's Walk of Fame. The only other surviving Stooge, Joe DeRita, was too ill to attend, so Joe Besser and Larry's and Moe's children represented The Stooges. By this time, there was probably no one more appreciative than Joe Besser.

BIG BANDS

Vaudeville began to lose its intimacy when theatre owners in the 1910s and 1920s began constructing ever-larger houses. The stages grew wider, deeper and with more height and became more suitable for flash acts, tab shows and circus acts than the monologist, single woman and cross-talk comedy team.

Usually, the large showcases were designed to accommodate motion pictures as well. Having an auditorium that sat 3,000 people was not a drawback when performers appeared on a large screen and (after sound came in) had their voices amplified. A customer in the back row of the second balcony could see facial expressions and hear whispered dialogue on the larger-than-life projection screen.

Big bands were a sensible live booking for the larger theatres during the 1920s and 1930s when swing music was in the ascendant. Except for the vocalists and piano players, bands did not require amplification, and the instrumentalists, bandleader and singers filled the stage, where one- and two-person acts seemed engulfed by empty space. Joe Frisco, the stuttering comedian and eccentric dancer, was playing one of the behemoth theatres, the newly erected Roxy, soon to be famous for its huge stage. Another vaudevillian asked Joe how his act went in such a big house. Joe told it went fine, "but don't get c-c-caught on that stage without b-b-br-bread and water."

Phonograph recordings and network radio increased the appeal and box office of big bands and their singers. People were curious to see as well as hear their favorites. The downside for swing and dance-band enthusiasts was that there was not anyplace in the theatres to dance.

Some African American bands, like those run by King Oliver, Louis Armstrong, McKinney's Cotton Pickers, Cab Calloway, Duke Ellington, Erskine Hawkins, Andy Kirk, Earl Hines and Count Basie, had attracted the attention and loyalty of white as well as black jazz and swing fans. When they played vaudeville theatres, usually they were in those houses that catered to black audiences.

Earlier outfits like Jim Europe's played at private parties for the rich (Europe's orchestra also accompanied Vernon & Irene Castle's dance act in white vaudeville). Noble Sissle fronted black orchestras for a number of Negro musicals, gradually eschewing blues and jazz for society swing dancing.

Over the decades from the 1910s through the early 1940s, the list of white bands that played vaudeville ranged from the Original Dixieland Jazz Band to smooth-music orchestras or novelty bands named for and fronted by the likes of Ted Lewis, Paul Whiteman, Vincent Lopez, Rudy Vallee, Abe Lyman, Leo Reisman, Ted Weems, Hal Kemp, Fred Waring, Isham Jones, Kay Kyser, Sammy Kaye, Shep Fields, Horace Heidt and Guy Lombardo to jazzier outfits like those fronted by Ben Pollack, Glen Gray (Casa Loma), the Dorsey Brothers, Benny Goodman, Jimmie Lunceford, Freddy Martin, Artie Shaw, Harry James, Woody Herman, Charlie Barnet, Red Norvo, Claude Thornhill and Glenn Miller.

Most bands had a female singer or two, and they invariably traveled by automobile while the male instrumentalists and male dancers or dance teams went by chartered bus. Big bands often included rhythm tap dancers in their package: the Miller Brothers & Lois or Honi Coles. Benny Goodman sometimes featured the Condos Brothers. Count Basie had Baby Lawrence. Louis Jordan had Teddy Hale. Charlie Barnet brought Bunny Briggs. Those bookings could change by the season, and most dancers worked with several bands. Peg Leg Bates danced with a half dozen or more big-name bands.

When the United States of America belatedly joined the Allied cause in the Second World War, rapid conscription was required to build up the armed forces, and most bandleaders saw important band members get called up to serve in the army, navy or air force. There was heavy competition, and sometimes a bit of a bidding battle, to fill open slots in the band with competent musicians who proved exempt from the draft. There were good female instrumentalists available, but for reasons ranging from gender chauvinism to trepidation about the potential complications possible in a coed band, women usually had to work in all-female bands (Lil Hardin and Mary Lou Williams were exceptions).

BIG FOUR

The Big Four refers to the most prestigious vaudeville theatres for African American performers and audiences during the 1920s and 1930s: the Lafayette in New York, the Earle in Philadelphia, the Royal Theatre in Baltimore and the Howard in Washington, D.C. These theatres were not part of the Southern-based chain, the Theatre Owners' Booking Association (also known as TOBA or Toby time).

The Big Four often worked together to produce vaudeville revues. A show rehearsed one week and played its first week at the Lafayette. For its second week, it moved on to the Earle in Philadelphia (or if that theatre were not available, then the Pearl, the Standard or the Uptown). The show played the third week at the Royal in Baltimore and the fourth at the Howard in Washington, D.C. The company, sets and costumes then returned to New York, where the cast rehearsed a new show and the production was recycled. Meanwhile, other shows followed in rotation, so each theatre had a new show each week.

Other cities with substantial black populations had fine, independently booked theatres that catered to African American audiences. Among those theatres were the Gayety and Casino Theatres in Boston; the Orpheum in Newark, New Jersey; the Standard, Uptown and Pearl in Philadelphia; the Standard in Pittsburgh; the Washington Theatre in Indianapolis; and the Grand in Chicago. If one of the Big Four's shows proved an exceptional draw, instead of being shelved and its cast put into another show, the hit show was booked to other black theatres from Boston to Chicago to St. Louis and back.

Chicago was always Harlem's rival in black creativity. Occasionally a popular show, such as the all-black version of *Canary Cottage* (1920) that originated in Chicago, subsequently played the Big Four.

BIG-TIME VAUDEVILLE

Two-a-day vaudeville was known as big-time vaudeville, primarily Keith-Albee or Orpheum time. Although some small time, such as Loew's, had some top-notch theatres in their circuits, big-time vaudeville theatres consistently were better managed and more lavishly appointed; they paid better salaries, attracted more discriminating audiences and, with notable exceptions, treated the acts civilly.

Big-time vaudeville was synonymous with two-a-day because the policy was to offer only two shows a day, a matinee and an evening performance. Seats were sold for assigned seating at a price comparable to ticket prices for musical comedies and revues and at least twice what neighborhood vaudeville houses charged. In turn, ticket buyers confidently assumed that the show would be well worth the cost. By performing their acts only twice a day, performers were able and expected to perform with focus, energy and enthusiasm.

Whether run by independent owners who booked through the United Booking Office (UBO) and whose theatres functioned as part of Keith or Albee circuits or by hired management directly answerable to Keith or Orpheum headquarters, the owner or manager of a big-time vaudeville house was protective of his theatre's reputation, its clientele and its position in the community. Performers were expected to conduct themselves professionally, and they were urged to neither offend nor embarrass any member of the audience. The Keith-Albee circuit was called the Sunday School circuit because of the specificity and extent of their admonitions to performers.

Infractions by performers resulted in fines or a report to the home office, sometimes both. A performer's future bookings, salary and spot on the bill were jeopardized by unfavorable reports. The most serious offenses resulted in blackballing.

BILL

The vaudeville bill listed the acts and their order of presentation. Performers did not call the bill a programme. A programme was the paper handout given at some shows to identify scenes (or acts) and the personnel involved in the show, both onstage and off.

The bill also referred to the sign or poster listing the week's acts. Improperly referred to as a poster, these bills were displayed in front of the theatre or in its lobby and were pasted on fences and walls throughout the town.

BILLBOARD

Named for the colorful lithographic posters that ballyhooed circuses, carnivals and tent shows from roadside and rooftop signposts, *Billboard* has had the longest run of any show-business trade publication in America. Begun as a one-man operation in 1894 by William H. Donaldson, it has lasted for more than 100 years. Donaldson, himself a lithographer whose printing clients included many folks who ran or worked for minstrel shows, carnivals, circuses, Wild West shows and world's fairs, created *Billboard* as a voice for the outdoor branches of show business.

The weekly branched into films, a natural enough extension, as many of the early movie men carted their flickers around, town to town, playing in tents, storefronts and makeshift venues. Although *Variety* specialized in coverage of vaudeville, movies, and Broadway and its road shows, *Billboard* also extended its coverage to those areas.

After the Second World War, *Billboard* became the chronicler of record for the recording industry, a position it retains into the early twenty-first century due to its extensive coverage of the pop music industry, including news, reviews, sales charts, radio play and concert tours.

BILLBOARD

Bills (advertising the show) were affixed by paste or tacks to an outdoor wood panel called a billboard. Most theatres had billboards attached to exteriors, especially on the front side.

BILLING

A matter of great seriousness and contention to vaudevillians, billing referred to an act's position on the bill, the placards that were pasted around town or set up in the lobby or on the sidewalk outside the theatre. Performers were concerned about the size of the font and placement of their names and billing matter (the title of the act) in a prominent position on the bills on display in the lobby and outside the theatre.

In time, the concept of billing extended to all forms of show business—musical comedy, legitimate theatre, motion pictures and television—and expanded in meaning. Major stars (and their agents) fought to have their names *billed* above the title of the play or musical in advertising as well as positioned prominently and in large type on bills and programmes. Featured players negotiated for inclusion of their names on bills and programmes. In movies and television, the contest was similar: the actor's name in as much of the advertising as possible, but more important was the order of precedence in the opening credits of the movie or TV show. The struggle for professional recognition was taken up by authors, composers, the crafts (sound, photography, and so forth), directors and producers.

BILL MATTER

Often called billing, the identifying phrase used to describe a particular act, such as "Masters of Mirthful Melody" or "King of the Sharpshooters," was known more properly as the bill matter. These were considered trademarks not to be appropriated. Sometimes a dispute arose when two acts claimed similar billing matter, such as "The Tramp Juggler" and "The Original Tramp Juggler." At one point in his vaudeville career, Fred Allen billed himself as "The World's Worst Juggler," billing matter no other performers wished attached to their names.

BINDLESTIFF FAMILY CIRKUS

Mr. Pennygaff and Kinko the Clown

b: (Keith Nelson) 10 May 1970, Holden, MA

Mistress Philomena

b: (Stephanie Monseu) 23 April 1968, Queens, NY

The caravan of an equipment van and two cars, one with a trailer, had traveled 1,000 miles in 17 hours, carrying six performers, two musicians and a merchandise maven and earned a speeding ticket along the way. The previous evening, they played in Louisville, Kentucky; this night, with a few catnaps en route to sustain them, they played at the Lucky Dog Music Hall in Worcester, Massachusetts.

The spring 2003 *High Heels and Red Noses* tour by the Bindlestiff Family Cirkus zigzagged across the eastern United States from Brooklyn to upstate New York, down to Baltimore and Washington D.C., farther south for a string of gigs in the Carolinas, Georgia and Florida, west to New Orleans, then Austin, Texas, north to Cleveland and Columbus, Ohio, south to West Virginia and Knoxville, Tennessee, back north to Worcester, Massachusetts, then on to New London, Connecticut, by way of Cape Cod. After a couple of days respite in New York City, the last leg of the spring tour took them from Providence, Rhode Island, to Monmouth and Portland, Maine, with a final booking in Winooski, Vermont, 40 miles from the Canadian border. Along the way, Bindlestiff played every type of venue from rock and pop music bars to performance-art venues to old-time vaudeville theatres and logged 10,000 miles in six weeks.

This is the new vaudeville, yet some things have not changed since old vaudeville: the crazy-quilt bookings, packing and unloading, vehicle troubles, preposterous jumps between dates, eating and trying to do laundry on the run, one-night stands, crummy dressing rooms (if any), and the challenge to appear fresh and lively in performance when performers are worn and tired.

The Worcester audience was enthusiastic and relatively young, with a sprinkling of a few Gandalf and William Burroughs look-alikes and a small crew of sports-bar types, perhaps hoping to get lucky. The Bindlestiff gig at the Lucky Dog has become an annual

Bindlestiff Family Cirkus. Photo credit: Maike Schulz

event for a large crowd of regulars, male and female, casually dressed but sporting some pierced appendages and trendy tattoos.

Although the troupe can and does present a family show—granny and kids invited—the best time to catch the Bindlestiff Family Cirkus is late at night, at one of their 10:00 PM or midnight shows, when some performances merit an R rating. Local acts occasionally open for Bindlestiff, and this night it was three young women from Thru the Keyhole Burlesque, one of an increasing number of women-led burlesque-revival troupes cropping up across the USA.

During a break after the opening act, as recorded music played over the sound system, the customers wandered around, ordered from the bar, visited friends or stood clustered in conversation.

Without fanfare, Kinko the Clown ambled onstage. Conversations trailed off, and the crowd gathered, 10 or 12 deep, in a semicircle facing the stage. This bruised tramp is not a romantic re-creation of a silent-screen favorite, nor is he the hopeful hobo who inhabits theme parks and family circuses, begging for your smile. Kinko drinks and likely pees his pants. Turning to his audience, swaying, mute and without any expectation of success, he held out a sign that promised more than he was likely able to deliver: "Will work for food." Offer unmet, he unrolled his sign, a bit at a time, proposing a succession of alternatives to food, among them "Cash," "Sex," "Peace," "Health Insurance," "Scotch," "Joint" and "Applause." No takers to any but the last. Kinko, removed equally from disappointment or satisfaction, resumed drinking and performed several tricks, working slowly, with confidence. The act was low-key, gritty and all the more poignant for its lack of sentiment.

It was a daring way to open a show to a bar crowd used to high-decibel, high-energy bands. Not that the two-man Bindlestiff music accompaniment was languid. Raja Azar played keyboards and Tim Hoey drummed, and between them, throughout the show, they delivered a wall of sound.

The various turns came hard and fast, and each member of the troupe has several specialties. Ringmaster Philomena, a brisk mistress of ceremonies, took the stage and welcomed the audience. Striking, long-legged, lean, shapely and sexy, she exudes *brio* with a street-hard edge. Her top hat and platform boots constitute much of her costume; a lacy network of tat-

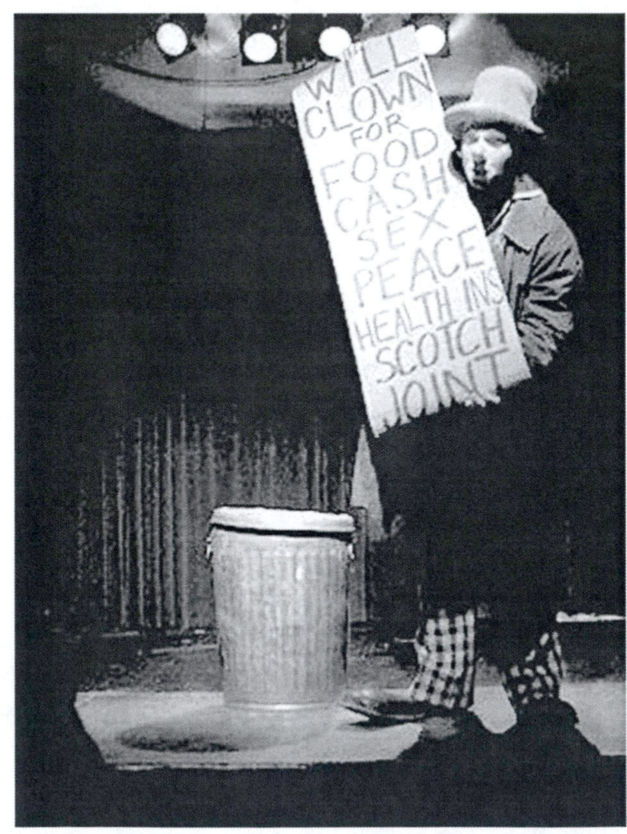

Bindlestiff Family Cirkus. Photo credit: Greg Costanzo

toos covers one arm. At various points in the show, she and two other young women rocked through a couple of fast numbers. Her specialty is a whip-cracking act. From the audience, she selected a volunteer who was given a long-stem rose and told to hold it out at arm's length. He did not say no to a lady cracking a ten-foot bullwhip. The club's low ceiling cramped Philomena's whip cracking style, but she sliced the rosebud off the stem. The volunteer next clenched the stem in his teeth, as directed. Slash by slash, the stem grew shorter until, with barely ten inches remaining, he was told to hold it between his thighs. Lots of laughter and a crack or two later, the stem was a twig.

Miss Saturn (Jenny McGowan) took the stage for a hula-hoop act. She began with a few hoops, but the volunteer Miss Saturn had plucked from the audience added so many of the florescent-colored hoops that she looked like Saturn rendered by a Las Vegas neon marquee. The Lucky Dog ceiling was too low to hang the rope netting for Tanya Gagne's Spanish Web act and barely high enough to accommodate her aerial rig, yet she gamely executed a balletic striptease from her trapeze.

Two silly billies, Adam Kuchler and Matthew Morgan, provided much of the comic relief. They teamed as the Slapinski Brothers, a bogus acrobatic duo inspired by two acrobat brothers named Woicheck & Woizek (pronounced the same) with whom Adam had worked when he was touring Russia. Later, Adam, a lithe acrobat, did a comic contortion turn and performed a cigar-box juggling routine reminiscent of W. C. Fields'.

In his solo spot, Matthew set up and manned a kissing booth, all mimed. It was an act of bravery until the audience got the point. Audience reactions vary from venue to venue, and Matthew has had to cope with all comers. Among the takers in Worcester was someone who brought his puppet up to Matthew. He nearly violated it.

One of the more anticipated acts on the Bindlestiff bill is Mr. Pennygaff, a slick, handsome son of the midway, who appears in the second half of the show and swallows swords and neon tubes. The danger of a 24-inch steel sword passing through Mr. Pennygaff's innards impresses even the most blasé. More dangerous is sliding the lit neon tube down into his stomach. "One hundred thousand dollars liberal arts education and this is what I do for a living."

The whole company joined for a musical number (the cleverly titled "Homeland Security Song and Dance") and the Big Juggle that provides the big finish for the two-hour show. Without breaking the pattern, one juggler at a time moved out into the audience and returned the clubs as fast as the other five served them, like a tennis player returning volleys from five opponents.

A Bindlestiff bill varies season to season, place to place, as acts leave and return, accommodating their Bindlestiff engagements to their solo careers. The constants of the Bindlestiff Family Cirkus are its leaders and partners, Stephanie Monseu and Keith Nelson. Monseu's stage persona is Mistress Philomena Bindlestiff, and Nelson performs as Kinko the Clown, Kinkette and Mr. Pennygaff. Keith and Stephanie met in 1994 while waiting on customers in a New York City restaurant. When business was slow, they slipped outside where Keith taught Stephanie fire-eating.

Stephanie has been performing since she was a child putting on shows in the back yard with her sister. Their mother was an exceptional pianist, and Stephanie learned to play piano and clarinet. There was always music in the home, classical as well as the swing jazz her father favored. It was a creative household, and the sisters were encouraged to make their own toys and entertainment.

Mom and Dad moved the family from Flushing to open a bread-and-breakfast in the Catskills, where the girls attended junior high and high school. Stephanie joined the drama club, the marching and concert bands, studied gymnastics and dance, and taught skiing.

After high school, she moved to New York City and branched in many directions, some at the same time: sign painting, studying graphic arts at the Fashion Institute of Technology, making jewelry, singing in a pop group and getting her real estate license. When Stephanie was 22, she was hit by an uninsured driver and suffered a severely broken right arm. A year later, she broke her left arm. Because of tendon damage, she could no longer do the detailed work that jewelry making required, so for artistic expression she turned to painting large canvasses. She searched for a way to combine painting, sculpture, costuming, movement and music. While keeping body and soul together by working as a waiter in a restaurant, Stephanie met Keith.

When he was three months old, Keith's parents moved from a small town in rural central Massachusetts to Winston-Salem, North Carolina. Nine years later, the family moved to a less urbanized area, where they lived at the end of a small airfield runway, where occasional barnstorming pilots and wing walkers amazed a young boy.

His dad was a New Yorker by birth and disposition. Keith's paternal grandfather had been a modernist architect, and his maternal grandfather a historian who carried on the family's horticulture business; they had brought the first African violets to the USA. The family was disposed to let Keith find his own way to his own niche.

Growing up, Keith joined the Boy Scouts and learned pyrotechnics, archery, knots, packing and cooking for large numbers, skills later essential to performing and touring. As an Eagle Scout, he taught archery and firearms and led kids in songfests and skits. According to Keith, all of his Scout buddies later turned toward alternative lifestyles.

When at 15 he attended his first Grateful Dead show, Keith was intrigued by the parking-lot scene where Dead heads came together in an impromptu community. By 18, he was a regular at Dead gatherings, followed Rainbow tours and had begun attending Hampshire College, where he lived in a clothing-optional dorm. He learned to juggle from a college friend, David Hunt, a slackropewalker and all-around performer who established the New Orleans School of Circus Arts.

The time between semesters sometimes extended into a hiatus—Keith earned his degree in five years—during which he jumped freights, hitched and once walked from Texas to New York City. As part of his studies, he interned at Autonomedia, a radical press in the Williamsburg section of Brooklyn, where he learned layout, editing, shipping and inventory. He also worked as a waiter and, for $150 a month, shared an apartment with an elderly lefty on the Lower East Side. After a six-month final act at Hampshire College that culminated with graduation, Keith returned to New York and Autonomedia, where he traded work for rent. He resumed waiting on tables, as well, and it was at his second restaurant job in Manhattan that he met Stephanie Monseu.

In their off-hours from working in the restaurant, Keith and Stephanie performed in alternative cabarets doing their fire-eating routine and juggling. Keith blockheaded (hammered nails up his nose) and manipulated devil sticks (juggling sticks aflame at both ends). Although many of Manhattan's cabarets remained mainstream venues primarily for singers and pianists, there was a burgeoning, especially on the Lower East Side and in the East Village, of alternative clubs, like the Blue Angel and the Pyramid Club, that were hospitable to more unconventional acts. Performing in the underground cabaret circuit was a good way to see what other acts were doing and get a feel for audiences. Stephanie claims that she and many others learned a lot about presentation and costuming from drag queens.

Following a jaunt to New Orleans to sample the street-performer scene, Keith and Stephanie returned to New York to find they no longer had their waiter jobs. The pair took the news as a spur to perform full time. In 1995, they journeyed to northwestern Nevada to participate in the annual Burning Man celebration in the middle of the Black Rock Desert. Out of that meeting of artists and anarchists grew an impromptu tour in 1996 with several others they had met at Burning Man. Like an old-time sideshow, the acts included lying on a bed of nails, blockheading and, of course, fire-eating. The wild and woolly tour with individualists pulling in various directions convinced Stephanie and Keith to organize and run their own show.

Bindlestiff Family Cirkus. Photo credit: Carl Saytor

Over the years since 1996, a pattern has emerged. Bindlestiff plays a winter season in Manhattan and Brooklyn, tours the eastern half of the USA in spring and the western half in autumn. During the winter 2003–05 season, Bindlestiff helped counter the Disneyfication of Times Square by opening a Palace of Varieties on 42nd Street in the chashama Arts Complex. They presented a daily exhibition as well as afternoon, evening and late night shows, with the early one geared to families with children and later shows to adults.

Over the years, they have performed at many New York City venues, including the Union Pool and Brooklyn Brewery, both in Williamsburg, the Theatorium on the Lower East Side, Chinatown's Mazer Theatre, Shine, Webster Hall, the Cutting Room in the Flatiron District, Coney Island, Theatre for a New City and two engagements at Lincoln Center.

The extended Bindlestiff Family embraces dozens of performers, past and present. Magic Brian does a grisly magic act, swallowing double-edged razor blades then regurgitating them strung together by dental floss. Angelo Iodice is a rope spinner from the Bronx. Scotty, the Blue Bunny, is a buffoon of sorts, "half man, half wild animal." Professor A. G. Gertsacov marshals a troupe of fleas through their acrobatic paces, truly an act of faith on the audience's part. Baby Dee, who describes herself as "the bilateral hermaphrodite in residence in a Coney Island Sideshow," plays concert harp and accordion while pedaling a high-rise tricycle. Ropewalker David Didd juggles razor-edged machetes, eats fire, walks on broken glass and swings on the trapeze.

During its existence, the Bindlestiff Family Cirkus has tilted more toward skill-based acts, although they have not forsaken the novelty turn; a Bindlestiff show would not be representative without a sensation or two. "We attract some of the most creative and original performers today, from the back end of the carnival lot to the stages of Broadway."

After a decade of working and living on the edge so familiar to artists, Keith says, "I can't imagine what else I would do. I enjoy spending hours and days working on goofy and otherwise useless skills, like balancing a shot glass on a coat hanger, throwing tops, catching a bottle of water on my head, not to mention juggling, sword swallowing, diablo, etcetera."

The *K* in Cirkus suggests a political agenda, but Bindlestiff is not political theatre in the old agitprop sense. They maintain a light hand, yet their work reflects the concerns of many of their generation: distrust of large concentrations of power in big government and the corporate world of big business, big art, mass communications and global commodities that seek to transform productive individuals into consumer-serfs.

BITS

Somewhat elastic, the term *bits* usually referred to parts of a comedy act (the seltzer squirt, a foot caught in a pail), but it has been used to mean an extended segment, especially in burlesque, in which a straight man and comic segue into a well-known skit or dialogue: courtroom scene (such as "Here Comes the Judge") or cross-talk bit (like "Who's on first?") or the straight man explaining to the comic how to make love to a woman. Not all bits were stock. Many comedians developed their own, and these became signature bits: Bea Lillie's slow, spiraling descent of a long string of pearls; Bobby Clark's expelling, catching and juggling his cigar; Edgar Kennedy's slow burn; and Billy Gilbert's extended sneeze.

BLACKFACE

Minstrelsy grew out of blackface. Perhaps the earliest use of blackface in American entertainment was by a journeyman clown, George Washington Dixon. When he first blackened his face in 1828 and sang "Coal Black Rose" in his approximation of plantation Negro dialect, he scored a hit, but his vogue in variety lasted only a few years.

The next entertainer to make his mark in blackface was Thomas D. Rice (1808–60). A native of Lower Manhattan's infamous Five Points slums, he left home with a touring stock company and worked his way up from stagehand and bit parts to a full-fledged actor. Variety turns between the acts of melodramas were added attractions, and, in 1828, Rice developed a blackface turn, "Jim Crow," that proved popular. In 1832, Rice brought his "Jim Crow" routine, which he expanded into as many verses as an audience might request, to The Bowery Theatre in Lower Manhattan. He made so great a hit that he was able to tour profitably for years.

Other performers took note, and Rice's success led to a proliferation of musical turns in blackface. By 1843, individual acts coalesced into evening-length minstrel shows, and blackface and minstrelsy remained intertwined for more than a half century. Even after the slow decline of minstrelsy by the turn of the twentieth century, individual performers continued to cork up. Al Jolson and Eddie Cantor continued the practice longer than most white song-and-dance men; Cantor persisted into the 1940s, and some Negro comedians blacked up until the years of the Second World War, when a younger generation of African American funnymen persuaded the older generation to forfeit their comic masks. Interestingly, in African American comedy acts, it was only the Negro comedian who blacked up; Negro straight men usually worked without black greasepaint.

Blacking up used various ingredients at various times. Often, white kids starting out in rough-and-tumble variety houses were advised, as a practical joke, to use coal dust to black up. It settled into their facial pores and was not easily cleaned away. Using burnt cork was a modest improvement, and black greasepaint was the choice of experienced professionals.

Blackface became a symbol of American and European ridicule of Africans. The dancing Golliwog, an adaptation of the grotesquely featured doll, was a display of skill by the contortionist who inhabited the costume and was tossed carelessly around the stage by his partners. The Golliwog was a severe caricature of Africans, with paws for hands, and it was treated as a thing, a being without sentience.

The tragic farce of supposed racial superiority and inferiority played out in the United States of America. Many European Americans regarded all African Americans and African Caribbeans as blacks, although many were part white—mostly white in more than a few cases. Some whites regarded anyone with darker skin, such as Italians and other Mediterranean people, as blacks or coloreds. The poison that judged quality by the darkness of skin color, hair texture and facial features unfortunately seeped into the attitude of some African Americans toward their own kind.

Most things that can be said about blackface, however, do not hold true universally. Although many blackfaced characterizations of Negroes were vicious, portraying them as savage and stupid creatures that could not exist, others presented the plantation darky as happy-go-lucky, uneducated, superstitious and dim-witted but harmless. Some white performers created benign blackface portrayals devoid of exaggerated speech or caricatured makeup or, like Eddie Cantor and Al Jolson, corked up as ebony Harlequins, wily servants hijacked from *commedia dell'arte.*

The blacked-up comic personas of African American comedians like Billy Kersands, Ernest Hogan, Bert Williams and Flournoy Miller & Aubrey Lyles were developed first for their African American audiences, and several generations of Negro comedians, like "Pigmeat" Markham, "Spider John" Mason and Dusty Fletcher, continued the tradition into the 1940s for black audiences.

All races and ethnicities were lampooned during periods of mass migration from the 1820s up to the First World War. Fresh-off-the-boat Irish were depicted as pugnacious drunks who wore knee breeches and had orange whiskers and red noses. Germans were invariably portrayed as loud, fat, thick-skulled and devoid of manners. Jews were presented as dirty and duplicitous and Italians as semibarbaric thieves and cutthroats.

Blackface persisted among whites as late as 1964, when the organizers and participants of Philadelphia's annual Mummers Parade were shamed into abandoning blackface. By that time, blackface existed solely as evidence of racial prejudice. It could not have been otherwise when the issue at hand was not only equality under the law but the recognition of the inherent dignity of African Americans.

BLACK HERMAN

b: (Benjamin Rucker) 1892, Amherst, VA—d: April 1934, Louisville, KY

A tall, imposing black man, Black Herman enjoyed a prosperous career for 20 years and left behind a legend. In his case, the word *legend* is not hyperbole. He made of himself a character that many believed superhuman. Black Herman crossed the line from stage conjurer to pretending to possess supernatural power.

He claimed to be a Zulu, born in Africa and brought to the USA as a boy to be educated. The truth was that he was working as a clerk or in a restaurant when he met Prince Herman, a traveling con artist who represented himself as a purveyor of an elixir. Prince Herman was a medicine-show huckster. He had mastered basic card tricks that attracted an audience and convinced naive country folk that he had abilities beyond their ken.

Benjamin was about 16 when Prince Herman invited him to join him on the road. In return for packing, driving, running errands and selling the elixir, Prince Herman taught him magic tricks, showmanship and how to make the *"secret African remedy"* from any old materials he found at hand plus a liberal amount of alcohol.

Prince Herman died about one year into their partnership, and young Benjamin took over. He was only 17 but physically imposing and grave in manner, so few realized that Black Herman was only a youth.

He chose his name as a nod to his two mentors: Prince Herman, who adopted him, and Alonzo Moore, the renowned African American stage magician whose work he had recently seen and admired. Alonzo Moore had been dubbed by the press as the Black Hermann [*sic*], a reference to the great, white stage conjurer.

Black Herman (Benjamin) was unschooled, and whatever literacy and skill he gained beyond Prince Herman's tutelage was a credit to his native intelligence and intuition. Instead of presenting himself as an entertainer and engaging in lighthearted banter, he adopted a more serious persona, an amalgam of preacher and professor. Most medicine-show men steered clear of local authorities and leading citizens. Black Herman cultivated their acquaintance. He invited local choirs to participate in his event, and a leading citizen was chosen to introduce him, reminding everyone that Black Herman's mission was to travel the world and that he would not return for seven years.

The truly unique aspect of Black Herman's presentation was that he evoked the authority and majesty of his audience's common heritage. His potion was derived from the knowledge of roots and herbs learned from Zulu witch doctors. He imitated the sounds of animals native to Africa and to the rural South. Even his escape act reinforced a bond of near kinship with his audience. He called upon three of the strongest-appearing men in the audience to bind him securely with rope. As he freed himself, he told his audience that was how his people escaped slave traders in Africa. When he presented the usual stage illusions, Black Herman related them to the miracles in the Christian Bible.

And then came the pitch. He had confederates planted in the audience: his brother, Andrew, and his chief assistant, Washington Reeves. One assistant was seized by the devil. With a cup full of elixir, Herman cast out the devil (usually a concealed and frightened snake or lizard that quickly scurried to escape the tent). Reminding everyone that he would not be back for seven years, Black Herman offered the miracle tonic. Those who bought several bottles were allowed a free consultation with Herman. Usually within their first few words, Herman got enough of an impression to divine their misfortune, and he then sold them an appropriate charm to turn good luck in their direction.

Washington and Andrew arrived in each town on their route before Herman. They scouted town records and newspapers and compiled names and dates from local cemeteries. As the act prospered, Black Herman created more elaborate illusions—the sword cabinet and sawing a lady in half—and engaged a mind reader, Madame Debora Sapphirra.

He was arrested several times for fortune telling, but he turned that to his credit. He implied that it was racially motivated and a frame-up and that he had simply walked out of prison each time because no jail had the power to hold him.

His most impressive stunt was a resurrection act. People paid to pass by the coffin in which Black Herman lay, his pulse stopped by applying pressure under his arm. As the coffin was covered and lowered into the ground, Herman slipped out of it and concealed himself. A week or so later, the coffin was exhumed, opened and Herman stepped out. In the days in between, Herman set up the same trick in other cities and returned in time to slip back into the coffin.

He settled in Harlem and went on the road less frequently. He set up several ancillary businesses. One was the sale of lucky charms and amulets; another was a series of potboiler adventures than purported to be the true adventures of Black Herman. Rather than employ a ghostwriter, Herman dictated the tales to a transcriber; he still could not read or write. Despite the devastating effect that the Great Depression of the 1930s had on most African Americans, Black Herman prospered. He owned a fleet of autos and a large and expensively appointed home.

When Black Herman did appear in public, it was at venues that accommodated 3,000 or 4,000 people that he was able to sell out for several weeks at a time. In April 1934, he was performing his elaborate show in Louisville, Kentucky, when he collapsed and died onstage. A doctor was called up from the audience, but Herman was dead at 42. Some fans refused to believe he was mortal. Others queued up at the funeral parlor—so many that his body was transferred to a commodious railway station. Viewers paid a dime to pass by his bier. Many of his followers believed that he would again resurrect. In a sense he did. A number of stage conjurers cashed in on Black Herman's fame and changed their names to some variant of Herman. His former assistant, Washington Reeves, billed himself as the Original Black Herman.

BLACKOUT

Strictly, a blackout was a stage instruction for all stage lights to be turned off abruptly and simultaneously. More practically, it was a term used in sketches to indicate that the lights must black out or go to black immediately after the concluding punch line.

BLACK PATTI

b: (Matilda Sissieretta Joyner Jones) 5 January 1869, Portsmouth, VA— d: 24 June 1933, Providence, RI

Often celebrated as black America's first recognized concert singer, Sissieretta Joyner was born into a family whose father was a minister in the African Methodist Church. In 1876, the family moved to Providence, Rhode Island, where Sissieretta attended school and sang at church. She married David Richmond Jones in 1883 when she was 14 and gave birth to one child, a baby girl who died before she turned two. Sissieretta and David moved to Boston, where she studied with professionals affiliated with the New England Conservatory of Music. Her husband became her manager and may have had a hand in arranging her participation at a benefit held in Boston at the Music Hall to raise money for Charles Stewart Parnell, the Irish revolutionary. At the time, the Music Hall was the home of the Boston Symphony Orchestra and the leading concert venue in town.

In 1888, Sissieretta Jones, her name shortened, gave her first concert, which was held in Steinway Hall in Manhattan. She was a critical and popular success, and her singing was likened to that of the famous Italian operatic soprano Adelina Patti. Faced with Sissieretta's formidable given name, audiences and chroniclers began referring to her as "The Black Patti." A tour was arranged, and she played dates in the West Indies. Upon her return to the mainland, Sissieretta was a major attraction of the Grand African Negro Jubilee at Madison Square Garden in 1892. That same year, Sissieretta sang at the White House for President Benjamin Harrison and auditioned at the Metropolitan Opera. There were announcements that she would sing *Aida* and *Le Africaine,* but those plans were quietly and quickly shelved.

Actually, there were earlier African American women concert singers, like Elizabeth Taylor Greenfield, well known in the 1850s, and Anna Madah Hyers and Emma Louise Hyers, two sisters active on concert stages in the 1860s and early 1870s. They all preceded Sissieretta Jones, but each had to abandon her concert career and switch to gospel music or popular entertainment to make a living.

In 1893, Sissieretta performed in Chicago at the Columbian Exposition, the fourth and largest world's fair thus far. Black Patti was not the only prominent Negro invited to participate; Frederick Douglass was there as well. From 1893 to 1896, Sissieretta was under contract to Major J. B. Pond, whose other clients included Mark Twain. Pond negotiated high fees for Sissieretta Jones, higher than those ever paid to any Negro entertainer. He booked her on a tour of Europe, Asia, Australia and

South America; in Europe, she sang for the kaiser of Germany and England's prince of Wales.

Sissieretta and David Jones began pulling apart. He had been dissipating the fortune his wife was acquiring and had effectively been sidelined by more professional managers. Conflicts between her husband and her managers may have induced her to sign with Voelckel & Nolan, white producers and managers, who conceived of building an entire show around Sissieretta, a show that appealed to the high brown and the low down. They called it Black Patti's Troubadours (Sissieretta disliked the nickname), listed themselves as proprietors and managers and launched it in 1896. Three years later, in 1899, Sissieretta divorced David, realizing that he had mismanaged her finances.

Over the next 20 years, Black Patti's Troubadours was the most prestigious African American show on the road, playing to both black and white audiences all over the country, north and south. Around 1908, the outfit was renamed the Black Patti Musical Comedy Company. Voelckel & Nolan owned the show's assets: scenery, costumes, equipment and contracts with Patti and other principal performers. Sissieretta auditioned and selected the talent as well as ran the show on the road, a company that sometimes numbered 50 performers, musicians and crew.

It was quite a show. The first half was a musical comedy (or farce or burlesque). For this section, original music was written, and Bob Cole & J. Rosamond Johnson were among the songwriters who created shows for Black Patti. The entire company, except Sissieretta, took part in the musical comedy, either as principals or as chorus. For one show, *Darktown's Circus Day,* the stage was populated with elephants, bears, monkeys, tumblers, jugglers, peanut vendors and candy butchers as well as the usual singers, comedians and dancers.

Following an intermission, seven or eight vaudeville acts played in front of the olio. It was in this section that Black Patti made her first appearance. The acts were as varied as one might have seen in white vaudeville at the time.

Immediately after the olio acts, the curtain rose (or parted) on the concert portion. A medley of operatic arias and light classics ensued. Black Patti sometimes sang the "Miserere" from *Il Trovatore* as well as quintets and sextets with other featured singers in the show or with the chorus. Before and after the show, the orchestra played popular songs of the day, march music, waltzes and the like. The show ran nearly three hours, and Sissieretta staged the production.

Sissieretta Jones left four legacies. First, she dispelled the notion that African Americans were capable only of vernacular entertainments. After Black Patti, black women and men could aspire to serious music, even if none made a living from it. Still, the pathway was marked out for Paul Robeson, Marian Anderson, William Warfield and Roland Hayes.

Second, the success of the Black Patti shows over a score of years proved that there was both a market for well-produced, expensive African American shows and there were black men and women who were capable and inventive entrepreneurs who knew how to run and promote those shows. There were many all-black minstrel companies touring the USA during the period before the Civil War, but Black Patti's annual show was not a blacked-up minstrel show. Black Patti lit the way for the Whitman Sisters (who doubled her record to 40 years on the road), Ma Rainey, Ida Cox and other African Americans to take control of their own show-business destinies.

Third, by eschewing the minstrel show in favor of musical comedy, vaudeville and concert formats in her shows, she moved black entertainment into those new forms, especially musical comedy, that were so ably exploited by Will Marion Cook, Bob Cole & J. Rosamond Johnson, Miller & Lyles and Sissle & Blake.

Fourth, her shows were an incubator of black talent: Ernest Hogan, Ada Overton and Billy Johnson were among the many alumni.

After her last season with her Troubadours in 1916, she retired to her home in Providence and became active in her church. By the time she died in 1933 at age 64, her savings were spent, and she was dependent upon the kindness of neighbors and friends.

HARRY BLACKSTONE

b: (Henri Bouton) 27 September 1883, Chicago, IL—d: 17 November 1965, Los Angeles, CA

The high priests of vaudeville magic were many, but few, possible Houdini alone, were as famous as "Blackstone, King of Magicians." He was deeply theatrical in voice and manner. Dapper, he dressed in white tie and tails, and his vigorous mane of white hair, black bushy eyebrows and riverboat gambler's mustache confirmed the look of the prototypical stage magician. Every cartoon drawn of some fictional magician seemed to resemble Blackstone.

Blackstone had come a long way since the days in Chicago when he, as a 17-year-old working in a Chicago cabinetmaker's shop, helped make trick boxes for a supplier of magic equipment. Harry was intrigued by magic; as a youngster, he watched the great stage magician Kellar at McVickers Theatre in Chicago.

For several years, Harry played local dates at small-time vaudeville houses, lodge halls and church events.

In 1908, he was added to an acrobatic act, the Famous Byrne Brothers, and assisted in some of the tumbling and performed sleight of hand. He got billing in his next endeavor, even though it was not in his own name. Marini & Maxmillian was a comedy magic act in which Bobby Landis, the fellow who owned the act, was the comic assistant and Harry assumed the role of Marini and did the serious magic tricks. The act must have enjoyed some success because Harry persuaded his brother, Peter, to put together their own vaudeville comedy magic act, "Harry Bouton & Co.: Straight and Crooked Magic." Harry, dressed formally, performed the tricks; Peter, dressed as a clown, provided comedy relief as a bumbling magician. They played the Midwest, Great Plains and Pacific Coast on Sullivan & Considine time for a couple of seasons, 1910–11 and 1911–12.

During the early period of Blackstone's vaudeville career, he employed a number of stage names: LeRoy Boughton, the Great Stanley, Beaumont the Great, C. Porter Norton and Fredrik the Great.

There are two versions of how Henri Bouton became Fredrik the Great. In both cases, Harry had bought from a printer, for pennies on the dollar, a large supply of playbills advertising Fredrik the Great, another magician who had defaulted on his order and failed to tour. Unknown is whether Blackstone first appeared as Fredrik the Great before or during the First World War (1914–18). In one version, Pete and Harry disbanded their act around 1913, and Harry then went out as Fredrik the Great. In a competing version, one advanced by his son, Harry Blackstone Jr., Harry Sr. did not appear as Fredrik the Great until the 1917–18 season. The latter report of events seems suspect because of the wartime hysteria about Huns and all things German. Entertainers across the USA with German names, like The Four Marx Brothers, were, for the duration, changing their names or the spelling to variants (Marks Brothers) that did not betray German origins. Harry would have endangered his growing popularity with a sizable portion of the American populace had he appeared as Fredrik the Great in 1917 and 1918.

Other sources confirm that it was at some point during the First World War that Harry assumed his final stage name, Blackstone. Even the choice of this name is freighted with conflicting explanations. At various times, he claimed it was his vgrandmother's maiden name; other times, he said he had admired the look and sound of the name upon seeing it adorning a hotel or a cigar box.

For 50 years, Blackstone, the Master Magician was a leading stage act. He inclined to the sensational, as had a predecessor, the Great Albini. Indeed, upon the latter's death in 1913, Harry purchased portions of Albini's apparatus and began expanding his act from prestidigitation to large-scale illusions that he invested with the trace of narrative. In one, he was abducted by the Ku Klux Klan (KKK), tied up in a sack, hoisted ten feet above the stage and then shot by a Klansman on horseback. The sack fell to the stage floor. The Klansman dismounted and crossed to the sack center stage, doffed his hood and revealed himself as Blackstone. Then the horse was led into a tent and made to vanish.

In another illusion, "The Living Miracle," he sawed a lady in half with a large buzz saw, like the Pearl White silent-movie serials of the time. (The first version of sawing a woman in two, as the trick was known, reportedly was devised by P. T. Selbit [Percy Thomas Tibbles], an inventor and magician; however, other claimants were Horace Goldin and the Great Leon.) The difference between Blackstone's act and other sawing-the-lady-in-half acts was that Blackstone did not encase her in a box but had her stretched out in view as the saw passed through her. The KKK routine is insensitive to modern sensibilities, just as the faked dismemberment by saws and piercing of young women by swords and florescent tubes seem tasteless a century later, but they were presented unabashedly at the time.

In place of the somber and deliberate demeanor of many of his predecessors, Blackstone performed with a quicker pace and adopted a lighter tone; the point of his presentation was fun mingled with surprise and awe. Illustrative of his tongue-in-cheek approach was when a young female assistant crawled out of view into a row of automobile tires. Blackstone reached in to pull her out, but all that emerged was the young lady's costume. Other assistants then removed and rolled each tire, one by one, to the other side of the stage and stacked them in a single column. A rope was lowered into the hole at the center of the tires, and when it was raised, there was the lady clothed in a different costume. In two versions of a disappearing act, Blackstone made a horse and a camel vanish. Blackstone was sometimes the victim as well as the perpetrator. He was "Blasted to Bits at the Mouth of a Canon," and as the noise ceased and the smoke cleared, the master himself walked onstage from the wings, immaculately dressed and groomed.

For all the trappings of his great illusions, Blackstone was also noted for his escape feats and his smaller magical illusions. Blackstone's two major rivals in vaudeville of the late 1910s and 1920s were Harry Houdini and Thurston. Houdini's ability to garner publicity was the envy of everyone in vaudeville. His successful escapes while chained and suspended from cranes, imprisoned in jails, handcuffed and locked in trunks or immersed in water tanks earned front-page notices in each city along his vaudeville route. Blackstone's escapes were similar. He was trussed, nailed into crates and lowered into harbors, among other ruses, to claim a share of the publicity. It worked, but Houdini was synonymous with escape.

Blackstone also scored heavily with audiences for his smaller-scale illusions. He invited children and adults onstage to observe close at hand as he made a dove vanish from its cage and reappear in "The Vanishing Bird Cage," turned a rabbit into a box of chocolates and back into a rabbit in the "Nest of Boxes," or made a handkerchief dance around the stage as "The Spirit Handkerchief." His appearances were very well produced, and Harry Blackstone did not miss a trick when it came to merchandising. He was among the first entertainers or producers to offer color souvenir brochures, as early as the 1920s, to retail books of parlor tricks for the aspiring amateur and to pen a serious essay on stage magic.

By 1930, after more than a decade as a vaudeville headliner, Blackstone was faced with the decline of vaudeville. Although this development ended or curtailed the careers of many stage magicians, Blackstone, like Thurston, took control of his fate and moved his act into the realm of evening-length entertainments.

Throughout the 1930s, Blackstone played in the better remaining vaudeville houses, new movie theatres, presentation houses and concert halls coast to coast, season after season. Blackstone had become the undisputed box-office draw in magic until Dante, who had come to the USA from Europe in 1940, built a challenging reputation. During the Second World War, Blackstone performed for servicemen and women through the auspices of the USO.

In the 1950s and 1960s, a Blackstone appearance was an occasion because he had more or less retired. He was not out of the public eye, however, and he was very friendly toward fans, old and new alike, often performing some card tricks at a moment's notice.

He married three times. His son, Harry Blackstone Jr., was born to Harry Sr. and his second wife. Harry retired with his third wife to Los Angeles, where he was welcomed as an honored member of the Magic Castle, an organization of fellow professionals and talented amateurs.

HARRY BLACKSTONE JR.

b: 30 June 1934, Three Rivers, MI— d: 14 May 1997, Loma Linda, CA

Unlike others who became stage magicians because as children they had been spellbound in a theatre as they watched their first illusionist, Harry Blackstone was not enthralled as he watched from the wings as his famous dad performed his act. Even if he had the urge to perform, there seemed little useful purpose in becoming a magician and risking unfavorable comparisons with his talented and experienced father. It was inevitable, however, that he learned tricks from his father and his uncle Peter (who had been his dad's first partner). His mother and father had divorced while Harry Jr. was still a youngster, and the father retained custody of the son. Off and on, young Harry accompanied his father on tour and occasionally assisted in the act. Harry Jr. went to college and earned a graduate degree before he took up the family profession.

Harry Jr. grew up during the 1940s. As a boy, he witnessed the demise of big-time vaudeville, the uncertainty of the Second World War and the cessation of hostilities. There was little room in the entertainment world in the 1950s and 1960s for large magic acts except in major nightclubs and casinos and in the occasional guest shots on TV variety shows. It was not an encouraging period for a budding magician.

Nightclubs, it is true, offered a place for the prestidigitator whose tricks were most impressive when performed close to the audience. Neither the limited stage space nor the salaries paid to nightclub acts could support large-scale illusions. After Las Vegas blossomed in the 1960s and the hotels and their performance rooms grew ever larger and grander, major illusion acts like Siegfried & Roy, David Copperfield and Doug Henning began to play there and on Broadway.

Even had Blackstone Jr. wished to follow his father's trade, he first had to deal with another war. After serving during the Korean War and finishing university, he found himself on the periphery of show business as a radio announcer, a tour manager for the national company of the musical *Hair* and working with the Smothers Brothers on their TV show.

After his father's death in 1965, Harry Jr. assembled the tricks he knew well into a nightclub act. He also performed it as part of the *Holiday on Ice* show of 1965. The Blackstone name was still a draw, but Harry Jr. had to prove himself a worthy successor, which he did through many performances on the then-vibrant Playboy Club circuit and appearances on late-night television shows, variety programs and eventually HBO specials.

In the mid-1970s, Harry Jr. decided to re-create in some measure his father's spectacular evening-length show. Some of the paraphernalia Harry Sr. had employed was still usable; other equipment had to be fabricated. It proved very expensive to produce and transport the show, and the worry of paying back the investment haunted Harry; however, the result rewarded his courage. The show toured more than 1,509 cities and then opened on 13 May 1980 on Broadway, where it ran for 118 performances. He had resurrected his father's buzz-saw illusion, the dancing handkerchief and floating lightbulb, the vanishing birdcage and the vanishing elephant.

In 1983, the Broadway show was adapted into a two-hour extravaganza, *Magic!!! Starring Blackstone,* filmed for PBS television. He also hosted and performed in a 13-part series on magic for Australian television.

During the 1980s and early 1990s, Harry Blackstone Jr. appeared on television occasionally, performed in industrial shows and took his act to Las Vegas. He was six weeks short of his 63rd birthday when he died of pancreatic cancer.

JAMES A. BLAND

b: 22 October 1854, Flushing, NY—
d: 5 May 1911, Philadelphia, PA

"Oh, Dem Golden Slippers," "Carry Me Back to Old Virginny," "Hand Me Down My Walking Cane" and "In the Evening by the Moonlight" were standards of minstrel shows, black and white, and were sung for more than a century after their composition by James A. Bland.

Not only was Jim Bland a trained musician who was graduated from Howard University, he was a second-generation college man, a rarity for a Negro in mid-nineteenth-century America. His father, Allan M. Bland, who was descended from a long line of free African Americans who had settled in Charlestown, South Carolina, held degrees from Wilberforce University and Oberlin College. Jim's mother came from Delaware, where her family, also freemen, had settled.

Like many others, though, the family moved north. When Allan Bland received an appointment to the U.S. Patent Office as an examiner, the first nonwhite to attain that position, he moved his family from Flushing, New York, where James was born, to Washington, D.C. The elder Bland later studied law at Howard at the same time that his son, James, was an undergraduate.

It was at Howard that Jim Bland became intrigued by nonclassical music. He was proficient on the banjo and began writing tunes based on what he heard sung by the former slaves who maintained the property and grounds at Howard. It did not please his family when James decided in 1873 that he preferred show business to the professional life his father had pioneered. The fact that minstrel-show work required Jim to black up must have been especially painful to his parents.

After an apprenticeship of sorts with lesser outfits, James, at age 24, was engaged by Sprague's Georgian Minstrels but barely worked a season before he switched to the most prestigious troupe of its time, Haverly's Genuine Colored Minstrels. Bland also enjoyed a string of songwriting successes. "Carry Me Back to Old Virginny" (1878) was a song well suited in melody, tempo and sentiment to a performer who played Uncle Tom roles in plantation scenes or in afterpieces condensed from the full-length *Uncle Tom's Cabin.* "Oh, Dem Golden Slippers" (1879) quickly became a standard for the walk-arounds of many minstrel shows. "In the Evening by the Moonlight" (1880), perfect for afterpieces, was soon known across the land.

Bland was at the height of his powers. He had developed into a versatile man of show business: a singer, dancer, comedian and actor but was best known for his songwriting and his humorous monologues that varied show to show. In 1881 the Haverly troupe left the USA for London. Although the company returned home after two rewarding seasons, Bland stayed until 1896, playing the music-halls in England and the occasional tour of Ireland and Germany. He became a pet of London's smart set and the English royal family, who delighted in many African American performers. Several times during his decade-and-a-half abroad, Bland returned to the USA for some engagements, but London was home.

The good life took precedence over his career. Work and reputation dwindled. By 1900, Bland's comic style was regarded as old-fashioned in comparison with the younger generation of comedians. Although he continued to write songs, his music seemed old-fashioned as well, as he wrote in the same minstrel style of a generation earlier and ignored the then-current ragtime rhythms. He spent the last decade of his life in the USA, touring black vaudeville and clubs when he could get engagements.

Even impoverished, Bland liked to put up a good front and continued to see friends like Eubie Blake and Tom Fletcher. When he could manage that pose no longer, he disappeared from view. Although his songs were still being sung, some often included in concerts of Negro spirituals, James Bland was forgotten. He was living in a Philadelphia rooming house when he died of pneumonia at age 56.

A generation after his death, black scholars restored Bland to his rightful place in popular music. He copyrighted about three dozen songs, three or four of which became lasting entries in minstrel and concert repertoires. His songs were as popular as Stephen Foster's, but Jim Bland never married and his family lost contact with him, so there was no one who could look after his copyrights. His music was copied and performed, often without crediting Bland as the composer and lyricist. In time, it was not uncommon for people to assume that "Carry Me Back to Old Virginny," "Oh, Dem Golden Slippers" and "In the Evening by the Moonlight" were penned by Stephen Foster.

BLOCK & SULLY

Jesse Block

b: 16 December 1900, New York, NY— d: 22 March 1983, New York, NY

Eve Sully

b: 1902, Atlantic City, NJ—d: 7 August 1990, New York, NY

Most comic characterizations are at least as venerable as their *commedia dell'arte* prototypes. One is more a symptom of its times: the smart, somewhat exasperated boyfriend and the dizzy girlfriend. This duo was a staple of vaudeville and radio from the 1920s through the 1940s, and it was the core of more than a few early television situation comedy series.

Block & Sully were among the best, but they failed to show sufficient interest or to make a deal to appear on network radio or in movies, so they faded from the collective memory sooner than Burns & Allen, Fred Allen and Portland Hoffa, Goodman & Jane Ace (The Easy Aces), Ken Murray and Marie Wilson (who starred on "My Friend Irma"), Lucille Ball & Desi Arnaz, or Joan Davis and Jim Backus (*I Married Joan*). Sponsors and moviemakers may have feared that Block & Sully were a bit too urban and Jewish for mass-media audiences.

Manhattan's Lower East Side at the turn of the twentieth century was likely the single largest incubator of successful vaudevillians in America. The list is long, and Jesse Block is on it. He began in amateur contests then played neighborhood vaudeville houses as a member of Nine Crazy Kids (a group that included Howie and Bert Gordon, the future Mad Russian of radio). The Gerry Society, powerful in New York City, hounded Nine Crazy Kids and other child acts out of town.

Jesse grabbed a few small parts in acts going on the road until, at 14, he successfully auditioned for a Gus Edwards' troupe. The subsequent tour on the big-time Orpheum circuit offered experiences that were typical of his age and the times: pretending to be younger than he was to qualify for discounted train fare, living in boardinghouses and sending money home when he did not lose his pay in craps games.

Unless boys or girls were quite small for their ages, reaching 15 or 16 meant leaving Gus Edwards' kiddy acts. Jesse was hired to join three other kids, including future Warner Brothers' utility player Frank McHugh, to tour in an act called "Sweeties." From 1922 to 1926, Jesse partnered with a young woman, Frances Dunlap. As Block & Dunlap, they made a living but did not break through to the front ranks. In 1926, old friend Bert Gordon introduced Jesse to Eve Sully.

Jesse Block and Eve Sully

Chroniclers remarked on the resemblance between the Block & Sully act and the Burns & Allen act. The two couples were dear and longtime friends. They swapped material and sometimes hired the same freelancers to write material for them. Jesse and George Burns were both accomplished straight men. George was not much taller than Gracie, but Jesse was a foot taller than Eve. From reports, Jesse's character was more patient with Eve than George's character was with Gracie, but Burns' character mellowed appreciably around 1940.

Both Eve Sully and Gracie Allen were petite attractive brunettes, and they could handle identical jokes. The difference was in motive and manner. Gracie Allen was always very ladylike and sincerely convinced of the logic that guided her. Eve was mischievous, and she had a "Noo Yawk" accent and a Jewish lilt to her delivery. After she teased Jesse with some tortured reasoning, she triumphantly giggled. Like Burns & Allen, Block & Sully topped off their cross-talk comedy with a song-and-dance finish.

Block & Sully

Block & Sully

Block & Sully reached the big time around 1928, as vaudeville was declining. They managed to play the Palace in 1929 and 1930 while it still boasted its two-a-day policy. They played big-time houses all over the USA, went to England, and played top variety theatres, including London's Palladium. When two-a-day vaudeville gave up the ghost and the larger houses converted to a presentation policy, Block & Sully headlined in them (Jesse sometimes doubled as emcee), and the pair earned a good income. In 1930, they married.

They appeared on radio, including the 25 March 1934 edition of Eddie Cantor's *Chase & Sanborn Hour,* and hosted their own show for a short time. Vitaphone, Paramount, Pathé and other studios filmed and released short subjects built around vaudeville acts. Sometimes the studio simply photographed a current act; other times they manufactured a slight plot and used elements of the stage act. There are reports that Block & Sully made several, but their claim to immortality rests on one feature film, *Kid Millions* (1934).

Eddie Cantor was the star, and he did a routine with Eve that was the most engaging in the entire movie. Jesse, who normally would have fed the lines to Eve, was relegated to a comparatively minor role as Eve's intended:

Eddie: "Where do I get a-hold of your father?"
Eve: "I dunno; he's awfully ticklish."
Eddie: "Go 'way. I can't talk to an idiot."
Eve: "C'm 'ere. I can." [cackle]

Block & Sully stayed in vaudeville through the 1930s. When the USO was formed, they volunteered to head overseas units. According to Marian Spitzer, author of *The Palace,* they engaged in covert activity for the United States government while entertaining the troops.

After the Second World War, they left show business. They had always been sensible and smart. Jesse worked in the stock market, rising to an executive position in the firm Bache and Company. Eve devoted her time to charity work. They continued to be part of the showbiz community. Jesse was admired for his dry wit. One time, he and Jack Benny decided to see America leisurely as they traveled from Los Angeles to New York. (Both had apartments in New York City.) Instead of taking the Super Chief train, they hired a chauffeured limousine and driver. As they were getting in the limousine, Jesse turned to Jack, "Let me sit near the door, I get out first."

Eve and Jesse remained married for 53 years until Jesse's death.

BLOOLIPS

Bette Bourne

b: (P. G. Bourne) September 1939, East London, UK

Precious Pearl

b: (Paul Shaw) ca. 1956, Little Hampton, UK

Diva Dan

b: (Danny Barratt) ca. 1945, Tyneside, UK—d: ca. 1988

Lavinia Co-op

b: (Vincent Fox) ca. 1956, London, England

Clockwise from top L: Lavina Co-op, Dottie Spot, Marge Mellow, Bette Bourne, Precious Pearl, and Diva Dan

Bloolips are "originals, not without sources, but without compare," as Laurie Stone observed in *Laughing in the Dark: A Decade of Subversive Laughter*, a compilation of pieces she wrote for *The Village Voice*. Bloolips (though they prefer all capitals) are unique because their sources are many. In their characterizations and performances are traces of panto dames, music-hall turns, American burlesque sketches, the spirit of Weimar cabaret, punked-out drag-queen antics, the bad-boy punning literacy of a Footlights Club show, and, just every once in a while in every show, the scent of something exquisite and sadly lovely.

Each Bloolips show is a collaboration of various talented people such as John Taylor (an Australian ideas man and original writer), Ray Dobbins, musicians Dick Cox of London and La Belle Martyn of New Zealand, and, of course, Bloolips founder Bette Bourne and other members of the troupe.

In the 1970s, Bette (pronounced "Betty") Bourne had been a professional actor with good credits when he got caught up in the Gay Liberation Front and sought an expression in performance more relevant to his life, work that would demand from himself more than that of a jobbing actor. Jimmy Camicia's Hot Peaches, an American troupe on tour in Europe in 1976, offered an alternative, and Bette joined the company for the remainder of the tour.

In 1977, rallying a few others, including Diva Dan and Precious Pearl, Bette and John Taylor founded Bloolips. Their earliest productions were *I'm Just Myself, The Ugly Duckling, Cheek, Vamp & Camp* and *Yum-Yum,* all performed within their first two seasons as a troupe.

They are proudly a drag act, a daft one. No attempt is made to portray women; they are queer men in frocks, but their welfare wardrobe will disappoint those who crave bugle-beaded trumpet gowns. Their costumes are oddly spiffed-up thrift-shop finds, like one of Bette's gowns that was trimmed with two dozen identical tea strainers dangling from the hem. Bloolips perform in whiteface—their features drawn in primary-colored daubs—and the result is midway between a Pierrot troupe and the faces in Max Beckman's post-war expressionist paintings. Audiences, gay as well as straight, that expect another *La Cage aux Folles* minstrel show or drag queens who channel Judy Garland and Marilyn Monroe, instead find clown faces and rubbish-bin wardrobe. Bloolips spoofs glamour.

During the quarter of a century that the Bloolips troupe has pulled itself together to present comedy and musical burlesks (with decreasing frequency, sadly), individual members of the group have come and gone, some wandering stars like Dottie Spot, Marge Mellow, Babs Yerankle and Naughty Knickers, but four held steady and remained paramount for most of Bloolips' existence.

Constant has been Bette Bourne. Offstage, his mien is that of a disciplined and serious classical actor, flinty and not patient with fatuity. His superb theatre voice, not put on, evokes Tallulah Bankhead on Quaaludes but less harsh and more musical. Onstage, he performs with physical economy and never is a note held too long or a line punched too hard. There is a dark, old-world cabaret quality about Bette—a bite. When he sang "Don't Give Nothin' Away," the bitterness was startling. Yet, in another scene, he simply ironed a garment in the half-light, occasionally cocking an ear to an "Ave Maria" hovering like birdsong in a garden—a poignant if ambiguous vignette.

When the troupe numbered a half dozen or so in the 1980s, Bette portrayed the theatrical star in the grand manner, contending with the squabbling of the gaggle of silly geese who shared his stage. Each member of the troupe was highly individual, but they orbited around Bette.

When not playing in Bloolips, Bette Bourne has acted in the theatres of the West End in London, film, television, Off-Broadway and on world tours in one-person shows. In addition to sharing several ensemble awards to Bloolips, including two Obies, Bette has won a clutch of individual awards for his performances in London and New York, among which were a 2000–01 season Obie for his portrayal of Quentin Crisp in the one-man drama *Resident Alien,* by Tim Fountain. Bourne's work is as varied as theatre productions of *The Importance of Being Earnest* and *Sarrasine,* an esoteric music drama by Bartlett and Bloomfield, and television's *The Avengers.*

Over a score of years, Precious Pearl (Paul Shaw) has come into his own as Bette Bourne's primary stage partner. His slightly off-kilter innocence is foil to Bette's elegant and world-weary decadence. Their onstage relationship of the worldly wise senior and his guileless junior is as old as burlesque comedy. Dressed in a cluster of bubbles with a dotty dollop of something atop his head, Pearl is childlike rather than angelic, as direct as Bette is devious.

At one point in their *BLOO Review: A Retrospectacle* (1997–98), Paul shucked his Pearl persona and drag to portray a not-quite-young male actor of disappointing prospects, whose customary work was tending bar at a theatre. In the monologue written expressly for Paul and drawn from playwright Neil Bartlett's *Night After Night,* the barman careens between resentment and a low assessment of self. At one point, Paul stepped toward the audience and offered a drink to a person in the front row; when it was accepted, he petulantly withdrew the proffered drink. It shocked because the pettiness of the new character was at odds with Pearl's personality. In the early 1990s, Paul took a male role in *Belle Reprieve,* a gender-bending take on Tennessee William's *A Streetcar Named Desire.* When not performing with Bloolips, or otherwise onstage, Mr. Shaw is a landscape architect.

Lavinia Co-op, as much dancer and mime as clown, was with Bloolips from 1977 for more than a decade. Although Lavinia could tear into a whirling queen of the Wilis, more usually he wafted about, looking as unworldly as an Arthur Rackham faerie. Like a swan among geese, he shunned his cast mates' bickering to search for Truth and Beauty. A *New York Times* review praised Lavinia as a "wonderfully eccentric comedian and mime." Early on, he studied at the London School of Contemporary Dance, and he was in his element in *Living Leg-ends* when he and the others, improbably cast as virginal Bennington dancers of the 1930s, genteelly frolicked with a billowing gauzy fabric to Debussy's "Clare de Lune." Looking more the grand dame in the 1990s, Lavinia has continued to perform in New York and London, often in cabaret, occasionally in plays, sometimes solo in performance works such as *Frock-Off* and *Installation InStilettos.*

For a number of seasons in the 1980s, Diva Dan was an audience favorite. Whatever inconvenience his profound deafness caused in his civilian life, in performance it seemed no handicap and, indeed, blessed him with a flat airy lisp and highly individual timing. Amid Pearl's prissiness, Lavinia's ethereality and the flurry of other Bloolips clucking around Bette, their mother duck superior, Dan picked his way along a skewed orbit. He looked working-class ordinary, something of the neighborhood biddy with a plain pudding face. Dan's stage character, however, regarded himself far more grandly.

Barmaid proud and sure of his allure and star quality, Dan veered from sweet and saintly to Beatrice Lillie hauteur. In each of the Bloolips shows, at least one song—such as "Star Quality"—was assigned solo to Diva Dan. Though he sang in straightforward manner instead of obviously trying to get laughs, he drifted in and out of pitch. His rendition brought down the house. As Bette Bourne noted, "but he felt the rhythms; that's why he was our best tap dancer."

Lust in Space (1978–80), a farce with music, won Bloolips critical plaudits, the first of their Obie awards from *The Village Voice,* and packed in smart audiences at alternative theatres in England and across the United States. *Lust in Space* was the show that introduced Bloolips to the USA. When asked why they were drawing sell-out houses in America's Midwest, Bette suggested, "Maybe it's because we're like vaudeville and there isn't a lot of vaudeville around."

Their follow-up show, *Living Leg-ends* (1981–83), artistically ambitious and so successful that it toured for several years, found Bette-"Bourne-Again" seeking spiritual balm. Bette's quest, which he foisted upon the rest of the troupe, took them from the Dawn of Chaos to the Age of Reason, but Bette quickly rejected that "elitist minority rubbish" and decided to find fulfillment through staging the biggest best seller of all time, *The Bible.* The project bogged down in Eden when Eve declined the apple proffered by the serpent, sending Genesis back for a rewrite: Diva Dan as Eve demurred, "Don't fancy it. Sets my teeth on edge." Time danced on, however, and so did Bloolips as a Greek Chorus, flagellant penitents, hippies in a time warp and boom-boom-room ballerinas.

Odds 'n' Sods (c. 1983) was a compilation revue of numbers and bits from previous shows that the troupe presented upon their return home to London. Much of it was the foundation for the revue *Sticky Buns* (1983–84). More Bloolips shows carried the troupe through the 1980s and into the 1990s: *Slungback and Strapless* (Bloolips meets Madame Mao), *Teenage Trash* (1987) "a very up tragedy" about the repression of youth, sexual and societal, and *Get-Hur* (1991–92), which depicted Rex and sex in the time of Hadrian.

Belle Reprieve (1992) earned an ensemble Obie for Bette (Blanche DuBois), Precious Pearl (billed as Paul Shaw), Peggy Shaw (Stanley Kowalski), and Lois Weaver (Stella) of Split Britches, a lesbian troupe. It was respected, confounded some of their fans and suggested that a Bloolips show was becoming a more occasional event.

Despite their considerable success and reputation, it was difficult to keep a full company with musicians together, though its members did not expect star fees. Unlike the days of music-hall, variety and vaudeville, there was no longer a clearly defined route on which a company set forth each year. In the 1980s and 1990s, bookings had to be patched together: London, New York, Boston, Chicago, Minneapolis, San Francisco, Seattle and Alaska. Doubtless, there was the tug between individual horizons and company goals.

For the 1994–95 season, Bloolips (minus Precious Pearl) was back, this time on *The Island of Lost Shoes.* Depressed with gathering age ("enough past the four dozen mark to make an omelet") and needing renewal, Bette rounded up his troupe and headed for the Greek Isles. On route, their plane began "losing attitude." Fortunately, it crashed harmlessly on *The Island of Lost Shoes.* Instead of palms, they found shoe trees, but there were no pairs because, "Well, they aren't pear trees." Wardrobe trunks washed ashore frequently enough that Bette, Lavinia and the others had enough costume changes for many musical numbers. A menacing monster was civilized with gifts of makeup—a triumph of diplomacy in foreign relations.

The final Bloolips show of the twentieth century was *BLOOLIPS: A Retrospectacle* (1997–98), alternatively titled *The BLOO Review,* a series of sketches, cross talk, songs and tap dances from previous shows that were routined into a vaudeville show. New items were added: Pearl/Paul's barman's monologue, a scene from Oscar Wilde's *The Importance of Being Earnest* with Paul as Jack Worthing and Bette as Lady Bracknell, a role he recently had toured in Britain, and Bette's rendition of "The Boy I Love Is up in the Balcony," a rowdy salute to music-hall favorite Marie Lloyd.

Bette and Pearl were joined by Nicolas Bloomfield, who wrote two of the songs, played the piano score and assisted in several bits, one of which is among the most loved Bloolips numbers. To a playback of a full orchestral recording of "The 1812 Overture," Nicolas and Pearl, as servants, helped Bette, as Marie Antoinette, don her duds. In a pool of warm stage light, Marie stood in her flimsies, still as a statue, as her servants dithered hither and yon for various garments and accessories, though they managed to dress her efficiently in time with the music. Together they lifted Marie onto foot-high platform shoes, and a wedding cake of a wig was plopped on her head. Panniers were brought forth, but this being Bloolips, two collapsible ironing boards, about three feet long, must serve. They were attached horizontally from her waist, like airplane wings, and draped with fabric. As the music built to its crescendo, Marie Antoinette was hooked into her gown, festooned with gewgaw jewelry and readied for empire. The stage business had been timed perfectly with the finale of the cannons roaring and the cymbals crashing, but instead of the expected blackout, harsh stage working lights were raised. There alone stood Bette, as the stage manager called over the sound system: "Sorry, Bette, that number's not 'till the second half." Bette's huge panniers block several attempts to exit the stage with dignity. Defeated, Bette hikes up his gown, snaps the ironing boards into a vertical position, turns and clumps off the stage.

Bette and Pearl returned later in the program as two grousing harpies in matted wigs and shapeless, soiled dresses. Clasped together in a death dance, they snarled hateful insults with the contempt of a familiarity that ensured dependency. They sketched within a few bars of music what Edward Albee detailed in two acts of *Who's Afraid of Virginia Woolf?*

During the 2004 and 2005 seasons, Bette Bourne acted in *Deep Rimming in Poplar,* another solo show written by Tim Fountain, and he followed that with *Theatre of Blood,* a farce staged at the National Theatre, that costarred Bette with Jim Broadbent.

BLUE

In relation to performance, the term *blue* means "off-color," referring to sexually suggestive or outright lewd routines. There were posted warnings in theatres, particularly in Keith houses, forbidding the use of profanity, sexual material and even some of the milder oaths. Doing blue material in vaudeville was cause for cancellation. In burlesque, it could get the show closed and the performers hauled off to the hoosegow.

There is some debate as to why the term blue came to be employed to denote material deemed lewd. After all, true *blue* and *blue book* point to acceptable, even preferred qualities and conditions. Some hold that early laws forbidding certain practices were originally written on blue paper and hence were referred to as blue laws. Others note that editors and censors used to employ blue ink and blue pencil to underline or cross out unwanted or objectionable words and phrases.

BEN BLUE

b: (Benjamin Bernstein) 12 September 1901, Montreal, QC—d: 7 March 1975, Hollywood, CA

George Burns said there were two comedians who could make him laugh just looking at them. W. C. Fields was one. Ben Blue was the other. Ben often had a wistful look, his mouth hanging slightly open, as though he were hoping to be scratched behind the ears or taken for a romp. When ignored and dismissed, he looked hurt and a bit cowed, like a puppy.

He moved like a lively puppy. A rail-thin natural-born dancer who never had a lesson in his life, Ben Blue became a vaudeville headliner. At age 13, Ben won several amateur-night shows in Baltimore, where his family had relocated from Montreal. He began picking up work as a chorus boy in his midteens and started traveling with shows. Having a natural bent for comedy, he put together the first of his vaudeville acts, combining eccentric dancing with comic pantomime. Years later, analyzing Ben Blue, Ed Wynn said he did not work hard enough at his act, and there is likely some truth in that. Physical things, pantomime and dancing, came easily to him, and he seems to have spent more energy trying to be a businessman. He was 20, and still appearing in vaudeville, when he opened several dance studios in the Midwest. Many years later, he tried to run nightclubs while appearing in them.

Ben Blue

Ben Blue belongs in the ranks of eccentric dancer comedians and pantomimists: Leon Errol, James Barton, Charlotte Greenwood and Ray Bolger. Unlike them, however, Blue did not have a strong comic characterization, a strong particular personality that suggested a certain type like Barton's drunk, Errol's philanderer or Bolger's clumsy suitor. After vaudeville slowed down and Ben Blue switched to movies, he became too much a utility player, and directors cast Ben as an amiable best buddy, a wise guy, a college boy, a taxi driver, a sailor, a stagehand, an artist, a hillbilly, a clown or a handyman. Sometimes Ben was the romantic male lead's best buddy, sometimes Blue was simply whatever uniform or costume he was given. Without much support from screenwriters or directors, Ben Blue enlivened movies with his rubber-legged pratfalls and dancing.

From 1932 until 1968, Ben made almost 40 movies in Hollywood, nearly half of which were two-reelers. In short films, he was first partnered with Billy Gilbert and then Shemp Howard. Despite excellent casts, the shorts were as unfunny and ill made as most that were ground out on a weekly basis in the 1930s and 1940s. He is probably best remembered in movies for playing the town drunk trying to emulate Paul Revere in *The Russians Are Coming, the Russians Are Coming* (1966).

Ben was among the first film stars to gravitate to television. He debuted on the *Ed Wynn Show* in 1950 and was given his own, eponymous half-hour series (with Wally Cox, Kenny Delmar and Arnold Stang in support), but it did not find an audience. Ben Blue's earliest appearances advertised him as being in the Charlie Chaplin tradition, but the large audience for Chaplin's pathos and comedy in mime had long passed, as networks discovered with Jimmy Savo.

In the 1949–50 season, Ben was engaged to provide comic relief (partnering Sid Fields) on the *Frank Sinatra Show,* an hour-long variety series during the 1950–51 season. He also had a couple of chances to become a rotating host on a comedy-variety show, but headlining single outings of *The All Star Revue* (1953) and *Saturday Night Revue* (1954) did not win him a permanent berth. Thereafter, his appearances were increasingly rare until the 1967–68 season, when he played a second lead in *Accidental Family,* a sitcom that failed.

In the late 1940s, Ben Blue got into the nightclub business as a performer and an owner-manager. He had some success with several clubs, including Ben Blue's Night Club in Santa Monica, but in the 1960s, the ventures landed him in tax trouble with the IRS. It is doubtful that he ever fully recovered financially, but he kept working as long as there was some demand for his services.

Ben Blue's one notable appearance in a Broadway revue was in the final edition of *George White's Scandals* (1939), which also starred or featured Willie & Eugene Howard, Ella Logan, The Three Stooges and Ann Miller.

Vaudeville gave him the best stage to perform his well-honed act of eccentric dancing and pantomime clowning. In a 1990 interview with an entertainment reporter, Eddie Rio, of the Rio Brothers, recalled a favorite bit by Ben Blue. Rio said when Ben worked a theatre where the orchestra pit was empty (because the house band was working on the stage that week), Ben would don a one-piece old-fashioned striped bathing suit and start dancing. When he made an exceptional move that motivated the audience to applaud, he stopped dancing and walked toward the footlights, applauding the audience for applauding his trick. Then he tripped over the footlights and fell face forward into the pit. All the audience could see were hands waving in the air and a spurt of water gushing up as if he were drowning. Then the hands disappeared and a giant periscope rose up over the edge of the pit and started scanning the audience left to right, then right to left. The periscope went down, and Ben popped up in the pit holding a giant rubber fish that appeared to be attacking him. After disposing of his aquatic adversary, Ben climbed over the front wall of the pit as the audience applauded, then sat in the lap of any guy or gal in the front row. He would look for a bald guy so he could kiss the top of his head, because that always got a laugh. Then he walked back to the stage and finished his act. Eddie Rio said that even when you knew what was coming you could not help laughing because that guy had such a remarkable face.

Throughout the 1920s and into the 1930s, Ben played the big time, including the Palace Theatre in its two-a-day incarnation and its post-1932 multiple-show format in which variety acts shared the bill with a movie.

In 1952, the 19 weeks that Judy Garland headlined her show gave Broadway the false hope that vaudeville was back, and the Palace tried to revive classic nine-act vaudeville bills. The week following Judy's closing, Ben Blue was prominently placed along with opera singer Lauritz Melchior and comedian Jean Carroll on a full bill of nine acts. The bill got good reviews, but it did not sell, nor did subsequent traditional nine-act bills. If vaudeville was indeed back at the Palace for a few years in the 1950s, it needed Judy Garland, Betty Hutton, Danny Kaye, Jerry Lewis or Harry Belafonte as drawing cards, and the bills were changed to give the superstar the entire second half of the show.

BOARDINGHOUSES AND HOTELS

While on the road, it was far more usual for vaudevillians—and actors and burlesquers—to stay in boardinghouses than in hotels. A major star might patronize a hotel, but decent hotels were often too expensive for show folk. Even if affordable, hotel management considered *civilians* more respectable than entertainers, and the suspicious atmosphere was inhibiting. Performers and actors usually relaxed more in the company of their own kind.

In small towns there was little choice; performers put up at the only digs available to them, a hotel or a boardinghouse, and if the performer had been wise or had enough notice, he booked ahead. For traveling troupes of actors and for burlesque companies, there was usually an advance agent who preceded the company en route and made all the arrangements, including accommodations. In vaudeville, accommodations, like travel arrangements and transport of equipment, were usually the responsibility and the expense of each act.

There were towns where it was a toss-up as to which was worse, the hotel or the boardinghouse. Bad food, small portions, dirty rooms, infested and badly soiled mattresses and linen, all for a price that far exceeded value were some of the marks of the worst boardinghouses (and hotels). If there were neither hotel nor boardinghouse, the railroad stationmaster probably knew which homes rented rooms to actors.

Invariably, the proprietors of boardinghouses were women, often widowed. The endless cleaning, cooking and dealing with the late hours, noise and occasional shenanigans of show folk were a trial for some unhappy souls, and they endured the hard work only to keep body and soul together. More than a few had been cheated by performers who had skipped out, owing their rent, and only the few saints among them had not hardened and grown mean.

It was an encouraging sign if a performer walked into a boardinghouse or hotel and found the public rooms filled with autographed photographs from other acts. The best boardinghouses were owned and run by retired performers or landladies who were drawn to the theatre. They were more sympathetic to their show-folk clientele, though not more gullible, and often there was a convivial atmosphere that was essential and healing to the emotional well-being of performers who moved from town to town, week after week, deprived of family and friends. The best of boardinghouses had tea ready when the act arrived after the train-wagon trip. Late at night, there were sandwiches ready in the kitchen when the acts returned from the theatre.

The difference between a boardinghouse and a hotel was not a matter of size; usually the former was smaller, but some large boardinghouses accommodated more guests than small hotels. Hotels were expected to be more impersonal than boardinghouses, but there were hotels whose managers actively encouraged the trade of theatre professionals and treated repeat guests like family. Yet the friendliest hotel could not equal the hospitality or price of the best theatrical boardinghouse, at which all the roomers sat around a very large dining room table, shared the same food and swapped tall tales and jokes without fear that civilians could eavesdrop or look askance.

AL BOASBERG

b: 5 December 1892, Buffalo, NY—d: 18 June 1937, Los Angeles, CA

Al Boasberg was a wholesale jewelry salesman in New York City when he made his first notable mark: he wrote for Jack Benny, who had mustered out of the U.S. Navy at the end of the First World War and needed a new act to resume his vaudeville career. Al became one of the most sought-after sketch writers in vaudeville, and he achieved long-lasting fame by writing the sketch "Lamb Chops" that made George Burns & Gracie Allen a star act.

With the decline of vaudeville, Boasberg began writing for radio comedians and for movies. He created intertitles (the on-screen printed words that carried on the narrative and spelled out dialogue) for silent films in the late 1920s and wrote dialogue for early talkies. Gradually, his credits grew to screenwriting, either solo or in partnership with others. Because of his sketch-writing experience in vaudeville, he was as adept devising physical gags as he was writing jokes and funny dialogue. Both talents were required in his Hollywood career. He wrote for comedians as diverse as the Duncan Sisters, Leon Errol, light comedian Jack Mulhall, Charlotte Greenwood, Buster Keaton, Jack Benny, Olsen & Johnson, Charlie Ruggles, Harpo Marx, Wheeler & Woolsey, Harold Lloyd, Ted Healy and The Three Stooges. He also directed nine short comedies, half of which starred Leon Errol.

BOFFO

Used to indicate a show was a big hit, *boff* or *boffo* is thought to be a condensation of *big* at the *box office*.

RAY BOLGER

b: (Raymond Wallace Bulcao) 10 January 1904, Boston, MA—d: 15 January 1987, Los Angeles, CA

A long, tall eccentric dancer and comedian who specialized in legomania, Ray Bolger was typical of many performers and actors who become typecast by a single characterization: Mary Pickford as Little Mary, Chaplin as the Tramp, James Cagney as a tough guy and Marilyn Monroe as a sexpot. In the extreme of typecasting, one role, usually on film, sometimes becomes so identified with a performer that neither role nor actor can be freed from the association.

In films, Ray Bolger remains famous for a single role, the Scarecrow in MGM's landmark movie musical, *The Wizard of Oz,* just as Bert Lahr will forever be linked to his role as the Cowardly Lion in the same film. So complete was the identification that Bolger eclipsed Fred Stone, an equally celebrated Scarecrow of 30 years earlier and Bolger's idol.

Like Lahr, Bolger enjoyed many other successes, several as brilliant as *The Wizard of Oz,* yet all but one have dimmed with time because they were never committed to film. The exception, and his greatest personal

Ray Bolger

triumph, was attained on the Broadway stage in *Where's Charley?,* a musical adaptation of *Charley's Aunt,* a comedy chestnut about deception and confused identity that had proved popular for a half century before it was set to music for Ray Bolger. A soft-shoe ballad, "Once in Love with Amy," from the show became Bolger's signature song. This stage show was adapted for the movies, but, when Warner Brothers decided to film it in 1952, the studio sent the star and crew to England, where the remaining roles were played by British actors unknown to American audiences. Warner Brothers did not have enough confidence in the project to give it strong production values or a truly cinematic treatment. Once *Where's Charley?* was released, the studio failed to hype their movie, and it fared poorly in comparison with other Hollywood musicals that year, especially Gene Kelly's *Singin' in the Rain.* Scarecrow and Charley provided the best roles of Bolger's career, but there were many good ones as well.

Ray Bolger was born and grew up in Dorchester, a working-class neighborhood in Boston. Unlike many male vaudeville dancers of his era, such as James Barton, John Bubbles, and Jack Donahue, Bolger took dance classes. In 1922, when he was 18, Ray made his public debut in a serious dance recital, and this led to an offer to join a tab show, grandly named the Bob Ott Musical Comedy and Repertoire Company. It toured small-time vaudeville in the northeastern United States.

Bolger partnered with Ralph Sanford in a short-lived two-man dance act, Sanford & Bolger, for vaudeville. Upon reaching New York City, Bolger was hired by Gus Edwards for one of his nonkiddie vaudeville acts, "Carlton Nights." Thereafter, Ray "Rubberlegs" Bolger went solo and did well enough in vaudeville to play the Palace Theatre in 1926.

Bolger was one of several dancers who appeared on the 27 November 1932 Radio City Music Hall's inaugural bill along with Patricia Bowman and the Radio City Corps de Ballet and the Roxyettes (later the Rockettes). Two other dancers, Martha Graham and Harald Kreuzberg, were less orthodox choices. The ill-sorted combination of dance, opera, high-wire act, choir music and vaudeville comedy made for a confused variety program, and management promptly instituted a second, more enduring, policy of a major motion picture coupled with an extravaganza-type stage show for its 6,200-seat house. Only Ray Bolger and humorist Doc Rockwell were held over for the transition to the new format.

Ray married Gwen Rickard in 1929, and they stayed together nearly 60 years until Ray's death in 1987. If the longevity of his marriage was unusual, so was his dancing style. At first blush, one is tempted to include Bolger with the great hoofers in vaudeville. Strictly speaking, a hoofer is a tapper, and Ray was never one of the great tappers. Instead, he seemed to bridge the eccentric dancing comedian, typified by Leon Errol, to the modern ballet dancer of the type who worked for Agnes DeMille, Michael Kidd and Jack Cole. Think of Bolger's "Slaughter on Tenth Avenue" dance choreographed by George Balanchine.

Bolger was also an actor and a character comedian, able to take part in a story rather than be slotted as a specialty act. Those who fashioned movies or produced musical comedies for the stage soon found that Ray Bolger was a useful addition to their casts. His first Broadway show was a Shubert revue, *A Night in Paris,* which opened on 5 January 1926 and ran for the larger portion of the year. Bolger was one among several vaudeville alumni in the show; other vaude veterans included Gertrude Hoffman and Jack Pearl.

Bolger next shared the stage with star Victor Moore in one of Rodgers & Hart's lesser musical comedies, *Heads Up!* Paul Gerard Smith, a well-known vaudeville sketch writer, was called in to punch up the libretto, and the show kept the lights on at the Alvin Theatre for 144 performances, beginning on 11 November 1929, despite the recent stock-market crash. The 1931 edition of *George White's Scandals* had a great cast headed by Willie & Eugene Howard, Ethel Merman, Rudy Vallee and Alice Faye as well as Ray Bolger. Its six-month run of 204 performances at the downtown Apollo Theater on 42nd Street was considered a solid success as the Great Depression deepened. In 1934, John Murray Anderson provided Broadway and the Shuberts with a first-class revue in *Life Begins at 8:40.* Bolger joined Bert Lahr, Frances Williams, Luella Gear, Dixie Dunbar and Brian Donlevy for 238 performances at the Winter Garden beginning on 27 August.

Ray was a star in the biggest hit of the 1935–36 season, *On Your Toes.* George Abbott beat the book into shape, Richard Rodgers and Larry Hart provided melodies and lyrics, and George Balanchine staged the dances. Balanchine's wife, ballerina Tamara Geva, was joined onstage by Ray Bolger, Monty Woolley and Luella Gear. Of all the hoofers on Broadway, Ray Bolger was likely the only name dancer who had the style and skill to partner Ms. Geva in the show's big production number, "Slaughter on Tenth Avenue." *On Your Toes* opened on 11 April 1936 and ran for 318 performances at the Imperial Theatre. Its success did not escape the notice of Hollywood's scouts on Broadway. Bolger already had experience in movies. He had made a Max Fleischer short in 1924, *Carrie of the Chorus,* and made an uncredited bit as a stagehand in *On with the Show* (1929), one of Warner Brothers' pioneer musicals.

In 1936 Ray signed with MGM, then emerging as Hollywood's most important and prestigious studio. He

Ray Bolger

was cast first to dance a specialty number in the fictionalized biomusical *The Great Ziegfeld* (1936), then drafted into *Rosalie* (1937) to provide a dancing partner for Eleanor Powell. Bolger performed much the same service in *Sweethearts* (1938) when he and Jeannette MacDonald sang and danced a wooden-shoes number.

His reward was to be cast in *The Wizard of Oz* (1939). Despite the film's great success, MGM did not make any meaningful attempt to keep Ray Bolger on its roster. He decided to go back to Broadway and to freelance in movies. *Keep off the Grass* (1940) was Bolger's first stage show since movie stardom. The revue had talent to spare in Bolger, Jimmy Durante, Ilka Chase, Larry Adler, Jane Froman, Virginia O'Brien and modern dance idol Jose Limon, but the material was weak, and *Keep off the Grass* did little to encourage people to come to the Broadhurst Theatre. Ray's next outing did not run long either, but it was fun; he joined Danny Kaye and Marty May for the *Lambs Annual Gambol* in 1941.

Ray Bolger, however, romped in success with Benay Venuta, Bertha Belmore, Vera-Ellen and Ronnie Graham in Rodgers & Hart's musical comedy *By Jupiter,* which opened on 3 June 1942. The best-remembered songs out of a clever score were "Ev'rything I've Got," "Wait Till You See Her" and "Nobody's Heart," the last of which provided Bolger with his biggest number in the show. After a year, the show was still pulling in customers when Bolger left the cast to entertain the troops abroad with the USO. It had been Bolger's third show for Rodgers & Hart and their last. It was a glorious finale for a brilliant partnership. Hart died the following year.

Three to Make Ready (1946) was a collaboration between Nancy Hamilton, who wrote the sketches and lyrics, and John Murray Anderson, who oversaw the production and staged the revue. Bolger danced the old soft shoe, Bibi Osterwald represented the new breed of revue performers, and Gordon MacRae and Arthur Godfrey were each two years away from stardom in, respectively, movies and television.

In 1946, Ray returned to Hollywood to work with Judy Garland again, this time in the film *The Harvey Girls.* Bolger made about two dozen movies over the half century between his first in 1924 and his last in 1979. Most of the latter half of them were made for television. Bolger never became a true movie star for several reasons. The immediate and enduring success of *The Wizard of Oz* was a short-term blessing; for a couple of years, Bolger was in every Hollywood producer's address book. *Oz* got him good roles in good films like *The Harvey Girls* and *Look for the Silver Lining* (1949), but horse-faced Ray Bolger did not look like a leading man. Neither did Fred Astaire, yet on screen Fred comported himself like a leading man. Bolger was a bit too much the clown to be more than the hero's best buddy, and there was a legion of such song-and-dance comedians waiting for a casting call: Jack Oakie, Ben Blue, Jack Haley, Phil Silvers, Donald O'Connor, Buddy Ebsen and Eddie Foy Jr. among them.

Astaire was not the dance star in the ascendant as the 1930s segued into the 1940s; Gene Kelly was. Gene was masculine and sexy, definitely a leading-man type in looks and manner, and his athletic and eclectic style of dance overlapped all but Bolger's most eccentric dancing. Ray's success in *The Wizard of Oz* was a bit of a fluke, as it was for Bert Lahr. After *Oz,* Bolger's movie roles gradually diminished in importance. So did Lahr's.

The same time that Godfrey was becoming ubiquitous on television and Gordon MacRae was starting to star in a series of musicals for Warner Brothers, Ray Bolger was back on Broadway for a role that gave him his greatest personal triumph onstage. *Where's Charley?* opened at the St. James Theatre on 11 October 1948 and ran just short of two years. On 29 January 1951, five months after it closed, *Where's Charley?* was revived at the Broadway Theatre, where it lingered six weeks. *Where's Charley?* provided Ray

Bolger with his best role on Broadway. It was also his last Broadway appearance of consequence.

Bolger was in his late 40s as his career unexpectedly and rather quickly waned. He was making the occasional minor feature film, and Broadway was in his past. Television guest shots paid poorly in the early years, but Lucille Ball, Robert Young, Robert Cummings and Ann Sothern had proved that B-picture stars could revive faltering careers through situation-comedy successes like *I Love Lucy* and *Father Knows Best.* Beyond that, Las Vegas was the new frontier in show business.

Bolger refused offers to appear in nightclubs. In 1952, the management of the Sahara Inn in Las Vegas explained that its new Congo Room had a fully equipped proscenium stage and was willing to pay $20,000 a week. The Sahara's Congo Room became a theatre, and Bolger opened it.

Bolger's agents, the William Morris Agency, represented many of the big-name variety entertainers in the 1950s. When the fledgling ABC-TV network was struggling to put together a full slate of programming to compete with the heavyweights, NBC and CBS, ABC engaged a number of William Morris acts. In one package deal, the agency made ABC take Danny Thomas when they wanted only Ray Bolger. Bolger's show, *Where's Raymond?,* lasted one season (1953–54). Danny Thomas set records with *Make Room for Daddy* (1953–71). Ray returned for a second season with a revamped *The Ray Bolger Show,* another situation comedy that, like its predecessor, concluded with a song-and-dance number by Bolger. It, too, lasted a single season (1954–55).

Ray Bolger went back to Broadway. *All American,* a weak entry in the 1961–62 season, eked out 80 performances at the Winter Garden, and *Come Summer* (1969) was a bigger flop.

Ray Bolger could always find work, most of it suitable even as his star dimmed. He was a surprisingly agile dancer for his age and a solid character actor, and he appeared in various productions for television and a few movies. He was called upon for various landmark shows like the Academy Awards and retrospectives. In 1985, two years before his death, Ray Bolger co-hosted with Liza Minnelli the retrospective film *That's Dancing.* His contributions to theatre were memorialized with the 1948–49 Tony Award and two Donaldson Awards. In 1980, the goofy dancer-actor was elected to the Theatre Hall of Fame.

BOOK

To book is to contract with an act for vaudeville appearances or engage a troupe or theatrical company of any kind to play a specific theatre or theatres. It derives from the act of entering the names of the acts in the manager's book.

A book, or, more properly, a libretto, refers to the script of written dialogue in a musical comedy.

BOOKERS

The agencies or individuals in vaudeville who represented management and dealt with the agents of the performers to contract the act—negotiate salary, devise routes and decide other particulars of employment—were known as bookers. In the small time, some local theatre owners or managers did their own booking and often dealt with the acts through an exchange of letters (in the early days) or telephone (later).

The method followed from the days of variety, when a diverse collection of performers were hired

ABERDEEN

TO THE ARTIST: Please read carefully before you sign.

Private Postal Wire — Phone Randolph 5170

Western Vaudeville Managers' Association

JOHN J. NASH, Business Manager

CHICAGO, ILL.

AGREEMENT, made MAY 16TH, 1923, between MC'CARTHY BROS., a Corporation, hereinafter called the "manager," and KEITH & PARKER hereinafter called the "artist."

1. Artist agrees to present a certain act with ... persons RATE $235 THREE SHOWS DAILY each day and once more at any extra holiday performance given during this engagement, including New Year's Eve and Election night, for TWO days commencing SAT. MAT. JUNE 2, 1923, 192.... at ORPHEUM Theatre, ABERDEEN, S.D., or any other place designated by the manager, for SIXTY SEVEN & 10/100 ($ 67.10) Dollars.

2. The manager shall pay any extra fares and excess baggage charges caused by change of place of performance; otherwise all transportation shall be paid by the artist. Where, however, the artist is routed over various theatres by the Western Vaudeville Managers' Association or its affiliations the manager shall be required to pay only for extra fares and baggage charges caused by change of place of performance when the aggregate amount of the fares and baggage charges over the entire route so rearranged exceeds the amount of such fares and charges on the route as originally laid out, and such excess shall be payable only upon presentation by the artist of itemized claim therefor, at the termination of the last engagement of such route.

3. If operation of theatre is prevented by fire, casualty, public authority, strikes or causes beyond manager's control, he shall only pay for performances given and pro rata.

A standard contract drawn between the Western Vaudeville Managers' Association and the act, Keith & Parker, for the Orpheum Theatre in Aberdeen, South Dakota, 1923 by an experienced and enterprising manager to tour as a package or a unit. The more successful managers had established reputations for dependability and providing entertainers who pleased audiences. So theatre owners welcomed the new offerings of the better-unit shows season after season, and the unit-show managers could prepare a route with shorter jumps and more play dates than a single act could manage on their own.

From the start of the twentieth century, however, vaudeville was in the ascendant and many new theatres opened. Lacking established relationships, the tendency was toward a concentration of business functions. A single independent theatre was at a disadvantage in obtaining desirable acts. If its owner contracted the booking function to an agency that was supplying a number of other theatres, there was more likelihood that the small independent would have access to better acts because a booker could offer a good act continuous work.

There was nothing constant in the affairs of bookers and booking agencies. A fluid business, it changed year by year, as did alliances between those who owned or managed enough theatres to influence the rules and the market rates for bookings. An agency that booked a small circuit one year could be replaced the next or swallowed whole by a larger agency, just as the independent theatre might be forced to sell or lease to a larger circuit.

IRENE BORDONI

b: 16 January 1895, Ajaccio, Corsica, France—d: 19 March 1953, New York, NY

Half French, half Italian, Irene Bordoni represented Parisian chic to Americans in the period between Anna Held and Maurice Chevalier. Like them, she was a product of French variety. Charm was more essential than talent to the success of all three. Bordoni more or less inherited the coquettish roles that the equally petite Anna Held once played.

A number of claims were made for her that may well be true: that the painter Millet was her granduncle, that she was educated in Paris at the Lycée de Jeunes Filles and the Conservatoire de Paris. Her first recorded appearance on a stage was made at the Théâtre des Variétés in Paris in 1907. Five years later, on 20 November 1912, she debuted on Broadway in a Shubert revue, *Broadway to Paris,* at the Winter Garden. The revue featured Doyle & Dixon, James C. Morton, Gertrude Hoffman and Louise Dresser, yet it ran only nine weeks. Still, audiences were intrigued by the tiny, saucer-eyed Bordoni and made her a vaudeville attraction.

Her basic act was simple: Irene and an onstage pianist who accompanied her singing. She changed piano players as fast as she changed gowns and songs and became famous among vaudevillians for going through eight different accompanists during the 1910s and 1920s. She shuttled between vaudeville, revue and musical comedy for a quarter of a century and occasionally played London and the Continent as well.

Her next Broadway show was Jerome Kern's *Miss Information* (1915), which flopped, sending both Bordoni and Elsie Janis back to vaudeville. A few years later, she tried Broadway again in an adaptation of Sacha Guitry's play *Sleeping Partners* (1918). It played nearly five months and qualified as a hit. So did the Raymond Hitchcock-Leon Errol revue *Hitchy Koo* (1919), which played Broadway for 220 performances. Bordoni was also in the following year's less fortunate edition of *Hitchy Koo,* which left town after eight weeks.

Bordoni's next four shows were all hits. *As You Were* (1920), a revue with Sam Bernard, Clifton Webb and Ruth Donnelly, ran for 142 performances. *The French Doll* (1922), a musical, played 120 shows, and *Little Miss Bluebeard* (1923) amused audiences 175 times. Irene proved she could carry a straight play when *Naughty Cinderella* (1925) ran for 125 performances, but she contradicted that conclusion when *Mozart* (1926) folded after a month. Cole Porter wrote words and music for *Paris* (1928), and Mlle Bordoni transported the Music Box Theatre from Broadway to Avenue de L'Opéra transported for six months.

In the late 1920s, Irene Bordoni made a few short sound movies and the first of her three feature-length films. She was one of the many vaudevillians in Warner Brothers' first filmed revue, *Show of Shows* (1928) and, in 1930, she made the film version of *Paris.*

An early Frederick Loewe musical, *Great Lady,* flopped in 1938, but Irving Berlin's big musical *Louisiana Purchase* (1940) was a smash, though it proved to be the last for Irene Bordoni. She was retained, along with Victor Moore and Vera Zorina, for the film version in 1942, which starred Bob Hope.

Swing-dance bands, boogie woogie, women in uniform or short skirts, gum chewing and jive talk ushered in the 1940s for America. Irene Bordoni's recherché charm needed more mannered times. Television provided a few opportunities to reappear before the American public, but she seemed an artifact from an artificial era.

In 1952, the year before she died, Irene Bordoni took a most uncharacteristic role; she played Bloody Mary in a national company of Rodgers & Hammerstein's smash hit *South Pacific.*

VICTOR BORGE

b: (Børge Rosenbaum) 3 January 1909, Copenhagen, Denmark—d: 23 December 2000, Greenwich, CT

For nearly a half century, Victor Borge had a very successful act as a serious musician with a delightful sense of fun. He turned concert halls into vaudeville theatres. Like the best of performers, he enjoyed an easy camaraderie with his audiences, and they loved him. Because he played concert music, he was considered by some to be a genteel comedian. That was due to his gentlemanly, old-world manner. Yet, within his evening-length show, he pulled hoary gags that had been the staple of burlesk comedians for a century. While executing a *grandioso* run up the keyboard, he slid off the bench and fell on the floor. At least once in a concert, the sounds tumbled out erratically as he began playing a piece, until he noticed that the sheet music was placed upside down. Rising to acknowledge applause, he placed his hand on the edge of his grand piano and the lid crashed down. This was the repertoire of a clown; that he made it hilarious each time was the work of a master clown.

Seldom did he play extended compositions. He opted for études and other short pieces for the piano. He played "Happy Birthday" in the styles of various masters from Mozart to Liszt. Sometimes he absent-mindedly segued from Chopin into a children's song or a television commercial. In his introductions to his musical selections, he offered anecdotes that detoured into bizarre associations of thoughts. Most of his jokes were understood by everyone, child or adult, music enthusiast or television viewer. A few were directed to music devotees, such as Borge's definition of a recitative: "the tune will be long any minute."

He had several famous verbal routines. One was inflationary language. Borge wondered if prices kept increasing, could wordage be far behind? He demonstrated what he meant by telling the story of a modern-day Jack and the Beanstalk: "Twice upon a time there lived a boy named Jack in the twoderful land of Califivenia. Two day, Jack, a double-minded lad, decided three go fifth three seek his fivetune . . . and so on and so fifth." Like much of Borge's verbal humor, it devolved from his own difficulty in understanding the American and British idioms.

Perhaps the favorite with most people was phonetic punctuation. In this, Borge assigned a specific sound to each mark of punctuation, the better to dictate speech to a transcriber. Individual vocal sounds—some quite rude and therefore funny on their own—were assigned to commas, periods, dashes, colons, semicolons, question marks and the like. Naturally, Borge demonstrated by verbalizing a letter and pronouncing each punctuation mark with whatever had been established. It was unfailingly hilarious.

His violinist father, according to Borge, "played for 35 years with Denmark's Royal Opera Orchestra, and when he came home, my mother did not recognize him." Borge began his own career as an organist at Copenhagen funerals but made his concert debut by 1922 and played throughout the Low Countries and Scandinavia. In 1934, he performed in a musical revue. He played in sketches and did physical comedy in addition to playing his instrument. He quickly became one of Denmark's leading performers and made several movies before the Nazi invasions led to the Second World War.

Hitler and his cohorts were frequent targets of Borge's comedy. Borge was a Jew. In 1940, the Nazis were at the border of Denmark while Borge was on tour. Because he was married to an American, Elsie Chilton, she was able to secure passage on one of the last ships to cross the Atlantic before war broke out among the European nations. They left their home, possessions and bank accounts behind and arrived in the USA with very little cash, few suitcases and their dog. They headed to California, then the headquarters of movie studios and radio networks. Elsie and Victor divorced sometime before 1950.

Victor Borge's (the name he chose for American audiences) first job of record in the USA was warming up the studio audience for the Rudy Vallee radio show in 1941. Vallee, despite his admiration for his own talent, was always appreciative of other talents. He may have introduced more future radio and television stars to national audiences than any other performer of the first half of the twentieth century. Bing Crosby's head writer, Carroll Carroll, got a phone call from Rudy Vallee urging him to show up before Rudy's broadcast to watch Borge work the audience. Rudy was sure that Borge would be a sensation on Bing's *Kraft Music Hall* radio program. Vallee's format did not allow for a proper use of Borge. Carroll went and was delighted. Borge was signed for a guest spot on Bing's show and was asked again for the following week.

Borge performed on radio before he mastered the language. He learned his lines phonetically, and the tiny uncertain pauses that became his trademark were the result. His approach to study was unorthodox but effective. When not working, Victor attended movies all day, day after day, to grasp the American version of the English language. Borge ended up performing on the *Kraft Music Hall* for 56 weeks, after which he got his own five-minute spot on NBC. These appearances gave Borge the visibility to get nightclub bookings.

In 1945, Borge was the summer replacement for the *Fibber McGee & Molly Show.* That autumn, he was given his own half-hour *Victor Borge Show,* with Benny Goodman, but Victor was more effective as a guest than a weekly host.

He had appeared in four Danish-language films between 1937 and 1940. In 1944, Victor Borge made his first Hollywood movies. One was an unbilled walk-on, but he had a featured role in *Higher and Higher* (1943), a flat comedy that never took off despite capable talent: Frank Sinatra, Leon Errol, Jack Haley, Michèle Morgan, Mary Wickes, Dooley Wilson, Paul & Grace Hartman and Mel Tormé.

Borge had achieved enough visibility by 1945 for concert management to chance booking him on a tour in the USA. This led to his TV debut on Ed Sullivan's *Toast of the Town* in 1949. That appearance and others won Borge his own half-hour comedy-variety TV show in 1951. His television experience was the same as on radio. He was better in guest spots than having his own show. (In 1965, Frederick DeCordova, Johnny Carson's longtime producer, filmed a pilot television show, *Mr. Belvedere,* with Borge in the role originated in the movies by Clifton Webb. The pilot did not sell.)

Early in 1953, he fashioned a more comedic version of his concert as *Comedy in Music.* He tried it out in Seattle, toured for a year, and then opened on Broadway at the intimate John Golden Theatre for a few weeks' run starting on 5 October 1953. It lasted 849 performances. His Broadway engagement ran into early 1956 and set a record for a one-person show. For the remainder of his long career, he toured with a version of his comedy concert. Sometimes the tour name was altered, but what sold it was his name. The material changed with each tour, yet the format and some favorite stage business stayed the same. For one tour he added a soprano whom he turned into a stooge.

Borge toured until he was 88 and made a few select appearances even at age 90. He never lost his game as he aged. The wit still sparkled. His timing was faultless, and his taste was intact. Borge looked and acted 20 years younger than he was. He made one concession to age: he eliminated falling off the piano bench after he turned 83.

Most of his bookings were in concert halls across the USA and Europe. He was aware of the difficulties some halls had staying profitable. Often, a Victor Borge concert was the only sold-out event a concert hall enjoyed all year. Victor began to do benefits for symphony orchestras: playing piano, chatting with the audience and musicians, joking and conducting the orchestras. Even as the maestro, he engaged in pranks. There was the bit in which the first violinist played a beat behind the orchestra. Borge stopped the music and banished the offending violinist off the stage. A few seconds after he exited, a single pistol shot was heard. Borge glared at the orchestra and ordered the violinists to move up one seat.

Not long before he died, he appeared at a National Press Club conference and noted that euthanasia advocate Dr. Jack Kevorkian had been their guest a few weeks earlier. "I expected to be speaking to an empty hall." In 1999, Borge was one of five performers selected for the Kennedy Center Honors. He had already received comparable awards from other nations and had been knighted by several. Sanna Sarabel Borge, whom Victor wed in 1953, died in September 2000. Borge died a few months later, at 91.

Borge's career spanned 75 years. For all of the last 50 of those years he was a star.

BORSCHT BELT

Centered in the Catskill Mountains, northwest of New York City, the Borscht Belt was the nickname given to a cluster of resorts that catered, almost exclusively, to a Jewish clientele, primarily Jewish immigrants from Eastern Europe and their American-born families. The name comes from *borscht,* the beet soup favored by Russian Jewry: hence Borscht Belt. Also known as the Jewish Alps and Sour Cream Sierras, the lodgings there ranged from small boardinghouses to bungalows to country club–style family resorts. There were accommodations to suit Jews from the most traditional to the least, from the orthodox to the secular and from the oldest to the youngest.

The larger resorts (Jenny Grossinger's, the Nevele, the Concord, Kutcher's Country Club, President Hotel, Flagler Hotel, the Laurels Country Club, Youngs Gap Hotel, Beerkill Lodge, Kiamesha Lake Inn, the Waldmere, Camp Tamiment and the like) offered entertainment every night. The afternoon and evening activities were the province of the tummler (social director), whose responsibility was to ensure that each guest had as good a time as he wanted and his disposition allowed. Soon, the tummlers needed assistants.

Young performers, hired by social directors before the summer season began, quickly found out that their duties included more than performing in a weekly Saturday-night show. The young, eager talents may have thought of themselves as future stars of Broadway and Hollywood, but the tummlers hired them to entertain in the broader sense of that word, and that meant dancing with the guests—especially the older ones and the young ones who had failed to blossom into swans—teaching them the newest steps, chatting up the lonely, bored or ignored guests, playing tennis and ping pong with them, conducting talent nights and treasure hunts, leading community song fests on campfire night, giving swimming lessons, losing believably to the guests on games nights and, oh, yes, dancing, dancing, dancing with the guests every evening.

In some of the smaller resorts, the musicians, the songstress, the dance duo and the comedian also carried the luggage, waited on tables and set up the games. Hanky-panky was discouraged if it involved young, marriageable maidens, but management often turned a winking eye toward after-hours activities between customers and hired help. Although the fathers and older sons and sons-in-law often commuted to work weekdays, it was hard to be discreet in a Borscht Belt resort peopled by a community bound together by layers of generations, cousins and in-laws.

The Jewish resorts in the Catskills (originally the Kaatskills) began as Jews from Eastern Europe, especially Poland, Lithuania and Russia, scraped together enough money to flee the urban confines of the Lower East Side and purchase upstate farms that reminded them of their homelands.

In 1898, in Fallsburgh, a Mrs. Fleischer, her husband and his partner, Mr. Morgenstern, who were peddlers, opened the Fleischer home as a hotel. Fifty years later it had grown into the famed Flagler Hotel. A year later, another peddler and his wife, the Sussmans, converted their Woodbridge home into a village inn, which decades later expanded into the Windsor Hotel. And so it went; a generation of old-world farmers turned peddlers turned hoteliers, their modest houses turned into resorts: Slutcky's Farmhouse into the Nevele Hotel. The Borscht circuit was not contained by Sullivan County or the Catskills. According to some, it spread westward and eastward across the Adirondacks and Berkshire Mountains and down into the Poconos, wherever Jewish hoteliers catered to Jewish guests.

Originally, the lure was fresh, clean air, wholesome kosher cooking and a sense of community. Gradually, both guests and hosts wanted more. If it was too chilly for a dip in the lake or too rainy for a walk in the meadow, the guests wanted some organized fun. Youngsters wanted to meet each other. As families prospered, they expected vacations to be more magical than quiet nights in the woods. Hotels added theatres, supper clubs, swimming pools and golf courses.

The hotels competed for prestige, fuller occupancy and better-heeled clientele. Families looked forward to their two weeks upstate. New cars and clothes were bought, and expectations were high. There was among some families a rivalry to appear prosperous. Young women hoped to find a wider range of potential beaux than was available back in the neighborhood. Young men were on the lookout for opportunity, a summer fling or true love coupled with upward mobility.

The demand for ever more professional and prestigious entertainment grew amid other escalating expectations of the guests. The hotels competed, and resort managers began hiring professional acts when guests complained of seeing the same young comedians, dancers and singers day after day and the same skits and routines week after week. Instead of being yoked to one hotel for an entire summer, a comedian or a dance act played a different resort each week: fresh material for the audiences and fresh audiences for the performers. Soon, agents devised circuits of sorts, and vaudeville was back in business, at least for the summers of the late 1930s through the 1960s.

The Second World War both helped and hurt. On the plus side, the hoteliers had to compete with the local draft boards for eligible young men. The hotels' staff of young performers, waiters and bellboys were pressed into new uniforms as buck privates. Ex-vaudevillians, exempt from the armed forces because of age or minor infirmities, got a second lease on their careers. On the debit side, gasoline was soon rationed, and upstate Sullivan County was a long hike from the Grand Concourse.

For agents, getting their entertainers work was the easier part. Getting the acts to their work was harder. This led to packaged shows. It was a lot easier if an agent could send all his acts to one place in one car. The problem for the entertainer was that he worked for the agent not the hotelier. The agent negotiated a price for the entire show and then hired the acts. Some agents made a lot more this way than their usual percentage. The act with both a car and a full gasoline ration book, however, was king.

During the late 1960s and the 1970s, however, decline set in. Air travel was faster and more affordable; the Caribbean and Florida promised exotic locales, more predictable and pleasanter weather. Families were no longer as cohesive. Young people preferred vacationing with their own age set, and in some cases older people preferred it as well. The importance of clan diminished. For many Jews, *community* had assumed a less parochial interpretation.

Although the Borscht circuit was Jewish, it was not ethnically unique. Peg Leg Bates, who like Buck & Bubbles was a black dance act that performed in Jewish resorts, decided in 1951 to open a resort for African Americans in the Catskills. It, too, prospered for a couple of decades, providing food, service and entertainment that appealed to its clientele, until the same factors in decline afflicted the Peg Leg Bates Country Club. Like the Jews, successive generations of African Americans no longer felt the need, out of choice or fear, to spend their holidays in homogeneous environs. Up in Boston, the Irish who could afford it established the Irish Riviera on the coast just south of the Hub. New England Yankees had long established their own enclaves away from the madding crowd.

During the several decades when the Catskills provided a coda to vaudeville, many big names and soon-to-be-big names in show business played its various resorts.

The roster of Borscht circuit alumni was formidable. Among the established acts were Willie Howard, Bob Hope, Belle Baker, Eddie Cantor, Milton Berle, Molly Picon, George Jessel, Ethel Merman, Cab Calloway, the Ritz Brothers, Lou Holtz, Joe E. Lewis, Tony Martin, Rose Marie and Arthur Tracy. Among those who got some of their training and experience playing the Sour Cream Sierras were Imogene Coca, Jerry Lewis, Danny Kaye, Sid Caesar, Jackie Gleason, Morey Amsterdam, Phyllis Diller, Joan Rivers, Moss Hart, Shelley Winters, Henny Youngman, Max Liebman, Mata & Hari, Myron Cohen, Joey Adams, Sam Levine, Zero Mostel, Jan Murray, Van Johnson, Don Rickles, Rodney Dangerfield, Jack E. Leonard and Buddy Hackett.

The golden age of the Borscht Belt ended when Miami, Vegas and other oases in the Sunbelt enticed vacationers, and some guests became year-round residents of the Southeast and Southwest. The Catskill resorts lingered on, more or less, as did the economies of some of the towns in which they were situated, but the land proved more valuable than the buildings, and grand hotels yielded to housing.

BOSTON VERSION

Primarily applicable to burlesque, but the term *Boston version* also was used, contemptuously, by vaudevillians annoyed at the strict rules governing which words (not just curses) could not be uttered on a B. F. Keith stage. The Boston version of a skit, song lyric or dance is one purged of all words and actions deemed objectionable by puritanical theatre managers or the Boston city censors, who earned a reputation as the most strict in the land. By extension, the Boston version referred to expurgated versions wherever they were performed.

BOSWELL SISTERS

Connee (Connie) Boswell

b: 1907, New Orleans, LA—d: 1976

Martha Boswell

b: 1908, New Orleans, LA—d: 1958

Helvetia Boswell

b: 1909, New Orleans, LA—d: 1988

Vaudeville provided the first and final stages for the Boswell Sisters as a trio. Born in New Orleans, the girls debuted in their midteens around 1923 in a hometown vaudeville house. This led to local radio appearances and then their own show, five days a week. They played light classical and popular music on their program: Connie, the musical leader of the trio and its arranger, sang and played cello, saxophone, piano and guitar; Martha was the group's swinging pianist; and Helvetia, or Vet, as she was more often called, played violin and tap danced.

All three were tutored in the classics but influenced by New Orleans jazz as well. The Boswells' mother took them occasionally to a black vaudeville, where custom permitted whites on Friday nights only. There Connie saw Mamie Smith, a singer who blended blues and ragtime into a popular sound. Connie later claimed that she tried to sing like Mamie.

The combination of training and influences stimulated the Boswells to employ rapid changes in tempo, close harmonies and modulations, which gave their pop songs a genteel but genuine jazz flavor and beat. Usually, they performed a number fairly straight the first time through, but jazzed up succeeding choruses.

Both radio and the recording industry were growing, and the Boswell Sisters found their fame through both. Successively, Victor Records and Brunswick contracted with them; in those days, the record company told the singer what to sing. The Boswells toured to promote their recordings.

They were getting work, but none of it paid well. Radio expected performers to play unpaid until sponsorship was secured; even when a sponsor signed on, the firm was local, as was the station before networks came into being, so the budgets were small. Recording companies generally paid a fixed (small) fee for each session, and there was no such thing as royalties at the time.

Vaudeville paid a bit better, but it was mostly small time for the Boswells until 1930, when the act began to catch fire. Big-time vaudeville beckoned when it was clear that fans of their records and radio appearances were willing to pay to see the trio in person. The Boswell Sisters scored their first major triumph in 1931 at New York's Paramount Theatre, a presentation house. They were then in a better position to demand better pay and to decide what songs to record. They recorded 60 or 70 sides with top jazzmen such as Bunny Berigan, the Dorsey Brothers, Eddie Lang and Manny Klein (mostly the same men who accompanied Ruth Etting and Ethel Waters). They were also in demand for stage and network radio performances.

The trio retired during the 1935–36 season, when both Martha and Vet married. Connee, who had changed the spelling of her first name about this time, continued with distinction as a solo act, and she was a frequent guest on the Kraft Music Hall on NBC radio in the 1940s, when Bing Crosby hosted the weekly show.

Connee had become paralyzed from the waist down when she was three years old. Thus, she always was shown seated, whether onstage, on-screen, on television or in publicity photos. It was difficult for her to move around with ease; nevertheless, during the Second World War, she visited servicemen in Stateside hospitals and sang at training camps. Connee requested to go overseas with a USO show, but, given her condition, the armed forces brass was unwilling to assume the risk. She died of stomach cancer in 1976, a year after her final public performance at a Carnegie Hall concert starring Benny Goodman.

BOX HOUSES

Related to honky-tonks, the box house was more narrowly defined. It offered the same mix of booze and entertainment, sometimes with gambling added, and the male-only clientele was catered to by serving girls, some of whom doubled as performers. Onstage, they sang and danced (showing their linen and limbs), but their primary duty was to hustle customers. This they did by sitting with the men at tables and encouraging them to buy drinks, for which the women received a chit. At the end of the evening, the women were paid a percentage for every drink they pushed. In the more forsaken of the honky-tonks, as the women lined up to redeem their chits, the male customers, who had money left and were still relatively conscious, were encouraged to make further arrangements with the women.

The more promising marks were encouraged to pay to sit in one of the boxes that made up the three sides of a low balcony. The boxes functioned as many of the boxes in theatres on the Continent. They had private access from the rear, a few seats and a small table, and, facing the stage, a curtain that could be drawn to afford privacy. Most of the big spenders lured to the boxes liked to be seen with a showgirl in their lap. If management policy and the local constabulary permitted, more intimate activity could be curtained off from view.

According to one of the most authoritative chroniclers of the era, Bernard Sobel, "often the girls were not girls, but female impersonators." The trick for the boys was to keep floating from box to box and stay no longer than a quick lap dance. Those who lingered too long, and whose charms were found to be counterfeit, risked being thrashed or shot unless the management's bouncers reached the trouble spot in time to intervene.

Although the renowned female impersonator Julian Eltinge provided few specifics about his earliest days in show business, it is known that his father had moved the family to Butte Montana and that, while there, Eltinge, then in his early teens, began dancing in drag in the town's saloons. It is unlikely that Butte, rough and ready in the 1890s, was sufficiently in advance of American society elsewhere, so young Mr. Eltinge, not yet the image of butch respectability he assiduously promoted throughout his adult career, was likely precocious and daring and one of the boys masking as women, hustling men. Bert Savoy also started his career as a female impersonator hustling men in the Wild West.

The box-house shows began about 9:00 in the evening and lasted for hours. In a typical, good-size box house, the entertainment opened with all the women and other performers assembled onstage for a musical number. Then the women, dozens of them, departed the stage to take their places at tables and especially in the boxes. They emptied bottles surreptitiously and called other women over to the box so that the sucker felt obligated to order more drinks all around. Through various ruses, the women tried to avoid drinking themselves; they emptied their glasses on the floor when the man was not looking, or insisted on whiskey, which arrived as cold tea in shot glasses.

Meanwhile, male performers sang, danced, did comedy bits and kept the show going. Most performers traveled from town to town. Along the route, they picked up standard bits of scenes, songs and dances. When the entertainers performed a three-act play, the stage manager or other performers provided a rundown of the action and furnished crucial bits of dialogue, but for the most part it was left to the inventiveness (and memory) of the performers to improvise dialogue and keep the action moving.

Between the acts, each performer did his specialty: sang, danced, tumbled or clowned. At various spots in the evening's bill, the women, wearing tights topped with low-cut bodices or tunics and knee-length skirts, deserted the boxes, with a promise to soon return, and clambered onto the stage to attempt ersatz cancans or military drills.

When a woman was not actually performing onstage, she was expected to assist in the boxes, even if she were married. Husband-and-wife teams were threatened with dismissal if they did not conform. It took nerve to buck the management out West, where most of the box houses were located and where decisions sometimes were rendered with beatings or bullets. The honky-tonks of the urban East operated in much the same fashion, although many were cellar joints, where the seating area tended to be smaller and there was no room for a balcony of boxes. More likely, a door at one end of the saloon led to an upper level or a building next door that housed cribs of the type found in brothels.

ARTURO BRACHETTI

b: 13 October 1964, Turin, Italy

The figure onstage, garbed in a black suit, stood downstage center. A white mask, as expressionless as a mannequin, covered his face. Each time he removed it there was another, identical mask beneath, and another, and 100 more—or so it seemed—for he whisked them off and magically disposed of them in a continuous flow of hands. This opening scene of *Arturo Brachetti, the Man of a Thousand Faces,* introduced to the USA in 2002 both the one-man show and the young man reputed to be the fastest quick-change actor of the late twentieth and early twenty-first centuries.

Rather than 1,000, Brachetti transformed into 100 fully costumed characters in 100 minutes, among them a Royal Canadian Mounted Police officer, a circus clown, a showgirl, a bumblebee, the four seasons of the year, a magician in mandarin costume, a preposterous flower, a Kabuki actor and all the stock roles of a Western movie—the good guy, the villain, the gunslinger, the dance-hall hostess, the bartender and the grizzled prospector—in a farce of hasty exits and slamming doors. As soon as Arturo exited in one guise, he popped up a few seconds later as another. The changes were not only of costume but, through posture and expression, a quick sketch of character.

A quicksilver sprite, Brachetti managed his transformations from one elaborate costume into another in the space of two or three seconds. At one point in the show, he entered in a black suit, turned to one side, and the suit was white; faced forward and it was black on one side and white on the other, turned again and it was solid white, yet all done before one's eyes in what seemed like split seconds. The international press has dubbed him the "Italian Chameleon," "the King of Metamorphoses" and "Man of a Thousand Faces."

After developing this theatre piece in Canada, where it first played at the Just for Laughs Festival in Montreal, the show then moved to Paris, where Arturo won the Molière Award in 2000. His show returned to North America and toured from Montreal into major U.S. cities.

In contrast to the rest of the production, which was lavish, one of the more charming routines was simple in presentation. Standing downstage left, Arturo extended his hands into a beam of light to cast a rapid series of shadow images of elephants, swans, dogs, birds, the Eiffel Tower and the like on a large movie screen. In another routine that was a nod to the variety acts of the past (the "Chapeau de Tabarin"), he suggested a cast of characters by fashioning a simple circular brim of a hat into dozens of shapes, among them a tricorne, bishop's miter, dunce cap, cloche and halo. It is during this last routine that Arturo talked to the audience, addressing them in a hearty, presentational tone like a circus ringmaster and reminiscent of his countryman, Roberto Benigni.

Arturo Brachetti. Photo credit: Pascalito of Paris

In a salute to Hollywood, Arturo flashed through a jump-cut pastiche of Hollywood images that had possessed him since childhood: Gene Kelly singing and dancing in the rain, King Kong, Scarlet O'Hara, Darth Vadar, Julie Andrews, James Bond, Charlie Chaplin, Esther Williams, Charlton Heston as Moses, Liza Minnelli in *Cabaret* appearing from Judy Garland in *The Wizard of Oz.* Arturo's tributes, however, were reserved for two of his countrymen, both of whom he reveres.

In a land where transformation acts were particularly popular, where they had originated in the Italian *commedia dell'arte,* Leopoldo Fregoli rose above all. His career spanned the late nineteenth and early twentieth centuries, and he combined ventriloquism, magic and mimicry with his quick-change skills. Brachetti is considered Fregoli's artistic heir, and Arturo celebrated Fregoli by reimagining some of his characters.

Brachetti's homage to film director Federico Fellini capped the second act of the show, and it was evident that Brachetti's respect and affection for the master were as sincere as his affinity was tangible. The scene was a dream state in which Nino Rota's original film music scored each succeeding vignette, opening with Fellini slumped midcenter of the stage. Arturo rose out of Fellini's body and became the various characters that Fellini put into his films, assuming the appearance of Guiletta Massina in *La Strada,* Marcello Mastroianni, the clowns, grotesques and voluptuous movie queens—each character a denizen of Rome born in Fellini's imagination and embodied by Brachetti.

The production *Arturo Brachetti, the Man of a Thousand Faces* was sumptuous like a Broadway musical or a Las Vegas show, a spectacle of lighting, sound and settings requiring a staff and crew of 18 people. In the center of the stage, a huge cabin-sized packing crate revolved, opening up in various ways like a puzzle to expose a new scene and a new Brachetti transformation. The show was produced like a David Copperfield or Siegfried & Roy spectacle, appropriately so, because Arturo Brachetti's transformations were the stuff of stage magic: objects materialized and disappeared; props he touched turned from one thing into another. Indeed, it was the study of magic that led to his career.

Born in a village near Turin in the foothills of the Italian Alps, Arturo was 11 years old when his parents sent him to a nearby Roman Catholic seminary. He was a bright student, and, instead of playing soccer, as was expected of all Italian schoolboys, Arturo's body, mind and soul were captured by magic. One of the resident priests, Father Silvio Mantelli, was an amateur magician. He had collected books and the tools of illusion, and these he shared with Arturo. Every few months the students put on a show. By the time he was 15, Arturo had worked out a transformation act combining magic tricks with three costume changes. A knowledgeable person in attendance suggested to Arturo that he read a biography of Leopoldo Fregoli, and the biography provided direction to Arturo's ambition and a sense of what could be accomplished artistically.

At 17, he left the seminary; his vocation was not the one expected by his father. Arturo won an amateur contest with an act that featured six costume changes, and he had the fortune to be seen by French magic star Gérard Majax, who advised him to audition in Paris for Jean-Marie Rivière, who ran the Paradis Latin, which Arturo has described as "Paris craziest cabaret."

Paradis Latin was his university and Rivière his mentor. Through observing and helping out where he could in the productions, both backstage and onstage, he gained skill and became an important part of shows at Paradis Latin. Arturo learned music-hall performance traditions as well as the mechanics of performance, learned to invest his characters with a quality that made his act more than a series of tricks.

He learned well; when Brachetti felt the time had come to go out on his own, he was engaged for a two-year tour of Austria and Germany as the emcee and star of *Flic-Flac,* an extravaganza production sponsored by the Austrian government. The show was created and directed by Andre Heller, who introduced Arturo to surrealism and German symbolism.

Brachetti made his debut in London as the creator and star of *Y,* a musical in the style of Folies du Music-Hall. His various roles in the show captured a nomination as best newcomer from the Society of West End Theatres, a guest appearance at the Royal Variety Show at Covent Garden Opera House, and a Christmas Charity Performance sponsored by the royal family. The year was 1984 and Arturo was 20.

He returned to Italy in 1985 to guest star on network television (a series of ten installments of *Al Paradise* for Italian National TV, RAI) and in several stage productions, including *Varieta* (1986), a re-creation of the golden age of Italian variety, the musical *Amani Arturo* (1987) and the first of his one-man shows, *Principio Arturo* (1988–89).

In 1990, just turning 26, Brachetti demonstrated his quality as a serious actor and his ability to play female and androgynous characters with the role of Sung Li-Ling, the Chinese spy, in the Italian production of *M. Butterfly.* Over the next few years Arturo acted in serious drama—Stravinsky's *L'Histoire du Soldat* (1991) and *Il Mistero dei Bastardi Assassini* (1993)—and took roles in several films.

Back in Britain, he cohosted a special Thames TV show, *The Best of Magic,* and acted the role of a shell-shocked First World War doughboy in *Square Rounds,* a drama by Tony Harrison produced by the National Theatre. This was followed by the telecast of *Disney Night of Magic,* which Arturo cohosted with Mickey Mouse, presenting a bill of international magicians including Harry Blackstone Jr. and the Pendragons.

In 1990, Brachetti began taking on directorial work, including two assignments for shows in which he starred: *I Massibilli* (1990) in Paris and *Fantasissimo* (1994) in Berlin. He also directed *Thousand Nights* (1995) in Berlin, *I Corti* (ca. 1997) and *Tel Chi El Telun* (1999), a comedy show featuring Italy's most popular comedians: Aldo, Giovanni and Giacomo. Arturo also directed several music and dance concerts and episodes of television programs.

Arturo's next acting engagement proved a highlight of his career. In 1994, he starred in the musical *Fregoli,* under the direction of Saverio Marconi, portraying both the legendary transformation actor Fregoli and his double, Romolo. For Brachetti, it was a wish fulfilled; for everyone involved with the show, it was a critical success and played to 280,000 people, making it the best-selling theatrical event in Italy's 1994–95 season. Meanwhile, Brachetti and Marconi were again collaborating in the writing of another show in which Arturo would star and Marconi would direct. *Brachetti in Technicolor* hurled Arturo to the future year 2095 and into a repository of Hollywood film classics where he caused havoc. He essayed 60 characters in full costume, and the production played to 250,000 customers between 1996 and 1998, thus repeating the success of their earlier collaboration.

Overseas jaunts were fitted in between seasons of *Brachetti in Technicolor.* Arturo participated in a Tokyo festival of Western culture and accepted the first of three invitations to appear in Montreal at the Just for Laughs Comedy Festival in the summer of 1997.

He returned to the Italian theatre in 1999 for a production of Shakespeare's *A Midsummer Night's Dream,* which placed the classic in the subculture of contemporary dance clubs. According to Arturo, he flew around the stage as Puck as "an end of the Millennium elf." Later that year, Brachetti was back in North America. On TV's *The Drew Carey Show,* he played an unsuccessful job applicant who, undaunted, tried and tried again, each time in a different guise.

In 1997, Brachetti was a big hit at the Just for Laughs Comedy Festival in Montreal. The festival's creator, Gilbert Rozon, convinced Arturo to put together many of the routines he had developed for various shows over the past decade into a full-length, one-man variety show. Brachetti used the narrative of his own life as the spine on which to string various routines, including introductory filmed sequences that presented him as a small child. *Arturo Brachetti, the Man of a Thousand Faces* played on two continents between 1999 and 2003, racking up 600,000 tickets in Paris, where it played three theatres in two years, before it toured the USA.

Out of costume, Arturo Brachetti is a spare, handsome man with a mime's physique and bright, dark eyes. His intensely focused energy and direct and articulate speech are balanced by a friendly, open manner. In civilian attire, he could pass for a university student if not for his trademark forelock waxed into a horn, though even offstage there is still the whiff about him of magic, a unicorn visitor to the earthly plane.

Arturo Brachetti speaks English with a light accent. His grammar is nearly faultless, and he speaks fluently with a impressive breadth of vocabulary, so it comes as a surprise when he halts for a moment during an interview, seeking an appropriate word. English is a second language—or fourth or fifth—as he also is fluent in Italian (his native language), French, German, and, according to a friend, is studying Japanese.

In the course of his 20-year career he has never been without work and often has juggled overlapping assignments. The energy an audience sees displayed onstage is surpassed by that expended during the moments he hurriedly changes backstage while a filmed segment or the spin of the set distracts the audience. The frantic rush has brought injuries to both Arturo and his longtime assistant and dresser, Massimo Sarzi. During a performance of *Fregoli,* Arturo broke his arm yet reappeared onstage. Highly disciplined, Arturo maintains a steady weight just under 150 pounds (he stands about five feet, ten inches tall) and gets eight hours of sleep each night. "I don't smoke or drink or take drugs, so I'm left with sex and chocolate. And lately I've cut out the chocolate as well."

BREAK-IN DATES

Established vaudevillians sought break-in dates when they changed their acts substantially. Performers who had a new act they wished to break in simply wanted a few weeks in front of audiences to test what worked and did not work. They did not wish to attract undue attention from trade-paper reviewers or managers and bookers until they had their act tightly routined, polished and ready to show.

A performer might take a new partner, or a partner might decide to go out alone as a single. A single woman, who generally traveled only with a pianist who was her accompanist and music director, might decide to carry her own instrumental quintet and expand her act from 13 to 20 minutes. Or, conversely, when bookings for her six-person act began to thin because of the price tag of the act, she might decide to revamp her act into a solo turn, retaining only her accompanist and music director.

Even if the personnel in the act did not change but the material did, that was reason enough for some tryout dates. A rope spinner like Will Rogers might find that a few offhand comments got solid laughs and decide to accent the humorous storytelling and cut back on the lariat tricks that first won him notice. Dancers might wish to add singing to their act.

Theatre managers and bookers always cried out for novelty and complained when performers did not change their acts for years on end, yet they were cautious about booking an old favorite who had changed his act radically. No one was more concerned than the performers themselves. They had no wish to risk professional reputations that had been built over the course of many hard years. So when they changed their acts or partners or decided to go solo, they sought bookings in out-of-the-way houses until they tested the new material with a number of audiences to discover what was well received, what should be jettisoned and in which order to routine the various bits and pieces of their material. Once they worked out the kinks, routined effectively and felt comfortable in the act, they invited bookers to see the new act performed in front of a paying vaudeville audience. Those showings were known as tryout dates.

EL BRENDEL

b: (Elmer Goodfellow Brendel) 25 March 1891, Philadelphia, PA—d: 9 April 1964, Los Angeles, CA

With a recorded legacy comprising six dozen or more motion pictures, mostly features for Fox, on which his reputation is inevitably based, El Brendel barely qualifies as a minor comedian. In his vaudeville days, he was regarded as a fine comedian, and, as one half of Brendel & Burt, he played the better small time and the big time. Flo Burt sang, danced a bit and played straight; El Brendel sang and danced some and was the comedian.

El Brendel married his partner, (Sophie) Flo Burt, and they played vaudeville for a few years, starting in 1913 as Brendel & Burt. At first, their act didn't quite jell, and they failed to win steady work in vaudeville, so they split professionally, although both went into burlesque for a season. They reteamed in 1917 with more successful results.

When Brendel began in vaudeville, it was as a German dialect comedian. The First World War and the rising anti-German fervor in the United States caused him to modify his accent to Swedish. "Yumping Yimminy" was one of the expressions he coined. By Christmas week 1927, Brendel & Burt were performing an act called "Waiting for Her" at the Davis Theatre in Pittsburgh on a bill with Fay Templeton, Lulu McConnell & Grant Simpson and Theodore Kosloff.

El Brendel

Spurred by the growing popularity in the late 1910s of phonographs and phonograph records, El Brendel began to include pantomiming to records in his act with Flo Burt. Show-business historians Joe Laurie Jr. and Joe Franklin claim El Brendel was the first to do it. Thirty years later, it was a standard bit for nightclub comedians across the USA.

In 1920, Flo Burt went into musical comedy, *Cinderella on Broadway,* which played four months at the Shubert's Winter Garden. Georgie Price was also in the cast. El Brendel followed suit by joining the cast (Mae West, Cliff Edwards) of *The Mimic World of 1921,* but it closed within a month. El Brendel had no better luck with *Hitchy-Koo* of 1922, which closed out of town despite Raymond Hitchcock in the star position and comedian Jack Pearl.

El Brendel & Flo Burt had better luck in vaudeville, and played the Palace Theatre several times and as late as 1929. While in New York, El Brendel made his first appearances in movies. He made eight features in 1926 and 1927, including the celebrated, Academy Award winning *Wings* (1927), starring Clara Bow, Gary Cooper and Richard Arlen. In 1929, Brendel began his career in talking pictures. Most of the movie studios preferred action and romantic dramas to comedy. At Fox, producers cast him as comic relief, but he was not given much in the way of decent material to work with; all that directors and producers wanted from Brendel was a "Yumping Yimminy" here and a slow-witted take there. Movies turned El Brendel into a dull, dim Scandinavian hick character. Frustrated that he could not gain star status and better parts in movies, he returned to vaudeville several times.

At first, he had more opportunity in short films. Two-reel comedies were not prestigious and had laughable budgets, but they were not supervised to death. Under some directors, there was a chance to display some originality. El Brendel's first two-reelers were made for Vitaphone and are regarded as superior to his later Columbia shorts directed by Jules White.

Flo Burt acted a few times in films. She appeared with her husband, El Brendel, in *I'm from Arkansas* (1944) and *The She-Creature* (1956). Gradually, they both faded from the screen. Occasionally, they returned to vaudeville as long as it lingered and to revues. El Brendel had two shining moments at the end of his career. He appeared in a first-rate film, *The Beautiful Blond from Bashful Bend,* and won the role of Joan Davis' father on her television series, *I Married Joan.*

FANNY BRICE

b: (Fannie Borach) 29 October 1891, New York, NY—d: 29 May 1951, Los Angeles, CA

Whether she was Becky "Back in the Ballet," a coughing Camille, a "Quainty, Dainty" concert artist, a dying swan, or spoofing other vaudeville headliners or avant-garde artists like Nijinsky or Martha Graham, Fanny's act was the essence of burlesk: parodying her classical betters. She was also an accomplished sketch comedian and a fine singer of Tin Pan Alley songs.

A favorite with both men and women, Fanny won over audiences because she seemed unpretentious and never took herself too seriously, yet she possessed a certain sex appeal. Offstage, she grew into an elegant, fashionable woman, poised yet animated, well-spoken yet not above punctuating an utterance with a stage leer or a cussword.

Her mother, Rose Stern, had emigrated from a village in Hungary, and her father, Charles Borach, from Strasbourg in the Alsace-Lorraine, a territory between Germany and France that belonged to whichever of the two countries had won it in the most recent conflict. Born on the Lower East Side, the family moved to Newark, New Jersey, when Fanny was just a tyke. She was the third of four children; Philip and Carolyn were older, Lew, a year younger. Rose ran the family.

Fanny Brice

Never shy or timid, Fanny and the neighborhood kids sang for coins from passersby. In 1905, she entered an amateur night at Keeney's Theatre, a vaudeville house on Fulton Street in Brooklyn. In those days, Fanny favored lachrymose ballads, and she could turn on the tears like waterworks. Impressed with her popularity, Frank Keeney, the owner and emcee, invited her to become a *professional amateur* at his two other theatres. According to her brother, Lew Brice, when Fanny sang, the customers tossed money onstage. So stagehands raised the bottom of the curtain off the floor to allow the coins to roll under, and Lew scuffled with the stagehands backstage to grab the throw money for Fanny.

In 1907, Fanny decided that it was time to turn professional. She tried to audition with a song but was hired, untested, as a dancer and was fired, unceremoniously, as a dancer. Fanny knew she had to learn how to dance and act as well as sing if she were to break into stage work. She took what work she could wangle, such as sewing costumes and playing an alligator in a theatrical stock company until it went bust. She was 16 when she decided to join a Hurtig & Seamon burlesque company to get the training she needed.

Not all chorus girls in burlesque were pretty, but they usually had sufficient curves to stir male customers. At the time Fanny was neither pretty nor curvy; she was adolescent and skinny. So "I sang way up in the balcony. I sang behind the scenes backstage, I sang in the shadow of the boxes, but the audience never got a glimpse of me."

She toured for one year each with *Transatlantic Burlesquers, The Girls from Happyland,* and *The College Girls.* Fanny admitted she bribed other chorus dancers and the dance directors to teach her the rudiments, step by step, of what passed for stage dancing in the 1910s. During her second season with Hurtig & Seamon, she changed her surname from Borach to Brice, the name of a family friend.

When Max Spiegel engaged Fanny in 1910 for *The College Girls,* he expected a specialty act from Fanny. Enter Irving Berlin, a young singing waiter and songwriter with Lower East Side roots, who had been trying to get producers to use his songs in their shows. Berlin provided Fanny with two songs, "Sadie Salome, Go Home!," a Yiddish dialect song that had been languishing in his trunk, and the ragtime "Grizzly Bear." Both songs demanded to be performed rather than simply sung, and Fanny delivered.

The experience of working out routines for both songs, playing to different audiences on the road and trying to keep her act seemingly spontaneous was great training. Less useful was her marriage to Frank White, a barber she met on tour. She soon divorced him.

The year 1910 marked a breakthrough for both Fanny Brice and Irving Berlin. Irving wrote his first big hit, "Alexander's Ragtime Band," and Fanny joined the cast of Ziegfeld's *Follies of 1910.* Just who recommended Brice to Ziegfeld is debated. The other notable debut in that edition of the *Follies* was Bert Williams.

Fanny Brice was a spindly 20-year-old when, for $75 a week, she first appeared in the *Follies.* Ziegfeld and his directors were preoccupied with the demands of designing the *Follies* and staging its spectacles. Successful *Follies* comics were those who brought their own routines. Bert Williams, Leon Errol, W. C. Fields, Ed Wynn and Will Rogers were able to devise most of their own material; Fanny Brice and Eddie Cantor needed good writers of songs and sketches, otherwise they were saddled with material that did not fit them. Marion Will Cook and Joe Jordan, a black songwriting team, provided Fanny with "Lovey Joe," a *coon song,* and Fanny performed it for its full worth.

When Fanny did not scout on her own for material and take pains to keep it fresh, her act suffered, as it did in the *Follies of 1911.* Critics complained about her weak material and her forced delivery.

After the 1911 *Follies* closed during March 1912, Brice entered vaudeville, taking a string of engagements mostly in and around New York City, starting with Hammerstein's Victoria. She joined a couple of revues. Al Jolson and Gaby Deslys continued to headline *The Whirl of Society* and *The Honeymoon Express* when those shows toured. Fanny was added to the road editions, but she failed to charm the critics. And so it went, from 1912 to 1916.

In 1914, Fanny worked for five months, with some success, in English revues and then played the Keith circuit with an 18-minute act that showcased her in five song numbers. The next season, she toured for two months in a straight comedy role in 1915's *Nobody Home.*

Fanny had been distracted from her career by Jules "Nicky" Arnstein, with whom she had been besotted since they had met in November 1912. Nicky became Fanny's second husband in 1918 and the father of her two children. When Nicky got into trouble, Fanny insisted he was a dupe, but other, less intimately involved observers believed him crooked, although a handsome, well-spoken, well-dressed and well-mannered crook. Among the less-partial observers were the juries and judges that consigned Arnstein to jail twice. Steadfast during Nicky's hearings, appeals and two years in Leavenworth, Fanny paid the bills. When she finally divorced Arnstein in 1927, due to his repeated infidelity, Fanny had spent about 15 years loving, obsessing and worrying about him.

If the first four years with Arnstein had distracted Fanny, the next four years focused her. She bore sole responsibility for her children's welfare. She worked hard, paid attention to her material, demanded top dollar and reached greatness through a series of revues and vaudeville engagements.

Fanny Brice, 1920

A reviewer for *The Dramatic Mirror* pronounced Fanny Brice "rehabilitated" from the "rut" into which she had slipped. The occasion was the debut of her new 16-minute vaudeville act at the Palace Theatre in Manhattan. (She had reverted to Fannie for her billing.) A two-a-day tour on the Orpheum circuit lasted three months, until she returned to the *Follies.*

Fannie Brice appeared in the *Ziegfeld Follies of 1916, 1917, 1920, 1921* and *1923* as well as the posthumous *Follies* produced by the Shuberts in 1934 and 1936. She also performed in the 1918, 1919 and 1920 editions of *Ziegfeld's Midnight Frolics* and the *Nine O'Clock Frolics* of 1918 and 1920. She had found people who could write for her: Blanche Merrill and the team of Gene Buck & Dave Stamper. From 1916 to 1923, Fanny trotted out burlesks of Nijinsky, Pavlova, Theda Bara, Ruth St. Denis (as Egypta), Martha Graham ("Rewolt!") and Camille (K'Meel: "I've been a bad, bad voman, but awfully good company, nu?"). Her only misstep in this productive period was made in 1918 when she tried straight comedy in *Why Worry,* a hackneyed Yiddish hodgepodge that costarred the Avon Comedy Four. Despite adding two of

Fanny's best vaudeville numbers, the show did not last a month.

Fanny Brice had become a superb burlesker, reassuring the bourgeoisie that they need not be ashamed at their lack of appreciation of the arts and that opera, art song, ballet and modern dance were pretentious and ridiculous. She mocked herself as well; her glinting squint, rolling eyes and rubbery grimaces said to the audience, "Isn't it absurd for me to be playing a dancer, an artist, a courtesan, a vamp?"

In performance, her clown's body assumed a series of contrasting angles: crossed eyes, mouth stretched wide, head forward, shoulders back, elbows out, knees and toes turned in or bowed out. When she sang "My Man," she stood still and let her beautiful voice sing the lyrics and the tune; she became a woman, and the song seemed to be code for her life with Nicky Arnstein.

In 1926, David Belasco enticed Brice into a play, *Fanny*, which flopped. *Hollywood Music Box Revue* in 1927 also flopped, but this time the failure occurred in Los Angeles, far from New York notice. A new vaudeville act written by Billy Rose worked very well, and her marriage to Billy Rose in 1929 worked for a while. Billy was the opposite of Nick. They both wanted to be big shots, but Billy was willing to work hard for success. Fanny now had someone who shared the show-business life with her and was smart to boot.

There were more shows, more vaudeville and a few films for Fanny Brice. Her stage shows were all revues. The dull *Fioretta* managed 111 performances at the Earl Carroll Theatre in 1929. A year later, Billy mounted *Corned Beef and Roses,* which the critics panned, so he changed its title first to *Sweet and Low* for 1930 then trotted it out anew in 1931 as *Billy Rose's Crazy Quilt.*

Fanny made six feature films. None made her a movie star, but they served to capture her routines on film. In *My Man* (1928) she sang the title song, "I'm an Indian," "Second Hand Rose," "I Was a Floradora Baby," "I'd Rather Be Blue," "If You Want a Rainbow" and "Mrs. Cohen at the Beach." Her second flick, *Be Yourself* (1930), featured "When a Woman Loves a Man," "Kicking a Hole in the Sky," "Sasha the Passion of the Pasha" and the great "Cookin' Breakfast for the One I Love." Fanny simply had cameos in three more film appearances: *Crime without Passion* (unbilled, 1934), *The Great Ziegfeld* (1936) and *Ziegfeld Follies* (1946). Brice had a substantial role in *Everybody Sing* (1938), which was quite enjoyable, although Fanny only got two numbers: "Quainty, Dainty Me" and "Why? Because," a Baby Snooks patter song performed with Judy Garland.

Although Brice alternated between movies and the stage in the 1930s, her future was in network radio.

Paper cutout toy with instructions on the back for making a dancing Baby Snooks, one of Fanny Brice's characters

Sunny California was becoming home to a lot of show folk, and network radio was shifting to the Hollywood talent pool. Fanny's first adventure on the airwaves was singing with George Olson's Orchestra in 1932. *The Ziegfeld Follies of the Air* followed in 1936 but was short-lived, even though the program introduced Baby Snooks to the radio public. Her Baby Snooks portrayal had debuted in *Sweet and Low* and was revived and renamed for the *Ziegfeld Follies of 1936.* Fanny claimed she had played a baby character in her early burlesque and vaudeville days, and perhaps she had, but she may have been a bit defensive about reminders that Ray Dooley had created the basis for the Snooks character when Dooley was in the *Follies* in the 1910s.

Fanny Brice had never really loved Billy Rose, and she divorced him in 1938 when it was apparent that he had fallen for swim star Eleanor Holm. That same year, Baby Snooks joined the cast of a third network show, NBC's hour-long *Good News of 1938.* After the first year, the *Good News* show was cut to 30 minutes, renamed *Maxwell House Coffee Time,* and divided in half with one segment starring Frank Morgan and the other with Fanny Brice as Snooks. The odd pairing lasted five years, and during that time Snooks picked up Hanley Stafford as Daddy and Arlene Harris as Mommy. Mommy and Daddy argued, and Snooks fanned the flames. For this she was paid $6,500 per broadcast and lived very well.

In 1944, a half-hour *Baby Snooks Show* appeared on the CBS radio lineup and stayed there until 1948, when Brice signed with NBC. Fanny had suffered a serious heart attack in 1945, but *The Baby Snooks Show* ran strong until 1951. That same year, Fanny brought Snooks and Hanley Stafford to television for one 15-minute show for Popsicle. Her Baby Snooks character transferred to television very successfully. Then, suddenly, Fanny Brice died. A cerebral hemorrhage took her away a few months short of her 60th birthday.

BUNNY BRIGGS

b: 26 February 1922, Harlem, NY

From the age of three or four, Bunny Briggs' mother brought him to stage shows, often to watch his aunt, who was a chorus girl. He was fascinated from the start, but it was Bill Robinson's appearance that turned Bunny's fascination into a commitment to be in show business himself. Briggs learned to tap by watching others and practicing. Still a child, he began dancing in a record shop for the love of it. Although the throw money came in handy, unlike many other black youngsters, his family was not poor.

At five, he was dancing in clubs and dance halls with an older dancer named Porkchops. Soon, by adding two other youngsters, they built an act of sorts called "Porkchops, Navy, Rice and Beans," but they were still playing for throw money, and that was the way it stayed for the next five or six years. Early in the 1930s, Charles "Luckey" Roberts, a jazz pianist and a society bandleader, spotted Briggs and signed him. Roberts' band did not play boisterous dance halls or nightclubs; they were hired for grand house parties and society events. This environment, more genteel than clubs and theatres, encouraged Briggs' soft sound in his tapping and a loose, debonair style of movement.

When the Great Depression dampened enthusiasm for parties among society's 400, Briggs got a job as a singer with Lucky Millinder's band. For much of the 1930s, however, he performed as a dancer with big bands like Erskine Hawkins and the 'Bama State Collegians (at Harlem's Ubangi Club) and later with Earl Hines' band (at Kelly's Stables). It was probably in the late 1930s when a teenaged Briggs toured with one of the last annual shows produced by and starring the Whitman Sisters. Briggs remembered, "You sang one week, danced the next and sold peanuts the next, and if you got caught breaking any of the rules they shipped you home in a hurry." Nightclubs hosted most of Briggs' later work.

In 1963, Bunny and his good friend, Baby Laurence, both soloed and teamed for their appearance with Duke Ellington's Orchestra at the Newport Jazz Festival. Briggs worked again with the Duke in 1965, when Ellington conducted his sacred-music concerts in New York, Chicago, San Francisco and London. In 1988, 70 years after his vaudeville apprenticeship, Bunny Briggs was featured in the phenomenally successful Broadway revue *Black and Blue.*

BROADWAY

In its larger sense, Broadway represents big-time American theatre, the ultimate in well-financed, polished, live performance productions that boast star players and established producers, directors, playwrights, composers, lyricists, choreographers and musical directors.

Over the twentieth century, the theatre district crawled up Broadway, south to north, as builders looked for less expensive land while trying to anticipate the flow of residential and commercial real estate. At the turn of the twentieth century, several theatres had located around 14th Street and Union Square, whereas others moved still farther uptown to Herald Square at West 34th and 35th Streets. By the 1910s, some adventurous entrepreneurs were building their new theatres as far north as the Long Acre, as the double triangle where Broadway crosses Seventh Avenue was known. When the *New York Times* moved into one of the triangles, the area was named after the newspaper: Times Square. The Broadway district is centered on Broadway, Seventh Avenue and West 42nd Street. It spans Times and Duffy Squares up to West 53rd and extends east to Sixth Avenue and west to Eighth and, on some streets, Ninth Avenues.

With the rise of Off-Broadway and Off-Off-Broadway theatres and productions, the term *Broadway* has yielded to other and less flatteringly grand connotations that range from mainstream and traditional to middle class and middlebrow to ossified and overblown commercial entertainment.

In the mythic sense, Broadway, like Hollywood, is a focus of dreams and aspiration.

HELEN BRODERICK

b: 11 August 1891, Philadelphia, PA—
d: 25 September 1959, Beverly Hills, CA

Helen was born into a theatrical family that did not wish her to enter show business. At age 14, however, she became a chorus girl in Boston, the city to which her family had moved from Philadelphia. Helen remained in the chorus through a stint in *The Follies of 1907,* the first of what became Ziegfeld's annual reviews, and she appeared the following season in her first musical comedy, *The Girl Question.*

Helen didn't return to the legitimate stage for 15 years. Instead, she went into vaudeville, where she and her partner-husband, Lester J. Crawford, built themselves into a popular two-a-day act. Eventually, their young son, Broderick Crawford (1911–86), joined the act, although it is difficult to picture filmland's gruff future tough guy as a child comic.

Contemporaries recalled the vaudeville comedy team of Crawford & Broderick as one of the best of its day, but Helen began to get solo work in revues and musical comedies as well as straight comedies. Her first Broadway show was *Nifties of 1923,* a revue produced by Charles Dillingham with sketches written by two Weberfields alumni, William Collier and Sam Bernard, who starred. It closed in little over a month, but Helen's work was well regarded, and she got cast in *The Wild Westcotts,* a comedy. *Puzzles of 1925* was a return to revue, but it managed a more respectable run of more than three months; Cyril Ritchard and Walter Pidgeon were in the cast. *Mama Loves Papa* (1926) was another straight comedy, and, later that season, *Oh, Please!* (1926) was a musical comedy starring Beatrice Lillie and Charles Winninger. The show eked out ten weeks on Bea Lillie's name alone; Helen, featured in the billing, got good notices.

Fifty Million Frenchmen (1929) could not be wrong, and songwriter Cole Porter and director Monty Woolley earned 254 performances for the musical comedy. Helen introduced Porter's "Tale of an Oyster."

The Band Wagon (1931) starred Fred & Adele Astaire, Tilly Losch, Frank Morgan and Helen Broderick, and Helen enjoyed another fine musical comedy with a season-long run. *Earl Carroll's Vanities of 1932,* did poorly, artistically and financially, despite staging by Vincente Minnelli and featuring the talents of Helen Broderick, Harriet Hoctor, Milton Berle, Patsy Kelly, Robert Cummings and two top-notch British comedians, Will Fyffe and Max Wall.

Helen Broderick's final Broadway venture was her most distinguished and successful. Irving Berlin's *As Thousands Cheer* opened on 30 September 1933 at his Music Box Theatre. The stars were Marilyn Miller and Clifton Webb; Ethel Waters and Helen Broderick were billed next. Others in the cast were black comedian Hamtree Harrington, modern dancer Jose Limon and comic actor Jerome Cowan. The revue ran 390 performances and was the talk of the town. Only quality or sensation could survive the economics times.

When Hollywood decided in 1931 to film *Fifty Million Frenchmen,* it signed Helen and William Gaxton to repeat their stage roles; husband Lester Crawford also appeared in the movie as did Olsen & Johnson. This was Helen's fourth film of the six she made between 1930 and 1931.

Broderick's movie partnership with Victor Moore nearly eclipsed Helen's vaudeville partnership with husband Lester Crawford. So well did Broderick and Moore work together in their initial outing, *Swing Time* (1936), as comic supports for Ginger Rogers and Fred Astaire, that the studios paired them in five more films in little more than a single year: *The Life of the Party, Meet the Missus, She's Got Everything, We, the Jury* (all released in 1937) and *Radio City Revels* (1938). Network radio executives tried to transfer the Broderick and Moore combination to the airwaves, but the resulting series, *Twin Stars,* was short lived.

Helen, however was popular on her own, as was Victor Moore. In her mid-40s, when she left Broadway for good, she became one of dozens of delightful character actors who carried many movies. Like the best, Broderick found a particular niche: relaxed, wise and wry. When she played society matrons, there was a touch of the dame in them, as if she had jumped the traces once or twice before settling down on Park Avenue.

SHELTON BROOKS

b: 4 May 1886, Amherstburg, ON—
d: 6 September 1975, Los Angeles, CA

Successful in vaudeville, musical revue and comedy as a singer-comedian, Shelton Brooks' lasting fame rested on his songwriting. Many African American performers—from Cole & Johnson and Ernest Hogan to Noble Sissle & Eubie Blake and Fats Waller—wrote songs for themselves and others to sing. Indeed, most successful songwriters, white or black, were performers. It took the mass production of sheet music and sound recordings for the phonograph to make the writing of popular music a profitable specialization that led to the formation of Tin Pan Alley, a marketplace, literal and figurative, where performers shopped for songs and special material appropriate for their specific vocal styles and stage personalities.

Shelton was both African American and Native American. To take up a post in Cleveland, Ohio, his father, a minister, moved the family from Canada to the USA. Musically inclined as a boy, Shelton taught himself to play the church pump organ and moved from that to the family piano. His path soon diverged from his father's. In the early 1900s, teenage Shelton found work playing piano in restaurants, clubs and nickelodeons. On his own, he moved to Chicago and played piano in theatres and clubs and also performed as a singing comedian. He was greatly influenced by Bert Williams and was frank enough to consider himself a Williams' imitator. Brooks' first published song, "You Ain't Talking to Me," was a comic piece inspired by Bert Williams, which Shelton wrote for his own act, but it failed to sell as sheet music.

Shelton's second published song, "Some of These Days," sold 2 million copies and perhaps a million or two more in the 50 years that it was Sophie Tucker's theme song and the capstone of her every performance. In 1910, Sophie was a vaudeville headliner besieged by songwriters hoping to get her to use one of their songs in her act. Fortunately, Shelton knew Tucker's maid and dresser, Mollie Elkins, and Mollie persuaded Sophie to grant Shelton a few minutes to play his song. Sophie, a superb judge of her own material and always happy to work with African Americans, adopted "Some of These Days" immediately, and Shelton Brooks was made professionally.

Brooks could have left for New York, but he had no guarantee that any of his next songs would equal the success of "Some of These Days," so he chose to remain in Chicago, where he was a good-size frog in a good-size pond. Comedian and producer Jesse A. Shipp cast Shelton Brooks in a couple of his touring shows, *Dr. Herb's Prescription, Or It Happened in a Dream* (1911) and *The Lime Kiln* (1912). Charles Gilpin was in the cast of *Dr. Herb's Prescription.*

In 1913, another Brooks song, "I Wonder Where My Easy Rider's Gone," proved its popularity by sheet music sales and its durability when Mae West sang it in her first starring film, *She Done Him Wrong* (1933). In 1917, "The Darktown Strutters Ball" was introduced by a vaudeville trio that Blossom Seeley soon incorporated into her act: Benny Davis, Jack Salisbury and Benny Fields (whom Blossom soon promoted to partner and spouse).

Shelton was a handsome man. His career in musical comedy had changed from comedy singer to leading man, and he did well. The Panama Amusement Company engaged Brooks for leading roles in *Canary Cottage, Miss Nobody from Starland* and *September Morn,* former Broadway shows, all cheaply produced in 1920 with black casts, that played the Avenue Theatre in Chicago. *Canary Cottage* was the most successful of the trio and went on to play the Lafayette in Harlem and the Earle in Philadelphia.

Shelton Brooks made the move to Broadway in 1922 when he was engaged by Lew Leslie as the emcee for the *Plantation Revue* (1922). Lew culled some of the more effective musical numbers and comedy routines that he had mounted during the past several seasons at the Plantation Club in Harlem: the result was a revue that made Florence Mills a star. After its Broadway run, the revue was shortened to one act and paired in London with a one-act English revue, and the two halves were passed off as *Dover Street to Dixie.* When the *Dixie* half returned to Times Square, it was matched up with a one-act white revue, and that paired show was titled *Dixie to Broadway.* Brooks and Mills (and her husband, dancer U. S. Thompson) survived all three incarnations, and then they went into *Lew Leslie's Blackbirds of 1926.* Oddly, despite his twin reputations as a songwriter and a musical performer, no producer created a Shelton Brooks revue.

In 1928, Brooks decided to put his own show together; he called it *Nifties of 1928.* Lena Wilson was the biggest name in the cast. With himself as the star, Brooks toured the show but did not bring it to Broadway. He appeared in one more Broadway show, *Brown Buddies* (1930), which starred Bill Robinson, Adelaide Hall, John "Spider Bruce" Mason and Ada Brown and ran 14 weeks at the Liberty Theatre.

Shelton continued to write songs and played much of the 1930s as a singer in vaudeville. He performed on radio, made a few records for OKeh and filmed a Vitaphone short, *Gayety* (1929), with Hamtree Harrington.

A black-cast movie, *Double Deal* (1939), and a few dates in the early 1940s at the Apollo Theater seemed to spell the end of the trail for Shelton Brooks as an entertainer until he moved to Hollywood and became part of *Ken Murray's Blackouts.*

Brooks finished his career as one of the grand old black men of popular song. One of his last appearances was with Ethel Waters on *Johnny Carson's Sun City Scandals* on 13 March 1972. He died a few years later at 89.

BROWN & HOWARD

Mae Brown

Garland Howard

African American song-and-dance and comedy act Brown & Howard toured for years in various shows in the 1910s and 1920s, including *Darktown Affairs,* a 1929 revue, for which they wrote the book, lyrics and music and staged the dances.

BUSTER BROWN

b: (James Brown) 17 March 1913, Baltimore, MD—d: 7 May 2002, New York, NY

Buster Brown was inspired by Pops Whitman, son of two extraordinary tappers, Alice Whitman (of the Whitman Sisters) and Aaron Palmer. Buster Brown was about six years older than ten-year-old Pops, who was a star tap dancer even as a kid. Sixteen-year-old Buster lost no time preparing himself for a professional career as a dancer. He and his Baltimore buddies watched all the dancers who came to town, and then they taught themselves the steps they had witnessed onstage at the black vaudeville theatres.

Perhaps Buster's first professional work was in a tap trio that danced in a unit show, *Brown Skin Models* (1931), and traveled the black vaudeville circuit. Between the Theatre Owners' Booking Association (TOBA) circuit and independent black theatres that dotted the USA from cities in the Northeast to the Southwest and the West Coast, a good black show could play two or three years on the road. In the mid-1930s, Brown formed his own act, a trio called Three Speed Kings. In the style of the time, the trio was highly energetic and acrobatic like their contemporaries, the Four Step Brothers and the Nicholas Brothers. Buster himself developed a reputation as a fast, jazz dancer; he also employed legomania in his act.

Like others before him, Brown tired of playing the segregated South and Border States, where most Theatre Owners' Booking Association (TOBA) black theatres were located. He first came to prominence as a solo dancing act on tour with the Duke Ellington Orchestra. He later worked with other top black bands such as those led by Cab Calloway, Count Basie and Dizzy Gillespie. In the early 1950s, he toured Europe, Africa and Asia with several great jazz orchestras. Buster settled in Harlem during the mid-1950s, and he became a founding member of the Copasetics, a social and benevolent group of veteran tap dancers who chose their name in honor of Bill Robinson.

With the rise of rock and roll and the decline of tap dancing in musical comedy, there ceased to be enough dependable tap-dance gigs. Often, Brown worked outside the profession in a series of menial jobs. He had to support his wife and two children and help his mother and some of his seven sisters in Baltimore. Despite the downturn in tap-dance fortunes, Brown and a few other dancers of his era formed a group they defiantly called the Diehards, and they played hotels, dance halls and nightclubs, often without pay.

Nostalgia took hold in the mid- and late 1960s and early 1970s. Silent films were reissued, as were old blues and jazz recordings. Musical comedies from the 1920s and early 1930s were remounted on Broadway following the surprising success of *No, No, Nanette* and *Little Mary Sunshine.* Buster accepted an offer to appear on Broadway in *Bubblin' Brown Sugar* (1976) and remained with the show for three years of steady paychecks.

Unlike some other black dancers of the 1930s, there is some filmed evidence of Brown's dancing. His first feature film was *Something to Shout About* (1943). He had a small part in *The Cotton Club* (1984) and made a 30-minute video in 1987 called *Cookie's Scrapbook,* in which Buster and Charles "Cookie" Cook talked about their vaudeville days. In 1989, Buster made two important appearances. Buster was part of the all-star tap-dance lineup (Honi Coles, Bunny Briggs, Jimmy Slyde and Savion Glover) for the PBS documentary *Dance in America: Tap* (1989). This salute was narrated by Gregory Hines, but is not to be confused with the feature film *Tap,* released that same year, that also starred Gregory Hines and Savion Glover and featured Buster along with Steve Condos, Sandman Sims and Sammy Davis Jr. as members of a fictional version of the famed Hoofer's Club in Harlem.

Later that same year, Buster capped his performing career in *Black and Blue,* the long-running show (824 performances) that brought a number of old, yet still commanding, hoofers, such as Bunny Briggs, Isaiah "Lon" Chaney and Jimmy Slyde as well as Buster, back to Broadway.

Buster Brown did not lament the passing of black vaudeville and the old days. He made more money later in his life in Broadway shows, and he was in demand as a teacher. Savion Glover was among his students. Brown also taught at Harvard, Duke and New York University. He remained active until his death at age 89.

COLONEL T. ALLSTON BROWN

b: 1836, Newburyport, MA—d: 1918

Mike Leavitt, a prominent showman of the nineteenth century, claimed that Colonel T. Allston Brown "was the first agent of his time and the recognized historian of the American stage." Among the Colonel's chronicles is his *History of the American Stage,* begun in 1858 and published in 1870.

Brown began his professional life as the Philadelphia correspondent for the *New York Clipper,* then the premier show-business trade publication. He worked for other papers, including his own trade, *The Tattler.* He switched sides in 1860 when he became an advance agent for the Henry Cooper English Opera Company. Then he became the treasurer or box-office manager for Gardner & Madigan's Circus.

T. Allston Brown won his honorary title when, at the last minute, he substituted in Blondine's act. Blondine, a ropewalker, began his act by climbing a rope from the stage to the upper balcony, carrying a man on his back. When the assistant failed to show up, Brown substituted. For his daring, *The Baltimore Press* dubbed him "Colonel." A sensible promoter, Brown saw no reason to discard the honorific.

In 1863, he returned to journalism as the dramatic editor for the *New York Clipper,* where he stayed for nearly a decade. He resigned in 1872 to set up as an agent for actors and performers. At one point, Brown represented female impersonator Ernest Byne, previously known as Ernest Boulton, a man convicted for homosexual behavior, and booked Byne into the Theatre Comique and Tony Pastor's house.

Brown took to personal management of some favored acts, like the Hanlon Brothers and Mlle. Marie Aimee, and became a partner in Simmonds & Brown Dramatic Agency, which he took over upon the death of his partner and operated until he decided to retire in 1906 to devote himself to further writings about the history of American show business.

JOE E. BROWN

b: (Joseph Evan Brown) 28 July 1892, Holgate, OH—d: 6 July 1973, Los Angeles, CA

Few comedians were as beloved in their day as Joe E. Brown, and women seemed to enjoy him as much as men. He became Warner Brothers' principal comedy star of the 1930s, a top box-office attraction who drew well above The Marx Brothers, W. C. Fields and Laurel & Hardy, the other comedians representing the best of the early talkie era. Between 1927 and 1963, Brown made 67 feature films, including 14 silents, and at least one Vitaphone short, yet Brown's long film career was only a portion of his 70 years in show business. He began as a child acrobat in the circus and became one of the most accomplished in show business.

Earning money was not simply a lark for young Joe; there were too many mouths to feed at home. At seven, Joe (then called Evan) started hawking newspapers and shining shoes in Toledo. He got his first laugh selling papers in a saloon, and it hurt. A drunk pointed him out: "Look at the funny puss on that kid." Although in time Joe came to understand that his narrow-slit eyes and his wide mouth were partners with his talent in comedy, he never grew comfortable with the remarks people made about his features. In his starring years, no feature article about Joe E. Brown was complete without a sometimes gratuitous reference to his cavernous mouth, as though it defined the man and accounted solely for his ability to generate laughter. We will never know how he truly felt about his looks, but, to the end of his life, Joe E. Brown maintained an enviably athletic physique, carried himself with grace and was always seen impeccably groomed and nattily dressed.

Like many youngsters, Joe could do handstands, jumps and flips, but he pushed it further. A neighborhood boy, a few years older than Joe, had been engaged by Billy Ashe for his troupe. Joe pestered the boy until he persuaded Ashe to grant Joe an audition. Joe had mastered enough essentials to win a spot in the troupe, but what impressed the boss most was Joe's refusal to let a fall deter him. Joe began his professional life, at $1.50 per week, as the youngest member of The Five Marvelous Ashtons. Being the smallest, weighing less than 70 pounds, Joe became the flyer, the acrobat tossed between the two catchers.

They played the Sells & Downs Circus and the Busby Brothers Circus. Billy Ashe, born of several generations of circus clowns, was a good teacher but a tough master. Mistakes were punished by a drubbing, and there was a lot of turnover among the acrobats. Accommodations were mean, and the menu, often bread and soup twice a day, was meager fare for hardworking athletes, especially a growing boy. Joe made his first circus friends in clown alley, where long-forgotten, old pros like One-Eye Murphy told him stories and taught him pantomime.

Early on, young Joe broke his jaw hitting the rough safety net. Joe's ankles and wrists were constantly swollen and bleeding from the grabbing by the catchers who tossed him back and forth 40 feet above the ground several shows a day, six days a week. During his second season, Joe was raised to $2.50 a week when the Ashtons went on the road with the John Robinson Circus, the Floto Circus and some carnivals. At one of the carnivals, Joe met another kid, Bobby Clark, who was just entering show business in a tumbling act with his partner, Paul McCullough. Joe and Bobby would remain lifelong friends.

After the circus engagements, Ashe led the troupe out to the West Coast through a series of bookings in honky-tonk saloons featuring booze and floozies. Joe found them sad and shameful after what he considered the high standards of circus folk. The situation somewhat improved when the tour reached the Pantages' vaudeville house in Seattle and D. J. Grauman's Unique Theatre in San Francisco. The small-time vaudeville schedule of four or more shows a day exacerbated Joe's problems with his ankles and wrists. During Joe's fourth season with the troupe, the Ashton's were still in small-time vaudeville, playing the Haymarket Music Hall on Mason Street in San Fran-

Joe E. Brown

cisco, when the infamous earthquake hit at 5:12 in the morning on 18 April 1906.

Much as Joe loved showbiz, he had tired of Billy Ashe's harsh ways and probably had begun to realize that he had been the star attraction of the Ashtons without the compensation of adequate pay or respect. Joe, not yet 15 years old, began playing semiprofessional baseball in 1907 in the trolley leagues (so named because the players could ride to any game on the system of trolleys that linked the neighborhoods). A friend of Joe's with connections in both baseball and vaudeville had gotten Joe into baseball. Now he sent out letters to get Joe back into show business. Joe hooked up with Tommy Bell and Frank Prevost at $7.50 a week.

Frank Leroy Guise had been the only non-family member of the Prevost Brothers and the understander in the act; he caught the others. The new trio did not last long; Ashe had been stern, Bell was vicious. One day, instead of catching Joe as he came down from a high somersault, Bell knowingly walked off the stage, and Joe broke his leg as he landed. Joe was gathered up by Frank and taken to the home he shared with his wife, Greta Leroy, to heal.

While recuperating, Joe and Frank put together a comic acrobat act to be billed as the Prevost Brothers. The two got good reviews in the trade papers and pulled down $60 a week for the act in burlesque. During the summer layoff, Joe returned to baseball, his second love, and broke another leg. He returned to burlesque for the 1909 season. By that time, the act had changed its name to Prevost & Brown. Finally, Joe got billing. The show's press agent dubbed Joe "The Corkscrew Kid" and claimed Joe was the only acrobat in the world to do a double body twist and back somersault in one leap.

Brown and Frank "Prevost" Guise stayed partners for about nine years. While they were playing the big-time Orpheum circuit, Joe met his future wife, Kathryn McGraw. They were married in 1915 and stayed so for the rest of their lives. Joe was devoted to his family, the two boys to whom Kathryn gave birth, and the two younger girls they adopted.

Even when Provost & Brown eventually played the Palace, they were relegated to the closing spot because they were acrobats. Burlesque was more democratic than vaudeville, and Joe was never ashamed that he played burlesque, yet he wanted everyone to know he never used blue material on any stage.

Joe's good friend, mentor and partner, Frank Guise, no longer had the energy to sustain a full acrobatic act, so Joe invented some comedy business to give him a rest. The comedy made their act more popular, and, in 1919, Joe got the chance to take over the comic lead in an established Broadway hit, *Listen Lester.* The night he took over, Actors Equity called their strike. Although Joe had a young family to support and his father had just died, leaving more family to help, Joe did not cross the picket line. Losing the role in *Listen Lester* and with no season's booking in vaudeville, Joe was reduced to taking short gigs where he could, including baseball, which led to an offer from the New York Yankees. In those days, showbiz paid better than baseball.

After the strike, Joe was back in *Listen Lester* but in the road company. Until *Listen Lester,* Brown had always worked in costume, a rube outfit. The laughs did not diminish when he switched to tailored street clothes. Broadway beckoned again in 1920 with *Jim Jam Jems,* and Joe joined a cast of great funnymen: Harry Langdon, Frank Fay, Ned Sparks and Joe Miller. *Jim Jam Jems* became *Hello Lester!* when it went on the road.

In following seasons, Joe was featured in three editions of John Murray Anderson's *Greenwich Village Follies* (1921, 1922 and 1923). Brown resigned three weeks into the 1923 edition in a dispute over material and played the rest of the season in vaudeville on the Orpheum circuit in a sketch, "Arrest Me." Joe returned to Broadway in *Betty Lee* (1924), *Captain Jinks* (1925) and *Twinkle, Twinkle* (1926). *Twinkle, Twinkle* went on tour and brought Joe to the West Coast and Hollywood in 1927.

Joe had made many screen tests before 1927. Each was rejected (his small, light blue eyes did not photograph well, or his mouth photographed too well). All he had to show for it was a one-reel Vitaphone, *Don't Be Jealous.* Finally, FBO (soon to be RKO) signed Brown without a test. Between 1928 and 1929, Brown worked at three studios and made a total of nine movies, the first six of which were dramas!

When sound hit Hollywood, Joe was Johnny-on-the spot: he was stage trained, experienced in dialogue as well as physical comedy, but still a new face. He acquitted himself nicely as a comedian and an eccentric dancer in Warner Brothers' first fully sound musical, *On with the Show.* The studio offered him Bert Lahr's stage hit, *Hold Everything,* and Joe scored in that, too.

Joe E. Brown did not play just one type in films. Sometimes he was a romantic lead and other times a clown. He could swagger with macho pride and a few minutes later flutter without embarrassment. If he was often cast as a dim hayseed, he occasionally played the sly fox. In some films, he was brave, faithful and modest, yet in others, he was a cowardly and lying braggart. His film roles ranged from Shakespeare to melodrama to musicals, light farce and slapstick comedies. In film versions of various stage hits, Brown took roles assigned to Broadway talents as diverse as Bert Lahr and Walter Huston.

Among Joe's more fondly remembered films are *Hold Everything* (1930), *You Said a Mouthful* and *Elmer the Great* (both 1932), *Son of a Sailor* (1933), *Six Day Bike Rider* (1934), *Alibi Ike* and *Midsummer Night's Dream* (both 1935), *Earthworm Tractors* (1936) and *Some Like It Hot* (1960).

Throughout his film career, Joe returned to vaudeville and presentation houses for personal appearances and to the legitimate stage for productions of *Elmer the Great* (1931) and *Square Crooks* (1932). After an ill-advised move away from Warner Brothers to freelance in 1936, his movies became consistently second rate, and his stage work more important. When his movie career faltered, he retained audiences nationwide that had grown up with him, and they turned out for his stage appearances in *The Show-Off* (1940), *Rio Rita* (1941) in the Robert Woolsey role, *Harvey* (off and on from 1944 to 1959), *Courtin' Time* (1951) and several tours as Captain Andy in *Show Boat* in 1960 and 1961. His portrayal of Elwood P. Dowd in *Harvey* and the title role of Aubrey Piper in Elmer Rice's *Show Off* were welcomed touring attractions for years, including long runs on Broadway.

Joe started entertaining troops with an unauthorized tour of Alaskan bases in 1941. Then, after his oldest son was killed in a routine training flight, Joe undertook a 30-month, 200,000-mile trek to the front lines from North Africa to the South Pacific. Joe E. Brown was awarded, among many citations, the Bronze Star, one of only two civilians so honored. The other was newsman Ernie Pyle.

In 1959, Joe capped his career in *Some Like It Hot* with a splendid turn as Osgood Fielding, the aging playboy bewitched by Jack Lemmon, who was disguised in drag and fleeing gangsters. The long chase climaxed in the final reel as Tony Curtis, Marilyn Monroe, Brown and Lemmon got away on a speedboat. Brown is outlining a connubial future to Lemmon. Jack explains he can not cook, can not have children. Brown does not care. When Jack whips off his wig and tells Joe that he is a man, Joe placidly replies, "Nobody's perfect."

BOTHWELL BROWNE

b: (Walter Bothwell Bruhn) 7 March 1877, Copenhagen, Denmark—d: 12 December 1947, Los Angeles, CA

Bothwell Browne, who entered the American vaudeville scene in the 1900s, first came to notice in one of (George M.) Cohan's & (Sam) Harris' minstrel touring units. Bothwell did not possess a distinguished singing voice but was an able actor, playing various characters rather than a single role.

A trained dancer, Bothwell made some theatre managers and audiences nervous, especially when he essayed the like of Cleopatra or Salome. The average audience enjoyed or at least tolerated female impersonation when the character was either demure and inoffensive or grotesque and funny. Bothwell Browne's sinuous dances were viewed by some as too seductive and unsettling.

He spent money to produce elaborate and effective vaudeville acts. His gowns attracted a lot of attention, and he hired actors and chorus dancers for his flash acts. At one point, he and male impersonator Kathleen Clifford did an act together in vaudeville.

In 1911, Browne appeared on Broadway at the Herald Square Theatre. He starred, designed the costumes and choreographed *Miss Jack,* but the show barely lasted two weeks. His attempt at a movie career also fell short of his vaudeville triumphs.

Julian Eltinge was the only female impersonator to find any degree of success in films. Most studios saw no gain in making movies featuring cross-dressers or female impersonators. Doubtless, many producers were at best uncomfortable with both impersonators and the idea of men impersonating women unless it was as unmistakably farcical as *Charley's Aunt.* Bothwell Brown at least got the opportunity to make one movie, however: *Yankee Doodle in Berlin* (1919) (also known as *The Kaiser's Last Squeal*), a five-reel feature-length Mack Sennett comedy.

Bothwell Browne played Captain Bob White, whose mission to infiltrate Germany required a disguise as a woman. Sennett regulars in this film included Ford Sterling as Kaiser Wilhelm, Ben Turpin and Chester Conklin as military officers, Bert Roach as von Hindenburg, Charlie Murray as an Irish infantryman, and Marie Prevost and Phyllis Haver. Bothwell Browne and some of the Mack Sennett Bathing Beauties toured big-time vaudeville theatres to promote the movie. *Yankee Doodle in Berlin* did not lead to a demand for Bothwell's future services in film, however.

As big-time vaudeville began to wane in the second half of the 1920s, and he was reaching his late 40s, Browne began to teach dance and to produce nightclub revues.

BROX SISTERS

Dagmar Brox

b: (Dagmar Josephine Brock) ca. 1898, Memphis, TN—d: 2 May 1999, Glen Falls, NY

Lorayne Brox

b: (Lorayne Eunice Brock) 11 November 1900, Memphis, TN—d: 14 June 1993, Los Angeles, CA

Kathleen Brox

b: (Kathleen Patricia Brock) ca. 1896, Winchester, KY—d: 1988

One of the earliest female singing trios, the Brox Sisters entered show business through small-time vaudeville, as was customary in their time. The highlights of their career bracketed the 1920s. They appeared in the first, third and fourth editions of Irving Berlin's *Music Box Revues* (1921, 1923 and 1924) and then closed the decade with two major movies, the big-budget, all-star musical extravaganzas *The Hollywood Revue of 1929* and *The King of Jazz* (1930).

The Brox singing style, although not as harmonically complex as the Boswell Sisters, foreshadowed the Boswells. The Brox Sisters sang quite a few novelty tunes, like "Monkey Doodle Doo" and "Red Hot Mama," as well as ersatz jazz tunes, like "School House Blues," "Bring on the Pepper" and "Everybody Step." They were a success on early radio, and their recordings were popular. The song they are most closely identified with is "Singing in the Rain," which they and Cliff Edwards introduced in the movie *The Hollywood Revue of 1929.*

That Irving Berlin chose them to sing his songs in his *Music Box Revues* is a solid tribute to the Brox Sisters' musicianship. Doubtless, Berlin was instrumental in hiring them for a specialty appearance in *The Cocoanuts* (1925), the only Irving Berlin show that failed to yield a hit song (as if any could be heard while Groucho, Chico, Zeppo and Harpo were cavorting onstage!). The Brox Sisters' next Broadway show was the equally prestigious *The Ziegfeld Follies of 1927,* in which they shared the stage with Eddie Cantor, Ruth Etting, Dan Healy and Irene Delroy.

WILLIE BRYANT

b: 30 August 1908, New Orleans, LA—d: 9 February 1964, Los Angeles, CA

Willie Bryant was 17 when he joined the Whitman Sisters for their annual tour in 1926. In a Whitman revue, most performers did several things. In one part of the show, Willie Bryant partnered two of the sisters, Bert and Alice, in a production number. Elsewhere in the program, Willie was paired with the diminutive dance star Princess Pee Wee. Less than 40 inches tall, Princess Pee Wee would tap under and between Bryant's long dancing legs, a routine later adapted for an early Shirley Temple and Bill Robinson film.

By the 1927–28 season, Bryant was in Harlem, where he met Leonard Reed. Bryant was a tall, muscular six footer; Reed was short and slim. The contrast in physiques worked for Reed & Bryant as it had for Bryant dancing with Princess Pee Wee.

Years later, Leonard Reed claimed that Willie Bryant was one of the most talented dancers and comedians, white or black, in the business, and it was true that Willie was a better dancer than Leonard, but it was the chemistry between them, the casual patter and slick moves, that quickly made them a success. Reed & Bryant billed themselves as "Brains as Well as Feet" in an act that took them to the heights of vaudeville during the three years they danced together.

Both Leonard Reed and Willie Bryant were fair skinned, and they could play white vaudeville theatres without discovery. They did not claim to be white, but few managers or other acts asked them or cared. Reed refused to be limited by matters of race, but Bryant refused more and more to pass as white. The choice was soon taken from them when, in the early 1930s, the national economy and vaudeville soured, and the team disbanded in 1933. Before that happened, however, Reed & Bryant enjoyed several years in big-time vaudeville. They played the Palace in 1930.

From the mid-1930s onward, Bryant restricted himself to black show business and developed into an all-around performer. After he and Reed split on good terms, Bryant became a bandleader for a time, taking over Lucky Millinder's outfit, which included, at the time, Teddy Wilson, Benny Carter, Ben Webster and Cozy Cole. Bryant taught the musicians some basic showmanship, even a few jive dance steps, so when Willie brought musicians off the bandstand to the front of the stage, they joined him dancing the *shim sham.*

In the 1950s, during his many years as an emcee, Willie was a great favorite with Apollo audiences, and he sometimes reteamed with his old partner, Leonard Reed, for a comedy skit.

(LIEUTENANT) J. TIM BRYMN

b: 1881—d: 1946

A graduate of Shaw University and the National Conservatory of Music in New York, J. Tim Brymn became a prolific songwriter who wrote for Bert Williams & George Walker, collaborated with W. C. Handy ("Aunt Hagar's Blues") and was a bandleader of note.

Brymn was an important figure in African American music of the first three decades of the twentieth century. He was the manager of an important black music publishing business, Williams & Piron, as well as musical director for several Broadway shows, including Williams & Walker's *Sons of Ham* (1900) and *Abyssinia* (1906).

He composed music for *Huckleberry Finn* (1902), *Happy Hooligan's Trip around the World* (1906), Sherman H. Dudley's musical *Black Politician,* which toured the Theatre Owners' Booking Association (TOBA) circuit in 1907, *Panama* (1908) and the Broadway show *His Honor, the Barber* (1909). He wrote the lyrics for Aubrey Lyles' show *The Husband* (1909).

Later, he led his own band and was one of the bandleaders who followed James Reese Europe's lead to form the Clef Club, the black musicians' union. During the First World War, like Jim Europe, Brymn earned his U.S. Army commission and military title by leading one of the American Expeditionary Force bands.

BUCK & BUBBLES

Buck

b: (Ford Lee Washington) 16 October 1903 (or 1906), Louisville, KY— d: 31 January 1955, New York, NY

Bubbles

b: (John William Sublett) 19 February 1902, Louisville, KY—d: 18 May 1986, New York, NY

They were cool before there was cool. They smiled, but their smiles were sly and knowing, not the "Golly, gee, we're just so happy you came to see us and hope you like what we do" grins sported by so many tappers anxious to ingratiate themselves with an audience. Buck & Bubbles knew they were good, better than very good, especially the long, tall, cocky dude called Bubbles. His smile, his stance and his manner said, "Yeah, we *know* we are fine. Catch what you can because I'm dancing for those who are hip to it."

There were hundreds of good tap dancers working from the 1910s though the 1950s. There were even a few dozen great ones. Any attempt to narrow the field to a list of the top ten courted debate, then as now. What set the best apart was an individuality married to great skill. Style, memorable style, was essential. Indisputably, on everyone's list of the very great tap dancers was John Bubbles, and that remains true at the turn of the twenty-first century.

Equally true is that Buck & Bubbles was one of the great song-and-dance acts. The humor and nonchalance they exhibited onstage made it all—exquisite timing, sophisticated musicianship and masterful dancing—seemed so easy. Bubbles came across as a sharpie, a persona that inspired George Gershwin to create a role just for him. Buck, the sharpie's buddy, gave the impression of being the lookout, distracting the audience with some funny business while his partner pulled off the sleight of hand—and feet. There was a hint of the con artist in their personalities, but their comic riffs diffused any apprehension about their primary commitment to being entertainers.

Much the shorter of the pair and built low to the ground, Buck looked badly fit in his fancy-dress suits and like a disguised thug in his newsboy, bootblack or Little Lord Fauntleroy costumes. He played piano in the act, often stop time for the dancing, so that between his piano and Bubbles' taps there was a call and response, a dialogue in rhythm. They both sang, Buck's raspy baritone anticipating bebop and harmonizing with

John Bubbles

Bubbles' breathy, almost hoarse and higher-pitched sound. Buck also danced; at some point in the act, the two swapped places for a few bars, Bubbles gliding to the piano as Buck rose to dance for a few bars. Compared to the fleet-footed Bubbles, Buck was rooted to the ground like a tree stump. Although his repertoire of a few flat-footed taps, slides, shuffles and turns was limited, Buck's rhythm was unerring, and his routine added comedy to the act. More relaxed than Bubbles, Buck pretended to fall off his piano bench, crouch on the floor beneath the piano keys as a gag, and lackadaisically reach up to hit a few keys at the precise moment they were needed. Or, with his hat, he fanned Bubbles' flashing feet burning up the stage floor.

Buck's stunt work at the piano belied his talent and skill. He was a solid jazz pianist, trumpeter and singer. Independently, he wrote a few jazz tunes and recorded with Louis Armstrong (1930), Bessie Smith (1933) and Coleman Hawkins (1934), among others.

Bubbles is credited with inventing rhythm tap dancing. Eddie Rector made tap dance move; instead of pounding the floor standing in place, the way many jigs were performed, Rector traveled across the stage. Thereafter, most tap dancers followed. Bill Robinson refined tap by bringing the toe of the foot into play, dancing close to the floor and carefully articulating each tap. Bubbles tapped with both his toes and heels, rolling and sliding between them. He also slowed the tempo of his accompaniment, which let him double the amount of steps, and changed forever the rhythm of tap. Continually shifting among precise toe taps, percussive raps of the heels, brushes and slides, and a tripping step that segued into a figure-eight crossover, he produced a variety of sounds like those of a drummer. His steps were as varied as his sound, and Bubbles varied his attack dramatically. What might begin with a strut, followed by a few seemingly casual and light-footed combinations, would suddenly erupt in a burst of staccato steps topped by a swirl of flashy moves and on-the-dime stops.

The surprise and brilliance of the execution made audiences catch their breath and wonder later just what they had seen. The theatregoing public was not alone in that wonder. Fellow tap dancers had a hard time figuring out those split-second combinations, and Bubbles was not about to give them a second chance.

Bubbles was not always a master. He first came to New York in 1919, a 17-year-old singer whose nickname at the time was Bubber. His voice had changed, and he had decided to add dancing to his act. Although he had learned the basics of clog, buck and tap, that was not enough to earn the respect of Harlem's hot dancers, as he found out when he visited the Hoofers Club. He was laughed off the floor and shamed out the door. He and his partner, Buck, continued their vaudeville tour, going back to the Midwest and on to California. Dancing for Bubber became a serious skill to master, not merely an added diversion in the act. Between performances, he practiced constantly and began to erase the gap between what he could do and what he wanted to do. Bubber was determined to be the best. When he and Buck returned to New York and the Hoofers Club a year later in 1920, Bubber was a competitor; by 1922 he was a master.

John William Sublett had met Ford Lee Washington around 1912, when both were kids earning money as pin boys in an Indianapolis bowling alley. Their families had moved from Louisville, Kentucky. A few sources peg Buck's birth year as 1906, four years Bubber's junior. Although it is possible that a six-year-old black boy could have been setting up pins in a bowling alley and that a ten-year old boy would choose a six-year-old for a good friend, it is more likely that they were born only a year apart. Bubber had been singing since he was seven, and Buck proved to be a piano prodigy. Along with the usual assortment of jobs that most kids tried, Buck and Bubber rounded up gigs in local saloons, demonstrated sheet music in a hometown five-and-dime store, and began to appear in amateur contests in small-time vaudeville houses.

Buck and Bubber won enough amateur contests to get some small-time bookings. For the next few years, roughly 1915 to 1917, it was catch-as-catch-can, doing whatever paid. The bookings they got were mostly in the Border States and the Midwest: Louisville and Indianapolis leading to gigs farther away from home, such as Detroit, Michigan. Colored acts were expected to don blackface, especially when playing white vaudeville houses, and usually an audience's assumption was that the blacked-up act was white. It was demeaning for African Americans to have to pass in this way, but at least they were working.

Gradually, Bubber's and Buck's experience and confidence grew; their song-and-dance act got sharper and more entertaining. Buck recalled that they both played the act for comedy as much as for music, emphasizing the disparity in their height: shoes too big, Buck's pants too short, and Bubber's too long. They were only 15 and 17, respectively, when Buck and Bubber played New York for the first time. They must have seen a fair number of buck and clog dancers on the circuits, and Bubbles acknowledged Harland Dixon, of Dixon & Doyle, as an inspiration.

Buck & Bubbles

Somewhere along the way, Bubber became Bubbles. By 1921, the duo generally opened their act with Buck playing piano, Bubbles singing and strutting, the two of them kidding around, keeping it light even though the act was well rehearsed and fast paced. With Buck pumping the piano, Bubbles laid down some fancy footwork. Buck left the piano to pick up the challenge, executing his little flat-footed dance, and then Bubbles joined him for a short dance duet. Buck returned to his piano as Bubbles launched into his solo dance that built into a rousing closing for the act. Bubbles—and the dancers who watched him expectantly—claimed he never did steps quite the same way twice. This frustrated those seeking to figure out his combinations, and the variations gave Bubbles his reputation as the best ad-lib dancer of the era.

By 1922, Buck & Bubbles were on Keith and Orpheum time and had played the Palace Theatre, reputedly the first African American act to do so. According to Marian Spitzer, chronicler of the Palace's golden years, Buck & Bubbles was about the only memorable and important act to be discovered at the Palace's Thursday-morning auditions. Although Buck & Bubbles played a lot of mainstream white time, they sometimes signed on as added attractions in black shows playing the northern black theatres. Hurtig & Seamon's black burlesque revues of the 1920s regularly began at the Lafayette or Alhambra in Harlem and circled around the Middle Atlantic states, usually playing the Royal in Baltimore, the Howard in Washington, D.C., the Earle or the Standard in Philadelphia, and sometimes heading north to Boston, either to the Gayety or Casino Theatres, and west to theatres in Pittsburgh, Cincinnati, Cleveland, Columbus, Detroit and Chicago.

Many of the black and integrated shows that played northern theatres were financed by one of the many producers whose shows played Columbia Burlesque. The Columbia wheel was the Tiffany of burlesque circuits; the owners did not tolerate smuttiness, and their theatres were carefully maintained. Acts like Buck & Bubbles were added to traveling black revues to provide the show with punch. Although Buck & Bubbles did not have to participate in the show other than doing their act, they often made more than the star comics and dancers who got top billing.

The Lafayette Theatre was home base in New York. When Buck & Bubbles played vaudeville or revues in Manhattan, they doubled by appearing in a matinee or a midnight show up in Harlem's Lafayette, or they closed the late show at one of the bigger nightclubs. In big-time, mainstream vaudeville, Buck & Bubbles were earning $1,500 to $2,000 a week in the 1920s. Doubling added another $500 or more to their weekly take. Unlike some black acts, Bubbles performed much the same for blacks as he did for whites. "Do the same act. If you do it right you didn't have to change the act neither place. Keep the same material." Jazz and tap-dance historian Marshall Stearns reported that Bubbles did admit that, although the material stayed the same, his style changed a bit: "I danced loose and rhythmic uptown—flop and flang-flang; simple and distinct downtown."

Buck & Bubbles was one of the most critically acclaimed and popular black acts in vaudeville. When they played the Palace for the week of 24 September 1928, they were billed as "Clever Colored Comedians," an indication that, in addition to being regarded as a premier song-and-dance act, they had established themselves as funnymen and all-around entertainers. They played the Palace many times between their debut in 1922 and 1935, when the Palace went wholly in the motion-picture exhibition business. Fortunately, there were many other bids for Buck & Bubbles' services toward the end of the 1920s, when vaudeville began to offer fewer weeks as the popularity of network radio and talking motion pictures claimed ever larger shares of the American audience.

Blackbirds of 1930, the fourth edition of Lew Leslie's well-worn franchise, ran only eight weeks, despite such stunning stars as Ethel Waters, the Berry Brothers, Flournoy Miller & Mantan Moreland, as well as Buck & Bubbles, yet the Great Depression years of the 1930s proved profitable for the team. They starred in top night spots like the Grand Terrace in Chicago and the Cotton Club in Harlem, where on various occasions they shared the bill with Duke Ellington, Ethel Waters and the young Nicholas Brothers.

Buck & Bubbles began their recording career in 1927 with a test pressing for Victor. Between 1930 and 1934, as the Great Depression worsened, most black entertainers, other than Ethel Waters, could not get recorded. Columbia Records, realizing that Buck & Bubbles, like Waters, had a white audience, contracted with the team to record nine sides during that period, including "Oh, Lady Be Good" and "He's Long Gone from Bowling Green," plus six recordings made in London in 1936. Curiously, some of their Columbia sides seem never to have been issued until resurrected, decades later, on vinyl LPs (long-playing, 33 rpm) reissues.

Their film careers began in 1929 in a series of two reel musicals for Pathé: *Black Narcissus, Fowl* [sic] *Play* and *In and Out* (all 1929), *Darktown Follies, High Toned* and *Honest Crooks* (all 1930), *Black Cat Tales* and *Night in a Nightclub* (both 1934), and *Harlem Bound* (1935). Later, they made full-length features.

Back onstage, Buck & Bubbles were signed to perform in the *Ziegfeld Follies of 1931,* the last one that Florenz Ziegfeld lived to produce. Fittingly, it played the theatre named after Ziegfeld rather than its usual home, the New Amsterdam, which at the time was hosting the hit musical *The Band Wagon.* In Ziegfeld shows, only industrious and entrepreneurial performers survived. First, an act could not rely upon the creative staff that Ziegfeld hired to provide material, music or dance routines; an act needed to find good material for itself. Second, the act had to score well with the out-of-town audiences to be spared the cuts that pared the overlong tryout performances into the final version of the show that reached Broadway. Every edition of the Follies was invariably stuffed with the production numbers of which Ziegfeld and his creative teams were so fond. The comedians and specialty acts had to fight for their time and space, and they were the first candidates for cutting. Hal Leroy and Mitzi Mayfair, accomplished white tappers, were also signed for the 1931 Follies, so there was a goodly amount of dancing in the show.

Some of the white performers (not Hal Leroy, who respected black dancers and was in turn respected by them) sniffed at working in a show with Buck & Bubbles. During rehearsals, Buck & Bubbles were ordered to cut their routine from 14 to 8 minutes. Opening night on the road, in Pittsburgh, they stopped the show. Because of the backstage unpleasantness, their manager, Nat Nazarro, forbade Buck & Bubbles to return to the stage to accept the audience's call. Reportedly, the applause lasted ten minutes. Before the *Follies* reached Broadway, Buck & Bubbles had been switched to several positions in the revue, but the audience reception killed whichever number followed them. Finally, by opening night on Broadway, Buck & Bubbles were slotted in the closing spot, despite the presence in the cast of New York favorites Helen Morgan, Ruth Etting and Harry Richman. This edition of the Follies ran about five months, not quite good enough to return investors' money, but it was a great success for Buck & Bubbles.

They toured Britain and France after the *Follies* closed, and their London reception ensured their return five years later. Buck & Bubbles reached a coast-to-coast American radio audience on Rudy Vallee's *The Fleischmann Hour* on 13 December 1934. In addition to Buck & Bubbles, the show's guests included Beatrice Lillie, Henry Fonda, Cole Porter and the legendary silent-movie cowboy William S. Hart.

When George Gershwin wrote the music for *Porgy and Bess,* the landmark folk opera that opened on Broadway in 1935, Gershwin did so with the intention that John Bubbles play the lead role of Sportin' Life. This change in medium suited Buck far less than Bubbles, who was easier to cast in musicals. Buck ended up with minor parts onstage, as in *Porgy and Bess,* and on screen, as in *Cabin in the Sky.*

The dance team returned to England for the 1936–37 season to appear in a revue and make a British film, *Transatlantic Rhythm,* the producers of which hoped its American stars, Ruth Etting, Buck & Bubbles and Lou Holtz, would entice Londoners to the theatre. Another English revue, *Calling All Stars,* paired English favorites Evelyn Dall, Carroll Gibbons and Ambrose & His Orchestra with Yankee imports Buck & Bubbles,

Larry Adler, the Nicholas Brothers and American expatriate Elisabeth Welch. On 2 November 1936, the first broadcast of the BBC Television Service included Buck & Bubbles in a variety show.

Back in the USA, they returned to Broadway, but only for a short time. The 1937 musical *Virginia* had a good composer in Arthur Schwartz, a good librettist in Laurence Stallings and a good cast going for it. It also had a lot going against it. According to musical-theatre authority Gerald Bordman, *Virginia* was, at its core, a thoughtful musical with a historical theme that was booked into the Center Theatre, a venue more fit for extravaganza than plot-driven musicals. Owen Davis was called in to bring grandeur and sweep, but 60 performances later, *Virginia* closed.

In the late 1930s, Buck & Bubbles appeared in feature-length films. For the most part, they contributed little other than their highly polished act. This was not unusual for African American variety acts, which often were added to the film but not the plots so that their specialty could be snipped out of the movie print that was exhibited in many white movie houses in the South. *Varsity Show* (1937), a flaccid college-kids confection of a musical, was redeemed only by Buck & Bubbles re-creation of their vaudeville act at the film's finish. *Cabin in the Sky* (1943) was the only important film the team made. Neither Buck nor Bubbles was in the stage version, but Bubbles assumed the role of the seductive villain. The highlight of the film was Bubbles' jitterbug with a stocky, but still game, Ethel Waters, followed by a dashing solo dance. Buck was barely on screen but played piano for Bubbles in the nightclub scene. The producers of *I Dood It* (1943), which starred Red Skelton, must have had it in for tap dancers; co-star Eleanor Powell was assigned a wretched role, and her numbers were among the weakest of her career. Buck & Bubbles were throwaways and were not given screen credit. *Atlantic City* (1944) was weighted down with a stodgy narrative, a stiff male lead and poor direction, but it sported a number of delightful specialties, including Joe Frisco, Belle Baker, Gallagher (actually Joe Kenney) & Shean, Paul Whiteman and Van & Schenck (actually Charles Marsh). The Buck & Bubbles routine was crammed onto a small stage already filled by Louis Armstrong, his band, Dorothy Dandridge and too much furniture. The team's next two films were cheapies made for distribution to theatres patronized by black audiences: *Laff Jamboree* (1945) and *Mantan Messes Up* (a Mantan Moreland vehicle of 1946). *A Song Is Born* (1948) was a misfire for star Danny Kaye, producer Samuel Goldwyn and releasing studio RKO. Buck & Bubbles were not even billed in the cast of this, their final, film.

The glory years were over. Although they had remained friends throughout their joint career, the team split in 1953, and Buck joined Timmie Rogers, an up-and-coming black comedian, songwriter and bandleader. Drugs were in well-publicized use among jazz musicians of the 1950s. Buck died in 1955, a drug overdose reportedly the cause. The choreography Agnes DeMille brought to Broadway in the mid-1940s changed theatrical dance for a generation. Modern ballet was in; tap was out. Hollywood followed the trend: Gene Kelly was in; the Nicholas Brothers and Ann Miller were out. Television was inhospitable. Ed Sullivan hosted Peg Leg Bates and other tappers on his Sunday-night program, but most TV producers found tap too much trouble. Camera technicians, trained to capture facial expressions with close-ups, often focused on the dancers' smiles instead of their legs and feet. The floors in TV studios were not built for tap dancers, and television sound engineers could not balance the music and the taps.

Still, John W. Bubbles (he had long ago officially changed his name from Sublett) got more attention than most tappers. Some of it was unpleasant. In the understandable zeal to project positive images of black people, some in the civil rights movement struck out at an older generation of black entertainers like Ethel Waters, John Bubbles, Tim Moore and the cast of the all-black TV version of *Amos 'n' Andy*. They were accused of Uncle Tomming. Bubbles rebuked his critics at a 1961 NAACP meeting. He told them he did what he had to do as a black entertainer at that time to make a living. That was too modest a retort for Bubbles, who had achieved so much. It was also too restrained in support of other old black entertainers. It was they who had been the public faces of black America, helping white Americans realize that African Americans were talented and were blessed and cursed by the same emotions, desires and foibles as whites.

Bubbles' grandest engagements in those uneasy years were when he returned to the Palace Theatre, the scene of so many professional triumphs for him and his pal and partner. In 1951, the Palace, several decades past its splendor, began offering vaudeville bills headed by well-known Hollywood musical and comedy stars like Judy Garland, Betty Hutton, Danny Kaye and Jerry Lewis. The remainder of the bills was split between newcomers and vaudeville veterans like Bubbles.

During the 1950s and 1960s, Bubbles toured with Bob Hope (to Vietnam), Caterina Valente, Anna Maria Alberghetti and Eddie Fisher; appeared on TV variety shows starring Steve Allen, Perry Como, Dean Martin and Bob Hope; played Las Vegas with Johnny Carson; and was reportedly the first black entertainer to appear on Carson's *Tonight Show*. He recorded an album of songs, *Bubbles, John W., That Is* for VeeJay, guest starred on a pair of 1962 episodes of the *Lucille Ball*

Show, and performed on a Barbra Streisand TV special, *Belle of 14th Street,* in 1967.

John Bubbles suffered a stroke in 1967 and considered himself retired. Gradually, however, he began accepting invitations to appear, rather than to perform. By 1979–80, he was performing again, appearing at the Newport Jazz Festival, making a new record album (*Back on Broadway* for Uptown Records), appearing in the filmed documentary *No Maps on My Taps* (with fellow tappers Chuck Green and Sandman Sims) and singing in the Broadway revue *Black Broadway.*

In 1986, after 70 years in show business, John Bubbles suffered a cerebral hemorrhage and died. He was not forgotten. In 1992, BBC television broadcast *Black and White in Colour,* which documented contributions to British variety in the 1930s and 1940s by black American entertainers such as Adelaide Hall, Buck & Bubbles and Elisabeth Welch. Though forgotten by American audiences, Bubbles remains an icon to each new generation of tap dancers.

BUMP

A bump is a quick pelvic snap forward, usually performed by strippers in burlesque to simulate a sexual act. It often follows a slower, sexual windup called a grind. Most often, the two movements are paired and known as the bump-and-grind.

JOHN BUNNY

b: 21 September 1863, New York, NY—d: 26 April 1915, Brooklyn, NY

John Bunny made his silent-screen debut in 1909 and became the first comedian to be accorded star billing in the movies. Flora Finch often played the wife in their Vitagraph movie shorts and so may be considered the first female star comedian of movies. (In 1896, May Irwin, the vaudeville and stage comedian, appeared in the notorious *The Kiss,* but that flicker was little more than a novelty.)

Bunny was born on Mott Street in lower Manahattan, the area that became Chinatown. He was the son of a seafaring man and reputedly the first of his family in many generations to turn his back on the sea. Bunny was probably about 20 when, after finishing high school and quitting his job as a grocery clerk, he ran off with a small-time minstrel show.

He graduated to touring stock companies, whose repertoire was melodrama and comedy, and, as was usual in that era, he traveled much of his first 25 years in show business. Like most journeyman stage actors, he did whatever was necessary to keep employed. Sometimes he was a stage manager, other times a character actor. Comedy proved his forte. At five feet, four inches in height and weighing more than 250 pounds, he was a natural choice for Santa Claus and Dickensian characters like Mr. Pickwick, both of which he portrayed on screen, but movies were a long way off.

Bunny's first recorded performance in Manhattan was the Bijou Theatre in *Aunt Hannah* (1900). He made it to the famed Wallacks' Theatre with *Easy Dawson* (1905), in which Bunny costarred with Raymond Hitchcock. The show then toured. Two years later, he starred in London in *Tom Jones* (1907), a musicalization of the Henry Fielding novel that reached the Astor Theatre on Broadway before going out on tour. *Fluffy Ruffles* (1908), based on a then-popular comic strip, was Bunny's next Broadway show; in a small role was young singer Mabel Mercer, future cabaret doyenne. John Bunny was featured in *Old Dutch* (1909) with Lew Fields, Vernon Castle and a very young Helen Hayes. He showboated his role as costar Vernon Castle's father, and his reviews were not his best. During the day, he was making his first films at the Vitagraph studios.

The number of films, mostly one reel in length, that John Bunny made is estimated between 200 and 250. Most are lost, but his broad reactive style turned his film roles into a recognizable character that quickly became a favorite with audiences. When he began with Vitagraph, he made about $40 a week, far less than the reputed $150 weekly salary he expected to draw on Broadway. Soon, however, his screen salary surpassed what he could make on the stage and eliminated the need to tour. He bought a home in Brooklyn and stayed as close to New York as was practical.

He made films until late 1914 or early 1915. Most comedians started in vaudeville. That is where Bunny's career ended. He organized a unit show, "Bunny in Funnyland," that debuted in March 1915 in New York City. Among those on the undercard were a clog dancer and a midget troupe. Bunny did an impersonation of Teddy Roosevelt and performed in a skit based on a day at a film studio. New York critics slammed the show, and its tour was cut short in Philadelphia. Despite the reviews, John Bunny was announced for a Chautauqua tour in summer 1915, but he fell ill. He likely had not been feeling well during "Bunny in Funnyland." On 26 April, he died of liver disease and was survived by his wife of 25 years, Clara Scallan.

HOVEY BURGESS

b: 8 September, 1940, Middlebury, VT

Hovey Burgess has brought together two worlds that traditionally functioned independently of each other:

master teacher, academic, author and editor on the one hand; juggler, equilibrist, acrobat and clown on the other. Perhaps more importantly, Burgess became one of the godfathers in the revival of interest in variety skills and performance.

His chemist father had taught Hovey to juggle when he was a young boy. As he grew up, Hovey entertained thoughts of becoming a circus clown and going on to higher education to secure a degree in veterinary medicine. (Perhaps he would not have to choose between a vagabond and a professional life; he could become a circus veterinarian.)

By the mid-1950s, the big-top circus extravaganza had pretty much passed from the scene. Gone was the excitement of its parades, steam calliopes, live band music and the ritual of setting up tents and booths, temporarily turning a vacant lot into several acres of wonders. Television borrowed circus acts from the big top and satisfied some of the public taste for spectacle with annual broadcasts of the Macy's Thanksgiving Day and the Tournament of Roses Parades. The big-time Ringling Bros. and Barnum & Bailey shows borrowed some of the flash and production values of Broadway for the arena, an innovation that tended to submerge the skills of individual performers within a whirl of color, noise and spectacle.

Hovey and his family were living in Battle Creek, Michigan, when he went off with a small circus for the summer prior to entering the Pasadena Playhouse College of Theatre Arts. At college, Hovey discovered a second enduring love, *commedia dell'arte,* a form of comic acting and clowning that grew out of Renaissance-era street performances and was adapted to the stage as farce. He traveled to Paris in 1965 to experience the old-style European circus, but its heyday had passed a few years earlier. Street performance, however, was thriving throughout Europe, and Hovey paid his way by juggling.

Back in the USA, Hovey began teaching juggling and other circus skills to budding actors and graduate students at New York University's School of Arts. In the East Village, a new club opened called the Electric Circus, a mad mix of rock music, light show, circus acts and party animals. There Hovey Burgess met Larry Pisoni, later a founder of the Pickle Family Circus. At the same time, New York University students Barry Bostwick, Judy Finelli and Cecil MacKinnon were students of Hovey's and had demonstrated an interest in circus. Burgess brought Pisoni, Bostwick, Finelli and MacKinnon together to form Circo dell'Arte, so-called because Burgess sought to marry *commedia dell'arte,* circus acts and busking into a street troupe.

After a couple of seasons in New York, Burgess, Finelli and Pisoni headed to the West Coast to see what the San Francisco Mime Troupe (SFMT) was doing. Pisoni ended up teaching classes to SFMT members, and Burgess taught students at William Ball's American Conservatory Theatre. Hovey went on to teach at Ringling Brothers Clown College, providing its students with skills more substantial than the usual courses in clown makeup.

His work was divided among performing with circuses (Clyde Beatty-Cole Brothers Circus and Patterson Brothers Circus), serving as president of the International Jugglers Association and teaching at Juilliard, the National Theatre School of Canada and Sarah Lawrence College. Hollywood director Robert Altman hired Burgess to choreograph the circus sequences for *Popeye* (1980); Burgess also performed in it alongside talented friends and students Judy Finelli, Larry Pisoni, Peggy Snider, Geoff Hoyle and Bill Irwin.

Hovey Burgess has taught circus techniques to all students enrolled in New York University's Tisch School of the Arts Graduate Acting Program from the time when it was incorporated into the curriculum in 1966. Hovey has continued to perform since 1991 with Circus Flora, based in St. Louis. He is the author of *Circus Techniques* (1976) and serves as a mentor for many individuals and performance groups.

BURLESK

An arbitrary choice has been made to use *burlesk* to differentiate the earlier, travesty form of burlesque from the burlesque of female minstrel shows of the nineteenth century and their successors that brought burlesque into the striptease era. Throughout the history of burlesque, however, the two spellings have been used to indicate both forms.

See Burlesque

BURLESQUE

For more than a century, chroniclers, critics, busybodies and bluenoses exhorted producers to elevate burlesque. Those who heeded the admonition and tried to market burlesque as a slightly saucy sister to vaudeville failed. It was not variety the burlesque audience craved, it was sex, salacious sex, and more of the same.

Sexual titillation was what distinguished burlesque from its rivals. Like vaudeville, comic opera, revue and musical comedy, burlesque had to be taken on its own terms. Dullness and lack of originality were sins to avoid in all forms of theatre. An additional sin for burlesque was respectability. The forbidden and brazen were the great allures of burlesque. The scorn for the moral posture of a conformist community and the public jousting with civil authorities endowed burlesque

Jeanette Alabassi

with an outlaw mystique that appealed compellingly to men (and some women). To men, burlesque offered an ideal of sex: dirty, ever fresh in its variety and free of consequence, responsibility or small talk. For the women exhibiting themselves onstage (or projecting themselves from the audience), it allowed them to be the focus of desire, to entice and taunt yet remain in command of the seduction: glamorous, tempting, yet safe from harm.

The enduring images of burlesque are of stripteasers. Rightly so, for these female entertainers were, for most of the audience, the dominant element and chief drawing cards of burlesque from the First World War through the Korean War. Comic acts were important in burlesque, but not quite as important. The straight men, comics, talking women and stooges who performed the sketches were appreciated by a brotherhood of aficionados, but for most patrons, the laugh makers were agreeable fillers between the exotic dance specialties, enjoyable to the degree of their ribaldry.

The ladies of chorus were a mixed lot. A burlesque producer usually had to choose between a modicum of attractiveness and a modicum of dancing ability. Young women blessed with both looks and ability usually hoped for more in their careers than being herded around a burlesque stage in their flimsies, six days a week, four shows a day, plus rehearsals, all for the lowest wages in show business outside of a sideshow. Except in a few top notch houses and in the later burlesque revues brought to Broadway by producers like Earl Carroll, Billy Rose and Mike Todd, burlesque chorus lines were apt to be ragtag assemblies too poorly trained, underrehearsed and poorly paid to give more than a perfunctory performance. The chorines often deviated sufficiently from classic proportions so as to seem, when lined up, too short, too tall, too scrawny, too bloated, too dissipated or too old to give rise to lust in the audience.

Another staple of classic burlesque was the candy butcher, admired only by quirky cognoscenti. The candy butchers stalked the aisles between the acts and during intermission to sell stale candy and items of bogus prurience. The best of them were glib successors to the medicine-show pitchmen of yore: hucksters, orotund and oracular in their delivery, profligate and obfuscatory with counterfeit promises of illicit delights.

The Great Depression put a damper on most live entertainment in the USA, including burlesque, but ticket prices cheaper than vaudeville or Broadway revues had a lot to do with burlesque's survival in the 1930s. More important was a lack of competition. After the suppression of the concert saloons and box houses of the nineteenth century, only burlesque provided dirty jokes and sexy dames.

Producers of Broadway revues, such as Florenz Ziegfeld, John Murray Anderson, Irving Berlin, George White and Earl Carroll, had hired burlesque comics and had trotted out their own version of female nudity to attract a wider audience. The comics won new admirers from intellectuals to uptown ticket buyers while keeping their old fans, but the regal hauteur of elegantly draped, perfectly proportioned showgirls made them seem unattainable to the common man, who could fantasize with more confidence in the bouncy, earthy presence of the cheeky burlesque chorus cuties. Only Earl Carroll's smutty *Vanities* delivered the kind of laughs and thrills burlesque audiences preferred, but why expect most guys to pay $2 for a ticket to the *Vanities* when they could get the same thing at Minsky's for 50 cents?

When revue and musical-comedy producers could not beat the burlesque producers at their own game, they tried to banish them from Broadway. The League of New York Theatres got religion and persuaded newly elected reform mayor Fiorello LaGuardia to action. In 1933, stripping was banned in New York City. By 1942, burlesque was chased out of the city and under the Hudson River into Union City, New Jersey.

How burlesque fared in other cities depended upon local activism. Left alone, it continued to draw audiences and was a great favorite with servicemen away from home. After the Second World War, however, burlesque faced a new competitor: nightclubs. Burlesque had beaten revues and musical comedies because burlesque could be raunchy and was cheaper to produce.

Nightclubs that sported girlie shows were an even leaner operation than burlesque, and usually the clubs did not attract as much adverse attention as long as they made regular donations to municipal watchdogs and did not run afoul of the liquor-licensing laws. Clubs also had great advantages. The customers were closer to the bump-and-grind. The clubs could sell booze to their customers, which the burlesque theatres could not, and it was easier to sell booze than tickets.

Organized burlesque and its queens and comics went into eclipse in the 1960s. The beat generation of the 1950s and the hippie generation of the 1960s had tossed off social constraints along with their more restrictive garments. Language was earthy or coarse, depending upon the listener's viewpoint. Nudity was on public display. Sex had ceased to be a furtive pursuit and was readily available and expected.

The Old Howard in Boston, Massachusetts

By the 1970s, burlesque performance was stripped to the bare essentials in the nude-dancing clubs, and the dancing style simulated sex acts. Denied elaborate costumes, flattering lighting effects and the distance that enhanced their allure, the strippers were no longer in charge of their acts. Male customers called to them as if they were counter help, stuffed dollar bills in their bikini bottoms and expected the women to sit beside them on bar stools when they were not dancing.

The tease had become too tame; suggestiveness was trumped by the blatant. The burlesque comedy acts of Ann Corio's 1980s revival revue, *This Was Burlesque,* were quaint compared with offerings by music videos. Nude-dancing bars, comedy clubs, girlie magazines and explicit Web sites raised expectations beyond anything that burlesque could deliver.

Oddly, by the turn of the twenty-first century, there was a sustained and extensive, if small-scaled, burlesque revival in the USA. The revival was successful because it restored humor and the teasing element to the sexual exhibition, and the women dancers again performed on a stage instead of writhing in the laps of the men in their audience. New burlesque attracted young people with a blend of pop music, re-created strip routines and vaudeville acts. If the performances lacked the polish of classic burlesque, they did foster a sense of community with their audience, and once more women were in control of the seduction.

Pop-culture historians profess that burlesque was both goddess worship and the worthy heir to the classic comedy of the ancient Greeks. Watching a striptease was more likely a manifestation of eternal lust. As regards burlesque comedy, it relied upon travesty, not satire or parody, and was built with physical action, wordplay, mistaken identities, surprises, tricks and the frustrations of lovers. Similar devices of comic construction did not elevate Billy "Cheese 'n' Crackers" Hagan into the same league as Aristophanes, Plautus, Grimaldi, Richard Brinsley Sheridan, Gilbert & Sullivan, Karl Valentin or George S. Kaufman. Burlesque's new apologists do well to remember that burlesque had few pretensions and liked it that way.

There remains the question of how far back burlesque can be traced before a clear line of influence is lost. There are two forms: travesties and girlie shows. To differentiate between these two distinct developments sharing a single name, it is useful, yet not exact, to refer to the earlier form based on travesty as *burlesk* and to the sex-themed shows as *burlesque.*

In truth, only by its extremes were burlesk and burlesque sharply differentiated. The travesties, variety shows and comic opera enhanced their appeal with cavorting young ladies in tights. In turn, the girlie shows knew they needed comedy sketches and variety turns to alleviate the pall induced by a repetitive flow of one torso-twister after another. That said, it was the extremes of the burlesque form that prospered. The stuff too close to the middle was rejected as ersatz vaudeville or revue.

Travesty had been a mainstay of the American stage from the early nineteenth century; several generations of audiences delighted in irreverent send-ups of books or classic and contemporary dramas. Source material was merely a takeoff point for a spoof spiked with song, dance, topical observations and caricatures of the powerful and famous. The popularity of travesties continued through minstrel shows.

Over the last half of the nineteenth century, there were as many variations of burlesk as there were producers and practitioners: William Mitchell, John Brougham, George L. Fox, Dion Boucicault, Charles H. Hoyt, Harrigan & Hart, George Lederer and Weber & Fields to mention some of the more influential. The differences in approach were individual, but, in common, burleskers chose the familiar—popular plays, books and stories—as a scaffold for sketches and full-length shows that targeted pomposity and pretension. The producers made inspiration flesh by employing music, dance, songs, eccentric costuming and makeup, physical comedy and wordplay, and a chorus line of lovelies to keep the show smartly paced and the audience amused.

Girlie shows arrived after the Civil War. Doubtless there were earlier, more clandestine displays of the female form in action, some in carnivals and cellar saloons, others in the brothels that offered varied entertainments, but these have passed largely unrecorded as theatre history. What did not pass unnoticed was *The Black Crook* at Niblo's Garden in New York in 1866. The play was dull, and its producers knew that. When an engagement for the opera *La Biche au Bois* fell through at the Academy of Music and stranded the 100 female members of the corps de ballet, *The Black Crook* producers quickly engaged the ladies of the ballet to spice up the play by dancing in flesh-colored silk tights and short skirts. New York audiences were shocked, some more pleasantly than others. The show was a smashing financial success, and hourglass-shaped chorus girls became a fixture of the musical stage for several decades.

Two years later, in 1868, Lydia Thompson and Her Imported British Blondes came to Woods' Museum and Menagerie in Manhattan, where they enlivened another flat production, *Ixion.* The chorus for *The Black Crook* had been just that, a largely anonymous chorus. Lydia Thompson's Blondes performed as individual acts and were publicized by name. They sang risqué songs, danced and played a variety of Roman gods and goddesses. Their success won them an engagement at Niblo's Garden, a more prestigious theatre, where they appeared in *Forty Thieves,* a show in which they had appeared in London. There were a couple of men in the troupe as well as the famous female buxom blonds. The men sometimes played women, and a few of the women took men's roles.

Lydia Thompson's troupe established an early formula for burlesque: a female minstrel show of sorts. The ladies performed as individuals and in ensemble. Dance numbers like the cancan ensured a thorough airing of their laundry and the display of more leg than had ever been seen on an American stage. After Lydia proved that sex sells, even at advanced prices, there were all manner of stage experiments by producers hoping to cash in on the display of the female form. The one constant was blonde; otherwise the imitations were a hodgepodge of farce, variety turns, spectacle, music and sketches. Within a few years, producers settled on the minstrel show for form, following the formula adapted by M. B. "Mike" Leavitt, the self-proclaimed and probable inventor of American burlesque. The mold was set, and most troupes surrounded their star performers with a line of chorus girls and added a few comedians to vary the tone and pace.

In the decades after the Civil War, theatrical producers of every stripe began to focus their efforts in New York, Chicago and other cities that were growing into centers of finance, trade, industry, transportation, retail and daily newspapers. A show that had won success in New York or Chicago was far easier to sell on the road than one that arrived unheralded. Producers began to move away from forms of entertainments that once had appealed largely to rural audiences and began to cater to urban tastes at the same time that rural and urban tastes were moving closer. The growth of railroads, the draw of manufacturing jobs in the cities, daily newspapers, catalogs of nationally distributed products, and increasing frequency of tours by shows that were conceived in New York or Chicago were the first steps in the creation of a mass culture.

As a nod to first-generation Americans and immigrants, ethnic impersonations began to challenge the hegemony of blackface. Harrigan & Hart (and Harrigan's musical collaborator, David Braham) were a classic illustration of burlesk for new urban, largely immigrant audiences. Like the blackface minstrel shows that made fun of uneducated African Americans supposedly trying to imitate the upper classes, Harrigan targeted the newly arrived underclass of Irish immigrants. Starting with musical sketches in 1871, Harrigan began writing full-evening plays that spoofed the pretensions of the lower classes, the very Irish who constituted his audience base! The Harrigan shows, however, lacked the lovely and talented dance choruses that later adorned the Weber & Fields spoofs.

A few titles of the Weber & Fields Music Hall shows during the 1890s illustrate how closely they hewed to

Unknown performer at the Old Howard in Boston, Massachusetts

classic burlesk: *The Geezer (The Geisha), Cyranose de Bric-aBrac* and *Quo Vas Is?* Blackface had been dismissed at the Weber & Fields Music Hall, and the Irish impersonations by Pete Dailey and John T. Kelly were a generation removed from Harrigan's fresh-off-the-boat good-old b'hoys. Most of the comic characterizations were Dutch (Germans) and Jewish.

Roughly contemporary with Harrigan & Hart, Hoyt, Lederer and Weber & Fields were the works of William S. Gilbert and Arthur S. Sullivan. Although the literacy of his wit placed Gilbert several steps above his American competition, and Sullivan's melodies earned them classification as operetta, the Gilbert & Sullivan stage shows were travesties occasionally reaching to satire. So extraordinarily popular did most Gilbert & Sullivan shows prove in London that they were exported to the United States. Nearly as soon as they reached New York in the form of legitimate productions, unscrupulous American producers were staging their own bootleg productions of Gilbert & Sullivan, abbreviated and tarted up. Even burlesks were burlesked.

There were few inviolable patterns for burlesk or travesty by the turn of the twentieth century, although most of them shared the basics. The shows were driven by comic writing, comic performers, impish soubrettes, fast-paced staging and lovely ladies of the chorus who dressed up the stage and got off some lively dancing. The songs had lyrics that were easily understood and melodies that were easily remembered. As added attractions, a few variety turns might entertain between the acts. In short, one branch of burlesque, the travesty, had approached comic opera and was on its way to setting the mold for musical comedy. Burlesk sketches became a staple of vaudeville and revue, and musical comedies made sure to integrate several comic sketches into their storylines to keep the show lively. If burlesk, as a full-length show, was rarely seen by the start of the twenty-first century, the burlesk sketch remained alive, well and universal onstage and in movies and television.

When the female minstrel show, the other branch of burlesque, emerged, its competition was the entertainments of the honky-tonk theatres and saloons. For most of burlesque's existence, the saloon-speakeasy-nightclub was its low-end rival. The main purpose of honky-tonks, however, was to make money from the sale of liquor and, in some, gambling. The primary role of women in most honky-tonks was to serve drinks and wheedle or challenge the male customers to buy more drinks and to lose their money gambling.

At first, almost as an afterthought, the employees were rounded up to perform. The waiters attempted a sort of barbershop harmony, and the hostesses attempted to dance and show their linen. If well heeled, the audience tossed coins or gold nuggets to the girls as they danced. The women, first and foremost, however, were engaged to push drinks. Except in the gold-rush towns, there was neither enough applause nor money to encourage a woman to remain in this line of work unless she had no other options. Women stuck in honky-tonks earned extra by picking pockets or offering private services after work.

Many saloons separated their show enterprise from their basic function by creating a separate performance space beside, above or below the barroom. Here the show developed into full-fledged variety, with one turn following another, singers, comedians, dancers, novelty acts and prize fights.

The burlesque show differed from the saloon show because it was created to entertain first and last, and it derived its income from ticket sales. For these reasons, the level of performance was expected to be professional, the production replete with sets, lights, costumes and musicians, the comedians funny, the women passably young and attractive and as scantily clad as the law of the day permitted.

When, in 1869, M. B. Leavitt introduced the first American burlesque company, Mme Rentz's Female Minstrels, he did not fail to credit Lydia Thompson for inspiration. Leavitt's general manager was a teenage

George Lederer, who later produced the glory years at New York's Casino Theatre during the decade between 1893 and 1903, when the Casino was chief rival to Weber & Fields Music Hall. It is generally conceded that Leavitt's outfit, later renamed Rentz-Santley to accommodate the popularity of its star, Mabel Santley, was the first burlesque show. With their long hair worn up or down as required by character, the ladies of early burlesque wore the equivalent of a modern one-piece bathing suit over leggings and corsets that remolded their natural figures into wasp-waisted Rubenesques. Mock jewels, sequins and fringe adorned tunics and headpieces, trying to entice as well as approximate some sense of the period and character: ancient Greek goddesses, nymphs of a bucolic paradise, geisha girls, Amazon warriors and the like.

Mike Leavitt's Rentz-Santley shows held sway for the decade of the 1870s. Although the shows declined after 1880, they managed to be profitable until 1890. Meanwhile, others were following Leavitt's lead: Ida Siddons Burlesque & Novelty Company, Ada Richmond's Burlesquers, Victoria Loftus Troupe of British Blondes, Mary Fiske's British Blondes, Rose Sydell & Her London Belles and Ada Kennedy's African Blonde Minstrels [!] among the more prominent.

Leavitt had developed the leg-show burlesques by incorporating various elements of existing forms. He took his opening from the minstrel show in which all the members of the company were arrayed in a half circle onstage as they traded jokes and sang songs: women took the end men's places. The second section of the show was straight variety: the olio, as it was called. Various members of the company stepped forward in front of the front drop, each to perform one in a series of specialties as the stage behind was reset and redressed for the third act. The third and final section was more flexible in form. Sometimes, it combined the walk-around of the minstrel show with a production number; other times it adapted the traditional afterpiece into a musical farce.

Helen Leach-Wallace Trio

Leavitt's finale was similar to the afterpieces that E. E. Rice used to close his extravaganzas such as *Adonis* (which also featured bodies beautiful, including Henry E. Dixey's). It is ironic that both E. E. Rice and Mike Leavitt, the originator and popularizer of the American burlesque show, should have been born and begun their careers in Boston, the city that gave birth to the phrase "banned in Boston" and the Boston version of burlesque.

Even in the 1880s and 1890s, however, some women wielded power in burlesque. May Howard, one of the first burlesque queens, starred in her own, self-named company beginning in 1888. Her husband, comedian Harry Morris, helped manage the May Howard Company on the road as well as served as its star comedian. May was a fine singer and introduced a number of popular songs, but flesh, well-rounded mounds of it were the feature attraction of the May Howard Company. She favored a full figure for herself as well as the chorus girls, and none weighed less than 150 pounds.

Throughout its century-long run, burlesque battled with limits. As the style in street clothes grew more daring, with skirts raised nearly to the knee, and Broadway revues featured artistically' draped nudes, burlesque was forced to be more audaciously explicit. In the words of Cole Porter, "In olden days a glimpse of stocking was looked on as something shocking, now, heaven knows, anything goes." The stakes escalated between Broadway and burlesque. If the tired businessman could see nearly everything there was to see of a woman's body on a Broadway stage, the next level had to approach the sex act. Burlesque was equal to the challenge.

In Manhattan, Sam T. Jack ballyhooed in high-flown language the delights of Sam T. Jack's Tenderloin Company, stressing his tantalizing living statues clothed in nothing more than flesh-colored tights and the daring of the young ladies who danced the cancan. Denounced

"A chorus of youth, grace, and beauty," from a 1910 touring burlesque revue at the Gaiety Theatre in Boston, Massachusetts

regularly from various pulpits in New York, this son of the Pennsylvania oil fields relocated to the more relaxed atmosphere of Chicago and prospered. He hiked the stakes when he hired Little Egypt to appear at his Chicago Theatre; she was fresh from her notorious success at the 1893 World's Columbian Exhibition. From that point on, Jack was an unapologetic producer of ever-rawer burlesque, reaching a level of lascivious display heretofore attempted only by the fly-by-night *turkey-show* troupes.

Koster & Bial's Concert Hall at 23rd Street and Sixth Avenue in New York had begun as a honky-tonk; many of its patrons were prostitutes. The partners tried to match Sam T. Jack and made a good deal of money, but police raids wore them down. When, inspired by Tony Pastor's success, Koster and Bial switched to more respectable vaudeville, the partners began to fade away as significant producers of either burlesque or vaudeville.

By the 1890s, there was a definite split in the ranks, with some producers trying to gain respectability and decrying the tawdriness of shows produced by their more shameless competitors. Public demands by newspapers and churches ebbed and flowed over the decades. There were clamors in the 1890s, again in 1915, and they became nearly constant by the 1920s.

As burlesque grew in popularity and politicians realized that the producers needed at least their tacit acquiescence, politicians began to acquire theatres. Big Tim Sullivan, a Tammany Hall stalwart, acquired a few and eventually partnered John Considine, who had begun as a box-house owner in Seattle and San Francisco.

There was no coordinating booking agency; traveling burlesque producers of the 1890s wildcatted, arranging, as efficiently as they were able, play dates at various theatres on the road. Mike Leavitt had an advantage because his brother Abe acted as his booker and established a route of sorts that the Rentz-Santley shows plied each season.

Among the other successful burlesque producers of the day were Gus Hill, Fred Irwin (Irwin Brothers), Al Reeves, Billy "Beef Trust" Watson and Jules Hurtig & Harry Seamon.

In 1900, the Traveling Variety Managers' Association was formed in Manhattan. Shortly after, the Eastern Circuit of House Managers organized. The two groups merged after a fashion, and their agenda was to reach agreements about territorial limits, actions against contract violators, as well as a way to provide a system of orderly bookings. There had been a growing rivalry between eastern and western burlesque producers, a process that afflicted vaudeville a few years later in the case of Keith versus Orpheum time.

The western burlesque producers and theatre managers pulled themselves together into what they named the Empire Association. The eastern forces did the same, and, almost immediately, the two groups merged. In 1900, the producer of a successful burlesque revue had 40 weeks of potential engagements in one season on the combined circuit, or wheel, as they were called in burlesque.

By 1905, the old rivalry split the organization into the Columbia circuit (or Eastern wheel) and the Empire Association (or Western wheel). By 1913, they were together again, or rather the Empire was absorbed by the Columbia Amusement Company. Columbia promoted clean burlesque, or at least burlesque that was not too risqué, and its policy was to draw a fair number of women into the audience. They were also trying to knock out stock burlesque (nontouring resident troupes, generally of lesser quality and baser entertainment). In 1908, the Columbia wheel, under the leadership of Samuel Scribner, Gus Hill and L. Lawrence Weber, banned wrestling and prize fighting from the circuit.

In 1914, nearly 80 shows were touring the Columbia circuit of 81 theatres that stretched form New York to Omaha, amusing 700,000 customers annually. There was another upstart to deal with, however, when the Progressive circuit debuted. The Columbia bosses immediately created the No. 2 circuit and went head to head with the Progressive. The fight ended in a year with the Progressive defunct.

The next year, 1915, Columbia set up a sham competitor by renaming the No. 2 circuit the American Burlesque Association and put Isadore H. Herk in charge; he was a smart workhorse management type with little show experience. Thus, the participating producers of the Columbia Amusement Company had it both ways until 1922: the Columbia wheel offered so-called approved burlesque, the more opulent and respectable shows, whereas the American played standard burlesque, employing runways and featuring the hootchy-kootchy dancers and raunchy comedians that the Columbia wheel officially disdained.

The decline of the Columbia circuit began in 1920. They faced competition in many forms. Free of transportation costs, stock burlesque was cheaper to produce. The movie industry, not yet hampered by censorship and reaching its silent zenith as an art form, produced a fair amount of product featuring pretty women, sexual titillation and passionate embraces, even the occasional bared breast. Broadway revues had long featured attractive women in the near nude. Most threatening of all, perhaps, was the emergence of the Mutual wheel. I. H. Herk, who had helmed the American wheel, was hired to run Mutual. He created an efficient operation. Gone were niceties like attractive scenery and costuming. Salaries were appallingly low in an industry in which $75 a week was star pay. Critics said the Mutual shows were cheap and dirty, and they were. Mutual lasted ten years but was not cheap enough to ride out the Great Depression.

Following vaudeville, which included the occasional colored act like Buck & Bubbles, Ethel Waters or Bill Robinson on otherwise all-white bills playing two-a-day white vaudeville, burlesque was next to employ African Americans. As early at the 1920s, it was not unusual to see integrated burlesque revues playing the fading Columbia wheel or the rising Mutual wheel. In some cases, the shows boasted black-and-white chorus cuties and specialty acts; in other cases, a top-notch act like Buck & Bubbles was added to an existing review as an extra added attraction to put a bang in the box office.

Comedians such as Hamtree Harrington and Pigmeat Markham played Minsky burlesque, and the Minskys occasionally added a black dancing act to their stock burlesque shows playing New York City. Stock burlesque companies were more viable than touring productions. Production values were not important, except with the Minskys, and sleaze was the crucial ingredient.

The stock-company policy began as early as 1903, when a number of theatre owners met because they objected to the dictatorial methods of the Western (Empire) wheel. Over the years, the general management of the circuits tried to enforce various rules that resident managers felt put them at a disadvantage. One rule was that a troupe traveling under the banner, say, of the Empire circuit would be blacklisted if it played independent or opposition theatres. This caused some independents to engage their own stock companies. This approach at the time was considered a defeat for the independents, but it proved to be the wave of the future, and by the post–Second World War years, economics dictated adoption of the stock-company policy.

There were four Minsky brothers but only one Billy Minsky. He was the sparkplug of a rather conservative family. Although Billy died in 1932, his brothers carried on burlesque in an increasingly hostile municipal environment. Throughout the 1930s, the Minsky organization seemed to spend as much time defending their business operations in court as they did running their theatres and shows. They won some trials and lost others, including, eventually, the right to do business. Burlesque was chased out of New York just as America went to war. Herbert K. Minsky filed for bankruptcy in 1942.

A few cities continued to tolerate burlesque: Boston, Newark, Los Angeles and Detroit, but the theatres were in full-time battle with city censors. The Second World War drafted a generation of young men and stuck them in various rural training camps until they were shipped overseas to do battle. If they were stationed in an army base or a navy shipyard near a city that hosted a burlesque house, the servicemen became a valuable part of the 1940 girly-show audience. Burlesque was also a rite of passage for college boys. White collar or blue—or red, white and blue—young men supported burlesque.

On one side of the burlesque game were the authorities who forbade smut and nudity. On the other side were the customers who sought both. Management and performers tried to trick the police with a system of warning lights and buzzers and often succeeded. They tried to trick the customers into believing they saw more than they actually did and often succeeded. Boys and men would swear to their friends that they caught a glimpse, that the stripper flashed it all. In truth, strippers were known to crochet the crotches of their garments. The women claimed to the magistrates that they were simply covering themselves. The guys in the audience thought the embroidery was pubic hair.

It was all about gimmicks. If the law decreed that a stripper could not caress herself, she worked with a trained monkey or a few birds that did it for her. If the law deemed that the pasties that were intended to cover nipples were not apparent or large enough, the stripper added tassels and twirled them to ensure that everyone in the audience saw them.

Some burlesque queens set themselves apart by doing a classy turn instead of the basic strip, bump and grind. Some of the later ones resorted to surgical enhancements. The best of the burlesque queens became top attractions with a nationwide following: Carrie Finnell, Hinda Wassau, Gypsy Rose Lee, Margie Hart, Ann Corio, Georgia Southern, Lois DeFee, Rosita Royce, Rose La Rose, Sally Keith, Lili St. Cyr, Blaze Starr, Tempest Storm and Sherry Britton.

Among the later generations of comedians who trained in burlesque and went on to Broadway and Hollywood were Leon Errol, W. C. Fields, Fanny Brice, Bert Lahr, Bud Abbott & Lou Costello, Red Skelton, Rags Ragland, Phil Silvers and Red Buttons. Most of the comics and straight men in burlesque stayed there, however, no matter how good they were, and their names have faded from memory and the record.

George Lowe, a burlesque alumnus known as Les Carter in his days as a specialty dancer with the Old Howard's 1950s stock company in Boston, recalled that the resident company included a dance corps and dance director. The dancers numbered four men and ten women. To augment the resident company at the Old Howard and other burlesque theatres, a different road troupe joined the resident company each Monday to present a new show.

The Old Howard's formula applied to many-burlesque houses. The road troupes brought two strippers and two comedy acts. Their turns were coordinated with the resident company, but, other than an afterpiece, there was not a great deal of onstage interaction between the two groups. The Old Howard dance director, Bunny Weldon, made each week's costumes, devised new routines and rehearsed his dance troupe after the final shows on Tuesday, Wednesday and Thursday nights.

On Friday and Saturday nights, a fourth show was added at midnight to the usual noon, 3 P.M. and 8 P.M. showings. Each weekly show was routined in much the same sequence. Although there were acts such as jugglers and acrobats that might be engaged to give the show more variety, the basic template of the mid-twentieth-century burlesque show combined strippers and comedy with a bit of song and dance.

As Lowe recalled, the overture brought on the stock company of dancers in a production number. Next was a specialty number that featured one or two of the resident dancers. Often, this was an exotic dance, but it could also be a dance duet between a boy and girl dancer: ballroom dance, tap, apache. A comedy act from the road crew took the third spot and was followed by one of the road crew's strippers. The full dance ensemble reprised to close the first half of the show.

The intermission gave the candy butcher his own spot in the show. He spieled from the front of the audience and moved up and down the aisles. Although he might appear between the acts to sell his wares, the length of the intermission permitted him to expound upon his offerings, and the best of them turned their pitch into an act. After the intermission, a brief overture again ushered in the dance ensemble. Next was another strip act by one of the resident female dancers, who in turn was followed by the second comedy act from the road crew. The next-to-closing spot was reserved for the star stripper of the road crew. The show closed with an afterpiece. Road and resident, the company came together in one hastily rehearsed number in which the stock company dancers and orchestra were the backbone. The stars and featured acts came out one at a time to perform a final gag, blow kisses, flash a leg or dance a few steps.

Meanwhile, across the street in several Scollay Square bars that aspired to be nightclubs, other strippers and comics were working on postage-stamp stages, and liquor was once again part of the show. This scene was replicated across America, but not for long. Soon there was just a TV set flickering above the bar.

THE BURLESQUE CLUB

Located on West 48th Street in Manhattan, the Burlesque Club was sort of a Friar's Club for burlesque folk in the 1920s and 1930s. One had to be voted into membership.

BURLESQUE COMEDIANS

After the Civil War, burlesque branched in two directions. The original intent, that of travesty, emphasized the comedy and hewed more to a narrative structure. Harrigan & Hart and Weber & Fields were among the producer-comedians who followed that course and added to the foundation on which was built the musical comedy. The other branch, influenced by the success of the various British Blondes, opted to glorify limbs, bosoms and buttocks and produced the ancestor of the girlie show.

The girlie show of the mid- to late nineteenth century had ambitions neither to spoof the topics or personalities of the day nor to grow out of itself. The goals were to titillate and amuse, so any theatrical structure sufficed that provided a platform on which to parade the female form.

Despite the emphasis on flesh, comedy was essential to the appeal of burlesque. Those burlesque comedians of the 1880s, 1890s and 1900s who built reputations based on talent, popularity, tenacity and the ability to take charge of a troupe became masters of their fates. Many of them organized and wrote, or at least helped to write, their own shows. Each season, they packaged shows around themselves by hiring other performers to add variety and went on tour. Theatre owners and managers welcomed these comedy stars because their shows were usually successful and filled the seats in their theatres.

The writer-producer-comedian often performed as compere of a sort as well as engaged in cross-talk humor, physical comedy sketches and musical numbers. Their shows featured, of course, saucy soubrettes and dancing choruses of females. The pairing of feminine allure and masculine antics remained constant in burlesque's century of entertaining mostly male audiences.

Burlesque comedy in the late minstrel era was often racial and ethnic, and the only standard was getting laughs as big and as continually as possible. The comic ethnic characterizations were similar to those in vaudeville at the time, but the stock situations demanded by burlesque comedy did not permit refined types. The Dutch comics (German) were played as stupid, coarse, blustering barbarians in loud checkered suits. The smart-mouthed Irish comic wore chin whiskers, and the level of his courage or cowardice was commensurate with his liquor intake. Jews were represented by shuffling, bearded older men worried about holding onto their money and making more. Negroes were portrayed by white men in blackface and Chinese by white men in pajamas with a pigtail trailing from under their caps; both were as peripheral to the plots of the sketches as they were to mainstream American life, serving in sketches as waiters, shoe-shine boys or laundrymen when they were not handling a razor, a pair of dice or an opium pipe. There was another category of comic called the dude, a sissy represented as a timid, bespectacled mama's boy afraid of women or, in the parlance of the day, a pansy, who swished and lisped his way through sketches.

As was true in vaudeville, some of the more talented and imaginative burlesque comedians pushed beyond the confines of the stereotypes. They did not necessarily surrender all traces of ethnicity, but they found in themselves the core of their comedy character and no longer needed to assume stock characters.

As important as the comedian was the straight man. He was always slick: sometimes a shifty sharpie of the type that Bud Abbott made most famous or else a stylistic cousin to the Kickapoo Juice pitchman, pretending to erudition with fancy airs and multisyllabic words. It was possible for the straight man to be attractive to women, but the comic was invariably sexually unattractive, because he was either old or grotesque, yet he had the instincts of a yard dog sniffing after a bitch in heat. Women in the person of the *talking woman* treated him haughtily or made it plain that their favors came with a price tag. Although individual burlesque comics differed in style, shape and characterization, they all were society's little guys, losers hoping against experience to dodge their usual fate.

Irving Benson

Max Furman

Many of the better burlesque comics went on to star on other stages. Among the earliest were Weber & Fields, Sam Bernard, Montgomery & Stone, Leon Errol, W. C. Fields, Willie & Eugene Howard and Sophie Tucker, who found favor and much larger salaries on Broadway and in big-time vaudeville in the late nineteenth century. David Warfield spent three years in burlesque before joining Weber & Fields and then became one of the great dramatic stars of the legitimate stage.

Early in the twentieth century, Roscoe "Fatty" Arbuckle apprenticed in burlesque with Leon Errol before becoming one of the first silent movie clowns, and Joe E. Brown, Fannie Brice, James Barton, Bert Lahr, Eddie Cantor, Clark & McCullough, Hamtree Harrington, Jack Haley, Lulu McConnell, Jack Pearl, Ted Healy, Lew Hearn and Jimmy Savo spent some of their formative years in burlesque before moving into vaudeville, Broadway revues and musical comedies.

Mid-twentieth-century burlesque graduates included Abbott & Costello, Red Skelton, Phil Silvers, Red Buttons, Pinkie Lee, Jerry Lester, Danny Thomas, Joey Faye, Rags Ragland and Jackie Gleason, who became top box-office draws in nightclubs, radio and television.

The majority of burlesque comedians, however, spent most, if not all, their careers in burlesque. Many of them were not lesser talents than their more famous brethren, and some were comic geniuses, according to those who saw them. Some recorded parts of their act on film, a few made a television appearance or two, and several were around long enough to participate in revivals such as Ann Corio's *This Was Burlesque,* which toured on and off from 1962 until 1981, or *Sugar Babies,* which was a hit on Broadway from 1979 until 1982. Even in their day, the best of the burlesque comics never became well-known, but, among their own kind and in the opinions of appreciative audiences, they were the best of laugh-makers: Joe Welch, Ben Welch, Dave Marion (also known as Snuffy the Cabman), Bozo Snyder, Harry K. Morton, Tom Howard, George Shelton, Joe Yule, the Watson Sisters, Chaz Chase, Steve Mills, Charlie Robinson, Billy "Scratch" Wallace, Billy Arlington, Jimmy Dugan, Shorty McAllister & Johnny Weber, the husband-and-wife team of Mike Sachs and Alice Kennedy, and straight man Connie Ryan.

CAROL BURNETT

b: (Carol Creighton Burnett) 26 April 1933, San Antonio, TX

The first generation of great female comedy stars on television—Imogene Coca, Martha Raye, Lucille Ball and Joan Davis—came to the medium with years of vaudeville, revue, radio and movie experience. Only Imogene had failed to find stardom before she costarred in *Your Show of Shows.* Carol Burnett, of the second generation of television's female clowns, never played vaudeville, but she had a few years experience in industrial shows, summer resorts and cabaret before she made her reputation with a television variety show. Her major mark in show business was as the star of a superb weekly television variety program, *The Carol Burnett Show,* on which Carol and her fine supporting cast presented a bill of sketch comedy and musical numbers every week for 11 years; a vaudeville revue, if you will.

Growing up, Carol had no reason to believe or even hope that life would so quickly make her successful and famous. Her mother and father were ill suited parents, unfocused and alcoholic. She was raised by her maternal grandmother, Nanny, who was willful and manipulative, but she assumed responsibility for Carol and, later, her half sister Christine.

Nanny, Mama, Daddy and Carol were living in Los Angeles when Carol was still in grade school and Christine was born. They survived on welfare. In high school, Carol, seeing herself as gawky, toothsome, tall and skinny, felt ill at ease, but she was a diligent student and got accepted to UCLA. The tuition at the state university was less than $50, but $50 dollars more than she or her grandmother had. Mysteriously, an envelope arrived with the cash in it. Carol never learned the identity of her benefactor.

Burnett attended college with the announced intention of majoring in English and journalism, but she gravitated toward the theatre and music departments. At UCLA, talent made her popular. She lived at home, supported herself with part-time jobs and grabbed every opportunity to sing, act and clown onstage. At one event, a rich couple took a liking to Carol and her onstage partner, Don Saroyan. They staked Carol and Don to $1,000 each to make it on the musical stage in New York City. It was a loan to be paid back; if they found success, they were to stake some other talented people to their dreams. Carol and Don upheld their pledge.

In Manhattan, Carol met the same casual indifference and bumped into the same cold shoulders as other hopefuls had. When she asked an agent how to break the catch-22 of not being able to get a job until she got an agent and not being able to get an agent until she got a job, he suggested she produce her own showcase. At the time, Carol roomed in the Rehearsal Club, an inexpensive hostelry for young women trying to break into the theatre. The Rehearsal Club was the model for the play *Stage Door* written by Edna Ferber and George S. Kaufman that Morrie Ryskind adapted for the film of the same name.

First lady of the American theatre Katherine Cornell signed the invitations that were sent out to agents, directors, playwrights and anyone else Carol and her cohorts thought could give them a job. The Rehearsal Club revue was staged by Don, and it got Carol an agent and work. It had been eight months since she arrived in Manhattan with no professional experience.

She married Don Saroyan, who was trying to make his way in New York as a director. Carol worked summers in the Catskills and got 13 weeks on television with the *Paul Winchell & Jerry Mahoney Show* (1956), a featured spot on Buddy Hackett's flop TV sitcom *Stanley* (1956–57) and guest shots on Garry Moore's morning show whenever she had new material. Between the Catskills and Garry Moore, Carol began to lean in the direction of cabaret rather than cracking Broadway.

In her first engagement at the famed Blue Angel, in 1959, Carol introduced a song that became her calling card. Sung as a teenage fan, "I Made a Fool of Myself over John Foster Dulles" (President Eisenhower's dour secretary of state) made Burnett the sensation of the Manhattan cabaret scene.

Burnett's big breaks came in 1959. The first one came from Garry Moore, one of the pioneers of the laid-back television style and a fixture in television programming since 1950. Moore had started an hour-long weekly, nighttime variety show (*The Garry Moore Show,* 1958–67) that featured comedians Marion Lorne and Durwood Kirby. With only two days notice, Garry asked Carol to substitute for guest star Martha Raye, who was ill with influenza. Carol succeeded, won the praise of Martha Raye and the admiration of Moore. She became a regular and stayed with his show until 1962.

The second break came from George Abbott (1887–1995), the dean of Broadway writer-directors and a fixture on Broadway since the 1910s. (He remained active on Broadway into his 100th year.) Abbott hired Burnett for a six-month pre-Broadway run of *Once Upon a Mattress* (1959–60). Abbott and Burnett made the show a success. Carol and Don separated soon after Carol got both of these breaks. Their marriage and breakup was friendly. Careers separated them. Also, with the death of her parents, Carol had assumed the responsibility for her half sister.

Burnett made her movie debut in the Dean Martin movie *Who's Been Sleeping in My Bed?* (1963). When *Once Upon a Mattress* was adapted for television in 1964, she re-created her role as Princess Winnifred the Woebegone. Carol also married Joe Hamilton, who produced Carol's first television special, *Calamity Jane* (1963). They stayed married for 20 years, and he produced her television series and specials. Somebody at CBS-TV got the brilliant idea to package a rotating roster of brilliant young comedians (Carol Burnett, Bob Newhart, Tessie O'Shea, Ruth Buzzi and Dom DeLuise) into an hour-long vaudeville revue. The producers neglected to hire capable writers or think of a better title than *The Entertainers.* The series limped through the 1964–65 season.

Because Carol was in *Once Upon a Mattress* before it played Broadway, *Fade In, Fade Out* (1964–65), which costarred Jack Cassidy, Lou Jacobi and Tiger Haynes, qualifies as her Broadway debut. It proved one of Jule Styne's and Comden & Green's lesser shows. People in the business criticized Carol for leaving the musical after a single season; the show closed when the producers failed to find a comedian of equal ability and drawing power to take Carol's place. She did not return to Broadway for 30 years. When she did come back, it was to costar with Philip Bosco in *Moon Over Buffalo* (1995–96), a popular farce by Ken J. Ludwig, and to star in a revue of Stephen Sondheim songs, *Putting It All Together* (1999–2000), which was later filmed for television.

Carol Burnett's reputation is grounded in the 11-year run of *The Carol Burnett Show* (1967–79) on CBS-TV. Molded in the image of *Caesar's Hour,* the Sid Caesar variety show of more than a decade earlier, Carol surrounded herself with a superior supporting cast. Harvey Korman was Carol's Carl Reiner, a versatile and alert comedy actor who could both play straight man and lead comic. Lyle Wagoner was a handsome announcer whose deft parody of glamorous hunks was underappreciated. Vicki Lawrence began the show as a look-alike sister to Carol but blossomed into a fine character comedian.

Carol's guests were always top drawer: Nanette Fabray, Imogene Coca, Martha Raye, Sid Caesar, Gloria Swanson, Mickey Rooney, Jonathan Winters, Art Carney, Gwen Verdon, Marilyn Horne, Eileen Farrell, Peggy Lee, Dinah Shore, Ella Fitzgerald, Edie Adams, Pat Carroll, Nancy Wilson, Jim Nabors, Mama Cass Elliot, Rita Hayworth, Carol Channing, the Pointer Sisters, Maggie Smith, Paul Sand and Emmett Kelly.

In 1975, midway through the series' run, Tim Conway joined the cast. He was a gifted zany (perhaps the only comedian of Jonathan Winters' generation who was a worthy rival in off-the-wall antics), and his presence on the show and Carol's willingness to showcase him added years to the show's life.

Carol Burnett was both a clown and a comedy actor. She had a Broadway belter's singing voice and a warm personality that engaged the folks watching her show at home. She did not dance well, nor was she adept as a monologist (neither were Jackie Gleason, Imogene Coca nor Sid Caesar).

Carol Burnett represented the third wave of television variety. The first had been led by veterans like Ed Wynn, Jimmy Durante, Eddie Cantor and Milton Berle, whose ability to survive the experimental years of live television was due to their experience of performing for decades in vaudeville and revue and on network radio. The second wave brought newer faces like Jackie Gleason, Imogene Coca and Sid Caesar to the fore, and they headed the top shows of the 1950s.

By the 1960s, many suspected that variety could no longer play on prime-time television. Popular music had become so amplified and heated that it created an imbalance with the rest of the bill such as comedy monologues and sketches. Yet there were as many successful variety hours as there had ever been on television: *The Hollywood Palace* (1964–70), *The Dean Martin Show* (1965–74), *The Smothers Brothers*

Comedy Hour (1967–75), *Rowan & Martin's Laugh-In* (1968–73) and *The Flip Wilson Show* (1970–74).

Of course the all-time champs were Ed Sullivan's *Toast of the Town* (also known as the *Ed Sullivan Show,* 1948–71), which ran for 23 years on CBS; *The Lawrence Welk Show,* whose 16 years (1955–71) on ABC-TV was followed by another 11 years (1971–82) as a syndicated show; and *The Red Skelton Show* (1951–71), which usually placed in the top 20 most popular shows on television and was still in the top 20 when it was canceled because sponsors believed that the average age of Red's viewers were too old to be frequent purchasers of their products.

Carol Burnett returned to television many times in dramas, musical specials (particularly with Julie Andrews) and several revivals of her variety hour and its cast. The revivals never quite caught fire. Perhaps everyone was older or had lost the ensemble feel. This was true of Jackie Gleason's and Sid Caesar's attempts as well.

Carol Burnett continued to be a presence in American theatre, films and television. Her ambitions have both diminished and grown with the years. On one hand, there is little left to prove. On the other, she ripened into a fine dramatic actor without losing her skill at comedy.

Burns & Allen

BURNS & ALLEN

George Burns

b: (Nathan Birnbaum) 20 January 1896, New York, NY—d: 9 March 1996, Los Angeles, CA

Gracie Allen

b: (Grace Ethel Cecile Rosalie Allen) 26 July 1908, San Francisco— d: 27 August 1964, Los Angeles, CA

George Burns was one of a handful of actors and performers who worked and maintained their star status into their 90s; Eubie Blake, Lillian Gish, Milton Berle and John Gielgud are most of the others. For his first 20 years in show business, Burns had no reason to expect such a long career.

George was eight when he and three friends working in a candy factory were taught to sing harmony by the local mailman who then found them a few jobs as the "Peewee Quartet." When they copped first prize on amateur night at the neighborhood movie house, George knew it had to be show business or nothing for him. George quit the quartet to become half of the Burns Brothers, a dance act that debuted at Seiden's Theatre in 1905.

Things were rough at home. His widowed mother had nine other children to feed, clothe and house. Those who could take care of themselves did. George did, but it was rough. He left school in the fifth grade and never his entire life was truly comfortable reading. As buck-and-wing dancers, the Burns Brothers laid off more than they worked. By 1912, then 16-year-old George was more out than in show business. He joined a kid act and soon outgrew it. He fancied himself a song-and-dance man, but it was a minority opinion.

Instead of changing his profession, he changed his act and stage names. He tried exhibition ballroom dancing, roller-skating and working with animals. He was Willie Saks, Glide of Goldie, Fields & Glide, Jed Jackson of Jackson & Malone, Jack Harris of Harris & Kelly, Phil Baxter of Baxter & Bates, José of José & Dolores and of José & Smith, Pedro of Pedro Lopez & Conchita, Burns of Burns & Gary, Maurice of Maurice Valenti & His Wonder Dog, Friend of Flipper & Friend, and on different occasions he was both Brown and Williams of Brown & Williams. In later reminiscence, the rejections and failures were burnished into comic adventures that he enjoyed telling. He also remembered every song he sang and every act he saw.

Twenty years into the business and 27 years old in 1923, George was still a small-time act, one half of a song-and-dance act, Burns & Lorraine, that was breaking up. Then he met Gracie Allen.

Gracie was also looking for a partner when Rena Arnold, a roughhouse comic on the same bill with Burns & Lorraine, introduced Gracie to Billy and George. George won, not knowing that Gracie had a boyfriend, Benny Ryan, successfully playing the big time as half of Ryan & Lee. George pitched Gracie the idea of a talking *mixed-double* act, or *flirtation act.*

Born into a showbiz family, Gracie's father was a clog dancer who taught his four girls and a boy to dance. He arranged Gracie's debut when she was three, and four years later she was a professional starting out with her sisters as a singing quartet. Their act was good enough to keep them working for ten years, most recently as the "company" part of Larry Reilly & Co. Her sisters left the vaudeville road to settle down teaching in the dance school they established in their hometown of San Francisco.

It is well known that at first George was the comic and Gracie the *feed.* George was a great raconteur, even then, but inexperienced as a stage comic. The change was made during a fill-in booking at a small-time house in Newark, New Jersey. According to the legend George Burns carefully passed down, they flopped the first show: Gracie got titters with her straight lines, George shot blanks. He reversed their roles for the second show, and the act wowed the audience. For the first time in his career, George had a good act, a hit act. In the audience was a new friend, one who would become his best friend for life, Jack Benny. Jack was already a solid act as a monologist with a casual air.

George may not have found himself yet as a comic, but, as a serious student of showbiz, he knew how to structure an act and quickly developed the confidence to write the act instead of cribbing old gags from joke books. It was all quite fast. Within a week, Burns & Allen had an act, an agent and more bookings, including six months on the Keith circuit, if only as a disappointment act, which meant keeping your bags packed and being ready to fill in where another act has fallen out.

When George's and Gracie's paths crossed Benny Ryan's, Gracie and Benny renewed their romance. George also was smitten with Gracie, and he did not want to lose his only successful act. By 1924, Burns & Allen were playing the better small time, the lesser houses and cities on the Keith and Orpheum circuits. Their patter had progressed from disjointed jokes to a connected dialogue, often about Gracie's bizarre family:

George: "This family of yours, do they all live together?"

Gracie: "Yes, my father, my uncle, my cousin, my brother and my nephew used to sleep in one bed, and. . ."

George: "I'm surprised your grandfather didn't sleep with them."

Gracie: "He did, but he died and they made him get up."

George always gave Gracie the credit for their tremendous success, and everyone admired her many gifts. Her delivery was faultless, she sang passably, danced better and connected with audiences. Those in the business also gave George credit for creating, writing and managing the act. They also appreciated the worth of a good feed. Although the public always applauds the comic, they probably do not appreciate how the feed or straight man paces the act and points the jokes and bits of business.

Meanwhile, Gracie had decided to quit the act and marry Benny Ryan. George worked hard to persuade Gracie on both counts; George had 20 years of experience dealing with rejection. The act was doing well, and they were part of a circle of successful friends who were either married or close to it: Jack and Mary Benny, Jesse Block and Eva Sully, Blossom and Benny Fields. Gracie decided to choose George, and they were married on 7 January 1926. It was a good year for George.

Burns & Allen made it into big-time, two-a-day vaudeville in 1925. They were not stars yet, and they did not have a good spot on the bill—yet. While touring Orpheum time out of Chicago, George had commissioned a sketch writer (either Al Boasberg or John Medbury) to write a new act for them. It was called "Lamb Chops," and George was tightening it. "Lamb Chops" made them headliners. The Keith and Orpheum jointly booked them for five years. George Burns had finally arrived, and at the Palace, too, on Broadway.

George: "Do you care about love?"

Gracie: "No."

George: "Do you like to kiss?'

Gracie: "No. (giggle)"

George: "What do you like?"

Gracie: "Lamb Chops."

George: "I bet a little girl like you couldn't eat two big lamb chops alone."

Gracie: "Not alone I couldn't. With mashed potatoes and peas I could."

Gracie was very believable. George insisted she was an actress more than a comedian, and that made her character and dialogue seem real.

In 1929, just before they sailed for England, where they would play a season in English variety and make their radio debut on the BBC, Fred Allen (no relation to Gracie) got sick and was unable to film his act as contracted by Vitaphone at their Astoria, Long Island, studio. George and Gracie stepped in and filmed *Lamb Chops* as their first motion-picture short. They made $1,700 for the nine-minute short. They filmed ten one-reel comedies between 1929 and 1933. Each was a vaudeville routine, mostly scripted by George and adapted for filming.

They repeated at the Palace in 1930 and 1931, played a couple of guest spots on both Eddie Cantor's and Rudy Vallee's radio shows, then joined the weekly *Guy Lombardo Show* on CBS for two years. They started their own series in 1933, which lasted until 1949, and made their first feature, *The Big Broadcast,* for Paramount Pictures in 1932. In all, they made 14 features, all but their two best for Paramount. Most of their roles in the feature films were similar to their one-reel efforts, but the routine was broken into segments and threaded throughout the feature. The one film they made for RKO, *A Damsel in Distress* (1937), starring Fred Astaire, presented George and Gracie at their best. Fred, George and Gracie performed the "Whisk Broom" dance. (George had the dance taught to him by one of the originators then showed it to Fred.) Later, Gracie appeared in three well-received films without George. George and Gracie's last film together was *Honolulu* for MGM in 1939, which starred Eleanor Powell and featured a charming song-and-dance duet between Eleanor and Gracie.

Their weekly radio show was the basis of the team's stardom. By 1942, after watching their high ratings sink, bit by bit, George modified the act. George and Gracie began playing a married couple, more appropriate roles for a woman in her mid-30s and a man more than a decade older. Another change, never spoken of, was that George's character mellowed. He stopped being the exasperated boyfriend and started evolving into the bemused husband. This new relationship made their transition in 1950 to television a success and their show one of the new medium's most creative. George would step through the fourth wall to wryly comment to the audience on Gracie's latest scheme.

Far less enamored of showbiz than George, Gracie was weary by 1958. She retired, which meant that Burns & Allen were retired—permanently. Six years later, in 1964, Gracie died unexpectedly. George was lost for a decade. Gracie was his great love. She was also, he was certain, the sole reason for their success. Despite his doubts about his ability to hold an audience, George was one of those comedians whom other comics think is hilarious. He got his laughs offstage. Also, he enjoyed great success as a television producer with several hit series to his credit.

Once a month, he would visit Gracie's grave at Forest Lawn Cemetery and tell her what he was doing. "I don't know if she hears me, but it makes me feel better." Show business was his religion and his life. It is what he believed in. He loved to perform. Because it had been such a struggle at the start, he was loath to give up. "I'm going to stay in show business until I'm the only one left." And for most of his 100 years on Earth, George Burns did just that. "I can't die. I'm booked."

At first he floundered a bit on his own, trying various new partners like Carol Channing, playing nightspots and TV variety shows. It was only after the death of his dearest friend, Jack Benny, that George Burns discovered that he could be a success solo. Jack had been cast as the quiet partner in *The Sunshine Boys,* the film version of Neil Simon's hit play about a vaudeville comedy team. When Jack unexpectedly died before shooting began, George was drafted into the role; it started a whole new career for George, who picked up the 1975 Academy Award for best supporting actor.

From his 80s onward, Burns worked steadily, making movies, appearing on TV, performing live in theatres, nightclubs and casinos, and writing books. He usually earned between $25,000 and $50,000 a week and sometimes that much or more for a single appearance. Beginning with *The Sunshine Boys* in 1975, Burns starred in a dozen films and as many TV specials.

Unlike many aging comedians, George Burns never lost his ability to time a joke or pace a routine until 1994, when he began to fail. Burns was 98! A fall dashed the hopes of many that George would celebrate his 100th birthday onstage. Irving Fein, the agent extraordinaire whom Jack Benny had "bequeathed" to his dear friend, had lined up a number of engagements, but, given Burns' health, there was no way he could fulfill those bookings, and all but one of them was canceled. One well-wisher promised George he would be at Caesar's Palace to see Burns perform on his 100th birthday, capping it to say he would be there a year later to see George perform on his 101st. George managed to crack "That's if they're still in business."

On 9 March 1996, George joined his beloved Gracie. At Forest Lawn the marker's brass letters read, "Gracie Allen and George Burns—Together Again." George had long wished Gracie to have top billing.

LANCE BURTON

b: (William Lance Burton) 10 March 1960, Louisville, KY

He was inspired by the great classic illusionists of the twentieth century: Channing Pollock, Dante and Thurston. He first saw a stage magician when he was five and, like many youngsters, decided to become one himself. The difference was that Lance Burton followed through, reading books that explained standard tricks and practicing daily. A locally based magician, Harry Collins, thought Lance had talent and determination, and he generously tutored the boy. Meanwhile, Lance went to school and worked at odd jobs; his earnings were spent on magic paraphernalia.

Burton built his act in his Southland homeland before bringing it to the land of illusion, Las Vegas. At first he offered a sleight-of-hand act, featuring the manipulation of cards and coins and the production of white doves from bits of paper. Like his mentor and other illusionists he admired, Burton dressed formally for his performances. He won first prize in a competition for junior magicians when he was 17, a gold medal at age 20 from the International Brotherhood of Magicians, and the Grand Prix of Magic at 22 from the Fédération Internationale des Sociétés Magiques.

He was raven haired, shirt-model handsome, debonair and impeccably tailored, but perhaps because he eschewed the theatrical flair and high-tech illusions of David Copperfield and Siegfried & Roy, Burton was pigeonholed as a supporting act for the Folies Bergère floor show in Las Vegas from 1982 through 1990. Growing respect from other stage magicians and a generous spot on Johnny Carson's *Tonight Show* did much to boost Lance's professional stature.

The turning point came in 1991, when Lance invested in a more elaborate, evening-length act. His new act was booked into the Hacienda Hotel. He kept part of his old act: the close-up manipulations that he presented in the classic magicians' attire of a tuxedo. The new effects were spectacular illusions: Lance floated aloft like an aerialist, with a lovely female assistant riding astride him; chorus girls materialized from a suitcase and dissolved into a flock of doves; another assistant seemed to penetrate his torso and exit from his back. Lance exchanged his formal attire for garb more swashbuckling and revealing. He stripped to the waist to display his buffed physique in a magical sword-fight illusion.

In 1995, Lance signed a long-term contract with the Monte Carlo Resort, proof that he was established as one of Las Vegas' premier drawing cards. During the 1990s and 2000s, he filmed a half dozen television specials. In 1994, however, Lance Burton received what many consider the greatest recognition that can be conferred upon an illusionist: the Mantle of Magic. Originally held by Harry Kellar, it was passed from him to Howard Thurston in 1908, from Thurston to Dante in 1936, and from Dante to Lee Grabel in 1995. Grabel presented the Mantle to Lance Burton.

FRANK BUSH

b: ca. 1860—d: 1930

A pioneer conversational comedian who finally became a top attraction toward the turn of the twentieth century, Frank Bush was a product, like Sam Bernard, of the Grand Duke Theatre of the 1870s, a rough Five Points entertainment venue run by the gang called the Baxter Street Dudes. He played variety and vaudeville into the 1910s.

In his landmark history, *American Vaudeville: Its Life and Times,* Douglas Gilbert described Bush's act. Like Weber & Fields and other near contemporaries, Bush portrayed a number of ethnic personalities: Jewish, Yankee and German. Instead of roughhouse comedy, Bush offered stories that depended upon his ability to create a character familiar to his audience rather than stringing jokes together. When imitating people whose native language was other than English, Bush peppered his gibberish with recognizable words of German or Yiddish, as required by the story.

After the Civil War, many comedians performed in blackface or donned Irish or German costumes and makeup. Frank Bush began to specialize in the Jew and the Yankee. He made his reputation as the solemn and bespectacled Isaac Levy Solomon Moses. Dressed in a long black peddler's coat and sporting a pointed beard, he set the standard for benign Jewish characterizations on the stage. Other comedians, who followed Bush's lead in devising a benign Jewish stage persona, were Ben Welch, Julian Rose, Joe Welch and, later, Willie Howard.

Bush was a storyteller, and his leisurely monologues stressed character. When the pace of contemporary performance quickened with the times, Frank Bush's popularity in vaudeville declined. As vaudeville drew audiences from a wider cross section of society than the urban poor and recent immigrants, Frank Bush exchanged his peddler's garb for a dinner jacket, but his style of presentation was passé.

BUSINESS

Among performers, the word *business* refers to stage business rather than finance, and it corresponds in a sense to *bits.* More specifically it refers to particular movements by an actor and the practiced handling of props or clothing. The script may state that the actor retrieves his hat in a certain scene. How that is accomplished is not detailed by the author but is left to the actor and director to devise.

For a dramatic actor, the action of getting his hat may be straightforward and understated so as not to divert attention from the dialogue. For a comedian, the removal of a hat may be the comic highlight of the scene. If the character is angry and imperious, he will snatch his hat. If he is more tentative or flustered, he could create a merry mix-up that culminates with a number of other people putting on the wrong hats. The business must be in harmony with the character and with the tone and incidents of the sketch. How the character executes the business helps the audience understand his nature, state of mind and motive.

BUSKERS

The English term *buskers* refers to the entertainers who performed on the street, often outside theatres, restaurants and saloons. They passed the hat among passersby or picked up the throw money and then divided the collection (or *take*) among themselves.

Taverns and saloons were preferred spots for buskers. The convivial customer was more likely to be generous. Buskers generally sang, danced, played instruments, juggled or performed bits of illusion.

There are a variety of roots for busker. Some scholars like to trace it to sandals worn by Greek actors. Joe Laurie Jr. was probably closer to the mark when he guessed that busker and busking referred to its nautical meaning: "to cruise as a pirate," because buskers operated outside the law (unlicensed) and cruised around from town to town, corner to corner.

Speculation suggests that innkeepers appreciated the better buskers as added attractions and likely invited inside those who found favor with their customers. This was a step along the way to the creation of music-halls. First, the innkeeper let certain buskers know they were welcome to come inside where, in turn for a song or two, customers stood them to drinks and the owner offered them a meal. The more popular buskers became successful by making similar arrangements with several taverns.

Unlike vaudevillians who appeared at a single theatre, music-hall performers had the option to appear at several in a single evening. When saloon keepers and innkeepers realized that the entertainers were the primary draw for their establishments, they built halls next to their barrooms, set up tables, chairs and a stage, invited womenfolk, and created a new form of theatre—music-hall—which offered a series of turns by various performers in an evening. Those entertainers who were not invited in likely set up near the entrance and busked.

BUTTERBEANS & SUSIE

Butterbeans

b: (Jodie Edwards) 19 July 1895, Marietta, GA—d: 28 October 1967, Bloomingdale, IL

Susie

b: (Susie Hawthorne Edwards) 1896, Pensacola, FL—d: 5 December 1963, Bloomingdale, IL

In Greenville, South Carolina, on 15 May 1917, Jodie Edwards married Susie Hawthorne on the stage of the local Theatre Owners' Booking Association (TOBA) theatre. Their partnership lasted a half century, a team onstage and off. To the delight of their black audiences, they sang, danced and never stopped complaining about each other.

Susie had been in the chorus of *Smart Girl*, a revue, when Jodie, a song-and-dance man talked her into joining him in a mixed-double act. For more than a decade they were billed as Edwards & Edwards. Then, when Jodie was inducted into the army during the First World War, Susie teamed up with an older performer, Butler "Stringbeans" May, until after the war, when Jodie and Sue reunited. Sometimes, they found themselves on the same bill with Stringbeans and Sweetie May, his partner and wife. When Butler May died in 1929, Jodie was persuaded by a booker to adopt Stringbeans' character and name. Jodie took on the *monkey-man* persona, tilted their act more to comedy, and they went out as Butterbeans & Susie, billing they kept for the rest of their lives.

Dozens of bluesmen and women sang plaints of cheating and abusing mates, but usually they did it solo. Butterbeans and Susie made their laments into a statement of particulars, each side prosecuting the other before the court of public opinion whose verdict was knowing laughter and applause. Neither possessed great vocal range, but Susie had a warm tone and a pleasant vibrato, and Beans had great timing with a dry, breathy sound, a bit like John Bubbles.

Susie dressed conventionally for the stage in a long gown, but Beans came onstage attired in a monkey-man outfit with an undersized hat perched atop his head and tight pants riding up his shins. The costume signified to the audience that he was unmanly and a wimp, easily dominated by women. After their battle of the sexes rendered in cross talk and song, they ended the

Butterbeans & Susie

act with Susie offering peace and loving in a song and Butterbeans doing his frantic "Itch" dance.

They addressed each other as "Sue" and "Butter" or "Mama" and "Papa," but behind the blues music and the familiar domestic comedy of put-upon lovers, there was a threat of violence. Their patter and songs told of sexual wanderings, black eyes and razors.

> "Sue, how come you don't open your door and let me in?"
>
> "How come you don't go back where you been?"
>
> "Well, if I don't get in, nobody better come out."
>
> "Listen, there been some changes made since you been gone. Your key don't fit my lock no more."
>
> "Mama, did you change your lock?"
>
> "Yessir, now back yourself out of my front door!"

Susie tormented Beans about his sexual inadequacies. When Beans responded with his own accusations and promises to do her in, Susie upped the ante with a few threats of her own. Her frustrations and complaints were coded within their songs about handymen and machinery that did not function.

I want a hot dog without bread, you see,
'Cause I carry my bread with me.
I want it hot, I don't want it cold,
I want it so it will fit my roll.

Some among the emerging black middle class, proud of the black writers and artists who led the Harlem Renaissance and the African American intellectuals who spoke of the New Negro, were chagrined by acts like Butterbeans and Susie. They hoped the achievements of black Americans would give the lie to white supremacist propaganda, and they feared that the low, sexual comedy that whites saw on their slumming expeditions into Harlem would reinforce the stereotype of base, ignorant blacks. The truth was that Butterbeans & Susie—and Tim Moore, Pigmeat Markham, Spider Bruce Mason and Dusty Fletcher, who followed them—did not set out to present an accurate portrayal of black people any more than Laurel & Hardy or The Three Stooges intended to represent white people. The point was to be funny, and 'Beans & Susie accomplished that by portraying fringe characters, just like Chaplin and The Marx Brothers.

In the course of a half century, Beans and Sue performed in shows with the big stars of each succeeding era. They traveled in minstrel and tent shows with great blues queens like Ma Rainey and Trixie Smith and in vaudeville with Ethel Waters. Beans and Sue headlined with Bessie Smith in all-black revues at Harlem's Lafayette Theatre and played Harlem hot spots like the Cotton Club with the Nicholas Brothers. During the 1950s and 1960s, they appeared on bills at the Apollo Theater in Harlem along with the much younger rhythm & blues and Motown recording stars.

Butterbeans & Susie were well liked within show business, and other entertainers found them professional, easy to work with and reliable. Ethel Waters often hired them for her touring revues, and they appeared with her in the Broadway musical *Cabin in the Sky* (1940).

Working the black circuit exclusively, they earned less than was paid in white show business. When work became scarce, especially as the African American theatregoing public's taste began to change after the Second World War and the civil rights movement discouraged negative portrayals of the Negro, they needed to take whatever work was available, frequently performing solo.

W. S. Butterfield

Semiretired in the Chicago area from 1945 until 1950, they worked more outside show business than in, but the 1950s brought some revival of interest, and they worked together somewhat regularly onstage until Susie died in 1963. Beans kept going for the few years he had left. He died on 28 October 1967 as he walked onstage at the Dorchester Inn, outside Chicago.

BUTTERFIELD TIME

W. S. Butterfield headed a self-named circuit that was centered in and around Michigan. His office was in Battle Creek. In 1916, he made the decision to book films on the states-right plan. Butterfield time included 15 theatres devoted to vaudeville or movies.

JOE BYRD

Active during the first half of the twentieth century, Joe Byrd was an African American comedian who toured with many shows, including Porter Granger and Freddie Johnson's *Aces & Queens* (1925) and Earl Dancer's and Donald Heywood's *Black Rhythm Revue,* which played the Comedy Theatre on Broadway in 1936. Much of Byrd's work was in packaged shows that played black theatres and some lesser white houses that booked vaudeville and burlesque, including black shows.

C

SID CAESAR

b: 8 September 1922, Yonkers, NY

Sid Caesar's career is inseparable from the early days of television. When television became available to the general public a few years after the close of the Second World War, it began as the stepchild of network radio. There were not many television receivers in American homes in 1947–48. They were relatively expensive and had small screens, many no larger than eight inches in diameter. Reception was spotty, flawed and pretty much clustered in a few urban areas. Few sponsors with national products were willing to risk investment in television. Gillette, Texaco and Kraft were among the exceptions.

Wrestling, boxing and 1930s black-and-white Westerns were broadcast three or four nights a week in 1948, and barrooms were among the first purchasers of television receivers. Taverns became salesrooms for television. At the time, most full-time wage earners were male, and it was they who bought the family's first TV set, often as a Christmas present for their families in 1948, 1949 or 1950.

Small budgets, small screens and small audiences did not tempt big stars or big sponsors. If the stars were in radio, most took a wait-and-see approach. If they were in the movies, they viewed television both as a threat to their industry that would keep people home and away from movie houses and as a comedown from the big screen: if a movie star appeared on television it was tantamount to admitting they were falling stars whose film careers were in trouble.

Television executives, potential sponsors and advertising agencies had to settle for has-beens and unknowns; it proved to be a fortuitous choice. The has-been barrel included old vaudevillians who were quickly able to adapt to live television and had a career's worth of jokes and sketches that kept them supplied for several seasons on TV. The unknowns were not inexperienced, but they were comparatively young performers who worked in Borscht Belt, in small Off-Broadway revues, cabarets, nightclubs and the few remaining vaudeville theatres.

Both the old-timers and the newcomers had experience working in front of live audiences, whereas many movie actors had not and were unaccustomed to a format that relied upon improvisation rather than retakes. Among the veterans were Ed Sullivan, Milton Berle, Gertrude Berg, Fred Waring, Ed Wynn, Ted Mack and his Amateur Hour, Boris Karloff, Joe Howard and Olsen & Johnson. Among the new faces were Julie Harris, Paul Newman, James Dean, Kim Stanley, Arthur Godfrey, Allen Funt, Dave Garroway, Jack Carter, Faye Emerson, Jerry Lester, Dagmar, Jackie Gleason, Larry Storch, Steve Allen, Imogene Coca and Sid Caesar.

Some lasted and became enduring stars of the new medium. Many, both veterans and newcomers, quickly faded. Big-name stars like Groucho Marx, Lucille Ball, Red Skelton, Martin & Lewis, Bob Hope and Loretta Young came in 1950–51 or later, once television had proved itself. Television was a great leveler. Some big stars bombed; some newcomers flourished. Talent, personality, suitability for the medium and a decent program in a decent time slot were the only guarantees of success.

No show in television history deserves and is given more credit for setting the benchmark for quality and originality in variety programming in television than

Your Show of Shows. Everyone associated with it was a newcomer. The show began during the 1949 season as the *Admiral Broadway Revue*. Its sponsor, makers of Admiral television sets, dropped the show after 18 weeks because Admiral, an undercapitalized but rapidly growing company, had to choose between investing in their manufacturing capacity or sponsorship. They had sold their entire inventory in a few months and were backed up in meeting demand for more sets.

Revamped as *Your Show of Shows*, Max Liebman's revue aired on Saturdays from 9:00 P.M. until 10:30 P.M. Each week, the talent created a new 90-minute revue, which was almost equivalent to producing a new Broadway show every week. Producer Max Liebman brought Sid Caesar, Imogene Coca and dancers Mata & Hari to television. He had known them though his days as the entertainment director for Camp Tamiment in the Catskills and later as producer of a couple of intimate revues on Broadway. Max was staging *Tars and Spars* for the U.S. Coast Guard when he met Sid Caesar, who became the chief comic of the production.

Singing and dancing production numbers consumed half of *Your Show of Shows'* time. Comedy spots filled up the rest of the time. Sid Caesar took primary responsibility for the comedy, and Liebman produced the musical numbers. Dancers on *Your Show of Shows* included James Starbuck and Bambi Lynn & Rod Alexander. Some of the singers were Robert Merrill of the Metropolitan Opera, Marguerite Piazza, the Billy Williams Quartet and Bill Hayes.

Sid helped write *Your Show of Shows*, and he and Max found supremely clever writers who later became famous as playwrights and comedians themselves: Mel Tolkin, Larry Gelbart, Lucille Kallen, Danny and Neil Simon, Tony Webster, Mel Brooks, Joe Stein and Woody Allen.

Carl Reiner was originally hired because he was an established straight man and comedian. At six feet, two inches, he was an inch taller than Sid, and Max insisted that the straight man had to be taller than the comic. Carl was hired as Sid's feed, but he quickly took a hand in the writing, so the show got a writer, a comic and a straight man all in one. Howard Morris was hired because he was very funny and small enough that Sid could lift him by his lapels with one hand.

Fifty years later, aging fans and those who had seen subsequent reissues of scenes from *Your Show of Shows* could recall favorite routines. Sid's specialties were gibberish talk in various European accents and his deft teaming with superb comedian Imogene Coca, a ladylike but pixilated foil to Sid's super-masculine, aggressive style of sketch comedy. They paired in domestic comedy as the Hickenloopers; in burlesks of opera, ballet and method acting; and in spoofs of movie genres like costume flicks, Italian neorealist films, war movies, Westerns and silent-screen dramas. Carl Reiner and Howard Morris joined Sid and Imogene in the sketches. One of their best-remembered turns was as metal statues in a medieval Bavarian clock. At the hour, the mechanical figures (Sid, Imogene, Howard and Carl) revolved out of the clock tower and then back in. After a few turns, the mechanism went haywire and the figures began swinging their swords and axes and crashed into each other.

It was offbeat material that made Sid Caesar special. He played a housefly looking for food in a kitchen, a man dragged unwillingly onto the stage as the subject of a *This Is Your Life* show, and an airplane pilot and the plane in an air battle. One of his most familiar bits was as the European professor, an authority on nothing, a character not unlike Irwin Corey's.

Sid Caesar bridged two generations of great sketch comedians. His immediate predecessors were Beatrice Lillie, Victor Moore, Bobby Clark, Willie Howard and Bert Lahr. Sid's performance style was as ferociously energetic as Bert's and as original as Bobby's. His ability to immerse himself in character reminded one of Bea Lillie and Victor Moore, and Sid was as versatile as Willie Howard. Sid's successors were the various improvisational crews like Second City and bizarre comedy ensembles like Britain's Beyond the Fringe and Monty Python. At its best, television's *Saturday Night Live!* follows the lead laid down by Caesar and company.

As a youngster, Sid Caesar did not burn with show-business dreams. He was the youngest and remained the smallest of three brothers. His brothers were 15 to 20 years older than Sid, so he grew up much like an only child.

By the time he entered junior high school, the Great Depression was impoverishing much of the American populace. Sid's father, a Polish Jewish immigrant, had done well to own some rental property and a cafeteria, but the workers he depended upon for patronage were losing their jobs when the factories closed. A tenant had skedaddled without paying his rent but left an old saxophone behind. This was given to Sid, who quickly learned how to play it. He and a few friends formed a junior high school dance band and made a few dollars playing dances and weddings. He advanced to a small professional combo that played in bars. Summers, Sid played in resort bands and volunteered to help out with skits, often playing the stooge or patsy in a burlesque sketch.

When he finished high school at 16, he moved to Manhattan and joined the local branch of the musicians' union. Because of his size and grown-up looks, it was assumed he was 21. Between gigs as a sax player, he studied music and worked as an usher then a doorman at the Capital Theatre. He got the doorman's job because he was the only usher large enough to fit into the uniform. He audited (sneaked into) classes at Julliard and learned quite a bit about serious concert music. By the time he landed a regular job with the Shep Fields Orchestra, it was clear that the USA was going to enter the war in Europe and that he was a prime candidate (right age and unmarried) to be drafted, so he remained in New York when Shep Fields went on tour. Sid got occasional gigs with bands led by Claude Thornhill and Charlie Spivak while awaiting the call from the Selective Service Board.

In summer 1939, Sid Caesar was hired as a saxophonist in the band at a Catskill resort called Vacationland. He volunteered to help in the sketches as well, so they were happy to have him back in 1940. The director of the entertainment, Don Appel, took Sid along when he switched to Kutschers Hotel in Monticello in 1941 and then in 1942 to Avon Lodge in Woodridge. Before Sid went to Avon, he had enlisted in the coast guard.

It was at Avon that Sid met and fell in love with Florence Levy, the niece of the hotel's owner. He found her beautiful and smart. She found him manly, talented and self-educated. That fall, when Sid joined the coast guard, he was pleasantly surprised to be sent to Manhattan Beach, near Coney Island, for basic training and delighted when, after boot camp, he was assigned to the coast guard docks in Brooklyn. Thus, his courtship of Florence continued.

Caesar was allowed to organize a band to play for well-chaperoned dances at the base. Another enlistee, composer Vernon Duke, wrote out the orchestrations and became Sid's good friend. The success of the dances led to putting on a camp show, in which Sid and Vernon took charge. The show pleased their superior officers, and other posts asked for it. Vernon Duke returned to civilian life temporarily. Florence and Sid married in 1943.

Sid was transferred to Palm Beach, Florida. Waiting to greet him was Vernon Duke, who was back with the coast guard to write and produce a show to be called *Tars and Spars.* A civilian, Max Liebman, had been hired to direct. The army had their show, *This Is the Army,* and the other branches were planning theirs, so the coast guard did not wish to be left out. These servicemen shows bolstered morale, increased enlistment and created goodwill.

Sid showed Max some of the comedy bits he had done in the Catskills. Max recognized Sid's raw talent and originality and helped polish the bits into gems. As the show toured presentation houses, Caesar did more and more bits in the show, and he was becoming exhausted. One night, after a couple of months on the road, he reacted violently in a run-in with coast guard brass. He was confined to a hospital for observation, where he got into another scrap with some anti-Semitic marines. After ten days observation, he was back touring with the show. No incarceration, no court martial, no punishment. Sid later observed that too much came his way too soon and too young, and that he was always protected from the consequences of his rash behavior.

Fellow cast members Victor Mature and Gower Champion were not in *Tars and Spars* when it was made into a movie, but Caesar was. Despite excellent reviews for his performance in *Tars and Spars* (1946), it led only to one more movie role—a bit part—so Sid played pic-vaude houses and nightclubs. Less than four years after boot camp, Sid Caesar was getting paid $3,500 a week for his act at the Roxy. He got a fraction of that for *Make Mine Manhattan* (1948), a revue that ran a year, but it provided an excellent showcase for his talents.

Early in 1949, Max Liebman brought Sid Caesar to television. When NBC gave the green light to *The Admiral Broadway Revue,* Sid was joined by Imogene Coca and Mary McCarthy in the cast. The next season, an expanded show was called *Your Show of Shows.* Sid Caesar became a famous star barely five years after playing Kutscher's in the Catskills.

The strain of turning out a new live revue every week was felt by all. It was probably hardest for Sid because of his volatile nature. Petty matters became magnified into crises. The explosive outbursts that fitted his characters in his television sketches were carefully contained versions of what went on behind doors between shows. At home, he was sullen or argumentative. At the studio, he worked too hard and was unpredictable. One famous anecdote concerns Mel Brooks, who complained to Sid that he did not feel like sitting around while Sid drank. "Let's go out," said Mel. Sid obliged him by dangling Mel out the high rise window. During the shows, he was totally professional and sober. Encouraged by his wife, who remained married to him, Caesar went to psychiatrists periodically but did not feel they were useful in helping him control his rage or his drinking and pill taking.

Sid was a large man, six feet, one inch and usually around 240 pounds. He could absorb a lot of alcohol. He did not get hangovers, yet his sleep was deep but troubled. The only time his kids saw him was when he crawled home after writing, rehearsing or performing all day, dog tired and drunk.

At the end of the 1953–54 season, NBC decided to split up its Saturday-night wealth of talent. Imogene was put into a couple of ill-conceived shows that failed. Max Liebman was contracted to produce occasional *specials,* as they were called then. Sid, Howie Morris and Carl Reiner were given *Caesar's Hour,* retaining two-thirds of their old 90-minute time slot on Saturday nights. The writers were split up the same way, and Nanette Fabray became Sid's new female foil.

Caesar's Hour did very well for several seasons, but it began to sag a bit in the ratings by 1958. Sid later said that when he viewed the videotapes from that final year, he was able to see the first signs of deterioration in his performance.

The public never heard about Sid's manic episodes, his drinking, his collapses and his hospitalizations. NBC saw to that. A year or so later, however, when the network ended its obligation to Sid, the pit of despair and rage deepened, and there was no organization to shield him. Of course, within the showbiz profession, his problems were known. He was only 36 years old when, after eight years at the top of his profession, it seemed to be all over. He was free of the debilitating grind, but his depression continued for many years.

Sid Caesar had a few professional triumphs left in his career. One of Sid's former writers, Neil Simon, who amassed the longest string of hit comedies in modern Broadway history, acquired the Patrick Dennis book *Little Me* and adapted it for Broadway. In *Little Me* (1962–63) Simon gave Sid the opportunity to play seven roles. Sid's energetic and versatile performance reminded many critics that Sid Caesar was still a great and original comedian. He followed that with a major role in Stanley Kramer's star-stuffed and overlong *It's a Mad, Mad, Mad, Mad World* (1963). Sid later made a couple of films for Mel Brooks and Neil Simon among the nearly three dozen more that took his movie career into the twenty-first century.

Caesar performed on a few more television shows, and often he appeared in dinner theatre, but he was shifting into character comedy in featured and cameo roles on film. He quit liquor and sedatives, grew more comfortable emotionally, and adopted a healthy diet and exercise program that made him look 15 years younger than his 70 years when he and Imogene Coca resurrected some of their old skits for a tour of theatres in the 1992–93 season. Sid, like his contemporary in sketch comedy, Jackie Gleason, was never good at stand-up comedy, but in this tour, Sid seemed relaxed and comfortable with the role of host. Still not a one-line joke teller, he nevertheless handled the hosting duties smoothly and talked to his audience. Sid and Imogene, then in her early 80s, still had the talent and the power to make audiences laugh.

JAMES CAGNEY

b: 17 July 1899, New York, NY— d: 30 March 1986, Stanfordville, NY

Manhattan's slums produced a fair measure of the generation of performers who cut their teeth scrapping on the street, sometimes singing for pennies, grew up in vaudeville, and, if talented and successful, became the Broadway and Hollywood stars of the 1920s, 1930s and 1940s. The turn-of-the-twentieth-century alumni of Five Points, Hell's Kitchen, the Tenderloin, Yorkville and Germantown included Fanny Brice, Eddie Cantor, The Marx Brothers, George Burns, George Raft and Moe, Shemp and Curly Howard. Jews had washed ashore on Manhattan in a tidal wave of immigration much as the Irish had a generation or two earlier.

The Cagneys had been part of the great escape from Ireland's miserable poverty, and the current generation was still part of the resident polyglot that inhabited Five Points when Carrie and James Francis Cagney Sr. welcomed their second-born son, James Cagney Jr., in 1899. The Cagneys moved to Yorkville, where two more boys were born. A fifth child, Grace, died in infancy. Much later, in 1916, a last child, Robert, was still a baby when he died.

Although the Cagneys were poor in material matters (James Sr.'s liquor bill was a major item in their budget), they were a close and boisterously happy family. Pop, "a gentle and charming man," according to son Jim, was a natural comedian, good enough at least to win the laughter and applause of his children.

James Cagney

The mother, Carrie, was a strong, practical woman who loved her sons and her husband. She taught the boys to box; Jimmy, the smallest, proved the most willing and adept. The youngest boy, William (1904–88), was as fearless as Jimmy but far more intent on making a buck. Jimmy and Bill later proved a complementary pair, and Bill took over management of Jimmy Cagney's career and finances. The two even looked alike.

Jimmy was small, but every inch of his body was filled with natural gifts: intelligence, fearlessness tempered by common sense, the ability and lightning-fast reflexes to fight, play sports, dance and act. Talent, curiosity, diligence and a strong and supportive family made the difference in outcomes between Jim's life and those of most kids in his neighborhood. Young Cagney played baseball well enough to be asked to join a semi-professional team. He fought well enough to turn pro, but his mother spiked that plan. Jim got grades good enough to encourage him to attend high school, drew and painted well, and was tough enough to flatten any bully twice his size who made the mistake of teasing Jim about sketching, reading and studying.

It was not all genes and luck. Jimmy never ran with the yapping pack. Although he showed respect to everyone and was reliable in a jam, Cagney, from boy to man, was a loner.

Cagney wanted money to lift himself and his family out of poverty. After he refused a chance to box professionally, he cast about for other work that paid more than his library job. He became a bellhop at the Friars Club and was impressed with the tips actors and performers shelled out and even more impressed when he learned the amount of money they earned. Free tickets were plentiful, and Jim, who had given little thought or time to the theatre, used the freebies to finance a few dates.

It was at the Lenox Hill settlement house that Jim got the opportunity to act and design for the stage, a small, amateur stage though it was. The Lenox Hill volunteers were idealists, and their integrity awoke in him a sense of a larger world and his own artistic aspirations. His first professional job was as a female impersonator in a vaudeville act called "Every Sailor," then playing Keith's Eighty-Sixth Street Theatre in 1919. The musical act grew out of the entertainments put on by soldiers and sailors during the First World War. In those male-only shows, doughboys assumed the roles of soubrettes and chorus girls, much to the hooting enjoyment of their buddies. Upon demobilization, vaudeville audiences were treated to comic displays of awkwardly butch prancing by bewigged and rouged men.

Jim had bluffed his way into the act; he became a replacement for a departing actor. He claimed he could sing and dance. Jim's voice was never tuneful, but he had the instincts of the embryonic actor, so he knew how to sell a song, and as a fighter he was nimble in his footwork and able to mimic any basic step he was shown. His strong male sense was discomfited by playing a woman, but the weekly paycheck of $35 was persuasive salve.

Rather than tour with "Every Sailor," Cagney auditioned for the dance chorus in a Broadway musical, *Pitter Patter* (1920). One of the chorus girls was Willard Vernon (1899–1994), a farmer's strong-willed daughter who calmly but firmly defied her parents' wishes and went into show business. It was not her first rebellion. She disliked her given name, Willard, so in her early teens, she reduced its importance by prefixing it with Frances. She admired Jim for his growing erudition, his serious purpose yet comradely mien, and his devotion to and support of his family. Jim liked her for her spirit, candor and down-to-earth qualities.

Mrs. Cagney, recently widowed, had the last of her seven children to support. Two were dead, as was her husband, but there was baby Jeanne (1919–84) to raise. Son Harry was in college, son Edward was about to follow him, and Bill was still in high school (although he never ceased to add to the family's coffers). Jim's primary obligation, as he saw it, was to his birth family; Jim's marriage to "My Bill," as he called Frances, was deferred until 1922. They stayed together until Jim's death in 1984. Frances lived to age 95.

When *Pitter Patter* closed, Jim got work in several short-lived vaudeville acts: Midge Miller & Her Boy Friends, several sketch acts such as "Dot's My Boy," Harry Ormonds & Company, and Parker, Rand & Cagney (formerly known as Parker, Rand & Leach; Cagney replaced Archie Leach, the future Cary Grant). By this time, Jimmy Cagney had moved out of the chorus and was working as a featured specialty act. Both Jim and Frances got dancing jobs (she in the chorus) in *Lew Fields' Ritz Girls of 1922,* a touring show that did disappointing business because audiences expected but did not see Lew Fields, who was then in a show on Broadway.

The years immediately preceding and following their marriage were hard, and Jim and Frances scraped along. According to Cagney's biographer, John McCabe, Jim sent much of what they both earned home to the Cagney household, yet, despite Frances' contributions, Mrs. Cagney never took to her daughter-in-law. Neither did Jim's three brothers. Perhaps his mother, Carrie, was disappointed that Jim chose show business over a profession; yet had he not, there would not have been the money to support Carrie's household while the other sons went to college and built their careers. Yet, even when Jim could not find work, Frances was contributing to the Cagney coffers. Frances and future film star Wynne Gibson did a double act when Jim and she could not get bookings for their mixed double. Throughout their courtship and marriage, Frances was treated as an unwelcome outsider.

While Frances and Wynne Gibson played vaudeville dates out of town, Jimmy was hired as a featured performer for *Lew Fields' Snapshots of 1923.* Jim was singled out for good reviews, but good reviews did not guarantee work, and the next season was one of chasing rainbows to Hollywood and Chicago. Back in Manhattan in 1925, Cagney was hired to act in a drama, *Outside Looking In,* by Maxwell Anderson; it ran four months on Broadway.

When Cagney went back to vaudeville, it was not in someone else's act. He and Frances had already begun to work together in a series of *flirtation acts*. The boy-meets-girl, boy-tries-to-pick-up-girl formula was fitted out with smart cross talk and a song and dance. Jean Dalrymple wrote them an act called "In the Park." For the most part, the Cagney bookings were small time, like Poli and Delmar houses. Later, Paul Gerard Smith cast them in one of his scripts known alternately as "Lonesome Manor" and "At the Newsstand." (The latter sketch had a long life: Pat Rooney Jr. & Marion Bent also played it in vaudeville, and Jack Benny used it as the basis for a Vitaphone short.) The Cagneys played the act with relish on the better small-time and some big-time dates.

Cagney almost landed the lead role for the London company of George Abbott's hit production of *Broadway* (1926), but backstage machinations deprived him of the chance to create the role of a song-and-dance man. *Women Go on Forever* (1927), starring Mary Boland in a rare dramatic role, was not quite a consolation prize, but it provided three months' steady work on Broadway. During the previous season or two, James Cagney became friends with two actors, Pat O'Brien and Frank McHugh, and the three remained lifelong buddies.

Jimmy again donned his dancing shoes in 1928 and 1929 for two consecutive editions of the *Grand Street Follies.* Originally mounted at the Neighborhood Playhouse by theatrically talented individuals associated with the Henry Street Settlement House, *The Grand Street Follies of 1927* was the first in what became an annual Broadway show for eight years. Jim choreographed and performed in the 1928 show and performed in the 1929 edition.

Later in 1929, Cagney costarred with Joan Blondell in *Maggie the Magnificent,* by George Kelly. It was a four-week flop, but it lasted long enough for Joan and Jimmy to become fast fiends and admirers of each other's talents. William Keighley (1889–1984), the stage actor and director and future film director, saw the show. Jimmy and Joan were exactly the young actors he was seeking for *Penny Arcade.*

Penny Arcade was another flop, but Al Jolson saw it, liked it and optioned it to sell to Warner Brothers. When Jack Warner saw the show, he was impressed with Cagney for his part as a sniveling killer and Joan Blondell for her wisecracking dame role. Warner signed Cagney, Blondell and Pat O'Brien (who was in a different Broadway show) to long-term contracts in Hollywood. Keighley, Blondell, Cagney, O'Brien, McHugh and George Raft (already in Hollywood) soon became the workhorses in the Warner Brothers' stable.

Penny Arcade was remade for the screen as *Sinner's Holiday,* and Jimmy and Joan repeated their roles. So began one of the more illustrious careers in Hollywood. James Cagney was made for talking pictures. He had a distinct vocal style, a rat-a-tat-tat that greatly helped pace his movies. His enunciation was unstagey yet clear enough for people in every region to understand what he said in spite of the rapid rush of words. His decade of experience as a song-and-dance man in vaudeville and a few musical revues gave a pulse and clean definition to his movement. No gesture was wasted, and none failed to achieve its effect. He paced the other actors in scenes with him.

In retrospect, Warner Brothers was a blessing and a curse for his career. Warner Brothers was the upstart that against long odds became a major studio. More than any other film company, it defined the style of gangster movies. Along with MGM and RKO, Warner Brothers defined the movie musical, at least for the 1930s. Both genres were perfect for Cagney (and Raft), but Warner Brothers gave Jimmy only two real shots at starring in musicals: *Footlight Parade* (1933) and *Yankee Doodle Dandy* (1942), for which he won the Academy Award.

Mostly, however, Warner Brothers assigned him the starring parts in gangster movies. His fifth film, *The Public Enemy* (1931), made his reputation. Within two years, Cagney was one of the ten top box-office draws. Among the three dozen movies Cagney made for Warner Brothers, a surprising number are superior by anyone's standards: *The Public Enemy* (1931), *Blond Crazy* (1931), *Hard to Handle* (1933), *Picture Snatcher* (1933), *Footlight Parade* (1933), *Lady Killer* (1933), *Here Comes the Navy* (1934), *G-Men* (1935), *A Midsummer Night's Dream* (1935), *Angels with Dirty Faces* (1938), *Each Dawn I Die* (1938), *The Roaring Twenties* (1939) and *Yankee Doodle Dandy* (1942).

Cagney constantly battled Warner Brothers for better pay and better projects. He was forced to make one stinker for them, and he looked ridiculous in the ill-suited part of *The Oklahoma Kid* (1939). He was not the only actor trying to battle his way out of servitude under Warner Brothers. Bette Davis and

Olivia de Havilland took on the studio; Davis lost, DeHavilland won, and neither result was without cost to those actors.

After winning his Oscar, Jim and brother Bill formed their own production company, and Jim freelanced, making the rest of his movies for various studios, including Warner Brothers. The films were fewer, roughly 20 over a period of 20 years. The general quality declined as well, but *White Heat* (1949), *Come Fill the Cup* (1951), *Mister Roberts* (1953) and *Shake Hands with the Devil* (1959) are among the best of his career.

By the time he made *Shake Hands with the Devil,* Cagney was no longer the vibrant actor he once had been. He was still forceful, but he lacked his former ease and had become harsh, and when he made Billy Wilder's *One, Two, Three* (1961), he was heavy-handed and no longer adept with comedy. He seemed to have trouble hearing himself, or maybe he simply lost interest. Cagney soon quit films and retired to his farms: one in Martha's Vineyard, one off the coast of New England and the other in California. Ever since he first visited a farm as a boy, he had seriously wished to study agriculture and become a farmer. He spent the last 25 years of his life on farms, raising horses, reading, writing and painting in oils. He developed into an accomplished writer and painter.

Cagney made a celebrated return to movies when he appeared in a featured role in *Ragtime* (1981). He was diabetic and had suffered a few minor strokes and had misgivings about acting again. The attention he received from the screenland community, the press and the public was a tribute for one of the last stars of Hollywood's studio era. His performance in the film was acceptable but did not add to his artistic reputation.

A made-for-television movie, *Terrible Joe Moran* (1984), paired Jim with Art Carney. Jim behaved like a professional despite increasing infirmity; he was much too ill to be mobile in his acting and most if not all his lines had to be dubbed in later by a Cagney impersonator. Still, Jim enjoyed the experience, and it gave his spirits a lift to be working again. He could no longer see well enough to read, write or paint. Even his physical movement was severely constricted. His decline continued for the remaining two years of his life. Cagney died at 86.

At various times during his film career, James Cagney acknowledged his affection and debt to vaudeville. In his autobiography he wrote, "I still think of myself as essentially a vaudevillian, a song-and-dance man. The vaudevillians I knew were marvelous people. Ninety percent of them had no schooling, but they had a vivid something or other about them that absolutely riveted an audience's attention. . . . I learned much from them because I studied them all and tried to take away from each something of the skill and persistence that characterized their best work."

MARIE CAHILL

b: 7 February 1870, Brooklyn, NY— d: 23 August 1933, New York, NY

"When I was down in Texas, I saw a baptism. There was one Negro, a great poker player, that came within the minister's grasp. As he was led out into the water, the ace of diamonds floated out of his vest, then the king, queen, jack and ten. The preacher's eyes bulged wide. 'Man, if that hand doesn't save you, there's no use bein' baptized!' "

Stories like this and an inclination toward songs like "Under the Bamboo Tree," "If You Like Me and I Like You" and "When I First Began to Marry, Years Ago" made Marie Cahill a natural for vaudeville, a singing comedian. She only ventured into vaudeville, however, during the last phase of her career, from 1919 to 1926.

Her large head and short neck were at odds with her short, chubby and corseted doll-like figure. According to contemporary observers, Cahill played strong-willed, no-nonsense American women, and she molded

Marie Cahill

each part to her own personality, like a vaudeville or revue performer, yet critics seldom complained. Some managers felt otherwise; Cahill was strong-willed in contract negotiations and fully aware of her professional status. More important to Cahill than creating a characterization was finding good songs to sing, having strong comedy scenes and protecting her position as a star.

When she played vaudeville in the 1920s, it was at the best of the big-time houses, like the Palace Theatre on Broadway. One of her final engagements at the Palace was during the week of 20 April 1925, when Marie shared a celebrated old-timers bill with Cissie Loftus, Weber & Fields, Emma Trentini and youngsters Bill Robinson, Doc Rockwell and Blossom Seeley & Benny Fields. The bill was so popular that it was held over for an additional two weeks. Cahill had insisted on the star dressing room at the stage level, but, with so many stars on the bill competing for prestige, Eddie Darling, booker for the Palace, devised a ruse that became famous: He had the stage-level dressing rooms closed and put painters to work in them. All the stars had to settle for upper-level dressing rooms of indeterminate rank.

Cahill had worked with Lew Fields years earlier; she costarred with Lew in his production of *It Happened in Nordland* in 1904, not long after Lew and Joe Weber set aside their partnership. She was quite at home in farce and burlesque. Early in her career, she appeared in straight comedies for Augustin Daly and farces, such as *A Tin Soldier* (1886) by Charles Hoyt. During the late 1890s, Marie performed in several musical spoofs for George Lederer, shortly before his death. She also starred in several productions devised by Robert A. Barnet, Boston's Extravaganza King. His productions combined humor redolent of Hasty Pudding Club spoofs, songs reminiscent of British music-hall, and the delightful mishmash of English pantomime. Cahill starred in three Barnet shows: *Excelsior, Jr.* (1895), *The Merry-Go-Round* (1896) and *Three Little Lambs* (1899).

For 20 years, from her first featured role in 1899 *(Three Little Lambs)* to 1919 *(Just Around the Corner),* Marie Cahill appeared in 14 plays, musicals and revues. During that time, there were few Broadway seasons without a Marie Cahill show. In 1902, she interpolated a song, "Nancy Brown," into the musical *The Wild Rose.* So popular became the song that the next season Cahill headed her own company in a new musical called *Nancy Brown.* The shows and the song made her a star.

It was determination partnered with talent that made Marie a star. She grew up in a strict Roman Catholic family, yet she was able to prevail upon them for dance and singing lessons. Given her plain face, plump form and natural bent for comedy, she was cast as soubrettes, but Marie and her family made sure that her soubrettes were chaste and fully clothed.

The New Yorkers (1930) was her last show. In sharing the spotlight and story line with new stars like Ann

Marie Cahill

Pennington, Frances Williams, and Clayton, Jackson & Durante, the Victorian era met the jazz age. Marie Cahill retired and died three years later at age 63.

CAKES

When an entertainer was engaged in a performance place that served food, the compensation might be stated as *salary and cakes*. In addition to the specified wage, the performer would receive his meals free of charge. At a resort or on a showboat, the added compensation was called *cabins and cakes*. In America, *and cakes* was used as late as the mid-twentieth century.

The term *cakes* is old and probably was first used in British taverns and inns. The earliest cakes were likely solid and substantial mixtures, heavy on the fats and more like bread than confections. They were intended to satisfy hunger with bulk rather than be enjoyed as gustatory delights.

CAKEWALK

The cakewalk was originated by African Americans on plantations in the southern United States. It was a high quickstep strut in 4/4 time, a mock-elegant parody of the types of promenades and grand marches that white plantation owners and their families engaged in at balls. The black cakewalk dancers were dressed in their hand-me-down finery, and they danced in a formation, at times changing partners. Men and women held their heads aloft, arched their backs and exaggerated polite manners as they strode high and grandly, slipping in the odd, idiosyncratic quickstep here and there. The white plantation owners often held contests in which their best black dancers competed against others. It is assumed that the whites did not perceive the parody and regarded the variations as vulgar but amusing distortions by blacks who could not perform with more dignity.

Away from white eyes, the cakewalk was looser, with more pelvic movement, becoming a comment on the stiff hypocrisy of whites during the social-sexual act of dance. This has led some researchers to speak of the influence of West African tribal movements as a source for the cakewalk. Others have suggested Seminole dances as an influence.

Some variant of the cakewalk appeared in minstrel shows along with quadrilles, reels and polkas. Black dancers in vaudeville and musical revue performed more personal versions of the cakewalk by the early 1890s, combining intricate patterns with jumps, kicks, turnarounds and improvisations devised by individual dancers. George W. Walker, Ada Overton Walker and Bert Williams made a great splash when they brought the cakewalk to Broadway. Soon it was a feature of most turn-of-the-twentieth-century black shows, and cakewalk contests abounded. Even social lions like the Vanderbilts hired black dancers—Tom Fletcher was a favorite—to teach them the dance in the privacy of their Manhattan salons. John Philip Sousa arranged cakewalk dance music for his marching band to play in his tours of Europe. In turn, Debussy sent the musical gift back in the form of his composition "Golliwog's Cakewalk."

CALL

A call is an instruction of some kind to the performers or actors. A curtain call is a summons from the audience to receive and acknowledge its applause (*See "Curtain Call" and "Taking a Call"*). An orchestra or band call (*See "Orchestra Rehearsals" and "Band Call"*) calls vaudeville acts to review their music, all sound and lighting cues with the pit band and the electrician. Calls were also made by the stage manager to alert the performers in their dressing rooms to be ready for their entrances. After the late 1930s, speaker systems were set up in many theatres linking the backstage with dressing rooms (also light booth and front office), and the stage manager made his call through the speaker system. Prior to the electronic call, theatres hired call boys (pages of a sort) to deliver the same alerts by knocking on dressing-room doors and announcing, variously, "half hour," "15 minutes," "5 minutes" or "orchestra and beginners, please." Beginners referred not to experience but to those performers or actors who opened the show.

CALL BOY

A quarterly published by the British Music Hall Society in London, *Call Boy* features articles about performers who played music-hall and variety as well as book reviews, interviews, reports from regional music-hall and variety clubs throughout Britain, and reproductions of vintage photographs, bills, posters and the like.

Contact information for the publication is, *Call Boy,* c/o Patrick Newley, BMHS, 45A Kingcourt Road, London, SW16 1JA, UK.

CAB CALLOWAY

b: (Cabell Calloway III) 25 December 1907, Rochester, NY—d: 18 November 1994, Hockessin, DE

Suave, handsome, hip, flamboyant and slightly dangerous. That was the image Cab Calloway projected from the stage. Out of the spotlight, he was smart, a tough businessman and, admittedly, a loner. He became interested in music while in high school and learned to play drums. Even as a teenager, however, singing was his forte, and he studied voice with several teachers. As a drummer, Cab played with small musical combos in speakeasies and appeared in vaudeville with an act comprised of youngsters like himself. At the same time, he played baseball in the Negro leagues.

Cab's sister, Blanche Calloway, was touring in the road company of *Plantation Days* when, in 1927, the show reached Baltimore, where Cab and his parents had been living since his early teen years. The tenor in the show's male singing quartet took ill, and Cab prevailed on his sister to intercede on his behalf. Cab got the job and left on tour, ending up in Chicago. His mother had given her consent with the proviso that he enroll in college that fall. After the show closed, Cab tried to balance college with singing in nightclubs. A new wife and high living competed for his energy and attention. Nightclub work quickly took over his life as he advanced from a boy singer to an emcee to a bandleader. He was inspired by the big-time African American bandleaders in 1920s Chicago nightlife: Carroll Dickerson, Louis Armstrong and Earl Hines.

Fronting his first band, Cab and the Alabamians toured out of Chicago. They worked a series of Midwest dates on their way to New York, where they flopped in their first engagement at the Savoy Ballroom; the band was not tight or musically hip enough to interest sophisticated New York audiences. Calloway split with the band and went solo; he was hired as a cast replacement for a downtown show, *Hot Chocolates,* while he looked for another band gig. He was hired to front another band, the Missourians, at the Savoy; Cab's contract and those of the individual musicians were held by an agent, Moe Gale. The Missourians were a better ensemble, and both it and Cab attracted notice. Soon, when Duke Ellington and His Orchestra needed a leave of absence from the Cotton Club in Harlem so Duke and the boys could make a film in Hollywood, Cab Calloway and the Missourians became Duke's replacement band at the Cotton Club, at the time the most prestigious show-business address in Harlem.

The Missourians were a corporate band, which meant that each member had a voice and a vote in the conduct of its affairs. Increasingly, Cab was taking control of the band instead of merely fronting it. It began when the mobsters who managed the Cotton Club informed Cab that he and the Missourians were to leave the Savoy and come to their club; they also informed Moe Gale that they were buying out his contracts with the band and Cab. The Cotton Club's management doubled Cab's pay and dealt with him as the band's leader. Thus empowered, Cab strove for a swinging sound and professionalism and did not hesitate to replace instrumentalists who failed to meet his standards of performance, reliability or cooperation.

Within the music business, Cab became respected as a tough disciplinarian who ran a first-rate jazz band and paid good money for top musicians. Among the public, he was regarded more as a showy entertainer than a musician, and it was Cab who was the band's drawing card. There were live radio broadcasts from the Cotton Club several times a week, so Duke's and Cab's reputations were growing beyond New York. Duke's association with the Cotton Club had led to recording deals and a few movies arranged by Irving Mills, who was a combination talent scout, agent and record producer. When Duke returned to his Cotton Club bandstand in 1930, Mills booked a tour for the Cab Calloway Cotton Club Orchestra in a series of vaudeville dates and nightclubs, mostly in and around New York. Cab and the boys played the Valencia in Queens, the Paradise in Brooklyn, Loew's in Jersey City, the Jefferson in Greenwich Village, the Roseland in Brooklyn and the Lafayette in Harlem. Most of these theatres played to white audiences who had heard Cab and the band on radio.

In 1931, Mills booked Cab and his band for a series of dates in the South. It was a tough call for the band members, many of whom had been born in the South and left it as soon as they could. It was an era of hostility toward blacks by those in authority. At the least they could expect dismal accommodations and petty hassles; far worse was the epidemic of terror and lynchings still perpetrated by the Ku Klux Klan. The band undertook the tour—Virginia to Florida and back—and there were a few bright spots and a few barriers that they broke to mitigate against the expected indignities that were more usual.

Until the Cotton Club closed its Harlem operation in 1936, the pattern for Cab Calloway and His Cotton Club Orchestra was a seasonal residence in Harlem at the club (alternating with aggregations led by Ellington and Jimmy Lunceford), going on the road, making records, appearing on network radio, and making several two-reel shorts and doing a specialty turn in a couple of feature films.

No African American entertainer was as savvy about self-promotion as Cab. He created a stage personality as well known and sharply defined as any of the day: Laurel & Hardy, Shirley Temple, Mae West or Fred Astaire & Ginger Rogers. Cab sang in a good, strong, tuneful voice, but his material was conceived to reinforce his image as the *heppest cat* in white or black America. His songs were ersatz blues about Harlem drug culture and lowlife personified by Minnie the Moocher and Smoky Joe, filled with jive talk and carried along by extended scatting. He epitomized swing-era energy, and his trademark long, black, wavy hair fell across his handsome, animated face as he frenetically conducted his band. His was the most successful black orchestra in the 1930s, earning more than Duke Ellington, Jimmy Lunceford, Count Basie, Earl Hines or Andy Kirk.

There are two views of Cab Calloway as a musician. One regards him as a pretender who could not read music well, was limited as a singer, and was a bandleader who left the day-to-day rehearsal and direction of the band to Eddie Barefield. Another view accepts those limitations but points out that it was Cab who molded the Missourians into a topflight band by firing and hiring personnel, and that Cab was the deal maker who got the band prestigious gigs and top pay. Cab may not have traveled on the bus with the band, he may have been tough and even downright pugnacious, but whether he governed from the rehearsal hall or from afar, he was in charge. Benny Payne, the band's pianist, recalled, "That band was like being in school all the time. We learned about music, we learned about the responsibility of being professionals, and we learned about life. . . . Occasionally, when Cab didn't rehearse the band, he would sit on a stool by the side, half crocked . . . while we worked our tails off. . . . It didn't bother us. We knew that while we were taking it easy, Cab would be stone cold sober negotiating contracts, figuring the books, or getting a new show organized with some producer." The list of jazzmen who were part of the Calloway bands of the 1930s and 1940s is impressive: Ben Webster, Chu Berry, Milt Hinton, Don Redman, Dizzy Gillespie, Doc Cheatham, Jonah Jones, Tyree Glenn and Cozy Cole.

The good times lasted until after the Second World War. By 1947, it was no longer feasible for Calloway to maintain a band. Bebop had replaced swing as authentic jazz, and *hipsters* had replaced *hep cats.* Nightclubs were hiring small combos, not big bands. All too soon, the stars of the nightclubs were the strippers and the small television set above the bar.

Cab's first marriage, long strained, was over. He married again, a lifetime love match, and had a great piece of luck in 1950 when he played Sportin' Life in a first-class revival of George and Ira Gershwin's *Porgy and Bess,* starring Leontyne Price and William Warfield. The show ran three seasons, including one in London. In the mid-1950s, Cab formed a small combo to tour the USA, South America, the Caribbean and Europe.

During the 1967–68 season, Cab costarred with Pearl Bailey in one of the many cast changes that kept *Hello, Dolly!* in front of Broadway audiences for a decade. He was back on Broadway for a 1974 revival of *The Pajama Game.* By then, Cab Calloway was an institution. High school kids of the 1980s and 1990s could identify him from his roles in music videos and the movie the *Blues Brothers* (1980). He had a good marriage, two daughters in show business, no financial worries and was a legend. Cab Calloway was five weeks short of his 87th birthday when he died.

CANCELLATION CLAUSE

A contentious matter between vaudevillian and management, a cancellation clause allowed a theatre manager to cancel an act after the first show. The canceled act, which had paid its own transportation to get there, was let go without payment for the one show they performed.

Gus Sun, whose name was almost synonymous with small, small-time vaudeville, is blamed for introducing the cancellation clause. To his credit, he put it in writing, and an act knew the bad bargain it had accepted.

Contracts meant little to some independent managers who ran part-time theatres or a saloon or a tent show in the sparsely settled regions of the Great Plains and Rocky Mountain states. A vaudeville act, scraping along a wilderness trail, could work several days and not receive a cent, and local law enforcement was not on the vaudevillian's side.

It was worse in some black vaudeville theatres in the South and the border states. Not only did some white managers renege on their agreements but waited until the weekend of performances were concluded; then they refused to pay a black act that had failed to please. The local sheriff let the act know that it had a couple of hours to get out of town.

CANDY BUTCHER

A fixture in burlesque, this pitchman emerged during the intermissions to hawk candies, so-called French postcards, and supposedly salacious, but actually quite tame booklets. A good candy butcher was nearly as entertaining as the stage performers; his delivery was fast, fluid and (to those who knew the nature and quality of his goods) funny. Before burlesque, candy butchers worked in circuses and carnivals and were a variation of the outside talkers (often erroneously called barkers) of circus and carnival shows.

JUDY CANOVA

b: (Juliette or Julia Etta Canova) 20 November 1916, Starke, FL— d: 5 August 1983, Los Angeles, CA

Judy Canova was the youngest of Joe and Henrietta Canova's eight children (four survived infancy). The family lived within spitting distance of the Okefenokee

Judy Canova

Swamp, but neither Judy's mother nor father fit the image of country folk that Judy and her sister and two brothers presented onstage in their hillbilly comedy and music act. Henrietta Perry had been a concert singer before she wed Joseph Canova, a cotton broker turned construction firm owner.

Judy began performing at age three, according to family lore, getting up and singing in front of folks at country fairs. When traveling shows came into town, they often auditioned locals for small roles. It saved on payroll and traveling expenses and provided publicity. Judy was 11 years old when she made her professional debut in just such a circumstance; she played an old lady in a production that hit the Canova's hometown of Starke, Florida, in 1928. The experience whetted her appetite for more, and Judy and another young lady began appearing in amateur-night contests and on the local radio station.

Judy's partner did not have the same level of interest, and the girl dropped out of the act. Henrietta, a former professional herself, realized that Judy had an abundance of talent and drive. Mother Canova drafted Judy's sister Diane and brother Leon, and the Canova Cracker Trio was launched. Juliette was turned into Judy, Diane became Ann, and Leon changed to Zeke. From the start, the Canova kids combined genuine music making with tap dancing and comedy. Their hillbilly characters and put-on accents were based on the people they heard and watched while on vacation in North Carolina with their parents.

Few of Judy Canova's later fans realized that she once had operatic aspirations and a voice good enough to achieve some measure of success as a concert singer. Her plan upon leaving high school was to study at the Cincinnati Conservatory of Music, but Mr. Canova died in the early 1930s, and family finances were not as they had been.

Judy tried to break into New York show business twice, as a single in 1930 and with Ann and Zeke in 1932. They offered a blend of light classics and some country clowning numbers replete with yodels and hog calls. They got work in nightclubs like Jimmy Kelly's and the Village Barn, both notable spots, and then were signed for a couple of guest spots on Rudy Vallee's network radio show. When Paul Whiteman brought his orchestra to radio, he hired Judy, Ann and Zeke as regulars.

Ann and Zeke were the more serious instrumentalists, and Judy was the comedian and audience favorite. Her antics and sunny personality won bookings, and she moved to the front of the act as the more serious music was shunted aside.

Vaudeville was well on the wane by 1933–34, but radio listeners wanted to see what their favorite stars of the airwaves looked like in person. Rudy Vallee, Vaughn DeLeath, Arthur Tracy and Kate Smith were offered huge sums to perform live for audiences in vaudeville houses across the USA. The Canova kids cashed in on vaudeville, too. Some radio stars were lifeless on the stage; they sang to their microphones instead of their audiences. The Canovas' act had visual appeal. Judy was a passable hoofer and a good physical comedian, and she wore her long auburn hair in pigtails, dressed in a checkered blouse, short skirt and oversized boots. The trio cavorted around the stage and made a favorable impression with audiences and critics.

Country-bumpkin music acts were quite new at the time. The best known of other rube headliners, Chic Sale, was a laid-back cornpone teller of tall tales, and music was not a part of his act. Variously called bluegrass, Ozark or Appalachian music, it was a regional phenomenon in the 1930s before the days when *Grand Ole Opry* became a national favorite. Later, the popular brand of country music joined up with its neighbor as country & western, a precursor of the country pop that won big audiences all over the USA in the last decades of the twentieth century.

The Canova Trio turned into a quartet when brother Pete joined the family act. By 1934, Henrietta and her four children lived in New York City. The Canova Family (minus mother) performed in their first show on Broadway when they were featured along with Lou Holtz, Phil Baker, Martha Raye, Ella Logan, Gertrude Niesen, Jack Whiting, Mitzi Mayfair and Harry McNaughton in *Calling All Stars* (1934). The show opened in Boston and died on Broadway. Warner Brothers had financed the show; perhaps to salvage something, Warner Brothers signed the Canova Family to a contract.

It took awhile for Judy Canova to sign with an appropriate studio. Warner Brothers, home to crime dramas, was no place for a farm girl and her siblings, and they went packing after they had performed specialty numbers in two musicals and Judy, solo, had played a dull-witted serving girl in a third.

Her next studio, Paramount, usually offered sophisticated, occasionally naughty fare and eccentric comedy; it hardly seemed the place for feedlot folks. Brother Pete left the act to enter business and eventually became Judy's savvy business manager. The three Canovas appeared in two Paramount movies in which they performed comedy-and-music turns to pep up the plots, and Judy was paired with Ben Blue as a second-string comedy couple at their best in *Artists and Models* (1937).

Between her contracts at Warner Brothers and Paramount, Judy went back to Broadway as a featured performer in the *Ziegfeld Follies of 1936*. Despite the presence of Fanny Brice, Josephine Baker, Bob Hope, the Nicholas Brothers and Eve Arden, most critics admitted they found Judy Canova's singing a delight and her antics fresh and funny standouts in the revue. Judy left the show at the close of the 1935–36 season and got married. That fall, she went into radio with Ann and Zeke, but NBC's *Rippling Rhythm Revue* ran only a single season.

Judy signed with Republic Pictures, an oddball studio. Judy chose Republic because she thought she would be the medium-size frog in a small pond instead of a tadpole in a big studio awash with bankable stars. According to exhibitors, Republic's four biggest stars were John Wayne, Gene Autry, Roy Rogers and Judy Canova.

Republic's largest shareholder, Herbert J. Yates, ran his studio like a plantation. Like William Randolph Hearst, Yates had a Pygmalion complex. He wanted to make his studio's biggest female star into his sweetheart or his sweetheart into the studio's biggest star. Canova's first Republic films were decent programmers until Yates' made Judy into the object of his romantic advances. When she rebuffed him, he cut the budgets of her films. He then turned to Vera Hruba Ralston, married her and put his energy into a futile effort to make Vera a public favorite.

Judy accepted a Broadway offer to costar in *Yokel Boy* (1939–40), which ran for 208 performances at the Majestic Theatre. Phil Silvers and Buddy Ebsen costarred.

Judy Canova

Other major players included Lew Hearn, Dixie Dunbar, Almira Sessions, and Ann and Zeke Canova.

Judy's greatest success was in network radio. Her radio career took off in 1943 with *The Judy Canova Show* on Tuesday nights for CBS. It was a situation comedy, usually in two parts, and Canova sang two numbers. It was a saucy bit of comedy and very popular. The show was broadcast for ten years and made her very rich. *Variety* opined that it "was a hybrid of the stuff that tickles the tall pine folk [mixed with] hot-off-the-cob witticisms from Hollywood and Vine." Canova's excellent supporting cast included Verna Felton, Hans Conried, Ruby Dandridge, Sheldon Leonard and Mel Blanc (who played a variety of roles for Judy that rivaled his contributions to the *Jack Benny Show*).

While performing on radio, Canova continued to make films and stayed at Republic from 1940 until 1955, although she made a couple of movies on other lots. She and Yates had reached an understanding. They both knew she was responsible for a good chunk of Republic's earnings, so Judy demanded and won approval over her writers, directors and casts as long as the production stayed within the assigned budget.

By the mid-1950s, Judy was no longer doing her country girl on radio or in movies. She worked up a nightclub act and appeared on a number of television shows. The accent shifted to straight singing, with just enough of her aw-shucks hayseed character to remind viewers who she was. Judy was not quite pretty, but she had a voluptuous figure and the talent and style to become a great delineator of popular song. After a quarter of a century of identification as a country bumpkin, however, it was impossible to move into a class with Helen Forrest, Margaret Whiting and Rosemary Clooney.

When given the opportunity in her nightclub act or on a variety show, Canova demonstrated a vibrant, well-trained voice with nearly a three-octave reach that exceeded the usual contralto range in both directions. Occasionally, in the past, she had sung several bars of operatic arias and surprised audiences and reviewers with her quality before turning her solo into the comic number that was expected.

Canova made one last movie, *Huckleberry Finn* (1960), an MGM all-star adaptation of the often-filmed Mark Twain classic. It was her first A movie since her Paramount days. Judy effectively had retired by the mid-1960s, although she agreed in 1971 to tour with the nostalgic revival of the 1920s musical comedy *No, No, Nanette* in the part of the maid played by Patsy Kelly on Broadway. Her daughter, Diane Canova, was only a few years away from emerging as a star, and Judy had invested profitably, so touring with *No, No, Nanette* pretty much marked the end of her career.

Canova was engaged several times and married four times. All ended in divorce. To folks who knew her, Judy did not always seem a happy person, and she admitted as much in rare interviews. She passed off her moodiness as typical of clowns.

Eddie Cantor

EDDIE CANTOR

b: (Israel Iskowitz) 22 or 23 September 1892, New York, NY—d: 10 October 1964, Beverly Hills, CA

At the time of his death, Eddie Cantor's star had been dimming, and, in the decades since, its residual glow has been outshone by many of his contemporaries who became the darlings of early movie enthusiasts and the college film societies.

For some people, then and now, Cantor's comic character seemed to lack a place in a relevant social context. From the 1950s onward, new, younger, college-educated audiences adopted some of the older comedians as heroes: Buster Keaton as the modern Everyman, Mae West as a sexual revolutionary, W. C. Fields for his contrary individualism, and The Marx Brothers as insurgent anarchists. Yet had the fascination with the golden age of comedy continued widespread into the 1980s, Eddie Cantor might have been better appreciated for his neurotic, sexually stirred, cowardly but calculating boy on the threshold of manhood, a forefather of sorts to three later generations of funny men—Danny Kaye, Woody Allen and Martin Short among them—who continued to play some variant of the hyperkinetic nebbish character a century after Eddie Cantor introduced it.

Eddie Cantor was arguably the most successful all-around entertainer of the first half of the twentieth century, but there is debate about how to classify him. Was he a minstrel, a song-and-dance man or a comedian? Some simply dismissed him as an entertainer. Yet calling any vaudevillian an entertainer was not derogatory. Cantor was a superlative entertainer.

Blackface marked a line between a minstrel man and a song-and-dance man, although both were expected to sing and dance and, maybe, handle funny lines and business. Like Al Jolson, Eddie Cantor persisted in employing blackface far longer than most people wished to see it, and that remains a prominent demerit in most assessments of Cantor's work. His blackface characters, however, were smart, urban and did not shuffle and drawl.

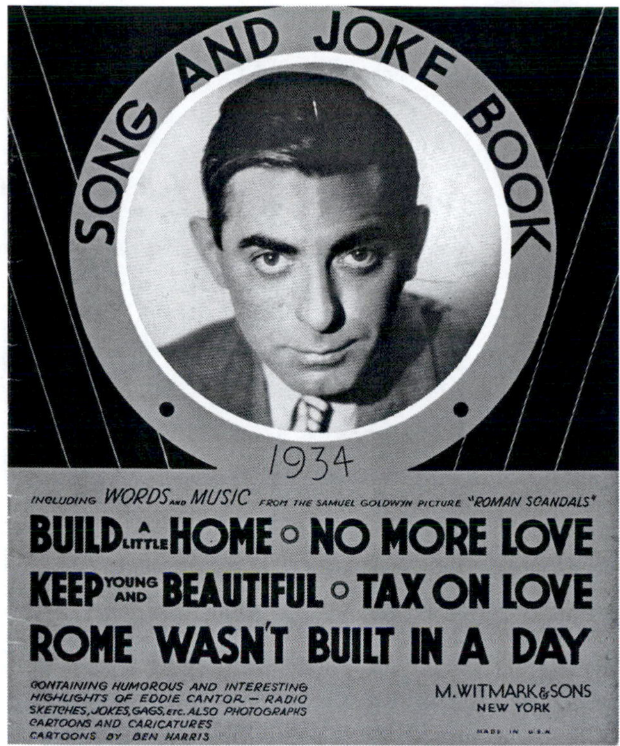

Eddie Cantor in his early Ziegfeld days

Cantor definitely was a song-and-dance man. Eddie's singing voice was odd; it was thin but strong, not particularly mellifluous but musically on target. His recordings outsold many romantic singers. The image of Cantor prancing around the stage suggests that he was more of a dancer than he was. Like any top vaudeville or revue performer, Eddie was capable of basic time steps but more enthusiastic than accomplished or graceful. Was Cantor a comedian? That question has been raised by several of his own generation of comedians and critics and later by performing-arts historians. The answers have not always been unbiased.

Milton Berle remarked that "Eddie Cantor was not really a comedian. . . . He had to fight for his laughs." Great comedy playwright George S. Kaufman opined that "Cantor's humor is painted on like his blackface." Motion-picture historian James Robert Parrish wrote that Cantor, within the strictest sense of the concept, was not a comedian. "He neither created a lasting image . . . nor established a permanent reputation as a wit. . . . Eddie was basically a song-and-dance man who vigorously pursued comedy." Parish did allow that Cantor's "expert timing of jokes was equaled only by Bob Hope's."

They were partly correct. Eddie Cantor was not a wit. Some comedians are at their funniest while relaxing with other comics, trading quips, telling stories and trying to top each other. Few of Cantor's ripostes made the record. If he said something funny offstage, the well-grounded suspicion was that a couple of his writers prepared him with a few jokes in the event he got the chance to spring them. Charlie Chaplin, Bert Williams and Ed Wynn were not particularly funny offstage either, but in their heydays, no comedian ever got more laughs from more audiences than Chaplin, Williams, Wynn and Cantor.

What is forgotten is that Eddie Cantor was a top-notch sketch comedian and equally skilled at playing straight or comic opposite a male or female partner. When Cantor played straight opposite Gracie Allen (of Burns & Allen) on his early radio show and opposite Eva Sully (of Block & Sully) in his movie *Kid Millions,* he was funny, too, getting laughs from his well-delivered straight lines.

In the early talkie *Glorifying the American Girl,* Eddie Cantor and stooge Sam Hearn re-created the classic tailor-shop sketch, "Belt in the Back." Instead of his callow and shy youth or sickly coward, this Eddie was an unscrupulous and cocky tailor, not above bullying his customer: "Look, you *know* you are not getting out of here without buying a suit, don't you?" Eddie Cantor was a fine sketch comedian, if not on par with Willie Howard, Bea Lillie, Bobby Clark, Charlotte Greenwood, Victor Moore and Bert Lahr, and, although he didn't fire off a series of one-liners when he did a bit of stand-up in vaudeville or, much later, on the *Colgate Comedy Hour,* he generated a feeling of fun more capably than most sketch comedians or song-and-dance men.

There are many rags-to-riches stories in show business. Eddie Cantor's was one of them. His childhood deprivation was as extreme as that suffered by anyone, black or white. As he matured, he not only sought the security of wealth and the comfort of a home and family, he also donated money and actively campaigned for the unfortunate. He took on causes even when it hurt his career.

Tradition has it that Eddie was born during Rosh Hashanah in 1892. Deserted by his father and orphaned at age two by his mother, he was raised in cold, filthy, miserable poverty by his aging Russian immigrant grandmother. He was malnourished and dressed in rags; he and his bubba had few hopes or expectations.

Eddie was a late bloomer; survival was foremost. Early on, he learned to make the bullies laugh to deflect beatings. As he grew older, he also learned, by his own admission, to steal, lie and run with a gang, and, by the time he was 15, he was living in sin with a woman four years his senior. Meeting Ida Tobias, his future wife, ended his illicit affair. Like so many other vaudevillians and comedians of his time, Eddie's home was on Manhattan's Lower East Side. For several generations, Weber & Fields, Fanny Brice, George Burns and many more youngsters from that neighborhood gravitated toward show business.

Except for a few amateur-night contests over the years, Eddie did not go onstage until he was 16 years old. It took him a while to commit to the stage as a career. Once he focused, within six years Cantor rose to become a featured performer for Florenz Ziegfeld. About six weeks of those first six years were spent in burlesque with Frank B. Carr's Indian Maidens, Eddie's first truly professional engagement. Then he dropped out of show business for more than a year to take on menial jobs at which he failed because he clowned around.

Eddie had left show business to earn the right to court Ida Tobias, whose father had withheld approval of the young, streetwise ragamuffin. After a long courtship, Ida became his lifelong helpmate and the mother of the five famous Cantor daughters. She was Eddie's steady rudder, a counterbalance to his exuberance and emotional swings. She taught him grooming and how to dress. Gradually, he grew from an ugly duckling into a presentable young man. Eddie returned to show business as a small-time vaudevillian.

His problem was not lack of talent as much as lack of an act. Small-time vaudeville gave Cantor the opportunity to pull together the rudiments of an act: a few jokes, a few songs. He billed himself as a dialectician. Because he did not have enough material for a new act, which he needed to play the same theatres a second time, he did what Weber & Fields had done a generation earlier. He kept the same act and changed the accent—from Italian to German to Jewish to blackface—and sometimes he changed his name as well. Eddie was well suited to blackface. His large pop eyes contrasted with the black greasepaint, and Eddie's slight build, quick movements and quick-witted remarks were markedly different from blackface acts that commonly employed malapropisms and lazy gaits.

Eddie progressed from the People's Theatres, a small-time circuit run by some future showbiz magnates (Adolph Zukor, Marcus Loew, and Nick and Joe Schenck), to big-time vaudeville as the unbilled third member of Bedini & Arthur's act. With Bedini, Eddie's role evolved from stooge to comedian. After learning all he could and making decent money, Cantor switched for more money to *Gus Edwards' Kid Kabaret,* one of the several Gus Edwards troupes plying the big time with a musical sketch. Eddie was 20 at the time, several years older than the rest of the kids, but Eddie looked as young because he was small and thin.

Unlike many young men with money in their pockets for the first time, Eddie was frugal. Each week he sent money home to help his *bubbeh* (grandmother) and to Ida to save for their life together. Once, when his friend from Gus Edwards' days, Georgie Jessel, noticed an evangelical church sign that proclaimed "Jesus Saves," Jessel countered, "Not like Cantor!"

Eddie Cantor

Soon Eddie was earning more money than his future father-in-law, Mr. Tobias. When he married Ida, Eddie was on the threshold of success, but his grandmother, Esther Kantrowitz, was slowly fading from the world. She never understood what her boychik did for a living and did not live to see him a star.

After nearly two years with Edwards, Cantor tried a two-man act—twice. Looking for a partner, he first hooked up with Sammy Kessler. They got an engagement in England, where they flopped, but the trip also served as a honeymoon, and Eddie got a few weeks of work, without Sammy, as an added attraction in a London revue. Back in the USA, Eddie found a new partner in Al Lee, Ed Wynn's former straight man. In their new act, "Master and Servant," Eddie portrayed a sissified, impudent, blackfaced comic. The act played the big time and earned Cantor good reviews that acknowledged he was offering something fresh in blackface.

While Eddie was on the road, Ida gave birth to their first daughter, Marjorie. In time, Margie would become her father's closest confidante. In 1916, after about a year-and-a-half as an act, Cantor split with Lee and took a small comedy role in *Canary Cottage,* a musical comedy playing San Diego, Los Angeles and San Francisco prior to attempting Broadway. Eddie violated professional good manners when he upstaged the star, Trixie Friganza, with unrehearsed and unsanctioned vaudeville shtick but walked away with the opening-night notices.

Cantor made it to New York but not with *Canary Cottage.* His agent sold Florenz Ziegfeld and his right-hand creative man, Gene Buck, on Eddie, and Cantor found himself added to the *Midnight Frolics* on the roof of the New Amsterdam Theatre. His success kept him working in the *Frolics* for six months, but his *Bubbeh* died just as he signed a two-year, $400-a-week contract with Ziegfeld.

From the *Frolics,* Cantor was signed for the *Ziegfeld Follies of 1917.* Over the course of his contracts with Ziegfeld, Eddie shared the *Follies* stages with many of the top comedians of the twentieth century: Bert Williams, Will Rogers, W. C. Fields, Fanny Brice and Walter Catlett. In one pairing that worked well but in retrospect seems insensitive, Cantor (in blackface) played Bert Williams' sissified son.

Eddie had lost his grandmother, but he had found his three great mentors: Bert Williams, Will Rogers and W. C. Fields. He learned the niceties of timing and proportion from these men. He also drew from their humanity, maturity and awareness of the world. From these men, Eddie learned, sometimes as the butt of a prank, to temper his brashness and widen his perspective.

Eddie Cantor entered his glory years with the *Ziegfeld Follies.* His importance to the success of the *Follies* grew with each edition: 1917, 1918, 1919 and 1920. Although Cantor liked, respected and was grateful to Florenz Ziegfeld, Eddie was also a businessman, anxious to get ahead. When Ziegfeld failed to fulfill his promise to star Eddie in a musical comedy, Cantor balked. They tore up their contract, and Cantor hitched up with the Shuberts. As a stopgap, Cantor joined the Shubert-produced *George LeMaire's Broadway Brevities,* where he reunited with his *Follies* chum Bert Williams, who also had differences with Ziegfeld.

Despite wishing to work New York stages so he could be close to his growing family, Cantor agreed to headline a national tour from late 1920 to early 1922 of the *Midnight Rounders of 1920.* The show was the late-night version of the *Century Revue.* Eddie returned with the show to Broadway in 1922 for a few weeks in the month of February. Immediately thereafter, Cantor was on the road again for the Shuberts in another revue, *Make It Snappy,* which returned to play several months on Broadway.

When the show laid off for the summer, Eddie filled in with some big-time vaudeville dates on Keith time, including the Palace. While he played the Palace, he also doubled in the *Ziegfeld Follies of 1922,* in which he replaced Will Rogers, who had taken leave to fulfill a Hollywood commitment.

Obviously, Ziegfeld and Cantor were again doing business with each other. Cantor came back because Ziegfeld finally committed to starring Cantor in a musical. After six weeks of tryouts on the road, *Kid Boots* opened on 31 December 1923 and ran on Broadway at the Earl Carroll Theatre for 479 performances until the end of August 1924, when the show switched to the Selwyn Theatre, where it remained a tenant until 21 February 1925. *Kid Boots* then went on the road into May 1926. Eddie Cantor had reached the top, where he remained for more than a decade.

Between stage shows, sound recordings, personal appearances and movies, Eddie Cantor was on the run. Some of it was ambition, the need to prove himself, and some was an excess of energy. But the Apostle of Pep had another, more pressing motive by 1929. The stock market crash had wiped him out. Nobody made more money from show business than Eddie Cantor, but he left it to unqualified people to invest and manage his wealth. His wife, Ida, should have managed the money. The stock market crash left him half a million dollars in debt!

In continuous succession over the previous five years, Eddie Cantor had made his silent feature-film debut in *Kid Boots* during summer 1926. Back in 1913, Eddie had made a single, experimental one-reel film for Edison, but *Kid Boots* must be considered his first movie. Though the film retained the title of his stage hit, all else was jettisoned; a singing-and-joke-filled stage show does not translate successfully into a silent picture. Eddie's debut was blessed by having a good studio, Sam Goldwyn's, a top director in Frank Tuttle, and a hot, young costar, Clara Bow.

As Cantor's biographer, Herbert G. Goldman, perceptively noted, Eddie was an accomplished pantomimist. Although deprived of his trademark singing and joke-telling skills in his transition from the musical stage into silent film, he adapted masterfully and in a matter of weeks. Cantor's facial expressions, gestures and movement stimulated admiration and predictions of great success as a movie clown.

Unfortunately, his second feature failed to live up to expectations. *Special Delivery* (1927) was beset with many problems, and it matched neither the box-office tally nor the good notices of *Kid Boots.* Also in 1927, Cantor starred on Broadway in the *Ziegfeld Follies of 1927,* sandwiched important vaudeville dates between movies and stage shows, made several short sound films and appeared in the talkie feature *Glorifying the American Girl.* Most importantly, Eddie Cantor created his greatest role as the cowardly hypochondriac in *Whoopee,* his last stage show for Ziegfeld. It ran a year on Broadway, beginning late in 1928, and toured for four months into 1930. That summer, Cantor made his first sound feature, *Whoopee* (with Ethel Shutta), for Sam Goldwyn. It remains his greatest film.

Eddie followed it in 1931 with *Palmy Days* (with Charlotte Greenwood), *The Kid from Spain* (with Lyda Roberti) in 1932, *Roman Scandals* (with Ruth Etting) in 1933 and *Kid Millions* in 1934. This last film boasted Ethel Merman, Ann Sothern, George Murphy and Block & Sully. These movies were conscientiously and lavishly produced by the Sam Goldwyn Studios. Scriptwriters included George S. Kaufman, Robert Sherwood, Nunnally Johnson, Nat Perrin, Arthur Sheekman and Morrie Ryskind, the cleverest comedy writers of their generation. The directors numbered many of the better comedy helmsmen available in Hollywood: Frank Tuttle, Roscoe "Fatty" Arbuckle, Leo McCarey, Eddie Sutherland and Roy Del Ruth. Although all the early Cantor films were well made, only two or three approached the standard of *Whoopee.* By the time *Strike Me Pink* was made in 1936 and *Ali Baba Goes to Town* in 1937, some of the quality and verve were dissipated, and Cantor's great starring days in Hollywood were over.

Coincident with his stardom on the silver screen was Cantor's trailblazing and subsequent eminence in network radio. Rudy Vallee was the first star of a big variety show that introduced many fine comedians to a national audience, but Cantor was the first comedian to take on the challenge of finding new material to amuse audiences week after week. Cantor and his browbeaten writing staff created a top-rated radio show from 1931 until 1939. Although Cantor began to lose ground in both radio and movies by 1937, he still was earning about $200,000 per film and $7,000 per week for his radio show, so there was salve aplenty for any slippage in box office and ratings.

Ever the practical showman, Eddie produced and starred in various vaudeville units during his years on radio. As the units played cities across the nation, Eddie used each engagement to plug his movies, his books and his future appearances. He also broadcast his weekly radio show from these theatres, bonding with local audiences who turned out in numbers unseen by other performers during the Great Depression.

Eddie Cantor

When not performing, Eddie Cantor was serious—dour and stubborn, some said—a hardheaded businessman who cut his own movie and network radio deals and used agents simply to tie up loose ends. He negotiated the contracts he had with performers and writers on his radio shows, often raking off a 10-percent commission for managing them.

He was cavalier with comedy writers, reportedly buying their services on the cheap, discarding them at will, failing to show writers appreciation or respect, and claiming (or sharing) credit for their creations. Top writers were well treated by smart comics like Jack Benny; consequently, Cantor's radio show did not evolve from gags to more sophisticated, character-driven situation comedy. There was little incentive to innovate, and the quality dropped.

Out of the limelight, Eddie lacked the bonhomie that radiated from him onstage. It was not that Eddie was humble or lacked the driving ego of other comedians; he was unable to engage in the quick-witted bantering that passed as sociability among comedians gathered at the Friar's Club and other fraternal settings. He did share a wandering eye with some of his fellow comics. Rumors persisted through the years of several affairs. They caused more comment because they were so contrary to his public image as a family man.

By the mid-1930s, the entrepreneurial and humanitarian sides of Cantor had come to dominate the funnyman. Twenty years earlier, W. C. Fields had introduced an untutored Cantor to the world of books. Not much interested in literature, Cantor consumed books of history and biography and regularly read the more serious newspapers. Eddie was a man of passionate and unshakable moral convictions. His own pathetic childhood and his identity as a Jew led him to labor for the unfortunates and the oppressed of the world. He endowed a summer camp for unfortunate kids, and he gave his money, time and talent to myriad causes.

Cantor risked the ire of producers by actively and publicly working to extend the protection of unions to the most vulnerable people in show business. Eddie served as president of the Screen Actors Guild, American Federation of Radio Artists, and American Guild of Variety Artists, and he was an officer of Actors Equity and the American Federation of Actors.

When the White House announced, during the pit of the Great Depression, a campaign against polio—the disease that had struck President Franklin Delano Roosevelt—Cantor came up with the idea of a March of Dimes that would enlist millions of children, women and men through their 10-cent contributions. By 1936,

Eddie was speaking out publicly and forcefully against Adolf Hitler and the increase of pro-Nazi and anti-Jewish propaganda in the USA.

He took on the most powerful demagogue of the day, Father Coughlin, the Roman Catholic priest turned rabid radio commentator, who swayed millions of Americans to his anti-Jewish, anti–New Deal, anti-immigrant cant. Letters from Coughlin's followers flooded the network and Cantor's sponsors. Their campaign cost him his network radio show in 1939.

Cantor traveled the USA and England to raise money to rescue Jewish children stranded in Europe. During and after the Second World War, Eddie sold U.S. war bonds, visited the troops on the *purple-heart circuit,* raised money for the new Israeli state and hosted a one-man charity radio marathon that raised $40 million in 33 hours! The record still stands.

When Cantor's career began to disintegrate in the late 1930s, he was not alone. The careers of Charlie Chaplin, Buster Keaton, The Marx Brothers, Joe E. Brown, W. C. Fields, Mae West and other comedy stars of his generation experienced similar slumps. In Cantor's case, it was more visible because he had been in the public eye continuously with a weekly radio series, nearly a movie a year in release, and on tour, fronting his annual packaged vaudeville shows.

Vaudeville became synonymous with old hat, and its great performers found themselves sidelined. Some, like James Barton, June Havoc and Walter Huston, became renowned legitimate actors. A few, like Elsie Janis, Willie Covan and Trixie Friganza, taught, coached or worked behind the scenes. Others, like Jesse Block & Eva Sully, Lou Holtz and Jack Haley, saw the writing on the backstage wall, turned their talents to other ventures and prospered. Less fortunate were those like Blossom Seeley and Benny Fields and a legion of others who saw their names drift off marquees into forlorn scrapbooks while they waited for vaudeville to come back.

Eddie Cantor, Sophie Tucker, Ted Lewis and Georgie Jessel appointed themselves drum majors for the golden age of vaudeville and Broadway, and they tried to lead audiences down memory lane. Cantor, Lewis and Tucker, who had cultivated their fan base, continued to attract loyal, if aging, audiences, but after the Second World War, the parade turned a corner and left the drum majors all dressed up and facing the past instead of the future.

Cantor was better off than most stars of the 1920s and 1930s. He had four starring movies in release between 1940 and 1948, was back on radio every year from 1941 to 1950, and enjoyed a few years as a top television star.

Eddie Cantor became NBC's workhorse on their Sunday-night *Colgate Comedy Hour* opposite Ed Sullivan's *Toast of the Town.* Originally, Cantor, Bobby Clark, Fred Allen and Martin & Lewis were supposed to rotate as stars. As the plan played out, Bobby Clark was lost in the shuffle, Fred Allen found television uncongenial, and Martin & Lewis, then at the peak of their fame, had far better paying movies and personal appearances to make, so Cantor did half of the shows during the first two years. The pace nearly killed Cantor until Abbott & Costello and Donald O'Connor were added to flesh out the roster.

In radio, Eddie had huddled with his writing staff and broadcast once a week, reading from the script. On television, he again had to help write, but he also had to memorize lines, engage in physical comedy and perform live. There had been several indications that Cantor's health was not up to the challenge. By the second season, Cantor was running out of material and had failed to assemble a loyal cadre of good new writers. By the third season, he suffered a major heart attack. He barely fulfilled his contract, often filming his segments, and left the show in 1954 with more heart problems.

Only Cantor had rivaled Al Jolson as a powerhouse entertainer able to carry a musical show alone. In Ziegfeld's heaven of electrically lit stars over Broadway, none burned longer, more brightly or steadily than Eddie Cantor. He was a successful pioneer, often the first big star to risk his reputation in the new mediums of sound movies, network radio and television. His recordings sold by the carload and made him a lot of money: "If You Knew Susie," "Ma, He's Making Eyes at Me," "Margie," "Ida, Sweet as Apple Cider," "Mandy," "Yes, We Have No Bananas Blues," "Charley, My Boy," "You'd Be Surprised," "Don't Put a Tax on the Beautiful Girls," "Making Whoopee," "When They're Old Enough to Know Better," "I Don't Want to Get Well (I'm in Love with the Pharmacist's Mate)," "What a Perfect Combination," "Yes, Sir, That's My Baby," "We're Having a Baby (My Baby and Me)," "Josephina, Please No Lean-a on the Bell" and "(Potatoes Are Cheaper, Tomatoes Are Cheaper) Now's the Time to Fall in Love." Few entertainers were more popular between the two world wars.

By the 1950s, however, his character no longer made sense. It is hard to be a naive and saucy juvenile when one is over 50 years old. For decades, Eddie Cantor had held age at bay. He seemed 25 until he turned 50. Then he began to grow old. His face got puffy, and he dyed his thinning grey hair black. His risqué material became unseemly. Bob Hope and Mickey Rooney were similarly afflicted by the accumulating years. What was spunky, cheeky and funny in a young man became tiresome and tasteless in a middle-aged man.

Sadly, Eddie Cantor outlived his talent and vitality. No one had worked harder onstage and off. Since the 1920s, he was frequently ill or in need of a rest. His voice had lost luster. Heart attacks had curtailed his mobility and spontaneity. His last decade was sad. Medical care for Ida and himself, charity donations and bad investments cost him much of his fortune. Eddie Cantor had earned an enormous amount of money in his day. He ended up well off but no longer a multimillionaire.

Eddie cowrote several books and had a magazine column to keep busy, but the life that had defined the Apostle of Pep was over, and he knew it. Ida, his steady rock, died before Eddie, as did his daughter Margie, his best friend. Margie had selflessly devoted her life to taking care of the family. By the time death came to an exhausted Eddie Cantor, he reportedly wished he had accomplished less and smelled more flowers.

In retrospective assessment, Eddie had been belittled as mawkish, dismissed as a nostalgia pitchman and pegged simply as a personality by critics who did not discern his talent or skill. Four decades after his death, Cantor still attracted admirers who formed fan clubs, but some fans admired him more as a symbol of family values and good, old-fashioned entertainment than for the individuality and extent of his talent. This is unfortunate because it credits him for his artificial image and shortchanges him for his talents, his phenomenal career, his charity and his social conscience.

CARDINI

b: (Richard Valentine Pitchford) 24 November 1899, Mumbles, Wales— d: 11 November 1973, Kingston, NY

Although noted for his deft manipulations and comic pantomime rather than grand illusions, "The Suave Deceiver" was the master of one great transformation: that of changing himself from a Welsh lad from the factories into his stage depiction of a debonair, upper-class Britisher confounded by a profusion of cards, handkerchiefs, billiard balls and lit cigarettes. It was not a transformation quickly accomplished.

His hometown village in Wales was a bit off the route of most variety performers, and it may be that he did not see a stage magician until later in his teens. Like many youths, he tried to learn small tricks, making coins and cards disappear. With little besides mines, slaughterhouses and menial labor available in his neck of the Welsh woods, young Pitchford enlisted in the British army, quite in time to be sent to become cannon fodder in the trenches of the First World War. To keep his fingers from freezing, he practiced card tricks. Because of the cold, he kept his gloves on, and because that did not allow him to materialize specific cards, he did develop dexterity in producing entire fully fanned decks. When an officer commented that he had not seen any magician do that, the young doughboy took note. He also fixed in his mind the officer's manner and bearing, and later he modeled his stage personality on the officer.

At the midpoint of the war, 1916, young Pitchford was injured at the front, so seriously that at first he was believed dead. Someone detected slight breathing, and he was transported to a field hospital. For his convalescence, he was shipped to a Southampton hospital. To while away the time, he asked for and was given a deck of cards. When he insisted on handling the cards with his gloves on, it was feared he had suffered emotional trauma. He was dispatched to a mental institution to mend mentally and physically. The hospital staff became his first audience outside the trenches to admire his card tricks.

Upon demobilization, he accepted work selling magic tricks at the magic counter in Gamage's department store while he tried, with little success, to get work in British variety. He found, as others had, that there was a difference between having talent and skill and having an act. Unwilling to settle for a humdrum existence, he signed on as crew aboard a tramp steamer and sailed around the world. When he returned to London, he was still unable to break into variety, so once again he took to the sea, heading for a new start in Australia.

Billed as Val Raymond, he played some small-time music halls Down Under. He earned a show date and grabbed the attention of a booker, who suggested a name change. Because his manipulation act was built around cards, and because Houdini possessed the most famous name in magic, R. V. Pitchford/Val Raymond became Cardini.

It was in Australia that Cardini developed his act. In jacket and trousers, he presented a relaxed persona and engaged the audience in a line of jocular chatter as he performed his tricks. He came to America in the mid-1920s, most likely through San Francisco, the portal most often used by visitors from Australia. He worked his way across the USA in vaudeville and hotel supper clubs. En route, he met Swan Walker, a nonprofessional, and they married almost immediately and stayed so for 47 years until Cardini's death.

By the time he played the Palace Theatre in Manhattan, Cardini had replaced his patter with comic pantomime. The British officer from the trenches had become a stage character, vague and a trifle tipsy, yet ever the well-bred gentleman. He was pronounced a success in the capital of big-time vaudeville.

He had been working with long stretches of silks and a variety of materials from thimbles to balls. As other magicians copied his act, Cardini refined it to its inimitable essentials: the exquisite manipulation of cards, cigarettes and billiard balls. His wife, now his onstage assistant as well, dressed as a hotel bellhop, opened the act by paging "Mr. Cardini." The spotlight picked him up as he sauntered onstage in elegant attire, holding a newspaper in his white-gloved hands and reading it through his monocle.

He handed his newspaper to the hotel page, but a fan full of playing cards got in the way. He grew irritated as one fanned deck after another appeared at his fingertips as fast as he could dump them into the outstretched newspaper.

Freeing himself of the endless packs of cards, Cardini handed his top hat, cane and cape to the page, but then ping-pong sized balls began appearing in his outstretched hands. He tossed ball after ball offstage as still more appeared and in greater profusion.

At last the balls ceased. A bit bushed, he tried to relax with a cigarette. Still slightly inebriated, he had difficulty fitting his cigarette into the holder he clenched between his teeth. The cigarette kept disappearing and reappearing until he captured and lit it. Then dozens of lit cigarettes began appearing from the ether. For every one he stamped out beneath his shoe, more appeared in his hands until, at the finish, the cigarettes gave way to a lit cigar, which in turn vanished and was replaced by a lit pipe. Mollified, Cardini exited the stage, smoking his pipe.

He was tops in his field of manipulation, but what made him a vaudeville star, a headliner at the Palace on Broadway and at London's Palladium, was his equally deft hand at comedy and his delightful impersonation of the elegant, vague, but unruffled, British upper-class man.

When American vaudeville waned after the 1920s and the onset of the Second World War in 1940 made overseas travel to English variety dangerous, Cardini switched to the better supper clubs. His act was perfect for the intimate yet occasionally noisy atmosphere. He needed to be seen, not heard, and because he eschewed large-scale illusions, he had no need to radically restage his vaudeville act for the smaller stages and closer audiences of nightclubs.

One pitfall that awaited vaudeville conjurers when they played nightclubs was the matter of sight lines. On a proscenium stage, the act was blocked, or staged, so as to be angle proof. Even far downstage center, the angle open to an audience was less than 180 degrees. If positioned farther upstage, the audience was able to see only the front of the stage magician facing it. In a nightclub, the playing area was often a three-quarter thrust so that customers seated on either side of the playing area were facing the magician at an angle from which they could see behind him, and it was more difficult to conceal some manipulations. According to other conjurers, Cardini so masterfully controlled his moves that even nightclub audiences did not spot him reaching for or disposing of items.

While active in vaudeville, the Cardinis based themselves in Jamaica on Long Island, New York, where they raised two children. They retired to Kingston in the Hudson Valley of upstate New York.

RICHARD CARLE

b: (Charles Nicholas Carleton) 7 July 1871, Somerville, MA—d: 28 June 1941, Los Angeles, CA

Tall, lean and good looking, Richard Carle was one of the busiest men in show business during the half century between 1890 and 1940. Carle was a theatrical wonder of his day, a skilled comedian, actor, dancer, singer, producer, playwright, lyricist, composer, dance director and show director. He performed almost every season in musical comedy from the 1890s until 1930, and he appeared in Hollywood movies from 1915 until his death in 1941. He made a few silent shorts and about eight features; his costars included Clara Bow, Lon Chaney, Jack Oakie and Laurel & Hardy. He shared billing in more than 100 talking pictures with John Gilbert, Constance Bennett, Charlotte Greenwood, Bert Lahr, Edward G. Robinson, Joe E. Brown, Maurice Chevalier, Jeannette MacDonald, Wheeler & Woolsey, Katherine Hepburn, Jimmy Durante, Spencer Tracy, W. C. Fields, Hal Leroy, Marlene Dietrich, Jimmy Stewart, Abbott & Costello and Greta Garbo.

He began his career as a monologist who specialized in bogus stump speeches and funny stories. Billed as a "Platform Humorist," Carle traveled throughout New England in his act, gradually accumulating the observations, timing and experience that made him an all-around talent who was effective in straight plays, variety, revues and musical comedy.

Carle's first appearance in New York City placed him onstage with another newcomer, Peter F. Dailey, when both were in support of John T. Powers in *A Straight Tip* (1891). Carle followed that with *Niobe* (1891), *Star Gazer* (1893) and *Excelsior, Jr.* (1895). *The Lady Slavey* (1896) allowed young Carle his first substantial opportunity in a production, and he made it a success. Thereafter, he played leads in *One Round of Pleasure* (1897), *Yankee Doodle Dandy* (1897), *In Gotham* (1898), *A Dangerous Maid* (1898) and *A Greek Slave* (1899). His debut as a dramatic actor in *Children of the Ghetto* (1899) was hailed as a success equal to his comedies.

In 1900, Richard Carle traveled to London in *An American Beauty;* the show did not appeal, so *The Casino Girl* was quickly substituted, and Carle became a favorite with West End audiences.

Back in the USA, Richard starred in *Ladies of Paradise* (1901); meanwhile, he had been readying his own work for the stage. Carle produced, starred in and served as librettist and lyricist for *Mam'selle 'Awkins* (1900), a quadruple duty he repeated in *The Tenderfoot* (1904), a show he opened in Chicago, *The Maid and the Mummy* (1904, with Annie Yeamans), *The Mayor of Tokio* (1905) and *The Spring Chicken* (1906). Carle's shows did better in

Richard Carle

Chicago and on the road than they did in New York, where critics faulted him for his risqué double entendres. Still, he mounted a show nearly every season, and his vaudeville days seemed well behind him.

The programme for *The Hurdy-Gurdy Girl* (1907) reminded audiences that the "Entire production [was] staged under the personal supervision of Richard Carle," and that the "Dances [were] arranged by Richard Carle." Carle went one better with his production of *Mary's Lamb* (1908); he composed the music as well as lyrics and the book, directed and starred. Carle's frothy, funny musicals continued each season: *The Boy and the Girl* (1909), *Jumping Jupiter* (1911), *The Girl from Montmartre* (1912) and *The Doll Girl* (1913).

Richard Carle removed his producer's hat and took a break from composing and writing when he appeared in *90 in the Shade* (1915), *The Cohan Revue of 1916* and *Words and Music* (1917) but supplied lyrics as well as his comedy presence in *The Broadway Whirl* (1921). Carle left the writing and directing to others when he starred in *Adrienne* (1923), which ran seven months at George M. Cohan's Theatre.

In those years, when he did not write, produce, star and tour in his shows, he made occasional appearances in vaudeville. He was a capable singer and comedian, of course, but he was also ranked among the better eccentric dancers, a skill that came in handy in vaudeville as well as musical comedy.

Cole Porter's *The New Yorkers* (1930) sported an exceptional cast, including Charles King, Hope Williams, Jimmy Durante and Fred Waring & His Pennsylvanians. Also costarred were Marie Cahill and 60-year-old Richard Carle, both of whom were making their last Broadway appearances. Thereafter, Richard Carle frequently appeared in character parts in movies until his death.

LEO CARRILLO

b: (Leopoldo Antonio Carrillo) 6 August 1881, Los Angeles, CA—d: 10 September 1961, Santa Monica, CA

In movies, he played gangsters, always with an accent; on television, he was Pancho, the Cisco Kid's sidekick. So thoroughly was Leo Carrillo submerged in his identity as Pancho and as a movie character comedian that his substantial and respected career in vaudeville has been forgotten. What has been remembered is the ranch land he bequeathed to the people of California as parkland and that Señor Carrillo, of Castilian ancestry, was a descendant on his father's side of one of California's first families. There were mayors, judges, even a governor of California among the Carrillos. His father was once, during a lifetime of many pursuits, Los Angeles' chief of police. His mother's family was the socially prominent Danas of Boston. They had been clipper captains and merchants. Before California became one of the United States of America, the Carrillo cattle barons owned immense tracts of the California coast and its islands and great ranches and beaches that eventually became cities like Santa Monica.

Leo's immediate family, however, struggled to live comfortably. Their grandfather had lost all his money on a horse race, but his sons prospered in time. Although the Carrillos and other first families of California held their family honor in high value, the times and the society of the newly admitted state of California were often barbaric, given the lynchings and massacres of Chinese and native people, a reported high incidence of abandoned mistresses and bastard children, claim-jumping, gunfights, bear and bullfights and other blood sports.

Two of Leo's talents made themselves known early in life: drawing and languages. He had grown up near a Chinese neighborhood, and the family employed Chinese helpers. Leo learned Chinese first, Spanish second and English third. His first job was as a Chinese and English interpreter and teacher of both languages to the Chinese laborers on the railroad and to their English-speaking supervisors. He moved to San Francisco, where he got a job in the art department of a newspaper and then became a cartoonist and reporter. His facility with languages now included Japanese and Italian.

Newsman and theatre critic Ashton Stevens encouraged Carrillo to develop a vaudeville act incorporating the various characters he had met and whose ethnic palaver he could imitate. First he joined another young colleague, Eddie Bowes, who was trying to raise money for a fraternal organization by producing an amateur show. Eddie became quite good as an impresario; later he was known as Major Bowes, the originator and host of *The Original Amateur Hour* on radio.

On the recommendation of Walter C. Kelly, one of vaudeville's top monologists who was known as the Virginia Judge, Carrillo got booked on the Orpheum circuit. For his first show, Pat Rooney Jr.'s wife helped Leo put on makeup he had never before used. Carrillo's monologue, told in various dialects, was a collection of vignettes about the people he had met in San Francisco and Los Angeles.

> A lady in San Francisco needed extra help for a dinner party she was giving for her bishop. She went to a local employment agency and engaged a young Chinese boy. His name was very difficult for her to pronounce and his grasp of English was limited, so she told him that "the bishop will probably ask you three questions: your name, your age and where do bad boys go." To the first question you must answer "John." To the second question, say "15 years." To the last question, just point downwards. That night the bishop came and, as expected, asked the Chinese boy his name. Nervously, the boy answered all three at once: "John, 15 year, go to hell."

Another story involved the Irish and Italians. "Tony was digging a ditch, and he had an Irish boss. An Irish priest came along one day and asked Tony 'How do you like your Irish boss?' 'He's okay. How do you like your Italian boss?'"

From the Orpheum in San Francisco he went to the Orpheum in Los Angeles. There was a dry spell for a short while until Walter C. Kelly finagled a date for Leo at the Haymarket Theatre in Chicago. Leo arrived as a blizzard swept the Windy City and killed theatre business for his opening night. Faced with an empty house, the theatre manager decided on a publicity stunt and had the theatre filled with Indians from a nearby encampment. Carrillo, doubly nervous, went out and told his stories to a silent audience. As Leo persisted, a quartet of people in a box began to applaud and then cheer. One of them whooped the Indians into applause as well. The man in the box turned out to be James J. Corbett, former prizefighter, a headlining vaudeville monologist himself and a friend of Walter Kelly.

Leo's triumph raised interest, and he was booked for six weeks in Manhattan at the Union Square Theatre, a new house that was a joint venture by the recent (and short-lived) partnership of B. F. Keith and F. F. Proctor. On the bill was an unknown trick roper, the Cherokee Kid, who later changed his name to Will Rogers.

Leo also met Edith Haeselbarth, whom he married. Their only child was called Antoinette. Edith died in 1953, several years before her husband.

Carrillo never really played small-time vaudeville. He went straight into the big time, which was an unheard-of situation for someone who was not experienced as a vaudevillian or famous as a celebrity. He played vaudeville up to the years of the First World War, when Oliver Morosco lured Leo from vaudeville to the legitimate stage by casting Carrillo in several plays. *Upstairs and Down* ran the full 1916–17 season. *Lombardi, Ltd.* (1917–18), in which Leo played Italian, proved an equal hit and ran for a year on Broadway and then toured another two across the USA before playing a year in Australia and New Zealand. The next six plays were flops, however, and he never again appeared on Broadway. Another production closed out of town.

Vaudeville was always there to offer Carrillo bookings when plays closed sooner than hoped. A Vitaphone short in 1927 provided his entry in the movies. He got his first work in a feature in 1929, and he went on to make about 90 full-length movies, most of them profitable, none of them remarkable. But Hollywood gave Leo Carrillo the chance to make a good living in the land he loved best.

There he built a beautiful and quite authentic adobe hacienda and continued his education, becoming expert in his state's history. His last role of note was in the very popular 1950 television series *The Cisco Kid.* Duncan Renaldo played the title character, and Leo played Pancho, a popularized version of Cervantes' Sancho Panza.

Carrillo purchased land, tract by tract, and eventually donated his holdings to the people of California. Leo served on the state parks commission, held titles as grand marshal and honorary mayor, and finished his life as a spirited public citizen of California.

CARROLL & HOWE

Jean Carroll

b: ca. 1918, Bronx, NY

Buddy Howe

b: (Zolitan) ca. 1910, Brooklyn, NY— d: 4 March 1981, Miami, FL

Independently, Jean Carroll and Buddy Howe entered show business as dancers, the tail end of the last generation to work big-time vaudeville.

Buddy and a friend of his, Buddy Soloff, began as 15-year-old kids rehearsing with an eye to breaking into vaudeville as a dance team when they were asked to audition for a flash act, Patti Moore & Band. The boys were hired. It was a lucky introduction to show business because the act, Patti Moore & Band with Sammy Lewis and Bud & Buddy, as it eventually was billed, toured Fox, Keith and Orpheum time for two years from 1926 to 1927, playing the Palace and other top two-a-day houses several times. (Buddy Howe was called Bud, and Buddy Soloff was Buddy.) In addition to Patti, Sammy, Bud and Buddy, there was a seven-piece band. The boys went from $50 a week to $75 in their second season, which was good money at the time for couple of kids new to show business.

Vaudeville had been up and down throughout the 1920s; by 1925, the golden age of silent movies was taking a serious bite of vaudeville's business. Talkies took a bigger bite a few years later. Buddy, by 1929, was playing dates as a single. In a reminiscence, published in 1976 along with other interviews compiled by Bill Smith and called *The Vaudevillians,* Buddy claimed his stage name was accidentally conferred on him by an emcee who could not or would not remember Buddy's surname, Zolitan, and introduced him as "Buddy—and how he can dance." Buddy took the name Howe and played around with his billing matter, trying various versions of "Buddy Howe and How He Can Dance."

As a single, Howe was more likely to be working in the Fanchon & Marco prologue units playing in presentation houses or doing a single in small-time vaudeville than the Keith and Orpheum time in which he had started. Then Buddy put together an act with a young tap dancer, Leonard Lebitsky, who changed his name to Jack Leonard, and Buddy engaged a young toe dancer, Alyce McLaughlin, to complete the song-and-dance package. For three years, the act did pretty well, considering the Great Depression was settling in for a long run. They played straight vaudeville dates and some presentation houses. In 1933, Alyce married Charles Correll of Amos 'n' Andy, Jack was on his way to becoming one of the first insult comics, "Fat" Jack E. Leonard, and Buddy Howe met Jean Carroll.

An agent from MCA had seen Jean Carroll in a Bronx amateur show and got her her first professional work as part of a two-girl and two-boy unison dancing quartet packaged by MCA for the 1933–34 season. The Gerry Society was a problem, always on the lookout for youngsters dancing or clowning. (They did not object much to teens in drama.) Jean was 14 or 15 at the time, so the act played dates away from New York City and Chicago, where the Gerry Society was more active.

The two boys were another problem and were more interested in playing at being sharpies than perfecting their act. After a squabble, the two girls were stranded when the boys took off with their costumes and sides (music arrangements). Fortunately, the boys were never heard of again. The theatre manager at the act's next date let the girls go on as a double act, but that was a stopgap that bought them train tickets home.

Jean joined a variety of other acts. One was a band outfit; this time she was left stranded by the bandleader, who took the act's money and ran. Jean had been in the business for about three years when she met Marty May, a well-known comic. He saw Jean while she was part of a short-lived comedy act, Saranoff & Carroll, and noted her good looks and ready wit. May introduced Jean Carroll to Buddy Howe.

Buddy and Jean liked each other, but their motivation at the time was to build an act. They did a comedy dance act. The burden for the dancing was largely on Buddy, who was an acrobatic dancer. Jean wrote the comedy dialogue, and Buddy learned to feed lines. It took the usual series of out-of-town dates to shake down the act. If the theatre, stage and crowd were small, they concentrated on the man-woman comedy talk. If they were playing on an outdoor stage at a fair, no one could hear them, so they both danced, solo and paired.

Once the act was set, they decided they were in love, and they married and stayed together for the rest of their lives. In 1935, the depth of the Great Depression, Carroll & Howe played presentation houses and the better small time. The next season, they got the opportunity to play British variety. They went over for a three-week engagement, hoping to build on that. They stayed for three years. In 1939, when England went to war, Jean and Buddy returned to the USA. Dates were thin until, in 1941, the United Service Organizations (USO) began gearing up for the USA's entry into the Second World War and recruited entertainers to play armed forces camps. Carroll & Howe worked the USO time for a couple of years until Buddy was drafted into the service.

Almost from the start, back in 1935, Jean had introduced monologues into their act. Buddy did not like doing dialogue, so their cross talk was composed of short feed lines from Buddy, and Jean got the laughs with her extended answers. Moms Mabley had been doing stand-up comedy for years in black vaudeville houses, Irene Franklin, Elsie Janis and other vaudeville *single women* talked to their audiences, and Ruth Draper had been telling stories and acting all the roles in her elegant character sketches at soirees and in small playhouses, but very few women did comedy monologues. Jean Carroll was often spoken of as a pioneer in the field.

With Buddy in the service by 1943, Jean ditched the dancing and did straight stand-up. She was an excellent comedy writer; she had created all the Carroll & Howe material. The 1940s and early 1950s were her peak years. Upon his discharge from the armed services in 1945, Buddy discovered that Jean Carroll had become a star solo act, and he decided against returning to the stage and became a talent agent.

The idea of a woman monologist was startling enough, but Jean Carroll was attractive and sophisticated. She tailored her delivery but not her material to her audiences, working a bit slower for rural folks. Jean believed there was no need to condescend; she simply adjusted the speed of her delivery. Her bits were about family and everyday life. Even with such conservative subject matter, there were complaints about Carroll using her husband and children as the butt of her jokes.

Buddy and Jean had appeared as guests on radio shows, and Jean began writing scripts for others while Buddy did two years at Camp Lee in the USA. Not everything Jean wrote was comedy; she turned out the scripts for the seminal radio soap opera *Our Gal Sunday* for 14 years, beginning in 1945 up through the final broadcast in January 1959.

Jean moved into television, but not quite fast enough. Usually a guest star—she appeared no fewer than ten times on Ed Sullivan's show—she finally got a chance at her own show. It was a combination monologue and sitcom show, a bit like the Burns & Allen format for TV, but she was canceled in three months. Imogene Coca, Martha Raye, Lucille Ball and Joan Davis had brought physical zaniness to television and raised expectations for female comedians. By the end of the 1950s, Phyllis Diller had taken Jean Carroll's themes of housework, husbands and children and made Carroll's treatment seem genteel.

Buddy Howe was a great success as an agent and was appointed board chairman of a major talent agency, Creative Management Agency, before he retired. When Jean retired, there were her children, grandchildren and a loving husband to entertain.

CARRYING THE BANNER

Another term for being out of work, or *at liberty,* in show business.

FRANK CARTER

b: ca. 1888, Kansas City, MO—
d: 1921, Wheeling, WV

Famous as the love of Marilyn Miller's life, Frank was a singer who had a solid career in vaudeville at home and variety abroad. He began as a child passing out programmes in a hometown vaudeville theatre and occasionally taking bit parts and walk-ons in shows that passed through Kansas City.

Frank took whatever jobs came his way as long as they were in show business. He performed as an ill-trained, 16-year-old daredevil in a carnival, diving from a 90-foot platform into a tub of water twice a day for a year until he suffered a concussion. Then Frank moved to Chicago and got work in nickelodeons singing to song slides, occasionally dancing. His singing drew full houses, and he launched into a vaudeville career that quickly took him to the premier vaudeville house of its time, Hammerstein's Victoria in Manhattan. This led to an engagement in London and a tour of Britain's music halls. He stayed abroad, traveling and working through Europe and Asia until the threat of the First World War brought him back to the USA in 1914.

Over the next few seasons, Carter reestablished himself as a vaudeville attraction in America. He may have appeared in a few touring shows for the Shuberts as well. Frank was hired for the *Ziegfeld Follies of 1918,* in which he met dancing star Marilyn Miller, one of Ziegfeld's favorites. The Miller-Carter romance was carried on as quietly as one can in the gossiping corridors of show business, and both Frank and Marilyn were engaged for the next season's *Follies.* When Ziegfeld learned of their marriage, he fired Frank before the show opened. Frank went into a musical comedy, *See-saw* (1919), that played about nine weeks in Manhattan before going out on the road.

Separated by Ziegfeld, who had a crush on Miller, Carter was rushing after a performance to meet his bride in Philadelphia when he lost control of his Packard touring car on a curve in Wheeling, West Virginia. His death was a blow to Marilyn from which she never fully recovered.

CARTOONISTS, CARICATURISTS, LIGHTNING-SKETCH ACTS

Some cartoonists, who gained national fame through the syndication of their popular comic strips in newspapers across the USA, relinquished their pens, pencils, brushes and paper when they worked on the vaudeville stage and became successful as humorous storytellers.

Others, who may or may not have had print experience, drew caricatures or cartoons to accompany their monologues. Although it was less used, *lightning-sketch act* was a more correct term because their drawings had to be executed in a lightning-fast fashion to keep the act moving at a quick pace. The sketches also had to be rendered in simple, bold lines so that they were clearly discernible from balcony seats.

Among those who enjoyed a vogue in vaudeville were Windsor McKay (*Little Nemo* and *Gertie the Dinosaur*), George McManus (*Bringing Up Father,* also known as *Maggie & Jiggs*), Bud Fisher *(Mutt & Jeff),* Richard Oucault *(Buster Brown),* Rube Goldberg and many others. Some were nationally known through syndication, whereas others were enjoyed by regional readers; some played vaudeville for several seasons, yet others only succeeded a few weeks. Among the last of the lightning-sketch acts to play vaudeville, clubs and television was Roger Price.

THE MORAL SONG WITH A BLESSING
The Curse of An Aching Heart
SOUVENIR
EMMA CARUS
VAUDEVILLE'S "FIRST LADY OF THE LAND"

Emma Carus

EMMA CARUS

b: 18 March 1879, Berlin, Germany— d: 18 November 1927, New York, NY

Born into a concert music family, Emma Carus' mother, Henrietta Rowland, was "a prima donna of some note" (according to Browne and Koch's *Who's Who on the Stage, 1908*), and her father, Carl Carus, a concert manager. Emma always claimed that she made her debut at six and that the family remained in Berlin while Emma completed her education and voice training.

The accepted biography is a bit at odds with other received facts or subsequent circumstances. The Carus family arrived in the USA prior to Emma's 15th birthday, and Emma was working in a hotel (according to Edward B. Marks in his memoir) when she was discovered and encouraged by Monroe H. "Rosie" Rosenfeld, a successful songwriter who had been charmed by her speaking voice.

It is difficult to understand what events or conditions could have brought the Carus family to the USA. Carl and Henrietta were unable to transfer their Berlin success to America. Their daughter, Emma, was younger than 15 when she worked in a hotel until she made her professional American debut in 1894. (Emma had been married twice by 1905.) Perhaps Emma Carus had advanced her birth date to 1879 or overstated her family's accomplishments.

Carus' star career in vaudeville and on the musical stage is beyond question; the facts remain on the record. After getting professional experience playing and singing minor parts in several operettas of the day, she won her first major role, as Lady Muriel, when she replaced May Yohe in *The Giddy Throng* in 1900 at the New York Theatre. Her success in the role resulted in being hired as a member of the New York Theatre's musical stock company (which included Marie Dressler, Lou Harrison, Adele Ritchie, Amelia Summerville and Charles H. Prince). While in that company, Emma notably created the roles of Nancy in *The King's Carnival* (1901) and Jane Bollingbrook in *The Hall of Fame* (1902). All in all, Carus remained with the company nearly three years.

Carus has been described as a deep-voiced vaudeville belter. A soubrette of a style then much in favor, she was pudgy and had a large pleasant pudding face. As she strode on to each vaudeville stage, she introduced herself: "I'm not pretty, but I'm good to my family." Her songs were character pieces, rather than hits of the day. Emma winkingly impersonated young girls, haughty society dames and good ol' gals, all with affection.

At some point in her early career, Carus wed N. S. Mattson, the son of a former Minnesota governor.

Emma Carus

It was not a successful marriage. July 1902 found Emma Carus in the starring role of Mrs. Jack Orchard in the Herald Square Theatre's production of *The Defender.* She then appeared as the Countess von Lahn in *The Wild Rose* (1902). As she is not listed among the opening-night cast, she must have replaced Marie Cahill during the show's 136-performance run.

Carus performed in two productions in the Crystal Gardens atop the Broadway Theatre. She shared the stage with Trixie Friganza, Pat Rooney Jr. and Junie McCree in *Mid Summer Night's Fancies: The Darling of the Gallery Gods* (1903), a spoof of *The Darling of the Gods.* The following season, 1904, Emma went downstairs into the Broadway Theatre proper to star in *The Medal and the Maid.*

In 1905, Emma married Harry James Everall, a Gotham businessman. She was also the star of *Woodland* (1904–05), which played half its 166 performance run at the New York Theatre and was switched into the Herald Square Theatre for the remainder.

Emma was among the cast of notables enticed from vaudeville and its relatively higher salaries to the lower-paying *The Follies of 1907* at the New York Theatre Roof Garden (renamed Jardin de Paris for the occasion).

The cut in pay that the *Follies* presented did not deter performers who toured most of the year away from their families. The opportunity to live at home or in a rented apartment in New York rather than traipse around the country from one hotel to another was worth it. Carus was joined in *The Follies of 1907* by vaudeville veterans Grace La Rue, Mlle Dazie, Charlie Ross and Harry Watson Jr. The first edition of what became Florenz Ziegfeld's annual revue ran a respectable 70 performances, during which time it transferred to the Liberty Theatre for a fortnight and to the Grand Opera House for a final week.

Carus' next two shows were produced by Lew Fields in partnership with the Shuberts. *Up and Down Broadway* (1910) costarred Emma with the legendary Eddie Foy. As the Greek muse of tragedy, Emma descended from her heavenly perch to civilize the denizens of Broadway. Yet it was Emma the muse who was corrupted by Broadway's lighthearted delights. *The Wife Hunters* (1911) barely lasted four weeks and marked her final Broadway show. Thereafter, Emma Carus chose to work in vaudeville, which she did until she retired in the 1920s.

CHARLIE CASE

b: ca. 1860—d: 1916, New York, NY

According to those who were old-timers even before vaudeville peaked, Charlie Case was one of the finest storytellers in vaudeville. Little is known about him, and what is comes from three chronicles: *Vaudeville: From the Honky-Tonks to the Palace* by Joe Laurie Jr., *American Vaudeville: Its Life and Times* by Douglas Gilbert, and *One Hundred Years of the Negro in Show Business* by Tom Fletcher. So little is known about Case that Tom Fletcher cites Case as an example of a white comedian in blackface; Douglas Gilbert speaks of Case as a Negro; and Joe Laurie Jr. explains that Case's father was Irish and his mother was African American.

Case began his days in variety working the tough concert saloons of the 1870s, yet he did not employ the violent roughhouse of the two-man physical comics that was a mainstay of barroom entertainment nor the coarse language and leering jokes of the usual monologist playing slabs and dumps. Instead, once out on the stage, he drew up a chair, sat down and fidgeted with a piece of string as he began talking. At one time, some of Case's monologues were published. Posterity is indebted to Gilbert for putting a portion of one of them in his book, *American Vaudeville.* In part, it reads: "Father was a peculiar man. Us children never understood him. Mother understood him. Mother could always tell when father'd been drinking. We couldn't tell. We used to think he was dead."

As was the custom of the time, he blacked up. Toward the end of his career, around 1910, he ceased applying black greasepaint. He played small-time vaudeville while other, younger black vaudevillians like Bert Williams and Ernest Hogan were starring in the *Follies* or in musical comedy.

Reports of his death differ widely. According to Gilbert, Charlie Case died of tuberculosis. Gilbert does allow that Case was melancholy; he was easily depressed by an inattentive or indifferent audience, and his manager had to coax Case into returning to the stage for his next performance.

According to Joe Laurie Jr., Case was working Loew's time when he died in his midtown Manhattan hotel room. Laurie wrote that the official report stated that Charlie was killed while cleaning his revolver, often a cover story for suicide. At home in Larchmont, outside New York City, his wife dropped dead at the news.

CASINO THEATRE

In 1882, when the Casino was built on Broadway at the corner of 39th Street in Manhattan, it was considered too far uptown to attract clientele. By the time it was torn down in 1930, there were 80 theatres closer to Times Square, the new center of theatrical life, and the Casino was considered too far downtown to do business.

Its seven- or eight-story tower, designed like a squat minaret, made the Casino the most exotic theatre that New York had ever seen. Its Moorish-influenced design carried through its interior as well as its terracotta facade. The building housed a 1,300-seat theatre, a café and the first known roof garden in the USA. Inside, the plaster ornamentation was painted in gold and studded with fake gemstones.

The Casino hosted everything from grand opera and operetta to musical comedy, revue and polite vaudeville, but vaudeville of any disposition played a small role in the 50 years that the Casino existed.

The Casino's true connection with vaudeville was as a home for musical comedy and revue. Many performers graduated from supporting roles in Casino productions to headliners' salaries in vaudeville: Lillian Russell, David Warfield, Fay Templeton, Francis Wilson and Marie Dressler among them.

The Casino started off wobbly. Construction was not finished when the audience arrived for the opening production, an operetta. After a decade of admirable yet not always successful productions of operetta, Rudolph Aronson, the resident manager-producer, instituted polite vaudeville, which also failed to draw. The owners brought in the management team of Canary & Lederer. The more active partner, George Lederer, began as a sketch writer for vaudeville, moved to the other side of the game as a reviewer for the *New York Journal,* then turned to production and management with a couple of partners, Thomas Canary, the best known.

During the decade that Lederer ran the house (and sometimes directed its shows), the Casino Theatre set a standard for revues (*The Passing Show,* 1894) and advanced the form of the American musical comedy (*The Belle of New York,* 1897). The Lederer shows were Weberfields' greatest competition. In 1899, Lederer produced *Floradora,* one of the most famous shows in Broadway history.

In 1903, the Shubert organization took control of the Casino and ran it for a quarter of a century until they demolished it. Two years into their management, the Casino was badly burned and needed to be reconstructed.

VERNON & IRENE CASTLE

Vernon Castle

b: (Vernon Blyth) 2 May 1887, Norwich, England—d: 15 February 1918, Fort Worth, TX

Irene Castle

b: (Irene Foote) 7 April 1893, New Rochelle, NY—d: 25 January 1969, Eureka Springs, AK

The dancing Castles enjoyed meteoric, brief but fantastic success. Until they danced onto the scene, ballroom dance was suspect in certain circles that laid claim to respectability. There was the misgiving that women who waltzed publicly were flamboyant at best and the men unmanly.

The Castles shattered that perception. Irene set the fashion for women of most classes: no corsets, little or no jewelry, flowing gowns, bobbed hair. Although not as good looking as his wife, Vernon was down to earth, manly and debonair all at once: what women hoped for in a man, what many men tried to be. Their dance band, including the leader, was made up of African American musicians, all of whom were permitted to dress and act as serious musicians, not minstrel clowns. The Castles and their musicians drew the patronage of high society and the applause of audiences in vaudeville.

Marrying in 1911 and teaming in 1912, the Castles represented a lighthearted but real image of American society that was leaving the Victorian and Edwardian eras to history and embracing a new American culture that accommodated the *new woman,* the *new Negro,* the *new psychology,* an acknowledgement of sexuality, and the interplay between the high and low of art and society. Vernon and Irene were entertainers, not social critics or revolutionaries, and that is why they succeeded. They were agents of change for the sake of change. The rush to be a new something was an expression of optimism and joy toward the modern world, not a preachment of how to achieve a better society.

Vernon Castle, a well-regarded dancer and comedian, was born and raised in England. Vernon had a degree in engineering but longed for the stage. After he arrived in New York, his brother-in-law, Laurence Grossmith, urged Vernon to audition for the chorus in *About Town* (1906), a Lew Fields show in which Grossmith was a featured player. Lew Fields, a fine physical comedian, saw that Vernon possessed an antic sense as well as dancing ability and expanded Vernon's part. Not only was Fields a mentor, as Broadway's busiest producer, his shows were a source of regular and well-paid employment. The two men became friends, and Vernon Castle remained with Lew Fields for four seasons.

Vernon was a reliable eccentric dancer, whose tipsy souse routines were guaranteed audience pleasers, and a comedy actor specializing in silly-billy roles. Among Vernon's appearances in Lew Fields' shows were *The Girl Behind the Counter* (1907), *The Midnight Sons* (1908), *Old Dutch* (1909) and *The Summer Widowers* (1910).

Irene had almost no stage experience when she met Vernon. She pestered him to arrange an audition for her with Lew Fields. Vernon arranged the audition, but Irene did not impress Fields. When a woman in a bit role left *The Summer Widowers,* Irene became her replacement very late in the show's run. She had a few lines, no songs and no dances. This was the first show in which Vernon and Irene appeared together. Vernon was a star. Irene was low on the totem pole. She shared a dressing room with another youngster, Helen Hayes, who became a future First Lady of the American Theatre. Vernon and Irene were about to tour in the show when Lee Shubert, Fields' financial partner, pulled the show off the road and mothballed it.

The Hen Pecks (1911) was Vernon's last show under his mentor's management. At the end of its first season's run, Vernon and Irene were married and went to England to visit his family. Unlike her husband, who combined flair with good humor, his folks were plain and gentle folk; his dad ran the local pub. Irene, in her memoir, confessed she was a spoiled brat whose first impressions were of dowdily dressed Englishwomen and homely houses. The Castles returned to New York in time to ready themselves for the August reopening of *The Hen Pecks.* Once again, Irene was a cast replacement.

Irene, a New Rochelle debutante, thought herself modern and grew up in a relatively liberal family. Still, she wanted no part of low comedy, and she was disappointed that Vernon had spent five years playing second fiddle to Lew Fields in farces. Irene wanted glamour and dance, like her idol, Bessie McCoy. During the tour of *The Hen Pecks* later that autumn, Vernon was offered a role in a revue in Paris. Vernon accepted with the proviso that Irene be included.

The trip to Paris in 1912 was part vacation because of the long wait for the producers to start rehearsals. Their time with the show—appropriately titled *Enfin . . . une Revue (Finally . . . a Revue)*—was short. The Castles went into the famed Café de Paris as a specialty dance act, faking their way through the latest American dance crazes such as the turkey trot, grizzly bear and the Texas Tommy. They were well received, invited to the races and soirees, and treated like guests at posh shindigs even when they were paid to perform.

They had left the USA as Vernon Castle and wife; they returned as Vernon and Irene, the Dancing Castles. The Castles were hardly American household names in 1912 and 1913, but the international set certainly knew them and could be counted on to attend their performances in Manhattan at Café de l'Opéra. They became the darlings of New York's café society.

Vernon provided the energy and dash; Irene was the trendsetter and the one who handled business. When she bobbed her hair, it started a trend. She was lithe; her figure foreshadowed the flapper's and replaced the buxom beauties typified by Lillian Russell. She had to be able to dance in the dresses she wore, so she wore simplified, softly draped gowns. When her bob did not stay flat against her head, she improvised a headband. Within a month, so did millions of young women. Everything she did started a fashion.

Vernon could sing, act and play comedy very well. Irene could not. They both danced divinely, but the disparity in their other talents made integrating both of them into a musical comedy script difficult. Irene's parts were never integral to the plot. To their repertoire of ragtime dances and waltzes and trots, they added the tango and created the (one-step, up-on-your-toes) Castle walk. Everything they danced became a fad. Famous, they returned to Paris and Deauville in 1913 for extended engagements.

Although Irene, holding a perfumed handkerchief to her nose, denied that the Castles performed much in vaudeville, the facts differ. At one time, in 1914, they were doubling at Hammerstein's Victoria and the Palace, a few blocks apart on Broadway. In their vaudeville days, they had their own 12-piece band. Vernon had hired James Reese Europe to assemble and lead it. When the musicians in the Victoria pit band refused to yield their places to Negro musicians, Vernon installed Reese and company up center on the stage. Once again, the Castles started a fad; having a black band onstage became quite the vogue for white vaudeville singers and dance acts. (Ford Dabney and his black orchestra succeeded Jim Europe's with the Castles.)

Irene had a good reason for looking down at vaudeville. She had seen too many animal acts in which the bears, monkeys, dogs or other animals were beaten and kept caged all day until showtime. Irene and Vernon purchased a number of these abused animals and placed them in better homes. Often even a zoo was a better alternative than vaudeville for an animal. Later in her life, Irene Castle became active in animal welfare, although, oddly, she continued to wear feathers and furs.

So strong a draw in 1914 were the Castles that they commanded $31,000 for one week of one-night stands. That same year, they opened Castle House, where they, or rather their staff, taught ballroom dancing to the hoi polloi. The Castles themselves gave private instruction to social lions and lionesses for fabulous fees that rivaled or surpassed their vaudeville and café earnings. They also opened a resort, Castles by the Sea, which they promoted by incorporating the place into a silent film *(Castles by the Sea)* that they made in 1914. Confirmed urban denizens could patronize the Castles' supper club, the Sans Souci, in Times Square.

Vernon & Irene Castle played the Palace again in 1915. The years 1914 and 1915 were their heyday. There were many ballroom dance teams in vaudeville, but the Castles had a way of keeping the public's attention and affection. There were those public voices of church, state and private soapboxes that decried ballroom dancing. The Castles were never targeted. They were chaste even when dancing the tango.

When, in the summer of 1914, Vernon and Irene had returned to holiday in France, the atmosphere had changed markedly. There was frisson in the air. Troops on their way toward some anticipated front were clogging the railways and roadways.

They had to return to New York that autumn to fulfill their contract with Charles Dillingham to appear in Irving Berlin's first Broadway show, *Watch Your Step.* It opened in December 1914 and ran through spring 1915 and then went on tour. The revue or musical comedy (the critics could not make up their minds about *Watch Your Step*) allowed Vernon to show more of his talent than his participation in the dance team, yet he was distracted. The European war consumed him. He decided to enlist when his obligation with the show permitted, and he took flying lessons with the hope he would take part in aerial combat in France.

Vernon and Irene's marriage was odd in some particulars. Both had their admirers with whom they used to dine and dance, but although Mrs. Castle was frank in her autobiography about the matter, it is not quite clear how innocent these flirtations became. They split their salaries, and each managed his own finances, which is to say Irene spent and saved and Vernon spent or gave away his share. When Vernon enlisted, he was broke, yet he had earned a few thousand dollars a week in *Watch Your Step.* A farewell concert was arranged with John Philip Sousa; Vernon needed the cash, although Irene made him a present of several thousand dollars.

Vernon went to England, was given his wings as an airman and spent six months flying battle sorties over the enemy lines. Irene made a movie, one of the adventure serials, like *The Perils of Pauline,* that had proved so popular. During his leave, they met in London and were pressed into being one of the acts on a benefit bill. It was their last dance together.

Vernon was sent back to the United States to teach flying in Fort Worth, Texas. Training young flyers meant suffering through accidents small and serious. Vernon survived one serious accident; he died in the next crash.

Had he lived, it is doubtful the Castles could have revived and long sustained the public's enthusiasm for their careers. The years following the First World War were vastly different from the Castles heyday, and the coming jazz age was not a tolerant host to genteel dance acts. Optimism about the new everything had died on battlefields. Innocent exuberance was supplanted in some people by wary cynicism and in others by angry righteousness.

When Irene tried to revive her career as a solo act or with a new partner, there was not much interest. In 1939, RKO made a film about their lives and careers, *The Story of Vernon and Irene Castle.* Fred Astaire was a natural to play Vernon; physically and stylistically there was a strong resemblance. Ginger Rogers took the role of Irene. Irene did not approve, and she was right. Ginger was a great dancer, actor and comedian, but she was not like Irene Castle and did not try to be in the movie.

CATCHER

In an aerial or acrobatic act, the catcher is the partner who catches the flyer, and is usually the strongest member of the act.

CATCHING FLIES

A term most often used among comedians and comedy actors to describe a certain type of unprofessional behavior by another actor or comedian, *catching flies* refers to the often deliberate fidgeting with hands or props by one performer to take the attention away from another performer or actor who has the lines at the moment. Rightly, this was considered unethical because it undermined rather than supported the performer who was speaking. Musical-comedy stars also employed the term to complain about restless or careless movement by chorus people while the star was performing a number.

WALTER CATLETT

b: 4 February 1889, San Francisco, CA—d: 4 November 1960, Los Angeles, CA

Walter Catlett was one of the more memorable character actors in Hollywood movies in a day when character actors were among the most valuable assets possessed by any studio.

Balding, bespectacled, fidgety Walter Catlett was tucked into a Hollywood casting type of blustery, larcenous windbags that included Edward Arnold, Guy Kibbee, Frank Morgan, Raymond Walburn and Charlie Winninger.

Catlett was far more versatile than Hollywood gave him the opportunity to demonstrate, but that was true of most former vaudevillians who went to movie land and discovered if they concentrated on offering a particular characterization that producers remembered them when they were casting similar roles. Brand names always sold well to producers and audiences. It was hardly a sacrifice, though, for many had done some variant of the same act for years in vaudeville, and the movies paid well.

Walter Catlett was tall, rather funereal looking, like a somber Ed Wynn. His large, bright eyes clearly conveyed triumph, delight, suspicion, confusion or fear. His voice sounded as though it once had been rich and melodic but had coarsened from too many cigars.

Indeed, his voice had been his mainstay when, as a child, he began in show business singing and acting in Gilbert & Sullivan operettas. When his voice changed, he turned to boxing only long enough to be discouraged and bunged up. He then washed out of the U.S. Marine Corps when his eyesight began to deteriorate, perhaps from too many blows to the noggin. He went back into show business, determined to make it to Broadway, which he did in 1911 at the Lyric Theatre in *The Prince of Pilsen.* Walter appeared in vaudeville between his Broadway shows. In the course of 16 years between 1911 and 1927, Catlett appeared in more than a dozen operettas and musical comedies. The more successful included *So Long, Letty* (1916), which starred Charlotte Greenwood; *The Ziegfeld Follies of 1917,* with Fanny Brice, W. C. Fields, Bert Williams and Eddie Cantor; *Sally* (1920), with Marilyn Miller and Leon Errol; *Lady Be Good* (1924), starring Fred & Adele Astaire (Catlett sang the title song); and *Rio Rita* (1927), in which he replaced Robert Woolsey, who was rather an imitation of Catlett instead of the other way round.

No doubt, Walter Catlett endeared himself to many performers when, during rehearsals for *Little Miss Simplicity* (1918), J. J. Shubert clambered onto the stage to holler and take a swing at Walter. Instead, former boxer Catlett slugged Jake Shubert and knocked him into the orchestra pit. Many a director, comedian, dancer, singer or musician who had been abused by the youngest Shubert brother must have been cheered that Walter Catlett had made a down payment on their revenge.

Offstage, Walter Catlett was a gregarious and amusing companion. Joe Laurie Jr. related that a certain vaudevillian, proud of his capacity, bragged to Catlett that he drank a fifth of whiskey a day, Walter brought him up short: "I spill that much."

As Hollywood began making movies that talked, Walter Catlett decided that might be the place for him; after years of good performances on Broadway, he still was not commanding lead comedy roles. He had made three silent features in New York, so Catlett was not unfamiliar with the medium. Once in Hollywood, he hung out his shingle as a dialogue writer as well as a character comedian and got work as both.

It proved a profitable move for him. In the three decades between 1929 and 1957, Walter played featured roles in 138 movies that ranged from slapstick to screwball comedy to musicals to dramas. Among the more important films that Catlett helped spark were *The Front Page* (1931), *Platinum Blonde* (1931), *Back Street* (1932), *Rain* (1932), *A Tale of Two Cities* (1935), *Mr. Deeds Goes to Town* (1936), *Cain and Mabel* (1936), *Bringing Up Baby* (1938), *Yankee Doodle Dandy* (1942) and *Friendly Persuasion* (1956).

Catlett was seen at his best in smaller-scale comedies in which his larger roles allowed him a chance to flesh out his character and engage in good comic business with other top comedians. He was memorable as a nightclub emcee in *Every Night at Eight* (1935), added to the Ritz Brothers' mayhem in *On the Avenue* (1937), crossed wisecracks with Ned Sparks in *Wake Up and Live* (1937)—Walter's third film with Alice Faye, traded dialogue with Mae West in *Every Day's a Holiday* (1937), supported Bob Hope in *They Got*

Me Covered (1943) and Danny Kaye in both *Up in Arms* (1943) and *The Inspector General* (1949), tried to con Olsen & Johnson in *Ghost Catchers* (1944), and gave a fine impersonation of Governor Al Smith (whom he closely resembled) in *Beau James* (1957), in which Bob Hope portrayed Mayor Jimmy Walker of New York.

Walter Catlett never stopped working from the year he arrived in Hollywood until his last role as Al Smith. He died three years later after a stroke.

JOSEPH CAWTHORN

b: 29 March 1868, New York, NY— d: 21 January 1949, Los Angeles, CA

Born into a minstrel-show family, Joseph Cawthorn was three years old when he first corked up to appear as a pickaninny in a minstrel show at Robinson's Hall in Manhattan. Certainly, neither he nor his brother Herbert were old enough to travel on their own after being engaged to tour as picks in Haverly's Mastodon Minstrels, so a parent was likely in the show as well. In 1876, eight-year-old Joseph was still with Haverly's when the minstrels traveled to England for engagements in music-halls and in Christmas pantomimes.

Joseph and Herbert returned to the USA in 1880, and the two brothers formed a blackface act to play vaudeville for the next three or four seasons. It was based on their minstrel work: some singing and dancing and a growing amount of comic byplay. The two boys were then hired to take *Little Nugget,* a musical, on tour in 1883.

Joseph went into burlesque during the mid-1880s, first as the lead comedian in Patti Rosa's company, then in the same position for the Gladys Wallis Company. Thereafter, he starred or was featured in a series of 27 musical comedies and spoofs from 1899 until 1922. He starred in touring shows like *A Fool for Luck* (1895), *Excelsior, Jr.* (1896) and *Miss Philadelphia* (1897).

In 1897, Cawthorn won a leading role in his first Broadway show in *Nature,* a production that played the Academy of Music. His next Broadway show, *The Fortune Teller* (1898), did little for him, but two Casino Theatre productions under the guidance of George Lederer, *The Rounders* (a comic opera by John Philip Sousa) and *The Singing Girl* (both 1899), were good showcases if not long runs. Those were followed by two extravaganzas. *The Sleeping Beauty and the Beast* (1901) was a substantial hit in its time, racking up 241 performances. *Mother Goose* (1903) lasted 105 performances. Cawthorn's specialty had become playing star comedy roles in musical comedy and comic opera.

Fritz in Tammany Hall (1905) and *The Free Lance* (1906) did not last long. Nor did *The Hoyden* (1907), but that show was notable for its early appearances of two great stars of the future: Elsie Janis and Mae Murray. Joe wrote lyrics for several songs in the show. Victor Herbert's musicalization of Windsor McKay's popular comic strip *Little Nemo* ran three months at the New Amsterdam in 1908. *Girlies* (1910) that followed was of small consequence.

The Slim Princess, produced by Dillingham, reunited Cawthorn with Elsie Janis and marked the first show that Joe played with his wife, Queenie Vassar. It ran three months at the Globe Theatre.

Cawthorn was a bit overshadowed in *The Sunshine Girl* (1913) by the dance team of Vernon & Irene Castle, then entering into the height of their fame. *The Girl from Utah* (1914) gave Joe a solid 15-week run at the Knickerbocker Theatre and teamed him with Julia Sanderson, with whom he shared the stage in *Sybil* (1916), another modest run. *Rambler Rose* (1917) lasted two months, but *The Canary* (1918, with Dixon & Doyle) kept the box office busy for five months. Joe did not appear on Broadway again until 1920, when *The Half Moon* kept him on the boards for six weeks. In 1920, he returned again to the Great White Way for four weeks at the Selwyn in *The Blue Kitten* (1922, with Robert Woolsey).

In 1927, 60-year-old Joe Cawthorn got a bit of a jump on other Broadwayites and vaudevillians who headed to Hollywood once sound revolutionized the motion-picture industry. Joe appeared in five silents and was established as a featured player when studios began to grind out talking programmers. Often playing German businessmen, he appeared in another 50 pictures between 1928 and 1942, and he made his home in Hollywood for the last 20 years of his life. His best-known roles were as Gremio, Katherine's elderly suitor in Shakespeare's (and Mary Pickford's, Douglas Fairbanks Sr.'s and Sam Taylor's) *The Taming of the Shrew* (1929); in *Love Me Tonight* (1932), with Maurice Chevalier and Jeanette MacDonald; *Naughty Marietta* (1935), with Nelson Eddy and Jeanette MacDonald; *Gold Diggers of 1935; The Great Ziegfeld* (1936), playing Florenz Ziegfeld's father; and as conductor Walter Damrosch in the biopic *Lillian Russell* (1940).

When he died of a stroke, two months shy of his 81st birthday, Joseph Cawthorn left behind his 79-year-old wife, Queenie Vassar, a former musical star of the 1890s. Vassar did not make any movies until the 1940s, when in her 70s she appeared in three. She died two weeks short of her 90th birthday.

CHANG & ENG

b: 11 May 1811, Meklong, Siam (Thailand)—d: 17 January 1874, White Plains, NC

Born near Bangkok, the conjoined twins were three quarters Chinese and one quarter Siamese. As children, they worked, as did their eight sisters and brothers, especially after the death of their father in 1819. Chang and Eng sold coconuts and eggs to ships that entered the Bangkok port. In 1824, a Scottish trader spotted the twins, who were joined at the chest, and told Abel Coffin, a showman, about them. In 1829, Coffin persuaded the twins to accompany him to Europe and North America and exhibit themselves for money.

The brothers made a lot of money and never seemed to regret their choice. They did not have an act, and never appeared in vaudeville, but they were one of the most famous attractions in nineteenth-century show business. They shared only one organ, the liver, and medical professionals claim that the two men could have been separated successfully had they lived in the twenty-first century. In their day, however, that was not a viable option.

They were first exhibited in Boston as "The Chinese Twins," and for the next half-dozen years or so, they traveled in Europe and the USA and reputedly had made $60,000 by 1839. They took their earnings and bought two adjoining tobacco plantations in North Carolina, where Change and Eng married two sisters, Adelaide and Sarah Yates, respectively, and produced 21 children between the two families. Chang and Eng became citizens of the USA in 1844 and assumed the surname of Bunker.

P. T. Barnum persuaded Chang and Eng to resume their exhibition careers under his banner. When, by 1860, the brothers needed money to educate their many children, they agreed to work for Barnum, and they appeared at his American Museum in Manhattan. Conflicts arose. Chang was the dominant brother and was argumentative. At the conclusion of their six-week contract, Chang & Eng retired to their farms, but the ruin of the southern economy by the end of the Civil War forced them to work again for Barnum. A tour of England followed in 1868.

In 1870, Chang, a heavy drinker, suffered a stroke, and Eng assumed the burden of physically supporting his brother's body and weight. Chang contracted what was thought to be pneumonia, and he died on 17 January 1874. Three to four hours later, Eng died.

CHAPEAUGRAPHY

The skill of manipulating hats, either juggling them as Gus Kiralfo did or twisting them into various shapes and styles.

CHARLIE CHAPLIN

b: (Charles Spencer Chaplin) 16 April 1889, London, England—d: 25 December 1977, Vevey, Switzerland

Charlie Chaplin remains a hallmark of popular entertainment made into art. He was a brilliant performer whose work deeply touched a broad range of people, from the untutored to the intelligentsia. In the 1910s and 1920s, when he was at his peak as a comedian, his comedy directly and indirectly addressed the human condition without becoming propaganda or preachment. Later, that changed.

The adventures of Chaplin's Tramp shone the spotlight on the contradictions and conflicts that had existed before the American century and continued to abound in the USA until the New Deal: robber barons of industry prospering amid Dickensian social conditions, Victorian certitude versus freethinking, and widely held racist and nativist sentiments in a nation of immigrants. Charlie's Tramp was not a revolutionary or agent for social change; he was old world in appearance and manner. The primary motivations of "The Little Fellow," as Charlie also called his character, were saving his skin and stuffing a decent meal under it. Once safe and fed, he became a more complex fellow: one part romantic poet, deeply desiring beauty and love, at odds with both social convention and modernity, and another part outlaw, defying authority and lying, scrapping, cheating and stealing to survive and remain an individual.

Most people understood Charlie's Tramp, and he served as a cinematic surrogate. Ordinary people everywhere yearned for the exquisite feelings that truth, beauty, selfless love and compassion prompted in the Tramp, but more often their daily struggles and their limits, like the Tramp's, evoked the baser instincts for survival, competition, sex, carefree fun and revenge for the humiliations to which they were regularly subjected.

The Little Fellow was in Chaplin's marrow. Chaplin was born in London, south of the Thames, in modest circumstances that grew dire. His parents were music-hall performers, rather successful by Charlie's

Charlie Chaplin

account. Before Charlie was born, his father, for whom Charlie later was named, had known Charlie's mother, Hannah Hill, personally as well as professionally, before she married someone else and moved to South Africa, where she gave birth to Charlie's half brother, Sydney (1885–1965). After she returned to London husbandless, Charles and Hannah resumed their romance and were married, according to Charlie, in 1886. By 1894, Charlie's fifth year, their lives turned mean.

Over the years, Chaplin told the story of his childhood several times, including in his early ghostwritten and unauthentic memoirs and his much later book, *My Autobiography.* Charlie claimed to recall occasions when Hannah and Charles would bring fellow entertainers home at night and rouse little Charlie, then two or three years old, to perform for the adults. His parents separated about this same time.

Hannah continued to work the halls as a singer until she began to have problems with her voice. By the time Charlie was five (and Syd was nine), Hannah could no longer perform and was reduced to taking in sewing to support her family. Charles Sr. was supposed to contribute weekly to their support, but payments from him grew less regular and finally ceased as he, too, gradually became unemployable.

Hannah's increasing incapacity was a blend of the psychological and the physical. Charlie described his mother's last stage appearance, which was his first. Her voice gave way midturn, and the manager pulled Charlie onstage to complete her spot. Chaplin remembered that he scored a success and that the stage was showered with money. Yet the family's situation continued to deteriorate. Had young Charlie been a success, Hannah would have been able to secure other bookings for him, because child performers, if they had a measure of charm and talent, were received sympathetically by music-hall audiences.

Instead, the family situation worsened. They moved to ever-smaller quarters, ending in a small garret room. Finally, Hannah applied to have all three of them admitted to the Lambeth Workhouse, a Dickensian institution that segregated the boys from their mother. The misery increased when the boys were sent to an orphanage. Charlie was six.

The next few years were dreadful. Hannah was committed to the Cane Hill lunatic asylum, and the court ordered Charles Sr. to assume care and custody of the boys. Living with another woman and father to her son, Charles Sr. spent most of his time at a tavern, and his mate, also a drunk, was obliged to accept Charlie and Syd into her home. Fortunately, Hannah rallied and reclaimed Syd and Charlie.

Charles Sr. arranged Charlie's official debut on the stage as one of "John W. Jackson's Eight Lancashire Lads," a young troupe of clog dancers. Young Charlie toured with the act for a while and appeared in a Christmas pantomime, but, when the job ended, he drifted into a series of minor civilian jobs, much like the type his older brother Sydney was working.

Charlie's father, severely alcoholic, died at age 37. Impoverished and malnourished, the boys' mother again broke down and again was committed. Charlie was 12.

A few months later, Sydney returned to London after working a cruise ship and falling ill in Cape Town. He confided to Charlie that he intended to become an actor. Charlie decided that he, too, would return to the stage. Against the odds, Charlie was hired to play important parts in two touring plays; one was a summer tour and the other was in *Sherlock Holmes,* starring H. A. Saintsbury. As Charlie's education had been sketchy, Syd had to read the part to Charlie so that he could memorize his cues and lines. Later, Sydney joined the cast in a small role. The first tour lasted 40 weeks, and then there was a second and third tour.

Hannah temporarily returned to health, and the boys were now able to support her, but she had lapses, and eventually they paid for her care in a private sanatorium until, located in Hollywood and at the peak of their careers in 1920, Syd and Charlie brought her to Los Angeles, where she lived comfortably until her death around 1927.

Meanwhile, in 1905, Charlie was summoned to London to act in a William Gillette curtain raiser. When the main play failed, Gillette, a prominent American actor, revived his most popular production for the London stage. It was *Sherlock Holmes,* and Charlie played Billy. He was 16 years old and had arrived as a featured player in London's West End, but, after the run ended, he was out of stage work for nearly a year.

Syd, however, had joined a knockabout comedy act headed by Charlie Manon. In this company, he was spotted by Fred Karno and hired for one of Karno's troupes. For many years, Fred Karno's was the standard in physical comedy acts. He discovered and engaged some of the top comedians of his era for his dozen or more companies that played music-hall and pantomime.

At last, Charlie got work in a small-time act, Casey's Circus, as one of the juveniles in a sketch called "Casey's Court." Once Syd was secure in his job with Karno, he arranged for Karno to see his brother in the Casey act. Karno was impressed enough to engage Charlie for a trial period. It was 1907, and Charlie was 18. Both Syd and Charlie stayed with Karno for a few years but in different companies. In 1909, Charlie went with Karno's Speechless Comedians troupe to Paris; the lead comic was the great Dan Leno, who was a major influence on Charlie. In 1910, Chaplin headed another company that went to America.

Chaplin arrived determined to stay in the USA. The Karno company's bookings did not extend beyond several weeks at Proctor vaudeville houses in and around Manhattan, however. It was not the first time a Karno company had played vaudeville in the USA, so the expectation was that other bookings would follow, but management had chosen a repertoire of comic acts that were too English in expression and dialogue for Americans to much enjoy. After six weeks, the Karno company moved on to Sullivan & Considine time, a chain of theatres out West. Along the route were Cleveland, Chicago, St. Louis, Kansas City, Denver, Minneapolis, St. Paul, Winnipeg, Billings, Butte, Vancouver, Seattle, Tacoma, Portland, San Francisco, Los Angeles and Salt Lake City, after which they returned to New York City. By this time, they had refined their repertoire and jettisoned those sketches that proved difficult for American audiences.

A surprise awaited them in New York. Instead of returning to England, they were given six weeks in William Morris' theatres, then 20 weeks again playing Sullivan & Considine. Of the several sketches in their repertoire that they played at Morris' theatres, one of them, "A Night in an English Music Hall" (known in Britain as the "Mumming Birds"), piqued Mack Sennett's interest. Sennett was working for film director D. W. Griffith and had yet to start his Keystone fun factory in Hollywood, but after Sennett saw the Karno troupe at Morris' American Theatre, he made a mental note of Charlie Chaplin.

Until he joined Karno, much of Chaplin's theatre work had been dramatic acting. Karno was his comedy college. In the four years that Charlie remained with Karno, he learned a lot from the many fine older comedians in the company, especially Fred Kitchen, and Charlie had the opportunity to be inventive, following his own impulses onstage and learning from the results.

After a return to England and a reunion with Syd, who had played the English provinces with another Karno troupe, Charlie returned to America in 1913. This time, he received an offer from the Keystone film company. Charlie signed a contract to make three movie shorts each week, for which he was paid $150 a week (twice his Karno salary). He began filming at Keystone in 1914. It took him a while to find a character. At first, he played sly and deceitful villains. Seeking to develop a recognizable character that would establish him at the box office, he gradually arrived at the Tramp look. He began snipping the ends off the Fu Manchu mustache he had been wearing until it was cropped into his trademark brush mustache. Both Charlie and legend insist that he borrowed Roscoe "Fatty" Arbuckle's too-large trousers; the too-small coat and hat as well as the large slap shoes and the cane were found elsewhere in dressing rooms.

There are many versions of Chaplin's relations with the Sennett funny farm (the studio was situated in a complex of former farm buildings). Mack's comics were outgoing comics who had come into films as circus clowns and ex-prizefighters or started as stunt men. Boiled down, some of the Keystone folks, especially Sennett's directors, found Chaplin a bit too standoffish and too eager to stand out as an individual than to perform as a member of a team. Chaplin, in turn, considered the Keystone lot a factory that ground out frantic pictures with crude mechanistic gags. Although Sennett was a firm boss, if a comedian was as determined as Chaplin to control his own work and had the talent and skill to deliver a funny picture, Keystone was a good place to learn how to make movies. After a slow start at Keystone, Chaplin turned into their biggest moneymaker, but Charlie had gotten a better offer. After one year with Keystone, making three dozen shorts, Charlie switched studios. Before he gave notice, he got Syd a job with Sennett. Syd and his wife moved to Los Angeles.

In November that same year, Charlie Chaplin signed with Essanay Pictures for $1,250 per week to make 14 films during 1915. He was now in charge of preparing, directing and starring in his own films. The Essanay flickers were an artistic step forward from the Keystone product, but Charlie hit his zenith at Mutual Film Corporation during the following two years, 1916 and 1917. He turned out 12 comedies, most of which were brilliant and funnier than any comedies that anyone else in Hollywood was making. *The Floorwalker, The Rink, One A.M., The Cure, Easy Street* and *The Immigrant* became classics. For his golden dozen Mutual two-reelers, Charlie was paid $10,000 per week plus a signing bonus of $150,000. In the span of two years, Chaplin's salary had skyrocketed from less than $10,000 for his year at Keystone to $675,000 annually at Mutual.

Then, in 1917, he left Mutual for First National Pictures, where he was paid $1,075,000 a year for a trio of two-reelers (*A Day's Pleasure, The Idle Class* and *Pay Day*), three shorts at three reels (*A Dog's Life, Shoulder Arms* and *Sunnyside*), one at four reels *(The Pilgrim),* and his first feature, *The Kid,* at six reels. *The Kid* marked a turning point for Chaplin. It combined melodrama, pathos and comedy—perhaps more successfully than the later features—and Chaplin allowed Jackie Coogan in the title role to be as important in the film as the Tramp, something that never happened again. (In 1914, Chaplin had appeared in a Keystone feature, *Tillie's Punctured Romance,* but Marie Dressler was the star of that movie, and Charlie was one of several supporting players.)

Charlie Chaplin

Chaplin's fame was so universal that the Tramp became the lead character in a comic strip, a dozen or so songs made mention of him, products such as statuettes and toys were made with his visage on them, and any amateur contest between 1915 and 1925 was sure to attract at least one Chaplin imitator. He captured the public imagination the way Elvis Presley and the Beatles did several generations later, but Chaplin's Tramp became a public icon without the power of mass-communications marketing that propelled Elvis and the Beatles into worldwide commodities. In the French-speaking world, he was called Charlot; in Spanish-speaking countries, he was known as Carlito. He became a figure and face familiar to audiences from Shanghai to Cape Town to Mexico City.

Sydney Chaplin also made a number of films, including a well-received *Charley's Aunt,* and he became Charlie's business manager and confidante as well. The half brothers had been close ever since they were children, and Charlie trusted no one as he trusted Syd.

In 1919, Chaplin joined with Mary Pickford, Douglas Fairbanks Sr. and D. W. Griffith to form United Artists. They were at the end or nearing the end of their contracts with other studios. Movies made by Mary, Doug and Charlie were the biggest box-office earners in Hollywood, and each of the three knew their worth. They decided to control the distribution of their films and thus receive a greater share of their films' earnings. Unfortunately, all three were winding down in productivity. It was a couple of years before United Artists had films to release, and the pipeline was never full of enough product to carry a studio's overhead and earn a substantial profit. All of Chaplin's future movies were released through United Artists—at ever greater invervals—except for *The Countess from Hong Kong,* his last movie. It was made in 1968 for Universal and starred Marlon Brando and Sophia Loren. Chaplin wrote and directed the film and took only a bit role. It was a dud.

The Gold Rush (1925) vies with *City Lights* (1931) as Chaplin's masterpiece in the view of many. *The Circus* (1928) was a good film, but because it was made between *The Gold Rush* and *City Lights,* some critics then and later tended to rate it as minor Chaplin.

Fifteen years after his film debut, the Tramp made his final appearance on the screen in *City Lights* (1931).

Chaplin was 42 when it was released, and the United States had changed markedly since the Tramp first appeared on film. It was time for Chaplin to experiment; recording technology had made sound a must for movies, and radio was nothing but sound, but for this movie Chaplin held to the formula. *City Lights* was silent, and the Tramp's character and situation remained unchanged. Some observers felt a lessening of verve and a continuing creep of sentimentality at the expense of bite and pace. After Mutual, the Tramp got scrubbed up. He looked cleaner and lost his brash manner and vulgar habits.

Many had felt that he had peaked with his short films for Mutual, but the establishment opinion, however, was that *City Lights* was Chaplin's masterpiece. This judgment was ratified a generation later, when, in 1951, a group of big-city critics selected it, upon its rerelease, as the best motion picture of the year. The critics' award was interpreted as a slap at the philistines at the Academy of Motion Pictures Arts & Sciences who had ignored Charlie during his career and at those in the press and federal government who had hounded Chaplin out of the USA.

The Tramp was laid to rest during the lingering Great Depression and buried during the Second World War. The American economy recovered only by revving up the machinery of war. News of death camps extinguished hope that the contrary individual could survive in a military-industrial economy, governed by laws rather than justice, and done so with the acquiescence of a complicit public.

By the mid-1930s, when Chaplin was in the thick of middle age, he had grown ruefully philosophic. A thoughtful man, he understood that the ghosts of his past were not exorcised by success or the most extravagant praise. No longer hopefully or anxiously excited about his future, he knew how the plot of his life had turned out. He had been rich for 20 years and discovered that, despite his egalitarian political stance, he preferred the companionship of young, nubile women and the acquaintance of people who were rich, famous and accepting of their privilege.

The open question for Chaplin was how to extend his career. The Tramp was his alter ego, albeit once or twice removed in time and station. Chaplin's solution was to put the Little Fellow to work in *Modern Times.* As to be expected in a Chaplin film, there were laugh-filled inventive comedy scenes as the Little Fellow (the name Chaplin preferred to call his screen character) tried to survive in the dehumanizing machinery of mass production, and there was the delight of hearing Chaplin, for the first time in a film, as he performed a gibberish music-hall number. By the time he made *The Great Dictator* (1940), he could not stop talking, and some critics spoke of dullness and self-indulgence while praising him for what was seen as a daring burlesk of Hitler, racism and totalitarianism. Actually, The Three Stooges were the first American movie comedians to spoof Hitler (Moe), Mussolini (Curley) and company, but the Stooges had been dismissed as unworthy of critical notice.

Like other major film comedians, Chaplin grew into his role as a writer and director in addition to being a comedian and the star of his films. Understandably, Chaplin, as a blossoming filmmaker, wished to make features; most comedians did. Length allowed a situation to develop into a story, and other characters and subplots took on some of the burden of carrying the story and provided a counterpoint to the required four or five comedy sequences that enlivened a 70- or 80-minute feature. Short films, even three or four reels in length, require taut stories and compact scenes; feature-length pictures gave Chaplin the chance to sprawl, and there were dull stretches in his features.

The dark and harsh look of his short films conveyed the desperation and scheming of the characters along with the milieu. As the features opened up and added scenes from the posh side of the tracks, the bargain look did not suit some scenes. Although there are isolated scenes of pictorial interest in Chaplin's feature films, too much of the scenery betrayed cheesiness redolent of Columbia two-reelers, and some uses of technology seemed primitive. The music Chaplin composed almost begged for tears.

There is a midpoint between moviemaking by committee and the auteur approach. Buster Keaton and Harold Lloyd assembled small teams of creative collaborators who could enhance a film's professional polish and curb its star's potential excesses. Chaplin did the same, but, as time passed, he listened less to his team, and he made films to please himself and those who urged him to fulfill himself as an artist, it seemed, more than for his audiences.

Even in his short films, Charlie introduced melodrama to good effect, balancing pathos with comedy. Once Chaplin began releasing films longer than six reels (approximately 60 minutes), however, he was pulled toward drama. No one faulted Chaplin for wanting to tell his stories in a more serious way, using comedy scenes as leavening rather than the primary element. One problem was that Charlie Chaplin was far better at crafting funny scenes and playing them than he was at drama; another was that his audience wanted to laugh.

Age was a factor. Although he remained in excellent shape physically and could perform comic stunts, the lightning quality of his movement had waned as he duckwalked into his 40s and 50s. Even at 60, he could manage a somersault on the floor, slide into a split and rise as he did in *Limelight,* but those delights accounted for less than a minute in that two-and-a-half-hour film.

Chaplin was too smart about himself as a performer to compete against his younger, lithe self. After *City Lights* and *Modern Times,* an older Chaplin needed to replace his superlative and once-continual whirl of movement with something else. He chose talk, finally and increasingly. Once he found his voice on screen, he grew indulgent. So intent was he to philosophize that he neglected to couch his thoughts into manageable dialogue, so much of the colloquy sounded like a call and response of "Thoughts of the Day."

At the same time, Chaplin slipped out of synchronicity with a public that worshipped at two altars: personal prosperity and enforced standards of community propriety. In the late 1930s and throughout the 1940s, Chaplin's philosophic utterances and his sexual activity began to attract disparaging scrutiny. The opportunistic charge that Charlie Chaplin was a communist was made by incautious politicians of minor talent and major ambition. Politicians and the press successfully sold to the American public this bogus bill of goods wrapped and trimmed with accumulated sexual scandal. His antagonists were abetted by Chaplin himself, who at various times in his life acted heedlessly, either tone-deaf or dismissive of public opinion.

Sharing the wealth was inconsistent with Chaplin's desire for personal wealth. He admitted as much. He was a committed capitalist who recognized that his ambition had been well served by capitalism. Chaplin's attraction to socialist ideals was rather like the average Christian's attraction to Jesus' ideals: lovely sentiments but unlikely to make most self-professed Christians give away their worldly goods. Chaplin trusted more in Switzerland, with its confidential banking codes, than any Soviet paradise promised by Stalin.

Early on, Chaplin had explained to a reporter, "My desire to make money came at an early age when I was growing up in poverty in Lambeth, on the south side of the Thames. I didn't starve, but I didn't know a regular bed. When I was small I had a terrific inferiority complex. Success helped me out of it and gave me confidence. The truth is that I went into the movie business for money. Art just sort of grew out of it."

During the hysteria of the First World War, some Americans questioned his patriotism, despite his efforts to sell war bonds, because he had not applied for citizenship in the USA, whereas some Britons accused him of cowardice and disloyalty by remaining safe in Hollywood. A quarter of a century later, his film *The Great Dictator* (1940) was a case of being anti-Nazi too soon, as improbable as that seemed to later generations. Chaplin's contempt for Hitler and his support for Russia troops—that were defending their nation against the Nazi invaders—quickened the suspicions of J. Edgar Hoover, founder and longtime chief of the FBI.

Suspicions about Chaplin's patriotism were paired with a certainty that he was enjoying too much licentious fun. Between the two world wars, the public had learned of Charlie's numerous romantic affairs with women, some less than half his age. He married four of them. Three ended in divorce: Mildred Harris (1918–20), whose one child with Charlie died in infancy; Lita Grey (1924–27), with whom he had two sons, Charles Chaplin Jr. and Sydney Chaplin; and Paulette Goddard (1936–42). Although a blood test proved that Chaplin was not the father of a child as claimed by its mother, Joan Barry, the court in 1943 refused such evidence, and Chaplin was convicted. He did not go to jail and was compelled only to pay a modest continuing sum for the child's support, but the damage was done. As though to further infuriate the public, that same year, 54-year-old Charlie wed 18-year-old Oona O'Neill, daughter of playwright Eugene O'Neill. They defied expectation and stayed wed until Charlie's death. Oona gave birth to eight of Charlie's 11 children.

By then, few cared or remembered why he had seemed so important. Since *The Great Dictator,* Chaplin, the artistic icon, had gathered dust. His first movie after *The Great Dictator* was *Monsieur Verdoux,* arriving in theatres in 1947. Despite the determination of many arbiters to declare it a masterpiece, others found it charmless and clumsy. His costar, Martha Raye, got better reviews from some critics than Chaplin did. A large segment of the public was dismayed by what they were assured was black comedy. Perhaps audiences found Monsieur Henri Verdoux was more like the real Chaplin, a man they had come to suspect as a libertine, than was the Little Fellow.

The Tramp had yielded to time, but Calvero was plausible. *Limelight* (1952) was the story of the fading days of Calvero, an old music-hall performer. Once a darling of the Victorian and Edwardian halls, he had been reduced to busking for his bread and board. The film is a melodrama punctuated with comedy scenes, the last of which is masterful turn onstage by Calvero and an erstwhile partner, played by Buster Keaton. It was Chaplin's funniest single scene since he made *Modern Times* in 1936. The film had two strikes against it, however. It was overlong; various cuts ran between 140 minutes and three hours, twice as long as most successful comedies. Its release was fumbled. United Artists was no longer the powerhouse distributor it had been, and Charlie and Mary Pickford, its majority stockholders, were trying to sell their shares at an advantage, so they stalemated. Each lost money, and United Artists films did not hit the market effectively.

At the same time, Chaplin had more problems with the federal government that manifested as tax claims and questions about his immigration status. Charlie and Oona suspected that the federal authorities might not let them return to the USA. They left the USA, took a long sojourn abroad and secretly transferred their assets to Europe. When the government and the public found out, Charlie became *persona non grata,* and the chances for *Limelight's* box-office success in America further diminished. The film debuted in England, where it was affectionately received, but it never got the systematic release with concerted publicity that a potential hit required in the USA. Instead, the film dribbled into the public arena with scattered art-house showings. By the time it went into general release, it was old news, and public opinion had once again set against Charles Chaplin.

As the scandals ebbed and the public had been distracted by newer and more titillating dirt, Chaplin received a knighthood from the British queen and, in 1972, was awarded a special Oscar for his body of work. He tinkered with his old films, adding gratuitous narration to *The Gold Rush* and creating musical soundtracks for many, yet Charlie Chaplin was no longer a working actor. To younger moviegoers, he was just an old-time movie star who was still famous for movies that most people had not seen in a generation or more. Laurel & Hardy and The Three Stooges had been syndicated to television for decades. The Marx Brothers, Mae West and W. C. Fields were iconoclastic heroes for college-age youth, their movies in constant rerelease. Buster Keaton, Chaplin's artistic rival, was newly celebrated as a revered modern Everyman.

It was during the Second World War and its triumphalist aftermath that national conformity drove individualism underground in the land of the victors. By the time individualism resurfaced in the mid-1950s, it was cursing and spouting streams of consciousness poetry while riding a motorcycle to the sounds of Charlie Parker, Gerry Mulligan, Gil Evans, Miles Davis, Paul Desmond, Thelonious Monk and Chuck Berry. The Tramp had been laid to rest, and Sir Charles Spencer Chaplin was no longer the spirit of rebellion. For decades thereafter, however, whenever discussion turned to the great comedians of the twentieth century, it was likely that Chaplin's name was the first invoked.

CHAZ CHASE

b: 6 March 1901, Russia—
d: 4 August 1983, Los Angeles, CA

Everyone remembered his act. Few remembered his name. If they did, they probably stumbled over Chaz, thinking it was a misspelled abbreviation for Charles. An eccentric comedian, Chaz Chase entertained vaudeville, variety, burlesque, nightclub and musical-comedy audiences in the USA, Great Britain, France and Australia for more than 65 years. His last Broadway appearance was with Mickey Rooney, Ann Miller and Mickey Deems in the smash salute to burlesque, *Sugar Babies.* Chase was touring in the national company headed by Carol Channing and Robert Morse in 1983, just before he died.

Chaz danced and played sketch comedy, but best remembered was his habit of eating inedible things. Without a word, he entered the stage and began walking in a circle. He pulled out a cigarette, lit a match, lit his cigarette and ate the match, but not before he lit the entire book of matches and popped it in his mouth, still flaming. He ate his cigarette, his boutonniere and the cardboard dickey, or dress bib, that he wore.

March music of a sort played as Chaz, wearing a long overcoat, circled the stage while eating. With each circle, he seemed to go farther into the ground. He did this by crouching ever more with each circuit. It was tough on the legs, feet and lower back, but upon entering a new town, Chaz located the best chiropractor available for weekly adjustments.

Sometimes he did a mock striptease, other times a mad dance. Often he dressed in the loud wide check suits with baggy pants of a burlesque comedian. It was the kind of physical comedy that played well in any venue from small nightclubs to large theatres and

Chaz Chase

even circus rings. After spending his early years in vaudeville and burlesque, Chase made his Broadway debut in *Ballyhoo of 1930,* a revue that ran a couple of months. Also in the show were W. C. Fields, Grace Hayes and the Slate Brothers.

Chaz's next Broadway show was *Saluta* (1934), an unsuccessful musical comedy that starred Milton Berle and Thelma White. In 1941, George Jessel and Bert Kalmar & Harry Ruby produced a vaudeville revue, *High Kickers* (1941–42), headlined by Jessel and Sophie Tucker and featured Chaz; it played five months on Broadway and then toured. His next tours were with several camp shows for the USO during the Second World War. One of the tours was headed by Bob Hope.

Chaz Chase followed one European theatre with another when he began what became an eight-year run at the Crazy Horse Saloon in Paris in the 1950s, and he was a favorite at the Latin Quarter in New York and other top-notch supper clubs and nighteries. Chaz Chase appeared on several television variety shows in the 1950s. Rediscovered through his performance in *Sugar Babies,* he made the rounds of talk shows like Johnny Carson's *Tonight Show.* Hosts and audiences were surprised at how agile the clown was in his 70s and early 80s.

His film credits number at least six. Three of them were Vitaphone shorts, including *Chaz Chase, the Unique Comedian* (1928) and *Public Jitterbug Number One* (1939), in which he performed portions of his vaudeville acts. Chaz played a music-hall performer in Tod Browning's 1928 film *West of Zanzibar,* one of Lon Chaney's last. In 1938, Chaz had a small role in *Start Cheering,* with Charles Starrett, Hal Leroy and Jimmy Durante. He played a waiter in the 1950 thriller *The Man on the Eiffel Tower.* Chase's last film was *Démons de midi* (1979), a Belgian, French and Spanish collaboration. According to his obituary, Chaz Chase was survived by a daughter, seven grandchildren and one great-grandchild.

DAVE CHASEN

b: 18 July 1898, Odessa, Russia— d: 16 June 1973, Los Angeles, CA

If the name Dave Chasen is recalled by the showbiz community, it is likely for the restaurant he opened in Beverly Hills in 1936. Among comedy aficionados, however, it is his decade-plus stint with Joe Cook that is fondly remembered. The combination was an effective matchup. Joe Cook was the most competent performer on the American stage; Dave Chasen was its prime bumbler. In Joe Cook's world, that made Chasen the perfect assistant.

Although Cook could juggle, tumble, do a Risley act, walk a slack wire, sing, dance, and perform monologues and sketch comedy, Chasen could do nothing right; he could not even hand Joe a prop without dropping it. With a wide vacant smile, Dave Chasen would smile at the audience and slowly and stiffly wave (reminiscent of Harry Langdon's wave but less tentative), turn, trip over his own feet and fall. He would get up, grinning, confident that the audience had forgiven him, and then louse up the next chore.

Genial as Joe generally was, occasionally he would bounce a few tricks off Dave, but none of them—being dunked in a tank of water or falling through a trapdoor—ever fazed the ever-genial Chasen. Dave Chasen left the act in the mid-1930s to move to Hollywood, where he opened a barbeque joint in Beverly Hills and fell in with the renegade New York theatre crowd that included W. C. Fields, John Barrymore, Errol Flynn and Humphrey Bogart. With 30 such cronies, his restaurant's success was guaranteed. It became Chasen's, one of the movie colony's places to be seen.

CHASERS

By vaudeville's heyday, a rather standard order had evolved in the presentation of acts on a bill. Earlier, there had been considerable experimentation and variation. Certain acts developed into star turns, the type of acts that sold tickets on the strength of their appearance alone. Audiences came to feel that the rest of the bill led up to the headliner, so few acts wished to be put into the thankless position on the bill that followed the headliner. Those acts that were forced into the closing spot were neither highly regarded nor well rewarded.

Before the start of the twentieth century, people began taking primitive motion pictures of phenomena like waterfalls, geysers, erupting volcanoes, and raging fires or man-made wonders such as locomotives pulling into stations, ships being launched and men building bridges, tunnels and 14-story skyscrapers. These short films were less expensive to show than another live act, and theatre managers began closing their programs with them. The novelty of motion pictures enchanted audiences.

Until the infrastructure was developed to rent and distribute motion pictures, it was customary to buy prints of each film. Thus, a theatre exhibitor might show the same few movies repeatedly. Soon these plotless, flickering films began to pall and to chase the audience out of the theatres at the end of a vaudeville show. Upon consideration, theatre managers decided this was desirable, as it allowed them to fill seats with new paying customers for the succeeding show. So managers used these early movies as chasers to discourage people from staying to see the vaudeville show a second time. The title of a short film that closed a 1903 bill at Case's Theatre in Washington, D.C., suggests that many films of that era proved to be effective chasers: "The American Vitagraph Will Present a Natural History Study Showing 15 Phases of Bee Culture."

As the movies began to tell stories, however short, and technical improvements smoothed the uneven, jerky unspooling of the films, the public once again was in thrall. By the mid-1910s, the reason some fans went to the nickelodeon or a vaudeville show was for the one-reel film that starred a favorite such as Florence Lawrence, the Biograph Girl; Little Mary (Pickford), America's Sweetheart; Bronco Billy Anderson; or the Keystone Cops. As silent motion pictures became America's favorite entertainment, vaudeville managers advertised on marquees or sandwich boards that a short with Fatty Arbuckle or, later, Laurel & Hardy was on the bill (were the managers fortunate enough to secure the rental).

When silent movies improved and became an attraction on vaudeville bills, new *chasers* needed to be found. The dullest act on the bill was chosen to close it. They were not always lacking in merit, but were simply of a nature that did not engage the public's interest after a turn by the headliner. The new *chasers* tended to be acts like harp soloists and dumb acts.

Eventually, the tail began to wag the dog when talking motion pictures became the rage. The movie still closed the program, but the five or so live acts were prelude to a feature motion picture by a major studio.

Patrons of top-notch big-time theatres paid considerably more for a ticket than small time audiences, so the big-time audience expected quality entertainment throughout the entire bill, so the closing act might be a fast-moving flash act or acrobatic turn.

CHAUTAUQUA CIRCUIT

If the Chautauqua circuit has any descendants, it is likely the adult education programs that strive to engender intellectual curiosity and make lifetime learning an entertaining part of every adult's journey. Chautauqua provided outdoor summer stages and indoor winter halls for a traveling series of lectures, debates, musical performances and higher-type vaudeville.

In its heyday, the early 1920s, 40 million people were estimated to attend Chautauqua events in 10,000 communities nationwide. In truth, the bulk of the host communities was centered in the Mid-Atlantic, Midwest and farm-belt states, although communities and programs were scattered into New England, the southeastern states and the Prairie states. Every one of the 48 states that then made up the USA had at least one community.

In another sense, the Chautauqua experience was not unlike the summer resorts of the Borscht circuit in that performers played for a group of families brought together for an entire community encounter. The acts performed four shows a day and were expected to represent the high standards of the Chautauqua community.

CHERRY SISTERS

Addie

b: 1859—d: 1942

Effie

b: 1865—d: 1944

Lizzie

b: ca. 1870—d: 1936

Ella

dates unknown

Jessie

b: ca. 1882—d: 1903

They were the most ridiculed act in vaudeville. Some audiences found them so bad that they laughed and cheered more than they would for a genuine comedian. Others, including performers who felt tarnished by finding themselves on the same bill with the Cherry Sisters, wanted them chased out of town. If one takes the Cherry Sisters at face value, they led sad lives.

The family lived in semi-isolation on a farm outside Marion, Iowa, then a small town near and northeast of Cedar Rapids. Five sisters and one or two brothers were born over a period exceeding 20 years. Their parents died, probably in the mid-1880s, leaving the older children with at least one infant sister and another barely in her teens plus a farm with no resources to maintain it or coax a living from except their own elbow grease. According to family lore, a brother quit the farm and lit out for Chicago in 1885, perhaps shortly after the death of their parents. He is named Nathan in one report and Isaac in another. Perhaps there were two brothers, both bent on fleeing the farm.

Four of the five sisters decided to visit Chicago's world's fair, the World's Columbian Exposition of 1893, and to find their brother. Needing money to travel and a continuing way to support themselves, they hit on the idea of giving performances. They had seen a little in the way of shows: the odd melodrama, phrenology demonstration, concertizing and recitation passing through town. The sisters devised their own material, writing songs of an old-fashioned style, moralistic playlets, poems and speeches for recitation. They presented themselves in a full-evening's program to their fellow townspeople at the Marion Opera House in 1893.

Mistaking the kind encouragement of their neighbors for a successful debut, they went on to Chicago. Although they never located their brother, nor did he surface during the years of their notoriety, they did find a booking agent who agreed to audition them. None of the sisters was handsome or shapely, and they dressed in home-sewn gingham dresses, so he must have sensed the potential of novelty. He hired them for a touring package whose performers acted in a short melodrama and doubled as specialty acts. Even on a junior *death trail* that took them to a series of small farming communities throughout Iowa and neighboring states, people were sophisticated enough to be offended by the Cherry Sister's gall to perform as professionals. Along the route, audiences jeered them.

As word spread, people bearing decayed farm produce showed up at the theatres, and they liberally peppered the stage with tomatoes, cabbages, turnips and rotting eggs. The menu soon included animals' livers, old shoes, buckets and busted tools. On at least one occasion, Addie had to resort to brandishing her shotgun to stave off rowdies in an audience.

By 1894–95, the Cherry Sisters' performance had made it impossible for them to continue with the unit show, and they struck out on their own, sometimes renting theatre space themselves. One manager dropped a mesh across the stage when the Cherry Sisters appeared, as much to garner more publicity as to protect the women. Others managers repeated the ploy, although the sisters claimed that a screen was never needed.

As more people came to their shows for the express purpose of hurling abuse and increasingly dangerous objects, the Cherry Sisters' notoriety reached Willie Hammerstein in New York City, and he sent one of his assistants to investigate. The returning word was that the Cherry Sisters were so bad that they were good. Willie was then assisting his father, Oscar, in trying to make the Olympia Roof Garden profitable. The Olympia, built in 1895, was a huge complex of two theatres (the Lyric and the Music Hall), a smaller Concert Hall, the Roof Garden, a café and a billiards parlor. The complex took up the entire block on Broadway between West 44th and 45th Streets. Unfortunately, the area, Long Acre Square, better known as Thieves Lair and not yet rechristened Times Square, was not a place fashionable folks wished to visit despite a richly ornamented building, elegant interior furnishings and appointments, and top talent onstage. Because he could not draw customers to the Olympia with the best available shows and vaudeville acts, Willie gambled on the worst.

He quickly brought the Cherry Sisters to New York, except for Ella, who gave up the stage to remain at the family homestead in charge of the farm. She was joined at various periods by Lizzie, as Elizabeth was called. Over the years, the Cherry Sisters usually appeared as a quartet but sometimes as a trio.

When the four Cherry Sisters appeared on the Olympia's stage in November 1896, Willie, too, dropped a protective screen, probably made of fish netting. Their act consisted of several solos and a few groups songs, and Lizzie pounded a piano while Jessie thumped a big bass drum. A reviewer reported that the four "grim-faced" Cherry Sisters sang a variety of songs intended to be sentimental, patriotic, and in some approximation of dialect as well as performing a gypsy song-and-dance number. For a finish, they posed in tableaux vivant, depicting Jesus hanging from a cross.

As expected, even hoped, members of the New York audience behaved like their Iowa cousins and tossed fruits, vegetables and trash at the Cherry Sisters. Willie Hammerstein probably instigated the disturbance to give the newspapers something juicy to print and thereby stimulate attendance.

Willie somewhat pacified the Cherry Sisters by telling them that the produce barrage was the work of other acts that were so jealous of the sisters' popularity that they hired claques to ruin the Cherry Sisters' performance. Manhattan audiences soon picked up on the joke, and the Cherry Sisters became a must-see event in town. They were held over and played for a total of four weeks and then played another two weeks at Proctor's Pleasure Palace.

Despite being a hit act, the talk of the town, and making more money than they ever imagined, they lived like ascetic nuns, leaving their hotel only for work in the theatre, an occasional ride in Central Park or a visit to a restaurant. Hidebound fundamentalists in religious belief, they shied away from places where they might find immodest dress, language or behavior, smoking or drinking.

Several good researchers, Jack El-Hai and Irwin Chusid among them, have pondered the reasons the Cherry Sisters were willing to put up with the abuse that attended their vaudeville careers. Most observers ranged between two poles of opinion: those who held that the Cherry Sisters knew what they were doing and to some degree were complicit and those who maintained that the sisters were talentless naïfs ignorant of how bad they were.

When they began in show business, Addie, Effie, Lizzie, Jessie and Ella were destitute and in danger of losing the family farm. Their parents' deaths and their brother's desertion must have dismayed them. Their rock-ribbed puritanism suggests that they were ill prepared to earn a living in any conventional way. Perhaps they surveyed their situation and felt their only chance was to sing for their suppers. Maybe they rationalized their involvement with vaudeville as their way of presenting wholesome entertainment at a time they saw declining moral standards.

Surely they grew more savvy with experience in show business, but any acquired sophistication did not attach to a blossoming of talent or technique. Eventually, they must have understood that it was their unsuitability for the stage that brought in the customers. Public humiliation may have seemed the preferred alternative to poverty.

The audiences' contempt was matched by the Cherry Sisters' resilience. They refused to be discouraged, even by reviews that began to appear in local newspapers, damning them not only for a lack of talent but also for their looks. Reviews were vicious, comparing them to ugly, shapeless, graceless witches. One critic wrote that the "mouths of their rancid features opened like caverns, and sounds like the wailing of damned souls" issued forth.

They were touring the Midwest and Canada when, in 1901, the above comment was made by a home-state theatre critic. The Cherry Sisters sued the *Des Moines Leader* newspaper for reprinting the review. To counter the alleged slander, the Cherry Sisters performed their act in court. The judge ruled that the critic's comment was not libelous. On appeal, the Iowa Supreme Court upheld his decision.

Despite the condemnation of the press and the abuse from audiences, the Cherry Sisters soldiered on in vaudeville for a few more years until 1903, when the youngest of them, Jessie, died of typhoid fever. They retired to their hometown and opened a bakery that specialized in cherry pie. It failed. Effie ran for mayor in their hometown. She lost both times. She wrote a novel that no one would publish.

After playing vaudeville for nearly seven years and living most frugally, the sisters were reported to have saved about $200,000, a figure that seems improbable. The best acts at the turn of the twentieth century were fortunate to earn $500 a week. It is doubtful that the Cherry Sisters ever earned more than that, and they certainly earned a lot less most of their years on the road. Still, vaudeville was the only thing that sustained them. Everything else they set their hands to turned to ashes.

Indeed, the Cherry Sisters were near poverty for all of their lives except their few seasons in vaudeville. The surviving sisters tried for a comeback in 1913 and failed. Addie and Effie tried again in a 1935 Gay Nineties nostalgia revue in Manhattan, but the sight of two old ladies (75 and 70 years old), who had not improved with age, no longer amused. As each sister died, obituaries recounted their notoriety as the worst act in show business. All the Cherry sisters died unmarried, childless and unmourned.

ALBERT CHEVALIER

b: (Albert Onésime Britannicus Gwathveoyd Louis Chevalier) 21 March 1861, London, England—d: 11 July 1923, London, England

When he was described as a coster comedian, no one was less pleased than Albert Chevalier. Others might deny him the title because he was an actor, dismiss him as a fake, unlike the beloved Gus Elan, but Chevalier considered himself an actor, a more glorious calling. It was simply the question of authenticity; no one denied that Albert Chevalier was a consummate performer and entertainer.

Perhaps comparing him to Gus Elan was unfair. In addition to singing, Chevalier was a storyteller who made his characters come alive. Music-hall chronicler Ernest Short noted his gift and placed him in the company of Yvette Guilbert (with whom Chevalier once toured) and Ruth Draper.

When he went on the stage, he jettisoned all but his first and last names. His full name was a tribute to his mother's Welsh heritage and his father's French.

Albert Chevalier

Albert's effectiveness was due to early training as an actor. He first attracted attention as a child actor, most notably at the Prince of Wales Theatre under Squire Bancroft and his wife, Marie Wilton (the future Lady Bancroft, after the squire became the second actor-manager to be knighted). Albert joined John Hare's company at the Court Theatre, where he played in Pinero's earlier farces.

All told, he spent more than 15 years, boy and young man, in legitimate theatre without feeling secure in his profession. A tireless worker and ambitious for a higher salary and more recognition, Chevalier appeared in Christmas pantomimes and began singing songs of his own composition at the Savage Club's Saturday Nights. His success as an entertainer won him music-hall bookings, including the London Palladium in 1891. Another early and prominent London booking was at the Tivoli in the Strand. Charles Morton, newly retired from the Alhambra, had taken over the Tivoli, a former beer hall, where he engaged Chevalier among other new, young music-hall talents.

Chevalier mastered a Cockney accent and idiom that passed muster with most and costumed himself to suit each of his characters. Some felt he lacked the salt of a true coster singer and possessed a dollop too much of sentiment, as when he portrayed an old Cockney singing of his wife, whom he called "My Old Dutch:"

I've got a pal, a reg'lar out-an'-outer,
She's a dear old pal, I'll tell you all about 'er!
It's many years since fust we met,
Er 'air was then as black as jet;
It's whiter now, but she don't fret—
Not my old gal!

Chorus:
We've been together now for forty years,
An' it don't seem a day too much;
There ain't a lady livin' in the land
As I'd swop for my dear old Dutch.

During his early years in music-hall, Albert married another performer, Florrie Leybourne, daughter of George Leybourne (a legend of the halls so identified with his most famous song that he was familiarly known by its title, "Champagne Charlie.")

Chevalier's attitude toward his work and music-hall was well known. He never grew comfortable with the informal, tavernlike atmosphere of a music-hall and an audience that chatted and called for more ale even during turns they enjoyed. This supposed snobbishness did not endear him to fellow performers. Chevalier's preferred venue was the concert hall. He gave recitations and sang songs at a series of concerts in the intimate Queen's Hall. Occasionally, he added another act, such as the plump singing Cockney comedian Connie Ediss or Pelissier's Follies, a Pierrot troupe.

Early on, Albert Chevalier became a favorite in American vaudeville. He made his debut in 1896 at Koster & Bial's in Lower Manhattan. When genuine coster singers, like Alec Hurley or Gus Elan, subsequently appeared in front of American vaudeville audiences, they were compared to Chevalier and sometimes dismissed for not being as authentic as Chevalier.

At first blush, sharing the bill with Yvette Guilbert for another American vaudeville tour in 1906 seemed odd, but both were actor-singers, each etched detailed characters, and the pairing worked well. Although Chevalier received credit for writing most of his material, in some cases it was shared. He probably wrote the lyrics, but his accompanist, Alfred West, or Albert's brother, Charles Ingle, likely composed the music.

Chevalier made several other tours of vaudeville in America, perhaps as many as six all told. For his 1909 bookings on Keith time, he was paid $1,600 a week. Variety had become a profitable turn for Mr. Chevalier and raised his reputation as well as developed his audiences on both sides of the Atlantic. In his later years, because of his music-hall and vaudeville fame, he was able to return to the legitimate stage both in London and New York.

He wrote scenarios for a handful of silent films for British studios during 1915–16, most of them based on well-known songs from his repertoire. He acted in *My Old Dutch* (1915), *The Middleman* (1915), *The Bottle* (1915) and *A Fallen Star* (1916). *A Fallen Star,* both the song and the movie, was a melodramatic and sentimental tale of an old actor recalling his glory years.

At age 62, Albert Chevalier died in 1923, shortly after he had announced his retirement from the stage. His most famous work, *Old Dutch*, continued to be performed as a song and as a play. It was filmed in 1926 with May McAvoy as Old Dutch and Pat O'Malley in the Chevalier role. A re-make in 1936 starred Betty Balfour as Old Dutch.

CHICAGO WORLD'S FAIR OF 1893

The World's Columbian Exposition, as the Chicago world's fair of 1893 was properly known, marked the 400th anniversary of Columbus' voyages to the Americas. Produced on a grand scale possible only during an era of low wages, the exposition was optimistic and congratulatory; it celebrated innovation and enterprise, acknowledged the cultural yearnings of some

Americans and satisfied the desire for thrills and novelty of the great majority.

There had been earlier world's fairs staged in New York City, Philadelphia, New Orleans and St. Louis, Chicago's however, was the first to attempt to equal or surpass those that had been mounted in London and Paris. In 1851, London had hosted the first, which it confidently called the Great Exposition of the Works of Industry of All Nations, and housed it in the specially constructed marvel known as the Crystal Palace. It remained unrivalled until 1889 when Paris produced the Exposition Universelle.

The emphasis at the World's Columbian Exposition was the same as other nineteenth-century world's fairs: exhibits boasting invention, manufacturing and commerce were housed in most of the 14 large Beaux Arts–style buildings and 200 smaller structures spread over the 600 acres. Other tenants were a zoo, gardens, restaurants and merchant stalls.

For six months, all roads led to Chicago, and many of those were railroads, capping Chicago's claim as the hub of the USA railroad system. The fair attracted 27 million people, about one fourth of the population of the USA, but at least a small percentage of the visitors came from other lands, and some of these were performers.

The exposition presented diverse attractions, none attracting more eager audiences than performances at temporary stages set up in the Midway Plaisance, where belly dancer Little Egypt started a craze that imitators would exploit for a score of years. Acrobats and jugglers were among the many entertainers from abroad and the USA who entertained thousands for weeks on end. A reconstructed harem on the fairgrounds and sensational and unsubstantiated reports of opium dens and sexual slavery inspired a rash of lurid novels and melodramas. The Columbian Orchestra and Chorus gave concerts on the lakefront—originally a swampland—and Buffalo Bill's Wild West Show played at an adjacent fairground. In addition to all manner of performances, the fine arts were served by exhibitions by American artists, Japanese painting and Egyptian design motifs that nudged Art Nouveau toward Art Deco.

Adjacent were the city's notorious stockyards and some hastily constructed brothels. Though fair managers neither publicized the slaughterhouses or sanctioned the bordellos, their presence became well known, one by odor and the other by word of mouth.

More elevated programs were presented through a series of world's congresses. Among the topics were education, science, music, social reform and religion. The participants included many of the most well-regarded and famous jurists, lecturers, authors, scientists and artists of the day. The World's Congress of Religion drew representatives from all the major religions of Asia, the Near East, Europe and the Americas and ran for weeks.

CHILDREN IN VAUDEVILLE

The experience of being a child performer was as varied as the personalities and their circumstances. There were children—Joe Weber, Lew Fields, Fanny Brice, Bessie Smith, Eddie Cantor and George Burns a few among the more luminous—who, with or without their parents' approval, made their own way in show business, usually beginning with sidewalk busking. Other kids, like Lotta Crabtree, The Marx Brothers, Elsie Janis, Alice Whitman and Milton Berle, were put onstage by their parents. Some children liked it, some did not. Some were cruelly exploited, none more so than the Hiltons Sisters. As newborns, the conjoined twins were sold to the midwife, held captive and exhibited as freaks until adulthood. Though both were talented, they had little hope of a conventional career or normal lives.

On farms and in the cities, it was usual and necessary among the lower and the lower-middle classes—the vast majority of households—for children to work from age six or seven onward if a family was to make ends meet. On farms, owned or tenanted, there were countless chores requiring varying levels of skills, enough for all the family children of school age. At harvest time, farm kids did not go to school and had little time to play. Indeed, the school year was largely scheduled around the need for rural children to be on hand from planting season through harvest.

In the cities, many of the poorest children, especially girls, labored in sweatshops; the comparatively lucky kids ran errands, collected and sold scrap metal, glass and paper. Girls retailed flowers in the streets; boys shined shoes and peddled newspapers. Many of the street children had been abandoned or had run away from mistreatment at the hands of parents or guardians. The youngsters who dressed up, wore shiny shoes and performed on the stage were the envy of kids scraping out a living on mean streets and alleyways.

Indeed, most children in the vaudeville era worked at least part-time and school-age kids continued to work through the Great Depression and until after the Second World War.

During the middle and last decades of the nineteenth century, the Industrial Revolution was synonymous with national purpose, yet the apostles of social betterment were not quite drowned out by the engines of material progress. Slavery abolished, moral indignation turned to the ills of poverty, drink, disease and violence. Among those responding to societal ills was the Society for the Prevention of Cruelty to Children (SPCC), founded in 1875 by Elbridge T. Gerry, a lawyer and descendant of a prominent, political New England family.

The SPCC was known simply as the Gerry Society to people in vaudeville. Gerry's avowed purpose was to liberate children younger than 16 from exploitation. Youngsters working long hours, six days a week, in factories, mines and mills attracted Mr. Gerry's attention less than those who performed two, three or four times a day onstage. Working with potentially dangerous machinery seemed less of a threat to the safety of children in Mr. Gerry's mind than singing, dancing, clowning or tumbling.

The level of education attained by kids in vaudeville largely depended on the education of their parents. Home schooling was the rule. Even the least schooled youngster learned how to count and read his billing matter. There were vaudeville kids who longed for a home, a neighborhood, a school and other youngsters to pal around. Others enjoyed the constant travel, meeting new and different types of people, mixing with adults as a fellow performer, and getting applause. Buster Keaton claimed he had a single day of school. He, who had performed on the stage as long as he could remember, was allowed, perhaps encouraged, to leave school. It seems he regarded the teacher as a straight man and his classmates as an audience. Groucho Marx resented that he, the only book lover in his family, had to leave school when still a boy to earn his living on long, lonesome tours of small, small-time vaudeville.

For those children who loved show business, or knew no life but showbiz, unseen difficulties came as they grew from lovable tots into gangly and ungainly teens. Love, approval and applause were withdrawn. June Havoc, a vaudeville headliner at four, discovered at 14 that she was no longer a draw, no longer baby cute and remarkably untrained despite more than a decade in vaudeville. She started at the bottom rung of show business as an adult and grew into a much-respected actor and director.

Milton Berle was his mother's creation. She had looked over her husband and sons and decided that Milton was the most promising of the lot. While his brothers stayed home, went to school, grew into a family with their father and went on dates, baby Milton was acting in silent films and teenage Milton was appearing at the Palace Theatre. Dating led to marriage, reasoned his mother, so when she became aware of her growing boy's needs, she arranged dates for Milton, one-night stands, sometimes with *professionals* of another sort.

Ethel Waters' ambition was to become a lady's maid, a giant step upward from being an eight-year-old lookout for prostitutes and thieves. Her talent made vaudeville an easier proposition than rising above her teenage position as a hotel chambermaid.

Fayard Nicholas delighted in show business from the first. From his crib parked near his mother's piano in the orchestra pit, he watched all the great black performers of the day. The Standard Theatre was his academy. He passed on to his sister and brother the dance steps that he learned, and the talented tots became a successful act. Fayard and Harold grew into the famous Nicholas Brothers.

Children of vaudevillians who did not take to the stage often were parked with relatives—grandparents, or an aunt and uncle, while the kids' parents toured season after season. The kids were schooled and cared for under the values and precepts of the fostering family. If the act had earned enough money during the September-to-June season, the children rejoined their parents for the summer.

This was not peculiar to show business. In many families, the primary wage earner had to go to sea, join the armed services or travel from town to town as a salesperson. Sometimes, misunderstandings and resentments festered and led to lifelong estrangements. Children felt denied, unloved and unvalued. In turn, showbiz parents were conflicted and felt alien to their *civilian* children's bourgeois longings, needs so foreign to their own youthful lust for independence and adventure. As a consequence, vaudeville scrapbooks were not always cherished and preserved.

Much has been made of being a child star and finding that one was washed up by puberty. For some children, this became the central paralyzing fact of their lives. Others found new professional lives and adapted to civilian life or stayed in show business and found new roles behind the scenes or in front of audiences. The outcomes were as varied as the mix of nature, nurture and luck.

CHING LING FOO

b: (Chee Ling Qua) 1854, Beijing, China—d: 1922, China

America's enduring enchantment with Orientalia dates from Colonial times when sea captains first brought artifacts back to their New England homes from Asian ports of call. Interest grew through the mid-eighteenth century and swelled by the end of the Gilded Age. In the three decades between the 1893 World's Columbian Exhibition in Chicago and the 1922 discovery in Egypt of the tomb of King Tut (Tutankhamen), Americans experienced a world opened wider by faster and safer ships, motion pictures, the press and popular literature.

Heading a small company of Chinese musicians and conjurer's assistants, Ching Ling Foo, entering through the port of San Francisco, came to the USA as part of a world tour. Billing himself as "The World's Greatest Conjurer," he performed in 1898 at the Trans-Mississippi

Exposition in Omaha, Nebraska. After four successful months, Ching was approached by bookers and agreed to perform in vaudeville. Provincial-minded officials tried to deport the Chinese under the federal Exclusion Act but lost their case when Ching and the others were deemed artists rather than laborers as covered by the law.

Much of his act consisted of producing objects from behind or under a cloth, both sides of which he showed the audience. One object, a six-inch pole, was employed to balance and whirl food-laden plates. According to observers, his most effective trick was making a huge glass bowl appear. The bowl held several pails of water and was said to weigh 80 to 95 pounds. Carrying it around the stage and passing his cloth over the bowl, he caused nuts, fruits, live chickens, even his baby daughter, Chee Toy, to appear (except where the Gerry Society was able to forbid the child's participation in the show).

Toward the end of his act, Ching drew from his mouth streamers that ignited and crackled like fireworks. He finished with a trick of regurgitation, packing his mouth with sawdust, chewing Chinese punk: (dried Fungi used to ignite fuses of firecrackers), drinking a glass of water and then emitting smoke, which was followed by balls of fire that he spat into the air. He concluded by drawing dry tissue from his mouth to dry his face and then spat one last fireball into a metal container filled with fireworks that blazed into a spectacular finale.

Ching Ling Foo began his career in the mercantile business, practicing conjuring as a hobby to amuse friends and business associates. Through his work, he mixed with government, industry and trade officials, including those from nations outside China. He found himself in demand to entertain at various parties and events for his former colleagues and quickly became successful as a professional illusionist. A good businessman, he parlayed success in China into a world tour.

Members of his troupe included his wife, who tottered about on bound feet as his assistant, his daughter, his son, who juggled and tumbled, and a comedian who bumbled about, made a few wisecracks in English and unexpectedly executed a few tricks. In each country, he engaged a person of Chinese ancestry to interpret and handle press. Ching may also have carried a few traditional Chinese musicians in his company. Ching Ling Foo's act played big-time vaudeville like Keith's time and headlined on the better small time, like Loew's, where he earned $2,000 a week for his troupe during the 1910s.

Ching Ling Foo's vaudeville appearances began a craze for Oriental conjuring and attracted more than casual interest. Other magicians noted his success, and within a year there were a number of three-syllable-named "Chinese" conjurers playing the vaudeville circuits. With no exceptions, it seems, all Ching's imitators were European or American born, and few were regarded as good as Ching.

One, Chung Ling Soo (William E. Robinson), was as good or better. He especially annoyed Ching because he had the nerve to take Ching up on his boast that no challenger could perform all of Ching's illusions. It certainly made bad feelings worse that Ching's rival had the audacity to select a name so similar it was bound to confuse bookers, theatre owners and audiences.

Ching refused to meet and compete with him. The issue for Ching was that Robinson was passing as a Chinese conjurer, and Ching regarded that as unacceptable and unworthy of recognition. Robinson, believing himself unfairly dismissed, pursued Ching.

Ching renewed his challenge when both men were playing London in 1914. Unfortunately for Ching, the press was not interested in who was or was not truly Chinese, and Ching refused to show up for the face-off. The press reported the event to Ching's detriment. His engagement at the Empire Theatre lasted four weeks, whereas Robinson, still billing himself as Chung Ling Soo, was held over at London's Hippodrome. The gathering war clouds burst over Europe and the First World War began, making it impossible for performers to continue touring Europe. Ching Ling Foo faded from the international scene and reportedly died in his homeland.

CHOP SUEY CIRCUIT

The flippant name for the various theatres, nightclubs and supper clubs that presented Asian and Asian American performers was the Chop Suey circuit. The individual venues in the "circuit" were owned and operated by Chinese, primarily, and a few Filipinos and Japanese entrepreneurs.

The restaurants and clubs began emerging after the repeal of Prohibition in 1933 and were located in the Chinatowns of San Francisco, Seattle, Portland, Chicago, New York, Boston and a few points in between. Like most nightclubs and theatres, two or more shows were presented nightly, and the work provided the best opportunities for Asian American entertainers to earn their livings. The clubs catered to a Caucasian tourist trade attracted to the supposed exoticism of all-Asian revues, although the stage shows also drew customers from their own Asian communities.

Singers and dancers tended to mimic popular white American acts and wear tuxedos and Western-style dress gowns. The acts of magicians, contortionists, jugglers and acrobats were rooted in traditional old-country skills and usually adopted some flashy variant of Asian costuming to enhance the connection with the mysterious Far East.

CHORINES

Chorines were also known as chorus girls. Dancing in the chorus was often the point of entry (and departure) for women starting in variety, burlesque and musical comedy. The level of talent and training required in the nineteenth century and early part of the twentieth was extremely modest.

As Frankie Bailey put it in 1912, the choice was between a guarantee of 40 weeks' paid work in burlesque and the likelihood in musical comedy of "spending half your life rehearsing without pay shows that half the time are no sooner on than they are off." The pay for chorus girls was extremely low: bad in musical comedy, worse in burlesque. Only those whose skills were severely limited stayed in the chorus.

The expectations of dance directors were superseded by the demands of later choreographers, and the capabilities of women and men of the chorus improved with each decade since the 1920s. A chorus dancer, male or female, in the late twentieth century was likely to be more adept than a featured dancer of the 1920s except in percussive dancing.

CHUNG LING SOO

b: (William Epsworth Robinson) 2 April 1861, New York, NY—d: 24 March 1918, London, England

Chung Ling Soo was the professional name of William E. Robinson, and he had bedeviled Ching Ling Foo ever since the Chinese magician had made a name for himself during his first vaudeville tour of the USA in 1898. Part of the publicity strategy of the times was for performers with highly developed skills or tricks to issue challenges to others to try to duplicate stage feats. The point of the challenge for the person who issued it or the people who accepted the dare was not to win the $500 or $1,000 prize but to use the contest to drum up free publicity.

Whether one was an aerialist, acrobat, escape artist, mentalist or illusionist, it was a pretty safe bet that few competitors, even if they had unlocked the secrets of how the trick worked, had the same precise set of skills (or tools) as the originator of the original feat, trick or stunt or had put in sufficient training time to duplicate it. Mr. Robinson, however, had so trained, and he tried to collect a $1,000 challenge issued by Ching Ling Foo. Mr. Robinson did not collect.

Robinson taught himself magic tricks and manipulations when he was a boy. At 14, in 1875, he gave his first show. He turned professional shortly thereafter, but it was many years before he was able to earn a decent living as a stage illusionist. By 1887, he had assumed the stage name of Achmed Ben Ali and was performing a black-art illusion. He had copied the trick from a German conjurer, Max Auzinger, whose stage name was Ben Ali Bey. Obviously, Robinson availed himself of Max's stage name as well. Auzinger performed his black-art act on the Continent but never brought it to America. In Robinson's version, he stood in an open recess ringed with lights directed toward the audience. An alcove or recess was placed against theatre blacks (dull black fabric used to mask light). Achmed Ben Ali was garbed in white and his assistant in black. Even when he moved, the assistant could not be detected against the black curtains. Also draped in black cloth were various objects. When Achmed waved his wand, the assistant removed the black covering from the indicated object and, presto, a vase or some other object magically appeared.

Talent and skill were not enough for an illusionist to succeed, even when he was brazen enough to steal other acts. Many stage magicians were inspired by their competitors to work out similar effects and add their own stamp to the routine, but Robinson was one of those who sometimes imported with little change another performer's creation. What Robinson had trouble doing was raising the money to engineer and construct the class of illusions that would bring him into big-time vaudeville as a headliner.

He got a good leg up by working for two stage magicians, Harry Kellar and Herrmann the Great, while they performed in America. Originally, Kellar hired Robinson to perform his "Black Art" illusion within the Kellar show, and Robinson soon added another illusion to the show: "Astarte, the Maid of the Moon," a levitation act in which a young woman rose into the air and spun head over feet. Kellar's great rival was Herrmann the Great, and Herrmann enticed Robinson away from Kellar, increased his salary and gave him a spot in the Herrmann show to perform "How to Get Rid of Your Wife." A woman was seated in a suspended chair and shot at with a pistol; she vanished instantly in midair and the chair fell to the stage floor. After Alexander Herrmann's death in 1896, Robinson assumed an important spot in the successor show, Adelaide & Leon Herrmann (Alexander's widow and nephew), and served as company road manager. Working for Harry Kellar and Alexander Herrmann was the best training any ambitious stage illusionist could want.

Robinson made his first move after he left Adelaide Herrmann's act. It was then that he learned of the $1,000 challenge from Ching Ling Foo and tried to win it, but the older Chinese illusionist refused to meet him. That rankled Robinson. Later, when an agent was looking for a less-expensive Chinese illusionist to play a date at the Folies Bergère in 1900, Robinson eagerly accepted. He cobbled together an act based on Ching Ling Foo's, dressed in Chinese garb, shaved his head and face, and presented himself as Hop Ling Soo.

By the time he left Paris to play his next engagement in London at the Alhambra, he had perfected his act and renamed himself Chung Ling Soo, the stage name he was to keep until the end. Over the next 18 years, Robinson, as Chung Ling Soo, performed his act all over Britain, the Continent, the USA and Australia.

In 1905, he was back in London for an engagement at the Hippodrome. Also appearing in London was Ching Ling Foo. If the Chinese illusionist had annoyed Robinson, Robinson returned the insult. He pretended to be genuinely Chinese, using a bogus interpreter to reinforce the deception. Ching hoped to expose Chung as fake Chinese, so he agreed to his promoter's suggestion to defy Robinson to duplicate at least half of his repertoire of illusions. Robinson, assuming the guise of Chung Ling Soo, accepted. The press was alerted, and it was arranged for the two conjurers to meet at the offices of *The Weekly Dispatch* in London. When Ching Ling Foo realized that the press was not interested in who really was or was not Chinese, Ching was indignant and decided not to attend. Chung Ling Soo, alias William E. Robinson, was delighted that Ching was seen to have backed out of the contest, and he entertained the press with portions of his act.

The press reported that Ching Ling Foo, the supposed one and only true Chinese conjurer, did not show up, and the event proved an embarrassment for Ching Ling Foo, whose engagement at the Empire Theatre lasted only four weeks. Robinson played the Hippodrome for three months. In retrospect, Robinson, too, should have been ashamed that he deliberately duplicated another man's persona and act and closely approximated that performer's name in the pursuit of his own stage fame and fortune.

Reputedly, Robinson was a master stage magician, but one wonders what kind of man he was. His initial response in London to Ching's challenge was to denigrate the true Chinese master as a mere street performer and claim imperial patronage for himself. This misrepresentation was at the core of Ching Ling Foo's prideful objection. Robinson played Chung Ling Soo for the next 13 years. The end, when it came, was spectacular.

It came on Saturday night, 23 March 1923, at the Wood Green Empire Theatre in North London. Among the stunts he performed was the gun trick. Robinson called his version "Condemned to Death by the Boxers—Defying Their Bullets." Trading on the public's scant but inflamed and faulty knowledge about the 1900 Boxer Rebellion in China, Chung Ling Soo demonstrated how he purportedly escaped from Boxer rebels. Two members of the audience were called onto the stage. Both had been British soldiers who had served during the First World War. They inspected the old-style, muzzle-loading rifles. Other ticket holders cut identifying marks of their own choosing into the two bullets that were to be fired. Robinson ignited a sampling of the gunpowder to prove it was real. The loaded rifles were handed to Robinson's assistants, who were costumed as Boxer rebels. They fired, and Robinson was supposed to catch the bullets in his teeth. The audience roared until it realized that Chung Ling Soo was prostrate on the stage floor. One of the guns had misfired. William E. Robinson, still dressed in his handsomely embroidered Chung Ling Soo robes, was rushed to the hospital, where he died early the following morning.

CINQUEVALLI

b: (Emile Otto Lehmann-Braun) 30 June 1859, Lissa, Poland—d: 14 July 1918, London, England

At the time the future juggling great Cinquevalli was born, his birthplace of Lissa, a town in the province of Posen, was under Prussian rule. Later, the family moved to Berlin. In school, young Emile practiced gymnastics and tossed objects in the air and caught them for the amusement of his fellow students. He also practiced sleight-of-hand coin and card tricks.

In planning his son's future, his father decided to send Emile to train as a Russian Orthodox priest, but Emile's vocation was the circus not the church. At 14 he ran off with an Italian aerial troupe led by Guiseppe Ciese-Cinquevalli. In homage, Emile changed his stage name to Paul Cinquevalli. The troupe was on tour, and, by the time it reached St. Petersburg in Russia, Paul Cinquevalli was a full-fledged member of the aerial team.

In an interview that he gave years later, Paul explained the fateful accident that changed the course of his career. In St. Petersburg, the troupe performed in the open-air Zoological Gardens. The trapeze rigging was set high above the ground, and the aerialists performed some 60 or 70 feet in the air without a net. The attendant who was supposed to clean, wipe dry and reset the trapeze between shows was neither sober nor particularly careful; he failed to wipe the grease and sweat from one of the trapeze bars. As Paul swung forward on one bar and flew in midair toward a second bar, he grabbed it only to have his hands lose their grip on the slick-coated second bar. Paul hurtled to the ground, trying to break his fall with a series of somersaults until he slammed into a guy wire. He spent eight months recuperating in the hospital at St. Petersburg. One of his wrists never healed properly.

Fortunately, he had been experimenting with balancing and juggling balls between shows, and he practiced his coin manipulations during his recuperation When he recovered sufficiently to return to work, it was as a juggler. He retained, however, the costume of the aerialist-acrobat, the skintight sheath designed by Jules Léotard. Cinquevalli overlaid his leotards with snug vests and abbreviated trunks, brocaded and set with sparkling stones, and wore soft, slipperlike shoes such as those worn in ballet.

His costuming symbolized his individual approach to juggling. He originated most of his tricks and worked with an astonishing range of objects: common items like coins, matches, cigars, cigar holders, umbrellas, canes, hats, knives, forks and vegetables, as well as more traditional things like billiard balls, plates, bowls, cups, chairs and clubs. Mastering those, he turned to outsized tables, whiskey barrels, cannonballs and a 40-pound wooden tub that was four or five feet in diameter.

While balancing and spinning the large wooden tub, he wore a spiked imperial helmet. He spun the large tub on a sturdy pole. After he set the tub spinning like a plate, Cinquevalli fastened other sections to the pole until the tub was whirling 25 feet high in the air. Paul then quickly removed the long pole, and the tub crashed down onto the spike on his head. It had to be perfectly centered or the blow would crack his neck and the velocity of the spin could send him flying into the wing space.

Most of his tricks were less spectacular but not less demanding of skill. In one, Cinquevalli balanced a glass of water on the base of an inverted pyramid. The point of the pyramid was balanced on the tip of a billiard cue and then spun in place. When finished, the glass was still filled with water.

Perhaps his most difficult trick with billiard balls was one that he claimed took him eight years to perfect. In his mouth he held a stemmed glass upright, like an egg cup, in which was set a billiard ball. Atop the ball he balanced a pool cue, narrow end down and handle up. Crowning the upper end of the cue stick were two more billiard balls, one balanced on top of the other. He called them tricks but allowed that was an inadequate description for effects he achieved through constant practice and without any deception.

Not all went well all the time. He sustained injuries during several performances. At the Empire Theatre in Newcastle-on-Tyne, England, the plate he used to catch balls in the air shattered, the shards cut deeply into his hands, and the ball dropped onto his slippered feet and smashed his toes. Still, Cinquevalli finished his act.

Cinquevalli was a handsome, finely built man who excited female admiration. Five feet, six inches tall, he weighed about 150 pounds. He waxed his trim moustache into upwardly tilted points, but his hair was not his own. Bald, he wore a dark-blonde wavy wig. Extremely strong with quick reflexes, he kept in shape by lifting weights.

Cinquevalli went to London to appear at Covent Garden in a Christmas circus. He quickly became a star act in the United Kingdom and a favorite of royalty, including the prince of Wales. In the USA, he made early appearances at Howard's Athenaeum in Boston and Koster & Bial's Thirty-Fourth Street Theatre in Manhattan. He returned to vaudeville in the USA with great success in 1894, 1901, 1904 and 1907, playing big-time houses such as the Union Square and Hammerstein's Victoria in Manhattan and other major theatres on both Orpheum and Keith time. Unlike most dumb acts in American vaudeville, Cinquevalli headlined the bills where he played.

Cinquevalli's fame extended across several oceans. He toured Australia and British outposts in South Africa, India and Singapore, as well as South America and Mexico. Paul Cinquevalli made four visits to Australia between 1899 and 1914. His act was a rousing success on each occasion. One of his favorite venues was the Tivoli circuit in Australia. Two of his feats especially pleased Australians. From about seven feet above him, his assistant dropped a 50-pound cannonball that Cinquevalli caught on his spine. In another routine, he made himself into "The Human Billiard Table" by donning a green felt tunic on which there were affixed pockets at his shoulders and fore and aft of his hips. Tossed into the air, billiard balls ricocheted, landed on his neck and back, and fell into pockets.

Walter Burford was his assistant from 1899 until 1909. Burford played the stooge who registered dismay or nervousness when Cinquevalli attempted an apparently dangerous trick, such as when Cinquevalli juggled billiard balls while he held between his teeth a table on which Burford was perched nervously in a chair. In addition to Burford's comedy, Cinquevalli charmed audiences with a line of patter. He told amusing stories while balancing and juggling. He spoke several languages well.

In 1909, Cinquevalli, who had been widowed the previous year, wed Dora Knowles, an Englishwoman. That same year, Walter Burford, his stage assistant who had become a close friend, suffered several violent epileptic episodes that necessitated leaving Cinquevalli's employ and entering a sanatorium, where he died.

Cinquevalli inspired many young men, among them W. C. Fields, to become jugglers. There was no fear that any of them would duplicate the master's tricks.

He had rivals, certainly, and several of them, Kara and Salerno, were as accomplished and as big draws.

Like his contemporary, Harry Houdini, Cinquevalli was very conscious of the need to keep his name in print and was nearly as adept at securing publicity as was Houdini. Yet all the years of cultivating newspapermen, favoring them with gifts and fostering favorable public relations failed Cinquevalli when he most needed support. During the First World War, public sentiment in Britain turned against all things German, including Cinquevalli. Although he had been born in a territory claimed by Poland and his stage name was Italian, the public fastened on the accident of his birth during Prussian rule and his real surname, the Teutonic-sounding Lehmann-Braun.

Forgotten was the fact that he had been a favorite of English royalty and a loyal citizen of the Crown for 20 years. Cinquevalli was dismayed by hostile receptions by his former fans. He retreated from the public, grew melancholic and died in 1918. He was 59.

CIRCUITS AND THEATRES

Like supermarket chains, vaudeville theatres grouped together in geographic circuits to facilitate bookings, lessen expenses and increase profits for their owners. Some of the individual theatres in a circuit were owned outright, a number were leased, and a few simply had entered into a cooperative arrangement of some sort. Individual owners might be intensely involved in the operation and booking of their theatres or little more than absentee landlords. Some owners contracted with savvy showmen like William Morris to book their shows, but most vaudeville entrepreneurs, like Keith and Albee, the Shuberts, Pantages, Proctor, Loew and the like, kept firm control of their theatres and tried to bring ever more theatres under their banner to increase their power to stop competition and increase profitability through economics of scale. Booking agents, once the servant of theatres and circuits, changed into their masters when the United Booking Office, dominated by E. F. Albee, grew to siphon the individual power of theatre owners and managers.

Before the era of vaudeville circuits, established company managers had worked out informal routes with theatre managers along the way. Invariably, theatre managers welcomed successful producers and acts and encouraged them to return another season. In this way, informal routes were set up. In the 1880s, this network did not yet extend very far westward, but there were enough theatres on the East Coast and in the Midwest to provide a local popular act with a decent living. With luck and diligence, one might book a route that lessened the amount of time and travel between engagements: Manhattan, Brooklyn, Paterson, Philadelphia, Baltimore, Washington, D.C., Harrisburg, Pittsburgh, Cincinnati, Indianapolis, St. Louis, Chicago, Milwaukee, Cleveland, Buffalo, Rochester, Syracuse, Albany, Springfield, Hartford, Worcester, Boston, Providence and back to New York City.

The start of formal circuits was more haphazard than their development. When trolley lines began to bring people to work in the center of a city and take them back to their homes on the outskirts, vaudeville theatres were built along the routes amid budding shopping districts. In large, heavily populated eastern urban areas like New York City, an act could work for a number of weeks simply taking trolleys and trains to various downtown theatres and those in the outlying neighborhoods. Some circuits were comprised of a number of theatres clustered in adjacent neighborhoods or towns. More extensive circuits tended to link larger population centers over a wider region, such as the Pacific Coast states or those in New England and the Mid-Atlantic states.

The core city business and shopping district drew patrons from a large surrounding area, and the theatres in these districts were fancier, higher priced and played better acts to more cosmopolitan audiences. The theatres in the outer neighborhoods tended to be more modest; they were plainer, less expensive and booked acts that appealed to the class and ethnicity of their particular neighborhood.

As the population and business center of New York gradually moved northward along Broadway, the center of theatrical activity moved with it, sometimes leading the way. Although neighborhoods did not move, the people who lived in them did, and fortunes of the district changed. A theatre that once relied upon a German American audience would have to rethink its booking practice if the neighborhood turned Irish, Jewish or African American or if their customers became less or more educated or prosperous.

Circuits were no more permanent and unchanging than the theatres they embraced. The leases or ownership of theatres in a particular circuit changed with the stroke of a pen and the transfer of a mortgage. What had been built as a vaudeville house might become a legitimate theatre a few years later after some unprofitable seasons hosting vaudeville. Still later, it could revert to variety or switch to motion pictures. Similarly, a circuit put together by one entrepreneur might be taken over by another or the ownership of several independent theatres could decide to cast its lot, for a time, with a larger theatre booking operation. For instance, Marcus Loew took over many of the American Theatres booked by William Morris, and a few years later, during the First World War, Loew and Pantages vied to pick up many of the Sullivan & Considine theatres when that circuit came up short financially.

The establishment and growth of circuits was not restricted to vaudeville. They were the engines for legitimate theatre and burlesque as well. Charles Frohman, Al Hayman and Abe Erlanger were the principal architects of the Theatrical Syndicate (also known as the Theatrical Trust), and the Shubert Brothers were their only major rivals. The more modest Stair & Havlin circuit focused on the popular-priced drama houses. In burlesque, there were several wheels, as burlesque circuits were called, and those were geographically organized like the vaudeville circuits.

Vaudeville circuits were either big time or small time, although in practice it was more a matter of big time, good small time and bad small time. Performers usually referred to circuits as *time,* playing Pantages time, Gus Sun time or, heaven forbid, Butterfield, Crescent or Fally Markus time. The start and growth of circuits were a boon to performers and theatre owners alike; they brought stability to the process of planning and booking a season. The performer no longer needed to write ahead to dozens, perhaps hundreds, of theatres and then try to fashion a schedule that was coherent in terms of the calendar and geography. The theatre owner, in turn, got access to a reliable supply of acts and was able to book a balanced bill of fare throughout the season.

In time, the booking operations were subsumed by the largest circuits. Power became concentrated in the hands of the few, who dictated salaries and routes. The option for all but the very most popular performers was take it or leave it. This led to the rise of the union movement in vaudeville and the legitimate stage.

The two-a-day policy of the big-time theatres did not long survive the success of sound movies or the collapse of the economy in the late 1920s and early 1930s. The once grand flagships of the premier circuits could no longer afford the high weekly talent costs and the overhead because their audiences could no longer afford high ticket prices. Theatres turned either to a grind policy of four to six shows a day or they brought in motion pictures. Some majestic vaudeville houses adopted a presentation-house policy, offering four or five acts of vaudeville preceding a major motion picture.

Acts that had become accustomed to 40 weeks a year of big-time vaudeville bookings learned to accept the reality that relatively steady work in vaudeville meant going back to the (good) small time like Loew's. Eventually, that option shrank, and, as circuits and individual theatres abandoned vaudeville to book movies, acts either found something else to do in show business or they relied upon independent agents to find them work. For many, it was a case of taking whatever was offered, often a single night's booking at a fraternal hall. Cans filled with reels of Hollywood movies were playing the circuits of theatres by then.

CIRCUS

Most forms of theatre and the vernacular shows can claim roots in antiquity, but few have roots as apparent as circus. The circular or oval shape of the audience seating was carried over from the pageants and entertainments of the Roman Empire. In the earlier Roman Republic, however, the shape of the outdoor arena was very much like modern racetracks; indeed, chariot races were the primary reason for the elongated shape.

As the variety of the presentations grew from the days of the Roman Republic through the centuries of the empire, the oval shape tightened into a circle to accommodate demonstrations of athletic contests, armed battle among mounted horsemen and canned hunts (animals from the wild were trapped within the arena and then systematically slaughtered by spear,

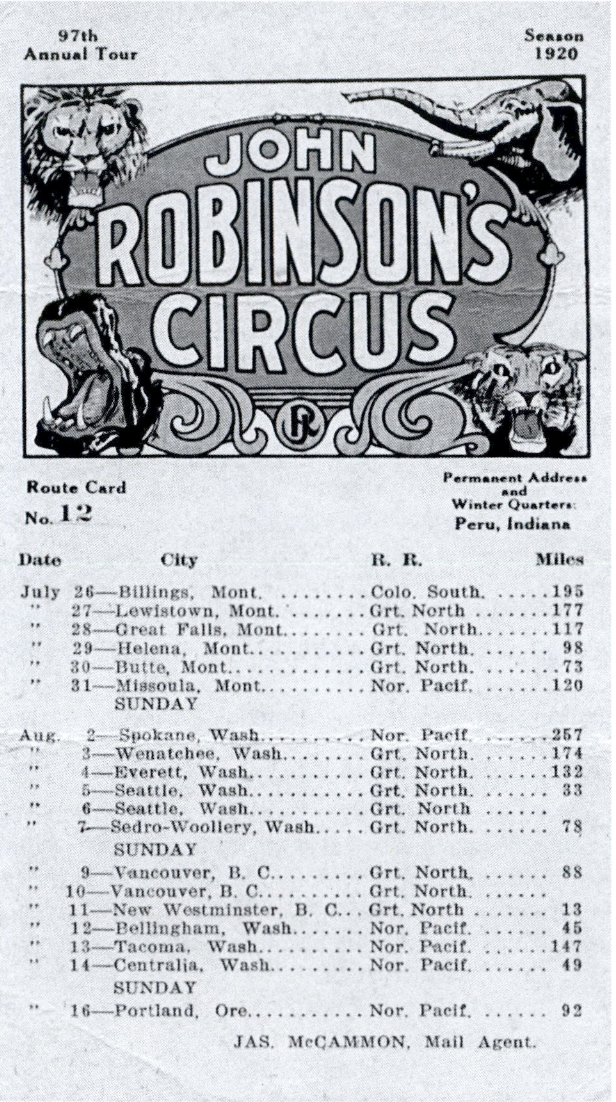
97th Annual Tour

Season 1920

JOHN ROBINSON'S CIRCUS

Route Card No. 12

Permanent Address and Winter Quarters: Peru, Indiana

Date	City	R. R.	Miles
July 26	Billings, Mont.	Colo. South.	195
" 27	Lewistown, Mont.	Grt. North	177
" 28	Great Falls, Mont.	Grt. North.	117
" 29	Helena, Mont.	Grt. North.	98
" 30	Butte, Mont.	Grt. North.	73
" 31	Missoula, Mont.	Nor. Pacif.	120
	SUNDAY		
Aug. 2	Spokane, Wash.	Nor. Pacif.	257
" 3	Wenatchee, Wash.	Grt. North.	174
" 4	Everett, Wash.	Grt. North.	132
" 5	Seattle, Wash.	Grt. North.	33
" 6	Seattle, Wash.	Grt. North	
" 7	Sedro-Woollery, Wash.	Grt. North.	78
	SUNDAY		
" 9	Vancouver, B. C.	Grt. North.	88
" 10	Vancouver, B. C.	Grt. North.	
" 11	New Westminster, B. C.	Grt. North	13
" 12	Bellingham, Wash.	Nor. Pacif.	45
" 13	Tacoma, Wash.	Nor. Pacif.	147
" 14	Centralia, Wash.	Nor. Pacif.	49
	SUNDAY		
" 16	Portland, Ore.	Nor. Pacif.	92

JAS. McCAMMON, Mail Agent.

Route card, 1920

bow and arrow, and sword). The larger arenas hosted re-creations of famous battles. Several were capable of holding water in order to reenact sea battles.

The Roman circus endures most truly in the shapes of the playing fields of modern sport. The flattened oval of the racetrack remains the model for football stadiums, track meets, auto racing and figure skating, and the circle continues to serve for some blood sports like bullfights, dogfights and cockfights and the squared ring for prizefights. Even baseball, basketball and hockey are witnessed from fans seated in a distended circle or oval around the game.

Beyond its housing and the traditional raised ring, called the curb, that marks the boundary between show and spectators, the Roman circus is nearly unrecognizable from its incarnation in the nineteenth and twentieth centuries. Without empire to focus and sustain it, the circus spread in different forms beyond the boundaries of the declining empire. Throughout the period after the Romans, the menagerie shows persisted. Wild animals were captured, caged and carted from town to town, sometimes the breadth of continents, to the wonder of onlookers who had never seen giraffes, lions, elephants, crocodiles and other denizens of far-off lands. Acrobats, jugglers, fire-eaters and sword swallowers were among the performers who either worked their way into the shows or busked on the sidelines wherever the menagerie set up camp.

Acrobats occupied pride of place in the Chinese circus, which evolved contemporaneously with that of Rome. The Chinese circus may even predate those seen during the Roman Republic, and the relative lack (not absence) of emphasis on animals in the Chinese circus may be due to a Buddhist ethic.

Because India lacked the organizational coherence of Rome and China, it is difficult to pin down when circus first emerged there. Probably, it began informally and small enough not to be noticed, much as it developed in Europe from the Dark Ages through the Renaissance. All manner of performers had entertained in marketplaces and courts of India from time immemorial. Conjurers, snake charmers, jugglers, dancers, ropewalkers and illusionists frequented every marketplace and village where there was money, food and lodging to be found. Some form of circus, carnival, menagerie or horse racing as a show of spectacle can be found in the histories of Asia from Arabia to Burma to Mongolia to Japan.

Armed combat between jousting warriors was adopted as both entertainment and as a manifestation of the chivalric code during the late medieval era until the end of the Crusades ushered in a Renaissance that looked for its ideals to ancient Athens and Rome rather than ecclesiastical Rome. The breeding of horses for purposes other than the pulling of plows, carts and carriages led to the military riding academies of the seventeenth and eighteenth centuries. Precision-riding drills gave birth to the equestrian shows of the mid-eighteenth century. In 1768, Philip Astley, who could ride horses while standing atop them, created England's first arena for displays of equestrian skill, and he presented trained animal acts and clowns as well, thus making the first true step beyond horsemanship toward the variety of acts that became the hallmark of the European and American circuses.

Influenced by Astley, an Italian family, Antonio Franconi and his sons, established an indoor circus in France, whereas Charles Hughes, another owner of an English equestrian show, carried the concept to Russia. By the early 1790s, John Bill Ricketts had set up something similar in Philadelphia and New York City.

Originally stationed in buildings either adapted or constructed for equestrian exhibition, the American circus was thought too cumbersome to travel like medicine shows and acting troupes. The construction of the circus tent, credited to the American John Bill Ricketts, probably was an effort to avoid or defer the building of a permanent theatre. Some circuses traveled by wagons. The penned carts served as cages for the animals captured from the wild. Other wagons converted into ticket booths and performers' living quarters or carried equipment.

The rapid expansion of railroads made circus transport easier and more reliable. Unpaved roads in rain and snow became impassable for heavily freighted wagons pulled by horses or oxen. Railway cars were capable of carrying more equipment in most types of weather.

Until the harnessing of steam inside locomotives, the railroads in the early 1800s were largely the same as they were in the 1500s and 1600s: carts drawn over track by cattle, ponies, mules and men, primarily to carry ore out of mines. England led the way in the broader applications of the rails and had put in place the beginnings of a national system of rail transport by 1835. The USA was not far behind, although it had enormous territory to cover. A vast amount of track was laid before the Civil War, and more was added at an ever-escalating pace throughout the conflict and afterward, particularly during the great push westward.

The crafts of maritime commerce had provided many of the tools for theatre. It did the same for circus, with the manufacture of masts, canvas and rope rigging among the more obvious contributions. With canvas at the ready, the circus was able to barnstorm America by rail or wagon. The larger circuses traveled the rails in the late 1860s into the mid-1930s, when the automotive industry devised trucks powerful and large enough to transport large loads, and roadways were expanded and macadamized to accommodate motor vehicles.

Over the decades, tents grew larger, and the possibilities afforded by their breadth and height attracted aerial acts that soon challenged the equestrian acts for status as the royalty of the circus. Greater variety attracted larger audiences, and all through the decades since the Civil War, the American circus has reinvented itself to keep its audiences through changing times.

Acrobats, jugglers, balancers, Risley acts and such could work in vaudeville during the winter layoff of the circus. No matter how accomplished they were, though, the circus acts were largely relegated to opening and closing spots on a vaudeville bill, and they never earned the respect accorded them in the world of circus.

Like all forms of show business during the twentieth century, star power was a growing asset and liability. Advertisements ballyhooed the most popular acts, turning the performers into highly paid stars. Ringling Bros. and Barnum & Bailey paid silent-film Western star Tom Mix $10,000 a week for a season in the 1920s and reckoned he was worth it in drawing power.

The big circuses competed for the most popular acts. As disparity in salaries grew, the top attractions priced themselves beyond what small-time circuses could pay. Over the course of the nineteenth century, the large number of small circuses plying the American byways shrank in number. Entrepreneurs like P. T. Barnum, James A. Bailey and John Ringling were intent on owning the biggest show in the land—and the only show. In the early years of the 1900s, at least 30 circuses traveled by train. Barnum & Bailey, before it was acquired by the Ringling Brothers in 1907, needed 84 railway cars to transport the show. The Ringlings needed the same number to carry their circus. Some of their competitors needed as many as 50 railway cars; others required as few as two or three.

Franz Ebert, lead comedian of the Liliputians

In 1910, a dozen circus owners convened to create a circus owners association. Purportedly, the aim was to drive unsavory owners out of the industry and to institute a code of fair practices. The real agenda was to consolidate power, control wages and eliminate competition. Among the signers were the principals from Ringling Bros., Forepaugh-Sells (which had been owned by John Ringling since 1906), Barnum & Bailey, Sells-Floto, Buffalo Bill, Gollmar Bros., John Robinson, Miller Bros., Gentry Bros. and Hagenbeck-Wallace.

The number of hyphens in the foregoing list indicates the degree of consolidation prior to formation of the circus owners association. The powerhouses that survived consolidation formed a syndicate that coincided in time, and mirrored in purpose, the Erlanger-led Theatrical Trust, which held a grip on legitimate theatres, and the Keith-Albee–dominated United Booking Office, which effectively controlled vaudeville.

At the close of the 1918 season, Barnum & Bailey Greatest Show on Earth merged with Ringling Brothers World's Greatest Shows & Spectacle. When the consolidated debuted in 1919, it became the sole big-time operator and advertised itself as "The Ringling Bros. and Barnum & Bailey Combined Circus, the Greatest Show on Earth."

For brief periods over the next decades, upstart outfits tried to play the same cities as the Ringling Bros. and Barnum & Bailey show but never made much of the dent in the behemoth's box-office take. Shows like the Hunt Brothers Circus lasted for 70 years because they stayed close to their small-time audiences. Clyde Beatty promoted his image as a great white hunter who bent to his will supposedly wild animals, especially big cats. Beatty was a star attraction with a number of circuses including Ringling Bros. and Barnum & Bailey before he went on his own as Clyde Beatty-Cole Bros. Circus. He managed to make a good living but never threatened the supremacy of the Ringling Bros. and Barnum & Bailey show. Most of the upstart, would-be competitors faded back into the small-time circuits after failing to siphon business from the Ringling Bros. and Barnum & Bailey big show. The first two decades of the twentieth century were the golden years for the combined Ringling Bros. and Barnum & Bailey operation.

During the Second World War, John Ringling North brought in Broadway set designer Norman Bel Geddes, Broadway musical revue director John Murray Anderson, modern ballet choreographer

George Balanchine and even modernist composer Igor Stravinsky to move the circus toward art. It was a one-season experiment. In 1956, Ringling Bros. and Barnum & Bailey folded its big-top tent and made the business decision to play only indoor arenas.

By the 1960s, Ringling Bros. and Barnum & Bailey had weathered several decades of tough times, but it emerged as a reduced operation, carrying about 30% to 40% of the performers and equipment it had boasted in its prime. Ownership within the Ringling family had fragmented. In the 1950s and 1960s, financial mismanagement and tax liabilities dogged Ringling staff (but not the Ringling Brothers), and television, far more able to quickly respond to changes in public taste, had become the greatest show on Earth.

Circus underwent another major transformation in the late twentieth century as small, innovative, and alternative outfits attracted audiences that were not charmed by mammoth spectacle and sought more intimate and interactive experiences. European-type affairs like the Pickle Family Circus, with its emphasis on clowns and skilled acrobats, partnered with local sponsors and established firsthand connections with audiences. The success of small circuses (which resembled vaudeville units) was due as much to the ethics of a counterculture as it was to the refreshing absence of corporate showbiz gloss.

These new circuses did not spring up without roots. A number of people like Hovey Burgess, Judy Finelli, Cecil MacKinnon, Larry Pisoni and Paul Binder—were inspired by the European circuses that showcased the talents of its performers and promoted a connection with the audience. Unlike previous generations of circus folk, Burgess and his compatriots were middle-class kids who had studied many forms of theatre and performance work. They were as much influenced by the Open Theatre, San Francisco Mime Troupe, black-box experimental theatre and carnival sideshows as they had been by the Ringling Brothers' mammoth show. Their fresh and informed eyes saw a vision of the new American circus. From this generation of new circus people came Electric Circus, Circo dell'Arte, Pickle Family Circus, Circus Flora, the Big Apple Circus and Cirque du Soleil.

During the late twentieth and the early twenty-first centuries, some of the small collectives and experimental operations disbanded, either for economic and organizational reasons or because its members wished to move on to other projects. The traditional circuses underwent the same winnowing process. Those that did not fold their tents bypassed the large cities and cut their shows down to an economically manageable size.

The alternative circuses, regardless of their individual fortunes, had changed circus in America because they had won the new generations of audiences. There were several reasons. People wanted to be awed by human mastery of skills and rekindle their intimate connection with the circus, and animal-rights groups exposed the cruelties and harmful conditions inflicted on captive animals in traditional circuses.

Cirque du Soleil, which became the most successful circus operation on the planet, never permits animal acts in its shows. The accent is on beautiful, young people of all ethnicities performing daring stunts gracefully. Circus mystique is reimagined by promoting an aural and visual design evocative of world cultures. A sense of wonder and magic is reclaimed through dramatic theatrical lighting and pace.

Clowns and individual specialty acts are best spotlighted at smaller circuses that offer a closer connection with its audience by means of the single-ring European circus that was popular in France, Italy, and Germany in the first half of the twentieth century.

CIVILIAN

Show folks referred to people outside the *profession* as *civilians*. The term was adapted by some to characterize nonshowbiz places, customs and attitudes as well. *Civilian* appears to be a neutral term, but show folk might employ it in much the same way as those in the military do.

BOBBY CLARK & PAUL MCCULLOUGH

Bobby Clark

b: (Robert Edwin Clark) 16 June 1888, Springfield, OH—d: 12 February 1960

Paul McCullough

b: 1883—d: 25 March 1936, Medford, MA

They were like two neighborhoods dogs: the smaller of the two, Clark, always in the lead and McCullough following, sniffing everything that Clark had sniffed. Their romps took them up alleyways and into people's yards, where they trotted around with a purpose unfathomed by humans, then abruptly left for the next yard. At the end of the day, when Clark & McCullough rested from their labors like dogs stretched out for a nap, they knew they had accomplished what dogs were set on Earth to do.

And that pretty much was the point of their sketches. They were the most indescribable of comedy teams. Although Bobby Clark occasionally punned, most of

Bobby Clark & Paul McCullough

his funny lines were random oddball observations to which McCullough assented. Few of their adventures climaxed with wild chases. Generally, they simply surveyed the chaos they had created and, as satisfied as a couple of mutts who have tipped over a garbage pail, scampered on to their next encounter. Their reactions were never in the ordinary mind proportionate to the matter. They tore around the stage, and, in pursuit of an errant collar button, left destruction in their wake.

Paul McCullough looked like a 1920s frat boy who, overnight, had turned into a lodge member—men with a secret handshake—a conventioneer who, mildly intoxicated and bored with his bourgeois world, was happy to hook up for a night's high jinks with a bizarre fellow who promised to kick over the traces the way they never did back home in Muncie, Indiana.

In 1897, Paul and Bobby met at their hometown YMCA in Springfield, Ohio, where Paul encouraged Bobby to join a tumbling class with him. Paul was larger and heavier as well as four years older than Bobby, so Paul may have trained as an understander and singled out Bobby because he was small and light enough to support or manipulate in a Risley act. Whatever the reasoning, they both worked together, became friends and, around 1900, decided they were good enough to turn professional. There was not much call for acrobats and gymnasts in Springfield, Ohio, however. Although the boys were skilled, that was not the same as having an act to perform in vaudeville, so they hooked up with a minstrel show passing though town.

The pay was meager but the work nearly constant in a series of one- and two-night stands. The boys, who had learned to bugle at the YMCA, tooted in the grand parade of minstrels as the troupe entered each town. In the opening scene of the minstrel show, they sang and danced. During the olio between the second and third parts of the show, they gave an exhibition of tumbling. In the afterpiece, they juggled. After the show, they and the rest of the company helped pull the outfit together to travel on to the next town. Paul and Bobby lived up to their end of the contracts, but the owners of the show defaulted. The boys were left without pay by several small-time minstrel troupes.

After a season or two of unrewarding minstrelsy, Bobby and Paul switched to the Hagenbach-Wallace circus, which hired them as tumbling clowns. Gradually, they developed a two-man act that presaged much of their later work. They brought a table and chair into the ring, and Paul jumped up on top of the table. Bobby tried to pass him the chair, but each time it caught on the edge of the table. Bobby paused to take stock of the situation. "Complicated, isn't it?," he asked the audience, then prowled the perimeter surveying the problem from all angles. "Really a problem for a scientist, *but* we will attempt it." In the process, they took off their coats, rolled up their sleeves, then shed most of the rest of their clothing, broke the chair, assaulted each other and destroyed the table. It was the first time that the boy gymnasts-clowns talked in public, and the lines went to Bobby Clark.

They had devised a successful act, switched the emphasis from tumbling to comedy and thus shifted the workload to Clark. In 1906, they were hired as a featured act, The Jazzbo Brothers, by Ringling Brothers, then a premier circus. They traveled with circuses until 1912, when they took their chair-and-table act into vaudeville. Actually, they had developed several routines during their time with circuses, and those were tailored into vaudeville acts.

By leaving the big arena for the more intimate confines of a vaudeville theatre, they moved away from Paul's strength as an acrobat into comedy in which Bobby assumed an ever-growing role. Bobby Clark was a sprightly acrobat as well as a quick-thinking comedian who was funny with words and without them. Even in the mid-1930s, when he was in his late 40s, he was agile and able to jump three feet straight up into the air.

During Clark & McCullough's five years in vaudeville, they employed more dialogue, the acrobatics diminished, and they solidified their stage characters and costumes.

Their costumes were not always the same. Often, Paul McCullough donned a raccoon coat, spats and derby, and Bobby Clark wore a flat porkpie hat and a baggy coat, yet they also favored elaborate costumes like flashy uniforms. Paul was never without his stuck-on toothbrush mustache, and Bobby always carried a cigar and a cane and drew greasepaint eyeglasses on his face.

In 1917, they accepted an offer from Jean Bedini to appear in burlesque. In addition to being the lead performer in a popular comedy-juggling vaudeville act (Bedini & Arthur), Bedini was a producing manager for the Columbia burlesque wheel. Clark once reminisced about burlesque comedy and noted, "We had a lot of good people then. It would be hard to pick out the best. Maybe Joe Welch with his Jewish comedy, or his brother Ben Welch, or Dave Marion, or maybe Frank Tinney. I used to catch them all whenever I could. They were good . . . better than anybody today, I think. Real funny fellows. Make you laugh like you meant it."

They spent as much time in burlesque as they had in either circus or vaudeville, about five years. One burlesque revue, *Peek-a-Boo!,* in which they costarred with another nut comedian and acrobat, Joe Cook, played all over the Columbia wheel from 1920 into 1922. British producer Charles B. Cochran needed a new, low-cost show in a hurry for a theatre he had leased in London's West End. His previous show had closed due to the illness of his star, and Cochran was losing money without a production to pay the rent. Cochran knew Jean Bedini and respected him as a responsible showman. He made a deal with Bedini to bring *Peek-a-Boo!* to London posthaste. *Peek-a-Boo!* was renamed *Chuckles of 1922* and became a big hit.

Irving Berlin, in London at the time, caught Clark & McCullough's performance. Impressed, he signed them for his new *Music Box Revue* scheduled to open on 23 October 1922 on Broadway. The boys, along with Charlotte Greenwood and William Gaxton, contributed to the second edition of Irving's *Music Box Revue,* which ran nine months on Broadway. At the end of its Broadway stand, the show toured, and Clark & McCullough went with it. They had earned sufficient fame to receive offers to play vaudeville dates at two Albee houses, the Hippodrome (by then reduced in glory), the Palace and other big-time venues.

Clark & McCullough returned for the fourth edition of the *Music Box Revue* in 1924. The revue had declined in popularity with each subsequent season, and the fourth edition (despite Bobby Clark and Fanny Brice as Adam and Eve) proved to be the end of the series. It was in this revue that Bobby Clark, in addition to the sketches he played with McCullough, also appeared in two other sketches without Paul. Reviews raved about Bobby Clark, but Paul McCullough's notices were almost embarrassed afterthoughts.

By this time, Bobby Clark's stage characterization had thoroughly evolved. In burlesque, his character developed a randy quality, and good-natured lechery became part of Clark's muttlike character. He was compared to Groucho Marx; both had a swift, crouched walk, toyed with prop cigars and spouted non sequiturs. Groucho had a greasepaint mustache and eyebrows; Bobby had greasepaint eyeglasses. Both were members of a madcap comedy team with an anarchist bent. Groucho's character, however, was deceitful, cynical, occasionally morose and a low-grade gigolo in search of an easy life. Clark's was a carefree, libidinous sprite whose pursuit of sexy women was prompted solely by his libido.

Up to this point, Clark & McCullough had been riffing on the many bits and skits they had developed during their dozen years in vaudeville and burlesque. *The Ramblers* (1926) was a book show, a Kalmar & Ruby musical comedy with the semblance of an evening-long narrative. Clark was a phony spiritualist, and McCullough, predictably, was his assistant. Newcomer Bob Hope was in the cast. The show, one of the first of Broadway's 1926–27 season, was more popular with the public than the critics, and it ran the full season. Reviewers, however, did praise Clark & McCullough, especially for the finale that the duo turned into an overheated operatic farewell to each other, to the rest of the cast and chorus, and, finally, as the boys piled into the theatre aisles, to the audience. It was a bravura tour de force that only they or The Marx Brothers or Olsen & Johnson were capable of pulling off.

At the time, Hollywood scouts were roaming Broadway in search of potential stars for the new talking pictures. Unfortunately, Clark & McCullough signed with Fox Films, a studio intent on capturing all Clark & McCullough's old material and stretching it out to 30 or 40 minutes in all but the first few of the 14 films they made for that studio. There was little inclination on Fox's part to create new material for the team. Although Bobby and Paul were not pleased with the Fox experience, they liked the Hollywood *shushy* (money), so, between 1931 and 1935, the team made 22 two-reelers for another studio, RKO. Years later, Sam Goldwyn enticed Clark back to Hollywood to make his only full feature-length film. *The Goldwyn Follies* (1938) was so stuffed with talent (Clark, the Ritz Brothers, Edgar Bergen & Charlie McCarthy, Ella Logan, Kenny Baker, Vera Zorina and Phil Baker) that only the Ritzes and some undeserving starlets got enough screen time to show what they could do. Clark was even denied the use of his greasepaint glasses, although Groucho Marx had proved that a greasepaint mustache was acceptable to movie audiences.

In the meantime, Broadway offered them a major production. George and Ira Gershwin wrote music and

Clark & McCullough

lyrics, and George S. Kaufman wrote the book for *Strike Up the Band* (1930). What started out three years earlier as political satire with an antiwar message flopped in Philadelphia, thereby giving proof to Kaufman's definition of satire as "something that closes on Saturday night." Morrie Ryskind was called in to change satire to spoof, and the Gershwins obliged the producers with some new songs. The cast was changed, and Clark & McCullough starred. Clark played the lead and McCullough, his assistant. Blanche Ring had a featured role. The show ran six months, a solid hit in a bad year for Broadway.

They went back to England in 1931 for *C. B. Cochran's Review* [sic], but neither luck nor audiences were with them that time. Although the provinces enjoyed the show, Londoners stayed away. Back home that same season, Clark & McCullough's next show, *Here Goes the Bride* (1931), lasted one week at the Forty-Sixth Street Theatre. Because Clark played the valet, Paul was cast as the valet's valet.

Walk a Little Faster (1932), a revue, costarred Beatrice Lillie with Clark & McCullough. Even three of the finest comedians on Broadway needed good material, which they did not get from S. J. Perelman, a celebrated humorist who wrote more successfully for light comedians than true clowns like The Marx Brothers or Wheeler & Woolsey. Still, Bea Lillie and Clark & McCullough were able to draw customers for three months. *Thumbs Up!* (1934), another revue, came along with promise. John Murray Anderson directed and Robert Alton choreographed. Eddie Dowling produced and appeared in the show; his wife Ray Dooley walked away with the best reviews. Jack Cole, Paul Draper and Hal Leroy ensured that the dancing was tops. The show kept the St. James Theatre lit for four months, which was a lot better than some Depression-era shows were faring.

Musical theatre historian Stanley Green noted that *Thumbs Up!* was the first show in which Clark & McCullough dispensed with their customary opening gag: Clark used to do a quick juggle with his stogie, drop it and then beat McCullough into retrieving it by snapping his cane at him. Also, Paul appeared only in two sketches, whereas Bobby appeared in most of them, and Bobby was writing some of the dialogue.

During the summers, between their Broadway assignments, Clark & McCullough sojourned in Hollywood, where they made their two-reel shorts for RKO. After they finished the last batch that was released in 1935, they agreed to head up the touring cast of a *George White Scandals* revue until it returned to New York.

Upon reaching the East Coast, Paul McCullough entered a Massachusetts sanatorium for what was reported as a rest for nervous exhaustion. A friend picked Paul up at the hospital upon his release in March 1936 to drive him back to Manhattan. While passing through Medford, Massachusetts, Paul told the driver he wanted to stop for a professional shave. Paul walked into a barber shop and chatted up the barber. The next moment, Paul grabbed the barber's straight razor, slit his own wrists and then his neck. Rushed to a local hospital, he died a few days later.

No definitive explanation has ever been published about why and by whom Paul McCullough was downgraded in the partnership or why he killed himself. All Bobby Clark would say is that, "I think it was just something Paul couldn't help. Something that had been with him a long time and he didn't know it." Several explanations were bandied about. Some thought that Clark so completely dominated the partnership on and offstage that McCullough grew unsure of his own talents and became despondent. Others held that Paul's diminishing activity in the act was due to growing nervousness, anxiety or mental illness. It had been no secret that several people in the business, cozying up to Bobby Clark, had suggested that he dump his partner, but Bobby always dismissed such talk. Perhaps feeling slighted led to anxiety, and anxiety precluded full participation in the act. Whatever the case, Bobby Clark was too crushed to say more and went into seclusion until he knew it was best to return to work.

Return he did in the fall revision of the *Ziegfeld Follies of 1936.* Originally, the show opened in January 1936, but in May, Fanny Brice, its chief individual attraction, took ill. When the show reopened in the fall, Bobby Clark and Gypsy Rose Lee replaced Bob Hope, Josephine Baker and others, and the critics approved. Clark refurbished an old burlesque sketch for Gypsy and himself. She was the demure but seductive and leggy witness on the stand; he was the leering and lecherous judge. After the show closed on Broadway, Clark toured it.

It was too readily conceded that Bobby Clark was the whole show because Paul was a capable feed and had his own charming way of telling a joke. McCullough also offered a connection between the mundane and the mad. Bobby Clark was mad. A madder hatter than Bobby Clark there never was on Broadway.

Clark was as successful without McCullough as he had been with him. Part of the reason is that Clark's character worked as well or better playing against female comedians like Fanny Brice, Gypsy Rose Lee and Mary Boland. As a solo star, Bobby Clark appeared on Broadway in nearly ten shows over the remaining 20 years of his career. Two long runs were revues: *The Streets of Paris* (1939, with Carmen Miranda, Abbott & Costello and Gower Champion & Jeanne Tyler), which ran for nearly nine months and gave Bobby the chance to do a quick-change routine that unraveled, and *Star and Garter* (1942, with Gypsy Rose Lee and Georgia Southern), Mike Todd's top-dollar burlesque show that racked up 609 performances.

Between those two old-reliable, ribald and risible shows, Bobby Clark ventured into new territory. He acted in the Players Club's production of William Congreve's Restoration comedy *Love for Love* (1940). The other members of the cast were distinguished stars of the legitimate stage: Cornelia Otis Skinner, Peggy Wood, Dudley Digges and Dorothy Gish. The idea of low-down Bobby Clark acting in a classic English comedy first produced in 1695 ensured packed houses for all of its limited one-week run. It was his first stage appearance in decades without his trademark painted-on glasses. Clark's next stage venture was a straight play with a contemporary setting. Unlike the Players Club's *Love for Love* of the previous season, *All Men Are Alike* (1941) had a short run that was unintentional.

He reverted to classic English comedy of manners by acting in Richard Brinsley Sheridan's *The Rivals* (1942) for the Theatre Guild. Clark played Bob Acres; Mary Boland was Mrs. Malaprop. Director Eva LeGallienne, of the legitimate theatre but no stranger to vaudeville, famously said to Bobby, "Mr. Clark, I'll do my best to keep the other actors out of your way." The distinguished Walter Hampden was one of the other actors.

Star and Garter (1942–43) brought Bobby Clark back to girls and gags; at one point in the proceedings he quipped to the audience, "And to think I left the Theatre Guild for this." Clark followed that commercial success with another. *Mexican Hayride* (1944), a musical comedy, gave Bobby a Cole Porter gem to sing ("Robert the Roué"), made a star out of June Havoc and ran for 481 performances.

Bobby Clark had been so well received critically in the classic roles that he attempted one more. With an uncredited collaborator, Clark adapted a Molière classic, *The Would Be Gentleman* (1946). Bobby cavorted in wigs and period costumes and got a lot of mileage out of props. Purists quibbled, but others felt Clark's fresh approach gave Molière's play a lively production instead of carefully presenting it as a musty museum piece. It ran nine weeks, which was a commendable Broadway run for a 300-year-old play (it debuted in 1670 in Paris). Just as amazing was that Mike Todd produced it.

Bobby enjoyed another long run with a revival of Victor Herbert's *Sweethearts* (1947) at the Shubert Theatre. Although only 35 years old, the operetta seemed antique in the post–Second World War era of jivey pop music. That Bobby Clark made the show run nearly the entire season surprised the Broadway wise guys. He also reverted to his greasepaint glasses, cigar and sawed-off cane. At one point in the doings, Clark turned to the audience, "I'll convince Lady Lucy that I'm her long-lost husband, find out which girl is the adopted daughter, and become the big shot of Zilania—and that's all the plot you'll get out of me!"

As the Girls Go (1948) marked Bobby Clark's last Broadway appearance. Mike Todd again produced, and it appeared that he had a major flop on his hands. In desperation, Mike turned the show over to Bobby, who turned it into a riot that stayed on Broadway for more than a year. In 1950, Clark directed the sketches for *Mike Todd's Peep Show* but did not perform. A revival of *Flahooley,* retitled *Jollyanna* (1952) did not make it out of Los Angeles and San Francisco, and the company of *Damn Yankees* (1956) that Bobby headed on the national tour was not the Broadway cast. Critics were divided as to whether Clark made an evil enough devil.

Damn Yankees was Clark's last show. He made a few television appearances, including a maddeningly dull William Saroyan playlet on *Omnibus* in which Bobby and Bert Lahr were directed to sit still on stools and spout pseudo-French.

More appropriately, he hosted a single edition of NBC's *Colgate Comedy Hour* (1950) and played the Ugly Duchess in a televised version of *Alice in Wonderland* (1955) that costarred Eva LeGallienne (it was her adaptation and production), Martyn Green, Reginald Gardiner, Elsa Lanchester, and Burr Tillstrom and his marionettes. After the death of Bobby Clark in 1960, only Beatrice Lillie and Bert Lahr remained of the last great generation of Broadway sketch comedians.

Offstage, Bobby Clark was the opposite of his performing self. He was wed once, to Angele Gaignat, and the marriage lasted for nearly 40 years until his death. Fellow cast members, who expected a lively prankster at rehearsals, were usually surprised to discover he was a quiet, serious man. Clark was conscientious about his craft. He experimented and worked diligently to create material and business that allowed him to perform with brio and seeming spontaneity.

BESSIE CLAYTON

b: ca. 1888—d: 1950?

According to contemporaries, Bessie Clayton was the finest acrobatic dancer of her day. She performed mainly on pointe, and was noted for balancing on one toe as she kicked backward and touched the back of her head while staying perfectly balanced. As Caroline Caffin observed in 1912, "What a marvelous whirl of energy is Bessie Clayton. Her suppleness and absolute control [of] muscle and the lightning speed of her movements leave one gasping. She is here, there and everywhere, and always buoyant, light-hearted, inconsequential and full of that restless, tireless nervous energy that animates so much of American life."

Like William Collier and Frankie Bailey, she came to Weberfields after several years' apprenticeship with the Charles Hoyt farces, such as *A Trip to Chinatown* (she replaced Loie Fuller in 1892) and *A Black Sheep and How It Came to Washington* (1895). Clayton was usually the lead dancer in shows (unless Frankie Bailey or Bessie McCoy was also cast and shared honors). Clayton was a leggy delight for the men, a symbol of charm for the women and a lighthearted delight for all.

Bessie joined Weber & Fields Music Hall when her husband, Julian Mitchell, was hired to stage the shows, and she left when he did. For five-and-a-half of the Weberfields seasons, from 1897 through 1902, Bessie Clayton remained a mainstay, appearing in most of the Weberfields shows, including *Hurly Burly* (1898), *Helter Skelter* and *Catherine* (both 1899), *Fiddle-dee-dee* (1900), *Hoity Toity* (1901) and *Twirly Whirly* (1902).

In 1900, she took a break from Weber & Fields Music Hall to support Marie Dressler in *Miss Prinnt*, an expensive flop. After her Weberfields seasons, Bessie costarred in Victor Herbert's *It Happened in Nordland* (1904) with Lew Fields, Marie Cahill and May Robson; *Wonderland* (1905); *The Belle of Mayfair* (1906); *Hip, Hip Hooray* (1907) and *The Merry Widow Burlesque* (1908), both with Joe Weber (the latter show also boasted Weberfields alumni Charlie Ross, Mabel Fenton and Peter F. Dailey); the final Weber & Fields reunion show, *Roly Poly* (1912), with Marie Dressler, Nora Bayes and Jack Norworth; and the *Ziegfeld Follies of 1909*. Many of these shows were directed by her husband. Alone, she joined the Joe Weber & Lew Fields reunion show of 1912, *Hokey-Pokey*, along with Fay Templeton, Lillian Russell, Willie Collier and John T. Kelly.

In 1913, Bessie danced at the Palace Theatre; it was the sixth week of its first year and the first bill to show a profit. Having Ethel Barrymore as the headliner brought in the customers. Bessie Clayton's last appearances were in vaudeville. She toured the Orpheum circuit in 1915 with "a lavishly costumed act" and added to her turn by performing "Ballin' the Jack" on pointe. Bessie's act in 1919 included a dance duo, the Casinos, whose daughter grew up to be Rita Hayworth. Two seasons later, Bessie Clayton was next to closing on the bill at the Palace for the week of 28 November 1921. She retired soon thereafter.

CLEF CLUB

Until well after the First World War, black musicians were generally excluded by the musicians' union from good-paying jobs in theatre orchestras and all-white dance bands. In 1910, James Reese Europe, among the most prominent Negroes in the American music business, decided to create a black response to the New York City union shop, local 310 of the American Federation of Musicians.

Reese brought together his brother John, a teacher; bandleaders Tim Brymn, Ford Dabney, Joe Jordan and James Vaughn; arrangers Will Tylers and Will Vodery; and songwriters Henry Creamer, Al Johns and Tom Lemonier to create the Clef Club. They were determined to raise the profile of black musical ensembles and to establish the professional credentials of black musicians with mainstream America. Within a month, membership grew to number more than 100 Negro musicians.

The Clef Club functioned as a clearinghouse for the African American instrumentalists and for potential employers. The former were assured of receiving a fair wage plus expenses, and the latter were guaranteed that the musicians sent to them through the Clef Club were trained and capable musicians who would appear punctually in appropriate attire. The various bookings through the Clef Club greatly enhanced the reputations of black musicians.

People assumed that they were getting Jim Europe along with the orchestra, so Europe made the rounds each evening and conducted at least one number at each engagement. By 1911, that meant Reese put in appearances at as many as a dozen dances, hotels and private parties.

Many black musical groups came together out of the Clef Club, both small combos and larger orchestras. They gained experience as ensemble players and parlayed that into appearances in nightclubs, black revues and black vaudeville.

A keystone of Europe's agenda for the organization was realized on 2 May 1912, when he produced the first Clef Club concert at Carnegie Hall as a benefit for the Music School Settlement for Colored People. The enormous orchestra numbered more than 130 musicians. Many of them were string instrumentalists, 14 of them played pianos, and the orchestra was augmented by a choir. Three thousand people attended, and the event was repeated in February 1913.

So strong was the impact of the Clef Club that the American Federation of Musicians local hall in New York voted to admit black musicians to membership. The Clef Club continued another 20 years as a benevolent association.

MAGGIE CLINE

b: 1 January 1857, Haverhill, MA—
d: 11 June 1934, Fair Haven, NJ

"'The Bowery Brunhilde' strode to the footlights with the easy assurance of one who had arrived and conquered," a critic noted in 1891. Maggie Cline was a star by then, and she dressed like one. Tall, plain, friendly faced and quite plump, she engaged in some friendly repartee with the music director and the musicians in the orchestra pit: "What do you think I weigh, George?" The leader offered a diplomatic answer of 135 pounds, but the drummer thwacked his bass drum. "How dare you!," snapped Maggie. "If I were to take one fall onto you, Mr. Hammerstein would lose his handsome little drummer. You're jealous of me 'cause you knew me before I wore these," pointing to large diamond brooches glittering on her bosom. Turning away from the drummer, she announced, "Now, ladies and gentlemen, I will sing the dainty and pathetic little ballad that drove me into this business." Looking to the gallery, she gave a belligerent hitch to her waistband and, in her powerful contralto, launched into the song she could never escape. She bobbed, jabbed and feinted as she belted out "Thrown Him Down, McCloskey," a tribute to the bare-knuckle brawls of the day that passed for boxing.

'Twas down at Dan McDevitt's at the corner of the street,
There was to be a prize fight, and the parties were to meet
To make all the arrangements, see everything was right
'T'row him down McCloskey,' was to be the battle cry,
(A startling crash was heard from backstage as stagehands dropped wooden beams to the floor for sound effects.)
'T'row him down McCloskey, you can lick him if you try.'
And future generations with wonder and delight
Will read in history's pages of the great McCloskey fight.

According to Cline, she got the idea to use the stagehands to create the clatter from some local newsboys. "McCloskey" was one of their favorites. The lads who could not afford the dime for a balcony seat crowded the stage door in the alley to hear Maggie. When she reached the chorus, all the gallery gods chimed in the singing. Outside the newsboys added their lusty voices and banged an assortment of metal trash-can covers and whatever else was at the ready.

At the end of "McCloskey," Maggie always brought the stagehands onstage for a bow. They were known to their neighbors in the audience and were kin to some, so Maggie's gesture always brought an extra round of hearty applause and hollers.

Her theme song was written by a fellow Irishman and vaudeville performer, J. W. Kelly, "The Rolling Mill Man." Kelly picked up a few extra dollars writing songs for other acts; it helped pay his bar bills. No one had wanted "McCloskey," so when, in 1890, Maggie Cline asked Kelly if he had something in her line, he offered her the song, and she sang it throughout the remaining 27 years of her career.

She had not started out in life as a singing comedian. Her parents were immigrants from Ireland who settled in the factory town of Haverhill on the Merrimac River, north of Boston. Her dad rose to foreman in a local shoe factory, where he got his teenaged daughter Maggie a job. Maggie liked neither work nor home, and she ran away a few times before her family faced the inevitable and helped her get a job with a traveling troupe of players and performers, Snellbaker & Benson's Majestics. One of the company's next stops was at the Old Howard Theatre in Boston. She remained with Snellbaker & Benson as the troupe toured the Midwest but decided that she would get ahead as a solo act.

At first, she inclined to romantic and wistful ballads but found she earned more applause when she sang Irish songs. She began costuming as a stage conception of an Irish colleen. She grew heavier with each season and decided that ballads were no longer appropriate. Ever with an eye out for new, humorous material, she gave a fair number of songs a trial. Several made it into her repertoire and stayed there for seasons: "Mary Ann Kehoe," "The Pitcher of Beer," "How McNulty Carved the Duck," "Nothing's Too Good for the Irish," "Choke Him, Casey, Choke Him," "Slide, Kelly, Slide" and "Down Went McGinty to the Bottom of the Sea." All were good songs for Maggie, but not one of them equaled "Throw Him Down, McCloskey" in popularity with the lads in the gallery.

Maggie Cline, "The Irish Queen," was a creature of vaudeville. There was immediacy between her and her audiences. If a gallery god called out to her, she answered him in kind. There was a publike atmosphere when Maggie Cline presided on the vaudeville stage. Even with the informality, her act never sagged; it was earthy, peppy and funny. After an encore, she might call for a drink, and a stagehand would bring her a glass of water. Looking up at the boys in the balcony, she sniffed the water. "And this is what they give me when I'm just dying for a glass of beer."

Although she was dolled up onstage, her fans knew that Maggie was one of them, and if matters got too rough, there was no doubt that Maggie herself could sort it out. "When I go to a place to sing there's nothing can stop me but the police, and they're on my side to a patrolman."

Nevertheless, she decided to try Broadway and starred in two productions, *The Prodigal Butler* (1893) and *On Broadway* (1896). Both were middling successes that could not showcase Maggie's strength: playing to an audience. Maggie realized that her place was in vaudeville, and there she stayed until she retired. She played the Palace in 1914. Maggie's audiences thought they knew her, but she kept her private life to herself. Few knew she had married a tavern owner, John Ryan, in 1888 and had a home sequestered in the small Hudson Valley town of Red Bank. In Red Bank, she was known as Mrs. John Ryan.

After her retirement in 1917, she lived full time in Red Bank. She had made and held on to more than enough money to live in comfort, and she resisted all attempts to return to the stage. In 1928, Maggie and John sold their holdings and moved to Fair Haven, New Jersey. It was there she fell ill in 1933 and died the next year. Maggie Cline and big-time vaudeville started and ended together.

CLIQUOT

In America, sword swallowers were found more frequently in old variety halls, circus sideshows and fairs than in theatres, but, if an act was daring and sensational, certain vaudeville theatres in the late 1890s and early 1900s booked it.

Cliquot was such a performer. He was born in Chicago, and his real name was Frederick McLand, but he billed himself as "Chevalier Cliquot" and claimed to be French Canadian. He was active as a performer during the period from 1875 to 1900 or so.

In his act, Cliquot swallowed swords with blades as long as 22 inches, and he could fit more than a dozen 19-inch bayonets down his throat at one time. For a novelty, he swallowed an electric bulb attached by a cord to a battery. His most famous trick was to swallow a sword attached to a crossbar from which hung two 18-pound dumbbells.

Repeatedly, he suffered injuries onstage. They were often from the misguided efforts of people in the audience, such as doctors, who rushed onto the stage to extract what they assumed must be injuring him. Unfortunately, their extractions were more harmful than Cliquot's feats. He reached his peak of fame in the 1890s; thereafter, he took up residence in England, where he became an agent for music-hall performers.

CLOSING IN ONE

Most acts in vaudeville played their entire act *in one, two* or full stage. Some acts could perform part of their act in a larger space, then come forward and play the end of their act downstage, in front of the dress curtain or traveler, thereby allowing the crew to set the stage behind them for the next act. That was called *closing in one.*

George Burns and Gracie Allen were able to finish their act *in one.* After performing a sketch and a song and dance *in two,* they briefly retired to the wings as the audience clapped and the front tabs closed. When they returned to the stage, ostensibly to acknowledge their applause, they emerged in front of the house curtain and played the balance of their act *in one.* George asked Gracie about her relatives, and the ensuing patter took several minutes. "Say Goodnight, Gracie," was the cue for their exit music.

CLOTHS

Drops, or drop curtains, that had scenes painted on them were known as cloths. Most theatres worth the designation had a selection of these cloths. A few acts carried their own scenic cloths, but many relied upon the selection that most vaudeville houses had on hand.

When lowered, the scenery or plain drop was framed or masked by a teaser, (a short drop like a household window valance) that masked or framed the top of the scenic drop. From both wings, tabs (like window drapes) extended a foot or so onto the stage and masked the drop on the sides. Similarly, a strip of black material was attached along the bottom of the drop, on its backside, that hung a couple of inches lower than the bottom edge of the drop. This blocked out light that might peek under the drop. The teaser and the tabs extended beyond the audience's view and prevented backstage light escaping around the borders of the drop.

Capable scenic painters were in demand to create cloths. Most rendered highly realistic scenes such as gardens and ballrooms (suited to acrobats, dance acts and some sketches), street settings (a storefront on a corner, for instance, that worked well for comedy acts), and an interior of a home (humble rather than grand, which could serve as a setting for melodramas).

From the 1920s onward, however, some scenic artists offered more stylized paintings; some were influenced by newspaper cartoons, whereas others cautiously experimented with newer trends in painting. On the whole, realism was preferred, yet cartooned and impressionistically painted cloths were welcomed in the more artistic and adventurous revues.

Cloths were actually canvas. They were secured to wooded battens from which ropes and pulleys raised and lowered them. As needed, the cloths were *flown in* and *out* of scenes from above the stage. Wooden battens affixed to the bottom of the cloths helped them to hang straight.

Providing these scenic drops for theatres was an offshoot of sail making. In the seventeenth and early eighteenth centuries, both in England and the USA, many, if not most, theatres were built in port cities near the dock areas. They were sited cheek by jowl with shipping warehouses and sail lofts (some of which were converted to theatres). Much of the early theatre technology was adapted from the shipbuilding business. Firms that had the equipment and know-how to fabricate canvas sails used exactly the same skills to provide canvas drops. The scenic painting, however, was an acquired skill done by artists who had learned to paint scenes that were representational when viewed at a distance and withstood the distorting illumination of oil, then gas, lighting.

See Ropes and Rigging

COAST DEFENDERS

Acts that did not venture far from the family hearth were known as *coast defenders.* For a variety of reasons, some acts would not travel. Many had family responsibilities that did not permit spending more than a day or two away from home, other hated the bother of travel. The choice to travel or not depended more upon the nature of the act than the preference of the performer. If an act was an accomplished piano player who sang pleasantly, he was able to work for months at the same hotel, supper club or café. On the other hand, if the act was a monologist, his material quickly became familiar either because people had heard the act or another comic had stolen the jokes and used them in his act in the same locality.

The term *coast defender* was adapted from armed-forces terminology that described those who never shipped out to other posts and were assigned to guard local populations and targets. Applied to show business, it was faintly derogatory, implying fair to poor acts that probably could not make the grade nationally. However, there were some good acts who made the choice to stay close to their home base despite national potential.

COATES & GRUNDY

Coates & Grundy's *Watermelon Trust* was popular with black and white audiences from 1900 until the act broke up in 1914, when Sherman Coates retired. The act included two married couples. They were among the favored black acts that played white vaudeville, appearing on Keith and Orpheum big time and the better small time: Loew's, Poli and Pantages.

According to contemporaries, Grundy, the comedian of the act, was older than Coates. Coates was the straight man who did a dance specialty; he won the admiration of other black dancers who later recalled him as the first acrobatic dancer they ever saw. Their wives sang and danced in the act. When the act split in 1914, Lulu Coates went out on her own with an act called Lulu Coates and Her Crackerjacks. Evidently, the parting was on good terms because Mrs. Grundy recommended a brilliant young dancer, Archie Ware, to Mrs. Coates. That goodwill continued when Lulu retired and encouraged Archie to take over the Crackerjacks as a dance act.

IMOGENE COCA

b: 18 November 1908, Philadelphia, PA—d: 2 June 2001, Westport, CT

From 1990 through 1991, Imogene Coca, Sid Caesar and a third actor took a two-act live show, *Sid Caesar & Imogene Coca, Together Again,* around various theatres and cities, re-creating some of their sketches from the fabled weekly television revue, *Your Show of Shows.* It had been four decades since the skits were first written and performed. Sid was 70 years old; Imogene was nearing 83. Sid Caesar had long ago laid to rest the demons and addictions that had both fueled his dynamic performances and bedeviled his personal life and career. The 1991 Caesar was a healthy, relaxed man who had traded away some of his manic edge. He appeared in all eight sketches.

Imogene appeared only in four, and she made her first entrance slightly dragging one leg, the result of a serious car accident nearly 20 years earlier that cost her the sight in one eye, broke her cheekbone, tore her leg open and fractured her ankle. As soon as she ripped into her first line of dialogue, however, her energy never flagged for an instant. Sid and Imogene re-created skits featuring the bickering married Hickenloopers; the put-upon woman customer who, in a movie theatre, finds herself seated next to an intimidating oaf; and the Italian star in one of their spoofs of European art films. With a huge mop of unruly black hair, wild gesticulation, and spouting a volcano of overwrought gibberish, Imogene Coca was both a fiery caricature of Anna Magnani and the comedian of 40 years earlier still at the top of her game. It was a rare bravura performance and a last hurrah for Imogene. She received a full measure of credit for a performance incredible in a person of her years, yet within a couple of years she retired to a home for actors, where she lived until Alzheimer's disease claimed her, and death came at age 92.

It was odd that Imogene Coca's contributions to the success of *Your Show of Shows* were given short shrift in the various celebrations of Sid Caesar and his writers. A stage play, a movie and a documentary about the show all managed to ignore Ms. Coca. The show boasted television's finest comedy writers, including Danny and Neil Simon, Larry Gelbart, Carl Reiner, Mel Brooks and Woody Allen, but they were smart-assed and obstreperous egoists accustomed to writing wild antic material for men. Often, Imogene had to supply her own solo numbers.

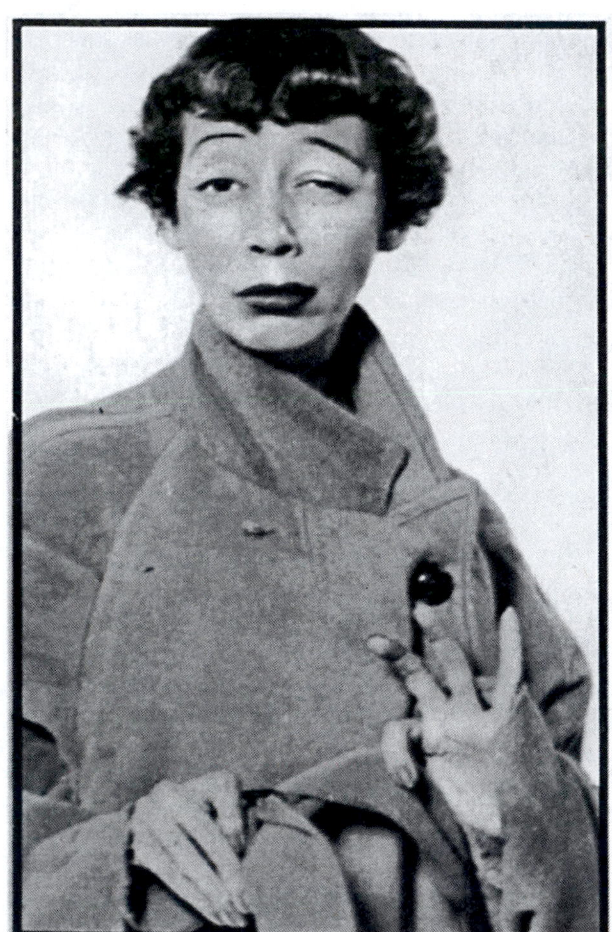

Imogene Coca

The problem began in 1949 when Imogene and Sid, along with Mary McCarthy, Marge & Gower Champion and other stage performers, were hired separately for the *Admiral Broadway Revue* produced by Max Liebman. The writers provided no material for her until she found herself cast in a skit with Sid. She resurrected all the routines she could remember from performing in vaudeville and cabaret.

The next season, Liebman and NBC expanded the show to 90 minutes, renamed it *Your Show of Shows,* moved it from Friday to Saturday night and retained only Caesar and Coca. Liebman added Carl Reiner and a dozen dancers and singers to the cast the first season and Howard Morris the next. Although the dancers and singers were both female and male, Imogene was the only female comedian. The group of 20-something writers, clever as they were, did not know how to write for her and failed to appreciate her approach to comedy.

Imogene was petite; interviewers and critics often spoke of her as elfin. She could dance and sing and play characters from harridans to silent-screen stars to meek, birdlike women and was an exceptional mime. Her dancing tramp was an innocent delight. Perhaps her most engaging bit was a small one that millions of viewers tried in their bathroom mirrors; she slowly closed one eyelid while keeping the other eye wide open.

The reasons *Your Show of Shows* was canceled remain unclear and contested. Was a slight slippage in ratings the cause for a network decision? Did NBC wish to attract more audiences and sponsors by splitting Sid and Imogene and starring each in their own show? Or did Caesar wish to be in charge of his own show? For whatever reasons, the team of Sid and Imogene separated after four successful years.

In fairness, Sid Caesar had the nerve and determination to fight for what he believed he needed: good scripts, a decent time slot, a sufficient budget and control of his own destiny. Imogene was temperamentally opposite to Sid. She was an extremely shy and private person. Imogene claimed that Sid was shy as well, but Sid, with a few drinks in him, would take on the world and claim his rightful due. Imogene seemed always to regard herself as an actor for hire and never a star who could control her own destiny. As a consequence, she earned $10,000 per show, only 40% of what Sid was paid. His $25,000-per-week salary was for both performing and helping to write the show.

Had Imogene not been born into a show-business family, it is likely that she never would have gone on the stage. Her Puerto Rican father, José Fernandez Coca (Joseph Coca) taught music and conducted a pit orchestra in a Philadelphia vaudeville house. Her Irish American mother, Sadie Brady, had run away from home to join Howard Thurston's magic show and became a vaudeville dancer. Imogene, from an early age, was drilled in dancing, singing and piano lessons and was expected to perform in school plays and in amateur shows for which the primary charm was cuteness rather than talent and skill.

Imogene made the transition to professional when, age nine, she began to get local vaudeville dates as both a tap dancer and a singer. Her parents, always supportive of a show-business career, allowed a 14-year-old Imogene the choice of continuing her formal education in high school or going full time on the stage. An indifferent student, Imogene chose the stage. It proved to be a very hard and discouraging life for more than 25 years.

Imogene Coca tried to piece together a career from small-time vaudeville dates, speakeasy shows and work as a chorus girl in musicals and revues. She lived a near-destitute existence from the mid-1920s, when she began looking for work in New York, through the Great Depression years of the 1930s, sometimes sleeping in railway stations and often going without food.

Her first vaudeville partner was dancer Leonard Sillman (1908–82), who later played an important role in her life. Her next partner was Solly Ward (1890–1942), a comedian, whom she married in the 1920s and divorced sometime before the mid-1930s. By 1930, vaudeville, withering, offered less and less to aspiring professionals, and the repeal of Prohibition in 1933 shuttered or transformed the hundreds of speakeasies in Manhattan that had offered work to variety acts. Imogene again tried musicals and revues.

Earlier, Imogene had risen from the chorus into a small role in *When You Smile* (1925), which kept her working little more than a month. The *Garrick Gaieties* (1930), with Sterling Holloway, Philip Loeb and Jack Whiting, ran 155 performances on Broadway before setting out on tour. Imogene earned good notices and kept the wolf from the door that season. Columnist and reviewer Heywood Broun pulled a number of associates together to produce, write and design *Shoot the Works* (1931). His intent was to produce work for some unemployed actors and performers, and he did that, at least for 87 performances. Then, Imogene won a spot in *Flying Colors* (1932), a chic, modernist revue. She was a relative small fry in a revue packed with big-name talent: Clifton Webb, Tamara Geva, Philip Loeb, Buddy & Vilma Ebsen, Charles Butterworth, Patsy Kelly, Monette Moore and Larry Adler. The cast gave 181 performances, but because the show was expensive, it barely managed to return its investment.

In 1934, her old friend Leonard Sillman had somehow pulled together enough money to produce *Low and Behold,* an intimate revue on a shoestring budget. He tried to put a positive spin on a negative—the absence of a star or even a recognizable name in his cast—by renaming it *New Faces.* Charles Dillingham, a grand, old-line producer, was on his uppers. Although he had no money to invest and many of his old-time backers were little better off than he was, the name Charles Dillingham still lent credibility to a production. Sillman pulled off a second coup when he talked Elsie Janis into directing his show. Nancy Hamilton wrote some of the special material as well as being among a cast that included Leonard Sillman himself and future stars Henry Fonda, Hildegarde (Halliday) and Imogene Coca. The show managed a respectable run of 148 performances at the Fulton Theatre. Later that year, on Christmas Day, Sillman opened *Fools Rush In,* another revue produced on the cheap, using some of the *New Faces* talent, including Ms. Coca. It closed in two weeks. Two years later, Sillman again begged, borrowed and stole enough to produce *New Faces of 1936.* Again, Imogene was in his cast, along with Van Johnson. To boost a sagging box office during the run, Sillman added two old faces, the Duncan Sisters, to propel the show into 192 performances (six months) at the Vanderbilt Theatre. In 1935, Coca made a pedestrian comic short about ballet for Educational Films. That same year, Imogene Coca wed actor Robert Burton, and their marriage lasted until his death in 1955.

Elsa Maxwell was the nominal producer of *Who's Who* (1938), Coca's fourth show with Sillman. Presumably, Elsa tapped some of her café society friends for production money, but as the show came and went in three weeks, they got nothing in return except a few house seats.

In 1939, Imogene took a summer-long job in the Catskills; it paid room and board and sent her home with whatever she did not spend of her season's salary of $700. Like everyone else who worked the Borscht Belt, Coca was overworked making guests merry. The *toomler,* or activities director, was Max Liebman, and he had assembled a cast of bright young performers, including Imogene Coca, her husband, Robert Burton, Danny Kaye, Sylvia Fine, Alfred Drake and dancers Jerome Robbins, Mata & Hari and James Shelton, to entertain the resort guests. At summer's end, Liebman and his cast brought *The Straw Hat Revue* to Broadway. Imogene spoofed Carmen Miranda and a Libby Holman–type torch singer. It ran only ten weeks, but a decade hence the experience paid off handsomely for Imogene Coca; Liebman hired many of the Straw Hats performers for *Your Show of Shows.*

Her husband, Robert Burton, soon left show business to join the U.S. armed forces to fight the Second World War. Coca joined Sillman for the fifth time in his production of *All in Fun* (1941), a show that, despite the presence of Bill Robinson in the cast, gave the lie to its title and closed in two days. Once more, Imogene had appeared in a flop. It had been nearly 20 years since Imogene Coca set out on a stage career in 1923. Although she had won good reviews, in all that time Imogene had not made a strong impression on Broadway. Intensely shy, she did not push herself forward or seek work with a variety of producers; consequently, she was still living below the poverty line.

New York cabaret began to change when, in the late 1930s, Barney Josephson, Julius Monk and others began to offer smart and offbeat entertainment for audiences that were adventurous and educated. These cabaret entertainments attracted the smart set, the bohemian and the political types. The cabarets provided Coca with another source of work. The pay was miserable, although it was all the owners could afford given the tiny venues and the small number of people they could hold. James Gavin, in *Intimate Nights,* the definitive history of Manhattan cabaret, records Imogene's ambivalence at the time: "I'm spending three-fourths of my life out of work, and the rest of it among people so chic you can hardly understand them." Gavin credits Coca with pioneering the type of female singer-comedian who relied on warmth, sophisticated material, and a certain off-kilter and subtle humor to charm cabaret audiences.

In an effort to increase the size of her paycheck, Coca joined Jerome Robbins again in *Concert Varieties* (1945), a vaudeville revue that also starred Zero Mostel, the Salici Puppets and Eddie Mayehoff. It opened the first of June at the Ziegfeld Theatre and did not last the summer. It was back to the cabarets: Café Society, Le Rueben Bleu, Blue Angel and others. The money was a joke, but for the first time, Imogene Coca was making a sustained impression among New York audiences and showbiz professionals.

When Max Liebman wished to hire Imogene in 1949 for the *Admiral Broadway Revue,* network executives and ad agencies demurred. Most of them had seen and enjoyed her act, but they felt she was too subtle and sophisticated for the *great unwashed* who made up television's audiences in Tallahassee, Topeka and Tulsa. As proof, they cited her participation in *Buzzy Wuzzy,* a television show of the previous (1948) season that lasted only four weeks. Nevertheless, Liebman prevailed.

The four years, 1950 to 1954, that *Your Show of Shows* ran on NBC on Saturday nights created a high point in their careers that neither Imogene nor Sid could equal or repeat. Indeed, performers and writers like Carl Reiner, Mel Brooks, Woody Allen and Neil Simon were the show's alumni who went on to great success because, as writers and supporting actors, they were less encumbered by legend.

After NBC split the team, Imogene was put into several formats that did not work no matter how much they were revised. The death of her husband, Robert, doubtless sapped some of her will to fight for a good show. Five years later, Imogene Coca married King Donovan (1918–87), a marvelous pint-size comedy actor. Together they starred with Peggy Wood in *The Girls in 509,* which ran 117 performances, from 15 October 1958 until 24 January 1959. Coca and Donovan also performed in summer stock and dinner theatres and stayed married until his death.

Over the years, Imogene made occasional movies and guest appearances on various television shows. She also signed on to several short-lived television series and joined in two attempts to re-create television success by reuniting with Sid, Carl and Howard.

Two highlights were left in Imogene's professional life. First was the success of a major musical comedy. *On the Twentieth Century* (1978–79) was a musicalization of a 1930s comedy stage hit written by Ben Hecht and Charlie MacArthur. For the new version, Betty Comden, Adolph Green and Cy Coleman contributed words and music, respectively. John Cullum and Madeline Kahn starred, and Imogene was billed third in a smallish role, and a superb young physical comedian, Kevin Kline, made a great hit in his featured role. The show ran 449 performances. More than a decade later, the final spotlight shone on *Sid Caesar & Imogene Coca: Together Again.*

Imogene's career stretched almost 70 years, and, although there was a lot of down time, she appeared in many revues, nightclubs, Broadway musical comedies, TV shows and movies. One production rises above the rest: *Your Show of Shows,* one of television's finer achievements. Imogene Coca remains among the great comedians of twentieth century America.

COFFEE-AND-CAKE CIRCUIT

Talking pictures and network radio were clearly ascendant by 1930. Big-time vaudeville was reduced to a dozen theatres, mostly in the Northeast, and there were about 150 or so independent theatres plus various other venues such as fairs and summer resorts that still offered vaudeville.

Consequently, competition was keen among vaudevillians, and bookers did not need to offer much money to attract good acts. Performers, looking at the money they had left over after expenses, derisively referred to their salaries as coffee-and-cake money.

Hence, the remaining small-time theatres were tagged as the coffee-and-cake circuit or the C & C circuit.

GEORGE M. AND THE FOUR COHANS

Jerry Cohan

b: (Jeremiah Keohane) 31 January 1848, Boston, MA—d: 1917

Nellie Cohan

b: (Helen "Nellie" Frances Costigan) ca. 1855, Providence, RI—d: 1928

Josie Cohan

b: (Josephine "Josie" Cohan Niblo) 1876—d: 12 July 1916, New York, NY

George M. Cohan

b: (George Michael Cohan) 4 July 1878, Providence, RI—d: 5 November 1942, New York, NY

The Four Cohans (clockwise from top, George, Jerry, Josie and Nellie)

Largely through Jimmy Cagney's performance in *Yankee Doodle Dandy,* one of the few successful biopics of an entertainer, George M. Cohan still lives in the public memory. Cagney's impersonation has outlived all of Cohan's works except a handful of tunes: "Yankee Doodle Boy," "Over There," "Mary," "You're a Grand Old Flag" and "Give My Regards to Broadway." The Cohan musicals and plays that once invigorated American theatre are seldom revived. His few movies—three silents and two talkies—were unable to represent George M. Cohan as effectively as he appeared in person.

Cohan was honored in his own time for his impact on American theatre. That alone assured him a place in theatre history. He wrote and produced and often starred in more than 60 musicals, plays and revues between 1901 and 1940, and his creation of an Irish American image was a breakthrough in popular characterization. When Cohan was in vaudeville, the popular stage in the United States was still populated by racial and ethnic types. In a country where immigrants were a majority, stage characterization was commonly denoted by costume and dialect.

George M. Cohan was not the first but among the first to present himself not as an immigrant but as an American of Irish heritage. He shed the knobby shillelagh, the cheek whiskers and the "begorra" accent. Young Cohan presented himself as the Yankee Doodle Boy. When he wore a derby, it was tipped jauntily to the side, and his cane was a slim, sleek walking stick. Cohan was clean-shaven and nattily garbed. He spoke and wrote contemporary American spiced with slang instead of the King's English or stage Irish. That made his dialogue accessible and real to audiences and provoked hidebound drama critics.

Asked by critic Ashton Stevens, "Who's the biggest man in the American theater," actor-comedian William Collier replied, "Georgie Cohan . . . he's not the best actor or author or composer or dancer or playwright, but he can dance better than any other author, write better than any other actor, compose better than any other manager and manage better than any other playwright—and that makes him a very great man."

For the first ten years of his career, George was the least popular of the Four Cohans. His gentle and easygoing father, Jerry or Jere, went into show business after a few harrowing years as a surgeon's orderly on the battlefields of the Civil War. When Jerry took to the boards, he simplified his Irish surname, Keohane, into Cohan and pronounced it "Co-HAN." George was the only family member to pronounce it as "CO-en." Jerry was introduced to his future bride in 1874 by his family. Nellie Costigan was witty, easygoing and seldom ruffled by upsets. They soon married. Nellie accompanied her husband on the road, but she did not perform until a leading lady walked out of the company and Nellie was pressed into service. She had heard the part so often that she was letter perfect in the role. Mr. & Mrs. Jerry Cohan, as they were first billed, played in comedy sketches that

George M. Cohan

Jerry wrote. Through the births of three children and the death of one in infancy, Nellie never left the stage until after the death of her husband in 1917.

Nellie and Jerry always took their children on the road with them. If Josie and George were shorted a formal education, they made up for it by mixing with adults in vaudeville and following their own curiosity. Josephine was a graceful, amiable and talented child who soon picked up dancing. At eight years old, she joined the act and did high kicks and handsprings. This developed into a contortion act. Later, as she blossomed, she developed a classy dance act.

George was seven when he joined the family act, but, although he was a good impromptu mimic, any other talents were less discernible. His father encouraged him to study violin, but George had little patience for teachers and incessant scales. At one point, Jerry and Nellie even sent him to stay with relatives and encouraged him to think abut a *civilian* life. That did not work out, and George was soon back with the family, playing second violin in the band and selling songbooks.

The Cohan Mirth Makers, or whatever Jerry might name his company, presented an act that expanded to a full evening, when the bookings called for it, and they hired a few extra acts and musicians. When it was only the four of them with a piano player and George on violin, they shortened the act to about 20 minutes. Nellie and Jerry were the backbone of the sketches, Josie had a dance solo, and Jerry took a solo turn as "The Dancing Philosopher." Georgie attempted baton twirling, juggling and delivering a recitation, but he was little more than a filler to allow the others to make costume changes. He was, however, learning a lot about show business, both ends of it: how to make money and what entertained audiences.

In the 1880s, the Four Cohans accepted offers on several occasions from B. F. Keith. Keith was an unlovely and stingy creature and his wife a sanctimonious cheat. Keith paid as little as he could get away with despite demanding five or six shows a day, but he kept an act employed for several weeks, and that was a godsend to a starving act. Mrs. Keith took one third of the salary back for the board and room she supplied: meager meals and a dormitory filled with sleeping cots partitioned by hanging sheets.

Keith's was not the only hellish booking. Many were in the 1880s. Once the Cohans got six months' straight work, but it demanded six shows a day, six days every week, and every Sunday was rehearsal. Another time, they traveled westward and did one-nighters, traveling to and playing a different town every night for almost a year. Vaudeville was not for delicate constitutions, the faint of heart or thin skinned.

George's first success was as Peck's Bad Boy. Out of the blue, the Cohans were asked to come to New York to act in a production of *Peck's Bad Boy and His Pa.* George played Hennery, the title character, and Jerry and Nellie were his Pa and Ma. Sister Josie was cast as Hennery's girlfriend. Unfortunately, George proved as obstreperous and swellheaded as his character, and all did not run smoothly. The show prospered for 35 weeks, but the Cohans were given their walking papers when George proved the reason for too many complaints from stagehands and electricians whom George thought could do their jobs better. Diplomatic he was not. Right he was.

As George settled into his teens, he took in every show he could, analyzing its weaknesses and strengths. He also began writing songs and sketches for the family act. Soon, he got requests from other vaudevillians to write sketches and special material.

Jerry had inherited the ethic of the nineteenth-century troupers: touring spread the gospel of theatre. George wanted to conquer New York and stop the endless travel. In 1893, after the Four Cohans earned acknowledgement as a favorite act among audiences across the eastern USA, George was determined to try to crack Broadway, even if he had to leave the family. Jerry got wind of his plans and decided to follow his son's hunch. George had emerged as the manager of the Four Cohans. He was 15.

The first breakthrough in Manhattan was an offer for Josie to dance solo at Koster & Bial's for the same salary as the family earned jointly. She was the top performer in the family act. George got a few songs published, but the only offer the Four Cohans received was from comedian Gus Williams for all four to tour in a play. They were lucky to get a season's work, even if it were on the road, but George began criticizing the script and tampering with his role, and the Cohans were dropped after 35 weeks.

The Four Cohans toured vaudeville for several more seasons in the mid-1890s, and George developed into an eccentric dancer and made a hit with audiences. He never had a good singing voice, but he could sell a song because he was a fine actor. At one event, the popular comedian Julius Tannen offered an imitation of George, ending it with an ad-libbed "My mother thanks you, my father thanks you, my sister thanks you, and I thank you." George appropriated the tagline for his own thereafter.

While on the road, they received a telegram from Hyde & Behman to return to New York to replace an act. They were a great success, and George's performances were met with enthusiastic applause. From that point onward, George wrote the act and handled the business, and the Four Cohans developed into one of the top vaudeville acts of their type and time, earning $1,000 a week by 1890.

Josie and George were no longer kids. George was 20 when he married Ethel Levey, a talented soubrette. With her in the Cohan act, there was competition between Ethel and Josie for the same parts and musical numbers. Josie met and married Fred Niblo, a comedy monologist and future film director, and then newlyweds Josie and Fred formed their own act.

George expanded his sketches into full-length plays, such as they were, and began to craft leading roles for himself. Ethel Levey played opposite, and Jerry and Nellie, then about 52 and 35, respectively, took supporting roles.

By 1903, the Four Cohans were no longer in vaudeville. George's first few plays failed to impress the critics and did not particularly excite theatregoers, but *Little Johnny Jones* (1904), was a winner. It was his fifth full-length play and the first not to be expanded from a vaudeville sketch that George originally wrote for the family act. It was the third Cohan play to reach Broadway and the first play he coproduced with Sam Harris, who became one of Broadway's most beloved producers. *Little Johnny Jones* included two of Cohan's most famous songs: "Yankee Doodle Boy" and "Give My Regards to Broadway."

Among Cohan's other 50-some-odd productions were *Forty-Five Minutes from Broadway* (1906), *George Washington, Jr.* (1906), *The Man Who Owns Broadway* (1909), *Get-Rich-Quick Wallingford* (1910), *The Little Millionaire* (1911–12), *Broadway Jones* (1912), *Seven Keys to Baldpate* (1913), *The Tavern* (1921) and *The Song and Dance Man* (1923). During those years, George lost his family. He and Ethel Levey divorced in 1907. Both were decent to each other but strong willed and focused on their careers. They had one daughter, Georgette. Sister Josie died of a damaged heart in 1916. Jerry died in 1917, Nellie in 1928.

Not all George M. Cohan's shows were hits. He had a goodly share of flops, and there were times when he seemed to fall out of favor. Whether a Cohan show was a hit or a miss, he was saluted as "Broadway's favorite son" because he, more than any other producer and playwright, through sheer fecundity, kept alive vernacular American theatre during a time when Broadway had been recolonized by Europe through a flood of operettas.

Cohan wed Agnes Mary Nolan right after his divorce from Ethel. They had three children. George had only a few close friends, and his life was contained in his work and his family. The Actors' Equity strike in 1919 was a difficult and signal event in Cohan's life and career. As a performer, he did not equate himself with a laborer and felt unions were not for actors. As a manager, he opposed unions. Performers and actors considered that George M. Cohan, whom they had known since he was a cocky kid, had broken faith with them. George felt much the same.

As he grew older, Cohan did not write, produce or direct as much. He felt time had passed him by. Harris & Cohan revived some of Cohan's earlier shows with younger men in Cohan's roles. George won praise on new fronts. He became a character actor with his performance in Eugene O'Neill's comedy *Ah, Wilderness!* (1933), which ran for nine months, and a character comedian in *I'd Rather Be Right* (1937–38), a musical comedy from George S. Kaufman & Moss Hart and Richard Rodgers & Larry Hart. It ran for nearly ten months. They were the last major successes of his career.

In 1940, as the USA tilted toward a Second World War, Congress honored Cohan with a special citation for his anthem from the First World War, "Over There," which was about to see new duty. The great man of theatre was suffering from cancer and died two years later, but only after he had the satisfaction of seeing *Yankee Doodle Dandy* become a hit movie and enjoying Jimmy Cagney's impersonation. A quarter of a century later, the man, his family and his music were the subjects of a new Broadway musical comedy, *George M!,* that ran for more than a year at the Palace Theatre.

COLE & JOHNSON

Bob Cole

b: (Robert Allen Cole) 1 July 1868, Athens, GA—d: 2 August 1911, Catskills, NY

Billy Johnson

b: (William Johnson) 1858—
d: 12 September 1916, Chicago, IL

J. Rosamond Johnson

b: 11 August 1873, Jacksonville, FL—
d: 11 November 1954, New York, NY

James Weldon Johnson

b: 17 June 1871, Jacksonville, FL—
d: 26 June 1938, Wiscasset, ME

Bob Cole, Rosamond Johnson and James Weldon Johnson were as important to American theatre, not just African American theatre, as Ned Harrigan. They changed the style of black performance from grotesquerie into more realistic and nuanced comedy just as Ned Harrigan had deepened the comic Irish stage character from the earlier mechanical knockabout. Bob Cole and J. Rosamond Johnson were also one of the first black acts, along with Williams & Walker, to play big-time vaudeville.

A comedian, actor, singer, dancer, instrumentalist, stage director, playwright and songwriter, Bob Cole was the black equivalent in versatility to George M. Cohan and Noël Coward. Rosamond and James Weldon Johnson became two of the more distinguished cultural figures of their day, with Rosamond in music and James as a writer and historian.

Cole's parents were better off than most black families but were not part of the small, emerging professional class of doctors, educators and lawyers. The Coles were all musical, and family and friends gathered to sing and play various instruments, including the piano. For some reason, Bob was sent to live with family in Jacksonville, Florida, around 1882. Perhaps it was there he first met James and Rosamond Johnson.

Bob rejoined his family before they moved to Atlanta, where he completed prep school and made a stab at Atlanta University. Around 1888, however, he headed to Harlem with hopes of a show-business career and wound up in Chicago in time to get employment with Sam T. Jack's *Creole Show* in 1899. Bob stayed with the show several seasons, progressing to a principal member of the troupe—singer, dancer and comedian—and staging the later editions of the show.

Cole married Stella Wiley, another principal in the company. Although they kept their ties to Sam T. Jack, they played vaudeville dates as a mixed double when the *Creole Show* was not booked. In 1894, the couple moved to New York, where Cole tried get his songs published and make a success of the Worth Museum's All Star Stock Company, a small Negro ensemble based in Worth's dime museum and curio hall. Cole tried to expand its scope by offering classes. It was thus that he met Billy Johnson.

There were two teams billed as Cole & Johnson. Bob Cole was the comedian in both. His partner from 1895 to 1899 was known as Billy Johnson. Billy was a veteran of minstrel shows when he met Bob. Although ten years younger, Bob was experienced as a comedian, singer, dancer, songwriter and stage director. Billy had appeared with the small-time Hicks-Sawyers Minstrels; later he toured with John and Will Isham's *The Octoroons* company for a season and then was hired for Black Patti's Troubadours, where he again encountered Bob Cole and Stella Wiley.

Together, Cole and Johnson wrote a number of the songs for the Black Patti show and the one-act sketch they performed in the show. Their comic characters followed the template of the times. Johnson played the con artist, Jim Flimflammer, and Cole played Willy Wayside, a tramp. According to David A. Jasen and Gene Jones, coauthors of the estimable *Spreadin' Rhythm Around,* Cole clowned in whiteface and red beard. Although whiteface had long been common for Caucasian clowns, there is little in the record about black performers in whiteface.

Cole was ambitious and unafraid of demanding what he saw as his due. A request for a salary raise was refused by Voelckel & Nolan, the white producers of Black Patti's show. Cole left the company and took his music with him; that included all the orchestrations—the *sides* that individual band musicians played for the show. A lawsuit ensued. Although Voelckel & Nolan were allowed to continue to play Cole's and Johnson's songs, Bob and Billy were awarded royalties. That ended the matter legally but not practically.

Cole & Johnson created their own show, *A Trip to Coontown,* around their characters, Willy Wayside and Jim Flimflammer, and organized their own troupe. Voelckel & Nolan threatened to blackball performers who went to work for Cole & Johnson and told theatre managers on the road that if they played a Cole & Johnson show, they would not get to play Black Patti's Troubadours, the most successful black company in the USA at the time.

A Trip to Coontown had a rough time at first getting play dates, but word of mouth was positive and bookings improved. The show opened on 4 April 1898 at the Third Avenue Theatre—way Off-Broadway—where it played a few weeks before going back on the road and then coming to New York again, this time at the Grand Opera House at Eighth Avenue and West 23rd Street and retitled as *The Kings of Koon-dom.*

Bob Cole started writing a few songs with James and Rosamond Johnson (no relation to Billy) in 1899, soon after the brothers moved from Jacksonville to Manhattan. Cole and Billy Johnson still had some vaudeville dates to fulfill, which they did. The reason for their break-up was debated: financial disagreements, Billy's drinking or Cole's ambition. Perhaps Cole felt he needed better educated and more creative partners such as James and Rosamond Johnson, both college educated and determined to improve conditions for African Americans. Cole had met Will Marion Cook and heard his arguments for art over mere entertainment. Cole was a practical man. He knew the limitations that show business placed on artistic aspiration, but meeting Cook and the Johnson brothers must have raised his sights.

Before they left Florida, the Johnson boys had enjoyed the benefits of being born into an educated family with a strong sense of purpose. Rosamond was a skilled pianist who had studied with teachers at the New England Conservatory, but, to earn a living, he found work with a John Isham show, *Oriental America* (1896).

James was a black school principal at 23 and the publisher and editor of the first black daily newspaper in the USA by age 24. A few years later, James became the first black lawyer to be admitted to the Florida bar. He also played guitar.

In 1902, J. Rosamond Johnson, younger brother of author James Weldon Johnson, became Bob Cole's new stage partner. Theirs was very different from the Bob Cole & Billy Johnson act. Bob and Rosamond did a 30-minute act dressed in evening clothes and without blackface. They engaged in some casual patter about what kind of music they should perform. Rosamond played a concert selection or two, but Cole persuaded him to play one of their own popular songs. Bob took the melody, and Rosamond harmonized and accompanied on the piano. Cole segued into the Virginia essence or its later version, the soft shoe.

Both James and Rosamond collaborated in writing music on their own and with Bob Cole. Bob Cole and the Johnson brothers wrote mainstream ragtime for white vaudevillians and musical-comedy performers like May Irwin, the Rogers Brothers, Peter Dailey, Anna Held, Marie Cahill, Eddie Foy and Lillian Russell. They also wrote songs sung by black performers Ernest Hogan and Bert Williams & George Walker. Some of their songs, like "Under the Bamboo Tree" and "Aba Daba Honeymoon," were remembered a century later. Cole and the Johnson brothers were the first African Americans to be consistently employed by white producers like Abe Erlanger to create songs for shows. Sheet-music sales paid them thousands of dollars in royalties each year during the early 1900s.

In 1904, Abe Erlanger gave Cole and the Johnson brothers the opportunity to create the entire score for Klaw & Erlanger's new show, *Humpty Dumpty.* It had a middling success, enough for Erlanger to offer them another show, *In Newport* (1904), but that fared poorly. Cole persuaded Rosamond and James that they should produce and write their own show. The plan was to play vaudeville dates in the USA and variety dates in Britain and save the money to invest in a show. James Weldon Johnson, however, was appointed U.S. consul to Venezuela by President Theodore Roosevelt in 1906. That left Bob and Rosamond as a show-business team.

Their first show was *Shoo-Fly Regiment,* and they appeared in it as well. The show dragged on for a year on the road and drained their finances. They had written a second show, *Red Moon,* which they hoped would be more of a success. Again, they had a hard time meeting expenses. Acting the lead roles, keeping the company together and soliciting bookings took a toll.

Red Moon closed in 1910 without making its creators any money, so Cole & Johnson signed to play Keith-Albee time to replenish their coffers. On the final night of their booking at Keith's Fifth Avenue Theatre, Bob collapsed during their act. It was reported that he was exhausted and had suffered a nervous breakdown. Actually, he had entered the paretic stage of syphilis. After a number of weeks in a mental hospital, his mother had him moved to a sanatorium in the Catskills.

One day, ten months after his collapse onstage, Bob Cole, while swimming with other patients, slipped under the water and drowned. There was no public evidence that he had a stroke or heart attack. It was presumed that he chose to end his life. With his death, the theatre world lost its third African American giant in a row: Ernest Hogan (May 1909), George Walker (January 1911), and Bob Cole (August 1911).

Rosamond Johnson needed to keep working. He helped write a revue and then joined Dan Avery & Charlie Hart's vaudeville act. The trio went to England and expanded their act into a revue, *Come Over Here* (1912). Johnson stayed after Avery & Hart returned to the USA.

When Rosamond came back to America, he was appointed music director for a Harlem settlement house. Rosamond's brother, James Weldon Johnson, was an author and social activist, and Rosamond inclined in his direction. He was turning to music scholarship in the black tradition, and he arranged concerts of traditional African American music, work songs and spirituals.

After 1930, his career was checkered. He scored music for several black-themed movies, employing the lush, respectable sounds of overly orchestrated choirs that drained the vitality from the blues and popular music he scored. His heart was in music anthology, and he took movie and revue chores to pay the bills. Once he had been in the forefront of revitalizing the American musical with black melody and rhythm, but he had long been working in other musical directions when he died at 84.

Sixteen years earlier, in 1938, Rosamond's older brother, James Weldon Johnson, died in an automobile accident near his summer home in Maine. He was one of the more famous and honored African Americans of his era. He had become known as a statesman, poet, author of fiction and nonfiction—especially his study of Negroes in New York, *Black Manhattan*—and had been a top-echelon officer of the National Association for the Advancement of Colored People, the premier civil rights organization.

WILLIAM COLLIER

b: 12 November 1866, New York, NY—
d: 3 January 1944, Los Angeles, CA

Born into a theatrical family that tried to dissuade him from a stage career until his education was complete, William Collier, affectionately known to all as Willie, resolved to follow his father's path. Instead of becoming an English tragedian like Edmund Collier, however, Willie developed into a versatile comedian. He became a major star of the legitimate stage, vaudeville and revue; a playwright; a stalwart of the Lambs and the Players theatrical clubs; popular among his fellows; and a noted toastmaster and wit. When someone suggested that good parts made good actors, Collier observed if that were so, then "everyone would be playing Hamlet—that's a pretty good part."

Even at ten years old, his determination for the stage was undeniable, and he ran away from home to join J. H. Haverly's Juvenile Company, a blackface minstrel outfit, on tour with a burlesk of *H. M. S. Pinafore*. The adventure gave him 14 months on the road, after which he agreed to finish grammar school. He lasted barely a year at St. John's Parish School, and his father resignedly arranged in 1882 for Willie to be apprenticed to Augustin Daly's Theatre, where the lad spent five years playing bit parts and learning from the most talented actors of the time.

Eventually, Willie's two sisters also took to the stage, as had their father, mother and an uncle before them. Collier claimed later in life also to have been part of a "pretty bad" youthful quartet that included future New York City mayor Jimmy Walker and future New York governor Al Smith.

In 1889, Collier joined John Russell's company; they performed farces by Charles H. Hoyt, which were very popular at the time. Although some thought him a cut below, Hoyt was Ned Harrigan's only serious rival in satire, and Willie got the chance to play a series of eccentric and extravagant characters. Collier attracted favorable notice in *The City Directory,* one of the 1890–91 season's hits and the first of a series of successes for Collier. In 1897, *The Man from Mexico* made him star. For the 1901–02 season, he appeared in the Augustus Thomas' comedy success *On the Quiet.*

William Collier was dapper, slim, five foot, ten inches tall, with brown hair and eyes. He could play subtle farce or broad burlesk. At first unable to dance, when a part called for it he practiced until he became one of the most original dancers on the stage of his day. He was among that generation of actors—John Drew, William Gillette, Gerald DuMaurier—that strove for an appearance of naturalism on the stage. Even with the broadest comedy, he tended to underplay a bit, holding to a quiet, deadpan technique.

Collier and his first wife, Louise Allen, were engaged by Joe Weber and Lew Fields for their 7th season in 1902–03 when De Wolf Hopper left the Weberfields Music Hall to head his own company in a production of *Mr. Pickwick.* Weber & Fields had to pay $15,000 to Jacob D. Litt to secure Collier's release from his contract, and Collier negotiated one of the largest salaries paid by Weber and Fields to appear in *Twirly Whirly.*

Collier wrote a comedy scene that he played in a Weberfields show. The laughs were in the way it was played as the two actors, including Collier, hemmed and hawed and finally dueled:

He: "Mary, I've got something to say to you."
She: "You've got something to say to me?"
He: "Yes, I've got something to say to you."
She: "Something to say to me?"
He: "Something to say to you."

She: "To say to me?
He: "To say to you!"
She: "Say to me?"
He: "Say to you!"
She: "To me?
He: "To you!"
She: "Me?"
He: "You!"

After a single but very successful season with Weber & Fields, Collier left to star in *The Dictator* (which featured John Barrymore) in 1904 and then formed his own company for a two-year tour in England with a revival of *On the Quiet.* While in London in 1905, he and his first wife, Louise Allen, who often played in shows with Collier, separated. The divorce emotionally taxed both Collier and Allen and drained his assets. The tepid response to his next play in New York, *Caught in the Rain,* of which he was coauthor, did not improve either the financial or emotional atmosphere. So, Collier accepted a year's bookings in Australia. On route to Australia, Willie played a San Francisco engagement, made more exciting than usual by the earthquake of 1906.

In 1908, William Collier successfully returned to the New York stage in *The Patriot,* a farce he cowrote with J. Hartley Manners. (In 1912, Manners authored the smash hit *Peg o' My Heart* for his wife, Laurette Taylor.) In *The Patriot*'s cast was William Collier Jr., who, billed as Buster Collier, was making his debut. William "Buster" Collier Jr. (1904–87) enjoyed a successful stage and film career.

Louise Allen died in 1909, and in 1910 Collier married Paula Marr, an actor. In 1914, Collier formally adopted her son by a previous marriage.

After *The Patriot,* William Collier starred in *The Man from Mexico* (a 1908 revival), *A Lucky Star* (1910) with his wife, Paula Marr, *Take My Advice* (1911), the Weber & Fields Jubilee reunion in 1912, as well as *Never Say Die* with Buster Collier that same year. In 1913, he was listed in *Who's Who.* William Collier got the opportunity to act with both his wife and their son, now billed as William Collier Jr., in *A Little Water on the Side* (1914).

Willie Collier mastered the sly, deft touch needed for contemporary comedies, the mannered style that enlivened classic comedies like Sheridan's *The Rivals,* and the broader comedy of revues. One of those revues was George M. Cohan's *Hello Broadway* in 1914, which costarred Collier with Cohan, his dear friend, and featured the lovely soprano Peggy Wood long before her television days in *I Remember Mama.* In an affectionate nod to Weber & Fields, Cohan's revue, at Collier's suggestion, burlesked the current crop of Broadway plays and musicals. Throughout a jumble of skits, musical numbers and asides to the audience, Collier walked into various scenes with an unexplained hatbox under his arm. At the final curtain, Collier's hatbox was revealed to be empty.

Nothing But the Truth was a substantial hit for Collier in 1916. *Nothing But Lies* kept him busy in 1918, and, in 1920, he cowrote and starred in *The Hottentot.* Collier performed in the first edition of Irving Berlin's and Sam Harris' *Music Box Revue,* which opened Berlin's Music Box Theatre in 1921. It ran for 313 performances and costarred another Weberfields alumnus, Sam Bernard. Collier ended his stage career after the revue *Nifties of 1923* (again with Sam Bernard plus Hazel Dawn) and the popular musical *Merry-Go-Round,* which costarred him with Marie Cahill in 1927.

William Collier had been dabbling in films since 1915, when, as a member of Mack Sennett's Keystone Company, he was on the books for $2,500 a week. Although neither Collier nor any of the other Weberfields alumni signed by Sennett proved to have sustainable silent comedy careers in films, Collier made the transition to Hollywood as a valuable featured character actor and worked in films until 1941, a few years before his death. One of his early appearances in a sound movie was a guest shot in the musical *Free and Easy,* the first talkie feature for Buster Keaton, his son's great and good friend.

JOSÉ COLLINS

b: 23 May 1887, London, England—
d: 6 December 1958, London, England

José Collins was the daughter of Lottie Collins, and, with her mother's guidance, she began her career on the music-hall stage when she was no more than ten. Her first stage engagement of note was in *Scotch Bluebell* (1900), when she was 13. She danced in a tartan skirt and Glengarry while Harry Lauder sang "I Love a Lassie."

Despite her lineage and that auspicious start to her career, it was not until 1904 that the striking 17-year-old beauty next attracted notice; she sang "I've Built a Bamboo Bungalow for You" at the London Pavilion. That led to a tour with Gaby Deslys, and their travels took them to the USA. Within a few years, José Collins was a singing star on both sides of the Atlantic Ocean.

Collins had a lovely singing voice and a natural manner of rendering both songs and dialogue. She was tall, graceful and had a commanding personality

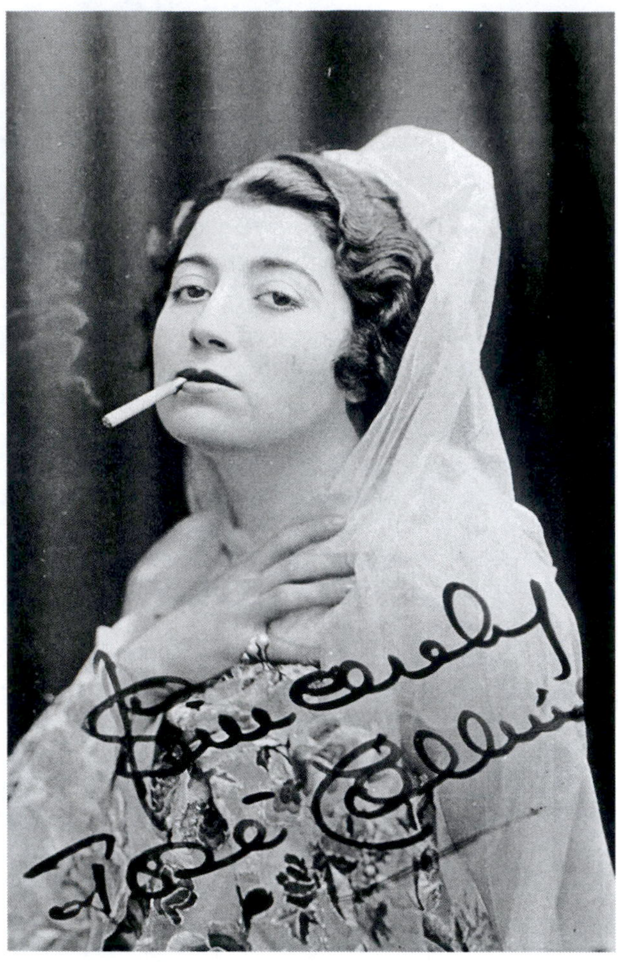

José Collins

onstage. She found easy success with American audiences and enjoyed one Broadway hit after another: *Vera Violetta* (1911) was part of an oddball tripartite entertainment that opened at the Shuberts' Winter Garden with an abbreviated vaudeville bill and closed with a performance of sorts by Annette Kellerman in *Ondine.* In between was *Vera Violetta.* The star was Al Jolson, but José Collins charmed the American public, after an opening night of jitters, as did Gaby Deslys and her raffish partner, Harry von Pilcer, when they performed their dance number, "The Gaby Glide."

Jolson made such a hit that the Shuberts rushed him into another three-part program: *A Night with the Pierrots* (sort of a whiteface minstrel show), *Whirl of Society* (a revue with a semblance of a plot) and *Sesostra,* "an operatic mimodrama," Jake Shubert's thudding attempt at artiness. Jolson was the whole show, but Collins won enough favor to be cast as the Countess Rosalinda Cliquot in *The Merry Countess* (1912), a reworking of *Die Fledermaus* that told its story in English and tried to capitalize on the success of *The Merry Widow* at the same time.

Collins' stage successes conferred star status, and big-time vaudeville beckoned. Assisted by Maurice Farkoa, José was on the bill at the Palace Theatre in 1913, during the fifth week (starting on Monday, 28 April) of its first season. After a few more weeks of vaudeville bookings, Florenz Ziegfeld engaged Collins for the *Ziegfeld Follies of 1913,* which ran at the New Amsterdam Theatre from 16 June to 6 September 1913 before going out on the road. José's best spot in the *Follies* was when she sang "Isle d'Amour."

The Shuberts brought Collins back to the Winter Garden the following season for *The Passing Show of 1914.* It ran a respectable four months. An operetta, *Suzi,* which opened on 3 November that same year, closed by Christmas. *Alone at Last,* a musical comedy was better received. It opened on 14 October 1915, with a Franz Lehar score that José Collins and John Charles Thomas sang well.

José was enticed back to Britain in 1916 to play in *The Happy Day.* In England, she married Lord Robert Innes-Ker. Further travel between the United States and Europe was out of the question as the First World War was fought on the Atlantic Ocean as well as in the trenches on the Continent. She spent the rest of the wartime years in a single show on the London stage after she was given the plum role in *The Maid of the Mountains* (1917).

The show played Daly's Theatre in London, proved a colossal hit with the public and made its investors very happy as it racked up three years of performances. On the last of 1,352 nights of singing, José finally lost her voice. *The Maid of the Mountains* toured Britain, and José headed the cast that brought the *Maid* to Broadway, where it failed dismally within a month!

José Collins never duplicated the phenomenal success of *The Maid of the Mountains.* She starred in *A Southern Maid* (1920), *Sybil* (1921), *The Last Waltz* (1922), *Catherine* (1923), *Our Nell* (1924) and *Frasquita* (1925). Several were respectable hits but hardly blockbusters like *The Maid of the Mountains.*

The American import *Lew Leslie's Blackbirds* was a surprise success when it played the London Pavilion for nearly the entire 1926–27 season, and its African American star, Florence Mills, became the toast of the town. An inexperienced English producer, more suited to his usual business in Yorkshire, financed a response, a revue called *White Birds.* José Collins, Maisie Gay and Maurice Chevalier were gathered to star, and the revue was booked at His Majesty's Theatre, where it flopped.

José's marriage was not as warm as once it was, and she found herself bankrupt in 1926. She had reached

40 years of age by the time *White Birds* closed, and though she remained a tall, dark-haired beauty with a fine singing voice, romantic leads were awarded younger, less expensive stars. Collins still enjoyed a faithful following, so she played music-hall and revue and turned to acting in stage dramas in the mid-1930s.

According to Marjorie Farnsworth, the Ziegfeld Girls' chronicler, José's most faithful devotee was Frank Curzon, wealthy racehorse owner and breeder, who in 1927 bestowed on José an annual income of $100,000. José Collins and Lord Innes-Ker were divorced in 1935.

Collins married again, without success, and talking pictures seemingly ignored her. All but one of the dozen movies José Collins made was silent, and it is odd that a singer with a good speaking voice would not have made more. Perhaps, during the postwar 1920s, public taste changed so markedly that the demand was for younger, spritelike musical stars and peppy scores.

José's third marriage proved a charm. She wed a Doctor Kirkland, and, during the Second World War, she quit the stage to serve as his nurse. They had a happy, rewarding life together. José died first, and her husband did not long survive her.

LOTTIE COLLINS

b: 1866, England—d: 1 May 1910, London, England

Only ten years old in 1877 when she made her debut as a rope-skipping dancer in music-hall, Lottie Collins soon joined her sisters in a musical act. The music-halls became her primary stages even when she went on as a single turn, but throughout her career she took a few flyers in musicals. The first of those was in 1886, when she was engaged as a dancer in a burlesque, *Monte Cristo Junior,* at the Gaiety Theatre in London. Others in the cast included Fred Leslie and the American star Fay Templeton.

Her first appearance in the USA is believed to have been during the mid-1880s at the Howard Athenaeum (the Old Howard) in Boston, then a variety house, where she was billed as Lottie Collins, the "Originator of Skirt Dancing." So successful was the bill that it transferred, almost intact, to variety houses in New York City.

Lottie Collins' fame came when, in her early 20s, she began to emphasize singing and comedy in her act. Not particularly pretty, she did have a fine figure and moved well as she sang. When she returned to England in 1891, she titillated audiences in London's Gaiety Theatre with a bawdy-house song she had learned and first performed in America as a song-and-dance number. The dark-haired, strong-featured, tall and sensual Lottie expunged its vulgarity but kept its naughtiness:

A sweet tuxedo girl you see,
A queen of swell society.
Fond of fun as fond can be,
When it's on the strict Q.T.
I'm not too young, I'm not too old,
Not too timid, not too bold.
Just the kind you'd like to hold,
Just the kind for sport I'm told.
[chorus]
Ta-ra-ra Boom-de-ré
Ta-ra-ra Boom-de-ré
Ta-ra-ra Boom-de-ré
Ta-ra-ra Boom-de-ré
Ta-ra-ra Boom-de-ré
Ta-ra-ra Boom-de-ré
Ta-ra-ra Boom-de-ré
Ta-ra-ra Boom-de-ré
I'm a blushing bud of innocence,
Papa says at big expense.
Old maids say I have no sense,
Boys declare I'm just immense.
Before my song I do conclude,
I want it strictly understood,
Though fond of fun, I'm never rude,
Though not too bad, I'm not too good.
[chorus]
Ta-ra-ra Boom-de-ré [etc.]

No singer was ever more associated with a particular song than Lottie Collins was with "Ta-Ra-Ra Boom-De-Ré," but many found the lyrics too close to the song's bordello beginnings. Others claimed it was a distorted version of an old British *coon song* of the 1880s. By the time it was issued, later that year, as sheet music with the title spelled "Ta-Ra-Ra Boom-De-Ay!" the lyrics had been laundered by Henry J. Sayers for publication as sheet music, the "sweet tuxedo girl, you see" had been turned into "a smart and stylish girl, you see," and although she was still "not too timid, not too bold," she was no longer "just the kind for sport I'm told."

"Ta-Ra-Ra Boom-De-Ay!" followed Lottie though all of her engagements in music-hall, and she was expected to sing it at every performance. She wore a large, wide Gainsborough hat, a short red corseted tunic, and skirt that failed to hide a wealth of petticoats. She sang the verse for its comedy and characterization, then, as she launched into the chorus, hands on hips, singing "Ta-ra-ra . . . ," from the pit orchestra came a crash of cymbals on the "Boom!," and Lottie threw herself into a frenzied whirl of fast waltz steps and high kicks as she and the audience yelled out the chorus and the band thundered away.

The song also opened the musical-comedy stage to her. In 1892, she appeared in another burlesque, *Cinder-Ellen Up Too Late,* performing "Ta-Ra-Ra Boom-De-Ré" as an interpolation. Doubtless, she was doubling during the show's run, appearing elsewhere in London in music-hall.

In 1896, Lottie was one of the stars, along with Agnes Delaporte, John L. Shine and J. J. Dallas, in *The New Barmaid,* a musical comedy. Collins had the soubrette role and performed a comic song and dance with the show's comedians, Shine and Dallas.

She was married three times, and her career continued during the decade between 1900 and 1910, but Lottie never had another success like "Ta-Ra-Ra Boom-De-Ay!" Oddly, Lottie's daughter, José Collins, had a similar fantastic success, a three-year run in an operetta, *The Maid of the Mountains* (1917–20). She, too, never scored another comparable success.

Lottie's health declined due to a heart condition that some believed was caused by the constant repetition of her frenetic song and dance routine. Lottie Collins died at 44 in 1910.

COLONIAL THEATRE, NEW YORK

Most vaudevillians agreed that the Colonial Theatre in New York City had the toughest of audiences. The gallery boys (and men) regarded a vaudeville bill much as Caligula and his cohort regarded the appearance of Christians at the Roman Coliseum. The Colonial's audience found malevolent pleasure in drowning out acts with a steady unified clap until the performer fled the stage. Seldom was the dreaded theatre mentioned by vaudevillians without noting the "Colonial Clap."

COLUMBIA WHEEL

When the light shines, it shines for all, even if it is just a light bulb snapping on over a cartoon noggin.

In 1896, a group of legitimate theatre owners met and decided that, for the good of the American theatre, the task fell to them to organize the industry they had nurtured and to bring order out of chaos. The problem was clear. So was the solution. Abe Erlanger, Marc Klaw, Charles Frohman, Al Hayman, Samuel F. Nixon and Fred Zimmerman were in agreement; they created the Theatrical Trust to systematize the bookings of theatres.

In effect, they attempted—and were successful for nearly 15 years—to decide what got produced and where it played. Because among them, they owned, leased or controlled by contract about 75% of the legitimate theatres and had the deep pockets to finance productions, they had the power and were going to use it to serve art and commerce.

That was too nifty a plan not to get around. E. F. Albee, B. F. Keith and a couple of other vaudeville theatre owners had a similar idea almost immediately. Albee and Keith had already spearheaded the creation of the Vaudeville Managers Association (VMA), supposedly to enforce uniform ethical practices within the trade. Like Erlanger's Theatre Syndicate, the VMA's goal was to protect territorial rights of theatre owners and to present a united front that would hold the line on vaudevillians' salaries. The United Booking Office was the next step. It was promoted as a clearing house to ensure that theatres had a steady supply of respectable and talented performers and that performers and their agents did not have to waste time trying to piece together a schedule of bookings that gave them more employment and less travel time. Out of necessity, of course, there were commissions attending these services and a passel of non-negotiable rules and regulation.

By 1898 burlesque producers were discussing similar matters and clucking their tongues at upstart producers—which they once had been—who were besmirching the fair name of burlesque with *turkey shows,* shows that were not only cheesy but nearly pornographic. A Traveling Variety Managers Association (TVMA) was envisioned, one that brought together theatre owners and those who produced shows. The object was to feed their theatres an orderly progression of approved burlesque shows that met an acceptable level in production values and taste. The first order of business, however, was to subordinate the competition among the owners and the producers to the greater goal. This was not resolved.

The TVMA floundered and divided into two geographic entities, one east of the Mississippi River and the other in the western part of the USA. Each wheel—for each show followed a largely circuitous route until the troupe returned to home base and, fitted out with an ostensibly new production, began playing the wheel again—provided a steady stream of shows, one predictably following another, keeping theatres booked and show producers earning income. But, also predictably, show producers and theatre owners were sure the other party was getting a better deal.

By 1900, some of the more established managers and producers tired of warfare that diverted energy from making money and were even wearier of hotheads; they withdrew from the TVMA and created the Columbia Amusement Company. The principals were a mixture of theatre managers and show producers. Some were both and some were also performers. All were experienced: Samuel A. Scribner, who was first among equals, William S. Campbell, William S. Drew, Gus Hill, J. Herbert Mack, Harry Morris, L. Lawrence Weber and A. H. Woodhull. Power was not held by office alone. A comedian producer like, Fred Irwin and Al Reeves, or theatre managers like Hurtig & Seamon and Tom Miner did not have to belong to the inner circle to have weight. If they consistently produced well-received and profitable shows, or put up their money behind a smart producer, theirs was a voice to be heeded at any table.

As the participants in the Columbia wheel had their theatres in the East, their organization and their theatres soon were informally called the Eastern wheel. Correspondingly, the folks in the west formed the Empire circuit, or Western wheel.

The Columbia wheel regarded itself as an association of clean burlesque operators. To them, the ideal of burlesque was to produce shows that were affordable to every man and woman in town, and clean enough (but just clean enough) not to offend. They still featured sly comedians and a line of young women kicking and flouncing.

The great dividing issue in burlesque always threatened to become an internal division as well. In each wheel, the advocates of wholesome shows were derided for trying to compete with vaudeville and revue. The argument was that they could not. Burlesque was entertainment for the lunch bucket crowd, and the optimum price for tickets did not allow for vaudeville's big name salaries or revue's splendid costumes and settings. And since Ziegfeld was giving his two-dollar customers glimpses of naked breasts, burlesque producers better give their guys in the 25-cent seats two naked breasts and a grind and a bump because they wanted something they weren't going to get in a family show.

Those who held out for wholesome shows reminded their cohorts, who favored skin shows and smutty comedy, that their strategy was a fast race to the bottom where district attorneys, do-gooders and city censors lay in wait, and if burlesque appealed only to the men, it ignored at least half its potential customers, women and maybe some children.

Despite the tug of war between profit and respectability that dragged dirt over the threshold occasionally, the Columbia Amusement Company prospered for about 20 years. None of the other wheels survived as long or prospered even though their shows were dirtier. In 1921 that changed. Profits dropped markedly, an intramural dispute with a low-rent subsidiary operation, the American Burlesque Association broke into a court case and the federal government was following up on accusations that the Columbia Amusement Company was a monopoly.

By the mid-1920s, Columbia's shows were far more sedate than any revue on Broadway. The chorus girls still wore body stockings! Billy Minsky and Minsky burlesque were redefining burlesque as striptease.

Columbia's show producers flailed about. Some staged dirtier shows; others started putting up the money for colored and black and white revues—packaged vaudeville revues produced and written by African Americans with African American or white and black casts. The Columbia franchise holders who owned theatres tried vaudeville and then movies—anything to pay the mortgage and the staff. By 1927, it was over for the Columbia wheel. Many of its original theatre owners and show producers retired from the fray, and the once proud Tiffany of burlesque circuits merged with its hated rival, the raunchier Mutual wheel.

COMBINATION

The dance term *combination* refers to a series of individual dance steps connected into a progression.

COMEDIANS AND COMEDY TEAMS

Professional comedians, critics and academics stumble over themselves and each other trying to explain the difference between comedians, comic actors, comics and clowns. The debate then turns to whether a given comedian can be further classified as a light comedian, eccentric comedian, sketch (or book) comedian or prop comedian. Critics and writers, searching for a fitting image, use words like droll, zany, knockabout, madcap, anarchic or romantic, all of which suggest tone more than type.

Ed Wynn and Milton Berle were two who should know. Wynn defined humor as the truth and wit as an exaggeration of the truth. His further definition implied a distinction between the creative and the less so: "A comedian is not a man who says funny things; a comedian is a man who says things funny." Berle distinguished between a comic and a comedian: A comic does jokes; a comedian does material that fits his character. "A comic is a guy who depends solely upon the joke; the comedian can get a laugh before he opens his mouth." Attractive and convenient as Berle's and Wynn's definitions seem, they do not lend themselves to a systematic survey of comedians.

Essentially, people are funny because they say something or do something to amuse. Comedians can

Walking Brothers

be considered by style, but categories such as light, romantic, slapstick, knockabout, eccentric and so forth are limiting. They do not describe versatility (the comedian being discussed may also do a song-and-dance act), and one person's eccentric comedian may be another's slapstick. Is there a clear line between eccentric comedy and comedy of manners? If so, on which side of the line fall Bea Lillie, Leon Errol, W. C. Fields, The Marx Brothers, Olsen & Johnson, Joan Davis and Bert Lahr?

If the light comedian and the slapstick comedian are at opposite ends of the spectrum, were Marie Dressler, Joe E. Brown, Bob Hope and Jack Lemmon light comedians or slapstick?

In the broadest sense, people amuse us because they are tricksters or bumblers. Ed Wynn, Charlie Chaplin, Buster Keaton, Bobby Clark, Mae West, Joe Cook, The Marx Brothers, Tim Moore, Moms Mabley and Pigmeat Markham were tricksters. Victor Moore, Leon Errol, Harry Langdon, Dusty Fletcher, Jack Benny, the Ritz Brothers, the Three Stooges, Mantan Moreland, Martha Raye, Joan Davis and Lucille Ball were bumblers. Marie Dressler, Bert Lahr, W. C. Fields, Harold Lloyd, Joe E. Brown, Jimmy Savo, Bob Hope, Jackie Gleason and Sid Caesar were both at various times. The rule applied to comedy teams. Lew Fields, George W. Walker, Bud Abbott and Dean Martin were tricksters; Joe Weber, Bert Williams, Lou Costello and Jerry Lewis were bumblers. Laurel and Hardy were both bumblers. Olsen and Johnson were both tricksters. Storyteller and stand-up comedians are usually tricksters. Clowns and stooges are usually bumblers.

Neater classifications are seldom satisfactory, but they remain useful. When the visual and aural evidence is missing, printed descriptions must rely upon words that are precise, well chosen and agreed upon.

Differentiating by performance method offers a less knotty system of categorization. Usually, a particular skill dominates in a comedy act, and the comedian finds himself regarded by producers and audiences as a monologist, a comedy actor or a clown. Admittedly, few performers depend solely on either verbal or physical methods (Harpo Marx never spoke, yet he whistled and used coach horns to "talk"), and few monologists simply stand there and talk without expression or gestures to sell their performance.

In practice (when not limited by silent film, radio or sound-only recordings), most comedians combine elements of verbal and physical comedy. Many, past and present, do stand-up, act in sketches and perform physically, whether taking falls or executing an eccentric dance. Versatility and contradictions acknowledged, all performers, including comedians, find themselves advertised and characterized by category. Some find this useful in marketing themselves, others feel constrained, but vaudeville's categories were broad.

In vaudeville, monologists (storytellers or stand-up comics) talked to us, the audience. Sketch comedians (comedy actors) usually talked to or at each other; sometimes they punctuated their exchange physically. Clowns expressed themselves physically through movement, gesture and the expression on their faces; they may have made sounds, even talked or hollered, but the dialogue or sound was primarily counterpoint to the action.

Comedy teams have as many options as comedians who work as singles. They tell stories or do stand-up but with dialogue, like Weber & Fields, Miller & Lyles, Burns & Allen and Abbott & Costello. Some teams, like The Marx Brothers, Clark & McCullough, Peter Cook & Dudley Moore and Monty Python, found the sketch format more suitable, keeping for themselves the primary roles rather than adding ad hoc to their casts. Still others, like the Three Keatons and Willie, West & McGinty, were essentially clowns whose acts were largely physical.

MONOLOGISTS: STORYTELLERS AND STAND-UP COMICS

Some vaudeville observers differentiated between monologists and storytellers, holding that the monologist told a single story that had a beginning, a middle and an end, whereas a storyteller talked about various topics that may or may not have been connected. Since the rise of what is now called stand-up comedy in the late twentieth century, it seems more useful to consider monologists and storytellers to be alike: performers who rely on character, follow a dramatic line in the telling and, for the most part, eschew a series of one- or two-line jokes.

Stand-up comics string together a variety of tenuously related topics and dispatch them in swift, telling strokes. If a particular series of jokes does not find audience favor, the comic can segue to other material. Although the storyteller achieves a quickening pace through an accumulation of humorous detail, the stand-up comic builds pace through a series of jokes, each pared to a minimum of carefully chosen words or even syllables.

Both forms rely primarily on verbal humor, although dressing in character is an option for each, especially the storyteller. Each style of monologist requires a performer who can bravely manage and hold an audience, yet the delivery skills differ with the form. A storyteller must convince the audience of the authenticity of his character and situation. In contrast, the stand-up comic must persuade, even bully, an audience to accept his point of view.

Perhaps that is why, in the past, women have been more accepted as storytellers. They depended more upon nuance and an appeal to an audience's sensibilities, cajoling an audience into warming to the characters. The stand-up comic deals with types not complex characters, with struggles rather than evolving stories.

In performance, the difference may be muted. Some storytellers, like Walter C. Kelly as the Virginia Judge, captured the course of a single court session by stringing together two-line jokes about each in a series of defendants. Some more recent stand-up comics, like George Carlin, pursue a theme with a succession of related jokes. In general, a storyteller emphasizes the journey, and the stand-up comic contrasts the start from the finish.

Storytellers

Storytelling is to the stage what a short story or a narrative poem is to the page. The storyteller may be at the center of the story, stand as an observer who reports thoughts and actions of others, or play a variety of roles. He tells the story through narration and dialogue and may choose either the objective voice of the reporter or the subjective voices of various characters. To the extent that the narrator's voice dominates, the storyteller resembles the stand-up comic in technique, yet the qualifying difference is a single plot as opposed to the stand-up's multiple targets.

The storyteller who voices the characters in his plot resembles the comedy actor who plays a particular character, although the storyteller is more likely to break through the fourth wall to engage the audience. The storyteller elicits a response from an audience similar to what an actor receives, but the role played by a comedy actor is neither born of the actor's personality nor endowed with his viewpoint, and that is one crucial divide between the storyteller and the comedy actor.

Another is that the storyteller is a cast of one, regardless how many roles he voices. Depending upon the nature of his act, the storyteller has several options for dress. He may choose everyday clothes if he remains the narrator, or he can employ an array of accessories to suggest the cast of characters who people the story. Each ticket holder is there as an individual, relating the story to his own experiences and sympathies; only when the storytelling performance is over does the audience applaud.

Stand-Up Comics

The stand-up comedian addresses his audience more directly than the storyteller. The storyteller is an actor; the stand-up comedian is a politician, a preacher, an agitator whose success depends upon persuading his audience to his point of view. He is the descendant of the stump orator who flatters, cajoles, challenges and confronts the audience with the aim of making himself the spokesperson for everyone listening to him.

At first, each joke is a potential land mine. The comic gauges the audience's reaction: he discards material, changes course and ad-libs as the audience guides him. He adjusts tempo, tone, volume and manner to meet his audience. Once he finds the pulse, comic and audience work in synchronicity.

If the comic is not well known, each stand-up session begins as a blind date during which the comic must prove himself. If the comic succeeds, he will win the contest of wills, or, by paying close attention, he will shift gears and adopt the audience's attitude. He then rallies his listeners and leads them through a litany of grievances, observations and affirmations.

If the stand-up comic does not move from blind date to interesting prospect, he can neither impose his will nor discern his audience's viewpoint, and the encounter sours. When it all works, the comic's one-liners alternate with the audience's laughter, cheers and applause, and the rhythm resembles the call and response of revival meetings, and the energy is that of a rousing motivational session.

SKETCH ACTORS AND SKETCH COMEDIANS

The number three spot on the vaudeville bill was often reserved for the sketch act. A short one-act melodrama or comedy filled the bill. The melodrama employed actors usually more at home on the legitimate stage than vaudeville. The comedy sketch, on the other hand, was played either by legit actors or comedians whose usual stage was vaudeville, revue or burlesque.

Comedy scripts were written to be cast or written to order. In vaudeville, there were producers who were also sketch writers, like Paul Gerard Smith, who could fashion a comic sketch that might play multiple seasons in vaudeville. Smith often hired two casts, and each company played different routes. Sometimes, he revived the script another season and cast it with other performers.

In other cases, writers could be hired by an established comedy act to create a sketch specifically tailored to the comic personalities and particular talents of the comedians. Many sketch comedians, such as Willie Howard and Bert Lahr, played a variety of characters, but versatility was more useful in revue than vaudeville because a sketch comedian might perform several skits in a revue but only one on a vaudeville bill.

Most dramatic actors went back to the legitimate theatre after vaudeville tours. Such actors as David Warfield, Alfred Lunt and Walter Huston, however, played drama or comedy with equal ease and effectiveness and found vaudeville hospitable and rewarding. Warfield, for one, developed a comic stage character. Had his later career as a tragedian not overtaken his reputation for playing comic characters, one could regard him as a sketch comic.

Sketch Actors

The vaudeville sketch actor was engaged to play either melodrama or comedy. The primary talent required was the ability to realize the author's intent and play the piece for all it was worth. A vaudeville audience expected excitement and vigorous performances.

If the sketch were melodrama, actors might be directed to work a bit faster and to forgo some subtleties common to the legitimate stage in order to score with audiences more accustomed to variety than drama and in houses larger than most legitimate theatres.

To act in comic sketches did not require the antic mentality and comic view of the world that inspired most comedians and clowns. Comic actors were interpretive rather than creative. They did, however, need many of the same performance skills: timing, phrasing, emphasis, the ability to react, and the capacity to surprise and express surprise.

Actors who played in melodramatic skits usually found vaudeville less rewarding in the creative sense than the legitimate stage. A dramatic actor finds fulfillment in the arc of character development within a full-length play. Some had assorted reasons for enjoying vaudeville: shorter performances for a larger paycheck and the possibility of future bookings without undergoing unpaid periods in play rehearsals or while searching for new jobs. More often, an announcement in the trade press gave the reason: "*Ruggles of Red Gap,* which was not destined to make much theatrical history [!], has closed. Ralph Herz, who had been the star of the organization, has gone into vaudeville" (1916).

Some comedy actors who found employment in sketches for vaudeville (or burlesque) also discovered that the short form suited their energies and abilities. Some who showed conspicuous aptitude in comedy sketches chose to change course, moving away from the legitimate stage to vaudeville. They became sketch comedians in scripts written to exploit their personalities and display their individual talents. If they spent too much time in vaudeville, there was the likelihood that producers forgot they were actors first and sketch comics second.

Most actors who made their living appearing in comedy sketches were journeymen actors who took work in vaudeville when they could not get hired for the legitimate stage. In either situation, they were expected to fill roles, not define them.

Sketch Comedians

From the advent of variety, through the golden age of vaudeville and revue, into the heyday of network radio and studio moviemaking, many accomplished sketch comedians started as something else: a noncomedy act singing, dancing or juggling. It was unlikely that a budding comedian would have the resources to spring onto a stage full blown as a sketch comedian. Even those who began as comics often first appeared as a song-and-dance performer or a monologist or as part of a team. It was a natural development for comedy teams to expand their cross talk into sketches. Sketch comedy became a vital staple of vaudeville and revue, an integral part of the scripts for musical comedies and comedy films, and a mainstay of network radio (where it was adapted for the ear alone) and television.

There were certain stock roles: the hero, a young man looking for adventure; the heroine, a young woman looking for romance; the best friends of the hero and the heroine, who were usually less conventionally attractive and much funnier; and the older authority figure (a boss, a father, a cop) who tried to thwart the hero. There were other types as well—the matriarch, the conniving servant, and so forth—and all of them descended from *commedia dell'arte,* at the least, and likely from universal prototypes found the world over from ancient times.

The script of a comedy sketch did not always provide all the jokes. Experienced comedy writers created situations that invited sketch comedians to invent comic "business." The sketch actor interpreted; the sketch comedian created.

Clowns

Clowns have found a home in the circus but have never been limited to that province. Historically, the clown is one of the oldest and most universal of stage characters, a participant in religious, political and social ceremonies. From the farces of Ancient Rome to *commedia dell'arte,* clowns were the conniving servants of the master, the rebellious daughter seeking her own choice in love and her adventurous and often impecunious suitor.

In royal courts, kings allowed the jester's jibes at the royal person only because the jester represented the outcast whose continued presence and existence was clearly and solely at royal whim. Even in the circus, the earthbound clowns are excluded from the privileged society of aerialists, equestrians and other heroes of the ring. On the stage, clown roles vary from boob to trickster to anarchist.

Debased, the clown has become a shill for a consumer culture—hawking fast food and sales days—a role quite at odds with clowns' traditional function as social critics. In latter-day experimental theatre and performance work, clowns have been exalted to a station of wise fools. Something of the latter imbued vaudeville and revue clowns who behaved like angels gone haywire, their behavior an amalgam of mortal flaws and poetic transcendence.

The stylized costume of the stage clown marks them as odd fellows and helps fix their character, status and situation. They are misfits in the larger society. Clowns dash about, take falls, throw things and mimic their betters with childish glee, and their reliance upon physical comedy accentuates their distance from society's more discreet, codified and often hypocritical behavior. The clown's stumbling missteps in society become transformed into art through the deftness of his movement and soulfulness of his characterization.

STOOGES

The pairing of a comic with a stooge affords the stand-up comic an antagonist who is present in the theatre rather than visualized by an audience. The stooge is not a partner to the comic and never gets cobilling; sometimes the stooge is unnamed on the bill. Unlike a straight man and comedian team, the stooge is only part of the act, an assistant to the star.

In vaudeville, a stooge often was planted in the audience, perhaps in a box, where he was easily spotted as he disrupted the comic's act. Unlike hecklers, who were unplanned and usually unwanted, the stooge's role was a scripted part of the act and played to the comic's strength. If the comic's humor was combative, the stooge would heckle him, and a mock battle of wits ensued, easily won by the comic. If the comic's style was reactive, the stooge engaged in a disruptive pantomime—dropping things, crawling over people, falling drunkenly out of the box, wandering around the theatre aisles—while the star performer, depending upon his persona, acted amused, loftily dismissive or exasperated by the stooge's antics.

Less frequently, a comedian worked a stooge into a sketch, but putting a stooge onstage accorded him higher status, elevating the stooge to sketch comic and nearly teaming him with the lead comedian.

SONG-AND-DANCE COMEDIANS

Not all song-and-dance acts in vaudeville employed comedy, but those that did often gave as much emphasis to the laughs as to singing and dancing. Although the song-and-dance act might engage in cross-talk, the primary outlet for their comedy was through patter songs or eccentric dance. In the late nineteenth and early twentieth centuries in America, it was common to see performers like Al Jolson billed as comedians. A century later, they are pigeonholed as singers.

Eddie Cantor neatly typified the song-and-dance comic. Although he was a fine sketch comedian, his funny business was more often tied to his singing and dancing. The same may be said of Ed Gallagher & Al Shean, Bert Williams & George W. Walker, Beatrice Lillie, Fanny Brice, the Ritz Brothers, Danny Kaye, Donald O'Connor and Pinky Lee.

COMIC MUSICIANS

Many vaudeville comedians were musicians. The Marx Brothers, among them, played a dozen instruments. Joe Cook could play nearly as many by himself. Despite

The Bizzarro Brothers

their musical skill, the Marxes were known primarily as sketch comedians, and Cook may be regarded as a sketch comedian, a storyteller or prop comedian. A case can be made that comic musicians, as well as most of the comedians mentioned elsewhere, could be classified in other ways. They were primarily musicians who, like Herb Williams, the Wiere Brothers, Victor Borge, Spike Jones' aggregation and Tom Lehrer, also excelled at comedy.

IMPRESSIONISTS

Not all impressionists are comedians, just many of them. Although most of the ensuing laughter depends upon the quality of the impressionist's material, his audience is rather like a crowd watching a seaside caricaturist, and the laughter begins with recognition.

Like the caricaturist, the impressionist usually does not offer a mirror image of his subject (as does an impersonator) but selects salient traits—vocal inflections, facial expressions, posture and gait—to economically sketch, with sure emphasis, those habits of speech and movement that unmistakably capture the subject.

Some vaudeville impressionists worked with props that embellished their portrayal: hats, glasses, scarves, cigarettes, even costumes. Those who used costumes slid into the arena of quick-change artists, rapidly shedding, donning or reversing one set of accessories for the next. Other impressionists, like Frank Gorshin, Larry Storch and Rich Little, eschewed most props and all changes of garments and preferred to create the picture of the original in the audience's collective eye.

Exaggeration and proportion were key. The degree of exaggeration must suit both the target and the impressionist. Impressions of Jimmy Cagney, Bette Davis or Jimmy Durante were catnip to boisterous impressionists, whereas the more subdued barely lifted an eyebrow while clipping Noël Coward's inflections or while purring a Mae West line.

No vaudeville bill was complete without a comedy act. Yet comedians, verbal or physical, retailed a product with a limited shelf life. Audiences often wanted singers to perform old favorites, and dancers could be sure that no one in the audience would remember the dance routine from their last time around on the circuit (except other dancers in the audience who were there to learn and steal the steps).

Jokes, sight gags and sketches, however, relied on surprise. Once the punch was gone, so was the laugh. Comedians were and always will be thirsty for new material. A good routine might last an entire season in vaudeville as the comedy act moved from city to city, unless someone stole the routine and played it in a theatre before the originators got there.

Moving pictures, phonograph recordings and network radio severely shortened the shelf life of a comedy routine, and the wise comedian did not commit his act to film, wax or a broadcast until he had finished with it in vaudeville.

COMERFORD TIME

Comerford was a small-time circuit of the late vaudeville era created by M. E. Comerford. He had theatres in Binghamton, New York, and Scranton, Wilkes-Barre, Hazelton, and Pottsville, Pennsylvania.

M. E. Comerford

COMIC OPERA

Also termed *opéra bouffe,* comic opera led—along with operetta, burlesks and vaudeville—to the development of the American musical comedy. Unlike grand opera, the plots were romantic romps, the music was light and the dialogue was spoken, not sung. The characters and plots often were formed from those of the *commedia dell'arte:* young lovers, often from different stations in society, aided by comic male and female servants, thwart the will of the maiden's father and the desires of an old, rich merchant. Comic opera attracted composers like David Braham and Reginald De Koven.

Burlesque producers sometimes tried to pass off their offerings as comic opera, but the distinction was settled, at least in legal terms, in a courtroom back in the 1880s. Camille D'Arville had signed to star in a show produced by E. E. Rice, a producer noted for his extravaganzas like *Evangeline*. Ms. D'Arville refused to fulfill her contract with Rice when she saw a rehearsal of his new show. She told him flatly that she refused to appear in burlesque. Rice maintained it was a comic opera. The court agreed with Ms. D'Arville that comic opera ceased to be such when specialties or variety turns were introduced into the show.

COMMEDIA DELL'ARTE

The very name *commedia dell'arte* roughly connotes professional comedy and served notice that the entertainments were not the amateur enterprises so popular at the time. The sketches were set pieces with a variety of roles that encouraged individual improvisation (though the actors were partially masked). The characters were universal to European politics and society so that traveling troupes played beyond the borders of their own countries; barriers of language were surmounted through pantomime.

Over the decades, France, Germany and England adapted *commedia dell'arte* to their own peculiar institutions and languages, and the basics survived the passing of centuries, emerging in the spirit of French farce, French and German cabaret, English Punch and Judy shows, comedies of manners, pantomimes and music-hall, and American variety, burlesque and musical comedy.

Commedia dell'arte evolved from various sources. Scholars trace it back to Roman times, citing the comic plays of Plautus (whose plots and style inspired the American musical *A Funny Thing Happened on the Way to the Forum*). A more contemporary source was the fifteenth-century Italian religious celebrations that commemorated holy days like Christ's Resurrection and Ascension. The reenactments of those events required transformation scenes that led to a revolution in stage technology. Stages were constructed with trapdoors, puppets were fashioned to resemble fantastical creatures from hell, and elaborate machinery was devised to create the illusion of miracles, flying angels, Christ's rise into heaven and the visitation of the Holy Ghost.

Commedia dell'arte characters gradually replaced their masks with makeup. The plethora of zany characters *(zanni)* settled into a few stock characters that remain the basis for most comic situations: a lovely maiden budding into womanhood and the object of desire for men, young and old (the *innamorata,* Isabella). She was the daughter of the petty-minded patriarch of stinted charity, Pantalone (or Pantaloon). The servants included the wily, amorous and sometimes abused Arlecchino (or Harlequin), the lovesick and less earthy clown (Pedrolino, Pierrot, Joey) and the wisecracking soubrette (Columbia, Columbine) who was often paired with Harlequin. Other characters included the pompous pedant (Dotore, Professor), the gross bully (Pulcinella, Punch), the swaggering military man or policeman (Capitano, Beadle), and the gossipy and frustrated widow. Most comedians of the stage and screen, male or female, old or young, of any ethnicity, portray some variation of the stock characters of *commedia dell'arte* and their descendants.

COMMONWEALTH SHOWS

When work was scarce, a few acts might decide to combine their acts and resources into a commonwealth show. This was the collective equivalent of a performer producing his own show. In the commonwealth show, the booking details, advertising and production duties were divided among the performers. Although they were all at liberty (out of work), each act needed to contribute some share of funds to the common pot to produce the show. After expenses and the payback of monies advanced, the pot was split evenly among the individuals or acts, however agreed.

Generally, the show was a packaged full-length variety show. In addition to each participant performing in their own act, they doubled as needed in other acts or sketches and group musical numbers cobbled together to provide contrast to the individual turns.

There were several dangers with a commonwealth act. One was that individual members were apt to leave it as soon as their agent got them a vaudeville booking or a spot in a revue, thereby leaving a hole in the show. The second was a matter of leadership versus independence. Unlike actors in straight plays or even musical comedies, vaudevillians were used to being their own directors. That meant there were as many potential directors to stage the show and determine the order of play as there were acts in it. What act willingly agreed to open the show? Whoever was responsible for staging the show and determining the order of the bill found himself in a position of herding cats.

COMPERE

A term that preceded master of ceremonies, *compere* was not well received in the United States but was a familiar term in British music-hall and survived into television. The word derives from the Latin through the French: *com* and *père*, meaning "with father." Its adoption as an entertainment term proceeds from the same notion that gave rise to master of ceremonies: one who guides the ceremonies and introduces the principals.

COMPING

Short for accompanying, *comping* is a term reserved for musicians, particularly pianists and bassists, who accompany singers in performance, following the singer's lead as to pace, volume and emphasis.

Comping also refers to the practice of supplying free (complimentary) tickets to press, certain members of the "profession" and as payment for donations in kind.

CONCERT SALOONS

Concert rooms, box houses, dives, slabs, the shades, honky-tonks, and free and easies were more alike than unalike. All those protonightclubs served liquor and provided variety entertainment; some offered gambling and prostitutes as well. They differed in particulars—some had separate rooms for the bar and the entertainment—but the terms overlapped and were sometimes carelessly applied. Box houses were more prevalent in the port cities on the West Coast; concert saloons were more likely found in port cities of the Northeast.

In the USA, the concert saloons emerged in the 1850s and flourished during the Civil War. They were a primary showcase for variety acts in the generation before vaudeville and burlesque became big time.

Despite the many names attached to these drinking and performance places, most differences between them were matters of local law and custom and the ambition of the saloon keeper. Many concert saloons were fetid holes; others were clean, tightly run and handsomely appointed. Some were a cover for nefarious activity, whereas others steered clear of blatant criminality.

In the early days of the concert saloon, the administration of law and justice was local, capricious and far from uniform. What was allowed in one city was forbidden in another, and the rules changed depending upon where in a city an establishment was located. In the mid-eighteenth century, there were competing police forces in many American cities and towns. A holdover from Colonial days was the constabulary and its marshals, usually appointed by a mayor, and the watchmen and ward men, largely volunteer, who were appointed by governors and councils. The ward men kept order during the day; the watchmen kept guard at night. The two often competed for supremacy, and both were rivals of the constabulary. There were also the self-appointed militias that formed out of demobilized soldiers, fraternal organizations and gangs that were the basis for the ragtag corps so neatly satirized by Ned Harrigan in his Mulligan Guard plays.

Drinking establishments had existed since Colonial times in America. They grew out of the inns and taverns that had provided sleeping accommodations, food and drink for travelers, stables for their horses and coaches, and a distribution point for the transport of mail. The English inn remained the model for post-Colonial USA. As postal responsibilities switched from a private matter to a government responsibility, the taverns and inns of the new nation either remained focused on travelers or courted the local population, and they diverged into inns and hotels or taverns and saloons.

Saloons catered to male-only clientele. Where authorities allowed or turned a blind eye, entertainment included gambling, prostitution, liquor and performances provided by the help. Waiters and bartenders formed quartets or sang solo when not taking orders or dispensing libation. A holdover from bordellos was a piano player who, alone or with another instrumentalist or two, provided the music and set the mood. Serving girls danced and showed their linen when not otherwise engaged serving drinks and egging on customers to buy drinks.

Serving girls as entertainers evolved in two directions, sometimes both at the same time. Some women's talents were in demand only in private chambers, but those who could lift a tune (if not carry it) and knew their right leg from their left were drafted by the management to put on a show. For this the women got the throw money that landed on the stage. This, added to their commissions, was a lot more rewarding than working a 12-hour shift, six days a week, in a textile mill or garment factory.

In fact, the throw money added so significantly to their meager income that saloon managers banned the women from picking up the throw money while they were performing because it was not dignified! Instead, the managers collected it themselves and began paying the performers a salary. This held true for the waiters who doubled as singing quartets. Intervention by managers between performers and the paying public was a major turn toward modern show business. The manager interceded as a middleman between those who tossed the coins and the performers, and it led to the star system. Those performers who drew the most throw money could threaten to leave and work at a competing honky-tonk.

Professional performers sometimes augmented the bill. Pairs of minstrel players, who were tired of the road, put together the rudiments of an act with a few comic songs, a jig or a clog dance and some scraps of dialogue. Often the same routine was fitted out with different dialects and costumes. Whether the performers wore blackface and nappy wigs or Irish red noses and sideburns or German chin whiskers and costumes to match, a few bickering lines of dialect dialogue quickly led to boisterous disagreement and then exploded in a rowdy and rough demonstration of knockabout comedy. More serious mayhem was also in demand, and 30-round, bare-knuckle fights were very popular as well, especially when the victor was a neighborhood lad.

The Civil War gave rise to the mass transport of soldiers. Concert saloons provided many pleasures to men on their way to or from the battle lines, and it was during the early 1860s that chroniclers began attaching the many names by which the concert saloon was known.

The more ambitious owners, like their British cousins, enlarged their concert saloons into music-halls or melodeons: taverns or saloons with an attached performance hall. In them, casual entertainment formalized into variety shows, and the offerings onstage were as much or more of an inducement to customers as the quality or price of liquor and the generosity of its measure. The concert saloon presaged the theatres that presented variety shows, vaudeville bills and burlesque revues.

The popularity of concert saloons persisted through the 1880s, diminished some in the 1890s, and went into the shadows until the federally enacted Volstead Act of 1919 banned alcoholic beverages but not a national thirst for them. Taverns and concert saloons were reinvented as speakeasies.

CONDOS BROTHERS

Frank Condos

b: ca. 1906

Nick Condos

**b: 26 January 1915, Pittsburgh, PA—
d: 8 July 1988, Los Angeles, CA**

Steve Condos

**b: 12 October 1918, Pittsburgh, PA—
d: 6 September 1990, Lyon, France**

Harry Condos

dates unknown

Their father owned the Standard Restaurant at the corner of Eleventh and South Streets, across from the Standard Theatre, an African American vaudeville house in Pittsburgh. Because of the theatre, South Street was a place that drew dancers from the surrounding neighborhoods.

The eldest of the Condos brothers, Frank, was the first to go onstage. Beginning around 1923, he and Mateo Olvera, a young friend from their Pittsburgh neighborhood, partnered in vaudeville as King & King. They were much admired by other dancers, black and white, but as Frank modestly told Marshal Stearns later, "from the waist up we did not have much personality."

From the waist down, however, they astonished other tap dancers, largely because of their ability to perform five-tap wings. Dazzlingly fast, a dancer jumps, raising one leg up and to the rear while the other leg rapidly raps five distinct taps on the floor before resting that foot on the floor and switching legs to jump and repeat the five taps with the other foot.

Frank and Mateo split the act in 1929. Mateo and two of his brothers created a new act called King, King & King, and they were quickly engaged for the revue *Broadway Nights* (1929). Frank Condos teamed with brothers Harry and Nick as the Condos Brothers. Usually it was one brother at any one time. Although the brothers in the act changed over the years, and occasionally included three instead of two, the Condos Brothers remained the name of the act.

Frank and Harry, as the Condos Brothers, were among the featured acts in *Earl Carroll's Vanities of 1930.* More usually, Frank seemed to work with Nick, whom many thought was the master of the five-tap wings. The average audience, however, was unable to properly appreciate the difference between a one-tap and a five-tap wing. They saw a dancer leap in the air, leaving one foot on the ground, then swap legs and leap again, landing on the other foot. Frank with his various partners, Mateo, Nick and Harry, knocked themselves out with strenuous routines in vaudeville that left them breathless and exhausted once the curtain closed. Other dancers congratulated them, but those same dancers saved their strenuous steps for the end of their routines and garnered as much applause.

Nick Condos performed solo in the movie *Dancing Feet* (1936) and then went out on his own in 1937, although he teamed with the youngest brother, Steve, in the movie *Happy Landing* (1938). Two seldom-seen films, *The Broadway Buckaroo* (1939), a Vitaphone short, and *Hey Rookie* (1944), carried the Condos Brothers in their cast lists but without identifying them by their first names.

Frank worked with brother Harry, especially for movie work. They danced in *Abbott and Costello in the Navy* (1941), *Moon over Miami* (1941), *Pin Up Girl* (1944), *Song of the Open Road* (1944), in which Steve joined Frank and Harry, and *The Time, the Place and the Girl* (1946).

Frank became a dance director during the 1940s, but, in 1952, he took employment as a welder in a shipyard, an occupation he seemed to have stayed with until retirement. Nick married Martha Raye, and they stayed wed from 1946 to 1953. Even after their divorce, Nick remained Martha's friend and managed her career until his death. Nick's advice to dancers has been much quoted: "If you fall down, do it again two more times. They'll think it's part of the choreography."

Very little information about Harry Condos has remained on the public record. Steve, the youngest, stayed with dancing throughout his life. He began dancing professionally in 1936, when he was about 17, and he spent the first decade of his career in vaudeville. He, like his brothers, switched to nightclub work in the 1950s. Steve's first film was as a third Condos Brother (with Frank and Harry) in *Song of the Open Road* (1944), but he was on his own in the short *Thrills of Music: Buddy Rich & His Orchestra* (1948). Steve partnered with Jerry Brandow as a pair of stage hoofers in the Betty Grable movie musical comedy *Meet Me after the Show* (1951).

On Broadway, Steve Condos danced in *Say, Darling* (1953), a play with music that ran for 332 performances, and *Sugar* (1972–73),v a musical comedy that racked up 505 performances.

Steve Condos returned to movies for *Tap!* (1989), a salute to hoofers that starred Gregory Hines and featured Condos along with Sammy Davis Jr., Savion Glover, Harold Nicholas, Bunny Briggs, Sandman Sims, Jimmy Slyde and Buster Brown. It was a last hurrah for most of the older dancers, but, in 1990, Steve collaborated with jazz tenor saxophonist Jay Corre in *Sax 'n' Taps,* a performance that was billed as a "conversation between two improvisers."

Tap dancer Brenda Bufalino recalled, "Steve would go out on to a stage, start hitting and did not leave till he felt he had said what needed to be said—as pure a tap dancer that ever lived." All the Condos Brothers garnered glowing accolades. Whatever praise each earned, the uniform opinion by other hoofers was that they had "legs of iron."

CONE TIME

A small-time circuit, Cone booked six cities in Wisconsin.

CONJURER

Akin to a prestidigitator, a stage conjurer seems to make things appear and disappear. The term was brandished in advertisements where it evoked its original meaning of the medieval sorcerer and the Native American shaman, one who calls upon spirits. There were some within the profession who balked at the term and preferred to be admired for their skill than to pass the credit onto spirits.

CONNIE'S INN

Located in the basement quarters of the Lafayette Theatre Building on 131st Street at Seventh Avenue in Harlem, Connie's Inn had once been a rough saloon called Shuffle Inn. The sensational success on Broadway of musical comedies, such as *Shuffle Along,* written by and starring African Americans, turned white interest toward Harlem. Connie Immerman was a white Harlem bootlegger who, with his brother George, owned several delicatessens that they converted into speakeasies during Prohibition. Connie acquired the Shuffle Inn and converted it to Connie's Inn in 1923. The club seated 500, and the generously proportioned stage could hold more than 30 performers and musicians. Unlike the garish Cotton Club racial motif, the decor at Connie's was elegant, designed and built by black artists and workmen.

Connie's Inn offered the tops in talent, invariably performers who had honed their acts in black vaudeville. Although it did not get the press its rival got, Connie's Inn was well established before the Cotton Club opened, and some folks thought it offered better shows. In addition to the eventual rivalry, Connie's Inn and the Cotton Club shared a racist policy; they were Harlem clubs that offered black entertainers for the delectation of white customers come uptown for forbidden thrills, but they denied entrance to the black citizens of Harlem. Very few blacks, only the rich and famous ones, could gain admittance to Connie's Inn or the Cotton Club. Even Charles Gilpin, the black Jack Barrymore, was turned away from Connie's.

None of the white gangster-owned clubs were welcomed by the black intelligentsia, Harlem's newspapers (*Amsterdam News* and *New York Age*), its businessmen (Colored Cabaret Owners Association) or community leaders. They were united against the spread of white gangsters from downtown Manhattan into Harlem.

There was a difference, however, in the motives for racism. Connie Immerman was a bootlegger like Owney Maddon, the mobster who owned the rival Cotton Club, yet Connie was not a bigoted man, unlike Maddon, nor as cold-bloodedly vicious. Connie's reasons for an exclusionary policy were strictly a matter of profit; he assumed that his downtown white clientele did not wish to sit, cheek by jowl, with African Americans, yet whites were willing to pay exorbitant prices to watch them cavort onstage.

Connie Immerman gave African American composers and stage directors the chance to create the shows. Leonard Harper, a black man, staged the first shows. Fats Waller and Andy Razaf were the house composer and lyricist.

Top talent at Connie's Inn included, at various times, dancers Osceola Banks and Peg Leg Bates, comic Jackie "Moms" Mabley, Fats Waller, who often supplied intermission music at the piano, and bandleaders Wilbur Sweatman, Louis Armstrong and Fletcher Henderson. Connie's Inn shows were sophisticated, fast-moving productions that rivaled the Cotton Club's.

The most successful show ever mounted at Connie's Inn was *Hot Chocolates,* a revue that went into several editions and enjoyed a success that outgrew Connie's Inn. Music and lyrics were by Waller & Razaf, and among its stars were Louis Armstrong and Edith Wilson. *Hot Chocolates* enjoyed a good run on Broadway in 1929 and went on tour.

Other big-time Harlem clubs were determined to succeed with Connie Immerman's formula: black entertainers for white audiences and 50-cent drinks selling for $5 a pop. Those that thrived included the Cotton Club and Small's Paradise.

Connie's Inn closed in 1933. Rampant gangsterism and the accompanying shakedowns resulted in the kidnapping of George Immerman, Connie's brother, which convinced Connie that bootlegging rivalries had gotten out of hand. When Prohibition ended in 1933, eliminating much of the profit in booze and nightclubs, the writing was clearly on the wall: "Premises for lease." At least Connie got the chance to retire without any penalties. Owney Maddon, who closed down the Harlem location of his Cotton Club that same year, got a brief spell in jail.

JOHN W. CONSIDINE

b: 29 September 1863, Chicago, IL— d: 11 February 1943, Los Angeles, CA

After a few terms of college at St. Mary's in Xavier, Kansas, and the University of Kansas at Lawrence, John Considine headed west as a junior actor in a traveling stock company, arriving in Seattle in 1889. Not in demand as a thespian, he found work dealing faro and other card games in a Seattle box house, the Theater-Comique. Within a year or two John was manager of another box house, the People's Theater at Second and Washington Streets.

Considine was admirably suited to his work. An intelligent and muscular man, he was able to charm or intimidate as needed. He became the baron of box houses in Seattle despite being a teetotaler and devout Roman Catholic. Whether impelled by his moral or business sense, he decided to upgrade the box house. He reasoned that if the liquor and the gambling games were the same in all, the only way one box house could distinguish itself from its rivals was to improve the stage show. This he did by recruiting women who could sing and dance; that relieved others, whose talents were more personal, from stage work.

The People's Theater prospered, but not without incident and only until the next financial panic hit the West Coast and the nation in 1893. Among the more usual incidents were brawls and accusations of being drugged, beaten and robbed. One of the more colorful events was a three-day battle between the queen of the People's Theater, Kitty Goodwin, and Lillian Masterson, who was being groomed by Considine to replace the aging Goodwin. The two ladies met at the bar, as the *Seattle Telegraph* reported it, "to discuss each other's virtues." They were quickly separated when a beer mug was brought into play, and the meeting adjourned. The next day's conference began with the slapping of rouged cheeks, the pulling of blondined hair and a demonstration of high kicks. The weaponry escalated to a knife with which Kitty tattooed Lillian's arm. Considine, playing peacemaker, got his expensive suit slashed. Charges were dropped by all, but the drumbeat of criticism from concerned citizens did not dim, and, in 1894, Seattle passed a law forbidding the sale of liquor in theatres.

Considine headed to Spokane, where he managed another People's Theater for three years until history repeated itself. In 1897, the Spokane lawmakers forbade women to work in box houses. John Considine returned to Seattle and arrived just as thousands of other men did, because Seattle had become a port of departure for the gold rush to Alaska's Klondike. Seattle's town fathers, never ones to thwart progress, turned a blind eye to the revival of box houses. After all, this time it was not their citizens who were being victimized, bilked and shanghaied, and the city fathers reasoned that Seattle owed its paying visitors some hospitality.

Upon returning to Seattle, Considine found the People's Theater thriving, as were all the other box houses. John moved quickly to undercut the current management by reaching a deal that was more attractive to the People's Theater's absentee owners. To mark his 1898 return to Seattle with triumph, Considine imported from New York the infamous belly dancer Little Egypt, the sensation of the World's Columbian Exhibition in Chicago in 1893. Little Egypt had scandalized and tantalized audiences throughout America. More recently, she had been acquitted of indecency by a New York City court, and she drew handsomely for Considine.

The corner of Second and Washington Street became the center of Seattle's entertainment for the masses. Rival box houses put on free sidewalk shows to attract customers, and the Salvation Army brass band marched to compete. The spielers in front of the saloons extolled the pleasures within, while the Soldiers of the Lord trumpeted the virtues of salvation, and a good time was had by the onlookers.

Considine became wealthy by investing wisely in real estate, financially backing the Metropole saloon and a gambling parlor. He also became a political power. Considine needed all his influence when he ran afoul of a newspaper editor and a police chief. Both reminded Considine that the ban on box theatres was still on the books. In turn, Considine reminded them that he no longer had any closed boxes and asked why they did not go after those establishments that were flouting the law.

As each side maneuvered, the stakes were hiked, and the police chief was dismissed for graft. He may not have been guilty, but few were innocent during those wild days in Seattle, and there were many who detected Considine's hand in the matter.

The police chief swore "that this town isn't big enough for both of us" and took after Considine. Like a movie-land Western, the fracas culminated in a gunfight that injured Considine but killed the police chief. John Considine was brought to trial for murder, and the town split between those who wanted an open town and those who wanted a clean Seattle. When John was acquitted, he turned to the movies.

Movies had been introduced to Seattle in 1894, but these were plotless novelties, and the folks who presented them traveled from town to town to set up in grange halls, general stores and saloons, wherever a merchant was willing to split the gate. In time, some of the merchants found more profit in showing films than in selling their products, and they converted their shops into bare-bones operations with benches for viewers and a sheet standing in for a projection screen. Given the modesty of their presentation, they became known as nickel Odeons.

Considine bought a half interest in Edison's Unique Theatre in Seattle. The plan was to book vaudeville and movies. John would supply the live acts, and the Edison people would provide their filmed product. Their end of the bargain was easier to effect than John's. He partially solved his problem by opening theatres in Spokane, Yakima, Portland, Bellingham, Everett, Vancouver and Victoria. Together with the Unique in Seattle, he could offer an act four- to eight-weeks' work. That was enough to induce some big-name acts to venture west.

Boasting that his circuit was "the first legitimate, popular-priced vaudeville chain in the world: admission ten cents," Considine topped his previous successes. He publicly turned his back on his honky-tonk beginnings—although he may have kept a covert hand in their operations—and became a founder of the Fraternal Order of Eagles (along with John Cort, a vaudevillian turned burlesk producer and then legitimate-theatre impresario). The steady expansion of Eagles' lodges throughout the USA brought Considine to Manhattan on occasion. In 1906, Considine teamed with Tammany Hall boss "Big Tim" Sullivan to create a New York–based booking agency and to ensure a steady supply of talent for their new Sullivan & Considine circuit.

Cut from similar cloth as John Considine, Timothy D. Sullivan was a physically imposing man who was a state senator and political boss of the Lower East Side of Manhattan. Sullivan brought political and financial connections to his several businesses and partnerships, some of which were theatrical. His relationship with Considine was the same: Sullivan smoothed the way, and John Considine ran the theatre business.

Armed with Sullivan's foreknowledge, a speculator could anticipate changes in zoning and transportation and be guided past regulations and permit officials. Oddly, "Big Tim's" connections proved of minimal use to the Sullivan & Considine circuit. Although it extended from British Columbia through California and from the Pacific Coast eastward to Louisville, Kentucky, it never reached New York City. By 1911 Sullivan & Considine had made a deal with Marcus Loew, who owned 20 theatres in New York and its environs. The alliance meant that S&C was the first circuit in the West to be able to offer an act 70 straight weeks of work on a national vaudeville circuit.

For several years, however, Considine had been shadowed by an aggressive West Coast rival, Alexander Pantages, who was determined to beat Considine at his own game. Considine enjoyed the better reputation among acts. Indeed, because of his policy of never canceling an act, he was regarded more favorably than most vaudeville tyrants. The contest, however, was decided on economic grounds, and Pantages was the better businessman.

Considine's primacy waned within two years. He lost his New York anchor and finance man in 1913 when Big Tim Sullivan was declared insane. Each new theatre in their chain had been built by mortgaging an earlier acquisition. It was a line of dominos ready to topple. Considine was not unaware of the precariousness of his financial position, so he tried to make a deal in 1914 to sell his circuit to Marcus Loew, but Loew backed off when the USA entered the First World War and the future of the economy became uncertain.

Desperately, Considine tried to hold his circuit together, but he could not keep a step ahead of his creditors. Foreclosures against his theatres began in 1915, and both Pantages and Loew were on hand to pick up the theatres, one by one. Considine was not a candidate for the poor house. He had other business interests in boxing, racing and bars. Gradually, he made his way back into the entertainment field when he and his son, John Jr., entered the movie business. John Jr. racked up producer credits during the 1930s and 1940s at MGM for *Puttin' on the Ritz* (1930), *The Gay Bride* (1934), *Broadway Melody of 1936* (1935) and *Boy's Town* (1938) among others. For most of the twentieth century, there was a Considine working behind or in front of the Hollywood movie and television cameras.

A nice irony rounds out the story. Both John Considine Sr. and Alexander Pantages retired to Los Angeles. It was there that Carmen Pantages, Alexander's daughter, married John W. Considine Jr.

CONTINUOUS VAUDEVILLE

First introduced in 1898 by B. F. Keith at his first real vaudeville theatre in Boston, the Bijou, the format of continuous vaudeville was devised to appeal to pedestrians who wished to while away some time watching a show. The potential customers either had later appointments or were not sufficiently intrigued to wait until the start of the next show, so Albee and Keith advertised that patrons could "Come when you please, and stay as long as you like."

The acts were hired to perform as many as ten performances a day, six days a week. Shows started each midmorning and continued until late night. There was no break in the performance; once the last act had performed, the cycle began all over again as the first act repeated its earlier performance.

In 1899, F. F. Proctor imported the idea to his theatres in New York City. He introduced continuous vaudeville at his Twenty-Third Street Theatre. His ads read, "After breakfast, go to Proctors—after Proctor's, go to bed." The idea then spread to other cities.

Without a break between shows, the performers were hard pressed to get rest and eat a decent meal before they were called again to the stage. Even as shows grew longer, and the repetitions for an act dwindled to a more manageable six or eight shows, the acts still got stale and tired, their performances flagged and the bill lost its shape and thrust. As one act followed another into a 12-hour loop, there was no opening, no buildup and no climax to the show.

CONTORTIONIST

An act that performs a form of acrobatics, in which the performer bends and twists his body into such improbable positions that he seems boneless or double-jointed. The contortionist often, but not always, worked solo and usually to musical accompaniment, like a dance. Contortionists learned how to dislocate various joints in order to contort their bodies into various shapes. The act could be done straight or as a fantasy, such as the Human Spider act performed by Hector Napier and, later, his daughter, Valantyne, or by Mankin the Frog Man. Many Asian acrobatic acts included a contortionist, frequently young, within their troupe. This was not as true of European or American acrobat acts.

JOE COOK

b: (Joseph Lopez) 29 March 1890, Evansville, IN—d: 16 May 1959, Clinton Hollow, NY

"Next to Leonardo da Vinci, Joe Cook is the most versatile man known to recorded times." That famous judgment, made by the usually levelheaded, highly respected and longtime theatre critic for the *New York Times,* Brooks Atkinson, was not far off the mark and certainly not a wit exaggerated if the arena were shrunk to the world of entertainment. Because of his versatility, Joe Cook is nearly impossible to categorize.

Joe Cook excelled as a storyteller and was famous for his routine "Why I will not imitate four Hawaiians." Originally an ad-lib during his vaudeville act around 1915, over the years his explanation grew, varied some, and eventually became the title of a book, but its essentials are:

> I will give an imitation of three Hawaiians. This is one. [Joe whistles.] This is another. [Joe plays a ukulele or a mandolin.] This is the third. [He taps out the time with his foot.] I could imitate four Hawaiians just as easily but I will tell you the reason why I don't do it. You see, I bought a horse for $50 and it turned out to be a running horse. I was offered $15,000 for him and I took it. I built a house with the $15,000 and when it was finished a neighbor offered me $100,000 for it. He said my house stood right where he wanted to dig a well. So I took the $100,000 to accommodate him. I invested the $100,000 in peanuts and that year there was a peanut famine so I sold the peanuts for $350,000. Now why should a man with $350,000 bother to imitate four Hawaiians?

With that he exited the stage. Like most stories, it was all in the telling.

Joe was also a one-man circus act: a superior juggler, Risley tumbler, slack-wire walker, unicycle rider, sharpshooter, ball-walker, cartoonist, knife thrower and magician. He played several musical instruments (string, brass and piano) and could sing and dance. And he could act. Any one of his skills would have kept him working. The combination made him a phenomenon.

Joe Cook

Joe and his brothers had been orphaned when Joe was three. His father drowned, and his mother died of grief. The Lopez children were adopted by neighbors, the Cooks. Aged 15, Joe left for New York City vaudeville and immediately secured small-time bookings as a juggler. Within a few months, he had added patter to his juggling and played the big time at Hammerstein's Victoria. At 15 he was a vaudeville headliner able to boast in his billing and live up to it, that Joe Cook was "A One-Man Vaudeville Show."

Although his first legitimate revue, *Half Past Eight,* closed out of town in 1918 and his next show, *Hitchy-Koo of 1919,* lasted only 56 performances, Cook would prove one of Broadway's favorite revue comics. Cook appeared with Moran & Mack in *Earl Carroll's Vanities of 1923,* which ran for 204 performances, and with Sophie Tucker in *Earl Carroll's Vanities of 1924,* which played 134 performances. In the 1924 edition, Joe was elevated to featured billing, and Dave Chasen became his stooge.

In these revues, Joe introduced another aspect of his talent. He created complex and comically bizarre apparatus to perform insignificant tasks. Reviewers likened the contraptions to Rube Goldberg inventions. In one revue, Joe sounded a saxophone that startled a monkey seated in a scenery tree. The monkey dropped a coconut on a native below. The native let fly with the arrow he had cocked in his bow and hit a missionary, causing him to drop a piece of pottery on Dave Chasen's head. This subtle cue was sufficient to bestir the addled Chasen to sound his musical triangle in time to punctuate Joe Cook's musical phrase on the sax. These contraptions were a visual delight that audiences came to expect from each new Joe Cook show.

How's the King, a book show, closed out of town in 1925, and Joe returned to vaudeville. Joe's greatest hit, *Rain or Shine,* a musical, opened in 1928 and ran for 360 performances. A year later, Frank Capra made it into a film. Capra junked the musical score but preserved the best record of the Joe Cook personality and the only record of his one-man vaudeville act. In 1930, back on Broadway, *Fine and Dandy,* with Eleanor Powell and Dave Chasen in the cast, was another winner, toting up with 246 performances at the Erlanger.

Inexplicably, the Capra-Cook film did not lead to more features for Joe, although Capra claimed it cleaned up at the box office. Joe Cook did make several less successful and inferior shorts for Educational Films in the early 1930s. The shorts provide little sense of the man or the range of his talent.

In the trough of the Great Depression, 1933, Joe and Jake Shubert produced *Hold Your Horses,* which survived for 88 shows at the Winter Garden. It was Dave Chasen's last show with Joe Cook. Radio was at its peak of popularity, and Joe made appearances on various network shows. In 1936, Joe, as a small-time circus man, wandered into a Western movie, *Arizona Mahoney,* in time to give Buster Crabbe a hand in his fight against the rustlers.

Joe tried Broadway again in 1939, when Max Liebman, not yet a producer-director, cowrote a straight comedy, *Off to Buffalo.* Critics praised Hume Cronyn, but audiences expected a Joe Cook vehicle, which it was not, and the show died after seven performances on Broadway. *It Happens on Ice,* in 1940, proved to be Joe's final show. It was a Sonja Henie ice-skating show, and, although Joe learned to skate passably, his act had no reason to be on ice.

Another problem was becoming apparent: Joe was fumbling a few of his tricks. Joe left the show midway in 1941 when he learned that he had Parkinson's disease. He took a small ad in *Variety* in 1942 to acknowledge that he had "been on the sick list for some time" and was retiring from show business. He lived in increasing pain for another 17 years.

COON SONGS

Ragtime songs whose lyrics were written and sung with a rural Southern Negro dialect were known as *coon songs.* Despite the label, which has been acknowledged as pejorative for generations, these ragtime ditties were not always intended to be offensive. Black composers as well as white used the term. Akin to character songs about the Irish, Cockneys, Scottish, Germans and Jews, all of them relying on stereotypical accents and situations, *coon songs* persisted after most other ethnic songs faded from popularity. In the main, Negro, Jewish and Italian ditties were the only dialect songs to last into the 1920s.

Historians point to May Irwin as the first to sing *coon songs,* and the first one she sang was "The Bully Song." She never corked up to sing these songs as many other white men and women did. Almost any female singer of the nineteenth and early twentieth centuries felt entitled, even obligated, to include a *coon song* or two in her act, and many male singers continued to cork up when they sang *coon songs.* In most cases, there was little thought given to appropriateness of the situation, to hurt feelings or to presenting a rounded characterization.

JIMMY COOPER

Prolific producer Jimmy Cooper created major black-and-white and all-colored revues such as *Darktown Frolics* (1926), *Black & White Revue* (1926–27), *Jimmy Cooper's Revue* (1927), *Okeh Revue* (1927), *Jimmy Cooper's 1928 Revue* (1927) and *Jimmy Cooper's High Jinks Revue* (1928).

Cooper's shows played an informal northern circuit of theatres in the USA, known as *round-the-world,* whose core circuit comprised of the Lafayette in Harlem, the Empire in Brooklyn, the Earle in Philadelphia, the Royal in Baltimore and the Howard in Washington, D.C. If shows were successful, the tour extended to Brooklyn, Boston, Pittsburgh, Cleveland, Chicago, Detroit, Toronto and westward.

COOTCH DANCERS

See Hootchy-Kootchy

JAMES J. CORBETT

b: (James John Corbett) 1 September 1866, San Francisco, CA—d: 18 February 1933, Bayside, NY

Jim Corbett was a first-generation Irish American whose father first settled in New Orleans. Patrick Corbett married, and the couple relocated to San Francisco in 1854, where Jim was born. A smart lad, Jim graduated at 16 from Sacred Heart College and secured a position as a clerk in the Nevada Bank. Much of his free time was spent boxing at the Olympia Athletic Club. Jim was focused and disciplined, but he displayed an easygoing, humorous manner that made him popular with members. Soon he was managing the facility. Older members noticed his proficiency as a boxer and encouraged him to turn pro. Corbett was a good bet. At six feet, one inch, he weighed about 185 pounds and was a scientific boxer who relied on skill rather than simple force.

Jim fought his way up to the rank of a heavyweight contender, and, a few days following his 26th birthday, he knocked out the popular reigning champion, John L. Sullivan, on 7 September 1892. The victory took 21 rounds. The previous year, William A. Brady, an agent and a producer, talked Corbett into letting him become his manager, with a show-business career as the goal. Once Corbett defeated Sullivan and became champ, Brady put Jim into a series of quickly produced stage farces and helped devise a vaudeville act for Jim.

Jim acted in various hokum plays that capitalized on his heroic image. According to vaudeville comedian and writer Will Cressy, who witnessed the event, one night the expected confrontation between Corbett and the villain misfired. As the villain snarled, "Then die, you dog," he pulled the trigger on his stage gun, and Jim slumped to the floor. Unfortunately, there was no sound of a bullet being fired. The villain stood stock-still in shock, forgetting to try again in the hope that practice might make perfect. So it was left to Jim to rescue the scene. He lifted himself onto one elbow and in pained tones blurted, "My God, shot with an air gun!"

There was a contingent in vaudeville audiences that enjoyed the personal appearances of sports stars. Occasionally, a swimming star, witness Annette Kellerman, or even a tennis player, Bill Tilden, could bring in a crowd, but the most popular were baseball players and boxers. Generally, the ballplayers and boxers talked a bit about their careers or their biggest wins. It was exciting stuff, but only to fans. Giants pitcher Rube Marquard had a good act that played for several years, and he managed to sing and do a soft shoe, but it was his girlfriend, later wife, singer Blossom Seeley who made the act big time.

Jim Corbett did not need anyone to make him a good act. He was a natural storyteller and wit. One of his first engagements was at the World's Columbian Exposition in Chicago in 1893. Corbett gave boxing demonstrations on the Midway. It was experience for the time when, after hanging up his gloves, Corbett made a good living and a fine reputation as a monologist. He eschewed jokes. Instead he capitalized on the Irish tradition of storytelling, offering short, self-deflating stories about his former ring prowess and ironic anecdotes that presented him as a celebrity with the common touch.

Gentleman Jim Corbett

Much of his material was written for him by Billy V. Van, a vaudeville and burlesque comedian who was in demand as a writer of comedy material. Jim was capable, as well, of providing some of his own material, as his Steve Brodie story proves.

> Shortly after one of my ring battles, I met Steve Brodie, the man who jumped off the Brooklyn Bridge. I told my father about him, and suggested that he come with me and be introduced to Brodie. I told him that it would be a nice thing to say that he had met and talked to the only man who ever jumped off the Brooklyn Bridge, so finally the old man grudgingly consented.
>
> When the introduction was effected, the old man looked Brodie over from crown to toe. "And you the felly that jumped over the Brooklyn Bridge?," he said. "No, Mr. Corbett," Brodie hastened to correct him. "I didn't jump over. I jumped off!" "Jumped off!," exclaimed father. "Any dang fool could do that!"

Corbett held the heavyweight title from 1892 until 1897, when he lost it to Bob Fitzsimmons. He tried to reclaim it, but for the most part his pugilistic career was over; the stage provided his new arena. In 1898, Corbett received bizarre and unhappy news from his brother Harry. Their mother had been shot and killed by their father, Patrick, who then killed himself.

Jim made many friends in show business; two of his dearest, Eddie Foy and Fred Stone, were at the top of their profession. Foy was a whimsical musical comedian who in his later years turned to vaudeville with his "Seven Little Foys," and Stone was an extraordinary athlete and half of the top comedy team of the 1910s, Montgomery & Stone. Corbett worked with Fred to develop the comic prizefight that Montgomery & Stone made famous.

Corbett took an active part in the duties of his profession. After the White Rats were formed, Jim was in the first group of performers to become members. He took a lead in producing various benefits for the White Rats. He became a member of the Lambs, as well. Jim was twice wed. He was 20 when he married Olive Lake in 1886. They divorced in 1895, at which time he wed Jessie Taylor; he later divorced her. His popularity was not hurt by the first divorce or the second marriage soon thereafter, even though he was Roman Catholic.

In some eyes, his reputation was stained when he was drawn into the racist cabal to fund a Great White Hope to reclaim the heavyweight boxing title from Jack Johnson, a proud African American whose romances with white women stirred the ire of bigots. Authors Jack London and Rex Beach, both rabid racists, encouraged an overweight, out-of-shape and alcoholic Jim Jeffries to take on Johnson in 1910. Jim Corbett was persuaded to train Jeffries. Johnson won.

Corbett earned his soubriquet, Gentleman Jim, because he behaved modestly and kindly. In 1902, two young comics had teamed up but were having no luck getting a manager to look at their act. One of them, Al Lewis, had a nodding acquaintance with Jim Corbett and knew that Jim was emceeing a benefit up in Harlem, then a white area. It was a rough audience until Jim satisfied the crowd by telling his stories and jokes. He concluded by introducing the next act and telling the audience they were fine fellows from the West Coast and to give them a warm welcome. The crowd did, and they laughed all through the act. When Al Lewis and his partner Ed Wynn left the stage, there were agents waiting in the wings to sign and handle them.

Corbett ventured onto Broadway in 1906 when he appeared, along with Margaret Wycherly and May Tully, in a revival of *Cashel Brown.* The play provided Corbett with one of the shortest counts in his career; it closed after 16 performances. His second attempt on Broadway was in a Shubert revue, *Doing Our Bit* (1917), with Herman Timberg; it lasted 130 performances.

In a sense, Corbett was one of the first American movie stars. Motion pictures of *Corbett and Courtney Before the Kinetograph* (1894), *The Corbett-Fitzsimmons Fight* (1897) and the *Corbett and Sharkey*

Fight (1898) captured moments from his ring battles on film, and Corbett, Courtney, Fitzsimmons and Sharkey were watched by great numbers of people. As a performer, however, Jim's storytelling had little to offer a silent screen, but he was cast in several silent comedies, made a few cameo appearances as himself, starred in *The Midnight Man* (1919), an 18-episode adventure serial, and played the lead in a Western flick, *The Man from the Golden West* (1913).

After talkies entered the scene, Jim Corbett appeared in a couple of shorts, one for Movietone and another for Vitaphone, in which he and other theatrical notables played themselves. His most notable later appearance was in the feature film *Happy Days* (1929), a minstrel show wrapped up in a flimsy narrative. Willie Collier, Georgie Jessel, Tom Patricola, Walter Catlett, Will Rogers, Ann Pennington, Rex Bell and other stars played themselves. In the concluding minstrel show, Jim Corbett handled the duties of the interlocutor and the minstrel chorus was made up of whatever stars were in town, from legends like Harry Lauder to teenage starlet Betty Grable.

His autobiography, *The Roar of the Crowd,* was published in 1925, and Jim Corbett played the Palace in 1928, providing two grand hurrahs for Gentleman Jim. In his last years, Jim suffered a long battle with cancer. The once-fine athlete slowly crumbled into an old, weak man. He died at 66 in 1933. His life story was fictionalized in a film, *Gentleman Jim* (1942), and Errol Flynn portrayed him.

ALAN CORELLI

b: ca. 1895—d: 1980

The range of the acts that one saw in vaudeville was far greater than in burlesque, revue, musical comedy and other types of live entertainment. A person could make a living from vaudeville tearing paper into designs, juggling handkerchiefs, playing melodies by rubbing the rims of drinking glasses, or just challenging people to lift him. That is what Alan Corelli did.

He never intended to go into show business. His primary interest was bodybuilding. When the USA entered the First World War, Alan joined the service as an ambulance driver. He continued to exercise and experimented with a form of muscle control that negated the possibility that anyone, even those who outmatched him in size and weight, could lift him off the ground. Alan regarded his talent only as an amusing trick to play on other guys in the service or, later, at parties and in bars.

After the war, like a lot of ex-servicemen, Corelli continued to see the world, from Paris to Utah and San Francisco, working at various jobs. In San Francisco, after demonstrating his trick at a party, a local theatre owner offered him a three-night gig. The money was better than anything Alan had been earning, so he accepted. He opened his routine with some muscle poses in a white leotard and then challenged the audience to try to lift him. His success led to other Bay Area bookings and still more up and down the coast.

After one show, John Ringling made Alan an offer to join the Ringling Brothers Circus. Alan accepted, and he and his new bride joined the tour. Afterward, he set out on his own, working out deals with various theatre owners and fair-grounds managers in Texas. Alan was asked to appear at the Texas State Fair because the local women's and citizens' groups would not permit the intended headliner, Roscoe "Fatty" Arbuckle, to appear (although he had been cleared of charges in three successive trials).

From Texas, he headed through the South on the Delmar vaudeville circuit. Corelli worked his way up the East Coast into New York—Buffalo, Syracuse, Binghamton, Elmira, Rochester, then over to New England. It was mostly small time with a few big-time dates in larger cities like Montreal, Boston and Baltimore. In a number of places, he was paid more for entertaining at private parties and fraternal clubs than in vaudeville.

When, in the early 1930s, he got the chance to play Italy, he grabbed it. The booking that started with dates in Milan, Genoa, Rome and Bologna was extended into France, Germany and England. As Corelli had done in the USA, he made arrangements with the managers of the theatres he played to promote his shows with stunts. Much was made in the press about his challenges to fire stations, sports teams and local strongmen to lift him. That boosted the box office as people attended to see if it could be done. The problem for Corelli was that his act was built around one trick. Once you had seen it, there was no need to come again. He did other feats of strength, but they were merely a prelude to the big trick.

The gathering conflict in Europe precluded further work there. In the USA, vaudeville was reduced to small-time venues that paid bottom dollar and offered most acts only a one- or two-day booking. Alan Corelli bowed to the inevitable when, in the 1940s, he went to work for the Theatre Authority, a body formed by a consortium of theatrical unions that ruled whether charity events could waive union rules for the occasion.

CORK UP

Corking up, or putting on blackface, was synonymous with blacking up but specifically referred to using Burnt corks to darken the face. Burnt cork took the place of coal dust, and, in turn, it was replaced by black greasepaint.

In most minstrel shows, it was customary for all performers, save the interlocutor, to work in blackface. This was true of black as well as white minstrel performers. The comic characters of Mr. Bones and Mr. Tambo carried over into variety, vaudeville, musical comedy and revue; comedy teams, white or black, adopted the give-and-take of the minstrel end men, and the formula served them from vaudeville through movies and into early television.

Some white comedy teams, notably McIntyre & Heath and Moran & Mack, continued to use blackface in vaudeville and musical shows, but the vast majority of white comedy teams retained little of the minstrel-show impersonation of Bones and Tambo except the comic mechanics and some of the hoary jokes. Blackface endured in black vaudeville into the 1940s until pressure from a new generation demanded more dignified portrayals of African Americans by Negro comedians. There were always exceptions, such as movies that included blackface (or tan) musical numbers, even after the Second World War.

JULIAN COSTELLO

African American female impersonator Julian Costello worked Toby time with a song-and-dance act about the same time as Julian Eltinge was in big-time vaudeville.

COSTER SINGERS

Costermongers were familiar sights in London's open-air fruit and vegetable markets. The word *coster* derives from *costard,* a large cooking apple, and *monger* means "vendor." By the early nineteenth century, costermongers had evolved into a particular and identifiable caste. Henry Mayhew, a contemporary chronicler of London's poor, estimated the number of costers in the Metropolitan London of 1851 at 30,000, including women and children.

The costers of that day had developed a distinctive style of dress that already featured the ubiquitous pearl and abalone buttons. The men favored worsted or plush caps, corduroy waistcoats (with pearl buttons) and corduroy trousers cut wide at the ankles. Coster women generally wore clean, white aprons over fitted bodices and full skirts. Pearl buttons took the place of jewelry for many poor Londoners. Dressy costers and members of various fund-raising clubs began to decorate their clothing with pearl and abalone buttons: some moderately, some covering nearly every inch of their clothing in a smother pattern.

Costers also fashioned their own dialect, a back slang that coded "Look at the police" as "Cool the esclop." This progressed into a rhyming slang.

I was sitting alone by the fireside one night,
A-warming me plates of meat [feet];
When wot should I 'ear but a knowck on the door
Which caused me old raspberry [raspberry tart, heart]
to beat.

COTTON CLUB

Situated on the second floor atop the Douglas Theatre at 142nd Street at Lenox Avenue, the Cotton Club was a safari stop for white audiences looking for exoticism without encountering any of Harlem's earthy reality. Strictly speaking, the Cotton Club had nothing to do with vaudeville. It was a Harlem nightclub with a floor show that changed significantly twice a year. Yet the best of black vaudeville performed in those floor shows.

The well-put-together revues featured top bands like Duke Ellington (in residence from 1928 to 1931) and Cab Calloway (in residence from 1929 to 1933), who alternated. If both Duke and Cab were on tour, then either Jimmy Lunceford or Lucky Millinder took over. Singers included Ethel Waters, Aïda Ward, George Dewey Washington, Nina Mae McKinney, June Richmond, the Dandridge Sisters and singer-dancer Cora La Redd. Dancers were always central to a Cotton Club show, and over the years Eddie Rector, Bill Robinson, Tip, Tap & Toe, the Step Brothers, Henri Wessels, the Berry Brothers, Carolynne Snowden, Earl "Snakehips" Tucker, the Nicholas Brothers and Whyte's Lindy Hoppers were featured.

Owney Maddon bankrolled the operation; his rule was black onstage, white running the show backstage. Lew Leslie staged the shows. Songsmiths Harold Arlen and Ted Koehler wrote some of their most memorable songs for the Cotton Club. Resident choreographers Clarence Robinson and Elida Webb made sure that the club's renowned chorus line of bronze cuties, the Copper Colored Gals, were good dancers, well-rehearsed as well as an eyeful in their skimpy costumes. The showgirls were called "Tall, Tan and Terrific," and if they did not dance much, who noticed?

As emcee, Dan Healy paced the show, engaged the audience and introduced the more famous of the ringsiders. Tallulah Bankhead, Marlene Dietrich, Harry Richman, Clara Bow, George Raft, Mayor Jimmy Walker, J. Edgar Hoover, Jesse Owens, Joe Louis, William Saroyan, Erich Maria Remarque, Doris Duke, and Lord and Lady Mountbatten were Cotton Club regulars, part of a mix of cosmopolitan personalities drawn from theatre, movies, politics, sports, literature, and moneyed and titled society.

Although the Cotton Club starred top African American singers, dancers and bands, such as Duke

Ellington, Ethel Waters and Cab Calloway, blacks were not allowed as customers unless they were very famous.

Indeed, the very atmosphere of the Cotton Club was an insult to African Americans. The stage was framed to resemble the front portico of an antebellum Southern mansion. The backdrop pictured a plantation and its slave quarters. Chandeliers hung from the ceiling. The entire place had been designed by Joseph Urban, most famous for his sumptuous sets for the *Ziegfeld Follies.* Black waiters, dressed in red tuxedoes, were expected to behave as if they were back in "massa's" employ. The chorus dancers were all quite light. The African American specialty performers were not permitted to mix with the customers, even if they were friends.

Originally, the premises had housed Douglas Hall, a large auditorium. In 1923, it was converted into the New Douglas Casino and then, a year later, refurbished and reopened as DeLuxe Cabaret. Ex-heavyweight boxing champion Jack Johnson fronted the club for white bootleggers, who were the true investors and owners. They hoped to snare some of the rich, white and adventurous who were coming to Connie's Inn and other Harlem clubs for exotic entertainment of one sort or another.

Shortly after Urban redesigned the club in motifs that spanned the jungle and the plantation, that most private of gangsters, Owney Madden, assumed control of the 700-seat cabaret, renamed Club DeLuxe. He also owned the Stork Club during Prohibition and other speakeasies downtown, including those hosted by Texas Guinan.

Madden's lieutenants had the advantage of being able to coerce the performers they wanted into working for them, to provide the bootleg booze (which they owned), and to protect the club and its illustrious clientele (like Mayor Jimmy Walker and J. Edgar Hoover) from embarrassing visits by the police or federal agents (some of whom they owned).

A particular element of the press, typified by columnists Walter Winchell, Louis Sobol, Abel Green and Ed Sullivan, lionized the Cotton Club, as Madden renamed it, and wrote items about the well-known writers, actors, performers, prizefighters, movie stars and socialites who patronized it. Winchell, however, was paid by Madden not to write about him.

The gangster management misread its clientele's prejudice. There was little if any objection on the part of its white customers to mixing with black entertainers and sports figures. Indeed, talented and good-looking black women and men were a major attraction for white café society that simply did not wish to mix with the hoi polloi, white or black.

Opinion was divided as to whether the shows at the Cotton Club or Connie's Inn were the best. By the end of 1935, it mattered little. The Great Depression had devastated Harlem; four out of five adult workers were unemployed. The atmosphere was too glum to entice slumming parties from downtown so, in February 1936, management closed Harlem's Cotton Club. In autumn that year, they opened another Cotton Club on the top floor of a building at Broadway and 48th Street. The new Cotton Club stayed in business until 1940, presenting ever-bigger name acts in ever-faster and flashier productions. By the time it shuttered, and despite its nefarious owners and segregated policy, the Cotton Club had given a stage to the finest African American talents of the vaudeville, revue, blues, boogie-woogie and swing eras.

WILLIE COVAN

b: 4 March 1897, Atlanta or Savannah, GA—d: 7 May 1989, Los Angeles, CA

In turn-of-the-twentieth-century variety and vaudeville, it was fashionable for white women *coon singers* to add inexpensively to their acts by hiring a group of young black singing dancers, between ages 6 and 12, officially known in theatrical circles as *pickaninnies,* or *picks,* for short. Eva Tanguay, Nora Bayes, Sophie Tucker and Blossom Seeley all employed *picks* at one time, as did black women entertainers such as the Whitman Sisters.

The positive aspect of this seemingly demeaning exploitation was that it provided an excellent opportunity for a young black child to get training, experience and a foothold in both black and white show business. The practice was not too different from the custom in the 1970s and 1980s for white pop singers to use black onstage backup singers.

Willie Covan was six when he began dancing in local minstrel shows. Soon after his birth, Willie's family had followed one of the established northern migration routes to Chicago, and there he spent his childhood. Chicago was a bustling city, a center of transcontinental transportation, a major entertainment center and the starting spot for entertainment troupes heading westward.

In 1908, he went on the road with Canadian Indian entertainer Cosie Smith & Her Six Pickaninnies. Willie's mother granted permission for him and his brother Dewey to travel in Ms. Smith's act on its tour of Los Angeles, San Francisco, Seattle, Portland and lesser western cities and towns. Sometimes, in the northern Rocky Mountain states, the Covan brothers and the other *picks* were the first colored people that their cowboy and miner audiences had ever seen. Covan recalled that the entertainment-starved audiences sometimes invited the *picks* to entertain in the saloons for throw money, which often was far more than they earned in the act.

Ambitious to develop as a dancer, Willie entered amateur contests that minstrel shows and vaudeville theatres used to stimulate neighborhood ticket sales. These contests were either held after the show or on the bill's day off. A dance competition customarily employed judges rather than relying on audience applause. Several dancers were placed below the stage to judge whether the contestants' execution was rhythmic. Other dancers-judges, placed in the wings, gauged timing, and those in the orchestra pit looked for style and appearance. Covan made a fair amount of money from his winnings.

Willie also worked in white minstrel shows as did other African American performers. With the black performers corked up like the white performers, audiences supposed they were seeing white-only minstrelsy and were none the wiser.

Sometime before the First World War, Covan teamed with Ulysses S. "Slow Kid" Thompson, who, older than Willie, had been a performer since the late 1880s and was the better known. Influenced by Thompson, who had closely observed the troupes of Russian dancers that toured the USA early in the twentieth century, Willie developed an athletic and muscular style of tap. Covan himself watched the Japanese and Arab acrobatic acts that appeared in vaudeville, and from them he found added inspiration. On occasion, the spelling of Willie's surname was changed to Kovan. It remains conjecture if this was the correct spelling of his family name, a frequent accident of misspelling, or both an effort to sound more exotic and an homage to the dancers and acrobats around the world who had inspired him.

Willie Covan proved a good pupil; a generation later, he proved a great teacher. He could do it all. Many dancers did some or most of it well, but all his contemporaries and his generations of students agreed that Willie Covan did it all very well: soft shoe, buck-and-wing, rhythm, acrobatic, flash. Covan was a lithe and dapper dancer, quite sensual, confident, slick and quick.

Even in his later performances during the 1950s for *Willie Covan's Annual Dance Studio Revue,* when the master took the stage, he still demonstrated the polish that distinguished his dancing. He was among the first tap dancers to strive for the grace and flair that became the hallmark of a generation of tap dancers from Fred Astaire to the Nicholas Bothers. In his prime, Covan was capable of dazzling with quicksilver high kicks, knee drops and a step that no one else could do: an *around the world* with no hands. This last step was adapted from the Russian dancers who, in a crouch, rapidly rotated one leg then the other under their bodies, supporting themselves with one hand and then the other. Willie Covan did it so fast he did not use his hands or anything else to support his body.

The career record for Willie Covan is thin generations later. It seems Willie Covan was half of three acts and the organizer of a fourth. On occasion, he worked as a single. It is likely that he took the best work offered, whether it was pairing with either his wife or his brother, appearing in the Four Covans or working alone. Some sources say he put the family act together in 1917, but the Four Covans (Willie, Dewey and their wives) were playing dates as late as 1932 (although, by 1933, John "Jack" Jackson had replaced Dewey in the act). Willie teamed with his brother Dewey early on, beginning as kids, then Willie joined "Slow Kid" as Thompson & Covan. A later double act, Covan & Ruffin, was formed in the early 1920s.

Leonard Ruffin was a highly regarded soft-shoe dancer, and the Covan & Ruffin act, "Every Move a Picture," played the top houses in white vaudeville during the 1920s, including the Palace in 1926. Their ability was their curse; because their act drew heavy and prolonged applause, other acts complained about following them. Throughout their engagements, theatre managers would continue to juggle the bill to find a spot for Covan & Ruffin that would not blow the other acts off the bill. Once, for this reason, they were canceled at the Palace and immediately hired by its rival, the Hippodrome, and then fired from there for the same reason: upsetting the balance of the bill. Many black dancers worked hard and fast, the best of them creating an excitement that often stopped the show. Not only exciting, Covan & Ruffin were elegant and musical, setting a standard of polish for other tap-dancing acts.

In 1923, Covan & Ruffin were featured in George White's 1923 hit musical *Runnin' Wild.* Not only one of the better Negro musicals of the era, *Runnin' Wild* also produced both the song and the dance craze "The Charleston," which came to symbolize the exuberant 1920s. The show starred singer Adelaide Hall and comedy team Flournoy E. Miller & Aubrey Lyles (who also wrote the show).

By the mid-1920s, Willie had reunited with his brother Dewey and formed an act with their wives, Florence Covan and Carita Harbert. The Four Covans played major vaudeville and club dates. Whether, after a half-dozen or more years, the Four Covans tired of being on the road or Willie had the foresight to understand where show business was headed, the act moved to Hollywood just as musicals were becoming the rage of early sound movies.

The Four Covans appeared in several spots in *On with the Show,* one of Warner Brothers' 1929 entries in the all-star musical stakes. The Covans' tight and fast precision dancing shamed the lackluster white dance chorus behind them. Elsewhere in the film, Ethel Waters in her "Birmingham Bertha" spot is backed up by a solo dancer. Physically, he resembles Dewey more than Willie. Other sources claim that this was an uncredited appearance by John Bubbles, yet the dancer in question neither looks like Bubbles nor dances like him. It remains a mystery. *Duke Is Tops,* a 1938 short, and *Gang War* (1940), a low-budget feature made by a small studio, gave Covan a last opportunity to lay it down for posterity. In the latter film he is partnered with dancer Marie Bryant.

By 1930, Willie Covan had opened a dance studio on 41st Street in East Los Angeles. It was across from the predominantly black Jefferson High School, so black and white schoolchildren attended Willie's classes along with movie stars. Willie's reputation had preceded him and ensured success. Perhaps Eleanor Powell was Covan's biggest booster, because she demanded that MGM hire him as resident choreographer and chief dance instructor at MGM.

Although he never earned a screen credit for his work with MGM's star players, he made a fine living coaching and training stars such as Eleanor Powell, Mickey Rooney, Judy Garland and Ann Miller. It has been noted that the glorious MGM musicals would not have been so glorious without Willie Covan devising choreography for the films and coaching the stars to give their best performance. In Hollywood, they know that not all the major talent is on screen.

NOËL COWARD

b: (Noël Peirce Coward) 16 December 1899, Teddington, England—d: 26 March 1973, Jamaica, British West Indies

At first blush, the master of merry wit and rueful sentiment seemed the polar opposite to a vaudevillian purveyor of insouciant Irish charm and brash. Yet Noël Coward was to London's Strand what George M. Cohan had been to Broadway a generation earlier, an entertainer who, imbued with the Zeitgeist of his generation, brought to the stage the characteristics that his audiences wished to see in themselves. English theatre critic Kenneth Tynan remarked of Coward, "He was the instant projection of a new kind of human being, which has never before existed in print or paint." Designer-photographer Cecil Beaton wrote that "all sorts of men suddenly wanted to look like Noël Coward—sleek . . . clipped and well-groomed, with cigarette . . . or cocktail in hand."

Like George M. Cohan, Coward was an all-around man of the theatre: playwright, songwriter, director, actor and variety performer. Music-hall historian Christopher Pulling argued:

> The theatrical phenomenon of the [post–First World War] epoch, Noël Coward, for all his achievements as a serious dramatist, belongs primarily to vaudeville. Like Ivor Novello, he was an actor as well as author and composer, with an inborn sense of the theatre which gave their productions a telling unity; but whereas Ivor Novello was above all emotional, Noël Coward was brittle, slick and sophisticated. If he could not claim to be a great musician, he had a gift for melody, and wrote brilliantly witty lyrics.

He was vaudevillian in that his guide was not a Muse but the perfect vaudeville act: the union of a performer and his material. One of his biographers, Philip Hoare, explained that he changed English comedy "by allying English humour to American pace."

The greatest difference between Cohan and Coward was that Cohan's musicals and plays have seldom been revived since his death, but, since Noël's passing, the best of Coward's plays and new revues, composed wholly of Coward's songs, have been staged almost without lapse throughout the English-speaking world and sometimes beyond.

Noël Coward grew up delighted by Christmas pantomimes and music-hall performances. He sang, learned to play piano and took dancing lessons, all of which proved useful when he had to help support the family through his appearances on the stage. From his father he inherited his talent, from his mother he got his drive and confidence.

Noël's slow professional ascent was typical of other child actors. His mother, needing to augment family finances, brought ten-year-old Noël to an audition, and the boy made his debut in *The Goldfish.* He appeared in fantasies like *Peter Pan,* acted small roles in drama, and, in 1912, played music-hall in a sketch, *A Little Fowl Play,* starring Sir Charles Hawtrey. Noël loved music-hall for the opportunity to watch consummate performers like George Robey and Nellie Wallace. In 1913, Noël was on the variety bill at the London Palladium, where he had the lead in a sketch, *War in the Air,* an uncanny forecast.

Even at 15, Noël was at home in the bohemia of show business and surefooted among the fashionable elite. He began writing songs that melded romance, hard-boiled humor and world-weariness. Noël served a nine-month hitch in his majesty's army but was back in civilian life in time to have his first play produced in 1917 and his second in 1918. Noël was 18. From then on, there was seldom a season in which Noël Coward did not have a play in production; he wrote a total of 50 during his lifetime.

By the time Noël was 25, he had several hit plays to his credit—*I'll Leave It to You* (1920), *The*

Vortex (1924) and *Fallen Angels* (1925)—wrote songs and starred with another one-time child performer, Gertrude Lawrence, in André Charlot's revue *London Calling* (1923).

The Vortex, a drama about drug addiction with Coward in the lead role, caused a sensation, and Coward rode the crest. His best-known plays, all great successes and smart comedies, have never gone out of style: *Hay Fever* (1925), *Private Lives* (1930), *Design for Living* (1933), *Blithe Spirit* (1941) and *Present Laughter* (1942). He wrote dozens of songs still sung in cabaret and revues that he originally penned for *London Calling* (1925), *On with the Dance* (1925), *This Year of Grace* (1928), *Words and Music* (1932), *Set to Music* (1939) and *Sigh No More* (1945). His musicals included *Bittersweet* (1929), *Conversation Piece* (1934), *Operette* (1938) and *Pacific 1860* (1946). Coward also composed songs for other of his stage pieces such as *Cavalcade* (1931) and *Tonight at 8:30* (1936), which contained the one-acter "Red Peppers" that was essentially a music-hall turn.

For 50 years, Noël Coward sold sophistication as surely as Mae West sold sex. Ms. West's frankness was regarded as salutarily American; Mr. Coward's smartness was considered the essence of being English. Both reached their zenith in the 1920s and 1930s. They created characters that presented themselves as they wished to be seen and admired. Each was its author's greatest creation. So commanding was the creation that it subsumed the creator. Noël Coward, like Mae West, never lost the vaudevillian's understanding that his act exalted him. He took the most amusing, most confident and most agreeable pieces of himself and created Noël Coward.

Behind the curtain, Coward was a practical man who worked diligently at his craft, yet his better straight plays took less than a week to write, once the plot and characters had settled in his mind. It took far longer to pull together plot, dialogue, lyrics and melodies for his musical comedies and operettas.

As a performer and actor, Coward displayed an airy grace and confidence onstage that came as a result of sure craft, experience, and diligent study and rehearsal. Noël never allowed the effort to show because that would have undermined his public reputation as a wunderkind. The one serious flaw was his inability to spark the necessary juice between himself and his leading ladies that was required to make real his heterosexual lead roles. As long as Coward was discreet, unfailingly polite to the world, petted the press and did not discuss his homosexuality, it was the unspoken bargain of the times that the press would not raise the issue.

His discipline and obligation to entertain extended to his behavior toward press and public. Even when he endured the inevitable rough patches in his life or career, he never confessed to obstacles in his path, ill health, worry or doubt. Interviewers were left certain that he was truly a witty, carefree, glittering gallant.

Coward devoted himself to Britain's war effort during the Second World War. In addition to entertaining the troops, Noël produced, wrote, directed and starred in England's most thoughtful propaganda film, *In Which We Serve* (1942).

After the grave toll of the Second World War and lingering postwar austerity, Coward came to be regarded as a superficial farceur and an apologist for the crown and the ossified upper crust. He went without a hit from 1945 to 1955, and his career seemed at its end. With the emergence of a few angry, young playwrights, who were as unfairly dismissed as "kitchen sink dramatists" as they arrogantly denigrated the crafters of well-made plays, there was the nearly unanimous prediction that Noël Coward would slouch into oblivion, to be followed in short order by Terrance Rattigan and the rest who wrote of brave behavior and civil obligations rather than crippling personal needs and society's faults.

In 1961, in a three-part series in the *London Times,* Noël allowed himself a few public opinions that faulted contemporary theatre and dramatists, forgetting that his own early work had been condemned as "dust-bin drama" by Gerald DeMaurier. Noël did admire, however, certain new playwrights such as Harold Pinter, whom he praised as an original and authentic voice. Perhaps what drew him to Pinter was precise dialogue. Like Coward's, Pinter's dialogue required acute timing and was easily undermined by overplaying.

Most of Coward's plays of the same period seemed ordinary and were not as enjoyable or memorable as his earlier work. Youthful self-centered characters in a play can be fun to watch as long as there is the hope they will come to their senses and redeem themselves. In middle age, when there is little promise left, self-centered characters are seen as shallow and unlovely. Coward's bright young things had become hard and hollow.

Noël's gifts as an entertainer, however, had not the least dimmed. With cabaret stands at Café de Paris in London (1951) and the Desert Inn in Las Vegas (1955), Noël Coward was reborn, reinvigorated as a variety artist, and in demand. Recordings were made of his one-man nightclub shows. CBS-Television contracted with Noël to create and perform in three specials, beginning in 1955.

His early plays from *Vortex* (1924) to *Present Laughter* (1939) were being revived by the early 1960s. Coward wrote three new one-act plays that he presented as *Suite In Three Keys* (1966) that earned him considerable praise. A half century later, most of Coward's plays were still revived, if not always well, and his work showed little likelihood to fall out of favor as did the plays of many of those who had damned him. As late as the turn of the twenty-first century, still in print were all of his plays, his three-volume autobiography, at least ten biographies, his songbook, and collections of his short stories, verse and witticisms.

Until late in the twentieth century, much of the popular music that was a hit on the British stage and heard on radio was American. Not that there were not capable, even superior, songwriters in the United Kingdom, but, allowing exceptions such as Ivor Novello and Noël Coward, few could make themselves heard amid the ubiquitous American imports.

Noël Coward's compositions varied widely from operetta to music-hall ditties. He wrote words and music that were romantic, even sentimental ("I'll See You Again," "Some Day I'll Find You," "If Love Were All" and I'll Follow My Secret Heart), cynical ("Twentieth Century Blues," "World Weary"), sprightly dance tunes ("Poor Little Rich Girl," "Dance Little Lady"), and, of course, funny, which occupied a spot between Gilbert & Sullivan patter songs and the character comedy ditties that were the glory of music-hall: "Mad Dogs and Englishmen," "(Don't Put Your Daughter on the Stage) Mrs. Worthington," "A Bar at the Piccolo Marina" and "I Went to a Marvelous Party," to name a few.

Advice was also among his legacy. As a playwright, Coward knew that a competently written script held most of what an actor needed to know about a role and that an actor's motivation was not necessarily his character's: "Your motivation? Your motivation is your pay packet on Friday. Now get on with it." An added admonition was "Play it fast."

> I wonder why it is that my plays are such traps for directors, as my lyrics are for singers. Nobody seems capable of leaving well enough alone and allowing the words to take care of themselves. Neither my lyrics nor my dialogue need decoration; all they do require are clarity, diction and intention and the minimum of gesture and business.

Noël Coward followed his own advice.

LOTTA CRABTREE

b: (Charlotte Mignon Crabtree) 7 November 1847, New York, NY—d: 25 September 1925, Boston, MA

Around 1830, Samuel Livesey and three of his four sons set sail for India. Their ship sank, and they perished. Mrs. Livesey, at home in Cheshire, England, faced two choices: genteel poverty in England or the gamble for a better station in America. She, her four daughters and young son set sail to New York in the early 1830s.

Mother Livesey set up housekeeping in a flat in Lower Manhattan and, with her daughter Mary Ann, ran a small upholstery business from their home. Mary Ann met a fellow immigrant from the old country, John Ashworth Crabtree, a bookseller and a charming loafer. They were married in 1844, and their first child, Harriet, was born in 1846 and died soon after. A second daughter, Lotta, arrived in 1847.

John Crabtree craved adventure, not hard work. When gold was discovered in California, reports about the *forty-niners* who struck it rich fired John's imagination. He sold his bookstore and, without his family, headed for California. In 1852, John wrote his family to join him in San Francisco. Mary Ann was no longer naive about John's ability to support them, but she determined to get to San Francisco as soon as possible. Travel to California in 1852 was a choice between a five-month journey by wagon train, a three-month sail around Cape Horn, or a combination sail and trek that

Lotta Crabtree

would carry them through the jungles of Panama. Each route was perilous. Shortest was the Panama route, and that is the one Mary Ann elected to take. Among their shipmates were men who were heading to the goldfields and women who were joining husbands. Not all the travelers were coming to San Francisco to mine the ore. Some—prostitutes, gamblers and con artists—were going to dig the gold out of the miners.

In her quest for reasonable and safe lodgings in San Francisco, Mary Ann settled in a boardinghouse for actors. In their company, she realized the possibility of earning money through Lotta. Mary Ann enrolled her daughter in dancing school just as her husband reentered the picture with plans to run a boardinghouse in a mining camp called Grass Valley in the foothills of the Sierra Nevadas. It was spring 1853, and Grass Valley was a society in transition. Its 3,500 residents ranged from churchgoers to gunmen. Minstrel troupes, stock companies, one-man shows and variety entertainers tried to find favor as they toured mining camps like Rabbit Creek.

The most famous and admired fairy star of the day was Sue Ann Robinson. When Miss Robinson arrived in Rabbit Creek, she and her promoter-father discovered that a local theatre owner had advertised Lotta Crabtree as her rival. Lotta played in the theatre while Sue Ann held forth at a saloon directly across the street. Lotta was the hometown favorite. She danced a jig for her mostly Irish audience and followed that with a series of sentimental ballads. Mary Ann, who carefully picked up all the coins and gold pieces tossed onstage, left a note for her once-again errant husband and went on the road with Lotta and Matt Taylor, the theatre owner.

To the child, strapped to the back of a mule for safety, the tour was a romantic adventure that Lotta recalled later in life. The adults who accompanied Lotta must have been far less sanguine as they wound along precarious mountain trails to rough settlements and camps called muslin towns. The saloons, schoolhouses, and dry-goods or grocery stores that, off hours, served as performance spaces were often tents. Canvas walls and roof were stretched above a dirt floor. A gunshot fired in one establishment could tear through several others before coming to a stop in something solid. The performers sang, danced and clowned upon a few rough planks placed on sawhorses as a stage, and blankets were rigged as a curtains. The audiences were miners, eager to throw coins and nuggets if they were entertained and just as eager to chase out of town those who displeased them.

The Crabtrees spent three years in the camps. When they returned to San Francisco, they found it had grown rapidly and wildly. Lola Montez, an old friend from Grass Valley, back from her Australian tour, was there to greet them. So, too, were more sophisticated audiences; people were turning out for Edwin Booth in Shakespeare, Beethoven violin concerts (unfortunately backed by a ragtag orchestra recruited from dance halls, bars, brothels, amusement parks and variety theatres), and increasingly clever entertainments of the variety stage.

After more tours of camps, Mary Ann engaged a professional agent in 1862 who arranged a full season of performances in San Francisco theatres. Lotta played in variety and began performing in one-act comedies and dramas, often in trouser roles. To be regarded as a serious actor by San Franciscans of that era, however, one had to demonstrate protean abilities and play many roles in the same play. This Lotta did in a farce, *Object of Interest,* and five of her nine roles were male.

Mary Ann sheltered Lotta from the social life of her fellow performers yet allowed the little girl to work melodeons alongside comics, jugglers, acrobats and corked-up minstrels, not all of whom performed material suitable for the discriminating family audience. The most flirtatious Lotta got was with a song like "The Captain and His Whiskers Gave a Sly Wink to Me."

Lotta had red hair and eyes that seemed black. According to newspaper notices of the day, she exuded a sense of fun and displayed more energy and dancing ability than her peers. Lotta's act was a little bit of a lot of things: playing banjo, dancing Irish jigs, Scottish flings, sailor hornpipes, polkas and shuffles, singing simple sentimental ballads or cute, seriocomic songs, and playing end man in a minstrel number.

Sixteen-year-old Lotta Crabtree had become the toast of the town by 1864, the year Mary Ann decided it was time to conquer New York City while Lotta was at the peak of her San Francisco popularity. New York proved too difficult to crack, so Lotta took part in an extravaganza, *The Seven Sisters,* which opened in Chicago. She portrayed a variety of roles, danced, sang and clowned. With a Chicago hit to her credit, Lotta got into a New York repertory company. By 1865, Lotta was touring on her own, acting with local stock companies from Albany to St. Louis. She played the lead in her repertoire of 11 plays, including *Fanchon* and *Po-Co-Han-Tas.*

In Boston, she played the Howard Athenaeum. In a total of 19 performances, Lotta performed in 13 different plays, taking on as many as six different roles in the same play (with the resident stock company in support)! Her repertoire ranged from Dion Boucicault's *Irish Assurance* and *Yankee Modesty* to *Uncle Tom's Cabin* (played straight). In most of her plays, there were opportunities for Lotta to dance and sing.

Three years after her failure to find favor in Manhattan, Lotta braved New York again, this time with a new agent. Mary Ann put up the money for six weeks at Wallack's Theatre for Lotta to play several shows in repertory. Mary Ann and Lotta were guaranteed half the gross. Lotta's competition was formidable. *The Black Crook,* which featured the novelty of Rubenesque ladies in tights, was stirring the wrath of the clergy. The clergy, railing from their pulpits, ensured the show's success. Lotta countered with a bit of sensation in one of her own shows. She said "Damn it!" onstage. She was a smash in New York and, thereafter, everywhere else she performed.

The pattern was set, and successes accumulated. Whether Lotta was playing in *Little Nell,* Cigarette in *Firefly* (an adaptation of *Under Two Flags*), *Uncle Tom's Cabin, The Ticket of Leave Man, Little Detective, Musette, La Cigale, Heartsease* or *Faint Heart,* the latter of which Lotta acted in for 30 years, the charm of her performances was not in the faithful portrayal of her character but in the naturalness of her acting style and the skills she learned as a variety artist: the dancing, the banjo playing, the sprightly comedy. Songs were named after her. Her public appearances found her mobbed by fans. She packed theatres that sat 3,000 to 4,000 customers.

In 1869, Lotta returned to San Francisco by way of the new transcontinental rail. The journey took ten days. Welcomed in high style, Lotta was booked at the new California Theatre. When Lotta left after six sold-out weeks, she was swamped with stacks of love letters, a pair of golden eagles and a diamond-studded tiara. Mary Ann stood between Lotta and any suitors, however.

Lotta was still in her early 20s when she found her second career as a humanitarian and philanthropist. Often playing urchins herself (she was a shade under five feet tall), she found a soft spot for the real-life versions, and they loved her in return. She built the fountain in San Francisco that provided water to humans, horses and dogs; she visited inmates in jail. The Crabtree fortune grew as Lotta earned fabulous sums and Mary Ann bought theatres, real estate and stocks. There was whispered speculation about Lotta's virginity and occasional rumors of secret marriages.

Lotta and Mary Ann occasionally toured Europe for pleasure, as well as an occasional play date, and Lotta spent the time studying music and languages. Some critics felt that she was losing the common touch, but she remained an audience favorite with the boys in the balcony as well as the swells in the dress circle. In 1879, Lotta began an extended round of farewell tours. When Lotta chose to retire in 1891, she was only 43, but Mary Ann was in her 60s, and the rigors of the road were a trial. Lotta attempted a comeback two years later but severely injured her back in a fall and left the stage for good. At age 45 she was the richest actor in America.

Lotta went into near seclusion when her mother, Mary Ann, died in 1905. Her father, long peripheral, had retired to England, where he died. Lotta studied painting and traveled a great deal over the years until a growing weariness sapped her energy. Fortunately, she had learned to manage her investments. It was said that she disliked growing old but that, at 70, she looked barely 40. She was not afraid to shock the conventional: Lotta smoked long, black cigars, and, from the 1890s onward, she had her skirts shortened each year until, by 1900, they were 16 inches above the ground at a time when other women swept the sidewalks with their hems.

With fellow actor Minnie Maddern Fiske, she shared a strong concern for the welfare of animals. Ms. Fiske had saved the egret population by convincing women to shun plumed hats. Lotta was horrified by barbarous experiments on captive animals and left a sizable bequest to antivivisection as well as trusts to provide food, fuel and hospitalization for the poor, help for released convicts, support for indigent actors, aid to young graduates of agricultural colleges, and relief for needy veterans of the First World War.

THE CRACKERJACKS

The Crackerjacks acrobatic and tap ensemble stepped onto the stage under their own banner in 1922. They had begun dancing in an act called Lulu Coates and Her Crackerjacks. Mrs. Coates, the star of the troupe, surrounded herself with young, fast-stepping dancers who developed into a tight ensemble. Archie Ware (born 1892) was the first of several acrobatic dancers hired for the act. Clifford Carter, Harry Irons and Raymond Thomas followed. These four dancers became the nucleus of the Crackerjacks.

This was the third flowering of an act that had begun before 1900 as Coates & Grundy's Watermelon Trust, a quartet composed of two married couples. Mrs. Coates wish to continue her career after the men retired in 1914.

In 1908, Archie Ware joined Maxie McCree, Willie and Dewey Covan as pickaninnies dancing in vaudeville acts. In the 1910s, he traveled to Europe with acts starring Mayme Remington and then Belle Davis. He returned to the USA in 1914, just as the First World War erupted, and it was around this time he joined Mrs. Coates as she organized her new act, Lulu Coates & Her Crackerjacks.

Eight years later, when Lulu Coates decided to retire, she encouraged Archie and the other dancers to go out on their own as The Crackerjacks. Archie served as director of the group as well as one of the dancers. He emphasized acrobatics as much as dancing and marshaled the dancers into a highly novel act that endured, with various personnel changes, until 1952.

According to Marshall Stearns, the act increased in numbers from four to six, and later members were Wilfred Blanks, Dayton Boyce (born 1913), Joe Chism, George "Tosh" Hammid, Walter Humphrey, Lloyd MacDonald and George Staten. Most were experienced acrobats or gymnasts.

Depending upon the booking, the fast-paced act ran from 10 to 15 minutes. It began with a precision ensemble tap number, followed by Bobby Goins' acrobatic and contortion dance with a chair. The third routine was another ensemble act in which the company dressed as old, bearded Civil War veterans who quickly progressed from tottering to tumbling. Another dancer did a specialty turn, and then, for a finale, they reverted to their Old Man (Civil War) number.

Archie and the others felt that they were fortunate to have Morris Greenwald as their manager. He was honest, supportive and worked hard to book them at the best money he could command. Consequently, The Crackerjacks stayed with Greenwald for the entire life of the act. He booked them in top white nightclubs, Chicago and Harlem hot spots, European tours, five years on Loew's time and several Broadway shows, including *Plantation Days* (1925), *Heebie Jeebies* (1927), *Hot Chocolates* (1929), and they were added to the show during the run of Olsen & Johnson's *Hellzapoppin* (1939–42).

RICHIE CRAIG JR.

b: ca. 1903—d: 1 November 1934

Possibly no comedian so highly regarded by his peers has been so thoroughly forgotten as Richie Craig Jr. Milton Berle placed Richie Craig Jr. on his short list of most admired comedians, describing him as "undeservedly forgotten . . . slender and always well-groomed . . . a gentile alien in a Semitic world. . . . [Craig] worked slowly, deliberately, preferring to score big but as if by accident." Berle's analysis differed from Joe Besser's. Joe remembered that his one-time partner, Richie, "slayed audiences with a rapid fire delivery of jokes."

What fellow funnymen agreed upon was that Richie Craig was the equal of better-remembered stand-up comedians and emcees who used sophisticated material: Frank Fay, Jack Benny and Bob Hope. Many felt Bob Hope patterned himself after Craig.

Richie was the son of a burlesque comedian, Richard Craig Sr., who later performed in musical comedy and produced stage shows. Like all talented children of vaudeville and burlesque, Richie Jr. could dance and sing as well as do comedy. His theatrical family did not encourage his stage aspirations, so Richie, age 16 or 17, ran away from boarding school to try his luck in small-time vaudeville. Within a year he was playing the big time, and at 19 he played the Palace. Over the years, his name changed: Richie Craig Jr., Richy Craig Jr. and Ritchy Craig.

Craig, not venturing far or long from New York City, played vaudeville and speakeasies. Gradually, he concentrated upon being a monologist, using his dancing only as a short break in his act. Richie was so light on his feet that he placed a wax 78-rpm phonograph record on the floor, tap danced on it and did not break it. He also worked out of the spotlight, writing special material for other acts and for Broadway revues.

His first role in a Broadway show was in *Dear Sir* (1924), which came and went within a fortnight despite a score by Jerome Kern. Craig had better luck with *The Ramblers* (1926), in which top liners Bobby Clark & Paul McCullough made audiences happy for a full season on Broadway.

In 1928, Richie was working as an emcee at Loew's in Brooklyn when Joe Besser appeared on the bill. The two hit it off with some improvised business; Richie was a fine feed as well as a joke teller. Bookers for Paramount/Public caught Craig's and Besser's act and packaged a unit around them, giving Craig and Besser a year's bookings, most welcomed in the economic downturn.

When Craig returned to Broadway it was in *Hey Nonny Nonny!* (1932), a 38-performance flop for the Shuberts and everyone concerned. According to some records, Richie was in the cast of *Tattle Tales* (1933), but it seems more likely that he merely contributed material to the show's star and producer, Frank Fay. Craig was on the bill the final week, 9 July 1932, that straight vaudeville played the Palace Theatre on Broadway. Thereafter, the Palace offered movies plus a few live acts.

Part of Craig's strategy to remain in Manhattan was working in radio. His last work was on a variety show with singer Aileen Stanley. Doubtless, Richie Craig's early death at age 30, or thereabouts, and the lack of a filmed record of his work have contributed to his gradual slippage out of the pages of vaudeville history.

CREAMER & LAYTON

Henry S. Creamer

b: 21 June 1879, Richmond, VA—
d: 14 October 1930, New York, NY

J. Turner Layton

b: 2 July 1894, Washington, D.C.—
d: 6 February 1978, London, England

A lot of songwriting teams and sketch writers not only wrote material for others to perform but also went into vaudeville with their own acts. Creamer & Layton, much like Noble Sissle & Eubie Blake, wrote many songs and appeared in vaudeville and in revues to sing and play some of their own compositions. Unlike Sissle & Blake, Creamer & Layton were together for only six years, from 1918 to 1924. In that time, they wrote "After You've Gone" (1918) and "Strut Miss Lizzie" (1921), both the title tune and the show, "Childhood Days" (1922), "Liza Jane" (1918) and "Way Down Yonder in New Orleans" (1922).

Creamer was the lyricist. He had various jobs in theatre, including working as an eccentric dancer, before he began writing songs with Tom Lemonier, Lester A. Walton, Will Vodery, Ernest Hogan, S. H. Dudley, Jim Europe and Bert Williams. Most of the shows that Creamer contributed to proved unprofitable.

By 1912, Creamer was a founding member of the Clef Club and the Negro Players Company and had joined the Frogs, a fraternal association of black performers. Much of his performing seems to have been in annual shows produced by several organizations to which he belonged. Creamer, at 36, was 15 years older than Layton when they met in 1916 through Jim Europe and the Clef Club. Layton's father was a music director for Washington, D.C.'s Negro public schools and for his church. Turner had attended college but decided to try his luck as a musician in New York. Because he was a trained pianist and could sight-read music, he was taken on by James Reese Europe for his musical organization that fielded orchestras and dance bands, many for white society events.

Creamer and Layton soon teamed and got a song accepted into a Shubert show, and then Bert Williams agreed to sing a pair of their songs in the *Ziegfeld Follies of 1917.* They created several hits sung and recorded by white vaudeville singers Marion Harris, Billy Murray, Lucille Hegamin, Charlotte Greenwood, Al Jolson and Sophie Tucker. Their first big hit, "After You've Gone," was recorded over the decades by Paul Whiteman, Sophie Tucker, Marion Harris, Louis Armstrong and Benny Goodman.

Creamer mounted their own show, *Strut Miss Lizzie,* but he had insufficient resources to produce it properly, and it debuted in a little theatre in Harlem. He made a costly deal with burlesque impresario Billy Minsky, who took a hefty percentage of the box office to play *Strut Miss Lizzie* in his Houston Street theatre, the Old National Winter Garden. Layton was not part of the production team, but deals to keep the show afloat (it did manage a few weeks at the Times Square Theatre at last) were depriving Layton of royalties and playing loose with his copyrights. The show split the team. Creamer continued to write songs with various partners, but the big Broadway show hit eluded him, and Henry Creamer died in 1930.

Although he continued to write a few songs, Turner Layton was more interested in playing and performing. He found a new partner, the older Clarence "Tandy" Johnstone, in 1922. They played at society gatherings and in vaudeville. In 1924, Layton & Johnstone went to Europe for successful flings in Parisian revue and London variety. They wowed the English and became fixtures in British variety, radio and cabaret.

In 1935, Johnstone became involved in a marital scandal. The Layton & Johnstone act dissolved, Johnstone fled to the USA and Layton remained a solo performer for two decades. He retired as a pub owner.

CRESCENT TIME

As small time as small time could get, Crescent time involved a few theatres clustered around New York City's outskirts. Performers new to vaudeville could expect to play *toilets* like these, but if a seasoned vaudevillian could get work only in a Crescent-booked theatre, it was time to quit.

CRESSY & DAYNE

Will Cressy

b: (William M. Cressy) 20 October 1863, Bradford, NH—d: 7 May 1930, St. Petersburg, FL

Blanche Dayne

b: 25 December ca. 1871, Troy, NY—d: 27 June 1944, Hackensack, NJ

A farm boy from New Hampshire, Will Cressy took the rube character and made it his trademark for decades in variety and vaudeville. In his late teens, he left the family farm and tried his hand as a carpenter, machinist, marine engineer, watchmaker, traveling salesman and hotel clerk before deciding that the actor's life was for him.

In 1899, Will made his professional debut in Norwalk, Connecticut, as the junior member of Frost & Fanshawe, a "ten-twent-thirt" traveling show. He moved on to other companies and joined Denham Thompson's outfit that was touring with his Broadway success *The Old Homestead.* It was the signal event in Cressy's young life. Will was greatly influenced in style by Denham Thompson, also from New Hampshire, whose specialty was playing true-to-life portrayals of the New England farmer. The company's leading lady was Blanche Dayne, whom Will courted and married on 19 January 1890.

Blanche began as a child performer, singing with Emma Abbott and then playing the inevitable child roles of Topsy or Little Eva in some of the ubiquitous Tom shows. By the age of 16, she was the ingenue and leading female player with Frost & Fanshawe. For six years, she played in *The Old Homestead.* It was this show (and as likely, Miss Dayne) that convinced Will that acting should be his life's work. He joined the company and worked up to a lead.

Cressy & Dayne became a popular sketch-comedy act from the early 1890s and lasted into the early 1920s. They played the Palace during its first year of operation, 1913. Will wrote at least one new sketch every season, so he and Blanche always had fresh material for each annual tour of vaudeville. Managers and audiences knew that if Cressy & Dayne were in town, they would have a new act.

Will's sketches were both humorous and sentimental, and Will took the role of a rube, usually an elderly one. It was not a caricature. Instead it was an affectionate and admiring portrait based on men around whom he had grown up. Blanche Dayne played straight in the act. In one, as reported by Douglas Gilbert, the scene was a rural crossroads grocery store. The old proprietor, played by Will, got a letter explaining that an old friend had died, and his baby girl was on her way to him for his care and protection. The old proprietor consults a book in his stock called *Advice to Mothers,* and this gives Will a number of comic lines to mutter.

His research is interrupted by the arrival of the baby girl, who is, unexpectedly, a grown young woman played by Dayne. The crib he has prepared is out of the question.

> "I don't know where I can put you to sleep, unless you don't mind bunkin' in with the station agent."
>
> "Sir, I am a lady!"
>
> "So is the station agent."

His sketches were much admired in the business because they combined rib ticklers with tugs at the heartstrings. Other vaudeville actors kept Will profitably busy writing sketches for them. He became one of the most prolific and successful sketch writers in vaudeville. According to Will's own reckoning, he wrote his first 100 sketches by the year 1907. Among the better known in their days were "Grasping an Opportunity," "The Key of C," "Bill Biffin's Baby," "The New Depot," "Town Hall" and "The Wyoming Whoop."

Cressy & Dayne were vaudeville through and through. Unlike other acts, they seldom attempted to work in musical comedy or revue. The short 15- to 20-minute sketch suited their talents as actors and Will's as an economical playwright.

One Broadway experience may have decided it for them. Will cowrote (with James Clarence Harvey) and costarred with Blanche Dayne in *The Village Lawyer* (1908), a full-length drama with a substantial cast that was produced by the Shuberts. It closed after 17 performances. In the 1910s, they ventured briefly into films. In 1915, Will wrote and he and Blanche acted in the two-reel *Fifty Dollars a Kiss,* and, in 1919, Will wrote the scenario for another silent film, *Stateroom Secrets.*

When the Vaudeville Comedy Club was formed in 1906, Will Cressy was elected president. It began as a social affair but soon branched into benevolent work and the support of actors' rights. As the club expanded, it lost focus and closed shop in 1914.

When the USA entered the First World War, there was no United Service Organizations in place to entertain the troops. The YMCA first assumed the responsibility, and a number of vaudevillians rallied to the call to put on shows for the doughboys. Will Cressy was among those who put their careers on hold and went overseas to perform.

Cressy always kept his ties to his home town of Bradford in the Lake Sunapee region of New Hampshire. He had retained an interest, along with his brothers, in the operation of the family farm and its hay and grain business and maintained a home in Concord, New Hampshire.

During the summer season, when Will and Blanche laid off from vaudeville, they repaired to their cottage on Cressy Island in Blaisdell Lake. In addition to visiting the farm and lending a hand, Will could be found cruising the lake in his boat.

Cressy's and Dayne's careers wound down, as did vaudeville. They spent summers in New Hampshire and winters in Florida, where Will died in 1930. Ms. Dayne survived her husband by 14 years and was 72 when she died in New Jersey.

CROONER

A late development in vaudeville, crooners were men, who specialized in romantic ballads and delivered them in a more intimate fashion than minstrels or song-and-dance men. Examples include Benny Fields and Bing Crosby. Often they sang with large dance and swing bands.

BING CROSBY

b: (Harry Lillis Crosby) 3 May 1903, Tacoma, WA—d: 14 October 1977, Madrid, Spain

That Bing Crosby is regarded as an American superstar stems not so much from any single talent or style he showed as from uniting into a single entertainer so many superior talents and presenting them in an original style. He was almost unique among romantic male singers, except for Frank Sinatra, in that Bing was liked equally by men and women. Men liked to think that Bing was their stand-in as a regular guy who paired a self-deprecating sense of humor with confidence. Women liked him for the same reasons. His nicknames included Der Bingle and the Groaner.

He was not the first crooner; Benny Fields and Rudy Vallee are among those who vie for that claim. Indeed, although Crosby was often called a crooner, he truly was not, at least not until after the mid-1930s, when he simplified his singing style. The crooning style was minimalist; the accusation being it was a mumbling, humming sort of sound rather than real—as in full-out—singing. In his early recordings and movies, Crosby displayed an ornamented singing style, more in the tradition of Al Jolson and Harry Richman. Later, he simplified his style, and that extended his vogue.

Crosby's relaxed manner of playing roles recalled Gerald DuMaurier and the naturalistic English actors, like George Arliss, who followed. The early male actors in American talking pictures gave high-energy, edgy performances of Americans like John Barrymore, Richard Bennett, Edward G. Robinson, James Cagney and Lee Tracy. By the time Crosby took on dramatic roles, he shared the understated style of contemporaries Spencer Tracy, Robert Montgomery, William Holden and Robert Ryan.

Bing Crosby

As a comedian, Bing had a breezy style of comic patter that was reminiscent of Frank Tinney and Frank Fay, who turned their audiences into a gathering of intimates. Like any good vaudevillian, Bing could hoof his way through a dance routine. He knew better than to try to dazzle. He had fun hoofing and his audience had fun watching him, and when the snappy patter and song and dance were done, his audience felt they had shared a good-natured evening with an amiable and widely talented host who was not the least taken with himself. If there was anything jumped up about Bing Crosby, it was never apparent to his fans.

Unlike the balladeers who sang of the old country or told jokes about Angus, Pat, Abe, Gus or Rufus, there was no racial or immigrant quality about Crosby. His style and talents, save for the occasional Irish ballad, were emblematic of the new American who had no ties to the old world or any class system of society. Bing—even his name was as American as the comic strip character for which Bing was nicknamed—was the guy next door, the good buddy, an amusing date, a companionable husband, a sensible father and a model American: modest, down to earth, capable.

He grew up in Tacoma, a city on Puget Sound, and went to Gonzaga College, in Spokane, at the opposite end of Washington State, where it nudges Idaho. His intent was to study law. He fell into music and bought a set of drums. As a singer and drummer, Bing was good enough by local standards to try to earn a few bucks playing with a local band, the Musicaladeers, managed by Al Rinker, brother of singer Mildred Bailey (1907–51). Actually, he was better than he thought, and he and the band made enough money that Bing decided to make show business, not law, his career. The Musicaladeers did not last beyond a single school year and summer. Most of the others in the band were high school seniors headed for college. For them, playing in the band had been a lucrative lark. Al Rinker, however, shared Bing's dream.

Rinker's sister, Mildred Bailey, had already left "nowheresville," her term for any city or town that did not jump with music and musicians, and had moved to Los Angeles with her second husband, a bootlegger. In October 1925, Al and Bing left Spokane to join Mildred in Los Angeles, and she put them up at her house. Al and Bing put together a snappy double singing act; there were a lot of them in vaudeville at the time, most notably Van & Schenck. It was the era of pic-vaude combinations and stage shows preceding major motion pictures in presentation houses. Paul Whiteman, then the leader of the most popular pop music orchestra, caught Bing and Al's act on the bill at the Metropolitan Theatre in Los Angeles, and he hired them for his stage act.

Once the boys had completed their bookings, they joined the Whiteman outfit in Chicago for an engagement at the Tivoli Theatre. Rinker and Crosby were not the success hoped for, and Whiteman let them go after the orchestra's booking at the Paramount Theatre. The problem was that Al and Bing were used to performing in vaudeville houses, not the much larger ballrooms and presentation houses that Paul Whiteman and His Orchestra played. Amplification was not available, and Bing and Al could not be heard at the back of the house. One of Whiteman's sidemen, Matty Malneck, suggested that Harry Barris join them. Barris had written a novelty jump tune, "Mississippi Mud," and the three boys worked out a crowd-pleasing arrangement. They were hired back by Whiteman, and he billed them as the Rhythm Boys.

Crosby was a hell-raiser in those days. He drank a lot and was even arrested once or twice for driving under the influence. This did not sit well with Paul Whiteman, who managed his orchestra like a well-run business. The Rhythm Boys left Whiteman in 1930 for Gus Arnheim's band in 1931. Arnheim broadcast on radio direct from his bandstand in the Cocoanut Grove in Los Angeles' Ambassador Hotel. Once again, Barris came through with a good song. By this time, Crosby was singing lead in the trio, and he won his first hit with Barris' "I Surrender, Dear." Crosby began concentrating on his solo career, and he left Arnheim to make short films for Mack Sennett, who was impressed with Bing's natural manner. The Rhythm Boys were no more. In addition to movies, Bing sang on radio and made recordings.

Bing made 21 gold records for the Decca label, including "White Christmas," "Silent Night," "Pistol Packin' Mama" and "Jingle Bells" (both with the Andrews Sisters), "Swinging on a Star," "Too-Ra-Loo-Ra-Loo-Ral" and "Don't Fence Me In" (with the Andrews Sisters).

He was responsible for making a lot of other songs into hits: "Just One More Chance" (1931), "Please" (1932), "Brother Can You Spare A Dime" and "You're Getting to Be a Habit with Me" (both 1933), "It's Easy to Remember (and So Hard to Forget)" and "Red Sails in the Sunset" (both 1935), "Pennies from Heaven" (1936), "Sweet Leilani" and "Too Marvelous for Words" (both in 1937), "Alexander's Ragtime Band" (1938) with Connie Boswell, "You Must Have Been a Beautiful Baby" (1938), "Moonlight Becomes You" (1943), "I'll Be Seeing You" (1944) with the Andrews Sisters, "Far Away Places" (1948), "Now Is the Hour" (1949) and "Play a Simple Melody" (1950). Every one reached the top position on the charts except the last, which only climbed to number two. Bing Crosby scored the most number-one hits ever: 38, compared with 24 by the Beatles and 18 by Elvis Presley.

His popularity in the movies and on records ensured that he would be the top-ranked singer in the history of network radio. Between 1931 and 1958, Bing was on radio with his own show every single season. The longest-running of Bing's radio shows was *The Kraft Music Hall* (1935–46) on NBC.

Crosby's movie career has faded with time. Video recordings of movies made by Bing's contemporaries John Wayne, Cary Grant, Bob Hope, Abbott & Costello, Katherine Hepburn, Humphrey Bogart, James Cagney, Judy Garland and Fred Astaire continue to be sold decades after their deaths, and cable television channels regularly schedule their films. With the exception of the "Road" pictures Bing made with Bob Hope and Dorothy Lamour, there is less call for Crosby films on tape and DVD than expected, given that for 20 years (1934–54) Bing Crosby ranked among the top-ten box-office draws 15 times!

Crosby's first films were six Mack Sennett sound two-reelers made in 1931 and 1932. The following year, he went to Paramount and made two more shorts. The difference was that Paramount was the biggest studio in Hollywood and able to make Crosby a star; Sennett's was a small operation, a ghost of his former Keystone studio, and without the promise.

The comedy training, however, made him a natural for musical-comedy films. His 17 starring features for Paramount between 1932 and 1940 teamed him with various comedians like Burns & Allen, Jack Oakie, Ned Sparks, Leon Errol, Roland Young, Mary Boland, W. C. Fields, Beatrice Lillie, Martha Raye, Bob Burns and Joan Blondell. Moviegoers paid to see Crosby, but the quantity of songs (usually four but as many as eight per 70-minute feature) clogged the plot, and the comedians were not always well served. Still, with few exceptions, Bing's 1930s Paramount films were lighthearted and pleasant.

In 1940, Paramount teamed Bob Hope and Dorothy Lamour with Bing. The black-and-white *Road to Singapore* was a bigger hit than expected, and it led to five very profitable sequels that took the trio to Zanzibar, Morocco, Utopia, Rio and Bali between 1941 and 1953. The screen relationship between Bing and Bob was not unlike that of Bud Abbott's and Lou Costello's. Bud and Bing always took advantage of Lou and Bob, but Bing also got the girl; Bud got Lou. A seventh Road picture sent Bing and Bob, both then about 60, to Hong Kong in 1962, but the moment had passed. Crosby also teamed with Fred Astaire for *Holiday Inn* (1942).

Crosby played a priest in two sentimental favorites directed by the great Leo McCarey, *Going My Way* with Barry Fitzgerald (1944), for which Bing won the Academy Award as best actor, and *The Bells of St. Mary's*

(1945) with Ingrid Bergman. Crosby's last important films were *White Christmas* (1954) with Danny Kaye, Vera-Ellen and Rosemary Clooney, *The Country Girl* (1954) with Grace Kelly and William Holden, and *High Society* (1956) with Kelly, Frank Sinatra, Louis Armstrong and Celeste Holm.

Crosby proved to be a power behind the scenes. It was he who financed the development of magnetic audiotape and visual-recording tape that revolutionized the recording industry and television. Performances could be made piecemeal and spliced together. This leveled the playing field between inexperienced performers and actors and experienced pros who could perform whole scenes and songs in one take.

Although he occasionally worked in television up to the year of his death hosting Christmas specials and other variety shows, he lost some of his insouciance and warmth as he aged. His singing voice was in prime condition during the 1930s and 1940s, but he let it rust a bit in the 1950s and 1960s. He worked to bring it back, but, although it was a fine singing voice for a man in his 60s and early 70s, it was lower and lacked the suppleness and rich tonality of his golden years.

Crosby had interests other than show business. He made money with the Minute Maid Orange Juice company and lost money on his racehorses. Golf was a favorite pastime, partly because he could keep a hat on and not wear the hated toupee he donned for movies, television and concerts. He and some friends were headed for the 19th hole on a golf course in Madrid, Spain, when he suffered a massive heart attack and died.

Much has been written about Crosby the person. Older brother Everett was his manager for part of his career. Younger brother Bob was a singer and bandleader. Married twice, Bing had four sons with Dixie Lee and two sons and a daughter with Kathryn Grant. He was faulted for being emotionally remote and too strict with his children. Three of his sons with Dixie had emotional and mental problems. Some performers found him cold and unresponsive. Others, like Peggy Lee and Rosemary Clooney, thought the world of Bing. He was a private person who kept his good works to himself. He was ready when needed by folks who amused him, like Joe Frisco, or whom he considered old friends, like Mildred Bailey. If and when things got tough for him, he kept that to himself.

CROSSOVER

A device often used in vaudeville and burlesque comedy acts: two comedians or a straight man and a comedian, who entered the stage from opposite wings and greeted, ignored or confronted each other. If they entered together from the same side, they obviously knew each other and that limited possibilities. When they entered from opposite sides of the stage, they might or might not know each other, be friends or enemies, or a con man meeting his mark.

In burlesque, this often led to a series of gags. The straight man entered unencumbered, but the comedian brought props with each successive entrance.

> [Straightman enters stage right and begins to address the audience when comedian enters from other side, carrying a suitcase.]
>
> **Straight man:** "Where are you going?"
>
> **Comedian:** "I'm taking my case to court."
>
> [Comedian exits stage right and straightman resumes his talk to the audience. In a few second he is distracted by the comedian re-entering the stage, this time carrying a stepladder as well as his suitcase.]
>
> **Straight man:** "What now?"
>
> **Comedian:** "I'm taking my case to a higher court!"

CRUMIT & SANDERSON

Frank Crumit

b: 18 May 1888, Jackson, OH—
d: 7 September 1943, New York, NY

Julia Sanderson

b: (Julia Sackett) 20 August 1884 or 1887, Springfield, MA—d: 27 January 1975, Springfield, MA

The daughter of a popular actor of the time, Albert Sackett, Julia entered the family trade in Philadelphia as a junior member of the Forepaugh stock company, in which her father was a principal actor. She remained with the company for five years, balancing rehearsals and performances with school studies. Summers were spent mostly in Springfield, Massachusetts.

As she matured from a child actor into ingenue roles, she developed a rich singing voice, so she switched from drama to musical comedy and vaudeville. In 1904, she was understudy to lead Paula Edwardes and danced in the chorus of *Winsome Winnie*. During the run, when Ms. Lawrence became indisposed, Julia stepped into the female lead. As a result, De Wolf Hopper engaged Julia Sanderson, as she was known professionally, to be a principal in the musical *Wang* (1905). In 1907, she married a famous jockey, James Todhunter Sloan, familiarly called Tod.

During the years from 1904 through 1921, Sanderson performed in 17 musical comedies, averaging one per year. Between the runs of her various musicals, the pretty, dark-haired, fair-skinned Sanderson played vaudeville in and around New York City with a song-and-dance act.

By 1915, she was under Charles Frohman's management and played opposite luminaries like Joseph Cawthorn. She had divorced Tod Sloane, and, in 1916, she married Lt. Bradford Barnette, a marriage that also ended in divorce. Among her many hits for Frohman were *The Girl from Utah* (1914), *Rambler Rose* (1917) and *The Canary* (1918). In 1921, she appeared in *Tangerine* opposite Frank Crumit, who wrote the words and music for "Sweet Lady," one of her numbers in the show.

There were no actors in Frank Crumit's family. His father was a banker who ensured that his son was well educated. Frank attended Culver Military Academy and graduated from Ohio University with a degree in engineering. By the age of 25, however, Frank had decided that his future was in show business. Untrained but confident and relaxed, Crumit won himself small-time vaudeville bookings as a song-and-patter man. He formed a larger act with Paul Beise. It seems to have been a flash act, in which Frank and Paul were the primary performers.

In 1919, Frank began making sound recordings for Columbia Records but soon switched to Victor. Much like his vaudeville material, the songs were humorous, and Frank's delivery was droll. As early as 1920, two Crumit records, "Abdul Abul Bul Amir," a novelty, and "Frankie and Johnny," sold 2 million copies each. To Victor's and his own delight, Crumit delivered hit upon hit record.

Crumit continued to play vaudeville. His vaudeville appearances promoted his recordings, and the more records he sold, the bigger draw he became in vaudeville. Frank was a relaxed personality onstage. He strolled out and told the pit musicians they could join the card games backstage while he was on. Accompanying himself on the ukulele, Frank sang humorous songs and chatted with the audience.

In musical comedy and revue he shared billing with Bert Savoy & Jay Brennan in the *Greenwich Village Follies* (1920), and he was part of the big-star line-up of Sam Bernard, Helen Broderick, William Collier, Hazel Dawn, Ray Dooley, Van & Schenck and the Tiller Girls in the *Nifties of 1923.*

More important to his future, personally and professionally, was joining the cast of *Tangerine* (1921), which played ten months at the Casino. In the cast were Julia Sanderson and Joseph Cawthorn. Although they became romantically involved, Frank and Julia did not marry for several years.

Both played in various stage shows apart from each other until 1928, when Julia and Frank were engaged for the 1928 revival of George and Ira Gershwin's *Oh, Kay!* They filled the lead roles originated two years earlier by Gertrude Lawrence and Oscar Shaw. The original 1926 production ran eight months; the 1928 revival with Sanderson and Crumit lasted two weeks. They went back to vaudeville for several seasons, where they were known as a class act, never vulgar, always smoothly professional, and had a great rapport with their audiences. During 1932, they were well up on the bill at the Palace as they had been in previous years, only this time it was the Palace's last season of two-a-day shows.

Radio was on their horizon. After years of touring in vaudeville and musical comedy, network radio allowed them to live in one place and reach many parts of the USA. Julia had a lovely singing voice and was the bigger stage star, but Frank had sold a lot of records and was as big as Julia in vaudeville. Their first joint performances on radio were singing spots on local stations in New York City.

In 1929, Frank Crumit and Julia Sanderson launched their own Tuesday-night show, *Blackstone Plantation,* on CBS. Their show moved to NBC, where it stayed until 1933. The two stars sang and exchanged banter. Music and gab with guests in their breezy and humorous style characterized their programs. Crumit had written many songs and collected thousands. Since 1917, when he began making sound records, he had recorded various old-time songs and folk tunes. Radio allowed him to further his study of popular music dating back a century and more and present the songs to his on-air audiences. In a sense, his work paralleled the research of Alan Lomax and other musicologists who sought to preserve American folk music.

Frank and Julia went back to CBS in 1933 for a late Sunday-afternoon show for Bond Bread. This, too, lasted three years. In 1938, they joined an NBC quiz show, *The Battle of the Sexes,* and in 1942 they hosted their own, *The Crumit and Anderson Quiz.* They had just begun their daytime *Singing Sweethearts* show for CBS when, in January 1943, Frank dropped dead due to a massive heart attack. Julia took on a ladies' program, *Let's Be Charming,* later that year but soon retired to their home in Longmeadow, Massachusetts, where she lived for more than 30 years. She died at 87. There had been no children to survive her.

CUES

A cue is a signal to others when the next response, action, sound or music should begin. It may be a written notation, a spoken word, or simply a gesture or movement.

Among performers, a cue is an agreed-upon sign or phrase by which one performer alerts another to make their reply or take a specific action. For actors, cues are usually designated in their scripts or added by a director.

Cues from performers to musicians take the form of notations in the musical charts, or *sides,* to signal the pit bandleader and musicians when to come in with music or a sound effect. The music may be the introduction to the next song, a signal to vamp or play stop-time, or just a note to punctuate a joke (a wah-wah sound from the trombonist or a rim shot from the drummer).

Cues were also specified to the electrician to indicate where certain light changes should occur (spotlight, blackout or dimming) and to the backstage crew to let them know when a curtain should close or open.

Cycle acts

CURTAIN

The term usually refers to the front curtain or to the various tabs that, when closed, block off sections of the stage, from one wing to the other. The front tabs or dress curtain remained closed until the bill began and closed again after the show. Usually a deep color (often red) in a plush fabric, the front tabs parted in the middle and were sometimes drawn into the wings. More often the front tabs or dress curtains were flown up and down; if a stage was set with lightweight props and the curtains or travelers were drawn aside, they created a draft that blew papers and other items off their places in the set (*See "Front Traveler or House Curtain" and "Tabs"*).

In the earliest days of variety and vaudeville, the curtains were rolled up and down by hand. Later, counterweights were used to help lower and raise the drops.

CURTAIN CALL

After the curtain closed at the end of an act or the show, a satisfied audience then applauded and summoned, or called, the actors or performers back onstage to accept and acknowledge the applause.

See Taking a Call

Jimmy Valdare & Duffy

CYCLISTS

As there was insufficient space on vaudeville stages for an exhibition of speed, most cycling acts concentrated on comedy and tricks. Cycles of all types were used: tricycles, bicycles, unicycles, large-wheeled cycles, small-wheeled cycles and cycles that fell apart.

The cycling act might feature a solo performer or one with an assistant (often a spouse) who simply brought on and took off the various cycles, or there might be several persons in the act, sometimes adding balancing feats to the trick cycling, as when troupes formed human pyramids perched atop a single cycle.

Clown cyclist

CYCLORAMA

Related to the sky cloth, the cyclorama was curved forward at either end and gave an illusion of great depth when properly lit. Cycloramas tended to be larger than the standard drop and fixed in place against the rear stage wall instead of being dropped in and out of the stage scene.

See Sky Cloth

D

PETER F. DAILEY

b: 1868, New York, NY—d: 1908, New York, NY

For Peter F. Dailey, the rotund yet nimble singing comic, life was a party. Show business suited him because he could sleep most of the day—except when he had rehearsals—then perform for a couple of hours onstage before engaging in the evening frivolities that brought him through the night and into the morning. Performing was not a chore because Dailey kept it fresh with ad-libs and impromptu business. Immediately after his performance, he uncorked a bottle of champagne, opened a quart of whiskey and proceeded to empty both bottles, using the champagne as a chaser. He then set out on his nightly rounds, apparently still sober!

Peter married and, surprisingly, remained so. When his wife complained that she saw little of him, he invited her to keep him company on his nightly rounds. After three nights, she gave in and, legend has it, never complained again about seeing so little of him. When he did go to bed, he left orders not to be disturbed, and his wife stood guard until the appointed hour, even if some harried emissary from a theatre wanted him at the rehearsals for which Dailey was always late and reluctant.

Pete Dailey was an unpretentious and gregarious soul who loved good stories and good liquor; perhaps he inherited much of his personality from his father, an auctioneer and politician. Dailey debuted as a child dancer at the Globe Museum in 1876 and followed that with a short fling in the circus. He found more congenial success as a member of the American Four, an act popular in vaudeville for a number of seasons. Dailey first met Weber & Fields when they joined a summer troupe featuring the American Four.

By 1884, Peter F. Dailey could be enjoyed in Boston at the Howard Athenaeum, where he remained for three years. Returning to Broadway in 1891, he was a featured player in *A Straight Tip,* and critics claimed Dailey stole the show from its star, John T. Powers. So pleased with his performance was the play's author, J. J. McNally, that McNally wrote several starring vehicles for Pete: *A Mad Bargain* (1893), *A Country Sport* (1893), which costarred Dailey with May Irwin, *The Night Clerk* (1895) and *A Good Thing* (1896).

When Weber and Fields engaged Dailey for their second season in 1897, Pete joined a cast that included Sam Bernard, John T. Kelly and Bessie Clayton. Pete stayed for a third and fourth season. Despite weighing 250 pounds, Pete was an acrobatic dancer as well as a singer and quick-witted farceur. He was also an incorrigible ad-libber and practical joker.

In 1903, during the next-to-last Weberfields season, Pete played in *The Stickiness of Gelatine* (1903), a spoof of Clyde Fitch's *The Stubbornness of Geraldine,* which took place onboard a yacht. Pete Dailey and William Collier had an amusing scene on the deck. While leaning on the railing and supposedly staring at the sea, they faced the audience, and each night they ad-libbed comments about the musicians in the orchestra and members of the audience. The scene was supposed to end when Charles Bigelow ran onstage to yell that his wife had fallen overboard. Then Willie and Pete rushed offstage with Bigelow.

One night when Bigelow rushed onstage, however, Pete and Willie decided to ignore him. When Bigelow

Peter F. Dailey

yelled, they continued chatting amiably. Bigelow was confounded; he yelled at them that his wife was drowning. He yelled some more. Still, Pete and Willie adlibbed to each other. In desperation, Bigelow begged, "Oh, for the love of Lee Shubert, come and help a feller, will you?!" At this point, Pete and Willie turned and sauntered off deck toward the wings, arm in arm. Collier paused and told Dailey he thought he had heard someone yelling "help." Dailey and Collier shrugged and exited. Bigelow was left standing onstage. For a minute he did not move. Then he hollered after them, "Well, say, you know, I don't give a damn either," and stamped offstage. It was probably the only time anyone got a bigger laugh than Pete Dailey and at his expense.

Dailey evened the score. A short while later, the entire Weberfields cast was directed, immediately after the show, to attend a midnight Park Avenue function hosted by some backers. Charles, who was always a bit late, found the others had gone but left a note instructing him that everyone was to black up before arriving, as they were to present a minstrel interlude. Dailey smeared some black greasepaint around the sink and on towels in the dressing room.

Bigelow quickly blacked up, grabbed a cab and arrived at the Fifth Avenue address after everyone else—the Weberfields contingent and the society guests—had arrived. No entertainment had been expected. Instead, Pete and the rest of the cast were impeccably attired in their formal bibs and tuckers and seated at the huge formal dining table when Bigelow rushed in.

When, in 1900, Dailey temporarily left Weberfields for a musical comedy, *Hodge, Podge, and Co.,* it took a superlative and versatile talent to replace him: De Wolfe Hopper. Pete Dailey joined his fellow Weberfields trouper Fay Templeton in a pair of vaudeville revues, *A Little Bit of Everything* and *In Newport,* both failures in 1904. Pete recouped with *The Press Agent,* a hit in 1905.

Dailey's association with Weber & Fields had come near the end of his short career. Even after Weber and Fields went their separate ways, he continued his association, first with Lew Fields, performing in his 1906 revue *About Town,* then with Joe Weber in *The Merry Widow Burlesque* in 1908. Pete Dailey died that same year. He was 40 years old.

CASS DALEY

b: (Catherine Dailey) 17 July 1915, Philadelphia, PA—d: 22 March 1975, Los Angeles, CA

Whenever Hollywood producers had a Martha Raye or Joan Davis role to fill but could not afford Davis' or Raye's fees, they turned to either Judy Canova or Cass Daley. Eventually, Judy Canova's price tag rose with the popularity of her radio show, so Cass Daley was regarded as the low-rent, man-chasing soubrette.

Cass Daley was thin as a yard of pump water, and in motion she jutted out at all angles, from her buckteeth to her elbows to her rear end. She developed her familiar characterization in nightclubs and performed it though nine years of vaudeville into radio and motion pictures. In person, she was a quiet, attractive lady. Her comic character was not an extension of her personality but was based on how she felt she had been seen as a child. In the poor, blue-collar neighborhoods she grew up in, Philadelphia and Camden, New Jersey, Cass was teased about her teeth and skinny body.

Despite the taunting, Cass had the gumption to enter amateur-night contests and often won one of the modest prizes the theatre management offered. When she was 14, she dropped out of school to help support the family. Like most of her neighbors, she found work in the local factories, wrapping candy and trimming fabric. The Great Depression was beginning, but it would take a few years before people realized its disastrous dimensions.

Like a lot of kids who were the butt of cruel jokes, Cass developed a sense for comedy. She won acceptance by clowning. One night, at a party, a nightclub owner heard her sing and hired her for double duty as a hatcheck girl and vocalist at the Old Mill in Camden, New Jersey. She was 17 and within a year or two was the family breadwinner.

Cass had a good, strong voice. She sang the songs of the day while strumming a ukulele. It would be a few years before she was willing to offer herself as a clown. One night, she was booked as an intermission act during a dance marathon. Midway during her song, the audience began to laugh. The emcee behind her was shining a light through her dress, revealing Cass' silhouette (Red Skelton is supposed to have been the emcee). It was not Cass' choice to go in for low comedy, but she realized comedy might get her more and better-paying work.

Shortly after this incident, Cass met Frank Kinsella, a would-be agent and part-time salesman. He persuaded her to stress the comedy and to let him manage her career. Comedy was not as natural to Cass Daley as it was to Fanny Brice, Charlotte Greenwood, Martha Raye or Joan Davis. Cass worked out several song numbers that she punctuated with various facial contortions. Those that got laughs were kept in the act. She developed her act in the noisy, boozy milieu of nightclubs. Subtlety was out; blue was in.

Despite economic conditions, Cass and her manager made a decent living in the 1930s. She worked presentation houses and what was left of vaudeville and even made it to Broadway as a replacement for Judy Canova, who had left her featured spot in the *Ziegfeld Follies of 1936*. In 1938, Cass accepted an offer to play British music-halls. She cavorted and mugged, shrieked her songs, throttled the microphone with her hands and rode it like a hobbyhorse, and swung from the velvet curtains. The audiences loved it. All in all, after a decade in vaudeville and clubs, the good times had arrived.

Cass Daley made eight feature films during the 1940s. Her roles in most of them were interchangeable. She belted songs while distending her body, chased men and bared her teeth. It was what the producers and directors wanted. One of her better opportunities came with a double role in Olsen & Johnson's *Crazy House* (1943). Unlike the roles Joan Davis, Judy Canova or Martha Raye played, the Cass Daley roles were not always written to win the affection or the sympathy of audiences. Because Ms. Daley was unable or failed to insist on some humanizing elements in her scripts, she did not develop beyond a frenzied caricature, and audiences did not root for her character. This was fatal for a comedian who aspired to move from stooge parts to star parts.

Daley guested on a number of popular network radio shows. In 1944, she signed on as a featured regular on the *Frank Morgan Show,* which folded in a year. The next year, 1945, she was engaged as a member of the *Fitch Bandwagon,* but a year later the show was retooled as the *Alice Faye–Phil Harris Show,* and Cass was dropped. In 1950, she won her own program, *The Cass Daley Show,* but by that time, television was the place to be.

Cass Daley did not think so. Instead, at the peak of her earning power, she retired to raise her son in Newport Beach. Fifteen or so years later, Cass needed to earn a living and tried to revive her career. Her son was grown, and Cass and her husband had divorced. It proved too late; those 15 years in Newport Beach had been a lifetime away from Hollywood.

Whether she had left show business in the early 1950s or not, the decline of her career may have been inevitable. Cass Daley had been overexposed through the 1940s by weekly radio shows and eight films made and released between 1942 and 1947. In few of her appearances had she moved beyond her basic act. Times had changed as well. Joan Davis had died in the mid-1950s, Martha Raye's television career had ebbed, and Judy Canova had retired. Lucille Ball and Carol Burnett had humanized the clown, and Phyllis Diller had updated the ugly duckling. The Cass Daley niche had been filled.

Spending all that time away from movies and foregoing television during the decade the small screen asserted its primacy over all of show business meant starting over again with producers who were too young to remember when Cass Daley was a star. She won a few guest shots on television, several small parts in films, and some stage and nightclub work, but none led to a new career. Cass Daley was a vaudeville turn in an era when the Beatles, the Vegas Rat Pack, go-go girls and James Bond defined show business.

On 22 March 1975, in what was described as a freak accident, Cass Daley fell in her home, breaking her glass coffee table. Somehow, a piece of glass cut her throat, and she bled to death.

JEAN DALRYMPLE

b: (Jean Van Kirk Dalrymple) 2 September 1902, Morristown, NJ—d: 15 November 1998, New York, NY

Jean Dalrymple was a *civilian,* working on Wall Street, when her boyfriend at the time, Don Jarrett, persuaded her to try vaudeville. He was one of the actors in a dramatic-sketch act that belonged to Thomas E. Shea, a legitimate actor. When a young lady in the cast left to marry, Shea okayed Dalrymple for the part, even though she had never been onstage.

Both she and Jarrett became adept at writing sketches for themselves and others. In their own acts, they played big-time and the best of small-time vaudeville for years. Dalrymple wrote a number of acts that she and Jarrett and another partner produced. They cast the parts and then sold the acts to bookers. James Cagney and Cary Grant were among the unknowns hired. Some acts played the big time, but most played small time.

It was in the legitimate theatre that Dalrymple became a force. In the early 1930s, she went to work for producer John Golden as an assistant with many portfolios from play doctoring to producing, but she found her initial fame on Broadway as a publicist. She was one of the founding members of the American Theatre Wing and was long involved with the American National Theatre and Academy. By 1945, she had become a Broadway producer, one of three women (along with Cheryl Crawford and Irene Selznick), as well as a publicist. Over the decades she amassed an enviable string of credits.

Dalrymple was married to theatre critic and author Ward Morehouse from 1932 to 1937, and then, in 1951, she married Major General Philip de Witt Ginder, to whom she stayed wed until his death in 1968.

From the late 1940s through the 1960s, she was a power at New York's City Center, where she produced revivals of musicals and classic plays. Dalrymple had extended her interest to the concert stage at City Center when the U.S. State Department asked her to arrange overseas tours and appearances for American concert artists.

DANCE

Dance was always an important part of any vaudeville bill. Most vaudevillians could manage a soft shoe, and more than a few could execute a buck-and-wing in addition to their primary skills as comedians, singers and specialty acts, but only a hopeful beginner would try to make a career out of modest dance skill. As a rule, the quality of dancing that appeared on a big-time bill was superior to that which played the small time. Over several decades, percussive dancers improved markedly and rapidly; technique that might have earned an act bookings in top-notch vaudeville houses in the 1890s would have been at best ordinary in small-time houses of the 1920s. As the twentieth century progressed, the audience for dance swelled and there was increasingly expert training in all sorts of dance, producing evermore skilled and versatile dancers.

Tap dance was the predominant image of vaudeville dancing—*tap* being employed in its broadest sense

Deno & Rochells, "America's Foremost Exponent of the Apache"

to include buck, clog and other variants of percussive dance—but vaudeville bills also featured dancers performing waltzes, trots, the Charleston, tango, Apache, eccentric dances, Cossack routines, acrobatic ballet, classical ballet, interpretive dance, the shimmy-sha-wobble and all manner of movement.

Very likely, the average chorus gypsy dancing in the twenty-first-century American musicals, whether on Broadway or out on tour, is a more accomplished and versatile performer than most of the solo dancers between the two world wars, but it is equally likely that the star tap dancers of vaudeville and revue have never been surpassed in technique, speed, originality or appeal.

The only thing that all dancing has in common is the body. Ballet evolved from the ballroom dances of European Renaissance courts. The aesthetic of the Renaissance was to find beauty through perfect form: perfect bodies, perfectly trained, that maintained classical lines and moved through formal patterns to make a poetry of form and movement that was pantomimic. The dancers were earthly gods elevating the body to an ideal state. The dances provided evidence that there was harmony and order above the chaotic and sordid mortal sphere. In common with dances of antiquity all over the world, the dances of the European Renaissance were expressions of earthly wonder at heavenly powers. The ballet established its heaven on Earth.

The formal patterns and codified behavior of the court dances lived on in the ceremonial balls of the aristocracy and the merely wealthy who imitated them. The customs of the dance fit nicely with social customs that reinforced rigid boundaries that kept everyone in his inherited place. As ballet increased in professionalism, it required talent—a gift that was not always inherited—and training—a discipline that was at odds with the aims of the leisure class.

The laboring class brought to the show-business repertoire hornpipes, clogs, jigs, reels and other dances that were fanciful takes on individual forms of work or grew from celebratory events such as harvests and weddings. As the work or wedding dance grew less spontaneous and more complicated through inevitable competition, the essential requirements of those vernacular dances were mastery of the craft by its performers and the enjoyment of the performance by its audiences. Unlike the court dances that led to ballet and ballroom dancing and emphasized the grace and lightness needed to rise about the earthly plane of travails, the working-class dances were dug into the hard ground they trod, tilled and marched, celebrating the stamina, speed and occasional faster-than-the-eye trickery it took to claim and hold their place on earth.

European traditions, either upper or lower class, were not the only forms of dance to be enjoyed, as U.S. audiences discovered in the late nineteenth century. Little Egypt gave the nation a wriggling eyeful at the Columbia Exhibition in 1893 in Chicago, the first world's fair that proved that the USA could host an extravagant and self-congratulatory celebration with as much *brio* as Paris, Vienna and London.

There were many developments in dance in the late nineteenth century. Loie Fuller, Isadora Duncan and Ruth St. Denis exhilarated and confounded the expectations of dance critics and audiences through their interpretive dancing. The inventiveness and syncopation of a generation of African American percussive dancers astonished white Americans. Anna Pavlova's tours convinced American mommas to put their little girls into tutus.

A generation later, just before the First World War and despite religion's long campaign against dance as a licentious exercise, Vernon & Irene Castle stimulated a national craze for exhibition ballroom dancing.

Other vaudeville favorites early in the twentieth century included Ted Shawn; Salome dancer Gertrude Hoffman; percussive dancers U. S. Thompson, Willie Covan, George Primrose, Alice Whitman, Eddie Rector and Bill Robinson; and dozens of others, including troupes from Arabia, Spain, Japan and other nations. All of them had to push for their time and space on American stages.

In the nineteenth century, opera productions had offered ballet dancers the opportunity to perform, and saloon and sideshow audiences approved of dancing when it was done by women with as few garments as the law allowed and did not stray far from sexual enticement. For nonclassical dancers or the experimental dancers who moved more than their midways, however, the dime museum, variety and vaudeville stages were at first the only hospitable venues to earn a living and develop as skilled performers. The serious young dancers who found their first consistent employment in vaudeville also learned about stagecraft and audiences. When the concert stage finally beckoned, they were more likely to make a success.

Interpretive dance, as it was known in Victorian and Edwardian times—moved along what modern-dance pioneer Martha Graham called the "inner landscape of the mind." As quicksilver a landscape as that of dreams, the dance was beholden to neither narrative nor meaning and limited only by imagination. The dancer tore across the stage frantically or stayed still as a stone. Sights and sounds were not always in harmony or lockstep.

Ballet, on the other hand, required strict adherence to rules of posture, musical time and movement. The literal mime gestures of the royal courts were left behind, so the arc of an arm no longer meant the rise of the sun or the flight of a bird but was intended as a beautiful movement shorn of literal meaning. Ballet found few admirers among vaudeville audiences, despite Pavlova's following, but ballet postures, gestures and moves were adopted by generations of contortionists, acrobats, tap dancers, roller skaters, cyclists and tableaux acts to lend class to their routines.

Ballroom dance, another descendant of the court dances, was far more successful in vaudeville, but only after Vernon & Irene Castle made it respectable for a man and woman to dance together in public embrace. Ballroom dance outlasted vaudeville, was a staple of chic supper-club entertainments into the 1960s, and, together with tap dance, ballet, and interpretive and modern dance, was a major influence in stage dancing for musicals.

In percussive dance, feet beat out rhythms or responses to rhythms. The beat could be as metronomic as marching, or it could fiddle with the steady tick-tock of time by rushing, slowing or alternating the rhythm. Instead of being a simple visualization of the music, percussive dance was part of the music. Ballet and ballroom dancing were mostly about romantic love. Interpretive and modern dance were explorations. Percussive dance was an athletic contest, either challenging others or challenging self. Many of its more inventive and athletic exponents were, however,

Three Little Maids, "Those Different Dancers"

African American, and race barred them from many opportunities.

Because dance displayed the human form frankly, and was often about love, was employed as a metaphor for lovemaking and required public physical contact, its reception by audiences varied community to community. On the whole, urban, secular audiences were more receptive than rural, rock-ribbed religionists. Onstage couples who were well dressed and favored flowing movement such as ballroom dances and kept the sexual metaphor at a remove were safe for vaudeville, as were the challenge dances of men. In duos, trios or quartettes, men could dance in the same act as long as they tried to outdo each other. If it were an all-women act, they usually danced in unison. Has the contrast in temperament and expectations between men and women ever been made manifest so clearly?

At another level, there was considerable freedom. Regardless of the type of dancing, the vaudeville stage gave dancers the opportunity to explore. In revue or musical comedy, dance directors set out the steps, and dancers were expected to execute them. In vaudeville, the dance was one's own creation, and that experience gave rise to a generation of brilliant dancers and inventive choreographers.

See Tap Dancing, Oriental Dancers, Tableau Vivant, Adagio Act, Belly Dancers, Cakewalk, Chorines, Combination, Denishawn Dancers, Eccentric Dancing, Exotic Dancers, Bump, Hoofer, Hootchy-Kootchy or Kootch (Cootch) Dancers, Hoofers Club, Interpretive Dance and Muscle Dance

DANCE CONTESTS

In the nineteenth century, the jig, clog, buck and tap dancing were dominated by male dancers who treated the routines more as athletic contests than an art form. The most accomplished set out challenges and took on all comers.

The rules for these contests were formal. There were three judges, one each for style, time and execution. The style judge sat in the audience, just in front of the orchestra pit, where he had the best view of the dancer. The time judge sat in the wings, stage right, where he closely observed the footwork. The execution judge sat beneath the stage, where he would not notice anything the dancer did except the sounds of the taps, rolls, shuffles, scrapes and the like. The three judges used a point system, conferred and named the winner, but sometimes the judges were overruled by an excited and unconvinced audience, and the judges wisely deferred to the voice of the people. A century later, the identical form of judging was still in use.

During the Great Depression in the USA, dance contests had a second connotation: dance marathons, which were endurance events.

See Dance Marathons

DANCE DIRECTORS

More customary in burlesque, revue and musical comedy, a dance director might be engaged by a vaudeville act to pull together a flash act or a tab show or simply to devise a dance routine for a dance act. Ned Wayburn, among the few famous dance directors of his time, created dance routines for hundreds of vaudeville acts, including Adele & Fred Astaire's first real vaudeville act.

In burlesque, revue and the emergent musical comedy, dance directors acted as traffic cops, relying greatly on quasi-military drills and striving for some measure of precision from their dancers. In vaudeville, however, the great majority of dance acts worked out their own routines. As individual dancers showed audiences what really good dancers could do, revue and burlesque producers were forced to make a choice in the fact of greater expectations by their audiences. Some permitted their dance directors to hire better-trained dancers and give them more sophisticated routines to perform. Others countered by ordering their costumers to reveal as much of the physical charms of their chorus dancers as the law allowed.

In vaudeville, the apogee of dance direction was seen in the revues staged by Fanchon & Marco. Vaudeville dancers themselves, the former brother and sister duo developed into producers of unit shows for which they negotiated contractual arrangements, devised the themes, chose music and costuming, and directed the dances. Like Ned Wayburn, Fanchon & Marco established schools for dancing.

Generally, the better dance directors were not content to merely marshal ill-trained and ill-paid chorines in drills, and the best of dance directors worked to create dances that demanded more than marching in time and punctuating the music with lame kicks, slow turns and a tap-shuffle-shuffle-tap. Dance directors who had imagination, talent and determination evolved into choreographers.

The term *choreographer* originated in ballet and dated from the beginning of the eighteenth century. It was accorded to those who recorded the work of the ballet masters (dance notation): the particular steps danced by principals and the corps de ballet and the order in which they flowed. Over time, the term was extended to include those who composed movement to music and chose which dancers performed specific routines.

By the late 1930s, creative and ambitious dance directors for the musical stage often had formal training in ballet or modern dance. They began to call themselves choreographers, and producers gradually acknowledged them as *choreographers* in programmes and advertising.

DANCE MARATHONS

A craze of the 1930s, dance marathons were run like traveling shows, going from city to city, inviting the locals to compete for prizes. Those who survived the punishing challenge emerged as the winners. Couples tried to outlast each other on the dance floor as a dispirited band pumped out the popular music of the day and the emcee tried to enliven the tedium with announcements of minicontests and specialty numbers. The contestants danced around the clock, stopping only for periodic rests imposed by authorities in local municipalities. There were breaks for food, restrooms and cursory medical attention to blisters, sprains, corns and other minor ailments.

Dance marathons go back centuries but became part of American folklore in the early 1920s when contests lasted three or four days. A decade later, with the Great Depression hard upon the USA, weeks-long dance marathons offered the hope of prize money and a daily meal to many of the unemployed. Some youngsters may have entertained dreams of being discovered and making a career in show business, but the ranks of the marathons were already peopled with dancers, actors and other performers who could no longer find work on the stage.

In addition to locals who participated—out of desperation, dreams, or the desire to exhibit themselves—there were the professional contestants. They began as amateur contestants but showed themselves game and able to elicit audience attention. The management encouraged them to travel along with the show, gave them specialty spots (which might be rewarded with throw money from the audience), and often rigged the event slightly to ensure that one of the professional couples won the prize money. If there were several professional couples, as was usual, they took turns winning. The pros who lasted made sure that they stayed on the good side of the manager and emcee. Splitting their prize money with him was one way to stay in favor.

Although there were similarities, not all dance marathons were identical. Most of those during the Great Depression ran for a couple of weeks; a few ran for as long as three or four months. Some had good-size bands to play music; the smaller outfits used recordings. Each marathon producer and road company tried to find a hook or novelty that would engender publicity and keep the audiences coming, night after night. The ghouls who attended these affairs were looking for something dramatic: a peppy young kid with lots of personality setting the pace, a fight (staged or not) between contestants or the collapse of an old favorite worn out. A novelty was cute, a fistfight exciting, but a heart attack was better.

The marathon kept customers coming back, night after night, to cheer on their favorites. Some people just came at night because they had no place to sleep, whereas others, who still had money, came liquored up after an evening's entertainment like witnesses to a blood sport. It also had elements of a soap opera (so popular on radio at the time). Everyone had a story that was still unfolding. Couples met, and couples broke apart. If one partner dropped out, the other hoped to find another partner newly split.

The phenomenon has been the subject of memoirs, plays and movies. June Havoc, after she left the family act, kept body and soul together by one-stepping the dance-marathon trail around the country for a year or two. *They Shoot Horses, Don't They?* (1969) was the most celebrated of several films on the subject. Eventually, the public tired of dance marathons, and municipalities outlawed them.

EDDIE DARLING

Of all the people associated over the years with the Palace Theatre—Martin Beck, E. F. Albee, Marian Spitzer, J. J. Murdock—none was more indelibly linked to its history and reputation than Eddie Darling, its chief booker. Albee, the czar of vaudeville, was the boss of the Keith-Albee circuit, J. J. Murdock was his Richelieu, Spitzer served in the publicity department and later became the theatre's historian, but it was Eddie Darling who set the tone.

The Palace was not just the flagship of big-time vaudeville, it was also the heart of the most important circuit in vaudeville. Albee, Murdock and Darling had their offices on the sixth floor of the office building over the theatre's front half, but Darling managed to run the Palace with a fair amount of autonomy.

Darling was a handsome, studious-looking chap who was ever mindful of what his job required. At first blush, it was to provide interesting, well-balanced bills that drew an audience willing, even eager, to pay top vaudeville dollar for tickets. This he had to accomplish within a tight, unyielding budget. Equally important, he developed into a diplomat: reasonable, calm and courteous but firm. Reputations were at stake when performers played the Palace. Ego was a major factor, but so, too, was professional standing. To be able to claim and prove that one headlined at the Palace was to set apart an act and ensure its ability to command top billing and increased salary in the future.

Top billing, the next-to-closing position on the bill and the star dressing room were indications of an act's stature and affected its financial future. The prerequisites of a star also caused temper tantrums that were flare-ups of self-importance, jealousy or selfish ego. Darling was considered a master at salving bruised egos, calming insecurities and resolving conflicts. He seemed to have kept his own ego in check and did not allow his own injured feelings or resentments to get in the way of running the Palace.

Eddie Darling

Sometimes, it was enough for Darling to have a quiet talk with the more malleable of two stars contesting the top spot, first-floor dressing room and accompanying honor. Other situations required more indirect tactics. One famous story tells of two single women claiming top honors, specifically the star dressing room on the stage floor. Realizing that neither would yield, Darling had ladders and paint cloths set up in the headliner's dressing room to indicate that the star dressing room was unavailable to anyone. This maneuver allowed both performers to save face. Sometimes, nothing could be done about a situation. A clash between Darling and George M. Cohan was never resolved, and, forever after it occurred, Cohan always refused to play the Palace.

As well known as Darling was in show business, there were some people who always confused him with Eddie Dowling. The story is told that when Darling was being honored for his years of service to the Palace and to the parent organization, someone requested a song.

LES DASSIES (DASSIE BROTHERS)

b: ca. 1930, France

From Paris, Les Dassies was an extraordinarily vigorous and fast-paced tumbling act that played a number of engagements in the USA during the early 1950s. Dressed in sailor outfits, the two men tossed, slapped and kicked each other. The accent on roughhouse clowning did not obscure their tight timing, strength, quick reflexes and deft acrobatics.

Brothers or not, they began as teenagers in France, working in nightclubs, circuses and revues. Their first North American engagement was in Montreal, where their long run attracted the attention of producers in the USA and from the Palladium Theatre in London.

Chief among their American appearances were the *All Star Summer Revue* (1952, NBC), hosted by Jan Murray and headlined by Jimmy Savo, and as the opening act at the Palace Theatre on Broadway, on a bill (11 April 1952) headlined by Betty Hutton and featuring Herb Shriner, Borra Minevitch's Harmonica Rascals, the Skylarks, humorist Herb Shriner, and Andre, Andree & Bonnie, "The Dancing Mannequins."

DATES

The more usual term among professionals for bookings on specified dates.

E. D. DAVIES

Ventriloquist who performed with various puppets in the mid-nineteenth century, most notably in the third act of the Black Crook extravaganza in 1866.

JOAN DAVIS

b: (Madonna Josephine Davis) 29 June 1907, Saint Paul, MN—d: 22 May 1961, Palm Springs, CA

Her nose was a bit long and her knees were a trifle knobby, but Joan Davis was a handsome woman whose curves, fore and aft, were what and where they should have been. Dolled up, as in her 1946 film *She Wrote the Book,* she appeared as glamorous as most of the leading ladies who worked at the same movie studios.

Joan Davis

Seeing her move and talk on the screen, however, presented a mix of contradictions. With the same attention to the camera angles, makeup, hair and clothes given to the glamour girls, Davis looked sophisticated, yet her voice was a flat, low-pitched Midwestern twang that she cranked up to a howl or lowered to a baritone mutter.

She was a better physical comedian than all but two or three of the very best male clowns, and she threw herself wholeheartedly into pratfalls, funny walks, stumbles and double takes. Often, though, it was simply the tilt of her head, a sidelong glance, or the slightest and subtlest of takes that earned a laugh. Just the way she stood was funny; she could hold herself so that her clothes appeared to be on a hanger, not her. Although the stage characters of Bea Lillie and Joan Davis were a style and social class apart, there was a similarity of technique.

Davis was a cutup from the time she was a toddler. Her family recalled that three-year-old baby Joan impersonated a cupid using a wire coat hanger for her bow. At six, she entered an amateur show, but, in the middle of her serious recitation, she was hooted off the stage. A barrage of squishy vegetables hastened her exit. Her father, a railroad dispatcher, advised her, "Better be funny, not serious. Keep moving! It spoils their aim." Vaudeville and burlesque audiences could be tough, and amateur night was close to blood sport, but pelting a six-year-old with rotten produce seems more a good showbiz story, exaggerated for laughs. The following week she came out with a comic song, "I Ain't Nobody's Darling."

By 1913, small-time vaudeville had invaded every outpost in America, and a Twin Cities agent spotted Joan, helped her form an act and, with her family's permission, booked her on Pantages time as "The Toy Comedienne." Her mother went on the road with Joan. Some seasons later, her billing was changed to the "Cyclonic Josephine Davis." In her 15-minute act, she sang comic songs, did eccentric dancing and clowned. A good portion of her attraction as an act was the novelty of watching a child cavort and sing funny songs. By 16, she began to look like a young adult, and her kid act no longer fit.

Joan retired from vaudeville after nearly a decade and went back to high school full time to earn her diploma. Despite having had to fit her studies into her travel and performance schedule all through grade school and two years of high school, Joan was graduated class valedictorian from St. Paul's Mechanical Arts High School.

She tried to walk the straight and narrow as a salesclerk in a department store but found her legs fell into their old routines of slipping, sliding, shaking and tripping as she toted purchases to the packing counter. Customers and fellow workers laughed, managers did not. A taste of civilian life convinced Joan that vaudeville was her calling.

By 1923, when Davis returned to the boards as "The Youthful Fit of Wit," vaudeville was slipping. Silent movies were attaining the peak of their artistry, and most small-time vaudeville bills were halved to accommodate a feature-length picture from Hollywood. Had she been located on either coast, or even headquartered herself in Chicago, Joan might have worked into the better small time and the big time.

Vaudeville dates were filled out with one-night engagements at special events, and, during the summers, she worked resorts and amusement parks. In an effort to class up her act, Joan teamed up with another vaudevillian, Si Wills, whose career was in the doldrums. Si and Joan shared the same agent, who suggested, in 1931, that they work together. The problem was both were comedians. Serenus "Si" Wills (1896–1977) was a baggy-pants comic specializing in slapstick hokum. Joan wore similarly clownish costumes, like outrageous hats and ruffled bloomers that sagged down to her ankles. Both streamlined their presentation; their physical comedy was still present, mostly in Joan's performance, but they dressed more conventionally and employed cross talk, with Si setting up the gags as the wise-guy straightman and Joan playing the gawky, inept boob.

They married while playing Pantages time, and their daughter, Beverly, was born in 1933. Raising a child on the road was difficult. Joan knew that first-hand. Schooling was sporadic, and there was little chance for children to make friends their own age. Joan and Si understood that vaudeville was not going to recover, so they headed to Hollywood. Wills & Davis ended their vaudeville dates in Los Angeles, settled in an apartment and threw a party, to which Joan and Si invited their vaudeville friends who had also headed west.

Joan shrewdly invited Mack Sennett as well. Sennett was no longer king of the Keystone Kops, as he had been in the 1910s, but he peddled a formula for short films that blended comedy, musical numbers and pretty girls in a vain attempt to woo back some of the two-reeler business he had lost to Hal Roach (who had two moneymaking series: Laurel & Hardy and the Our Gang comedies). The new Sennett formula had been fairly successful in 1931–32 when he released a half-dozen shorts starring Bing Crosby.

Sennett put Davis in a hick pic, *Way Up Thar* (1935). Myra Keaton, Buster's mother, played Joan's hillbilly mom, and the Sons of the Pioneers played the Sons of the Pioneers. In the film's 20 minutes, Joan sang three comic numbers (including "That's Why I Stutter") and reprised her vaudeville classic of carrying a tall and precariously perched pile of dishes on the brink of crashing to the floor.

It was not art, but the short comedy was a calling card that got her into agents' offices and provided two reels of audition film that showed some of what she could do. Davis soon got work, the start of 45 feature films that kept her increasingly well paid between 1936 and 1952.

Davis signed with RKO and made one feature. While awaiting further assignments, Wills & Davis took some vaudeville dates, beginning in 1936, at the once prestigious Palace Theatre on Broadway. They flopped. Their agent quickly shunted them into the Academy of Music in Manhattan, where they began a series of vaudeville dates. When RKO did not come up with any follow-up features, Joan and the studio tore up her contract, and she went to work for Darryl F. Zanuck, who had taken over Fox Films.

Beginning with her third feature, Joan spent five years with Twentieth Century Fox, making 24 movies in which she bobbed and weaved around the romantic couple at the center of the plot. Also involved in one or more of the same films were other deft comic talents: Fred Allen, Binnie Barnes, John Barrymore, Milton Berle, Ben Bernie, El Brendel, Walter Catlett, William Demarest, Jimmy Durante, Buddy Ebsen, Jack Haley, Bert Lahr, Joe E. Lewis, Franklin Pangborn, Nat Pendleton, the Ritz Brothers, Sig Ruman, Ned Sparks, Arthur Treacher and Cora Witherspoon.

Several of the Fox films in which Joan Davis appeared were both genuinely funny and gave her opportunities to shine. Her tentative wooing of Nat Pendleton in *Life Begins at College* (1937) was a delight, and she was given a fair amount of time and decent material to work with in *Thin Ice* (1937), *Sally, Irene and Mary* (1938), *My Lucky Star* (1938) and *Hold That Co-Ed* (1938). Still, Fox was not giving her lead roles, and she knew she was able to carry the lead in a comedy film. When her contract with Fox was up in 1940, Davis declined to renew.

After averaging five films a year for five years at Fox, Joan decided that freelancing would allow her to be choosier and to negotiate her price picture by picture. The year 1941 proved a good one for Joan Davis. She won the second comedy lead in *Hold That Ghost,* one of Abbott & Costello's better films. She showed she was in the same class as Lou Costello, and they shared a hilarious dance duet.

That same year, Joan Davis made an appearance as a besotted fan of Rudy Vallee on his self-named network radio show for Sealtest Ice Cream. She made such a hit that Vallee, ever a keen judge of talent, brought her back as a regular cast member. Vallee was committed to active duty with the U.S. Coast Guard during the Second World War, so he made the transition from his show over a period of months, gradually shifting the focus to Davis while he underwent further military training.

After Vallee left his show and time spot, the show was retooled as *Sealtest Village Store,* and Joan took over as proprietor. Physical clown Gil Lamb and character comedian Verna Felton were added in support. Audiences stayed loyal, but the sponsor got nervous. Vallee was a major star and a man. Joan Davis, in their view, was a stooge, and women seldom starred in top-rated, prime-time radio programs. As insurance, the network and sponsor hired Jack Haley to be her costar. Davis left in 1945, when she had driven the show into radio's top five and earned her reward as radio's highest-paid female star.

Haley and Eve Arden became Sealtest's new leads. Then Haley left the show, and Jack Carson became the final proprietor of the *Sealtest Village Store.* Eve Arden left the shuttered shop for the opportunity to teach high school as *Our Miss Brooks.*

In 1945, the CBS network eagerly offered to star Joan on her own in *The Joan Davis Show.* Her salary was $1 million per year. Four years later, CBS and Joan agreed to revamp the format into straight situation comedy. Called *I Married Joan*, it kicked off for the 1949–50 season. The show transferred to television for the 1952–55 seasons.

Meanwhile, she made about two movies per year at her price of $50,000 per picture. The studios that hired her, Columbia, RKO, Republic and Universal, seldom invested budgets, time, good writers or directors into her pictures. Among the more interesting were two films, *Show Business* (1944) and *If You Knew Susie* (1948), that were produced by and starred Eddie Cantor. His costar in both films was Joan Davis. *Show Business* was a low-budget but fairly lively and believable vaudeville story in black and white that was a lot closer to the truth than the Technicolor confections that George Jessel was about to produce for Fox. *She Wrote the Book* (1946) gave plain Joan the chance to doll up in fashions and play a professor who impersonates a best-selling author of a steamy novel. None of her movies ever truly fulfilled her promise as a great clown, yet she combined the vulnerability and physical ability that makes for great clowns, and she was expert with dialogue.

Unfortunately, Joan Davis is more likely remembered for her television series, *I Married Joan,* than for her films. If she had a professional weakness, it may have been as a judge of comedy material, given the film roles she assumed and the eventual shape of her television series, or she may simply have been exhausted by the fight to get better material and took the money instead.

I Married Joan (1952–55, NBC-TV) compares unfavorably with *I Love Lucy* (1951–55 in its original format). Joan Davis probably had the edge on Lucy as a farceur, but Lucy's writers were tops, and Joan's writers were not. Lucy played a showbiz-crazy, emotional and rather immature wife married to a bandleader and nightclub performer. The premise was not improbable; Ricky was not the first bandleader to wed a ditzy redhead. Joan played a whacky, bumbling, 40-year-old housewife who created exactly two disasters per show and embarrassed her husband, a judge. Huh? Judges do not marry social misfits, or, if they do, they do not stay married to them for 20 years. *I Married Joan* did Joan Davis' reputation little good.

Joan Davis was 45 when she began her television situation-comedy series and near 50 when it ended. Perhaps she should have tried variety and become one of the rotating hosts of the *All Star Revue* or *Colgate Comedy Hour,* both NBC shows. The comic characters Charlotte Greenwood, Gracie Allen and Martha Raye aged well; Joan's did not. She was too old to play a silly bride. Gracie, in her later years, changed her youthful dizzy self into an eccentric but normal-appearing middle-aged woman who behaved as she should except in matters of reasoning.

Like Eve Arden, Joan Davis' character in movies had a self-deprecatory sense of humor, and both delivered their remarks in a similar flat voice, but Arden's character was upscale and her delivery a tad more wry. Fanny Brice, a comedian at the opposite end of the spectrum from Eve Arden, was once asked who she would want to see play Fanny Brice if they made a movie of her life. (They did decades later, with Barbra Streisand.) Fanny famously replied, "There's one dame who could play me; that's Joan Davis."

Joan was often compared with Martha Raye, who was her equal in physical comedy. Joan cultivated a plain-Jane look. Despite a good, if lean, figure, she was almost always costumed to hide her curves and look like a bag of bones. Martha hid nothing. She was a juicily voluptuous bubble of energy and sexual aggressiveness. Martha knew what men wanted, and she was more than willing to give it. If Joan Davis knew what men wanted, she was sure it was not her.

After *I Married Joan* faded out, Joan went into semiretirement while new series were announced for her and pilots were filmed. A few years went by, but no projects got off the ground. Joan was well-off with homes in Palm Springs and Bel Air, so she did not have to work. She made news when she filed assault-and-battery charges against prospective husband number two in 1959. Two years later, at her Palm Springs home, she was rushed to the hospital, complaining of severe back pain. With her mother and a priest in attendance, she died of a heart attack, one month short of her 54th birthday.

Joan died intestate, so her former husband, Si Wills, whom she had divorced in 1948, sued for a share. He received a settlement, but the bulk of Davis' reputed $1-million-dollar estate went to their daughter, Beverly. Two-and-a-half years later, in October 1963,

Beverly fell asleep while smoking. She, her two sons and grandmother died in the all-consuming blaze.

SAMMY DAVIS JR.

b: 8 December 1925, New York, NY—d: 16 May 1990, Los Angeles, CA

George Burns thought Sammy Davis was the best all-around entertainer of his day and equal to the greatest of vaudevillians. Sammy grew up in vaudeville. According to his recollection, he performed professionally before he turned three years old. Unfortunately, Sammy lost most of the materials related to his early career, so his memories of vaudeville were more atmospheric than detailed by theatres and dates played.

Sammy's mother, Elvera "Baby" Sanchez, left Sam Davis soon after Sammy Jr.'s birth. It was not calculated callousness, although Elvera, a chorus girl, did not wish to work in the same traveling show as her ex-mate. In show business, people had to go where jobs took them.

Their son was raised for the first two years of his life by his grandmother, Rosa B. Davis, then Sam took little Sammy on the road with him. Sam, a good tap dancer, worked for Will Mastin, a dancer with an entrepreneurial bent. Sammy called him "Uncle Will"; he was an old friend of Sam's but not a blood relation. In turn, Will and Sam called Sammy "Poppa."

When Will Mastin could promote the money and bookings, he expanded his vaudeville act into a full-length show numbering 30 or 40 people. The titles changed—*Holiday in Dixieland, Shake Your Feet* or *Struttin' Hannah from Savannah*—but the formula was constant: music, girls, gags and hoofing.

When times were harder than usual, Will tried to hustle vaudeville bookings for an act comprised of himself, Sam, Sammy and maybe a couple of young women: "Will Mastin's Gang, Featuring Little Sammy." Little Sammy was eight when his name was featured in the act alongside Will Mastin's.

Sometimes the act was pared down to the Will Mastin Trio. Sammy did not realize until later that it was largely because of him that the Will Mastin Trio got good bookings. It was not that Will or his father were indifferent dancers—they were fine, athletic tappers—but there were many excellent black dancers vying for a limited number of jobs, and precocious, undersized Sammy, the little wonder who did impressions, danced up a firestorm, sang and mugged, gave the Will Mastin Trio an edge.

Sammy never had formal lessons in singing or dancing. By the time he was five or six, he could perform intricate tap steps, mimic everybody else's routine and

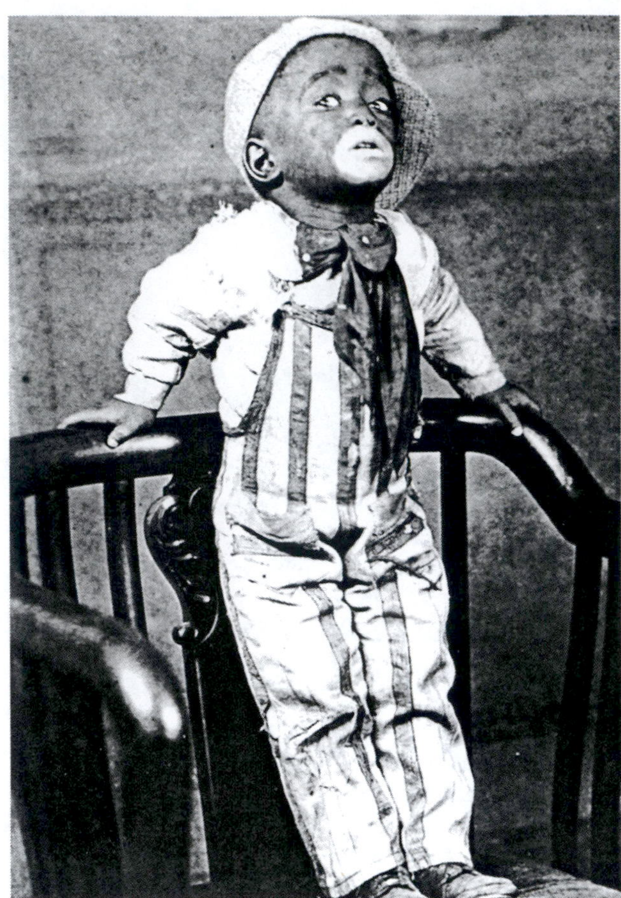

Sammy Davis Jr.

mug for laughs. Will and Sam put blackface on him and outlined his mouth in white greasepaint so that he looked like a miniature minstrel clown. Will Mastin coached Sammy from behind the wings. It was a game they had played on trains and in dressing rooms, and now it was paying off in shtick. When Will rolled his eyes, Sammy rolled his but looked straight at the audience or at the other person in the scene.

Grandmother Davis worried about Sammy's welfare and health on the road, but Sammy loved performing, and Sam and Will went hungry before they skimped on Sammy. Within a couple of years, by the time Sammy was six or so, he was vital to the act.

The act was good; it may have been great, but times got tough. The Great Depression moved from Europe to the USA, where it hung low over those on the margins. Jobs were lost. There were few extra coins for fripperies like vaudeville and burlesque. When someone had the odd nickel or dime, it was more likely spent to see a double feature at the movie house. Bookings dried up. Acts folded.

Six-year-old Sammy Davis Jr. won an audition and made his first movie in 1932. It was a two-reel musical fantasy called *Rufus Jones for President.* It starred

Ethel Waters and featured Hamtree Harrington and Dusty Fletcher, and Sammy was Rufus at the center of the plot. He did not make another movie for nearly 15 years.

Sammy Davis Jr. later reckoned that between the ages of three (in 1928) and 1944, when he entered the U.S. Army to fight in the closing days of the Second World War, he had traveled back and forth across Canada and the USA more than a couple of dozen times. Nearly all of his life was spent in the cocoon of show business where, by and large, he, his father and "uncle" worked with and had friends among white acts as well as black.

The outside world of segregated lunchrooms, inhospitable rooming houses and snarled remarks was *civilian,* often hostile, territory. For a while, Sammy thought he, Sam and Will had second-class standing because they were in show business. Will and Sam encouraged that assumption. Sometimes, Sammy thought it was because he was ugly. Girls laughed at him. He grew up without formal schooling or friends of his own age. To the extent he could read, it was show-business trade papers that provided news of a slightly larger world. He learned about life from older men and women on the bill.

During his stint in the U.S. Army, Sammy Davis Jr. had many fights, and his nose was broken a few times when he stood up to taunts. The white bigots learned that he fought back, so they ganged up on him, coated him in white paint and then painted in black the words *coon* and *nigger* on his face and body. Half naked, Sammy was forced to dance. Each time he faltered, he was beaten again.

Eventually, his talent and professional experience led to a transfer into the Special Services. He entertained in camp shows for eight months until the war's end. Sammy left the U.S. Army wiser in many ways; he had encountered evil, hatred and indifference. He had also met people—a sergeant who supplied him with selected books—who helped Sammy become the man he wished to be. Sammy read ambitiously and eagerly. At 20, he sounded so cultivated that he was accused of putting on an English accent.

Sammy rejoined the act after his hitch in the army. Mostly, the Will Mastin Trio with Sammy Davis Jr. was still stuck in the prewar Great Depression, whereas the rest of America seemed to be enjoying the new prosperity, but occasionally they got a few important gigs here and there. They joined a unit headed by Mickey Rooney, and Mickey gave their act, specifically Sammy, more time onstage. Frank Sinatra remembered the prewar days when he and Sammy were both struggling. At last able to call his own shots, Sinatra insisted that Sammy be on the bill with him when Frank played the Capitol Theatre in Manhattan. Sammy believed that he needed to become a star to win respect. When he won stardom and respect, the dynamics within the trio changed.

Both Mickey and Frank treated Sammy like a friend, and he watched to see what made them special onstage. Will and Sam came from the era of vaudeville in which the act was all important. The new postwar model of show business success, it seemed to Sammy, was built more on personal connection with the audience.

This had been true, of course, of old vaudeville, but after decades of doing an act, concentrating on making the dance steps more intricate and dancing faster, yet weary with travel to one-night stands, the danger was that the connection with the audience was reduced to a painted-on smile. Frank Sinatra and Mickey Rooney understood that audiences wanted the intimacy of a nightclub act, no matter how large the theatre. Realizing that made the difference for Sammy.

Will and Sam reluctantly followed Sammy's lead, and soon the act was pulling in more than $500 a week. Increasingly, Sammy was the center of the act. He danced, sang, did impressions of famous entertainers and actors, told jokes and talked to the audience. Will did not want Sammy doing impressions, and Sam followed Will's lead. Sammy did impersonations anyway, and some were of white actors and performers. Everyone worried because no black entertainer had ever attempted that, yet white audiences seemed to have no problem with Sammy Davis Jr. as Jimmy Cagney and Ronald Colman.

Sammy was 25 in 1950 and had been in show business for 22 years. Sam was 50 years old, and Will was about 65 or so (he did not reveal his age); they framed the act. The trio opened fast with dancing, then Sammy did his impressions and sang, and Will and Sam piled in from the wings for a fast, flashy dance finish. Sammy's portion of the show kept getting longer, and during it Will and Sam held to the back of the stage, like backup singers, keeping time and smiling.

They played Las Vegas and Hollywood, and Sammy scored with the big names in the show business of his generation. As an act, the Will Mastin Trio had arrived; their price had shot to $1,500 a week, and they were working full time at top nightclubs from Hollywood to Manhattan: Ciro's, the Rivera, the Copacabana, the Beachcomber. As an entertainer, Sammy Davis Jr. was on the brink of stardom. The trio appeared on Ed Sullivan's television show, *Toast of the Town,* and won national notice. Newspaper columnists were tagging Sammy Davis Jr. as the hottest new entertainer in the country.

With Sammy's fame and confidence, women discovered that he was attractive. Most people ignored their own bias for a brush with celebrity. Will still acted as the trio's manager, so he was Sammy's de facto manager. Sam was relatively ignored. Still, he and Will were astonished at the $3,500 to which the act's salary had vaulted, and they were happy to be splitting it three equal ways. Show business had not been that good since the 1920s, if then.

As Sammy's star rose higher, Will had to surrender a measure of leadership to the kid he had helped raise, bathe, feed and comfort. Sammy was the baby they cared for and protected, even when Will and Sam had nothing, not even hope. They remembered the bad times better than Sammy. Will and Sam wanted to lay money away for future bad times, which had never failed to visit. Old age was just around the corner, and retirement was only a heart attack or a broken ankle away. Sammy wanted to play "Charley Star," as he later called it. He spent every dollar of his share of the act's take.

Milton Berle, Jerry Lewis and Jack Benny gave him solid professional advice and introduced him to the right people. Eddie Cantor risked what remained of his career when he booked the Will Mastin Trio's for a guest shot on his television show. After the Will Mastin Trio's turn, Eddie joked with Sammy and wiped his sweaty face with his own handkerchief. The gesture triggered a flood of hate mail. Cantor's response to hate mail and threats was to sign Sammy for the three remaining shows in that season's schedule.

Every success was balanced by a setback, every victory with a defeat. A car accident in 1954 cost Sammy an eye. He wore an eye patch until he was able to accommodate an artificial eyeball. The study of Judaism helped him deal with the loss. Sammy refused to play venues where Negroes were not admitted into the audience, and he broke racial barriers in Las Vegas on the biggest stages and in hotel accommodations. When Davis refused to play hotels in Miami Beach and casinos in Las Vegas unless he were allowed to stay in those same hotels, those two cities' hotels and dining places were integrated. Despite this major feat, Sammy was faulted for not staying in black-owned rooming houses.

When Sammy chummed around with Frank Sinatra, the black press accused him of turning his back on his old friends in Harlem. Sammy did not have old friends in Harlem, except his grandmother, and he moved her into her own home in California. The Harlem boys and girls whom Sammy met on his rare trips home from playing vaudeville on the road had made fun of him when he attempted to be friendly. Sammy's social life was integrated, and he was doing his best to break down racial barriers for himself and other entertainers.

Sammy wanted Broadway; Will Mastin wanted the steady $25,000-a-week nightclub gigs that the trio was earning in the late 1950s. The weekly salary continued to be split three ways. Sammy prevailed, and a Broadway show, *Mr. Wonderful,* was crafted around his talents. Will insisted, however, on the old billing: "The Will Mastin Trio Starring Sammy Davis Jr." Their arguments should have been about the show's music, conception and construction. Through doggedness, the producers and Sammy kept it running from 22 March 1956 until 23 February 1957. Harlemites filled the balconies, but not enough rich folks bought orchestra seats, and the show did not return its investment. Due to his profligacy, Sammy fell deeper in debt each week the show ran, and he had nothing to satisfy the demands of the tax man.

Mr. Wonderful had a positive payoff for Sammy; it settled who was the star, if not boss, of the Will Mastin Trio. When Sammy got ill a few months after the show opened, everyone, including Will Mastin, understood without a doubt that without Sammy there were no ticket sales, no salaries to be split three ways. Without Sammy, there was no act.

It was hard for each member of the trio. Sam and Will had been his parents and mentors. They gave him a career. Sammy took their careers to a height they never imagined, and he was a 40-year-old man and a star. Audiences did not wish to pay homage any longer to Will and Sam, "who taught me everything I know." People were paying expensive cover charges and buying overpriced drinks to watch Sammy. Television producers wanted Sammy for variety shows, but the spots were five minutes or so, so they did not want to yield a single moment of that precious, sponsor-supported time on camera to Will and Sam. Producers demanded Sammy alone.

Mr. Wonderful presented nightclub Sammy, not an actor. Much of the second act was the Will Mastin Trio's nightclub routine. Sammy's next Broadway show, *Golden Boy* (1964–66) was a play with music. Clifford Odets' Great Depression–era drama about an Italian boxer was adapted for Sammy. The change made sense; African Americans were a dominant force in the prizefight ring.

Clifford Odets died while he adapted his script for a musical treatment. The result was a mishmash cobbled together by several writers, a couple of directors and two choreographers. It played Philadelphia, Boston, Detroit and other cities for six months before opening in New York. Critics were kind to the show and raved about Sammy, so the show ran 569 performances, about a year and a half on Broadway.

Sammy's troubles, some of his own making, were catching up with him. Living well beyond his means left him seriously behind in taxes. He had developed a cocaine habit—hardly an economical vice—and he was catching flak from some blacks and a lot of whites for dating white women. *Golden Boy* should have established Sammy as an actor. Gossip about his personal life drowned out discussion of his merit as a thespian.

Sammy Davis Jr. became inseparable from the swinging hipster image that engulfed him, along with Frank Sinatra, Dean Martin, Peter Lawford and Joey Bishop.

They had been the core of the cast of *Oceans Eleven* (1960), the crime caper and buddy movie they made together. With Sinatra at the center, they melded into a self-congratulatory cohort called the "Rat Pack." A lot of fans loved the Rat Pack, their kidding about "broads, booze and stiffing any criticism with their credo, 'living well is the best revenge.'" Other folks thought they were sexist, phony in sentiment and sophistication, and a waste of good talent, and Sammy was being dismissed for his unctuous stage behavior by a public who once had championed him. His personality and personal life overshadowed his performing talent.

He married three times. Once to a black woman, Loray White, a marriage many thought was intended to stop talk about Sammy's passion for white blondes. Loray and Sammy divorced within several months. His second marriage (1960–68) to blonde Swedish movie star Mai Britt could not survive more than six years of death threats, racial hatred and the unceasing glare of prurient publicity. His third wife, an African American, Altovise Gore, stayed with him from 1970 until his death, despite all the accumulated trouble.

Sammy Davis Jr. worked often in television, especially well as a frequent guest on *Rowan & Martin's Laugh-In,* and he continued to draw in Vegas. His first TV series failed. Most of Sammy's movies were not bad, simply unmemorable. *Anna Lucasta* (1959), *Sweet Charity* (1969) and *Tap* (1989) were among the exceptions. He craved a big record hit, but his voice became unreliable when abused (he smoked five packs of cigarettes a day). The biggest record hit that Sammy ever had was "Candy Man," a song he despised for its banality, yet one he was expected to sing for years.

In 1974, Sammy brought a touch of vaudeville back to Broadway for two weeks. Various acts opened for what was largely a one-man show, appropriately named *Sammy.* Four years later, he starred in his final Broadway show. It was a three-week revival of the Leslie Bricusse and Anthony Newley musical *Stop the World—I Want to Get Off* (1978).

The final decade of Sammy's career was less eventful. He worked frequently but never got out of the tax hole he passed on to his estate. He came to the sorry conclusion that he had largely squandered his talents. It wasn't a matter of arrogance or indifference; Sammy Davis was a decent man who simply had come into the world with as much unfortunate baggage as talent. He could dance, sing, clown, do impressions, play several instruments and act, yet he was as much remembered as a celebrity, famous for being famous, than as the greatest entertainer of his generation, as many hailed him.

In the movie *Tap,* one of his final efforts, he acted and danced among his peers: Bunny Briggs, Harold Nicholas, Steve Condos, Sandman Sims, Buster Brown and Jimmy Slyde, and with two top hoofers from two succeeding generations, Gregory Hines and Savion Glover. It was good work. In his maturity, Sammy Davis Jr. said he wished he had done more of it and less of the hipster shtick.

DEAD-LINE

The correct level at which cloths, trapezes or webs were hung. The ends of the *lines* (ropes) that lowered and raised cloths and equipment in and out of the stage area were secured backstage on cleats attached to the curtain rail. (In earlier days, wooden pegs were used instead of metal cleats.)

The cloths and equipment were attached to battens, then raised by ropes into place, and then tied off at the point where they hung properly. Once the stage crew got the cloths or equipment hanging straight—one end not higher than the other—and at the right height with no space between the bottom of the cloth and the stage floor, the lines were tied around a second set of cleats up in the flies. Thus, at showtime, when cloths or an act's equipment needed to be quickly lowered from the flies into place, they stopped at the point where they had been tied off. Until the time a cloth or a piece of equipment was needed and lowered onto the stage, it was flown up into the fly space above the stage, where it remained out of the way.

DEADPAN

A straight-faced expression betraying no intense emotion or reaction; poker-faced. Literally, a "dead face" (*pan* meaning "face"). Buster Keaton made inspired use of a deadpan.

SIDNEY DEAN AND DANIEL DEAN

Sidney Dean

b: (Sydney Taradash) ca. 1911, Louisville, KY

Daniel Dean

b: (Daniel Taradash) 29 January 1913, Louisville, KY—d: 22 February 2003, Los Angeles, CA

Sidney began in vaudeville in a comedy act with his brother, Daniel, whose career soon turned onto a different path. Reverting to their family name, Taradash, Daniel chose to write, and enjoyed great success penning the stories and screenplays for *Golden Boy, Knock on Any Door, Rancho Notorious, From Here to Eternity* (for which he won an Academy Award), *Desiree, Picnic, Storm Center* (which he also directed), *Bell Book & Candle, Morituri, Hawaii* and *The Other Side of Midnight,* among others. In 1971, Daniel became president of the Academy of Motion Picture Arts and Sciences, and in 1977 he was chosen president of the Writers' Guild of America.

Sidney married Bonnie of the Reed Sisters and formed a trio that, for a time, was billed as Reed, Dean & Reed. All three were engaged by Olsen & Johnson for their vaudeville revue *Hellzapoppin,* which provided Sidney Dean with his most enduring role as one of the many second bananas who helped make the show a riotous funhouse. Unlike the other clowns who scampered about, he played a disengaged audience member who, instead of watching the show, wandered through the house trying to find adequate light by which to read his newspaper. Finally, he walked up onto the stage and sat off to the side, reading beneath the proscenium lights while the Reed Sisters and others performed their routines. After *Hellzapoppin*'s three-and-a-half-year run (1938–41), Sidney and Bonnie Reed worked as Reed & Dean, a double act, comedy and music, in USO shows. Eventually, they divorced.

The Dean brothers may have been related to an earlier performer, Sydney Deane, who appeared in a number of musicals during the 1900–04 New York seasons: *The Knickerbocker Girl, Floradora, The Mocking Bird* and *My Lady Molly.*

See Reed Sisters

LAWRENCE DEAS

Dancer, singer, songwriter and choreographer Larry Deas was a standard act of the 1890s and 1900s in black vaudeville, both as Deas & Wilson ("Jack the Bear" Wilson) and as Deas, Reed & Deas. One of Deas & Wilson's songs, "All I Want Is My Chicken," was popularized by Bert Williams.

By the 1920s, Deas was more active behind the curtain, and he staged several *colored* shows. His most famous contribution was as dance director (with Charles Davis) for *Shuffle Along* (1921), the great hit black show. His other Broadway credit was as cochoreographer with Speedy Smith for *Change Your Luck* (1930), a flop.

DEATH TRAIL

So called because the theatres along this route tested the mettle of the performers who performed in them, the Death Trail meandered through the Dakotas, Montana, Idaho and the Canadian provinces of Manitoba, Saskatchewan and Alberta. The working conditions were often crude, the pay insulting, and the audiences were often native peoples for whom English was at best a rudimentary second language. Most bookings were only for a *split week* (an engagement from one to three days at a week's end) because of the long distances between dates and the hazards of travel during the winter (which claimed more days in the year than the other three seasons put together).

The Death Trail was a patchwork of theatres on several small, small-time circuits, such as Ackerman & Harris and Webster's. George Webster sometimes booked only one live act and one film and demanded as many as ten shows a day. Among the Canadian outposts on the Death Trail were Winnipeg, Regina, Moose Jaw, Saskatoon, Medicine Hat, Calgary and Edmonton. The situation on the USA side of the border was not much better, with dates in garden spots like Fargo, Jamestown and Deadwood in the Dakotas, Duluth in Minnesota, Butte and Missoula in Montana and Coeur d'Alene in Idaho.

MICKEY DEEMS

b: 22 April 1925, Englewood, NJ

Mickey Deems was part of the last generation of comedians who worked in vaudeville. Not the vaudeville of two-a-day shows in the big time and 30 or 40 weeks a year every year in the better small time, but vaudeville in its last decade, when it held on here and there across the USA, often booked for weekend nights only, and usually sharing the bill with a feature film.

The other alternatives for comedians were burlesque and nightclubs. After the Second World War and well into the 1950s, burlesque still attracted loyal audiences, and nightclubs, from small dens to large supper clubs, required comedians who were able to *do time*—carry the bulk of the show with jokes, impersonations, a bit of song and dance, and introduce the female singers and dancers.

Mickey Deems began as a drummer in many house bands and then segued into comedy. From small clubs, he moved into the top nighteries of the age: the Copacabana, Blue Angel and Latin Quarter in Manhattan; the Palmer House in Chicago; and several of the casino-based club rooms in Las Vegas.

In 1950, the 24-year-old Mickey Deems appeared on Broadway in *Alive and Kicking,* a Winter Garden revue with a young cast that soon claimed marquee space in other shows. Comedians David Burns, Jack Guilford, Carl Reiner, Lenore Lonergan and Mickey Deems;

dancers Jack Cole, Gwen Verdon and Bobby Van; and singer Jack Cassidy did not get strong-enough support from the song and sketch departments to push the show beyond eight weeks. Later in the decade, Mickey and Maria Karnilova were the best known of the performers in *Kaleidoscope* (1957), a more intimate revue in Greenwich Village's Provincetown Playhouse.

Mickey took the Bert Lahr role in *Waiting for Godot* (1960), an Off-(and Off-Off-) Broadway venture met mixed notices. More successful was another Off-Broadway revival, *Anything Goes* (1962) in which Deems shared honors with Hal Linden.

Deems moved uptown to the Great White Way for a straight comedy, *Golden Fleecing* (1959), which ran a couple of months, and for *Vintage '60* (1960), which did not. In 1962, Mickey was chosen to play opposite Sid Caesar in the musical comedy *Little Me,* an attempt to turn Patrick Dennis' spoof of a celebrity gold digger, Belle Poitrine, into a stage success for Sid Caesar. One of Sid's chief television writers, Neil Simon, wrote the book and changed the focus from Belle to her seven different conquests, each one played by Sid Caesar. Mickey understudied Sid and played five roles. The show ran from mid-November 1962 to the end of June 1963.

At first blush, *Royal Flash* had promise. June Havoc was the director and Jack Cole was brought in to choreograph. But Cole was replaced by Martin Green, the Gilbert & Sullivan stalwart, and Green was replaced by Martin Beaumont. The show closed out of town.

In 1963, network television brought Mickey Deems and Joey Faye together as *Mack & Myer for Hire,* two blundering handymen. Unfortunately, the show was aimed at a kiddie audience. The creativity came from Mickey's and Joey's talent and memory of old routines. It might have fared better if the TV producers had trusted *Mack & Myer* to an adult audience and provided some comedy writers.

When another perennial number-two comedian, Don Knotts, got his own self-named variety hour on NBC-TV in 1970, he wisely engaged Mickey Deems in support. All in all, Deems was a regular on several short-lived television series and a guest star on many popular evergreens. He appeared on *Car 54, Where Are You* (1950s) at least seven times and on *Three's Company* (1970s) no less than four. He also directed a number of *Car 54* episodes.

Mickey played featured roles in a number of movies popular in their day: *Diary of a Bachelor* (1964), *Hold On!* (1966), *The St. Valentine's Day Massacre* (1967), *The Busy Body* (1967), *The Spirit Is Willing* (1967), *Who's Minding the Mint?* (1967) and *With Six You Get Eggroll* (1968).

In the mid-1980s, Mickey Deems toured with Ann Miller and Mickey Rooney in the much-beloved and greatly successful valentine to burlesque, *Sugar Babies.* One of the featured specialty acts in the cast was 22-year-old comedian and juggler Daniel Rosen. Years later, Rosen spoke of his good fortune to work with both Rooney and Deems. He never missed watching him from the wings and greatly enjoyed talking with Mickey Deems, a man he claimed as his comedy mentor.

CARTER DE HAVEN

b: (Francis O'Callaghan) 5 October 1886, Chicago, IL—d: 20 July 1977, Woodland Hills, CA

Driven by a stage mother, Carter De Haven performed in vaudeville from 1896 onward, appearing as a nine-year-old child actor and entertainer. In 1904, Carter appeared in the final season of the Weber & Fields Music Hall along with Lillian Russell, Pete Dailey, John T. Kelly, Louis Mann and the McCoy sisters. Carter played the juvenile role in *Whoop-De-Doo* (1904), then the 17-year-old returned to vaudeville to sing and dance in his own flash act.

Epes W. Sargent, writing as "Chicot" in *Broadway Weekly* of 21 September 1904, observed of a subsequent vaudeville outing:

> The Carter De Haven Sextette is a surprise in one way. It shows that De Haven's season at Weber & Fields under a stage manager instead of his doting mother's direction has whipped some of the nonsense out of his head and placed him in line for better things. If he keeps it up he will make a good actor when he attains maturity.

Indeed, he did make good. He acted, sang and danced in Broadway musicals such as *The Queen of the Moulin Rouge,* which, because of a helping of vintage 1908 cheesecake, managed a good run despite the critics.

When Joe Weber and Lew Fields reunited in 1911 for a Friars' Club benefit, Carter was among the entertainers who joined Joe and Lew for the occasion.

De Haven was a handsome song-and-dance man. No longer typed as a juvenile, he was playing romantic leads by the time he was hired by Lew Fields for his productions of *Hanky Panky,* which opened in Chicago in 1911, and *All Aboard,* which toured in 1913. Carter was especially valued for his ability to sell a song, and in *All Aboard,* the now-debonair Mr. De Haven sang "In a Garden of Eden for Two" and danced with his wife, Flora Parker De Haven. In between the two Lew Fields shows, De Haven was seen in *Exceeding the Speed Limit* (1912), which ran neither fast nor long, and *The Passing Show of 1913,* which proved to have legs.

The film business, based in and around New York City, was trying to prove its artistic merit by hiring stage actors. Carter De Haven and his wife, Flora, made a number of early silent films and over the coming decades increasingly shifted their work to the movies. Carter even learned the business well enough to try his hand as a producer.

Onstage, he starred in *His Little Widows* (1917), which gave him another opportunity to sing and do a soft shoe. When the show quickly closed, despite a grand cast and good reviews, Carter went back to movieland.

Carter De Haven lived long enough to see two subsequent generations of De Havens find success in the picture business. Carter's son and some grandchildren also worked in the motion-picture business, but behind the scenes. Gloria De Haven, his granddaughter, was a popular romantic lead in 1940s film musicals and an entertainer into the 1980s. Carter De Haven reached his 90th birthday before he died.

DELANEY CIRCUIT

This group of theatres in Pennsylvania offered small-time bookings.

MILLIE DE LEON

b: ca. 1885—d: 1940

A tall, leggy dancer of better-than-usual face and figure, she began her career in burlesque as Mlle. De Leon, but the semiliterate patrons of burlesque looked more at the photographs on display in the lobby and slighted or misread the names. Her pictures warranted a longer glance than her name, and Millie De Leon she became.

In 1909, Millie was one of the bright stars of burlesque. Her goal was to be the most famous. The *New York Telegraph* described her as a "statuesque brunette, with dark eyes suggestive of the Odalisque of the East," but the patrons of burlesque were not buying *odalisque* any more than they had *mademoiselle.*

Millie and her manager, Lew Rose, knew that highfalutin' talk did not fill burlesque houses; notoriety did, so they courted scandal. In fact, Millie reveled in it. Although she was a draw, burlesque-house managers worried that her antics would bring the police and arouse the indignation of the surrounding community.

She was arrested on occasion for forgetting to don her body stocking before appearing onstage, and she steamed local bluenoses when she removed her garter onstage and tossed it to a man in the audience. That was hot stuff in 1904. When men tried to interpret such actions as invitations, her indignation was expressed with an uppercut.

Millie De Leon took an Eva Tanguay sensibility into burlesque and lowered the bar for other dancers. She made her stomach muscles rotate and roll, she quivered, she shivered, she shook in a mounting frenzy as her gulps of breath turned into moans, then tiny yelps. Male audiences drowned out the musical accompaniment with yells and cheers of their own. After the climax of her performance, she tossed garters to the audience, no longer just one but a dozen or more, and then called a few men onstage to kiss them.

In 1915, she was the primary reason police raided the show at Daly's Theatre in New York. By then, she was allowing selected customers to remove her garters for her. With an act like that, Millie De Leon did not have to look for work; producers engaged her as an added attraction, which meant she had her own solo spot toward the end of the show and was spared having to appear in sketches or production numbers. She worked with the biggest producer-comedians: Al Reeves, L. Lawrence Weber, Barney Gerard, Fred Irwin and Hurtig & Seamon.

DELIVERY

Refers to the way comedians and comedy actors speak lines whether the actor is performing a monologue or engaging in a dialogue. Delivery can be quick, slow, loud, soft, bold, subtle, fluent or stumbling. There is no one right way to speak a line in every situation. There is no right way for a particular actor to speak any line. There is a right way for a particular character to say a particular line in a particular situation. A good actor finds that way.

A comedian's delivery makes lines his own. Groucho jousted with his lines, Jack Benny mulled them over, and Eddie Cantor served them with a feigned innocence. Mae West made her dialogue undulate. Bea Lillie clipped it. W. C. Fields orated, and Bert Lahr sputtered. Jimmy Durante chopped his way through a jungle of words, stumbling in the rough patches.

Delivery is, or should be, as individual as the comedian's character, makeup, costume and movement; it illumines character as well as situation. Delivery differs from pacing, which is concerned with maintaining the rhythm and momentum of a scene. Together, delivery and pacing illumine character, set up the situation and propel the scene.

DELMAR CIRCUIT

Delmar was a small-time circuit in the Deep South centered in Alabama.

TONY DE MARCO

b: (Antonio De Marco) 1 January 1898, Buffalo, NY—d: 14 November 1965, Palm Beach, FL

Tony De Marco did not start the craze for ballroom dancing; Vernon & Irene Castle take the bow for that, and other dancers were performing exhibition ballroom dances in vaudeville before the Castles or Tony. Adelaide & Hughes, Mae Murray & Clifton Webb, Maurice & Florence Walton, Harry Fox & Jenny Dolly and Martin Brown & Rosie Dolly were a few of the many dancers who teamed up for the light fantastic before and after the Castles made it respectable and popular in 1914.

Tony De Marco, however, through a long career, established the look and style that endured. Tony revived the Rudolph Valentino image of the sensuous seducer. He even reverted to his given name of Antonio in the 1930s. De Marco's contemporaries, Veloz & Yolanda, trotted much the same path.

Tony did not spring onto the dance floor in a tuxedo. He spent many years doing various types of dancing in burlesque, speakeasies and vaudeville, performing solo at first and then with a succession of now-forgotten partners. According to some sources, he had six to eight partners; he married three of them. His first wife was Helen "Nina" Kroner. His second was known only by her professional name, Renee. Sally Craven was his third wife and his partner at the peak of their joint careers. Each marriage ended in divorce.

Sally and Tony De Marco

Tony De Marco first attracted big-time attention in *George White's Scandals* (1924). In 1929, Antonio was the dance director for *Harry Carroll's Revue* (1929). The next year, Antonio & Renee De Marco had specialty dance spots in *Girl Crazy* (1930), a hit musical that scored 272 performances at the Alvin Theatre with a cast topped by Willie Howard, Ethel Merman, Ginger Rogers, Lew Parker, Benny Goodman, Jimmy Dorsey, Jack Teagarden, Gene Krupa, Glenn Miller and the Red Nichols Orchestra. The next Broadway showcase for Antonio & Renee De Marco was in Ziegfeld's *Hotcha!* (1932), which starred Bert Lahr, Gypsy Rose Lee, Eleanor Powell and Lupe Velez and ran four months at Ziegfeld's self-named theatre.

Antonio directed the dances for Cole Porter's *Jubilee,* which lasted 21 weeks during the 1935–36 season. A good show, relying on Mary Boland for much of its appeal, it opened two days after *Porgy & Bess* and never found its way out of the shadow of Gershwin's street opera. Shortly thereafter, Antonio reverted to Tony.

Sally Craven was listed as Tony's dance partner in the movie *In Caliente* (1935), but thereafter his professional work was solo until 1940. In 1935, he still was married to Renee, although the status of their onstage partnership is unclear by the mid-1930s. Tony made an unbilled solo appearance in the film *The Shining Hour* (1938) as Joan Crawford's dance partner; the film's producers also gave him a credit as dance arranger.

Sally Craven appeared without Tony in *Very Warm for May* (1939), a musical that ran seven weeks at the Alvin Theatre on Broadway. Sally next joined Tony De Marco in two more Broadway shows: *Boys and Girls Together* (1940–41), which lasted most of the season at the Broadhurst, and *Banjo Eyes* (1941–42), the Eddie Cantor musical that ran 16 weeks at the 51st Street Theatre (later the Mark Hellinger). Tony and Sally married early in the 1940s and thereafter were billed as Tony & Sally De Marco.

His next opportunities in film came back to back. Tony appeared without Sally in Busby Berkeley's *The Gang's All Here* (1943) and with Sally in Olsen & Johnson's *Crazy House* (1943) and the Carmen Miranda musical *Greenwich Village* (1944).

The De Marco heyday came in the 1940s with the growth of posh supper clubs in major cities across the USA. San Francisco, Los Angeles, Reno, Chicago, Philadelphia, Manhattan, Boston, Palm Beach and Miami boasted hotels and supper clubs that sported top-notch floor shows that suited ballroom dancing duos. The De Marcos commanded as much as $4,000 per week.

Tony De Marco (partner unknown)

Undeniably, exhibition ballroom dance was far more popular among women than men. Men were unlikely to be pleased when they had to fumble through a foxtrot after Tony De Marco, ever lithe and masterful, had provided a fantasy for wives. Sally's haute-couture gowns were also a draw for the female audience.

Ballroom dance lost most of its general appeal after the rise of rock and roll. Nevertheless, Tony and his partner appeared no fewer than five times on Ed Sullivan's *Toast of the Town,* the CBS-TV variety show. Alone, as an actor, he also accepted a few small acting parts on television, including stints as a news vendor in *Adventures of Superman* (1956) and a waiter on *Route 66* in 1962. Tony De Marco died a few years later in the motion-picture industry's retirement residence in Woodland Hills, California.

WILLIAM DEMAREST

b: 27 February 1892, St. Paul, MN—d: 28 December 1983, Palm Springs, CA

Many vaudeville performers made the transition to character acting in talking pictures, but few were as successful as William Demarest. He enjoyed a film and television career for more than 50 years as a gruff, hard-boiled, even cantankerous tough guy. The roles varied from humorless, sometimes dim, cops to fast-talking reporters, politicians, military men, bartenders and even priests. He brought superior comic timing and a yappy bark to his dialogue.

At 12, William was the youngest of the three Demarestio Brothers (probably their real surname), who did a blackface song-and-dance act. Somehow, Bill had learned to play the cello and brought it along on his travels. Some reports claim he even played it for throw money on the streets of Manhattan when vaudeville dates were hard to get.

Bill tried a number of acts but was best remembered for performing a *nut act.* He remained a small-time vaudeville comedian until he was nearly 25, when he met, formed an act with and wed Estelle Collette. By 1917, Demarest & Collette were playing the better small time, and the next year they made it to the Palace on Broadway, the pinnacle of big-time dates.

By 1925, Bill and Estelle were playing the Palace on Broadway the week of 1 November. Joe Cook, "The One Man Vaudeville Show," was the headliner, and a Hal Roach comedy short, *Should Sailors Marry?,* with Clyde Cook, was a forecast of things to come. Demarest & Collette "returned by popular demand" to play their comedy sketch, "String and Stringers."

Demarest & Collette were back at the Palace on the sad occasion of its last two-a-day bill on 7 May 1932. Bill emceed the show and did a sketch with Estelle Collette. Other acts on the bill were Rosetta Duncan (as a single because sister Vivian was giving birth), *sepia* singer Ada Brown, knockabout comics Mitchell & Durant, Dave Apollon with his Filipino Orchestra and the Albertina Rasch (dancing) Girls.

Bill began making movies in the late silent era in 1926. All told, he made nearly 150 feature films and three television series, of which *My Three Sons* (1965–

William Demarest & Estelle Collette

72) was his best known. He also appeared as a guest star in many of the more popular dramatic, detective and Western series. Few of his films will make anyone's 100-best list, except perhaps for Preston Sturgis' *Hail the Conquering Hero* (1944), but most were competently crafted and enjoyable, not the least because William Demarest helped to pace them.

JACK DEMPSEY

b: (William Harrison Dempsey) 24 June 1895, Manassa, CO—d: 31 May 1983, New York, NY

Jack Dempsey, the heavyweight prizefighter, fought 78 fights in the ring, knocked out his opponent in 49 bouts, and in 25 of the matches the knockout was scored in the first round.

He left home at 16 to ride the rails and hobo. It was a tough challenge for a kid, and he had to learn to handle himself. He did so well, he became a brawler who fought in the western mining camps for chump change. Jack "Doc" Kearns became his manager and guided Dempsey to a profitable boxing career. In 1919, Jack Dempsey defeated heavyweight champion Jess Willard and then took on all qualified challenges, including Georges Carpentier and Luis Angel Firpo.

His fame made Dempsey a natural for some vaudeville theatres, and he scored in several different acts. Jack and Doc Kearns did a lame cross-talk act at the Hippodrome in Manhattan in 1922, but fans loved it, and Dempsey earned a bundle. With his wife, Estelle Taylor, he worked up a comedy sketch, "The Big Fight," that played extensively and profitably on Keith-Albee-Orpheum time.

Playing vaudeville much of 1922 to 1925 did not keep the champ in top shape. Gene Tunney defeated Dempsey in 1926. A rematch in 1927 produced the same result, but controversy developed over the so-called "long count" that allowed Tunney to recover after a near TKO. The referee delayed the start of the count until Dempsey complied with his order to retire to his corner.

After his second defeat by Tunney, Jack left boxing to younger lads. He stayed in the public eye by staging a series of exhibition fights that brought in some comedy in the person of Tom Kennedy, a well-known burlesque and vaudeville comedian.

Dempsey stayed famous because of his remarkable win-loss record. He opened a few restaurants during his long retirement, but his celebrity was never dependent upon playing the maître d' for customers.

DENISHAWN DANCERS

Originally, *Denishawn* was a word coined by a theatregoing contestant in a publicity campaign to name a dance. During their first joint tour, 1914–15, Ruth St. Denis and her new partner and husband, Ted Shawn, appeared with their company at a Portland, Oregon, vaudeville theatre. The manager decided to spark box-office business by holding a name-that-dance contest in advance of Ruth and Ted's opening a week hence.

The St. Denis-Shawn program presented a sampler of dance. Ruth performed one of her exotic solos—Hindu or Egyptian—Ted danced a solo to Saint-Saëns and then executed a few exhibition ballroom dances. The chore for contestants was to name the new mazurka. The winning entry was "The Denishawn Rose Mazurka"; the rose was the City of Portland's official flower.

Shortly thereafter, Ruth and Ted opened their dance school in Los Angeles. Newspaper reporters flocked because the school attracted Broadway and silent-screen stars, including Lillian Gish, Mabel Normand, Blanche Sweet, Ruth Chatterton, Carol Dempster, Ina Claire, Louise Glaum and Roszika Dolly (of the Dolly Sisters). Even the stars took their dance classes on the outdoor dance floor for all the Denishawn neighbors to see. Their practice costumes covered less flesh than did swimsuits of the day. When reporters wrote up the bohemian and arty doings at the Ruth St. Denis School of Dancing and Related Arts, they referred to the operation and place as Denishawn. On the company's next vaudeville tour, the four young intern members were billed as the Denishawn Dancers.

Neither Ted nor Ruth objected to the new name, although Ruth had reservations about submerging her independence as a woman, a star and a major international leader of interpretive dance. Certainly, Loie Fuller, Gertrude Hoffman and Isadora Duncan would not have done it. Ted was Ruth's equal in ambition and, although 23 to her 35 years old, he was as well read and nearly able to keep up with Ruth in discussions of philosophy and spirituality.

Misgivings aside, the unplanned branding of the company as Denishawn proved useful. According to the terms of the bookings, the company swelled and contracted. Ted and Brother St. Denis (Ruth's actual brother, who sometimes, as René St. Denis, doubled as a ballroom dancer) often had more than one group on the road in vaudeville. Brother and Ted offered bookers smaller groups of two to four dancers (without Ruth and Ted) as well as the entire company: Ruth, Ted and four to six members of the dance corps, plus music director and company manager (Brother St. Denis).

When one of the better dancers, Florence Andrews, went out on her own, it was felt she needed a more exotic name. Florence of Denishawn was suggested and agreed to, but a typesetter rechristened her with printers' ink as Florence O' Denishawn, and that name stayed with her throughout her career.

It was expensive for the full Denishawn company to travel. Granted, the company commanded a couple of thousand dollars per week, but spread among eight or ten performers and staff, railway tickets, meals and lodging, there was seldom any money left in the grouch bag at the end of a tour. Ted groused, 40 years later, that vaudeville managers were coarse, abusive philistines who complained that their act was too high-toned. Ted sniffed that vaudeville audiences in many parts of the country that "spent hard-earned quarters to watch a seal twirl a trumpet were not always receptive to the dances of Denishawn." Yet he took justified pride that Ruth and he had introduced Americans all over the country, not just in big cities, to new horizons in dance.

At Christmastime 1914, the troupe reached Manhattan from Los Angeles after a wearying series of one-night stands. The company was in debt, and the only work it had booked was a series of matinees at the Hudson Theatre. Brother talked some bookers into attending the matinees. Among the few who accepted was a representative of the United Booking Office (UBO), an operation dominated by the Keith-Albee empire and thus the most important booking agency in all vaudeville. He signed them for the Palace.

Ruth and the Denishawn company were such a success at New York's Palace Theatre in January 1915 that they were the only act at the time, other than Sara Bernhardt, to be held over for a second week. This led to 16 weeks on Keith-Albee time that finished up the season and got them at least partway back to the West Coast. During the summer, they looked forward to teaching, knowing they had signed contracts in their possession for a full 40-week season, 1915–16, playing mostly top-drawer Keith-Albee theatres. Full-week engagements were a welcomed change from the one-night and weekend stands of the previous season.

After proving a sensational draw at the Palace Theatre and doing quite well on the Keith-Albee circuit, the Denishawn company turned over the performance schedule to a respected concert manager, and from that point forward they played concert venues with evening-length programs rather than the 30-minute act they did in vaudeville. Beginning with the 1922–23 season, the Denishawn company toured regularly. They danced 28 weeks a year for three seasons and maintained a fairly intense schedule of bookings through the following three seasons. Summers were for teaching at the Los Angeles and the new Manhattan schools.

In 1925, the Denishawn company made a tour of Japan, the Philippines, China, Singapore, Java, Cambodia, Burma, and India and repeated some countries, including Japan. The tour lasted about 18 months. A 1927 tour of the USA brought Ruth, Ted and company to New York, where they joined in the *Ziegfeld Follies of 1927* on a tour of 38 weeks that paid them $3,500 per week.

The *Follies* tour was, practically speaking, the end of Denishawn. There were several reasons. Vaudeville itself was on the wane, and there was no longer two-a-day big-time vaudeville to rescue Denishawn finances after a concert tour that was a critical and box-office success yet paid so much less than vaudeville that there was never money left over after expenditures for costumes, transportation and lodging.

Ruth St. Denis and Ted Shawn had led separate personal and romantic lives for some time. Their union, as represented by the name Denishawn, had endured as a dance business, and it was over. The Great Depression precluded either of them from ever yielding as they always had in the past to spending vast amounts of money on costumes, settings, and lighting or touring with a 25-person company as they had done. By 1930, Ruth St. Denis had passed her 50th birthday. Her interests in dance, always both spiritual and sensual, had evolved more toward a type of temple dance worship she called Rhythmic Choir pageants. As Ted approached 40, he established himself as a solo star and turned ever more to the idea of an all-male dance company.

DEUCE SPOT, DEUCER

A number-two act. Deuce spot is second place on the bill.

DEVIL STICKS

Juggling tools consisting of three slender sticks or rods. The two shorter sticks (about 18 inches) are held in either hand to juggle and balance a third stick (approximately two feet long), which is the one actually called the devil stick. Touching the devil stick with the two handheld sticks only, the juggler tosses it in the air, back and forth, spins it and does whatever else the juggler's imagination can conjure. Originally simple wood sticks that originated centuries ago in China, modern devil sticks are made out of a range of materials: natural woods, metals, fiberglass, and so forth. Some are designed to glow in the dark; others can be lit on both ends like torches for alfresco performances at night.

Juggler and clown Keith Nelson noted that some people were offended by the age-old name of *devil* sticks and began calling them angel sticks, flower sticks, hippie sticks and rhythm sticks.

BILLY DE WOLFE

b: (William Andrew Jones) 18 February 1907, Wollaston (Quincy), MA—d: 5 March 1974, Los Angeles, CA

Bill Jones was an unsuitable name for a young entertainer about to embark on a career that placed him in the stylistic company of prissy Franklin Pangborn, the eccentric madcap Reginald Gardiner and the stuffy droll Arthur Treacher. When Bill made his debut as a dancer in a revue at the small-time vaudeville house in Quincy, Massachusetts, where he ushered, he appropriated the theatre manager's name and billed himself as Billy De Wolfe.

Billy left home to tour theatres as a dancer. He was part of a packaged show starring Jimmy O'Connor's dance band. In Manhattan, Billy teamed with two female dancers and devised an act for vaudeville. They accepted a four-week booking in England that extended into five years for Billy. While in London, he grew into a singing-and-dancing revue comedian in several of Charles Cochran's revues. As the Nazis made known their territorial ambitions, Europe crept toward a war footing. De Wolfe returned to America, where he parlayed his reputation and experience in revue into a series of cabaret bookings from Montreal to Boston to Manhattan. His style by this time was signaled by his Noël Coward impersonation, which was a centerpiece of De Wolfe's act at the Rainbow Room.

Billy enlisted in the navy when the USA allied with England and Russia in the Second World War. He had featured roles in a few Hollywood movies before his tour with the navy, and after the war he returned to Hollywood for more picture assignments.

John Murray Anderson's Almanac (1953–54) was Billy's first Broadway show. He was costarred with Hermione Gingold above the title. His London reputation from the Cochran revues of the 1930s and his success in post–Second World War cabaret in the USA gave producers the nerve to star him. Ed Sullivan was so taken with the show that he invited both Hermione and Billy on his *Toast of the Town* television variety show many times to perform bits of their sketches from the show during its run. The highlight of their pairing was Hermione and Billy's impersonation of two elderly genteel ladies taking a respite from shopping and getting crocked on sherry.

De Wolfe was recruited by the producers of the *Ziegfeld Follies of 1957,* a cheapjack production that failed to evoke the visual splendor of the original *Follies.* The talent was fine. The revue's most valuable asset was Beatrice Lillie. Billy was assigned witless material that included an Elvis Presley imitation. Harold Lang and Carol Lawrence likewise did what they could with second-rate music and lyrics. In 1964, De Wolfe replaced Rudy Vallee in the long-running musical comedy *How to Succeed in Business without Really Trying.*

Billy De Wolfe made nearly two dozen films between 1943 and 1974, usually playing the prissy and officious fussbudget and killjoy roles that once were the province of Franklin Pangborn. One of his better opportunities came with the film version of Irving Berlin's musical comedy vehicle for Ethel Merman, *Call Me Madam* (1953).

De Wolfe's best-known television venture was as a regular from 1969 to 1973 on *The Doris Day Show,* and he was a frequent guest on Johnny Carson's *Tonight Show.* In his later years, he developed lung cancer and died at 67 in Hollywood.

DIABOLOS

Hand sticks attached to a length of cord or string (like a jump rope) are used to manipulate a diabolo. Diabolos roughly resemble hourglasses. Some liken them to giant butterfly yo-yos or barbells, four to six inches in diameter, in which the connecting bar has been reduced to a groove between the two disklike bells, or ends.

The juggler uses the sticks to toss the diabolo into the air and maneuver the connecting rope so that, on the diabolo's return, it catches it in its groove. Moving his hands quickly and deftly, the juggler can make the diabolo run up and down the cord like a monorail train, balance into a cat's cradle, and do a number of other tricks by varying his speed, slackening or tightening the tension in the string, and controlling the arcs of the string. Some jugglers manipulate more than one diabolo with a single string.

DIALECT COMEDIAN

The usual basis for a two-man comedy act was one sharpie (often the feed) and one patsy (the target of physical and verbal abuse). In lieu of any real plot, this pairing prompted an exchange of insults and body blows. When the pair assumed the guise of immigrants, their comedy was compounded by misinterpretation.

In variety, many if not most comedy acts were presented as ethnic and racial characterizations. A budding comedian or comedy duo often experimented with various ethnic and racial impersonations—blackface, Irish, Jewish and Dutch (meaning German)—before finding the one that best suited the act. Often, the content of the comic dialogue and situation differed little from one racial or ethnic impersonation to the next, except in feigned accents and mispronunciations.

To increase their chances of getting bookings in and around New York City, Weber & Fields sold themselves in much the same act simply by changing their appearance and accents from blackface to Irish to Dutch. The pair still played the same aggressor and patsy combination no matter whether they adopted blackened faces and gloved hands and sputtered in minstrel *"darky"* talk, wore Irish costumes and red muttonchops and spouted a brogue of sorts, or donned German suits and chin whiskers and jabbered in some approximation of a Teutonic accent.

Coinciding with the rise in Irish and German immigration between 1820 and 1860 and the popularity of blackface minstrel shows, dialect comedy was very popular for at least 70 years. It endured even after the First World War, although it was far less prevalent; people were increasingly identifying themselves as Americans rather than by their ancestral homelands.

In the nineteenth century, and persisting into the twentieth, portrayals were often mean-spirited and demeaning; however, it is also necessary to insist that not all characterizations, even of Negroes and Jews, were not wholly unsympathetic. Insulting caricatures of Negroes and Jews did continue into the 1930s, however, whereas Germans and Irish were targeted less by unflattering impersonations as their numbers swelled in the ranks of voters and they gained power and position.

As late as the 1920s and 1930s, Al Jolson, Eddie Cantor, Rosetta Duncan and Tess Gardella often worked in blackface; Chico Marx maintained an Italian accent; Lou Holtz, Minerva Pious and Artie Auerbach told Jewish dialect stories; Jack Pearl played Baron von Munchausen; Bert Gordon was the Mad Russian; and Mel Blanc was heard on radio as a Mexican. When network television became host to variety, a major shtick in Sid Caesar's comic arsenal was his mastery of dialect gibberish, and Myron Cohen continued to tell Jewish stories. By the 1970s, dialect comedy was again ascendant. Sometimes its practitioners were exaggerating the sound of their own minority groups, whereas others took on Greek, Japanese, Chicano, Italian, English, Arab and Hindu personas and accents. Again, there was a disparity in sensitivity.

JOHNNY DIAMOND

b: ca. 1823, New York, NY (?)—d: 20 October 1857, Philadelphia, PA

Johnny Diamond was a young busker who danced for throw money at New York's old Fly Market (fly was pronounced *flee,* after the Dutch word *vlie,* meaning "valley").

Master John Diamond won his fame early, while still in his teens, by 1840. He was billed as an accomplished dancer of "Negro Camptown Hornpipe, Ole Virginny Breakdown, Smokehouse Dance and Five Mile Out of Town Dance," names designed to confirm his versatility and advertise his threat to all who would contest his primacy as a dancer.

P. T. Barnum engaged Johnny to perform at the Vauxhall Garden sometime around 1840. Johnny Diamond (it is unknown whether that was a family or stage name) was 17 or so years of age. He proved such an attraction that Barnum engaged him for his traveling show. Diamond's dance act was typical for the time. Rather than a fixed performance, it was advertised as sporting events of a sort—a "Negro breakdown"—and local dancers were challenged to try to beat him.

John Diamond was a small man, rather sharp tempered, and a chronic alcoholic, which was not unusual for the era but a barrier to a long dancing career. He was considered the only rival to Master Juba, a black dancer, but Juba bested Diamond in two out of three meets, with one ending in a draw.

DICTY

Term once used among African Americans to denote those of their race who did not hide the fact that they regarded themselves as more respectable, cultured and educated than other blacks.

DIED

Failed to please the audience and garner applause. When an act *died,* it produced a funereal atmosphere, cooled off the stage and made it hard for the next act to reengage the audience.

DIGS

Accommodations for the performers: a boardinghouse, a hotel or even a private home that would let rooms to transient performers. Finding digs was a major concern for African American performers who, throughout the vaudeville era and beyond, were often denied public accommodations near the theatres in which they were appearing.

See Boardinghouses and Hotels

PHYLLIS DILLER

b: (Phyllis Ada Driver or Diller) 17 July 1917, Lima, OH

There had been few successful female monologists before Phyllis Diller popped onto the scene in the mid-1950s. Earlier, Moms Mabley had been a fixture on the black vaudeville and club circuit since the 1930s, and Jean Carroll made her name as a stand-up comedian after starting in vaudeville as a child dancer. In 1955, when Diller began in comedy clubs, she had several advantages over her predecessors.

Society was changing radically. The USA was on the verge of social upheaval, and the clubs that nurtured Diller's development and career were the new, hip alternatives like San Francisco's Purple Onion and the Hungry I. They were part of an informal network of clubs, mostly located on either coast, that appealed to a better-educated audience with folk and blues singers, jazz combos and social-commentary comedians like Dick Gregory, Mort Sahl and Lenny Bruce, and oddballs like Irwin Corey and Lord Buckley. The traditional nightclubs relied upon the familiar male comics who assailed mothers-in-law and their wives' cooking, then introduced the girl singer and the stripper or belly dancer, and demanded little of their boozy audiences.

America, especially its women, was ready for Phyllis' onstage character. Many women had resented the idea that they could only go to public places with a male escort. They found a voice in Diller, who rejected the traditional role as wife and helpmate. Phyllis preached the gospel of the escaped housewife, hell-bent on liberation. She fled from a husband she called "Fang," a homemaking career she saw as a life sentence, and the manufactured glamour expected of women.

In some ways, her stage routine paralleled her personal life. In 1939, Phyllis left three years of classical-music studies at Chicago's Sherwood Music Conservatory for a senior year at Blufton College. She left Blufton to elope with Sherwood Anderson Diller. She spent the next 15 years raising their children and moving several times, lastly to the Bay Area of California. She cleaned house and took care of their paying boarders. Unlike most comedians, Diller started out as a long-married, middle-aged woman, mother to three daughters and two sons. Her only experience since her college days had been writing for local newspapers, ad agencies and radio stations, performing at local social functions, and cleaning, cooking and ironing.

Onstage, early in her career, she used a lot of props. Holding up an ad in Vogue magazine, she indicted the male designers who fashioned hats that made a model's head look as if it had exploded.

Although he never earned enough to support their family, her husband encouraged her to turn professional, and eventually he became her business manager. She was 37 when she got her first real gig, a substitute engagement at the Purple Onion in 1955. The club quickly brought her back, and she stayed nearly two years, honing her act with every performance. In 1957, she and Sherwood left the kids with relatives and embarked on a two-year odyssey, playing all sorts of clubs. Bob Hope saw her and encouraged her. She recorded her first comedy album in 1959. Jack Paar took a liking to her, and in 1961 she appeared on his *Tonight Show,* the first of 30 appearances. She sharpened her act, eliminating all props but her costume, a cigarette holder and hair that looked coifed by a typhoon.

Cosmetic surgery held particular fascination for her, at once a form of mutilation and a pathway to greater self-esteem. Of a film star, she noted, "She's had her face lifted so many times that there's a knot on top of her head." Of herself, she claimed that, in his initial consultation, her plastic surgeon simply recommended adding a tail. Diller punctuated each gag with a mad cackle, which allowed the audience to catch up. She also sang—and well—but gradually eliminated singing from her act.

Phyllis was not an in-your-face revolutionary, but rather than simply confide to her audience that her girdle hurt, she bragged about using it to bundle firewood. As she won more of a mainstream audience, her offbeat attire became clownishly bizarre: the Clown Alley version of a fashion model's. In another view, she was no different from earlier women who got laughs from their size, their shapelessness and their lack of sex appeal.

Diller made dozens of appearances on many TV variety shows and starred with Bob Hope in three films at the sagging end of his movie career. In 1966, she replaced Beatrice Lillie, who had declined the role, as the eccentric lady of the mansion in the TV series *The Pruitts of Southampton.* Despite the presence of such slyly arch players as Reginald Gardiner and Gypsy Rose Lee and reliable character actors Charles Lane and Grady Sutton, the scripts and direction did not live up to the original idea. Nor was Diller ideally suited to embody a character designed for Bea Lillie. The show limped along for one season. It did not hurt Diller a bit. She had been a comedy star for 10 years and remained one for 30 more.

Phyllis was her own best comedy writer, and perhaps only Totie Fields and a few men like Bob Hope rivaled Diller for effective timing in monologues. Diller never smothered a joke nor hung on too long.

She debuted on Broadway in 1970 as one of the dozen or so women who played the title role in *Hello,*

Dolly! People were astonished that she could sing. She also starred in a string of ineptly written movies. Her many record albums were better because they were essentially her stand-up act. Her most fortunate appearances on television were as a monologist; sketch comedy was not one of her strengths.

She divorced her first husband, Sherwood, in 1965. In the 1970s, she was briefly married to Warde Donovan. She enjoyed a decade of happiness with the love of her life, Robert Hastings, an attorney, until he died in 1991. Offstage, Phyllis was attractive, elegant and cultured. In later years, a series of surgical adjustments to her face and figure grew at odds with her onstage persona as an ugly duckling.

In 1971, Phyllis Diller made her debut as a concert pianist. She played Beethoven's First Piano Concerto with the Dallas Symphony Orchestra. Over the next 20 years, Diller performed as a piano soloist with 100 symphony orchestras across the USA.

Although Phyllis, by then a grandmother, continued in the 1980s to perform as a stand-up comedian, her appearances became rarer. At 81, she had a pacemaker implanted. Three years later, in May 2002, nearly 85 years old, she announced her retirement.

DIME MUSEUMS

Situated in many of the East Coast's larger cities, dime museums appeared before the Civil War and were one of vaudeville's early, seedy antecedents. Some of the older states and commonwealths clung to the blue laws of Colonial times that forbade many forms of entertainment other than uplifting drama and concert music. Smart showmen got around the law by imitating their betters. They, too, opened *museums,* advertised them as educational—even though their exhibits tended to the fraudulent and sensational—and housed them in storefronts in highly trafficked downtown areas.

Instead of Pre-Raphaelite paintings and Roman copies of Greek statuary, they exhibited human and nonhuman animals born with one too few or one too many limbs along with albinos or the skinniest or fattest or smallest human and jarred or stuffed specimens of anything that would shock the viewers.

On their upper floors, they presented "for the public's edification" an "educational demonstration" of the occult, the arts of Muses Euterpe and Terpsichore, and superhuman strength. Translated to the vernacular, this meant a magician, a motley duo or trio of musicians, a skirt dancer in scanty clothes and a muscleman in scanty clothes. Although their demonstrations often scraped the bottom of the show-business barrel, the dime museums gave early performers as diverse and talented as Ruth St. Denis and Weber & Fields their first opportunities.

DISAPPOINTMENT ACT

An act who works only when others do not. Often unable to win regular bookings on their own, disappointment acts were on call by various agents to substitute for another act in the area that failed to show up for an engagement, got sick or was canceled. In fairness, it must be acknowledged that some acts that were quite good refused bookings because of family obligations or other such reasons. Because variety was essential when booking, there were a limited number of dates a local act could play in a metropolitan area before the public tired of them. Often, a reasonable alternative was to offer themselves as disappointment acts.

DIVE

Many towns situated along railroad lines throughout the frontier territories of the USA sported opium parlors that were patronized by cattlemen and miners as well as Chinese rail workers. Opium came ashore on the Barbary Coast of San Francisco, and a network of smugglers masquerading as tradesmen and salesmen dispersed the drug inland. The opium parlors were called *dives* because they were furnished chockablock with *divans* for their soon-to-be recumbent clientele.

With usage, the term *dive* was expanded to refer to any low-down or nefarious establishment that specialized in intoxicants.

DIXON & FREEMAN

Jessica Dixon

b: 18 November 1888

Frank Freeman

b: 1884

Kathleen Freeman

b: 17 February 1919, Chicago, IL—d: 23 August 2001, New York, NY

Dixon & Freeman were a *black-and-tan, mixed-double,* or *flirtation act.* Jessica Dixon wore tan makeup, and Frank Freeman blacked up. In several ways, they were representative of a majority of vaudevillians. They did not change their act except in particulars, performing in blackface after it had fallen out of public favor, and they stayed in vaudeville until the bitter end.

Dixon & Freeman

Frank Freeman started his career in minstrelsy around 1890 and worked up to being an end man in Lew Dockstader's Minstrels:

Interlocutor: "I understand you are anxious to join the army. What branch of the army would you prefer?

End Man: "Oh, the Infantry, by all means."

Interlocutor: "Infantry, eh? I should think you would have preferred some other branch, for instance the cavalry. Just picture yourself galloping along on a noble steed, charging right up to the enemy trenches."

End Man: "Dat's all right. Dat's all right. I know all about that 'charging the enemy on a noble steed' stuff, but say, when they sound 'the retreat,' I don't want to be hindered by draggin' no old hoss along with me, no sir."

Jessica Dixon's earliest performances were a world away from Frank's. She began singing around 1910 as a professional soloist for two Methodist churches in Los Angeles, and she appeared from 1912 to 1916 in the annual mission play. Her concert career was extensive. As "Miss Dixon, Dramatic Soprano," she appeared with philharmonic orchestras and in recital.

She moved into vaudeville on Bert Levy time, bookings that allowed her to remain in California. When the USA began to train men for the impending First World War, the Over There Theatre League petitioned the YMCA, which ran the entertainment programs for the American Expeditionary Forces (AEF), to recruit Jessica to lead a concert party (a troupe) to the battle zones.

When Dixon went overseas, her concert party, the Philharmonic Four, included pianist Kathleen Morris, violinist Harriet Gates and reader Florence Redfield. Their repertoire included art songs, operatic arias and recitations. They played 250 concerts in 18 months, and Jessica received the following AEF commendation: "Miss Dixon, Prima Donna Soprano, during the late war, sang to more than two hundred thousand of our boys in England and France and with the Army of Occupation."

Upon her return, she worked Pantages time, filling in jumps with low-paying Bert Levy gigs. Around 1920, perhaps realizing that vaudeville was not quite the place for soprano renditions of an aria from Charpentier's opera *Le Pui du Jour* or of genteel ballads like "Rose of My Heart" and "The Spirit Flower," Jessica went into a musical comedy, *Hello Papa, or The Ambassador's Reception,* starring Joe Kemper.

Jessica then entered vaudeville as "The Overseas Girl," playing decent circuits like Orpheum, Pantages and Shubert Advanced, as well as smaller, more marginal circuits like Junior Orpheum and Interstate, and the Ackerman & Harris *Death Trail.*

Meanwhile, Frank was half of a singing double act billed as Freeman & Dunham. Because Frank was later associated with veterans' groups, he may have served in the First World War and met Jessica Dixon during his service. Whatever the circumstances of their meeting, they were married by the war's end in 1918.

When Jessica and Frank first teamed in vaudeville, the act was billed as "Jessica Dixon, The Overseas Girl, assisted by Frank Freeman, The Minstrel Man." By 1922, they had altered their billing to "Dixon & Freeman, The Overseas Girl and The Minstrel Man." By 1924, it read "Dixon & Freeman, Black & Tan Song & Comedy Sketch."

A 1922 review judged, "Headline honors must be divided between Dixon & Freeman, of whom Miss Jessica Dixon, an overseas entertainer, is the feature who gives several songs in splendid voice and charming personality. However, it is the knowledge that she spent 18 months singing before the doughboys on the other side that makes her particularly interesting. With her is a partner who sings several songs in blackface and makes a good mimic of Eddie Cantor."

A sense of their act can be gleaned from the following communication:

Hotel Irving
Philadelphia, PA
September 22nd, 1924

Henry Chesterfield, Secretary,
National Vaudeville Artists,
229 West 46th Street,
New York City, N.Y.

Dear Mr. Chesterfield:

The following is a description with continuity of act of DIXON & FREEMAN, "THE SINGER and THE MINSTREL", which we wish to register with your organization, the N.V.A.

Man and woman, black and white. Thirteen minutes in one, six changes of wardrobe. Open with two slides. One announcing and the other gives reason. Lady follows with number, "My Hero" from *Chocolate Soldier,* exit. Two . . . Man working in pit, colored preacher number, "Oh Death Where Is Thy Sting," special business. Three . . . Slide reading Miss Dixon's Idea of How She Would Have Looked and Sung To The Boys Of 1861. Lady follows slide singing a medley of period "61" numbers. Four . . . man enters using two stories and goes into medley popular numbers of to-day. Five . . . N.B. This idea for our finish please note. Lady sings [undecipherable] Faust . . . after singing a repeat of twelve bars . . . effect of lightning and thunder, man laughing off stage and then enters character of Mephisto (BLACK) using words "Ye Gods," one for Spot, continuing with "I HAD A DEVILISH TIME GETTING HERE" follow with special chorus of "I AM A DEVIL," closing double with Lady singing last eight bars of this and man doing pantomime and heavy laugh.

We have been doing the above act for three years but have not been into New York with same and while we know of no others doing anything near the routine we will feel better satisfied and more comfortable by apprising you of the foregoing details.

Thanking you for any interest you make take in the matter, beg to remain,

Very Truly Yours
DIXON & FREEMAN

Dixon & Freeman were a number-two act and averaged $25 per night to $225 a week from the early 1920s up to 1925, when their salary began to drop. By 1927, Jessica and Frank earned as high as $15 and as low as $10 per night, minus 5%.

By 1929, one- and two-night stands were standard. The booking slips gave in cryptic language the where and when: "Rivoli Theatre, Bergenline Ave. & 13th Street, West New York, N.J. for two days, three shows daily, salary $18.00, minus 5%, fare & baggage by artist, piano only." That translated to: the only music accompaniment was a piano, and out of the $17.10 net, they had to pay for transportation.

By 1930, bookings were scarce as hens' teeth, and it was difficult to put together a coherent route of dates. A 9 January communication from the White Entertainment Bureau in Times Square read in part: "I note that you are accepting the Bridgeport date, and I shall make every effort to place the 7th, but of course, this is a strange business, and it may be that I will have no requests for that date. Should you have the opportunity of filling it, do not hesitate to do so."

At the end of the trail, Frank Freeman was working as an editor for the *Ad Age,* the weekly bulletin of the San Francisco Advertising Club, and in office positions for the California Artists' Protective Association and the International Alliance of Theatre Stage Employees (IATSE). He kept his hand in show business by producing special-event shows for various charities, especially veterans associations of which he was a member.

There are Second World War rationing books extant for Kathleen Freeman, their daughter, Frank Freeman and Mildred Ruth Freeman, all sharing the same Los Angeles address, so it is not clear whether Jessica Dixon's and Frank Freeman's marriage weathered the bad times of the 1930s, if he remarried, or even if Jessica Dixon Freeman was still alive by 1940.

Their daughter, Kathleen Freeman (1919–2001), worked in the family act from the age of two until she was ten. By then, vaudeville was a shadow of what it had been in its prime, and young Kathleen left vaudeville to attend public school. At the University of California at Los Angeles (UCLA) she studied piano and composition.

Kathleen Freeman became one of Hollywood's most beloved and recognizable character comedians for 50 years, advancing from bit parts in *Naked City* (1948) and *Mr. Belvedere Goes to College* (1949) to a voice-over for *Shrek* (2001). She had the distinction of appearing in two versions of the *Nutty Professor* (1963 and 2000) and two of the *Blues Brothers* (1980 and 2001), in which she played Mother Mary Stigmata.

Among the television series on which she was a recurring character were *Topper, The Beverly Hillbillies, Hogan's Heroes, Married with Children* (voice of Peg Bundy's mother), and *Caroline in the City.* On the stage, Kathleen Freeman was accepted as a serious actor. She appeared in many dramas and coached students in university workshops. Freeman was one of the nominees for the 2001 Tony Award for best featured actress in a musical for her performance as Jeanette Burmeister, the role she originated, in the Broadway production of *The Full Monty.* She died that year while in the show.

DOCK

Section of the backstage area where scenery is stored. It is located as near as possible to dock doors through which scenery and large furnishings are loaded to and from conveyances.

LEW DOCKSTADER

b: (George Alfred Clapp) 7 August 1856, Hartford, CT—d: 26 October 1924, New York, NY

He was one of the last great minstrel men, an entertainer who preferred the tradition and format of refined minstrelsy to vaudeville, yet, late in his career, Lew Dockstader turned to the two-a-day.

He was still called George Clapp when he began singing in public, and he did so with local amateur groups who put on minstrel shows in his hometown of Hartford, Connecticut. In 1873, the 16-year-old Clapp was paired with Frank Lawton in a song-and-dance double act that caught the eye of Larry Bloodgood, who invited Lew to join Bloodgood's Comic Alliance. That was Clapp's first professional job. Many others followed, including a tour with Wood's Minstrels, in which Clapp distinguished himself with his drag burlesque of Camille in *La Dame aux Camélias,* and with Whitmore & Clark's Minstrels.

Upon reaching Manhattan in 1878, Clapp joined Charles Dockstader, an older minstrel, in an act called the Dockstader Brothers, and George Clapp became Lew Dockstader. Upon the death of Charles, he retained his stage name of Lew Dockstader.

Managing a minstrel company was an uneven adventure. Sometimes Lew was flush with a bankroll; other times he was scraping near empty coffers for coins. He dissolved his own company and joined others, including Carncross' Minstrels, a Philadelphia institution, in 1885. Evidently, he was soon flush again because, in 1886, he established his own resident minstrel company in Manhattan, which prospered for three seasons before Lew took a troupe on the road from coast to coast.

In 1898, Lew partnered with George Primrose, another of the remaining big minstrelsy names, as Primrose & Dockstader's Minstrel Men. Both Primrose and

Lew Dockstader

Dockstader probably preferred running their own show, but their partnership revived flagging public interest in minstrelsy, and the two men maintained their joint company for six years. Dockstader kept some of the company under his own banner, and others went with Primrose.

Lew managed to keep a company working for several seasons, and it provided an incubator for talent that soon headlined in vaudeville and starred in revue. Lew attracted dancers like Harland Dixon, Jack Corcoran and Jimmy Doyle to his troupe, but it was hard to keep top performers with a minstrel wage of $20 per week when vaudeville offered double or better (even if the work was not as consistent). In 1909, he hired a young fellow named Al Jolson. Solo spots in a minstrel show were for stars, such as Dockstader, but Jolson pestered Lew until he gave in. So popular did Jolson prove that Lew yielded his star spot in the show to Al.

Lew must have realized that show business was changing. Jolson, although he worked in blackface, personified the move from the old-style Stephen Foster plantation harmonies and dances to the ragtime and early jazz eras. Dockstader had come into minstrelsy when it was one of the most popular of theatrical entertainments in America. By 1900, the momentum was with vaudeville and the blossoming musical comedy and revue. By 1910, he made occasional appearances as a monologist in vaudeville.

Lew was well suited to vaudeville, although he was more fond of and attuned to minstrelsy. In addition to being a fine singer, Lew had developed a stump speech, a specific type of comic monologue much in favor in the 1890s and 1900s. The stump speeches were humbug parodies of politicians (and occasionally preachers), and Lew's specialty was his imitation of Teddy Roosevelt, vice president and president at the time.

Lew gave up minstrelsy but not blackface when he went into vaudeville full time in 1913. He spent most of his remaining career in two-a-day on Keith time. He brought his most famous song, "Everybody Works but Father," from minstrelsy to vaudeville and finally to the new phenomenon that was sound recordings. In his last years as an entertainer, he abandoned blackface and singing—he was in his 60s—to concentrate upon his comic monologues. Lew's career spanned 50 years, and he did not fully retire until a few years before his death at 68.

DODGERS

Printed on cheap-grade paper, dodgers were handbills or flyers, more often tossed around the streets and sidewalks than handed out. They advertised the fun and frolic at various melodeons and concert saloons.

DOLLY SISTERS

Rosie Dolly

b: (Roszika Deutsch) 25 October 1892, Budapest, Hungary—d: 1 February 1970, New York, NY

Jenny Dolly

b: (Janszieka "Yancsi" Deutsch) 25 October 1892, Budapest, Hungary—d: 1 June 1941, Hollywood, CA

The Dolly Sisters were identical twins, brunette beauties from Hungary. Their almond-shaped eyes, olive skin, and perfectly molded faces and figures represented exotic allure to audiences in Europe and the USA. They came as children to America and were still young when they worked up a dance act for vaudeville. Although their first vaudeville date of record is 1909 at Keith's Union Square Theatre at 14th Street, it seems likely that they had honed their act in less famous theatres.

The next season, producer Charles Dillingham signed Rosy and Jenny for the musical *The Echo.* Bessie McCoy and George White starred, and the music was composed by Deems Taylor. The show opened in mid-August and closed by the end of October 1910.

The Dolly Twin Sisters made their first revue appearance in the *Ziegfeld Follies of 1911.* Bessie McCoy and George White went with the Dolly Sisters to the *Ziegfeld Follies.* Among the more prominent in that season's edition were Bert Williams, Leon Errol and Fanny Brice. The Dolly Sisters' dance number represented them as conjoined twins, a bizarre idea that audiences of the day found charming. With their next musical, *The Merry Countess* (1912), Rosie and Jenny enjoyed a four-month run at the Casino, then under Shubert management and in the shadow of its more glorious past.

They were graceful dancers, but their routines were no more intricate or demanding of athleticism than ballroom dances. They did not sing or act, and they changed costumes and jewelry more often than their dance steps. Their success was founded in glamour and the novelty of twinned beauty; few could tell them apart. The most adventurous part of their lives was offstage. They juggled male admirers and accepted jewels, luxury automobiles and other expensive gifts without embarrassment. Occasionally, they married.

Rosie married songwriter Jean Schwartz in 1913. He wrote the music for her ballroom-dance act with Martin Brown. Between 1913 and 1915, the two sisters tried separate careers. Rosie appeared without a partner in *The Whirl of the World* (1914). Willie & Eugene Howard toplined the cast, and the show ran from January though May. At the same time, Jenny paired with dancer Harry Fox onstage and off. They were part of an all-star cast in the Winter Garden extravaganza *Honeymoon Express* (1914), and they played the Palace in 1914. (She divorced Fox in 1921, the same year that Rosie shed Jean Schwartz.)

Hollywood beckoned. Jennie made *The Call of the Dance* (1915), and Rosie appeared in *The Lily and the Rose* (1915). Earlier that year, Rosie performed in a George M. Cohan show, *Hello Broadway* (1914–15), which starred Cohan, William Collier, Louise Dresser, Florence Moore and Peggy Wood. In January 1916, the Dolly Sisters danced together in the *Ziegfeld Midnight Frolic* and played their first vaudeville date as a sister act at the Palace. By this time, they commanded $2,000 per week. *His Bridal Night* (1916), although it included one song, was a play. It ran for 77 performances and proved that the Dolly Sisters should be seen but not heard.

The Dolly Sisters appeared in their only film as a team when they made the purportedly autobiographical *The Million Dollar Dollies* (1918). Later that year, they headed the touring company of *Oh, Look!* Harry Fox was a holdover from the Broadway company.

At the close of the First World War, the Dolly Sisters bought a château in Fontainebleau, toured Europe, and starred at the Casino de Paris in London, where they taught the *haute monde* all the latest naughty American dances like the Charleston and Black Bottom.

They found, however, that performing in shows and vaudeville cut into their earning power. Gift-bearing millionaires of Monte Carlo, Deauville, London and Paris were standing in line. King Christian of Denmark, King Carol of Romania, King Alfonzo of Spain and the prince of Wales courted them. Their admirers bought the chips in gambling casinos, and Rosie and Jenny pocketed all the earnings and suffered few of the losses. The twins pulled in nearly $1 million from the casinos at Cannes. When the Moulin Rouge offered them 5,000 francs per day (more than the star Mistinguette received), they accepted. When Mistinguette threatened to quit, the Moulin Rouge backed out of their contract with the twins. Rosie and Jenny sued and collected. They no longer had to perform to collect a salary.

Perhaps they needed the exercise when they accepted a bid to star in the *Greenwich Village Follies of 1924*. The Dolly Sisters were given a number, "The Dollies and the Collies." As Rosie and Jenny moved about the stage, trained collies mimicked the Dolly Sisters' movements. It was probably easier for choreographer Larry Ceballos to train the collies to imitate the twins than for the sisters to mimic the collies.

In 1927, Rosie married Mortimer Davis, the son of a Canadian tobacco millionaire, but Davis' dad cut Rosie off from a possible inheritance, and in 1931 that marriage, too, failed. Rosie wed prominent merchant Irving Netcher the following year and stayed married to him until his death in 1943.

In 1931, Jenny was mad for Max Constant, a dashing French flyboy, but her 51-carat, square-cut diamond ring, emerald necklace, diamond necklace and other sparklers were in danger of losing their collective reputation as the most valuable privately owned jewel collection. H. Gordon Selfridge, owner of the self-named London department store, offered Jenny $10 million to marry him in 1933.

What was a young woman to do? Jenny tested her love by running off for a last weekend thrill with Max. On their way back to Paris, Max accidentally crashed the sports car he was driving. Jenny was so seriously injured that it took many surgical procedures to patch her together. She underwent plastic surgery to restore her face. Selfridge, a gallant, paid the bills. Jenny was emotionally crushed, and marriage no longer was on the agenda.

Rosie and her husband, Irving Netcher, brought Jenny to their home in Chicago and introduced her to wealthy lawyer Bernard Vinissky. Jenny and Bernard wed in 1935, but her melancholy increased rather than lessened. In 1941, in Hollywood, Jenny hanged herself from a shower rod. Exactly one year later, in 1942, Max Constant died in a plane crash.

Both sisters had displayed charitable impulses, and Jennie left behind two Hungarian war orphans she had adopted after the First World War. After their retirement from the stage in the late 1920s, Rosie began to shun the spotlight. Never as madcap as Jenny, Rosie spent a good deal of the money she had accumulated in providing for the children of her defeated and ruined homeland, Hungary.

DOMINIQUE

b: (Dominique Risbourg) April 1932, Paris, France

Starting out as a child actor in Paris, Dominique Risbourg quickly developed a passion for magic and ventriloquism. The son of the chief engineer of the Suez Canal, he declined a university education in order to become a professional entertainer. As a way to make his audiences laugh, the teenage magician added a pickpocket routine in his act, with which he toured the nightclubs of postwar Europe. A favorable French newspaper write-up led to a booking at the Moulin Rouge in Paris. He soon dropped the magic and was starred in the show as a pickpocket and comedian.

The owner of the venue decided to produce a revue in the USA; soon Dominique was performing in America. A four-page spread in *Life* magazine about his act sparked a sensational career in top nightclubs, including a record-breaking four-month starring run at the Latin Quarter in New York. For the next few decades, he was the starring act in many major production shows in Las Vegas and appeared on virtually every television variety program in the world. In the early 1990s he decided to retire to Paris, France, with his wife and family.

At its peak, Dominique's act was a whirlwind of brash comedy that began as he entered the stage through the audience, shaking hands with everyone in sight while at the same time lifting wallets, watches, keys, pens and combs. By the time he made his way onto the stage, his pockets were bulging. He then had his assistant return the goods to the spectators while he coaxed a half-dozen male volunteers to join him onstage and proceeded to relieve them of their personal goods, such as watches and wallets and even belts, suspenders and shirts! He would then have this committee of spectators sit down on seemingly unprepared chairs that would jolt the men up onto their feet as if they were hit by an electric shock, which would cause gales of laughter.

As a counterpoint, he also performed a beautiful magic trick in which he played classical guitar, and while the orchestra accompanied him, he took a break to wipe his brow with a couple of small paper napkins. The napkins then suddenly came alive and wafted about in the air as if they were butterflies. Two or three came to rest on a single rosebud that protruded from the tuning pegs of his guitar. His other trademark was a sensational magic trick in which he changed a woman in the audience into a goat.

JACK DONAHUE

b: 1892, Boston, MA—d: 1 October 1930, New York, NY

Vaudeville offered Jack Donahue the chance to escape a lifetime as a laborer at the Charlestown Navy Yard that provided blue-collar employment for most of the men in Jack's Irish neighborhood. He was a streetwise kid with an easy charm, and he picked up dancing the way the other neighborhood boys did, by watching the hoofers at the local vaudeville houses. The boys then tried to recall and figure out the steps they had seen.

In *Letters from a Hoofer to His Ma,* Jack Donahue left a humorous record of his experience as a single in 1910, playing the small time in New England. Earlier, around 1902, Jack, then a lad of 10, ran away from home with a medicine show. For a spell, he traveled with the Young & Adams Repertory Company; he danced in the olio between acts of the melodrama or farce. There were nearly 350 such theatrical companies barnstorming various regions of America at the time. The odds were high on small road-show companies failing, and the odds were no better that, upon failing, managers would abscond with a week's box-office take and leave their players stranded. When this happened to Jack in Chicago, he hitched up with a burlesque company and worked his way back east.

By 1910, Donahue had added a line of patter and jokes to his hoofing. He was getting $20 to $30 per week, minus an agent's fee and booking levy that skimmed $2.50 to $4.00 off the top. Depending on the length of the jump between dates, train fares each way hovered between $1 and $2. Rooms were $1 to $1.50 per night, and, if one was smart, tips were in order: 15 cents to a porter and a dime to a bellboy. Provided Jack did not get ill or canceled, he netted $10 to $20 a week, which he tossed away on food, laundry, shoe repair, postage stamps, phone calls, paying off old debts and mailing a dollar or two to the old folks back home. By season's end, though, Jack's salary had risen to $35 a week.

Even in 1910, movies were a big part of the small, small-time vaudeville bill. Sometimes it was a gymnast who opened the show, followed by Jack in the number-two spot, and a couple of short silent flickers until, at the last, the *pièce de résistance,* a contest to select the prettiest girl worker at the local factory. In the better small time, there were five acts on a bill; among them might be a contortionist, opera singers, jugglers, an acrobat with a barrel-jumping finish, a singing sisters and hoop-rolling act, a ventriloquist, a school act comprised of three fellows and three young women, a musical act with xylophone and drums, a fire- and glass-eater, a whistler performing bird imitations, trick cyclists or any of the many small timers who fancied themselves singers or comedians.

In addition to listing the type of acts to be found on a small-time New England bill, Jack's memoir detailed a typical route (made up mostly of split weeks and few full weeks). A small-time act took the dates he got even if the jumps required a miracle to arrive on time. His route for the 12-week period between 18 April and 2 July 1910 was:

Manchester, NH, Bijou Theatre
South Framingham, MA, Princess Theatre
Taunton, MA, Broadway Theatre
Hathaway's New Bedford Theatre
Newport, RI, Opera House
Westerly, RI, Star Theatre
Lynn, MA, Comique Theatre
Salem, MA, Salem Theatre
Lowell, MA, Opera House
Woonsocket, RI, Family Theatre
Biddeford, ME, Opera House
Sanford, ME, Comique Theatre
Lewiston, ME, Empire Theatre
Portland, ME, Jefferson Theatre
North Attleboro, MA, Lyric Theatre
Rutland, VT, Grand Theatre

Jack met, wed and developed an act with Alice Stewart. Their performance was typical of the time: a double act with comedy and eccentric dancing. Alice Stewart retired after a couple of seasons, and Jack reverted to his dancing-and-patter single. By 1915, Jack Donahue had broken into the big time and had been booked at the Palace on a bill with Weber & Fields, Herb Williams, Lew Hearn (all comedians), dancer Gertrude Hoffman, and song-and-dance man Eddie Leonard. Donahue returned to the Palace on several occasions in the early 1920s.

His style, like all dancers before and after him, was modeled on the previous generation of dancers and his own contemporaries. Critics and dancers, who knew and praised Jack Donahue's work, also saw the strong influence of Harland Dixon, and Jack admitted his admiration for Dixon. Critics praised Donahue's "lissome vaulting" and his clowning, and he had an endearing stage personality as well as talent and skill.

Jack's first featured role in a revue was not on Broadway. He was hired for the road show of *Hitchy-Koo of 1918,* the second edition of an annual series starring Raymond Hitchcock. Jack probably took the place of Leon Errol, a comedian and eccentric dancer, who had costarred and staged the first two, *Hitchy-Koo of 1917* and *Hitchy-Koo of 1918.*

Donahue made it to Broadway, if only for 57 performances, when *Angel Face,* a musical comedy, opened on 29 December 1919. He had better luck in the *Ziegfeld Follies of 1920* and *Molly Darling,* another musical that tried out in Washington, D.C., before it opened on 1 September 1922 on Broadway and ran for 101 performances. *Be Yourself,* with a book by Marc Connolly & George S. Kaufman, disappointed cast and producers when it scored only 93 performances after its opening on 22 September 1924. On 18 November 1922, Jack joined dozens of Broadway luminaries, among whom were Ethel Barrymore, Savoy & Brennan, Vivienne Segal and Laurette Taylor, for *The Midnight Jollies,* a benefit at the Hotel Astor for Actors' Equity.

By the time he reached his 30th birthday, Jack Donahue's health was failing. He was beset by physical problems stemming from heart disease, high blood pressure and kidney disease. He gave up his energetic dancing and relied more on his gift for comedy. Charles Dillingham's musical comedy *Sunny,* a vehicle for Marilyn Miller, presented Jack in a featured role. Opening on 22 September 1925, it racked up an astonishing 517 performances. Marilyn Miller was starred again for Ziegfeld when she appeared in *Rosalie,* which opened on 10 January 1928. The musical comedy played 327 performances, and Jack had the comic lead, cast as an air cadet afraid to fly.

To lessen the strain on his body, Jack explored other show-business options. He gave his name to a dancing school in Manhattan. Most of the instruction was given by dance director John Boyle, and Eleanor Powell became its most celebrated alumnus. Donahue also began to write and produce for the stage.

He produced, cowrote the book and starred in *Sons O' Guns.* It opened on 26 November 1929 with Lily Damita and William Frawley in support. After giving 297 shows on Broadway, the show went on tour. Also as a producer, Jack was readying a straight play, *Lost Sheep,* slated to open on Broadway on 5 May 1930. Jack Donahue had been working nonstop for a decade, and with both *Sons O' Guns* and *Lost Sheep* claiming his attention, he was overworked and physically drained. His heart gave out and he died on 1 October 1930. He was 38 years old.

KITTY DONER

b: (Catherine Donohue) ca. 1894, Chicago, IL—d: 26 August 1988, Los Angeles, CA

According to contemporary reviewers, Kitty Doner excelled as a dancer as well as being the equal of any male impersonator, American or British. The acts of most male impersonators, like Vesta Tilley, Ella Shields and Hetty King, emphasized comic character songs embellished with good humor and a few dance steps. Doner also sang and created characterizations, but her dancing distinguished her from the rest.

In what was thought to be a compliment, Doner's dancing was praised as masculine. Kitty explained that was because she was trained by her father, Joe Doner, an eccentric vaudeville dancer whose turns combined character impressions with a virile style of dancing. Kitty made her debut in the family act. Her mother, Nellie, often performed as a principal boy in British pantomimes, so the cross-dressing tradition was well established in the family.

Kitty was born in Chicago while Joe and Nellie were playing American vaudeville. Tall and lanky as a youngster, Kitty was costumed by her father as a

Kitty Doner

Kitty Doner

male in the family act. Later, she played both female and male characters in her own act. Kitty Doner was still a teen when the Shuberts engaged her for the replacement cast of *The Passing Show of 1913.* Evidently, she worked out well because the Shuberts signed her as a featured player in three musicals that showcased Al Jolson: *Dancing Around* (1914), *Robinson Crusoe, Jr.* (1916) and *Sinbad* (1918). There were rumors that a casual romance developed between Doner and Jolson. Some folks believed that Jolson started the rumor.

After five years back in England, Kitty returned to Broadway in *The Dancing Girl* (1923), another Shubert show, in which she danced with her brother, Ted Doner (1896–1979). The musical comedy also starred Marie Dressler and Jack Pearl and ran for four months at the large Winter Garden theatre.

Kitty made two one-reel Vitaphone shorts back to back in 1928: *A Famous Male Impersonator* and *A Bit of Scotch.* Increasingly, her professional time was spent in American vaudeville, including appearances on the bills at the Palace for 1919, 1926, 1928 and 1932.

When it was apparent that vaudeville was unable to rebound after losing popularity to network radio and Hollywood talking pictures, Kitty, then approaching 40, moved behind the scenes as a dance director before she retired. It is an intriguing coincidence that longevity blessed most of the well-known male impersonators: Vesta Tilley (88), Ella Shields (73), Hetty King (89) and Kitty Doner (93).

DON'T SEND OUT YOUR LAUNDRY

A manager might cancel an act after the first matinee performance, so acts were advised verbally and by signs posted backstage not to send out their laundry until they were sure they would be retained on the bill by the manager of the local theatre.

RAY DOOLEY

b: (Rachel Rice Dooley) 30 October 1896, Glasgow, Scotland—d: 28 January 1984, East Hampton, NY

The Dooley family grew up in show business. The father, Robert Rogers Dooley, was a circus performer turned minstrel man, and Ray was a youngster when she began performing in her father's minstrel act. At various times during her early vaudeville career, she went out as a single or formed an act with one of her brothers. Billed as "The Live Wire," Ray Dooley made her initial appearance at the Palace Theatre in 1917 with her brother Gordon, a dancing comedian. Ray appeared at the Palace several times between her debut with her brother and the act she did with her husband, Eddie Dowling, in 1932. She also had her own act, Ray Dooley and Her Metropolitan Minstrels.

Even as an adult, Ray was slight and barely five feet tall. She was able to play children in comedy sketches even in her 20s, and it was her impersonation of a mischievous child that secured her fame in the *Ziegfeld Follies.*

Of all the lead comedians who appeared with some frequency in the *Follies* produced by Ziegfeld, only two were women: Fanny Brice and Ray Dooley. (The Duncan Sisters appeared in *Ziegfeld's Midnight Frolics,* and Tallulah Bankhead and Beatrice Lillie starred in posthumous productions of the *Ziegfeld Follies.*) Fanny is remembered with great affection because movies, phonograph recordings and especially network radio extended her fame and preserved some of her performances. Ray Dooley, one of her era's top comedians, is known to have appeared only once in a movie, a presumably lost Paramount picture, *Honeymoon Lane* (1931), that starred Eddie Dowling and was adapted from his Broadway show of the same name. Consequently, Ray Dooley has not been included in most books about comedians.

Most of what remains in the record about Ray Dooley is connected to the five editions of the *Ziegfeld Follies* in which she appeared (1919, 1920, 1921, 1925 and 1926 (which was also known as *No Foolin'*).

Bert Williams, Marilyn Miller and Eddie Cantor were the big names in the *Ziegfeld Follies of 1919.* Shortly before Ray first joined the *Follies* in 1919, Ray married Eddie Dowling.

Ray and her brother Johnny were recruited from *Hitchy-Koo of 1918,* but Eddie Dowling did not have to move. He was in the cast of Erlanger's *The Velvet Lady* that was closing at the New Amsterdam, where the *Follies* was slotted as the incoming production. Ray, Johnny and Eddie appeared along with Bert Williams and Eddie Cantor in the minstrel number that closed the first act of the *Ziegfeld Follies of 1919.*

Ray also showed to good advantage in the 1920 edition of the *Follies.* She played the daughter of W. C. Fields and Fanny Brice in one skit and appeared in a park scene as a squalling baby who got drunk on the spiked milk she was given to quiet her. Ray appeared in no fewer than three sketches in the 1921 *Follies,* two as her patented brat and one with Fanny Brice in a ladies' impersonation of a boxing match.

Ray left the *Follies* for a couple of seasons. During that time, she played big-time vaudeville and performed in *Nifties of 1923,* a six-week disappointment written by and starring old Weberfields alumni Sam Bernard and William Collier. Helen Broderick, Van & Schenck and Hazel Dawn were also in that Dillingham-produced revue.

Both Ray and W. C. Fields joined the cast in 1925 for the second season of the *Ziegfield Follies of 1924.* Fields came into the *Follies* straight from the failure of *The Comic Supplement,* a revue intended to showcase Fields. It never reached Broadway, so Fields took his best material from the wreckage and brought it into the *Follies.*

Ray Dooley joined Fields in four skits. Ray played his daughter in "A Back Porch," in which all manner of noises and interruptions disturb Fields' nap; this scene became one of the funnier sequences in Fields' feature-length talkie *It's a Gift* (1934). Dooley and Fields also partnered in "A Road," a skit about a traffic cop and a collapsible car, "The Drug Store," which Fields later turned into a short talkie, and as a ballroom-dance team in "The Waltz of Love."

Adult comedians playing children was not new on the stage, and no one can point to the first. Fanny Brice introduced her impish child in the *Ziegfeld Follies of 1934* and revived it for radio a decade later as Baby Snooks. Because of the reach of a radio broadcast and the show's recordings, Brice's brat eclipsed Ray Dooley's kid character that she introduced to Broadway in *Hitchy-Koo of 1918.*

Ray Dooley worked with Eddie Dowling in *Sidewalks of New York* (1927), another Dillingham venture, for which Dowling cowrote the book and the songs. She performed with brother Gordon Dooley in *Earl Carroll's Vanities* (1928) along with her partner from the *Follies,* W. C. Fields.

Ray and husband Eddie costarred in the Broadway show, *Thumbs Up* (1934–35), which Dowling produced. The show opened on 27 December and ran through the rest of the 1934–35 season. After the show closed, Ray retired to raise their two children, a daughter and a son. Ray and Eddie lost their son in the Second World War.

In May 1948, Ray Dooley and Eddie Dowling acted for the last time together on Broadway. Eddie Dowling and the American National Theatre and Academy presented a limited run of three short plays in a program titled *Hope's the Thing.* Ray and Eddie took the lead roles in one of the plays, *Home Life of a Buffalo.*

Ray was the lone survivor of a talented brood. Her comic singing and dancing brothers died young: Johnny (1887–1928), Gordon (1899–1930) and William (1882–1921). Ray outlived her husband, Eddie, and died at 87, a great female clown, unfortunately forgotten.

DOUBLE ACT

When an act was made up of two people it was called a double act—the logical extension of a single (one-person) act. The two partners in a double act were usually of the same gender. When the combination was male and female, it was tagged a *mixed double.* A two-person act could be defined further as a *singing double* (Van & Schenck), a *taking double act* (Abbott & Costello) or a *mixed comedy, song-and-dance double* (Burns & Allen).

DOUBLING

Essentially, doubling meant working two places at the same time. If an act was playing vaudeville, they appeared only once during each show; this gave the enterprising act the opportunity to do a turn in a nearby speakeasy or nightclub between shows. It was more difficult if an act was in revue or appearing in a musical comedy, unless they were an added attraction that performed only once nightly. If an act had a role in a musical's plot, then the doubling had to wait until after the show ended, and they were free to appear in a midnight floor show.

Most producers and managers tried to discourage the practice, believing that doubling hurt ticket sales. If the star was important and popular, he could negotiate his contract to allow him to double.

Black acts often did not need to negotiate or tell management that they were doubling. If they were, chances are it was in Harlem, for an entirely different audience, and a white producer or manager would never know.

EDDIE DOWLING

b: (Joseph Nelson Goucher) 11 December 1894, Woonsocket, RI—d: 18 February 1976, Smithfield, RI

The future actor and director of the legitimate stage and producer of the Pulitzer Prize-winning play *The Time of Your Life* began his career as a singer in small-time Rhode Island vaudeville theatres in 1909. His day job was as a cabin boy on the Fall River Steamship Line. Eddie also sang in St. Paul's Cathedral Choir in nearby Providence, and, in 1911, he was among the choirboys who went to London to perform.

Back home, he worked as a song plugger, convincing visiting vaudeville acts to use his company's songs and sometimes singing the songs himself from a well-positioned spot in the gallery or balcony. This exposure led to an offer to join a vaudeville act, and Eddie was on his way. He adopted his mother's maiden name for the stage.

Dowling was never a son of vaudeville alone; as early as 1914–15 he played drama in a traveling theatre troupe in New England. It was likely this experience that prompted Eddie to create a dramatic sketch, "The Stowaway," that he performed for a season in vaudeville. A review of Eddie's act at Fay's Theatre in Providence, dated 4 June 1917, shows his tilt toward drama continued: "Eddie Dowling, a local young man made a great success and responded to many encores. His principal offering is a story of the war told in the dialects of the various countries engaged."

It was as a vaudeville song-and-dance man, however, that he was invited to join the *Ziegfeld Follies of 1918* on tour. The *Follies* stint led to his Broadway debut in *The Velvet Lady* (1919), a Victor Herbert operetta. Eddie and Ray Dooley, a fellow vaudevillian, got married in 1919, just before Eddie and Ray joined the Broadway cast of the *Ziegfeld Follies of 1919.* The revue played from 16 June to 12 August, when the Actors Equity strike closed the shows on Broadway. The *Ziegfeld Follies of 1919* reopened on 10 September and ran until 6 December 1919. The show's opening number was a "Follies Salad," with Dowling as a chef. He sang as he assembled showgirls onstage, each dressed as an ingredient: Lettuce, Oil, and Salt and Pepper (the Fairbanks Twins). Eddie and his wife, Ray Dooley, appeared in a minstrel number, "Mandy," with Bert Williams, Eddie Cantor, Van & Schenck and John Steele.

Eddie toured in another Victor Herbert musical, *The Girl in the Spotlight* (1921), until he got his first chance to work as part of the creative team of a Broadway show. He and Cyrus Wood collaborated on the libretto for *Sally, Irene and Mary,* which ran 313 performances, the entire 1922–23 season on Broadway. Eddie also had a principal role and toured with the show through 1924.

Sally, Irene and Mary marked the beginning of Eddie Dowling's emergence as a major figure on Broadway. During the three-plus decades between 1919 and 1955, he was a principal in 30 Broadway productions. He produced many of those shows, acted in some, directed a few, and wrote librettos and songs for more than a few.

Dowling and James Hanley cowrote the book, music and lyrics for *Honeymoon Lane* (1926); Eddie Dowling starred, and the show was adapted for the screen in 1931 for Paramount. Ray Dooley appeared with Eddie in the movie (her only film) but did not appear in the stage version. Dillingham produced *Sidewalks of New York,* for which Dowling cowrote the music, lyrics and book. Ray Dooley headed the cast, but the show ran only 14 weeks on Broadway before touring.

Ray and Eddie worked together in vaudeville and appeared at the Palace in 1932, its final season of hosting two-a-day vaudeville. In 1934, Eddie and Ray were back on Broadway with *Thumbs Up* (1934), a Depression-era revue produced by Dowling. The lineup also included Bobby Clark & Paul McCullough, Hal Leroy, Eunice Healy, J. Harold Murray and Jack Cole. Considering the dire economic situation, the show did well, running 20 weeks at the St. James on Broadway. After that show closed, his wife, Ray, left show business to raise their daughter and son. Eddie took a hand in helping the Democratic Party and Franklin Delano Roosevelt's campaign teams frame their messages for network radio and other media during the presidential campaigns of 1932, 1936 and 1940 and for the Democrats during the midterm Congressional campaign of 1934.

In 1937, Eddie Dowling coproduced Shakespeare's *Richard II* that Margaret Webster directed with Maurice Evans in the title role. It ran the last four months of the 1936–37 season then opened the 1937–38 season and eked out another five weeks of performances, which was a major run for Shakespeare on Broadway. Critics tumbled over themselves with accolades for Evans. Critic John Mason Brown proclaimed, "It is one of the finest Shakespearean performances the modern theatre has seen." With that production, Eddie Dowling established himself in serious theatre, and greater successes were to follow, but not before he produced four failures, each a straight drama, one of which starred him, *Here Come the Clowns* (1938). In 1939, he toured briefly as the Stage Manager in Thornton Wilder's *Our Town.*

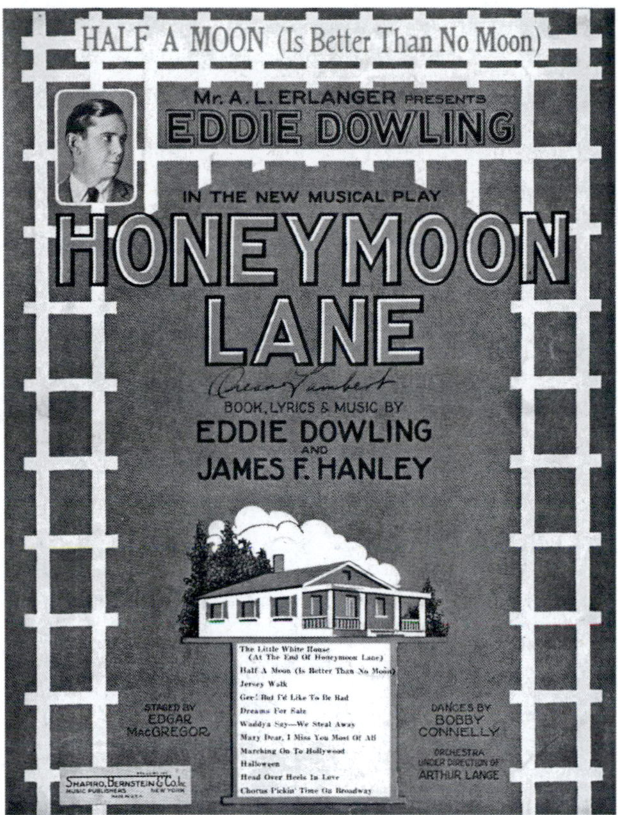

Eddie Dowling

The Time of Your Life (1940), written by William Saroyan, made up for recent disappointments. It won a Pulitzer Prize and three New York Dramatic Critics awards. The credit reads that the play was "produced by the Theatre Guild in association with Dowling," but it was he who pulled the show together, staged most of it and acted its leading role. Opening on 25 October 1939, it ran a profitable 185 performances through the rest of the season and closed on 6 April 1940. It reopened in autumn 1940 and ran another four weeks.

If only to prove he had not lost his vaudevillian touch, Eddie staged Olsen & Johnson's *Sons o' Fun* (1941–43), a madcap revue little different from its predecessor, *Hellzapoppin.* It kept the money pouring into Shubert Brothers' box offices for 743 performances. Close to President Franklin Roosevelt, Dowling was instrumental in getting FDR's backing for the United Service Organizations (USO). During the Second World War, Eddie Dowling served as the first director of the USO camp shows. He also lost his only son, John Graham Dowling, to the war.

Dowling's next two stage triumphs came back to back. He produced, directed and costarred with Laurette Taylor (in her comeback role) in *The Glass Menagerie* (1945). It was Tennessee William's first hit on Broadway, and it established him as a serious playwright. Hailed by critics, it ran 561 performances.

That was followed by *The Iceman Cometh* by Eugene O'Neill, which was produced in 1947 under the Theatre Guild banner at the Martin Beck Theatre. Dowling and Louis A. Lotito shared the odd credit for staging (Dowling) and direction (Lotito). At the time, the play was deemed a lesser effort by O'Neill, yet any play by O'Neill was given due respect, especially after an absence from the stage of a dozen years. The play's four-hour running time discouraged many and tried the patience of others; its run was limited to 136 performances. The star, James Barton, a former song-and-dance man like Dowling, was replaced during the run by E. G. Marshall.

Dowling replaced Barton during the run of *Paint Your Wagon* (1951–52), a musical by Alan Jay Lerner & Frederick Loewe that had a decent run but did not pay back its investment. It was Eddie's first appearances onstage in a musical since *Thumbs Up* (1934). He produced a few more modest successes: *Angel in the Pawnshop* (1951), a straight comedy in which he acted, and *The Righteous Are Bold* (1956), a drama that he directed.

Less well known was Dowling's work in movies and television. Two of his half-dozen feature films were adaptations of his stage successes: *Honeymoon Lane* (1931) and *Sally, Irene and Mary* (1938). The only films he acted in were *Rainbow Man* (1929) and *Honeymoon Lane* (with his wife, Ray Dooley). Eddie appeared on Ed Sullivan's *Toast of the Town* variety hour four times in the 1950s, and he acted in a public-service health series in 1952. His last appearance as an actor was as P. J. O'Hara in "The Ascent of P. J. O'Hara" (1956), a half-hour playlet on the drama anthology series *Star Tonight.* When Dowling retired from theatre, he was only in his early 60s, despite a huge body of work. He lived another 20 years and was survived by Ray Dooley, his wife of 57 years.

NELSON DOWNS

b: (Thomas Nelson Downs) 26 March 1867, Montour, IA—d: 1938

The "King of Koins" was regarded by stage magicians and vaudevillians alike as the first great manipulator of coins. Early on, Nelson Downs worked for a railway company as a telegrapher in Marshalltown, Iowa. Telegraphy and handling money during his work hours made his fingers nimble, and he spent free time hiding and producing coins.

Downs entered variety where he devised an act based upon close-up demonstrations of his ability to make coins disappear, reappear, multiply and vanish. He moved into vaudeville as it grew in importance and spread over the land. He was reported to be the highest-paid variety and vaudeville performer by 1900. Downs was recalled by Joe Laurie Jr. as the greatest of the coin men, admired as much for his showmanship as his dexterity and ability to break new ground in an ancient practice.

He traveled all over America and went to Europe for the first time in 1899; he played Berlin's Wintergarten, and he stayed in London for six months performing his coin act that he called "The Miser's Dream." He was given a five-year contract to return to the Palace Theatre in London each season for ten weeks.

Nelson Downs invested wisely and was able to retire a rich man by the start of the First World War. He devoted the remaining quarter century of his life to cultivating his knowledge about the history of stage magic, its practitioners and the secrets behind illusions. He dictated to John Northern Hilliard the material for the book that was published by the authors as *The Art of Magic* and wrote *Modern Coin Manipulation* himself.

DOWNSTAGE

The portion of the stage nearest the audience. So called because in Europe, Australia and South America, the stages were often raked (slanted down toward the footlights). Raked stages allowed everyone in the orchestra level of the theatre to have a relatively unobstructed view of the performers' feet, particularly the audience down front (which was the lowest part of the theatre and where the viewers' eyes might be level with or below the stage floor). Though a benefit for viewers of dance, it was sometimes treacherous for dancers and acrobats unused to the slant.

DOYLE & DIXON

James Doyle

b: ca. 1888, Halifax, NS—d: 13 June 1927, New York, NY

Harland Dixon

b: 4 November 1885, Toronto, ON—d: 27 June 1969, New York, NY

"The classiest dancing act of its kind" was the opinion of one vaudeville theatre manager, and doubtless he spoke for many others. Doyle & Dixon "work in evening clothes, making an excellent appearance. . . . Their dancing was tremendous and their conversation-songs and bits of chatter scored solidly." The boys teamed for nine years in vaudeville and Broadway musicals. Harland Dixon on his own proved a most versatile tap dancer, able to mimic almost anyone's style, quickly picking up their steps. He was a gentleman and well thought of personally and professionally by other tap dancers, both black and white.

Although other budding tap dancers began dancing in the streets for pennies from passersby, Harland Dixon was carefully shepherded by strict religionist parents in a strict religionist community. He was allowed to visit the Young Men's Christian Association (YMCA), and there he took gymnastics. Intrigued by another boy's slapping sounds, Harland began to explore the various sounds he could make with his feet. He then became friendly with a local newsboy who taught him a time step and the basics of clog dancing.

Any hopes his family had that Harland would trod the straight and narrow were dissipated by their son's inability to hold a straight job. He slipped off to vaudeville shows when able, and the percussive dancers on the bill always earned Harland's rapt attention.

Dixon entered amateur contests doing imitations of the dancers he had seen in vaudeville. Some musical shows included an amateur contest within the production. It was a sure device to arouse local interest, and the carelessly carpentered plots of early musicals could accommodate almost any interpolation. *In Old Kentucky* was a popular musical show of the 1890s. The principal roles were played by white actors, but the dance corps was black. The show toured for years, and, to drum up local interest en route, every Friday night's performance incorporated a dance contest that attracted the best local dancers, amateur and professional. Among the percussive dancers who got a leg up from *In Old Kentucky*'s dance contests were Willie Covan, George White and Harland Dixon.

Thus encouraged, Dixon left home for Buffalo, New York, then Boston, Massachusetts, and New York City, working as a busboy, elevator operator and checkroom clerk to pay for formal dance lessons. At some point, he hooked up with another young dancer, Jimmy Malone. They began dancing together in shows at men's clubs. In 1906, the pair introduced themselves to George Primrose in Manhattan, and he hired the lads as chorus dancers for Primrose's Minstrels. They were two of the eight chorus dancers. They toured with Primrose throughout the South.

Versatility was expected of dancers in a minstrel show; one needed to be able to perform the Virginia essence (precursor of the soft shoe), an updated soft shoe, clog and buck dancing. It was great training for two tyros. George Primrose, a graceful dancer whom many contemporaries as well as later historians regard as the great master of the soft shoe, became an early model for Harland Dixon. But Primrose, late of a partnership with Lew Dockstader and co-owner of Primrose & West's Minstrels for 30 years before that, was having a difficult time keeping his 40-person company profitable as minstrelsy faded in popularity.

After a year-and-a-half, Harland Dixon and Jimmy Malone left Primrose. Malone went home. Dixon signed with Lew Dockstader's minstrel show for a season. When he left Dockstader, Dixon teamed with Jack Corcoran, and Corcoran worked up a blackface comedy-dance act for the two of them that they performed on the Little Orpheum circuit in prairie waterholes like Paris, Texas.

The next season, Dixon went out as a solo dancer with a burlesque revue and was no longer corking up. Reaching New York, he met James Doyle at an actors' hangout. Jimmy Doyle was a few years younger than Dixon. Unlike Dixon, who, despite entering show business against his parents' wishes, eschewed drink, gambling and carousing, Doyle enthusiastically pursued all three. Both Doyle and Dixon were born in Canada, and both had matriculated through Lew Dockstader's minstrel troupe, although Jimmy left the year before Harland joined. In 1912, the two young men put together a dance act for vaudeville and burlesque, hoping to get noticed and hired for a Broadway show.

The acts they devised for vaudeville were based on a familiar device—a challenge dance—but they added comedy and framed the dancing with little stories, such as dentist and patient or two men-about-town. They started out with a soft shoe duet, and then each challenged the other with particular steps. The contest escalated as Doyle did a complex combination, and Dixon countered with an eccentric dance involving high kicks and other leg work.

That sort of character work attracted interest from Broadway producers who were looking for dancers who could act and sing and be part of the plot rather than an interpolated specialty number. Doyle & Dixon were added to the lineup of a burlesque revue, *Let George Do It* (1912), after it had opened in Manhattan. They were spotted by an agent, who invited Doyle & Dixon to perform at the Winter Garden during one of the Sunday concerts. They were an unknown act and surprised the sophisticated audience who had come to see Al Jolson (who was sort of the host of the Sunday concerts) and Nora Bayes, then a reigning diva of big-time vaudeville. The concert appearance made Doyle & Dixon, and they were hired for a specialty spot in the upcoming Winter Garden revue, *Broadway to Paris* (1912), headlining Gertrude Hoffman and featuring Irene Bordoni, Louise Dresser and James C. Morton.

Over the next nine years, Doyle & Dixon had their pick of Broadway musicals and revues as well as big-time vaudeville. Together, they danced in five Broadway shows: *The Honeymoon Express* (1913), *Dancing Around* (1914, starring Al Jolson), which closed out of town, *Stop! Look! Listen!* (1915), *The Century Girl* (1916, with Marie Dressler, Elsie Janis and Leon Errol) and *The Canary* (1918).

Al Jolson was the star of *The Honeymoon Express,* and he never expected another act or performer to stop the show. That is what Jolson expected to do. As Rae Samuels, Jolson's costar, recalled, Doyle & Dixon mischievously stopped the show whenever they wanted, and Al Jolson seethed. He did not permit their act to be scheduled during the show at any spot immediately before or following him.

They were just as successful in big-time vaudeville. By 1914, Doyle & Dixon were playing the Palace, and they were brought back the following year. They also proved to be favorites with English audiences. In 1916, they replaced Montgomery & Stone as the stars of *Chin Chin* when it toured. Offstage, the men had little to do with each other, except when Doyle, in high spirits and prankish, called Dixon in his hotel room late at night and pretended to be an incensed hotel detective or manager.

Dixon was either asleep or reading at those times. The next day, Dixon was dutifully rehearsing while Doyle was as the racetrack, sleeping late or otherwise engaged in his hotel room. Dixon learned or worked out the steps. Doyle, as quick a study as Dixon, showed up in time for a run-through with Dixon.

This behavior cost Doyle his career when, in 1921, he and Dixon were in a Charles Dillingham show, *Good Morning Dearie.* Dillingham fired Doyle for missing rehearsals and insisted that Dixon dance solo. Harland Dixon had already proved himself capable of keeping a show together when, a few months earlier, he had substituted at the last minute for Fred Stone, one of that era's most popular and beloved stars, when Stone broke his foot and was forced to drop out of *Tip Top.* With only four days notice and rehearsal, Harland filled in for Stone. The critics loved Dixon's performance, and the cast and Dillingham (the show's producer) were grateful that the show did not close.

Doyle appeared as a solo act in several shows on Broadway and continued in vaudeville as a single until there was no more big-time vaudeville. He opened a dance school but was unable to make a go of it and died a few years later.

Dixon continued to work in top-notch Broadway shows, such as *The Ziegfeld Follies of 1923* and *Kid Boots* (1923–25), starring Fanny Brice, Eddie Cantor, Bert & Betty Wheeler and Paul Whiteman). After the 1923 *Follies* show closed, both Harland Dixon and Paul Whiteman and His Orchestra were brought to Paris to headline a show at the Théâtre de Champs-Elysée. Seated in the dress circle were *le tout de Paris* and stars of French variety, including Mistinguette, Maurice Chevalier and the Dolly Sisters.

Back in the USA, Harland joined the casts of the Gershwins' *Oh Kay!* (1926, with Gertrude Lawrence and Victor Moore), George White's *Manhattan Mary* (1927, starring Ed Wynn, Lou Holtz and White), *Rainbow* (1928, a four-week flop) and *Top Speed* (1928–29), the last two of which had scores by Vincent Youmans and book and lyrics by Oscar Hammerstein II. Harland went on the road with most of these shows, toured in *Show Boat* in 1929–30, and played profitable vaudeville dates in between.

After 1929, when many investors lost their fortunes and livelihoods, few shows were truly profitable either on Broadway or on the road, so Dixon accepted a bid from London to choreograph *Charlot's Masquerade* (1930), a revue starring Bea Lillie, Florence Desmond and Anton Dolin. Back home, big-time vaudeville was fading away or changing into presentation revues in combination with big motion pictures, so Harland played nightclubs and devised dance routines for a few younger hoofers, including Jimmy Cagney.

Harland Dixon made a few attempts at the movie business. He danced in a musical two-reeler, *Du Barry Did All Right* (1937) starring Irene Bordoni and assisted as a choreographer for eight or ten movie musicals. One of those was *Something to Sing About* (1937), an independent feature starring James Cagney and produced by Cagney while he was battling Warner Brothers. Dixon danced in one of its scenes.

He also helped stage and direct dances for nightclub shows, including several at Billy Rose's Diamond Horseshoe. His last show on Broadway was the musical *A Tree Grows in Brooklyn.* Shirley Booth was the star, but 65-year-old Harland Dixon performed a dance number. He was able to dance even when, in the 1960s, he had to sit in a chair to perform. He was still a compelling performer although in his late 70s.

In his retirement, Harland Dixon was available to dance historians like Marshal Stearns. He spoke insightfully yet kindly about dancers of the past whose work he remembered clearly and admitted how much he learned from them. Yet other dancers like Jack Donahue pointed to Dixon as a great innovator. Dixon belonged to a great-books club and continued his lifelong practice of reading everything from philosophy to economics. He wed once, his childhood sweetheart, Charlotte Jean MacMullen, and they remained married until his death in 1969.

PATSY DOYLE

b: (Patrick Doyle) 1866, Utica (?), NY—d: 11 August 1930

He was something new in the monologist line, especially for an Irishman. Instead of spreading the charm and delighting in his own sly humor, Patsy Doyle simply walked out onstage, stood in one spot, his chubby body nearly immobile except for an occasional twitch of his finger, and stared like an iced haddock at the audience. "Patsy Boyle, who is back a second time leads the bill. His drollery, his inimitable humor gotten off without even a smile, his expression of stupidity, are irresistible. He kept his audience in a perfect uproar of laughter the entire time he occupied the boards, and had to respond to an encore." At the time of this review, he was headlining on the Orpheum circuit.

Offstage, dressed spiffily in a three-piece suit and wearing a straw boater, he looked like a solid businessman or a politician. Onstage, he wore a soft hat with the brim down, like a man's version of a cloche, straggly bangs spread across his forehead ear to ear. His stage suits tended to plaids or checks with a contrasting vest pulled tight across his bulging belly.

When his audience least expected it, Patsy broke into a dance, his grace and speed belying his 200 pounds. He began, as did most of the first-generation vaudevillians, especially those from the British Isles, in minstrelsy. Although a minstrel man, or boy, needed to sing, dance, tell jokes and play an instrument—at least a tambourine—Patsy Doyle specialized in high-stepping dancing. Joe Laurie Jr. remembered Doyle in his affectionate survey of vaudeville; he grouped Doyle with the finest dancers to emerge from minstrel shows: George Primrose, Barney Fagan, Eddie Foy Sr. and Eddie Leonard.

Patsy went into vaudeville around 1890 and enjoyed his greatest success during vaudeville's golden years throughout the 1900s and 1910s. Doyle was still working in show business in 1930 when he died unexpectedly.

RUTH DRAPER

b: 2 December 1884, New York, NY—d: 30 December 1956, New York, NY

The thought of setting Ruth Draper among vaudeville and variety performers would have dismayed patrons of legitimate theatre and puzzled vaudeville fans. Had she not possessed the social connections that allowed her to first present her character sketches in the salons of high society, however, vaudeville would have been far more hospitable to her talent and method of presentation than the legitimate theatre. Her legacy is that she became one of the more important influences in performance art.

In her day, the smaller playhouses booked her, and drama critics reviewed her performances and invariably admired Draper's telling dialogue and exquisite portrayals. Draper herself referred to her works as *dramas,* no matter how distilled or fragmentary, and called herself a *character actress.* That was her privilege and choice, yet she was more accurately described as a *diseuse,* an impersonator, a protean actor or a storyteller, and her stage pieces were more often and more truly character sketches than fully played-out dramas.

A mark of drama is a playability and relevance that endures apart from its creator. Although actors have revived her minidramas and monologues, the effect has been a tribute rather than a re-creation. What is certain is that few actors or performers have left such a lasting legacy as Draper. She inspired generations of other actors and performers who needed to create their own theatre pieces: Cornelia Otis Skinner, Joyce Grenfell, Lily Tomlin and John Leguizamo among the better known.

Draper did not invent the sketch with one actor playing multiple parts. The protean actor had enjoyed popularity in America from at least the 1870s, but she made a career of it. After appearing in one conventional play, *A Lady's Name* (1916), she decided never again.

She had always been an effective mimic who charmed friends and family with her vivid impersonations, and she had written since childhood. Expanding beyond her circle of friends, acquaintances and hired help, she studied people from many walks of life.

Though a Manhattanite by birth and a lifelong resident, Ruth Draper was bred of New England stock. Her father was a transplanted Vermonter, a distinguished doctor and an amateur musician. Her mother was a Dana, a clan of intellectuals and artists. Both sides of the family were well-off, and Ruth's childhood was spent in the company of governesses and private teachers. Ruth was not the only talented or famous child in the Draper household. Charles Dana Draper became a businessman and philanthropist. George Draper was an internationally honored specialist in heart disease and psychosomatic therapy (he originated the term). Dorothea and Alice raised families and were active participants in charitable works, and baby brother Paul was a concert singer and father of Paul Draper, the improvisational percussive dancer.

Until she was 30, and unlike her brothers and sisters, Ruth was unable to divine a direction for her life. She was an avid theatregoer, and she stored memories of people and devices she admired onstage. Seeing Beatrice Herford (1868–1952) onstage provided a model for Ruth. Beatrice worked as a conventional actor and as a monologist, sometimes appearing on the variety stage like Yvette Guilbert and Cissie Loftus. Vaudeville and variety provided Herford with appropriate stages and receptive audiences. Her sketches were essentially humorous, although the characters she represented were as similar and diverse as those Draper later impersonated.

Between her midteens and late 20s, Draper assembled a folio of character sketches. Her first audiences were family and friends. Soon, she was asked by society hostesses to present her sketches at luncheons and other social events. She was regarded as a talented postdebutante, an *amateur,* but she determined to become an artist and a professional. Like most of her class, Ruth visited England regularly. There, too, she performed her recitals, and she became a favorite of the royal family, Queen Mary, in particular.

The outbreak of the First World War in Europe ended her frequent sojourns to London for the duration. She set about making a professional career in the USA. Her first venues were often unlikely places like the Hippodrome (one of the largest stages and auditoriums in America for one of the most intimate of acts). Many of her first theatres were vaudeville houses from Kennebunk, Maine, to Tyrone, New Mexico. There were also engagements at universities and YMCAs. The YMCA engagements turned into overseas tours, because it was that organization that provided entertainment and homeland contact with the battlefield troops in the absence of the not-yet-formed United Services Organizations (USO), which took over the function during succeeding wars.

After the war, Draper gave what she described as concerts; her first was in London's Aeolian Hall in 1920. She appeared several times on a variety bill at London's Coliseum and Palladium. More often, as the 1920s progressed, she performed in playhouses. By 1929, she toured cities in America, played on Broadway, and then in London's West End. Every few years, from 1929 until 1956, the year of her death, she brought together a gallery of new characters. Each sketch took 15 to 30 minutes or so, and four to six would make up an evening. There were always humorous sketches, but what set Ruth Draper apart from most of those before her and after her was the inclusion of sketches that were tragic, bitterly satiric or sad.

Economy and restraint also distinguished her from most other protean actors. Often, the protean act was an occasion for bravura, a showy exercise as the actor transformed himself (sometimes with seemingly instantaneous changes in make-up and costuming) from one Shakespearean or Dickensian role to the next in a truncated version of the original play. Draper eschewed the grandiose and subtly detailed her characters, their thoughts and behavior.

Draper worked on a starkly curtained stage with a couple of chairs, a table, and perhaps a desk or sofa. She entered in a simple solid-colored dress that, augmented with a shawl, a cloak or a hat, lent itself to a succession of characters as diverse as immigrant country folk, society women and maids. She did not move much. She addressed various imagined people onstage, employing a different tone, pitch, accent and pace for each of her characters. Admirers insisted that Draper could convince an audience of 1,000 or more that they were seeing multiple characters on a stage with full sets representing gardens, art galleries, churches and drawing rooms.

LOUISE DRESSER

b: (Louise Josephine Kerlin) 5 October 1878, Evansville, IN—d: 24 April 1965, Los Angeles, CA

A top vaudeville performer in her day and a silent-picture star whose career spanned five decades, Louise Dresser was one of vaudeville's golden dozen or so single-women acts. Lula, as she was called, won an amateur contest at 16. The prize was a professional job with a comic opera company in Columbus, Ohio. The company was really a minor burlesque outfit, the type that combined comedy skits, palaver and songs with a line of luscious ladies. As soon as she earned enough money for a return ticket, Lula took a train home, but instead of returning straight to Evansville, she gave show business another try in Chicago.

According to Charles and Louise Samuels, the authors of *Once Upon a Stage: The Merry World of Vaudeville,* Louise Kerlin walked into the office of music publishers Howley, Haviland & Dresser, looking for songs to perform in vaudeville. Paul Dresser heard her announce her name to receptionists and wondered if the tall, blonde, handsome young woman was related to Bill Kerlin, a railway conductor who had befriended Paul when, as a boy, he hawked gum and candy on the trains. Paul returned the long-ago kindness by helping Bill's daughter.

To advance her career and spare her from gossip, Paul suggested that Louise adopt his last name and pose as his sister. As Paul Dresser was the brother of novelist Theodore Dreiser, the assumption throughout much of Louise's career was that she was sister to both. Paul called up a producer and arranged for his "kid sister, Louise Dresser" to audition and supplied her with a song he had just written, "My Gal Sal," which turned out to be one of his (and Louise's) biggest hits. According to author and Evansville historian Kenneth P. McCutchan, The Sal in the song was Paul's former love, Sallie Walker, the madam of Evansville's classiest bordello.

Paul provided Louise with a second great song, "On the Banks of the Wabash." With two numbers that allowed a strong emotional delivery, Louise Dresser had the makings of a solid single-woman vaudeville act.

The single woman was invariably a singer, usually a comedian as well, who brought as much personality, showmanship and humor to her act as she did musical ability. Good material—some ingratiating patter and good songs—and glamorous gowns were essential to the success of a single woman's act. Louise pulled all of it together as she played vaudeville out of Chicago. In a few years, she was ready to move on to New York.

Paul Dresser died in January 1906 while in New York. Louise's first New York City vaudeville date was a few months later. Perhaps they had come east together. Louise continued to climb in vaudeville. In addition to singing, she tried a sketch and acquitted herself well, an augury for her successful film career. In vaudeville, Louise was headlining by 1910. She played the Palace in 1914.

While in Chicago, Louise had married vaudeville singer, comedian and composer Jack Norworth in 1906. She may have met him through Paul, as both were members of the songwriting fraternity. Jack, however, strayed and took up with Trixie Friganza, and Louise divorced Norworth in 1908. In 1910, she wed actor Jack Gardner, a New York musical-comedy actor and singer, and they remained wed until he died in 1950.

Dresser also worked in musical comedy and revue, at an average of one show a year between 1906 and 1917. She obtained her first role in her first year in New York. Lew Fields hired her for *About Town* (1906), a revue disguised with a slim story line as a musical comedy that ran four months. Vernon Castle, Lew's favorite young comedian, Lew himself, May Irwin, Blanche Ring and Jack Norworth were in the cast. The following year Louise was in another hit show, *The Girl Behind the Counter* (1907), that ran 260 performances.

The next four or so shows barely qualified as successes, but *Potash and Perlmutter* (1913), a comedy without music, was a tremendous hit, running 882 performances, two full years. The producers nudged another 192 performances by changing the title to *Abe and Mauruss,* then *Abe and Mauruss: Potash and Perlmutter in Society* (1915), and changing theatres. Louise stayed in the show only for its first years but was lured back to *Abe and Mauruss: Potash and Perlmutter in Society.*

Have a Heart (1917) was Louise's final Broadway show. Despite music by Jerome Kern, lyrics by P. G. Wodehouse and a book by Wodehouse and Guy Bolton, it was not a hit although it garnered good reviews. In it, Dresser played a shopgirl turned movie star—a foreshadow. Louise Dresser concentrated on her vaudeville career for the next few years, often appearing in sketches with husband Jack Gardner.

In 1922, she began making silent movies, about 30 in all. Louise started out at $350 per week, a big comedown from her vaudeville salary that approached $2,000 per week, but a good investment in an industry new to her. In three years, her film salary increased tenfold.

She acted the parts of middle age, often selfish or cruel, but she did not always look, dress or act matronly. She was a versatile actor, even minus her voice—one of her strongest attributes—and she played in melodramas, comedies, Westerns and romances. In each, she was a principal player although never top billed. At least one of her silents is still available through videotape and DVD: *The Eagle* (1925), in which she portrayed Catherine the Great as a jealous czarina who desired the young army-officer-turned-Black-Eagle revolutionary played by Rudolph Valentino.

Louise made nearly 20 talkies between the dawn of sound and her retirement in 1937. Her characters were more often admirable in her sound films, such as those still available for home viewing or on cable television: *Mammy* (1930), starring Al Jolson, and five Will Rogers vehicles, *Lightnin'* (1930), *State Fair* (1933), *Doctor Bull* (1933), *Harum Scarum* (1934) and *The County Chairman* (1935). She reverted to unsympathetic types in several other films, notably the *Scarlet Empress* (1934), starring Marlene Dietrich. In 1929, Louise Dresser was nominated for an Academy Award for *A Ship Comes In* (1928).

After she retired at age 59, she volunteered at the Motion Picture Country House and Hospital in Woodland Hills, where she died at 86.

PAUL DRESSER

b: (Paul Dreiser) 21 April 1857, Terre Haute, IN—d: 30 January 1906, New York, NY

The songwriter brother of novelist Theodore Dreiser began working as a boy, selling candy and chewing gum to passengers on a railway line out of Chicago, while studying at a local school for boys preparing to enter a Catholic seminary. Instead of pursuing the priesthood, Paul at 16 hooked up with a medicine show.

Musical, he worked in many branches of show business. He sang and played in variety then vaudeville. By 1885, he was an end man in Billy Rice's Minstrels, a touring outfit. He also wrote songs and joined a sheet-music publisher as a song plugger. Eventually, he became a partner in Howley, Haviland & Dresser and, finally, his own self-named firm.

His two most famous songs, "My Gal Sal" and "On the Banks of the Wabash," were introduced by vaudeville singer Louise Dresser. She was not a relation, but Dresser was a friend of her father and helped get her started in show business under the fiction that Louise was his kid sister.

Many of Paul's songs were sentimental, even bathetic by standards a century removed, but they sold well in his day, and two of them have remained favorite examples of popular music before the ragtime era. "On the Banks of the Wabash" was used in no fewer than two movie musicals, and "My Gal Sal" has been heard in at least three movies and served as the theme song for one of Jackie Gleason's television sketch characters, Joe the Bartender. Paul Dresser was among the most successful songwriters of his day.

MARIE DRESSLER

b: (Leila Marie Koerber) 9 November 1868, Cobourg, ON—d: 28 July 1934, Santa Barbara, CA

Every article written about Marie Dressler during her lifetime, and every biography or article written since, begins with her appearance. Even Marie titled her first autobiography *The Life Story of an Ugly Duckling.* Dressler was taller than many women of her time, and her 200-plus pounds sturdily padded a large-boned frame. She was never ugly, rather she was homely in the truest and best sense of the word. Her deep, soulful green eyes radiated much larger than they were and flashed her intensity, while her lips signaled all manner of emotions from beatific reverie to motherly care to snarling disgust. Through her carriage and posture, Marie conveyed whatever was required by her role: great dignity and grace, clumsiness, bellicosity or battered defeat. Dressler was the complete physical clown, mastering everything in the comic repertoire from double takes to hand flutters to cartwheels and pratfalls.

Infatuated with the glamour of theatrical life and determined to get away from a father she nearly despised, 14-year-old Marie Dressler left home to join a third-rate touring theatre company. For six dollars a week, Marie played small parts until, six months after she had been hired, she lobbied for and landed the role of Cigarette, the Carmen-like charmer of *Under Two Flags.* If Marie was not quite as pretty as the authors had envisioned Cigarette, she brought to the role the hoydenish energy it required.

Three years later the company was stranded in Michigan, and Marie went on to a series of similar failing troupes. She acted in European operetta and *opéra bouffe,* playing a variety of parts, usually older women such as queens and occasionally older men such as

Marie Dressler

kings. It was rugged training. Sometimes, a cast had only a day to prepare a new play and went onstage armed with little more than a sense of the plot and the ability to bluff and improvise.

After nine years' apprenticeship, she tried her luck in Chicago, where she won a small role in *Little Robinson Crusoe,* which starred Eddie Foy, then went on the road with *The Tar and the Tartan.* Marie decided in 1892 to brave New York City. Unable to get stage work there, she turned to singing in beer parlors and rough vaudeville houses. Thrifty, Marie conscientiously sent half her salary home to her parents; soon she would provide a measure of support for other relatives in tough times.

After playing a small part in Maurice Barrymore's musical burlesk *The Robber of the Rhine* in 1892, Marie was told by Barrymore that comedy was her forte and she should not go against fate by pursuing dramatic roles. This was good advice at the time, yet in her late film years, Marie would realize her ambition to play drama as well. In 1893, Marie won a role in *Princess Nicotine* at the Casino Theatre, important to her only as the start of her friendship with the show's star, Lillian Russell. Lillian became Marie's mentor and friend.

Dressler's first star part came in *The Lady Slavey,* imported in 1896 from England with its London star, Dan Daly. Marie's height and girth contrasted with Daly's short, slight build, and the hit of the show was a vigorous dance through which Marie propelled Dan. The show had a respectable New York run before it went on tour for the balance of two years. When the tour laid off for the summer, Marie tried burlesque at Proctor's Pleasure Palace at East 58th Street in Manhattan and entered vaudeville with a sketch called "Tess of the Vaudevilles," a travesty of the Thomas Hardy novel.

Dressler had a run-in with Abe Erlanger, one of *The Lady Slavey's* producers. As a result, Erlanger limited the type and amount of work Dressler got for the next few seasons. He put her into a touring show, *Courted in to Court,* as Dottie Dimple. It was a vaudeville revue of sorts, and when the show debuted in New York, Erlanger replaced Dressler with May Irwin. That much penance behind her, Dressler was permitted to open in New York in a dim revival of *The Lady Slavey.* In 1898, fully absolved, Marie appeared at the Herald Square Theatre in *Hotel Topsy Turvy* before she and Eddie Foy took it on tour.

Marie learned the value of publicity, and the press was usually a compliant partner. Every enthusiasm or disappointment Marie encountered was turned into a campaign trumpeted by the press. Sometimes, the publicity focused on one of Marie's more serious and sustained passions, such as racial equality, fair labor conditions for girls or, later, rallying support for the First World War.

In 1899, Dressler appeared prominently in a box at a theatre accompanied by two friends, one of them her African American maid Jenny. Jenny (whose surname is unrecorded) was there socially, not as a maid, dressed for the theatre and sharing refreshments with her companions. Marie's commitment to racial equality was more than a posture. In 1901, she had a fellow actress fired for insulting a black laundress. Occasionally, the press showed Dressler's other side when, for example, she got into a fistfight with another actress.

Between 1898 and 1904, although Broadway teemed with success, Marie's career went up and down. Her New York successes were *The Man in the Moon* (1899) and *The King's Carnival* (1901). Her failures included the foray into management with *Miss Prinnt* (1900–01), which bankrupted her. Vaudeville and burlesque engagements revived her, but the most serious low point was a severe bout with typhoid fever in 1902. Her weight dropped from 210 to 130 pounds! During her illness, which lasted into 1903, her mother died of heart problems. As Marie recuperated, she accepted limited vaudeville engagements, mostly on Percy Williams' circuit of theatres around New York, to keep the wolf from the door.

After Joe Weber and Lew Fields split in 1904, Joe Weber mounted *Higgledy-Piggledy* that year and engaged Marie Dressler. She was unhappy at the Weber Music Hall and complained to the press and through them to her public that she was tired of slapstick, tired of the Weberfields formula (as was Lew Fields), tired of show business, tired of touring and tired of playing New York. Some of her fans and the press were getting a bit tired of Marie's complaints in the face of their loyal support.

Next season, she returned to vaudeville and earned nearly twice the $600 per week Weber had paid her. Her act included bits and pieces from various productions, including the song "A Great Big Girl Like Me" and her impressions of various dramatic leading ladies. Sustained success was thwarted by meeting Jim Dalton, however, an obsequious fraud who for more than a decade lived off Marie. He enraged producers and nearly ruined her financially. Marie, 30 years old at the time, became a partner to her own deception.

Dalton escorted Dressler to England to play variety. She began her act at the piano. Sitting down and finding the piano too far away, she simply jerked the instrument toward her rather than shift her stool and herself. It won the audience. She also did a song routine, "The Bonnet Store-y," donning a variety of hats to match a variety of verses. Her success was interrupted by bronchitis, and a larynx operation made her a contralto. She returned to the USA to play vaudeville for Percy Williams for three months.

Back in England, Marie performed in variety at the rate of $2,500 per week while she took another stab at management. She had no talent for organization, and the hash called *Philopoena* opened and quickly flopped in 1909. As creditors were the only ones waiting in line to see her, Dressler left town, bad-mouthing London theatre. Once again Marie went into American vaudeville to rescue her finances and career.

Vaudeville bookings pulled Dressler out of hock, but an operation for growths on her tonsils and an attack of blood poisoning sidelined her again. Despite commanding a vaudeville salary of $2,000 per week, her debts, her illnesses and her ill-conceived business schemes drove her, for the second time, into bankruptcy in 1910. This time it was Lew Fields to the rescue.

Lew Fields had made a success as a producer, director and character comedian since his split with Weber. Lew's associates in 1910 included the Shuberts and Ned Wayburn. Together they presented Marie Dressler with her most enduring success. As the household drudge, Tillie Blobbs, she introduced the anthem "Heaven Will Protect the Working Girl." Then came more trouble: a throat operation a month after the opening, an attack of ptomaine poisoning and the death of her beloved maid, Jenny. Eventually, Marie recovered and Tillie racked up 753 performances on tour. While playing San Francisco, Marie met a young reporter, Frances Marion, who later would lead Marie to the most productive and satisfying years of her career, her time in Hollywood at MGM.

Marie made a few cylinder sound recordings for Thomas Edison and a couple of experimental sound flickers for his film company. Those were early efforts at synchronizing silent movies with wax recordings. Stage producers had grown leery of hiring Dressler because her husband, Jim Dalton, gummed up deals and was suspected of a bit of larceny. Lew Fields took a chance again in 1912 when he and Weber reunited for *Roly-Poly* and *Without the Law,* a burlesk and a sketch with Weber & Fields, Nora Bayes and Bessie Clayton. Marie was engaged, but the production fell apart when Dressler began feuding with both Weber and Fields.

An offer from Mack Sennett to star in a feature film, *Tillie's Punctured Romance,* brought Marie Dressler back to the movies. Mabel Normand, Mack Swain, Chester Conklin and newcomer Charlie Chaplin were cast in support, and Marie's first released film was an extraordinary success. It was 1914, and the movies were becoming vaudeville's biggest threat. More Dressler films, poorly made and poorly distributed, ended her silent-film career.

Nor were her next stage shows great successes. The year 1916 began a decade of failure, and Marie Dressler was nearing 50 years old. Marie threw herself into selling war bonds to promote the Allied cause and appeared at charity bazaars, auctions and banquets. After the war, Marie visited hospitals to sing to the war's wounded and entertained at benefits for the Red Cross and women's groups.

When Actors Equity called a strike in 1919, Marie rallied to the standard. She organized chorus girls, and thus was born the Chorus Equity Association. Marie won them a decent salary, some expenses and employment protection.

Her stage career was nearly finished by then; the decade of the 1920s proved her lowest point. Her activism alienated the few remaining producers who would tolerate her demands or her husband's interference. The jazz age had dawned, and Miss Dressler was consigned to yesterday's fashion bin. The producers of her heyday were retired or dead. Her husband confessed to bigamy and embezzlement, and then he suffered a stroke and was left paralyzed. Still, Marie took responsibility for him. Unable to afford a nurse, she dragged Jim around the vaudeville circuits with her until he died in 1921.

She took stage roles when offered, small parts in *Cinderella on Broadway* and *The Passing Show of 1921,* a 20-week tour called *Moments from the Winter Garden* (1922) and *The Dancing Girl* (1923). Her last Broadway engagement of note was in vaudeville at the Palace in Manhattan. Called *Old Timers' Week,* the bill played the week of 19 October 1925 and headlined Dressler, Cissie Loftus, May Irwin and Marie Cahill. Dressler filled in the rest of this slack time with the first of her biographies, *The Life Story of an Ugly Duckling.*

Dressler despaired of finding work until movie director Allen Dwan offered her a cameo role in *The Joy Girl* (1927), shooting in Florida. A bit later, Frances Marion came through, convincing Irving Thalberg to team Marie with MGM contract player Polly Moran in *The Callahans and the Murphys* (1927). Preview audiences loved the movie. Critics loved it. The Hibernian Society hated it. They claimed it depicted the Irish as continuously drunken and fighting. The film was withdrawn from release.

Marie had nowhere to go, so she stayed in Hollywood. No further film offers were forthcoming, so she entertained at private parties for $150 per appearance until small roles materialized: *Breakfast at Sunrise* (1927), *The Patsy* (1928) and *The Divine Lady* (1929). In 1928, MGM had decided it would try a sanitized version of *The Callahans and the Murphys;* Polly Moran and J. Farrell MacDonald played Maggie and Jiggs in the film of the popular comic strip *Bringing up Father*; Marie played their maid.

All told, Dressler made six silent feature films until sound made her useful to studios. In 1929, she made *The Hollywood Revue of 1929* and *Chasing Rainbows* for MGM and *Vagabond Lover* for RKO; 1930 brought *One Romantic Night* at United Artists and *Let Us Be Gay* at MGM. Finally, Hollywood had noticed that Dressler delivered the goods. Then the stock market crashed. This time, Dressler did not go back to vaudeville. Vaudeville was no help to anyone. Instead, Frances Marion came to the rescue.

MGM had no greater problem in the conversion to sound than Greta Garbo. Thalberg chose Eugene O'Neill's stage play *Anna Christie* for Garbo's first sound vehicle. The Swedish characters allowed for Garbo's accent. Frances Marion enlarged the part of the blowsy wharf rat to create a memorable role for Dressler. The 1930 film proved a great success for everyone involved.

MGM reteamed Marie with Polly Moran in *The Girl Said No* and *Caught Short,* both in 1930. Lost is the 1930 mishmash *The March of Time*, which featured Dressler, Fay Templeton, William Collier, De Wolf Hopper and Weber & Fields. Now that Marie was under exclusive contract, MGM kept her working. *Min and Bill* (1930) won her the Academy Award for best actress, yet MGM returned her and Polly Moran to the slapstick formula for three more cheapies: *Reducing, Politics* (both 1931) and *Prosperity* (1932). *Emma* allowed Marie a more serious role in 1932; however, Marie had become very ill, diagnosed with cancer in 1931. Louis B. Mayer, MGM's studio chief, who knew that she had abdominal cancer, tempted her with a bonus to complete three films during summer 1933 and arranged the schedule so that Marie would work only three hours daily.

Two of these films capped her reputation. *Tugboat Annie* was a blockbusting sentimental sister to the more caustic *Min and Bill,* and *Dinner at Eight* gave a dozen of MGM's finest the chance to act in the film that defines MGM at its best. *Christopher Bean* was her final film.

Dressler could dance and sing, and few comedians or actors had her range, although perhaps she relied too often on a stockpile of favorite double takes, muggings, fidgets and lurches. She was equally believable as a grand dame and a guttersnipe. Her voice was musical and expressive, giving her low-life characters dignity, just as her antic facial expressions humanized her haughtier portraits.

Marie Dressler was thrilled to have a movie career and as astonished as MGM and the rest of the movie colony when she was crowned "Queen Marie of the Movies, America's Most Beloved Star." But by the time success returned to Marie, she had the will, but illness robbed her of strength. When the time came for her exit, Marie Dressler left the stage like a trouper.

DROPS

See Cloths and Ropes and Rigging

S. H. DUDLEY

b: (Sherman H. Dudley) 1870, Dallas, TX—d: 1 March 1940, Oxon Hill, MD

Remembered as the African American entrepreneur who became the owner or lessee of many theatres and parlayed them into a powerful position in the Theatre Owners' Booking Association (TOBA, Toby time), S. H. Dudley first gained prominence as a good musician and a better comedian, two essentials for an end man in minstrelsy.

He traveled and performed with the McCabe & Young Minstrels around 1890. At a benefit, he teamed up with a fellow named Dude Kelly, and they subsequently worked for Richard & Pringle's and Rusco & Holland's Georgia Minstrels. Around 1896, he struck out on his own with Dudley's Georgia Minstrels.

In 1904, Dudley costarred with Billy Kersands in *King Rastus,* a musical farce, but the show quickly folded. That same year Dudley took over management of a company called the Smart Set, a hardy perennial that had been on the road since 1896. Over the life of the company, the star comedians of the Smart Set included Kersands, Ernest Hogan and Tom McIntosh. Upon McIntosh's death, Dudley became the lead comic, and his costar was Ada Overton Walker, the future wife of George Walker, Bert Williams' partner.

It was in the Smart Set that Dudley introduced the comedy act most associated with him. His partner was a mule named Pat, who nodded his head in agreement or shook it in dispute. Dudley was famous for lines like "I'm so proud of the fact that I came from Texas that I'm going to stay away." Among the shows that the Smart Set performed were *The Black Politician* and *His Honor, the Barber.* Later, Dudley took his mule act into vaudeville.

The White Rats strike in 1901 was a failure for white vaudevillians, but it opened the door for blacks to mainstream (white) vaudeville audiences. Until then, with the exceptions of adventurous whites who attended black shows featuring Cole & Johnson, Ernest Hogan and Walker & Williams, most whites' impressions of black entertainers were filtered through the blackface performances of white men in minstrel shows. When white vaudevillians went on strike, Keith & Albee, Loew's and other circuits began hiring black acts to fill their bills. The larger American public discovered that blacks could perform monologues (like Dudley), juggle, roller-skate, perform magic and ventriloquism, as well as sing, dance and clown. Because the White Rats had excluded black vaudevillians from membership, there was no ethical question of fraternal solidarity.

Dudley was one of those who brought together other black performers to create the Colored Actors' Union around 1902. George Walker took the lead in organizing the Colored Actors Beneficial Association in 1907, which metamorphosed into the Frogs. The Dudley-led group probably disbanded before then.

By 1913, Dudley had retired from performing and had begun to concentrate on buying and leasing theatres in Washington, D.C., Virginia and westward. All the houses he acquired were in the border states. The theatres that Dudley booked numbered between 21 and 28. They provided a geographical bridge between the black theatres of the Old South and Southwest that were controlled by TOBA, or smaller white-owned circuits in the South, and those independently run black houses in the Northeast and Midwest.

Although he began as an independent and operated his theatres as the Dudley circuit, he entered the TOBA around 1920. If the whites who ran TOBA thought that business would continue as usual, they were mistaken. Dudley controlled enough theatres to make him a powerful force in what had been an organization whose primary purpose was to make as much money as possible from black audiences by hiring black talent with little care for either audiences or performers.

S. H. Dudley combined with other progressive voices in TOBA: Mr. Cummings, a white theatre owner in the South, and Martin Klein, a Jewish businessman and investor. The trio took control and instituted a number of reforms as well as expanded Toby time to encompass about 100 theatres by the mid-1920s. As the stock market crash turned into the Great Depression, Dudley sold his theatres and retired with his wife, Alberta Ormes, and their son to his farm in Maryland. It was a rather grand farm where he raised thoroughbred cattle and racehorses. There he died in 1940.

DUFFY & SWEENEY

Jimmy Duffy

b: (James Terrence Duffy) 1889—d: 30 March 1939, New York, NY

Freddie Sweeney

b: (Frederick Chase Sweeney) 1894, Harrisburg, PA—d: 10 December 1954, Sylmar, CA

Legends abound in show business. Longevity, box-office records, long runs and precedent-setting salaries are benchmarks for other shows and performers to surpass. Other legends are the stuff of gossip, passed down as delightful anecdotes. Most records get broken, most performers are forgotten, and the stories once told about them lose meaning as the protagonists fade from public memory.

When show folk gathered at the Friars or Lambs, they talked about their acts and show business in general. When talk turned to lighter matters, it needed to be funny to be heard, and show folk traded stories about the more colorful of their fellow performers. Someone always brought up Duffy & Sweeney.

Jimmy Duffy and Freddie Sweeney had a *nut act,* a style of comedy act popular in the 1920s and 1930s. The operating principal was "anything for a laugh," illustrated by the last of the nut comics, Ole Olsen and Chic Johnson, whose show *Hellzapoppin* (1938–41) wired the customers' seats for a buzz, had stooges running through rows of seating, and had chorus girls dancing with the audience and sitting in men's laps. Duffy & Sweeney were simpler.

Duffy's Irish parents were a music-hall song-and-dance act before they immigrated to America. In vaudeville, they were known as Duffy & Sawtelle before young Jimmy joined the act and made it Duffy, Sawtelle & Duffy. Like his parents, he sang and danced. With experience, he demonstrated a flair for light comedy and gave the family act a lift.

Around 1910, Jimmy Duffy married Mercedes Lorenz, a beauty with whom he formed an act. They were a bright romantic comedy act, two good-looking juveniles who could dance, sing and deliver comedy lines. Musical comedy and revue would have been the next step, but Duffy faltered. It was not unusual for some performers and actors to take to the bottle, but Duffy underwent a conversion and chose liquor over his career, wife and child. He still managed to get work, appearing in revues with Gertrude Hoffman and for the Shuberts.

When Jimmy and Mercedes split about 1917, he was growing puffy with continual drink and losing his looks, his nimble step and the ability to learn lines. The only way he could accommodate his addiction and continue to get work was to become a freewheeling, roughhouse comic. To help, he found Freddie Sweeney, who remembered whatever needed to be remembered, such as where they were going and how and when to get there.

Fred Sweeney came from a good middle-class family in Pennsylvania's capital city. He was a pageboy for the state legislature before he had reached high school, and throughout high school he was on track to study law and enter politics. Sometime around 1910, Freddie got sidetracked when he saw Charles Ahearn & His Bicycle Troupe at the local vaudeville theatre.

Ahearn did a trick cycling act, one of many comic bike acts that found receptive audiences and steady work in vaudeville during the 1910s and 1920s. The act featured various styles of cycles, including one or two that came apart as they were ridden. As part of the act, Ahearn challenged anyone in the audience to attempt to ride a particular cycle. Sweeney had ridden bikes since his childhood, and he accepted. Fred made the most of his moments onstage; so good was he that Ahearn invited him to join the act. He did. Charles Ahearn & His Bicycle Troupe did well, regularly playing two-a-day Keith time.

According to George Jessel, Fred Sweeney was an easygoing lad and not greatly ambitious, and Fred Astaire wrote of Sweeney that he was clever as well as an agreeable companion. Somehow, Sweeney passed eight years in show business before he met Duffy around 1918. Each seemed to be what the other was looking for. Duffy, nearing 30 and a vaudeville veteran of more than 20 years, found a young, agreeable man who drank but drank enough less than Duffy to see that their few bags were packed and they caught the right train. Sweeney, six years junior, was attracted by Duffy's warmth, wild good humor and fund of stories. When Duffy suggested they pair up in an act, Sweeney was willing.

Jimmy Duffy devised an act heavy on improvisation, and all Sweeney needed to do was follow Jimmy's lead. Duffy wore bagged and wrinkled tights and a dress coat over his bare chest, and Sweeney wore whatever was handy. That took care of having to worry about laundry. Duffy announced, "I and Mr. Sweeney will sing an impromptu song. Most people make up these songs as they go along. I and Mr. Sweeney will make them up as we come back." Then Sweeney began a shaggy-dog story, and Duffy nodded off. Startled, Duffy quickly awoke. Finding Sweeney still prattling, Duffy slapped him and then, bowing, apologized. The action spiraled: they slapped, shoved and kicked each other, followed by a few rounds of apologizing and bowing, until they collapsed in an exhausted heap.

One of their most famous bits had Duffy calling into the wing space, asking for a piano. After a grand piano was rolled out, Duffy and Sweeney would crawl under it and lay there, like two boys in makeshift clubhouse. They sucked on lollipops and batted a few screwball comments back and forth until Duffy announced, "This is too hard work. Tomorrow, let's stay at the hotel and phone the act over."

Fellow performers ate up the act and admired Duffy for making whole cloth out of nothing. They also admired the way Duffy pricked E. F. Albee, the czar of vaudeville, daring to do what others would not. Albee's house union, the National Vaudeville Association, advertised its $1,000 death benefit paid to an act's survivors. On one occasion when they were playing on the road, Duffy sent a telegram to Albee, "Died here at matinee, please send $1000."

Big-city audiences, filled with savvy veteran observers of many a vaudeville act, found the team hilarious, and they placed on the bill at many top big-time houses, including the Palace, where they were booked numerous times despite their growing reputation for unpredictability and drunkenness. Their infractions were reported back to the Keith Vaudeville Exchange, the successor to the United Booking Office (UBO), and Duffy had to plead and lie with promises to reform to get reinstated as an act acceptable to Keith-Albee management.

It was not just Duffy. Sweeney had become a drunk, but the younger man was unable to match the master. Joe Laurie Jr. recalled that, at the end of one long night of imbibing at a saloon, Sweeney slumped unconscious to the floor. Duffy turned to the bartender, "That's the thing about Sweeney, he knows when to stop."

Prompted by his devotion to his Roman Catholic faith and the need to keep body and soul together, Duffy periodically dried out. He was well regarded as a comedy writer, and he provided lyrics and gags for the *Ziegfeld Follies of 1922* (as well as, perhaps, some of Olsen & Johnson's material in that revue). He also wrote song lyrics and thought up gags for *Earl Carroll's Vanities of 1923* and *Earl Carroll's Vanities of 1924*. (Duffy also stooged a bit onstage for the 1924 edition.)

Joe Cook was chief comic for the 1924 *Vanities*, and Ted Healy was a star of the 1925 edition. Both Cook and Healy were fine nut comics, then at the top of their game, and doubtless Duffy's comic mind was in sync with theirs. In 1929, Duffy cowrote with Will Morrissey the lyrics for *Keep It Clean* (1929), a Broadway revue built around Morrissey and produced by William Duffy (who may have been a relative), but the show died after a fortnight at the Selwyn.

Despite being a hit act much of the time in big cities, Duffy and Sweeney died in many places outside of New York. Sometimes the audiences felt insulted and grew angry. The most famous incident occurred at one southern vaudeville house, alternately reported as Memphis and New Orleans, where they were hissed in the middle of their act, while lolling under the piano. Duffy, quite drunk, began talking back until the manager pulled them offstage, but Duffy got loose and staggered up to the footlights to announce, "And now, to show our appreciation for the way you've received our act, my partner, Mr. Sweeney, will pass among you with a baseball bat and beat the bejesus out of you."

Impromptu had become unpredictable, then unreliable and finally unbookable. Sweeney had watched as Duffy's wild humor occasionally turned into rage and then led to injuring himself. Their bookings slid from big time to small time, and Duffy often was barely coherent and barely able to stumble onstage. Sweeney watched as Duffy drank shaving lotion when there was no money for booze. The act was finished, and Sweeney was no longer in shape to help Duffy.

Sweeney heard the living was easy for old vaudevillians in movie land, and sometime in the 1930s he joined some of his old vaudeville pals, like Tom Dugan, Bill Grady and Dave Chasen, Joe Cook's stooge, on the West Coast. Gradually, Fred Sweeney got his drinking under control and managed to pick up a few bit roles in movies. He was nearly 60 when he succumbed to pneumonia.

For Jimmy Duffy, the 1930s were downhill. He never made it out of Manhattan and took occasional scraps of work—such as writing gags—that old friends entrusted to him. Vaudeville historian Douglas Gilbert reported that Duffy had begun to pull himself together and was given a contract to write for an NBC radio comedy show. Three weeks later, on one late winter's day in 1939, Jimmy Duffy was found dead in Times Square, a block from the Palace Theatre and Broadway.

TOM DUGAN

b: (Thomas J. Duggan) 1 January 1889, Dublin, Ireland—d: 7 March 1955, Redlands, CA

Better known within show-business circles than with ticket buyers—although his face became familiar to movie-goers of the 1930s and 1940s as one of Hollywood's most reliable characters, the actor-comedian, Tommy Dugan was renowned in show business as a practical joker. On a whim, he would attend a movie, read aloud the credits and titles until he had everyone in the audience shushing him. Escorted out by the management, Dugan protested that he was able to read only out loud and that he was being deprived of his rights. They always refunded his money and sent him on his way to his next prank.

Tom ran with the boozing-and-betting set, but on a vaudeville stage or on the movie set he was as reliable and disciplined as he was wild and unpredictable off. A lean, pasty-faced actor with a hard mien, Dugan looked as if he had lost too many fights and won too many drinking contests. He was a natural for Damon Runyon characters, whether criminals or cops. Between 1927 and his death in 1955, Tom Dugan, sometimes billed as Tom, Tommy or Tommie, and Dugan or Duggan, acted in supporting roles in more than 250 feature motion pictures plus a few shorts.

Before he entered the movies, however, Tom Dugan had a long, if not particularly distinguished career in vaudeville. He worked as a single and in several acts, but he became best known as half of Dugan & Raymond. Dugan & Raymond were one of dozens of comedy-sketch actors in vaudeville. "The Apple Tree" was their best-known act. Tom wrote the sketches for their acts, and he had a very active sideline as a sketch writer for hire. Little is known about Ms. Raymond; she appeared neither in Broadway shows nor films.

Billed as Thomas Duggan and Babette Raymond, they joined Aileen Stanley and William Rock in the revue *Silks and Satins,* which ran the summer of 1920 at George M. Cohan's Theatre. Tom wrote the sketches for the show.

Dugan managed during his frantic schedule in Hollywood to cowrite a play with Thomas Hogan; *The Barber Had Two Sons* (1943) was produced on Broadway and starred Blanche Yurka, but it closed inside of three weeks. Tom continued to appear in films until his death at 66 in a 1955 motor vehicle accident.

DUMB ACTS

Acts that did not use speech, either spoken or sung, were known as *dumb acts* and included a wide array of performers: jugglers, tumblers, aerialists, wire acts, cyclists, strongmen, balancing acts, contortionists and animal acts, among others. Unless the dumb act had attained near-headliner status, as did juggler Cinquevalli, trick cyclist Joe Jackson, rope spinner Will Rogers or escape artist Houdini, they were usually fated to fill either the opening or closing spot on a bill regardless of the quality of their act.

The opening and closing spots on the vaudeville bill were the toughest spots for a performer. Those opening the show had to deal with the interruptions of late arrivals and, at the same time, warm up the audience for the rest of the bill. Those closing the show complained they "played to haircuts" because much of the audience, after seeing the headliner in the next-to-closing spot, tried to beat the departing crowd by leaving during the closing act. Because dumb acts neither spoke nor sang, managers assumed their acts could best suffer late arrivals and early departures. Yet executing a dumb act required quiet from an audience and great concentration on the part of the performers, especially if they were performing dangerous stunts. Once you were tagged as an opening or a closing act, it was difficult to escape that placement on the bill and the connotation that you were second rate.

By 1905, the editors of *Broadway Weekly* were advising:

> Good acrobatic work is always in demand, especially if it be of the comedy persuasion. It is far better to know how to turn a new sort of somersault, than to be skilled at reading blank verse. A comedy act of the same value as the old Caron and Herbert turn, would be swamped with offers. Trick cyclists, on the other hand, are drugs [*sic*] on the market. Any reputable agent can supply such turns by the half-dozen, and the chances are some of them have been resting so long that they have eaten the tires off their wheels. If you can ride a bicycle up the wall or across the ceiling, cycle riding will be profitable, but where that bicycle now has to perform tricks that would stagger a horse, the ability to do a few saddle tricks will not pay board. Jugglers have to take up cannon balls or automobiles to command attention nowadays; a trick trying to the nervous system, and there is small market for big trapeze acts. They cannot in any case be swung out over the audience.

Creating and perfecting a successful dumb act required skills and discipline. Often these were family acts in which training and expertise were passed from one generation to the next. Beginning as young children, they put in many hours of practice each day. Yet, although performers began their professional lives at an early age, the strength and agility demanded by their acts and the prospect of injury meant that they would retire from the act in late middle age. So, many of these families had a commercial trade on the side to sustain their retired members.

There were pluses, too, to being a dumb act. Sight acts could work all over the world and never have to worry about a language barrier between them and their audiences. They were as welcome in circuses as they were on variety stages. If they wished or needed, they could work every season, everywhere. So, unlike many other acts on the vaudeville bill, when vaudeville declined, the dumb act still had places to work. When the dumb act worked in the circus, however, they were not relegated to opening or closing a show. Aerialists and wire acts in particular were only a rung or two below equestrians, the royalty of circuses.

DUMPS

See Honky-Tonks

DUNCAN SISTERS

Rosetta Duncan

b: 23 November 1897, Los Angeles, CA—
d: 4 December 1959, Acero, IL

Vivian Duncan

b: 17 June 1899, Los Angeles, CA—
d: 19 September 1986, Los Angeles, CA

The Duncan Sisters well represented vaudeville at its best. They performed a double singing act—a sister song-dance-and-patter act—one of the more prevalent types of acts in vaudeville. Rosetta and Vivian Duncan, however, were unique. Instead of dressing prettily and singing songs of the day, as many sister acts did, the Duncan Sisters' act reflected their peculiar talents and winning personalities.

They offered sentimental songs like "Remembering," "Side by Side" and "I'm Following You" and comic ditties like "It Must Be an Old Spanish Custom" and "In Sweet Onion Time." They sang in close harmony that was capped by Vivian trilling like a rare bird and Rosetta clowning. What they did was unlike anything done by anyone else.

Vivian was, if not quite ethereal, a bit pixilated and very feminine. Her long hair was perched precariously atop her head or floated around her face in Mary Pickford curls. She worked from her own special inner world, one whose orbit was slightly skewed. Occasionally, she seemed given to the vapors. Rosetta was tomboyish, earthbound and broader in style than Vivian, rather like a Peter Pan in an English pantomime, and she displayed the same showbiz energy that fueled Cantor and Jolson, grabbing an audience by its lapels and selling the act. She was also a physical clown

Rosetta and Vivian Duncan

who could take a fall, turn it into a somersault and end upright.

Rosetta and Vivian began their careers, probably around 1913, as a team with a yodeling-and-singing act in their native Los Angeles. Exactly how old they were is in question; it is not even certain which of the pair was the older. Most accounts agree there were two years separating them in age.

According to some reports, they were playing Pantages time by 1914. Their older sister, Evelyn, was already working in show business in the East. Rosetta and Vivian were reunited with Evelyn after a series of small-time routes brought them to New York City. They were playing a Coney Island vaudeville house when Evelyn either informed them of an audition for Gus Edwards or arranged for Mr. and Mrs. Edwards to see her younger sisters' act. In 1916, Rosetta and Vivian became part of a battalion of talented youngsters that toured in one or another of the various acts that Gus Edward sent into vaudeville. His better-known known troupes were "School Days" and "Kiddie Kabaret."

So speedy was the Duncan Sisters' ascent in East Coast vaudeville that by early 1917 the Duncans got a shot at the big time when they were booked at the 5th Avenue Theatre. They were not quite the hit they hoped but promising enough to win a spot in *Doing Our Bit,* a patriotic-themed Winter Garden extravaganza headlining Ed Wynn, Frank Tinney and James J. Corbett. Barely 20 but with nearly a decade of seasoning in vaudeville, they had developed an effective act and quickly became a popular drawing card on any bill.

Rosetta and Vivian brought their vaudeville sensibility into the Jerome Kern musical, *She's a Good Fellow* (1919), which ran from May until August 1919 when the actors' strike shut down Broadway. The following year, the Duncans again left vaudeville to appear in *Tip Top,* a revue stitched together by a wandering thread of a plot. It survived the critics and ran the season because of the talent and popularity of its star, Fred Stone, and the Duncans' growing favor with audiences.

In 1921, London called, and they played the Gaiety Theatre in *Pins and Needles,* a show that established them as English favorites. They returned to the USA for more vaudeville, including a 1922 booking at the Palace Theatre in New York, the vaudevillians' Olympus.

The Duncan Sisters starred for most of 1924 in *Topsy and Eva,* a musical farce they freely adapted from *Uncle Tom's Cabin* and for which they wrote all the songs. From the first, in 1853, Harriet Beecher Stowe's plaintive tale of the evils of slavery was more often adapted into a happyland burlesk minstrel than into serious drama. Either way, the play found an audience for nearly 80 years.

Rosetta and Vivian Duncan fashioned a sentimental and good-humored portrait of the Old South, similar to the Jolson confections, but their characters were not stock types. Rosetta was a blacked-up but lively and mischievous Topsy; Vivian was a lovely and mischievous Eva. Topsy refused to let anyone temper her enjoyment of life or throttle her spirit. Eva knew she was supposed to reform Topsy; instead, she was drawn to her bold and free spirit. Many critics were confounded. They could not decide whether *Topsy and Eva* was a burlesk, a farce, or a naive and sentimental musical.

It was all of that, and audiences accepted it at face value. The Duncans had taken Topsy and Eva, the two characters out of *Uncle Tom's Cabin* that interested them, fashioned them into suitable roles for themselves, and pushed them to the forefront of the plot and stage. Rosetta and Vivian were vaudevillians seeking to entertain, and their recipe had long required alternate portions of whimsy, tugs at the heartstrings, lovely singing and slapstick capers.

Topsy and Eva was such a success that it played Chicago for nearly a year and then played 20 weeks on Broadway. Over the years, Rosetta and Vivian revived *Topsy and Eva* and toured in both full productions and tab versions of their show. They returned to London in 1927 for a musical revue, *Clowns in Clover,* at the

Adelphi. In the USA, they successfully resumed playing *Topsy and Eva* coast to coast and then took it to England, France, Germany and South America. Back in Manhattan, they joined Helen Morgan, Lillian Roth, and Paul Whiteman and His Orchestra for the 1928 edition of the *Ziegfeld Midnight Frolic,* to which cast Maurice Chevalier was later added.

In the late 1920s, when the movies began to dance and sing, Hollywood studios were busily scouting Broadway and big-time vaudeville for performers appropriate for talking pictures. The Duncan Sisters were at the peak of their popularity in vaudeville and musicals. Because of commitments, however, they had to turn down Irving Thalberg's offer of the leads in MGM's first full-fledged musical, *The Broadway Melody* (1929).

Indeed, the story might have been suggested by the relationships and events in the Duncan Sisters' own lives, altered to fit the conventions of society and filmmaking. Anthony Slide reports in his *Encyclopedia of Vaudeville* that neither sister was particularly happy. Rosetta was a lesbian, and the effort to prevent her sexual orientation from harming their popularity may have led to alcoholism. Vivian was unhappily married to silent star Nils Asther, whose preference for sexual threesomes, including another man, caused Vivian to divorce him. Those themes were too strong for musicals of the 1930s or even later, so they were transformed into more acceptable melodramatic situations for *Broadway Melody.*

The Duncans were reported to have made two movie appearances before Thalberg's offer: a silent feature of their stage hit *Topsy & Eva* (1927), which still exists, and a guest spot in a W. C. Fields' silent, *Two Flaming Youths* (1927). Actually, only Vivian is listed in the cast, and her appearance was in a guest spot along with more than a dozen other well-known Broadway stars.

Thalberg's trust was reasonably placed in the Duncan Sisters, and theirs in him, as *It's a Great Life* (1929) proved. Few vaudeville acts have been so well served by a movie. Unfortunately, the film delivered MGM only a marginal profit.

The Duncan Sisters joined Lillian Russell, Fay Templeton and Weber & Fields in *March of Time* (1930), which MGM had intended as a sequel of sorts to the previous year's success, *The Hollywood Revue of 1929.* In fact, its working title was *The Hollywood Revue of 1930.*

The movie was shot but never released. The reasons are unclear. Some said it was poorly written and directed. Others claimed MGM feared glutting the market with another musical. Later, the film was cut up with portions stuck into other films, whereas the remainder,

Duncan Sisters, Vivian and Rosetta

Duncan Sisters, Vivian and Rosetta

it seems, was consigned to rot in storage. The Duncans' committed their Topsy & Eva act to a sound two-reeler called *Surprise!* (1935); it was their final movie.

During the last days of big-time, two-a-day vaudeville, Rosetta performed solo when she starred in *Tell a Vision* at Boston's Majestic Theatre. During the week of 7 May 1932, billed as Rosetta "Topsy" Duncan, she was booked into the fourth spot on the closing bill of two-a-day vaudeville at the Palace Theatre. At the time, Vivian, a new mother, tended to her baby daughter, Evelyn.

The Duncan Sisters are usually recalled for their Topsy and Eva turn, an act they continued to perform even into the 1950s when blackface was anathema to most audiences. The reviews of the time assured readers that there was nothing mean-spirited or mocking in Rosetta's spirited portrayal, yet the fact that the Duncans occasionally tried to revive their act long after the rejection of blackface suggests that they had drifted out of touch with the contemporary spirit.

On the other hand, audiences still turned out for the exercise in nostalgia. Vivian and Rosetta had lost all their money in the stock market crash of 1929, and they needed to continue working. In the public mind, they were Topsy and Eva, so they frequently revived those roles, even for network radio bookings.

Rosetta, always the more inventive half of the team, constantly changed their songs and comic business. Even though they still were playing Topsy and Eva, their material was fresh. Vivian was the more gregarious of the pair. She handled press interviews and enjoyed spoofing a show-business image by driving a gaudy automobile. Rosetta kept out of the public eye when not performing.

In the 1950s, Rosetta and Vivian continued to appear in nightclubs, occasionally on television, and they returned to vaudeville in 1957 when they were on a bill at the Palace Theatre, a few years after it revived its combination vaudeville and movie policy. After Rosetta's death in a 1959 automobile crash, Vivian continued as a solo act and played Australian variety one season. Sister Evelyn, long retired, had married and raised her family back home in Los Angeles. Vivian had married again in 1947 and lived comfortably in Atherton, California, not far from Menlo Park in the Bay Area.

DUNNINGER

b: (Joseph Dunninger) 28 April 1892, New York, NY—d: 9 March 1975, Cliffside Park, NJ

As a boy, the future "Master Mind of Mystery" attended vaudeville shows with his father, and young Dunninger quickly developed a fondness for magic acts. He saw Kellar, the Herrmanns, Houdini and Thurston, but Kellar and mind reader Anna Eva Fay were his inspiration.

He began his career, as many teenage performers did, by presenting card-manipulation demonstrations at local fraternal organizations and the like. One of his earliest professional engagements was at the Eden Musee, an old theatre and wax museum down on West 23rd Street, in the former theatre district. He performed a standard but well-executed and well-received program of magic tricks.

Even as early at 1915, Dunninger appreciated the value of promotion. He dressed with a theatrical flair and took a leaf from Houdini's book to create interest in his local appearances by initiating some newsworthy bit of sensation.

During the war-bond drives to support the USA's participation in the First World War, Dunninger found it more effective to demonstrate mind reading than deal with the props of a magic act in an uncontrolled, often outdoor, environment.

Dunninger set himself apart from most mind-reading acts because he worked alone, without an aisle man. He presented his act as a scientific demonstration (as had many) and assured his audience that mentalism had benefits, as yet untapped, for society, especially law enforcement and business transactions. He drew volunteers to distribute pencils and paper among the audience. They were instructed to write a name, a place, a date or a single word upon their paper, fold it, and place it in a pocket or purse. Another volunteer was asked to choose among those who had participated and gather their papers and place them in an envelope. Dunninger went upstage, sat at a desk with the unopened envelopes and revealed what had been written on each of the five pieces of paper.

Boston was the scene of several of his exploits; he gave a demonstration at the Parkman Bandstand on the Boston Common to a large gathering of the curious. A committee of leading citizens was chosen to identify one person who would be in the crowd that day. Without any obvious clues, Dunninger identified the man among the thousands present. Reports of his feat led to a series of well-attended one-man shows at Steinert Hall a block away on Boylston Street.

One fortuitous bit of mind reading led to one of Dunninger's most famous publicity coups. In the audience at a Boston mind-reading session, one of the persons whose message was selected to be divined by Dunninger was a forger and ex-convict named Charles K. Ponzi, famous for bilking naive investors of millions of dollars. The newspaper reports of Dunninger's demonstration included Ponzi's name and photo, and he was promptly arrested by police.

Dunninger probably made as much money from society swells in private performances as he did in vaudeville, but Keith time and Orpheum time offered as many dates as Dunninger wished to fill playing the two-a-day. He also presented a full-evening show for a while during the 1925–26 season, performing illusions in the first half of the show and his mentalist act in the second, but it was the demonstration of mind reading that attracted his audience.

Dunninger performed throughout the 1930s and tried radio. His second effort on NBC in 1943 was successful for a couple of seasons, but listening to a mentalist act without seeing it done was as improbable an attraction as appreciating a broadcast by a ventriloquist (unless he were Edgar Bergen).

The Amazing Dunninger was an early if brief attraction on television. He shared a biweekly spot with ventriloquist Paul Winchell and Jerry Mahoney and then had his own dedicated time slot. Doing it each week became repetitious, especially as Dunninger lacked the warmth of personality required by performers who enter the public's homes on the small screen. More successful was the Amazing Kreskin (George Kresge Jr., born 1935), who possessed more savvy about the television medium and projected a more engaging personality. His appropriation of Dunninger's methods distressed the older mentalist. Neither was a favorite with stage magicians whose ethics dictated that illusionists make clear to audiences that they had no extraordinary psychic power or extrasensory perception.

JIMMY DURANTE

b: (James Francis Durante) 10 February 1893, New York, NY—d: 29 January 1980, Santa Monica, CA

The antic spirit is frequently dispossessed in the middle-aged comedian by his gradual concession to a world that has refused to be reinvented or even reordered. Too often, the aging comedian's center of levity shifts from the rebellious mind of his youthful self to a compromised heart. Broken and grown cynical, or salved by success, the capitulating comedian may cut a deal with the world he once ridiculed. Defeated or co-opted, he loses his edge, his sense of the madness of life. Jimmy Durante kept his performer's heart pure.

If ever a young man seemed ill suited to the entertainment industry it was Jimmy Durante. He had not been favored, even as a baby, with an attractive face. No article was ever written that did not point to his nose: a large, Old World nose. Young Jimmy imagined people looking at him and thinking, "What an ugly kid! What a monster! And then I'd go home and cry. . . . [Even] when I'm out there on the stage laughin' and kiddin' about the nose, at no time was I ever happy about it." One of his biographers, Gene Fowler, claims that Jimmy vowed, because he was "hurt so deep, . . . never to hurt anybody else."

Time and a good spirit were on his side. If others wore out youthful good looks, Durante stayed in fine physical shape, and his face mellowed into impish and gentle nobility that shone with goodness. Fortunately, in one respect he never changed. Had he ever overcome his inability to properly memorize and enunciate long words, he might have been out of business. Yet Durante achieved eloquence by reaching for words that, though they were beyond his articulation, were expressions of the heart and soul of a frustrated poet.

The Durante family was musical. By the time Jimmy, the youngest of three boys and a girl, was in his early teens, the family could afford piano lessons for him, but Jimmy loved ragtime, and he preferred learning by ear. Leaving school after an unrewarding seven or eight years, he began playing piano for dances and losing a series of menial day jobs. Finally, Jimmy found a job he liked: playing barroom piano in Diamond Tony's at Coney Island. It was 1910, Jimmy was 17, and he worked seven nights a week

Jimmy Durante

from 8:00 P.M. until 6:00 A.M. Diamond Tony's was a typical beer hall, but neither dancing nor gambling was permitted. Prostitution was not permitted either, but sporting men knew where to go because Diamond Tony's waiters served more than the booze to favored customers.

When the summer season ended, Jimmy got work at the Chatham Club in Lower Manhattan's Chinatown. There was little to distinguish the Chatham Club from the nearby Jimmy Kelly's Mandarin Club or Nigger Mike's; all were dumps. Jimmy was finding his approach to life through working in these saloons. He got to know prostitutes, pickpockets, opium addicts, police, mobsters and lushes. He treated them all with respect, but for the most part he kept a safe but not alienating distance. Never judgmental and always ready with a handout, Jimmy Durante set his own course and steered a middle path between the gangsters and the police.

He started his second year in show business at Kerry Walsh's at Coney Island, where he met and became friends with Eddie Cantor, a singing waiter. In performance, they were well matched, each attuned to the other. No matter what song a customer requested, the young singer and the young piano player could fake it. Cantor was ambitious and focused, and he urged Jimmy to join him in vaudeville. Jimmy was passive and without goals except playing piano, happy to earn enough to support himself, help out at home and place a few bets.

Cantor moved on, but Durante willingly repeated his seasonal cycles for several years. During that time, he worked the Alamo, a cellar joint in Harlem, and played during the summers at the College Arms and later at the College Inn, places on Coney Island operated by the Alamo's owners. As the head of the house's five-piece band, Jimmy introduced the dance contests and hired the acts. One of the acts that tried out in 1915 was Eddie Jackson & Eddie Murray, but Jimmy did not hire them. When in 1917 Eddie Jackson tried out again, this time successfully, his partner was Dot Taylor, a singer and shimmy dancer.

In 1923, Durante, Jackson and another man opened a speakeasy, the Club Durant, so called because the sign painter forgot the final *e*. It was Prohibition, and speakeasies were making money hand over fist with bootleg booze—except the Club Durant. That changed soon after Lou Clayton walked through the door and took charge of the club and the act. Lou became the architect of Jimmy's success.

One of the most celebrated and rowdy acts in Prohibition-era speakeasies was comprised of Lou Clayton, tap dancer and monologist, Eddie Jackson, a cakewalking singer, and Jimmy Durante, a musical clown. They could have been called "Slide, Strut, and Stride" for the way they invaded a stage. Announced by the high-decibel blare of Jimmy's onstage band, Eddie Jackson, in top hat and tails, strutted onstage singing "Won't You Come Home, Bill Bailey." From the opposite direction, Lou Clayton slid across the stage in his tap dancing shoes. Then Jimmy Durante, in his stiff-legged gait, strode downstage between them, and the show was off to a rollicking start. What followed was a blur of songs, soft shoe, jokes and impromptu forays into the audience.

Eddie Jackson (1896–1980) was born in Brooklyn. The family name in the USA was Jacobs, changed from something an immigration officer could not pronounce or spell. After getting through as much school as he and the teachers could stand, Jackson got work in a bookbindery. One of his fellow workers always bet on the wrong horses, so Eddie kept loaning him money for lunch. It proved a good investment, especially when Clayton, Jackson & Durante played Chicago, where Eddie's friend, the erstwhile bookbinder, Al Capone, called the shots. During Jackson's first winter at the Alamo, he and Dot Taylor broke up. Jimmy kept Eddie on for the season then took him as a partner in the Club Durant. Jackson became a junior partner of sorts in the Durante act and stayed on 60 years.

Lou Clayton (1887–1950) was born Louis Finklestein. A poker-faced, hard-eyed character right out of Damon Runyon's stable of horse-playing hoods, Lou was already a vaudeville success when he visited the Club Durant one night with a friend. Lou obliged a request to sing. Impulsively, Durante asked him to join the operation. Lou agreed, provided he was the boss. That was okay with Jimmy, who just wanted to play piano and make a few bucks. Their 30-year contract was sealed with a handshake.

Lou's word was his bond, and he demanded the same from others. With his guidance, the club and the trio prospered, and Lou kept everyone in line. He and Jimmy were more than partners. Jimmy was the one man Lou trusted and loved like a brother; Lou handled the money and all the troublemakers: drunks, goons or feds.

The Club Durant became the place for Broadway's elite to meet. Mobsters mingled with the Park Avenue swells, and a good time was had by all until Lou discovered that their fourth partner was skimming. Lou, Eddie, and Jimmy pulled out and opened the Parody Club. Friendly press pumped the Parody, and the trio became famous enough for vaudeville bookers to make offers. Each time bookers countered with less than Lou asked for, he raised the price. When Clayton, Jackson & Durante finally debuted in vaudeville in 1927 at Loew's State, it was for $3,500 per week. When the Palace finally met Lou's terms in 1928, it cost the Palace $5,500 for a week, a good investment because Clayton, Jackson & Durante broke the box-office record.

Jimmy was an instinctual musician and better than was often credited. The songs he wrote for himself demonstrated that he had a canny grasp of his stage character: "Jimmy, the Well-Dressed Man," "I Ups to Him and He Ups to Me," "I Know I Can Do without Broadway, but Can Broadway Do without Me?," "Inka Dinka Do" and "Who'll Be with You when I'm Far Away?" Performing character-comedy songs like those, Jimmy Durante became the American equivalent of the coster singers of English music-hall.

Their most famous number was "Wood." Like Kipling's poem "Boots," it became a fevered chant as Jimmy extolled the virtues of wood, and the trio heaped the stage with everything wooden they could find, from toothpicks to pencils to chairs, poles, desks, trees, an outhouse and a piano they reduced to splinters.

Ziegfeld beckoned in 1929, and the trio was added to *Show Girl.* Their first film, *Roadhouse Nights* (1930), followed, after which they went into another stage show, *The New Yorkers,* in 1930. That led to a five-year contract for Durante with MGM. Clayton, Jackson & Durante were finished as an act except for rare occasions such as benefits.

Lou Clayton was content. No longer an entertainer, he made deals that protected Jimmy's interests. Eddie Jackson tagged along for the ride whenever there was a club date, otherwise he was poolside. The three each got a third of Durante's earnings. That's the way Jimmy wanted it, and Lou saw to it that they got top dollar for Jimmy's services.

MGM got Durante, but they did not know what to do with him, so they paired him with Buster Keaton in three poor films. Jimmy's and Buster's styles could not meld; Durante seemed overbearing, and Keaton looked as if he wanted to go home. For 20 years, film producers failed to discover a way to use Jimmy well, yet he made more than three dozen movies. *Jumbo,* made in 1962, was one of the better. On Broadway, Durante scored in *Strike Me Pink* (1933), *Jumbo* (1935), *Red, Hot and Blue* (1936) and *Stars in Your Eyes* (1939) but struck out with *Keep off the Grass* (1940).

The Second World War years were a bad time personally, as well as professionally. Jimmy's first wife, Jeanne, had grown increasingly morose about the intrusion of his career into their married life. Clayton was enduring a series of illnesses. Clayton, Jackson & Durante teamed for the final time in 1946 at Manhattan's Silver Slipper Café.

Radio costarred Jimmy with Gary Moore in 1943. It worked well. Moore was bright and a good contrast; Durante had begun to lay back a bit and unveiled his sentimental side, closing the weekly broadcast with the line, "Good night Mrs. Calabash, wherever you are."

Jimmy Durante

Mrs. Calabash was Jeanne, and 1943 was also the year she died.

Durante's rambunctious clowning had suited his raw youth and the loud clubs he played. The same act had seemed strained in a middle-aged man. He began to display warmth, decency and a bit of wisdom. As Jimmy mellowed, his performances became more sympathetic, and the studios began to give him better films, but it was television that best showcased the older Durante. Lou arranged Jimmy's triumphal television debut in 1950 and then succumbed to cancer.

Television and the older Durante were made for each other the way the young Schnozzola and nightclubs were. For his first four seasons, Jimmy appeared as one of the rotating stars of the hour-long *Four Star/All Star Revue,* a variety show. The next three years he starred in the *Jimmy Durante Show,* a hybrid of variety and situation comedy set in a disinfected Club Durant. Thereafter, he guest starred and did the occasional special broadcast. Although he never abandoned his novelty songs, Jimmy sang love songs plaintively and so well in his raspy voice that decades later his recordings were gracing film scores of the 1980s and 1990s.

Jimmy won an Emmy and a Peabody Award. He wore well on TV and was the most beloved of the old comics of the vaudeville era. Not only did his antic spirit not dim with age and stardom, he avoided sentimentality by never compromising his innocence and decency.

DUTCH COMICS

Comedians who played their routines as stage Germans were called Dutch comics. *Dutch* is likely a corruption of *Deutsch,* the German word for "German." A Dutch act was the same in most essentials as an Irish act, a blackface act or nearly any other stage ethnicity of the period from the 1870s through the 1910s. Usually two comedians paired in a Dutch act. They wore loud checked or striped clothes and chin whiskers. One portrayed the domineering trickster who bullied and took advantage of his slower, stooge-like partner. In truth, neither character was very smart.

When starting out, Weber & Fields were one of the many Dutch acts playing variety in beer halls, dime museums and small-time theatres. When Weber & Fields discovered they had been booked on a bill with another Dutch act, one that was more established, Joe and Lou readily switched to Irish or blackface. What changed were the costumes and the accents. The act's structure, its hectoring dialogue and physical abuse remained largely the same. The same act, minus the accents and costumes, survived as routines performed by the Three Stooges and Abbott & Costello.

E

EASTERN WHEEL

A burlesque circuit better known as the Columbia Wheel (*See "Columbia Wheel"*).

BUDDY & VILMA EBSEN

b: (Christian Rudolph Ebsen) 2 April 1908, Belleville, IL—d: 6 July 2003, Torrance, CA

b: (Vilma Ebsen) 1911, Belleview, IL

Buddy Ebsen was a tall, gangly scarecrow of a dancer. At 6 feet, 3 inches, he had grown used to slumping over in a world where everyone else was bound to be shorter. He brought his rag-doll posture into his dancing. Spine curved, legs akimbo, arms splayed and feet pointed every which way, his entire approach to dancing was a list of don'ts, yet it was an individual entry into the ranks of eccentric dancing, or, more precisely, legomania.

In contrast to her brother, Vilma Ebsen was a petite and quirky dancer, her movements more feminine and far less exaggerated than her brother's. They did not mirror each other's steps; they danced, as Vilma later explained, in counterpoint. Somehow it fit together, and they remained an act from 1929 until 1942.

Their father was a ballet teacher, trained in the Danish school of ballet, which differed from the Russian school in several ways. The Danes tended to choreograph to folkloric story plots, emphasized pantomime and character dancing (and acting), and gave equal, if not greater, roles to the premier *danseurs,* whereas most other Europeans, including the Russians, choreographed for their prima ballerinas and emphasized physical grace and beauty of movement and attitudes.

As kids, Buddy and Vilma moved with their parents to Orlando, Florida, where Buddy found his way to the stage doors of local theatres. He picked up some dance steps that he passed on to his sister. Soon they had an act—Vilma as a dance teacher and Buddy as the hick pupil—that played various dates in Florida. During a summer-long vacation in the Appalachians of western North Carolina, Vilma and Buddy, still in their teens, were hired by Arthur Murray to dance at teatime at the Grove Park Inn in Asheville, where the future famous ballroom dance teacher was the social director.

Buddy was finishing up college and Vilma was starting when the bust in Florida land speculation laid low the economy in 1928. Buddy decided to head to New York. Vilma was teaching dancing with her sister Norma at the Ebsen Dance Studios when Buddy urged her to come to New York. Vilma borrowed $50 from Norma and headed north. (They also had a sister Helga.)

Their dancing had been good enough for Florida and North Carolina, but New York City was tap-dance central. Being good was not good enough. Vilma studied at Jack Donahue's studio, and Buddy and Vilma swapped steps with other young hopefuls. In 1930, Buddy managed to get a Broadway job in the chorus of *Whoopee,* the Eddie Cantor hit. When the show was casting replacements for the road, Vilma was hired as well.

Cantor, who valued ambition, encouraged them as they spent free time practicing onstage between shows. After the show closed, they got work dancing in clubs. In Atlantic City, it was Vilma who landed the job first then wangled Buddy into the show. Walter Winchell, vaudevillian-turned-Broadway scribe, saw their act in Atlantic City and plugged the Ebsens in his column so repeatedly that they got dozens of offers.

Buddy and Vilma put together an act for vaudeville and started at the top, the Palace Theatre on Broadway. They also won featured or starring spots in Broadway shows. *Flying Colors* (1932) boasted music by Arthur Schwartz, lyrics by Howard Dietz (who also directed), book by Dietz and George S. Kaufman, and a great cast that included Clifton Webb, Tamara Geva, Imogene Coca, Charles Butterworth, Patsy Kelly, Monette Moore, Philip Loeb and Larry Adler, along with Buddy & Vilma.

In the *Ziegfeld Follies of 1934,* Vilma and Buddy attracted a lot of attention with their second-act, train-station number, "Stop That Clock." The stars of the revue were Fanny Brice and Willie Howard; Eve Arden, Jane Froman and the Preisser Sisters were the other newcomers. Vilma danced with Charles Walters in *Between the Devil* (1937), which starred Jack Buchanan and Evelyn Laye. *Yokel Boy* (1939) starred Buddy on his own in a cast that included Judy Canova, Phil Silvers, Dixie Dunbar and Lew Hearn. Hollywood called, and both Buddy and Vilma responded by making their debuts in *Broadway Melody of 1936.* They shared a charming tenement rooftop dance sequence with star Eleanor Powell, but, stylistically, the Ebsens and Powell were worlds apart. *Captain January* (1936) showed Buddy to good advantage; the disparity in height between Buddy Ebsen and tiny Shirley Temple served them well, and they dueted a good novelty song-and-dance number, "The Cod Fish Ball."

Making movies became Buddy's primary occupation, and he appeared in a dozen or so films until the USA joined the Allies in the Second World War and Buddy heeded the call of duty, His better films had come in the 1930s. Buddy's most famous movie was one he did not make: *The Wizard of Oz* (1939). When he developed an extreme allergic reaction to the metallic makeup, Ebsen was replaced by Jack Haley as the Tin Man.

Work thinned for Buddy Ebsen after the Second World War, but, by the early 1950s, he appeared fairly regularly in character roles in movie Westerns, took roles in several TV anthology and Western shows, and tried a couple of television series of his own. His big break came in 1962 when *The Beverly Hillbillies* started its run on television. It was among the most-watched series of its time and did not cease production until 1970. Despite his identification with the role of Jed Clampett in the series, a mere two years later Ebsen began another quite different series, *Barnaby Jones,* which also ran eight seasons.

Vilma retired to Pacific Palisades after the Second World War. Buddy never retired. He was active in conservative causes and, in his 80s, continued to pop up in television series, did some voice-overs and wrote an autobiography, *The Other Side of Oz* (1994). In 2001, at 93 years of age, he published a novel, *Kelly's Quest.*

ECCENTRIC DANCING

Around the turn of the twentieth century, a number of Arab and Japanese acrobatic troupes, contortionists and belly dancers played the USA. Their visits were part of their global tours or they came specifically to perform at world's fairs and expositions such as those held in New Orleans (1885), Chicago (1893), San Francisco (1894), Buffalo (1901), St. Louis (1904), Seattle (1909), and San Francisco and San Diego (1915).

Buck, clog and tap dancers became intrigued by the flips, jumps, twists and shakes they witnessed and vied with each other to incorporate some of the movements into their dancing. Already grounded by a basis in rhythmic movement, the dancers adapted the acrobatics and contortions into syncopated movements, adding style and speed.

The stiff torso of Celtic and Anglo-Saxon clogs and jigs had earlier been loosened in contact with African American dances. Eccentric dancing employed the entire body in ways that carried the dancer across the stage and encouraged them toward both floor work and leaps. Stylistically, it demanded that a dancer be original in his combinations, even to the point of grotesque, an extreme at which the eccentric dancer is hard to differentiate from the eccentric comedian. As tap-dance and jazz historians Marshall and Jean Stearns point out in their book *Jazz Dance*, "The term 'eccentric' is a catch-all for dancers who have [developed] their own non-standard movements."

Eccentric is used sometimes to describe the more bizarre of physical comedians and clowns, tumblers, jugglers and other entertainers, but in those cases it is a descriptive word, not a professional's term.

CLIFF EDWARDS (UKULELE IKE)

b: 14 June 1895, Hannibal, MO—d: 17 July 1971, Los Angeles, CA

In a decade when much adventurous and diverse music was being composed and performed, it is a bit foolhardy to suggest that there was an identifiable 1920s sound. Yet, if one asked Americans four generations beyond that decade to describe the sound of the 1920s, they would as likely as not burble "Boop-boop-a-doop" or mention the ubiquitous ukulele.

The ukulele was the guitar of its day, and Cliff Edwards was so identified with the instrument that he was better known to audiences by his nickname, Ukulele Ike. By 2000, both names were largely forgotten, and few people other than elders know that Cliff Edwards was the voice of Walt Disney's Jiminy Cricket, heard first in Disney's animated *Pinocchio* (1940). Jiminy Cricket's song, "When You Wish upon a Star," was revived in

1954 as the theme song for television's long-running *Disneyland* (also known as *Walt Disney's Wonderful World of Color*) program, and again in 1977, when the song was used during the closing credits of Steven Spielberg's movie, *Close Encounters of the Third Kind.* By the time that Spielberg's movie had been released, Cliff Edwards had been dead six years.

According to Edwards, he began singing as a boy to drum up business while selling newspapers. By 1909, age 14, he had chucked the newspapers, home and school, and worked his way southward on the Mississippi River to St. Louis. Cliff sang in saloons for nickels tossed by customers and learned that he could sing for his supper. A passing carnival offered a more reliable wage, so Cliff hit the road with carney shows for a few seasons. Although pay was steady, it was also poor. Saloons paid even lower wages, if any at all, but tips could be plentiful. Cliff learned to play the ukulele by the time he went to work professionally in saloons; many did not have pianos, so he carried a uke to accompany himself.

Cliff Edwards

When he felt he had developed enough material for an act, Edwards tried his luck in small-time vaudeville. He got along as best he could, playing night spots and small-time vaudeville, and then teamed up, around 1918 when he was 22 or 23, with piano player and singer, Bobby Carleton. Edwards and Carleton formed a musical act that helped both careers. Bobby composed "Ja-Da," a lilting nonsense song that Cliff helped make a hit. Cliff was tagged with the nickname "Ukulele Ike" at the Ansonia Café in Chicago. According to Cliff, one of the waiters, Spot, kept forgetting his name and called Cliff "Ike." Others began calling him Ike. Instead of fighting it, Cliff starting calling himself Ukulele Ike. The moniker stuck.

He began making sound recordings in 1919, but his first pressings were never released. He played drums and sang in Joe Frisco's act for a while and had several short-lived onstage partnerships: with dancer Lou Clayton (before Lou teamed with Jimmy Durante) and another with Pierce Keegan, a singer and dancer. Although Edwards & Keegan: "Jazz As Is" was successful, the partnership only lasted a couple of years before Cliff went out as a single. Cliff also got married for the first time in 1919, to a nonprofessional named Gertrude Ryrholm Benson. Their union produced a son.

Cliff was divorced by 1921 when his career as a solo act was in high gear. He costarred with Mae West and the husband-and-wife team El Brendel & Flo Burt in *The Mimic World of 1921.* It played the Century Roof for three weeks but gave Edwards bragging rights that he had made it to Broadway. Cliff Edwards recorded a number of sides for Pathé, then an important label, and some of his records became big hits, including "Sleepy Time Gal," "June Night," "I Cried for You" and "Toot, Toot, Tootsie! (Goodbye)," which he made famous before Al Jolson performed the same song.

Over the course of his career, Cliff Edwards sold about 75 million to 80 million records. His clear diction, soft high tenor, fluid rhythmic sense and vocal tricks made him distinctive. Having excellent musicians like Red Nichols and Eddie Lang backing him helped. Cliff Edwards and Gene Austin, another high tenor, predated Bing Crosby with a relaxed melodic style that grew into crooning.

In 1923, Edwards married Irene Wylie, a dancer from the *Ziegfeld Follies.* Two of his banner years were 1924 and 1925. He made his debut at the Palace in 1924, and, later that year, costarred with Fred & Adele Astaire and Walter Catlett in the musically innovative Gershwin hit *Lady Be Good,* which kept Cliff on Broadway from 1 December 1924 through 1925. Cliff did not figure much in the plot; he was trotted out for a song several times, one of which was the big hit "Fascinatin' Rhythm."

Edwards left the show to join Marilyn Miller, Jack Donahue, Clifton Webb, Joseph Cawthorn and Pert Kelton in an even bigger hit, Jerome Kern's and Oscar Hammerstein's *Sunny,* which played 517 performances, opening on 23 September 1925 and running for 15 months. Again, Edwards was not part of the plot but an interpolation that came onstage and performed a couple of numbers. He joined the *Ziegfeld Follies of 1927;* Eddie Cantor was the major star, but every night of its 167 performances, Ruth Etting earned her keep by "Shaking the Blues Away."

Edwards returned to vaudeville a headliner, and not just around New York City where he had triumphed in three Broadway shows in a row. Cliff played the best vaude houses across the country, like the Orpheum in Los Angeles in 1928. While there, he made his movie debut in MGM's filmed vaudeville show *The Hollywood Revue of 1929,* which sported one of the greatest all-star casts in film history. Cliff Edwards grabbed a lot of the attention as he led the rest of the cast through the big production number, "Singin' in the Rain."

Also in that film was Buster Keaton. Cliff supported Buster in several subsequent talking pictures, including *Doughboys* (1930), *Parlor, Bedroom and Bath* (1931) and *Sidewalks of New York* (1931). His duet with Buster in *Doughboys* was a joy, and his extended scene with Buster and Charlotte Greenwood in *Parlor, Bedroom and Bath* ranks as one of the funniest in film history.

In 1930, Irene Wylie divorced Cliff Edwards and won the right to one half of his earnings for the rest of his life. It was a sensational trial, but his ex-wife's triumph gradually turned to ashes after their divorce, when Ukulele Ike's career started its long decline, never to recover its former prominence or profitability. For the rest of his life, Cliff Edwards battled gambling, bankruptcy, creditors, drugs and booze. Before the slide, however, he married one last time, in 1932, to a young woman named Nancy Dover. He filed for bankruptcy in 1933. She filed for divorce in 1936. That same year, Edwards was back on Broadway in *George White's Scandals of 1936.* It ran 14 weeks with a cast headed by Willie Howard, Rudy Vallee and Bert Lahr.

In the movies, Cliff had begun as the best man's buddy, and his billing was usually third. By 1933, he had made two dozen films of declining merit and prestige, and his billing had slid to fourth or fifth. In the late 1930s, he was playing bit parts in decent films and featured roles in cheapie, bottom-half-of-a-double-bill quickies. From 1941 to 1943, Cliff played in a series of about 15 low-budget Westerns, first as the sidekick to Charles Starrett and Russell Hayden, then to Tim Holt. All told, he made about 75 live-action films between 1929 and 1947.

He voiced two memorable Disney characters in animated films: Jiminy Cricket in *Pinocchio* (1940) and, in *Dumbo* (1941), Jim Crow, a jive bird with a name that had unpleasant associations for many African Americans and whites.

In 1949 he tried television. He had his own 15-minute musical show that followed the *CBS Nightly News* on Mondays, Wednesdays and Fridays for a few months; later that season, he was one of a number of performers in *The Fifty-Fourth Street Revue.* The show was a swan song for Cliff Edwards, but Bob Fosse, Joan Diener and Carl Reiner moved on to great things.

Walt Disney had a soft spot for Cliff, and he used him to voice Jiminy Cricket for a series of short educational TV spots. Occasionally, Ukulele Ike Edwards, as he was often billed, played nightclubs. By the 1950s, the still melodic voice of Jiminy Cricket was competing with strippers in low-class nightclubs. The nostalgia boom of the 1960s pretty much passed him by. He spent his last years in poor health and died, almost unnoticed, in a nursing home. He was 75.

GUS EDWARDS

b: 18 August 1887, Hohensalza, Germany—d: 7 November 1945, Los Angeles, CA

The future songwriter of "School Days" and the man most identified with producing kiddie acts for vaudeville left Germany and came to the USA with his family in 1891. Gus Edwards became a boy singer in variety saloons and burlesque, where he supposedly was the first to sing from the galleries. That contrivance became a cliché after a while, much like the dancing *pickaninnies* that white and black singers employed to give their acts movement and spark. In the beginning, a star act would hire a young boy (usually) to sit in the balcony; when he got his cue, the youngster arose in place to add his voice to that of the onstage singer in a duet, or sometimes the boy sang his own solo from the audience. Of course, the lad was a plant, but until the practice became overused, most audiences accepted the supposedly impromptu interlude as genuine. It was a canny device to engage the audience and make them feel that the star was a gracious sport to let a young fellow interrupt and take part in the act.

Gustave was a 12-year-old boy soprano in the early 1890s when he began singing from the galleries in burlesque houses like Koster & Bial's, Hurtig & Seaman's and Miner's, and in variety theatres such as Tony Pastor's 14th Street Theatre. Among the star acts he

SONG SUCCESSES FROM
GUS EDWARDS' SONG REVUE
VAUDEVILLE'S GREATEST SENSATION
A Company of 30, Mostly Girls – All Beauties with
GUS EDWARDS, HIMSELF
6
LOOK OUT for JIMMY VALENTINE
Lyrics by
EDWARD MADDEN
Composed & Staged by
GUS EDWARDS

Gus Edwards

assisted were Lottie Gilson, Imogene Comer (a female baritone with whom he harmonized), Patsy Holmes and Helena Mora. The songs he warbled were of the sentimental sort: "A Mother's Plea for Her Son," "Only Me," "The Little Lost Child," "Don't Send My Boy to Prison" and, naturally, "The Song in the Gallery."

With his advance into his later teens and a voice change, Gus was no longer an engaging tadpole able to ring the audience's heartstrings, but agent James Hyde was impressed with Edwards and put him together with four other lads in an act Hyde billed as the Newsboy Quintet. Hyde managed to book the act in vaudeville two seasons, and it played all over the country. While playing vaudeville, Gus Edwards wrote his first successful song, "All I Want Is My Black Baby Back," which was introduced by May Irwin. In 1898, the Newsboy Quintet was entertaining troops at Camp Black in Nassau County on Long Island, New York, when he met his future and long-time songwriting partner, Will D. Cobb.

By 1899, in his 19th year, Gus Edwards was a song plugger. He told Bernard Sobel, a clear-eyed chronicler of American burlesque, "I plugged my songs everywhere, behind ten cent store counters, at the race track, from the stage, on the elevated [trains], on boat excursions. I sang without accompaniment, of course, and passed out printed copies of the choruses to the crowds. Sometimes we used stereopticon slides." In addition to promoting his own tunes, he plugged those of other songwriters whose works were handled by the music publishing firm Howley, Haviland & Dresser, for whom he worked. In those days, songs for burlesque revues, opera spoofs and musical comedies were gathered from various composers rather than having one songwriter or team compose an entire integrated score.

Gus recalled that the only perk that the singing stars and producers received in return was incorporating the star's photo on the cover of the sheet music as well as listing the name of the show (and sometimes its producers). The producers were also promised exclusive rights to the songs for which they contracted, but some song publishers were a bit forgetful and sold performance rights to other shows if they were far enough away. Even then, however, Gus was providing producers with suggestions for staging the songs, costuming and lighting as well as selling rights to use the songs. In 1904, still a song plugger, Gus joined Fay Templeton and Peter Dailey in the cast of *A Little Bit of Everything,* to which he also contributed two songs, as did George M. Cohan. The African American songwriting team Bob Cole & J. Rosamond Johnson had four of their songs in the show.

Edwards was always entrepreneurially minded, and in 1905 he established the Gus Edwards Music Publishing Company at 1512 Broadway in Manhattan. That same year, he got a boost professionally when Lillian Russell introduced a song Gus cowrote with Will Cobb, "Somebody's Sweetheart I Want to Be." He was also matrimonially minded in 1905, for he wed Lillian Boulanger, the woman who lived with him for the rest of his life. Lillian was also his partner, and she accompanied the various troupes of youngsters, at least until the end of the 1910s, acting as chaperone, confidant and referee.

Sheet-music sales had been growing since the mid-nineteenth century. Playing music at home was the indoor family entertainment of the era. It has been estimated that there were 1 million pianos in American households by 1900, and the population of the USA, at 75 million, was growing more slowly than the manufacture of pianos, so sheet-music publication was big business in the USA, rather like the music-recording business a century later. In 1914, Gus Edwards became a charter member of ASCAP (American Society of Composers, Authors and Publishers).

There was frenzied competition between music publishing houses, and the 1910s and 1920s saw the rise of Tin Pan Alley and American composers who became as famous as the stars who sang their songs: Harry Von Tilzer, Cole & Johnson, Irving Berlin, Jerome Kern,

Charles K. Harris, Sissle & Blake, Rodgers & Hart, Cole Porter, George Gershwin and Harold Arlen, among many. Sheet-music sales, along with sound recordings, grew through the 1920s but sank a bit, along with most other forms of show business, during various bank panics and economic recessions, especially the Great Depression that began in 1929.

Many of the songs Gus Edwards wrote—almost always with partners—became popular American classics that were remembered a century later: "By the Light of the Silvery Moon" (with Edward Madden), "In My Merry Oldsmobile" (with Vincent Bryan), "I Just Can't Make My Eyes Behave" (popularized by Anna Held) and the Gus Edwards theme song, "Schooldays," (with Will Cobb).

This last number was more than a song; it became the focus of a stage act that Gus Edwards created in 1907. He wrote the sketches and music for the act and cast it with lively and talented youngsters. In one version or another, the Gus Edwards' kiddie acts were a popular staple of vaudeville bills for 20 years, spanning the golden age of vaudeville. Earlier, in 1906, he produced an act called "Postal Telegraph Boys"—among the cast was a 16-year-old singer who later would be known as Groucho Marx—but it was with the "Schooldays" song that it all came together for Gus and company. The song provided Edwards with the nucleus of the act, which was titled "School Boys and Girls." It started a craze for school acts, and various vaudevillians built their acts around classrooms. Even The Marx Brothers cribbed the idea for their first comedy act "Fun in Hi Skule."

"School Boys and Girls" was so successful in vaudeville that Gus created a Broadway revue with the same theme and featured song, but *School Days* (1908) only managed to draw customers for a month at the Circle Theatre (at Columbus Circle, north of Times Square, an area wags called the Arctic Circle). It was a major disappointment because his previous show at the Circle, *Merry-Go-Round* (1908), with Mabel Hite and James J. Morton, had run three months and was the reason the theatre was temporarily renamed the Gus Edwards' Theatre.

Eventually, Edwards had a number of troupes traipsing over various vaudeville circuits. Gus appeared in some, like *Gus Edwards' Song Revue,* and played piano while his protégés took turns singing his songs or simply acting as props as Gus sang to them of ice-cream castles. In other of his kiddie acts, only youngsters appeared onstage, although there was always an adult watching from the wings or hovering around during the kids' free time.

Gus Edwards' acts became targets for imitators, but no one ever challenged his supremacy. The success of kiddie acts fueled many a parent's dream of their children becoming stars. For some youngsters, their time in a Gus Edwards' unit was a quick way station along the paths of their careers; for others, trouping under the Gus Edwards banner was the background that made them experienced professionals. Among the more notable of Gus Edwards alumni from his vaudeville units and his Broadway shows were comedians George Jessel, Groucho Marx, Bert Wheeler, Eddie Cantor, Georgie Price, Elsie Janis, Herman Timberg, Jack Pearl and Jesse Block; singer-comedians Rosetta and Vivian Duncan; chanteuse Hildegard; fan dancer Sally Rand; dancers Eleanor Powell and Ray Bolger; dramatic actor Helen Menken; bandleader Ina Ray Hutton; gossip columnist Walter Winchell; film stars Lila Lee, Ricardo Cortez and Mae Murray; and film directors Eddie Buzzell and Mervyn LeRoy.

Gus Edwards

Over the years, Edwards gave his touring shows various titles, like "Kid Kabaret," "Gus Edwards' Song Revue," "Gus Edwards' New Song Revue," "Kids in Candyland," "Yankee Doodle Scouts," "Gus Edwards' Song Revue of 1921" and "Gus Edwards' Bandbox Revue." The change of titles let the customers know it was a new act with new songs, but the same formula, by and large.

Occasionally, Edwards sent out an act with older casts instead of kids, such as "Gus Edwards' Matinee Girls," but for most vaudeville audiences, the name Gus Edwards was synonymous with the best in children's acts. Gus Edwards' revues were one of the most reliable draws on Keith and Orpheum time, and they frequently played the Palace Theatre—as early as 1913 and as late as 1932. Gus himself played the Palace in 1927, 1931 and 1932. He accompanied himself on the piano as he sang songs that he had written or cowritten.

From 1895 though 1936, Gus, with and without his songwriting partners, contributed songs to more than three dozen revues and musical comedies, including three editions of the *Ziegfeld Follies* (1907, 1909 and 1910). Edwards was one of a number of composers who contributed interpolated musical numbers to each of those editions of the *Follies*.

Gus Edwards is listed as the sole composer for *Breaking into Society* (musical comedy, 1905), *When We Were Forty-One* (musical comedy, 1905), *Hip! Hip! Hooray* (revue, 1907), *School Days* (revue, 1908), *The Merry-Go-Round* (musical comedy, 1908), *Out on Broadway* (musical comedy, 1913), *Sunbonnet Sue* (musical comedy, 1923) and *Broadway Sho-Window* (revue, 1936).

Gus Edwards saw the writing on the wall earlier than most, and he moved to Hollywood in 1928 just as talkies began to take over the silver screen and vaudeville continued to slump. At the studios, he tried his hand at nearly everything, directing a couple of shorts, appearing as an actor and performer in a couple of shorts and a couple of features—notably *The Hollywood Revue of 1929*—and contributed songs to six films. By 1933, it was apparent that he could not re-create his stage success on film, and, although his songs continued to be used in movies well past his death, Gus headed back to New York and played vaudeville as a solo when he wished.

He became seriously ill with cancer and retired in 1939, the same year Paramount Pictures released *The Star Maker,* a movie musical film of his life but more fiction than fact; Bing Crosby played Gus. Lillian cared for her invalid husband until he died in 1945.

GUS ELEN

b: (Ernest Augustus Elen) 22 July 1862, London, England—d: 17 February 1940, Balham, London, England

At the turn of the twentieth century, the still-Victorian audiences liked their entertainments brightened up with a bit of gay color and sugared with a dollop of sentiment. Perhaps Britons and Americans had too much of their lives chronicled as dark Dickensian realism. So it was when it came to depictions of the Cockneys of Dickens' East London. Many audiences preferred Albert Chevalier's romantic impersonation of a Cockney to Gus Elen's grittier, less fanciful portrayals. Chris Simmons, an American performer and expert in nineteenth-century theatre music of England, Ireland and the USA, researched Gus Elen and his music and contributed to the revival of interest in the coster singer—as have Tony Barker, Max Tyler and Richard Anthony Baker.

The character that Gus Elen presented onstage was kin to the people he met growing up and with whom he worked. Like all poor lads, Gus went to work at an early age, taking whatever job was available. Occasionally, he sang at *smokers* or busked in front of theatres and popular restaurants. His ambition was to work the *halls*.

In an interview some time after he became a star, Gus Elen recalled:

> Years before I entered the ranks of music-hall profession proper, I used to contribute to the programmes of the weekly 'sing songs' held at such places as Poppy Lords in Lisson Grove; the Magpie and Stump, Battersea; or the George Street Recital Hall. At the last-named hall, the salaries ranged from a shilling to three and sixpence a night with a cup of coffee and a bun thrown in by way of refreshment. In those days I often filled in a season on the 'waxeys' (on the seaside) at Margate and Ramsgate in a Negro minstrel troupe.

The military canteens at Aldershot also hosted entertainments, and young Elen sang in several canteens in 1883.

Gus found himself a partner named Daniels, and they performed a blackface act at the Old Marylebone Theatre in what was one of Gus' first appearances in music-hall. When Daniels died in a boating accident shortly after they had started as an act, the music-hall manager insisted that Elen perform solo. Evidently, Gus and his audiences were satisfied with the experiment; Gus Elen remained solo throughout his career. He was one of many comic vocalists of the 1880s, more talented than most but not yet differentiated in style. That began to change in 1891, when he purchased "Never Introduce Your Donah to a Pal" from songwriter A. E. Durandeau. (*Donah,* from the Italian *donna,* was Cockney slang for "girlfriend.") When Elen introduced the song on 4 June 1891, at Harewood's Varieties in Hoxton, he sang the song as he knew a Cockney would. A few months earlier, a stage actor, Albert Chevalier, made his music-hall debut at the London Pavilion singing "The Coster's Serenade." So began a friendly rivalry.

According to Simmons, "The coster dialect and the costumes offered natural and attractive opportunities to performers, and more than a few costers found performing quite natural and attractive. Costers remained a theatrical favorite for a century through many shows, including revivals of *Pygmalion* and its musical incarnation, *My Fair Lady.*"

"I made up my mind at the outset," as Gus Elen said later, "that my renderings of the coster character should be neither idealistic nor in the nature of a caricature, but just realistic." As the lyrics to one of Gus Elen's songs indicate, he was not above tweaking his rival's artifice:

It sounds so werry pretty
In a sweetly warbled ditty
With limelights and footlight
And pearlies to the ground.
But I gives you my word
It's a fable—what you've heard
For there ain't a coster like it
To be found!

Throughout the 1890s, Gus became ever more popular. His manner onstage was distinctly his own. He seemed a rather severe personality at first: tall, thin, unsmiling, in the clothes of an ordinary workman. He did not move much, and his gestures were economical, and all the more telling for that. He did not signal for laughs. He was a poker-faced humorist watching to see if his listeners had wit enough to understand the drollery: "If It Wasn't for the 'Ouses in Between" was subtitled "The Cockney's Garden" and addressed the crowded conditions in which they lived.

Oh! It really is a werry pretty garden,
And Chingford to the eastward could be seen;
Wiv a ladder and some glasses.
You could see to 'Ackney Marshes,
If it wasn't for the 'ouses in between.

Other songs in Gus' growing repertoire included "Me an' 'Er," "It's a Great Big Shame," "You Could See As 'Ow 'E Didn't Feel at 'Ome" and "The Golden Dustman." The success won by Gus Elan and Albert Chevalier brought other coster singers onstage, like Alec Hurley, Marie Lloyd's second husband, who was born and bred Cockney, Kate Carney, Harry Champion and Nat Travers.

Gus Elan kept separate his professional and private lives. He was thrifty and a bit of a homebody who tended his garden at his home in Balham. He enjoyed driving in the countryside, fishing, shooting and amateur photography. When interviewed, Gus never referred to his wife by name, and, if they had children, it was unknown to the press. He did not socialize much with fellow artistes from the halls. Although he had offers to cross the Channel, he refused them until 1907, when two events led him to the USA and vaudeville.

The first was his part in the leadership of the so-called Music-Hall Strike of 1907 to wring decent salaries out of management for the majority of acts that had not the clout that put him, Marie Lloyd, Chevalier and others in a position to negotiate top salaries. If there was not a blacklist, there was also little enthusiasm on the parts of managers to engage the very performers who had led the fight against them.

In 1907, the czar of the American legitimate theatre, Abe Erlanger, approached the equally ambitious Shuberts to form Advanced Vaudeville, intended as a threat to Keith-Albee's vaudeville hegemony in the eastern half of the USA. Erlanger had the money; Lee Shubert had acquired more theatres than he and brother Jake had shows to fill. They drew William Morris, a respected vaudeville man with experience as an agent, booker and theatre manager, into their scheme, not as a partner who knew their true goal was to shake down E. F. Albee and B. F. Keith, but as a salaried talent scout of sorts. Erlanger supplied him with a line of credit and sent Morris forth to sign as many vaudeville acts as possible. When the competition between Erlanger-Shubert and Keith-Albee resulted in raised vaudeville salaries across the board, Morris was sent to London to find music-hall attractions that would play well to American audiences. One of his discoveries was Gus Elen.

Albert Chevalier had already played the USA, so it was likely that performers like Marie Lloyd, Alec Hurley and Gus Elen would be successful, too. A critic for the *New York Dramatic News* noted that, "While his act is in a sense similar to that of Mr. [Albert] Chevalier, it is also radically different. Mr. Elen portrays the coster as he actually exists in his native element." Whether that observation was informed perception on the part of the critic or prepared publicity by William Morris, it was not disputed. The box office, however, showed that the public preferred Chevalier to Elen. Gus did not make the necessary adjustments that would have made his material more comprehensible to American audiences, nor did he play as broadly as comic singers were expected.

His reputation among English audiences was untouched. He continued for the next seven or eight years as a top attraction in the halls. He appeared onstage less after 1914, and, by 1916, after a 33-year career on the boards, Gus Elen decided to retire. The old world was changing. The First World War had sobered a nation used to glorying in empire. A generation of young men had been decimated in the trenches of France. English musicals and revues changed from fairy tales and operettas to mad ragtime whirls influenced by Broadway and Tin Pan Alley.

Gus took to retirement as one who had earned it. He did not seem to miss the stage until, 15 years later, he allowed himself to be coaxed into a comeback on the variety stage. London film companies were able to get him to perform several of his old songs in movie revues, and his performance was as crisp and tart as ever. In 1935, Gus Elen was among the select who entertained at a Royal Command Performance. Five years later, at the dawn of another world war, Gus Elen died at his Balham home at the age of 77.

JULIAN ELTINGE

b: (William J. Dalton) 14 May 1881, Newton, MA—d: 7 March 1941, New York, NY

While other female impersonators were dismissed or derided and were restricted to performing in variety, vaudeville and cabarets, Julian Eltinge performed his act in musical comedies and movies and had a Broadway theatre named in his honor. His public acceptance was based on the fiction that he was a heterosexual, a college man and a rugged he-man offstage. No one fostered that impression more assiduously than the former Billy Dalton.

Researcher and writer Mark Berger sorted fact from fiction to provide as true as possible a story of Julian Eltinge's life. The claim made of Eltinge making his debut in a Hasty Pudding Club annual, while attending Harvard College, was as bogus as his proficiency with fisticuffs. Billy's father, caught up in the promise of great and immediate wealth by the gold rush, ventured west from Massachusetts. He ended up running a barbershop in Butte, Montana, where his wife and son joined him in the 1890s.

Early on, Billy was drawn to dressing up, a fancy that his mother apparently indulged. In his early teens, Billy used to don women's apparel to perform in one or two of the melodeons and saloons in Butte. One might wonder at his reception with the male-only audiences; Butte in the 1890s was still a rugged mining town where gold and railroad building had lured the Irish workers from the East and defeated Confederate soldiers from the South and Chinese laborers from the Far West.

In territories where ranching, mining and railroad building drew large numbers of men and far fewer women, it was difficult to find attractive young women who were willing to work in saloons as entertainers or shills for liquor sales and gambling. There was a prevailing ethic, usually observed, that unless a woman made it clear that she permitted physical contact, she was to be regarded as respectable, even if she worked in a dance hall or saloon. Thus, it was not unknown for saloon keepers to hire pretty young boys to fill the ranks of dancing girls onstage. Those women who were willing to mix with the men in the audience, sit with them in boxes and encourage them to drink and gamble tended to be older women whose prospects for a respectable life had been brooked by circumstance and accident.

In 1899, Billy's father discovered that his teenage son was performing as a girl. After Billy was thrashed severely by his father, Billy's mother, Julia, sent Billy back to Massachusetts to live with her sister in Boston. Billy had no intention of renouncing show business. He studied dance at Mrs. Lilla Viles Wyman's dance studio, entered amateur contests and won a cakewalking competition.

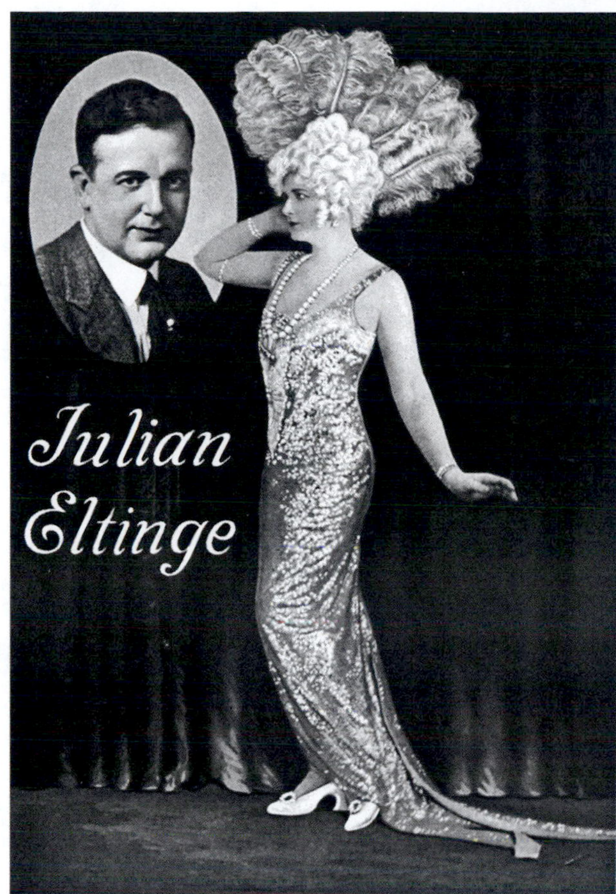

Julian Eltinge

Dalton made his professional debut at the Tremont Theater in Boston with the Cadet Theatricals, a group of theatrical amateurs directed by Robert A. Barnet, who also wrote their annual extravaganzas. The proceeds were devoted to the construction of a large armory. Mr. Barnet's granddaughter and biographer, Alison Barnet, discovered that the purpose for the castlelike fortress in Boston's Park Square was fear among the gentry of the rising numbers of immigrants settling in Boston.

The roles, both male and female, in the annual Cadet shows were played exclusively by young men, usually those of social station and with some formal connection to the cadet militia. Young Bill was recommended by his dance teacher, and Barnet engaged him to play the soubrette role in his 1900 original production of *Miladi and the Musketeer.* Because Bill demonstrated skill and a willingness to practice and work relentlessly, traits the more social and lighthearted members of the cast did not always share, he was given the choice role of Mignonette, the Machiavellian cardinal's spy. For his stage name, Bill adopted that of a close male friend he had left behind in Butte. Thereafter Julian Eltinge (rhymes with *impinge*) was his name and his identity. Given the amount of revenue his shows generated, Barnet was engaged by the Bank Officers' Association (BOA) in Boston to create a similar show for them.

Eltinge's success ensured his value to both the Cadets and the BOA, and he appeared as an ingenue in *Miss Simplicity* (1901) and *Baron Humbug* (1903).

Barnet's shows were closely watched by New York producers, and most of the Barnet shows were remounted with professional casts for Broadway and touring. The producer E. E. Rice saw Eltinge and engaged him for a musical comedy that had been successful in London. *Mr. Wix of Wickham* opened and closed on Broadway in five weeks. The plot provided the basic format that most of Eltinge's musical comedies and films followed: A young man is forced by the machinations of the plot to disguise himself as a woman. Although the show was not a success, critics praised Eltinge, and vaudeville bookers took notice.

Eltinge's first vaudeville dates were playing Keith's Union Square Theater and the Aerial Theater atop the New Amsterdam Theater, both in Manhattan. By the summer of 1905, Eltinge had embarked on a tour of Paris, Berlin, Vienna and London, which included a 1906 command performance at Windsor Castle for King Edward VII. Eltinge returned to the USA in February 1907 for a vaudeville bill at the Alhambra Theater. In his vaudeville act "The Sampson Girl," Eltinge parodied the Gibson Girl, an idealized woman of 1900 based on Charles Dana Gibson's illustrations. It was the combination of quick changes and characterization that appealed to press and public. *Variety* declared on 21 September 1907 that the "audience was completely deceived as to Eltinge's sex, until he removed his wig . . . his act is far and away above what is described as female impersonation."

Performing at a benefit for George Fuller Golden, founder of the White Rats of America, a union formed to protect white male vaudeville performers, Eltinge attracted the attention of George M. Cohan, who quickly hired him to perform with the Cohan and Harris Minstrels along with George Evans and the 100 Honey Boy Minstrels. Eltinge performed an exotic Salomé, a racy bathing girl and a kid specialty, all in blackface. By 1910, Eltinge was a vaudeville headliner. He took pains with his makeup and costuming and employed a Japanese dresser to assist with the quick changes. Sime Silverman, editor of *Variety,* praised Eltinge's great drawing power, sense of style and class, and concluded that he was "as great a performer as there is today," equal to Eva Tanguay, Nora Bayes, Harry Lauder, Ed Wynn and Fanny Brice.

Al H. Woods, a Broadway producer who had been following Eltinge's success, convinced Eltinge to move into full-length Broadway musicals on the legitimate stage. In October 1910, A. H. Woods, Martin Herman, Ferdinand Pinner and Julian Eltinge formed the Eltinge Company, Inc., "to conduct general theatrical, amusement and real estate business, to own and lease theaters, to sell, produce and manage dramatic and musical attractions." It was capitalized at $10,000. Their first production, *The Fascinating Widow,* starring Julian Eltinge, opened at the Liberty Theater in New York on 11 September 1911 and ran for 56 performances. Afterward, Eltinge toured the show, on and off, around the country until 1914, making changes to the numbers to keep the show fresh. In his vaudeville performances, Eltinge revealed his male identity only at the end of his act, as he took his last call. In his musical comedies, Eltinge played a young male hero who had to assume a woman's disguise in order to prevail or right some wrong.

Eltinge noted that reviews and articles praised him for acting manly when he played the hero and for giving a genteel, rather than simpering or campy, performance as a woman. Throughout his professional life, Eltinge sought to foster the illusion of heterosexual manliness. To reinforce Julian's bogus he-man image, he and his handlers staged stunts, such as an occasional barroom fight in which Eltinge handily defeated a man who insulted him. Many vaudevillians who met Eltinge assumed he was homosexual, despite the publicity.

Although the Julian Eltinge Theater opened on 11 September 1912, Eltinge himself never performed there, but he kept busy with a succession of shows such as *The Crinoline Girl* (1914) and *Cousin Lucy* (1915). Most of Eltinge's shows did not linger long on Broadway, but they proved profitable on the road.

This national fame prompted a call from Jesse Lasky of Paramount Pictures. Between 1917 and 1930, Eltinge made seven feature-length movies and a few short films. In 1917, *The Countess Charming* introduced Eltinge as a kind of male-to-female Robin Hood. Eltinge's film enhanced his fame; when he returned to vaudeville in 1918, he drew one of the highest salaries of any vaudeville star at the time, $3,500 a week. His debut at New York's Palace Theatre in January 1918 equaled the gross of Sarah Bernhard; his run at the Brooklyn Orpheum broke the season's record; and his performances at Chicago's Majestic Theater in March broke all previous box office records. In 1919, Eltinge put together his own vaudeville package, *Eltinge's Revue,* which toured the USA and then Europe. It included four of his most famous impersonations plus "His Night at the Club," a sketch written by June Mathis, who had appeared with Julian in *The Fascinating Widow.* (Mathis also wrote

The Four Horsemen of the Apocalypse and other films for Rudolph Valentino.)

Julian Eltinge's movies—*The Countess Charming* (1917), *The Clever Mrs. Fairfax* (1917), *Over the Rhine* (1918), *The Widow's Might* (1918), *Madam Behave* (1925) and *Maid to Order* (1931)—generally fell within the now well-developed plotline of an upstanding, clean-cut straight man who is forced into impersonating a woman to solve some personal or domestic problem. The formula was altered in *Over the Rhine*, a movie set amid the First World War; Eltinge played both Jack Perry, a patriotic young American, and Elsa von Bohn, a female spy in the employ of the U.S. Secret Service.

Eltinge continued to perform on vaudeville stages through the 1920s, with "The Elusive Lady" in 1922 and "The Black and White Revue" of 1923, as well as return engagements at the New York Palace in 1927 and 1929. He even published *The Fascinating Widow: The Julian Eltinge Magazine of Beauty Hints,* a periodical of articles, advice and advertisements.

Throughout his career, Eltinge often traveled with his mother, and she often shared his homes, including a ranch at Alpine, near San Diego, and the Villa Capistrano, a movie-star-styled home in Silver Lake, Los Angeles. The stock market crash caught Eltinge unprepared, however; he had spent extravagantly, and his investments had failed.

In July 1931, Eltinge opened in *The Nine O'Clock Revue* at the Music Box Theatre in Hollywood. That same year, he starred in his only musical comedy sound film, *Maid to Order,* portraying a private detective who disguises himself as a diamond-smuggling French chanteuse working in a New York nightclub. It was Eltinge's last starring role. Work grew scarce in the 1930s as the Great Depression worsened. Eltinge had grown portly. He was 50 years old by 1931 and no longer able to impersonate the svelte young ladies that had made him famous. Eltinge took to drink for solace.

The vogue for female impersonation had ebbed. It was no longer regarded as a lighthearted entertainment but rather a signal of perversion, and municipalities enacted laws against drag. Julian Eltinge was barely a memory by 1940. In need of money, he accepted a booking at a Los Angeles nightclub that had a gay clientele. A police ordinance, designed to crack down on homosexuals, forbade any man or woman from impersonating the opposite sex. Eltinge was restricted to wearing a tuxedo and forced to display his old costumes on a rack, describing the roles he had performed that were associated with each gown. There was little interest; the engagement was canceled.

Eltinge made a cameo appearance along with other bygone vaudeville stars, including Blanche Ring, Trixie Friganza and Eddie Leonard, in the Bing Crosby film *If I Had My Way* (1940). His novelty value earned him an offer of $110 a week to perform at Billy Rose's Diamond Horseshoe Jubilee in *Nights of Gladness,* his first New York engagement since 1927.

While performing at Billy Rose's Diamond Horseshoe in 1941, Eltinge died in his Manhattan apartment. His death was reported as a stroke, a heart attack, kidney and liver failure, and suicide. More than 300 people attended his funeral. The obituaries revived both fact and fiction: Eltinge had performed before royalty, headlined at the Palace, socialized with society swells and the elite of Broadway and Hollywood, brawled with thugs, had a theatre named in his honor, starred in films, made and lost three fortunes, and advised women how to retain their beauty. It was the fiction he cultivated.

EMCEE

The word *emcee* derives from the pronunciation of the two letters M and C, which stand for master (or mistress) of ceremonies. An emcee is also known as a compere (but that term had more currency abroad than in the USA).

Emcees were seldom used in vaudeville until its closing years when, occasionally, a monologist (or what later was called a stand-up comic) or a singer took on hosting chores for the entire bill, introducing the acts and bantering with them and with the audience. Unless briskly handled, the chore of introducing acts could slow down the desired pace of a vaudeville bill. The use of an emcee was more usual for talent nights.

EMPIRE CIRCUIT

The Empire Circuit was a burlesque circuit more commonly known as the Western Wheel (*See "Western Wheel"*).

EMPRESS CIRCUIT

See Sullivan & Considine Circuit

ENTERTAINMENT

Centuries ago, *entertainment* implied hospitality rather than shows. A place that offered entertainment was one that served food and drink and may have provided rooms to the traveler. When innkeepers, tavern owners and beer-garden proprietors added performances to their services, the term *entertainment* assumed a wider connotation. American concert saloons, beer halls and melodeons, like their British cousins, were drinking establishments that added performances to bolster sales of drink.

ENTREPRENEURS

Many of the men who became titans of vaudeville management were ruthless, grasping, coarse autocrats. They were typical of the late-nineteenth-century robber barons who clawed their way out of hardscrabble beginnings to build, by hook and crook, economic empires of mining, railroads, oil, steel, tobacco, shipping and banking. Social Darwinists in action, they beat up the competition and sacrificed partners when expedient. Power was the goal, monopoly and wealth the measure.

Some, like Andrew Carnegie, created monuments to culture during their lifetimes, after they had grabbed all the money they wanted. Others left it to their descendants to take an interest in the social betterment of the masses, to refund to society some small share of the interest on the fortunes they had amassed through the poorly paid labor of fellow citizens and the use of public lands, minerals and waterways.

Most giants of capital and industry were born in the United States of parents who had come from Scotland, Ireland, Holland, Germany and other northern European countries. A few were immigrants themselves; inspired by work-hard-and-get-rich stories, they arrived in the USA understanding little English and possessing little more than the clothes they wore. Whatever the origins of these robber barons or whether they triumphed in finance, manufacturing or show business, evidence of generosity, kindness and refinement was scant, whereas greed, ruthlessness and materialism manifestly governed their ambitions. In their defense, it must be said that they pulled together, in rapid time, the industrial engines that powered the USA into the front rank of nations. The ills they created or worsened, and left behind, are another of their legacies.

What the entrepreneurs brought to their respective industries was the ability to expand and make the economies of scale work for them. Their model was standardization. Railways could not become a national system until all regional trains ran on the same gauge track. Automobiles were made affordable by machines that standardized parts, allowing the replacement of worn parts and saving time in the manufacture and the assembly of parts into a whole product. Banking left small-town service behind to control the borrowing and lending of money on a large, impersonal scale.

Most powerful vaudeville entrepreneurs worked on somewhat smaller stages than those where Jay Gould, Andrew Carnegie, John D. Rockefeller or J. P. Morgan acted out their desires. But the bosses of vaudeville tried to follow the same road to success through a series of agreements made and broken, and by eliminating competition, monopolizing the means of production, distribution and exhibition, and standardizing the product.

The vaudeville entrepreneurs had great daring; they believed that if they sustained enormous losses or captured fabulous success one day, it would be a different contest tomorrow. They flourished because they fought for an exacting interpretation of what was due them, yet they held a liberal view of their own obligations toward the law, the public and vaudevillians. The moguls were feared and hated by vaudevillians and often by their own minions and each other.

Nevertheless, they fitted pieces together into a whole. They standardized the form of presentation, acquired theatres, contracted acts to play them and demanded a level of professionalism from the performers toward their audiences and their employers. They devised a method of booking that assured theatre owners a steady supply of reliable product at a price that was regulated for all but the foremost headliner. The acts, in return for a series of bookings that was more or less guaranteed, were forced to accept the managers' terms.

By this time, the booking agents were working more for the managers than for the acts they represented. Big-time vaudeville was run by regional emperors vying to forge a national monopoly. The chief rivals were E. F Albee, Abe Erlanger, Morris Meyerfield and Martin Beck, J. J. Murdock, F. F. Proctor, William Morris, Marcus Loew, and the Shuberts. To do business with one was to cross the others, although they did business with each other when they were not double-crossing their sometimes partners, sometimes rivals.

Less powerful entrepreneurs than Albee, Erlanger, the Shubert brothers, and Meyerfield and Beck had fewer choices in the game of survival. They had to be courageous and lucky enough to acquire theatres and assemble circuits and strong enough to resist takeover by the giants, or they had to be smart enough to do business with the giants but stay out from under their boots. In the end, size did not always determine wealth. Like speculators in every field, audacity and vision had to be balanced with timing and good sense. Some vaudeville entrepreneurs, major or minor, knew when to hold or fold. Some overreached.

LEON ERROL

b: (Leonce Errol Simms) 3 July 1876–81, Sydney, Australia—d: 12 October 1951, Los Angeles, CA

The usual assessment of Leon Errol is a dismissal: the guy with the rubber legs who always played a drunk, a low comic who parlayed a stock routine into secondary roles in dozens of feature films and a hundred two-reel comedies. The truth is that he was a versatile

Leon Errol

performer who enjoyed as extraordinary a career as his *Ziegfeld Follies* contemporaries Bert Williams, W. C. Fields, Will Rogers, Fanny Brice and Ed Wynn. Leon Errol's professional life spanned three continents, a half century, most forms of entertainment—circus, drama, Shakespeare, dancing, singing and comedy—and an assortment of roles in his profession, including producer, company manager, sketch writer, director, choreographer and, most importantly, comedian.

Born into a professional, middle-class household, Leon was apprenticed to a physician during high school and directed toward a career in medicine. While a premed student at Sydney University in his native Australia, Leon wrote a revue that was performed at various men's clubs in Sydney. In it, he played a red-nosed, knockabout comic. Buoyed by the reception, Leon wrote, directed and performed several more revues while in college. If the year 1881, usually given for Errol's birth, is to be believed, he would have been a 15-year-old college sophomore at the time. A more likely birth year is 1876.

Leon devised a vaudeville act to earn money to continue his studies, and, in 1896, he made his professional debut at the Standard, a vaudeville theatre in Sydney. In the process, the expedient became the new goal. Among his earliest engagements were a stint with the Martinettis, a teeterboard act that toured Australia and New Zealand, and a season as a clown and bareback rider in the circus. During his near decade of performing Down Under, Errol sang and danced in operettas; toured in repertory companies as a production manager, leading man and character actor; acted in Shakespearean drama (playing Edmund in King Lear, Macduff in Macbeth, even Juliet's nurse) with the George Rignold Company; and essayed contemporary dramatic roles with the Sydney Stock Company. "Whatever success I've had in comedy I owe to my training in tragedy," Errol said many years later. "In fact, you can't play low comedy at all without an understanding of tragedy."

When Leon Errol left Australia for the United States, probably in 1904, he was accompanied by his dance partner, Stella Chatelaine. They married in 1906. Leon got work as a singing waiter in San Francisco, then as a singing coster comic, but the American audiences could not understand the Australian's imitation of a Cockney accent. He had much better luck as an eccentric dancer. The American Northwest was booming, new variety and vaudeville theatres were mushrooming, and Errol soon promoted himself into vaudeville with a pantomime comedy sketch.

He also toured with burlesque troupes for which he wrote the shows, managed the company and starred as principal comedian. By 1905, he was in charge of a burlesque house in Portland, Oregon, where he hired 18-year-old Roscoe Arbuckle as the unit's singer for a company tour. Working in the Northwest and the Rockies meant long jumps between engagements, and the expenses of travel, food and lodging were often greater than box-office receipts. Errol's unit went bust in Boise, Idaho, and Arbuckle latched onto another burlesque outfit headed to the Southwest.

Back in San Francisco, Errol performed in burlesque operetta until the 1906 earthquake devastated the city. Realizing that it would be some time before San Francisco was able to rebuild its theatres, Errol once again hit the road, determined to find safe harbor and financial security in New York.

By 1908, Leon Errol and Stella Chatelaine were performing in *The Grafters,* a burlesque musical for which Errol was composer, lyricist and librettist. Leon also was star, composer, lyricist and librettist for *Dugan the Deputy,* but the date for that show is uncertain. Perhaps the two vehicles alternated in repertory. Neither show made it to New York City.

During the 1908 and 1909 seasons, Leon and Stella were touring with a burlesque unit known as *Jimmy*

Cooper's Jersey Lillies. Leon was manager, director, sketch writer and chief comic; Stella was billed as "The Little Ingénue." One of Leon's sketches was "She's a Darn Fine Woman." When the show reached New York, an ad in *Variety* ballyhooed it as "the best laughing spoke in the Eastern Wheel."

It is reported that Abe Erlanger caught his performance at the Columbia Theatre in New York and paid the then-hefty sum of $15,000 for Leon Errol's release from his contract. Erlanger signed Errol for a musical, *The Primrose Path,* that never got produced. As Erlanger owned one third of the *Follies* productions, Erlanger turned Errol over to Ziegfeld for his next show.

Most sources claim Errol did not play vaudeville until 1916, but time between bookings meant no paydays. Errol, who always strove to keep working, must have filled in with vaudeville and burlesque dates around New York between his engagements with Ziegfeld.

Leon Errol starred in the *Ziegfeld Follies* from 1911 through 1915. The cast list for the 1911 *Follies* boasted Fanny Brice and Bert Williams as well as Errol for comedy, and it was the teaming of Leon Errol with Bert Williams that critics and audiences judged the hit of the show.

It is odd that historians make little of the breakthrough teaming of Bert Williams and Leon Errol. If there were other black-and-white comedy teams in show business before them or at the same time, they worked on stages far from Broadway and remain unknown to most historians. Even more remarkable is the viewpoint of the skit and its wholehearted acceptance by the audience. Leon was always the customer, Bert was the service provider, yet their master and servant roles did not define them, their capabilities did.

In the "Upper and Lower Level" skit that the two comics devised (and constantly ad-libbed) for the *Ziegfeld Follies of 1911,* Leon Errol portrayed Major Waterbrush, a bewildered and besotted tourist who has arrived in Grand Central Station amid the construction of the subway being built beneath. Bert Williams is Rufus Redcap, the porter who tries to guide Errol through this obstacle course.

To steady his nervous, wobbly-kneed customer, Bert ties a rope between Leon and himself and leads the way as they climb out onto girders. The rope helps steady Errol as he slips and slides until, distracted, he steps off into the abyss from a girder labeled "160 foot drop." Hand over hand, Bert hauls Leon back up.

Barely regaining his balance and composure, Leon asks the redcap for a match. Bert lets the rope go to search his pockets, and Leon drops again. Exhaustedly, Williams hoists up Errol for a second time. As Errol again reaches their perch, he tells Williams, "Never mind, porter, I broke my pipe." The two chat while catching their breath:

Leon Errol

"You have a wife and children I suppose?"

"Oh, yes, sir; I'se married and I'se got three child'un."

"Is that so? Ah, that's very commendable. What are the names of your children?"

"Well, I names 'em out of de bible. Dar's Hannah and den dar's Samuel, and de las' I names Iwilla."

"Iwilla? I don't remember that name in the bible."

"Sure 'tis. Don't you 'member where it say 'I willa rise'?"

Uncertain whether his leg has just been pulled, Leon resumes his upward climb, led by Bert. Errol continues to stumble and, during another respite, he knocks over the redcap's lunch. To make amends, Leon promises the porter a big tip—five cents! Williams withers him with such a scornful look that Errol again tumbles off a girder, this one marked "288 foot drop." Bert watches the rope run through his hands, unties it from his waist, mutters "Five cents!" and drops the rope after Leon. For good measure, he tosses Leon's luggage after him, too. A second or two passes, then there is an explosion. With his eyes, Bert follows Errol's trajectory high into the sky, drolly reporting to the audience: "There he goes. Now he's near the Metropolitan Tower; if he can only grab that little gold knob on top . . . Uh, um! . . . He muffed it."

Bert Williams and Leon Errol again teamed for the *Ziegfeld Follies of 1912.* This time, Bert was a hansom-cab driver with a broken-down, two-man comedy horse (played by vaudeville comedy team, LeBrun & Queen). The setting was the street corner of Seventh Avenue and Forty-Seventh Street. Leon was the smartly dressed drunk trying to get to Seventh Avenue—where he already was!

> "Where do you want to go, boss?"
>
> "I wanna go to Sebaloobaloo."
>
> "Oh, you want to go to Seventh Avenue?"
>
> "Yeah, I wanna go to Sebalabaloo. Y'know where that is?"
>
> "Oh, yes, Ah know where it is. Get in and Ah'll drive you dar. Ah know where it is. It's fur!"

The horse, tired and old, overhears Bert's intention to take Errol for a long, roundabout and expensive ride. The horse balks, sits, crosses its legs and refuses to budge. Bert tries to prod the poor old nag upright as Errol counterpoints, drunkenly tottering around the stage, trying to get into the carriage, buckling at the knees and ankles. Bert finally seats his customer in the carriage and gains the cooperation of his horse with the promise of "Oats, Nicodemus, oats!" The sketch captured the comedy honors of the evening.

Stella Chatelaine joined her husband in the *Follies* from 1911 through 1914. Their dance number, "Turkish Trottishness," in the 1913 edition was "the show's big hit," according to historian Gerald Bordman. The audience roared as Leon struggled nightly to hold up his pants while he tried to teach the dance routine to the entire cast. Bert Williams was absent from this *Follies*, so Leon partnered with Frank Tinney as a pair of bumbling robbers in a sketch. Leon never wrote funny lines for himself. His dialogue had no jokes in it. He got his laughs by garbling his lines and with ahems, wheezes, coughs and sputters as he tried to avert embarrassment.

Not only did Leon Errol perform in the *Ziegfeld Follies of 1914,* but Ziegfeld, after a spat with Julian Mitchell, assigned Errol to direct the entire production. Errol was Ziegfeld's third most frequent director of the *Follies* and *Midnight Revels;* Mitchell and Ned Wayburn were first and second. Errol again teamed with Bert Williams in the 1914 *Follies*. In one skit they were a golfer and his caddy; in the other they were two steelworkers struggling to put a huge, careening beam in place on the 1,313th story of a skyscraper. The *Washington Star* deemed this skit the "big hit" of the 1914 *Follies. The Ziegfeld Follies of 1915* was Leon's last, and he codirected it with Julian Mitchell. The cast featured Leon Errol along with Bert Williams, W. C. Fields, Ed Wynn, Ina Claire, Mae Murray, Ann Pennington and George White. Despite the great cast, the critics focused their praise on Joseph Urban's debut as the *Follies'* designer. It was Leon Errol's last opportunity to work with his friend Bert Williams. When Bert died seven years later in 1922, he was given both a private and a public funeral, the latter of which was held at St. Phillip's Episcopal Church in Harlem. Leon Errol was the only one of the 12 pallbearers who was white.

Leon Errol

On 16 September 1917, Leon Errol joined Weber & Fields, Will Rogers, Irene Franklin, Harry Houdini, Nat Wills and Belle Baker in a benefit for the Army Athletic Fund, two of several benefits held at New York's Hippodrome. Leon and his *Hitchy-Koo* partner, Raymond Hitchcock, jointly emceed a similar Hippodrome benefit for the Naval Relief Society.

Leon Errol was riding high. Ziegfeld signed him to codirect with Ned Wayburn *The Century Girl* in 1916 at the grand Century Theatre. The cast included Hazel Dawn, Van & Schenk, Marie Dressler, Elsie Janis, Sam Bernard, Frank Tinney, Harry Langdon, Doyle & Dixon and Errol. Urban designed the production, and Irving Berlin and Victor Herbert wrote the songs. Ziegfeld's coproducer was Charles Dillingham, Ziegfeld's foremost rival in taste and critical success.

Leon did no fewer than 21 shows (and one in London) in 18 years on Broadway. Each was a hit by the standards of the era, especially *The Century Girl* in 1916–17 (although it failed to return all of its investment), *Hitchy-Koo* in 1917, *Sally* from 1920 to 1921, and *Louie the 14th* in 1925. In some cases, Leon was acting and directing, in others he was only acting or directing or choreographing. He even wrote libretto, lyrics and music on a few occasions.

When he was not on Broadway, he took vaudeville engagements. One of Errol's more memorable vaudeville bookings must have been when he headed the Palace Theatre's New Year's Eve bill of 1920. One assumes that Leon again did his drunk act to salute the occasion.

Leon worked in movies as well. He made a couple of shorts in New York before he went to Hollywood to re-create his character in *Sally,* a 1925 silent with Colleen Moore in the Marilyn Miller stage role. From that point onward, Errol worked more in film and less on the stage. He was nearing 50 years old and was an avid golfer, which it was easier to be in Hollywood than on Broadway. Of his 56 feature films, few are memorable beyond specific comedy scenes. Because he freelanced, studios did not have the incentive to exploit his talent and invest in his career; he slid into supporting character roles.

Leon Errol's character, like W. C. Fields', was that of a reprobate. Yet, whereas Fields was seldom guilty of more than sharing drinks, tall tales and choruses of "Sweet Adeline" with the boys, Errol's character was a philandering, lying, lecherous sot who shared himself with women other than his wife. Only the threat of being found out prompted remorse. His was not the sort of character around whom Hollywood wished to build a major film, although they considered him fine for supporting roles. Most movie comics grew more avuncular as they grew older; Errol never forswore his liquor or lechery.

The Mexican Spitfire series paired two Leon Errols with Lupe Velez. In these films, a compromise was struck with Leon's character. As lovable Uncle Matt, he was a misunderstood husband always getting into jams, whereas as Lord Epping he indulged in his wayward ways.

Oddly, Leon Errol the man seems quite at odds with his stage persona. His coworkers described him as "a dear man." He was affable, polite, intelligent, educated, and hardworking yet all business on the set. He preferred a quiet home life, except for golf and fishing, and was devoted to his wife.

Instead of being honored for his stage career, Errol has been judged by his films. The lack of esteem may also be due to the 98 two-reel domestic comedies Errol made between 1933 and 1951. Major comedians were not supposed to trifle with two-reel comedies, yet shorts often are better suited to comedians than features. Along with the Mexican Spitfire series, ever-smaller roles in other features, and Monogram's Joe Palooka series, these shorts represent Leon Errol's output during the last two decades of his life.

It is in some of Errol's short films that his talents are best displayed. One of his early two-reelers, *Should Wives Work?,* was nominated for an Academy Award. Each one of his short films was an essay of the late middle-aged crisis of a man trying to recapture his youth, an updating of the curmudgeonly figure of farce descended from Pantaloon. Leon Errol was at his best in *Jitters,* re-creating his drunk eccentric dance act from a generation earlier.

Errol patented a particular role: the straying married man who is found out despite all his flustered alibis. Leon did not portray a happy drunk; instead, his tippling and swaying inebriate frowned and fuddled in confusion. Confronted, his expression soured. Trying to speak, he sputtered. Moving, his legs jerked, his arms flapped and his head pecked forward like a disgruntled rooster.

The year Leon Errol died, 1951, he had completed his 98th two-reeler and was planning a television series with Dorothy Grainger, his on screen wife from many of his two-reelers. Had he lived a bit longer, one wishes Leon Errol would have had the opportunity and accepted the challenge, as did Bert Lahr and Bobby Clark, to play the classic comedies of the seventeenth and eighteenth centuries: Ben Jonson, Molière, Congreve, Goldoni and Sheridan. After all, Leon Errol was trained in Shakespeare. Think of him as Malvolio or cranky Peter Teazle in *School for Scandal,* the scheming Volpone, the nervous Boniface in Feydeau's *Hotel Paradiso,* or even Vladimir in Samuel Beckett's *Waiting for Godot.*

ESCAPE ACTS

Essentially, all escape and release tricks fit into one of three categories: ties, locks and containers. *Escape* refers to the illusion; *release* is the method or technique employed to effect that illusion. Often, volunteers were called up onstage from the audience to verify what the audience thought it witnessed.

Ties: volunteers were usually restricted to helping the act's assistant tie up the escapist. The trick is in the way the escapist maneuvers during the binding process to allow his arms some play. After the delegation from the audience is satisfied and publicly attests to the fastness of the ropes or cords, a curtain is drawn, behind which the escapist frees himself. The straightjacket is a variation, with clasps replacing rope knots.

Locks: handcuffs and chains secured by padlocks are usual. The method of release is effected by either of two methods: picking the lock with a tiny tool that has been concealed from the audience or, if the lock is susceptible, dismantling its mechanism. Again, audience members were singled out to serve as onstage witnesses, but the escapist usually released himself behind a screen or curtain.

Containers: rather than simply being tied up or being chained and locked by a key, some escapists devised what seemed to be a more daring feat—an escape from inside a bag, a trunk, a large milk can or some other container that was locked from the outside. When this became a favorite trick and audiences began to learn of false bottoms and trapdoors, escapists went to the next level, and the container was suspended in the air or submerged in a tank of water.

If the escapist were especially renowned, such as Harry Houdini, local police and fire chiefs often came to the theatre and gave onstage testimony that the containers and locks were escape proof. Houdini's appearances, after he achieved stardom, generated extensive press coverage wherever he performed, and local dignitaries were often eager to share Houdini's spotlight. Volunteers from the audience served the same purpose for less-famous escape acts.

The task for the escapist was to unfasten the lock from the inside without revealing the method. Sometimes, to increase the drama, the performer would be shackled by rope or locked in chains before being encased in the container, which, in turn, was locked. Whether the escapist was bound inside and the container was locked from outside or not, the essentials of the release were the same. The container had some concealed mechanism that yielded to the performer, and the performer had concealed either keys or lock picks and, while being bound, held his arms in such a way as to permit some wiggle room to later manipulate his hands.

The earliest escape act in modern era show business may have been part of a phony spiritualist act being performed during the Civil War by the Davenport Brothers. Séances were of great interest in the USA at the time, and the point of the escape act was for the performers to seem to act as conduits for mystical forces. In one of the early, rudimentary demonstrations, the performers were bound, tied and shut away in a cabinet amid various objects. Once the performers were sequestered, the objects began to fly forth from an opening in the cabinet. Another variation was emanation of sounds, such as musical instruments, and this was performed by the Davenport Brothers during the Civil War era. They not only played the instruments but tossed them out as well.

In those acts, the escapists had managed to wriggle free of their bonds, toss out the objects, then twist their arms and hands back into the tied ropes by the end of the act just as the cabinet opened. In the view of the enchanted audience, the performers were found, still bound, as they had been at the start.

Debunkers of séances, like the Davenports' contemporary, John Nevil Maskelyne, made their careers by performing much the same illusions but insisting they were accomplished by human ingenuity rather than spiritual force.

GRAINGER ESCH

b: ca. 1967, Texas

Eccentric dancer and clown, Grainger Esch left Duke University, where theatre activities had engaged him, to attend Ringling Bros. and Barnum & Bailey Clown College. He was graduated with the class of 1988 and toured with Ringling Bros. and Barnum & Bailey's circus for the next two seasons and again in 1995.

Esch moved to Los Angeles, where he found various outlets for his skills. He was the percussionist, banjo and ukulele player with a stilt-walking novelty band, Lou Wow & the Poi Boys, impersonated Stan Laurel at Universal Pictures theme park, clowned onstage and in circuses and worked in the film industry.

In 2000, Grainger Esch played the role of Near Miss Who in the film *How the Grinch Stole Christmas*. During the making of the film, Grainger met his future wife, Penny Mathis. They moved to Texas, where they founded the Salado Silver Spur, a theatre dedicated to filmed and live variety performances.

RUTH ETTING

b: 23 November 1896, David City, NE—
d: 24 September 1978, Colorado Springs, CO

The term *torch singer* is not heard much anymore, but once upon a time it meant a sad-eyed lady pausing for absinthe and a lament on her way to a harsh destiny. Between the two world wars, there was a legion of the warbling wounded, singing songs of loss and longing. Actually, *torch singer* was as artificial a designation as *song stylist* would be a generation later, a shorthand convenience for marketers and reviewers. Most of those who sang torch songs are forgotten today, but the image persists of a delicate yet debased creature throbbing her brokenhearted ballads in a low and husky voice, a vision somewhere between the Dark Lady of Shakespeare's sonnets and Shanghai Sal.

Yet the best of them, the few that are remembered, really did not fit that image. Belle Baker had just the right voice and coloring, but she was also earthy and robust enough to earn her the alternate billing as a Red Hot Mama. Helen Morgan, although she looked and acted like the quintessential torch singer, brunette, tiny, and tragic, she sang in a shimmering soprano. Libby Holman cultivated the deeper torchy sound and soulful look, yet she seemed about as vulnerable as the Spider Woman. Ruth Etting was crowned "Queen of All Torch Singers" by press agents, but she was too inventive a singer to be so simply typecast, and she was healthy and blonde, to boot.

Born in a small town in Nebraska, Ruth demonstrated an artistic bent as a youngster, and she moved north in her late teens to attend classes at Chicago's Academy of Fine Arts while she worked in a millinery shop. Ruth got her first show-business job as a chorus girl at the Rainbow Gardens, where she was also allowed to do a bit of singing. She spent about eight years in Chicago as a chorus girl and singer, gradually working the better clubs and hotels, performing in vaudeville and singing on radio. Her first performance over WLS radio station in Chicago drew so much fan mail that she was signed to appear on WLS twice weekly for a year. Meanwhile, Balaban & Katz starred her in their presentation house, McVickers Theatre, where live acts preceded the film.

Ruth Etting was never wrapped up in her career. Her friends knew that she was in show business primarily because it promised the most likely chance to earn enough money to buy a small country spread. Ruth was shy and modest, and her career would have stalled had she not been talented and beautiful and pushed by friends. Of those people who gave Ruth Etting's career a nudge, one went far beyond that. In 1922, Ruth had married an abrasive demihood named Martin "Moe the Gimp" Snyder. He took full charge of her career and in a short period pumped her weekly salary from $25 to $2,500. Moe was rude and ruthless and eventually was barred from the very places he booked Etting. He measured his own stature by how successful he was in managing Ruth, and for the 12 years their marriage prevailed, he dominated her personally and professionally.

Still in Chicago, Ruth began recording in 1926. For the next ten years, even bridging the trough of the Great Depression, she continued to record, changing with the times from a flapper ebullience to a less ornamented, almost somber style. Her records, from first to last, displayed a voice almost immune to the distortions of the early recording technology. Her tone at the top was full and bell-like, rich and mellow in her middle range, and her low notes were dark and elegant. She modulated superbly throughout. Ruth's enunciation and sustaining power were among the best, her pitch true. Yet it is a smallish thing that steals your heart: her *s* sound was perfect.

Ruth's vaudeville act was simple and straightforward. She usually went on as a single, with her accompanist onstage, backed by the pit band, and sang three numbers. Even when she moved her base of operations from Chicago to New York, her presentation remained the same. If "Sam, the Old Accordion Man" was on tap for the evening, an accordionist might share her spotlight, standing just to the side and rear of her, but otherwise she just sang quietly but compellingly without a lot of production. She knew she was not an actor, and, although she might sashay, she did not dance. She was a musician more than a performer.

Onstage and on record, Ruth Etting introduced and made popular many top pop standards, some of which endure today in other repertoires: "Ten Cents a Dance," "Mean to Me," "Take Me in Your Arms," "Varsity Drag," "I'll Never Be the Same," "It All Depends on You," "Glad Rag Doll," "You're the Cream in My Coffee," "Button Up Your Overcoat," "All of Me," "Everything I Have Is Yours," "Body and Soul," "What About Me?," "Just One More Chance" and, of course, "Love Me or Leave Me."

In 1927, Etting went to New York City for engagements with the *Ziegfeld Follies* and Paul Whiteman and His Orchestra. Irving Berlin, who was writing the music and lyrics for the *Ziegfeld Follies of 1927,* had heard Etting's recordings and suggested her to Florenz Ziegfeld, who signed her for the 21st edition of the *Follies* along with Eddie Cantor, Cliff Edwards, the Brox Sisters and Claire Luce. As Venus "Shaking the Blues Away," Ruth Etting made such a hit that she remained with Florenz Ziegfeld for five years. She appeared in his productions of *Whoopee* in 1928 starring Eddie Cantor, the 1930 Rodgers & Hart vehicle for Ed Wynn titled *Simple Simon,* and Ziegfeld's final and ill-fated *Ziegfeld Follies of 1931* with Helen Morgan, Harry Richman and Jack Pearl, which was memorable for Ruth's revival of Nora Bayes' signature song, "Shine on, Harvest Moon."

Ruth Etting abruptly turned away from her stellar career to escape the public and press that hounded her after the (not fatal) shooting of her second husband, Myrl, by her first, Moe the Gimp. Myrl Alderman had been Ruth's accompanist, and it was with him that Ruth would enjoy the rest of her life. She was 40 when, together, they retreated into the anonymity of small-town America that she had known in her childhood. This time it was Colorado Springs, where she would spend the second half of her life until her death.

Rumor pictured her as a recluse after her retirement. Instead, she cherished her marriage with Myrl, traveled a lot, kept in touch with old friends and even performed a bit again in the mid-1940s. Equally untrue was the

Hollywood musical-bio *Love Me or Leave Me,* with Doris Day portraying Ms. Etting. Neither the singing style of the mid-1950s nor Doris Day's sound was at all evocative of Etting and her music. Ruth was more troubled by the movie's emphasis upon her nightmare years with the Gimp, played by Jimmy Cagney. "It's a shame that the most beautiful part, my twenty-eight year marriage to Myrl Alderman, was left out because that was the real highlight of my life."

Her recorded legacy lay buried until 1955, when Columbia reprised 12 of Etting's original hits, an LP timed to coincide with the release of *Love Me or Leave Me.* The success of the Ruth Etting reissue was one of the first signals to record companies that a revival market existed. Ruth never received a nickel in royalties from Columbia, but Biograph's 1973 reissues gave her residuals. Ms. Etting was astounded that anyone was interested. She had not kept many of her own records and had not heard some of them for nearly 40 years. A year after her death, Take Two Records brought out more Ruth Etting standards.

In her 20s, Ruth had a girlish, buoyant quality and often sang novelty tunes. She took liberties with her phrasing but always kept inside the time (*rubato*). Within the measure, she varied the beat's accent, alternated melody and harmony. Ruth was an ensemble musician and enjoyed simpatico partnerships with pianist Rube Bloom and a bit later with the jazz guitar and violin team of Eddie Lang and Joe Venuti. Not only was she musical and experienced, she was a near-legend for her one-take recordings. This meant the instrumentalists could use the remainder of the booked studio time to record their own material.

Critic Whitney Balliett points to Etting along with Ethel Waters, Louis Armstrong and Bing Crosby as pioneers of an authentic American singing style. But Ruth never took herself that seriously. Indeed, when the 1950s, 1960s and 1970s brought renewed attention, interviewers were surprised at how little she recalled of her career. It simply did not mean that much to her.

Only Ruth Etting outlived the myth of the torch singers. Helen Morgan drank and died at age 41. Belle Baker, widowed and twice divorced, seemed to drift away along with vaudeville, occasionally appearing on a revival bill. Libby Holman found scandal, was crushed by news stories and barely escaped conviction for murder. Billie Holiday, who invested the torch song with a blues and jazz aesthetic, died at age 44, a victim of racism, drink and drugs. Twenty years after her debut, Ruth Etting retired, as she always had intended, with a man she loved to their home "where the mountains meet the meadow." Myrl Alderman died in 1968; Ruth passed away ten years later.

JAMES REESE EUROPE

b: 22 February 1880, Mobile, AL—
d: 9 May 1919, Boston, MA

The future bandleader and composer James Reese Europe was born into a middle-class African American family that moved, in 1889, to Washington, D.C., where James' father had accepted an appointment as a supervisor in the U.S. Post Office. Young Jim Europe attended good colored schools and studied various instruments, primarily violin and piano.

James Reese Europe was a tall, handsome, well-spoken, impeccably dressed and groomed gentleman who negotiated the various strata of class and race more easily than most African Americans of his day. He moved to New York City when he was 22. Although he first supported himself playing piano in honky-tonks, he forged connections with the upper class and soon was leading a string quartet at parties hosted by the city's elite. In time, the James Reese Society Orchestra was a favorite among society's 400 and one of the first black ensembles to record.

At the same time, he found employment leading theatrical orchestras and choruses and worked with many of the great names of black musical theatre: Ernest Hogan, Will Marion Cook, Bert Williams & George Walker, Bob Cole & J. Rosamond Johnson. Europe's importance as a musician was equaled by his efforts on behalf of Negro musicians. Various local union chapters of the American Federation of Musicians refused to allow Negro musicians to join. Black musicians were excluded from good-paying jobs in Broadway pit orchestras and dance bands, and they had no protection against unscrupulous employers. Joined by various prominent black bandleaders and songwriters, Europe spearheaded the effort to establish the Clef Club, a union hall and fraternity of sorts.

Europe favored strong string sections in his orchestras, and his various ensembles dispelled the notion that Negro musicians could play only banjos and tambourines. Several annual Carnegie Hall concerts, planned and conducted by Jim Europe, also verified the high level of black musicianship. The first, on 2 May 1912, featured music by Will Marion Cook and J. Rosamond Johnson and James Reese Europe, plus an aria from Saint-Saens' *Samson et Delilah.* Carnegie Hall's 3,000 seats were sold out; the audience was integrated. More than 20 years before others claimed the glory with a swing-to-gospel concert, the James Reese Europe–led affairs were the first jazz events at Carnegie Hall. The success of the Clef Club motivated the local chapter of the American Federation of Musicians in 1914 to finally admit black instrumentalists. Europe quickly moved on.

Through one of his society gigs, he impressed Vernon and Irene Castle, the ballroom dance darlings of the American stage. The Castles erased any taint of sinfulness attached to ballroom dancing and made it fashionable. Jim Europe became their music director, a job that required him to assemble musical aggregations for the various Castles ventures: Castle House, an East Side townhouse converted into a posh dance club, and San Souci, a chic supper club. Europe also composed and arranged the music as well as hired and led the 11-piece, all-Negro dance orchestra that sat onstage and accompanied Vernon & Irene Castle in their tours of vaudeville from 1914 to 1916. Jim managed several Europe Society Orchestras playing in and around New York. Noble Sissle was hired as a singer and associate bandleader, and Eubie Blake, his partner, soon followed him into the Europe organization as a pianist, arranger and conductor.

In 1916, James Reese Europe enlisted in the 15th Infantry Regiment of the National Guard, a segregated Negro outfit. His fame had reached the armed services, and he was directed to create a top-level army band. He was given carte blanche. He auditioned and selected the instrumentalists and quickly made them into a great band. They played a number of civilian engagements, starting with the Manhattan Casino in Harlem, and then a variety of military dates before shipping overseas in 1918. Sent to France, they played a number of goodwill dates for the French people as well as entertaining the American troops. In the closing months of the war, they were attached to a French unit. Renamed the 369th Infantry Regiment (all Negro), and fondly nicknamed the Harlem Hellfighters, they exchanged musical instruments for guns and fought on the front lines. Europe was made an officer.

The 369th Regiment returned to the USA early in 1919. Europe was swamped with offers. He took his recently demobilized Hellfighters on an extensive and phenomenally successful concert tour throughout the Northeast and Midwest, made recordings with the band and made plans to collaborate with Eubie Blake and Noble Sissle in a Broadway show. The orchestra returned to Boston to play Mechanics Hall on 9 May 1919 because their previous Boston concerts had been sold out and people were still clamoring to see and hear them. During the intermission, a mentally disturbed member of the band attacked Jim Europe and stabbed him in the neck with a jackknife. Jim was rushed to Boston City Hospital; he died before doctors could help him.

No other African American entertainer had achieved such professional success, done more to advance the position of black musicians or won the affection of so many Americans of all races and ethnicities, from Park Avenue to Harlem, from Carnegie Hall and Hammerstein's Opera House to vaudeville stages and the trenches of the First World War.

James Reese Europe enjoyed most types of music: European concert music, opera, Negro spirituals, ragtime and jazz. He was nearly 40 when he died. Had he lived longer, he could have accomplished far more for himself, black musicians, the musical theatre and the concert stage.

EVANS & HOOEY

Charles E. Evans

b: 6 September 1856, Rochester, NY—d. 16 April 1945, Santa Monica, CA

William Hooey

b: ca. 1850—d: 1897

Charlie Evans enjoyed a long career that carried him from concert saloons and rough-and-tumble variety to vaudeville and Broadway. Like many comedians of his era, Evans began with racial and ethnic characterizations, performing blackface the first time around in Lower Manhattan and Brooklyn theatres, only to change makeup, costume and accent and reappear in the same places as a Dutch or an Irish comedian. Vaudeville historian Douglas Gilbert notes that Evans' first partner was James Niles and that they were a successful act that played Tony Pastor's on the Bowery in 1874. They then teamed with another male double act, Bryant & Hooey, and the comedy quartet was an act for several seasons.

In 1882, Evans and Hooey decided to shuck their other partners and work up their own act, and they engaged the French Twin Sisters to dance and sing in "Book Agent," an adaptation of an infamously naughty afterpiece by Frank Dumont. The twins, Minnie and Helen French, married, respectively, Evans and Hooey. The act was so successful that Evans and Hooey commissioned farceur Charles H. Hoyt to turn the act into a full evening's entertainment.

Hoyt created a musical farce out of "Book Agent" and named it *A Parlor Match*. The show opened in 1884 and ran for eight seasons at the Bijou Theatre in Lower Manhattan. It became Evans & Hooey's most notable success as a team. The reason the show remained a perennial favorite was that Evans & Hooey changed the comedy bits and their songs each year. It was in the final season of 1892–93 that an English music-hall song, "The Man Who Broke the Bank at Monte Carlo," was added to the show.

English songwriter Fred Gilbert had been inspired by a gentleman, impressively named Arthur DeCourcey Bower, who arrived unknown into the midst of London's smart set, in 1891, and spent and tipped lavishly, explaining he had won his boodle on the gambling tables of Monte Carlo. When DeCourcey Bower died impoverished many years later, word leaked out that his publicized spree had been an early and highly successful example of marketing, one which had been bankrolled by the since-famous Casino to boost tourist attendance. Before he was exposed, however, Gilbert wrote the song and offered it to music-hall favorite Charles Coborn, for whom it became a signature song that he performed into his 90s, nearly a half century after he introduced it. In the USA, Bill Hooey's jaunty rendition of "The Man Who Broke the Bank at Monte Carlo" in *A Parlor Match* caused a mild sensation, and the song was inevitably requested of him until his death in 1897. Charlie Evans once estimated that he and Bill had netted about $400,000 from their years of playing in *A Parlor Match* and their ownership of the show.

After Hooey's passing in 1897, Evans appeared on his own in plays, musical comedies and revues, notably *There and Back* (1903), *The Sho-Gun* (1904), *Marie Dressler's All Star Gambol* (1913), and *Sick-a-Bed* (1918). Evans left New York for Southern California, where he kept a hand in show business by playing old men in 17 talking pictures made between 1929 and 1939. Nine of them were First National and Warner Brothers films starring George Arliss. Otherwise, he remained socially active in comfortable semiretirement with his second wife, Helena Phillips.

GEORGE "HONEY BOY" EVANS

b: 10 March 1870, Pontlottyn, Wales— d: 12 March 1915, New York, NY

Sometime in the 1870s, when George was still a boy, the Evans family immigrated to the USA. Eventually, they settled in Steator, Illinois. Evans was blessed with the beautiful voice expected of Welsh singers, yet it seems he did not turn professional until the relatively old age of 21, when, as Anthony Slide reports, George made his debut as a member of the Columbia Quartette at Balser's Music Hall in Canton, Ohio.

That same year of 1891, he joined Haverly's Minstrels in Chicago, but the following season he toured with Cleveland's Minstrels. Each move pushed him further up the minstrel ranks from one of many in the chorus to an end man and to a specialty act in the olio. By 1893, George was a principal with Primrose & West's Minstrels until he returned to Haverly's the following year.

Working in a solo spot during the olio, the middle part of the minstrel show, was perfect preparation for vaudeville. George spent a bit more than a decade in vaudeville, from the mid-1890s to 1908. He was well liked, an amiable gentleman with a sense of fun. His close friends included other performers who liked to write songs. Most of what they wrote, parodies and nonsense ditties, was never intended to be published. On one famous occasion, however, a chance remark by Evans about the good old summertime prompted his friend Ren Shields to suggest some lyrics, and Evans provided a tune. Vaudeville headliner Blanche Ring asked to perform "In the Good Old Summertime" in her first Broadway show, *The Defenders* (1902), and Evans and Shields gladly consented.

In time, Evans forewent blackface, yet his act did not falter in popularity. It was a combination of singing and storytelling, a relaxed, informal act typical of the period when theatres were small and the relationship between performer and audience was intimate. A singer often spelled his numbers with good-natured patter and anecdotes, a style that was no longer possible when theatres surpassed 1,000 seats and audiences expected a snappy pace.

During the 1906–07 season, Evans played the week of 29 October at Keith's New Theatre in Boston as "George Evans (New Bits of Wit and Wisdom by Vaudeville's Greatest Monologuist)." He shared the bill with "Will Rogers (His Pard, His Horse and His Lariats in Cowboy Stunts)," "Josephine Gassman & Her Pickaninnies (Droll Doings by Darktown Youngsters)," "The Uessems (The Equilibristic Marvel)" and "The Mozarts (in the Novel Terpsichorean Skit, 'A Cobbler's Dream')," among others.

In 1907, friend, vaudevillian and fellow tunesmith Jack Norworth composed "Honey Boy" for Evans. George's rendition made it a favorite in his repertoire, and it quickly became his theme song. Seldom if ever in the seasons ahead would Evans be billed as anything but George "Honey Boy" Evans.

George left vaudeville and its higher salary of $1,500 a week to star in *Cohan and Harris Minstrels* (1908). Although the show boasted other star acts like Eddie Leonard, Julian Eltinge and Rice & Provost, it had only a short run on Broadway before heading out on tour. It came back to Broadway in 1909, minus most of its stars except Evans. His heart had always been in minstrelsy, so he bought the name and rights to *Cohan & Harris Minstrels* and toured it from 1910.

George was too easy a touch, generous to a fault, and ill prepared for rainy days, despite the big money he made in vaudeville. Perhaps running his minstrel show and keeping it booked was a strain. It was reported that when he died five years later in 1914, just 45, he was broke.

EXCESS BAGGAGE

Civilian (nonprofessional) spouses who traveled the vaudeville or burlesque circuits with their wives or husbands were known as excess baggage. Often, performers would try to incorporate the spouse because another person in the act usually entitled the act to a few more dollars. A reasonably attractive wife could be costumed as an assistant to a magician, a juggler or any other act that required the handing over of props and the clearing of discarded items. A presentable husband, appropriately attired, might join his singing or dancing wife onstage as her partner in a simple fox trot and help her quick change between numbers in her act. A spouse unable or unwilling to perform such simple tasks was deemed to be excess baggage.

EXOTIC DANCERS

Essentially strippers, they were advertised as exotic dancers by the post–Second World War nightclubs in which they worked to suggest something more modern and, yes, exotic than the strippers of dear old dad's day as well as to circumvent municipal prohibitions against striptease. The term endures for those dancers who, a half century later, perform the customary shakes, bumps and grinds but, topless and bottomless, have nothing to strip.

FAIRY STARS

Fairy Stars were child performers who charmed the USA for nearly a century. The craze began with the westward expansion of the American empire and the gold rushes that turned northern California and Alaska into tent towns whose inhabitants were in thrall to the promise of a golden future. In those years, small companies of performers picked their way through a trail of port cities and mining encampments, performing for the prospectors and the people who made a living from them.

Primarily girls, the Fairy Stars were prodigies who could act the classics, sing, dance and impersonate. Most popular in the West, the Fairy Stars had childlike qualities and an innocence that appealed to the sentiments of miners, especially those in their cups and estranged from their families. The young boys were billed as Master, such as Master Billy who acted Shylock at five and Master Gus Howard who danced and played several instruments. The girls were particular favorites: La Petite Clorinda danced and sang, Miss Anna Maria Quinn essayed Hamlet and other trouser roles, and, of course, Lotta Crabtree danced, clowned, played banjo and sang. There was also a troupe of girl and boy wonders billed as The Fairy Minstrels who sang and danced.

The Civil War intensified the desire for Fairy Stars, and if they no longer were called such, there was another generation of children brought to the stage to assure the nation that innocence could be regained, at least for the duration of a show.

America's fascination with child stars continued throughout the remainder of the nineteenth century. Once motion pictures began to tell stories in the early 1900s, child characters became an essential part of filmed melodramas. Not all the youngsters played children, however. Because early film technology tended to photograph its subjects harshly, the first generation of female silent screen stars were young teenagers like Mary Pickford, Marguerite Clark, Mae Marsh and the Gish Sisters. The public's affection for them was based on the virginal child-woman roles they played. They were the Fairy Stars of the early twentieth century.

A generation later, Americans suffering through the Great Depression needed Fairy Stars again, and Shirley Temple was there, up on the silver screen to prove there was still goodness, purity and hope in the world. Perhaps the last of the breed were Bobby Breen and Deanna Durbin.

FALLY MARKUS TIME

Infamous and often the butt of bitter jokes and sour reminiscence, Fally Markus time was the option of last resort. An act willingly took a booking on Fally Markus time only when it wanted to break in a new act without attracting notice. More often there was little choice: the act was desperate and all other possibilities had been denied them. The theatres that Mr. Markus booked were located in and around New York City. The pay was as insulting as the facilities and the audiences, yet Fally Marcus dates provided a temporary safety net for a vaudevillian with no where to go but down.

FANCHON & MARCO

Fanchon

b: (Fanchon Wolff Simon) May 1892, Los Angeles, CA—d: February 1965, Los Angeles, CA

Marco

b: (Marco Wolff) April 1894, Los Angeles, CA—d: October 1977, Los Angeles, CA

The most famous producers of live stage prologues for moving pictures began in vaudeville as a sister-and-brother dance act, Fanchon & Marco. Originally, before they turned professional, there were three performing siblings: the sister was Fanchon and her brothers were Rube, the eldest, and Marco, the youngest of the trio. All sang and were trained musicians. Rube studied trumpet, Fanchon, piano, and Marco, violin.

When as teenagers they began their professional careers, Rube ventured forth as a musician, and Fanchon & Marco devised a ballroom-dance act, very popular in the 1910s, for vaudeville. They sang and demonstrated various dances, rather like the Castles, and, for a finish, Marco deftly hoisted Fanchon to his shoulder, and they waltzed offstage while Marco played the violin.

Fanchon & Marco, anticipating what was evident to only an astute few—the limited future viability of vaudeville—turned producers in 1919. Silent films were no longer restricted to one- and two-reel shorts; they had matured into features five and more reels in length, occasionally as many as ten. Many were artfully produced, and, by the early 1920s, the silent film was acknowledged to be an exciting art form.

The silent-film industry had progressed mightily in a single generation from plotless novelty to crude narrative to stirring pantomimes of drama and comedy. In the early nickelodeons, local music teachers or the piano students used to play whatever songs they knew on battered upright pianos, but by the early 1920s the better movie houses employed full orchestras to perform original scores that accompanied many first-rate films.

The businessmen who founded the film industry were driven by competition to create ever-better-made products, and they sought to showcase their quality. Movie studios began to debut their features with glittering premier exhibitions to stimulate the interest of press and public. Celebrities, klieg lights and radio broadcasts were part of the ceremonies attending these openings, and studio moguls sought to outdo rivals with grander promotions.

The trick was to extend the newsworthiness of each feature film beyond its premier. Stars like Douglas Fairbanks, Gloria Swanson and Rudolph Valentino ensured audience anticipation, but only a few films were graced by such insurance. Between 1923 and 1934, Fanchon & Marco prologues stimulated added interest in the film they preceded. Mae Murray, former *Follies* dancing star and one of the more *outré* screen idols of the 1920s, saw the success of prologues and demanded that her studio allow her to film her own prologues to accompany her feature pictures.

Fanchon & Marco were not the only producers of stage prologues or revues that preceded feature films, but they were the best known and most prolific of the producers. Their success was due to talent, organization and branding their product. By 1923, Fanchon & Marco had settled on calling their stage revues *Ideas.* Each *Idea* revolved around a specific theme. The themes were as varied as the color blue, Mother Goose, Christmas, fashions, flamenco, spring, rivers, vegetables, pirates and whatnot. Their first was *Ideas: Love Tales,* and it opened at the Warfield Theatre in San Francisco on 13 October 1923.

The Fanchon & Marco prologues were one-act revues, attractively set and costumed, with specific music scored for a full orchestra. The larger theatres boasted as many as 18 to 24 musicians in the pit; the smaller ones usually had a minimum of seven or eight.

Older brother Rube Wolf [*sic*] assumed the post of orchestra leader in several California houses: the Warfield and Loew's State in Los Angeles. Another brother, Roy, eventually became the manager of Los Angeles' Manchester Theatre, which became the tryout house for new Fanchon & Marco revues.

Fanchon & Marco churned out a new *Idea* every week, and the range of theatres for which they produced prologues grew from San Francisco to Oakland, Sacramento, Los Angeles, Long Beach and San Diego. The dancers, often all girls, performed in unison, perhaps as a chorus line or a mock military drill, as well as in a production number. Most of the girls danced a specialty as well. The prologues played three to six shows daily. Smaller theatres frequently were one-night bookings, so at the end of a tiring day, the dancers had to decamp and head for the next town and theatre. Sleep and food were catch-as-catch-can.

In 1926, Fanchon and Marco were servicing Pacific Coast theatres from San Diego to Vancouver. By 1929, Fanchon & Marco prologues had spread across the USA through the Fox, Pantages, Keith-Orpheum, Paramount/Public and Loew's circuits.

Fanchon & Marco was a major organization by 1932. They had 5,000 employees and often staged two productions per week. View Busby Berkeley's 1933 backstage movie musical, *Footlight Parade* (1933), to get a sense of the energy and personnel required to maintain such a schedule.

This expansion required precise administration, efficient production, reliable transportation and standardized training geared to Fanchon & Marco staging. Their school specialized in ballet, acrobatic and tap dance. It provided a farm system that fed dancers into the performing companies, and it generated income from students who never turned professional.

When it became apparent that the Great Depression was going to set records for a long run, the prologues became an expense eliminated as movie studios somewhat trimmed costs. Fanchon helped staged various dance sequences for movie musicals and later for Shipstad & Johnson's Ice Follies. She married William Simon, a successful restaurateur. Marco became a movie-theatre owner both independently and with his sister. Marco ended his career as the owner of a large chain of movie houses and as a Christian Science practitioner.

ANNA EVA FAY

b: (Ann Heathman) ca. 1850, Southington, OH—d: ca. 1930

A very successful vaudeville performer until she retired in 1924, Anna Eva Fay began her career a half century earlier. She conducted séances in lecture rooms and concert halls. As she moved into vaudeville in the 1890s, Anna performed some larger-scale illusions like the spirit cabinet, comparable to the one the Davenport Brothers devised and John Neville Maskelyne adapted for his act.

Anna Eva Fay was bound hands and feet and placed in a cabinet with bells and musical instruments. As far as the audience knew, the magician was unable to reach any of the instruments, yet, once inside, bells, horns and other sounds issued forth. When the doors were opened, Fay remained bound as she had been when placed inside. She also presented a spirit dancing handkerchief and a levitation illusion, all of which were to foster the belief that she possessed supernatural powers.

Anna Eva Fay attracted audiences more for the advice she dispensed during the psychic segment of her act than for the illusions she performed. Her two husbands, Mr. Fay, the first, and David H. Pingree, his successor, did the advance research she needed before she arrived in town to play the local theatre. Through diligent research, showmanship, her ability to intuit and the codes worked out between Fay and her aisle men, the small, fair-haired lady became a highly paid vaudeville attraction.

Fellow conjurers and mentalists faulted Fay for failing to make clear that she was a dealer in illusion. Instead, she presented herself as a psychic. Her son, John Fay, married Anna Norman but committed suicide in 1908 after ten years of marriage. His widow, billing herself as Eva Fay, "The High Priestess of Mystery," entered vaudeville and provided spirited competition for her mother-in-law.

FRANK FAY

b: (Francis Anthony Fay) 17 November 1897, San Francisco, CA—d: 25 September 1961, Santa Monica, CA

Nobody in his field was more respected and less liked than Frank Fay. Debonair, natty, well-groomed, he possessed a handsome, somewhat delicate and open Irish face dominated by a mane of wavy auburn hair and large blue eyes. Fay presented a charming and casual front that masked a contentious wise guy. It was said that he was bigoted against Jews and African Americans and was misogynist to boot, but that ignores the range of Fay's contempt, for there is little evidence that he respected anyone except himself. Called to testify in court and asked to identify himself, he replied, assured of his charm, that he was Frank Fay, world's greatest comedian. Later, when Fay's counsel remonstrated, Frank explained that, being under oath, he had been obliged to tell the truth. There was as much conviction as humor in his remark.

No one was safe from Frank Fay's suave but stinging observations, including himself. Often, he turned his wit on himself, making fun of his self-absorption: "Careful, you're talking about the man I love."

Faysie, as he was called, was acknowledged by other great monologists to be their model. Rather than opt for a series of one-line insult jokes, Frank displayed his mastery of the storytelling form by conjuring up the people who figured in his droll, rambling stories. He got many of his laughs not from gag lines but from the surprise aptness of his observations. Or he would sing a few lines of the ballads of the day and then dissect them for their banality or lachrymosity. A silly passage in "Tea for Two" earned his scorn:

> "Day will break, and you'll awake, and start to bake a sugar cake,"—
>
> That poor woman. What a future. She hops out of bed at dawn and—bang!—she runs to the oven.
>
> "For me to take for all the boys to see—"

> Imagine. A guy going down to the poolroom to see his side pocket pals. "Guess what I got! … No, not a new set of tires. No, not a TV set." Then he whips out his cake—lemon chiffon!

It was all in the way he told it.

Faysie was a big-city favorite. He was too sly and too full of himself for rural audiences, who admired the concealed canniness of a not-as-dumb-as-he-looks hick funnyman to a boastful big-city boulevardier. So Frank stuck, as much as he could, to vaudeville and revue bookings in New York, Boston, Philadelphia, Chicago, San Francisco and Los Angeles.

Fay, born into a showbiz family, traveled from infancy with his parents, Will and Molly Fay, as they toured. Baby Frank's first role was a carry-on in *Quo Vadis,* performed in Chicago, when he was a year old. Little more than a baby, he appeared in small roles, such as the page in *When Knighthood Was in Flower.* His experience ranged from Shakespeare to melodrama, extravaganza and variety. Fay claimed to have appeared in his youth with Henry Irving, E. H. Sothern and Rose Stahl. By 15, Frank Fay was a veteran trouper.

Switching from acting and singing (he had a fine ballad voice) to comedy, Frank teamed up with Johnny Dyer and, as Dyer & Fay, played small-time vaudeville for a couple of seasons in a comedy act Fay came to loathe as crude. It soured Fay on low comedy and clowns forever.

By the age of 20, Fay was professionally secure in showbiz as a monologist. For a couple of seasons, he offered himself to vaudeville audiences as a sketch comic, even once in a dramatic sketch, but Frank's followers wanted Faysie, the breezy wit.

In 1918, Fay got a role in a book musical, but *Girl O' Mine* closed after 48 performances. Later that same year, he opened in *The Passing Show of 1918,* an all-star revue with Willie & Eugene Howard, Charles Ruggles, Lou Clayton, Nita Naldi and Fred & Adele Astaire. This edition of the annual Shubert revue scored 124 shows at the Winter Garden. Fay saw his future on Broadway. After some big-time vaudeville, including a 1919 engagement at the Palace Theatre, he tried musicals again, but *Oh, What a Girl,* another book show, managed only 68 performances in 1919.

Jim Jam Jems did better with 105 performances at the Broadway Theater in 1920 before it went on the road. Its stars, Frank Fay, Harry Langdon and Ned Sparks, refused the tour, and a second-string comic, Joe E. Brown, was the only featured member of the cast to accompany the show on the road. (A quarter century later, Brown replaced Fay in *Harvey.*) *Frank Fay's Fables* (1922), written and directed by Fay, closed after 32 performances at the Park Theatre, in plenty of time for Frank to try, later that year, another revue, *Raymond Hitchcock's Pinwheel,* but it folded after 35 performances.

When the Shuberts put Frank Fay into *Artists and Models* in 1923, it changed his luck; the show racked up 312 shows at the Broadway Theater. For the next couple of years, Frank played big-time vaudeville, repeating at the Palace in 1924.

In 1927, a solid cast of comedians (Bert Lahr, Winnie Lightner, Frank Fay and Patsy Kelly) pushed *Harry Delmar's Revels* to 114 shows at the Shubert. Yet vaudeville and vaudeville revues were losing their audiences. *Tattle Tales* (1933), a revue that Fay also wrote and directed as well as costarred in with Barbara Stanwyck (who reportedly bankrolled the production), failed after 28 performances at the Broadhurst. It was a dismal season for most Broadway shows.

In 1939, Fay tried to cover all bases but failed to score a home run with *Frank Fay Vaudeville.* Elsie Janis, Smith & Dale and Fay represented the traditional headliner acts of vaudeville; legitimate actor Eva LeGallienne was brought in to transform the Romeo and Juliet balcony scene into a vaudeville turn, and stripper Maxine de Shone was engaged as an antidote.

Among Frank Fay's more ignoble acts was his treatment of the great actor Eva LeGallienne. First he withheld a substantial portion of her salary, although the revue *Frank Fay Vaudeville* was breaking even during its two-month stand in Manhattan. He knew her financial situation was desperate, and she could not afford to quit the show. Years later, at a 1947 meeting of Actors Equity, agitated by the communist conspiracy allegations that propelled several political careers, Frank Fay publicly accused Margaret Webster (and, by association, Eva LeGallienne, Webster's dear friend) of being a communist. LeGallienne was nonpolitical. Perhaps Fay was motivated by his contempt for lesbians.

Perhaps because of the grim news from the battlefronts, the 1943–44 Broadway season was host to lightweight revues that traded partly on nostalgia. *Laugh Time* (1943), was only one of several old style shows. A Shubert show that originated in California and transferred to Broadway, boasted a superior cast of vaudeville veterans, not much past their prime, who pushed the tired format to 126 performances. *Laugh Time Bright Lights of 1944* starred James Barton, Frances White and Smith & Dale. *All for All* temporarily brought Jack Pearl back into the spotlight. *Artists and Models* was the final tired entry in the 20-year-old Shubert franchise. It failed to attract despite up-and-coming performers Jane Frohman and Jackie Gleason.

Other tepidly received revues starred Jimmy Savo, Ethel Shutta and Hazel Dawn. *Voice of the Turtle,*

Carmen Jones and *One Touch of Venus* were in the season's vanguard. *Something for the Boys* and the *Ziegfeld Follies of 1943* were hybrid hits—old bottles filled with new spirits. *Something for the Boys* supported old Broadway hands Ethel Merman, Mike Todd, Cole Porter, Herbert and Dorothy Fields with newcomers like Paula Lawrence, Betty Garrett and choreographer Jack Cole. The 1943 *Follies*—the longest-running *Follies* ever—sported fresh faces Milton Berle, Ilona Massey, Jack Cole and the Bill & Cora Baird's Puppets. All in all, however, it seemed as though producers had not figured out how to blend old and new as had *Oklahoma,* the big hit of the previous season, which had combined the form of operetta and a nostalgic setting with a serious book and modern ballet.

Fay tried his hand at a book musical when, in 1951, he wrote the book and lyrics, composed the music, directed and starred in *If You Please.* The show did not even make it to Broadway.

These failures were a contrast to Fay's glory days in big-time vaudeville. He was one of the first and best of vaudeville's masters of ceremonies, a term he is credited with coining. Traditionally, vaudeville did not employ emcees, but in the waning years of big-time vaudeville, the novelty of having Fay, Florence Moore, Jack Benny, Georgie Jessel, Eddie Cantor, Julius Tannen, Lou Holtz, Benny Rubin or Jack Haley introduce the acts at the Palace Theatre, as well as perform their own, gave the box office a needed spike. Fay headlined the Palace bill for eight weeks in a single season. Faysie did not simply introduce other acts. He toyed with them, engaged the audience and told stories between the acts; in short, he dominated the bill. So successful was he that other comics, whether they realized it or not, copied some of his bits. Milton Berle, although no fan of Fay—nor Fay of Berle—handled the emcee chore much as Fay did, butting into acts and generally commanding the proceedings. Jack Benny, another superb emcee, assumed much the same persona as Fay, but Jack emphasized the self-deprecatory aspect. Fay also could handle a gag: "Mayor Frank Hague promised to get the prostitutes out of Jersey City. He's a man of his word. Last night I saw him driving two of them to Philadelphia."

Fay was formidable in repartee. Those who tried to best him usually lost. In the audience at one show, Milton Berle, whose rapid delivery generally overwhelmed hecklers, challenged Fay to a duel of wits. "All right, Milton, but I want you to know it's against my principles to fight an unarmed man." On another occasion, Groucho Marx evidently thought he could fare better and tossed a few barbs from the safety of his seat in the audience until Fay invited him onto the stage. Groucho demurred. Frank dismissed him with, "See, Groucho, you really did need Zeppo."

Offstage, Frank Fay was less successful and less in control. His first two marriages did not last as long as some of his bookings. Alcoholic and pugnacious, Frank was publicly embroiled in several drunken fights. When, in a restaurant, he punched his third wife, Ruby Stevens (who became Barbara Stanwyck), it was noted that it was one of the few fistfights Frank had ever won. Frank's sun set while Barbara Stanwyck's star grew ever brighter. When they divorced, one wag said it was the only nice thing he ever did for her. Yet when Fay was summoned to Hollywood, he brought her and insisted that Columbia Pictures sign her.

The best example of Frank Fay's style in performance available to us today is in the filmed revue *Show of Shows* (1929), an all-star affair that Fay emceed to the point of surfeit. Other films with Fay were far less successful, and he eked out a living in the late 1930s and early 1940s playing secondary roles in a few B movie dramas and trying to revive his stage career.

His comeback vehicle, when it finally arrived, owed little to his renown as a raconteur. *Harvey* was a gentle comedy about a gentle man, Elwood P. Dodd, who had a weakness for liquor and enjoyed the company of a large rabbit, Harvey, that no one else could see. *Harvey* was a long shot for Broadway success, and Frank Fay was neither first, second nor third choice for the lead role. After it opened on 1 November 1944, however, it ran for 1,774 performances, garnered lavish praise for its star and won the Pulitzer Prize. It was Fay's greatest success and his last.

JOEY FAYE

b: (Joseph Anthony Palladino) 12 July 1909, New York, NY—d: 26 April 1997, Englewood, NJ

Joey Faye had great timing onstage but not in his career. By the time he left amateur contests to try his luck in vaudeville, vaudeville was fading back into a jumble of low-paying, small-time dates. Joey left vaudeville for burlesque in 1931, just before New York City began to crack down seriously on burlesque in 1932 and 1933. For seven seasons, Joey Faye made good money as a lead comedian in burlesque, most regularly with Minsky's, but never knowing when other cities were going to outlaw his livelihood as had New York City. To hedge his bet, Joey was part of the summer exodus to the Sour Cream Sierras, where he and Danny Kaye, Red Buttons, Alan King, Phil Foster, Myron Cohen and Jack E. Leonard served as toomlers and made merry the customers at various Jewish resorts on the Borscht circuit.

Parts in Broadway shows started to come Joey's way when he took over a role midway during the 500-performance run of *Room Service* (1937). He was given lots of opportunities in his next Broadway show, *Sing Out the News* (1938), and he played roles as diverse as Japanese Emperor Hirohito and Harpo Marx. The revue's three-month run did not make expenses, and six months after *Sing Out the News* closed, Lou Costello made a huge hit in *Streets of Paris* (1939).

Joey Faye and Lou Costello were not unalike in appearance or stage character, but Costello, one of comedy's truly skilled physical clowns, shot to fame with his partner Bud Abbott through their Broadway appearance and a weekly spot on Kate Smith's popular radio series. Costello rivaled Bob Hope as America's favorite comedian in the 1940s and was earning a fabulous salary as a Hollywood and network radio star while Joey Faye was still a second banana playing medium-sized cities for a medium-sized paycheck.

Joey tried television early on, and he appeared on no fewer than five ill-conceived series from 1946 through 1951. Some ran as long as three months; two lasted only for two weeks each. Thereafter, Joey appeared less frequently as a guest star on television's more popular and better-produced variety hours, comedies and dramatic shows.

By the 1950s and early 1960s, when burlesque had come to seem harmless and nearly quaint, Joey tried to ride the celebratory revival of burlesque on Broadway, movies and television, but producers would not risk the investment without big-name stars like Phil Silvers engaged as the top banana. Joey Faye was stuck as the reliable, versatile second banana.

Not the least of Joey Faye's value as a second comedian was his encyclopedic collection of gags and burleycue routines. Even in high school, Joey had proved himself a writer, and he continued at that trade throughout his life, most notably in recording for posterity the burlesque comedy canon.

Although Joey did not break into the ranks of leading comedians, he made a very good living acting small parts in a couple of dozen movies between 1938 and 1991 and about half as many Broadway shows between 1937 and 1993. On Broadway, he supported Phil Silvers in *High Button Shoes* (1945–47) (for which Joey took over the lead role after Silvers departed the cast), and *Top Banana* (1951). He also supported Sid Caesar in *Little Me* (1962). In other shows, Faye had the opportunity to do comedy routines with other fine burlesque veterans like Mickey Deems and Jack Albertson. Joey Faye worked into his 80s; he was 87 when he died. Fittingly, his last appearance in front of the cameras was made the year of his death in *Vaudeville,* a documentary produced by KCTV Seattle for the PBS *American Masters* series.

FEATURED SPOT ON THE BILL

Next to closing was the featured spot on a vaudeville bill, and it was reserved, almost without exception, for the headliner. Infrequently, there might be another, lower-billed act that was so raucous or made such a hit with local audiences that the headliner complained that they could not effectively follow that act. In this case the headliner and manager might agree to move the headliner into another spot, such as fourth or fifth, the second to last, or the last spot on the bill before intermission.

Occasionally a major, two-a-day house like the Palace Theatre in New York might find itself with two headliners, perhaps one carried over from a previous week. In this case, one of the headliners would likely close the first half of the show in the fifth spot.

FEED

A feed is a straight man; it can also mean to set up the comedian's gag with the right attitude and words: volume, cadence and inflection. A good feed understands how to hold long enough between lines to allow the audience to laugh yet anticipate the end of laughter at that split second before it begins to fade. It is the straight man's or feed's job to allow the comedian enough latitude while keeping the act tight and without slumping spots. The best feeds divine their partner's intent and pace, knowing when and how long to let the comedian improvise and run with a gag, knowing when to pull the comedian back to the spine of the act, and being quick to cover for an unsuccessful line. To allow the comedian the freedom to be inventive, the superior straight man or feed needs to be in synchronicity with the audience's pulse as much or more than the comedian.

MAXINE FELDMAN

b: (Maxine Adele Feldman) 26 December 1944, Brooklyn, NY

One branch of show business—folk music—considered itself apart from the mother industry. Folk songs were considered to be the voice of the people; more realistically, they were songs for which the composer and lyricist were forgotten. A folk song was as likely to be a half-remembered version of some minstrel's ditty performed on market day for the receipt of a few coins as it was an outgrowth of a work gang's chant or a mother's impromptu lullaby.

Before the popular revival of interest in the late 1940s, a majority of American folksingers were old, rural and white, and their songs derived from earlier versions once heard in England, Scotland and the Celtic lands. Diligent musicologists sought out and captured their lyric memories on recordings made in the hills and hollows of their communities. They also made field recordings of old, rural black folks singing gospel and work songs.

During the political struggles of the 1930s, several well-known balladeers, like Burl Ives and Maybelle Carter and her family, emerged to become beloved entertainers. Others veered clear of the music industry as much as possible and, like Woody Guthrie, became the Walt Whitmans of their century.

By the latter half of the 1950s, folk music found devoted young audiences near college campuses and equally young balladeers eager to learn the love and work songs of previous generations. The watchword was authenticity. As folk music rapidly grew in popularity, black bluesmen were discovered and honored for their lives of hoboing and singing on the streets, alleys and byways of a romantic version of the American heartland. The bluesmen were happy to be engaged to play places where they had a roof over their head, an attentive audience and the prospect of payment. The blueswomen were largely ignored, their music dismissed as vaudeville blues.

The Weavers of the 1940s and 1950s, collectively and individually (Ronnie Gilbert, Lee Hays, Fred Hellerman and Pete Seeger), along with the legendary Guthrie, inspired a younger generation of protest singers like Phil Ochs and Bob Dylan. Susan Reed, a concert singer, endowed old ballads with a lovely voice and musicianship. Although Reed was seldom acknowledged, many young women seem to take her as their model, admittedly or not.

Boasting nearly three dozen universities and colleges, Boston and Cambridge, its neighbor across the Charles River, in Massachusetts, vied with Manhattan and Berkeley, California, for the number of coffeehouses receptive to folksingers. The Club 47, named after its original and brief residence at 47 Mount Auburn Street before it moved to its longtime home on Palmer Street in Harvard Square (where it is now known as Passim's), became the best known, but there were many others, including Tulla's Coffee Grinder, the Unicorn, the Turk's Head, the Golden Vanity, the Loft, Café Yana, the Salamander, the Rose and the Orleans (later called the Sword and the Stone).

Folksingers who appeared often enough during the late 1950s and early 1960s in the Boston and Cambridge area to be considered at least semiofficial residents included Joan Baez, Eric Von Schmidt, Dave Van Ronk, Jackie Washington, Mark Spoelstra, Tom Rush, Tim Hardin, Taj Mahal, Jim Kweskin's Jug Band, Geoff Muldaur, Maria Muldaur, Robert L. Jones and the Charles River Valley Boys. Each of them developed a following that brought them national fame, recording contracts, consistent bookings and, eventually, various outcomes in their lives. During their careers, protestations aside, they all moved into show business, playing a national if unofficial circuit of coffeehouses, hipster bars and, if they proved big-enough draws, theatres and folk festivals.

Folk music provided a simple way for a performer to try his wings as a performer. All a kid needed was the ability to play several chords on a guitar and a decent voice, to have rehearsed several old-time ballads and summon enough nerve to get on a coffeehouse stool and keep a small audience entertained.

Making a success in folk music, however, required the usual formula of talent, audience appeal and good breaks. There was also a measure of having the right look and stage personality. There were many talented folk performers all over the country who, like small-time vaudevillians before them, plied the coffeehouse circuit until, untouched by luck, they gave up and moved on.

Those who were successful exuded a romantic quality at odds with contemporary society, proving a vision of what audiences wished to see in themselves. Many young men adopted a "Ramblin" Jack Elliot style, whereas Joan Baez quickly set a "dark lady of the sonnets" standard for the women. A few, like Oscar Brand and Max Morath, who dug out old songs from less-visited sources, brought a sense of fun to folksinging. Maxine Feldman inclined more to the fun makers.

Brooklyn-born Maxine was Jewish, tall, robust and full of joy. No "Ballad of Barbara Allen" or "Farewell Angelina" for her. She had come to Boston to attend Emerson College and found herself drawn into the lively local folk scene that caught the attention of instrumentalists and singers looking for performing experience. Maxine already had racked up some credits; among her earliest was a bit part as a Girl Scout Brownie on Gertrude Berg's television show *The Goldbergs* (1956).

When Maxine was six, the Feldmans moved into a Manhattan apartment. One night, Maxine saw Pud Flanagan, a child actor who lived in the same building. There he was, on the television, acting in *Billy Budd* (1955). Convinced that she, too, could act and perform, despite a stutter, Maxine asked her parents for acting lessons. Hoping that training would help Maxine overcome her stutter, her parents consulted the Flanagans and enrolled Maxine in classes with Dora Wiseman, who played Mrs. Bloom on *The Goldbergs.* Training included singing and ballet, modern and tap dance as well as acting lessons. Maxine thought she was in heaven, although the reality was the Carnegie rehearsal halls: "I had the best couple of years in my life. I loved it! I got to learn different kinds of scripts, monologues, and I danced and sang."

The Feldmans moved to Queens for what they perceived as better schools, but, not long afterward, Maxine had to commute back into Manhattan after she won an audition to attend the Performing Arts High School.

> When my parents went for holidays to the Borscht Belt hotels in New York State and northern New Jersey, I was one of those obnoxious little kids who, when the emcees asked for talent from the audience, ran up on stage. I got the chance to sing with a band—songs like "Seventeen," "Faith, Hope and Charity" and "Flat Foot Floogie with a Floy, Floy." In the late 1940s and early 1950s, during the polio scare, my parents sent me out of the city to Twin Lakes summer camp because so many of my classmates were ending up in iron lungs. Of course, the counselors always staged summer productions, which I loved. I didn't get leads; I didn't care I was never the star 'cause I didn't look an ingénue, but I performed solos as well as performed as part of the group. Later, in my teens, I began re-writing lyrics of the popular rock 'n' roll songs for the shows.

During high school, Maxine performed professionally in children's theatre at weekend matinees at the Anderson Theatre, a one-time Yiddish theatre on Second Avenue that then was hosting evening performances of *Little Mary Sunshine.* Maxine felt her acting teacher at the Performing Arts High School, Mrs. Banks, was an inspiration, and after high school, Maxine moved to Boston to go to Emerson College as a theatre arts major. Maxine never hid that she was a lesbian, probably more in certainty than in practice at the time, but once Emerson officials were alerted, she was told to leave and not come back until she had a year of psychiatric care. Her parents sent her to a Dr. Bieber, who employed electroshock therapy. Because Maxine refused to continue with the treatment, her parents turned their backs on her.

"Folk music was real big at the time in Boston, and, by then, I had learned to play at least three chords on my small Martin." She worked as regularly as most folkies for three seasons, from 1963 to 1966, including an ongoing stint as the emcee at Orleans' weekly hootenanny, where, one night, Maxine introduced a young and unknown José Feliciano to one of his first audiences.

A local folk chronicler and disc jockey discovered that Maxine was gay and decided his mission was to warn all coffeehouse owners not to book her because she was likely to bring the wrong crowd to their establishments. Maxine was neither secretive nor flamboyant about her budding sexuality, but only the Rose coffeehouse, in one of Boston's more conservative enclaves, the North End, continued to book her regularly.

Her next gigs were sales clerking in a bookshop, stock clerking in a department store and tending bar at King Arthur's Tavern in the South End. Rents for a cold-water flat were $30 per month in those days.

Hoping that the situation was better elsewhere, in 1968 Maxine headed back to Manhattan and then to Los Angeles. She resumed her college education at El Camino College, where she helped organize a women's center on campus. Since the mid-1960s, when the USA took over France's colonial battle and mustered full force in the Vietnam War, Childe's Ballads had slipped off the song lists of folk musicians, replaced by singer-songwriters' protest songs against the war and for the struggle for civil rights and economic justice. In 1969, just prior to the Stonewall–Christopher Street gay rebellion against police harassment, Maxine had written her own protest song, "Angry Atthis"

I hate not being able
to hold my lovers hand
'cept under some dimly lit table,
afraid of being who I am.

I hate to tell lies,
live in the shadow of fear.
We've run half of our lives
from that damn word queer.

It's not your wife I want.
It's not your children I'm after.
It's not even my choice I want to flaunt.
Just wanna hear my lover's laughter.

—Excerpt from words and music by Maxine Feldman © 1969/1976 Atthis Music B.M.I.

Maxine met a feminist comedy team, Harrison & Tyler, when they performed on the El Camino campus during the 1970–71 season. At a get-together after their show, Robin Tyler heard Maxine perform "Angry Atthis," and Robin and Patty Harrison insisted that Maxine open for them for a season's tour of coffeehouses, college campuses and theatres across the USA. The song was recorded and is generally accepted to be the first anthem of the lesbian and gay liberation movement. Other songs by Maxine followed.

Women's issues, long ignored by male society, could no longer be denied when, in 1971–72, *Ms. Magazine* began its life as an independent periodical (very important to Maxine), Germaine Greer's *The Female Eunuch* was published and an English translation of Simone de Beauvoir's *Second Sex* appeared on American bookshelves for the first time.

Maxine found herself in demand for movement events, although some in the women's movement were uneasy with lesbianism. Many feared that discussion about it would detract from their gender-based struggle, and others worried that it could splinter their supporters. Most of Maxine's gigs were benefits, and she jokes that she is still looking for Benny Fitz to bill him.

Beginning in the early 1970s, Maxine reverted to being a variety performer. She sang, clowned, did stand-up comedy (often political) and performed magic tricks. Bookers for clubs were confused. They were used to performers who marketed themselves either as folksingers or comedians. Nevertheless, a national if informal circuit of colleges and coffeehouses opened up to Maxine, and she managed to scratch out a living for the next 15 years, except in places where her sexual orientation was a bar, despite the reputed liberality of the management, clientele and community.

Whenever performance dates dried up, as they did periodically, Maxine stepped off the road and into the Berkshires, where, for a number of years, she worked on and off for her friend Alice Brock at the famous Alice's Restaurant.

Among the many venues, large and small, that Feldman played, were the Village Gate and the Other End in New York City and Ash Grove in Los Angeles. She performed 15 times at the annual Michigan Women's Music Festival, and her song "Amazon" was played in the opening festivities for 30 years.

In 1974, Maxine was booked at Town Hall in Manhattan on a bill that included Yoko Ono and the band Isis. *Variety* reported, "Feldman was a smashing success, accompanying herself on six string acoustic guitar. She proved an impressive spokesman for lesbians with her voice, tunes, interpretation and sense of humor." *The National Review,* improbably reviewing the show, called Maxine "Jonathan Winters in drag," a compliment Maxine considers the highest.

Covering Maxine's 1976 engagement at the Troubadour in Los Angeles, Richard Cromelin reported in the *Los Angeles Times,* "Maxine Feldman has a wide ranging voice and a powerful, impassioned delivery (which suggests an admiration for Sophie Tucker). Her skillfully crafted songs go from the wildly humorous to the chillingly serious. Feldman makes her political points not with jargon but through sure and dignified personal expression. . . . Its essence involves the rejection of self deception."

It was not all accolades; at a concert in Houston, Texas, underwritten by the National Organization of Women to celebrate International Women's Year in 1977, the Secret Service, there to protect Rosalyn Carter, Betty Ford and Bella Abzug, insisted on special protection for Maxine if she insisted on performing. Although it was less to prevent harm to Maxine and more to avoid unpleasant publicity with presidents' wives in attendance, it was the first time Maxine, a veteran of civil rights demonstrations, could recall the police being on her side. Outside the hall, demonstrators carried signs proclaiming, "Kill all dykes, kikes, commies and abortionists." Inside the hall, Maxine quipped to her audience, "Well three outta four ain't bad."

Working on the fringes of show business did not allow for luxuries like health insurance. Maxine deferred treatment until she fell seriously ill in 1994. More than a decade later, various ailments continue to limit her activity, but she remains a vivid, amusing and friendly personality with a positive view of life. In more recent years, tribute has been paid. Her long-playing record album *Closet Sale* is a collector's item. Maxine Feldman has received recognition for her role as a foremother in women's music and she was saluted in Dee Mosbacher's film documentary *Radical Harmonies* (2002).

FEMALE IMPERSONATORS

In theatrical practice, there are two types of female impersonation: comedy characterizations, like the comic dames of English pantomime, not intended to be true representations of women but to make audiences laugh, and illusionists who, through skillful mimicry, attempt to make audiences forget they are watching a fake.

The distinction works best at the extremes. At one end, in the latter half of the twentieth century, were the screeching harridans of Monty Python. At the other end of the spectrum and roughly contemporary, illusionists like Jim Bailey and Jimmy Jones performed dead-ringer imitations of Judy Garland and Marilyn Monroe.

There were many strands of female impersonation in American variety since minstrel days. Although some actors portrayed elderly crones, comic and otherwise, most impersonated desirable women. Those like Julian Eltinge, who presented a decorous picture of maidenly young womanhood on the stage, were applauded by public and press for their skill and taste. Others, such as Bert Savoy, who camped and dished like ladies of the evening, found favor with the public, especially urban audiences, but some critics tarred them as nance acts and refused them good notices regardless of their talent or ability to amuse.

Most female impersonators fell somewhere in the continuum between uncanny mimicry and broad comedy characters. In the case of imitators, some regarded themselves as character actors who presented an impression of a specific female or a particular archetype by exaggerating certain mannerisms and vocal patterns, thus moving from imitation toward impression. Comic actors and clowns, although focused primarily on caricature, chose to foster to some degree an illusion that they were women—witness the Englishman, Arthur Lucan (Old Mother Riley), and the Australian, Barry Humphries (Dame Edna Everage)—but the primary goal of comic actors and clowns was and is to be funny.

On Old World stages, the custom of boys imitating young women grew from laws that prohibited and customs that discouraged the theatrical exhibition of women. It is likely most boys, whether young actors in drama or *castrati* in opera, strove to inhabit their roles. It is from this point that the tradition of imitating women proceeds.

Although boys occasionally played young women's and girls' parts in American theatre from Colonial times into the nineteenth century, it was a matter of convenience and economy rather than tradition; the lads and men were often members of the same family troupe. Generally, impersonations of the opposite sex were not the only theatrical roles these fellows assumed.

In the 1840s, the gold rush lured adventurers to the California goldfields well before transportation, by land or sea, made the journey tolerable. Settlements gathered on the fringes of mine operations, logging camps and railroad construction sites, and the populations were largely male. Some men made a living cooking or doing laundry for other men.

Even allowing for the shortage of women in the settlements, it is still surprising that some managers of box houses hired feminine-looking teenaged boys to pretend to be women. Padded, dressed and made up, they augmented the staff of genuine female hostesses. Some of the boys in drag served drinks, mingled with the male clientele, urged the men to buy more liquor, flirted with them and even sat in their laps. The boys had to be careful; their impersonations had to be convincing and their behavior conservative. Discovery of their true gender meant a thrashing, sometimes death. It was in the box houses of Butte, Montana, that a teenaged Julian Eltinge first impersonated women. In his case, his father discovered, before the saloon's customers did, that his son was dressing up; it was his father who punished Julian.

Julian Eltinge performed subtly onstage and behaved circumspectly in public. On the vaudeville stage, Eltinge and most of his rivals, only a bit less chaste—Bothwell Browne, Karyl Norman and Francis Renault foremost among them—impersonated respectable women or less respectable but historic or royal women. It was the glorious gowns that women came to see. Any newspaper story of that time about a female impersonator made much of his gowns, wigs and jewelry and the thousands of dollars he invested in his costuming. During the first half of the twentieth century, Eltinge and his rivals ushered in the heyday of female impersonation.

Stars, managers and publicity men all pretended that their cross-dressing clients were fine actors carrying on the tradition of Shakespeare. Their audiences, primarily women and male homosexuals, did not attend primarily to witness how musically the impersonators sang, how vigorously they danced, or how well they acted drama or comedy. The benchmark was how truly they looked, spoke and behaved as women, and what they wore.

In the box houses, female impersonators had to fool men; in vaudeville, they had to fool women. Women enjoyed female impersonation because most of the impersonators were credibly glamorous creatures who wore women's clothes with panache. Men long had been designing clothes, hats, jewelry and foundation garments and setting the standard for fashion. A few men in vaudeville demonstrated how best to inhabit the designs.

A rougher sort of female impersonator, Bert Savoy, hinted that he, too, began his career in a similar fashion to Eltinge's, in low circumstances. Unlike Eltinge and most of the others, Savoy began playing the coarser women of the Bowery. When he brought his act to vaudeville, Savoy was closer to the pantomime dame than the female imitator.

Producers felt that most female impersonators could not carry an entire show. Eltinge could. He starred in full-length Broadway shows but often employed the device of acting as a man who, later in the plot, had to assume the guise of a woman, thereby using cross-dressing and quick changes as a dramatic device within a larger show.

Vaudeville was a more suitable showcase for most female impersonators. They were one of eight or nine acts, and they sang, danced, changed costumes and departed the stage before the more red-blooded and easily embarrassed men in the audience grew too uncomfortable.

The 1920s occupy an early chapter in American sexual politics. Women won the right to vote and promptly bobbed their hair, hiked their skirts and smoked cigarettes in public. Young men, spared death or mutilation during the vicious First World War, returned home to pomade their hair, trim their mustaches into "eyebrows" above their lips and their muttonchops into Valentino sideburns. They even wore wristwatches! Scolds in pulpits and on editorials warned that sexual chaos was nigh.

Female impersonators had entered mainstream show business in the 1910s, and some became headliners in the 1920s, but by late that same decade the ball was over. The Wall Street crash exposed the first of the fault lines in the economy of the United States, and the Roaring Twenties segued to the worried, repentant, recriminating 1930s. The bluenoses equated moral decay with failed politics, and the crusade was on to rid society of sexual perverts, Mae West movies and burlesque. Female impersonators retreated to small clubs as had male impersonators. By the time female impersonators were playing nightclubs openly and traveling in vehicles like the Jewel Box Revue, vaudeville was moribund.

The early 1950s saw a revival of moral politics that condemned female impersonators along with communists. The post–Second World War period began with Red hunts and ended with civil rights laws. The momentum was with individual freedom, and drag made a comeback due to some very talented practitioners: Arthur Blake, Charles Pierce, Lynn Carter and Craig Russell. They kept the glamour and went for the laughs, for the most part, yet they explored the character and occasionally achieved poignancy. They were, however, lumped with less-talented brethren who simply wore large wigs, sequins, falsies, lots of makeup and strutted about as they mouthed lyrics to recordings.

The clown tradition in drag is ancient. In modern times, the grotesque dame was a tradition and an audience favorite in English panto, which made it to the USA in the form of pantomimes, extravaganzas and burlesks. In panto, the star male character comedians played Cinderella's ugly stepsisters, Mother Goose, the Old Woman who lived in a shoe and the Queen of Hearts.

As the roster of indigenous American comic characters grew, it included taciturn Yankees, southern gents and frontier free souls. A few mid-nineteenth-century male actors found favor playing women's roles, and it was regarded as an expression of versatility. The female characters were often domestics, elderly spinsters and widows (the latter revived even as late as the television era by Jonathan Winters, Cliff Arquette and Johnny Carson).

Among the most popular in the latter half of the nineteenth century was Tony Hart of Harrigan & Hart, who won enthusiastic audience approval for his female portrayals. A bit later, the Russell Brothers toured the USA for decades as Irish servant girls. Few comedians in silent pictures and early talkies failed to essay a female role at some point. Fatty Arbuckle, Charlie Chaplin, Syd Chaplin, Buster Keaton, Oliver Hardy and Stanley Laurel were especially successful. Among the stage comedians of the day, Bert Lahr, Ed Wynn, Charlie Ruggles and Bert Wheeler donned drag as needed. In vaudeville, there were comic tumbling and dance acts in which one partner dressed in women's clothes, but again it was not intended to be a representation but a clown act. Comedian and dancer Ray Bolger made a personal hit in *Where's Charlie?,* a musical-comedy version of the drag chestnut *Charlie's Aunt,* and Milton Berle made sure drag was on the bill when vaudeville moved into commercial television.

In the 1970s, prompted by the women's movement and gay liberation, there was a reaction against non-comic drag, the sort that promoted a male ideal of how women should dress and act. A countercultural drag sensibility emerged, one that had far more in common with the panto dames than with Julian Eltinge: glam rock acts (David Bowie), theatre (Charles Ludlam & Everett Quinton), new vaudeville (Bloolips), underground musicals *(The Rocky Horror Picture Show)* and countless numbers of Off-Off-Broadway spoofs from Boston to Los Angeles, Seattle to Key West. Female impersonation had outlived vaudeville.

FEMCEE

A term popularized in the 1930s to denote a female emcee, an unusual occurrence at the time.

STEPIN FETCHIT

b: (Lincoln Theodore Monroe Andrew Perry) 30 May 1902 (or 1892), Key West, FL—d: 19 November 1985, Woodland Hills, CA

It is doubtful that any performer of the first half of the twentieth century was more reviled than Stepin Fetchit. His slow, shuffling, mumbling, dissembling plantation "darky" fulfilled ignorant white expectations. Some in the black audience recognized, or hoped they did, the defensive inward retreat of a black serf in a white bigots' world.

The question is whether he winked at the audience as he played his roles. In some movies, his character seemed to be a retarded and confused servant or handyman who was incapable of getting things right. In other roles, the Stepin Fetchit character seemed to adopt that manner as a way of thwarting white masters. Being smarter than the white boss was a dead-end tactic. Being too dumb to be of much use was subversive.

Much of the scorn hurled against Stepin Fetchit was spawned by two generations of black and white civil rights activists, appalled by what they viewed as his portrayal of a stereotype that denigrated African Americans. Some of the contempt he suffered was stoked by his own ostentatiously extravagant and vulgar public life. His entire public posture was a parody, intentional or not, of the grandiose, self-enchanted lifestyle of white movie stars in Hollywood's golden age.

The press of the day was an accomplice. Publicity is oxygen to careers, and movie stars did what was expected of them in the battle for notice. Starlets posed, fetchingly they hoped, in bathing suits, comedians

Stepin Fetchit

mugged for the camera, leading men donned dressing gowns and ascots or sat on horseback in jeans and cowboy hats. Negro stars of the 1930s were similarly typecast; they were expected to reflect their screen images in interviews when, on those infrequent occasions, the press called.

Among Stepin Fetchit's better films were those in which he was paired with Will Rogers. In life as in business, Rogers was a humane man and a shrewd observer. This persona carried over to his film parts in the first half of the 1930s, before his accidental death in 1935. Fetchit had been on friendly terms with Will since they had appeared in vaudeville, and Will had sufficient clout to insist on scripts that gave Step good featured roles in four of his movies. That did not mean that onscreen Will's character treated Stepin's character as an equal, but Will's character was tolerant if paternalistic toward Fetchit's.

Although Stepin made two silent films, talking pictures afforded him the opportunity to add his distinctive whiny mutter to his pantomimic skills. He was a tall, lanky yard of pump water dressed in oversized overalls that stooped when he stood. His eyelids rode low on his eyeballs, and his mouth hung loose as he mumbled. None of his joints operated in unison, and his legs quivered as his big feet shambled forward. Stepin's shiny bald head tilted downward as he grumbled along, his hands fluttered, and his arms sometimes rose, bent and flopped in confusion, as though attached to tangled marionette strings. It was a lot of physical business all at once but well calibrated and executed ever so slowly. Stepin Fetchit scored quickly in films and made 42 movies between 1928 and 1939, the best of which may be one of his first, *Hearts in Dixie* (1929).

Long before he became Stepin Fetchit, Lincoln Perry was a 14-year-old student at a Catholic boarding school. He ran away with a traveling black minstrel revue, the Royal American Shows. His first job was probably as a *pickaninny* in the show because most black kids started out as "picks" in either black or white acts. The kids danced backup for the female star singer and added excitement to her act.

When he and another kid, Ed Lee, outgrew the cute "pick" stage, they formed a double act, Skeeter & Rastus, "Two Dancing Fools from Dixie." They changed their names to Step 'n' Fetchit. When asked where the name of their act came from, Step usually attributed it to a racehorse that they had backed. It was the type of stage name comics used in black vaudeville, burlesque and revue (Willie Best used to call himself "Sleep 'n' Eat"), a commonly heard insulting command or high-handed observation made about a black slave or poorly paid wage earner. The comedians took pride in turning it around into a symbol of subtle rebellion.

According to Mel Watkins, Step's characterization of the lazy no-account was a parody of his unreliable, lazy partner, Ed Lee. When Step went out as a single in black vaudeville, he appropriated the name Step 'n' Fetchit and adapted it. He had become a comedian, although he still performed a dance at the end of his act.

Black vaudeville during the 1910s was pretty rough. The largest circuit was the Theatre Owners' Booking Association (TOBA), which expanded from booking a handful of theatres in 1908 to nearly 100 by the mid-1920s. There were no vaudeville palaces among the TOBA houses. Audiences were either skirting or mired in poverty, ticket prices were dirt cheap, and the theatres were shabbily constructed and poorly maintained. Provided the white theatre managers paid them as agreed, black vaudevillians—except for headliners like the Whitman Sisters, Sissieretta Jones ("Black Patti") or Ma Rainey—barely earned enough to get to the next town.

Instead of trying to break out of the South and head to New York or Chicago, Step headed to Hollywood. He was playing a theatre in Los Angeles when he heard that MGM needed a "colored boy" for a film role. Unlike many of the locals who auditioned, Step had a polished act. He simply stayed in (dumb) character and got one laugh after another as he reacted to the directions at the audition. He was hired, but his calculated audition was thought by many white pros in Hollywood to be the real thing, not an act. When Step achieved more prominence than any black person had ever won in movies, press reports treated him as if he were his stage character.

Stepin Fetchit alternately rebelled against his image and was complicit in perpetuating it. On the one hand, he taunted the press and public with his high life and public flaunting of liveried servants, audaciously painted automobiles, his public brawls, and conspicuous and profligate spending. On the other hand, he hid the fact that he was literate and acquiesced to studio strategy that directed the press to render anything he said in proper grammar into "stage darky" talk for their readers.

Stepin Fetchit became a handful for his employer, Fox Studios, especially after Darryl Zanuck took over the studio. Mel Watkins, in his landmark study of black comedy, *On the Real Side,* reports that Stepin Fetchit created a mythical agent, Mr. Goldberg, to whom he referred all matters of business. This ploy gave Fetchit time to consider a proposition or a contract. It took a while before Zanuck, who had assumed that Step must have had professional help to guide his career, caught on that Step was managing himself and simply buying time with the fictitious Mr. Goldberg.

Supposedly, his pose of being dumb carried onto various movie sets, where even some directors thought Fetchit backward. He did not always abuse them of that notion, and many thought, erroneously, that Fetchit could not read. Rather than waste time directing him or giving him lines to say, directors often let Step play the scene his own way, and he usually got away with padding his part.

By the mid-1930s, a lot of things caught up with Stepin Fetchit and trapped him. Partial to Guinness stout, he sometimes drank while working on films, and his character's speech became so slurred on occasion that it was incoherent, and his shiftless, lazy screen image began to wear on the public. New black comedians like Mantan Moreland and Willie Best came to Hollywood and did a peppier and fresher, if as craven, version of Step's act, and they did it for less money. When Stepin Fetchit got arrested by police, it won him no sympathy from blacks or whites. Had Step been a white actor, he would have been shielded by his movie studio from negative publicity.

By the Second World War, there was little work for Step in Hollywood. He made only two feature films for Hollywood studios in the 1940s, two in the 1950s and nothing until the 1970s, when he had cameo roles in two films. During that period, he appeared in films created specifically for the African American market, but these were modest affairs hurt by meager budgets, primitive technology and some inexperienced people in front of and behind the cameras.

On Broadway, Step performed in a musical, *Walk with Music* (1940). The odd assortment of stars included Step, Kitty Carlisle, Mitzi Green and old-timer Frances Williams in a musical that tried to combine the down-to-earth songs of Hoagy Carmichael and Johnny Mercer with a libretto by Guy Bolton, the chronicler of the rich and ridiculous. Step was lost in the shuffle, and the show expired in about six weeks.

Stepin Fetchit developed an act for black vaudeville houses like the Apollo and black nightclubs. Sitting in a wheelchair, he was pushed onstage by a pretty girl. He stayed seated to tell some stories. At the end of his act, an assistant lifted Step's arm to help him wave goodbye. Not everyone got or appreciated the joke. Most of his dates during the 1950s and 1960s were on the so-called chitlin' circuit of small theatres and black clubs.

Significant numbers of black people did not approve of the lazy Negro caricature. Young comic Timmie Rodgers had launched an assault on blackface still worn by some of the older generation of comedians. Black service personnel had returned from the Second World War, and they wanted the college education and the professional jobs that systematically had been denied them and their forebears. The political agenda for activist African Americans was to project dignity, intelligence and competence. Those qualities were a death sentence to all types of comedy except the observational. If that agenda had been forced on white comedians, The Three Stooges, Abbott & Costello and Martin & Lewis would have been conspicuous casualties.

Throughout the decades of his decline, Stepin Fetchit filed for bankruptcy, converted to Islam, joined prizefighter Muhammad Ali's entourage and battled for what he maintained was his rightful place in black history. He insisted that it was he, Stepin Fetchit, who opened the doors of Hollywood to black performers; that other African Americans got the chance for careers in the movies because he proved he could attract whites to the box office.

Civil rights activists countered that he had won his place as the first black movie star by projecting an image that had been injurious to the reputation of black Americans. It was a divide without compromise, and it consigned to a purgatory of shame a generation of black comedians: Stepin Fetchit, Tim Moore, Mantan Moreland, Willie Best, Johnny Lee, Nicodemus and Flournoy Miller.

Despite his demand to be seen as a pathfinder and barrier buster for black entertainers, Stepin Fetchit was unable to reconcile the evidence of his screen portrayals with his claim. Every time his career seemed on the brink of revival, he would be held up as an example of the despised "darky" image. He suffered a stroke in 1976 after reading yet another article that blamed him for the stereotype. Broke, he was accepted into the Woodlawn Hills, California, home for retired movie actors. Although most actors paid their way, the trustees had provision for those who were poor and ill. Stepin Fetchit spent his last ten years there, without condemnation or commendation for his career.

GRACIE FIELDS

b: (Grace Stansfield) 9 January 1898, Rochdale, England—d: 27 September 1979, Capri, Italy

In Gracie Fields' heyday, only Caruso sold more records worldwide. The Palace Theatre billed her as the "funniest woman in the world," and in Great Britain she set a long-run record with *Mr. Tower of London,* a revue in which she starred for nine years; she gave more than 4,000 performances seen by more than 1 million people. A ship was named for her, as was a rose. She retired to a large estate on a hillside overlooking the Mediterranean Sea and died a dame of the British Empire.

Gracie Fields

Gracie Fields traveled the English-speaking world between the two world wars. She was as much at home with audiences in New York, Toronto, Vancouver, Sydney and Cape Town as she was in London. To one and all she was "Our Gracie." Although she became the highest-paid performer of her day, she never ceased to be a Lancashire mill-town lass grateful for the talent that gave her opportunity but neither ashamed nor regretful that as a girl she used to clean the neighbors' outdoor privies for a few extra pennies.

The key to her success, as was true for many of the best variety performers, was that she performed for 3,000 or 4,000 people the same way she would have for a handful. Gracie was able to make her performance before thousands as intimate as if she were sharing a few rounds with her pals in a Rochdale pub.

Rochdale was a sooty working-class town in Lancashire, and most of its folks considered themselves lucky to find work in the mills. Gracie, her parents, younger sisters and brother lived above a fish-and-chips shop owned by her paternal grandmother, Chip Sarah, who at six had begun her working life, slaving 12 hours a day as a door tender in the mines. Gracie did not begin to earn her living until she was seven, when she went to work in a local cotton mill. She enjoyed the camaraderie of the workers in the mill, but she hated getting up at 4:00 every morning. She worked from six to noon in the mill then spent the afternoons at school.

Her mother, an orphan, was stagestruck. She was set on her three girls going into show business, and in her cellar she rigged up a tiny theatre with a swath of fabric on curtain rings and told her children to play in it. Gracie's first job in the theatre was helping her mother scrub the stage of the Rochdale Hippodrome every Sunday. Gracie, the oldest of the children, also helped her mother do the actors' laundry, which they always delivered in time to watch the show from the wings. Gracie also earned a few pence cleaning her neighbors' outhouses; indoor plumbing was unknown in the Fields' section of Rochdale. Gracie sang while she scrubbed.

One day, a music-hall singer, Lily Turner, heard Gracie and coached her for an amateur-night contest at the Hippodrome. Gracie tied for first prize, and that led to several appearances at local smokers (entertainments at all-male private clubs) and a few appearances with Lily Turner. Gracie suffered a couple of false starts with two different juvenile troupes in which she was the youngest and most vulnerable. Haley's Garden of Girls proved to be a nest of teenage vipers, and Nine Dainty Tots were demonstrably past puberty. Gracie found a more suitable engagement with Charburn's

Young Stars, with whom she toured two years. Afterward, she joined a seaside Pierrot Concert Party, where she met her first mentor, comedian Fred Hutchins, who taught her how to set up, deliver the gag and hold for laughs. It was during this tour that she abbreviated her birth name Grace Stansfield to Gracie Fields.

More short engagements followed: pantomime, small music-halls and then a revue, *Yes, I Think So* (1915), which toured for a year-and-a-half. The chief comedian was Archie Pitt. He put together a revue, *It's a Bargain,* on a shoestring, but it kept him and Gracie employed for two-and-a-half years. By this time, Gracie's two sisters and her brother were in the show, and Archie's brother was the tour manager.

Archie Pitt and Gracie Fields came into their own with Archie's next revue, *Mr. Tower of London.* It played coal-mining villages in Wales and small factory towns for a more than a year before gradually working up to better provincial theatres. During its fifth year, Gracie, 25, married Archie, 43. Between the three revues, they had toured nonstop for nine years, and Archie had worn down Gracie's resistance to him and marriage. Because Gracie had first encountered him at 16, Archie had become Gracie's second mentor, a Svengali of sorts. *Mr. Tower of London* had grossed £250,000 during its six-and-a-half years in the provinces, and in 1925 it was brought in to London's West End, where it ran until 1928.

Gracie was 27, and the reviews confirmed that she had arrived. Critics loved the show. Although she was the star, Gracie had one spot in which she had 25 minutes offstage. The producer paid her £100 per week to use her time offstage to dash across the street and do a ten-minute turn at the Coliseum. Still performing in the revue and doing a music-hall turn, Gracie was engaged by the Café Royal to sing the midnight show. Many performers doubled, but Gracie was one of the few to triple.

In 1928, London's top leading man, the actor-manager Gerald du Maurier, asked Gracie to appear with him in his production of *S.O.S.* and play the part of a duchess, which she did to everyone's delight and satisfaction. If there was any remaining need to prove her versatility, she marked that paid when she substituted for Rosetta Duncan. The Duncan Sisters had brought their popular production of *Topsy and Eva* to London, but Rosetta fell ill, and, with only one day's notice, Gracie stepped into the role of Topsy—in blackface—until Rosetta recovered.

Early on, when Gracie began as a professional, she sang the songs she heard onstage and recordings, often melodramatic romantic songs. When she tired of them, she began to spoof some of them, and her audiences quickly warmed to her spunky humor. As a singer, she had remarkable range, both musical and dramatic. Her soprano was high and strong enough to tempt suggestions that she study opera. Grand diva Tetrazzini even offered to coach her, but Gracie knew her talents and her limits. Her voice was true in pitch and clear as a bell but a trifle piercing in its upper range. Gracie was never tempted to essay anything more classical than the Back-Gounod "Ave Maria."

Over the course of her 60-year career, Gracie Fields continued to sing romantic songs like "One Night of Love"; show tunes like "How Are Things in Glocca Morra?"; traditional songs like "Scarlet Ribbons (for Her Hair)," "Go 'Way from My Window," and "Danny Boy"; and sentimental ballads like "Little Old Lady" and "Now Is the Hour"; but her forte was the comedy character song. She continued the tradition of Marie Lloyd with "The Biggest Aspidistra in the World," "I Took My Harp to the Party (But Nobody Asked Me to Play)," "Walter, Walter (Lead Me to the Altar)," "Ee by Gum" and "Heaven Will Protect an Honest Girl."

In 1930, she accepted a bid from the Palace Theatre in New York for a two-week booking that did not go well at first. She was not the only performer from the *halls* that did not click with American audiences at first. The reverse was true as well. The Marx Brothers were only one of dozens of heavily touted acts that flopped with the Brits. Various accents were difficult for others to understand, and British and American humor touched at many points but not all. To compensate, visiting entertainers tried to substitute Americanisms for the English equivalents, and vice versa. Gracie overcompensated and later claimed she had needlessly tried too hard to be American. Her greatest charm was being herself, and she never erred in that way again, and she ended the New York engagement a success.

More immediately successful was her entry into films. This, of course, was engineered by her husband, Archie Pitt. Her first, *Sally in Our Alley* (1931), provided Gracie with her theme song, "Sally," and set the pattern that the rest of her films followed. Inexpensively produced, modest, comic and sentimental, the films showed Gracie to good advantage. Basil Dean was in charge of most of her early films: *Looking on the Bright Side* (1932), *Sing As We Go* (1934), *Love, Life and Laughter* (1934) and *Look up and Laugh* (1935). Invariably, Gracie was a working girl, a good, honest and plucky lass who saved the mill, the store or the shipyard and the day. The least of her films of this period was *This Week of Grace* (1933), made for an American outfit. It was a cheapjack quickie. All Gracie's movies proved very popular with the British public and earned Gracie about $4 million. She needed a good chunk of that because she had just purchased a property on the Isle of Capri that was sliding into the sea.

The 1930s were her busiest years. Although Britons were suffering through gloomy years of the economic depression that sank much of Europe and soon moved to the USA, Gracie's cheery, cheeky performances on film and in variety helped bolster spirits. By 1936, Gracie was back in American vaudeville, very successfully so. While she was on the West Coast, as a lark, she made an uncredited cameo appearance as a socialite in *My Man Godfrey* (1936), a screwball comedy for Universal Pictures that starred William Powell, Carole Lombard and Alice Brady.

Back home, harsh financial times did not prevent British filmmakers from offering Gracie $200,000 per picture for four films. The first, *Queen of Hearts* (1936), was directed by future husband Monty Banks. Now pushing 40, Gracie treated the British public to a somewhat glamorized version of herself as a working girl posing as a socialite. While in the mood to try other types of roles and forms of theatre, Gracie took her first serious stage role in *Her Last Affaire* (1936).

Gracie Fields was the highest-paid film star in the world in 1937. Whatever the role, her name in the script was Sally, Molly or Gracie. *The Show Goes On* (1937), however, was her first misstep in films, or, rather, Basil Dean's first miscalculation with his studio's most popular star. Seeing Gracie in melodrama, even melodic melodrama, was not what her public wanted. One poor English film did not close off Hollywood offers, however. *We're Going to Be Rich* (1938) was the first of her American films, and it looked as if it had been shot on dark soundstages after the studios had closed for the night. *Keep Smiling* (1938) turned out a bit better but did not pull at the box office; neither did *Shipyard Sally* (1939).

Gracie felt chronically tired. At first, she thought it was a result of her frantic schedule of variety performances and making movies and records. Just before the United Kingdom went to war to prevent Hitler from conquering the world, Gracie fell gravely ill from cancer of the cervix in 1939. She nearly died. Gracie faced a long recuperation following surgery. An estimated 500,000 cards were sent to her wishing her a speedy and complete recovery. One message was from the queen.

Instead of convalescing as her physicians had prescribed, Gracie set out on a concert tour of English-speaking nations to raise awareness and money for Britain's war against the Nazis. When her first concert for the war effort was broadcast by the BBC, parliament adjourned to listen. After a year of giving concerts throughout the USA and Canada, where she pleaded the cause of freedom, she turned over $1.5 million to the British war effort.

Her marriage to Archie Pitt had never been a love match on Gracie's part, and perhaps not on his part either. Pitt was ambitious and focused, Gracie was his star, and through their association both had risen to the top. He became an important producer, and Gracie's star continued to rise without his constant guidance. They separated in the early 1930s but did not divorce until 1940, when Gracie married her second husband, Monty Banks, a film actor and director.

Many of her countrymen turned against Gracie. Some because she married Banks, who was a French-born Italian citizen, at a time when Mussolini's Italy signed a pact with Hitler against the United Kingdom and France, which had quickly capitulated and set up the puppet Vichy regime in league with the Nazis. Others were hostile because Gracie chose to move to the USA so that her husband, Monty, could not be interred in England for the duration of the war. Gracie, still weak, used the war years to raise funds for the Allies. When, in 1941, she returned to Britain to undertake a tour of the factories, mines, shipyards and training camps to boost morale, Gracie was met with criticism by some English newspapers and citizens.

She made her last Hollywood film, *Paris Underground,* in 1945. Gracie costarred with Constance Bennett, who also produced the movie. Both proved capable actors in the espionage drama.

It was at the war's end that Gracie initiated a gesture that has become a pop- and rock-concert tradition. She was entertaining in the jungles of Borneo when the Japanese surrendered. She was asked to sing "The Lord's Prayer." It was dark, but she could see cigarettes burning in the field in front of her. She asked all the soldiers to light a match. She was humbled by the 30,000 flames before her. She asked the troops to turn around and again light matches so they could see the glorious sight. Together they all sang.

Five years of volunteering during the war had left both Gracie and Monty strapped for cash. He made a few films, and Gracie made records and toured variety theatres and gave concerts. She could still execute a high kick to punctuate a song. Sometimes, amid the exuberance of performance, she turned a cartwheel and showed her linen.

The good times came to an end in 1950 when Monty Banks died. Gracie retired to Capri and submersed herself in the lives of her sisters, brother and their children. In 1952, Gracie married Boris Alperovici, a local man who had repaired some electronic equipment for her at her home in Capri. Half Italian and half Russian, he had served with British forces during the war and spoke all three languages. They settled into a comfortable existence on Capri.

Occasionally, she got the urge to work. She appeared on both American and British television. She may have been the first actor to portray Agatha Christie's snoop sleuth Miss Marple when she headed the cast of

"Murder Is Announced" (1956) on *Goodyear Television Playhouse.* She had a featured role in "A Tale of Two Cities" on the *DuPont Show of the Month* (1958). A few weeks later, she starred in "Mrs. 'Arris Goes to Paris" (1958) for *Studio One.* On the variety front, Ed Sullivan invited her several times a year between 1953 and 1956 to sing on his *Toast of the Town* show.

Finances recouped, Gracie did not need the money, but she enjoyed performing. Her last years were spent in semiretirement with occasional concerts that she and her public enjoyed. Even in her late 70s, Gracie could charm an audience. After singing a well-known song through once, she would turn her audience into a choral group, and she would sing harmony to their melody.

She made her final recordings in 1975, when she was 77. They were issued in album form as "The Golden Years of Gracie Fields." While in London, she went to see Danny La Rue's latest show. He introduced her to the audience and bid her to stand up. As she acknowledged the applause, people called for her to sing. Danny invited her onstage, and Gracie obliged with a song. This led to several concerts. A few years later, a fan letter elicited a joyful response from Gracie, "I'm eighty years old, and I can still sing a damn fine song!"

Although her native land awarded Gracie Fields the title of Commander of the British Empire (CBE) in 1938, it failed to commemorate her wartime work. Belatedly, a few months before her death, the British crown and government made Gracie Fields a dame of the British Empire. Her fans had already crowned her.

SID FIELDS

b: (Sidney Fields) 5 February 1898, Milwaukee, WI—d: 28 September 1975, Las Vegas, NV

Well known as a comic foil to Bud Abbott & Lou Costello, Sid Fields was a versatile comedian and a comedy writer. His bald-headed, hard-boiled and aggravated persona was to Bud and Lou what Jimmy Finlayson was to Stan Laurel & Oliver Hardy.

Sid began as a teenaged comedy monologist in amateur shows and local, hometown vaudeville before leaving for a succession of medicine wagons and tent-show troupes. He teamed up with Jack Greenman to play vaudeville and burlesque, and the team made it to Minsky's in the 1920s. By the early 1930s, Minsky's burlesque was being hounded by New York City's municipal authorities, and Sid departed burlesque and his partner for a chance in network radio and Hollywood movies.

Fields worked far more steadily as a comedy writer than an actor, contributing jokes to scripts for Rudy Vallee (on radio) and Eddie Cantor (in films). He won supporting or comedy roles in Eddie Cantor's starring flick, *Strike Me Pink* (1936), in *Love Is News* (1937), *Sing and Be Happy* (1937), *Charlie Chan on Broadway* (1937), and in another Cantor film, *Ali Baba Goes to Town* (1937). Then he supported the Ritz Brothers in *Straight, Place and Show* (1938). Unfortunately, his roles were small and sometimes uncredited cameos as newspapermen, barkers and hecklers.

Sid seemed to disappear from the airwaves and silver screen during the early 1940s; he may have enlisted in the armed services, although he would have been in his early 40s. After the Second World War, Sid began his most profitable association. He was featured in a trio of movies with Abbott & Costello, then at the height of their popularity: *The Naughty Nineties* (1945), *Little Giant* (1946) and *Mexican Hayride* (1948).

When Frank Sinatra agreed to star in a weekly variety series for two seasons in 1951 and 1952, he engaged Sid Fields and Ben Blue as comic relief. Ben and Sid teamed temporarily but well. When Lou Costello and Bud Abbott decided to film a weekly syndicated series for television (1950–51), in addition to their contracted appearances on the *Colgate Comedy Hour* for NBC, they brought Sid with them as their exasperated landlord. He also assumed disguises to play other roles on the series.

Among Sid Fields' last television appearances were those for *Jackie Gleason and His American Scene Magazine.* During the show's four-year run, Sid Fields appeared during its last two seasons, from 1964 to 1966. Soon after, Sid relocated to Las Vegas, where he performed in Pat Moreno's *Artists & Models* revue. He died at age 77 of lung cancer.

W. C. FIELDS

b: (William Claude Duskinfield) 29 January 1880, Darby, PA—d: 25 December 1946, Pasadena, CA

Ah, yes, W. C. Fields was the forlorn tyke who persevered despite a loveless childhood and a hardscrabble world fraught with peril. Bedeviled by Nosey Parkers, mountebanks, knaves and the petty minions of law, the young lad rose above it all through a long and penurious apprenticeship. Portmanteau in hand, he traversed the farther reaches of the world and emerged a juggler extraordinaire, the great man of comedy. Not quite.

During his years in vaudeville, W. C. Fields regaled reporters and friends with fabrications that were another form of performance: storytelling. So well spun and true to his image, even today the fable of W. C. Fields has greater currency and appeal than honest biography. By the time he came to Hollywood to star in talking films, Fields' transformation was complete. Person, icon and commodity were all of a piece; the offstage man seemed an extension of the curmudgeonly coward he usually portrayed on the screen.

Fields' first biographer, Robert Lewis Taylor, drawing on material supplied by Gene Fowler and his son, Will Fowler, accepted the gospel according to W. C. Fields. The early chronicles reported Fields' version: a Dickensian childhood capped by running away from home and a Huck Finn adolescence replete with outlaw escapades and short stays in jail. By his own account, Fields matured, or was bent by the indignities inflicted upon him by venal people (especially women) and a conformist society, into the creature upon the screen. Even a publication as late as the 1971 memoir by Fields' last mistress, Carlotta Monti, whose source on Fields was the man himself, reports the same twaddle that Fields shoveled out to the press about his youth, even his birthday.

Likewise, the evolution of his performance style made good copy for lazy reporters and an easy digest for casual readers. From humble beginnings, the little, unloved lad trained himself into the Tramp Juggler, his ragged costume the result of penury, a pantomime artist who never spoke a word to the audience until a score of years after his debut. Balderdash!

It is ironic that W. C. Fields, who systematically obscured the personal and professional record, should have been subjected subsequently to thorough and critical research. His grandson, Ronald Fields, led the revisionist way, lovingly and admiringly, and his work has been continued through recent biographies.

According to current informed opinion, young Claude Fields, as he was then called, grew up in a lower-middle-class household, the eldest of four children. His mother, Kate Felton Fields, was a warm parent and the family wit. James, his father, was a no-nonsense provider, probably no more stern than most male parents of his day and certainly malleable enough to heed his wife's insistence that he give up his job as a bar manager so as not to set a bad example to his son.

Claude Fields had little use for schoolroom education and, in lieu of classes, took various jobs. Sometime during his early teens, young Claude began to teach himself to juggle. There were many vaudeville theatres in Philadelphia in the 1890s, and, because he was earning money, Claude was able to afford the ten-cent balcony ticket.

Fields often claimed it was Cinquevalli, "The World's Greatest Juggler," who inspired him. Undoubtedly he did, although he was probably not the first juggler to intrigue Claude. There were many good jugglers in vaudeville, and several of them wore tramp costumes. By his midteens in 1896, Claude, had arranged his juggling tricks into some semblance of an act and secured a few local bookings as a tramp juggler. He continued to live under his parents' roof.

During the first years of his professional career, he varied his name, trying out several: Wm. C. Felton, H. Fields, Wm. C. Fields, W. C. Fields and William C. Fields. The formal and legal change of name to W. C. Fields occurred a decade into his career.

When Fields left home in 1898, he was 18 years old, not 9 or 10, and he left with the family's good wishes. He began as a juggler with a line of patter. When performing with the touring burlesque troupes, he helped change scenery and participated in musical numbers as well. These burlesques were more akin to the shows that Harrigan & Hart and, later, Weber & Fields produced than striptease shows.

Within a year he had featured billing in a touring burlesque show, the Monte Carlo Girls Burlesquers. One of the young ladies in the show was Harriet "Hattie" Hughes. Far from the puritanical dragons that Fields later skewered, Hattie, born into a showbiz family, was free enough a spirit to play in burlesque and lovely enough to catch and keep W. C. Fields' eye. They married in 1900, about a year-and-a-half after they met. Later, Harriet was to engage in her own character embellishment when, at Fields' estate hearing, she claimed to have met him at a girls' school reception.

From burlesque, Fields accepted William Morris' offer to be booked on the big-time Orpheum vaudeville circuit. Fields was just 20 years old when he opened on 18 March 1900 at San Francisco's Orpheum with Hattie as his stage assistant. Fields' act blended deft juggling with comic patter. Morris booked Fields solidly, even during the summer months, on the Keith and Orpheum circuits. This after a mere two years in show business. So much for the long struggle.

Fields' pretense that his tramp costume was a result of penury does not hold up. He made decent money from the start. Billing himself as "The Tramp Juggler" and "Different from All the Rest" was a defense against allegations that Fields stole his look and billing from more senior members of the profession, including Nat Wills ("The Happy Tramp"), O. K. Sato ("Tramp Juggler") and James Harrigan ("The Tramp Juggler"). Later, in annoyed refutation of Fields' persistent claim, Harrigan billed himself "The First Tramp Juggler."

Variety had always been international, but it spiked as steamship travel became much safer and faster. Language was no barrier for specialty acts like jugglers; they could play anywhere in the world. The English-speaking world was vast, and the stages of England, Australia, the United States, Canada, South Africa and even Egypt, India and Hong Kong offered plenty of work.

On 12 December 1900, after less than one year in big-time vaudeville, just three years after turning professional and a month shy of his 21st birthday, Fields sailed for Germany to perform at Berlin's Wintergarten. Fields' act ran 13 minutes. He was held over.

We know his vaudeville juggling act because Fields resurrected it for one of his finest films, 1934's *The Old-Fashioned Way.* As the Great McGonigle, Fields portrayed the improvident actor-manager of a touring acting company. Fields inserted his juggling as a specialty turn between the acts of the melodrama, *The Drunkard,* performed by his troupe. Thirty years after his juggling prime, it was all there: craft, grace and precision.

Depending upon the physical style of a juggler, the performance can incline toward balletic movement or the sleight of hand of a magic act. Fields delighted in misdirection, and he achieved his effects—and got his laughs—by upending the audience's expectations, whether it was with a hat, four balls, a dowel or ten cigar boxes. Central to his performance was his prank of seeming to fumble a toss only to make a recovery twice as difficult as the trick. In feigned frustration, Fields might bounce a ball off his stooge's noggin or drop all of his cigar boxes (to show they were not held together) only to bring them all into an escalating pyramid.

Fields opened on 23 February 1901 at the new Royal English Opera House, renamed the Palace Theatre of Varieties a year later. He toured much of the United Kingdom and played the Folies Bergère in Paris before returning to the USA late in August 1901 for 11 months on the Keith circuit. By the following summer of 1902, Bill and Hattie were back in Berlin for August and September, Vienna in October, and Prague in November. As he was now performing in countries that could not furnish him with English-speaking audiences, Fields began to develop his comedy juggling act as a pantomime turn.

Mr. and Mrs. Fields doubled back to London to play the two-year-old Hippodrome. The Hippodrome was a technological marvel of its day, with a stage large enough to cover a swimming tank 230 feet in diameter, and it had hydraulic lifts to raise portions of the stage.

An international performer, Fields repeatedly toured European theatres and ventured to South Africa and Australia as well. As he sailed from one continent to another, Fields began to use his shipboard time to educate himself. Eventually, along with his equipment, he had to add a trunk to carry his books. One can speculate what reading Victorian authors did for his phrasing, intonation and vocabulary. In 1904, four years into their marriage, Hattie and Bill were expecting. Hattie returned to the USA.

Fields was working more outside the USA than in, so he paid for a continuing ad in the *New York Daily Mirror* to remind bookers and public alike that "W. C. Fields was touring the world," noting which city he was playing each week. Fields brought his father to England for the two months W. C. played there. So much for the legendary hatred of parent by abused son. News came that a son had been born, and Hattie and the newborn, Claude Jr., joined the new father and grandfather in England. Bill left his wife and son in London and continued his 1904 tour alone, playing dates on the Continent. He returned to England early in December to perform in a Christmas panto, *Cinderella,* in Manchester. This provided W. C. Fields with his first acting role since burlesque.

By July 1905, Fields had made a decision to leave vaudeville to make his debut in the featured role of Sherlock Baffles in a musical version of *The Ham Tree,* an expanded version of McIntyre & Heath's vaudeville act. The plan would allow Bill, Hattie and baby Claude Jr. to return to the USA and set up housekeeping in New York during a hoped-for long run. Instead, *The Ham Tree* musical ran for 90 performances at the New York Theatre before touring the USA through the 1906 season and into the first half of 1907. Once again, Bill was on the road alone. Gradually, the marriage began to sour. Fields, who had been a temperate drinker of alcohol, began drinking more.

After his stint in *The Ham Tree,* W. C. Fields went back to big-time American vaudeville with his juggling act. He had not reverted to talking in his act, yet he would not bill himself as "The Silent Humorist" until 1910.

Bill and Hattie were no longer living together, yet they could not divorce. Hattie had converted to Roman Catholicism and had baby Claude baptized. Perhaps, as his biographer Simon Louvish suggests, Fields worked more outside the USA than in because he could live and travel with a mistress more easily overseas.

His European tours, which totaled 11 between 1901 and 1914, became annual from 1908 until the First World War put an end to them. When the First World War exploded in 1914, Bill Fields was in Australia. This time, when he returned home, he never left the USA again. Change was everywhere. International vaudeville was on hold for the duration. New producers, songwriters and designers were propelling stage revues into showy, syncopated shows for the smart set.

W. C. Fields

W. C. Fields was never one of the diehard vaudevillians who were sure that vaudeville would triumph and were unaware of the larger world around them. At 34, Fields had reached some formal, permanent détente with his wife that acknowledged his financial obligation but permitted his personal freedom. Personally and professionally, he was looking to the future, and the future was at his doorstep.

Broadway beckoned. According to Fields himself, he encouraged the call. The adventure and charm of constant travel and hotels had faded with the years, so, ever since *The Ham Tree,* Fields had been trying to get a featured role on Broadway. He was hired in 1914 by Charles Dillingham to appear in *Watch Your Step,* the first show to boast a complete score by Irving Berlin.

Fields' contribution was an interpolation, doing his juggling act in an Automat setting. After opening night in the tryout town of Syracuse, the Automat was changed to the Palais de Fox Trot, and Fields' act went out with the old scenery. Supposedly, Gene Buck (Florenz Ziegfeld's lyricist, confidant and right-hand man) saw the Dillingham show on its first night and alerted Ziegfeld to engage Fields for the 1915 *Follies*.

Between *Watch Your Step* and the rehearsals for the *Follies*, which began in early May, Fields filled in with vaudeville bookings; his act now ran more than 20 minutes. In seven editions of the *Ziegfeld Follies,* he performed his vaudeville turns, juggling in most of the editions. Fields revived his trick billiard game for the 1915 and 1917 *Follies* and for his film debut, the 1915 short *Pool Sharks.* He adapted his vaudeville golf routine for the 1918 *Follies*, created a new act, his hassles with the family Ford, for the 1920 edition, and portrayed a minister distracted by a bratty child in the 1921 edition.

Fields starred in *Poppy,* another book show, which ran the entire 1923–24 season. It became a silent film in 1925 as *Sally of the Sawdust* and was revived in 1936 for sound as *Poppy.* Then Fields switched to a competitor but was so poorly served by the material given him for *George White's Scandals of 1922* that he went right back to Ziegfeld, who lived up to his earlier promise to build a musical comedy around Fields, *The Comic Supplement.* It failed out of town, but two routines from that 1925 show were quickly recycled, along with Fields, into the 1925 *Follies* (the 1925 edition was basically an update of the 1924 *Follies*). Both skits introduced themes that would inhabit the plot of many of Fields' sound films: the nagging wife, bratty child, and the constantly interrupted nap or reverie.

Fields joined the cast of *Earl Carroll Vanities of 1928.* Among Fields' sketches was "Dr. Pain," the dentist who would be immortalized in the 1932 two-reel film.

Between 1924 and 1928, whenever Fields was not engaged in a revue or making another of his ten feature-length silents, he was headlining in vaudeville, often with one of his famous revue sketches, such as "The Family Ford" or "The Golfer."

In August 1930, Fields played Cap'n Andy in a two-week revival of *Show Boat* at the St. Louis Municipal Opera House. His final book show, *Ballyhoo,* was a showcase for Fields. W. C. played Q. Q. Quale, a promoter who runs afoul of the law and crashes a Hollywood studio. He put many of his vaudeville and revue bits into the show to little avail, because the show became a casualty of diminished box office receipts during the growing Great Depression late in 1930.

W. C. Fields was 50 years old when he moved to Hollywood in 1931. It was a slow start, and his first Hollywood film, *Her Majesty Love,* did not trigger other offers (nor for Marilyn Miller and Leon Errol, his *Follies* costars also in Hollywood looking for work). Luckily, Hank and Joe Mankiewicz, producer and writer, tailored a role for Fields in their picture *Million Dollar Legs,* and Fields' future in sound films was assured. Between 1932 and 1936, W. C. Fields created 5 classic shorts, 1 for RKO, 4 for Mack Sennett, and 13 starring features for Paramount, more than half of which are very good and at least three are among the best comedies of the 1930s: *Million Dollar Legs* and *If I Had a Million* (both 1932), *International House* and *Tillie and Gus* (both 1933), *You're Telling Me, The Old Fashioned Way* and *It's a Gift* (all 1934) and *The Man on the Flying Trapeze* (1935).

At the height of his skill and box-office power, a series of accidents and Fields' drinking compromised his health and career. Warned that his consumption of alcohol would destroy his constitution, Fields allowed that "my constitution was ruined years ago; I'm now working on the bylaws." Other chestnuts included a doctor's warning to Fields that unless he gave up drinking he would lose his hearing. Fields replied, "The stuff I've been drinking is better than what I've been hearing." This, perhaps, was the first and last diagnosis that drinking led to deafness.

Accumulating afflictions included several back injuries, rosacea, double vision, insomnia, grippe and pneumonia, with arthritis and cirrhosis of the liver waiting in the wings. Radio offered a less-strenuous alternative to moviemaking, and in 1937 Fields appeared to good advantage on *The Chase & Sanborn Hour,* sparring with stars Edgar Bergen and Charlie McCarthy. In 1938, he was again on network radio, incongruously filling a weekly comedy spot on *Your Hit Parade!*

Fields still had four good films left in him, which he made for Universal: *You Can't Cheat an Honest Man* (1939), *My Little Chickadee* (1940), *The Bank Dick* (1940) and *Never Give a Sucker an Even Break* (1941).

The last five years of W. C. Fields' life offered no more starring roles. He lacked the stamina and memory to learn new material and play a lead. Indeed, he spent much of his time living in a cottage on the grounds of a sanatorium rather than at his home. Still, when health permitted and he received an offer, he worked. There were guest spots on radio—in 1943, he was back on the Bergen & McCarthy show as a semi-regular cast member—and, in 1944, he performed cameos in two films. In the better of them, *Follow the Boys,* he committed his vaudeville billiard routine to film. He had been a comedy star for nearly 50 years when he died on Christmas Day 1946.

FILLERS

Fillers, like *openers* and *chasers*, were short films, inexpensively rented to fill out a vaudeville bill or to cover an elaborate change on the full stage. Usually, the scenery and prop change could be made while another act played *in one* (in front of the dress curtain). In some cases, however, there were too many acts that needed to play *in two* or on the full stage, and no act on the bill that could play *in one*. So a screen was lowered downstage and the change was made while a short filler was shown. Fillers were far less common than openers or chasers, because most vaudeville bills were competently arranged to eliminate the need for fillers.

FINKLESTEIN & RUBIN TIME

A Midwest chain of small-time vaudeville houses.

FINK'S MULES

It was, reputably, a good opening act that could set an audience up for the rest of the bill. Although respected for that reason, Fink's Mules achieved legendary status, perhaps, because its name was so easy to recall. Although memorable, little real information about the act has survived except a few reviews.

In Sime's report in the 19 April 1918 edition of *Variety,* he indicated that the act worked on the full stage and employed a revolving table. In a simulated circus setting, "the Fink turn runs swiftly for 10 minutes, the comedy causes laughs and the monkeys [*sic*] are a new and novel assistance in the laughing department. Opening the Palace show at 8:05 [after the 8 p.m. overture] with a light house at that hour, the turn got over very strongly." Trained ponies and dogs provided other tricks, and a "colored boy" and a plant or two in the audience added to the comedy quotient.

FINN & HEIMAN TIME

A small-time circuit of eight theatres in the Midwest.

FIRE CURTAIN

The heavy steel and asbestos fire curtain was required in all theatres, especially after a series of devastating fires spread from stages to auditoriums at the turn of the twentieth century. The fire curtain hung between the audience and the stage and backstage area and was intended to confine any blaze that might occur. Fire departments required that it be in good working order (able to be raised and lowered), and many localities insisted that the fire curtain be raised and lowered before each show to demonstrate it remained in working order.

FIVE-PERCENTER

An actor's or performer's agent; so called because of the percentage of the act's salary the agent retained for his services. When the percentage rose to 10 percent, agents were call ten-percenters.

FLASH ACT

A flash act was essentially a song-and-dance act, usually either two men or a single male and female duo, that added some scenery and lighting effects along with a line of ill-paid chorus dancers to appear like a big production act. It was said the entertainers added *flash* to their act.

Top portion of letterhead used for booking correspondence

DUSTY FLETCHER

b: (Clinton Fletcher) ca. 1897—d: 15 March 1954

He was a lean, rather handsome man who wore a too-large top hat and threadbare black coat and trousers; his shoes were long crumpled slap shoes. Dusty Fletcher began in black vaudeville and burlesque; his first show of note was the *Mamie Smith Revue* of 1926. Fletcher and Mose Gaston were her lead comedians. Mamie was the first black popular singer to make a record ("Crazy Blues") in 1921, and she became a favorite among Negro audiences for much of the 1920s. The following season, Dusty joined Tim Moore's road show, *Southland Revue* (1927), and then took his own revue, *Harlem Strutters* (1927), on the road for the balance of the season.

Not to be confused with *Bamboula* (1921), *Bamboola* (1929) was a rather ordinary revue of the period that came and went in a month at the downtown Royale Theatre. The Royale often presented black revues and other productions, such as Mae West's *Diamond Lil* (1928), that some of the tonier Broadway theatres rejected. Dusty costarred with John "Spider Bruce" Mason in *Bamboola,* and they wrote much of their material, including "Strange Interfeud (with apologies to the Theatre Guild)" (but not to Eugene O'Neill, whose play they spoofed). "The Suicide" and "The Wall Between" were two more of their sketches.

The Joy Boat (1930), another of the ubiquitous black revues that toured for a season, paired Jackie (later "Moms") Mabley with Dusty. The following season, Dusty joined another touring revue, *Lucky to Me,* starring Ethel Waters and named after her song hit "You're Lucky to Me," written by Eubie Blake and Andy Razaf. *Fast and Furious* (1931) was a Broadway revue, and Dusty shared comedy billing with Jackie Mabley and Tim Moore. Unfortunately, it lasted only a week at the New Yorker Theatre.

In 1933, Dusty Fletcher and Hamtree Harrington provided the comedy in *Rufus Jones for President,* a musical short that starred Ethel Waters and introduced a small, six-year-old Sammy Davis Jr. Fletcher made his second film short the next year; Bill Robinson and Ernest Whitman were the stars and Fletcher was billed third in *King for a Day* (1934), a musical two-reeler.

Ubangi Club Follies (1935) had music and lyrics by Andy Razaf and was produced by Leonard Harper. In addition to Dusty, the traveling revue starred singers Billy Daniels and Velma Middleton along with Erskine Hawkins & His Bama State Collegians Orchestra. *Rhapsody in Rhythm* (1945) was another touring revue, one that starred Ethel Waters and Mantan Moreland and featured the Four Step Brothers plus Dusty and the young, up-and-coming comedian and musician Timmie Rogers.

For more than 20 years, Dusty Fletcher had been recognized as one of the top black comedians. He had a good voice, excellent delivery and was a talented physical comedian, but he was a secret known only to black audiences. That changed in 1947. For a short while, in the years following the Second World War, there was no more famous Negro comedian than Dusty Fletcher. Novelty tunes were all the rage, and "Open the Door, Richard" became a hit song of 1946–47 and a catchphrase that endured into the civil rights era, when it was revived by editorial writers and social activists to decry segregation in public facilities.

Dusty Fletcher

Not everyone connected Fletcher with the song. John "Spider Bruce" Mason claimed he originated the skit, and many agreed. Several versions of the song were recorded. Jack McVea was first; he recorded it as a jump tune sung by a zoot-suited hipster. Jack admitted he got the song from accompanying Dusty Fletcher in a stage show. Dusty recorded it next. Count Basie, the Charioteers, the Pied Pipers, Three Flames, Ted Heath, Hank Penny and Louis Jordan also scored hits with the song. More bizarre and obscure versions were committed to wax by Burl Ives, Lauritz Melchior and Molly Picon (in Yiddish), and some sources debate whether Billy Adams, Ernie Barton and Billy Riley recorded it.

There were legal tussles between Mason, Fletcher and McVea about ownership of the song. After it was ironed out, the sheet music credited lyrics to Dusty Fletcher and John Mason (known professionally as John "Spider Bruce" Mason) and music to Jack McVea and the fictitious Don Howell (a straw man stand-in for the music publisher's share).

Original authorship was always in doubt, but long before it was a hit song, "Open the Door, Richard" was a comedy routine, and, like other famous routines, it is impossible to know how long it has been in the comic repertoire and who first put it there. John Mason, a comedian who spanned the minstrel period to the heyday of the Apollo Theater, where he frequently worked with Fletcher, had performed "Open the Door, Richard" before Dusty, but how similar their versions can not be determined.

What is certain is that Dusty Fletcher made the comedy routine his own. His unnamed character, calling for Richard, is a drunk, but a three-dimensional drunk who presents a case study of an alcoholic as he undergoes a roundelay of injured pride, shame, regret, arrogance, defiance and self-pity. Fortunately, Fletcher's performance was captured on film as part of the Cab Calloway short *Hi-De-Ho* (1947) and recut as a one-reeler, *Open the Door, Richard.* Soon, a one-reel response, *Richard's Answer,* was released with Stepin Fetchit as the Richard who is not about to get out of bed to unlock the door.

The story line was simple. Fletcher got bounced out of a bar and tried to get into his apartment across the street, but his roommate will not respond to his pleas to "Open the door, Richard!" Combining pantomime, a balancing act, pratfalls and stumbles, and a long monologue that is a stream of consciousness rant, Fletcher made whole cloth from a single narrative thread.

He begged and demanded that Richard let him in, to no avail—not even a response. The urgency of his need pumps the comedy. Perhaps it was to sleep, but, although nothing was suggested, one got the impression that he needed to go to the bathroom. He found a tall ladder and attempted to maneuver it in place so that he could climb up to his window, but he and the ladder never made it to the wall and window at the same time. When he did climb the ladder, it was in the middle of the stage, and Dusty did a balancing act halfway up the unsupported ladder. More often, he and the ladder were falling over each other.

Indignant that he was evicted from the tavern and that Richard would not let him in, he noticed a nosy neighbor peering at him from behind her curtains. Defiantly, he turned to her and roared, "*Yes!* It's me, and I'm *dru-u-u-nk* again!" It became Dusty's tagline. Many of his comedy bits, at least during his days at the Apollo, had him impersonating an inebriate, and audiences demanded that tagline.

Open the Door, Richard, opened the door to more movies for Dusty. He costarred with Moms Mabley in *Killer Diller* (1948) and *Boarding House Blues* (1948), both films were made for Negro audiences, but the movies were a last hurrah.

Dusty, John "Spider Bruce" Mason and Pigmeat Markham were three of the Apollo Theater's more durable and popular comedians throughout the 1930s and into the early 1940s. A new breed of African American comedians was taking over, however, by the late 1940s, and there was tension between the two generations. It was a matter of professional competition or jealousy. The older comedians still wore their exaggerated costumes, as did Chaplin, Keaton, W. C. Fields and The Marx Brothers. And they still used blackface. Most did not exaggerate their mouths with white and pink, but they covered their faces with black greasepaint as they had for decades. It was their clown face. The new crop of comics wore crisp business suits and eschewed physical comedy, pleading, sometimes haranguing the older ones, telling them that they were perpetuating demeaning stereotypes.

By 1947, Dusty Fletcher's star had begun to fade when he made the record and the film of *Open the Door, Richard.* It revived his career for a few seasons, but eventually he and most of his contemporaries were replaced on Apollo bills by a new breed of stand-up comedians, such as Allen Drew, Redd Foxx, Timmie Rogers, Nipsey Russell and Slappy White, who in turn were supplanted by Richard Pryor, Godfrey Cambridge, Dick Gregory, Flip Wilson and Bill Cosby.

FLIER

The acrobat who does the somersaults and turns in the air and is tossed and caught by *catchers* is usually called the *flier*. The flier is usually the member of the act who is lightest in weight.

FLIES

The large, open space above the stage was fitted with a grid, ropes, battens and pulleys to which were attached stock scenery, trapeze bars, picture sheet (a screen for showing motion pictures) and other items, stored until needed. The space was called *flies* because curtains and scenery—affixed to battens—were flown up to the ceiling by means of pulleys and ropes. This area was concealed from the audience's view by the proscenium arch and *teasers*.

Drops and such were suspended in the flies by counterweights, such as sandbags, or the ropes *flying* the drops were tied off down below, secured to a scenery rail to hold them in position, either high and out of view or dropped into the stage for a particular act. If a batten was free—not already holding a piece of scenery—a sign marked "dead" was placed on the scenery rail; thus, when an act brought its own special backdrop to the theatre for hanging, the stage crew could tell by the signs which ropes among the jumble were tied to battens that were empty and available.

In the better theatres, a fly floor (a walkway) was installed off to one side and high above the stage. A strong metal rail ran parallel to the walkway, and it held large metal hooks or cleats to tie up suspended cloths and drops. The flyman pulled up and tied off drops or released and lowered them as required.

JAY C. FLIPPEN

b: 6 March 1899, Little Rock, AR—d: 3 February 1971, Los Angeles, CA

The term *craggy-faced* seemed to have been coined for Jay C. Flippen, whose seen-it-all eyes and cynical twist of mouth made him a natural for dozens of tough-guy roles in movies. This was not as limiting as it sounds, because among his roles were Broadway con men, Western sheriffs and outlaws, military officers, priests, policemen and bartenders. When he entered television, though, it was as the grizzled old-timer in big-sky Westerns or big-city crime shows.

Jay C. Flippen enjoyed success in all three rather distinct phases of his career. He worked in blackface from the time he first entered an amateur contest as a 14-year-old in Little Rock, Arkansas, and then joined the "Al G. Fields, Dean of Minstrelsy" show a year later. The Fields' minstrel troupe was in its last years but still welcomed throughout the country because its road show, which carried a variety of stage scenery and traveled in its own specially equipped railway cars, did not stint on production values. Young Jay C. (who sometimes used the alternate billing of J. C. Flippen) quickly became a principal performer in the Fields troupe, assuming the role of an end man (Tambo or Bones). Even as late as 1930, trade papers were praising Flippen for his burned-cork act, although by then he was no longer exclusively working in blackface.

In 1918, he went on tour with *Oh, Justine!,* the road-show edition of *Over the Top,* a Broadway revue, and in 1921 it is reported that he replaced Bert Williams when a scaled-down edition of *Broadway Brevities of 1920* went on the road. Thereafter, he played two years on the Columbia wheel in Lena Daley's burlesque show as a sketch comedian and spent most of the rest of the 1920s doing a single in vaudeville as a blackfaced monologist.

Jay C. Flippen

When he first played the Palace Theatre around 1924, he made enough of a success to be booked three more times that same season. J. J. Shubert caught Jay C. Flippen's act during one of these Palace engagements and signed Flippen to a three-year contract that put him in as many shows. *June Days* opened at the Astor in the doldrums of August 1925 and lasted only six weeks. *Hello Lola,* a reworking of Booth Tarkington's *Seventeen,* duplicated *June Days*'s feat almost to the day. Jake Shubert had more luck with *The Great Temptations,* which opened on 18 May 1926; a top-notch cast of Flippen, Jack Benny, Hazel Dawn and Flournoy Miller & Aubrey Lyles accounted for its run of 197 performances.

Less than a year later, on 5 July 1927, Flippen opened in *Padlocks of 1927,* one of Texas Guinan's attempts to escape the hazards of fronting a speakeasy. Flippen and a cast of little-known performers opened in *The Second Little Show,* which played the Royale Theatre for 63 performances beginning on 2 September 1930.

J. C. had been a vaudeville headliner since the mid-1920s, his seemingly informal wisecracking style going over big with audiences. As hard times threatened the economic viability of two-a-day vaudeville, Flippen could point with pride to the week he toplined the bill at the Palace, along with Weber & Fields (in one of their reunion appearances). It was Holy Week, traditionally bad for business, but the bill did exceptional box office, far better than the Palace was used to by 1932.

J. C. Flippen committed his vaudeville personality to at least a pair of one-reel shorts in 1932 and 1938; what made them a pair was that Flippen played an emcee aboard a cruise ship in both. He also played character roles in two feature films, yet he was only in his mid-30s at the time. Despite the decline of vaudeville, Flippen organized package shows in which he toured presentation houses, where his stage show alternated with the featured movie.

After it opened on Broadway on 22 September 1938, *Hellzapoppin* became the biggest smash show since Charles Dillingham's musical extravaganzas with Montgomery & Stone before the First World War. *Hellzapoppin* ran nearly three years and made its creators and stars, Ole Olsen and Chic Johnson, very much sought after for radio and movies. When Ole & Chic went to Hollywood to make a movie version of *Hellzapoppin,* Jay C. Flippen was hired to replace Ole in the stage hit. (Happy Fenton assumed Chic's part in the show.) When Olsen and Johnson returned to Broadway to assume their original roles, Jay C. Flippen stayed with the show. Over the years, Ole & Chic made periodic changes to the material and cast, so it was probably easy to create a new slot for Flippen.

In 1943, the American Theatre Wing recruited J. C. for *The Lunchtime Follies* (also known as *Lunch Hour Follies*), a revue that was sent to various manufacturing plants that were producing war matériel. During its several productions, the casts included some big names such as Shirley Booth, Vivienne Segal and Fredric March from the legitimate stage; Helen Tamiris from the modern dance world; and Milton Berle, Betty Garrett, Jack Albertson, David Burns, Joey Faye and Zero Mostel from variety stages.

Jay C. Flippen entered the third stage of his career after the Second World War. He became a reliable and popular character actor in Hollywood, appearing in more than 60 movies and more than two dozen television shows during the quarter century between 1947 and 1970. He was a member of the regular cast of TV's *Ensign O'Toole,* a sitcom that ran from 1962 to1964, and appeared several times each on *The Virginian, Rawhide* and *Burke's Law.* Even the amputation of his leg did not retire him; he simply acted in a wheelchair during the handful of films he made in his last four years. His 60-year career seemed to span an even longer period, from the days when the minstrel show came to town through the glory days at the Palace to series television and wide-screen motion pictures.

FLIRTATION ACT

Essentially a one man and one woman act in which neither partner is married, at least not to each other. The bantering crosstalk was often followed by a song-and-dance duet.

FLOODLIGHTS

Also called *floods,* these intense, bright lights flooded the stage with light. They were usually placed in a circle facing the stage and attached to vertical stands on either side of the stage and in the wings. It was only in the last years of vaudeville that *floods* came into use, sooner in some theatres than others. *Floods* were standard in large presentation houses and rare in small old-time vaudeville houses.

FLOP

As a verb it means "fail"; as a noun it means "failure." A performer flops when the jokes, songs and dances land with a thud and the bored or disinterested audience does not applaud—or even boo. A show is a flop when it earns bad reviews and can not lure customers to the box office.

FLYING ACT

A trapeze act with at least two hanging bars. The performers *flew* from one trapeze bar to the other or from one partner to the other. Because of the height needed, this act was more successful in a circus tent than on a theatre stage and, consequently, was infrequently seen in vaudeville.

FLYING KARAMAZOV BROTHERS

Dmitri

b: (Paul David Magid) 21 May 1954, Seattle, WA

Ivan

b: (Howard Jay Patterson) 25 June 1955, North Hollywood, CA

Alyosha

b: (Randall Edwin "Randy" Nelson) ca. 1953

Fyodor

b: (Timothy Daniel Furst) 19 March 1952

Smerdyakov

b: (Samuel Ross "Sam" Williams) 10 September 1953, Seattle, WA

Alexei

b: (Mark Ettinger) 20 April 1963, New York, NY

Pavel

b: (Roderick Kimball) 21 May 1970, Canada

Ratikin

b: (Michael Preston) 1959

The Flying Karamazov Brothers: from left, Ivan (Howard Jay Patterson), Pavel (Roderick Kimball), Dmitri (Paul David Magid) and Alexei (Mark Ettinger)

For many people, The Flying Karamazov Brothers launched, with flying clubs, the first signal that the vaudeville act was not dead. Variety performers had never been on hiatus, but they had grown fewer in number during the second half of the twentieth century and were eclipsed by press coverage devoted to rock and roll, movies, television, comedyless musicals and naturalistic drama. The press was not solely to blame.

Vaudeville as a business institution was dead and not a candidate for resurrection. In the main, live variety shows had been reduced into insipid re-creations of song-and-dance acts, as exercises in whitewashed nostalgia or as amateur events, the sole redeeming value of which was to raise money for charity. Television variety, once the last stage for vaudeville acts, narrowed to stand-up comedians, singers plugging new recordings, and chitchat with talk program hosts.

After the mid-1950s, some performers who drew on clowning, wire walking, juggling and tumbling found employment with circuses, ice-skating and industrial shows, but presentations began to incline toward extravaganza, scenic dazzle, canned music and large production ensembles. There was a small scale reaction as some creative theatre people searched for ways to renew their connection with the audience, invigorate their performance and have fun doing it.

The reinvention of the variety performer took root, as it always had, on street corners, in marketplaces and fairs but also on college campuses. At first blush, the university seems an unlikely hothouse, but, in dorm rooms, quads and gymnasiums, hundreds if not thousands of young folk took up juggling, acrobatics, card and coin manipulation, and puppetry, although more students bought guitars than Kehoe clubs and linking rings.

Most strumming or juggling college students decided that life as civil engineers, administrators, chemists and computer technicians was a safer and surer course, but the music and the performance forms continued to belong to them, and, collectively, they became keen, expectant audiences.

The Flying Karamazov Brothers met at the University of California at Santa Cruz. Howard Patterson, a biology major and music minor who had fallen ill, recuperated during the winter of 1972–73 by expanding and refining his juggling skills. When he returned to campus, he was evangelical about juggling; he converted dorm mate Paul Magid, an English-literature major and Muslim-history minor.

Juggling is what Howard and Paul had in common, that and performing for people. Paul inclined to acting in the theatre; Howard was a musician. When Paul won a role in *The Three Cuckolds,* a *commedia dell'arte* play, the director asked if anyone could perform a Renaissance period act. Paul volunteered himself and his friend Howard. To accompany their juggling, Howard dug out a bawdy Elizabethan song, and a partnership was born. Their act scored more favorably than the production. Thus emboldened, they decided to stage the "Question Game" from Tom Stoppard's *Rosencrantz and Guildenstern Are Dead* as a juggling routine.

To earn a few dollars before the start of the 1973–74 college year, they went to Los Angeles, where Howard already had a gig as part of a quartet that sang madrigals. He and Paul also found a spot to juggle and pass the hat. Late in the season, they joined a Renaissance Faire, and their hat spilleth over. It was there that they began juggling with objects that had chiseled blades and sharp points. Danger drew audiences and provided an incentive to improve.

Their 1973–74 college year provided a few more plays, time to practice their juggling and an occasional opportunity to demonstrate at Renaissance Faires. That summer, an old acquaintance of Paul's, Randy Nelson, a painter, ballet dancer and former actor turned student at San Jose University, joined Howard and Paul for a summer of busking and living the hippie life on the streets of San Francisco. Randy was not a juggler, but he could do a few magic tricks.

They discovered that they were not the first college kids to come to the City on the Bay with dreams of juggling. They set out for Expo '74 in Seattle. Up to that point, they had billed themselves, when asked, as Patterson & Magid, but Patterson, Magid & Nelson sounded like a law firm. After much debate, they adopted Howard's suggestion and called themselves The Flying Karamazov Brothers. It was more than a whimsical choice. They felt that they had personalities akin to those Dostoyevsky created for the brothers in the novel, so Howard, Paul and Randy adopted as stage names Ivan, Dmitri and Alyosha. It was also a perhaps unconscious tip of the foolscap to tradition. Nearly a century before they formed their juggling and comedy act, Russians were famous in American vaudeville for acrobatic and juggling acts.

Choosing a name was about all they accomplished that summer. They were not allowed to pass the hat at Expo '74, and Canada did not want them, so they rode the rails back to California. The trio split up for the rest of the summer. Dmitri went to Spain, 40 years too late for the Lincoln Brigade. Alyosha got a job at a Ford factory. Ivan juggled, returned to Santa Cruz, rejoined his madrigal group, renewed acquaintance with Sam Williams, a fellow alumnus of the Renaissance Faires, and met fellow juggler Tim Furst, a philosophy and architecture major, conscientious objector and motorcycle courier.

Enter Michael Mielnick (also known as the Flaming Zucchini and Reverend Chumleigh). In summer 1975, Chumleigh drew together some acts for a hippie event called the Oregon Country Fair in Veneta, at which Paul and Howard performed. Chumleigh's stage show was a success that led him to the next logical step: a boatload of street performers sailing around the world. The first leg was supposed to sail from Seattle to Alaska. The closest Howard and Paul got to that goal was juggling and passing the hat for a number of weeks on a ferryboat out of Seattle.

Having put in the effort and time to prepare a vaudeville show at the Oregon Country Fair, some performers felt frustrated that, just as the show jelled, it ended along with the fair. They decided to take the show on the road. The Flying Karamazov Brothers were the engine that made the ensuing tours happen annually for many years. After the first Oregon Country Fair, Tim Furst and Sam Williams joined Howard and Paul as Karamazov Brothers.

A new Chautauqua vaudeville circuit grew out of the Oregon Country Fair. Inspired by the original Chautauqua circuit (60 to 80 years earlier) that sent lecturers, debaters, musical aggregations and genteel variety acts throughout the Midwest and farm belt, the new Chautauqua traveling vaudeville show was guided by communal discussion, accompanied by classes (crafts, juggling, song sharing and other variety arts), discussions of spiritual matters and cultural issues, and the daily demonstration of social responsibility such as a semivegetarianism, ecology and recycling. In practice, the participants discovered that a symbolic big tent is heavy to haul; the process was as essential to some folks as training and rehearsal was to others.

A typical tour played out-of-the-way spots like Omak, Forks, Neah Bay, Spokane, Ellensburg, Port Townsend and Orcas Island in Washington State; Boise, Salmon and Sandpoint in Idaho; Browning in Montana; and Quadra Island near Vancouver Island. The performers and crew traveled in a caravan that included a lunch wagon, equipment truck and trailer, a bus and various automobiles. Many of the vehicles were held together with baling wire and chewing gum. The course over the rugged Rocky Mountains took them on byways (no superhighways), and they met with rain, mud, chills and road accidents.

In addition to juggling clubs, eggs, meat cleavers, fruit, torches, hunks of dry ice, balls and bottles of champagne, a couple of the Karamazovs emceed the shows and did comedy bits; others played musical instruments in the band. Ivan also led the band. They were never just jugglers.

Several of the Karamazov Brothers sought a larger context for their displays of skill. Agreement on direction was not always reached painlessly. The genesis for what did develop—evening-length performance pieces—according to Ivan (Howard Jay Patterson), "began around 1977, when we weren't good enough jugglers to keep a pattern going long, and got into the habit of throwing a *drop back in* instead of stopping: otherwise we'd have had to stop every few seconds."

When four or more people engage in a group juggle, the unplanned happens, but many big juggles are choreographed as tightly as possible to ensure smooth, error-free routines. The Flying Karamazov Brothers prefer the unexpected; they call their big juggle "Jazz" and intend it to be improvisational. The throws are unplanned and not without the intent to catch someone off guard. The result is more misses and more excitement. They bandy words as well as clubs. Some are cryptic references or reminders that have specific meaning within the group. Others are philosophical leftovers from their university years or shorthand for more recent debates and explorations. Many are puns, non sequiturs and jokes: "All for one!," "And three for a dollar."

Another juggling staple of the Karamazov act is juggling unalike objects at the same time. Other jugglers do this, but the Karamazov audiences show up with all manner of objects—heavy, slimy, crumbly, tiny or cumbersome—as potential juggling items. The challenge is never refused. By applause, like the old talent-show nights, the audience indicates its choices from among the various objects, always choosing the most disparate and disgusting among the offerings. Rejected by the Brothers are objects lighter than an ounce, heavier than ten pounds, bigger than a bread box, alive or too dangerous. The reigning champ among the Karamazovs juggles the assortment until they disintegrate or melt. Keeping them in motion a certain number of minutes qualifies as success.

Since the 1980s, The Flying Karamazov Brothers have undertaken eastern tours as well, without other acts. The shows take place mostly on indoor stages at universities or independent theatres. In 1983, The Flying Karamazov Brothers made it to Broadway; Ivan, Dmitri, Fyodor, Alyosha, Smerdyakov and two performing cats, Flutter and Wow, signed on for a limited engagement of five weeks at the Ritz Theatre in a show they called *Juggling and Cheap Theatrics.* The reviews were excellent.

Paul (Dmitri), Howard (Ivan), Randy (Alyosha), Sam (Smerdyakov) and Tim (Fyodor) appeared as Tarak, Barak, Karak, Arak and Sarak in *The Jewel of the Nile* (1985), the good-humored adventure film starring Michael Douglas, Kathleen Turner, Danny DeVito and an old Flying Karamazov Brothers' friend, Avner (the Eccentric) Eisenberg.

Back in the theatre in 1986, the five Brothers revived *Juggling and Cheap Theatrics* for a limited run at the Vivian Beaumont Theatre in Lincoln Center.

The first of their shows that expanded substantially beyond juggling was *L'Histoire du Soldat* (1986). It was part of the New Wave Festival at the Brooklyn Academy of Music, and it proved to be a useful experiment that forced them to deal with the difficulties of integrating juggling, music and comedy (that they did well) with narrative and dialogue.

Greg Mosher's production of Shakespeare's *The Comedy of Errors* was originally produced for Chicago's Goodman Theatre in 1983, then at the Los Angeles Olympic Arts Festival in 1984. When it reached the Vivian Beaumont in New York during the summer of 1987, the cast included Ivan (Howard Jay Patterson), Dmitri (Paul Magid), Fyodor (Timothy Daniel Furst), Smerdyakov (Sam Williams) and Alyosha (Randy Nelson), plus Gina Leishman, Steven "Flip" Bernstein, Douglas Weiselman and Bud Chase (who played parts as well as being members of The Flying Karamazov Brothers' music band, The Kamikaze Ground Crew).

The Comedy of Errors cast members outside The Flying Karamazov Brothers family included Jeff Raz, Mark Sackett and Danny Mankin (who had an act called Vaudeville Nouveau), Ethyl Eichelberger, a baton-twirler-turned-actor Sophie (Schwab) Hayden, trapeze aerialist Wendy Parkman, and the multiskilled clown Avner the Eccentric (Eisenberg). It was from the start a strange concept. Some folks had hoped to hear more of the Bard's words, but it was a production that fascinated. Filmed in 1987, *The Comedy of Errors* was telecast as an entry on the PBS series *Great Performances: Live from Lincoln Center.*

Randy Nelson, painter, calligrapher and ballet dancer, was one of the original three when the act changed from Patterson & Magid to The Flying Karamazov Brothers. In 1988, married with children, he left the act to be with his family. Sam Williams, a vaudevillian they had known for years, had already joined the act as Smerdyakov.

Tim Furst, perhaps The Flying Karamazov Brothers' most accomplished juggler, preferred variety to plays and left the group in 1992, although he periodically helped out his teammates by filling in for a missing Karamazov. English-born circus performer, actor and director Michael Preston joined The Flying Karamazov Brothers as Ratikin to replace Tim.

Professionally, The Flying Karamazov Brothers were very busy in 1994. They began the year by returning to New York, where they opened *Club Sandwich* in January. That summer, London audiences saw them perform *Juggle and Hyde* (1994). They closed out the year with *The Flying Karamazov Brothers Do the Impossible* (1994), which played six weeks at the Helen Hayes Theatre.

The composition of The Flying Karamazov Brothers had changed in persons and number. The five were now four: Dmitri, Ivan, Smerdyakov and new member, Michael (Ratikin) Preston. *Sharps, Flats & Accidentals* toured the West Coast before it opened at the New Victory Theatre in 1996 and again at the Alice Tully Hall in 1998. In between, they appeared on two television shows: *Ellen* (DeGeneres) and *Mister*

Rogers' Neighborhood, and, in 1997, they revived the 1930s stage farce *Room Service* in a production that played Seattle, the Arena in Washington, D.C., and the Mark Taper Forum in Los Angeles. In 1998, The Flying Karamazov Brothers filmed *Enable: People with Disabilities and Computers* (1999), a public-service piece, shot for Microsoft.

"Looneyverse" was the Brothers' nickname for *L'Universe* (2000), their ambitious multimedia collaboration with the Media Lab at Massachusetts Institute of Technology (MIT). The Flying Karamazov Brothers explored the universe by entering the greatest juggling act of all: the spinning, rotating planets. Their costars were visual and aural technology, like the upstage screen that enabled the Brothers' live and imaged selves to combine in performance.

Catch was the name of a 2002 show they played in Chicago and Washington, D.C., among other places, but The Flying Karamazov Brothers did not bring the production to New York. They made up for that omission in 2003 when they and the Cincinnati Pops Orchestra took their Cincinnati-based concert to Manhattan's Carnegie Hall.

The Flying Karamazov Brothers offered *Life: A Guide for the Perplexed* in 2004, although the premise primarily revolved around Dmitri's philosophical predicament. To resolve his midlife crises, Dmitri consults Maimonides' texts, and his brothers oblige with Shakespeare's *Seven Ages of Man* lobbed into the mix and the Hindu epic *Mahabharata* performed in Bollywood style with a grand, puppet-assisted finish. Former stage brother Michael Preston directed the show, and the Brothers for this show were Dmitri, Ivan, Alexei and Pavel.

Reviewers compare The Flying Karamazov Brothers to The Marx Brothers. Perhaps that is because both have the word *Brothers* in the name of their act or are the only two zany acts they can recall or there is at least one large black moustache in both acts. Actually, in style, deftness and coordination, The Flying Karamazov Brothers more resemble the Ritz Brothers or the Wiere Brothers. They exhibit the zaniness of the Ritzes, but like the Wieres they are jugglers and musicians as well as comedians. In appearance, the Karamazov Brothers look like silent-screen depictions of dark, bearded anarchists lobbing round bombs with fizzling fuses. One wonders in the years after 2001 whether the Karamazovs can pass through airport security without anxiety on both sides.

As Ivan, Howard Jay Patterson bounds onto the stage with the authority of a premier *danseur,* the sort of chap who engages the villain in swordplay with one hand while charming the crinolines off the fair damsel. An equally commanding presence onstage, Paul Magid, in his guise as Dmitri, resembles a tribal chieftain, veering between horse trader and seeker of truth and beauty. Mark Ettinger is the scampering, ever-cheerful Alexei, troubadour of joy and harmony. Sam Williams, when he played the bushy-bearded Smerdyakov, was the son-of-the-soil prankster. Roderick Kimball, youngest of the Brothers, past or present, plays the fresh-faced Pavel, eagerly complicit if occasionally confused.

Despite a few changes among the cast, The Flying Karamazov Brothers have remained, for more than three decades, one of the more durable, respected and popular acts. They bring something new in content, technique and technology to each production wherever they go, and their tours have taken them across the USA and to England, Scotland, Ireland, Australia, New Zealand, Hong Kong, Canada, Singapore, Bermuda, Israel, Germany and the Netherlands.

FOIL

Some commentators use *foil* and *stooge* interchangeably, but there is a nice distinction between their roles, their relationship to the lead comedian and their status in the act.

Whereas a stooge gets laughs by bumbling in his attempts to serve the comedian, the foil is closer to the role of a partner, usually an antagonistic one, like W. C. Fields' screen wives, the ferocious and gigantic Mack Swain playing against Chaplin's Little Tramp, Eddie "Rochester" Anderson and his impudent lack of responsiveness to his boss Jack Benny, or Gale Gordon exercising his exasperated bullying of Lucille Ball.

There is often insulting banter between the chief comedian and his foil. Even if the foil is a villain who gets his comeuppance in the final scene, the comedian and foil are usually more evenly matched in the script and stature than comedian and stooge.

It is often suggested that the stage use of the term *foil* extends from its connection to jewelry making. Metal foil was used to set off the jewel, hence the foil provides the setup for the comedian. An equally far-fetched theory suggests that the verbal jibes the foil directed to the comedian stung like the jabs of a fencing Foil. More likely it is because the foil's function is to 'foil' the comedian's plans.

FOLD

Close. Invariably the term refers to any type of show that closed due to poor business. Literally, folded up its tent and scenery.

FOOTLIGHTS

Seldom used in any form of theatre by the late twentieth century, footlights were installed at the edge of the stage apron with oil, gas and then electric lights positioned a few inches above floor level. These lit feet, legs and faces more fully, especially if the act wore hats, and footlights were said to give a warmer look to the performers and the stage.

The foots were angled upward 20 degrees to 45 degrees, depending upon the angle of the stage floor, if it was raked. The lamps were shielded from the audience by cans or opaque shells that directed the lights toward the performance. Footlights were jelled in sequence: white, red, blue and amber.

IDA FORSYNE

b: 1883, Chicago, IL—d: ca. 1967, Schenectady, NY (?)

She was regarded as the best female vernacular dancer of her generation and held on to her reputation among black dancers when Alice Whitman and Jeni Le Gon joined her in the pantheon. Despite her talent, several factors combined to abbreviate her career.

Ida was born into poverty; her father deserted the family when Ida was two, and her mother was a maid. Ida perched herself on the fire escape of a local theatre and taught herself how to dance, performing for pennies on street corners. Ida and her mother lived above a brothel, and the house piano player, Willie Mason, taught Ida more steps, enough to dance at rent parties and, when she was 14, to run off and earn her living with *The Black Bostonians,* a touring tab show. She sang and did an eccentric dance. Ida had the not-uncommon experience of being stranded in Butte, Montana, and working her way home.

In 1898, she joined Black Patti's Troubadours for several seasons. Forsyne developed her skills as a singer and dancer, and she traveled the breadth of the country. At 16, she landed in New York City and got work in clubs. She permanently strained her voice trying to sing above the noise in the boisterous clubs, but her reputation was made with her dancing.

Ida was tiny, barely five feet tall, and 100 pounds, with a very pretty dark face. She joined the Smart Set Company in 1902, when it was headed by Ernest Hogan. In 1904, she moved on to Will Marion Cook's *The Southerners,* then playing the New York Theatre Roof Garden. The show was one of the first to have an integrated cast—headed by white song-and-dance man Eddie Leonard—but the whites had all the speaking roles, and the blacks performed many of the specialty numbers. Then, in the 1905–06 season, she got the opportunity to tour Europe in an ensemble act called the Tennessee Students. Ida was featured along with comedian and dancer Ernest Hogan, singer Abbe Mitchell and fellow dancer Henry Williams.

Ida Forsyne stayed in Europe for nine years. She played the Moulin Rouge in Paris for a year and then toured British music-halls for several seasons before going to Germany, Russia and other countries. In Russia, she picked up their athletic dancing. She delighted Russian audiences with her energetic kazotsky, a dance Americans think of as Cossack, in which the dancer squats with his arms folded and rapidly kicks out his legs.

Ida was 22 when she left for Europe, and she was 31 when she returned to the USA in 1914. That was a long time to be away from American producers and audiences. She had spent her prime years as a performer abroad, and it proved to count for little when she began seeking work in the USA. Many things had changed in show business. Black producers had become very color conscious, and they wanted light-skinned women for their shows. Ida Forsyne was not the last to complain; Josephine Baker was turned down for black-run shows because she was black rather than tan. Other factors were Ida's dancing and performance style. Russian dancing, done to Russian music, was never much of a draw among black audiences. They preferred a ragtime, a blues or a jazz rhythm in their music. Russian dancing was Ida's specialty in an era when the shimmy was the rage, and Ida was not comfortable with a sexual exhibition.

When former star dancer Ida Forsyne got work, it was in an ensemble. Usually these were packaged vaudeville shows or musical farces playing TOBY time: *Darkydom* (1914–15), *Holiday in Dixie* (1916–17), *They're Off* (1919), *Beale Street to Broadway* (1920), *Strut Your Stuff* (1920) and *Town Top-Piks* (1920) among them. When Ida was allowed to perform her specialty, she was chided by confused and derisive audiences who expected sexual grinds and shakes.

Ida must have given up temporarily in 1920; she was engaged by Sophie Tucker as her traveling maid. A bit later, Sophie decided to put Ida in her act, and Ida's dancing helped give Sophie's act an energetic finish. Some theatres demanded that African American performers cork up. To her everlasting credit, Sophie refused to permit Ida Forsyne to be subjected to that indignity. Sophie remembered too well that, when she was starting her career, theatre owners insisted she wear blackface because they told her she was too fat and ugly to appear white. It was an insult to black and white women alike.

Forsyne later appeared with Mamie Smith in her traveling show (1924), with Dusty Fletcher in

Harlem Strutters (1925) and with Whitney & Tutt in *Rainbow Chasers* (1926). In 1928, Ida was hired by Bessie Smith as a chorus dancer, and Bessie made time in her act for Ida to perform her specialty. Ida was about 45, and, although still a fine dancer, she could not predict how long she could compete with younger dancers. Further, the economic situation got very bad, and black show business headed into the dumps. From 1930 onward, Ida spent much of the rest of her working life as a domestic servant and an elevator operator. There were few professional bright spots, but in 1936, she was cast as Mrs. Noah in the screen version of Marc Connelly's musical play *Green Pastures.*

Ida Forsyne lived long enough to be interviewed in 1965 and 1966 by Marshall Stearns, researcher and editor with his wife, Jean, of *Jazz Dance: The Story of American Vernacular Dance.*

FOUR DANCING FORDS

Johnny Ford

b: ca. 1876

Maxie Ford

b: ca. 1880

Edwin Ford

b: ca. 1882

Dora Ford

b: 1885—d: 1978, New York, NY

Mabel Ford

b: 1888, Ohio—d: 1982, New York, NY

Four of the five children born to John and Miriam Ford went into vaudeville as the Four Dancing Fords. With at least five performers in the family, their vaudeville acts seemed to constantly shift in their configuration, combining some siblings and outside partners one season and a different mix the next. No doubt this flexibility accommodated personal events such as marriages and births and those siblings who took a musical comedy role or desired to do a *single* in vaudeville. In 1913, they broke up for what seems to have been the final time.

Dora and Mabel continued as a sister act and accepted engagements in England and France in 1914. There, Dora married and gave birth to future stage magician Roy Benson. The First World War forced the Fords to sail home in 1916. Mabel & Dora Ford, as they were billed, continued to perform into the mid-1920s, often playing Orpheum time and Keith-Albee-Orpheum time.

In 1921, Milton Berle, at the time 12 years old and one half of Kennedy & Berle, was on a bill at the Palace Theatre with Dora and Mabel Ford. He later recalled that, although he had worked with dozens of dance acts by then, the Ford Sisters were the most polished he had seen.

Dora & Mabel Ford spent a lot of money on their act: they brought their own onstage band, their own special drop curtain and they made several changes of beautiful costumes. Dora and Mabel worked *in full* and were a sensational *closing act* for the big time.

Maxie, one of the better wing dancers of his day, astonished other dancers with his dance combinations, such as performing a wing on one foot while executing a roll with the other. He was the originator of a step called, variously, the Maxiford, the Maxie Ford, the Maxie or the Jackknife. It combined a leap, a brush step and then a toe jab by the opposite foot before landing and reversing the combination.

It is not certain how Edwin and Johnny fit into the family act. Around 1906, an act called The Ford Dancers was comprised of Edwin Ford, Lottie Ford (she may have been an in-law), Mayme Gehrue, Bob Adams and William Cutty. When they played the Orpheum in San Francisco, they were on the undercard of a bill headed by James C. Morton and a sketch comedy troupe whose star was Franklin Ardell.

Most sources list Johnny as one of the Four Dancing Fords, but family historian Liane Curtis writes that it was Edwin, Mabel, Dora and Max who danced as the Four Fords and the Four Dancing Fords. After the Four Fords drifted apart professionally, however, Johnny was a solo act for much of his career, especially during the early 1900s. Both Max and Johnny were esteemed by other tappers, and Harland Dixon spoke highly of them. Sometime in the late 1890s or very early 1900s, Johnny won the Fox Medal for buck dancing in a contest held at Tammany Hall in Manhattan.

Johnny appeared in a Wilbur Mack musical, *Lovers and Lunatics* (1906), in which he partnered Mayme Gehrue in several dance numbers. That was about the same season that Mayme Gehrue worked with Edwin Ford in a five-person act. Johnny married Eva Tanguay in 1914, but their marriage did not last. In 1919, Johnny Ford costarred with Charlie Ruggles, Peggy O'Neill and Zelda Sears in *Tumble Inn,* a Rudolph Friml & Otto Harbach musical.

FOUR STEP BROTHERS

Al Williams

b: 29 August 1911, Arizona—d: 30 June 1981, San Francisco, CA

Maceo Anderson

b: 3 September 1910, Charleston, SC—d: 4 July 2001, Los Angeles, CA

Red Gordon

Sherman Robinson

Sylvester "Happy" Johnson

Freddie James

Flash McDonald

b: (Rufus McDonald) 16 March 1919, St. Louis, MO—d: 15 July 1988, Hollywood, CA

Sunshine Sammy Morrison

b: (Frederick Ernest Morrison) 20 December 1912, New Orleans, LA—d: 24 July 1989, Lynwood, CA

Prince Spencer

b: 3 October 1917, Jenkinsville, SC

The careers of individual dancers last as long as audiences want them and the dancers' will, desire, hips, knees and feet permit. Dance groups, however, struggle with the additional factors of individual personal lives and ambitions and the economics of a multiperson act.

It was hard to keep three or four individuals content and working with each other while touring in vaudeville. Dissatisfaction usually stemmed from personal conflicts, disruptive work habits, poor performance or disputes about finances. Any change in personnel meant breaking in a new dancer and teaching him dance routines that originally were set on the departing dancer whose physiognomy and specific skills were different from those of the incoming member of the act.

Four Step Brothers: clockwise from top, Maceo Anderson, Al Williams, Prince Spencer and Flash McDonald

A booker or a manager needed to be convinced that a trio of dancers was worth more than a single dancer. Did it make any difference to ticket buyers whether one act on the bill was a solo hoofer or a trio? How could a manager justify paying two or three times what a single tapper earned unless there was a demonstrable increase in box-office take? A dancer's cut of a salary paid to all but the very top trios and quartets made many dancers wonder if they could earn more as soloists. One group of dancers that, for the most part, seemed to handle these matters in stride was the Four Step Brothers

Despite the name of their act, they were not brothers, not even stepbrothers. In 1925–26, Al Williams, Maceo Anderson and Red Gordon organized the act first as a trio. As boys, each had come north to Harlem with his family. They met at the Hoofers Club, where they picked up steps from the masters. Individually, they discovered they sold more newspapers when they called attention to themselves by dancing at their corner stand. Dancing usually won them the attention of passersby and a few extra sales.

Maceo's mother rigged up a dance floor in the basement of the building where the family lived, and he, Al and Red gathered there to practice. They entered amateur contests, but quickly got their first professional job in a touring black revue, *Moon over Alabama.*

According to Maceo, the act was called Anderson, Williams & Walker because Williams & Walker were still a well-remembered act. In 1927, they took on a fourth member, Sherman Robinson, and changed the name of the act to the Four Step Brothers.

The Cotton Club, although it did not permit black customers, paid black acts top salaries to perform. The boys pestered Duke Ellington, whose band was in residence at the time, to let them dance in the show. Finally, he agreed to put them on at the break between shows. The four boys scored and performed at the Cotton Club, off and on, from 1928 for four years. The Cotton Club shows usually changed twice a year, but if one dance act or band was on tour, the management brought in another. When the Four Step Brothers went on tour with Ellington, as they did several times, the Berry Brothers or the Nicholas Brothers, if available, replaced the Four Step Brothers. Sometimes it was the other way around. All three acts were sensational, and, although competitors, they easily filled in for each other if they were in town and had some open dates while the others were on tour or making a movie in Hollywood.

From the late 1920s onward, the Four Step Brothers played black vaudeville and revue as well as big-time vaudeville like the Keith-Albee circuit. In vaudeville, they did a 30-minute act; in presentation houses, they cut the act to 13 minutes.

When the Four Step Brothers switched from black clubs and small-time vaudeville to white clubs and big-time vaudeville, there was the problem of music. Pit bands in black theatres knew the rhythms and accents necessary to the tap act. Even if they did not know the music, they were able to fake it, playing appropriate musical phrases that matched the tap rhythms or playing stop-time and letting the tappers lay down the percussion themselves. White bands usually expected *sides* (musical arrangements for each instrument) with the accents clearly laid out. The Four Step Brothers had not invested in musical arrangements.

They did not have that problem, however, when they traveled with big bands like Ellington's that had a resident arranger. During the 1930s, swing bands, both black and white, were at the peak of their popularity and perfect for the big presentation houses that paired a stage show with a first-run motion picture. The band members filled the back of the stage. Individual instrumentalists stepped forward for their solos, and, to vary the presentation, the band unit also included a singer or two and a dance act.

In any act of three of more people, there was bound to be turnover. Of the three founding members of the act, Maceo Anderson and Al Williams remained the longest. The first great dance influence in Al William's young life was King Rastus Brown. Al met King Rastus at the Hoofers Club, and the older man generously taught the youngster some *fly* steps. Williams was usually considered the leader of the act, although it seems Anderson had more than a little authority.

Maceo Anderson started in show business when, age six, he got a job in Ida Mae Chadwick's act, shortly after he and his mother moved from South Carolina to Harlem. Ida Mae formed her own act after years performing with her mother and father. To add excitement, she hired some *pickaninnies*. Vaudeville audiences loved to watch a bunch of energetic, happy kids dancing up a storm. They enlivened the act and did their own turn while the singer changed costumes offstage. After Maceo outgrew the "cute pick" stage, he came back to Harlem. Still bitten by the dancing bug, Maceo attended vaudeville shows whenever he could and hung around the Hoofers Club, when they let him and met his future dance partners, Al and Rod.

During the 1930s, Sylvester "Happy" Johnson and Freddie James replaced Red Gordon and Sherman Robinson. Freddie's stage work extended back into his childhood, when he was a member of his family's vaudeville unit on Toby time. Freddie James was already much admired by other percussive dancers when he joined the Four Step Brothers; he had been a member of another deservedly famous dance act, Tip, Tap & Toe. Al Williams, Maceo Anderson, Sylvester Johnson and Freddie James were the Four Step Brothers who danced in the movie *When Johnny Comes Marching Home,* which was made in 1941 and released in 1942.

Freddie James played several instruments, and his acrobatic work included splits, flips, knee drops and spins. For the several years he was with the act, Freddie stimulated the Four Step Brothers into performing some of their flashiest work. Unfortunately, Freddie was addicted to the high life, and he became too ill to dance.

Freddie James had brought Prince Spencer into the act around 1942. Early on, Spencer's family had moved from his South Carolina birthplace to Boston and then to Toledo, Ohio, where Prince grew up. Prince was another who was impressed by King Rastus Brown, but Prince learned percussive dance on the sidewalks along with other neighborhood kids. He got work in local shows where he was spotted by a scout for Ben Bernie. Prince left home to tour with Bernie's band, then he continued on the road with *Major Bowes' Dixie Jubilee.*

Like Gus Edwards a generation earlier, Major Bowes sent troupes of youngsters on the road in various packaged shows. Bowes found some of his talent among those who applied to perform on his popular radio *Amateur Hour,* but others, like Prince, were pros masquerading as amateurs. For four years, Prince traveled with various Bowes' units in vaudeville and sang and tap danced on Bowes' radio show.

When Ted Mack took over the operation, Prince continued with him before working the better small time and Keith-Orpheum big time as a single. As vaudeville declined, Prince played nightclubs, doing vocal impressions as well as singing and dancing. He was playing the Club Alabam in Los Angeles in 1942 about the time that Maceo Anderson joined the U.S. Army. Freddie James invited him to join him, Al Williams and Happy Johnson as the Four Step Brothers.

Prince Spencer brought Flash McDonald into the act a year later. Flash had a similar story to the other Step Brothers: tap dancing on street corners with his mates, selling newspapers and dancing to call attention to his wares. Like the others, he made more in tips than in newspaper sales commissions, so he switched to working local clubs on weekend nights and making a good week's pay in salary and tips. In 1940, he left St. Louis for Chicago, quickly got work, traveled with Louis Jordan's hot band and played the Apollo in Harlem. More bookings followed. Flash was working in the Jungle Room in Los Angeles while the Step Brothers were looking for a new member, and Prince spotted him.

After Maceo was inducted into the army in 1941, Sammy Morrison joined the group for a short while. Maceo had become the group's comedian, and Sammy was every bit as able to get laughs. He had an impressive career beginning as an infant *extra* in films. A few years later, Hal Roach signed Sammy, which made Sammy quite likely the first African American signed to a term contract rather than for a single picture. Sammy worked with Harold Lloyd and Snub Pollard and then was cast as one of the kids in the very popular silent-film Our Gang Comedies. At 11, he had grown too old for the series, and he went into vaudeville in 1924. The Our Gang Comedies proved adaptable to sound, but the cast from the silent comedies was replaced by younger kids.

In 1940, Sammy became the first Negro member of the East Side Kids, starring Leo Gorcey and Huntz Hall, although Sammy was only briefly with the series. The following year, he joined the Four Step Brothers and appeared with them in the Technicolor movie musical *Greenwich Village* (1944). Morrison quit the act when Maceo returned from the war. Sammy then went into *civilian* life, where he remained for 30 years until he made one more film in 1976.

After the Second World War, when the act played Las Vegas and toured Europe, the personnel were Al Williams, Maceo Anderson, Prince Spencer and Flash McDonald. There were several reasons why the act did not have more problems than it did when there were changes in personnel. The act commanded a high salary, and, more often than most black acts, the Four Step Brothers were booked in movies, top nightclubs and theatres, and, eventually, on television, so there were many wonderful black dancers willing to join the act. Also, a dancer did not need to submerge his style or personality when he became a Step Brother. Several of them sang well, a couple proved capable of generating laughter, and others expanded the act's basic acrobatic tap style with Afro-Caribbean dance moves. Most could play a musical instrument. The act actually grew stronger from the early 1930s to the early 1940s.

Once an act had a good routine, other, lesser acts were apt to steal and perform it, as best as they could, without making some effort to change the routine. The Four Step Brothers retained the challenge dance from their days when they were just kids learning how to dance, busking and trading steps on street corners. The dancing was fueled both by rivalry and support. The dancers, in their solo spots, tried to outdo each other, but they also stood by and clapped out a rhythm to spur the others to perform their best.

The Four Step Brothers brought a version of the street act onto the stage and made it the centerpiece. This gave everyone in the act a chance to shine at their own specialty and to improvise. The unpredictability and the intensely personal styles of the Four Step Brothers made their act difficult to copy. While one Step Brother did his specialty, the others kept time and had a chance to catch their breath.

The Four Step Brothers lasted more than 40 years, from vaudeville in the mid-1920s to the Cotton Club to Hollywood musicals to Ed Sullivan's *Toast of the Town* television show to the top performance venues in Europe in the late 1960s.

FOURTH WALL

Usually, this term refers to a convention of theatre wherein the drama is played as if there were no audience, only a fourth wall at the stage edge. Members of the audience become witnesses to the drama rather than participants in the performance. The fourth wall was an article of faith for the naturalistic theatre of the late nineteenth century and first half of the twentieth century. Around the same time, however, there arose other styles and approaches to drama that did not accept the immutable virtue of a fourth wall. To some, in certain styles of drama and comedy, it was absurd not to acknowledge the audience as participants.

In variety, vaudeville and revue, the performer plays to the audience. The process works; the audience demonstrates its approval through laughter and applause, under the best of circumstances, and does its part to keep the pace and circuit of energy flowing back and forth between stage and audience. Music, song and dance, tumbling, juggling—even sketch comedy—require a presentational performance in which entertainer and audience are in tune with each other.

FOX & WARD

Joseph Fox

b: (Joseph F. Fox) 7 May 1852 (?), Ogdensburg, NY

William Ward

b: (William H. Ward) 17 September 1852, Canandaigua, NY

By the time Fox & Ward appeared on Percy G. Williams' Old Timers' Bill at his Colonial Theatre in Manhattan, they claimed to be "The Record Minstrel and Vaudeville Team of the World: 1868–1911."

The boys began their careers in the Hudson River and Ohio River Valley territories, making their debut, playing with the Worrell Sisters, in 1868 at the Woods Theatre in Cincinnati, Ohio. Their earliest photographs show Fox & Ward dressed as clog dancers and tumblers, and they capitalized on a pedestal dance they advertised as the "Silver Statue Clog." Fox was the slenderer of the pair, and Ward was more robust and doubtless the understander in the act.

They traveled west and played the Winter Garden, the only variety house at the time in Chicago, where they introduced a dance variation they promoted as the marble pedestal clog. The boys enjoyed an enthusiastic reception by Windy City audiences that kept them employed there for much of the 1869–70 season.

Next, they joined Dupres & Benedict's Minstrels as that troupe toured westward into the Rocky Mountain states and the up and down Pacific Coast; it was reputably the first theatrical company to make a transcontinental trip on the newly constructed Union and Central Pacific Railroads. This tour consumed nine years of Fox & Ward's career until they were engaged by the management of Barlow, Wilson, Primrose and West's Minstrels for the seasons of 1879–80 and 1880–81.

The following year, Joseph and William formed Fox & Ward's Minstrels, but they disbanded the outfit to return to vaudeville in 1883. Under the management of Rich & Harris, Fox & Ward appeared at Boston's Old Howard Athenaeum. They continued to play vaudeville, crossing the USA and returning to California in 1886.

In their later years, Fox & Ward performed a patter, song-and-dance act, and were billed as "The Minstrel Men: Those Mighty Masters of Mirth Who Move the Moody and Morose to Much Merriment," often, though not always, appearing in blackface.

GEORGE L. FOX

b: (George Washington Lafayette Fox) 3 July 1825, Boston, MA—d: 24 October 1877, Cambridge, MA

He was the firstborn of Emily Watt Fox and George Howe Fox and was called Laff throughout his early years. Although he grew into one of the most esteemed comedians of his era, George L. Fox was considered less promising as a stage performer than several of the other five surviving Fox children. His parents worked for the Tremont Theatre, and children were often in demand as supernumeraries in pageants or for small roles in plays. Nearly a century before the Gerry Society (Society for the Prevention of Cruelty to Children) tried to banish children from the immoral stage, Puritan Boston regarded children as a purifying element in otherwise corrupted entertainments.

As the oldest Fox child, Laff was the first to take to the stage around 1830, but younger siblings James, Caddie (born Caroline) and Charles soon proved to be more attractive, charming and consistent performers, and when Laff grew into his teens, he was apprenticed to a tradesman. James and Caddie became child stars and appeared often at Boston's Tremont Theatre in the 1830s and on several bills at the Vaudeville Saloon in Boston during summer 1840.

James, the youngest of the three, continued as an actor even as he studied law at Harvard University. He gave up the stage for a successful law practice, married into a socially prominent family and eventually became a four-term mayor of Cambridge, Massachusetts. Caddie, a great audience favorite as a child actor-dancer, married actor George Howard, and they began their own theatrical dynasty. Off and on over the years, the Fox-Howard clan was a prominent presence on the American stage.

By the time Laff was 20 or so, he had failed in his attempts in the trades and in commerce. He was back in the family business billed as L. Fox and assigned secondary character and comic roles in the Fox-Howard tours. Fox was at once the odd man out yet free to develop on his own. The company toured in summertime and during the winter seasons sought a residency, which they found successively in Providence, Rhode Island, and Worcester, Massachusetts, before ending up in Manhattan in 1850. Late that year, Laff Fox left the family company to accept a slot as a low comedian at the Bowery's National Theatre.

Bowery audiences liked their entertainment coarse and pointed, whether toward laughs or thrills. Laff's style, which had been faulted for being less refined and charming than Caroline's and James', was well suited to the taste of the National's boisterous patrons. Within a season, George L. Fox became a Bowery favorite. He remained under the National's banner for seven years and spent nearly all of the remainder of his career in Lower East Side theatres. Bowery theatres did not cater to Manhattan's carriage trade that lived, worked, and socialized farther uptown, an ever-northward expanding frontier for the ambitious, speculative and successful.

As Fox's biographer, Laurence Senelick, points out, one of Laff's early successes was more than a theatrical triumph. There were many stage versions of *Uncle Tom's Cabin,* and dramatizations of Harriet Beecher Stowe's story were not always true to the spirit of her antislavery theme. Some *Tom shows* were crude burlesks that caricatured the victims depicted in the novel. Sentiment in the Bowery was pro-Democrat, and in the years of the widening schism leading up to the Civil War that meant pro-South and anti-Abolitionist.

Racism was prevalent and overt among white lower classes; resentment was even stronger. Recent white immigrants, largely Irish and Roman Catholic, were abjectly poor and hanging onto the bottom rung of the economic ladder. They feared that free Negroes, scrambling for their own purchase on the ladder of economic democracy, would displace the tenuous grip of the Irish. The marvel was that, in 1853, George L. Fox directed his cousin's (George Aiken) adaptation of *Uncle Tom's Cabin* in such a way that, for the moment at least, audiences' sympathies were with slaves yearning to be free. The National went so far as to accommodate Negro patrons in one section of the theatre.

Another element of his success was Laff's amalgamation of the rural Jonathan character, popularized by comic actors like Joseph Jefferson, with the amusingly cynical urban wise guy much loved by the "Bowery Bhoys" in the balcony.

Productions were becoming more splendid and inventive. The Ravels, a French family troupe, had won great favor with American audiences in Boston, New York City and Philadelphia and had done much by the mid-1850s to establish Niblo's Gardens reputation. George L. Fox could not have been unaware of their impact in the theatrical scene. Fox's popularity tilted the National Theatre to specialize in burlesk, pantomime and extravaganza, and he had the support of cousin George Aiken, Laff's younger brother Charles, a fine comedian and character actor, and an increasingly skilled company of comedians and acrobats. Whereas newspaper critics hurrahed over each return of the elegant Ravels to Niblo's, they often turned up their noses at what they presumed to be the common entertainments of the Bowery houses.

From 1858 onward, Fox was his own manager. He took over the lease at the Old Bowery Theatre and then built the New Bowery in 1859 and managed the theatre until the outset of the Civil War. He served as an officer, rising to the rank of major, in the Union Army during the Civil War. When he returned, he quickly resumed his production of pantomimes. P. T. Barnum enticed Fox and leading members of his company to play at Barnum's American Museum, where uptown critics saw and admired him.

George L. Fox's gaunt, angular body was not especially suited to the balletlike pantomime that evolved from *commedia dell'arte,* in which the Ravels excelled. Nor did he follow Grimaldi and the jolly, silly-billy British clowns. His success was not as an acrobatic Harlequin, a wistful Pierrot or a buffoon. He had moved a few steps away from the tumbling clown toward the comedian who thought before he acted and let his thoughts mold his countenance before he reacted. Fox won his laughs with words as well as movement and facial expression. Chroniclers commented upon the *American* quality of his character, one with a bit of an edge. It may have been a reflection of the man; Fox was often described as ungracious, a hard man to work for and quick to take offense.

As an entrepreneur, Fox was less successful. He spent carelessly to achieve the effects he desired onstage and a level of production that pleased him. According to Laurence Senelick, he seems to have accorded scant attention to the bottom line. Even when productions sold out or were extended, he was hard-pressed to make income match outgo. His last decade, from the cessation of the Civil War until his forced retirement, was spent performing in several great successes and trying to stay afloat financially. Losing the New Bowery in a fire was a demoralizing trial.

Laff had grown famous with his burlesk of *Hamlet* and fanciful representations from fairy tales, the most notable of which was *Humpty Dumpty,* a role that Fox first played in 1867 at the Olympic Theatre. The show combined slapstick, ballet, music and stage illusions and ran for more than a year. Humpty Dumpty is the role with which George L. Fox is still identified.

During his last decade, whenever a show misfired, Fox reverted to an updated *Humpty Dumpty.* The Hanlon Brothers had replaced the Ravels as rivals. The Hanlon's spectacular pantomimes were chock-full of breathtaking acrobatics and sensational illusions. New and younger players were coming to the fore, and Fox began to work for managements that had other stars on hand. Complicating matters was the financial panic of 1873.

Fox's last stab at management was undermined by a deceitful partner who promised him a greater share of profits in turn for a lower salary. For at least the fifth time, he revived *Humpty Dumpty* in 1875 and added vaudeville turns to it. The refurbished show provided him with a vehicle that toured New England, the Midwest and the South for more than a year. He was star, company manager and coproducer, but he never saw much in the way of profits, although the show earned them.

The strain exhausted Fox. He suffered a few accidents onstage, and his mental and physical health declined. He grew erratic in his behavior onstage and off. At the same time he drew crowds on tour, rumors flared about his mental state. Soon he could no longer function dependably onstage, and he was committed to an asylum. Many reasons were offered for his madness, including general paresis, dementia and poisoning from the white lead in his face makeup. Strokes followed, and George L. Fox was moved to Cambridge, where he spent his final days among family.

Few American actors of his time left so valued a legacy. With neither film nor sound recordings to preserve his reputation, the name of George L. Fox remains familiar, due in large measure to Professor Senelick and actor Bill Irwin.

HARRY FOX

b: (Arthur Carringford) 25 May 1882, Pomona, CA—d: 20 July 1959, Los Angeles, CA

An all-around talent was much admired in show business. A versatile performer had more opportunities to get work if he could tell jokes, read lines, sing and dance. Harry Fox was all that. He picked up his skills along the route from circus to vaudeville.

So many show-business stories began as Harry's did: he ran away from home in 1897 to join the circus. he tried his hand playing semiprofessional baseball, then went to work as a song plugger for a sheet-music publisher and sang songs from the balconies of vaudeville theatres. This led to an opportunity to join a burlesque troupe that toured in and around northern California. He worked up an act with Flora and Lillian, the Millership Sisters, for vaudeville and then achieved a personal success in a musical comedy, *Mr. Frisky of Frisco* (1904), which played San Francisco and then toured.

After the earthquake of 1906 that wiped out theatres along with most businesses in San Francisco, Harry Fox headed east. Within a year or two, he had made his mark in vaudeville as a singing comedian who did a bit of dancing for a finish. Fox carried his own pianist in his act; this was a great benefit to performers who could afford it. A pianist also served as the act's music director. On Monday morning, at each new theatre, the accompanists and music directors went over the music with the orchestra leader and his musicians to ensure that the music was played at the correct tempos and the various cues were understood.

Onstage, the performer and accompanist worked out signals to follow if the singer decided to change direction in the middle of the act or add an extra chorus. Harry had several good accompanists, among whom were Harry De Costa, Lew Pollack and Harry Weber. They learned to anticipate any change of Harry's direction in performance, which was very important to a singing comedian.

Harry teamed with Beatrice Curtis around 1907. They married as well as partnered in a male-female flirtation-comedy act. They were probably split as a couple onstage and offstage by 1912, because Harry was cast without Beatrice in *The Passing Show of 1912,* a revue headlined by Trixie Friganza, Willie & Eugene Howard, Charlotte Greenwood and dance team Adelaide & Hughes. The show ran four months at the Winter Garden. Watching Adelaide & Hughes may have inspired Harry Fox to concentrate for a while on ballroom dancing in his act. If so, he and Jenny Dolly found each other at the right time.

The Dolly Sisters had fair success as youngsters in a twin-sisters act by the 1909–10 season. When in their teens, they split up their act and sought male partners for their individual dance acts. Harry met Jenny in 1914. They formed a vaudeville team and got married. The ballroom-dance craze had begun to build along with the popularity of Vernon & Irene Castle, so Harry and Jenny made exhibition dance the centerpiece of what had been Harry's comedy-singing act. Jenny Dolly's beauty became the talk of the town. She and Harry appeared in a Winter Garden extravaganza, *Honeymoon Express* (1914) and played the Palace Theatre that same year.

In later years, the claim was made that Harry introduced the fox-trot in the *Ziegfeld Follies of 1913* or the *Ziegfeld Follies of 1914.* He may have joined either edition when it opened or when it went on tour, but he was not among the opening-night principals for either show when it began its Broadway run. At the time, Fox was several storeys above the New York Theatre, performing on its rooftop, the Jardin de Danse. Some dance-history sources say that Harry did perform a dance he called the fox-trot, but it was a jerky, comic number, quite unlike the quickstep glide that became known as the fox-trot. It was the fashion of the time to name dances after animals: grizzly bear, turkey trot, monkey dance, the horse trot, the bunny hug and the kangaroo dip.

Harry was one of many acts in *Maid in America* (1915), which ran three months at the Winter Garden. The show toplined Nora Bayes, Joe Jackson and Mlle. Dazie; newcomers Blossom Seeley and Lew Brice were also on hand. On Christmas day of that year, Harry opened in *Stop! Look! Listen!,* a revue at the Globe Theatre that ran three months into 1916 with Gaby Deslys, dance team Doyle & Dixon and Joe Santley. In neither production was Harry partnered with Jenny Dolly. Jenny and her sister, Rosie, had pooled their most valuable assets—their exotic beauty and the ability to wear clothes—and formed the Dolly Sisters, an act that made them international favorites of the idle rich. Jenny belatedly divorced Harry Fox in 1921.

In 1916, Harry ventured into films for a 13-part silent film serial, *Beatrice Fairfax* (1916), in which he played a leading role as a reporter. Thereafter, however, he returned to the stage, mostly in vaudeville and occasionally on the musical stage. He was in the cast of *Oh, Look!* (1918), a musical comedy that ran two months. According to show-business historian Anthony Slide, Harry Fox and his former wife, Beatrice Curtis, reunited as a vaudeville team in the early 1920s. Curtis, however, was not with Fox when he appeared in his last two stage shows. *Round the Town* (1924) was a revue starring Julius Tannen, Irene Delroy and Jack Haley that lasted only two weeks on Broadway. *George White's Scandals* (1925), with Helen Morgan, Tom Patricola and Harry Fox, enjoyed a healthy run of five months.

Harry Fox concentrated on vaudeville during the latter half of the 1920s, and Vitaphone recorded three of Harry's vaudeville acts on film: *Harry Fox and His Six American Beauties* (1929), *Harry Fox & Bee Curtis* (1929) and *The Fox & the Bee* (1929). Curtis & Fox made one more film together, another short, *The Play Boy* (1930).

Harry's film career did not build. In 1930, he supported Ole Olsen & Chic Johnson in the film adaptation of a stage musical, *Fifty Million Frenchmen* (1931), and then he waited another three years for a film role. When it came, it was an unbilled appearance. He made a dozen films in the 14 years between 1934 and 1948. In only three films did he receive billing, one of which was his last picture, *The Easter Parade* (1948). All the other appearances were as an extra. Sensibly, however, he also worked as a technician in the airplane-manufacturing industry. He married movie star Evelyn Brent in the 1930s, and they stayed wed until his death in 1959 at the Actors' Home in Woodland Hills, California.

WILL H. FOX

b: ca. 1840—d: 1915

Active in circus, variety and vaudeville from the early 1850s through the turn of the twentieth century, Willie Fox debuted as a boy tenor in what was likely an amateur night at the Opera House in Louisville, Kentucky. Willie's singing and dancing appealed to the audience but not his parents, so Willie took "leg bail" and ran away with the Henning, Cooper & Whitby's Circus. In those days, circuses often offered a variety bill between the halves of the circus, much as minstrel shows presented specialty acts during the olio between acts.

The circus ended its season under canvas in Cincinnati, and Will Fox auditioned for H. J. Sargent, who managed the National Theatre. Will, then doing a "Dutch" song-and-dance act, made the grade and performed at the National. Sargent was one of vaudeville's pioneers. Like the impresarios who sent out minstrel and burlesque companies, Sargent packaged a bunch of acts together in a unit and toured as vaudeville starting in the early 1870s. Will Fox may have joined one of these troupes. In any case, he ended up at Boston's Old Howard Athenaeum, then under the management of John Stetson.

John D. Hopkins, owner of the Theatre Comique and other theatrical enterprises in Providence, was expanding westward across the country. Hopkins saw Fox at the Old Howard and engaged him for his theatres.

When Fox began to have problems with his singing voice, he turned to songwriting to earn a living. In the style of the time, he composed the well-remembered standard "Heart of My Heart" as well as 50 or so other tunes, including "Perhaps," "Stepping Stones of Life," "Who Knows" and "A Broken Home."

When Will H. Fox returned to vaudeville as a performer, he did so in a comedy act with a piano fitted with trick mechanics, perhaps a precursor of an act performed later by Herb Williams. As late at 1911, Will H. Fox, "World's Greatest Piano Player," performed in Percy G. Williams' vaudeville theatres.

WILLIAM FOX

b: (Wilhelm Fried) 1 January 1879, Tulchva, Hungary—d: 8 May 1952, New York, NY

William Fox is the least celebrated of vaudeville and movie pioneers, yet the name Fox is famous in film and television, and it has lasted since 1914. Fox was a granddaddy among Hollywood film factories. Among many competing systems of sound recording for movies, it was Fox Movietone that emerged triumphant.

In 1935, the 20-year-old Fox Films merged with the young pup of studios, Daryl Zanuck's independent operation Twentieth Century, and the tail wagged the dog. Twentieth Century Fox endured all the crises that bedeviled movie studios, and it launched, against great odds and amid predictions of doom, a popular television network.

Fox Film was never ambitious artistically. Neither was Fox vaudeville. William Fox was a businessman making entertainment at the lowest possible cost for audiences of little learning and modest dreams.

Working since he was a boy, William Fox held small jobs and dabbled in various enterprises until age 25, when he bought his first nickelodeon in Brooklyn. As was common with curio museums and sideshows, Fox employed a *talker* to extol the wonders of motion pictures and lure customers into his small theatre. During his first years of operation, he hired vaudeville acts to help draw customers. He parlayed his first success in Brooklyn into a string of nickelodeons.

In the early days, a nickelodeon operator bought or traded film prints; a national rental and booking system for movies was in the future. The shortage of filmed product spurred Fox in two directions. The first was adding vaudeville acts to fill out the bills at his theatres. Fox did not much care whether the acts were good as long as they were inexpensive. His second option was to make his own movies.

William Fox

As an exhibitor, Fox had several battles with Motion Picture Patents Company, as did his fellow film pioneers Carl Laemmle and Adolph Zukor. He was unwilling to submit to the broad restrictions that Thomas Edison sought to impose on anyone who used motion-picture equipment. Eventually, Edison patents failed to hold up under counterclaims by those who had made their own inventive contributions to film cameras and projectors.

In 1913, Fox became the first vaudeville magnate to become a budding film mogul. To ensure a steady supply of movies for his theatres, Fox established Box Office Attractions (BOA). The Fox theatres and booking operation became the nucleus of the Fox Motion Picture Corporation, as BOA was reorganized. Over the decades, Fox's big stars were vamp Theda Bara, vaudeville humorist Will Rogers, child star Shirley Temple, director John Ford and a succession of Fox blondes: Alice Faye, Sonja Henie, Betty Grable and Marilyn Monroe.

Fox's major rival in vaudeville and film was Marcus Loew. Both men had assembled vital small-time circuits in vaudeville. Early on, the two recognized the importance of motion pictures and regularly included movies with vaudeville at their theatres. Marcus Loew died in 1927 with a superb organization in place to run Loew's and its nascent Metro-Goldwyn-Mayer film company.

For much of his career as a movie mogul, Fox preferred not to live on the West Coast; his lieutenant in charge of the day-to-day operations at the studio was a young man, Sol Wurtzel, who started as Fox's personal secretary. William Fox lived until 1952 and saw his studio pass into the hands of Daryl Zanuck, whereas he, Fox, became an outcast in Hollywood. A 1936 bankruptcy process was part of the merger of Fox and Twentieth Century. A few years later, William Fox was tried and convicted of bribing a judge. Fox served a year in jail. When he was freed in 1943, he did not need to earn a living; he still held many movie-technology patents that allowed a comfortable life, but he was shunned by the filmland community. His worst sin was that he had gotten caught and added another scandal to Hollywood's reputation. When he died, aged 73, in Manhattan, Hollywood ignored his funeral.

WILLIAM FOX CIRCUIT

Joe Leo, William Fox's son-in-law, was the first booker for the Fox Theatres. Located in and around New York City, this small-time circuit was able to offer a total of 15 weeks to acts. Unlike the merit-plus-popularity system that governed the pay of acts in most booking agencies, the acts that Fox hired were paid set fees regardless of worth. A single got $20 per week, $40 for a double, $60 for a trio, $80 for a quartet. Any additional people in the act warranted only an extra $5. The first Fox theatres included the Dewey, Gotham, Nemo, Star and Family in Manhattan and the Comedy and Folly in Brooklyn.

Fox and Leo ran the operation from their Dewey Theatre office across from Tony Pastor's Fourteenth Street Theatre. Fox was not highly regarded due to his business practices, and he was odd man out for a time with the United Booking Office. After Joe Leo, Bill Fox relied upon a Mr. Norris, then Edgar Allen, and, finally, Jack Loeb to handle bookings. Fox later acquired several small circuits, including that owned by Sylvester Z. Poli. By 1914, Fox was busy with his East and West Coast film studios. He manufactured Theda Bara, the first movie vamp, out of a plump 30-year-old Theodosia Goodman and set her loose in a profitable series of potboilers that financed the building of what became one of filmland's largest and most enduring studios.

EDDIE FOY

b: (Edwin Fitzgerald) 9 March 1856, New York, NY—d: 16 February 1928, Kansas City, MO

Greenwich Village in Lower Manhattan was a slum when Eddie Fitzgerald was born. Families were crammed into squalid, often windowless rooms. It was, however, several steps up in livability and safety from the Bowery, where the Fitzgerald family first lived after they arrived from Ireland in 1855. Like tens of thousands of other men and women, Richard, Mary and their firstborn, daughter Catherine, fled the starvation that was the fate of many who remained in the Old Country.

Conditions in New York City proved a bit better than in Ireland. The local Roman Catholic church referred a newcomer to the local political office of the city's Democratic Party. The bosses tried to find jobs for as many men as possible; in turn, one was expected to vote "early and often" to ensure that their benefactors held on to power. If an immigrant fellow did not find a job, there was the option of stealing. In Ireland, there had been nothing left to steal.

Most of the time, the Fitzgeralds had a roof over their heads, clothes on their backs and some food on the table until Richard went mad in 1862. He was confined to an insane asylum, where that same year he died from paresis, the advanced state of syphilis. He left destitute his wife and four children, ranging in age from 11 to 3.

Eddie Foy

A relative in Chicago took pity on the Fitzgeralds and staked them to railway fares to relocate. Once there, Mrs. Fitzgerald and her two daughters found work at meager wages in sweatshops, and Eddie shined shoes and sold newspapers. There was no time for schooling. Like most paperboys, Eddie picked up dancing.

It helped fill the time between potential customers and was a way to compete with other boys, and occasionally a few dance steps earned a tip.

Some of the big cities had newsboys' foundations. Generally endowed by rich benefactors, a foundation converted a building into a haven for newsboys, many of whom had no other place to live. The facility provided a place where boys could clean up, get a decent basic meal and find a safe place to sleep. Some facilities included a gymnasium and auditorium where boys climbed ropes or tossed a medicine ball or Indian clubs. When the hall was not used for sport and exercise, the boys put on talent shows.

Supervision was strict in all matters, and some boys preferred life on the streets. Eddie, however, enjoyed the regular meals, which were not always available at home because his mother and older sisters were busy working in factories. The talent nights gave Eddie his first taste of performing, and he decided the stage was preferable to bootblacking and hawking newspapers.

Armond Fields, Eddie Foy's biographer, has written a stirring account of Eddie's experiences as a boy confronted with the Manhattan race riots over conscription for the Civil War and the great fire in Chicago that left the Fitzgeralds with nothing but the clothes on their backs. Life got better when his mother was engaged to look after President Abraham Lincoln's widow, whose mental health had caused a decline in her physical well-being.

Eddie, then 16, decided that dancing could save him from a life of drudgery. He and Jack Finnegan, a friend his own age, decided to form a double act in 1872. Although they patterned themselves after other Irish acts they had watched in variety, they adopted less obviously Irish names for the stage and sought booking as Edwards & Foy. Why they did this was a mystery. They wore the costumes of stage Irishmen: whiskers, plug hats and knee britches and warbled Irish songs and danced Irish jigs and clogs.

Playing beer halls in Chicago, Edwards & Foy stepped onto the lowest rung of variety entertainment. The act did not last long. Edwards fought with a manager, and Foy learned how hard it was to work as a solo act. Eddie teamed up with Ben Collins, another friend with some show experience.

Live entertainment in an 1870s beer hall functioned much like a television set in a twenty-first-century barroom: it fostered a sense of shared community and kept the tavern's patrons drinking. Customers could either watch the entertainment or not, and there was no need to keep their voice down in deference to the act or other customers. There was a limit to how many times even drunks would watch the same thing, and it was easier to change acts than for the current act to continually conjure up new jokes or write parodic ditties. Management generally forced the issue, so Collins & Foy spent as much time at liberty as engaged.

When they got the chance to join a small circus, they took it for the promise of steady work. Traveling with a circus around the Midwest was probably exciting for two boys in their midteens. Certainly, they learned a lot. Ben and Eddie did their acrobatic act, mixed with circus folk and learned circus lingo and rules. They helped to set up and strike the circus every day during a two-month series of one-nighters, sold programmes to customers, and did whatever chores needed to be done that fell to two new recruits. The tour ended when the circus owner bailed out of his struggling venture and took the box-office receipts with him.

Stranded, the circus folk devised various strategies to work their ways home. A more experienced man, one with whom they had grown friendly, suggested to Eddie and Ben that they throw in with him. His proposition was to buy a horse and wagon to tour the northern backcountry of Illinois with a three-man minstrel show, with Eddie and Ben as end men and their new partner as interlocutor. Their itinerary was planned so that eventually they would get back to Chicago.

It seemed the only sensible solution to their dilemma, and Eddie liked the prospect of being a blackface minstrel man, but it took the boys longer to work their way home than they had spent on the road with the circus. The trio barely earned enough to keep body and spirit together, but Eddie got the chance to experiment with song, dance and comedy.

They arrived in Chicago in 1876, desperate for money and with no wardrobe to dress a variety act. Because they had experience in show business, Ben and Eddie wangled jobs as supers (supernumeraries) at McVickers Theatre, a well-equipped and prestigious establishment that played host to important stage stars. Supers were the bit players of the stage. They were spear-carriers, milled about in crowd scenes and got the occasional one-line part ("All hail to the king!"). The pay was small change, but McVickers provided Ben and Eddie with the chance to watch Edwin Booth and Joseph Jefferson, two great actors of the age who appeared at McVickers while the boys worked there.

Booth was a supreme classical actor, a tragedian, and Jefferson, a comedian, was as popular an actor as existed in America. Eddie and Ben played in a repertory of Shakespeare productions with Booth and in *Rip Van Winkle,* Joe Jefferson's signature piece. For intelligent and watchful tyros, the experience was a master class in stagecraft and acting.

Eddie Foy had turned 21, and Ben was about the same age. Both were anxious to build careers but had different goals. They parted friends after their season at McVickers. Ben went into minstrelsy; Eddie turned to variety with another partner. It did not work out for either of them. Eddie persuaded Ben to create a variety act together, and they played the small time in small towns. Ben again went back to minstrelsy, whereas Eddie tried his luck as a single. He found another partner in Jim Thompson, a handsome singer and dancer. They stuck together from 1878 through 1883 and shared many adventures.

When Foy & Thompson teamed, west of the Mississippi River was still the American frontier. While performing in Chicago, they received a generous offer to play St. Louis and Kansas City, Missouri. The western part of Missouri was frontier land. Foy & Thompson were successful in Missouri and accepted an offer to play Dodge City, Kansas. They found a rapidly growing, crowded, slapped-up town of wooden shacks and sidewalks and a rutted main thoroughfare that turned to mud when it rained; it was a stockyards crossroads of cattle and railroad. There they met Bat Masterson, Doc Holliday and Wyatt Earp. The local theatre was a saloon where liquor, gambling, prostitution and fights competed with the stage. Everyone wore guns except Eddie and Jim.

Eddie and Jim sang lively tunes and danced acrobatic versions of the clogs and jigs familiar to the cowboys. Their tumbling degenerated into knockabout clowning, and the cowboys and town folks loved the act. Even old jokes worked, especially if they were slightly blue. Foy & Thompson worked about ten weeks there before moving farther into lawless land in Leadville and Denver, Colorado. Inviting them to return each season, the three frontier cities kept Foy & Thomson booked and well paid from 1878 into 1881.

Eddie and his partner sometimes found themselves on a bill with the Howland Sisters, a dance act. Eddie and Rose Howland took a fancy to each other. They married in 1879, and Rose Howland traveled with Foy & Thompson and played the same dates but as a solo act. Traveling by train was bad enough; one either had closed windows and stifling heat or open windows and soot that permeated hair, face and clothing. Traveling by wagon was worse and often perilous. Impassable roads in bad weather required performing three or four months in a single town.

Thompson met and married an actor, Millie Thomas, so when Eddie and Jim accepted an offer to go to San Francisco to play in a stock company, the four of them went to California together. Millie and Rose were hired as well. They alternated in melodramas, comedies and occasional variety shows at the Adelphi Theatre during the season, then joined Emerson's California Minstrels. Billy Emerson, the owner and star, had long been Eddie's idol, so Eddie jumped at the chance, and the others followed.

Late in 1882, the four of them left Emerson to head back east. It was not the best-conceived plan or route that took them through Virginia City, Nevada; Butte, Montana; and Chicago en route to Philadelphia, where they joined Carncross' Minstrels after discovering that Foy & Thompson's big-name status in the Wild West did not open doors in the East. Thompson headed back west. Eddie and Rose stayed in Chicago because she was pregnant.

Eddie worked his way up in the Carncross' Minstrels troupe during the 1882–83 season and returned during the summer layoff to his family in Chicago. His wife was faring poorly. Rose and their baby died at childbirth. Eddie was late reporting to Carncross, and he had not the heart to perform so he left for a few months. When he came back to Carncross' Minstrels, he stayed a couple more seasons.

From 1885 to 1888, Foy spread his performing wings, acting in farce with several touring troupes. In 1887, he was back in San Francisco, where he and Lola Sefton spent time together. Both had careers, and they never married as far as researchers can discover, but they remained a couple for nearly ten years until her death in 1894. Lola and Eddie had a daughter. They named her Catherine, perhaps after Eddie's oldest sister, but the girl was raised by Eddie's other sister, Mary.

In 1888, Foy joined David Henderson's company and became its leading comedian. Over a period from early 1888 through the 1893–94 season, Henderson produced a series of splendidly mounted extravaganzas based on fabled adventures: *The Crystal Palace* (1888–89), *Bluebeard, Jr.* (1889–90), *Sinbad* (1891–92) and *Ali Baba* (1892–94). Each show played a Chicago season and then toured.

In 1894, Eddie went into the managerial business as the star of his own company. *Off the Earth* toured off and on from 1894 to 1897 but was a long time putting any money in Foy's pockets. Eddie's second show, *Little Robinson Crusoe* (1895), had trouble from start to finish. *The Strange Adventures of Miss Brown* (1896) fared no better. Eddie Foy gave up his company.

Foy had waited two years after Lola's death before marrying his company's lead dancer, Madeline Morando. She gave birth to Bryan Foy on 8 December 1896. Eddie took a show, *In Gay New York* (1898–1900), on the road for Klaw & Erlanger, the two instigators of the Theatrical Trust. It was steady work but under harsh conditions with untrustworthy employers. Eddie had steady work. During the run, Madeline gave birth to their second child, Charles, on 12 June 1898.

Eddie moved the family from Chicago to New York City because the latter city had become the center of show business. From 1899 through 1903, Foy appeared in a half-dozen shows: *In Gay New York* (1898), *Hotel Topsy Turvy* (1899), *An Arabian Girl and Forty Thieves* (later in 1899, a flop), *A Night in Town* (1900), *The Strollers* (1901–02) and *The Wild Rose* (1902–03).

The 1903–04 season was memorable—and not for Eddie Foy alone. During a tour in *Mr. Bluebeard* (1903), Eddie and the rest of the company inaugurated the new Iroquois Theatre in Chicago. On 30 December 1903, the backstage caught fire. Eddie came to the stage after most of the crew, cast and several musicians had fled; Eddie walked to the front of the stage and calmly pled with the audience to leave calmly and orderly. Panic caused the deaths of 600 of the 1,700 theatre patrons. Eddie escaped at the last minute through a sewer. His calm courage won him greater fame and the love of American theatre audiences.

Foy needed work. He had never been one to save money, although he earned a lot. He made his first venture into vaudeville in February 1904. He was 48. In the 1870s and 1880s, Eddie had performed in variety, but vaudeville was becoming more widespread and, in a few years, a more tightly controlled operation.

From 1904 through 1911, Eddie spent part of nearly every season in vaudeville, alternating with work in travesties and musical comedies. Each show opened outside New York and worked out the kinks before coming to Broadway for a few months' run. Then it went on tour, sometimes for two seasons. The Shuberts offered Eddie musical comedies, and E. F. Albee proposed eight to ten weeks at a time of big-time vaudeville bookings on Keith time. A vaudeville salary was invariably higher than that earned in musical comedy.

Eddie Foy still costumed for the stage much as theatre clowns had a half century earlier. He wore whiteface or something close to it, usually a small hat cocked preposterously to one side of his head, and leggings or pantaloons. He frequently clowned in drag. His makeup emphasized his U-shaped mouth, and he spoke out of the side of his mouth in a rasp. He worked with a lot of props.

For the Shuberts, Eddie starred in the musical farces *Piff! Paff! Pouf!* (1904–05), *The Earl and the Girl* (1905–07) and *The Orchid* (1907–08). Eddie played vaudeville whenever there was an open spot in his schedule, usually between musical shows or during the late spring and early summer after his show had closed for the season. In vaudeville, he clowned in sketches and performed his impersonations. At the end of the 1907–08 Broadway season, Foy returned to vaudeville with a burlesque of *Hamlet*'s grave digger. It was good publicity for his next Shubert show, *Mr. Hamlet on Broadway* (1908–10). He did just enough straight to impress the critics, but most of Eddie's acting of the role was a spoof.

Eddie bought a 20-room house on nine acres of land in New Rochelle, just north of New York City. In addition to Eddie, Madeline and their seven children, his

Eddie Foy

daughter Catherine, who had been raised by Eddie's sister Mary, lived there, too. The house was large enough to accommodate a steady flow of visiting relatives. Foy worked the situation into his act and press interviews. One of several jokes was that the population of New Rochelle doubled when the Foys became residents.

Madeline, who had birthed six children and suffered three miscarriages, was warned not to get pregnant again. She was quite ill, as she had been during earlier pregnancies, when she gave birth to their last child, Irving, on 26 August 1908.

Eddie Foy's last stage shows in the 1910s included a revue, *Up and Down Broadway* (1910–11), and two musicals, *The Pet of the Petticoats* (1911, a flop) and *Over the River* (1911–13). *Over the River* marked the first time that Eddie put his seven children by Madeline onto a stage. Catherine, his daughter with Lola, did not appear onstage.

In 1912, Eddie Foy and the Seven Little Foys made their debut in vaudeville in an act that, for its novelty, overshadowed, to a degree, all of Eddie's other triumphs. Irving, the youngest Foy, was four and able to take direction. Bryan, the oldest, was 16. Eddie took the first half of the act himself, singing and clowning, dressed as various characters. In the second part, six of the Foys marched onstage in a line, and Eddie followed carrying a carpetbag, out of which little Irving jumped. Eddie introduced each son or

Eddie Foy and the Seven Little Foys

daughter in turn, and each performed a few dance steps and bowed. Eddie and his brood performed a couple of numbers together and then marched offstage to great applause. Predictably, the Gerry Society was on hand to demand that the police arrest Eddie for exploiting his children. Eddie and the Gerrys battled it out until his retirement.

His act with the Seven Little Foys came at the right time in Eddie's career. He was nearing 60, and, despite his scoring well with several musicals since 1910, the stage was changing and he was not. By the early 1920s, the new crop of Tin Pan Alley composers like Irving Berlin were influenced by ragtime and early jazz. Whiz-bang black shows had sped up the pace of white musical comedies and revues, even vaudeville. Comedians in vaudeville were emphasizing verbal humor and dressing in suits. Physical comedy enjoyed greater scope in movies, from the Keystone Kops in the mid 1910s to the early 1920s when Roscoe "Fatty" Arbuckle, Charlie Chaplin, Harold Lloyd and Buster Keaton were doing stunts that involved automobile chases or hanging from cliffs and skyscrapers.

Eddie Foy had appeared as himself in two shorts for Mack Sennett: *Actors' Fund Field Day* (1910) and *A Favorite Fool* (1915). In this last flicker, he was supported by all Seven Little Foys. Foy got so disgusted with Sennett's studio's slam-bang style that he walked out of his contract after this picture but returned four years later, perhaps as a patriotic gesture, to play a character in Mack Sennett's six-reeler *Yankee Doodle in Berlin* (1919). Female impersonator Bothwell Browne played Captain Bob White, who disguises himself as a woman to penetrate enemy lines. Most of Sennett's current roster and a few alumni were on hand to enliven this propaganda comedy: Ford Sterling (as the Kaiser), Bert Roach, Ben Turpin, Charlie Murray, Marie Prevost, Chester Conklin, Heinie Conklin, Phyllis Haver, James Finlayson, Harry Gribbon, Edgar Kennedy and Tom Kennedy.

In 1918, Eddie's wife, Madeline, died of pneumonia after a prolonged illness. Eddie and his children kept the act going. By this time, it did not need to coast on novelty. The Seven Little Foys were talented, and they had their own specialties. After Madeline's death, however, Bryan left the act to join the navy. When he returned, he went into the business end of the motion-picture industry. The act without Bryan was renamed Eddie Foy and the Younger Foys.

By 1924, Eddie Foy had worked a half century on the stage. He retired and married again. He was coaxed back to vaudeville in 1927 to act in a nostalgic sketch as an old doorman of a theatre who reminisces about the old times. Eddie sang, did a few impressions and danced. His heart had been weakened by a few mild attacks. He suffered a fatal heart attack while playing a vaudeville date in Kansas City. A beloved man as well as star, Eddie was given a grand send-off by friends and the press.

Eddie's oldest daughter, Catherine, never appeared in the family act. She had been adopted as a baby by his sister, Mary Fitzgerald Doyle. Catherine left the New Rochelle home at 18 in 1912 to move on her own to New York City. Bryan Foy became a Hollywood producer and died on 20 April 1977 in Los Angeles, California. Charlie ran a nightclub near Hollywood and was a character actor in movies. He died on 22 August 1984 in Los Angeles, California. Richard followed Bryan into movies but ended up in Dallas, Texas, where he died on 4 April 1947. Mary left show business; she died on 13 December 1987 in Los Angeles, California. Madeline made a few movies but left show business as well and died on 5 July 1988 in Los Angeles, California.

Eddie Foy Jr. found his own success in the theatre. On Broadway, Eddie was featured in *Show Girl* (1929), starred in Jerome Kern's *The Cat and the Fiddle* (1931), the 1945 revival of Victor Herbert's *The Red Mill,* and *Rumple* (1957). He was a standout in the

Broadway musical comedy *The Pajama Game* (1954) and played his same role for the film version in 1957. Eddie Foy Jr. made 60 movies, including *Yankee Doodle Dandy* (1942), in which he portrayed his father, and the movie version of *Bells Are Ringing* (1960). He appeared many times on television. Eddie Foy Jr. died in Hollywood on 15 July 1983.

Irving Foy, the baby, moved in 1944 to New Mexico, where he ran movie theatres. He lived to be 95 and died on 20 April 2003 in Albuquerque, New Mexico.

IRENE FRANKLIN

b: 13 July 1876, St. Louis, MO—d: 16 June 1941, Englewood, NJ

Burton Green

b: ca. 1870—d: 17 November 1922, Mount Vernon, NY

Irene Franklin's parents were actors in a theatrical stock company. They carried their six-month-old baby girl onto the stage as part of the action in a melodrama, *Hearts of Oak.* Having conquered legitimate drama, baby Irene went into retirement until age three, when she emerged to perform a song-and-dance routine.

When her mother decided, around 1890, to visit her family in Australia, she took Irene with her as well as a younger daughter. In Australia, Irene played variety engagements, but the journey was marred by the death of her mother. Presumably, the family took care of funeral arrangements and the care of Irene's young sister. Irene returned to her father in the USA. By the time she returned, she discovered that he, too, had died.

Irene tried to find work on her own. According to show-business historian Anthony Slide, she appeared in London variety theatres in 1894, but when she came back to the USA she struggled along. Her most frequent source of work was from Tony Pastor, who used her to fill in when he needed a disappointment act. Reportedly, Irene's weekly salary from any manager did not exceed $25 until she teamed up with Burt Green.

It was Pastor who diagnosed her problem. Irene was a talented actor-singer-comedian, but she had not yet harnessed her gifts to make an effective presentation. Pastor hooked her up with Green, who had been the piano accompanist at Tony Pastor's Fourteenth Street Theatre until a few years earlier. Green was as popular with the audience as the acts. He provided enough sound to cover the defects or errors of marginal acts and was able to anticipate truly good singers, who appreciated Burt's improvisations. Green spurred many a singer to extemporize and give their best performances at Tony Pastor's.

Irene Franklin

Burton Green began his adult working life as a hardware salesman, but his talent as a self-taught musician allowed him to turn professional. He had married Helen van Campen, a columnist for New York City's *Morning Telegraph,* and taken up selling advertising in the same newspaper to better support their family of eventually two children.

Burton watched Irene work onstage, liked her and agreed to help her with her act. They wrote special material together that suited her better than the Tin Pan Alley product because she was less a singer than an impressionist. Irene was quite taken with Burt and wanted him to take over her career and become her stage partner; she was also in love with him. Burt's wife, a liberated soul if ever there was one in the 1900s, believed that spouses owed little to each other but honesty, kindness and love. A daredevil journalist, she was often the only woman on adventures everywhere from the Artic to the jungles. Helen admired and liked Irene, and when she realized that her husband was in love with Irene, she promised him a divorce if he married

Irene. Helen turned the romantic triangle into a magazine article.

Elsie Janis and Cissy Loftus impersonated famous people of the stage in their acts, but Irene presented a gallery of ordinary folks: little girls ("I'm Nobody's Baby Now" and "Somebody Ought to Put the Old Man Wise"), farm wives, chambermaids, spinsters ("If I Don't Lock My Father Up, It's the Old Maid's Home for Me"), old ladies, waitresses, suffragettes ("The Woman Policeman"), infatuated teenagers ("At the Dasant") and schoolteachers.

Irene and (primarily) Burt wrote all her material: the songs and short monologues that were character sketches. Irene used her voice, expression and posture to suggest each one. The 1907 song "Expression" was a tour de force in which she used her face to present a range of emotions. Often, these character studies were enhanced only by the change of a single article of clothing, such as a shawl, a hat or an apron. Sometimes, especially when she impersonated one of her little girls, she appeared in full costume, like rompers or a nightgown. When she left the stage for a full costume change, Burt performed a solo at the piano. Other times, she forwent any change in garb and simply used her hair. She had waist-length red hair that, while onstage chatting with the audience, she deftly rolled up into a bun, gathered it into a curly top, pulled it forward over both shoulders like a schoolgirl, or swayed it seductively when she did a naughty number, as she did during Prohibition when people carried concealed liquor flasks, "What Have You Got on Your Hip? You Don't Seem to Bulge Where a Gentleman Ought To."

Her crowning glory became the subject of her theme song, "Redhead." It told the story of a little girl who is teased by being called "carrot top," "copperhead" and other names. She was often affectionately referred to as "the Redhead," and there is no indication she minded.

Irene Franklin became a vaudeville headliner. She claimed it was due to Burt's songs and guidance. (He was a superb musician, and the orchestrations he made of her songs enhanced her act.) Burt, in turn, told interviewers that he was "just part of the scenery of Irene Franklin's act."

The singing *single women* of vaudeville worked very hard and determinedly to reach the top of their profession. They guarded their status as vaudeville's royalty. Most were not without an ego and a combative spirit. When a prerogative of a headliner, such as top billing, placement on the bill, or star dressing room, was at risk, that hard-won privilege was defended with a flash of temperament and the demand that every condition of her contract be honored. Instead, Irene Franklin was known for her courtesy, professionalism and willingness to yield primacy to benefit the bill. Managers and other acts loved her for that.

Irene Franklin sings
"I've got the mumps"
for the Edison
The mumps are "catching," but not so catching as this song, not so catching as Irene Franklin nor so contagious as the pleasure which she brings to your home on the
EDISON PHONOGRAPH
Irene Franklin, newest and brightest headliner on the vaudeville circuit, joins the great array of stars already making records for the Edison—Lauder, Stella Mayhew, Marie Dressler, Marshall P. Wilder, Digby Bell, Sophie Tucker, Anna Chandler, Billy Murray and Ada Jones, of vaudeville fame; Slezak, Carmen Melis, Constantino, Martin, Marguerita Sylva, Carl Jorn and Marie Delna, of the Grand Opera stage; Victor Herbert's Orchestra, Sousa's Band and innumerable others almost equally famous.
Irene Franklin and all these other great stars are at your command *whenever you want them* when you own an Edison Phonograph.
Hear the new Irene Franklin Records at your Edison dealer's today:
"I've got the mumps," "The talkative waitress," and "I want to be a janitor's child." These are Amberol Records—which means *all* the verses of each song, no cutting, no hurrying.
Thomas A. Edison, Inc.
11 Lakeside Avenue Orange, N. J.

Irene Franklin

Irene was primarily a vaudeville performer, and her first appearance at the Palace was during its second season, 1914. She was most effective in intimate contact with her audience. Nonetheless, she appeared in several stage shows. She had a small role in *The Orchid* (1907), her first Broadway show. By the time she again appeared on Broadway, Burt Green was in the shows with her: *The Summer Widowers* (1910) ran 140 performances, *Hands Up* (1915) ran seven weeks, and *The Passing Show of 1917* played 25 weeks before touring.

Burt suffered from Bright's disease, so he was unable to accompany Irene in *The Greenwich Village Follies* (1921) during the 21 weeks it ran. The malady claimed him in 1922. He was at least in his late 40s. Irene was devastated. It was not the loss of a beloved husband alone; it struck at her confidence because she always believed that Burt was responsible for her success.

The momentum of her career plus her talent and experience kept her a star of big-time vaudeville and the musical-comedy stage for the remainder of the 1920s. She tried several pianists but failed to find one that was as sympathetic an accompanist and as true a partner as Burton Green had been. Irene, a great favorite with Palace Theatre management as well as audiences, played there in 1925, 1926, 1929 and 1931. Her new accompanist on those Palace engagements was Jerry

Jarnagin, who proved the best of those who followed Green. Irene eventually married Jarnagin.

Irene's final Broadway show, *Sweet Adeline* (1929–30), provided her with her longest run, yet she was no longer the lead but a featured player. While in the show, Irene made her first sound movies for Vitaphone. She performed her vaudeville act for a one-reel sound short, *The American Comedienne* (1929), in which Irene was accompanied on piano by her second husband, Jerry Jarnagin, and also made *Those Were the Days* (1929). All told, Irene made 30 feature films between 1933 and 1939, none of which did anything for her career other than pay the rent.

Irene was in straightened circumstances for the last five or so years of her life, and there were several mysteries about her. Why did her second husband, Jerry Jarnagin, shoot himself fatally on an evening in 1934 when they had guests for dinner? What had happened to her money? Irene had earned a lot of money on Broadway and as a vaudeville headliner for 30 years. Was she estranged from her children? Irene raised her own two children with Burt Green plus his children from his earlier marriage to Helen Van Capen, yet Irene lived the final years of her life alone in poverty. She had worked for nearly a decade in the film industry, but instead of living at the Motion Picture Home in Woodland Hills, California, she went east to New Jersey, where she spent her last few years at the Actors' Fund Home in Englewood.

Totally forgotten by the public, the press and, it seems, her fellow vaudevillians, Irene sent a plaintive letter to New York gossip columnist and radio commentator Louis Sobol that read: "Irene Franklin speaking. Perhaps you remember her. She was born on July 13, Friday, and her name is spelled with 13 letters. Now another Friday, June 13, is near. Do you think anyone remembers or cares?"

Less than a week later, a cerebral hemorrhage claimed Irene Franklin.

FREAK ACT

In sideshows, the term *freak* had a derisive meaning. In vaudeville, it was also a belittling label but one that addressed a lack of talent and skill rather than physiognomic differences.

Although there were vaudevillians coarse and callous enough to use the word *freak* to refer to a person with a physical deformity, a *freak act* in vaudeville described people outside showbiz who had neither talent nor skill but were added to the bill solely because of their temporary notoriety.

The standard acts of vaudeville—professionals who took their work and reputations seriously—gave *freak acts* a collective cold shoulder. These included a man who had walked the breadth of the USA, or wrestlers, bicycle racers, Arctic explorers or the comely cause, like Evelyn Nesbit, of a murder. Probably because so many vaudevillians were fans, baseball players who appeared in vaudeville were exempt from the usual snubbing, although theirs, too, technically were *freak acts.*

As a freak attraction, Carrie Nation was among the best. An anti-alcoholic-beverage crusader, she took the opportunities that vaudeville bookings provided to rail against booze. Thrilling her audiences if not convincing them, she performed a sketch in which she demolished a barroom to the cheers of "wets" and "drys" alike.

In some cases, an act initially booked for its curiosity value proved to have lasting entertainment value. Hadji Ali was a regurgitator who swallowed a great quantity of water followed by kerosene. He emitted the kerosene, thoroughly spraying a model castle, and then put a match to it. After it flamed fully, he doused it with a continuous stream of the water he had ingested.

In some cases, like musicians Violet and Daisy Hilton, who were conjoined twins, the people in the act had considerable talent or were remarkable, like the accomplished deaf, dumb and blind Helen Keller for overcoming daunting obstacles to lead exemplary lives. Both Ms. Keller and the Hilton Sisters became standard acts and played vaudeville for many seasons.

Certain vaudeville managers, Willie Hammerstein most famously among them, reveled in the publicity and increased box-office receipts triggered by the latest sensation he had booked for the Victoria Theatre. One had to capitalize so quickly on notoriety that it was impossible to put together anything approaching an entertaining act. Willie Hammerstein sought people who had garnered a lot of recent news—a celebrated divorce case, a murder trial, a daring rescue from a disaster or a feat of endurance—any of whom ensured a large turnout of sensation seekers and the curiously morbid until the next titillating scandal. It was the vaudeville equivalent of *sweeps weeks* for television.

There were many people who were willing to exploit their own foolishness, cupidity or callousness in the spotlight. Most *freak acts* were flashes in the pan that lacked personality and ultimately disappointed the public by failing to repeat their crime onstage. The story is told of the man who offered to commit suicide on the Victoria stage for money. Obviously, he had not thought it through because Willie stumped him with two questions: How was he going to collect his fee, and, if his act was a success, what was he going to do for the second show?

Fifty years before it dawned on Andy Warhol that even the most ordinary of mortals could win 15 minutes of fame, Willie Hammerstein was doing his best to prove it and exploit each sensation's shelf life into at least a week's full house.

FREE-AND-EASIES

Located in the gamier quarters of cities, *free-and-easies* offered both liquor and entertainments and attracted a no-questions-asked kind of custom. These places were known by many names, including impressive terms like *concert halls* and *music-halls* and those more derogatory like *honky-tonks, dives* and *joints.* What differentiated the free-and-easies from melodeons and music-halls was free entertainment.

To a casual observer, the more aggressive free-and-easies might be mistaken for dime museums or curio halls. Obscuring the first-floor windows and tenting above the cellar entrance were canvas banners depicting the delights below. At the entrance, *talkers* called out to passersby, "Free to all, the great Evans and Block Concert Company" (or some such real or similarly fictitious troupe). "Free and easy every evening."

The show was free and the standards easy, but the proprietor's aim was to divest his customers of as much cash as possible through the sale of liquor. An incautious customer could rack up quite a bill if he did not resist the blandishments of flirtatious serving girls.

Free-and-easies were alike in structural matters; generally, they were long, narrow cellars in buildings that housed rooming houses or businesses on the upper floors. Other than that, they varied according to their proprietor's aims or the customers' preferences: cheap prices, anonymity, gaudiness of decor, conviviality of company, comeliness of waiter girls or the talent on the stage.

Free-and-easies and their like were an outgrowth of the centuries-old taverns. To keep their customers drinking more and longer, the saloon keepers offered various attractions like performers, gambling, hostesses and special rooms where a gent could find some privacy. The hostesses got a commission on every drink that they encouraged the johns to buy.

FREEZE

Extrapolated from belly dancing, the *freeze* is an overall shiver of the body. The dancer stands in place, without moving arms, torso or legs, and the entire body begins to quiver very rapidly. The freeze is distinct from the shimmy or shimmy-sha-wobble.

LEOPOLDO FREGOLI

b: 2 June 1867, Rome, Italy—d: 1936, Viareggio, Italy

There is no neat divide separating the magician, the actor and the quick-change artist. To be effective, the quick-change performer must be both actor and illusionist as well as master of whatever other skills his impersonations demand.

Leopoldo Fregoli brought many talents to the stage. He played several musical instruments, sang, danced, acted, juggled, performed magic, acrobatics and ventriloquism, and he was the fastest quick-change actor of his era. Fregoli performed in a surreal whirl, seeming to arrive onstage as a new character before he had departed as the old. His reputation was built as much on his ability as an actor capable of giving distinct personalities to his many characters as it was on his dazzling technical proficiency. Contemporary chroniclers described several portions of his various acts.

He entered the stage singing the tenor half of an operatic duet. Seemingly without pause or transition, he metamorphosed into the soprano and sang her part. Then, as he exited as the singer, he entered as an old man and headed for the piano, where he played a few bars of music until another soprano, a hefty and matronly soul, entered singing to the piano music. By the time the audience comprehended that the pianist was now a dummy, the stout soprano disappeared, and the very picture of a Victorian magician came onstage, formally attired, sporting a Vandyke beard and moustache. He showered the stage with suddenly appearing flowers as he crossed the stage and exited as, in wig and tutu, he danced on from the opposite wing.

Once upon a time, the quick-change actor was a marvel of the vaudeville stage. There were many in Europe, of whom Fregoli was paramount, and more than a few in America, like Charles T. Aldrich and Owen McGiveney. Some preferred to be billed as protean actors, which implied a dramatic skill beyond the mere ability to change quickly from one costume to another. That Fregoli was supreme in his field was the choice of his name in 1927 by French psychiatrists Courbon and Fail to describe a rare disorder. The *syndrome d'illusion de Fregoli* described a patient who held a delusional belief that one or more persons, strangers or otherwise, are actually other persons—a family member, friend or enemy—in disguise. The patient's assumption was that one set of familiar or famous persons was subsumed by other people with whom the patient came into contact.

Fregoli's first American performance probably was for Oscar Hammerstein (the first) at the Olympia Theatre in 1896, a few years before Oscar was forced to sell the combination theatre, roof garden, billiard parlor and café. Fregoli was a summertime attraction on the roof garden. Hammerstein brought Fregoli back to the USA in 1906 to perform his act at the Victoria. Joe Laurie Jr. reported that Fregoli proved such a substantial draw that "he put the roof on the Manhattan" Opera House that Hammerstein was erecting that year.

Essaying 60 characters in 60 minutes, Fregoli occupied the second half of a vaudeville bill. As in all illusionist and transformationalist acts, the crew and Fregoli's assistants needed every minute of the intermission to set up the act. It took as long to strike the stage, so no act could follow Fregoli unless it played *in one*.

A film pioneer, Fregoli made at least a dozen experimental movies between 1897 and 1899, at the same time as Louis Lumière and Georges Méliès. Fregoli sometimes offered, at the end of his hour-long variety and vaudeville appearances, a one- or two-reel film (Fregoligraf). Italian film historian Carlo Montanaro suggests that Fregoli the filmmaker was avant-garde, surrealist or futurist. Leopoldo Fregoli expanded the storytelling power of film by interspersing scenes of his assistants helping him change costume along with the act itself as seen from the stage. Other transformational effects included surreal trick scenes in which objects changed shape and color in his hands. Fregoli was among the first to realize that the medium of film allowed far greater artistic possibilities than simply recording events without intervention.

In addition to numerous appearances in vaudeville, variety and music-hall, Fregoli ventured into other performance forms. Among his most ambitious achievements was playing and singing all the roles in a 90-minute version of Gounod's opera *Faust*.

All transformationalists or quick-change actors required split-second precision backstage, where assistants helped them shed and put on costumes. Sometimes, the assistants doubled for them onstage, switching places with the actor so that he appeared to remain onstage at the same time he was entering in another guise. This was part of the illusionist's art of making the audience believe it was seeing something other than what was occurring.

Leopoldo Fregoli wrote a memoir, *Fregoli Told by Fregoli,* published in the year of his death, 1936, reflecting that "the art is life, and the life, transformation." He had this sentiment etched in stone as well, at the cemetery in the village of Viareggio, where Fregoli was interred. His epitaph reads: "Here Leopoldo Fregoli carried out his last transformation."

THE FRENCH TWIN SISTERS

Minnie French

Helen French

In an era fitfully in transition from rough variety to either vaudeville or burlesque, the French Twin Sisters were known as a class act. They were active during the 1880s and 1890s, and most of their careers were spent in vaudeville and musical comedy. The girls harmonized (one soprano, the other alto), and they danced with charm and grace. Their reputation as a class act notwithstanding, they joined Evans & Hooey in a bawdy variety act based on a notorious afterpiece called "The Book Agent," which was somewhat cleaned up to become a vaudeville act, "Book Agent." In turn, the act was expanded (and further refined) into a long-running musical farce, *A Parlor Match.* The sisters also married Evans & Hooey: Minnie and Charley Evans and Helen and Bill Hooey.

TRIXIE FRIGANZA

b: (Delia O'Callahan) 29 November 1870, Grenola, KS—d: 27 February 1955, Flintridge, CA

According to a Friganza-O'Callahan family historian, Franklin G. Jensen, Trixie and her family had moved from her birthplace in Kansas to Anna, Illinois, by 1876. The family then relocated by the mid-1880s to Cincinnati, Ohio, where Trixie's father worked for a railroad company. Legend had it that Trixie danced for coins on the sidewalks outside saloons, but this may have been exaggerations by hometown folks who wanted to impress others that they had known Trixie Friganza when she was just little Delia O'Callahan.

Surely busking, if it happened, was a passing thing, something that many kids of that era did to earn a bit of spending money or to bring the coins home if their family was needy. Trixie led an ordinary life, going to school and imagining a future. By 18, she was a bored and frustrated salesclerk in a local store. She may have had friends with similar ambitions, because she was tuned in to the show-business parade passing through Cincinnati.

When she learned that *The Pearl of Pekin,* a musical show then in town, was looking for a chorus girl or two, Trixie applied and ran off with the show without telling her family. She was just a month shy of her 19th birthday. Perhaps she had been waiting for the day when show business would bear her off to a future more glamorous and exciting than retail, for she already had chosen a stage name: her mother's maiden name, Friganza.

Her mother, Margaret, must have been a resourceful soul, for she quickly found out that Trixie had left town, under which name, with which show and where that show was headed. She promptly sent the local police to bring Trixie back. The constabulary was beyond its jurisdiction in Cleveland, where they located Trixie. When they reported to Margaret O'Callahan without Trixie in tow, they assured her that Trixie's virtue was as likely to remain unsullied in a well-chaperoned show as it was in the stockroom of a retail shop. It likely occurred to someone that her $18-a-week salary in *The Pearl of Pekin* was a marked improvement over the $3 per week she earned as a salesclerk.

The Pearl of Pekin was a popular and well-traveled adaptation of Charles Lecocq's Operetta, *La Fleur de Thé* with interpolations by Gustave Kerker. Later, much was made by publicists and interviewers that the mature Trixie Friganza, who had grown quite large, once had been a slim chorus dancer. Over the course of two years, Trixie worked her way out of the chorus and into small parts. In the 1890s, musical shows spent far longer touring than they did playing in Manhattan, and Trixie played the road for years. By the 1891–92 season, Trixie was a member of Henry E. Dixey's light-opera company that toured for months before opening in Manhattan with operetta in repertory: *The Mascot, Patience, Iolanthe* and a double bill of *Trial by Jury* and *The Sorcerer.*

Trixie was not yet a featured actor or performer; she played small roles. Throughout the 1890s, her parts began to get bigger, and so did Trixie. She appeared in *Venus* (1893) in Boston, then *The Little Trooper* (1894) and *Fleur de Lys* (1895–96) on the road. She played Henry, a featured role—likely a trouser role—in *La Poupee* (1897–98), a musical comedy adapted from the original by Edmond Audran. It was reported that Trixie was in the production headed by Anna Held at Hammerstein's Lyric Theatre, formerly the Olympia, but there was second production of the same musical at Daly's later that season.

Trixie was under George Lederer's management at the Casino Theatre during the 1899–1900 season. She was given featured roles in *The Rounders,* which played successfully through summer into fall, and in *The Belle of Bohemia* (1900).

Although *The Belle of Bohemia* only managed 55 performances at the Casino, it was brought in 1901 to the Apollo Theatre in London, where Trixie made a favorable impression. She stayed in England for *The Whirl of the Town* (1901). Her next show was a 1901 revival of a London show, *The Girl from Paris.* This was likely to have played in London, although it has been listed as an American production, one that toured rather than played Manhattan. *Sally in Our Alley* (1902) was also listed in some sources as a show with Trixie in the cast; however, Marie Cahill was the star, and Trixie was not listed in the cast programme. She may have taken the show out on the road following its New York engagement.

Friganza was in the Broadway cast of *The Chaperons* (1902), a short-lived musical that attracted attention primarily because Eva Tanguay brought the house to attention with her rendering of "My Sambo." Trixie Friganza was noted by critics, who remarked that she was a singing comedian in the style of Marie Dressler and May Irwin. This was praise indeed and a clue that Trixie was no longer the svelte showgirl. She was not yet hefty, but she was definitely buxom.

Trixie went on the road with *A Trip to Chinatown* in 1903. Originally staged in 1891, it played the old Madison Square Theatre for 657 performances, a long-run record that was not broken by any show until 1916. It then toured for several years and was revived several times, including the short run in 1903 in which Trixie played. *The Darling of the Gallery Gods* (1903) was half of a double bill with *The Dress Parade,* and Trixie was among the principal players. The show closed within a month.

Joe Weber and Lew Fields split up their 30-year partnership in 1904. Joe was the better businessman; Lew was the more imaginative producer. Lew was interested in exploring the new musical comedy; Joe was content to stick with the burlesks the Weber & Fields Music Hall had been producing for nearly a decade. Joe established the Weber Music Hall, went into a partnership of sorts with Florenz Ziegfeld, and hired Marie Dressler and Anna Held (Mrs. Ziegfeld) for his first season. *Higgledy-Piggledy* was the 1904 production, and Trixie Friganza replaced Anna Held in the show when it went on tour. Marie Dressler was the hit of the show. Mercurial Marie and no-nonsense Joe Weber did not get along, but they made a fine stage combination.

Some reports listed Trixie's appearance in two comic operas: *The Sho-Gun* (1904), perhaps another road tour that skirted Broadway, and *The Prince of Pilsen* (later in 1904), which was a London revival at the Shaftesbury Theatre. Early in 1906, back in the USA, Trixie was reunited with Joe Weber and Marie Dressler in *Twiddle-Twaddle.*

In summer of that year, Friganza made her vaudeville debut at Hammerstein's Victoria. It was her first experience without a script to guide her, and *Variety* thought her promising but underprepared and lacking top-notch material. Her impersonation of Marie Dressler was the highpoint of her act.

Trixie was in the cast when *His Honor the Mayor* played Philadelphia in March 1907 and was then back in Manhattan to open on 8 April 1907 in *The Orchid* with Eddie Foy and Irene Franklin. Foy was the star. *The Orchid* opened at the Herald Square Theatre, closed for summer, reopened at the Casino Theatre, where it ran for six months of the 1907–08 season, before it closed shop at the Academy of Music after a total of 178 performances. Trixie and Eddie Foy took the show to major cities, including Chicago, where Trixie was injured in an automobile accident. She was thrown 30 feet from the car, and doctors feared for her life.

One year later, Trixie was back on Broadway. She had a good role and a snappy song-and-dance number in *The American Idea* (1908). Her sister, Bessie

Friganza, was in the show's ensemble. It was one of George M. Cohan's less successful shows, but it made money on the road. Back in Chicago, Trixie appeared in *The Girl from Yama* (1909).

Chicago audiences kept Trixie and her next show, *The Sweetest Girl in Paris,* busy at the La Salle Theatre during the first half of the 1910–11 season. The census of 1910 showed that Trixie and her two sisters and one of their husbands were sharing a house. Both Trixie and Bessie were listed as divorced (Trixie had wed a W.J.M. Barry in 1900). In 1912, Trixie married again. Charles Goettler was a business manager in a theatrical firm. That same year, Trixie appeared in the Shuberts' *The Passing Show of 1912* at the Winter Garden for four months. Among her costars were Willie & Eugene Howard, Charlotte Greenwood, the dance team Adelaide & Hughes and Harry Fox.

From 1912 onward, Trixie was well enough known from her tours to be a promising act in big-time vaudeville. Her vaudeville salary was more than she earned on Broadway, and the work was less tiring with two acts a day that ran perhaps 25 minutes each. She called her act "My Little Bag o' Trix." By then a roly-poly, rollicking *nut* comedian and impersonator, her presence on any vaudeville bill promised fun and strong box office. Offstage, she divorced her second husband in 1914.

Ned Wayburn's Town Topics opened on 23 September 1915 for an eight-week run. Trixie was joined in the revue by Blossom Seeley, Clifton Webb and Lew Hearn. A decision was made to bring it to London. Despite the war in Europe, Trixie and Will Rogers sailed to London in 1915 to headline *Town Topics* at the Century Music-Hall.

By 1916, Friganza was back in the USA and all the way over on the West Coast for *Canary Cottage,* which began its tryouts in San Diego. Trixie was the star and lead character, and the show was headed to Broadway. She had worked more than 25 years for that opportunity. A loveable, easy-going talent, full of zany fun onstage, Trixie offstage was a savvy professional, protective of her career.

In *Canary Cottage* there were two flies in her cold cream. One was Lily Marr, a chorus girl whose unmistakable resemblance to Anna Held was noted by the press during rehearsals. Indeed, she was the daughter of Anna Held and Florenz Ziegfeld. Instead of interviewing Trixie Friganza, the star, the press wanted Lily Marr. Trixie had her removed from the show before it opened at its next stop, Los Angeles.

The second fly was more nettlesome. The young vaudevillian who was cast in the small part of Trixie's character's chauffeur had two songs. During rehearsals, he ad-libbed some funny business that made everyone laugh. Trixie ordered that he not improvise on the script or the songs. Eddie Cantor was too smart to show his hand. He waited until opening night and then unloosed a series of ad-libs and comic business that won laughs. The reviews the next day claimed he had stolen the show. Trixie told the producers to fire him. The producers told Trixie that he was staying with the show.

Somebody should have asked Eddie Cantor. He begged out, claiming family illness, so that he was free to accept a much better offer from Flo Ziegfeld. Eddie soon appeared in Ziegfeld's rooftop *Frolics,* the start of a long professional association between Ziegfeld and Cantor. Friganza, free of Cantor, took *Canary Cottage* on to Broadway, where it ran 14 weeks.

Trixie Friganza scored better when she brought her vaudeville act to the Palace the week of 22 April 1918. Assisted by Mae Welly and Melissa Ten Eyke, Trixie sang, danced and kidded as was expected. She also introduced one of her more famous bits, a seemingly improvisational percussive turn with a bass fiddle, which she thumped and spun.

Trixie was the type of personality that showed best in vaudeville. It was not simply her musical and comedic talent that made her a star, it was the warmth of her personality and her cockeyed sense of humor. The fourth wall of drama and musical comedy prevented Trixie from kidding with her audience. With one exception, Trixie left musical comedy behind and concentrated on her vaudeville career and tried her luck in silent and sound films.

The Trixie Friganza who was a vaudeville headliner in the mid-1920s was a large, jolly comedian in her mid-50s. She kidded about her size ("I'm a perfect 46") and wore several layers of clothes that exaggerated her 190 pounds. With each number she shed a layer instead of slipping offstage for a costume change between songs. She told audiences, "When I started in show business I was so thin that you could blow me through a keyhole. Now you have to take down the whole door to get me through." Or her instructions for fat women wishing to dance a shimmy: "walk fast and stop short."

Her first silent film, *Mind Over Motor* (1923), was her only starring vehicle, and her parts grew smaller in those that followed. She made five films in 1925 and four in 1926. One was a Cecil B. DeMille film, *The Road to Yesterday* (1925). The rest were respectable programmers of the time. Trixie appeared in three more films made in 1927 and 1928.

In 1929, she returned to the Palace Theatre in her vaudeville act and costarred with Jimmy Savo in (John) *Murray Anderson's Almanac* (1929). The show's highlight was the song "I May Be Wrong (But I Think You're Wonderful)," sung by the diminutive Savo to the tall and hefty Friganza. Jimmy wistfully gazed into her face as he tried to get his arms around her, and it was a pairing of two fine clowns that was long remembered. The show opened in mid-August and closed with the stock-market crash in October.

Big-time vaudeville still had a couple of years left in its run, and Trixie played part of the 1929–30 season in the big time. In 1930, she headed a Fanchon & Marco show called *Discoveries* that played Keith-Orpheum time. The then-50-year-old, 210-pound star fronted a line of 20 young dancers and singers.

Much of the remainder of Trixie Friganza's career was spent in California. She resumed picture making with MGM's *Free and Easy* (1930), an attempt to make over its most popular comedian, Buster Keaton, into something that studio bigwigs thought suitable for talkies. It is an interesting picture because it featured Trixie as an actor in a large role and because Buster demonstrated, under trying circumstances, why he was well suited to sound.

Most interesting of all of Trixie's films are two one-reel sound shorts that she made in 1930: *Strong and Willing* and *My Bag o' Trix,* her vaudeville act committed to film and completely restored in the 1990s. During the rest of the 1930s, she made five more films without adding to her reputation. A popular network radio series, *Myrt and Marge* (1933), was padded to feature-film length by bringing in a lot of top vaudeville talent: Trixie, Ted Healy & His Stooges (Moe, Larry, Curley, and Bonny Bonnell), Grace Hayes and Eddie Foy Jr.

Friganza played in a couple of Westerns, took a bit part as a waitress in *A Star Is Born* (1937), and joined Bing Crosby and former vaudevillians Charles Winninger, Julian Eltinge, Blanche Ring and Eddie Leonard in *If I Had My Way* (1940). Thereafter, Trixie Friganza retired.

Arthritis had pained her for some time, and it grew to seriously cripple her over the years. In 1940, Ms. Friganza made an arrangement with Flintridge (California) Academy of the Sacred Heart. Nearly 70, Trixie entrusted the school with her considerable assets and taught drama. In turn, the nuns provided a home on campus and cared for her through her final years. There was initial unease at the prospect of a vaudeville performer and divorcée coming to live among nuns and schoolchildren, but the concern was short lived. Trixie Friganza remained at the Sacred Heart Academy until 27 February 1955, when she died at 84.

JOE FRISCO

b: (Louis Wilson Joseph) 1890 (?), Milan, IL—d: 12 February 1958, Woodlawn Hills, CA

For nearly a half century, Joe Frisco was a legend among show folk; dozens of stories are still told and written about him. He was a character out of Damon Runyon's "Noo Yawk," where raffish performers, con artists, politicians, chorus cuties, old dolls, gamblers, prostitutes and bootleggers populated speakeasies and racetracks and the oldest established floating crap game ran longer than any Broadway musical. Joe Frisco was so typically Runyonesque that, as the saying goes, if Frisco had not existed, Runyon would have had to invent him.

There were lots of small-time hoofers and comics whose worlds were only wide enough to accommodate their act, the dope sheet and a few basic urges. Joe fit the outlines of that stereotype, but he had wit and talent as well. Although unschooled and functionally illiterate—except with a racing form—Frisco was street smart and the master of the quick retort.

As a vaudeville star, Joe commanded a salary of $1,500 to $3,500 per week, but he banked with the bookies and paid interest rather than earned it. He chose to live in third-rate hotels, and he danced and told jokes onstage only to earn enough money to pay off what he owed bookies. His act did not change much in 30 years. It was the one thing he got right.

The band jumped into "Darktown Strutters' Ball," and Frisco glided onstage, bent at the waist and knees, shuffling, turning, crossing his steps, deftly twirling his cigar

Joe Frisco

and juggling his black derby. A critic described Joe's dance as a "Jewish Charleston," and Joe himself called it jazz dancing, even billing himself as the "The World's First Jazz Dancer" despite ample contrary evidence.

Whatever critics called it, Joe's dancing fell into the category of eccentric dancing, a category broad enough to encompass the styles of Jigsaw Jackson, George M. Cohan, James Barton, Leon Errol, George Stamper, Harland Dixon, Earl "Snakehips" Tucker, Charlotte Greenwood, Clarence Dotson, Hal Leroy, Buddy Ebsen, Ray Bolger, Ben Wrigley, Marilyn Mason and Buster West. Joe put together an idiosyncratic and personal combination of a (pelvic) grind, shuffle-off-to-Buffalo (crisscross steps as the dancer moves sideways), falling-off-a-log (similar to Buffalo but with a leaning pause added, like logrolling), a camel walk, and a few bits of the old hands-in-the-pocket clog.

The Frisco jazz dance became a craze. F. Scott Fitzgerald mentions it in *The Great Gatsby,* and it supplanted Chaplin's Tramp as the costumed impersonation of choice. Gus Edwards, who always needed to fill his vaudeville troupes of kiddie acts, despaired that so many tykes auditioned with a Frisco imitation.

When Joe Frisco—named after a string of boxcars passing by his agent's window—first started out in show business, he was simply another hoofer with a limited bag of tricks. Even this was a world away from his beginnings on an Iowa farm.

It is uncertain when Joe Frisco was born. Indeed, most facts in Joe Frisco's life before he became famous are open to question. What is known is what little Joe divulged. As tales were retold, the punch lines doubtless became more important than circumstances. Even the biography of Joe Frisco written by Ed Lowry is third hand, based largely on the recollections of Charlie Foy, Joe's lifelong friend. Paul M. Leavitt, a professor at the University of Colorado, in turn, set about bringing order to reminiscence and separating fancy from fact.

By the time Joe was seven, he had learned to dance from his mother, who had a brief career in English panto before she married and came to the USA. She told Joe stories about her days as a dancer and taught him a Lancashire clog. A bit later, Joe picked up the essentials of the soft shoe. His mother had told him of the English buskers who entertained on the sidewalks outside theatres and pubs, so with a couple of neighborhood pals Joe began to dance for throw money outside Dubuque's theatres.

His father ridiculed Joe's stutter and assigned him the most menial farm chores. When Joe brought home a pair of shoes with taps on them, his father, furious at what he saw as a waste of money, threw the shoes into the potbellied stove. Joe flew at his father, knocked him over and then flew out of the house, never to return. He was probably about ten years old.

Joe set Chicago as his goal, but his next few years he meandered between riding the rails, working in horse stables and delivering messages for Western Union. He got work dancing in small-time vaudeville and dives as half of a soft-shoe act, Coffee & Doughnuts.

One day, Joe met Loretta McDermott, a petite, young beauty who caught his eye and held it for many years. He asked Loretta to join in a dance act with him. After a week's rehearsal, an agent booked them into the first of the many dumps they would play over the next few years.

Basing themselves in Chicago, they lived in theatrical hotels and rooming houses. Once he learned to spell Dubuque, whenever Joe had a sawbuck that either the bookie or the bartender missed, Joe wired it home to his mother.

One night, in New Orleans, yielding to Loretta's urge for a night on the town no matter how low they were on money, Joe and Loretta joined other couples on the dance floor of the Creole Café. On the bandstand was a band called the Dixieland Five. Their music was far jazzier than the piano-and-drums combos that accompanied Joe and Loretta in theatres. Carried away, Joe and Loretta improvised, and the other dancers cleared the floor for them. When they came back a second night, Joe cracked to the crowd, "Don't applaud, folks, just throw m-m-money." And they did. More than the team was used to earning for four shows a night.

Once McDermott & Frisco gelled as a team, an agent, Walter Meakin, began booking them. While playing Battle Creek, Michigan, on the Butterfield circuit, Joe and Loretta appeared on a bill with Bill Robinson. According to Joe, the great Bojangles watched him rehearsing and offered cogent advice: "You're trying to squeeze six pounds of sugar into a five pound bag." Robinson and Frisco shared several traits—both were nearly illiterate and both enjoyed the hustle—but Robinson showed Frisco the value of treating his act like the small business it was.

Joe talked his agent into promoting a new act: "Joe Frisco and the Dixieland Five assisted by Loretta McDermott." Frisco brought the band up from New Orleans and introduced the new act into Mike Fritzel's Café, a basement club in Chicago that Joe tagged "an upholstered sewer." They were such a success that soon there was turn-away business, and Frisco and company were doubling at local vaudeville theatres.

Things also started to go wrong. His dad died, his brother was accidentally shot and killed, and Loretta was keeping company with their act's singer. Joe bolted for New York. Whether Loretta went with him depends upon which report one accepts After a few trials and errors, Joe made a hit and won a booking as a single on the Keith circuit.

Vaudeville chroniclers Charles and Louise Samuels remember seeing Frisco at Keith's Theatre in Brooklyn at the time: "Frisco never uttered a word. [His] specialty was the wildest apache-like dance we'd ever seen. Right in the middle, with the savage music pounding, he stopped at the front of the stage, got down on one knee, twirled his derby and sent it rolling up one arm and down the other, while furiously puffing perfect smoke rings."

Frisco won a tryout with Gene Buck, then putting together the 1917 edition of Ziegfeld's *Midnight Frolics.* During the audition, Florenz Ziegfeld asked him, "Do you always stutter like that?" Frisco said, "No sir, only when I t-t-talk." The *Midnight Frolics* catapulted Joe Frisco, then in his mid- to late 20s, into the big time. He stayed on for the 1918 *Midnight Frolics* and the *Ziegfeld Follies of 1918* then came back in 1920 for another *Frolics.*

Sometime before the *Midnight Frolics,* Joe Frisco added patter to his act. He was now famous as much for his funny lines as he was for the Frisco dance. The steady topflight work, recognition and the generous salary did not much change Joe's style of living, except that the food and booze got better and the bets got bigger.

As a vaudeville headliner, Joe reportedly earned up to $3,500 per week. His usual salary seems to have hovered between $1,500 and $2,500 per week. In 1927, Frisco was booked into Keith's Palace Theatre. After Joe and his agent concluded the deal and left the office of E. F. Albee, the czar of the Keith circuit and the Palace, they had to thread their way through street excavation. Joe's agent wondered why they were digging up the street. Frisco opined, "Albee's kid lost his ball."

A Broadway habitué, Joe was not fond of taking his act on the road, but for the rest of the 1920s, Joe toured the Keith and Orpheum circuits. It was in Atlantic City that Joe found himself on the bill with Eddie Foy and the Seven Little Foys. Frisco and Charlie Foy began a friendship that lasted until Joe's death 40 years later.

The *Earl Carroll's Vanities of 1928* was Frisco's last Broadway revue. Vaudeville was collapsing, but Frisco still got high-paying club work into the mid-1930s. Fame never seemed to interest Frisco, only the payoff and the ponies. After nearly 15 years in the Broadway spotlight and headlining in vaudeville, Joe headed west. He chose to work in small clubs not too far from racetracks, where he could deposit his salary before the tax people could take it.

He settled in at a few favorite spots, working for friends—people who had been in the business, like Charlie Foy and Grace Hayes—occasionally traveling to some of the posher joints in Chicago, Florida and Palm Springs. Gradually, he faded as a headliner; his act stayed the same, although he relied more on comedy, working the tables and trading quips with the customers. He still danced the Frisco jazz dance to "Darktown Strutters' Ball," but he was losing a bit of his verve. He worked most of his last 15 or 20 years at Charlie Foy's club and shared Charlie's apartment above the club, which was close to the track.

Joe had a doughy face; the only even features were his store-bought teeth. He was short and slight, and if you took away his trademark derby and cigar, he might have been unrecognizable to anyone but his closest friends, bartenders and bookmakers. His stutter disarmed people, and when he let loose with a barb, his delivery and appearance did not raise the ire that another comic might have with the same crack.

Unlike his bets, his humor was based on probabilities and delivered poker-faced. Frisco's wit did not take flight into the absurd, instead he deflated the situation to street-corner logic. Once, when buying furnishings for his mother's house, an art dealer tried to sell Joe a copy of *The Last Supper* for $250. "No dice. T-t-tell you what. I'll give ya t-t-ten dollars a plate."

Frisco decided he needed a first name, and the 1926 National Vaudeville Association benefit show at the Palace marked the first time that Frisco was billed as Joe Frisco. He explained, "I think its un-dignified not to have a handle on my name."

Comedian Joey Adams recorded a number of Frisco barbs, including his favorite, which took place at a *Friars Frolic* in 1925. An all-star bill of Friars was on hand to salute Enrico Caruso. George M. Cohan was the toastmaster, John Barrymore and Al Jolson were among the entertainers, and everyone was in awe of Caruso. Except Joe Frisco. At a point in the evening's entertainment, Frisco found himself standing next to Caruso while both were waiting their turns. "Hey, Caruso, don't do 'D-D-Darktown Strutters' Ball.' That's my number and I follow you."

Joe did not know anything about grand opera, but he knew Caruso's act was opera, so his comment was not naive. Joe's observations were shrewd. In the 1920s, before the stock-market crash, Joe was taken to a stockbroker's office by Groucho Marx, who hoped to get Joe to invest in something besides races. The brokerage was appointed to impress, and the suite had a majestic view of New York Bay. The stockbroker pointed out the marina and told Joe that the yachts moored below belonged to brokers like himself. "Great," said Joe, "but where are the c-c-customers' yachts?"

One guy who did not find Frisco funny was Uncle Sam. For years, Joe had failed to pay taxes. He was making far less than in the vaudeville days, and his bookies had a rival—the tax man—for Joe's diminished weekly paycheck (down to $500).

Frisco appeared in eight or nine feature-length films, including *Atlantic City* (1944), in which Joe, 20 years past his prime, credibly re-creates the Frisco dance. He also did a few radio shots and appeared on local television talks shows. Years of high living and Joe's neglect of his health caught up with him. In 1958, while a resident of the Motion Picture Country House and Hospital in Woodlawn Hills, Joe Frisco died of cancer.

FROGS CLUB

In 1900, a group of white actors and performers had created the White Rats for the protection and benefit of their fellows. Although the notion of actors banding into a union of sorts, like common laborers, was radical and distasteful to some, most performers recognized the need for protection against a frequently rapacious management. Black performers and actors had long realized this was especially true for themselves. No one was more concerned than George W. Walker, Bert Williams' partner.

Walker, an energetic man, sought a way to advance the prestige and economic position of Negro stage artists. He wanted black capital to support black producers, enabling them to put on more black shows employing more black performers earning sufficient wages to support families and educate their children. Walker had joined the Black Business Men's League in 1905, yet he needed a group more responsive to the needs of black show-business professionals.

Walker courted trouble from both directions when he started to drum up support for an industry-wide Colored Actors Beneficial Association. This dream shrank a bit into a more focused operation, the Colored Vaudeville Benevolent Association (CVBA); still, it faced hostility from the white managers, who wanted a pool of quiescent colored acts who would take what they were given. The White Rats, who did not want to lose strength through splinter groups, also opposed the CVBA.

The White Rats leadership was as conservative as the times in a number of ways. No provision was made for women in the leadership. Chorus girls were not covered. Membership was theoretically open to Negro artists, but the White Rats supported the informal policy of allowing only one black act per vaudeville bill (and that, of course, did not mean every bill). Further, the White Rats endorsed the notion that no colored act should be billed above any white act.

Prodded by Walker, a dozen of the top professionals of the variety stages assembled on 18 July 1908 in Walker's Harlem home at 52 West 153rd Street. They elected officers among themselves. Walker became president, composer J. Rosamond Johnson was vice president, performer and librettist Jesse Shipp was treasurer, and lyricist Cecil Mack became secretary. The remaining charter members were Tom Brown (a dancer), Bob Cole (songwriter, performer and partner of J. Rosamond Johnson), Samuel Corker (business manager and advance agent), James Reese Europe (bandleader), Alex Rogers (lyricist), Lester Walton (critic and actors' agent) and Bert Williams (comedian and partner of Walker). Some sources list R. C. McPherson in place of Cecil Mack; they were the same person. McPherson began using "Cecil Mack" as his *nom de plume* after 1902.

The single event that had brought the Frogs together was reputed to be their individual participation in a salute to comedian Ernest Hogan. Mr. Hogan was a well-off, highly paid and famous comedian. He was at the top of his fame and earning power but ill. He died the next year. Two years later in 1911, the Frogs' guiding spirit, George W. Walker, died after a long illness. His partner, Bert Williams, hitherto the less active offstage of the duo, assumed the presidency of the Frogs in 1910.

Even as late as 1909, after Walker had retired from the stage, the White Rats formally protested the top billing at Hammerstein's Victoria Theatre given to Walker's erstwhile partner Bert Williams, even though some critics ranked Bert as the greatest comedian of the era.

The group produced an annual Frogs Frolic in the summer at the Manhattan Casino. It was a combination costume ball, party and vaudeville show. The 1913 show was so enthusiastically received that it was put on tour with the cream of Negro acts. It was reported that white audiences in Philadelphia, Baltimore, Richmond and Washington, D.C., anxious to see these shows, sat alongside blacks in the orchestra and balconies, a first for some of the theatres and cities.

Eventually a clubhouse was established at 111 West 132nd Street in Harlem. The Frogs held a respected and beloved position in Harlem society, and they attracted a number of professional and businesspeople in addition to theatrical people to their membership. A major thrust of the evolving organization was raising funds for various charities.

The Frogs were named, according to some sources, after the creatures who inhabited one of Aesop's fables and a comedy by Aristophanes. The frogs in the fable were deemed to have reasoned very cannily for untutored beings. Those in the comedy *The Frogs* were the croaking Greek chorus who, although not active participants in the affairs of men or gods, always knew who the players were and what the score was.

FRONT CLOTH

The drop curtain, hung farthest downstage, behind the house curtain and the front set of tabs. Usually the scene painted on the curtain was appropriate for a number-two act—a singing or song-and-dance act slotted into the second spot on the bill—or a single comedian or a two-person comedy team that relied on dialogue more than action.

FRONTED

Primarily used to designate a bandleader or at least the person in the outfit who stood in front of the band and seemingly conducted it. The terms *fronted* and *front man* usually implied figureheads, but a more flexible usage did not preclude real authority and leadership.

FRONT OF THE HOUSE

The area of the theatre exclusive of the stage and backstage areas; it was under the control of the house manager. In smaller houses, the theatre manager assumed house-manager duties as well. The front of the house encompassed the box office, the business offices, lobbies, the marquee and the auditorium. The house-manager had oversight of ticket takers and ushers and was the authority expected to persuade, when necessary, the audience to behave appropriately and to comply with safety regulations.

FRONT TRAVELER OR HOUSE CURTAIN

A dominant feature in a theatre's decor, the front traveler usually was plush masquerading as velvet, often red and tasseled with gold braid. It was the dress curtain that greeted the audience as it arrived. Hung immediately in back of the proscenium arch, it was parted in the center and was usually drawn toward the wings at the start of the show; the procedure reversed at the end of the show. Although parted in the center, the front curtain was flown when the setting behind the curtain contained papers and other lightweight items that could be blown away in the draft. Raising the curtain was less likely to cause a disturbing draft.

Also called *front tabs, front curtain,* and *house tabs* in British and Australian variety.

LOÏE FULLER

b: (Marie Louise Fuller) 1862, Fullersburg, IL—d: 1 January 1928, Paris, France

In the 1890s and 1900s, Loïe Fuller was the most famous dancer in the world, the first interpretive concert dancer of the modern era and the ubiquitous model for Art Nouveau. She ended her career as a scientist, but, in her early years, she was a typical variety performer.

As a child, Loïe acted in melodramas (often as a boy), offered recitations, gave temperance lectures and won dancing contests. In her teens, she worked as a Shakespearean reader and an actor, authored several plays and toured with burlesque troupes, the Felix A. Vincent Comedy Club, and Frank Mayo's Company. The burlesks were spoofs of current plays, not exhibitions of female anatomy. She was 19 when she joined a variety show starring Buffalo Bill Cody. Loïe played banjo and acted in a melodramatic sketch. She got almost as far as New York City with the company before she fell ill. Taking up the role of an entrepreneur for the first time, Loïe put together a singing group for touring early vaudeville.

In 1885, she appeared at the Boston Theatre in *Our Irish Visitors,* a play with interpolated songs and dances. Her uncorseted dance helped fill the theatre. She went to New York the next season to sing and act in *Humbug,* a comedy. The famous comedian Nat Goodwin noticed her and hired her for the title role in *Little Jack Sheppard,* a burlesque that put her back in trousers. Loïe was not pretty. Her wide, uptilted nose detracted some from soulful eyes and a friendly smile, and she continued to be cast in trouser roles as often as not, although her shapely form stimulated comment in the press. The press was less impressed with her acting, but Nat Goodwin continued to cast her in his productions for several more seasons. She was, however, willing to take falls and showed promise in physical stunts.

In 1889, she married a portly man nearly twice her age, William B. Hayes, the nephew of former President Rutherford B. Hayes. The union provided Loïe with a husband able to bankroll her theatrical endeavors, or so she thought. Hayes acquired a third wife, although it was later revealed that he had failed to divorce the previous two. Loïe Fuller made her debut on the London stage in 1889. From this point onward, Loïe's life was filled with great debts, much litigation and bizarre events, the first few of which were Hayes' abandonment of Loïe, the debts Hayes had left her and the suspected poisoning by Hayes of Loïe's father.

Stranded in London with her mother, Loïe gave several dance concerts and appeared in variety to bring in some money. While appearing at the Gaiety Theatre, Loïe must have realized that the Gaiety Girls (the chorus dancers) were that theatre's most reliable attraction. The Gaiety Girls performed a swirling skirt dance in flowing long gowns, but Loïe still thought of herself as an actor.

Finally able to afford ship passage, she and her mother returned to Manhattan in 1891, but the only job Loïe could get was in a touring farce, *Quack. M.D.* She had a small role and performed a skirt dance between the acts. She was almost 30 yet not well enough known to win lead roles. Rudolph Aronson, then manager of the Casino Theatre, engaged her to dance in one of his variety shows.

Her act, a collaboration between Fuller and Aronson that he named "The Serpentine Dance," had her draped in a white gown and manipulating the fabric as she danced in and out of darkness or shafts of white, blue, purple and red lights. Her dance was the hit of the show and set Loïe Fuller on her course as a dance pioneer and scientist.

Her "Banner of Light" act in vaudeville involved Fuller and seven other female dancers. They twirled around in gauzy fabric and bare legs on top of large sheets of glass set into the stage floor and lit from below. Fuller's act evidently required the services of all the backstage crew, including the stage doorman. None could be located backstage while Fuller was onstage. They were all watching the show through the transparent glass from below. Loïe's act was one of their favorites.

Offstage, her affairs were jumbled. There were several bigamy or perjury cases against her supposed husband, William Hayes, and Loïe launched a few legal actions herself against Aronson and a "Serpentine Dance" imitator. She escaped blame in the Hayes matter but lost her actions to protect ownership of her dance. The judge ruled that mere movement, unlike words, could not be copyrighted. In New York, her new dance was a much-applauded novelty act quickly copied by others; in Paris, it became an impressionistic dance, in tune with developments in French painting, sculpture and design.

First there was a trip to Berlin, and her play dates there were not fulfilling. Undaunted, Loïe, her mother, ailing and in decline, and her agent pressed on to Paris. She failed to get the engagement she sought from the Paris Opéra, so she persuaded the Folies Bergère to hire her to replace another woman who was performing a pallid version of a serpentine dance. Publicity was adroitly arranged, and Loïe Fuller became the sensation of Paris.

Among the other acts on the bill were Wallenda and His Great Danes, Techow and His Educated Cats, Fatima, a belly dancer, American blackface comics Sherman & Morrissey, and The Girards, a musical clown act. It was in Paris that she adopted the accented spelling of her first name. Without the diaeresis over the *i*, *loie* in French meant "goose," not a good name for a dancer.

Writers, artists, other distinguished persons and the merely rich began filling the stalls, despite the Folies Bergère's somewhat unsavory reputation. Thousands were turned away at the box office. Loïe Fuller became the most celebrated artist of the day in Paris. Composers created music for her. Poets wrote paeans to her artistry. The avant-garde adopted her as a kindred spirit. Loïe brought distinction to the Folies Bergère.

Over time, Loïe created many variations of her serpentine dance. Whatever the dances were called—"Violet," "White," or "Butterfly" ("Danse Fleur," "Danse Blanche," "Danse Papillon") or any of dozens of other names—they employed billowing costumes, wands, electric lights and colored gels (later chemical alloys added to the fabric of her costuming). She did not truly dance; she moved. Wearing a voluminous, gauzy garment and grasping a baton in each hand over which the fabric extended, she swayed, turned, skipped and waved her arms, creating swirls of fabric that changed color with the lighting.

She was booked for Russia but had to cancel when her mother grew seriously ill. Her contract had a forfeit clause requiring Fuller to pay $40,000. Thus began the financial hole out of which she had to climb and back into which she often slipped. Loïe's fame brought her bookings in London variety; then she decided to return to New York, where she worked every opportunity, but still the Russian forfeiture weighed oppressively.

Back in Paris, she lived with her mother and a young woman who dressed as a man and to whom Loïe developed a strong attachment. Professionally, she began to explore the possibilities of light and color to improve her act. Motivated at first to distance herself artistically from a pack of imitators, she discovered in herself a strong interest in the technology of electric light and color.

She stayed several steps ahead of other dancers who tried to imitate her. By the time they had purloined an effect or a portion of her act, Loïe had devised something new, and she kept secret her fabrics, chemical compounds and lighting effects. Not always did she lead. When the Salome fad invaded Europe, Fuller created her own version of the young lady with seven veils.

She returned to her native USA in 1896 to appear in vaudeville at Koster & Bial's in Lower Manhattan for a heretofore unheard of four-figure salary, one larger than that commanded by Yvette Guilbert or Lillian Russell. But Loïe soon went back to Paris, her adopted home, her artistic home, where she had emerged as a leader in the Art Nouveau movement. Edgar Degas and James McNeill Whistler were friends; craftspeople working in blown glass, bronze and wood consulted her. Her dances with their kaleidoscopic swirl of color became subjects for lithographs, lamp bases and glass vases in works by Gallé, Tiffany and Lalique. Loïe employed 15 to 20 electricians to manage the effects she chose, especially when they were as elaborate as her "Fire Dance," in which she appeared as a shimmering flame.

Loïe hosted performances by the visiting Japanese and Cambodian dance troupes in 1900, the same year that Ruth St. Denis, touring Europe, saw and was impressed by Loïe Fuller. As a result of her friendship with Marie and Pierre Curie and their experiments with radium, Loïe began to work with phosphorescent salts that gave off a fluorescent glow in the dark. This led to her "Radium Dance."

She grew knowledgeable about music, and her dances were set to music by Debussy, Berlioz, Gluck, Delibes, Wagner, Beethoven and others from the concert-hall repertoire. Though growing quite plump, she reigned as the toast of Continental painters, composers, writers and even scientists.

When she returned to the USA in 1909 and in 1910, it was not to play vaudeville theatres but opera houses in New York and Boston. Over the next few years, her performances were as likely to be in the salons of wealthy society, but when the First World War broke out, Loïe volunteered to entertain the troops. After the war, her professional appearances became less frequent as she neared 60 years of age.

France loved her because she was practical and modest. She was also generous to other dancers. Although Ruth St. Denis declined Loïe's invitation to join her tour, Maud Allan, then trying to make the change from a pianist to a dancer, gladly accepted. When Isadora Duncan sought *entrée* to European sponsors and producers, it was Loïe who took Isadora to Berlin, Vienna and Leipzig and introduced her to people of influence.

In addition to her scientific discoveries, Fuller also helped revolutionize stage design. Before Loïe, the emphasis was on realistic and elaborate sets, even for dance. Loïe discarded settings, furniture and props. Her stage was bare save for lighting cords, lights and an occasional glass-topped platform through which light was projected. Yet she was eclipsed by new generations of interpretive dancers like Duncan and St. Denis, by emerging modern dancers like Mary Wigman, and by jazz dancers like the young, captivating Josephine Baker.

Fuller was considered *passé* when she returned in 1925 to the USA, first in San Francisco then New York. She defied expectations by quickly training a group of 17 Loïe Fuller Dancers, who performed work choreographed by Fuller, including a sea dance in which the dancers undulated beneath a long length of fabric to create waves of color. Audiences and critics found her lighting effects astounding and enchanting. The company, however, was a large one with large expenses, and it was difficult to book with a profit either for Loïe or the theatre, so engagements were sporadic during the years from 1926 to 1928. Fuller made several experimental films as well. Perhaps her true heir was choreographer Alwin Nicholais.

Loïe Fuller continued to defy her debts and live well until, at 65, she died in Paris. There has never been an exhibition of Art Nouveau in which Loïe Fuller was not represented as the inspiration or the model for either a lamp or lithograph.

FULL STAGE

The entire playing area that was available to acts. Double the space *in two* and four times that *in one*, the playing area extended from the footlights on the apron downstage to the last drop curtain against the brick exterior wall upstage. Full stage was usually reserved for tab shows, flash acts, sketches with a goodly amount of scenery, illusionists and magic acts with paraphernalia, large animal acts and specialty acts with a lot of equipment and a range of movement, like trapeze artistes, wire and ropewalkers, and cyclists.

FUNAMBULIST

Derives from the Latin *funis* (meaning "rope") and *ambulare* (meaning "to walk"). The term was appropriated from the circus to denote a ropewalker.

See Wire Acts

J. AUSTIN FYNES

b: ca. 1855—d: 1920

A newspaperman who started at *The Boston Herald,* J. Austin Fynes became a stringer for the *New York Sun.* He fed reviews from Boston shows to the home office in Manhattan. He proved to have an excellent feel for theatre. The *New York Clipper* engaged him for its drama desk in 1884, and Fynes moved to Manhattan.

He became the *Clipper*'s managing editor in 1887, but he butted heads with the paper's business manager. In 1891, Fynes was offered the drama chair at the *Evening Sun* but ran into trouble with Arthur Brisbane, the *Sun*'s new editor. When the *Clipper* was put up for sale in 1893, Fynes raised the money to buy the *Clipper* with much help from B. F. Keith, whom he had known in Boston, but the paper's business manager went to the publisher's family and persuaded them not to sell.

Keith, who obviously thought highly of Fynes, hired him to manage Keith's Union Square Theatre in Manhattan, where Fynes introduced refined vaudeville. He proved himself to be among the more imaginative entrepreneurial types in vaudeville, but he never had the authority to will his ideas into policy. First, he had to persuade his boss to his point of view. He got along well with Keith, who gave Fynes his head, and Fynes paid temptingly high salaries to lure established stars of the legitimate theatre into vaudeville, thus doing much to establish high-class vaudeville. Among the first legitimate stars to accept Fynes offer were Sidney Drew and his wife and stage partner, Gladys Rankin. Drew was the cousin (perhaps half brother) of Lionel, Ethel and John Barrymore. Fynes made Keith's Union Square Theatre into one of Manhattan's more important vaudeville houses.

His success as an independent-minded manager put him on a collision course with E. F. Albee, who at the time was taking over the management of the Keith operation from Fynes' friend, B. F. Keith. Fynes was a snappish man, and his relations with his two major vaudeville employers, E. F. Albee and F. F. Proctor, were predictably combative. Albee brooked no rivals in the Keith operation, and Fynes' success made him a potential rival. After several confrontations, Fynes left Keith-Albee to become general manager of F. F. Proctor's theatres. Proctor irked Fynes, who could never get Proctor to spend the amount of money that Fynes thought necessary to assemble a first-class vaudeville bill.

Fynes' attitude toward his staff was the reverse. They admired him and were loyal because Fynes protected them and never passed the buck when anything went wrong, although it seldom did. When the White Rats went on strike in 1900, Fynes hired actors to form resident stock companies in a number of Proctor's vaudeville houses, and, until the crisis passed, the Proctor stock companies successfully played dramas and comedies that were produced by his assistant, Hugh Ford, a future film director.

Fynes decided to become his own boss. He had been one of the first vaudeville men to realize the growing importance of movies and the likelihood of their staying power. He began to acquire small churches and storefronts and set them up as movie houses. He then sold them at a solid profit. This he intended as a stepping-stone into film production, much as Marcus Loew, William Fox and others were doing. They were younger, however, and had access to venture capital. Fynes could not sell anyone on his idea to star big-name stage stars in silent films. Finally, he gave up and retired. A few years later, former vaudeville operators Adolph Zukor and Jesse Lasky established, respectively, Famous Players and Feature Plays, two movie studios geared to film legitimate stars in stage plays.

G

GAGGING UP THE MATERIAL

Akin to ad libbing but more self-indulgent, gagging went overboard. Heedless and undisciplined performers called attention to themselves or detracted from others onstage by padding their parts with unscripted lines and bits of business. Whereas a well-timed, clever ad lib could energize and freshen a scene, gagging usually threw off the others in a sketch because, unlike an ad lib, it did not come and go in a flash but was carried on too long and without regard to the mood, plot or pace of the act.

GAGS

Usually referring to verbal jokes, the term can also be stretched to include sight gags. Some historians claim the term came into stage use because originally it meant that a joke stopped a fellow actor or comedian, effectively gagging him until it ran its course with the audience. In British variety a gag was known as a *wheeze.*

GALLAGHER & SHEAN

Al Shean

b: (Abraham Elieser Adolph Schoenberg) 12 May 1868, Dornum, Prussia/Germany—d: 12 August 1949, New York, NY

Ed (Edward) Gallagher

b: 1876, San Francisco, CA—d: 28 May 1929, Astoria, NY

Sometime in the 1880s, Abraham Schoenberg changed his name to Al Shean, quit his garment factory job and found work in show business. It was not always onstage. After playing a small part in a show that rehearsed longer than it lasted in front of an audience, Al decided to take control of his destiny. He had a fine singing voice, so he and a friend, Sam Curtis, formed a singing act with George Brennan and Charley Harris. Male singing quartets had been a variety staple since concert saloons first appeared. Over the next seven or eight years, the act, billed as the Manhattan Quartet, offered sentimental and comedy songs to beer hall and variety theatre audiences.

As comedy rose to the fore in their act, they modified their name to the Manhattan Comedy Four around 1895. Short comedy skits, some written by Al, became part of their expanded act. The personnel changed as well; Ed Mack and Arthur Williams replaced Brennan and Harris while Shean and Curtis stayed with the act.

The Manhattan Comedy Four played variety, burlesque and vaudeville for five or six years and reached the top of the bill in big-time vaudeville. In 1899 the Manhattan Comedy Four were touring with Weber's Big Olympia Company (not Lew Weber). One of Al's comedy sketches, *A Tin Wedding: a Musical Burletta in One Act,* was part of Big Olympia's evening-length burlesque revue.

In 1900, Al and Sam Curtis broke up the act to pursue solo careers. Al took another partner, Charles L. Warren. They probably met when both were separately cast in the Harry von Tilzer operetta, *The Fisher Maiden* (1903). Al wrote the vaudeville material for Shean & Warren, and their sketches "Quo Vadis Upside Down" and "Kidding the Captain" proved vaudeville favorites for years. Punning and absurd leaps of logic in Al's scripts presaged a style of surreal humor that was built

Sheet music cover for Gallagher & Shean's famous Patter Song

on by other, later comedians like Clark & McCullough, Burns & Allen and The Marx Brothers (Al's nephews, for whom he wrote their first real comedy play, *Home Again,* during a period when he and his last partner, Ed Gallagher, were not speaking to each other or working together).

Al was nearly 40 when he dissolved the Shean & Warren act around 1904. Perhaps he tired of shuttling from one theatre to the next every week and longed to settle down. He had perfected his comic *Dutch* characterization and employed it throughout the 1900s and 1910s as a solo and double act in vaudeville. Leaving his wife in New York, Shean based his center of operations in Chicago, about the same time as did his sister, Minnie and her boys (The Marx Brothers). Al played vaudeville dates out of Chicago and appeared in musical comedies that originated there, such as *His Highness, the Bey* (1904) and *The Isle of Bong Bong* (1905).

Shean was back in Manhattan by 1910, where he teamed with a former burlesque straight man and comedian, Ed Gallagher, in a vaudeville act. Together they appeared in *The Rose Maid* (1912), but only Al was in the cast of *The Princess Pat* (1915).

Ed Gallagher hailed from the Bay Area of the Pacific coast. For 15 years, he teamed with Joe Barrett, another burlesque-trained comedian. In his landmark work, *The Encyclopedia of Vaudeville,* Anthony Slide notes that Gallagher & Barrett performed in a series of sketches that burlesqued the military. In burlesque, Gallagher was the straight man, a position with at least as much prestige as the comedian's.

In vaudeville, comedians got the recognition and straight men were regarded by some as little more than *feeds* who cued the comic with questions and otherwise simply stood there fingering a cigar while the funnyman acted up. This may not have been enough for Gallagher, who had developed into a capable comedian.

Gallagher teamed with Shean around 1910, and the two played vaudeville for three or four years. In 1914 they split up, each sure of a slight from the other. Both harbored grudges, and the two did not speak for six years. Gallagher appeared in a Broadway revue, *The Frivolities of 1920,* which lasted barely the first two months of that year. Minnie Marx persuaded them to reunite in 1920; their vaudeville act, "Gallagher & Shean In Egypt," featured the two men, garbed in bush jackets, doing their act *in one* in front of a drop of the pyramids. Gallagher wore a pith helmet and spats; Shean sported a fez and flowing cravat.

They are two funny men, the best I've ever seen.
One is Mister Gallagher, the other, Mister Shean.
When these two cronies meet, it sure is a treat.
The things they say, and the things they do, and
the funny way they greet.
Oh! Mister Gallagher, Oh! Mister Gallagher.
Hello, what's on your mind this morning, Mister
Shean?
Ev'rybody's making fun of the way our country's run,
All the papers say we'll soon live European.
Why, Mister Shean, Why Mister Shean,
On the day they took away our old canteen,
Cost of living went so high, that it's cheaper now
to die,
Positively Mister Gallagher, Absolutely, Mister Shean.

The team got snared by a contractual dispute with the Shubert Brothers and Florenz Ziegfeld that took more than a year to resolve. The producers contended separately that each had exclusive rights to Gallagher & Shean's services. The team went to court to preserve their independence. A partial victory required Gallagher & Shean to play some vaudeville dates for the Shuberts.

Al Shean and Ed Gallagher were booked for *The Ziegfeld Follies of 1922* solely on the strength of the vaudeville popularity of their Egypt act, and they performed "Mr. Gallagher & Mr. Shean" in the 1922 *Follies* and the summer edition of the 1922 *Follies*—about a full

Ed Gallagher and Al Shean

year's work. Their theme song followed them for the rest of their lives.

Once I think I saw you save a lady's life.
In a rowboat out to sea, you were a hero then to me,
And I thought perhaps you've made this girl your wife.
Why, Mister Shean, why Mister Shean,
As she sunk I dove down like a submarine.
Dragged her up upon the shore, now she's mine forever more.
Who, the lady, Mister Gallagher? No, the rowboat, Mister Shean.

Many verses were added, mostly in response to audiences that would not let them leave the stage without performing their signature song. Apart from its content and their delivery, it is remarkable in that the routine was birthed in 1922, a generation or two after that sort of patter song had enjoyed its greatest popularity in minstrelsy and variety.

In 1924, Al and Ed performed a vaudeville act appropriately called "In Dutch." Despite their success, the Gallagher & Shean partnership was not an easy one, and it did not survive the Shubert-ordered road tour of *The Greenwich Village Follies of 1925*. Perhaps the court squabble with the Shuberts added to the tension between the two personalities. Each one tried to go his own way, with diminished success.

Al Shean appeared in the musical comedy *Betsy* (1926) that flopped, a revival of *The Prince of Pilsen* (1930) that flopped, *Light Wines and Beer* (1930) that flopped, and *Music in the Air* (1932), a fine hit that ran from November through the summer of 1933. Between 1930 and 1943, Al acted character parts in about 30 movies. In only one of them, *Atlantic City* (1944, Republic), did Shean re-create his famed vaudeville routine, "Mister Gallagher and Mister Shean," with Jack Kenny performing the late Ed Gallagher's part.

As late as 1946, Al was performing in a musical comedy, *Windy City,* although it never played Broadway. In his 80th year, Al appeared in *Doctor Social* (1948), but it closed at the Booth Theatre in Times Square after five performances. Al Shean lost the bulk of his money in the stock market crash of 1929. So did Groucho Marx, but he was making big money on Broadway and was about to make a lot more in Hollywood. Al's career, however, had slid from his headlining days in vaudeville. He got work as a character actor—oddly, he was never hired for one of his nephews' motion pictures—but there were more layoffs than work during the last 20 years of his life. The Marx Brothers contributed to his support.

Ed Gallagher formed a short-lived partnership with Fifi D'Orsay for vaudeville, but he was buffeted by a divorce from his third wife. In 1925, Ed suffered a nervous collapse. In 1927, remarried, he was divorced again and committed to an institution. He died two years later at age 56.

GALLERY

Sometimes called the *galleries* or the *gods*, the gallery is the highest balcony in a theatre. In vaudeville houses and most legitimate theatres, the second balcony was the highest. *(See "Gallery Gods" and "Gods.")*

GALLERY GODS

While either word was used alone to refer to both the upper balcony or circle of a theatre, which held the least expensive seats, and the people who sat there, *gallery gods* referred only to the people who bought tickets for the balcony.

In the rowdier theatres of the nineteenth and early twentieth centuries, the gallery gods hooted and stamped their praise for or damnation of the performance. Thus there were twin meanings to the witty epithet *gallery gods*: they were seated high up in the theatre, and their shouted judgment often made or broke an act—even an entire show.

Theatres sited along a strand or a rialto attracted audiences because they were located in downtown neighborhoods that offered other desired destinations like department stores, restaurants and nightclubs. Few people patronized neighborhood variety and vaudeville theatres unless they lived in the vicinity. The local theatre became an important institution for the community, and patrons regarded the theatre as their own.

From the Civil War through the 1920s, the *gallery gods* often included a goodly number of newsboys who demanded their money's worth for their hard-earned nickel. If they liked a show, they told everyone about it, and they themselves came to so many performances that they knew the lines and the songs. Often, to the upset of greener performers, they sang along or hit the punch line before the actor onstage.

Savvy performers did not ignore the *gallery gods*, and some entertainers used them wisely. A singer was assured of applause if she beckoned or called to the house—the gallery in particular—to sing along on the chorus. Comedians, to ingratiate themselves and preserve their punch lines from premature utterance, often directed a lot of their jokes and ad libs to the gallery.

Occasionally and unexpectedly, a young boy popped up in the gallery to sing a familiar tune along with the woman or man onstage. Occasionally he was quite good and hoped to be hired by the theatre manager or discovered by an agent. These impromptu incidents soon became a ploy. Sheet music publishers and songwriters employed boys to sing, supposedly impromptu, from the gallery to stimulate sheet music sales. Singers adopted the ploy as an inexpensive way to add audience interest to their acts. Reacting hospitably to the intrusion helped make the singers seem like regular folks.

TESS "AUNT JEMIMA" GARDELLA

b: 1897, Wilkes-Barre, PA—d: 3 January 1950, Brooklyn, NY

One of the last female performers to wear blackface, Tess Gardella was a generously proportioned, jolly Italian American singer. In her only revue, *George White Scandals* (1921), she appeared in her patented role as Aunt Jemima, as she did in vaudeville. Just as often, though, she was billed simply as Tess Gardella. She played Queenie in the original production of *Show Boat* (1929) and its 1932 revival, the only cast member to wear blackface. Her only other musical of record, *The Little Dog Laughed* (1940), closed out of town.

When *Show Boat* was filmed in 1929, Gardella appeared—or was just heard singing—in the prologue (the restored film is not complete), and Gertrude Howard took the Queenie role in the film. Tess assumed her Aunt Jemima character in the Shirley Temple feature *Stand Up and Cheer!* (1934, Fox), but the better representation of Gardella's stage act was in the two-reeler *A Swing Opera* (1939), in which her makeup is lightened and she portrays the Gypsy Queen.

Tess Gardella was noted for a warm and peppy stage personality and a melodic contralto. Her smile was ever-present, and she swayed rather than danced. Not particularly effective on-screen and nearly absent from network radio, her reputation rests on reports of her ability to charm live audiences.

Gardella began singing at local events of various sorts, including patriotic rallies, and became professional in 1918 through small-time vaudeville, mostly in and around New York City. Tess quickly got good bookings and played Loew's time, where she was one of the four or five acts that preceded the featured silent movie. Her success moved her to the big time, and she played the Palace in 1922. She returned to the Palace in 1949 when, newly refurbished under the aegis of Sol Schwartz, the onetime flagship of American vaudeville returned to a policy of vaudeville (eight acts) plus feature film. It was Tess Gardella's last appearance. Long a diabetic, she died six month later.

JUDY GARLAND

b: (Frances Ethel Gumm) 10 June 1922, Grand Rapids, MN—d: 22 June 1969, London, England

The Gumm Sisters were already playing vaudeville when three-year-old Frances wandered onstage to join in the singing. The older girls were Mary Jane (1915–64) and Virginia (1917–77). Their mother was their accompanist. The girls' father, one of the illustrious Von Tilzer brothers who were in the music business with varying degrees of success, traveled with the act sometimes. It was he who carried Judy offstage after her unscheduled debut.

In 1929, when Judy was only six, the three Gumm Sisters appeared in a musical short film, *The Big Revue* (aka *The Starlet Revue*). They made three more shorts, all for Vitaphone, in 1930, *Bubbles, The Wedding of Jack and Jill* and *Holiday in Storyland.*

Judy was still a young girl when the Gumm Sisters were rechristened the Garland Sisters. While they were back playing vaudeville after their first brush with movieland, their new name was supplied by Georgie Jessel, who was the headliner on the same bill at a Chicago vaudeville theatre. According to legend, the immediate incentive was that they had finally gotten to see their name in lights, but the marquee read "Glumm Sisters." By that time it was apparent that vaudeville was no longer able to make stars, and that radio and movies were the dynamic new media.

When her husband died, Mrs. Gumm had three girls to support, and she was driven by a desire for fame and financial security. The trio had already made an appearance in an all-star musical Technicolor movie short, *La Fiesta de Santa Barbara* (1935) for MGM. Soon Judy emerged as the most promising of the Garland Sisters, and Mrs. Gumm focused on Judy as the family's best bet.

Louis B. Mayer, head of Metro-Goldwyn-Mayer (MGM), put Judy under contract and tried her out in a succession of movies, beginning with a musical short called *Every Sunday* (1936), in which she costarred with Deanna Durbin, a youngster who was making her film debut. Mayer pondered which youngster to keep on the payroll. Oddly, and despite MGM's pretensions of being the studio with class, he chose vaudeville singer Judy Garland. The classically trained Deanna was hired by Universal Pictures, which, despite the work of a few great directors like James Whale and some exceptional actors, was for the most part a lowbrow operation. At Universal, Deanna became the highest-paid youngster in the world while Judy proved a box-office bonanza for MGM.

Pigskin Parade (1936) was Judy's first feature, and public reception of her was good, but her next picture made her a star. *Broadway Melody of 1938* (1937) starred Eleanor Powell, Robert Taylor and George Murphy, but Judy Garland was given a great spot in the picture. She sang "Dear Mr. Gable" to a photograph of Clark Gable, then Hollywood's heartthrob and king of the box office. Mayer rewarded Judy with increasingly bigger and better parts, in *Thoroughbreds Don't Cry* (1937) with Mickey Rooney and Sophie Tucker; *Everybody Sing* (1938), in which she was cast with Fanny Brice, Billie Burke, Reginald Gardiner and Allan Jones; *Love Finds Andy Hardy* (1938), again with Mickey Rooney; and one ill-advised attempt to pair her with Freddie Bartholomew, *Listen, Darling* (1938). Even in her first feature, Judy acted and performed with instinctive savvy.

The Wizard of Oz (1939) represented the best of MGM. Only that studio had the depth of technical talent and the range within its musical department to pull off such a superb movie musical adaptation of Frank Baum's classic fantasy.

Larry Semon had made the Oz stories as silent comedies-cum-fantasies, but the enduring public memory was of the 1903 production that starred Fred Stone as the Scarecrow and Dave Montgomery as the Tin Man. The Montgomery & Stone show ran for many months on Broadway and toured for years. Fred Stone was Ray Bolger's idol, and Fred's Scarecrow provided Ray's inspiration.

The adage that too many cooks spoil the broth did not hold for the script, for there were three writers and many revisions. The score by Harold Arlen and Yip Harburg was a masterwork. The casting of Bert Lahr in the hitherto minor and nonspeaking role of the Cowardly Lion was a brilliant choice, and Lahr never found another movie role of its quality. Victor Fleming (among Hollywood's top and most versatile helmsmen) had a tight schedule for such a complicated production, and when MGM found it was unable to borrow Shirley Temple from Fox for the lead role of Dorothy, Fleming and the studio took a chance on Judy Garland. With her budding breasts bound, 16-year-old Judy Garland made everyone forget that another youngster had been the first choice for the role that Judy made her own.

Mickey Rooney and Judy Garland replaced Fred Astaire and Ginger Rogers as Hollywood's top song-and-dance team. Together, Mickey and Judy made entertaining musicals and topped box-office charts with *Babes in Arms* (1939), *Strike Up the Band* (1940), *Babes on Broadway* (1941) and *Girl Crazy* (1943), but Mayer insisted they also appear in B movies as well. Rooney continued in the Andy Hardy series of programmers, and Judy pulled duty in two of them.

Garland also got the chance to play grown-up opposite veteran song-and-dance man George Murphy in *Little Nellie Kelly* (1940) and opposite new movie song-and-dance man Gene Kelly in *For Me and My Gal* (1942). In terms of career achievements, the seven years between *The Wizard of Oz* in 1939 and *The Harvey Girls* in 1946 were Garland's glory years. They were crammed with constant work, and the pace and pressure grew horrid.

Her decline began in 1944. A few months after performing well in *For Me and My Gal,* Judy was ordered to replace the pregnant June Allyson in *Summer Stock* (1944). Judy looked plump and the film was lackluster. She soon slimmed down and gave several vibrant performances, including a dramatic turn in *The Clock.* Among her better musicals of the time were *Meet Me in St. Louis* (1944) and *The Harvey Girls* (1946), but the tension and unhappiness were beginning to register on the screen.

Judy Garland's hometown attractiveness fell short of Hollywood standards for glamour. She looked in the mirror and grew depressed that she did not see Lana Turner, Hedy Lamarr, Betty Grable or Rita Hayworth. Her mother was in cahoots with

Louis B. Mayer to keep Judy on track as a moneymaker. Judy had a tendency to gain weight. Diet pills were the answer. To keep her energy up, amphetamines were prescribed. To calm her down and make her sleep, she was given barbiturates.

Judy had been hooked on daily visits to psychiatrists as well as pills since 1945. That year, she divorced her first husband, composer David Rose, after he insisted on an abortion. She married director Vincente Minnelli next, and daughter Liza was born in 1946.

Her talent was affected. Garland had been a memorable singer—she was one of the last of the vaudeville women who could fill a theatre with a big sound and not lose tone, pitch or characterization. She hoofed well enough and was a capable actor with a comic sense and an aura of vulnerability.

By 1950, Garland had made 27 feature films during her 14 years at MGM. There had been problems with her behavior on the set of several of the later films, like *The Pirate* (1948), as well as rumors of a suicide attempt, and in 1949 she was fired from the movie version of Irving Berlin's blockbuster musical comedy *Annie Get Your Gun.* (Garland was replaced by Betty Hutton, soon to suffer a similar fall from grace.) Judy Garland became fodder for gossip columns, and the tabloids trumpeted every embarrassing misstep.

Between the late 1940s and 1955, her manner became somewhat distracted and arch, and her voice grew strident, a bit sour and wobbly. Her throbbing delivery inclined to the melodramatic and her movements became twitchy and mannered. Yet, in 1950, Judy Garland astonished the entertainment world with her appearance at the Palace Theatre on Broadway. Her performances electrified audiences and critics alike and gave rise to optimistic talk that vaudeville had made a comeback. Garland did inaugurate a new if short-lived era of big-time vaudeville, but it did not spread far beyond Broadway.

Equally miraculous was her own legendary comeback after being rejected by Hollywood and nearly imploding. Wisely, and prior to appearing at the Palace, Judy began her comeback with a four-month series of dates in European theatres that culminated in an extended engagement at London's Palladium. By the time she played London, Judy was in pretty good physical and musical shape, and her mood soared with the enthusiastic reception demonstrated by audiences.

Thus primed, she was more than ready when she was asked to reopen the newly refurbished Palace on 16 October 1951. *Judy Garland at the Palace Two-a-Day* ran for 19 weeks until 24 February 1952, although Judy missed a few shows during the fourth week when she collapsed onstage. The first half of the bill was an old-time vaudeville show, and among the acts were comedy perennials Smith and Dale and British variety comedian Max Bygraves, who sometime into the run was replaced by Señor Wences. The Nicholas Brothers also joined the bill during the run. The second half of the bill was a one-person tour de force by Judy; she sang, danced, joked and sat on the edge of the apron and talked with the audience.

Other powerhouse stars tried the same formula; Betty Hutton, Danny Kaye and Jerry Lewis followed over the next few years and did great box office, as did Harry Belafonte, who performed in concert, but others, like Liberace, failed to draw. Between those held-over engagements by the superstars, the Palace attempted traditional nine-act vaudeville bills, but, lacking a big name from Hollywood or television to head the bill, the traditional bills did not always pay the mortgage. Judy returned to the Palace 26 November 1956 and performed to great box office for 15 weeks, closing 8 January 1957.

Garland's manager, Sid Luft, had supervised Judy's personal appearances in Europe, at the Palladium and at the Palace. She married him in 1952 and they had two children, Lorna and Joey. He also produced Judy's comeback movie, the remake in 1954 of *A Star Is Born.* It garnered her an Oscar nomination and a hit song, "The Man That Got Away," but the box office did not compensate for a budget inflated by Judy's problems. Judy stayed wed to Sid for 13 years, but in the latter years they drifted apart. They divorced in 1965.

There was little of quality left in Judy Garland's career or life by the late 1950s, and that included her fourth and fifth husbands, whom she wed in the 1960s. Neither marriage lasted a year. The film *Judgment at Nuremberg* (1961) provided one of the few laurels that graced her last years.

Garland was portrayed as a lamb on the Hollywood altar sacrificed to the American dream. Certainly others had surmounted greater trials and deprivation. Judy Garland had been given abundant talent but not the ability to ride it. Alcohol and drug addiction coarsened her once-winsome and delicate femininity into the fragile self-obsession of a soap opera drama queen. She died a suicide, accidental or intended, at the age of 47 in London.

BETTY GARRETT

b: 23 May 1919, St. Joseph, MO

Betty Garrett and Larry Parks were a famous and handsome couple in the years just after the Second World War. She was a vivacious soubrette, reaching the zenith of her youthful career in a series of notable films: *Take Me Out to the Ball Game* (1948), *Neptune's Daughter* (1949), *On the Town* (1949) and *My Sister Eileen*

(1955). Larry Parks (13 December 1914, Olathe, KS—13 April 1975, Los Angeles, CA), a serious actor, found fame impersonating one of vaudeville's giants in a pair of films, *The Jolson Story* (1946) and *Jolson Sings Again* (1949).

Growing up, Betty moved with her family to various places in the Midwest and Northwest. On one occasion her father moved without them. By that time mother and daughter were both ready to fend for themselves.

Barely 16, Betty was already a go-getter, although she had only a couple of summers' dance lessons to her credit and negligible stage experience. On the plus side, her dance teachers had worked with Martha Graham, and as a favor Martha recommended Betty for a scholarship at the Neighborhood Playhouse. Betty's mother, entirely supportive, suggested an adventurous trip by sea and land that took them from Seattle to New Orleans to New York in 1936.

The Neighborhood Playhouse was a hothouse of stage training: dance classes taught by Martha Graham and Anna Sokolow, music taught by Lehman Engel, Shakespeare by Margaret Webster and Method acting by Sandy Meisner. Among the student body were Richard Conte, Edmund O'Brien, Lorne Greene and Gregory Peck.

Despite her build, long-waisted and proportionately shorter legs, Betty danced in the highly regarded Martha Graham Company and got a minor part in Orson Welles' production of *Danton's Death* for the Mercury Theater. Most of Betty's jobs were far less exalted. There were six full years of summer stock, expositions, the Borscht circuit, American Youth Theater, Unity House (a playhouse affiliated with the Garment Workers Union) and nightclub floor shows. In 1943, Betty landed a job on Broadway in *Something for the Boys,* a Cole Porter show starring Ethel Merman. Garrett had a single number but it was a showstopper. She also understudied Merman, who did her the favor of being sick for a week so Betty could play the lead.

Betty's next show, *Jackpot,* flopped, but Betty now had an act she could perform in intimate, tony nightclubs until she got a role in the Olsen & Johnson vaudeville revue, *Laffing Room Only,* in 1944. It lasted a year on Broadway and then went on an extensive tour. An even better year was 1946: Betty and Larry married and she got her big break when she starred in *Call Me Mister,* sang her exhausted lament, "South America, Take It Away!," and helped pilot the show to 700 performances.

With her success in *Call Me Mister,* Betty Garrett attracted a lot of attention both on Broadway and in Hollywood. She had joined the roster of slightly kooky girl-next-door soubrettes that included June Havoc, Celeste Holm, Nanette Fabray and Helen Gallagher. Meanwhile Larry Parks' career was peaking as well. After making 36 B movies in five years, he won the job of impersonating Jolson on the screen while Jolie dubbed the soundtrack of *The Jolson Story.* Columbia Pictures expected the movie to be a modest success. Instead it was tremendous. It revived Al Jolson's career and made Larry Parks a star. By the time he completed *Jolson Sings Again* three years later in 1949, Larry Parks was a household name. Unfortunately, the house was in Congress—the House Un-American Activities Committee (HUAC).

Larry became a test case of sorts. He received advice from every quarter: advice to comply, advice to defy, advice to give names, advice against giving names. He agreed to talk about his own activities and no one else's. He felt that if he could explain that he had joined the American Communist Party when he was a youth, when the USA and the USSR were allies against fascism, rational men and women would understand.

Few people were rational in the anticommunist hysteria that followed the Second World War. When Larry testified before HUAC, the left wing carped that he had complied with a panel of bozos out to subvert American freedoms. Yet he refused to give HUAC the names of other people who attended Communist Party meetings, so the right wing condemned him as a commie out to destroy American security. By 1950 Larry Parks was virtually unemployable in show business. It was the era when *Red Channels,* a booklet that listed suspected communists and *fellow travelers,* was compiled without evidence and distributed free to movie studios and broadcast networks. So afraid of being tarred themselves, the honchos of American media complied. A false rumor was enough to blacklist a performer.

Watching what happened to Parks prepared those who were to follow him to the HUAC stand: Lucille Ball, Sterling Hayden, Edward G. Robinson, Jose Ferrer and Lee J. Cobb, among others. Even Betty Garrett, who likewise had joined the Party as a youngster, was due to be subpoenaed, but she was pregnant at the time and HUAC wanted no sympathy for its witnesses.

Work dried up, so Betty and Larry devised a vaudeville act and spent several productive seasons in British variety. They were frequent headliners at London's Palladium and toured all over England and Scotland. To the Brits they were big American film stars, and their troubles with HUAC were of no account.

Gradually, people in the industry began to tire of *Red Channels* and to stand up to self-appointed judge advocates. First Danny Thomas hired Betty for a couple of his shows on the *All-Star Revue,* then more TV work followed when Ethel Barrymore and Carl Reiner stood up for Betty. Soon the blacklist evaporated for Betty and others, but Larry did not get a decent chance to resume his film career until 1962, when he played opposite Montgomery Clift in John Huston's film *Freud.*

Neither Betty nor Larry ever reclaimed star status, but they made a good living in truck and bus tours of Broadway comedies. Stress contributed to a series of ailments, and Larry Parks died in 1975. Betty Garrett found a place in TV history in the casts of two long runs, *Laverne and Shirley* and *All in the Family.* She also toured for years in her one-woman show, *Betty Garrett and Other Songs.*

ANTHONY GATTO

b: (Anthony Commarota) 14 April 1973, New York, NY

Known in the worldwide juggling community as a child prodigy, Anthony Gatto had an upbringing that has been compared to that of Wolfgang Amadeus Mozart. Raised and coached by his father, Nick Gatto, a vaudevillian and onetime member of a three-man acrobatic team called Los Gatos, Anthony started juggling at the age of four. While most children his age had trouble tying their shoelaces, Anthony already juggled three balls easily. When he turned five, he was able to juggle five balls, and from that point onward his skill accelerated. At eight, he entered his first international juggling competition and won a gold medal; he defeated jugglers with decades more experience.

His feat led to an appearance on the television show *That's Incredible*, which in turn led to an invitation to compete against the world's finest circus artists at the Festival Mondial in Paris, where he won his second gold medal. By age ten he was appearing at the Flamingo Hilton Casino in Las Vegas, and in his teens he claimed billing as "The World's Greatest Juggler."

In the 1990s and 2000s, Gatto split his time between performances in Las Vegas and the variety theatres in Europe. He effortlessly juggles nine rings, seven flaming torches and, when he wants to take it easy, seven balls in his hands while bouncing a soccer ball on his head.

WILLIAM GAXTON

b: (Arturo Antonio Gaxiola) 2 December 1890, San Francisco, CA—d: 2 February 1963, New York, NY

Bill Gaxton parlayed his vaudeville success into a spectacular career in Broadway musicals by Irving Berlin, George & Ira Gershwin and Cole Porter. Gaxton began in vaudeville as a song-and-dance man, added a line of chatter and ended up as a sketch actor–comedian. His first act of note was a flirtation act with his partner, Ann Laughlin. They sat on a bench, she fed him straight lines and they closed with a song.

Gaxton fared best on his own. His stage character had a bit of an edge. He was a no-nonsense singing comedian who became an excellent comedy actor, first in sketches for vaudeville and revue and then in musical comedy. Although as the lead he was cast as the hero in musicals, his stage characters were never sterling examples of American manhood. It was often a case of the slightly larcenous hero straightening out for the right girl. He would have made a good Sky Masterson in *Guys and Dolls.*

It was Palace booker Eddie Darling who recommended Bill Gaxton for Irving Berlin's *Music Box Revue of 1922.* It was a great start for a newcomer to Broadway. The revue boasted a superb lineup: Clark & McCullough, Charlotte Greenwood, Grace La Rue, John Steele and the Rath Brothers. Deservedly, it ran 330 performances between 23 October 1922 and 4 August 1923.

Gaxton did not desert vaudeville. He was in the big time and earning a headliner's salary. Late in the Palace's two-a-day heyday, Eddie Darling teamed Bill with Lou Holtz as co-emcees. The combination of Cantor and Jessel had been sensational, so Darling wanted to repeat the formula. Gaxton and Holtz did well, hosting for eight weeks, and more dual emcees followed, notably Jack Haley and Benny Rubin. Bill Gaxton found time to make a few movies. His first two were silents. *It's the Old Army Game* (1926) was a comedy vehicle for W.C. Fields. *Stepping Along* (1926) simply provided a paycheck.

Gaxton starred in the title role of *A Connecticut Yankee* (1927–28), a Lew Fields, Rodgers & Hart, Busby Berkeley musical that played from 3 November 1927 through 27 October 1928 at the Vanderbilt Theatre for a total of 421 performances. In 1931, Gaxton starred in what most observers regarded as one of America's great musical comedies; *Of Thee I Sing.* George S. Kaufman directed and cowrote the book with Morrie Ryskind, and music and lyrics were provided by George and Ira Gershwin. Gaxton did a fine job as president of the USA, but Victor Moore nearly stole the show as the vice president whom no one remembered. The show was a smash, critically and at the box office, where it kept cashiers counting from 26 December 1931 through 14 January 1933. It also won the Pulitzer Prize and toured profitably despite the Great Depression. *Let 'Em Eat Cake* (1933) was a sequel to *Of Thee I Sing.* The Gershwin brothers,

Kaufman, Ryskind, Gaxton and Moore were again teamed, but the musical's tone and the public's mood had changed. It closed in 12 weeks.

Between his stage successes, Gaxton again tried his luck in Hollywood. His first feature-length talkie was the film version of *Fifty Million Frenchmen* (1931). Gaxton and Helen Broderick were brought over from the stage show, but precious little else. The film proved that Broderick was a natural for feature films as a second lead, and it introduced vaudeville zanies Ole Olsen & Chic Johnson to movie audiences.

In 1932, Joe Santley, a former vaudeville and stage star, rounded up old friends William Gaxton, Victor Moore, Lois Moran, De Wolf Hopper, Charles King and Otto Kruger for a two-reel romp, *Ladies Not Allowed* (1932), an entry in what was planned as a Lambs Club Gambol series based on the famous theatrical club's annual stage events. (Gaxton later served as Shepherd of the Lambs Club.) *Their Big Moment* (1934) was a programmer, one of a bottom-of-the-bill series pairing ZaSu Pitts and Slim Summerville. After that one, Gaxton left films for nine years.

Anything Goes proved that Broadway still had a pulse in 1935. Ethel Merman, Bill Gaxton and Victor Moore paced the Cole Porter show to 420 performances. Howard Lindsay directed and cowrote the book with Russell Crouse. The show was Lindsay and Crouse's first collaboration and the beginning of a string of hits. *The White Horse Inn* (1936–37) was an operetta staged as an extravaganza at the cavernous Center Theatre in Rockefeller Center, where Gaxton, Kitty Carlisle and Robert Halliday could barely be seen and hardly be heard during their 233 performances.

Sophie Tucker and Mary Martin joined Gaxton & Moore for Cole Porter's *Leave It to Me!* (1938–39), a solid hit with 291 shows. Future star Mary Martin stole the show with her number "My Heart Belongs to Daddy." Gaxton won another plum the following season when he starred with Victor Moore, Vera Zorina and Irene Bordoni in *Louisiana Purchase* (1940–41), which ran for a year. Morrie Ryskind wrote the book and Irving Berlin supplied the songs. George Balanchine choreographed the ballets for Zorina, his wife.

It had been an amazing run for William Gaxton. Despite hard economic times, Gaxton starred in at least as many popular and critical successes during the 1930s as any other Broadway star, male or female. His next two shows were forgettable. In 1942, he joined a bill of Victor Moore, Paul & Grace Hartman, Hildegard, Jack Cole, Fred Sanborn and Zero Mostel for a vaudeville revue, *Keep 'Em Laughing*—which it did not. Gaxton & Moore left the show; Gracie Fields was brought in and the producers retitled the show *Top-Notchers,* but it still did not sell.

Gaxton's run of bad luck did not improve in Hollywood. After he got mired in one musical mediocrity, *Something to Shout About* (1943), produced and directed by Gregory Ratoff, it is astonishing that Bill was again inveigled, that same year, into another Ratoff shoestring movie musical muddle, *The Heat's On* (1943). Gaxton played a penurious Broadway producer who tried to con an investor (Victor Moore) into backing a nonexistent show with a star (Mae West) who refused to sign with him. It was remarkable that Gregory Ratoff did not see himself in the character. Only Victor Moore, Almira Sessions and Hazel Scott emerged from the wreckage with unsullied reputations.

William Gaxton redeemed himself in his final film, another musical, *Billy Rose's Diamond Horseshoe* (1945), which starred Betty Grable supported by Gaxton, Beatrice Kay, Dick Haymes and Phil Silvers. That same year, Gaxton and old partner Victor Moore returned to Broadway in the cast of *Hollywood Pinafore* (1945), the Gilbert & Sullivan operetta as adapted by George S. Kaufman. It was one of Kaufman's few failures and Billy Gaxton's last stage show.

Starting around 1950, a goodly number of movie stars past their glory years signed on to host network television series. Often the shows were drama anthologies, and the host did little more than appear at the top of the show to introduce that night's playlet. William Gaxton led the parade as host of *Nash Airflyte Theatre,* named for one of the sponsor's automobile brands. The scripts were varied and good, and fine actors agreed to star in the weekly dramas, but CBS exiled the show to the 10:30 slot on Thursday nights, where it followed an audience participation show, *Truth or Consequences,* and was opposite ABC's *Roller Derby,* Dumont's boxing and the schmaltz-waltz half-hour *Wayne King Show.* Bill's show eked out one season. A few years later, 1953, Gaxton acted in an hour-long *United States Steel Hour.* It was his swan song. He died of cancer, ten years later, at 73.

GELATINS

Commonly referred to as gels and sometimes misnamed jells, as in jellies, gelatins were transparent colored coverings cut to fit metal frames placed in front of lights and lamps. Different colors were used to change the mood of scenes, alter the color of a scene and costumes or combine with makeup to produce a flattering, frightening or comic effect. Originally these transparencies were made from sheets of hardened gelatins derived from animals. After the Second World War they were replaced by synthetic materials such as nonflammable plastics.

In vaudeville they were used infrequently, most often on the roving spotlight.

GERRY SOCIETY

The Gerry Society was the informal name for the Society for the Prevention of Cruelty to Children, founded in 1875 by Elbridge T. Gerry, grandson of a man who was a U.S. vice president and a Massachusetts governor. Governor Gerry had won notoriety in the early nineteenth century by dividing the state into awkward and barely contiguous districts so that his political party, the Democratic Republicans, had maximum influence in the selection of electors. This political maneuvering came to be known as gerrymandering. A hard G is used when pronouncing Gerry, although, over the years, the G has softened for Gerry mandering.

His descendant Elbridge T. Gerry took on the cause of exploited children under 16 years of age by establishing the SPCC. For 20 years he captured headlines as he made a social and political issue of child labor practices.

Gerry's attention was engaged more by children performing on the stage than youngsters laboring in factories or homeless urchins selling newspapers. Gerry railed against parents who exploited their children by exhibiting them and exposing them to what he saw as the pervading corruption of disreputable and semi-reputable theatre, but he gave short shrift to children living in the streets without homes or families or those laboring six days a week, ten hours a day in sweatshop factories. Geography was a factor: Gerry kept a watchful eye on shows in New York City, but his influence diminished with distance. Often acts and plays with children in them could perform throughout the USA with little interference until they reached New York City or a few other cities.

Gerry was either more flexible or less consistent, depending upon one's view, than his reputation allowed. Persuaded that Adele and Fred Astaire were being well cared for and educated, he reached an agreement with their mother that permitted Adele and Fred to work onstage in New York. However, he always tried to prevent Buster Keaton from working, perhaps because the family act was a punishing roughhouse. The Gerry Society also pursued Elsie Janis, Baby June (Havoc) and Sammy Davis Jr., whose acts were no more demanding than the Astaires'.

Adults in the acts were known to try to pass off minors as midgets. That ruse became a standard gag in plays and movies. Mickey Rooney and other kids appeared as underage performers, mimicking adult mannerisms and brandishing cigars to throw the bloodhounds off the trail.

GET BACK YOUR PICTURES

When a local theatre manager decided to tell an act it was canceled, he sometimes brought along the act's promotional photographs. Also to be returned was the act's music held by the pit band leader, but it was the sight of the manager heading backstage with photos under his arm that was the sure signal that all was not well. The phrase was used waggishly to refer to dying (in the literal as well as the showbiz sense).

GET OVER

To get over is to be appreciated by an audience, to score, to make a hit with them.

GHOST WALKED, THE

When the ghost walked on a Saturday evening, it meant that the company manager came around and paid all of the performers their due salary. Although the phrase gained currency throughout show business, from legit troupes and stock companies to vaudeville performers and burlesque companies, it likely was coined in the early nineteenth century by a member of a traveling theatrical company, one with a repertory that included Shakespeare, specifically *Hamlet.* The ghost refers to Hamlet's dead father.

To save the expense of carrying another actor in the troupe, the manager often doubled in bit parts, such as the apparition and voice belonging to the ghost of Hamlet's father. Supposedly, when the company manager, still wearing some vestige of his costume, came round with the pay packets immediately after the last Saturday performance, a wag greeted him, "Ah, the ghost walks!"

At least as likely and more amusing is the following anecdote. Typical of traveling companies, the tour turned out to be a rough row to hoe. Audiences were poor, and the company had not been paid for some weeks. The actor playing the ghost of Hamlet's father was fuming offstage when he heard Hamlet say of the ghost, "Perchance 'twill walk again." From the wings the ghost interjected, "No! I'll be damned if the ghost walks any more until our salaries are paid!"

GILLY OR GILLEY

A small fair or carnival with tented entertainment that traveled rural areas and set up wherever they could draw a crowd. A gilly was larger than a medicine show but smaller than most carnivals. The name derived from the type of wagons that carried the mechanical rides, game booths, show tent and other equipment.

CHARLES S. GILPIN

b: (Charles Sydney Gilpin) 20 November 1878, Richmond, VA—d: 6 May 1930, Trenton, NJ

Charles Gilpin was reputedly a great talent and the first Negro to attract critical mainstream notice as a great actor. Before he was able to take on dramatic roles, he spent nearly 30 years as a variety performer, mostly as a singer but dancing and doing comedy as well.

The play that brought Charles S. Gilpin to the Broadway stage was *The Emperor Jones* by Eugene O'Neill. The year was 1920, and Gilpin played Brutus Jones, the lead and title role. It took 30 years to get from Richmond, Virginia, to Manhattan's Great White Way.

One of 14 children, he managed to complete the eighth grade in the local Catholic parochial school before he was apprenticed to the printing trade. His first job was with the black newspaper *Richmond Planet.* How he began in show business is unclear, but even by his mid-teens he was heard singing in a fine baritone at various events.

By the time he reached 18, he had latched onto a minstrel show passing through town and took to the road as a performer. He sang with two outfits, the Big Spectacular Log Cabin Company and the Great Southern Minstrel Barnstorming Company; both proved to be less impressive than their names, and twice Gilpin was left stranded.

In 1897 Charles Gilpin wed Florence Howard and settled in Philadelphia, where he found work in a barbershop, in a boxing gym and as a janitor before going back into the printing business. They had one son, Paul Wilson, born in 1903. On the side, Charles sought and found some work as a singer. His first real break came in 1903 when he was engaged by another touring outfit, the Canadian Jubilee Singers, with whom he remained until midway through the 1905–06 season, when he got a job singing in the chorus of *Abyssinia,* the musical starring Bert Williams and George Walker.

Some sources claim that Gilpin assisted Williams & Walker in their act during one or more of their many vaudeville seasons. At the beginning of the 1906–07 season, Gilpin signed on with the Smart Set Company, an act that had been touring since 1902, when it starred Ernest Hogan and Billy McLain, who also produced and wrote the act.

For the 1907–08 season, he joined the Pekin Stock Company in Chicago under the producing hands of J. Ed Green. The shows were musicals: *Captain Rufus* and *The Husbands,* but at least Gilpin had featured roles that required him to act instead of being stuck in the chorus. Some of his roles called for blacking up and playing comedy. Despite the indignity, stock was excellent training because a new production was mounted every two weeks. Gilpin remained with the all-black Pekin Stock Company until 1909, when the company seems to have dissolved.

From 1911 to 1913 Gilpin barnstormed with the Pan American Octette. In 1913, he joined the Negro Players, one of the first black stock companies. Under that banner, Gilpin appeared in *The Old Man's Boy* (1913), which opened 12 May in Philadelphia and moved to New York in June. The story was peppered with song-and-dance numbers, but the third and final act was intended as straight drama. Gilpin was getting closer to his dramatic goal but still singing and dancing.

In 1915, he joined the Anita Bush Stock Company at Harlem's Lincoln Theatre. There Gilpin acted in what some believe was the first wholly prose play written and performed by professional Negro actors, *The Girl at the Fort.* The play and the company moved to the Lafayette Theatre that same year. Gilpin continued with the company and played the lead in *Southern Life,* but he quit the company in the spring of 1916 in a salary dispute. He moved to Cleveland, where he established the Gilpin Players in 1916. After the actor moved on, the African American company continued to perform and renamed itself Karamu Theatre.

In 1918, Charles Gilpin wrote music and lyrics for *The Bridal Not,* a musical put on by the Mask and Wig Club at the University of Pennsylvania. That Gilpin may have been a different person, but, as Gilpin continued to perform in vaudeville, singing and doing comedy, he may also have added to his earnings through songwriting.

At some point during the mid-1910s, Gilpin formed a vaudeville act with Lillian Woods. Perhaps this is where Eugene O'Neill spotted him, as O'Neill frequented vaudeville houses. More likely, O'Neill was alerted to attend Gilpin's performance on Broadway as the black minister in *Abraham Lincoln* (1919) by John Drinkwater.

O'Neill pressed for Gilpin to be engaged to play the lead in *The Emperor Jones,* which first opened November 1920 Off-Broadway at the Neighborhood Playhouse and moved uptown to Broadway on 29 January 1921, where it finished its run of 204 performances before touring nationally for two years.

The Drama League honored Gilpin as one of the ten persons who had distinguished the American theatre that year. Despite protests and threats of boycott by some whites, the Drama League invited Gilpin to the presentation banquet to receive his award.

Not everything was smooth behind the scenes, but it was not primarily a matter of race. Gilpin seems to have been impetuous and a bit imperious in his professional relations with both blacks and whites. O'Neill, who took himself as seriously as Gilpin took himself, objected when Gilpin changed lines he felt were racially offensive. Gilpin also drank to excess. O'Neill was hardly one to complain about drinking, but Gilpin was onstage while O'Neill stayed off it. Although O'Neill genuinely thought Gilpin a great talent, he did not offer Gilpin the role in the London company of *The Emperor Jones.* Instead, it was given to Paul Robeson. And it was Robeson who played the role when the play was revived on Broadway in 1924. Gilpin did play *The Emperor Jones* again in two short-lived revivals, both in 1926, one of which he directed.

After the Broadway run of *The Emperor Jones,* the production toured for a couple of seasons. Gilpin's critical and popular success in *The Emperor Jones* on Broadway and on the road increased offers (and salary) for him to resume his vaudeville bookings with Lillian Woods.

During the 1920s, the Lafayette Theatre, known proudly as the Uptown Palace, offered all types of stage shows, from Shakespeare to vaudeville. The management formed the Lafayette Players to present serious drama. Gilpin became a leading member of the company early on. The Players lasted until about 1932, performing a mix of classical works, including Shakespeare, and contemporary plays, but the Depression forced management to concentrate on shows that were more popular, such as vaudeville and burlesque revues. Historian Bill Reed claims that the Lafayette Players relocated to Los Angeles in 1928, but the players may have split into two struggling groups.

In March 1924, Gilpin appeared in an all-black cast revival of *Roseanne,* by Nan Bagby Stephens. His costar, Rose McClendon, garnered the lion's share of praise while Gilpin was faulted. Perhaps it was a matter of his increasing alcoholism.

There were reports that he lost his voice in 1926 and was operating an elevator. Little else is known about the last years of Gilpin's life. According to Tom Fletcher in the book *100 Years of the Negro in Show Business,* Gilpin again tried to form his own stock company but failed, then attempted to find work in vaudeville. When unable to get show work, Gilpin toiled as an elevator operator and a railroad porter.

A Charles Gilpin is listed as the composer and lyricist for a Shubert show, *Listen Dearie* (1926). This may or may not have been the same man. More certain is a film credit for that year: Gilpin played the lead, an alcoholic father, in *Ten Nights in a Barroom* (1926), which was produced and released by the Colored Players Company. He lost lead roles in Universal Pictures' *Uncle Tom's Cabin* (1927) and Fox's *Hearts in Dixie* (1929) for what the Fox studio charitably described as "carelessness and crankiness," more harshly and frankly reported as belligerence and drunkenness. In 1928, Gilpin was engaged for a featured role in Ben Hecht's and Charlie MacArthur's comedy drama *The Front Page,* but Gilpin arrived at rehearsals drunk and was dismissed from the cast.

His last few years were spent in drunken, anonymous poverty. He was found dead in Eldridge Park, near Trenton, New Jersey, and was buried nearby. His second wife, Alma Benjamin, survived him, but they had long been separated. It fell to Gilpin's old vaudeville partner, Lillian Woods, to have his body exhumed and brought to the Woodlawn Cemetery in New York City for reburial. Woods also arranged for a memorial service.

LOTTIE GILSON

b: (Lydia Deagon) 1862, Basel, Switzerland—d: 10 June 1912, New York, NY

Little is known about Lottie Gilson, who set the standard for the vaudeville soubrette along with Maggie Cline. Gilson's official debut was made at the Old National Theatre on the Bowery, then under the management of Mike Heneman. The year was 1884, and Lottie Gilson, as she was billed, was 21 or 22 years old and married for the first time.

She may have sung earlier in other venues, beer halls and the like, where all-male audiences, well in their cups, called for one lachrymose and banal ballad after the other. Or perhaps she first performed in her native country, Switzerland, and did not arrive in the USA until she was a young woman.

At the Old National, her repertoire was made up of sentimental ballads, but they were appreciated, and it was not long before she was engaged by other theatre managers. Lottie appeared at Miner's Theatre and Tony Pastor's new 14th Street Theatre in Lower Manhattan and Hyde & Behman's in Brooklyn. The melodramatic ballads soon yielded to character comedy songs like "You're Not the Only Pebble on the Beach," "Can't You Take It Back and Change It for a Boy?," "My Mother Was a Lady," "Games We Used to Play," "I Don't Blame You, Tom," and "The Sidewalks of New York" ("East Side, West Side"), which Lottie introduced from the stage of the Old London Theatre on the Bowery.

Lottie was a pert-looking lass, with dark hair and a fine figure, and according to contemporary reports, she knew how to engage an audience. In her breezy, friendly manner and her way with a naughty song, she was like many of the soubrettes of the English music-hall, such as Marie Lloyd and Vesta Victoria.

Lottie also knew how to make a little money on the side, and she was criticized for taking money from Tin Pan Alley promoters to plug songs that were fair to middling and did her no credit.

She also adopted a contrivance that later became a cliché in burlesque. She used a hand mirror to reflect the spotlight into the audience, preferably singling out older, bald men, while singing to them in a mock coquettish fashion. Lottie Gilson also claimed to be the first to employ a boy in the balcony or a box seat to join her in song. This began as a fluke, supposedly, when a boy unexpectedly stood up and sang, but more likely the boy was a plant from a sheet music publisher, and the boy was there to demonstrate to the audience how easily the song could be learned. Gus Edwards began his career in this way; in the employ of songsmiths, he sang from Bowery theatre balconies a repeat chorus to the songs that Lottie Gilson, Maggie Cline or Emma Carus had finished. Whether the initial outburst by a boy singer was a ruse or an unplanned event, Gilson quickly made the interpolation part of her act. Audiences loved it until it became hackneyed through overuse by many singers.

By the late 1890s, a few complained that some of her material was a trifle blue. The criticisms leveled against her for payola or suggestive songs were inconsequential. Lottie Gilson was a darling of vaudeville audiences, and theatre managers recognized the value of that. In praise of her drawing power at the box office, someone tagged her "a little magnet." Not one to miss an opportunity, the petite soubrette chose as her billing matter "Lottie Gilson, the Little Magnet."

Of the many songs associated with Gilson, none was requested more than "The Sunshine of Paradise Alley."

She's had offers to wed by the dozen, 'tis said,
Still she always refused them politely;
But of late she's been seen with young Tommy Killeen,
Going out for a promenade nightly.
We can all guess the rest, for the boy she loves best
Will soon change her name from McNally;
Though he may change her name, she'll be known
just the same
As the sunshine of Paradise Alley.

Over the years, Lottie Gilson married several times, abused her constitution and suffered depression and physical illness. She died at the age of 50, still popular, just as vaudeville was entering its golden decade.

BILLY GLASON

b: 10 September 1904, Boston, MA— d: unknown

A singer, comedian and songwriter, Glason segued into vaudeville by way of song plugging. Born into an immigrant Jewish family, he sold newspapers during his boyhood. Billy was in his early teens when he began singing to illustrated slides at small, small-time theatres in Boston and selling sheet music. Instead of demonstrating the sheet music in a music shop or the music department of a department store, Billy used to go to beach boardwalks, like Revere Beach, located north of Boston at the end of a long trolley car ride, and, with megaphone in hand, sing to people gathered in the ice cream parlors along the beach. Billy worked on his patter so the potential customers would understand that he was not simply singing for their enjoyment, but was selling the music he sang. By his mid-teens, Billy had the rudiments of a vaudeville act.

For a number of years he was a *coast defender*, filling in where needed as a *disappointment act*; later he began to get booked for split weeks in outlying cities like Lowell, Worcester and Springfield in Massachusetts and Providence, Rhode Island, all dates within a few hours' travel from Boston. Throughout the 1920s he played Keith-Orpheum houses on the big time and Poli, Proctor, Western Vaudeville, Interstate, Butterfield and Gus Sun on the small time.

Billy Glason was an assertive comedian like Milton Berle and an effective singer to boot. His musicality served him well, as he wrote a number of songs and special material for himself and others. He stayed in the business up through the presentation house era. Gradually, he was in demand by a younger crop of comedians for jokes and made a good living creating special material for others.

JACKIE GLEASON

b: (Herbert John Gleason) 26 February 1916, Brooklyn, NY—d: 24 June 1987, Fort Lauderdale, FL

No one expected young Jackie Gleason to become a star. Certainly not his fellow comedians who hung around with him between gigs. They knew Gleason was talented. In any group of off-duty comics having a few drinks or a bite to eat, Jackie was one of the funniest. He just was not very funny in front of audiences.

A lot about Jackie Gleason's life didn't follow the expected trajectory. In his younger years, he was very much the neighborhood guy—fat, coarse, a pool hustler, an occasional brawler, limited in his prospects but well-liked. What was extraordinary was the way his life evolved. He became one of the most beloved comedians in American history and blossomed into an intellectually curious man, well-read, articulate, complex and sophisticated, and yet he clung to a flashy gold standard of success, a Vegas-style conspicuous consumption of all that the top shelf of life had to offer—clothes, booze, food, women. The carefree, spendthrift bon vivant that audiences and offstage sociability brought out in Gleason was the reverse of the brooding private man. By turns jocular and melancholy, his personality verified the contradictions in the Black Irish stereotype.

Gleason's childhood neighborhood had been Bushwick, a section of Brooklyn inhabited by the Irish, Italians and Jews during the First World War and the 1920s. Jackie's mother, Mae, taught him to read, and he went to school with that advantage over most of his classmates. Jackie's dad, Herb, frequently took Jackie to the Halsey Theatre to catch the weekly vaudeville and movie bill. From his first Halsey show, Jackie knew he wanted to entertain. Both his parents were drinkers; home life was dreary, impoverished and filled with disappointments and recriminations. The family moved often. Once, the father moved without wife or son. Herb Gleason left, never to be heard from again, just before Jackie's ninth birthday.

Gleason quit school shortly after he began high school. For a time he bummed around with street-corner pals, but he scored well enough in a couple of amateur shows to win the once-a-week job of emceeing the Amateur Night at the Halsey. By 1935, Jackie's mother had grown ill and weary. Jackie looked after her as well as he knew how, but she weakened and died, only 49 years old. At age 19, Jackie found himself on his own. He moved to Manhattan, sharing a room with two other hopefuls, and scraped along, week by week, taking whatever work was offered. Within a year he married.

Jackie's jobs included boxing in carnivals, bouncing in saloons, exhibition diving at Atlantic City's Steel Pier and emceeing in burlesque and nightclubs when he could get that work. Most of his intermittent club work was in New Jersey, and one gig, at the Club Miami, familiarly known as the Bucket of Blood, stretched into a two-year engagement. At the start, Gleason purloined Milton Berle's act and performed it word for word, although without imitating Milton's delivery. Thus began a lifelong relationship between the two comics. Milton claimed friendship. Gleason did not. Yet, later, when both Berle and Gleason had become major television stars and someone criticized Berle, Jackie countered that no one could understand everything that Berle had to go through to get where he was in show business and what it took to stay there. Indeed, according to W.J. Weatherby, one of Gleason's biographers, Milton Berle was Gleason's most frequent guest star in his later shows and always engaged at Berle's top price.

Jackie Gleason was a natural for clubs because he enjoyed the atmosphere of booze and people out for a good time. He was at his best with the audience when his devil-may-care attitude took over. He was weakest as a monologist. Stand-up comedy was never his strength. His two years on the New Jersey nightclub battlefields seasoned him, and he shed his reputation as a sidewalk comedian when he began to score consistently with various audiences.

Jackie had been 20 when he married Genevieve Halford in a Roman Catholic ceremony. Their first daughter was born three years later in 1939, and their second in 1941. The roles of nightclub comedian, big spender, husband and father did not coalesce into one happy life, and Gleason chose career and high times over husband and father. There was more to the growing divide than Jackie's shortcomings. Genevieve was a devout believer in Catholicism. Jackie was a searcher; his reflective nature led him to read about other religions as his curiosity about life expanded into various fields. They continued to drift apart, or Jackie did the drifting; they separated in 1954 but did not divorce until 1970.

Professionally, he was growing more secure. His pay jumped from $100 to $300 a week. He sometimes doubled, playing two clubs at the same time, shuttling between them via a furiously wild cab ride. The legitimate stage beckoned in 1940 with a small role in *Keep Off the Grass,* a musical starring Jimmy Durante, Ray Bolger, Jane Froman and Larry Adler. It lasted only a month on Broadway. Gleason recalled with affectionate respect that Jane Froman drew him aside to kindheartedly advise him to drop his nightclub persona and habits like ad libbing and to stick to the script and immerse himself in character. It was Gleason's only acting class, and one that proved critical to his later success as a serious actor.

When his first big break arrived, it did not do him much good. Jack Warner had seen Gleason doing his nightclub act, signed him to a $250-a-week contract and sent him to the Warner Brothers' studios in Hollywood, where they had no idea what to do with the beefy unknown comic. Despite several small roles in comedies and gangster pictures, the only lasting impression Gleason seems to have made in filmland was as a second-string Jack Oakie.

Years later, detractors would claim that Jack Oakie was the original Jackie Gleason. Gleason readily admitted a resemblance to Oakie. Consciously or not,

Gleason was in the process of adapting from a monologist to a character and sketch comedian, and he credited Oakie and Edward Everett Horton, veterans of movie comedy, as superb models.

Though he made little headway in the film studios, the crème of the movie colony enthusiastically applauded Gleason's nighttime appearances at Slapsie Maxie's, a nighterie co-owned by Slapsie Maxie Rosenbloom, a former boxer turned character comedian.

No other movie offers followed the end of his Warner Brothers contract, and Gleason returned home, but only until the tension prompted him to resume his bachelor life. He contributed a smaller share of his earnings to his family's support than to the support of the various watering holes he called home.

His excessive weight exempted Jackie from the wartime conscription. While his weight remained steady, his career fluctuated. He got two jobs in 1943. First he toured in Chic Johnson's role in *Hellzapoppin'*, the Olsen & Johnson Broadway smash hit. In October and November of that year, he joined jazz singer Frances Faye and ballad singer Jane Froman (again) in the tryout tour and a three-week Broadway stand of the final edition of the six *Artists and Models* revues that the Shuberts produced between 1923 and 1943. The next year he returned to Broadway in *Follow the Girls,* which lasted 882 performances—his first big hit. Yet it was back to nightclubs, but at least they were in Manhattan and not Jersey. He did vaudeville of a sort when he played the opulent and cavernous Roxy Theatre for $3,000 a week. Jackie then appeared on radio for a fraction of that salary in several short-lived shows.

In 1949, Gleason managed to play Broadway again in *Along Fifth Avenue,* for which he won the George Jean Nathan Award. The show provided four months of work. A year earlier, the producer of the radio show *The Life of Riley* had seen Gleason when he appeared on Ed Sullivan's Sunday night *Toast of the Town.* Riley had been played on radio by William Bendix, whose movie contract forbade any television appearances. When *The Life of Riley* moved to TV for the 1949–50 season, Gleason was hired to play the title role. The show was dropped after one season until 1953, when Bendix was free to resume the role. In 1950 Hollywood made Gleason another offer, but his role as an Arab in *The Desert Hawk* turned out to be as bad as or worse than his previous roles in the nine films he made in the 1940s. Jackie did not go near Hollywood for a decade.

Television, however, was not through with Gleason, nor he with it; the underfinanced Dumont network hired Jackie to replace Jerry Lester as host of *Cavalcade of Stars,* four months into its second season, 1950–51. Jackie's Hollywood break had not panned out. Studios did not know how to use Gleason, and did not bother to figure it out, so he approached the DuMont show with few hopes and low expectations, although he had been surprised that his single season as Chester Riley did more for his public recognition than 15 years of Broadway and nightclubs. During its first two seasons (Jack Carter had been the star for the first season), the low-budget *Cavalcade of Stars* was slotted against NBC's *Your Show of Shows,* one of television's most professionally produced shows, a major hit that starred Sid Caesar and Imogene Coca.

Both Gleason and *Cavalcade of Stars* fared far better when the show was moved to Friday nights and gradually built its audience against NBC's *All Star Revue.* Gleason's television career was more checkered than is usually remembered. One thinks of the original variety hour and then the half-hour *The Honeymooners,* but there were many changes in formats and casts.

Gleason's initial contract with the DuMont network was for four weeks, and Jackie expected to return to Slapsie Maxie's once the four weeks ended. Instead, Gleason stayed with *Cavalcade* for one and a half seasons. During that time he displayed all his familiar characters: Reggie Van Gleason, the Poor Soul, Joe the Bartender, Fenwick Babbitt and Moriarty the Undertaker, among others, including, of course, Ralph Kramden.

It is doubtful that Gleason at first realized that he had found something universal in the Kramdens and Nortons. Creating them was a tip of Gleason's hat to Bushwick and the folks who struggled to make their lives in places where hope seldom had reason to bloom. Ralph Kramden portrayed by another comedian could have been repellent. Despite his blustering rages, Gleason conveyed the angst of the man. Reggie van Gleason and the Poor Soul were homage to the great physical comedians of silent films as well as extremes of Jackie's contrary view of himself: Reggie blessed with luck, the Poor Soul burdened with the Fates' disdain. Joe the Bartender was a dumbing down of Gleason holding forth at Toots Shor's bar, his favorite watering hole, owned by one of his dearest friends.

It was on *Cavalcade* that he first teamed with Art Carney and the June Taylor Dancers and put together the stable of scriptwriters who would move with him to CBS. William Paley, the founding ruler of CBS, lured Gleason away from DuMont by offering him $8,000 for each weekly variety show, a figure five times his DuMont pay. In succeeding seasons, that weekly salary escalated astronomically. The hour-long *Jackie Gleason Show* aired at 8 P.M. on Saturday nights for the first three seasons, 1952 through 1955. It shrunk to 30 minutes for the fourth season, when it was turned into a situation comedy, *The Honeymooners,* starring Gleason,

Carney, Audrey Meadows and Joyce Randolph. More successful in reruns than in its original broadcasts, *The Honeymooners* ran for only one year, a total of 39 episodes, because Jackie did not wish to grow stale in a situation comedy. Skits featuring Ralph Kramden, his wife, Alice, and neighbors Ed and Trixie Norton had appeared in past Gleason variety shows and would appear in future shows, and *The Honeymooners'* later popularity resulted in those skits being excerpted and reissued in the 1980s as "lost episodes" of *The Honeymooners.* They made Gleason quite wealthy. For the 1956–57 season, however, Gleason and company reverted to variety, after which Gleason and company took a year off. Although there were still successful shows and seasons ahead, the glory years of television were over for Jackie Gleason.

Jackie returned for the 1958–59 season with Buddy Hackett replacing Art Carney as second banana in a show that did not find favor. He had better luck on Broadway. He was given the lead role in a 1959 revival of William Saroyan's *The Time of Your Life.* Later that year, Jackie played the alcoholic brother-in-law in *Take Me Along,* a 1959 Broadway musical version of Eugene O'Neill's only comedy, the warmhearted *Ah Wilderness.*

Jackie tried weekly television again, this time with a quiz show that was so inane that he took the brave and unorthodox step of publicly apologizing for it on camera. The talk show format that replaced it did not find much of an audience either. In 1962, Gleason brought the variety format back to Saturday nights at 7:30 with the one-hour *Jackie Gleason Show: The American Scene Magazine,* which proved quite popular, although Jackie seemed less inspired, and neither the plots nor the chemistry equaled the legendary seasons. His new sidekicks included comedian Alice Ghostley, a revue comedian with a light, fey touch, and Frank Fontanne, a singing comic whose limited repertoire soon palled.

Gleason's attention was elsewhere. His third experience with Hollywood, a series of films made in the early 1960s, probably encouraged Jackie to think he had a future in films. The optimism began with *The Hustler* (1961) and his role as Minnesota Fats, a pool hustler, that earned Gleason an Academy Award nomination as best supporting actor. The optimism grew with another featured role in *Requiem for a Heavyweight* (1962) and the starring role in *Gigot* (1962), a movie largely his own creation in which he gave a pantomimic performance of comedy and sentiment. Optimism dimmed after *Soldier in the Rain* and *Papa's Delicate Condition* (both 1963). While these films were respectable successes, Gleason had failed to create a box-office demand in movie houses; the public was used to seeing him for free on TV.

In 1964, with more cast changes, Jackie moved his show and his base of operations to Miami Beach. George Jessel joined the variety format as a roving talent scout for young performers whose television debut was on Gleason's show. The 1966–67 season reunited Gleason with Art Carney after a nine-year absence. Sheila MacRae and Jane Kean (of the Kean Sisters) were the boys' new spouses. Although the new *Jackie Gleason Show* lasted four seasons, Gleason continued to experiment. Sometimes Jackie did a variety show; more than half the time it was an hour-long Honeymooners plot done either as straight comedy or as musical comedy.

Jackie chose big-band music, such as the Dorsey Brothers, to replace his show during the 13-week summer. Gleason had become very interested in the music. Soon he began making a series of long-playing records that featured romantic compositions written and conducted by Jackie Gleason. They surprised the industry and Gleason himself by proving very successful, and there were three dozen albums in all.

As Gleason neared the end of his TV series career, he was becoming more of a straight character actor than a comedian, and the lack of satisfaction that his career brought him was increasingly evident. In 1971 Gleason was canceled. His show still placed in the top 10 or 20 in the ratings, but he was a victim of demographics. Like Red Skelton's audience, Gleason's was middle-aged and older, not the buying public of young adults and teens that sponsors craved. So, despite top-ranked shows (Red was fifth), Skelton and Gleason were put out to pasture.

Jackie met the cancellation philosophically, outwardly at least. He spent more time golfing and less energy pushing his talent or career. More was occurring on the personal front. His 13-year romance with Honey Merrill, begun in 1959, had disintegrated by 1970 without the prospect of marriage. Some believed Honey to be the love of Gleason's life. He married a second time, in 1971, and divorced a second time in 1974. In 1975 Gleason married Marilyn Taylor, June Taylor's sister, on the second time around. Marilyn and Jackie had been a couple back in the early 1950s until Marilyn decided there was little future for their relationship since Gleason's first wife was unwilling to agree to a divorce.

In 1978, Gleason, then 62, agreed to return to the stage in *The Sly Fox,* an adaptation of Ben Johnson's *Volpone* by Larry Gelbart. While playing Chicago, Gleason suffered a severe heart attack and underwent a triple bypass. On the plus side, among another dozen films made for either exhibition or television, several caught the public's fancy. Jackie was handed the role of an apoplectic redneck sheriff opposite Burt Reynolds in *Smokey and the Bandit* (1977). So successful was the film that it prompted two sequels (1980 and 1983). These were followed by starring roles in *The Toy* (1982) and *The Sting II* (1983).

There was not much left to Gleason's career after the final Hollywood hurrah. He appeared in several movies, attracting attention with Laurence Olivier in the dull *Mr. Halpern and Mr. Johnson* (1983), an ill-prepared reunion with Art Carney as *Izzy and Moe* (1985) and opposite Tom Hanks in *Nothing in Common* (1986).

The Great One, as Orson Welles had tagged him, had lost zest. Over a hard-living lifetime his iron constitution had taken a great beating. Decades of overeating, heavy drinking and little sleep wore him down during his final decade. The television syndication of *The Honeymooners* reminded anyone who had forgotten that Jackie Gleason was a brilliant sketch comedian and beloved by his fans. When he died, age 72, from colon and liver cancer, the public was surprised. He had not publicized his illness. *The Honeymooners* remains popular even after the turn of the twenty-first century. That three biographies have been written about him attest to the continuing interest in Jackie Gleason.

GLOBE ACT

A form of acrobatics in which performers balanced atop large spheres. By moving their feet rapidly in small steps, they rolled the large balls and themselves about the stage, up and down ramps and over narrow planks. This act was at home in the circus as well as in vaudeville and variety. Joe Cook sometimes included it in his act, though more usually in a revue than in vaudeville.

SAVION GLOVER

b: 18 November 1973, Newark, NJ

Few tap dancers have had such a heavy burden of expectation placed on them as had Savion Glover. He was just 12 years old when he replaced Alfonso Ribeiro in the title role of Willie in *The Tap Dance Kid* (1984–85), and critics anointed him as the savior of the art form. He fulfilled his promise as an artist in a series of Broadway shows and performance tours. With each production he explored ways of putting foot and metal to wood and creating rhythm.

The interest in Savion Glover was considerably more ardent than for percussive dance in general. The larger audience for dance seemed content with highly theatrical versions of popular dances—ritualized courting—that they themselves practiced. The audience for percussive dance declined along with that of its musical soul mate, jazz.

As a boy, Savion Glover identified with the raw energy and athleticism of street dancing. Just as the vitality of early percussive dance (clog, buck and tap) came from generations of street kids who watched (and stole and adapted) the moves and combinations of older tappers, Savion's generation put together moves they had seen in martial arts, street mimes, acrobats, escape artists (who could bring their arms handcuffed behind them over their heads to the front and slip free)—even cartoons—and created an original and expanding form of dance.

With vitality came a rebel edge. Savion sought to disconnect himself from what he saw as the servile smiling faces and artificiality of the impeccable dress and gracefulness of the 1920s and 1930s tap masters. To some young percussive dancers, the tap dance performance style of the past was a perpetuation of the subservient characters of blackface minstrelsy and plantation shows, and tap had ceased to innovate.

There was something to be said for that argument. Despite the line of percussive dance masters who passed down, from one generation to the next, their commitment to innovation, some tap dance had become a museum exhibition in drill formation, an evocation of production numbers from the 1920s and 1930s. Tap dance had grown up with ragtime, blues and jazz, but by the 1920s and 1930s, much of percussive dance was following syncopated show music instead of jazz.

When Broadway turned to the less rhythmic music championed by Rodgers & Hammerstein and its companion Agnes DeMille–style choreography, tap was left in a dead end. Jazz had moved on to bebop, and drummers advanced from pulse- and time-keepers to soloists. But dancers like Baby Laurence, Buster Brown and Jimmy Slyde found a way to fit percussive dance back into jazz, and Savion Glover found a way to make it integral.

Savion eschewed the top-hatted, tuxedoed style of presentation, yet his antistyle became a performance style itself—a blend of ghetto and Che Guevara chic. Savion grew a beard and long hair fashioned into dreadlocks. The beard and downward angle of his head in performance often masked facial expression and in the early days put formal distance between him and his audience. Often he watched his feet and turned upstage or faced toward the wings, paying scant attention to his audience.

In place of gentlemanly grace, his presentation was gritty, even as compared to break-dancers busking in marketplaces. Savion did not seem to share the street dancers' sense of having fun with a job well done.

Instead, he connected with the disaffected, defiant attitude that rappers brought to performance, an attitude shared by young audiences bored with the shiny, smiling packaging that had kept so many acts tightly wrapped. Artist and audience wanted to keep it real—both determined not to lose their street creds.

After decades of show business smarm typified by Vegas acts, Savion Glover's attention to the essentials of performance was welcomed. He never failed to deliver craft. Meanwhile, he worked out the transition from being the Tap Dance Kid to becoming the mature percussive artist. He performed in one movie, *Tap* (1989), and two Broadway musicals where narrative or interaction with other cast members took care of the matter of performance: *Black and Blue* (1989–91), for which he received a Tony nomination, and *Jelly's Last Jam* (1992–93). In those films and shows, Savion was in the company of many tap greats, including Bunny Briggs, Diane Walker, Lon Chaney (not the horror film actor), Jimmy Slyde and his friend and model, Gregory Hines.

He gave five years (1990–95) of occasional appearances to *Sesame Street* on PBS and made several movies. With *Bring in Da Noise, Bring in Da Funk* (1996–99), Savion Glover remained a phenomenon and became an artist. With *Improvography,* he proved it was not a one-off. And he seemed to enjoy himself. If he played more to the musicians—his fellow musicians—than the audience, it was in the nature of the ensemble performance, and the audience was not ignored. He introduced his collaborators and offered some genuine smiles.

There is little acrobatic lift to his dancing. His footwork is the thing. Few tappers since King Rastus Brown have been so earthbound—or so piston legged. Savion digs into the ground, machine-guns the boards (or an amplified floorboard) with his size 12 1/2 EE tap shoes—that is a lot of iron to lay down, and he does it fast and energetically. He can dance close to the ground and toss off more clear taps per second that one can count or bring his feet high and pound out a rapid-fire barrage. He dances on his heels, his toes and the sides of his feet, sometimes scraping the floor with his feet—short brushes, longer rasps—all the while building rhythmic patterns that segue from straight-up jazz to Afro-Cuban to tango.

Savion and his dancers, Maurice Chestnut, Ashley DeForest and Cartier A. Williams, musical director Tommy James and distinguished jazz musicians Andy McCloud, Brian Grice and Patience Higgins undertook a 35-city tour in spring 2005 with *Improvography II.* For a matinee performance with no interval, Savion danced for two hours with one seven-minute break to change his sweat-soaked pants and shirts while his three companion dancers took over the floor. The octet of four instrumentalists and four tappers closed out the show with John Philip Sousa's "Stars and Stripes Forever (for Now)," and the smiling Savion Glover enjoyed a loose-limbed and witty romp with his fellow dancers.

In 2005, his occasional concerts, *Classical Savion,* signaled a new phase in the dancer's professional reach. Glover danced to Vivaldi, Bach, Mendelssohn, Bartók and the less-known Astor Piazzolla, as played by 10 classical musicians.

GODS

Gods was an affectionate term for both the level of seating known more properly in the USA as the second (or highest) balcony in a theatre as well as the people who sat in those seats. In British Commonwealth nations and in nineteenth-century America, this section was called the upper circle.

The *gods* held the theatre's least expensive seats, often filled by the true but impoverished aficionados, including people of the profession, students and retirees. Some actors preferred playing to the *gods,* where they believed their most knowledgeable and appreciative audiences sat. Done artlessly, this led to the accusation by those seated in the orchestra (also called the stalls) that an actor "played to the balcony," meaning that he gave a louder, less subtle performance than one desired if seated closer.

GEORGE FULLER GOLDEN

b: 1868, Alabaster, MI—d: 17 February 1912, Los Angeles, CA

Golden was one of many well-regarded monologists of early vaudeville. His chief enduring claims to fame were that he was central to the formation of the first union for performers and actors, the White Rats, and as the author of *My Lady Vaudeville and Her White Rats.*

J.C. Nugent, a contemporary monologist, wrote nearly 30 years after Golden's death, "He was distinctively an originator. He was the first great intellectual monologist, and, to me at least, is still the greatest monologist and the greatest man that the vaudevilles ever produced. . . . Peace to his ashes."

Before he earned such distinction and accolades, Golden left his small-town birthplace for Bay City, Michigan. He considered himself an urchin, an outcast, one of a pack of boys earning an honest dollar or two shining shoes and selling newspapers and earning a few dishonest ones when the opportunity arrived.

From the age of 14 onward, Golden earned his living as a prizefighter, circus acrobat and song-and-dance man. A romantic figure, a man's man, as they said in that day, he was a boxer, an enthusiastic dancer, a lover of poetry, handsome and, as Douglas Gilbert described him, "a voracious reader of the classics; a radical idealist."

Like many young men, George first fell in with a circus. He and another boy formed Golden & Quigg, an acrobatic act for the circus. Later, with another friend, James "Gypsy" Dolan, he put together a song-and-clog-dance double act for variety houses and saloons. They added some comic patter and then turned the act into a comedy sketch with a song-and-dance finish for vaudeville.

George became a self-directed student of literature and drama, and his education informed his social life and his stage work. Always a beguiling storyteller, George was encouraged to show that talent on the stage, He went solo in vaudeville as a monologist. His material was a series of short stories in which the telling was as much the point as the punch line. He decided to try his act in London's music-halls in 1899; he had a partner at the time, Cliff Ryland. They were a modest success for a couple of seasons.

Golden joined the Water Rats and got married in England. He wanted to leave music-hall and try his luck on the dramatic stage, but there were more than enough English actors to play Shakespeare, Sheridan and Shaw. He tried to return to the halls, but, as he later claimed, managers knew of his near desperate straits and paid him starvation wages. Unable to get ahead, he could not support his wife properly. He developed pneumonia and was unable to work.

The Water Rats came to his aid. They began as a group of music-hall performers in London that owned shares in a racehorse that won a number of purses. The performers decided to do good deeds with the money, and the first item of business was to take care of their own. They formed the Grand Order of Water Rats in 1889. It was the Water Rats who rescued Golden. They paid for George Fuller Golden's passage back to America and promised to take care of his wife until he could send for her.

Back home he was determined to establish an organization along the lines of the Water Rats. He rallied to his cause a number of his best-known vaudeville friends. He knew that their fame and stature promised success. His old partner, Gypsy Dolan, was among the earliest supporters, as were Fred Stone, Dave Montgomery, Tom Lewis, Charles Mason, Sam Morton, Mark Murphy and Sam J. Ryan.

He also revived his career in the USA, paid his debts in London and claimed his wife. In vaudeville he performed as a monologist. His sojourn in London provided Golden with one of his more famous anecdotes; it has been retold many times and appears in several old monologue books.

> "One day I was riding on top of a bus in London with my friend Casey when the chimes from Westminster Abbey burst forth in joyous melody. I said to Casey, 'Isn't that sublime? Those magnificent chimes. Do they not awaken tender memories of the past?' Casey leaned forward and said, 'I can't hear you, you'll have to talk louder.' I got as close as possible and said, 'Do you not hear the melodious pealing of the chimes? Don't they touch your heart with a feeling of pathos?' Casey put his mouth close to my ear and said, 'Those damn bells are making such a hell of a racket, George, I can't hear you!'"

In 1905, he again tried London, this time to great success, but when he returned to the USA, he developed consumption, as tuberculosis then was called. Through his belief in Christian Science he held his afflictions at bay and worked for five or more years. This time his fellow vaudevillians came to his aid. Many members of the profession underwrote the cost of publishing his history, *My Lady Vaudeville and Her White Rats.* Reportedly, George M. Cohan was a major benefactor, yet in a decade's time Cohan moved to the side of the managers in a labor dispute with actors. More surprising was a donation from Klaw & Erlanger, the legitimate theatre monopolists and eternal enemies of any actor. George Fuller Golden was residing in Southern California, perhaps for his health, when, early in 1912, he died at age 43.

HORACE GOLDIN

b: (Hyman Goldstein) 1873, Poland—d: 1939, USA

In 1899, when Horace Goldin came to the USA, he was 16 and spoke very little English. Several years later, he started his climb in show business in dime museums and carnival sideshows. As Goldin pulled together a magic act, he found work in small-time vaudeville. He soon decided to become a silent act because his heavy accent made it difficult for many in the audience to understand him.

By eliminating the setup palaver, he sped up the act and squeezed in far more illusions than other conjurers were presenting in the same amount of time. That took him into big-time vaudeville, where his act was advertised as "45 tricks in 17 minutes." The pace of his act made other illusionists' acts seem belabored and slow, and although it had not been his intention when he began his sped-up silent act, he made all his competitors tighten the pace of their presentations.

Within ten years Goldin was a top attraction in America and Europe. He stayed up-to-date by fashioning his illusions on current events. The illusions may not have been new or innovative in themselves, but his method of presentation gave them the sheen of novelty. He was best known for sawing a woman in half. He did not originate the stunt but wrought changes in its staging. When he had the box constructed so that the woman's head and legs protruded through openings at either end, others began to do the same. Goldin took back the initiative by taking out a large, publicity-engendering insurance policy on the woman and by employing a mechanical buzz saw.

In another illusion, "The Tiger God," he put a woman into a cage with a Bengal tiger. Before her rehearsed screams could inflame the tiger, Goldin made the animal disappear from view.

Over the years during his tours around the world, before and after the First World War, he amassed a collection of bejeweled stickpins given to him by reigning monarchs from King Edward VII of the United Kingdom to the king of Siam. Always one to capitalize on opportunity, he changed his billing to "Horace Goldin, the Royal Illusionist."

Nat Goodwin

NAT C. GOODWIN

b: (Nathaniel Carl Goodwin) 25 July 1857, Boston, MA—d: 31 January 1919, New York, NY

Many aspiring legitimate actors took work in vaudeville to gain experience and a paycheck. Developing a reliable and well-received act was a way to keep body and soul nourished until the big Broadway break. Nat Goodwin became known onstage for character roles in classical and contemporary comedy after a useful apprenticeship in vaudeville.

He began his career in Boston in 1874, cast as a bootblack in *Law in New York* at the Howard Athenaeum in the days before it became reviled as the Old Howard. During a well-planned foray into Manhattan, the 18-year-old Goodwin was singing and doing a few impressions at a local Elks social event when Tony Pastor heard him and signed Nat on the spot to play his theatre, perhaps the most famous variety house of its time in the land.

Goodwin's earliest acts featured his imitations of well-known stage stars, such as Edwin Booth. Although Nat stayed with Pastor long enough to appear in a comic sketch, "Jerry Clip, the Stage Struck Barber," he had found his foothold in New York theatre, playing several seasons in musicals for E. E. Rice.

In 1876 Goodwin spent a season with Haverly's Minstrels; then, in 1877, he organized his own company, Froliques, which specialized in farces. As he worked for other managements over the course of more than 40 years, his comic playing moderated, along with public taste, from grotesque knockabout to light comedy. Goodwin attempted a variety of roles, trying to balance dramatic parts like Shylock (not a success), Fagin and Nathan Hale with roles in contemporary comedies as well as Gilbert & Sullivan. At his peak in vaudeville, he commanded $2,500 a week.

Offstage he was notorious for high living and somewhat ridiculed for marrying five times. His third wife, the fine actor and great beauty Maxine Elliot, realized one of Goodwin's unfulfilled ambitions, having a theatre in Manhattan named after her.

Nat C. Goodwin enjoyed a successful career until he died at age 62 of apoplexy following the removal of an eye.

BERT GORDON

b: (Bernard "Barney" Gorodetsky) 8 April 1895, New York, NY—d: 30 November 1974, Duarte, CA

A first-generation comedian born in one of Manhattan's ethnic neighborhoods, Bert had his first experience with an audience at age six, when the boy soprano sang at Kessler's Thalia Theatre on the Bowery. Barney was 14 when he joined Gus Edwards' Newsboys Sextette. A bit later he went to work for an Edwards competitor, Joe Wood's Nine Crazy Kids—one of the many "skool daze" acts that were popular in the 1910s.

Some time during the process of finding a foothold in show business, Barney Gorodetsky traded his given name for Bert and his surname for Gordon. He formed a double dialect comedy act with his brother, and Harry & Bert Gordon lasted a few seasons as an act. Bert was able to do Jewish, Irish, German and, of course, Russian dialects.

After Harry, Bert partnered with Jean Ford, the first of the statuesque showgirls who proved fine foils for the diminutive jug-eared comic with the wild bush of hair. Bert's other showgirl partners included Alice Knowlot and Florence Shubert. One of Bert's favorite vaudeville acts was a sketch called "Desparate Sam," in which the undersized, dialect-spouting Bert played a gun-toting westerner.

It was with Jean Ford that Bert Gordon got his first big break; they were hired for the cast of the 1921 edition of *George White's Scandals.* Among the others in the revue were Lou Holtz, Ann Pennington, Charles King, Tess Gardella (billed as Aunt Jemima), Lester Allen, Harry Rose and George White. After the show closed, Bert Gordon took a few dates in Europe and stayed two seasons.

As opportunities in vaudeville faded, Bert signed on for *Billy Rose's Crazy Quilt* (1931). Even with Fanny Brice and Ted Healy toplining, the show eked out eight weeks. Meanwhile, Jack Benny introduced Bert Gordon to radio audiences. Network radio provided Bert Gordon his biggest break. In 1935 he was hired by Eddie Cantor as a character comedian for Eddie Cantor's radio show. The show's writers, working with Gordon, developed the Mad Russian character in 1936 for the show.

A weekly network radio show devoured a lot of comedy material, so the smarter comedians, like Eddie Cantor, Fred Allen and Jack Benny, spent at least half their airtime playing straight to various characters. Comic foils were less expensive than guest stars. Cantor had two reliable foils: Harry Einstein, who played a Greek named Parkyakarkus, and Bert Gordon, who, as the manic Mad Russian, startled everyone with his greeting, "How do you DO-O-O-O-O?!"

The Mad Russian and his tagline became so popular that Bert Gordon was in demand. In 1940, he returned to the stage in a featured role in *Hold on to Your Hats,* a musical comedy starring Al Jolson and Martha Raye. Hollywood called, and Bert played the Mad Russian or some variant in a series of movies including *New Faces of 1937*, *School for Swing* (1937), *Outside of Paradise* (1938), *Sing for Your Supper* (1941), *Laugh Your Blues Away* (1942), *Let's Have Fun* (1943) and, predictably, *How Do You Do?* (1946). Bert also made cameo appearances in an all-star Second World War rally morale picture, *Thank Your Lucky Stars* (1943) and an Eddie Cantor movie, *Show Business* (1944).

Bert Gordon was a Cantor radio regular, under Eddie's personal management, for ten years, until Cantor failed to renew his contract in 1945. Cantor's ratings had been dropping since the late 1930s but dropped even more in 1946, so the Mad Russian returned to the lineup until 1949, when Cantor switched to television.

Neither television nor the 1950s was hospitable to the old-line dialect comedians, and Bert Gordon was indelibly and forever identified with the Mad Russian. There was no escape and little work. One of his last performances, however, was on the television hit *The Dick Van Dyke Show* in 1961. This led to a nightclub engagement, but there his career ended.

CLIFF GORDON

b: (Morris Saltpeter) ca. 1880, New York, NY—d: 21 April 1913, Chicago, IL

His billing matter as "The German Senator" did more than hint that Cliff Gordon was a dialect storyteller who specialized in an updated version of the old minstrel show favorite, the stump speech. Garbed in tails, white vest and string tie, with his hair whitened and waved, Cliff began speaking in a normal tone of voice but worked up a lather that ended in a frenzy of garbled words and confusion.

> Friendtz and Vellor Voters: I am gladt to distress you beoples mit all the elephance dot is in me. Der furst remark vot I shall make eggsplanashun of will be capital. I am *not* against capital. In fact, I am for all I kin get of it. Dose dot are aginst idt are *up* against it. . . . Vot is more pee-u-tiful und perspiring don to look at der Statue of Liperty. Dot great peanuckrel of success, standting dere in New York harboor, mid a lemon in von hand und der ocean in der utter? . . . All men are cremated equal. But dey don't stay dot vay. President Teddy Roosevelt is der greatest president vot ve effer hadt. If you don't belief dat, read vat he says aboudt himself. In 1906 there vas more children porn dan in any odder year, and he takes *all* der credit for it.
>
> Congress always asks for money. In comes a Congressman and sez: 'Gut morning, Congress, let me have $60 million dollars. He don't never make no touch for a quarter or half a dollar.

Gordon was born on the Lower East Side of Manhattan, the oldest son of a Jewish immigrant family from Poland. His baby brother went into show business as well, adopting Cliff's stage name and became Broadway producer Max Gordon.

Cliff Gordon's success was quick and short-lived. Like all the other families in the neighborhood, the Saltpeters were poor. Neither mother nor father learned to speak English, and their Orthodox beliefs (no work on the Saturday Sabbath) limited employment opportunities. Morris had to leave school to help support the family. He had no intention, however, of building a *civilian* career; he hid from the family that he took part in amateur nights and entertained at local clubs and beer halls.

When he was sure enough of himself and his act, he entered small-time vaudeville, offering impressions of then popular comedians and finally securing a spot as second comedian in the Imperial Burlesque Company. When he informed the family that his pay was $75 a week, in an era when $15 or $20 was the most that their neighbors hoped for, family resistance crumbled, and Morris—Cliff Gordon for the stage—took on the responsibility of supporting his parents and siblings.

Cliff Gordon understood that talent needed equally good material to shine onstage. He developed a relationship with Aaron Hoffman, a first-rate sketch and monologue writer, to keep him supplied with material. The high point of his ambition was to produce his own show, which he did in the 1909–10 season with his partner, friend and fellow burlesque comedian, Bobby North. *The Merry Whirl* starred James C. Morton and Frank Moore (Morton & Moore, a burlesque team) and played three weeks on Broadway before touring nationally.

By 1913, Cliff Gordon was playing Keith time, appearing on several bills with Sarah Bernhardt and placed in the impossible position of closing the bill after Bernhardt's act. Gordon was not well at the time, complaining of headaches and feeling tired. On the afternoon of 21 April, at the Majestic Theatre, Bernhardt had wowed the audience and Cliff, in the throes of what may have been a severe migraine attack, was unable to get the audience's attention. He bombed in the closing spot, repaired to his hotel and left a call for 8 P.M. When he failed to respond to his call at the theatre dressing room, the stage manger called the Hotel Sherman. Unable to rouse Cliff, the staff forced the door and found him dead in his bathwater. The cause of death was listed as heart failure. Cliff Gordon was 32.

MAX GORDON

b: (Mechel Saltpeter) 28 June 1892, New York, NY—d: 2 November 1978, New York, NY

Younger brother of Cliff Gordon, "The German Senator," Max was the baby of a family of Polish Jews that settled on the Lower East Side. Bored by ordinary life and frustrated by dreams deferred, Max quit school in his last year of high school—against the wishes of the elder brother he idealized and whose world Max strove to share.

Following his brother Cliff, Max adopted the surname of Gordon when he began his career as a 17-year-old advance man for a Hyde & Behman burlesque revue. After a couple of seasons on the road, he formed a vaudeville agency with former vaudevillian and burlesquer Al Lewis. After the unexpected and early death of Cliff, the brother he revered and loved, Max and Al turned their agency into one of the most successful production shops of sketches for vaudeville.

Once Gordon showed what he could do, his late brother Cliff's favorite writer of stage material, Aaron Hoffman, bought into the production company, getting a 50% interest in the firm in exchange for turning over the extensive catalogue of scripts he had written for vaudeville.

The firm of Lewis & Gordon grew rapidly. Their sketches and casts played the Keith and Orpheum circuits, with at least one playlet getting booked into the Palace every month. The actors they employed in their sketches included Eddie Foy Sr. (at the end of his career), Judith Anderson, Theda Bara, Clara Kimball Young, Henry Hull and Roland Young.

In 1930, during the early years of the Great Depression when others were retrenching, Max Gordon decided to go on his own without partners. In his third season (1933–34) as an independent producer, Max had four hits running on Broadway at one time: *Roberta, Her Master's Voice, The Shining Hour* and *Dodsworth*—a musical comedy, a straight comedy and two dramas.

Over the course of a long and exceptionally successful career, Max Gordon produced many hits that included the revues *Three's a Crowd* and *The Band Wagon,* the musicals *Roberta, The Cat and the Fiddle* and *The Great Waltz,* and dramas and comedies such as *The Women, My Sister Eileen, Dodsworth, The Late George Apley, Junior Miss, The Solid Gold Cadillac* and *Born Yesterday.*

BILLY GOULD

b: ca. 1865

A former newspaperman, Billy Gould tried his luck in vaudeville as a song-and-dance man in the 1890s and became well known and popular into the 1910s. He created one of the first known flirtation acts, in which Billy and his partner, Nellie Burt, exchanged playful wisecracks and flirtatious cross talk while singing and dancing a soft shoe.

Around 1905, after his split with Burt, he teamed with Valeska Suratt, a future vaudeville headliner then virtually unknown. In their act, they performed an Apache dance and each did a solo specialty. Suratt went off on her own by 1908.

In 1912, Gould became a principal booster of the American Vaudeville Artists, a fraternal organization that quickly folded in competition with the better established White Rats. Billy Gould was fondly remembered by William Morris as a performer who generously came to his aid when Harry Lauder's ship was delayed reaching New York City's docks in 1911. At Morris' request, Billy Gould, Frank Tinney, the Empire City Quartet and Carter de Haven entertained the audience at the Manhattan Opera House until the Great Scot arrived.

MARTHA GRAHAM

b: 11 May 1894, Allegheny, PA—d: 1 April 1991, New York, NY

Martha Graham, who had toured in vaudeville as a Denishawn dancer, was asked why she did not provide brief explanatory notes for her dances in her concert programmes. She responded that if words could describe her intent, then there was little or no reason to make the dance. She could have added that she evolved as an artist in vaudeville and revue without the luxury of explaining her work in writing.

Martha Graham

She was born in a town near Pittsburgh, in what was in the 1890s the heartland of America. In 1908, when Martha was 12, her family relocated to Santa Barbara, California. Five years later, when Martha was 17, she first saw Ruth St. Denis in performance and was impressed by her theatrical presence. After high school, her first stage studies were in theatre. The courses emphasized the practical—lighting, mechanics and the like, as well as the visionary, such as the work and writings of the avant-gardist Gordon Craig. In 1915, Graham began taking dance classes in Los Angeles at the new Denishawn School, so named for its two founders, Ruth St. Denis and her new husband and partner, Ted Shawn.

St. Denis was a vaudeville veteran from its earlier days, when she performed eight shows a day in curio halls, euphemistically called museums, to her later annual tours of vaudeville theatres with a large dance company and elaborate sets.

Miss Ruth, as she was called, *inspired* students. It was up to Ted Shawn to teach students and manage the school and company. It was St. Denis who first presented a vision of what life and art on the stage could be to Graham, but it was Shawn to whom she gravitated as a student. Martha was 21 when she began dance class, well past the age when most girls started. From 1916 to 1918, Martha advanced at Denishawn from beginner to performer and teacher. She came to the fore in the Denishawn organization and dance company just as the organization was entering its most productive and popular period.

In 1920, Ted Shawn created a role for Martha opposite him in a Mayan-inspired piece he called "Xochitl." It was part of a program that played the Pantages circuit that season. Charles Weidman was also in the company and danced with Graham in "Xochitl." St. Denis, together with Louie Fuller, Genevieve Stebbins, Isadora Duncan and Maude Allan, represented the first generation of American interpretive dancers; Graham, Weidman and Doris Humphrey, who also taught and performed for Denishawn, became the bedrock of modern dance in America. The Denishawn music director and accompanist, Louis Horst, was nearly an equal creative partner with the other three, who were later hailed as the heroic generation of modern dance.

Meanwhile, there were usual vaudeville dates, along with the rare concert engagement, to fill during the October-to-April seasons that Denishawn toured. John Murray Anderson spotted Martha Graham while she was playing vaudeville during Denishawn's 1922–23 season. He engaged Martha for *The Greenwich Village Follies of 1923*. Anderson's *Follies* reflected his view of theatre and his experience; the shows were both inventive and vaudevillian, a salute to the future and the past. Martha was one of the lesser acts in the revue. She shared the stage with two-a-day veterans like Eva Puck & Sammy White, Daphne Pollard and the Cansinos, a ballroom dance team whose child became movie star Rita Hayworth.

Yet Anderson also staged artistic ballets to musically sophisticated scores by Louis Hirsch, Cole Porter and Harold Levey. One of the dance numbers, "Serenata Morisca," that Martha performed in the revue was created for her by Ted Shawn as a farewell present to a favorite student. In another number, "Spanish Fiesta," Martha danced one part and the Cansinos danced the remaining three. Martha appeared in a total of three numbers, the last of which was "The Garden of Kama [sic]," which was reminiscent of Ruth St. Denis' style. Anderson brought Martha Graham back for the 1924 edition.

Martha Graham was fortunate to perform for the diverse audiences of vaudeville and to teach Denishawn technique in Manhattan. She lived and worked in Greenwich Village when it was a center of great artistic stimulation. There she met many fellow artists, sympathetic souls and future producers and benefactors.

Like many painters, sculptors, writers, musicians and theatre people in New York, Graham found it a constant struggle to keep body and soul together. As a choreographer, she needed a group of dancers with whom to work regularly. Unlike a play script for which actors are then cast, choreographers fit movement to dancers. About seven years into her independent career as a concert dancer and choreographer, and desperate to keep her small band of dancers-believers intact, Martha accepted an invitation for her company to be part of the opening bill at Radio City Music Hall on 27 December 1932. Samuel L. ("Roxy") Rothafel, who initially managed and booked the new 6,000-seat theatre, had assembled a vaudeville bill that exceeded the tolerance and tried the patience of his audience. Among the mixed bag of acts on the bill were the Wallenda Family Acrobats, operatic tenor Jan Peerce, eccentric dancer Ray Bolger, German Expressionist concert dancer Harald Kreutzberg and slapstick comedy greats Weber & Fields. Martha Graham decided to present herself and her company in a new work she titled "Choric Dance for an Antique Greek Tragedy."

It was a long bill that began at 9 P.M. and ran nearly four hours. By the time Martha and her dancers took the stage well after midnight, many of the 6,000 seated in the audience had drifted out of the theatre. The Graham choreography accelerated the rate of departure. The weak box office following the opening night persuaded Roxy that high art had to be sacrificed. Although there was no cancellation clause, Martha and her dancers were dismissed from the bill.

Many years of touring vaudeville with Denishawn had made Martha Graham into a showbiz professional. She had high ideals for her art, but she also had a tough-mindedness that directed her to the Radio City Music Hall stage door each night of her engagement. Canceled or not, Martha was not going to violate her end of the contract. Modern dancers were poorer than all but the most wretched small-time vaudevillians; Martha and her dancers needed the very fine fee that Roxy had promised. Graham brought her entire company every night of their contract to Radio City Music Hall. Every night, they were told they were not needed. Every night, Martha replied, "We'll wait."

It took a few weeks for Martha to collect her fee, but she did. It was good practice for the decades to come. Thereafter, Graham accepted the fact that the more esoteric art became, the smaller its audience; she could not hope to survive on box-office receipts alone. Martha Graham molded herself into the most famous visionary in dance, a cultural icon and a hardened if reluctant rattler of the busker's tambourine. After cutting her teeth on vaudeville and revue producers like Roxy, she was better able to put the bite on the foundations and philanthropists that supported the Martha Graham Dance Company and school for the next half century.

Martha Graham was a superb actor and a keen dramatist as well as one of the more technically and artistically gifted dancers of the twentieth century. She created theatre pieces that had greater impact on the storytelling technique of drama than most if not all the American playwrights whose careers were contemporary with hers. She reenvisioned Greek tragedy for the modern stage. American experimental theatre flowed in great part from her creative wellspring; the spare décor she preferred became its hallmark. Her device of presenting multiple characters in the person of one actor or one character in the person of multiple actors was later adopted by playwrights such as Edward Albee.

It took more than 15 years for Martha Graham to become the doyenne of modern dance and to be able to sustain a company and a school through annual concert tours, foundation grants and generous patrons. It became accepted critical opinion that Martha Graham, like Pablo Picasso and Igor Stravinsky, was one of the few truly revolutionary geniuses in the Western world of art in the twentieth century. She danced well into her seventies and managed her company nearly to the end of her very long life.

NILS T. GRANLUND

b: 1882, Korpilombolo, Sweden—
d: 21 April 1957, Las Vegas, NV

NTG, as he was known, made Earl Carroll look classy. Some professionals noted that Granlund's initials also stood for Not Too Good, a much-employed epithet in showbiz. He had a varied career in vaudeville, nightclubs, radio and boxing, but mostly he was known for collecting and exhibiting impressionable young girls with stage aspirations.

His family moved to the USA when Nils was nine. He began his career as a newspaperman, then jumped into show business as a press agent for a touring burlesque revue, *Hanky Panky.* He was good as a publicity flak, and Marcus Loew's Theatres hired him to promote their vaudeville bills and movies. Granlund became chief of publicity for the theatre chain.

He got into radio, where he first made his name as a ringside announcer for blow-by-blow broadcasts of prizefights. During Prohibition he began producing revues for speakeasies, or at least rounding up the showgirls. Occasionally he took the floor himself as an emcee. Granlund became his own product to sell. He turned himself into a personality of sorts and found himself work as an emcee and radio host.

As an example of how badly vaudeville was faring in 1932, NTG made it to the stage of the Palace Theatre with a line of chorus girls. He talked, they danced and the men in the audience ogled the skimpily clad showgirls.

Granlund even appeared in four films during the 1930s and 1940s, always playing himself. By that time, he had relocated from Manhattan to Hollywood. Again, he parlayed his experience as a promoter into work for himself in radio. He had a hand in a couple of nightspots before taking a flyer in local television. He died in a car crash at age 74.

SID GRAUMAN

b: (Sidney Patrick Grauman) 17 March 1879, Indianapolis, IN—d: 5 March 1950, Hollywood, CA

Sid Grauman's father, D.J. Grauman, was the showman who first organized and toured a troupe of African American minstrels after the cessation of the Civil War. Settling in San Francisco, D.J. opened the city's first ten-cent vaudeville house and won a reputation for quality family entertainment, which he promoted as "polite vaudeville." Grauman also enjoyed a reputation for fair and considerate dealings with performers.

Sid Grauman

D.J.'s son, Sid, also went into show business. He began performing in San Jose, California, with a friend, Joel Whitehurst. Both were in their teens when they worked at a restaurant that sported an indoor pond. While a crowd gathered, Sid tossed 40 plates into the water. It was Joel's job to retrieve them. After making a big show of summoning his energy and gathering his breath, Joel dived into the pond. Minutes passed, perhaps five or more, and there was no sign of Joel or the plates. Off to one side was a clump of water reeds, where Joel had secreted himself to build up suspense. Just as the crowd began to grow restive with alarm, Joel picked up a stack of plates they had previously stacked on the floor of the pond and rose to the surface.

Encouraged by the reaction to this bit of hokum, Sid and Joel decided to devise an act for vaudeville. They tried to make a go of it as acrobats, but there were many better tumblers, balancers and strongmen already on the circuits. Joel's grandson, Joel Whitehurst, recalled that the young fellows contracted with the Edison electric company to build them a 10-by-12-foot electromagnetic grid that could be assembled onstage and held up by four steel corner posts. Hoisting themselves upward, Sid and Joel roller-skated upside down on the underside of the grid. It took a lot of practice, and the audience reaction in various vaudeville theatres was sensational.

During one performance in Dubuque, Iowa, they performed through a storm without incident until the end of their act. Sid released himself from the grid, flipped into an upright position and acknowledged the applause. Joel was a bit slow off the mark, and a bolt of lightning found the power line to their equipment and fried it. Without electrical juice, Joel was unceremoniously dumped on the stage, nose first. On the basis of a broken nose, Joel decided he had his fill of showbiz.

Sid, on the other hand, enjoyed a long career. He and his dad decided in 1898 to join the gold rush in the Yukon. It did not pan out for them. They returned to California and resumed, independently, their careers in show business.

Sid was doing well enough by 1918 to open his Million Dollar Theatre. He also acted occasionally in small film roles. His two most prestigious credits were for extra parts in *Ben-Hur* (1925) and *The Gold Rush* (1925). Although he was one of 36 founders of the Academy of Motion Picture Arts and Sciences, Sid's enduring fame is linked to several innovations in marketing.

He was among the first, and perhaps *was* the first in Hollywood, to present live prologues (as short as ten minutes or as long as an hour), in which the feature film was introduced by a sketch or a musical production that had some thematic relevance to the film. Sid was the first to institute lavish premieres that featured klieg lights, radio interviewers, Hollywood stars in their most glamorous duds and hordes of besotted fans.

Several generations of Americans knew the name Grauman because his name was attached to two of Hollywood's most exotic and famous movie palaces: Grauman's Egyptian Theatre (opened in 1922) and Grauman's Chinese Theatre (1927). Grauman's Chinese Theatre's tradition of movie stars setting the prints of their hands and feet in wet cement in the Forecourt to the Stars began with Mary Pickford and Doug Fairbanks, the acknowledged queen and king of movieland.

GILDA GRAY

b: (Marianna Michalska or Winchalska) 24 October 1901, Kraków, Poland—d: 22 December 1959, Hollywood, CA

The Shimmy Queen, Gilda Gray was discovered by Sophie Tucker during the Red Hot Mama's vaudeville tours in the mid-1910s. If Gray's claimed birth date is to be believed, she must have been a precocious lass, for her specialty, then and later, was shaking her breasts and hips in time with the music.

During the Jazz Age, from the late 1910s until the late 1920s, Gilda Gray, dressed mostly in beads and fringe, was a sensation. In 1924, she shook down Los Angeles' Metropolitan Theatre for $24,000, her percentage of the box office for the Christian Holy Week.

Marianna was eight when she and her parents immigrated to the USA, ending up in the suburbs of Milwaukee. Her father became a small-time politician. According to Gilda/Marianna, she was 14 when she married John Gorecki, the son of a local saloon keeper and ward politician; they had a son.

Gilda claimed that she was dancing professionally in her father-in-law's saloon—"shaking her chemise" (supposedly the source for the derivative slang term *shimmy-shaker*)—when she accidentally invented the dance that made her famous. Like one of her rivals, Bee Palmer, Gilda became defined by the novelty of the shimmy. Other vaudeville and nightclub stars claimed to have introduced the shimmy. Among them were Ethel Waters and Mae West, but they had many other talents to sustain them and dropped the shimmy-sha-wobble, as it was also known, before the novelty could leave them behind.

Gilda Gray

Marianna left home and family for show business and the high life of Chicago. She changed her name to Marci Gray and teamed in vaudeville and nightclubs with Mildred Vernon as a dance duo. Solo, she moved to New York. At New Jersey army camps, she entertained troops training to fight in the First World War.

Sophie Tucker's husband, Frank Westphal, took to Gilda, and Sophie kindly helped her into the big time and away from Frank. Sophie suggested Marci adopt a more glamorous name, and Marci Gray assumed her final professional name, Gilda Gray. The novelty and near nudity of the dance was enough to make Gilda Gray thousands of dollars a week in vaudeville and get her hired to perform onstage in *Shubert Gaieties of 1919, Hello Alexander* (1919), *Snapshots of 1921* and the *Ziegfeld Follies of 1922*. Everyone cashed in while the craze was hot.

Gilda made about eight movies in twice as many years, starting in 1919 with *A Virtuous Vamp*. Other films, equally provocatively titled, were *The Girl with the Jazz Heart* (1921), *Lawful Larceny* (1923), *Aloma of the South Seas* (1926), *Cabaret* (1927) and *The Devil Dancer* (1927). It took E. A. DuPont, A German director working in England, to deliver something steamier than an exotic title; *Piccadilly* (1929), despite its pedestrian name, was an arty and erotic snipe fest between Gilda and Anna May Wong.

Gilda was a creature of the Roaring Twenties; her fame and finances did not survive the harsh 1930s.

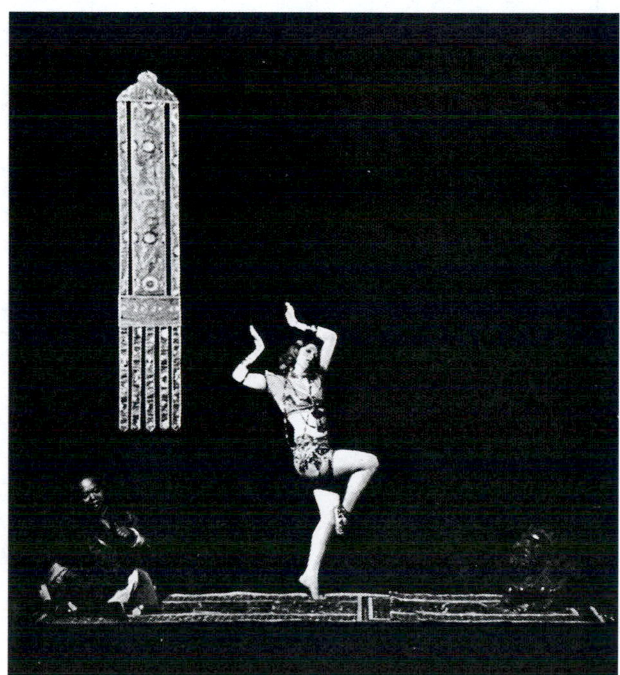

Gilda Gray

Gilda's one appearance in a sound flick was in a small role in *Rose-Marie* (1936), an "Indian Love Call" duet between America's singing sweethearts, Jeannette MacDonald and Nelson Eddy. A Canadian Mounties song saga was a strange place to find a fringe-clad shimmy shaker. It took a long time for Gilda to find her way back to an appreciative audience. MGM filmed her in several dance sequences for its forthcoming (and overlong) *The Great Ziegfeld* (1936), but her numbers were sliced out of the film before it was released.

Gilda Gray was one of several former stars whose dormant careers were revived through the television show *This Is Your Life*. Her comeback, a season or two in nightclubs, was briefer than her original short career. Gilda made a telling crack to newsmen covering her comeback: "Nowadays I need a trunk to pack my costumes. When I started out, a dove could've carried them."

GREASEPAINT

Originally an animal-based grease tinted with pigment and packaged into tubes for use as makeup. The color ranged from creams to pinks to tans, with browns and blacks for racial portrayals. The original greasepaint was replaced by cream-based formulas available in tubes and then cakes and liquids. Greasepaint was applied over cold cream, and all stage makeup was powdered to a matte finish to prevent shine under the lights.

GREAT DEPRESSION

There was little government protection against financial panics that occurred throughout the history of the United States. Until the sweeping regulations of the 1930s, banks could play broker to the financial markets. When a financial panic reared, banks could, with little heart and full attention to profits, call in loans. Stocks in the 1920s were heavily traded on margin, and when share prices collapsed, investors forfeited the shares pledged as collateral. When loans were called, farmers lost their farms and livelihood, and individuals, their houses and jobs.

The stock market crash of 1929 did not start the Great Depression; it merely exacerbated the excesses that had gone unchecked throughout the 1920s. Despite the Sherman antitrust law, big business had been allowed to do its thing and had gone unchecked. The Roaring Twenties were allowed to roar. Bootleg liquor, speakeasies, gangsters, rising hemlines and the decline in family values were the order of the day.

The Great Depression was a worldwide phenomenon. Banks failed in Austria and Germany before failures occurred in Britain, France and the United States. In Austria and Germany, rampant inflation was not held in check by central banks. In the United States, euphoria reigned, and the Federal Reserve failed to hold inflation in check.

Little is mentioned in textbooks about the substantial stock market recovery in 1930. Nevertheless, the USA was paralyzed—so, too, were France and England. Germany experienced a period of galloping inflation, and consumers with wheelbarrows filled with paper currency sought to buy a loaf of bread.

With the Great Depression, Broadway, that once fabulous industry, turned into the long-running *fabulous invalid.* Financing for all forms of entertainment was limited. The Great Depression added another nail in vaudeville's coffin, and capital that was available was invested in Hollywood and network radio, two more major contributors to vaudeville's demise. Ironically, at the depth of the Great Depression, the silver screen was top-heavy with films depicting a luxurious way of life—bejeweled women in furs, stately mansions, leading men in tails—all this when the unemployment rate in the country rose to 30%.

In response to the Great Depression, federal legislation of the 1930s revolutionized the way business was done in America and afforded protection to a populace long held captive by big business. While the economy eventually recovered, vaudeville was not as fortunate.

Great Small Works

GREAT SMALL WORKS

John Bell

b: 18 December 1951, Redwood City, CA

Trudi Cohen

b: 5 February 1950, New Haven, CT

Stephen Kaplin: 3 August 1957

Jenny Romaine

b: 1962, New York, NY

Roberto Rossi: ca. 1950

Mark Sussman

b: 8 May 1963, New York, NY

The use of wood, cloth and molded figures, masks and performing objects has been a central element of children's shows, television series, contemporary dance, performance art, political theatre and demonstrations. The scale may be as intimate as Great Small Works or as vast as Bread & Puppet Theater's annual *Our Domestic Resurrection Circus,* produced every summer from 1969 through 1998 by Peter Schumann and his colleagues, past and present.

Most of the founding members of Great Small Works (GSW) performed with Schumann's Bread & Puppet Theater. They came together again in the 1980s, a collective of artists who kept theatre at the heart of social life in Manhattan's East Village, where they participated in community vegetarian spaghetti dinners—Pasta & Puppets—that were part of neighborhood block parties on Ninth Street at First and Second Avenues.

In the late 1980s, rising rents forced Ninth Street Theatre out of its storefront and into an East Village community center, CHARAS/El Bohio. Members of Ninth Street Theater established GSW in 1995, and CHARAS was their first home. By that time, the group's spaghetti dinners had been established as a regular monthly event at Performance Space 122, one of the more respected venues for performance art in New York's Downtown art scene. As they have since the early 1980s, GSW continues the tradition of monthly spaghetti dinners and variety performances.

Through their individual and collective explorations, the founding members of GSW drew upon the centuries-long tradition of puppets, masks and performing objects prevalent in all cultures, but they were not hampered by a single popular style of puppetry because American theatre possessed no dominant style.

Since the early nineteenth century, creators of American theatre had drawn, as needed, on Punch and Judy shows and Victorian and Edwardian toy theatres from Britain and performing objects employed in European theatre from Baroque opera to pantomimes and extravaganzas. In the twentieth century the theatrical reach expanded to masks from African, Caribbean and Native American rituals and shadow puppets from the Near East and South Asia.

By the time television became an early influence in the childhoods of the founders of GSW, there was still no one dominant style of puppetry. Instead, with great discrimination but no snobbishness, they adapt both ancient and popular theatre techniques: toy theatre (*Papiertheater*), mask and object theatre, circus, sideshow and picture show (*cantastoria*—sort of a stump speech set to flip-chart pictures).

As they vowed at the outset, the company continues to perform in the streets as well as in schools, clubs, galleries, theatres and other centers of community. Members produce performance works ranging from outdoor pageants with giant puppets and hundreds of performers to miniature toy theatre.

Some of their performance pieces demand a high level of professionalism as puppeteers, musicians, singers and actors and a performance space with professional production capabilities. *The Man Who Was Thursday: A Nightmare* (1997–98), adapted from the novel by G. K. Chesterton, was directed and designed by Mark Sussman and presented at P.S. 122 in New York City. *The Memoirs of Glückel of Hameln* (1999–2000), directed by Jenny Romaine, was a collaboration with Yiddish music stars Adrienne Cooper and Frank London. *A Mammal's Notebook: The Erik Satie Cabaret* (2001) was created by the company in collaboration with pianist Margaret Leng Tan under the direction of John Bell. It was presented to sold-out houses at the LaMama Annex in New York. Other pieces, perhaps no less demanding of technique, can be played in living rooms, community centers, prisons, libraries, art galleries and other small and nontraditional settings for performance.

Olivier's Hamlet and *Toy Theater Faust,* two miniature classics, were staged as toy theatre presentations by John Bell and designer Stephen Kaplin. A noir handpuppet thriller, *New York Confidential: B.B. in L.A.,* was adapted from the Los Angeles journals of Bertolt Brecht and performed with objects and a live band. *The True Story of CHARAS* was described as a *cantastoria* about real estate on the Lower East Side. Two performance pieces were created especially for kids: *Our Kitchen,* created by Trudi Cohen, and *Kasper in Metropolis,* created by Roberto Rossi and George Konnoff.

Around 2000 at the Zeitgeist Gallery in Cambridge, Massachusetts, Bell, who is a thoughtful, quiet man offstage, gave a rousing song-and-dance (*cantastoria*) exposition of the history of toy theatre that spilled forth like a tongue-twisting Gilbert & Sullivan patter song.

Not every GSW production requires a complete cast of professionals or the professional polish of traditional theatre. The collective mission includes a social and political agenda as well as a theatrical one. GSW seeks to help their audiences renew, cultivate and strengthen their spirits by taking part in theatre as a model for participating in democracy. To that end, GSW creates large- and small-scale productions with community and school groups. GSW organizes workshops in puppetry, movement, stilt dancing, mask and banner making and the development of themes using all kinds of popular theatre traditions, such as pageantry, circus and toy theatre to encourage and enable participants of all ages and backgrounds to dramatically tell their own stories.

In 1996, GSW created *A History of Apizza in New Haven* for the first International Festival of Arts and Ideas in New Haven, Connecticut. The production involved hundreds of schoolchildren and volunteers from New Haven's diverse communities. Participants constructed giant puppets and masks, researched local history, wrote personal recollections, learned to dance on stilts and manipulate puppets, rehearsed and presented an outdoor circus history of the city. Performances took place on the town green during the festival.

In January 1998, GSW was invited by third-generation Mexican puppeteer Pablo Cueto to conduct workshops in toy theatre at the Museo de Cultures Populares in Coyoacan, Mexico City. Working with a group of theatre students, photographers, cartoonists and theatre and puppetry professionals, the company divided a group of 80 participants into teams, each creating a new theatre work over the course of one week.

Later that same year, GSW conducted a six-week workshop with teachers and students at the Bread & Roses Integrated Arts High School in Harlem, New York. The pageant was based on textile workers' Bread and Roses strike from which the school took its name. Workshops culminated in a free outdoor performance in a park across the street from the school.

In October 2001, GSW created *The Procession to End All Evil* for the DUMBO Arts Festival in downtown Brooklyn, New York. A project that incorporated working with local volunteers, the procession acted as a cathartic response to the events of 11 September 2001. During the countdown to the Gulf War in 1991, members of GSW, inspired by Walter Benjamin's notion of a culture in a permanent state of emergency, began performing a surreal serial drama. They used excerpted texts and images cut from the daily newspapers. *The Toy Theater of Terror as Usual* is ongoing and had surpassed a dozen episodes by 2005.

Members of GSW curate and produce the biennial Toy Theater Festival, including the Temporary Toy Theater Museum, a display that features the work of 75 artists, many working in the medium for the first time. Festivals have taken place at Theater for the New City in 1993 and 1994, the Los Kabayitos Puppet Theater in 1996 and 1998, and the HERE Arts Center in 2000. Touring versions of the festival have been presented at the Jim Henson Foundation's International Festival of Puppet Theater, the Museum of the City of New York, Fécamp Scène Nationale (France), the Hopkins Center at Dartmouth College, the Full-On Puppetry Festival in Philadelphia and the Rhode Island School of Design.

GSW received a 1997 *Village Voice* OBIE Award grant and a 1997 Union Interationale de la Marionnette (UNIMA) Citation for excellence in puppetry,

THE GREAT TOMSONI & COMPANY

John Max Thompson

b: 27 July 1934, Chicago, IL

Pamela Hayes

b: (Pamela Everest) 4 October 1936, Ridgewood, NJ

As a young man, John Thompson was passionate about magic, art and jazz music. While still a teenager, he became a master of the bass harmonica and played in Jerry Murad's Harmonicats, Johnny Puleo's Harmonica Gang and, later, his own band, the Harmonica Jazz Quartet. During the wane of the harmonica's popularity, he became a professional magician performing a very serious dove magic act, but following a tour of the Playboy clubs with the comic team of Lewis & Christie, he was instilled with a taste for comedy.

In 1969 he created an alter ego, a pompous Polish magician called The Great Tomsoni, The Wizard of Warsaw. His was a unique comedy magic act in which astounding tricks were executed perfectly, yet mistakes would happen in comedic fashion: while reaching under some scarves in search of a rabbit, instead the Great Tomsoni pulled out a bowling ball. To Tomsoni, this was an error, but audiences were left wondering from whence came a ten-pound bowling ball.

In 1976, Thompson's wife, actor Pamela Hayes, joined his act, playing a gum-chewing, disinterested assistant, and their act reached a new level of comedy. As a result, they soon were booked on all the major television variety programs of the day, including the Johnny Carson, Mike Douglas and Merv Griffin shows. The Great Tomsoni & Company has appeared in live venues all over the world and have starred at the Lido de Paris and the Folies Bergère in Las Vegas.

Among magicians of the late twentieth and early twenty-first centuries, Johnny Thompson is universally acknowledged as a master of serious stage magic, comedy magic, close-up magic, sleight of hand and grand illusions. He is sought after as a consultant and teacher to many of the world's finest magicians.

GREAT WHITE WAY

Specifically, the term refers to the electrified theatre marquees and signs that were lit by millions of white bulbs along Broadway, the theatre thoroughfare (also known as the Main Stem) in Manhattan.

See Broadway

ABEL GREEN

b: 3 June 1900, New York, NY—d: 10 May 1973, New York, NY

Although Sime Silverman was the founder and longtime editor of *Variety,* the showbiz bible (as it bragged), Abel Green was as important to its history. He was a 17-year-old cub reporter when he started work at *Variety.* He quickly demonstrated his value to the magazine by coining many additions to Varietese such as *biz, boffo* and *payola.* Green gets credit for *Variety*'s two most famous headlines, "WALL ST. LAYS AN EGG" (30 October 1929) and "STICKS NIX HICK PIX" (17 July 1935).

At 32, he succeeded Sime as *Variety*'s editor in 1933. It was not a healthy time for the beloved trade paper. Vaudeville had been its first love, but the public had given its collective heart to movies and network radio. Broadway was no longer offering dozens of new shows each season (and part of their advertising budget to *Variety*). The national economy had flopped.

Still, Abel Green managed to chart *Variety*'s course for more than three decades. He covered network radio and television, recognized the emerging importance to variety acts of the growing number of hotels in coastal Florida and, especially, Las Vegas. His best-known accomplishment is coauthoring with Joe Laurie Jr. *Show Biz: From Vaude to Video,* a 550-plus-page witty distillation of American show business from 1900 to 1950, as recorded by *Variety.*

MITZI GREEN

b: 22 October 1920, Bronx, NY—d: 24 May 1969, Huntington Beach, CA

Show business legend abounds with claims of being born in a trunk. Though these claims were not literally true, it was a fact that an open drawer in a theatrical trunk served as a cradle for many a second- or third-generation vaudevillian—at least until he or she was old enough to crawl onstage and add some measure of applause to the parents' acts.

Mitzi Green snoozed in a trunk drawer until she was three and joined her parents, Keno & Green, a light comic song-and-dance act. She soon proved the star of the act and was performing solo within a few years. Mitzi was born a bit too late for big-time vaudeville—it was dying out just as she was peaking as a child entertainer—but she was just in time for talking pictures. Paramount, the most sophisticated and prolific of the Hollywood film factories, signed Mitzi to a six-year contract, and the family moved west to Hollywood. Heretofore, she had offered impersonations of stage favorites of the day, male and female, but talking pictures provided her with better-known targets such as Greta Garbo, George Arliss and the Barrymores.

Although she made a dozen films in little more than three years, Paramount's producers and directors were uncertain about how to use her and lacked confidence in her box-office potential to fashion star vehicles for her. She was a capable actor in conventional roles in conventional films like *Tom Sawyer* (1930) and *Huckleberry Finn* (1931), but she appeared to better advantage in several contemporary comedies.

In *Finn and Hattie* (1931) she was the daughter and ironic observer of her parents, a pompous patsy well played by Leon Errol and a vapors-prone mother that was familiar territory for ZaSu Pitts. Mitzi was cast in the title role in *Little Orphan Annie* (1932), an inventive riff on the popular comic strip of the era; May Robson and Edgar Kennedy costarred and Mitzi added an impersonation of The Three Marx Brothers. The story was enlivened by imaginative technical innovations and an animated film sequence.

The film version of *Girl Crazy* (1932) was a star vehicle for Bert Wheeler & Robert Woolsey, but Mitzi got to perform a tap solo and show some of her other talents. By the time 14-year-old Mitzi appeared in *Transatlantic Merry-Go-Round* (1934), her star was waning and the cast was filled with bigger names like Jack Benny, Nancy Carroll, Patsy Kelly and Sidney Howard. With the competition for screen time, Mitzi's participation was limited to a series of impressions of famous folks.

Mitzi was never cuddly cute and seemed, even at age ten, to be a slightly undersized and intelligent adult. She outgrew her use to the film studios as she grew taller and more mature. Mitzi became an attractive

Mitzi Green

young woman, but of the sophisticated, wisecracking type along the lines of Eve Arden or Helen Broderick rather than a romantic lead.

Having matured into a young soubrette, Mitzi Green headed back to the East Coast for a series of vaudeville and nightclub dates and to appear in four Broadway shows during the late 1930s and early 1940s.

Babes in Arms opened 14 April 1937 and stayed on Broadway at the Shubert Theatre for 289 performances until 18 December of the same year. Alfred Drake, the Nicholas Brothers and Robert Rounesville were also featured. Despite the talents of songwriters Hoagy Carmichael and Johnny Mercer, the dully titled *Walk with Music* lasted about seven weeks on Broadway in 1940. A revue, *Let Freedom Sing* (1942), opened and closed in a week. *Billion Dollar Baby* (1945) costarred Helen Gallagher, Joan McCracken and David Burns with Mitzi, and they were blessed with a book by Betty Comden & Adolph Green and the tough-minded direction of George Abbott. It ran for 27 weeks and was Mitzi Green's last Broadway show.

Mitzi had wed Joseph Pevney in 1942. Their marriage lasted more than a quarter of a century, and she bore four children. They settled on the West Coast, and stage work took second place to family. Mitzi accepted show business work that did not require travel. Abbott & Costello's *Lost in Alaska* (1952) pleased few, and there was little that Mitzi Green could do except collect her paycheck, but she went right into *Bloodhounds of Broadway* (1952), a Damon Runyon confection that was her last motion picture.

In 1955, Mitzi Green became one of the four stars of a television series, *So This Is Hollywood,* about the early days of the film business. Mitzi played a savvy stuntwoman, and her costars were Virginia Gibson, Jimmy Lydon and Gordon Jones. The show was well written and produced, but it was scheduled against *The Jackie Gleason Show,* one of the top-rated shows of its time. Occasionally, Mitzi acted in anthology television shows or did impersonations that were as sharp and amusing as ever on variety shows, such as Ed Sullivan's, but essentially her career was over. Cancer claimed her at age 48.

CHARLOTTE GREENWOOD

b: (Frances Charlotte Greenwood) 25 June 1890, Philadelphia, PA—d: 18 January 1978, Beverly Hills, CA

"Manhattan's Pennsylvania Station has received and dispatched millions of young hopefuls, but none more than I looked as if she had stepped out of a comic strip. I was approaching 13 and I was five foot, nine inches. My ribs could have been used for a xylophone, and my chest bones threatened to pop through my skin at any moment. . . . Those hands of mine, dangling from my thin spindly arms, felt like a pair of five-fingered fern fronds on a string—and those long, narrow feet, like the roots of a sapling tree, shot out from under me. I might as well have been walking on skis." The foregoing appeared as "A Page Out of My Book" in *Variety,* the showbiz journal, part of a larger memoir that Charlotte Greenwood wrote but did not publish.

The year was 1904, and young Lottie Greenwood, feeling awkward and isolated among other teens, had left school to come to New York City and stay with her mother, who managed the Royal Arms, a hotel for theatrical people. Show folk at the Royal Arms came in all sizes and ages. Talent—or at least an ability to entertain—was all that was required for acceptance. Charlotte recalled that the queen of vaudeville, Eva Tanguay, quickly made her feel at home. Young Lottie had good musical sense, sang well and danced a bit.

By 1905, Lottie found work in the chorus of musical shows. Among her first, or perhaps her first, was *The White Cat,* staged by Ned Wayburn for producers

Charlotte Greenwood

Klaw & Erlanger. In this show Lottie met Eunice Burnham, and the two future vaudeville partners became friends. Lottie Greenwood, as she was billed, got her first featured role in *The Rogers Brothers in Panama* (1907), the last of the Rogers Brothers' annual shows that had begun in 1899. The show played from September into November 1907. At some point, Burnham suggested to Greenwood that they form a vaudeville duo, which they did in 1908. It was a wise decision; although Eunice, short and chubby, and Lottie, long and lean, contrasted well as a vaudeville act, neither conformed to the proportions usually expected of female singers and dancers.

"The Fisher Sisters: Two Girls and a Piano," as the pair first billed themselves, set out in 1908 on the small time. Theirs was a standard and unremarkable act at first; Greenwood sang and Burnham played piano and sang. Ever fearful of appearing gawky, Lottie reined in her natural high spirits and sang in a restrained and straightforward manner.

One evening, the audience tittered at an impromptu move—some reports say it was a simple twist of her body, others claim she slipped in a memento left by the preceding animal act. Eunice suggested that Lottie repeat the gaffe. In their next performance, Lottie loosened up. Buoyed and directed by the audience's laughter, she played to the laughs. As Lottie Greenwood and Eunice Burnham, then billed under their own names, they worked their way into big-time vaudeville. Lottie emerged as the star of the act. There was a sense of wholesome fun about her as she sang self-deprecatory ditties. Her long arms flew in every direction, and her longer legs kicked straight up and over her head sideways; critics and audiences described her as double-jointed.

After the young ladies split the act, Charlotte formed a partnership with Sydney Grant, who at five feet, two inches was in comic contrast to Charlotte, whose five-foot, nine-inch frame approached six feet in heels. Producers caught Greenwood and Grant in their New York vaudeville dates and offered them work in revues and musical comedies. The first of these was a Shubert annual, *The Passing Show of 1912,* in which Charlotte and Sydney joined comedians Trixie Friganza and Willie & Eugene Howard, dancers Adelaide & Hughes and Harry Fox, Jobyna Howland and Ernie Hare (a future Happiness Boy). The revue opened 22 July 1912 and closed in November after 136 performances at the Winter Garden.

Both Sydney Grant and Charlotte Greenwood were called back for the next edition, *The Passing Show of 1913.* A bit less successful, it opened 24 July 1913 and ran 116 performances. Between the two *Passing Shows,* the Shuberts put Charlotte and Sydney into *The Man with Three Wives,* a hybrid of musical comedy and operetta by Franz Lehar. The show opened at the new Weber & Fields Music Hall on 23 January 1913 and closed in less than two months.

Charlotte was enticed away from the Shuberts by producer Oliver Morosco for his musical comedy *The Pretty Mrs. Smith,* which opened 21 September 1914 and played two months at the Casino Theatre. Sydney Grant, Fritzi Scheff and Jimmy Gleason were in the cast. When the show began its national tour in Boston, its title was changed to *Long Legged Letty.* So popular did Charlotte's interpretation of the Letty Pepper character prove, it developed into a series of farces with song-and-dance numbers. *So Long Letty* was fashioned as a star vehicle and was so inexpensively produced that it could not fail to yield a profit. It ran from 23 October 1916 into January 1917. It was also the last time Charlotte teamed with Sydney Grant. *Linger Longer Letty* opened 20 November 1919 and ran for 69 performances, but *Let 'Er Go, Letty* opened and closed out of town in 1921, and *Letty Pepper,* which opened 10 April 1922, quickly closed after 32 shows. Letty was not finished; the character was put on ice until revived for an early talking picture and for another attempt on the stage in 1935, *Leaning on Letty.*

During the early Letty stage shows, Charlotte Greenwood married (1916) and divorced (1922) Cyril Ring, Blanche Ring's brother. A smash hit, the *Music Box Revue of 1922* helped assuage any unhappiness at either the end of Charlotte's marriage or the end of her Letty annuity. Bobby Clark & Paul McCullough, singer Grace La Rue, William Gaxton and dancer Ruth Page were among Charlotte's costars who helped propel the second edition of Irving Berlin's annual *Music Box Revues* to 330 performances. In 1924, Charlotte wed songwriter Martin Broomes, and their marriage lasted until his death in 1971.

Broomes was the songwriter for Hassard Short's *Ritz Revue* (1924) that costarred two fine comedians, Charlotte Greenwood and Raymond Hitchcock. The show was welcomed by critics and ran about four months in the small Ritz Theatre. Charlotte enacted "Her Morning Bath," one of the best sketches or numbers she ever performed. Wrapped in a towel, she is about to enter her bath when the phone rings. From this point, a succession of interruptions escalate as friends arrive, clothes are delivered, the meter man shows up and the iceman appears. Embarrassed, the iceman drops his block of ice and flees. Charlotte holds onto her towel with one hand and uses her other hand, long legs and feet to try to pick up the ice, open the icebox and get the ice inside. Accomplishing her task at last amid missteps and laughter, she clutches the towel about her and is about to reenter her bath when a burglar intrudes and demands, "Stick 'em up!"

Blackout. Between Broadway shows, Charlotte took the "Morning Bath" sketch into vaudeville. *Rufus LeMaire's Affairs* (1929) was another revue, lasting not quite two months despite a lineup of Charlotte, Ted Lewis and Sophie Tucker.

Charlotte had ventured a couple of times into silent films, but neither she nor a studio was, at the time, interested in a long-term contract. By 1930 things were changed all around. Charlotte was a star, a proven success who could sing, dance, talk and move funnily. Hollywood studios offered the hope of enough work for her to live without traveling. Charlotte was 40 years old, happily married and anxious to quit the road. Later in life, when other vaudevillians used to rosily reminisce about the good old days, Charlotte let everyone know she had been very happy to chuck it all for a home of her own in sunny California.

During the first years of the talkies, Charlotte made ten movies, three of which remain films of continuing interest. Her first talkie was the film adaptation of *So Long, Letty* (1929), shot with most of the music excised. Still, as the movie is essentially a filmed play, it offers a fair representation of Charlotte's stage technique and her most famous character. Her best opportunity to show her stuff to movie audiences came in a Buster Keaton sound feature, *Parlor, Bedroom and Bath* (1931). It sticks Keaton into a dull drawing room farce but, in the second half of the film, Buster, Charlotte and Cliff Edwards create a ten-minute scene that is one of the funnier and longer sustained comic scenes ever filmed. Buster is masquerading as a man of the world; in reality he is hapless and inexperienced in seduction. The scene opens with Buster arriving in the rain at a hotel with a young woman. Registering at the front desk, Buster creates a physical tangle that drags in Cliff Edwards. Once in the hotel room, there is amusing byplay between the sexually unawakened Keaton, who is supposed to act the seducer, and the young woman (played by Sally Eilers) who is there to make her sister take Buster away from her—or something like that; it really does not matter. The third and final portion of the scene is the payoff; Charlotte has been hired to teach Buster how to pitch woo. It is a superb comic match.

Charlotte Greenwood, ca. 1925

Charlotte next played opposite Robert Montgomery in a comedy of manners, *The Man in Possession* (1931), that was well regarded at the time of its initial release but was never reissued. Charlotte dropped to featured billing in *Palmy Days* (1931), her next notable talkie. She had a couple of good scenes in a good movie, but its star was Eddie Cantor, and it was his picture from first to last reel. *Flying High* (1931) again featured Charlotte in the loud screen adaptation of a stage hit. Bert Lahr, starring in his first film feature, re-created his stage role. One more major role for Charlotte followed; the film was *Cheaters at Play* (1932), but it failed to score.

Greenwood worked in England for much of 1932–34. She made an English film, *Orders Is Orders* (1933), and acted in two plays: *Wild Violets* (1932) and *Three Sisters,* a 1934 collaboration of Jerome Kern and Oscar Hammerstein that played London's Drury Lane for five weeks beginning 9 April. When Charlotte returned home, she did a bit as Tarzan's Jane in the all-star *Hollywood Party* (1934). She did not get billing and did not make another American film until 1940.

Charlotte turned to Letty Pepper to provide work in 1935. Lucile Watson had starred in *Post Road* on Broadway in 1934; marginal success, the farce thriller was retitled *Leaning on Letty,* and Charlotte Greenwood took it on the road. She earned rave reviews in cities like Chicago. Ashton Stevens, the dean of the Windy City's critics, wrote: "Two versions of Charlotte Greenwood—pre- and post-depression—were welcomed at the Selwyn last night (Nov. 22) where she played straight at being an undetected detective in *Leaning on Letty* and then threw herself into the old familiar curves, kicks and hip-slaps of the Charlotte Greenwood of the earlier Letties. She was a success both ways, so let's call it a double hit." Stevens was referring to Charlotte's curtain call that became a short vaudeville turn, with Charlotte "singing songs and executing her old buffoon dances," according to Lloyd Lewis of the *Chicago Daily News.*

She later toured in a national company of *I Remember Mama* in the starring role created by Peggy Wood on Broadway, but work was not as plentiful as it once had been. After a five-year Hollywood film drought—except for filming a few shorts—Charlotte was given a supporting role opposite Jack Oakie in *Young People,* the last profitable movie that starred Shirley Temple. Greenwood and Oakie played vaudevillians and Shirley was their daughter. It was Shirley's last film for Twentieth Century Fox, yet the first of many for Charlotte.

Charlotte Greenwood

From this film on, Charlotte was a star's mother, aunt or guardian, playing second banana to Betty Grable, Alice Faye, June Haver and Esther Williams. The films were Technicolor musicals such as *Down Argentine Way* (1940), *Moon Over Miami* (1941), *Springtime in the Rockies* (1942), *The Gang's All Here* (1943), *Oh, You Beautiful Doll* (1949) and *Dangerous When Wet* (1953).

Had Greenwood not been busy filming the Grable movies at Fox and committed to one of her two short-lived network radio series in 1943, she would have appeared on Broadway in *Oklahoma* in the role of Aunt Eller, which was written with her in mind by Oscar Hammerstein II. Rodgers & Hammerstein's hit show *Oklahoma* is regarded as a seminal Broadway musical. Charlotte was free to act the role when *Oklahoma* was filmed in 1955.

Perhaps the best remembered of Charlotte's stage hits, other than her Letty series, was Cole Porter's sophisticated musical comedy *Out of This World.* Critics felt the show about Roman gods and goddesses and their intrigues with each other and humans never quite jelled, and they were unhappy with some of the casting. Charlotte and David Burns were highly praised. On the verge of retirement, Charlotte was wooed to the role of Juno but fought a losing battle against some of the more risqué scenes. This marked a change in attitude for Charlotte, by then a committed Christian Scientist, because her early stage and film work sometimes bordered on the risqué for its era.

Based upon a Theatre Guild production, *Amphitryon 38,* a smart success for Alfred Lunt and Lynn Fontanne, *Out of This World* opened 21 December 1950 at the New Century Theatre and eked out 157 performances, closing 5 May 1951, a loss to its investors. It was a noble failure—the level of wit was high and the songs were good, even if they did not make the hit parade. There was much discussion as to why it failed: the Century Theatre was too far uptown; Cole Porter's score could not live up to his 1948 show, *Kiss Me Kate*—a previous adaptation of a Theatre Guild/Lunt and Fontanne success; the public wanted low-down shows like Olsen & Johnson's *Pardon Our French* or *Mike Todd's Peep Show;* or there were too many top-quality shows that season, such as *Call Me Madam, Guys and Dolls* and *The King and I.* Most of the informed blame went to the book's creators, Reginald Lawrence and Dwight Taylor, and to the show's director, Agnes DeMille.

Before Charlotte retired, she made two more films: *Glory* (1956), a programmer, and *The Opposite Sex* (1956), a dowdy musical remake of Claire Booth Luce's *The Women,* the smart stage and film hit of the

1930s. *The Opposite Sex* offered the opportunity to see a number of female stars near the end of their film careers: Joan Blondell, Ann Sheridan, June Allyson, Ann Miller and Agnes Moorehead.

After her retirement, Charlotte Greenwood and Martin Broomes lived graciously but not ostentatiously. At the time of her death, at age 87, most obits recalled the Letty stage series and the film of *Oklahoma*. Few made the case for her inclusion in any list of great comedians. She was more versatile than most, ranging from physical clowning to wisecracks and smart repartee to song and dance to straight dramatic acting. In a roll call of great female comedians, her name must be added to those of Marie Dressler, Trixie Friganza, Beatrice Lillie, Ray Dooley, Fanny Brice, Mae West, Rosetta Duncan, Hattie McDaniel, Martha Raye, Joan Davis, Imogene Coca, Lucille Ball and Carol Burnett.

GRID

Above the stage was a strong and solidly anchored grid work of iron, steel or wood beams (depending on when and how well the theatre was built) to which pulleys and ropes were attached to raise or lower equipment, scenery and drop curtains. This setup was critical to illusionists, aerial acts and other acrobats.

GRIND

Grind can refer to a dance movement, a booking policy or a theatre.

1. In dance, the grind is a rotating pelvic movement employed by both men and women. Male tap or eccentric dancers like Snake Hips Tucker and James Barton rotated their hips and pelvises, often wearing large glittering belt buckles that reflected the spotlight into the audience. It was an audacious movement and more often performed in nightclubs than in polite revue or vaudeville. Female burlesque dancers employed the grind in a more frankly sexual way because they usually topped it with a *bump*.
2. As an exhibition or performance policy, grind refers to repetitions of a program—vaudeville, burlesque or movies—advertised as "Continuous Performances" (vaudeville), "Always Something Doing" (burlesque) and "Continuous Showings" (movies). Shows were generally constructed to have an opening, a build-up and a finish. In a continuous loop of performances, the arc was lost and, in general, the shows sagged as dispirited and exhausted performers lost energy and keenness during the constant grind.
3. Referring to a theatre, a grind house, instead of having distinct shows at set times, such as a matinee and an evening performance, the theatre repeats its program with little time elapsed between the end of the previous show and the start of the next. Customers can drop in any time, without having to wait for a formal start time of show, and stay as long as they wish.

GROCK

b: (Karl Adrian Wettach) 10 January 1880, Bern, Switzerland—d: 14 July 1959, Imperia, Italy

Grock was billed as "The Emperor of Clowns." His reputation is as legendary as that of Grimaldi, George L. Fox, Dan Leno, Little Tich or Charlie Chaplin. Grock was a quintessential transition figure between the clowns of the old European-style circus and those of the music-hall and early vaudeville stage. He retained some of the elements of the entrée clowns—the white face and a modified Pierrot makeup—but his costume was less fanciful and more on the order of what Charlie Chaplin, The Marx Brothers or Jimmy Savo wore—ill-fitting street clothes.

Professionally, he began as a child playing fiddle at his family's inn. His father, an amateur musician and clockmaker, taught his son music and acrobatics. Young Karl joined his sister Jeanne in a series of local variety shows and then hitched on to a passing circus as an acrobat and musician. Karl switched to a band of Roma (Gypsy) entertainers. By his mid-teens, he performed in Fiame Wetzel's traveling circus.

When he partnered with another clown called Brick, Karl assumed the stage name Grock, which he would keep through the rest of his 70-year career. He became a star within a few years and took a new partner, an already famous clown called Antonet (Umberto Guillaume). Their aim was to create a variety act that could command salaries much greater than what circuses paid. Antonet & Grock failed to make the transition from a circus act to a music-hall attraction. As public response guided the development of their act, Antonet's role grew smaller as Grock became the audience favorite. They split. Grock toured the Continent with a new partner (Grock & Lole) until the outbreak of the First World War, when Grock made the United Kingdom his base of operations. In 1924, he returned to live and work on the Continent.

Offstage, he looked like a dignified professional man. Onstage, he had the gentlest and happiest of clown faces. His eyebrows were blotted out by the clown white makeup; his eyes, tightly rimmed in black to look small and smiling, and a blush of pink on his nose and cheeks contrasted with his long white chin. His most distinctive feature was his painted red, U-shaped smile.

Grock's clown-white face was skullcapped, so his head looked like an inverted eggcup and egg, and his two small ears stuck out like handles. He wore a long, oversized plaid coat that nearly reached his ankles and would have sloped off his shoulders had it not been buttoned across his chest. Loud plaid trousers bagged beneath his coat and over his small, flat, slippered feet.

His earliest routines grew out of his musical and acrobatic abilities. In one of them, he stumbled across a dozen or more musical instruments onstage. He fumbled with them as though he had never before seen such objects. Once the audience was convinced of his bumbling incompetence, Grock picked up each one and played it masterfully.

In another routine, Grock, a diminutive figure, trudged into the arena, toting a large trunk on his back. He paused every few steps to consider the possibility of putting down the trunk but could not decide where or how. Instead he went round and round, staggering under the weight. (The act worked best following the edge of the circus ring.) At last he set down the trunk, opened it, extracted a tiny violin and began to play a lovely tune.

He turned next to the grand piano, but the stool was too high and too far from the keyboard, so he spun the seat down to a comfortable height (as Harpo Marx later did in reverse) and pulled the piano toward him (as Marie Dressler and others later did). Once settled, Grock played masterfully. He played 17 musical instruments in all. Music was his passion as well as part of his profession.

Grock was a ventriloquist, juggler, acrobat, mime and actor as well as clown. Although he reputably spoke a dozen languages, his stage utterances were usually the nasal squeals and deep-throated growls of the ventriloquist's dummy. Sometimes in his act with a partner, they staged a squabble that led to upended chairs and tables, pratfalls, the destruction of the piano and tobogganing about the stage on the piano lid.

In 1924, Grock and his Italian-born wife moved to the Italian Riviera. Grock had always been an astute judge of his own worth and an able businessman. Even in the early 1900s, he commanded $3,000 a week, and his fees went higher throughout the 1910s and 1920s. He drew about $3,500 a week when he played the Palace Theatre in New York. When he retired, it was to the 50-room lakeside palace, the Villa Bianca, that he had built in the 1920s. In 1927, Grock made *What For?*, a silent movie for either an English or American film company, and two versions of *Grock* (1931), one in German and the other in French.

He refused to involve himself politically throughout the 1930s or during the Second World War and seemed to have steered clear of any involvement with Mussolini, Hitler or other fascist leaders. After the war, he resumed touring. He established his own circus in 1951 at age 70, and it played all over Europe until his last performance in 1954 in Hamburg, Germany.

After he officially retired, he made a film, *Au revoir M. Grock* (1949, also released in 1950 as *Clear the Ring*), and appeared on television several times in 1956. He was revered in Italy, England and the rest of Europe and by clowns and comedians the world over. Grock died in 1959, at age 79. Even in the twenty-first century, his name is well known to clowns, and he remains a legend.

YVETTE GUILBERT

b: (Emma Laure Esther Guilbert) 20 January 1865, Paris, France—d: 3 February 1944, Aix-en-Provence, France

Before there was Piaf and Patachou, there was Yvette Guilbert. Her importance to music and theatre is contained in her work in France; her success in American vaudeville is a footnote to her career and an indication of how diverse were American vaudeville audiences.

In Paris—indeed, in the major cities of Europe—Guilbert was a diseuse-chanteuse of renown. She had begun as a street child, the type that Parisians carelessly called street arabs. As she got older, she assisted her mother, who took in sewing. Although she was tall, skinny and not handsome of face, she had the ambition to star on the stage. The preferred style of café concert (cabaret) singers was rather like that of the English music-hall singers—buxom jolly women who kidded

Yvette Guilbert

sex, themselves and their audiences with risqué and comic character songs.

Yvette corseted herself, dyed her hair a defiant henna and emphasized the seriousness of her face with white powder and strongly drawn eyes. Her gowns were severe, and she wore long black gloves and little other ornament. She took pains with her diction and clipped her words as she half spoke, half sang her ironic, rueful, cynical, erotic (for the day) and sadly comic songs. Intelligent, she read widely and tried to make up for her lack of formal education. As she grew in artistry, she revolutionized Parisian song and singing.

Word of her increasing skill carried out of tiny cellar theatres off the Place Pigalle to the Moulin Rouge and Divan Japonais, and from there to the Nouveau Cirque (theatrical home to the Frattelinis and the clowns Footit and Chocolat, which was attended by audiences in formal attire). Even managers of leading theatres in London, Berlin, Rome and Paris heard of Guilbert and vied to book her.

Frisson seemed a word coined for Yvette. Reviewers wrote and fellow artists spoke of her "songs with a shiver." Guy de Maupassant supplied her first name, Yvette. Toulouse-Lautrec painted her. Aristide Bruant wrong songs for her.

Guilbert was important enough to catch the attention of American vaudeville entrepreneurs. Her vaudeville bookings in 1895, 1896, 1906 and 1909 were a success, one as unlikely as Sarah Bernhardt's. Both Yvette and Sarah performed in French. Both were paid top dollar: $7,000 a week for Bernhardt, from which she paid her leading man and assistants, and $4,000 a week for Yvette, who worked alone, save for an accompanist. Predictably, it was Oscar Hammerstein I who offered her $4,000 for each of four weeks she sang at his Olympia Theatre. His gamble paid off; the box office took in $60,000 during the four weeks. Her tour continued on to the Music Hall in Boston, then to Brooklyn, Washington, D.C., Philadelphia and Chicago.

A year later, she returned to Manhattan to appear (for a reported $6,000 per week) at Koster & Bial's Thirty-fourth Street house. To her usual French repertoire, Yvette added "My Pearl Is a Bowery Girl," "I Want You, Mah Honey," and "I Want to See the Old Home." This tour lasted into 1897, and she visited Chicago and parts of the South, including New Orleans. While large cities usually turned out appreciative audiences, smaller and more rural stops on the vaudeville route were less successful for managers.

When Guilbert retuned to the USA in 1905, it was following a command performance at Buckingham Palace for Queen Alexandria. Yvette's original itinerary was under the management of Charles Frohman, who arranged a series of art song concerts in Manhattan, Boston, Philadelphia and Baltimore. Upon fulfilling her contract for Frohman, she accepted vaudeville dates for F. F. Proctor. For both Frohman and Proctor dates she wore splendid gowns reminiscent of Pompadour fashions from the French monarchial court, and many of her songs dated from the same period.

Yvette accepted the offer of a joint tour across America, sharing star billing with English actor Albert Chevalier, who had taken to the *halls* with an act in which he played a Cockney and sang coster songs. The tour was not a success for its producers, and western audiences were hard-pressed to understand why they had shelled out good money to listen to people they could not understand.

In 1909, Yvette Guilbert returned to New York to begin a tour of Percy Williams' vaudeville houses. Unfortunately, the first theatre was his Colonial, a house notorious for impatient, rude audiences. It went no better in Brooklyn, Philadelphia or Pittsburgh.

Part of the problem was that Madame Guilbert, buoyed by extravagant praise from the cognoscenti, took herself too seriously. She had never been diplomatic, and the American press had for years published her critiques of American art and culture. When she began complaining about the audiences—the people who paid to see her—it was clear that this was her last vaudeville tour in the USA.

When she came again to America, it was in the 1915–16 series of 20 concerts in the Lyceum and Maxine Elliot theatres to select audiences. In 1917, she undertook a tour of recitals and lectures. The following year, 1918, Macmillan published her manual, *How to Sing a Song.* In it she described herself as "a comedian at the service of a singer without a singing voice, who demands an orchestra or piano to do her singing for her." It remains pithy and smart advice for other actor-singers.

As the years passed, Yvette did not settle into a style; she was always learning and growing as her musical instinct was buttressed by knowledge. She became interested in French songs from earlier centuries and developed into a musicologist. On the other hand, in 1937, at the age of 72, she played Mrs. Peachum in a French production of Bertolt Brecht's and Kurt Weill's *Threepenny Opera.*

She lived to be 78 years old, still married to Max Schiller, her devoted husband of many years, but their last years together were spent under Vichy and German rule. Politically unsophisticated, they had waited too long. By the time Max tried to line up some lectures for Yvette in America, the hostilities made travel impossible.

Max was Jewish; Yvette was suspected by the Nazis of being Jewish. There were three years of investigation, but Yvette and Max were too old to do anything but comply and try to survive. Yvette Guilbert died before the Allied invasion. Max brought Yvette's body back to Paris after the war.

TEXAS GUINAN

b: (Mary Louise Cecilia Guinan) 12 January 1884, Waco, TX—d: 5 November 1933, Vancouver, Canada

She presided over speakeasies like a madam at a brothel. Texas Guinan was loud and cheery, looked worse for the wear and was a capable quipster who was indulgent with drunks and took too many liberties with her audiences. They loved her for it. She was the nightclub hostess par excellence during Prohibition—a time when going out to someplace exciting meant sitting, drinking and dancing, under the threat of a police raid and in the same room with gangsters, industrialists, show folk, gossip columnists, lawyers, society swells and politicians.

"The Queen of the Night Clubs" hosted tacky floor shows with small-time acts, but part of Texas' genius was getting stars in the audience to get up and perform for free. George Raft proved he was the classiest and fastest Charleston dancer alive. Blanche Ring sang "Rings on My Fingers and Bells on My Toes." Sigmund Romberg obliged Tex by playing some of his compositions on the piano. Once Rudolph Valentino and his second wife, Natasha Rambova, took a break from their vaudeville tour, where they were paid thousands of dollars to play to thousands of adoring fans twice a day, to perform gratis at Guinan's for 200 people crammed into a space large enough for 80.

Tex reigned nearly ten years in speakeasies, and that was the final phase of her career. Before that, she played vaudeville and in numerous road shows of musical comedies and then went to Hollywood to become movieland's first hard-riding, two-gun cowgirl in a series of Westerns. She was also a queen of ballyhoo, a master of creating her public image. Whatever she told about herself was not to set the record straight, to create her posthumous monument, but to sell herself and her latest venture.

Texas Guinan was born in the already civilized town of Waco, not on a frontier ranch, as she claimed. As the oldest daughter, she was her mother's surrogate, tending the younger children and helping to cook, sew and clean, and she was schooled at the local Catholic convent. She already possessed a forceful personality as a child, and she was as much a mischievous adventurer as any lad her age in Waco.

One reason that wild adventure and mischief were part of her legend is because Texas made it so. Interviews and feature articles and her own fictionalized biography were intended to advance her public image, the persona that people paid her money to be. Perhaps few events made as much of an impression on her when she was young than the first stage show she ever witnessed. It was mounted at the Waco Opera House and she loved everything about it—the melodrama, the costumes and the outsized acting. It offered an exciting alternative to the mundane life of a wife and mother.

When Tex was 16, the family moved to Denver, Colorado, where her mother and father had family. She remained fascinated by theatre and may have sung and acted locally. In 1904, near her 20th birthday, she eloped to Chicago with a young Denver newspaperman, John J. Moynahan. Texas was not geared to be a housewife, and the two grew apart but not unfriendly. In 1906, Texas headed for New York City, vaguely determined that she would become an actor. She got her first job as a chorus girl and the show, an operetta, *The Girls of Holland,* took her out of town.

Guinan had enough confidence to jump into vaudeville as a singer of popular songs. She always claimed to have studied voice, and between her singing, her looks and her personality, she was a natural for vaudeville. By 1909 she had made the cover of the *New York Dramatic Mirror,* a sure indicator that hers was a popular act. At the same time, she took soubrette roles in musicals. During a tour with one of her shows, Texas met the love of her life, Julian Johnson, a theatre reviewer. He also became her cultural guide. She began to read seriously and cultivate her senses and taste. They did not marry but kept company for nearly ten years.

After a half dozen years constantly on the road in vaudeville or road shows, Texas grew ill and had to retire temporarily. She occasionally went on starvation diets and lost weight rapidly to get in shape for a show or a vaudeville tour. She battled chubbiness all her life; plump was attractive, chubby was not.

During the years that the USA was engaged in the war in Europe, Tex made movies. She liked the idea of settling down in Hollywood, where she could enjoy the trappings of a star. She was 34 by the time her first Western was issued in 1918. By all reports Texas was good; she rode very well and appeared to be able to handle a six-shooter. Perhaps the most telling critique was that instead of playing the traditional female in a Wild West–type role, she played a Western hero, just like screen idol William S. Hart.

Tex had not abandoned the stage; indeed, she used personal appearances to create publicity for her latest movies. She took over the marketing of her pictures and formed her own production company. Texas' last Western was issued in 1921. She was old for a silent star. The early cameras were not kind. Almost all the female stars of 1918—Mary Pickford, Lillian Gish, Mae Marsh, Mabel Normand and Norma and Constance Talmadge—were a decade younger than Texas. Even Theda Bara was six years younger. Marguerite Clark was the oldest—the same age as Tex; Clark looked like a waif, yet her career was finished by 1921. Texas' competition as female action stars, Pearl White and Ruth Roland, were both five years younger.

Fortunately for Texas Guinan, the USA, in a burst of morality in the midst of war, decided that drink was indeed distilled damnation. A constitutional amendment, ratified by the prerequisite number of states, banned booze. Underground drinking establishments came into being like toadstools after a rain. Gangsters supplied the booze and hired a proxy who leased the premises. Popular entertainers like Clayton, Jackson & (Jimmy) Durante, Helen Morgan and Harry Richman fronted some of the more respectable of the illegal establishments. No host or entertainer became more famous, more identified with speakeasies, than Texas Guinan.

Texas was pushing 40 when she accepted her first speakeasy job. She was getting too old-looking for movies. Her radical dieting had affected her health and appearance; her once attractively plump flesh sagged a bit under her arms and on her face. She had not made enough of a name in musical comedy to make a go of being an overage soubrette. So it made business sense to try to make the most of the opportunity that hosting a "speak" offered. She sent money home faithfully and was able to bring some of her family, including her ailing mother, to Manhattan. She hired her brother, Tommy, and he handled a lot of business matters for her.

She worked at a succession of speakeasies, all among the better ones. It was not easy work. Tex came to the club around midnight and was the last to leave. Besides picking the acts, she needed to know people's names (if she did not, she greeted them as Fred), stroke their egos, monitor everything going on in the room, prevent unpleasant situations, keep an eye out for government agents and make the evening exciting so that people returned often. There were nights to honor particular stars when they were in town, and audience participation games when the stars were not out on the town. If Tex sensed a lull, she urged her customers to use their noisemakers or get up and dance.

Every night was a New Year's Eve party. Years of yelling in smoky speakeasies had turned her lovely singing and speaking voice into a gravelly rasp. When she made her first appearance of the night, she shouted, "Hello, suckers!" It was the signal that the festivities had begun. She introduced the rich and famous to the rest of the audience and called by name as many as she could remember of those who wished they were rich and famous. She smoked cigarettes and drank coffee constantly, but she never drank liquor—even off duty.

On at least two occasions, probably after one speakeasy had been padlocked and another was readying to open, Texas took part in revues, *Gay Paree* (1925) and *Padlocks of 1927* (1927). She usually brought along some of her chorus girls, which at one time included future film star Ruby Keeler, future *Follies* girl Doris Vinton and future ambassador Claire Booth (Luce).

At dawn, after she closed her club for the night, about five in the morning, Tex went home to her apartment in Greenwich Village. Few people were invited there. Her private life was just that. She had partners and customers and she had friends. Seldom was one the other.

Life was not all champagne and roses. She was hauled into court and beat the rap for aiding and abetting the illegal sale of booze. Publicity-seeking public officials let murders slide by to concentrate on convicting Texas Guinan of something. Her club was closed, but the authorities were even angrier when she walked away from speakeasies for a while to take her show into vaudeville at $7,500 a week. Warner Brothers paid her $75,000 to make a movie, *Queen of the Night Clubs* (1929), and a newspaper paid her for her serialized life story.

On one occasion, late in the game, when Texas arrived at her club to find it padlocked, a newspaper photographer was on hand to snap her picture and record Tex's mock-indignant complaint: "Whaddya mean I sell bootleg booze!?" But the show was over. The 1920s segued into the 1930s. Prohibition was repealed. Texas grew tired and then ill. While touring her show in the Northwest, she underwent surgery. She died, at age 49, from a combination of peritonitis, colitis and a reaction to the anesthesia.

For all her mythmaking and exaggeration, Guinan seemed to possess a bedrock of common sense. A legacy, a reputation that would last beyond her death, seemed pointless to her. Tex saw herself as a hostess whose job it was to see that everyone else had fun. She worked hard to ensure that she did that job better than any of her competitors, and she knew when to let go and move on.

GUS SUN CIRCUIT

Gus Sun time was small time. The father-and-son team owned only eight theatres, but at the height of their success they booked over 100 theatres. However, an act was kept hopping because Gus Sun booked split weeks—a half week at one theatre in one town and the second half of the week in another theatre in another town. That meant a minimum of two days of travel during a single week.

In 1910, a Gus Sun route might start in upstate New York (New Savoy in Syracuse and Arcade in Niagara Falls) and move on to Pennsylvania (Liberty in East Liberty, Star in Monessen and an Orpheum each in Oil City and Franklin). Next in line were Gus Sun theatres in Ohio (New Sun in Springfield, the Grand in Hamilton, Arcade in Toledo, American in East Liverpool, the New Priscilla in Cleveland and a string of New Orpheums in Lima, Mansfield, Canton, Portsmouth, Newark and Marion). An act might continue west and north to Michigan, Illinois and Canada, or south to Indiana (Star in Muncie and New Murray in Richmond), West Virginia, Virginia and Kentucky. The jumps were often long and time-consuming, and the connections difficult to make.

Gus Sun (born Auguste Klotz) began his career in a juggling act with his brothers John, George and Pete, then tried various other forms of show business from medicine shows to circus. In addition to booking for their own circuit, Gus and his son added to their revenue by booking acts for other small-time chains between the East Coast and the Rockies. When vaudeville faded, the Suns segued into booking acts for carnivals, fairgrounds and amusement parks.

Gus Sun

As a manager and booker, Gus Sun got mixed reviews from vaudevillians. While many found him affable, he was cursed for introducing into contracts cancellation clauses that permitted managers to cancel an act after the first show—leaving the performers without work for the reminder of the week. Gus was cursed as well for introducing split weeks (which, more probably, he may have reintroduced and boosted into a trend).

Note: The list of the theatres attributed to this circuit is a composite of lists. It was culled from several sources, including *Julius Cahn's Official Theatrical Guides* (1910), *The [New York] Clipper Red Book & Date Book* (1910), Jack B. Shea's *Official Vaudeville Guide* (1928) and Herbert Lloyd's *Vaudeville Trails thru the West* (1919).

Theatre affiliations with circuits changed over time, however. A Proctor theatre later may have become a Keith-Albee house; a Pantages' or a Loew's theatre may have been a former Sullivan & Considine theatre; and independent circuits were often taken over by larger enterprises like Keith-Albee, Orpheum, Pantages or Loew's. Theatres were bought and sold, and names were changed entirely or simply altered to reflect their new owners.

Some theatres were specifically designed as opera houses or vaudeville theatres, but generally theatres were able to accommodate several types of show. A theatre could host vaudeville for several seasons and then change to exhibiting only motion pictures. A former burlesque house might be converted to vaudeville.

The following list of theatres is not a snapshot in time. It includes theatres that functioned at various times over a period of nearly 20 years; thus there will be duplications.

Muncie	Indiana	Star
Richmond	Indiana	New Murray
Niagara Falls	New York	Arcade
Syracuse	New York	New Savoy
Canton	Ohio	New Orpheum
Cleveland	Ohio	New Priscilla
East Liverpool	Ohio	American
Hamilton	Ohio	Grand
Lima	Ohio	New Orpheum
Mansfield	Ohio	New Orpheum
Marion	Ohio	New Orpheum
Newark	Ohio	New Orpheum
Portsmouth	Ohio	New Orpheum
Springfield	Ohio	New Sun
Toledo	Ohio	Arcade
East Liberty	Pennsylvania	Liberty
Franklin	Pennsylvania	Orpheum
Monessen	Pennsylvania	Star
Oil City	Pennsylvania	Orpheum

GUY ROPES OR GUY WIRES

Used to hold scenery and apparatus in position onstage. The ropes or wires are tightened through a system of pulleys and tied off. Aerialists, trapeze performers, ropewalkers and other acrobats used guy wires to secure the paraphernalia from which they swung, walked or climbed. Any carelessness in the matter of securing the equipment could cause a loss of balance and a fall, resulting in serious injury.

The term *guy* dates from the Elizabethan era and refers to chains or ropes that are attached to something that needs to be guided or braced in place, so *guy ropes* or *guy wires* are redundancies of a sort. It was said that *guy,* used as a synonym for man, proceeded from the term *guy ropes,* as in "He's the main guy," indicating that a particular man was essential to keeping things in place and operating.

H

BILLY "CHEESE AND CRACKERS" HAGAN

b: (William Hagandorn), 1888—d: 1986

Something unexpected happened onstage, and burleycue comic Billy Hagan caught himself just as he was about to utter forbidden words. Instead, he quickly switched to a phrase his father used in place of profanity. This accidental turn gave him his catchphrase, one of the most famous in the history of burlesque.

Billy Hagan spent much of his career at "the Troc" (the Trocadero) in Philadelphia. Unlike some burleycue comics, Billy did not don particularly distinguished makeup or costumes. What distinguished him was a high, squeaky voice that dropped to a lusty basso profundo when a sexy dame came into view. When a statuesque burlesque stripper sashayed across the stage and paused near Billy long enough to wind up a grind and snap his head off with a bump, Billy yelped "cheese and crackers!" and brought down the house. Before he went into show business, Billy had a short career as a boxer, an experience that stayed with him in the form of a large lumpy nose. When he switched to vaudeville, Billy played straight for his brother; they were billed as Billy had begun in vaudeville as one of the Hagan Brothers. Playing straight was an excellent way to gauge audiences and learn how to time jokes, and Billy soon decided that he wanted to be the funnyman. After he went solo, he found burlesque suited his style and sense of comedy. Hagan was unabashedly vulgar and won loyal audiences for that, but he skirted outright dirty words. His trick was to employ multisyllabic words as though they were dirty, as when Billy told the straightman that, on his way to the theatre, a crowd had gathered to watch

Billy "Cheese and Crackers" Hagan

a fire. Billy confided that when he looked up there was a woman standing on a window ledge and he saw her "predicament." Billy stayed in burlesque until the last curtain rang down.

JACK HALEY

b: (John Joseph Haley) 10 August 1898, Boston, MA—d: 6 June 1979, Los Angeles, CA

Often enthusiasts lament the absence of documentation of vaudeville stars whose acts were never captured by sound or visual recordings. In Jack Haley's case, it might be wished that the Hollywood evidence did not abound to puzzle those who have read of his great success in vaudeville and revue. Onscreen, few of Jack's nearly three dozen Hollywood features show him to exceptional advantage; often Haley's character seemed to stand still in wide-eyed confusion while more prepossessing and energetic performers grabbed Jack's scenes away from him.

On the plus side, Haley was a utility player, useful to producers and directors because of his clean-cut look, his light Irish tenor and his ability to dance and play both light romantic leads and comedy parts—a considerable package of talents. His best opportunity in films came as the Tin Man in MGM's 1939 classic version of *The Wizard of Oz.*

Jack Haley grew up in blue-collar Boston, where his only performing outlet was singing at community and church events. At age 17, faced with the need to learn a trade, he apprenticed as an electrician only long enough to save enough money to leave town. According to an interview he gave historian Bill Smith, Jack landed in Philadelphia, where he got a job as a bellhop and switchboard operator for the Philadelphia Club. He also took tap dancing lessons. Next, he worked as a song plugger for the McCarthy & Fischer Music Publishing Company but failed to help the company's sales.

His dance teacher, Ed Kramer, rescued him. Kramer was putting a six-girl chorus line through their paces for a flash act when he learned that the act's juvenile had not shown up. The act's star was Bayonne Whipple, then the wife and former vaudeville partner of Walter Huston. Jack got the job.

Haley jumped about in vaudeville, looking for an act that would lift him out of the small time. During one period he worked in an act called Alexander & the Lightner Sisters. One of the sisters was Winnie Lightner, who became a big Broadway and Hollywood star of the 1930s, and another 'sister' was Florence McFadden, whom Jack courted, then married in 1921.

In the early 1920s, Haley teamed with another Boston-born song-and-dance man, Charley Crafts, and they clicked as a team, at least enough to work steadily in the small time and break into big time. Crafts played straight for Haley, and they both sang and hoofed. It was a typical song-dance-and-comedy double act, but Crafts & Haley were good enough to make it to the Palace by 1924. Crafts and Haley were both cast in a Shubert revue, *Round the Town,* but it lasted only a fortnight.

In 1925, Jack Haley's new partner was Helen Eby Rock, William Rock's last partner and his widow. She played largely the same character for Haley that she did for Billy Rock—a dumb cluck, straight. Again, the act was solid, and they played the Palace in 1925.

Two more Shubert revues provided a reunion of sorts for Jack Haley and Winnie Lightner, both of whom were cast in *Gay Paree* (1925) and *Gay Paree* (1926). Each edition ran a good five months. Jack, married since 1921, wished to settle down into some semblance of home life. Revues that played Broadway for several months allowed this. But often, to earn his living, Jack went on the road with big-time vaudeville dates.

He appeared at the Palace a number of times, never more notably than when he partnered with Benny Rubin in 1932, during the last of the big-time days at vaudeville's flagship. Haley never talked much about it, and Rubin claimed it was he who set up the date, but Haley and Rubin were scheduled as co-emcees at the Palace, a tradition made successful by the pairing of Cantor and Jessel.

Rubin had little liking for Haley, but the two were held over for five additional weeks (at $5,000 for the pair), and then took their temporary partnership to other top-notch Keith-Albee-Orpheum theatres. They were due to play a return date at the Palace when Rubin got sick, so a mouthy 24-year-old comedian, Milton Berle, took Rubin's place and made his Palace debut as an adult. (He had appeared there in a kid act a decade earlier.)

Jack's first three Broadway musical comedies were produced (or coproduced) by Laurence Schwab. Both Schwab and Jack started off 1929 with *Follow Thru,* a musical comedy crafted by DeSylva, Brown & Henderson (with an assist by Schwab). Haley played the male comedy lead for the entire calendar year of 1929, and he and Zelma O'Neal shared the musical honors of the evening with a duet on "Button Up Your Overcoat." Hollywood bought the rights, and the film version of *Follow Thru* gave Jack Haley his first important film role.

In 1931, *Free for All* quickly added its cast, including Haley, to the nation's growing unemployment numbers. Schwab rallied in 1932, but started with a dud on his hands. He quickly closed down *Humpty Dumpty,* made some major changes in creative personnel and reopened the show as *Take a Chance.* People did, and the show ran from late November through the spring of 1933. Late in the run, the comedy crook roles originated by Haley and Sid Silvers were taken over by Ole Olsen & Chic Johnson.

With big-time vaudeville in a coma and too many Broadway shows running for less time than they rehearsed, Jack happily accepted Hollywood's invitation to make movies. He made no less than 20 features between 1932 and 1938. Most were B movie programmers and were successful at the box office. Among the better and better known were *Poor Little Rich Girl, Pigskin Parade, Hold That Co-Ed* and *Alexander's Ragtime Band* (all 1938), *Moon Over Miami* (1941) and *George White's Scandals* (1945).

Haley had his biggest Hollywood hit, *The Wizard of Oz,* fresh in the public memory when he opened in 1940 on Broadway in *Higher and Higher,* one of Rodgers & Hart's unsuccessful musicals. It lasted a mere ten weeks. Hollywood bought the film rights and a few years later made an equally unmemorable movie. Jack Haley was in that, too.

Jack was back on Broadway in 1943 when *Show Time* opened in September and ran most of the season. Other vaudeville revues had not fared as well, but this show, headed by Haley, George Jessel, singer Ella Logan and the dancing De Marcos, somehow found its public.

Haley's star had dimmed in Hollywood by the late 1940s; his roles were no longer starring parts. *Inside U.S.A.* was his last shining moment on Broadway. He was most fortunate that his costar was Beatrice Lillie, still accurately billed as "the funniest woman in the world." *Inside U.S.A.* opened 30 April 1948 and played through the summer and into 1949 for a total of ten months. Performances by singer Thelma Carpenter, dancers Valerie Bettis and Rod Alexander and supporting comedians Carl Reiner and Louis Nye contributed to the word of mouth that kept the box office humming. The cast was far better than their material.

Around this time, Haley gave several interviews that announced his retirement from show business. He claimed he enjoyed the real estate business (in which he had become a multimillionaire). It seemed to some in show business that Jack was simply acknowledging the facts of a career that had evaporated. His retirement did not prevent him from hosting television's *Ford Star Revue,* which lasted the single season of 1950–51, or appearing on summer replacement shows in the early 1950s. Finally, he gave up trying to be a star in a medium whose audiences were looking for crooners rather than song-and-dance men, and Jack settled for making the occasional guest appearance as a character actor in some established TV series during the 1950s and 1960s.

The public saw Jack Haley one last time—at the 1979 Academy Awards presentations, a month or so before he died. He joined his *Wizard of Oz* buddy and fellow Boston native son, Ray Bolger, to present an Oscar. Jack had been married for nearly 60 years to Florence McFadden when he died of a heart attack. His son, Jack Haley Jr. (1933–2001), had become a successful, Peabody Award–winning Hollywood producer of the 1960s, 1970s and 1980s. During the early 1970s, Jack Jr. was married to Liza Minnelli, the daughter of his dad's *Wizard of Oz* costar, Judy Garland.

HALF-AND-HALF ACT

Almost always a dance act, in a half-and-half act a solo performer was costumed and made up to appear as both a man and a woman. He appeared male as he faced the wings on one side of the stage and then female as he turned toward the opposite side of the stage—like two sides of a coin. The demarcation line was drawn down the center of the face to the crotch. If it was a dance act, the male side might wear half a tuxedo or bolero costume (one arm and one leg) and half a ball gown or blouse and skirt. As the performer danced, he made sharp, quick turns, keeping the profile toward the audience as much as possible to foster the illusion of two people dancing together.

A variation on the half-and-half dance act was to have a solo dancer with a flexible dummy. The dancer held the dummy by the hands and arms and the dummy and dancer were attached only at the toes so that their steps seemed coordinated. Although this was occasionally performed as a serious dance illusion, it was far more often a comedy act in which the flexibility, even floppiness, of the dummy permitted grotesque movements and wild gyrations.

It was rare but not unknown for a half-and-half performer to do a comic dialogue act. Rather than dance, the performer would pivot in position so it appeared that the man and the woman were exchanging questions and answers or quips and insults.

ADELAIDE HALL

b: (Adelaide Louise Hall) 20 October 1901, Brooklyn, NY—d: 7 November 1993, London, England

After the First World War, a handful of superb, musically well-rounded women singers emerged from black vaudeville, burlesque revue and musical comedy. They became welcomed and reliable acts in mainstream vaudeville, and they performed in black musical shows that drew white audiences. Their impeccable diction and their wish to sing various styles of popular music made them likelier candidates for white vaudeville than blues singers, whose success with black audiences was rooted in the black experience and a style of speech that was as indecipherable to most whites as Yiddish or Italian. However, many middle-class blacks, those

Blackbirds: Bill Robinson, Tim Moore, Mantan Moreland, Adelaide Hall and Peg Leg Bates

who found themselves represented as the *New Negro*, wanted to see performers of their own race break artistic as well as societal barriers.

Among the women singers who proved popular with white audiences, the most famous were Josephine Baker, Adelaide Hall, Florence Mills, Ethel Waters and Elizabeth Welch. Waters chose to make her career in the USA, although she made occasional tours in Europe. Mills was still a new success on Broadway and in London's West End when she died at 32. The others—Hall, Welch and Baker—were among the large number of black entertainers and musicians who found that working in France and England gave them wider professional opportunity and more personal respect than they were likely to find in the USA.

Adelaide Hall was born into a middle-class African American family in Brooklyn. Her mother was a music teacher. Adelaide studied voice and attended Pratt Institute in Brooklyn. The family later relocated to Harlem, which gave Adelaide the opportunity to get work as a singer and dancer. She won her first professional job as a dancer in the chorus of *Shuffle Along* (1921–22), the Miller-Lyles-Sissle-Blake musical comedy that revived black entertainment on Broadway and then went on tour. When Flournoy Miller & Aubrey Lyles put together their next show, *Runnin' Wild,* Adelaide was engaged for a featured role. Also in the cast was Elizabeth Welch. *Runnin' Wild* (1923–24), produced by white hoofer and budding producer George White, ran six months and then toured for another season. The show gave Hall her first hit, "Old-Fashioned Love."

While playing London in the cast of *Chocolate Kiddies* (1925), Adelaide wed a Trinidadian, Bert Hicks, who became her manager. Despite music composed by Luckey Roberts, Hall's next show, *My Magnolia* (1926), bloomed and faded in four days. In 1927 she worked with Duke Ellington & His Orchestra. They made vaudeville appearances on Keith time as well as sound recordings that included Duke's "Creole Love Song," an example of his "jungle jazz," and "The Blues I Love to Sing," a wordless exercise in vocalese by Adelaide.

The death of Florence Mills required last-minute changes to what was to have been her next starring revue, *Blackbirds of 1928.* Producer Lew Leslie engaged both Adelaide Hall and Aida Ward to perform the numbers originally assigned to Florence. The show, which also featured Elizabeth Welch, Bill Robinson, Mantan Moreland and Tim Moore, ran for 519 performances, from May 1928 into August 1929, and then played London and Paris. The show provided Adelaide three songs forever identified with her, "I Can't Give You Anything but Love (Baby)," "I Must Have That Man" and "Diga Diga Doo."

After her Broadway success, Adelaide received offers to appear in mainstream vaudeville. In 1930, she appeared on a bill at the Palace. As always, she dressed elegantly, sang a diverse group of songs and hoofed energetically. Later that year, she and Bill Robinson costarred in *Brown Buddies* (1930) with Ada Brown and John "Spider Bruce" Mason, but the show disappointed with a 14-week run.

In 1931, Adelaide and her husband, Bert, went to England for a series of performances. They stayed there for the better part of two seasons. When she returned to the USA, big-time vaudeville was being replaced by presentation house programming that paired a feature film with a one-act revue, several vaudeville acts or a big band with singers and dancers. Hall appeared on the Paramount/Publix circuit, joined the *Cotton Club Parade* (1934) and made two short films, *Dancers in the Dark* (1932) and *An All-Colored Vaudeville Show* (1935). These shorts show Adelaide Hall as she must have appeared live onstage in vaudeville, revue and night clubs. She made a sophisticated but friendly impression. Adelaide had a soprano range augmented by a low falsetto that she used for growls and trumpetlike sounds.

In 1936, Adelaide and Bert returned to Europe for an engagement at the Moulin Rouge. They managed their own Parisian nightclub, the Big Apple, until the Nazi invasion, when they fled to London. Because Bert was a British subject, it was probably easier for them to establish residence in London and for her to get work permits. She appeared in West End shows (Cole Porter's *The Sun Never Sets,* 1938), sang on radio, made more recordings and a few films (*The Thief of Bagdad,* 1940), performed in British variety and, with Bert, opened their own nightclub, The Florida, which was bombed during the Second World War. During the war, Adelaide entertained the troops at home and abroad, continuing to offer her services through ENSA (the British counterpart of the USO) after the cessation of hostilities.

Until the late 1950s, Adelaide remained abroad, singing and acting in two English productions of musicals, *Kiss Me Kate* (1952) and *Love from Judy* (1956) and one drama, *Someone to Talk To* (1957). She was also a favorite of BBC radio and television audiences. She returned to the USA to act in the musical *Jamaica* (1957), whose star, Lena Horne, had been a chorus girl at the Cotton Club when Adelaide was a star singer there.

Nearing 60, and with new styles of popular music in the ascendant, there was little work for Hall or her contemporaries throughout the 1960s and early 1970s. In 1976, Hall made a long-playing album of her more famous songs for Monmouth-Evergreen Records, and, in 1980, she performed in a New York Town Hall concert called *Black Broadway* (1980) that included dancer-singer John Bubbles and singers Elizabeth Welch and Edith Wilson. Thereafter Adelaide made appearances at celebrations such as Eubie Blake's 100th birthday. A documentary of her life and career, *Sophisticated Lady* (not to be confused with the revue *Sophisticated Ladies*) was released in 1989. Through her last years, even at age 90, Adelaide Hall continued to sing in concert, appear on television (mostly in England) and make music recordings.

HALLS

Chiefly British and short for music-halls, most often meaning the theatres rather than the institution, for example: "They played the halls exclusively between 1885 and 1890."

NAN HALPERIN

b: 1898, Odessa, Russia—d: 30 May 1963, New York, NY

A petite singing comedienne, Nan Halperin was described as "a riot" when she appeared at the Palace the week of 15 February 1915. Based on information gleaned from an interview Nan gave the *New York Dramatic Mirror* in 1915, Anthony Slide, author of *The Encyclopedia of Vaudeville*, reported that Ms. Halperin had a repertoire of 300 songs. If Halperin's given birth date of 1898 can be believed, she was 16 or 17 years old at the time and a remarkable prodigy. Given her birth in Odessa and her arrival in the USA as a child, there may not have been reliable birth records to contradict the birth date she claimed.

Nan Halperin

Her act, "In a Character Song Cycle," was a mix of impersonations and songs written expressly for her rather than as potential Tin Pan Alley hits. Her impersonations were not of famous people, like those performed by Elsie Janis, Florence Desmond and Mitzi Green. Instead, more like Irene Franklin, Halperin acted out characters like little girls (for which she was renowned), a young woman on her first date, a bride and several older characters. Her impersonations of children, unlike Ray Dooley's and Fanny Brice's, were not wholly comic. Halperin offered less broad portrayals and added poignant touches to her characters and their situations.

She married William Barr Friedlander, who made his name as a tunesmith and a writer of special material. Later, he turned out 20 musicals and plays between 1920 and 1944. In each production, W.B. Friedlander performed several tasks, often producing or directing as well as writing the show. During the 1910s and 1920s he created and produced various tab shows to play vaudeville. One of these was *The Suffragettes* (also billed later as *Nan Halperin and Her Suffragettes*), a very successful tab show that spotlighted his new bride.

Nan Halperin was primarily a creature of vaudeville, eventually a headliner on the big time. There is no record that she made any sound recordings or appeared in movies. She headlined with Eddie Cantor, J. Harold Murray and Lew Hearn at the Winter Garden in *Make It Snappy* (1922), a revue that managed about 90 performances between 13 April and 1 July. Five days after *Make It Snappy* closed, Nan Halperin and Lew Hearn, along with Georgie Price and Valeska Suratt, opened in another Winter Garden revue, *Spice of 1922,* that finished out the summer. Nan had far better luck the next year when she costarred with Miriam Hopkins in *Little Jessie James* (1923), a musical comedy that ran from mid-August through the entire 1923–24 season at the Longacre Theatre. Halperin closed out her career as vaudeville yielded to radio and talking pictures.

THE HAMMERSTEINS

Oscar Hammerstein I

b: 8 May ca. 1846–48, Stettin, Pomerania/ Prussia (now Szczecin, Poland)— d: 1 August 1919, New York, NY

Willie Hammerstein

b: ca. 1870–74—d: 10 July 1914, New York, NY

Arthur Hammerstein

b: ca. 21 December 1873, New York, NY— d: 12 October 1955, Palm Beach, FL

It is commonplace to say that television is the new vaudeville—with the viewer the new booker of acts, flicking channels to produce a fast-moving bill of confessional talk, sketch comedy, music videos, soap operas, bottom-of-the-ninth hitting rallies, cartoons and death-defying stunts. This facile observation ignores the centricity to vaudeville's success and its patrons' satisfaction of a balanced bill of polished, well-crafted acts.

Still, when the subject of vaudeville narrows to Willie Hammerstein and his Victoria Theatre at the famed corner of 42nd Street and Seventh Avenue, the *freak acts* that Willie often booked at the peak of their sensationalized fame are echoed nearly a century later as a new generation of shameless scandalizers are booked by television shlockmeisters.

Willie was first-generation American and second-generation showman. His father, Oscar, emigrated from Berlin and embarked upon a dazzling, often calamitous, sometimes profitable career. Oscar Hammerstein was one of the old-time showmen who, despite a certain roguery, loved theatre and music truly and well. To the Hammersteins, show business was an adventure, not a case study for an MBA. Oscar did not survey a potential audience to find out what it would support; he produced what he loved—opera and classic drama—and hoped his productions would draw audiences.

Sixteen-year-old Oscar came to the USA in the middle of the Civil War and established a foothold through tobacco. A budding violinist, flutist and pianist, he was unable to find work in music or to afford further training, so he turned to making cigars by hand. Along his way to becoming an impresario, he published a trade journal, became a superior publicist, played in and conducted orchestras, wrote music—including opera—and developed into a superb, if instinctive, acoustical engineer. Over his lifetime he earned more than 50 patents for various mechanical inventions, many of them cigar-making patents that made him wealthy and continued to bail him out of show business disasters.

He also fought publicly and physically with rivals and partners, landing in court and on prominent pages of newspapers. Some of his contemporaries viewed Oscar as a true renaissance man; others saw him as a belligerent and erratic rascal.

Oscar built a number of theatres in New York City, among which were the Hammerstein's Victoria Theatre, the Manhattan Opera House (the first in 1892, the second in 1906), the Harlem Opera House (1888), the Columbus (1889) and the Olympia. He also lost most of them because he was financially overextended. In the case of the Manhattan Opera House, the year after he built it, Oscar sold an interest to Koster & Bial, and the trio turned it into a music-hall. The ink on the partnership papers was barely dry when fists began to fly, and Koster & Bial bought out Oscar's remaining share.

With proceeds from the sale, Oscar made his boldest and longest-lasting move—uptown. Back in the days when Times Square was still gaslit Longacre Square (it was renamed in 1903 for the newly erected New York Times building), Oscar built three theatres: the

Olympia (1889) on the east side of Broadway between 44th and 45th streets, the Victoria (1899) at the corner of Broadway and 42nd Street, and the Belasco (1900) and the Republic (1900), both located on 42nd Street. Contrary to skeptical predictions, these long shots paid off for Oscar, even though he did not hold onto the rewards. Those four theatres proved that shows could attract patronage far uptown. Oscar's theatres provided the foundation for the famed Broadway theatre district that still existed a century later.

Although Oscar Hammerstein I produced plays, a few musicals and some vaudeville and established New York's first roof garden, opera was Oscar's lasting love. His sponsorship brought top-notch artists and new operas, like Debussy's *Pelléas et Mélisande* (premiered in Paris, 1902) and Richard Strauss' *Elektra* (premiered in 1909 in Dresden), to American audiences at the Manhattan Opera House, located between 34th and 35th streets. That theatre, however, was in competition with the Metropolitan Opera House for the patronage of society's opera-loving upper crust.

In 1910 the Metropolitan Opera cut a deal with Oscar to abandon competition with the Met for ten years. Hammerstein's Manhattan Opera House changed to vaudeville, and his newly constructed Lexington Opera House in New York became a movie theatre. The money Oscar got from the Met (reportedly in excess of $1.2 million) plus another $200,000 he took from E. F. Albee in another matter a few years later could have provided him security for life; instead he chose to gamble again. Having been beaten by the Met in New York, Oscar decided to go up against Covent Garden in London. Predictably, he failed.

Meanwhile, one of Oscar's legacies became, in the hands of his son Willie, the great vaudeville landmark of its day. Hammerstein's Victoria Theatre and Music Hall, which Oscar had built as a legit house in 1899, switched to big-time vaudeville in 1904, one year after he had lost his other theatres and hit bottom. Until 1915, Hammerstein's Victoria, as it was popularly known, remained the most famous vaude house since Tony Pastor's theatre in Tammany Hall on 14th Street. Like Pastor's, the Victoria bills reflected their manager's taste and personality, and Willie's were idiosyncratic.

No less a character than his father, Willie was far more practical and far less artistically ambitious. He had his beginnings as an advance man for touring shows and as a partner in a Harlem beer hall. Willie's booking choices caused the Victoria to become known as "the Nut House," because Willie inclined to the sensational.

He often booked right off the front page of tabloid news rags and sports pages. An assortment of beautiful women accused of shooting lovers who had forsaken them or who were the object of straying affections, like Evelyn Nesbit, paraded into the Victoria's stage along with newly minted boxing and wrestling champions and baseball stars flushed with victory. Willie tried to wrap his notorious headliners in some sort of an act ("The Singing Murderess"), but his attempts were strictly a pretense to let the public pay to gawk until the next scandal or sports champ captured the public's fancy.

"Sober Sue—You Can't Make Her Laugh" was given a spot in the Roof Garden, and Willie posted a challenge of $1,000 to disprove his claim. She was held over for nearly four months. Willie could hype an act with the best of them. To cash in on the publicity, some of New York's top comics accepted the challenge, so customers came back week after week to watch the great comedians do their routine (for no pay from Willie). No one won the $1,000 prize. Sober Sue's face was paralyzed. Willie paid her about $20 per week plus expenses and made a bundle.

Some of Willie's *freak acts* were professional only in the sense that they played vaudeville season after season. The Cherry Sisters were billed as "America's Worst Act," and the sisters fulfilled the boast, although they regarded themselves as accomplished singers. The remainder of the bill, however, was filled up with some of the finest acts of the day. Given the length of the bill—sometimes over four hours—there was something for everyone in the audience.

Contemporaries doubted that Willie ever saw any shows other than the acts that played the Victoria, and he did not see too much of them, either. He preferred to hang around the box office with a bunch of his cronies. He also observed civilian business hours that were totally at odds with show business schedules; he started work early in the mornings and left his theatre for home about halfway through the Victoria's bill. The performers tried to win a spot on the bill that was not at the end of the long night, when many patrons had followed Willie's example and gone home.

The Victoria, the most cheaply built of Oscar's theatres, returned to the Hammersteins their greatest profit. During its decade of operation, the Victoria yielded more than $300,000 a year profit, most of which Oscar diverted to his various failures in high art. Later, after E. F. Albee squeezed Martin Beck out of the newly built Palace Theatre in 1913, he discovered that it would cost him another $200,000 to pay off Oscar Hammerstein. Albee, whose sharp mind was clouded by his ire over Beck's effrontery in opening a theatre in Keith-Albee territory, forgot that Oscar still held a franchise that granted him exclusive rights to all United Booking Office acts for vaudeville in midtown Manhattan, an area that included the Palace. This meant that Albee could not book his own UBO acts into the newly acquired Palace.

Fortunately for Albee, Oscar Hammerstein always needed money, so he accepted the buyout.

Still, the Palace stumbled along for a year or so, while Willie broke records at the Victoria with Evelyn Nesbit. Nesbit had faded along with her newsworthiness, but Willie fanned the cooling embers of scandal and was coincidentally aided by the sensational escape from prison of Nesbit's husband, the socially prominent scion of industry Harry Thaw, whose role in the love triangle was to murder Evelyn's lover, the socially prominent architect Stanford White.

Unwilling to leave the golden goose alive, Oscar tried to sell the Victoria to the Shuberts, but his sons Willie and Arthur blocked the deal. Arthur Hammerstein had built the Victoria under Oscar's supervision, then took over Oscar's production of *Naughty Marietta* (1912). Arthur made a specialty and a success of producing operettas such as *The Firefly* (1912–13), *High Jinks* (1913), *Katinka* (1915), *Wildflower* (1923), *Rose-Marie* (1924), *Song of the Flame* (1925–26) and *Sweet Adeline* (1929–30) but also produced comedies, dramas and revues—a total of more than 30 productions.

From 1910 to the late 1920s Arthur had a good share of hits, but like his father and his own contemporaries Charles Dillingham and Florenz Ziegfeld, Arthur Hammerstein lived from one production to the next, and he had not the financial wherewithal to withstand the onset of the Great Depression. He gave his nephew and protégé, Oscar Hammerstein II, his first creative work in musical theatre and lived long enough to enjoy Oscar's success.

Oscar Hammerstein II (1895–1960) achieved the most lasting fame and legacy of anyone in the family. Librettist and lyricist, later a producer, playwright and director, Oscar II was still a teenager when his first musicals were produced by Arthur Hammerstein on Broadway. In the early half of Oscar's career he partnered writer Otto Harbach and composers Rudolf Friml, Jerome Kern and Sigmund Romberg. After a low period during the 1930s, he joined with composer Richard Rodgers, with whom he wrote and produced the most successful musical comedies of the mid-twentieth century.

HAMMERSTEIN'S VICTORIA

It came to be called the Corner because Hammerstein's Victoria Theatre and Music Hall was the dominant presence at the corner of West 42nd Street and Seventh Avenue in the newly rechristened Times Square. Just as Tony Pastor's 14th Street Theatre had been the most respected variety and vaudeville theatre from 1881 until the late 1890s, and as the Palace Theatre was to become while it played two-a-day vaudeville from 1913 to 1934, Hammerstein's Victoria, built in 1899 by Oscar Hammerstein, became the most celebrated vaudeville house of its day, from 1904 until 1915, under the management of Oscar's son Willie.

It was the fifth theatre that Oscar built, and he named it not for the British queen, as many supposed, but because he felt victorious in his accomplishment despite the naysayers. The exterior was a white- and gold-trimmed confection, looking rather like a well-proportioned five-layer cake. As it was sited on a corner, two sides were open to public view. Looking like giant spiders, iron fire escapes crisscrossed both sides.

Inside, the walls and ceilings were canary yellow and white relieved by wall hangings, gold accents, and red seats and carpeting (the last of which was salvaged from an ocean liner). The house seated 1,200, but the wide promenades that ran along the rear of the boxes and balconies accommodated up to 2,000 standees.

After Willie assumed control and changed the musical comedy policy to vaudeville, the theatre quickly became successful. Performers enjoyed playing there despite bills that sometimes ran more than four hours. Audiences, especially standees, often did not stay for the entire show, so acts that played the Victoria, instead of pleading for next-to-closing spots, angled to get on by the middle of the bill. Performers such as Will Rogers and Buster Keaton considered the Victoria the greatest of all vaudeville houses.

The Victoria earned two rather opposing reputations. On the one hand, it was saluted as a grand building where the finest acts in vaudeville played; on the other hand, it was notorious as the home of the *freak act*. If someone had scandalized the public enough, and newspapers had reported their moral lapse in large enough print, then Willie Hammerstein wanted to be sure that the public could demonstrate their disapproval close up, preferably in the 50-cent seats at the Victoria.

Love triangles that ended in one or more murders or suicides were top attractions, as long as at least one of the parties stayed alive and free on bail, and thus able to regale audiences with the details they craved. Absent scandal, novelty, if well exploited, helped fill the bill and attract the curious. Famous prizefighters and baseball players debuted at the Victoria; a few, like boxer James J. Corbett and Giants pitcher Rube Marquard, had enough talent and personality beyond their athleticism to succeed as vaudevillians. The Cherry Sisters, an act so bad that it was enjoyable, also found Victoria audiences more appreciative than elsewhere, thus adding to their firm belief that they were indeed a talented top act.

Willie Hammerstein, who ran his father's theatre, was not above wily deception to keep seats filled. Sober Sue was booked solely to challenge people to make her laugh. Since she had neither talent nor an act, the dour-visaged old woman simply sat onstage without cracking a smile as various people from the audience, lured by cash prizes if they could make her laugh, tried. What

Willie intended as a passing novelty turned into a substantial draw. To keep his goose laying golden eggs, Willie began inviting professional comedians to make Sober Sue cackle. Not only was Willie paying Sue a pittance, his challenge brought high-priced comedians to his stage free of any cost to the theatre. The pros wanted to succeed where their rivals had failed.

Eventually it was revealed that Sober Sue was infirm. Some said she had suffered paralysis of her facial muscles, whereas others contended that Sue was deaf and nearly blind, unable to hear the jokes or see the antics but glad to receive the $20 a week that Willie paid her.

The contradictions in the Victoria's policy were perhaps rooted in its construction. Oscar was broke, although he was never too broke to build another opera house, so the Victoria was constructed and furnished with secondhand materials. Oscar's other son, Arthur, who knew something about building, was able to make the odds and ends cohere into a handsome house praised by all.

In 1900, a year after building the Victoria, Oscar installed a roof garden atop the Victoria as a café and petting zoo, and he called it the Venetian Terrace Roof Garden. In 1902, after he won permission to erect a roof that could open and close to suit the weather and replaced tables and cages with theatre seats, he renamed it the Paradise Roof Garden Theatre. Still later it became Hammerstein's Roof Garden.

Roof garden theatres, Hammerstein's and others, had the advantage of being able to play vaudeville all year long. In the years before air cooling by ice and fans was truly effective, they were able to attract audiences during the hot summer months while conventional theatres shut down. Seventeen years after it was built and two years after the death of Willie, Hammerstein's Victoria Theatre and Music Hall was demolished by S.L. (Roxy) Rothafel, its new owner, who replaced it with Times Square's first movie palace, the Rialto.

HANDCUFFED AUDIENCE

The wry explanation given by a performer who failed to elicit applause from an audience.

HANLON BROTHERS (HANLON-LEES)

Thomas Hanlon

b: March 1833, Manchester, England—d: 5 April 1868, Harrisburg, PA

George Hanlon

b: 10 October 1835, Manchester, England—d: 5 November 1926, New York, NY

William Hanlon

b: 7 November 1839, Manchester, England—d: 7 February 1923, New York, NY

Alfred Hanlon

b: ca. 1843, Liverpool, England—d: 24 January 1886, Pasadena, CA

Edward Hanlon

b: 31 August 1845, Manchester, England—d: 9 March 1931, St. Petersburg, FL

Frederick Hanlon

b: ca. 1848—d: 6 April 1886, Nice, France

During the last decades of the twentieth century, variety performers of the mid- to late-nineteenth century stimulated much interest among academics, as attested by Laurence Senelick's biography of George L. Fox (1988), John A. McKinven's survey of the Hanlon Brothers' careers (1998), David Carlyon's study of Dan Rice (2001) and countless graduate school theses.

Employing a combination of pantomime, acting, ballet and acrobatics, theatrical families such as the Ravels, the Hanlons, the Martinettis and the Kiralfys influenced the Byrne Brothers, the Fratellinis and several succeeding generations of physical comedians, dancers, acrobats, jugglers and illusionists. The individual performers of each troupe varied in their talents, but all were versatile, and their multiple skills won public acclaim and advanced the rise and stature of the variety performer.

What set the Hanlons apart from—not above—their contemporaries was their eventual inventiveness in stage machinery. They created effects that allowed them to expand their original variety turn as Hanlon-Lees into elaborate productions featuring spectacular illusions and thrilling stunts, thus setting an example that found a cinematic response in the films of Georges Méliès and inspired many gags used by clowns of the silent cinema in the USA and Europe.

Their earliest venture on the professional stage was put together in 1846 by John Lees, a gymnast, who convinced Tom Hanlon Sr., a family friend and manager of a Manchester theatre, to let Hanlon's sons George, William and Alfred join Lees in an acrobatic act. Oldest brother Tom was already an acrobat, and his younger brothers had picked up the basics from him. John Lees and His Three Pupils toured the world for a decade until 1856, when Lees died in Cuba while on tour—an odyssey filled with adventure, exotic sights and perils.

To celebrate their late tutor, George, William and Alfred reconstituted the act as Hanlon-Lees, and returned to England, where brother Tom assumed leadership. Younger brothers Edward and Frederick were added to the Hanlon-Lees troupe, and Tom took what was basically a *Risley act* without its leader (John Lees) and drilled his five brothers into a star turn that developed while the act toured Britain, France, Russia and the USA. While in France, they observed the trapeze exploits of the young Jules Léotard, who set the bar for aerial work.

The Hanlons were not long in meeting his challenge, and while playing the Academy of Music in New York City in 1861, Tom, George and William created a sensation as they flew back and forth among three swinging trapezes spaced about 80 feet apart, from first to last, 20 feet over the heads of the audience. There were no safety nets in place.

Not all the principals in the various Hanlon shows were blood relatives. As a boy, Frederick Hanlon had been adopted by the Hanlon brothers' father and subsequently was regarded as a full member of the family. Tom adopted and trained a young boy, Little Bob, a child aerialist who performed with the six brothers during their first tour in America. Little Bob was only one of several youngsters who were more or less adopted and trained to perform in the act.

Throughout the first half of the 1860s, the Hanlon-Lees performed on variety bills in South America, Europe and the USA. They thrilled audiences as they formed human pyramids, did a balancing routine atop a ladder held below by one of the brothers, tumbled with abandon and swung from ropes.

Their daredevil routines were not without cost. William broke his arm in a fall from a trapeze. Far more serious was Tom's crash into gas footlights in 1865. For personal or economic reasons or both, the Hanlon act broke in two for a few years.

George, William and Alfred, who had been the original members of Hanlon-Lees, formed the Hanlon & Zanfretta Combination and explored the feasibility of moving away from straight acrobatics toward stage illusions. During his attempt to heal, Tom joined with the two younger brothers, Edward and Frederick, as the Hanlon Brothers. Tom's condition never improved, and he was placed in an asylum. After three years of enduring intense cranial pain, Tom killed himself. In 1867, Edward and Frederick hooked up with Henri Agoust, a superior juggler wise in the ways of theatre. Agoust became a leading and influential member of the Hanlon Brothers' company.

In 1868, the five surviving Hanlons came together for their "Re-Union and Farewell Tour." François, Julien and Victor were advertised as "adopted pupils." A year later, Little Bob returned to perform with Alfred and Frederick Hanlon in another leg of their prolonged and premature farewell tour. In a sense, however, the 1868 tour marked the turn of the Hanlons toward a new form of act. Henri Agoust, who had worked with the six Hanlons as early as 1865, suggested that they look to the pantomime form to supply both a story line and a context for their variety turns. Agoust worked with the Hanlons in the late 1860s and again in the late 1870s. In later years there were disputes as to whether it was the Hanlons or the genius of Agoust that was responsible for their great success in pantomime and extravaganza.

Though it was Agoust who urged the Hanlons to produce and perform full-length pantomimes, it was the Hanlons' ability as roughneck comedians and acrobats and their mechanical inventiveness that created a series of successful spectacles, culminating in *Le Voyage en Suisse (Voyage to Switzerland)* in 1879, *Fantasma* (1884) and *Superba* (1890). Each of these shows, especially the latter two, ran for decades. The brothers gradually withdrew from performance into production and, in residence in Cohasset, Massachusetts, and continually refreshed their productions with new and increasingly macabre and sensational illusions like shipwrecks, cyclones, explosions, bloody executions, underwater battles and ghostly apparitions.

These illusions were created mechanically, without the benefit of film sequences, sound recordings or electrically operated devices, and many were the inventive handiwork of William Hanlon. As early as 1869, the Hanlon brothers won patents for their modifications of the original French velocipede: an adjustable seat and pedals that permitted people of various height to ride it, mudguards and rubber tires for the wheels and rear-wheel brakes operated from the handlebars.

The Hanlon family grew large with offspring, and George's son, Fred, and William's son, William Jr., went into vaudeville, Broadway revues, and Ringling Brothers and Barnum & Bailey circus. George W. Hanlon Jr. took a hand in the mechanical inventions, wrote plays and joined comedian Fred Corwey in a vaudeville act billed as the Hanlons. Many performers who appeared in vaudeville and circus under the name Hanlon, however, were not blood members of the family but adopted; others purloined the Hanlon name, which remained a draw in show business for nearly a century.

POODLES HANNEFORD

b: (George Hanneford) 14 June 1891, Barnsby, England—d: 9 December 1967, Kattskill Bay, NY

Early on, the act was billed as the Hanneford Family, but it was the grown son Poodles Hanneford who made them a top equestrian and dog act in circus, extravaganza and vaudeville. The Hannefords were an English circus family; Poodles' dad taught him to ride bareback by blindfolding his son, forcing the boy to rely on the horse's sense of motion and balance rather than his own.

The Hanneford Family traveled with small English circuses like Bostock's until they came to North America. In the USA, they appeared with Ringling Brothers and Barnum & Bailey Circus, Tom Mix's combination circus and Wild West show, and on a bill at New York's Hippodrome, the massive auditorium that staged spectacles on its 200-by-110-foot stage and, depending on the specific need, could increase its usual 5,200 seats in the auditorium to 7,000.

With Ringling Brothers and Tom Mix, the Hanneford Family act was primarily equestrian, although Poodles did his own spots with a troupe of trained dogs—hence his nickname—and as a featured clown whose gags included subversive pants suspenders and trousers that kept falling. His part in the family's bareback riding act was to clown. Poodles had a shock of reddish hair that he topped off with a small derby perched to the side. A bow tie hung low below an open-collared white shirt. He wore an oversized patterned sport coat or topcoat, rather wide-legged trousers and large white spats over small, dark slippered shoes.

Poodles Hanneford

In the Hanneford equestrian act, Poodles rode bareback, but the fun of it was watching him slide around and finally off the horse's back. He never quite fell; instead he dropped below the horse's belly and dragged along the ground as he tried to pull himself aright. In his climb upward on the running horse, Poodles squeezed headfirst between the horse's rear legs and then crawled back on top. The audience watched a very funny routine, but professionals watched nervously because they understood the risk.

Poodles' dog act was more suitable for the smaller stages that were usual in vaudeville. His wife, Grace, acted as his assistant. In the family show, Grace played the role of ringmaster. With Poodles' individual success, the name of the family act was changed to Poodles Hanneford & Company.

The Hannefords were remembered for two shows in particular. The first was the Dillingham-produced extravaganza *Happy Days,* staged at the Hippodrome. It was scheduled to open in late August, as was usual for Hippodrome shows, but all was not smooth sailing. In 1919, conflicts over actors' and performers' rights came to a head between Actors' Equity and the Producers and Managers Association. The stagehands walked out on strike. That could be dealt with in a normal-sized vaudeville house, but the Hippodrome, home of spectacle, required 412 stagehands for the *Happy Days* show. The show's star, singer Belle Storey, organized the large dance chorus to apply for membership in Chorus Equity. The chorus girls got a raise from $25 to $35 a week, and *Happy Days* reopened 1 September 1919 and ran for 452 performances.

The next notable show for Poodles Hanneford was Billy Rose's *Jumbo* (1935). The show starred Jimmy Durante and boasted genius to spare: Ben Hecht and Charles MacArthur wrote the book, Richard Rodgers & Larry Hart created the score and John Murray Anderson directed. It was staged at the Hippodrome, a dozen years past its prime. Rose had the entire venue spruced up, and seating was arranged like a circus grandstand. The *Hipp's* restoration was spectacular, gaudy and very costly.

With 1,200 animals, many scenic effects, numerous specialty acts and restoration work providing ample distraction, *Jumbo* was a complicated and cumbersome show. Consequently, and despite the capable Murray Anderson, it was underrehearsed and ill-paced by the time critics reviewed it. Poodles, Durante and many of the other acts were applauded, as was the score, but the show eked out only 233 performances and closed. *Jumbo's* departure also posted the closing notice for the Hippodrome. Billy Rose took *Jumbo* to the Dallas Exposition, where he finally folded the tent, and his investors lost a lot of money.

Poodles appeared in a dozen or so movies, between 1927 and 1954. None were particularly memorable except *The Circus Kid* (1928), in which Poodles had a decent role opposite ten-year-old Frankie Darro in the title role and Joe E. Brown. Brown had been a circus acrobat, and Darro grew up in a circus family and had worked as an aerialist. In Poodles' other films, he did a turn as a clown, played a sidekick or appeared in uncredited bit roles.

The Hannefords returned to Ringling Brothers and Barnum & Bailey, and, as late as the 1950s, Poodles appeared on Ed Sullivan's *Toast of the Town* and other television variety shows. Perhaps the highest praise for Poodles came from a fellow clown who knew far better than any critic what it took to be a physical comedian. Buster Keaton did not consider himself, Fairbanks, Harold Lloyd or any of the Keystone Cops true acrobats. Keaton claimed that a trained acrobat taking a tumble always looked like an acrobat taking a fall rather than a comic character suffering an accident. Said Buster, "The only trained acrobat I ever saw who could take a fall and make it seem funny was Poodles Hanneford."

HARD-SHOE DANCING

Distinct from soft-shoe dancing in that the soles of the shoes worn by hard-shoe dancers, such as clog dancers, were wood or had metal plates affixed to them.

HARLEM

During the vaudeville era and the years before the Second World War, Harlem was both a place and a cultural identity, As a place, nearly all of its real estate was owned by absentee white landlords and real estate corporations. Its major businesses, whether furniture stores, groceries or theatres, were also owned by white outsiders; in the case of the more famous nightclubs, the men behind the paper names were gangsters.

Harlem, 50 blocks long and 8 blocks wide, was home to 250,000 African American and Caribbean Americans during the 1920s. Although Harlem had existed since the 1600s, when it was settled by the Dutch, it remained rural farmland divided into large estates until the early 1880s, when developers decided to turn Harlem into New York City's most fashionable district. Railroads connected it to Manhattan to make Harlem a bedroom community for businessmen. A yacht club, a philharmonic orchestra and Oscar Hammerstein's first Opera House were established there in the 1880s.

Financial panics in the 1890s and a collapse of the real estate market in the 1900s doomed developers' hopes. In an effort to recoup some of their investment, landlords began renting to Southern blacks migrating to New York City. Between 1905 and 1925, the black population of Harlem quintupled. Many white businesses simply faced facts and sold to the new black community, but more resisted and even refused to hire black employees. But, beyond 127th Street, the location of many white-owned businesses, Harlem was for African Americans.

Harlem grew into a semi-autonomous region given its physical distance from the centers of power in Manhattan and as the numbers of black residents grew after the First World War. A number of demobilized servicemen, incensed by the continuance of second-class citizenship after fighting in the First World War, decided that if they were to reman unequal, it might as well be in a place where they were dominant. Harlem drifted into benign neglect, for the most part, unless a racial incident stimulated white fears of a black rebellion and rioting.

Harlem possessed several cultural identities. Most folks were poor, undereducated and doing the best they could to raise families and, like most Americans, have a bit of fun. There was a criminal element that slipped back and forth between Philadelphia and Harlem to avoid capture for crimes committed. And there were numerous churchgoers; the largest churches became power centers of Harlem politics.

The comfort of a black majority in Harlem also attracted the African American and Caribbean American historians, fiction writers, journalists, painters, musicians, performers and entrepreneurs who created and fostered the Harlem Renaissance of the 1920s. The concentration of the best minds and talents of black America in Harlem gave birth to philosophical and political theory with a Negro perspective, and literary, exhibition and performance art that drew on a shared experience.

Another side of Harlem was evident in its nightclubs, juke joints, dance halls, hot music, uninhibited dancing and frank sexuality. The combination proved irresistible for whites on the prowl for hot music, exoticism and forbidden pleasures. Night spots like Small's Paradise, the Cotton Club, Gladys' Clam House, Connie's Inn, Log Cabin and Club Hot-Cha, owned by white gangsters, were closed to nonwhites, except top-echelon celebrities like prizefighters or the few blacks who had become Broadway stars. These clubs flourished, and it was there that greater numbers of whites began to witness the great black dancers and singers of the day. Most of the New York Negro entertainers of the age, however, were to be seen in vaudeville houses and small nightclubs that were not on the white slumming tour.

During the Great Depression Harlem declined rapidly. The white-owned nightclubs continued to survive into the late 1930s, but times were bad for most of Harlem's people and stayed that way. The Second World War provided an increase in employment, but landlords allowed the housing stock to deteriorate, sometimes to dangerous levels. In the 1980s, Harlem began a slow revival, but it was the speculators who profited. Still, benign neglect in Harlem meant that many of its fine century-old properties had been spared by the urban renewal bulldozers, and the once-gracious properties formed the core of a community on the threshold of revival a century after its habitation by African Americans.

HARMONICA RASCALS

Organized by Borrah Minevitch (1903–55), the Harmonica Rascals were one of several harmonica ensembles that were popular from the 1930s into the 1950s, but no harmonica group was better known. Minevitch began playing the instrument at age five in his native Kiev, Russia. By his teens he was expert. He attended the College of the City of New York in the USA, during which time he wrote a history of the harmonica that was published by a musical instrument manufacturer.

Minevitch played in several bands and orchestras that permitted his instrument. Generally, the harmonica was considered a blues instrument, and country blues at that. Minevitch was among the first who essayed a semiclassical repertoire, playing "Liebestraum," "Deep River," "Rhapsody in Blue," and other showy pieces that lent themselves to dramatic chord changes and glissandos. By 1925, he was on a bill at the Palace Theatre.

Borrah Minevitch and the Harmonica Rascals

According to Joe Laurie Jr., Minevitch had put together a harmonica orchestra composed of 32 youngsters. He asked $3,000 a week for the act in the late 1920s and got it from presentation houses. Obviously, because of its size and the age and number of the adolescents, this was not an act to play far and wide, so Minevitch put together a succession of smaller groups, each composed of about six harmonica players, for vaudeville. They were popular on radio and in nightclubs as well as in vaudeville. Soon, the Harmonica Rascals were hired as a specialty act for various theatres with a pic-vaude combination.

Borrah Minevitch was an entrepreneur. He owned a harmonica factory and had several other commercial interests in show business. Minevitch did not always front the band himself; sometimes he sold the Harmonica Rascals act to bookers minus his participation. It did not matter; the real star of the act was Johnny Puleo (1907–83), a weary-faced little person who was a natural clown.

The musicians played the widest assortment of harmonicas ever seen—big, small, long and short—and played them in a flashy, virtuosic manner. Little Johnny Puleo scrambled around the edges of the cohort, trying to squeeze in and play. The pushing, slapping and changing of positions never interfered with the rendition of the music, and that was part of the fun. The act proved as popular on 1950s television as it had onstage and in movies. After Minevitch's death, Puleo led the act.

LEONARD HARPER

b: (Leonard C. Harper) 19 April 1897 or 1899, Birmingham, AL—d: 10 February 1943, New York, NY

Dancer, choreographer, stage director and producer Leonard Harper started as so many black tap dancers had, as a child dancing to attract a crowd to the medicine show wagon. His father, William Harper, was a performer; he died when Leonard was ten. That was when Leonard hitched up with a medicine show that traveled throughout the South.

According to his grandson, Leonard saved the small troupe from being burned alive by the Ku Klux Klan in 1909 by dancing until the Klansmen who were holding them captive lost their fury and allowed them to live.

Leonard teamed up with comedian George Freeman for some theatre dates, and they connected with Dave Schaffer, Leonard's childhood friend and the then partner of Clarence Muse. The four young men threw in together as traveling stock players with *Mr. and Mrs. Brown* and *Stranded in Africa* (1912). Harper worked his way to New York City in 1915 but did not find enough work to stay there. He moved to Chicago, where he met the Blanks Sisters, another young act. Leonard and Osceola Blanks created a classy dance act modeled on the exhibition ballroom craze sweeping white vaudeville and revue. Harper & Blanks dressed formally and glamorously.

For several seasons, 1916 to 1920, Harper & Blanks played Toby time. When the Shuberts decided to get back into vaudeville around 1920–21, they needed acts. They reached out to African American performers, something they had not done before, and Harper & Blanks, "The Smart Set Couple," played white vaudeville for the first time.

Harper & Blanks brought their song-and-dance vaudeville turn to Noble Sissle's and Eubie Blake's revue, *Plantation Days* (1922–23) when it opened at the Lafayette Theatre in Harlem. Leonard Harper also staged the show. They appeared in several revues, such as *The Frolics* (1923) at the Lafayette. Romantically involved for years, Harper and Blanks decided to marry. Her real name was Arsceola Blanks and she was born in 1899, according to the New York City census. In June 1925 Osceola was 25 and two years younger than Leonard.

In addition to performing, Leonard worked with several white vaudeville acts to tighten up their routines and more effectively present the performers. Leonard staged the production of *Plantation Revue* that Lew Leslie brought to London in 1923 as one half of *Dover to Dixie.*

That same season, 1923–24, Leonard produced floor shows at both Connie's Inn in Harlem and the Kentucky Club (also known as the Hollywood Café) in Times Square at 203 West 49th Street and Broadway. Harper offered Duke Ellington and his orchestra, the Washingtonians, the opportunity to become the house band at either club—both were speakeasies. Duke chose the Kentucky Club and stayed there four years. He moved to the Cotton Club, where a white performer, Dan Healy (married to Helen Kane), directed the black stage shows. *Variety* gave Leonard Harper a boost when it compared his work to Dan Healy's shows at the Cotton Club—faulting the Cotton Club shows for being staged by whites.

By 1925, Leonard Harper was a small industry. He owned a dance studio in Times Square where black dancers taught black dance styles to white performers. He also made a deal with Hurtig & Seamon to produce integrated revues to play theatres on the Columbia burlesque wheel; these were not burlesque shows but vaudeville revues. *Black & White* shows toured the Northeast and Midwest. Harper continued to produce and stage revues, including *Brown Skin Quinan Revue* (1925), which was revised by Lew Leslie into *Blackbirds of 1926,* starring Florence Mills. Harper & Blanks danced in those shows; thereafter, the team retired from performing. Osceola Blanks Harper managed their domestic affairs, and Leonard concentrated on staging and choreographing revues and floor shows.

Leonard produced touring revues, *Midnight Steppers* and the *Pepper Pot Revue* with Bill Robinson (both in 1927) and the *Swanee Club Revue* (1928) at the Lafayette Theatre, and he staged vaudeville revues such as *Adam and Eve in Harlem* for Frank Schiffman at the Apollo Theatre and *Hot Chocolates* at the Hudson Theatre (both in 1929). Louis Armstrong made his revue debut in *Hot Chocolates*, and other performers included Jimmie Baskette, Eddie Green, Billy Higgins and Edith Wilson. Some of the songs from *Hot Chocolates* were quickly recycled into the floor show *Load of Coal* (1929) at Connie's Inn. Louis Armstrong was held over from *Hot Chocolates* to *Load of Coal.*

Billed as the first sound feature film made by African Americans, *The Exile* (1931), directed by Oscar Micheaux, was reported to be based on both Cecil B. DeMille's first film, *The Squaw Man* (1914), and Micheaux's own first film, *The Homesteader* (1919), which was an adaptation of his own first novel, *The Conquest* (1913). A musical sequence directed by Leonard Harper featured him with a line of chorus girls, a tap dancer, and Don Heywood and his band.

Back at Connie's Inn, Fats Waller wrote the music, Andy Razaf cooked up the lyrics and Leonard Harper staged *Hot Harlem* (1932) with the Four Mills Brothers and Don Redman and His Orchestra. Leonard Harper was forbidden to use dark-skinned dancers in his chorus girl lines at Connie's. Perhaps in subtle rebellion, he made it a practice to always include one café au lait transvestite in the line.

In 1934, Harper and songwriter Andy Razaf went to Chicago to create and stage *Rhythm for Sale,* a floor show at the landmark Grand Terrace Café. They stayed there for another show, *Chicago Rhythm,* with Earl Hines and His Orchestra. A bit later, back in Harlem, Harper staged several floor shows starring Gladys Bentley at the Ubangi Club in Harlem, including *Round 'n' Round in Rhythm* and *Ubangi Club Follies* (1935). Andy Razaf wrote most of the songs for those shows.

By the mid-1930s, Harper was working at the Cotton Club. He staged revues like the *Cotton Club*

Parade (1935) with Butterbeans & Susie, Lena Horne, Miller & Moreland and Nina Mae McKinney. But the public's taste was changing. They still wanted to listen to Duke Ellington, Louis Armstrong and Don Redman, but they did not want to sit still and watch chorus girls, tap dancers and singers. Customers in the clubs wanted to get up and dance themselves. If they wished to see a dance act, Whyte's Lindy Hoppers or a similar group filled the bill.

Harper's career declined due to the change in taste and never recovered. He had produced and staged more shows than almost anyone else, black or white, and then was reduced to choreographing chorus lines—when he was offered work. It was not just Harper; a lot of entertainers from the 1910s and 1920s found themselves sidelined.

Harlem Cavalcade (1942), produced by Ed Sullivan at the Ritz Theatre, directed by Noble Sissle, and with choreography by Harper, closed after 49 shows despite a top-shelf, once-in-a-lifetime company of old and new performers: Una Mae Carlisle, Tom Fletcher, Johnny Lee & Flournoy Miller, Moke and Poke, Tim Moore, the Peters Sisters, Pops (Whitman) & Louie (Williams), Amanda Randolph and Noble Sissle.

Leonard Harper died in 1943 of a heart attack while rehearsing his dancers at a Harlem nightclub called Murrain's.

HARRIGAN

b: (James Horrigan) ca. 1875–1940

Active in the 1890s and 1900s, Harrigan won fame as America's first "Tramp Juggler." He was also billed as "The Juggling Comedian." His best bit was his manipulation of cigar boxes, but he also juggled and balanced his top hat, ball, bottles and a piece of paper.

Both his characterization and his routine influenced W.C. Fields, who at the turn of the twentieth century was just getting started in burlesque and vaudeville. Fields later claimed to have originated the tramp juggler, as did others, but Harrigan's earlier claim still stands, and he had the foresight to copyright his act. Although he appeared to good reviews and audiences in the USA, Harrigan played British music-halls and European circuses with considerably frequency.

During his juggling act, Harrigan told jokes and sang ridiculously comic ditties. Later in his career, his act was primarily that of a monologist who performed magic and juggling tricks as part of his storytelling.

Jim Harrigan's brother, Barney Horrigan (1877–1948) was a well-known stage magician of the 1890s and 1910s; later he became a successful oilman in Tulsa, Oklahoma.

HARRIGAN & HART

Ned Harrigan

b: (Edward Harrigan) 26 October 1844, New York, NY—d: 6 June 1911, New York, NY

Tony Hart

b: (Anthony J. Cannon) 25 July 1855, Worcester, MA—d: 4 November 1891, Worcester, MA

The story of Harrigan & Hart is mostly the story of Ned Harrigan. Tony Hart was a bright and talented comedian, but his older partner, Harrigan, wrote their shows and had a far longer career.

Ned Harrigan, as everyone called him, was the paragon of the day, a self-made man who never forgot his origins. He was beloved by the lower classes and respected by men and women of letters and erudition. Harrigan, it was frequently boasted, was the Molière

Edward 'Ned' Harrigan

of the USA, the Yankee Dickens, and a Stateside Shakespeare. Though some of the loftier drama critics of the day viewed Harrigan's shows as boisterous trifles, his champions in the gallery, the swells in the orchestra seats and the elite of the Fourth Estate would no more miss a Harrigan & Hart show than they would opening day of the baseball season or opening night at the opera. Certainly no New Yorker with any claim to celebrity or power intentionally missed an opening of a Harrigan & Hart show.

Between 1840 and 1859 the total number of immigrants to the United States soared to 4,242,000; 40 percent were Irish, 32 percent German and 16 percent English. Most of these immigrants entered at the Port of New York and had little money to travel any farther.

The potato was the staple of poor people's diet in Ireland. When potato blight wiped out the crop in 1845, it started the Great Famine that decimated Ireland. Many died, many fled to the USA and many stayed and struggled for generations. The potato blight also afflicted parts of Germany, where the cost to lease a farm for a year was equal to that required to purchase the same amount of land in the midwestern USA. Unsuccessful revolts in parts of Germany had made the political situation as unstable as the economy.

The Irish settled in the poorer sections of Lower Manhattan, such as the notorious Five Points. The Germans set up their own bailiwick called Kleindeutschland, centered between Canal Street and Rivington. These two ethnic groups provided Edward Harrigan with most of his inspiration for his later sketches and plays. A third group, African Americans, who had been a presence in New York City since the Dutch colonial period, presented a further source of material. By 1860 black New Yorkers numbered approximately 12,000 and were concentrated in several isolated spots around lower Manhattan, including Five Points. The heaviest concentration, however, was located around Thompson Street.

Although it was assumed that Ned Harrigan was a purebred Irishman, he was born in Lower Manhattan, at Corlear's Hook, an elbow of land that juts out into the East River. His father came from Newfoundland, and they were Protestant, not Catholic as supposed. His mother was Protestant Yankee. Of the 13 children to whom Ned's mother gave birth, only four survived infancy:

The Lower East Side was a violent and dangerous place; gangs such as the primarily American-born Bowery B'hoys would often fight with their nemesis, the Irish Dead Rabbits. Rival fire companies often fought each other, rather than the fires they were sent to extinguish. Disputes between rival city police forces (at one time there were two) erupted in violence. Ned transformed these tussles for power and prestige into the sketches and plays he later presented at Harrigan and Hart's Theatre Comique.

Ned's father tried to apprentice him to several trades. His mother encouraged his music:

The many happy evenings I spent when but a lad,
On Paddy Duffy's lumber cart, quite safe away from dad;
It stood down on the corner, near the old lamplight,
You should see the congregation there, on every
  summer's night.

—"Paddy Duffy's Cart," lyric by Edward Harrigan,
music by David Braham, 1882

When Ned was 18, his father and mother divorced. Ned found work as a ship's caulker, his father's old trade. Caulking was an ongoing job while under sail and steam. After the Civil War, he shipped out for San Francisco, where he found plenty of work in the caulking trade. To pass time, Ned began to compose new lyrics for old tunes. His workmates encouraged him, and Harrigan made his first professional appearance at the Olympic Theatre in San Francisco and was a success. He remained at the Olympic until the end of the year (1867). Over the next few years he had a couple of partners, Alex O'Brien and Sam Rickey, at different times, and worked with Manning's Minstrels.

He met his third partner, Tony Hart, in Chicago, where they made their debut as a team. Harrigan built sketches around his songs when he worked with other partners, but with Hart the act really began to expand and succeed. Harrigan & Hart's first major engagement was in Boston at the Howard Athenaeum, a first-class theatre before it sank in status to become the notorious Old Howard after 1900. They performed there from spring through fall of 1871, and Ned made a friend in John Braham, the orchestra leader at the Howard Athenaeum. John provided Ned with a letter of introduction to his brother David in New York.

Harrigan's and Hart's six-month run at the Howard Athenaeum brought them bookings in Rhode Island, Connecticut, Massachusetts, New York State and Chicago, where they appeared with a traveling Tony Pastor troupe. When they returned to Manhattan in 1872, it was to play a brief engagement for Tony Pastor, who had discovered them at the Howard in Boston. Harrigan also met David Braham, and they began collaborating on songs immediately. In less than two years, Harrigan & Hart had quickly developed into a solid, popular act with a growing reputation.

Tony Hart was 11 years younger than Ned Harrigan. His parents were Catholic and born in Ireland. Tony was a rebellious fellow, at home and at school. His parents consigned him to a reformatory, but Tony slipped away and headed for Boston, his cap set for a career in musical theatre. He cleaned taverns and was allowed to sing for tips in return for room and board. Upon hearing Tony's sob-inducing soprano, M. B. Leavitt signed "Master Antonio" for his burlesque troupe, Madame Rentz Female Minstrels. The company was playing Chicago when Tony met Ned. They complemented each other. Ned was tall and serious looking; Tony, short and angelic. Ned, 26, sang tenor; Tony, not yet 16, sang soprano. Both danced in an eccentric fashion and could play comic business in lines and pantomime. After six months at the Howard Athenaeum, they agreed that they were a team.

Josh Hart (no relation to Tony) engaged Harrigan & Hart for his Theatre Comique in New York City at 514 Broadway. A typical Theatre Comique bill consisted of eight acts, of which as many as five might be sketches, and an afterpiece. Usually the sketches would be written by a house dramatist. Ned Harrigan filled this role during his tenure there. Fortunately, he was an industrious and purposeful man, equal to the demands of creating new material every few weeks as well as performing nightly. The Theatre Comique became the home of Harrigan & Hart for the next nine years, except for a short period on the road.

Harrigan courted David Braham's young daughter, Annie. They married in 1876 when Ned was 32 and Annie 17. Their marriage lasted until death, and they had ten children, seven of whom lived into adulthood.

At the end of the 1875–76 season, Josh Hart gave up the proprietorship of the Theatre Comique, and Harrigan and his business partner (and father-in-law) David Braham took over the lease. On 7 August 1876, the Theatre Comique became the home of Harrigan & Hart.

The pattern for success at the Theatre Comique had been laid earlier in 1873, when Harrigan & Hart had produced a song and sketch titled "The Mulligan Guard." The sketch began with a burlesque military drill—Harrigan as Captain Hussey and Tony Hart as his company of one. They paraded on the stage in cast-off military odds and ends. After Tony Hart's clumsy drill and Edward Harrigan's equally inept handling of the commands (with drill manual in one hand and sword in the other), the duo burst forth into song:

We crave your condescension, we'll tell you what we know
Of marching in the Mulligan Guard from Sligo Ward below.
Our Captain's name was Hussey, a Tipperary man,
He carried his sword like a Russian duke whenever he took command.
We shouldered guns, and marched and marched away.
From Baxter street, we marched to Avenue A,
With drums and fife, how sweetly they did play,
As we marched, marched, marched in the Mulligan Guard.

—"The Mulligan Guard," lyrics by Edward Harrigan, music by David Braham, 1873

Harrigan had written the song sketch as a spoof of the target companies that proliferated during the 1860s and 1870s among the Irish neighborhoods of the Lower East Side. As a writer recalled in 1926 in an article written for the *New York Herald Tribune:* "Frequently these target companies would arrange a target excursion, engage a brass band and—after obtaining the blessings of their local politicians—would proceed to the picnic ground. Trailing behind came the target borne by a sturdy Negro. [In *The Mulligans' Silver Wedding,* a small, young African American actor by the name of Morgan Benson brought up the Mulligan Guards' rear, dragging and occasionally hoisting their unwieldy target.] Although the outings were ostensibly arranged for target practice, they actually served as drinking sprees. In their inebriated condition they often mistook their comrades for the bull's-eye." It was an apt as well as amusing commentary on the state of competing police forces and independent militias at the time in Manhattan.

"The Mulligan Guard" proved to be more of a success than any previous Harrigan & Braham song to date. The melody traveled around the world and even into the pages of the Rudyard Kipling novel *Kim.*

Harrigan produced other Mulligan Guard sketches: "The Mulligan Guard Picnic" and "The Mulligan Guard Ball." The latter sketch was more of a play in seven scenes, and Harrigan had settled on several recurring characters that were played by variety actors he had met and admired in vaudeville. Harrigan played Dan Mulligan, an Irish immigrant who had served in the Irish Brigade during the American Civil War. Annie Yeamans, a veteran of burlesque, variety, farce and drama, played Cordelia Mulligan, Dan's wife. Tony Hart played the Mulligans' son, Tommy (and, later, the Mulligans' African American neighbor, Rebecca Allup, the much-married—and much-widowed—bookmaker). Johnny Wild made his reputation by playing Captain Sam Primrose, an urban African American, rather than the stereotype plantation minstrel type. Billy Gray, also in blackface, played the Reverend Palestine Puter and doubled with Wild as the officers of the rival Skidmore Guard. Harry Fisher and Annie Mack played the Mulligans' German neighbors, the butcher, Gustavus Lochmuller, and his wife. Michael Bradley took the role of Walsingham McSweeney, Dan Mulligan's longtime chum who ran the Wee Drop Saloon. There was also Ah Wung, who operated a combination laundry and flophouse.

When *The Mulligan Guard Ball* had grown into its full-length play form, it contained another of what was to become one of the more popular songs of the Harrigan & Braham oeuvre:

If you want for information, or in need of merriment,
Come over with me socially to Murphy's tenement;
He owns a row of houses in the First Ward near the dock,
Where Ireland's represented by the babies on our block.
There's the Phalens and the Whalens from the sweet Dunochadee,

They are sitting on the railings with their children on their knee,
All gossiping and talking with their neighbors in a flock,
Singing, "Little Sally Waters" with the babies on our block.

Oh, little Sally Waters sitting in the sun,
A-crying and weeping for a young man;
Oh, rise Sally, rise, wipe your eye out with your frock;
That's sung by the babies a-living on our block.

—"Babies on Our Block," lyrics by Edward Harrigan, music by David Braham, 1879

Other Mulligan plays followed in quick succession. *The Mulligan Guard Chowder* (1879), *The Mulligan Guard Christmas* (1879), *The Mulligan Guard Surprise* (1880), *The Mulligan Guard Picnic* (1880, an expansion of the earlier "Picnic" sketch), *The Mulligan Guard Nominee* (1880), *The Mulligans' Silver Wedding* (1881), and the two closing installments, *Cordelia's Aspirations* (1883) and *Dan's Tribulations* (1884).

An early-twentieth-century stage historian, J. Hobson Quinn, outlined Dan Mulligan's qualities as "honest, courageous, impulsive, irrational, likely to become drunk and disorderly at slight provocation, and while irascible and quarrelsome, is forgiving and generous even to his enemies. His mate, Cordelia is his prudent and frugal helpmeet."

Throughout the Mulligan cycle, Dan worked at a number of jobs: garbage contractor, saloon keeper and then—finally—he reached his apogee as alderman of the Fourteenth Ward. As Harrigan explained to a reporter in 1879: "I have just let the Mulligan family work out its own history naturally." The earlier Mulligan sketches had formed an afterpiece to an evening of variety, but they grew in length until they occupied an entire evening. The process was organic, as described by J. Hobson Quinn: "(The) sketches grew from mere song to a duet, to a dialogue, and then to a one-act play which (was) later developed into several scenes and then the final step . . . to a well articulated play."

The success of Harrigan & Hart's productions was due in great part to their subject matter: city low life and the portrayals of working-class life wedded to catchy songs and slangy dialogue. Working-class audiences filled most of the seats at the Theatre Comique. In Harrigan's plays (and in the earlier variety sketches), the Irish often fought with their German and African American neighbors—verbally and physically.

Although the ethnic groups in Harrigan's plays usually settled their differences and lived quietly together for a while, the Irish made it quite clear that they ruled the roost. In Harrigan's play *The O'Reagans* (1886), Paddy Kelso, "fresh off the boat," asked Bernard O'Reagan, "All Nationalities rule here?" "Yes," says O'Reagan, "the Italians rule the south of it [New York City], the Dutch rule the east of it, the Nagurs rule the west of it and the Irish rule the whole of it." "That plazes me," says Kelso. Replies O'Reagan, "And me too."

The company numbered more than three dozen players. In those days, actors rehearsed without pay, but the Harrigan & Hart company received half pay for rehearsals. Most of them had not been well known when they were first engaged, and starting salaries were modest. They melded into an intuitive troupe that played German, Irish or Negro roles as required. As the Harrigan & Hart seasons became ever more profitable, salaries increased for the actors and work was steady. Aware of their good fortune, the actors were loyal, and most remained with Harrigan for nearly two decades.

Harrigan was a man of the theatre to his core. When he was not at work at his theatre, he was home, working on new plays. A thorough professional, he expected the same behavior from those who worked for him, be they prop man or performer. Any contentions, however, were handled in a quiet, reasonable manner. Ned Harrigan earned his reputation as a gentleman. His wife, Annie, was the more dominant of the two. She ruled the roost at home and was not adverse, when she thought it necessary, to set things right at the theatre as well.

By 29 October 1881 the Harrigan & Hart Company had moved to a new home at 728 Broadway. The new theatre was called both Harrigan's & Hart's Theatre and the New Theatre Comique. It sat 1,200 patrons, and the location was nearer the more affluent uptown trade. Between 1881 and 1884, the New Theatre Comique hosted *The Major, Squatter Sovereignty, McNooney's Visit,* plus the two plays that formed the finale of the Mulligan cycle: *Cordelia's Aspirations* and *Dan's Tribulations.*

The move uptown had also attracted the notice of the critics of the legitimate theatre. Among the critics was William Dean Howells, novelist, poet and champion of realism in American literature. Howells praised Harrigan's portrayals of Lower East Side life, comparing him to Goldoni, the eighteenth-century Venetian dramatist: "The old Venetian filled his scene with the gondoliers, the serving-folk, the fish-women, the tradespeople, the quacks, the idlers, the gamesters, of his city; and Mr. Harrigan shows us the street-cleaners, and contractors, the grocery-men, the shysters, the politicians, the washer-women, the serving-girls, the truckmen, the policemen, the risen Irish man and Irish woman, of contemporary New York." Others had begun to speak of Ned Harrigan as the American Molière.

But dual tragedies soon struck. The bane of nineteenth-century theatres—fire—destroyed the New Theatre Comique on 23 December 1884. Five months later Tony Hart left the company, after about ten years with Harrigan, never to return. Still, Braham remained to create new stage works with Harrigan and to run the enterprise.

After the fire Harrigan leased the Park Theatre on 35th Street on 31 August 1885 and began his new season with a play that was to rival the Mulligan plays in popularity. *Old Lavender* was a substantial reworking of an earlier variety sketch of 1877 entitled, originally, "Old Lavender Water." The character Old Lavender, as played by 40-year-old Edward Harrigan, was a down-and-out character who had seen better days and hung about the docks in the company of a host of colorful characters. Harrigan was to play this role, off and on, for the next 11 years.

For five years at the Park Theatre, Harrigan produced a number of revivals (with actor Dan Collyer taking over Tony Hart's old roles), as well as a string of new plays, one of which, *Waddy Googan* (1888), was an attempt on Harrigan's part to portray the Italian immigrant; he had done this before in his early variety sketches such as "Ireland vs. Italy." At the time, the old Irish and German neighborhoods were being flooded by a new wave of immigrants: Jews, who were being driven from eastern Europe by repressive legislation and murderous pogroms, and Italians fleeing the poverty of southern Italy. *Waddy Googan* was a success due to Harrigan's protean performance of both Waddy Googan, a New York City hackney driver, and Joe Corello, an unwilling member of Mother Donnetti's criminal gang. However, Harrigan's portrayal of an Italian was less convincing.

As Harrigan's old neighborhoods were changing, so too were the theatrical tastes of his audience. The new generation did not know and therefore could not appreciate the Mulligan types. In 1889 Harrigan and his company left for California. They played six weeks at the Alcazar Theatre, San Francisco, the start of an extended road tour.

Upon returning to New York, Harrigan cast about for a site for a new theatre. He soon found an abandoned African American Methodist church at 35th Street and Sixth Avenue. In its place, Harrigan's Theatre opened 29 December 1890 with *Reilly and the 400,* his last unqualified success. Harrigan took part of his title from Ward McAllister's recently published book, *Society as I Found It,* which profiled the elite of New York City. The author conjectured that the number of New York's elite, 400, was dictated by the size of Delmonico's Ballroom, which held 400 people. Harrigan was in top form as pawnbroker Willy Reilly, who assumed the identity of an Irish baronet to insinuate himself into society.

From 1891 to 1895, Harrigan produced a number of revivals: *Squatter Sovereignty, Dan's Tribulation, Old Lavender, The Major* and *The Mulligan Guard Ball.* There also were new productions: *The Last of the Hogans* and *The Woolen Stocking.* The financial panics of the 1890s hurt business, and critics suggested that his heyday was passing.

Tony Hart fared much worse. He had married Gertie Granville, an ambitious and meddling actor. She and Tony toured but Hart, original and talented as he was, had worked under Harrigan's direction in Harrigan's plays and sang Harrigan's and Braham's songs, and his wife was unable to offer comparable support or good advice. Tony was ill much of the six years after he left Harrigan. He had contracted syphilis, and it had begun to affect his performances during his last season with Harrigan.

Tony's last years were pathetic. He found it difficult to speak, and his temper grew uneven and unpredictable because his brain was softening. The press discovered his ailment, and Tony was denied dignity or privacy. A benefit was held that provided him with some money to pay debts, but his last months were spent in the Worcester, Massachusetts, asylum for the insane. He was last seen in public when he left the institution to attend his wife's funeral and burial. He was silent and nearly paralyzed when he died a few months after his 36th birthday in 1891.

In the spring of 1897, Harrigan returned to where he had begun—variety, newly transformed into vaudeville. Harrigan headlined at Proctor's Twenty-Third Street Theatre, Koster & Bial's and Tony Pastor's in New York and the Gilmore in Philadelphia. He condensed his full-length play, *The Grip,* one of his few flops, for vaudeville. Harrigan's professional life had come full circle.

Harrigan's career took an up-and-down swing for its final decade. In some places he was joyously welcomed by those who remembered him. In other places, it was hit or miss. Touring in revivals of his own plays alternated with smaller parts in other people's productions.

The basis for his plays had been the acculturative process for immigrants of various nationalities and the struggles they underwent as they learned to live in a culturally diverse urban society after coming from homogenous, largely rural homelands. By 1900, Ned's ethnic New Yorkers were too busy trying to prosper and to educate their children to fight the old battles. There was still plenty of prejudice and poverty. But many immigrants who had arrived in the USA a generation or two earlier saw themselves differently, saw themselves as Americans.

Two of Harrigan's children followed him on the stage, William (1893–1966) and Nedda (1899–1989). Both prospered in show business, and Nedda married the well-known theatre director Joshua Logan.

In the spring of 1909 Harrigan made his last public appearance. He was to perform in blackface at the annual Lambs Club Gambol, but he collapsed during dress rehearsal from a probable mild heart attack. He did not recover. His deterioration over the next two years kept him housebound. While he was not rich in a grand manner, Harrigan's industry had ensured that he and Annie owned their home and lived comfortably. When he died at 66 in 1911, he believed that he had been forgotten. Upon his death, old friends and younger admirers formed the Ned Harrigan Club. He was toasted as the Dickens of New York, and he has been well honored by his researchers and biographers, Chris Simmons, E. J. Kahn and Richard Moody.

HAMTREE HARRINGTON

b: (James Carl Harrington) 1889, South Carolina—d: 1956

There are two explanations for Harrington's nickname, Hamtree. One claims he was tagged with it because of the oversized shoes he wore in his act; he looked like a tree growing out of two ham-sized feet. The second points to a skit he did on Toby time early in his career; he stole a ham and hid it under a tree. Neither claim is persuasive.

Harrington was a popular comedian who ran away from home in the early 1900s to join a carnival. Subsequently, he appeared in black vaudeville, revues and musical comedies. When there was no stage work, he worked as a barber. Most, probably all, of his vaudeville work was performed on Toby time stages, the circuit of theatres in the South and border states that catered to African American audiences. Very little data have been preserved from that circuit, which grew from a couple of dozen vaude houses to more than 100 by the mid-1920s.

He performed in a number of revues and musicals beginning in 1921 with *Put and Take,* a revival of a 1917 Irving C. Miller show, *Broadway Rastus.* Hamtree costarred with his vaudeville partner, Cora Green, and Perry Bradford, dancer Maxie McCree, singers Lillian Goodner, Mae Crowder, Earl Dancer and female impersonator Andrew Tibble. In both incarnations it totaled nearly a year on the road, including a three-week stand in Manhattan.

His next show was a vaudeville revue, *Strut Miss Lizzie* (1922), that started in Chicago, managed a couple of months in New York City between its Harlem tryout and a few weeks at the Old National Winter Garden, a burlesque house on Houston Street, and then played four weeks at the Times Square Theatre.

Hamtree Harrington and Cora Green were engaged for a Broadway revue, *Dixie to Broadway,* a production by Lew Leslie based on his Plantation Club revues, and a further adaptation of his London hit, *From Dover to Dixie* (1924). The cast included Florence Mills, Will Vodery, Shelton Brooks and dancers Covan & Thompson and Johnny Nit. It ran two months at the Broadhurst Theatre.

Cora Green & Hamtree Harrington played vaudeville during the 1925–28 period with their act "Nobody's Girl," a medley of song, dance and comedy. A small man sometimes billed as a "Vest Pocket Bert Williams," Hamtree played the gullible dupe onstage, and the few films that he made gave him a similar character to play.

His sound recordings betray a style clearly modeled after Bert Williams, and the titles tell the story: "Nobody Ever Let Me In On Nothin'," "You're Talkin' to the Wrong Man Now," and "If I Can't Come In, Don't Let Nobody Come Out." In each of his recordings, Hamtree sang-talked his way through them.

Hamtree toured with *Darktown Affairs* during the latter part of 1929. Slightly modified, the show opened at the George M. Cohan Theatre as *Change Your Luck* but lasted only two weeks. Hamtree was the star comic, and a rising young singer, Alberta Hunter, was in the show.

As vaudeville declined and the country's economic situation worsened, Hamtree looked to burlesque. He was one of the first black comedians, if not the first, to play white burlesque. Billy Minsky hired him, and burlesque provided a much-needed income until Mayor Fiorello La Guardia chased it into New Jersey.

Harrington joined Queenie Smith and Grace Hayes in *A Little Racketeer* (1932), a musical comedy that ran just six weeks. After that failure, Harrington joined a packaged vaudeville tour, *Old Kentucky* (1932), that starred blues singer Clara Smith and dancer George Dewey Washington.

A year earlier, the *Chicago Defender* reported Hamtree as saying, "It has taken about 75 years for the Race actor to emerge from what is known as a freak attraction to the real artist that he is considered today." His comment was in response to a challenge to permit exhibition of the Paramount motion picture *His Woman* (1931), which featured Harrington in support of Claudette Colbert and Gary Cooper. That same year, Hamtree made another feature, *Blind Cargo*. Those two movies were followed by several short films, *Rufus Jones for President* (1933), a two-reeler with Ethel Waters, Dusty Fletcher and Sammy Davis Jr., *Mills Blue Rhythm Band* (1934), a single-reel short with Fredi Washington, and another two-reeler, *Bubbling Over* (1934), with Waters.

Harrington's professional relationship with Ethel Waters began earlier than their two films together. Hamtree joined the cast of the biggest revue of the 1930s, *As Thousands Cheer* (1933–34), which starred Marilyn Miller, Clifton Webb, Helen Broderick and Ethel Waters. The revue stayed on Broadway for 50 weeks, then went on a long tour, with Dorothy Stone replacing Marilyn Miller. On 23 March 1935, the show played a date at the Tivoli Theatre in Chattanooga, Tennessee. Unknown to Waters or Harrigan until the day before the performance, the management of the Tivoli Theatre would not permit Negroes to buy tickets and attend. Both Waters and Harrington denounced the policy, but they were contracted to perform.

In 1938, Hamtree and Stepin Fetchit toured the South with Erskine Hawkins' swing band show. *Blackbirds of 1939,* the fifth and final edition of the Blackbirds series, starred a quartet of great black comedians—Hamtree, Dewey "Pigmeat" Markham, Tim Moore and Joe Byrd. Despite them, Lena Horne and Whitey's Lindy Hoppers (also billed variously as Whyte's Maniacs, Whitey's Maniacs, Whitey's Lindy Hoppers, Whyte's Lindy Hoppers and Arthur White's Lindy Hoppers), the show closed after nine performances at the Hudson Theatre.

Harrington made a few more movies, including a boxing flick, *Keep Punching* (1939), with boxing champ Henry Armstrong, Canada Lee, Dooley Wilson, Willie Bryant and J. Rosamond Johnson. *The Devil's Daughter* (1939) costarred Nina Mae McKinney, and a two-reeler, *Jittering Jitterbugs* (1943), paired Hamtree with Arthur White's Lindy Hoppers. Especially during the Great Depression, work often dried up; when it did, Hamtree opened a photography studio in Harlem.

There is little in the record about Harrington during the Second World War (he was probably too old for military duty) or the years following. His last credit is a sad one. *Shuffle Along* (1952) was a reunion for many 1920s greats. Noble Sissle & Eubie Blake composed lyrics and music; Flournoy Miller and Paul Gerard Smith wrote the book. Smith also staged the show, and Henry LeTang directed the dances. Hamtree was joined onstage by singer Thelma Carpenter, song-and-dance man Avon Long, Flournoy Miller and Sissle & Blake.

The premise was good—the adventures of black soldiers at the end of the Second World War—but the producers padded the show and slowed it down. Critics savaged the show as dull and tired, and it closed after four performances.

MARION HARRIS

b: (Mary Ellen Harrison) ca. 1896, Hendersen, KY (?)—d: 23 April 1944, New York, NY

For a vaudeville headliner and popular recording star, surprisingly little is known about Marion Harris. It seems she wanted it that way. Several researchers, including those who were fans and those who wrote biographical notes for the reissues of her sound recordings, have investigated the birthplace, birth date, family name and parents' given names offered by Marion Harris during her lifetime. No records on file supported any of her statements.

Consequently, contemporary press stories are cluttered with unsubstantiated assertions that include her being related to a president of the USA and a Civil War general and running away from a convent school at age 14 to enter show business. Some news articles reported that she began her career singing in nickelodeons to illustrated song slides, a modest and therefore believable claim.

More surprising is the quick, giant leap she seemed to make into the big time. One story had her discovered by Vernon Castle, then at the height of his fame in an exhibition dance act with his wife, Irene. Another version had Marion joining the cast of *Stop, Look and Listen,* an Irving Berlin revue of 1914. Both are suspect. Vernon Castle died during the First World War. The original cast of *Stop, Look and Listen* did not include Marion's name, yet she may have been a replacement later in the run.

What is certain is that she was a featured singer in Ziegfeld's *Midnight Frolic of 1916* and that she began her recording career in 1916. Fortunately, her recordings from 1916 to 1919 were for Victor, one of the fledgling recording companies that grew into a giant enterprise, so Marion's records from that period have been preserved.

During her Victor years, Marion was a popular vaudeville act that attracted favorable comment in the trades, so it is odd that so few photographs of her survive. Those that do show a poised woman wearing the type of fashionable clothing more appropriate for a woman a decade older. Her face is attractive and well sculpted by bone structure and lacks the plumpness of youth. Perhaps Marion was as much as a decade older than she admitted; if so, that may be one reason that birth records and family information have been so difficult to locate.

From her first recordings, supposedly made at age 15 or 16, her singing style was musically mature and more individual than one expects from a teenager. The clear tone of her soprano was evocative of Ruth Etting's, and Marion displayed rhythmic but occasionally unconventional phrasing akin to Blossom Seeley's. Marion's material covered ballads, novelty tunes and so-called blues. Among her more popular numbers were "I Ain't Got Nobody" (1916), "After You're Gone" (1918), "A Good Man Is Hard to Find" (1919), "Look for the Silver Lining" (1920), "St. Louis Blues" (1920), "I'm Nobody's Baby" (1921), "Carolina in the Morning" (1922), "It Had to Be You" (1924), "Who's Sorry Now" (1924), "There'll Be Some Changes Made" (1924), "I'll See You in My Dreams" (1925) and "The Man I Love" (1927).

Although she claimed to be from Tennessee and sang *darky dialect songs*, Marion, a white Southerner, promoted and recorded the work of African American songwriters like Eddie Green, Creamer & Layton, and Spencer Williams. It is unlikely that any other white star of the period recorded or included in her vaudeville act so many songs by black composers and lyricists.

By the mid-1920s, Marion was a vaudeville headliner. As part of touring Keith-Orpheum time, she played the Palace Theatre in 1926, 1927, 1928, 1930 and 1931. Accounts differ, but the record indicates that she was wed four times and divorced two or three times: Phil Goldberg, her piano accompanist in vaudeville, was her first husband. Robert Williams, an early film actor, died in 1931, at which time they may or may not have been wed. Her third marriage, to Rush Bissell Hughes, son of novelist Rupert Hughes, produced a daughter and a son but ended in divorce.

Marion Harris made several short films and two feature-length motion pictures that captured her sound and something of her performance style. The first feature was *Devil-May-Care* (1929), which starred Ramon Navarro. The second feature, *Falling in Love* (1935), was made in England; in it Marion played herself, although the rest of the actors assumed roles.

By the mid-1930s, Marion had moved to London, where she met and married Leonard Urry, a theatrical agent. According to reports, Marion and Leonard lived through the Second World War in London, and their home was bombed. Yet, it was also reported that Marion returned to the USA in 1944, a rather difficult time for nonessential travel across the Atlantic Ocean, and was admitted to a neurological sanitarium. Within a few weeks of her arrival in New York from London, Marion Harris died at the Hotel Le Marquis in Manhattan. The cause of death was asphyxiation and burns caused by falling asleep with a cigarette still burning.

PAUL & GRACE HARTMAN

Paul Hartman

b: 1 March 1904, San Francisco, CA—d: 2 October 1973, Los Angeles CA

Grace Hartman

b: (Grace Barrett) 7 January 1907, San Francisco, CA—d: 8 August 1955, Van Nuys, CA

Both Paul and Grace Hartman came out of vaudeville, and they developed into one of the more popular male-female comedy teams on Broadway, playing in revues of the 1930s, 1940s and 1950s. As a child, Paul was literally carried onstage. As he grew up, he continued in the family act as a dancer. He met, teamed with and married Grace Barrett sometime around the late 1920s, and they created a dance act for vaudeville and speakeasies that quickly took a comic twist. They satirized many forms of dance act: ballroom, apache and ballet.

Paul and Grace made their Broadway debut in *Ballyhoo of 1932,* a revue strong on comedians. Willie & Eugene Howard starred; Bob Hope, Lulu McConnell and Paul Hartman were featured and Grace Hartman had a couple of small parts. Despite all the laugh makers, the show folded in 11 weeks. The Hartmans had featured roles in *Red, Hot and Blue* (1936–37). The show ran 23 weeks and was heavy with star talent: Ethel Merman, Jimmy Durante and Bob Hope. Cole Porter wrote words and music, and Howard Lindsay and Russell Crouse wrote the libretto.

Despite comedians Victor Moore & William Gaxton, Paul & Grace Hartman and Zero Mostel, *Keep 'em Laughing* (1942), a vaudeville revue, did not live up to its title and closed in ten weeks. The producers changed the show's name to *Top-Notchers* (1942), replaced Gaxton & Moore and Hildegarde, brought in Gracie Fields, kept Paul and Grace and managed to eke out another six weeks.

The Hartmans' work predated but was akin to the type of music and sketch comedy that Sid Caesar made popular with Imogene Coca and Nanette Fabray on television in the 1950s. Grace and Paul handled dialogue very well, which is why television producers tried to fit them into situation comedies instead of giving them the freedom of a variety hour. Paul was tall and seemingly awkward, and he had a long, rubbery face. He always seemed confused and several paces and sentences behind Grace, who was crisp, pretty and alert.

All aspects of American life were fair game, and the Hartmans ridiculed Senate investigating committees, garden parties, theatre, exotic safaris, roller derby and the ballet. Trained dancers, the Hartmans brought a fine physical dimension to their burlesks. Movies and television noticed.

They had featured roles in two movies. Originally, *Sunny* was a stage musical written for the late Marilyn Miller; she also starred when it was first made into a movie in 1930. It was filmed again in 1942 with Anna Neagle in Miller's part and Grace and Paul in support, but the movie was not a success. *Higher and Higher* (1944) was a vehicle for Frank Sinatra in which Paul and Grace, Leon Errol, Mary Wickes, Dooley Wilson, Victor Borge and Mel Torme were wasted.

Wisely, the Hartmans returned to Broadway, where Paul and Grace were superbly presented in *Angel in the Wings* (1947). They helped write the sketches in the intimate revue, and both won 1948 Tony Awards for their performances—he as best actor and she as best actress in a musical. Also catching the attention of critics and audiences was a young woman, Elaine Stritch, who sang "Civilization" ("Bongo, bongo, bongo, I don't wanna leave the Congo, oh no no no no").

The Tony Awards made Paul & Grace Hartman hot prospects for television. They won their own series, *The Hartmans (at Home),* in 1949 on NBC, but it did not catch on with viewers. They were still wanted on Broadway. They signed up for *All for Love* (1949)—a dull, bloated affair, according to reviewers—a revue that wasted Bert Wheeler, Grace and Paul, ran for 121 performances and lost money.

Their next revue, *Tickets, Please!* (1950–51), returned to the oddball informality of *Angel in the Wings* and ran 245 performances. It showcased Grace, Paul, Roger Price, Jack Albertson, Patricia Bright and Bill Norvas. One of the show's featured dancers was Larry Kert, soon to become one of Broadway's top leading men in musicals such as *West Side Story.*

Grace and Paul continued to perform on Manhattan-based television shows as guests. They needed a variety program like *Your Show of Shows,* which starred Sid Caesar and Imogene Coca. *Showtime, U.S.A.* (1950–51) showed the Hartmans at their best, in a variety format with well-written material. It was a variety series that spotlighted scenes from current Broadway plays, musical comedies or revues. A different show was saluted each week. Like other guest hosts, the Hartmans were on the program only once, to present scenes from their hit, *Tickets, Please!*

They were at the height of their careers when Grace fell ill with cancer. Paul Hartman appeared without her in the revival *Of Thee I Sing* (1952). He played the vice president, a role originated by Victor Moore. Some critics liked it better than the public. Paul took television work while Grace was ill. They moved to Los Angeles, where a half dozen featured roles in movies and a television series, *Pride of the Family* (1953–55), with Natalie Wood and Fay Wray, allowed him to remain nearby. Grace Hartman died in 1955 at age 48.

In 1957, Paul went back to the Broadway stage in a revival of *The Pajama Game; Drink to Me Only* (1958) was Paul's last show on the Great White Way. Thereafter he moved back to Hollywood and concentrated on film and television work. Paul costarred with Wally Cox in *Alfred of the Amazon* (1967), a poorly received television series, but his luck quickly changed when he became a cast member of three very successful series. He spent two years (1967–68) on *The Andy Griffith Show* as Emmett Clark, a role he repeated from 1968 to 1971 for *Mayberry, R.F.D.* In between the two, he made occasional appearances on *Petticoat Junction* (1968–69) as Bert Smedley. Paul Hartman died of heart disease in 1973 at age 69.

HATHAWAY CIRCUIT

Small-time Massachusetts circuit of vaudeville theatres in secondary urban centers: Brockton, Fall River, Lynn, Malden and New Bedford.

JUNE HAVOC

b: (Ellen June Hovick) 8 November 1913, Vancouver, BC, Canada

In 1928, June Havoc had been a vaudeville veteran for 13 of her 15 years when she fled the family act and the collapse of vaudeville. She vowed to take what came—vaudeville, one-night stands, dance marathons.

June's lot was the endless, numbing misery of dance marathons, that sadomasochistic response to the Great Depression that rewarded the survivors of an elimination contest. Havoc has detailed the ordeals in her two autobiographies and her play. The contestants were a mix of professional marathoners and locals trying to hold body, mind and soul together as they went round and round for 1,000 hours, then 2,000 hours, until only the victorious couple was standing. Curiosity seekers, slumming parties, the bored, the rootless and the depraved dropped by, day and night, to cheer their favorites or to hope that they saw someone drop from exhaustion or a heart attack. June vowed to get off the merry-go-round as soon as she could, but marathons allowed her to survive the worst years of the Depression.

June Havoc's career was born of a few dancing lessons and her mother's determination to make a good

Baby June Havoc

future for herself and her two children. June picked up dancing *en pointe,* though she was far too young to safely practice toe dancing.

Encouraged by June's precocity and convinced that her newspaperman husband would never fulfill her expectations, Rose took her daughters to her grandmother's home. The two-year-old June made her toe-dancing debut at a local lodge. Some combination of native talent and toddler charm must have worked because Baby June progressed from this debut to a variety of engagements.

At one benefit the two-and-a-half-year-old Baby June played on the same bill as Anna Pavlova, the artist who brought ballet to world audiences. Rose asked the great Pavlova for her opinion of Baby June's dancing. Pavlova offered no comment other than that the child was too young to dance on toe. Rose dismissed any opinions that did not jibe with her own and began billing her daughter as "Baby June, the Pocket-Sized Pavlova."

June was taught to bite her lips red, pinch her cheeks rosy and smile endlessly for agents and producers as she auditioned her little song and dance. She won jobs as skinny waifs in silent films and stock theatre companies. At three, she was the family breadwinner.

Baby June's vaudeville act grew in popularity and earned enthusiastic reviews. When she appeared as Dainty June at New York's Majestic Theatre about 1923, *Variety* wrote: "A tiny blonde headed little tot grabs off the laurels of the bill this week with her versatility and cleverness. She is supported by five other youngsters as talented as they can be."

Schooling, bloody toes, mumps, measles and fever proved insufficient excuses to skip a performance. Only June's bout with German measles canceled an engagement. Havoc laughingly recalled her years as "Dainty June, the Darling of Vaudeville (Reg. U.S. Pat. Off.)" and the "squish, squish" sound her bloodied baby feet made in toe shoes.

In her autobiography *Early Havoc* (1959), June recalled, "I was raised, if you wish to call it that, in vaudeville, going from town to town, playing on a bill with musicians, acrobats, dancers, singers, even freaks. Some were famous, some nice, some tender, some vicious. Many were genuinely big-time, and you knew it the moment you were with them. Others were simply small-time human beings—petty, meager-minded, touchy, whiny, changing from week to week as we traveled from town to town."

Dainty June and Company (of seven) became a headline act for about half the dozen years they spent in vaudeville. Toward the end, June became restive as a series of rapid growth spurts signaled that her adolescence could not be denied. As vaudeville began to wither, June felt she was trapped in a museum piece she no longer fit and the curator, her mother, was unwilling to change. She was also keenly aware that as an adult entertainer she needed training.

When June bolted the act, Rose took a new look at her elder daughter, Rose Louise, and pushed her to become Gypsy Rose Lee. After Gypsy's career took off, Mother Rose had little time or interest in June.

In many ways, June Havoc's childhood and family mirrored that of other youthful stars and the families they supported. The lives of the Hovicks, somewhat conventional as vaudevillians, nevertheless veered between celebrity status and outlaw society. Even when comforted by lucrative bookings, Rose's custom-tailored moral sense overruled society's rules. She would trash a rival act's props and pilfer on impulse, able to square anything with her conscience.

Modest and proper in appearance and manner, over the course of her life Rose attracted and dismissed four husbands, several unsuccessful suitors and a number of female companions. As she grew older and more removed from the adult careers of her daughters, Rose extorted secretly and separately from each. Upon her death. June and Gypsy discovered multiples of television sets, furniture, clothing, jewelry and other gifts each had bestowed.

June and Gypsy became successful in their individual careers. The sisters were intelligent, elegant beauties who had cultivated lovely speaking voices and even shared a mocking innocence in performance. June developed into a skilled actor while Gypsy was essentially a personality welcomed for her sophistication in revues.

June's Broadway career began with *Forbidden Melody,* a Sigmund Romberg & Otto Harbach operetta that closed after 32 performances in 1936. June's first success, *Pal Joey,* a few years later, ran 374 performances in 1941. Havoc began rehearsals with one musical number and ended up with five.

Havoc left *Pal Joey* before it closed to make films, beginning with *Four Jacks and a Jill* (1941). Among the more interesting of her 44 films were *Hello, Frisco, Hello* (1943), *Brewster's Millions* (1945), *Gentlemen's Agreement* (1947) and *When My Baby Smiles at Me* (1948).

Back on the stage in 1944, June Havoc had her longest Broadway run with *Mexican Hayride,* which starred Bobby Clark in one of his last revues. Other shows included *Sadie Thompson* (1944), Gilbert Seldes' update of Aristophanes' comedy *Lysistrata* (1948), Jean Cocteau's re-creation of Sophocles' tragedy, *Infernal Machine* (1958) and Marc Blitzstein's adaptation of Shakespeare's *A Midsummer Night's Dream* that same year.

In 1963 June Havoc directed a cast of 55 in her play, *Marathon 33*, with Julie Harris playing the young Havoc. June returned to acting in 1966 in Tyrone Guthrie's revival of Kaufman & Hart's *Dinner at Eight* (1968), playing the rattled hostess, Mrs. Jordan.

As artistic director of the New Repertory New Orleans, 1969–71, Havoc staged *A Streetcar Named Desire, As You Like It, The Threepenny Opera* and *The Skin of Our Teeth* (she also starred as Sabrina). She toured *Sweeney Todd* in the early 1970s and came back to Broadway in Alan Bennett's *Habeas Corpus* (1976) and as Miss Hannigan in *Annie* (1977). On tour during the 1970s, she directed and starred in *A Delicate Balance* by Edward Albee, *The Effect of Gamma Rays on Man-in-the-Moon Marigolds, The Gingerbread Lady* and *Twigs.*

June Havoc starred in her own TV series, *Willy* (1954–55), and a syndicated talk show, *The June Havoc Show* (1964). In the years of live television Havoc acted in many dramas and a few musicals. Later she guest starred on many popular television series. June returned to her showbiz roots as a commentator for the 1997 PBS documentary *Vaudeville,* and she occasionally performed in her own one-woman show, *An Unexpected Evening with June Havoc.*

GRACE HAYES

b: 23 August 1895, Springfield, MO— d: 1 February 1989, Las Vegas, NV

A fine singer, a capable impersonator and a good comedian, Grace Hayes took quite a while to come into her own as an entertainer. She found her best audiences after her vaudeville and Broadway career. Those were the show business professionals who patronized Grace Hayes' Lodge when it was located in Los Angeles and later, after she moved it to Las Vegas. She was host and performer. Just as during her last days in vaudeville when he was part of her act, her son, Peter Lind Hayes, helped keep their customers jolly.

Grace worked both vaudeville and nightclubs. According to Charles and Louise Samuels in their vaudeville history *Once Upon a Stage* (1974), one of Grace's earlier jobs was working at Big Jim Colisimo's club in Chicago. They also mentioned that she could be a pepper pot, but it still is surprising that, with her classy looks, red hair, singing style and talent, she did not become a bigger star or rise more quickly to the top rank of single women.

She was half of Grace Hayes & Neville Fleeson, a vaude act. He wrote their songs, played them at the piano and sang them solo or in duet with Grace. Grace, of course, had a solo or two, but it was Neville's act. Later, she went out on her own. Her singing voice was a strong but mellow contralto, yet there is no evidence that she made sound recordings. She did, however, appear as a guest on several network radio shows.

Beginning around 1924, she added her son, nine-year-old Peter Lind Hayes, to her act. He was her son by an early first marriage before she was 20. In addition to singing in her own style, Grace included some of her impressions—especially Mae West—and Peter imitated the then famous child star Jackie Coogan.

Grace appeared in four musicals on Broadway. Her first was *The Merry World* (1926), which ran 11 weeks at the Imperial. *A Night in Spain* (1927) was more successful. Its cast included Ted & Betty Healy (with Shemp Howard stooging), Helen Kane, Sid Silver, Phil Baker and the team of Stanley Rogers (not the Rogers Brothers) & Jay Brennan, who were ably performing the old Bert Savoy & Jay Brennan act. *Ballyhoo of 1930* starred W.C. Fields, Chaz Chase and the Slate Brothers but lasted only eight weeks. *A Little Racketeer* (1932), with Hamtree Harrington and Queenie Smith, ran only four weeks.

Peter Lind (as he was then billed) was 15 when he joined his mother at the Palace Theatre in 1933 for a show that featured one bloody accident after another. Marion Spitzer tells the story in her history of the Palace

Theatre. The act immediately preceding Grace Hayes on the bill was a knockabout comedy dance act, Fritz & Jean Hubert. Fritz lost control during the act's finish and crashed into a piano hidden behind a stage curtain. He was bleeding, but the show had to go on, so they dragged him off and Grace began singing "Loveable" as she swept across the stage in a beautiful, long white gown that soon soaked up some of Fritz's blood. Grace called Peter onstage just after he cut himself on a prop and unknowingly sprinkled his own blood all over his white suit as he did an impersonation of Cab Calloway. The audience rewarded them with a big hand, and one of Grace's friends, who was sitting in a box, was ecstatic at Grace's calm control and solid professionalism throughout the ordeal. The friend applauded heartily, stood up abruptly and toppled out of the box. She had to be taken away in an ambulance.

Overall, business was slackening on Broadway, and Grace Hayes headed west, one of many vaudevillians who came to Hollywood in the early 1930s. She opened one of the most enjoyable nightclubs around Los Angeles. Instead of being in the heart of Hollywood, Grace Hayes' Lodge was in the San Fernando Valley. Grace was joined onstage not only by son Peter, but by his wife, Mary Healy, whom Peter married in 1940.

Grace also appeared in a few films, providing vaudeville enthusiasts with a record of her performance. Her first film, *The King of Jazz* (1930), an extravagant revue of sorts built around Paul Whiteman and His Orchestra, was her most notable. *Myrt and Marge* (1933) was a reunion for a number of superior vaudevillians. The film boasted Trixie Friganza, Ted Healy and the Three Stooges and Eddie Foy Jr. in addition to Grace Hayes and her son Peter, then 17. *Rainbow Over Broadway* (1933) was a low-budget programmer, and Hayes did not make another movie until the two-reeler *Maid for a Day* (1936), which also featured son Peter. Grace was one of many old vaudevillians who were wasted in MGM's big-budget *Babes in Arms* (1939) that starred Mickey Rooney and Judy Garland.

Both Grace and son Peter starred in an inane low-budget film, *Zis Boom Bah* (1941). Grace sang, and she emulated, without imitating, the confident and stately presence of Mae West as well as Mae's understated and relaxed style. Also cast was Mary Healy. *Always Leave Them Laughing* (1949) turned into a vehicle for Milton Berle; Hayes and Bert Lahr were wasted. Grace performed an uncredited bit as a prison matron in *Caged* (1950), a well-regarded so-called problem picture of the period.

By that time, Grace had gotten in on the desert floor in Las Vegas when she took over the Red Rooster club during the Second World War and changed its name to the Grace Hayes Lodge. She did not say no when the owners of the future Mirage hotel and casino wanted her spot on the Strip and offered her a very handsome price to sell. Grace continued to reside in Las Vegas, where she died in 1989 at the age of 93.

HEADLINER

The name of the star always *headlined,* or appeared at the top in the boldest and largest letters in the signs, handouts and ads that publicized the bill.

Even in big-time vaudeville, headliners were the only truly highly paid performers on the bill. If the headliner was a major star who commanded a large salary, perhaps in excess of $2,500 per week, management could not afford to pay the other acts on the bill more than $150 to $500 dollars a week. The total salary for a week's bill had to be added to other weekly costs of publicity, maintenance and house wages and still allow for a net profit. By the mid-1920s, tickets usually sold for between $1 and $2. To promote a new vaudeville house or to enhance the reputation of an existing one, a manager might intentionally book a bill, such as one headlined by Eva Tanguay or Sarah Bernhardt, that did not permit income to exceed expenses.

In the small time, salaries varied from the miserable to the modest, and the distinction in billing and salary between the headliner and an average act on the bill was not nearly as extreme. The pay for a small-time act was as low as $35 per week and might approach $500 for the act at the top of the bill. Of course, in the boondocks off the established circuits, an act took what it was lucky to get, sometimes in the worst situations working for little more than room and board, a percentage of the house (counted by the theatre owner) or throw money.

Salaries varied depending on the economic times, and they grew vastly for almost everyone on the bill between 1900 and 1920. Sometimes an act had to take a bit of a cut to work the big time when show business was in a slump, and at other times some theatres on small-time circuits paid as well as two-a-day houses comparable in size, condition and location, especially if the acts were expected to perform three or four shows a day.

TED HEALY

b: (Clarence Ernest Lee Nash) 1 October 1896, Kaufman, TX—d: 21 December 1937, Los Angeles, CA

Ted Healy is remembered for two things. He was the man who organized The Three Stooges, and he was the drunken comedian who died after a violent bar brawl. It is a shame because Ted Healy was one of the most original stand-up comedians of the vaudeville era.

Many of the great monologists in twentieth-century vaudeville, like Julius Tannen, Frank Fay and Jack Benny, had matured in style along similar lines and in reaction to the older-style dialect storytellers who appeared in costume. They were well tailored, casual and relaxed, and their patter displayed varying degrees of 1920s American sophistication.

When Ted Healy burst onto the vaudeville scene with his wife Betty in 1922, he flashed a harder edge. Even when simply waiting for a reaction, he was coiled with energy. He talked, rapid-fire, like a *mugg* sounding off in a barroom, ready to pounce on either agreement or argument.

Most monologists spoke to their audiences about life, love and the luck of the draw; they shared observations on the kinds of topics that were the stuff of daily life for ordinary people. The viewpoints of the generation of monologists that emerged in the 1920s were usually in tune with their audiences, but the comedians played a bit smarter. They dressed well, but not too flashily, acted down-to-earth but confident.

Ted Healy

Healy's onstage persona was no such symbol of genially held success. He was the show-off, a volatile kind of guy who bought the drinks when he was flush with cash and confidence and grew surly when broke and defeated, complaining that no one ever stood him to a drink. Frank Fay and Jack Benny were the kind of men whom many women in the audience wanted to be with, and whom men in the audience wanted to be like; Ted Healy was the guy many women were married to and many men in the audience actually were.

In style, Ted Healy was the most modern of his contemporaries.

Nearly six feet tall, often with a puffy morning-after face, Healy swaggered onstage in cheap suits with trousers that had shrunken at the cleaners and showed his white work socks. He wore his lived-in felt hat with the front of its brim turned up, and he removed the cigar stuck in his mouth only long enough to bark his lines.

Healy's wiseguy persona and delivery made him the idol of stand-up comedians of his day, and many of the stand-up comics from the late twentieth and early twenty-first centuries, whether they knew it or not, owed a lot of their cynical attitude and brash, rapid-fire style to Ted Healy. They got it not directly from Healy but from his successors like Milton Berle, Jackie Leonard, Jack Carter, Shecky Greene and Buddy Hackett, who, unlike Ted Healy, lived to appear on television.

Healy was the son of a well-off Catholic businessman and his wife. Around 1904, the family moved to Houston. By 1909, the family had either moved to New York or spent several summers in Brooklyn, where Healy met and cavorted on the beach at Coney Island with local kids Samuel (Shemp), Harry (Moe) and Jerry (Curley) Horwitz, who later changed their surname to Howard and became known as The Three Stooges.

According to some reports, someone spotted the kids at the beach in 1912 and gave them temporary jobs in the Annette Kellerman Diving Girls vaudeville act. One report tells of a fatal accident sustained by one of the diving girls that shut down the act. Or Kellerman's act moved on to its next booking in another city, where new young boys were recruited.

During his teens, Ted, influenced by his father, was torn between a career in business and going onto the stage. Evidently he decided that he could both clown around and make a lot of money, and that proved true. Unfortunately, Ted spent money as soon as he earned it, and sometimes before. His primary dependents were bookies and barkeeps, and the situation worsened as he grew into middle age.

For many young comedians who had not yet developed a character, working in blackface was an easy, temporary solution. Young Ted Healy followed the familiar "corked-up" route. He was also a capable singer and able to hoof a few steps, so his blackface impersonation was more as a comic song-and-dance man. As he got experience, he began telling jokes, discarded the blackface and changed his stage name to Ted Healy.

Around 1920, Healy met and married Betty Braun, a dancer; as Ted & Betty Healy, "The Philosopher and the Flapper," they performed a mixed double act, with Betty the beautiful singing and dancing straight woman and Ted a clowning song-and-dance man. Although he was a capable monologist, Ted worked better when he had a target for his comments. Initially he did that with Betty, but audiences did not want to watch a comic run down his lovely female partner.

Supposedly, Healy hired tumblers as stooges in the act, guys he could insult and knock around onstage. Once acrobats or stooges were added to their act, it took on various names, like Ted & Betty Healy and Family, with the pint-sized acrobats behaving as unruly children.

There are two different versions of how Shemp and Moe Howard, two of the future Three Stooges, joined their old friend's act.

In 1922, Ted was back in Brooklyn at the Prospect Theatre, doing his act with Betty and the acrobats. His old friends, Shemp and Moe Howard, who were laying off from their small-time act, stopped by to say hello. (The question is whether they would have known him as Ted Healy, as he was billed, or only by his real name, Lee Nash.) Later that day, Shemp, Moe and Jerry (later known as Curly) went to see the evening show. The upshot was that Ted invited the Howard boys onstage; they horsed around as they had a decade earlier, and they clicked. Ted hired them to join the Healys' act for next season's (1924) vaudeville bookings.

The second version has Ted's first acrobats, a German trio, giving their notice, and Ted taking out an ad in a theatrical weekly for three replacements. Shemp, Moe and Jerry showed up, and Ted suggested that they improvise a bit during that evening's show. At any rate, the Howards did not join the act until the following season, and then without Jerry.

There were two problems. First, friendship with Ted was one thing, but business was another. Ted regarded stooges as devices in his act, one step up from props. He was doing his boyhood buddies a favor by taking them into his successful act and giving them the first steady, 40-week season they had ever known. A paycheck, small as it was, was dependably paid to them each week (their mother forbid Jerry from going on the road, so only Shemp and Moe joined Ted). The other problem was that Shemp and Moe were not acrobats. They lacked the training to take falls, knocks and slaps. The physical abuse became a literal sore point, especially as Ted drank more and did not pull his punches.

For over a decade, Ted Healy, his wife, Betty (to whom he was frequently missing in action), and the Stooges lived in a love-and-hate situation. All five benefited by the association, but Ted's erratic and irresponsible behavior was the primary factor in things eventually falling apart.

Healy employed more than a dozen stooges at various times. The famous ones were Larry Fine and Shemp, Moe and Curly Howard, but there were also Fred Sanborn, Mousie Garner, Dick Hakins, Sammy Wolfe and Dave Chasen (later Joe Cook's stooge).

Healy tried to branch out from vaudeville to silent films and Broadway shows. His one effort in silent films, *Wise Guys Prefer Brunettes,* was directed by Stan Laurel for Hal Roach but stirred no further interest. Broadway was a different and more positive story.

Ted & Betty Healy were engaged for *Earl Carroll's Vanities of 1925.* Other comedians in the show included Julius Tannen and Jack Norton. A great success, the 1925 edition of the *Vanities* racked up 440 performances

Betty Healy, 1927

on Broadway and then toured, keeping everyone in the cast employed for a good part of two seasons.

The Shuberts grabbed Ted and Betty for their revue, *A Night in Spain,* which opened 3 May 1927. Ticket sales kept the Shuberts happy and the Century Theatre humming for five months. Then the show began the 1927–28 season with a national tour that started in Chicago. Betty chose not to tour with Ted, whose indiscretions were hurtful and embarrassing and whose problems with alcohol were felt more by his wife and stooges than by the show's management or audiences. A few years later, Betty divorced Ted.

Hoping the formula worked twice, the Shuberts engaged Ted for another revue, *A Night in Venice* (1929). Ted was the only star of this show, and Anne Seymour covered Betty's role. This show, too, played five months and then toured. The souring economy cut short the road show, and Ted pulled together his stooges for a vaudeville act, Ted Healy and His Racketeers (Shemp Howard, Moe Howard and Larry Fine). It played Keith time and paid Ted a top salary. The stooges saw only a fraction of Ted's weekly wages; they were, however, working steadily, and not every vaudevillian could claim that.

While Healy and company were playing the Palace, a scout from Fox arranged for Ted and His Racketeers to come to Hollywood and make a movie, *Soup to Nuts* (1930). A Rube Goldberg concoction, it was a good comedy but bizarre fare, unlike most Fox products, and the studio lost interest in Healy, and the Racketeers.

Healy, minus Howard-Fine-Howard, was in the filmed version of *A Night in Venice* (1931) with his leading lady from the stage, Anne Seymour. This may be a lost feature film. That same year, Ted appeared in a musical comedy, *The Gang's All Here.* Hal Leroy, Ted and the rest of the cast were, but the customers were absent. The show closed in three weeks. A few months later, Ted hooked up with a songwriter turned producer, Billy Rose.

A study in tenacity, Billy Rose starred the first of his five wives, Fanny Brice, in the first show he ever produced. This revue went through three incarnations: *Corned Beef and Roses* (1930), *Sweet and Low* (1930) and *Billy Rose's Crazy Quilt.* Fanny was the only major holdover in each show. Ted Healy was brought in to provide laughs in the third version, *Billy Rose's Crazy Quilt* (1931), but the shopworn show closed inside of two months.

Times were tough on Broadway and were not any better in the rest of the USA, and things were going to get worse. Healy was convinced of his future in Hollywood. He made a couple of shorts and flirted with some studios, especially MGM. His first role in an A picture was a Jean Harlow movie, *Bombshell* (1933), and his work caught MGM's attention.

Healy made two MGM features in 1933 with Larry Fine and two of the Howard Brothers, *Meet the Baron* (an attempt to make a film star out of Jack Pearl) and *Dancing Lady,* in support of two of the studio's top stars, Joan Crawford and Clark Gable. One of the Howards, however, was new to the act. Shemp never liked all the slapping around and had quit in disgust. Younger brother Jerry Howard replaced him, while Shemp began a profitable and respectable film career as a character comedian. Seldom starring but working as much as he wished, Shemp was cooperative and a conscientious and inventive pro that directors liked to have on hand for comedy insurance.

This was the last significant time that Ted Healy employed stooges. After some snarling back and forth, Moe Howard, who had emerged as the business leader for Larry Fine, Curly Howard and himself, got the trio some vaudeville dates, the right to use the name The Three Stooges and their old material (after a court battle that Ted lost), and a contract with a Poverty Row studio to make two-reel films. Columbia paid them twice what Healy did, but it was still peanuts and stayed that way until television. Before reaching Hollywood, Ted Healy had taken on a chorus dancer, Bonnie Bunnell, whom some people regarded as another stooge but simply played the Betty Healy role.

Healy made about three dozen movies in Hollywood between 1933 and 1938. He proved adept at drama as well as comedy, but MGM chose to use him as a featured character actor and character comedian. Few of his films were distinguished. Those that were bona fide *class* pictures were made at MGM, and Healy was billed fifth or below, as in *Bombshell* (1933), *Dancing Lady* (1933), *Reckless* (1935) and *San Francisco* (1936). He made a good pairing with Nat Pendleton in seven feature films. Their names in the scripts were Clip or Gabby (Healy) and Spud or Tiny (Pendleton). Healy might have fared better had Warner Brothers signed him in 1933 instead of MGM, where glamour was king. In the early 1930s, Warner Brothers specialized in fast-paced Busby Berkeley musical comedies and gangster pictures, and both of those genres might have made Ted a bigger movie star.

In the mid-1930s, Ted found network radio receptive to his kind of comedy. He even got his own short-lived series. This was fortunate, because he annoyed Louis B. Mayer, the chief of MGM. Mayer liked his ring kissed, and Healy was more likely to thumb his nose at authority. In 1937, Healy and MGM called it quits. Healy finally moved over to Warner Brothers, where he acted in *Varsity Show* (1937) and *Hollywood Hotel* (1938).

Just before signing with Warner Brothers, Healy met and married another Betty, Betty Hickman, a woman more than a few years younger than Ted. They had a son, John Nash, born 17 December 1937. According to those who knew him, Healy had wanted to be a father, and the birth of a son put him on top of the world. Ted had to tell the world, or at least Hollywood. He trumpeted the good news for several days and nights, making the rounds from one celebrity watering hole to the next. On 20 December 1937, he ended up at the Trocadero, well soused.

A fight started; Ted took it outside and found the odds three to one against him. A waiting cab took Ted, badly beaten, to a doctor. A hospital emergency ward would have attracted the press. Some say it was Joe Frisco who got the cab and took Healy to the doctor. But the Trocadero was not the kind of joint Frisco patronized, and he would not have worried about attracting the press if a friend needed a hospital. Details vary according to the telling.

The official story—and the big studios like MGM and Warner Brothers had "fixers" on the payroll who guided the hands that wrote the official story and news accounts—was that Ted tried to brush off some annoying and antagonistic troublemakers, college boys out on the town, who then took him outside and beat him.

Decades later, eyewitnesses broke their silence and said that Healy, drunk, had his run-in with another famous boozehound, Wallace Beery, who had a notorious temper and mean streak. Beery was with a gangster, Pasquale "Pat" DeCicco, and the future producer of the James Bond movie series, Albert "Cubby" Broccoli. The witnesses claimed that Beery, DeCicco and Broccoli fatally beat Ted Healy. Beery was one of MGM's big stars. Healy was new to Warner Brothers. Neither studio liked bad publicity. The fixers had done their work.

Ted died the next day, four days after the birth of his son. His body was quickly embalmed so no autopsy was possible. The cause of death was stated as organ failure aggravated by acute and chronic alcoholism and the beating. That is what studio fixers knew how to do.

BONITA & LEW HEARN

Lew Hearn

b: 15 February 1882, Poland 1965, New York, NY

Bonita Hearn

b: (Pauline L. Des Landes) 2 December 1886, Mennan, GA—d: unknown

Lew Hearn came to New York's Lower East Side from eastern Europe as a child. He began performing on New York's Bowery in places like the People's Theatre. Nothing is known about his beginnings except that which he told burlesque and vaudeville historian Bernard Sobel. Lew described his early days playing the honky-tonks in the Northwest. The point of the entertainment was to get all the men in the audience into a sporting party mood, spending freely.

Lew's work began with the early show at 9:00 P.M. that lasted until midnight, at which time the male-only clientele found their own amusement with the help of the hostesses. Meanwhile, Lew went back to his digs and slept until 5:00 A.M. or so, when he was roused to perform the final show at six in the morning. The audience for the sunrise show was filled with women who had finished work at the various dance halls, box houses and bordellos. It was their time to unwind, and they proved to be the more appreciative members of an audience otherwise peopled with men too drunk to find their way out or sleeping off the night's revels.

Lew hooked up with three other fellows and formed a quartet in a burlesque company headed East. His initiation as a comedian came when he realized he was too short to perform the dance drill assigned to the quartet, so he devised a comic quickstep that brought laughs. When the lead comedian fell ill, Lew begged for the chance to fill his slap shoes and convinced the company manager that he knew all the routines. He was successful, and the experience pointed him on his way as a comedian.

Bonita and Lew Hearn

Pauline des Landes used the single name Bonita for her stage appearances. Her sister also chose a show business career and adopted the name Artie Hall. Bonita began her career as a 12-year-old dancer in and around Atlanta, Georgia, and made her professional debut in a St. Louis, Missouri, vaudeville house. Within a season, she was performing at Koster & Bial's Theatre in Manhattan. In 1901, Bonita, then 14, was engaged by Mortimer M. Theise's Wine Women & Song burlesque company. She remained with the company for five years, by the end of which time she had risen to star billing.

During the 1905–06 season, Lew joined the Wine, Women and Song company, where he met Bonita, his future wife and stage partner. *Casino Girls on Smiling Island* was the name of the burlesque revue that the company presented that season. The title was an attempt to cash in on the popularity of the Casino Theatre shows in Manhattan. Under the direction of George Lederer, the Casino shows were Weber & Fields' rival.

According to reports, the cast of veteran vaudevillians and burlesquers pretty much created the material for *Casino Girl on Smiling Island* and directed the sketches. The result was a show that ran more on inspiration and nerve than on formula. Word of mouth kept the show on the boards at several theatres on Lower Broadway until Abe Erlanger arranged for *Casino Girls on Smiling Island* to be shipped uptown to the newly remodeled Circle Theatre at Columbus Circle.

Because of the theatre's location well north of the theatre district, in what some wits called the Arctic Circle, most producers were reluctant to book the show, but *Casino Girls on Smiling Island* kept the Circle box office busy for a year and a half and made a bigger star out of Bonita. The opening scene of the show was a masque ball on the lawn of the Asterbilt estate. Each of the performers took turns arriving as famous guests. Among Bonita's impersonations was Lillian Russell, a great beauty whom she resembled.

Like Lew, Bonita had played both burlesque and vaudeville. Hers was an important vaude act by the time the two met. During their partnership, both Bonita and Lew occasionally worked as singles, and, during the 1906–07 season, Bonita was accompanied by a small chorus of *pickaninnies* that included the future vaudeville and revue star Florence Mills.

Lew stayed in burlesque, where he worked as a comedian with Max Gordon, future Broadway producer. Max, then all of 15, did a Jewish dialect comedy routine, and Lew sang and worked in the sketches. They played theatres that booked burlesque revues in Spokane, Washington and Portland, Oregon, among other cities in the Northwest.

Briefly, Lew switched to vaudeville and formed a short-lived song-and-dance double act with Al Lewis. Lewis had acting ambitions, and he split from Hearn but had to turn back to burlesque, where he continued to make his living as a Dutch comedian. To make the circle complete, Max Gordon then joined Al Lewis in a vaudeville agency. Later Gordon became an important Broadway producer.

Bonita & Lew Hearn were in demand as a vaudeville act during the nine-year period between 1904 and 1914, but occasionally Bonita played musical comedy. She was still the more important performer, and sometimes, as in 1909, their vaudeville act was billed as "Bonita (late star of Wine Women and Song) assisted by Lew Hearn In an Original Travesty on *Three Weeks.*" She sang and fed Lew, who handled the gags. In 1911, they produced and toured in *Real Girl,* a musical with words and music by Irving Berlin, an early opportunity for the future master of the Broadway musical. *After the Girl* (1914) was the last show in which Bonita and Lew Hearn shared the stage. It was a London revue and lasted about three months. Bonita ceased to appear in Broadway shows and may have resumed her single in vaudeville. The last credits found for her are for five films in the mid-1930s, when she was at least 50. The only film in which she received billing was *The Virginia Judge* (1935), a not very successful attempt by Walter C. Kelly to fire up a screen career. Bonita's last known movie appearance was in Harold Lloyd's *The Milky Way* (1936).

By November 1914, Lew was working on his own, appearing in *Suzi,* an ill-fated Casino Theatre musical produced by Lew Fields. Many of the revues in which Lew Hearn appeared closed either out of town or shortly after they arrived on Broadway. *Ned Wayburn's Town Topics* (1915) fell short of a two-month run.

Make It Snappy (1922), a Shubert Winter Garden revue, put Lew in support of star Eddie Cantor with results that Cantor did not forget. Lew reached the pinnacle of his career, at least in terms of fame and recognition, when he joined the cast of the *Ziegfeld Follies of 1923.* Fanny Brice, Bert & Betty Wheeler and Eddie Cantor were the chief comedians, but Lew nearly stole the tailor sketch, "Belt in the Back." The sketch was transferred to film as one of the closing numbers of *Glorifying the American Girl* (1929) and Hearn played it in vaudeville for a time. Both Hearn and Cantor claimed authorship of the sketch, but it may have been a re-working of an older skit written by someone else.

Lew Hearn was a small, unprepossessing man, and although he could sing and probably dance some, he was consigned by appearance to secondary roles, playing the *schlimazel*—the little guy unblessed by fate, one of life's patsies. He was an excellent comedy actor in both his timing and his characterization, and he was able to portray both city and rural types, a skill few comedians had.

In "Belt in the Back," Lew is the hapless customer who wanders into a clothing shop (probably on Canal

Street, known as "the clothes-hunting street"), shopping for a jacket with a belt in the back, a piece of goods unknown in the store. As he is pressured into one inappropriate coat after another, Lew whines his wishes and objections in a high pitch that sounds as if it is coming out of an old gramophone. But both he and the salesman, Eddie Cantor, know that the only way Lew can leave is to buy something.

Hearn was on Broadway again in *Innocent Eyes* (1924), a Shubert Winter Garden revue that ran three months with Mistinguett and Frances Williams as stars. Thereafter, Lew did not attempt Broadway often. There was *Ned Wayburn's Gambols,* which flopped in 1929, and then nothing until 1939, when *Yokel Boy* placed Hearn in the comedic company of Phil Silvers, Jut Canova and Buddy Ebsen.

Lew Hearn remained professionally active into the mid-1950s. He recreated "Belt in the Back" with Milton Berle in Cantor's role on Berle's TV show, appeared in a few straight comedies on Broadway and about a dozen Hollywood movies, but the roles got smaller and the vehicles less distinguished. Considering that Lew and Bonita were a top vaudeville act, little remains on the record about them.

MARCUS HEIMAN

ca. 1880–1940

An alumnus of the Orpheum organization who survived the various internal intrigues of the Keith-Orpheum empire, Heiman succeeded Martin Beck as one of the many who booked the acts for the Palace Theatre until Eddie V. Darling took over. Along with J.J. Murdock, Marcus Heiman lasted into the days when Keith-Orpheum became RKO, and both Heiman and Murdock worked for Joe Kennedy.

ANNA HELD

b: (Helene Anna Held) 8 March 1873 (?), Warsaw, Poland—d: 12 August 1918, New York, NY

At the turn of the twentieth century, Anna Held was the toast of theatregoing bon vivants in Paris, London and New York City—the single most glamorous and feminine public figure of her day. Though she introduced the Parisian coquette to American audiences, she was also a transitional figure between the buxom and blonde Anglo-Saxon beauties of the Gilded Age—never more beautifully represented than by Lillian Russell—and the darker, more petite and sensual sirens, soon to be parodied as silent-screen vamps, who came from more exotic breeding grounds than Yorkshire dairy farms and America's Corn Belt.

Anna Held possessed a slenderized silhouette of the hourglass figure. She was still as bosomy as the figure on the prow of a clipper ship, but she was wasp waisted and leaner in the hips and thighs than the well-upholstered dream girls of the 1880s. Held entranced audiences by her enviable figure (her waist supposedly measured 18 inches), her expressive large brown eyes, a glorious mass of auburn hair, a French accent she made no effort to curb and an air of innocence compromised by sophisticated glamour and mischievous fun.

Her stage personality was well expressed in two songs with which she was identified. The first was "Won't You Come and Play With Me?," which she introduced at the Palace Music Hall in London around 1890, and "I Just Can't Make My Eyes Behave," which she sang in *The Parisian Model* (1906) in the USA.

I just can't make my eyes behave,
Two bad brown eyes, I am zheir slave.
My lips may say "run away from me,"
But my eyes say "come and play wiz me."

"I Just Can't Make My Eyes Behave," by Will D. Cobb & Gus Edwards

Anna Held

Anyone who had known Helene Anna Held as a girl would not have recognized her as a young woman. It is difficult to discern the exact facts, but it seems certain that Anna was the only one to survive childhood of between seven and ten children born to a father who was a Polish Jew and a mother who was a French gentile.

One of several periodic pogroms in Poland caused the family to flee to Paris in 1881, when Anna was between 7 and 12. Her father died that same year. Without any means of support, Anna took to singing in the streets and helping her mother earn money. For some reason, her French-born mother thought a move to London would improve their lot—perhaps there were relatives there. Within a few years (Anna was between 12 and 15) her mother died.

Even as a young girl, Anna was a vivacious performer, attractive and arresting rather than pretty. She had a lovely figure and was willing to show her legs and laundry, so she found work as a chorus girl. By advertising herself as French rather than Polish, she endeavored to add a modicum of glamour to her teenaged self.

Some accounts of her early life report that Anna became a protégé of the famed Jewish theatre star Jacob Adler, and that she toured with Adler, the founder of a Jewish-American acting dynasty, for five years, until the late 1880s. It was apparent to Anna, and perhaps Adler, that young Anna Held belonged on variety, not dramatic, stages.

For another five years, Anna Held toured in variety and in musical confections in France, the Low Countries, Germany and Russia. On the road, she met and was courted by Maximo Carrero, a Uruguayan playboy whose family boasted a long Spanish heritage. The family disapproved of Anna. Nevertheless, the couple married in 1894. She gave birth to a daughter, Liane. Cut off by his family, Carrero was drowning in gambling debts.

Anna Held was the only one bringing money into the household. She did not marry to be poor and support a husband. They separated without bitterness, and in later years, both Maximo and Anna visited their daughter on occasion. Maximo died in 1908.

Held was appearing at various Parisian music-halls like the Théâtre des Variétés and was scheduled to play the Folies Bergère when Florenz Ziegfeld decided that he must bring Anna Held to America and become her lover. Had her marriage been successful, it is doubtful that Held would have taken a chance on a neophyte producer from America. He offered her $1,500 a week (that he did not have) and, in 1896, when she could no longer think of any more reasons not to accept, Anna agreed. She placed Liane in a French convent school.

Ziegfeld's experience had been a few of years on the road managing Sandow the strong man. Now he intended to make Anna a Broadway star and himself a Broadway producer. Flo Ziegfeld managed to borrow enough money and sell shares in his revival production of a tried-and-true show, *A Parlor Match* (1896), in which Held made her Broadway debut in a featured, not starring, part. She introduced to American audiences what became a theme song of sorts, "Won't You Come and Play With Me?"

During his seasons with Sandow, Flo had developed into a master promoter, and he plied the press with all manner of ploys; he did the same to publicize Anna Held. One of Ziegfeld's most legendary stunts was conceived during the production of *A Parlor Match.* He arranged for a milkman to file suit against Anna for nonpayment of a bill for 40 gallons of milk. Why, demanded the press, did Anna Held require so much milk to be delivered? "Eeet iz for to take ze beauty bath." Thousands of American women began ordering milk by the cartload. It even took the press a while to realize it had been bamboozled.

Flo and Anna entered into a common-law marriage. Professionally, he built her into a top American attraction, as he had Sandow. She helped refine his taste in fabrics, color and line. After a few years, despite all the money they made, Anna realized that Flo was gambling away their earnings. She decided to hold onto her own cash, and while Ziegfeld always lived beyond his means, Anna Held saved her money and became a millionaire.

Ziegfeld, in partnership with various moneymen, continued to present Anna in a series of frothy musicals: *La Poupée* (a quick flop in 1897), *The French Maid* (1897, in which Anna appeared only during its final week on Broadway but toured with the show), *A Gay Deceiver* (1898, appearing as an added attraction), *The Cat and the Cherub* (1899), *Papa's Wife* (1899–1900), *The Little Duchess* (1901–02), *Mam'selle Napoleon* (1903–04) and *Higgledy-Piggledy* (1904–05, with Joe Weber and Marie Dressler). *A Parisian Model* (1906–07) was Ziegfeld and Held's most successful show thus far; it ran 30 weeks in New York and then toured. Oddly, other than acting in a filmed segment, Anna Held never appeared in any of the *Ziegfeld Follies,* which began in 1907, although it was she who suggested the format for annual revues that made the Ziegfeld name and reputation.

Ziegfeld began an affair with the actress Lillian Lorraine in 1909. Held tried to ignore the infidelity, but Flo moved his paramour into the same hotel in which he and Anna lived. Held expected the infatuation to pass, and it did. Yet, after Flo decided that Lillian was too willful and difficult, he turned his attentions to another actress, Billie Burke, whom he later married.

During that period, Held turned to vaudeville, where she quickly scored with audiences more effectively than she did in Ziegfeld's musical pastries. The setting was more intimate in vaudeville, and all Anna needed to do was charm and sing her slightly naughty songs rather than sustain an acting role. Soon, she was confident enough to appear in vaudeville sketches. She was a well-paid headliner in big-time vaudeville, toured British music-halls in 1910 and then played engagements in France and other nations on the Continent, her first appearance in those countries in 15 years. Back in the USA, she played the Palace Theatre in 1914 and 1915 and made her single silent feature, *Madame La Presidente,* in 1916.

During the First World War, when she was not working in American vaudeville, she traveled to France to perform for French soldiers. Anna Held also played many benefits to raise money for the French cause. If she was frightened when she visited the front lines of combat, she did not let on. When she returned to the USA, she was plumper and had lost much of her youthful freshness. Her health had been compromised; one night in 1918, she collapsed onstage. When Anna Held died a few months later, her age was given as 45, but she may have been a few years older. Flo Ziegfeld did not attend her funeral—he avoided all such events. The cause of death was reported as multiple myeloma, yet speculation ensued, including from some medical men, that the years of tight corseting had damaged her internal organs.

HELLFIGHTERS JAZZ BAND

Brought together under the baton of James Reese Europe as the 369th Infantry Jazz Band, the band toured vaudeville and made recordings under the nickname they earned during combat in the First World War. Accompanying the Negro 369th infantry outfit to which they were attached, the band participated in trench warfare; the entire outfit proved themselves brave warriors in a number of critical battles. Before reaching the front, the American Expeditionary Forces command had them tour civilian venues, and the band was warmly greeted, especially by the French, whom the band reportedly made "jazz mad."

Between its members' valor and its musical popularity, the 369th Infantry Jazz Band had a reputation that reached the USA. When the band returned home in February 1919 at war's end, the Hellfighters were prominent among those units who marched in victory up Fifth Avenue from Madison Square Garden into Harlem. The popularity of several of their tunes led to a contract to record for Pathé Freres Phonograph Company of Brooklyn in March and May of that same year. The two dozen tunes the band recorded included three W.C. Handy blues compositions, a couple of Dixieland jazz tunes, a few popular songs, several rags and numbers that today could be considered early jazz.

Their tumultuous greeting by the public and the success of the first batch of their recordings prompted a contract to tour vaudeville. On 10 May 1919, a few days after their May recording sessions and just after their vaudeville tour began in Boston, Massachusetts, Jim Europe was killed by a disgruntled band member. The band's vocalist, Noble Sissle, who had been Europe's assistant since the onset of the War, assumed the baton. Eubie Blake, a pianist and earlier partner of Sissle's, became his assistant. After the initial tour, which ended with an engagement at the Palace Theatre in Manhattan, Sissle and Blake resumed their partnership, formed a smaller outfit from the Hellfighters' roster and resumed playing vaudeville until their show *Shuffle Along* catapulted them onto Broadway.

HERSCHEL HENLERE

b: (Herschel Steinberg) 14 December 1890, Waterloo, Canada—d: 13 January 1968, London, England

Variety, to fulfill the promise of its meaning, required acts like Herschel Henlere's comedy piano act. He did not fit any precisely defined type of act. Like Victor Borge, who came on the scene a generation later, Herschel was both a gifted pianist and a comedian. He billed himself variously as "The Mirthful Music Master" and "The Poet of the Piano."

Among the earliest records of his time in vaudeville was his stint as Anna Held's accompanist. He made his name, however, with his own novelty music act. He took popular songs and played them in various musical styles (as did Borge with "Happy Birthday"), and Herschel was noted for dazzling audiences with quicksilver transitions from one composition to the next. He was popular in American vaudeville during the 1910s and capped his career in the United States with an appearance at the Palace in 1920. Herschel Henlere wrote a number of songs, including "Kismet, an Arabian Fox Trot," and made sound recordings and piano rolls.

By 1921, he had based himself in England and played variety theatres and appeared in a few films, such as *Soldiers of the King* (1934), which starred Cicely Courtneidge, and *Crazy People* (1934). According to his grandnephew, Peter Mones, who has chronicled Henlere's career, Herschel made a Vitaphone short around 1930.

He was still "working the halls" in 1956, only they were variety houses like Newcastle Empire. Henlere performed in *The Royal Variety Show* of 18 November 1957, a gala that boasted performers like the Crazy Gang, Gracie Fields, Vera Lynn, Max Bygraves, Judy Garland, Count Basie, Harry Secombe and the Tiller Girls.

JOHN & WINNIE HENNINGS

John Hennings

b: (John Henry Hennings) 26 November 1886, Baltimore, MD (?)—d: 8 November 1933, St. Joseph, MO

Winnie Hennings

b: (Winnetta Hamlet) 9 December 1882, Stanberry, MO—d: 12 July 1961, St. Joseph, MO

"The Kill Kare Kouple," as John & Winnie Hennings were billed, was what was called in the trade a mixed-double act. They sang, played musical instruments, danced and clowned. John and Winnie cannot be found in books about vaudeville, yet they were a popular and worthy act in their day. They played the number three spot on the Palace bill of 15 February 1915 and won glowing reviews. The headliners were singing comedian Nan Halperin in the next to closing spot, and Eddie Leonard & Mabelle Russell closing the first half of the show in the fifth spot. The trade paper *Variety*, not noted for overpraising, succinctly assessed the week's acts, giving top honors to Halperin—"a riot"—and noting that John & Winnie Hennings "went over very big."

While playing Orpheum time in 1913, they played on bills headed by Sarah Bernhardt (assisted by Lou Tellegen) at the Orpheum theatres in Sacramento, San Francisco and Los Angeles. Bernhardt's billing was bigger than the rest of the acts combined, but the Hennings were top billed among the rest.

John was the comic in the act. He was tall, handsome and well proportioned, but from the audience's viewpoint he appeared to be a thin chap with long, spidery legs. He fostered that illusion through his movement and tight clothes and by brushing his hair upright into spikes. His signature song was "Nobody Loves a Skinny Guy," one of several originals the couple wrote for their act. His wife and stage partner, Winnie, pretty and plump, provided the focus for John's larking, and she sang pleasingly. Together they performed what was called a flirtation act. Their daughter Nancy described it: "Winnie opened by singing a cute little ditty that had some clever patter. John entered and engaged in all kinds of silly antics, trying to get her attention, but she demurely gave him the cold shoulder. Rebuffed, John broke into 'Nobody Loves a Skinny Guy,' clowning as he crooned his lament. He won the audience from the start. Winnie, however, pretended to be unimpressed and played a tender cornet solo.

"The flirtation continued, and John tried to gain Winnie's attention by accompanying her on the piano. He demonstrated that he was a capable musician with hot ragtime 'licks' before the piano unexpectedly made a noise like an automobile 'backfiring' (backstage sound effects). This propelled John into a madcap bit, as he pretended to 'drive' the piano with its stool and mimicked the sounds of beeping horns and whistling birds. The bit ended when the piano-mobile finally blew up." John's high jinks won Winnie's attention. Encouraged by Winnie's coy response, John launched into his "grasshopper dance," his own version of eccentric dancing.

"Winnie softened, and gave him a big smile. He pulled out an old beat-up trombone and attempted to play it, but it kept falling apart. John explained to the audience that he slept in it. It almost seemed plausible with a body that thin and flexible, and the audience laughed. John told them he was so thin that he had to eat spaghetti one at a time." He finally hammered together the pieces of the trombone and played a solo. Winnie made it a duet when she joined in with her cornet.

"The act ended with the pair seated on camp stools back-to-back while they sang another of their own songs, 'Skid Daddle Daddle Dum.' This was one of those novelty ditties with a nonsense chorus and many funny verses that were sometimes topical or could be adapted to various localities."

The careers of John & Winnie Hennings neatly paralleled vaudeville. Both were in other acts when they met. Winnie was one of four children born to Mary Baker Hamlet and Charles Hamlet. The family moved from Nebraska to settle in St. Joseph, Missouri, in 1879. Mary, a musician herself, taught her children to play instruments. Eventually they formed the Hamlet Family Band. Winnie played cornet, Byrde, the trombone, Leola, the clarinet and Frank, the only son, played drums. Their father, Charles, learned to play bass just enough to get by and be part of the musical family. Charles' full-time job was working for the railroad. When he transferred to a small town in Kansas, the family, to earn extra money, opened a small music store. Winnie's cousin was bandmaster Arthur Pryor, son of musician Sam Pryor, with whom Winnie studied music.

"As a teenager, Winnie found her life in a small town monotonous," explained daughter Nancy. "At 16 she left home to become a cornet musician in a 'ladies orchestra.'" The Navassar Ladies Band consisted of 50 girls. They were well trained and looked after, and they wore nifty uniforms. They performed at amusement parks and community functions all over the country, even on the White House lawn. Winnie spent nine years touring with the orchestra. A half dozen or so of the young women were selected to form a smaller musical ensemble, Vassar Girls, for vaudeville.

John was traveling in a family act, Hennings, Lewis & Hennings, when he met Winnie Hamlet. The Hennings performed comedy and sang and danced. John was the latest in a long and wide theatrical dynasty. He and his sister Mamie, a few years John's senior, had been vaudeville veterans since they were children. John was four at the time of his debut—a small singing spot in an act with his cousins, Bessie and Nellie McCoy, two dancers who reached the first rank in vaudeville and revue.

John and Mamie joined their parents in a variety act in blackface. Later, they traveled with their father, John Bernard Hennings, as the Hennings Trio, "Comedians, Vocalists and Dancers." The promotional materials describe the act as "A Double Proposal: a high class comedy act, entirely devoid of gags." According to photos and reviews, they played as Dutch comics and as Irish at various times.

Earlier, John's mother and aunt had appeared in vaudeville as the Lee Sisters. (His aunt became the mother of Bessie and Nellie McCoy.) Eventually, after John's father became a legit actor, John and Mamie formed a mixed-double act as eccentric dancers. Ross Lewis was the manager for the Vanity Fair company, a tab show, when he married Mamie and joined their act.

Winnie Hamlet and John Hennings married 29 September 1908 in Chicago. Winnie traveled with John's trio until it completed its bookings on Western Vaudeville time; then Winnie and John put together an act and, as the Kill Kare Kouple, they made their debut June 1909 at the Kedzie Theatre in Chicago.

Winnie felt that John was the great talent, and the act was built around his capabilities as an eccentric dancer and clown. In some mixed doubles, the spouse was onstage simply to add another $50 or so to the act's salary and did little more than assist. But Winnie had a charming manner, sang well and developed into an able comedy partner for John. "Some of the married vaudeville teams," according to Nancy, "were perpetually 'nipping' at each other due to the difficulty of too much togetherness. That John's and Winnie's relationship ran quite smoothly was mostly due to John. He deplored an argument and simply walked away. Winnie had to fight any battles that developed with bookers, agents and stagehands. She was good at it. John never wanted to wrangle over money. Due to her efforts, the Kill Kare Kouple earned better and better billing and money."

The Kill Kare Kouple spent their first season on the better small time, like Sullivan & Considine and Loew's, before graduating to Orpheum and Keith-Albee time. Over the next four or five seasons, they played big-time theatres from Keith's New Theatre in Boston to the Orpheum in Los Angeles, appearing on bills with top headliners like Ed Wynn, The Three Keatons (at Hammerstein's Victoria), The Four Marx Bros., Mae West, Belle Storey, Jack Donahue, Belle Baker, Eddie Leonard, Pat Rooney Jr., the Avon Comedy Four (including Smith & Dale) and Sarah Bernhardt during her 1913 visit to America.

When John and Winnie embarked for London in 1915, Europe was already rumbling with the first battles of the First World War. Two weeks later, the *Lusitania* was torpedoed and sunk. John had been engaged for a musical at London's Hippodrome. He was billed as "Johnny Henning," and his role described as "an American Rube." *Push and Go* opened 15 May and did nicely, attracting the visiting king and queen of Belgium and Britain's King George V and Queen Mary despite the increasingly frequent zeppelin bombing raids on London by the German forces.

It was still two years before the USA entered the war, yet John and Winnie began visiting hospitals in England, bringing cheer to the war's first military casualties. John himself ventured deep into the battle zone to perform for the British troops on the front lines between Belgium and France. He was with the boys in the trenches at Ypres, Belgium, during the second battle of 22 April to 5 May 1915 and at Festubert, France, during the five days of 19–24 May, just after the battle of 15 May 1915. It was at Ypres that the Germans used poison gas.

The wartime attacks with chlorine gas may have affected John's lungs. When he tried to enlist in the American Expeditionary Forces, after the USA joined Britain and France, he was turned down because of weak lungs. Instead, Winnie and John visited the American troops in training camps and hospitals during the war, and they performed in benefits for the troops. Thereafter, John suffered frequent bouts of pneumonia.

Winnie and John resumed their vaudeville work after the USA entered the war, and their first post-London engagement was at Keith's Boston Theatre. Afterward, John went solo in a series of musicals, including *Take It from Me* (1919) and *Trial Honeymoon* (1924). Between the two shows, their first child, a baby boy, died at birth. Nancy was their second child.

"My mother, Winnie," according to Nancy, "hated being left out of show business and away from John. There were too many pretty girls in the show. Mother used to write songs and material for other acts as well as their own, and that talent provided a way to get back into the fray. I was six months old and healthy, so Mother wrote the manager of the show to tell him that she had written a parody of one of the show's songs, 'Petting Party,' and that she thought it would be a great bit if John sang the parody later as a reprise in the show while carrying his baby onto the stage. Amazingly, the manager said, 'Come on, Winnie, and bring the baby. We'll do it.' The show was flagging a bit at the time, so I guess he thought it might give a lift to the show."

When it comes to petting,
I was there as you can see.
I took every kiss, from a certain Miss,
Now we're married, haven't tarried;
Seven more like this.
[pointing to baby in his arms]

The reprise turned out to be a showstopper, and there were several verses to meet the audiences' demand for more.

The appearance of the six-month-old baby Nancy Hennings Tomlin onstage caused some controversy and a lot of publicity. It was the time when the Society for the Prevention of Cruelty to Children was crusading against children appearing onstage but doing little about the thousands of orphaned waifs and strays hawking newspapers or selling flowers. Many articles championed the Hennings, and several reviewers called baby Nancy the star of the show, despite her brief appearance onstage.

John's health fluctuated. He had good periods and those that were not good. By the mid-1920s, vaudeville was flagging and silent movies had reached their apogee in artistry and attracted huge weekly audiences. John decided to try his luck in filmdom. He made at least one feature film, *The Poor Millionaire* (1930), in which Richard Talmadge starred. John was featured.

"After Hollywood, John tried taking the act with Mother on the road again for a while. I remember hotels, theatres and dressing rooms as a kid. Mother would make me sit on her cornet case in the wings while they were doing their act. They taught me a few dance steps and worked me into the act. I was about four to six years old then, and Mom was homeschooling me with a correspondence course for actors' kids. The pace then was pretty tough, more shows and more travel until Dad's health declined again. When I was eight we came back to St. Joseph, Missouri, where I could go to a real school."

The prolonged Great Depression was as hard on vaudevillians as it was for the steelworkers, farmers, shopkeepers and office workers. Perhaps it was harder, for while factory workers and clerks knew that the struggle to survive would persist until industry and commerce revived, the vaudevillian knew—even if hope lingered in his heart—that his way of life was gone forever. The public had turned away from vaudeville toward radio and movies as it had from horse-drawn carriages to motorcars. A vaudevillian had spent his entire life developing and perfecting his act, only to find his skills unwanted, even when life grew better.

In John Hennings' case, theatre, music-hall, variety and minstrelsy were the family business, the only occupation known to four generations. John, like his father, grandfather and great-grandfather, had given his life to it. He had been happy as a husband and father, and he enjoyed a bit of fishing at their cottage at Put-in Bay, a vaudevillian summer colony on Lake Erie in Ohio, but, like many men before him and since, his work defined him. He was a vaudevillian, and vaudeville was dead.

His health never had been the same since the First World War. Long after the armistice, his own battles continued; bouts of pneumonia and melancholy dogged him for 15 years. He had seen men slaughtered on the battlefields, and his skills had been made obsolete by movies and radio. One day, late in autumn, in the middle of the Great Depression, after he had given a dance lesson to a young pupil, John Hennings went downtown to the theatre district. He walked up the alley to the stage door of the Orpheum Theatre, and there with a single pistol shot he ended his life.

Winnie never remarried. "She opened a restaurant—rather ironic, as she never cooked while living in theatres and hotels her whole previous life. My mother lived to be 80, saw her daughter raised and enjoyed her grandchildren." Winnie and John are buried side by side in St. Joseph, Missouri. Their headstone reads, "Kill Kare."

ISIDOR H. HERK

b: ca. 1880—d: 1945

He was known variously as I. Herk, Izzy and Napoleon; most called him Mr. Herk, and everyone admitted that he was as smart a burlesque operator as you could find in his day. Like other producer-managers who founded or later drifted to the Columbia wheel, Herk was a small-time producer when he joined the Columbia Amusement Company shortly after its establishment in 1905. His shows proved profitable. Ten to 20 years younger than Sam Scribner and the other leaders, Herk mastered the financial end of the business while rising in importance as a producer along with the organization. He quickly became right-hand man to Scribner, then the leader of the Columbia organization.

He earned his nickname Napoleon by being a strict supervisor. Although he made his way among the leaders through diplomacy and compromise, he never made it into the inner circle, yet he helped effect the merger of the Eastern and Western wheels.

To stave off competition from a rival who planned a cheaper brand of burlesque, the Columbia producers created the American Burlesque Association, a subsidiary that competed with the upstart on their own cut-rate and raunchy level. The elders chose Herk to run the American wheel.

But top management at Columbia was slow to change or prepare for new times and circumstance, and Herk was unable to crack through into the leadership council that ran the Columbia Amusement Company. Twice he tried to leave burlesque. The first time, in 1922, he allied with the Shuberts, who were making their second bid to deal themselves into the vaudeville business with their Affiliated Vaudeville. When the group's flirtation with vaudeville foundered, Herk bailed out of the campaign without recouping his losses, but he managed to get back in burlesque within the year.

Herk was a businessman, a bean counter more than a showman. Along with others dismayed at Columbia's reactionary leadership, Herk helped form and then headed the Mutual wheel, a circuit that inclined to shows that were faster paced, played funkier music and were dirtier. Perhaps to cover himself, he issued edicts similar to Columbia's, exhorting producers to clean up their shows, but the Mutual brand of raunchy burleycue sold well, and he built the circuit into 50 theatres with 50 shows touring them.

The Great Depression hit the poorest folks first, and burlesque, the workingman's choice in theatre, suffered along with him. When the Mutual wheel went kaput in 1931, Herk tried to revive the Columbia standard, but stock burlesque, as exemplified by the Minskys, was ascendant.

Herk's final effort in show business was to produce a Broadway revue, *Wine, Women and Song* (1942), that the Shuberts promoted as a "revue-vaudeville-burlesque show," a description that failed to draw those three constituencies, who preferred their favorite form undiluted.

Even with comedian Jimmy Savo and burlesque queen Margie Hart heading the ensemble, and a police raid to capture headlines, the show barely ran seven weeks with two shows a day. Herk was arraigned for producing an indecent show and sentenced to six months, of which he served three. His jail term lasted longer than his show. He died three years later.

HERMINES MIDGETS

An attraction billed as *Lilliput* opened in the spring of 1937 in the Prater, an amusement park in Vienna. A fanciful miniature village was populated by a dozen or so little people who came from Austria and the surrounding countries of Czecho-Slovakia, Yugo-Slavia and Hungary, as those nations were then known. *Lilliput* proved such a popular and financial success that it reopened the following spring. The little people were poorly paid and badly treated, so they agreed to decamp and work for another promoter, Bob Rebernigg.

A former circus performer turned electrician who had fashioned the lighting effects for the *midget village*, Rebernigg saw potential in transforming the exhibition into a performance. Doubtless he also realized that Austria and the rest of Europe might soon be engulfed in a war that would destroy the local economy.

Rebernigg formed a traveling troupe of midgets. He knew the business. Born into a circus family, Rebernigg's father, Jakob Staub (Rebernigg was his illegitimate son) owned a small circus in Vienna, Bob's uncle managed a large traveling tent operation.

Begining with Josef (Pepi) Krisch, his sister Maria (Mimi) Krisch, Mathilda (Hilda) Karollus and her brother Friederich (Butch) Karollus, Bob engaged ten of the Lilliput inhabitants for his troupe and drafted Bor's wife and her parents into the venture. His stepmother,

Hermines Midgets

Hermine, took over the task of creating their costumes as well as lending her name to the new company, Hermines Midgets. Bob Rebernigg changed the family name to Hermine.

Most of the little people doubled in the troupe, playing instruments in Bob Hermines Military and Midget Jazz Band as well as performing as acrobats, wire walkers and even pugilists, who sparred in exhibition boxing matches. Bob trained and built on the talents of his troupe.

Wisely, the company headed south into Italy, then a fascist nation on friendly terms with Austria, but one more likely to prove an easier point for further European travel than Austria, Czecho-Slovakia or Germany. The itinerary for Hermines Midgets was a familiar one of fairs, festivals and circuses, a route that took them from Venice to Milano, Turino, Genova, Pisa, the island of Elbe, Florence, Rome, Naples and Palermo in Sicily. They were joined in Italy by Jakob Straub and two midgets, Vilmos (Willi) Haasz and Elisabeth (Bözsi) Zöllner. During the tour, Mrs. Hermine fell ill and died in Merano, where she was buried.

The bookings in Italy had permitted the troupe to develop, and their good reception led to a circus engagement in Paris. Agents for the forthcoming 1939 World's Fair in New York were scouting attractions in Paris; they engaged Hermines Midgets to appear in a presentation called "Morris Gest's Little Miracle Town," an aggregation of 80 people who were reputed to be the smallest on Earth. The troupe was reengaged for the second season, 1940.

With a worldwide war looming, a return to Europe was neither feasible nor desirable. The troupe acquired an American agent, Dave Solti of Solti & Grund, and Hermines Midgets began touring the USA. Vaudeville was essentially dead, especially for a troupe that carried salaries for at least a dozen performers as well as Bob Hermine and his wife, but personal appearance tours and circuses provided employment.

They joined the Lone Ranger tour that played Chicago, Minneapolis, Detroit, Cleveland and Boston, among other cities, and were added to the Zuhra Shrine Circus bill for other warm-weather dates. Summers were not layoff time for the Hermines. During the 1942 and 1943 seasons they helped fill out bills headlined by Kate Smith and Peter Lorre on the Million Dollar Pier in Atlantic City, New Jersey. The next two summers they undertook extensive tours of all the eastern states from Maine to Georgia with the "World of Mirth Shows." Eventually, they played all but four of the United States in America, as well as Canada and parts of Latin America.

Although there was still a demand for the act through the 1940s and the Second World War, bookings began to thin. There were USO tours of Stateside armed services hospitals, one-shot appearances at war bond rallies and promotional events, scattered theatre dates, even the occasional nightclub engagement. After the conclusion of the war, it became difficult to piece together a coherent and sustained itinerary that was profitable, but members of the troupe toured and appeared on television and in movies into the 1970s, among their films are:

A postwar change in the public's taste led to a major shift in entertainment choices. Popular music and the recording industry became a far more important element of the entertainment industry, and the novelty of television kept potential ticket buyers home, fascinated by the unsteady images of the small screen.

Also developing was a turn away from entertainments that had the hint of the sideshow about them. On the one hand, the incipient sensibility that eventually led to a push for racial equality and civil liberties also led to a sense of embarrassment toward entertainments that presented people as objects of curiosity. On the other hand, show business afforded little people and other former carnival *exhibits* a decent living and the companionship of their special communities.

THE GREAT HERRMANNS

Carl

b: (Compars Herrmann) 23 January 1816, Hanover, Germany—d: 8 June 1887, Carlsbad, Vienna

Alexander

b: 11 February 1843, Paris, France—d: 11 December 1896, en route between Rochester, NY, and Bradford, PA

Adelaide

b: (Adelaide Scarcez) 1852, London, England—d: 19 February 1932, New York, NY

Leon

b: 1867—d: 16 May 1909, Paris, France

The Great Herrmanns were the most famous family in theatre magic in nineteenth-century Europe and America. Eldest brother Carl Herrmann performed from about 1840 until shortly before his death. He toured Europe frequently and made a tour of the USA beginning in New Orleans just as the Civil War erupted. He was persuaded to play major theatres in the northeastern states from 1861 to 1863 before returning to

Adelaide Herrmann, "Queen of Magic"

Europe. Carl Herrmann began his career with grand illusions, but midway he pared down his act to manipulation and witty commentary. He became rich from his theatrical appearances and from his investments, in which he was guided by one of the Rothschilds.

Younger than Carl by 27 years, Alexander Herrmann had built his own career by the time his more famous brother died. In 1869, Alexander capitalized on his brother Carl's appearances six years earlier to make a splash among New York City theatregoers. When Carl returned to the USA later in 1869, Alexander then took his act to London, where he set a record of a thousand consecutive nights of performances at Egyptian Hall. The brothers were friendly and cooperative. When one played Europe, the other took bookings in America. In 1877, Carl returned to Europe and Alexander went back to the USA. This time Alexander was accompanied by Adelaide Scarcez, a dancer, and they wed in New York that year. The Herrmanns continued to tour, and Alexander and Adelaide decided to become citizens of the USA.

Alexander specialized in *close magic,* pulling things from the air. His talent was not confined to the stage, where he obviously had control over the setting and circumstance; he could amaze people by making things materialize from under their noses. He did this at private dinners or for people he met for the first time, those who were famous, like presidents, or ordinary, like shopkeepers and hackney drivers.

Just as Carl simplified his act, Alexander began adding spectacular illusions to his sleight of hand. Adelaide was the subject of his "After the Ball" illusion, in which she disappeared in front of a full-length mirror. Alexander also devised a Svengali and Trilby levitation act, and the "Cremation" act, which saw Adelaide going up in smoke. As his illusions became more spectacular, Alexander Herrmann developed an ever more theatrical stage personality. He enjoyed adopting the personas of Svengali and a mad scientist (who decapitated a man). Alexander looked like his brother Carl. Both were lean with bony faces and wore moustaches and Vandyke beards that gave them a Mephistophelean look.

Unlike Carl, Alexander was a careless investor. He lived in the grand style; his home was palatial, his yacht, large and magnificently appointed, and he traveled to engagements in his luxurious private railway car that once belonged to Jenny Lind. Alexander's act, including his horses, required several more baggage and freight cars. Consequently, when he died en route between shows, Adelaide was left without income or savings. She sent an urgent message to Leon Herrmann, the 29-year-old nephew of both Carl and Alexander. Leon, once his uncle Carl's assistant, was making a name for himself in Europe as a gifted manipulator, and he was Alexander's acknowledged successor. Together with Leon, Adelaide hoped to keep the show on the road.

Leon looked like his uncles. The Herrmann name still meant box office to many theatre managers. The revived "Herrmann the Great Company" starred Adelaide, who performed several illusions and a serpentine dance, and featured Leon, who did his repertoire of tricks and joined Adelaide for a faux Japanese finale. Leon, however, soon demonstrated that he wished to be on his own, and he created an evening-length show that he made available to bookers as "Herrmann the Great." For economic reasons he pared down the act, and he continued to work in American vaudeville and European variety until his death at age 42 in 1909.

Adelaide Herrmann also discovered that she had the makings of a headline variety act in herself. Like her husband, she preferred living and working in the USA, but her elaborate show was a hit in the Folies Bergère, the Wintergarten in Berlin and London's Hippodrome. As she grew older, she grew plumper and ceased to dance. But she hired young women to add dancing to her own feats of illusion. Young women disappeared with a snap of her fingers; Satan materialized in a puff of smoke. A painting of a young woman came to life, danced and returned to canvas and oil. She used many animals in her act: cats, dogs and birds of many

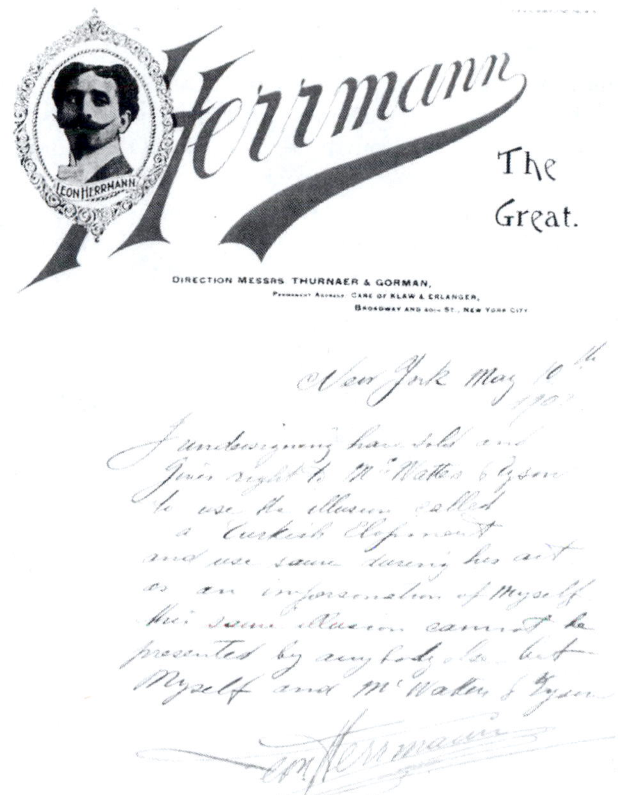

Herrmann The Great.

LEON HERRMANN

DIRECTION MESSRS. THURNAER & GORMAN,
PERMANENT ADDRESS: CARE OF KLAW & ERLANGER,
BROADWAY AND 40TH ST., NEW YORK CITY

New York May 10th 1902

I undersigning have sold and given right to McWatters & Tyson to use the illusion called a Turkish Elopement and use same during his act as an impersonation of Myself this same illusion cannot be presented by any body else but Myself and McWatters & Tyson

Leon Herrmann

1902 letter from Leon Herrmann to Arthur McWatters of McWatters & Tyson granting permission to use "Turkish Elopement"

types. They were caged in a warehouse in 1926 when it burned to the ground. All but three of the 60 animals died in the fire. The Queen of Magic, then in her early 70s, continued to perform her "Magic, Grace and Music" act until 1928 on the Keith-Orpheum circuit.

IRVIN HESS

b: 1894, Reading, PA—d: ca. 1970

The Alco Trio of stage acrobats was managed by Mr. and Mrs. Bard, who owned the act and performed in it. Irvin Hess was the third member. They did an acrobatic and balancing act and played small-time vaudeville and some big-time dates on the Orpheum, Little Orpheum, Interstate and other circuits from about 1910 until 1914, just before the First World War. Perhaps the act broke up when one or more members were inducted into the American Expeditionary Force.

After the war, Hess returned to his birthplace of Reading, Pennsylvania, and from the 1920s into the 1940s he appeared locally in a banjo and piano act.

CHARLES HICKS

b: ca. 1840—d: ca. 1902, Java

Although little is known about Mr. Hicks and no evidence exists that he was directly connected to vaudeville, he provided a place for innumerable African Americans to get their professional start in show business. Hicks, a black man, founded in 1865 what is thought to be the first successful minstrel show run by blacks. He managed to stay in business until 1872, and among his alumni were Billy Kersands, Sam Lucas, Bob Height, Pete Devonear and James A. Bland. Hicks himself was a versatile entertainer, a singer, dancer and comedian, but his history suggests that he was more interested in establishing a black-owned and black-run troupe than in performing himself.

Brooker & Clayton's Georgia Minstrels boasted that theirs was "The Only Simon Pure Negro Troupe in the World." The fact was that Negro jubilee singers and minstrel troupes had been on the road since the mid-1850s, but they failed to prosper or long endure. In 1865, Hicks organized the Brooker & Clayton operation, and he was its business manager during their first season. He quickly left to start his own Georgia Minstrels that same year. Due to Hick's success with his own company, a plethora of Georgia minstrel companies sprouted along the tour routes. It seemed that every former slave and future minstrel man once had worked plantations in Georgia.

Unlike many other black entrepreneurs, Hicks was experienced, and white competitors took serious notice of him. Hicks was the only advance man cited as among the best in his field by Mike Leavitt, a power in show business for 50 years. Many audiences were curious to see the *real Negro*, and Hicks not only capitalized on curiosity, but he also presented great talent.

He was a black man trying to operate in a white business world, but Hicks managed to tour his company across the USA and Canada several seasons and travel to Australia and New Zealand twice, in 1877 and 1888. In so doing, he carved out an international circuit that later was followed by Billy McClain and Ernest Hogan.

In 1872, after seven years of mixed results, Hicks was bought out by Charles Callender, a white impresario. Unlike white producers, Hicks had little access to financing to bridge bad times or expand his shows in good times, nor did he travel in circles that acquainted him with many of the whites who controlled the theatres. Callender was able to offer the Georgia Minstrels better production values and to arrange longer and regular bookings.

Thereafter, Hicks went back to managing various minstrel companies owned by others. Most of these were whites, including Charles Callender, but Hicks was ever eager to try to make black-owned outfits succeed, and he left more secure positions to manage short-lived companies headed by Billy Kersands, himself and others.

He died in 1902 while shepherding one of his now marginal minstrel troupes through Java.

BILLY HIGGINS

ca. 1880–1940

Higgins was listed by Langston Hughes and Milt Meltzer as one of the "Golden Dozen" of great African American comedians. Like Eddie Green, Sandy Burns and Eddie Hunter, Billy served as chief comedian in dozens of vaudeville units, burlesque revues and musicals that toured black theatres above and below the Mason-Dixon line without ever breaking through to white show business as had Bert Williams and Miller & Lyles.

Among the first shows Billy Higgins starred in was *Two Bills from Alaska* (1912–14). Billy King produced, wrote and, with Billy Higgins, played the title roles. Jack "Ginger" Wiggins was the featured hoofer.

Along with James P. Johnson, Gertrude Saunders and Dicky Wells, Higgins starred in the 1924 jazz revue *Cotton Land.* His most famous show was *Hot Chocolates,* also known as *Connie's Hot Chocolates* (1929–30 and revived in 1935), written by Eddie Green.

In 1934, Hurtig & Seamon revived *The Oyster Man,* written by Aubrey Lyles and Flournoy Miller, changed the title to *The Man from Baltimore* and engaged Billy Higgins to play the lead role originated by Ernest Hogan back in 1907–8.

GUS HILL

b: 1858, New York, NY—d: 20 April 1937, New York, NY

An amateur athlete, Gus Hill parlayed his abilities into an early career as a wrestler and then an Indian club twirler. (*Indian clubs* was the popular name for *Kehoe clubs,* so called after their manufacturer.) Hill's gimmick to build up box office was to challenge the locals to a juggling contest in each of the theatres he played as he traveled about the USA. Like a pool hustler, he let the locals win, and he awarded them a medal carrying some spurious citation. On his return route he would challenge past contestants to defend their titles and medals, thus assuring himself of another full house. The second time around, however, Gus Hill vanquished the local heroes, sometimes by trickery.

Hill eventually was awarded a title of questionable merit as "Champion Clubman of the World." He may well have deserved it at the time—some of his clubs were as long as 30 inches and very heavy—but it was known that he sometimes unscrewed the bottoms of his heavier clubs and removed concealed weights before tossing the clubs about with ease. Regardless of its merit, the "Champion Clubman of the World" title was effective billing for variety houses.

Smart, hardheaded and hardworking, early on Gus went into the business end of show business, even as he kept performing for a decade or more. From the 1880s into the 1920s, when Gus was a burlesque and vaudeville entrepreneur, his productions ranged from drama to musical comedy to vaudeville ("Gus Hill's Novelties") to burlesque (*Gus Hill's Aggregation* and *Gus Hill's Stars*). In when 1910s, Gus also underwrote several African American revues and troupes (the Smart Set).

Hill was a founding member of the Columbia Wheel in burlesque. He claimed that he was the pioneer who worked out a circuit of bookings, which included all the big towns in rotation, that became the template for the Columbia Wheel (and for vaudeville as well). At the same time, he had a reputation for producing on the cheap, sending out tacky shows with old costumes and scenery and performers who were inexpensive because they were either on their way up or on their way down.

Later, when the Columbia Wheel was in decline and sending out cut-rate burlesques of hoary old melodramas, Gus Hill created tab shows based on comic strip favorites such as *Mutt & Jeff* and *Bringing Up Father* (Maggie & Jiggs).

Hill insisted he was a burlesquer even though his burlesque shows featured more variety acts than most and consequently were cleaner. A number of top vaudevillians, like Weber & Fields, Montgomery & Stone and Eddie Cantor, got valuable experience playing in Hill shows.

HILTON SISTERS

b: (Violet and Daisy Skinner), 5 February 1908, Brighton, England—d: January 1969, Charlotte, NC

Violet and Daisy Hilton brought into sharp focus one side of the debate about children working in vaudeville. Perhaps no other child act illustrates the extreme of exploitation as does the Hilton Sisters.

At birth, the twins were joined at the hip and lower spine and shared the same blood supply. Their mother, Kate Skinner, an unmarried barmaid, was utterly

Hilton Sisters

unprepared for the responsibility of raising them. Kate sold them to a midwife, Mrs. Mary Hilton, when the babies were two weeks old.

Daisy was blonde and Violet was brunette. Both were beautiful and smart. Early on they learned that if one of them tried to go in one direction and the other went a different way, then neither of them went anywhere. Said Daisy, "I think there are lots of other people that ought to learn that lesson."

The baby girls were instructed to call Mr. and Mrs. Hilton "Sir" and "Auntie." Mrs. Hilton had them singing, reciting and reading at a very early age, and they were traveling and performing by the age of three in various circuses, carnivals and exhibitions. Violet was taught the piano and Daisy the violin, and both eventually received dance lessons. At four they toured Germany, and by five years old they had been to Australia. At age eight, the Hiltons moved to the United States of America.

Many show folk, among them Harry Houdini and Sophie Tucker, tried to befriend the twins, but the Hiltons kept them isolated and intimidated with threats of violence. When they were not touring, the girls lived with the Hilton family in a mansion, paid for by the girls' earnings, in San Antonio, Texas. By the time the girls were 17 they were playing the big-time Orpheum circuit, headlining on the better small time such as Loew's, and earning thousands of dollars a week.

Daisy and Violet saw none of the money, of course. Only when they showed Auntie's daughter, Edith, a critic's review complaining that the girls had outgrown their kiddie act were the young women allowed to go to a beauty parlor and be shorn of their demure little-girl curls. At the same time, they demanded a room of their own, and surprisingly their guardians assented. Violet and Daisy were finding their voices.

When Sir, Mary Hilton's fifth husband, died, Mary married again and became Mrs. Hilton-Meyers. When Mr. Meyers died, his place was filled by Auntie's son-in-law (her daughter Edith's husband), who immediately became the new Sir in the Hilton girls' lives—one they feared more than the original or even Auntie. Mary Hilton-Meyers died shortly thereafter, and Daisy and Violet were informed that Edith and her husband, the new Sir, were their new masters.

In 1931, when they were 23, Violet and Daisy were sued for a quarter of a million dollars as correspondents in a divorce suit involving the advance man for their act. The charge was flimsily based on a publicity photo they had signed with "love and best wishes" to the advance man. Stunned, Sir took them to an attorney, Martin J. Arnold, who, sensing something was wrong, insisted on seeing the twins alone. They jumped at this chance and told the lawyer of their bondage. The attorney managed to free them from their guardians and arranged a settlement of $100,000 for Violet and Daisy. They were free but inexperienced in making decisions.

Harry Houdini had taken a sustained interest in the twins and advised them that they must develop mental independence of each other. They took Houdini's advice and learned to live their own lives; they each had several engagements, and each married. Daisy's marriage ended after only ten days. Her spouse, Harold Estep (whose stage name was Buddy Sawyer), said, "As far as being a bridegroom . . . I suppose I am what you might call a hermit." Violet's marriage was done for publicity and was in name only, ending in annulment after lasting a few years. An earlier engagement of Violet's had ended when her fiancé, who was the act's orchestra leader, Maurice Lambert, was unable to obtain a marriage license. Twenty-one states told him such a marriage would be against morals.

At the height of their careers the Hilton Sisters broke house records and were reputed to earn as much as $5,000 per week, although this was probably an exaggeration. Many in the audience may have attended to gawk, but they applauded because the Hilton Sisters had talent and were a good musical act. They appeared in a classic film, *Freaks* (1932), and a generation later they starred in a cheapie called *Chained for Life* (1950).

The record is spotty toward the end of their stage careers, when they ceased to be a subject of public curiosity. After the Second World War they lived in Pittsburgh, where they may have owned a hotel. They headlined the RKO Palace Theatre in New York for the week of 24 August 1950. In the early 1960s they were reported to be running a fruit stand somewhere in Florida. In 1969, they were working a weighing counter in a suburban supermarket in Charlotte, North Carolina. After missing three days at work, police were sent to their home to investigate. Daisy and Violet were found lying together on the floor, victims of a deadly influenza.

THE HINES BROTHERS

Maurice Hines

b: 1 January 1943, New York, NY

Gregory Oliver Hines

b: 14 February 1946, New York, NY—d: 9 August 2003, Los Angeles, CA

Gregory Hines was the most famous tap dancer of his generation. It was extraordinary for a hoofer of his day—after vaudeville—to become a star, yet he got top billing in Broadway shows and Hollywood movies for a score of years. In the course of his career, Gregory demonstrated a talent for acting and comedy as well as dance.

His older brother Maurice was an equally talented dancer and performer. Both showed to excellent advantage in *Eubie* (1978–79), a Broadway revue celebrating Eubie Blake, the African American vaudevillian and composer. Maurice and Gregory were at home with the songs, skits and style of dancing in *Eubie* because they were part of the last flowering of the old vaudeville tradition.

When somebody offered free tap-dance lessons to kids in their neighborhood, their mother, Alma, encouraged Maurice to take them. He in turn passed on what he learned to his little brother, Gregory. The brothers went on to study with Henry LeTang, a top-notch dancer, choreographer and teacher.

Alma regarded the training as good discipline and a positive alternative to hanging out on the streets. Maurice and Gregory began dancing professionally at age eight and five, respectively, as the Hines Kids. They played black theatres on bills led by well-known bands, such as Lionel Hampton's, or recording stars. They are reputed to have performed at the Apollo on several occasions as the Hines Brothers. In 1964, when they were in their teens, their father, Maurice Sr., a drummer, joined them, and Hines, Hines & Dad played clubs and theatres.

Rhythm and blues and rock 'n' roll had supplanted jazz and Tin Pan Alley pop as the music of the times. Gregory grew increasingly interested in rock music and identified with the cultural changes of the 1960s. He also tired of the constant touring, and the act broke up. Gregory moved to upstate New York and to Venice, California, and made a life away from dance. For a while he tried writing rock music and performing with a band, Severance. Maurice, a jazz devotee, stayed in New York and worked Broadway shows.

Gregory discovered that the hippie lifestyle did not work for him, and he responded to his brother's suggestion that he return to Manhattan and try out for *The Last Minstrel Show.* It closed on the road, yet the experience was enough to refocus Gregory. Maurice and Gregory became prominent members in the cast of *Eubie* (1978–79) and *Sophisticated Ladies* (1981–83)—both shows choreographed by their former teacher, Henry LeTang. Those were not their first Broadway shows. Back in 1954, they had had small parts and a number in *The Girl in Pink Tights.*

By the 1980s, the two brothers again had individual careers. Gregory preferred working on the West Coast, although he came east for several Broadway shows, most notably *Jelly's Last Jam,* for which he won a Tony Award as best leading actor in a musical. His movies included Mel Brooks' *History of the World: Part I* (1981), *The Cotton Club* (1984) with Maurice, *White Nights* (1985), *Running Scared* (1986), *Tap* (1989) and *Bojangles* (2001), among the best remembered of more than three dozen films and several television series. He died of liver disease at 57, leaving behind several children, his father and his brother.

Third and fourth from the left, Maurice and Gregory Hines with Hines, Hines & Brown

Maurice remained a well-known Broadway performer, and he branched into teaching and devising choreography for Broadway musicals.

HIPPODROME

Various theatres in different places across the USA were called Hippodrome, but the one erected on Sixth Avenue that covered the entire 240-foot block between 43rd and 44th Streets was *the* Hippodrome. It was not New York's first; a far more modest hippodrome had existed in the nineteenth century near Madison Square. The popularity of circuses, spectacles, extravaganzas and pantomimes had caused other large theatres to be constructed in Manhattan, but the new Hippodrome that opened 12 April 1905 dwarfed all predecessors.

Press agents trumpeted the Hippodrome as the most spectacular theatre ever built, and for once the characterization was not hyperbole. The Hippodrome stage, 200 feet wide and 110 feet deep, was a dozen times larger than any other in New York at the time. It could support hundreds of performers plus automobiles and elephants, camels, horses, lions, bloodhounds and any other large animals that could be rounded up and added to the spectacle.

It was not merely monumental; the Hippodrome was revolutionary. Electric lights had already turned Manhattan's rialto into the Great White Way, but lighting at the Hippodrome was an indoor wonder as well. The lighting board was 30 feet tall; hydraulic lifts could raise or lower portions of the stage. The stage floor could be rolled back to reveal a water tank the size of an Olympic swimming pool into which lovely young ladies dove and were not seen again. (They swam out through chambers to emerge into the backstage.) The water scenes were both pastoral, as waterfalls cascaded into the pool, and dramatic, as machinery stirred the water into waves. Under the stage, in the bowels of the theatre, the animals were caged in lightless pens.

The exterior of the Hipp, as it was familiarly called, looked like a Victorian brick fortress topped with an Arabian Nights palace. Inside, the auditorium seating was divided into orchestra, mezzanine and balcony, and its 5,200 seats could be augmented to 7,000, as was the case when most of the stage was filled with audience members for a concert by John Charles Thomas, a baritone with a light classics repertoire and a tremendous following in the 1910s. Houdini, Bessie McCoy, Belle Story, Carmella Ponselle, Chaliapin and De Wolf Hopper all played Sunday concerts at the Hipp.

In addition to the theatre, there were arcades, cafés, lounges and lobbies. Spanning the entire theatre space was a huge shallow dome, studded with thousands of electric light bulbs, held in place by four enormous and concealed steel girders. An elephant's head provided a design motif that was repeated throughout the building; some had tusks that ended in electric bulbs.

The Hippodrome was a dream realized by Frederic Thompson, Elmer S. "Skip" Dundy, and John W. "Bet-a-Million" Gates. Thompson and Dundy were competitors turned partners in a series of expositions that had become popular drawing cards after the success of the Columbian Exposition at Chicago's 1893 World's Fair. Thompson, a rather private man, had trained as an architect and was skilled at turning fantastical notions into profitable exhibits. Dundy,

1918–19 Hippodrome souvenir program

The Hippodrome

a politician and canny businessman, was a forceful promoter and wheeler-dealer. They sunk every cent they had and could borrow into a venture on Coney Island they called Luna Park. Its success emboldened Dundy to look toward Broadway.

He attracted the backing of Gates. Initially reluctant but reassured by Gates' backing and the promise of realizing a new dream, Thompson designed a venue for extravaganza and spectacle based on the indoor European circuses or hippodromes but far more vast. It was Gates who financed the $4 million to build, equip and appoint—a tremendous expenditure at the turn of the twentieth century.

To keep the Hippodrome open, the estimated cost was more than $5,000 a day, and that without returning a cent of Gates' investment. The expenditure allowed little margin for error in judgment or management. Trouble came early on and John Wayne Gates fired Thompson and Dundy as managers; Thompson's parade of stupendous scenes of fairylands, outer space and gardens studded with dozens of water fountains failed to pay the bills.

The Shubert Brothers took over in 1906 and made the place profitable for the next nine years with a series of less lush spectacles (created by Arthur Voegtlin) that relied on the novelty of seeing ship battles, baseball exhibitions, dirigibles landing and balloons ascending.

The format for much of the Hippodrome's existence was the three-part show: a first act melodrama with special effects, a second act fancy ballet and an adventure fantasy to close. It was not a place for vaudeville, but some notable vaudevillians appeared on its stage. Marceline, a true European clown, was brought to the Hippodrome by Thompson and Dundy, and he stayed for a number of years. Toto, another of the great clowns, was a later favorite.

The water tank provided the perfect place for Annette Kellerman, her graceful swimming and her one-piece bathing suit. Pavlova danced in candy box settings of ballets. Vernon & Irene Castle danced to the full blare of John Philip Sousa's Marching Band. Nat Wills, the tramp comedian, almost lost in the wide-open spaces, told his shaggy dog stories.

The Shuberts had made the Hippodrome pay, but they had not invested in it. The need to refurbish the house was obvious to Charles B. Dillingham and his lieutenant, R.H. Burnside, who took over the lease. Burnside, with Dillingham's backing, proceeded to stage musicals, revues and wartime Sunday benefits despite the lack of intimacy and the crushing continuing expenses needed to keep the Hippodrome's doors open. Dillingham, who perennially flirted with bankruptcy, managed to hold on to the Hippodrome until 1923.

E. F. Albee took over and saved the Hippodrome for a few years. He gutted a lot of the hydraulics and the water tank and made the stage area smaller and more suitable for vaudeville. Albee booked a lot of circus acts—tumblers, aerialists, acrobats and animal acts—and staged production numbers with ballets or chorus lines. He added movies and installed a "Toytown" in the basement where kids could wander, supervised, while their parents watched the vaudeville show.

Hippodrome program

Albee lost control in 1928 and died in 1930. Management at RKO, the successor corporation to Keith-Albee Orpheum, had wrested control away from Albee and was not interested in live performance; it was in the business of talking motion pictures and network radio, among other new technologies. The Hippodrome was demolished in 1930.

RAYMOND HITCHCOCK

b: 22 October 1865, Auburn, NY— d: 24 November 1929, Beverly Hills, CA

Sometime around the year 1884, future vaudeville headliner, Broadway star and producer Raymond Hitchcock appeared in the very first Keith-Albee production, a cheapjack, hour-long tab show version of Gilbert & Sullivan's *Mikado* produced by the then newly forged team of Benjamin Franklin Keith and Edward Franklin

Raymond Hitchcock

Albee. At the time, Gilbert & Sullivan's scripts and music were not copyrighted in the USA, so, when their operettas proved popular with American audiences, the shows became game for the ambitious and the unscrupulous. Albee convinced Keith that throwing together a stripped-down and abbreviated *Mikado* and offering it for two bits would successfully bite into the business the nearby legitimate, full-length production was enjoying with seats at $1.50. For Keith and Albee it was a major step in their pursuit of a vaudeville empire. For Raymond, just a dancer in the *Mikado*'s chorus, the experience was one small first step on the small-time treadmill.

Working as a chorus dancer held little promise of stardom for anyone. For Hitch, as he was universally called, it frequently led to other employment—as a scrub man in a barbershop and a shoe store clerk. In an interview with critic Ashton Stevens, Hitch spoke about serving time in prison. So obscure, indifferently received and intermittent were Hitch's early efforts in show business that at least one notable and reliable theatre historian has written that Hitchcock did not begin his stage career until he was 25 in 1890.

That was the year the Casino Theatre sought to stimulate its sagging box-office takings by launching a program of revivals. Oddly, but successfully, they chose the fading form of opéra bouffe. Press and public interest was rekindled by richly mounted productions, stellar casts (with actors such as Lillian Russell), witty translation into English and lively direction that did not blink at impudent interpolations or a brisk farcical style.

Raymond Hitchcock first attracted attention in the Casino's production of Offenbach's *Les Brigands* (advertised as *The Brigands*) in 1890. When the star got sick and withdrew while the show was still on the road, Hitch was given the lead. He brought the show into New York with such success that he was offered a featured role in the new English import, *Charley's Aunt* (1893), by Brandon Thomas. The play became a hardy perennial on Broadway and in little theatres everywhere for many decades.

Two successful shows did nothing to insulate Hitch from some flops, but it did guarantee that he was cast in about one Broadway production a year between 1889 and 1916. Most toured for a while, ran a month or two on Broadway and, if successful, toured again, providing nearly a season's work in most cases. Several were hits, and they all starred Hitch: *King Dodo* (1902), *The Yankee Consul* (1904) and three shows for George M. Cohan, *The Man Who Owned Broadway* (1909), *The Red Widow* (1911–12) and *The Beauty Shop* (1914).

Cohan was the man Hitch most admired, both for George M.'s easy confidence on the stage and because he had taken charge of his career by becoming his own producer, playwright and songwriter. Hitch decided to emulate Cohan, and he produced his shows under the Cohen and Sam Harris umbrella. Between 1917 and 1920, Hitch raised the money to produce four revues. But before he produced those revues, he tried Hollywood.

At various times, Mack Sennett had under contract Roscoe Arbuckle, Mabel Normand, Charlie Chaplin, Polly Moran, Harold Lloyd, Louise Fazenda, Ben Turpin, Harry Langdon and most of the other physical comedians who invigorated movie comedies of the 1910s and early 1920s. None of the weekly salaries of these stars and future stars ever exceeded a few hundred dollars a week while in Sennett's employ, yet he repeatedly paid thousands of dollars a week to stage comedians like Eddie Foy, Weber & Fields, De Wolf Hopper, Marie Dressler and others to appear in his two-reelers. None of them proved nearly as successful as the homegrown Keystone comedians.

Although under contract to the Lubin motion picture studio, Hitch was apparently able to free himself and, in May 1915, he agreed to make several short comedies for Mack Sennett, an old acquaintance from Sennett's days on the stage. First, however, Hitchcock needed to fulfill a contract to appear in several shorts at the Lubin studio.

Raymond Hitchcock made five films for Sennett in 1915, and while some critics enjoyed them, there was no demand to make more. Hitch turned his attention to producing and starring in *Hitchy-Koo* (1917). As insurance, he hired Leon Errol as his costar and stage director. Errol had staged several revues for Ziegfeld, and for Hitchcock Leon devised choreography, directed the sketches and paced the overall revue.

Errol, then near the peak of his stage career, was not inexpensive, nor were other performers in the show: vaudeville team William Rock & Francis White, Irene Bordoni and Grace La Rue. *Hitchy-Koo* was a whopping success on Broadway (200 performances) and on the road—without La Rue and Rock & Williams, who chose not to tour. Talent costs were so high that even with full houses, Hitch did little but break even. Undeterred, Hitch produced five more shows, including three more editions of *Hitchy-Koo* (1918, 1919 and 1920). None of them fared well on Broadway, but on tour they recouped at least part of their investment.

Hitch's revues seemed more informal than they really were. There was a convivial quality about them, with Hitch gathering the audience to his bosom like a good host. He emceed his shows—talking to the audience and even leaving the stage to go into the audience to greet some friends or stray customers who caught his eye. Sometimes he joined the audience in an aisle seat from which he introduced a few acts. He seldom told jokes; he won his laughs with bemused commentary. His seemingly casual style carried over into his acting in the comedy sketches.

During the late 1910s and the 1920s, Hitchcock appeared more frequently in vaudeville than he had earlier in his career. He played the Palace several times between 1918 and 1927, but as the 1920s gathered pace, Hitch was judged to be a little too laid-back for the times.

In his mid-50s by 1920, Hitch let go of producing—after one last disastrous fling in 1922, *Raymond Hitchcock's Pinwheel.* He contented himself with drawing a reliable and fine salary as a star in the *Ziegfeld Follies of 1921* and *Hazard Short's Ritz Revue* (1924). He appeared in a few more Broadway productions that were not successes. With the exceptions of a few occasional appearances, Raymond Hitchcock retired with Flora Zabelle, his wife of 25 years, to his Los Angeles home, where he died at age 64.

HODGKINS LYRIC VAUDEVILLE CIRCUIT

Comprising about a dozen theatres in the Southwest, Hodgkins Lyric was among the smallest of small-time circuits.

GERTRUDE HOFFMAN

b: (Gertrude "Kitty" Hayes) ca. 1880, Canada or San Francisco, CA—d: ca. 1955

Billed as Kitty Hayes, the future Gertrude Hoffman made her debut in San Francisco as an "extra girl" at Frederic Belasco's Alcazar Theatre. She married music composer Max Hoffman, and they had a son, Max Jr. (1902–45), who later became a bit player in many Hollywood movies.

A patrician beauty and talented in many areas, Gertrude quickly made it to Broadway. By 1903, she shared the bill (as Gertrude Hay Hoffman) with Josie (Josephine) Sabel in *Punch Judy & Co.,* a revue promoted as an *extravaganza.* It played the Paradise Roof Garden atop Oscar Hammerstein's Victoria Theatre. Gertrude devised the dances for the show, and Oscar produced and wrote the words and music. Later in 1903, she joined Louis Harrison, Blanche Ring and Billy B. Van in George Lederer's production of *The Jersey Lily.* The musical comedy played a few weeks in September and October at Hammerstein's Victoria before going out on tour.

Gertrude composed the music for several songs for *When We Were Forty-One* (March 1905), a New York Theatre Roof revue that starred Elsie Janis, Emma Carus and Mlle. LaBelle Dazie. One song bore the intriguing title "Kindly Pass the Chloroform Along." In May she was engaged as dance director for a production of a musical, *Me Him and I,* that opened in Chicago (June 1905). That fall, Gertrude directed the dances for the Marie Cahill musical *Moonshine* (1905), which played the Liberty Theatre on Broadway from late November.

Gertrude danced "La Mattchiche" in the musical comedy *A Parisien Model* (1906), and her husband Max composed much of the music. Ziegfeld produced it as a showcase for his lover, Anna Held, and Julian Mitchell directed. Oddly, Gus Hoffman was listed as

Gertrude Hoffman

the lyricist for several songs and Gertrude wrote music for a few novelty songs. In 1907, Gertrude had a major role in George M. Cohan's musical *The Honeymooners,* which ran a couple of months.

Gertrude Hoffman created a sensation in 1909 when she became the first person to perform a Salomé dance in American vaudeville. That same year, Oscar Hammerstein had staged a production of Richard Strauss' one-act opera *Salomé.* Hoffman created the "Dance of Salomé" for bookings in vaudeville; she possessed the exotic appearance, dancing ability and theatricality needed to make it more than a tent show turn. Her version sparked an uproar: there was censure from the pulpits and a rush to the box office.

Many dancers, including good ones like Maud Alan and Ruth St. Denis, claimed to have performed the first Salomé dance, but if they did, it was while they toured in Europe. Maud Allan's claim is justified; she performed the dance a year earlier, 1908, in London. Vaude headliners Eva Tanguay and Aida Overton Walker did other early versions of Salomé. Many other claimants were just jumped-up hootchy-kootchy dancers. They would not have known Salomé from a salesman until they saw newspapers filled with publicity photos of Gertrude, but the ladies of the midway knew how to shed seven veils. The imitations grew so numerous that many theatre managers banned them, and trade papers called for their end.

Vaudeville meant touring away from her family. In Manhattan, Gertrude had a growing boy and a husband whose work was writing music for stage shows. To be with them, she agreed to join the cast of *Broadway to Paris* (1912), a revue with songs by Max Hoffman. The other stars were Louise Dresser, Doyle & Dixon, Irene Bordoni and James C. Morton. It ran for 77 performances.

She also took vaudeville dates close to home, such as the Palace, where she was billed as one of the top acts in 1915. Salomé was no longer part of Gertrude Hoffman's vaudeville act of the mid-1910s. She did impersonations of well-known stage personalities, an informal segment that brought her in closer contact with her audiences, but dance remained central to her act. Often she headed a flash act, surrounding herself with other dancers and a splendid-looking scenic drop and drapery.

Hoffman did several styles of dancing. The balletic turns that she choreographed for herself and a corps de ballet (the nucleus of the future Gertrude Hoffman Girls) were short and relied on familiar symbols of ballet like swans or the Grecian free form promoted by Isadora Duncan. Interpretive dances had been part of Gertrude's dance repertoire since her old Salomé number. Perhaps she was influenced by Ruth St. Denis and her dance meditations based on the arts and religions of Egypt, India and Japan. If so, it proves that Gertrude was more aware of a wider range of dance than most dancers and dance directors. Theatre dance of the 1910s was especially reliant on drill formations, which Hoffman dancers did exceedingly well.

Too much can be made of Gertrude's being influenced by other dancers. She has been called a copyist or even a plunderer of others' genius. Underlying that criticism in part was snobbishness. It was hard for those who looked to high art as the font of creativity to accept that anything artistic and original could come out of vaudeville. There is gray area between slavish imitation and being part of a movement toward a national dance style or exposing a national audience to dance from many cultures. After the fact, some balletomanes accused Hoffman of poaching on Serge Diaghilev's territory, of stealing the Ballets Russes' thunder by mounting, in concert with her manager Morris Gest (1881–1942), a touring program of Russian ballet before the arrival of the Ballets Russe in 1914. The Ballet Russe at the time was more a modern European company in its music, design and subject matter than it was a classical ballet company from the days of czarist Russia. The training and dance style of ballet remained mostly Russian, yet with a growing French influence, but the dance conceptions ranged ever wider—to Asia, Africa and Arabia—for inspiration. Serious dancers in the USA were interested in Russian Imperial ballet, and, conversely, Diaghilev's Ballets Russes was interested in the contemporary revolutions in music composition, painting and dance.

Gertrude Hoffman and her agent and sometimes partner, Morris Gest, tried for several years to bring some Russian company to the USA. Nothing got settled. The Metropolitan Opera negotiated with Diaghilev but his company was in turmoil. Nijinsky had married, and Diaghilev and Bakst in pique vowed to ban him. Massine replaced choreographer Fokine and dancer/choreographer Nijinsky.

The First World War in Europe made hash of Diaghilev's bookings and schedules, and Nijinsky, whom the American contracts specified must star, was interred in Austria, his wife's homeland. Neither the 1915 tour that began and ended at the Metropolitan Opera, after 15 play dates on the road, nor a subsequent USA tour, headed by Nijinsky, showed the Ballets Russes at its best. Ballets Russes experts Charles Spencer and Philip Dyer reported that "the [Nijinsky] season ended in chaos."

Gest and Hoffman hired their own Russian-trained dancers and put them on tour. They were greeted favorably: the "marvelous Russian ballet is truly a sporting speculation, and the biggest enterprise yet attempted in that line. The magnificence of its scenery and costumes and the accuracy of its realism make it a spectacular presentation of the highest order."

In 1917, Gertrude was back on less arty boards when she joined a stellar cast of Leon Errol, Joe Jackson and Van & Schenck for an Irving Berlin revue satirically titled *Dance and Grow Thin.* The revue was produced at the Cocoanut Grove, the Century Theatre's roof garden. After it closed, Hoffman seemed to disappear from view until 1923. Probably, Gertrude returned to vaudeville with her own act and toured for a few seasons.

Gertrude's next engagement to be found in the annals is a tour with Harry Lauder in his revue *Hello Everybody* (1923). By the mid-1920s, she was in her mid-40s, and she began concentrating on creating acts and revue numbers for a dance ensemble she called the Gertrude Hoffman Girls. They danced in *Artists and Models* (1925), a Shubert revue that played the huge Winter Garden from 24 June 1925 throughout the following 1925–26 season for a total of 416 performances. It was Gertrude's most successful show, even though she herself did not perform. The Winter Garden success led to two more productions for the Shuberts: the Gertrude Hoffman Girls danced in *A Night in Paris* (1926), which ran a year, and *A Night in Spain* (1927), which ran about six months.

Gertrude Hoffman slipped out of theatre history after the late 1920s. There were reports that she opened a school on the West Coast and coached some dancers. There has also been a great deal of confusion regarding three different women in show business with the same name. In addition to the vaudeville Gertrude, there was a character actor, Gertrude Hoffman (1871–1965), who sometimes used a middle initial of V or W to distinguish herself from "that kootchie dancer." Gertrude V. Hoffman entered Hollywood movies in 1933 at age 62, made three dozen films and a TV series, *My Little Margie,* and died in her 90s. The evidence for a third Gertrude Hoffman is less certain. She spelled her name *Hoffmann* and occasionally used *Trude* instead of *Gertrude;* she appeared in at least nine silent films made in Germany between 1918 and 1921. Oddly, these three years are the same years that vaudeville's Gertrude Hoffman's career in the USA seemed to be on hiatus.

THINK-A-DRINK-HOFFMAN

b: (Charles Hoffman) 1895—d: ca. 1965

Hoffman was a stage magician with a line of patter and a narrow specialty. Occasionally billed as "The Highest Paid Bartender in the World," he produced a variety of drinks on request for his audiences. From a single cocktail shaker he poured wines, beers and, according to his press materials, 80 different alcoholic drinks on demand. His stage equipment consisted of a small bar, over which he presided impeccably dressed in white tie and black tails. He looked every inch the stage magician, from his pomaded hair and trimmed mustache to sharply creased trousers and highly polished shoes.

Hoffman first came to prominence in the 1930s and remained a popular act in vaudeville during the 1940s, although little is known about him. He also appeared in nightclubs and revues, such as *Streets of Paris* (1939–40), which starred Bobby Clark and introduced Abbott & Costello to Broadway, and *Curtain Time* (1941), a West Coast revue.

There was a debate about how much of Hoffman's act was genuine. Like all magicians, he had tricks; one cocktail shaker could not produce liquids of varying colors and viscosity unless the shaker contained several compartments and mechanisms that released what was called for and held back the rest.

It was speculated that Hoffman employed plants in the audience to request specific drinks and then verify that what Hoffman produced was the real McCoy. This seems especially likely given that Hoffman, at some period in his career, added mind reading to his act and appeared to divine exactly the drink requested by given members of the audience.

Hoffman occasionally played British variety. He had a European rival, De Roze, who produced on request all manner of beverages—milk, soda pop and alcoholic mixed drinks—from pitchers of clear water.

ERNEST HOGAN

b: (Reuben Crowders or Crowdus) 1860 or 1865, Bowling Green, Kentucky—d: 20 May 1909, Lakewood, NJ

The first African American star on Broadway was not Bert Williams, as is popularly thought, but Ernest Hogan, a comedy star of several musicals for which he wrote some songs. One of those songs, "All Coons Look Alike to Me," written in 1896, was a great hit, but to the end of his days Hogan regretted writing it, despite the royalty of $10,000 that the sale of one million copies of sheet music earned him. The publisher, Witmark, claimed it was the first ragtime song to be available in sheet music, and its success prompted a rash of *coon songs* by black and white songsmiths.

According to Tom Fletcher, a contemporary black performer and esteemed chronicler of *100 Years of the Negro in Show Business*, "The fact remains, however, that ragtime was discovered, put on paper and introduced to the people of the United States by a colored man by the name of Reuben Crowders who was known to the world as Ernest Hogan."

Hogan's "coon song" was suggested by a ditty played and sung by a black piano player in a saloon. His girlfriend had dismissed him with the snipe that "all pimps look alike to me." Hogan adapted music and lyrics, changing one forbidden word for another that he thought less explosive. The song was a duet sung by a suitor and the "dusky damsel" who rejected him in favor of another, implying that all men other than her beloved looked alike. Among the three dozen or so Hogan songs that were published were "La Pas Ma La," "My Gal's de Town Talk," and "I Love My Honey," but it was his *coon song* that took ragtime in a new and often derogatory direction.

Ernest Hogan was a child when he first went traveling with shows: most likely in Uncle Tom companies or as a *pickaninny* with musical acts. Later he joined Black Patti's Troubadours and Pringle's Georgia Minstrels. Minstrel shows run by Negroes for Negroes were still rare when he entered show business, and indeed, some "colored" shows like Black Patti's had white producers. A few black minstrel shows had cautiously emerged out of the shadows before the Civil War, and the number began to multiply afterward. In those days an entertainer was expected to be able to dance, sing, speak lines and play the clown. It was good training for the complete performer and, before the rise of black vaudeville, the best work an aspiring Negro variety performer could get.

Although Reuben Crowders changed his name to Ernest Hogan because the most popular minstrel men were Irish, he played mostly in black-managed, all-Negro minstrel shows for many seasons until he was able to find stardom in black vaudeville and musical comedy. He was an eccentric dancer who evolved into a comedian and comic actor.

In the early 1890s, Hogan toured Negro theatres and tents each season. In 1891 he formed Eden & Hogan's Minstrels with a partner, and the show toured out of Chicago. In 1896 he moved to New York but went out on the road with the Georgia Graduates until late in 1897, when he was hired as the lead comedian in *Black Patti's Troubadours.* About this time Hogan began advertising himself as "The Unbleached American."

Hogan's greatest opportunity came when he returned to New York. On 5 July 1898, Hogan starred in the landmark musical comedy *Clorindy, or the Origin of the Cake Walk.* Originally conceived as a full-length piece for Williams & Walker, with music composed by Will Marion Cook and book and lyrics by black poet Paul Laurence Dunbar, it ended up as a 45-minute tab show, all songs and comedy without Dunbar's story.

Cook had tried to interest the Casino Theatre's new manager, Ed Rice, in *Clorindy.* Cook got the brush-off. With the help of the Casino's white musical director, John Braham, Cook and his cast auditioned their show. Not only did it get booked on the Casino's Roof, but Braham deferred to Cook to conduct the Casino orchestra.

Competing claims have been made for various black productions as the first to play Broadway. In 1896, *Oriental America* played the Palmer Theatre, a Broadway house, but the show was devised, owned and managed by a white man, John W. Isham. In 1897, Cole & Johnson wrote, produced and starred in *A Trip to Coontown,* which reached Jacob's Third Avenue Theatre in 1898, but Third Avenue was as much Broadway as a Harlem or Brooklyn theatre. A few months later in 1898, *Clorindy,* created by and starring African Americans, played the Casino Theatre's Roof. That was certainly on Broadway (though rather high above it), making *Clorindy, or the Origin of the Cake Walk* uncontested as the first truly black show to reach Broadway.

Hogan followed his success in *Clorindy* with a stint in John W. Isham's production of *Octoroons.* Then, in 1899, he went to Philadelphia to star in *Captain Kidd.* He was the only black actor among more than 100 white cast members.

Will Marion Cook and Paul Laurence Dunbar reunited for another one-act musical, *Jes Lak White Folks* (1900), which they intended as a vehicle for Ernest Hogan. At the time, however, Hogan was otherwise engaged. When M. B. Curtis, a producer, put together a revue to send to Australia, he persuaded Hogan to join Billy McClain as stars of his cast. Two weeks before the arrival of M. B. Curtis' African American Minstrels, however, Australia had already welcomed O. M. McAdoo's Minstrels and Cakewalkers, and other black minstrels were roaming Australia as well. The upshot was that the Curtis troupe, although critically successful, was following McAdoo's company along the circuits. Disappointing box office meant that Curtis could not pay salaries. McClain joined the competition, McAdoo, and Curtis fled with the remaining funds. Hogan was left holding the empty bag.

Ernest rallied, reorganized the troupe as Ernest Hogan's Minstrels and picked up enough play dates, primarily in Brisbane, throughout the winter to earn passage to Hawaii. In Honolulu, which they reached in March, they made enough money to buy their steamship tickets back to the USA. When their ship refused to allow them to board because they were Negroes, and the steamship line would not refund their tickets, the company again was stranded. Honolulu had seen their show, so Hogan buckled down and wrote three new shows, each playing two weeks, until they made enough for passage and found a ship that would transport them back to the USA. They had been away the better part of a year.

In 1900, Ernest Hogan headlined in white vaudeville at Hammerstein's Victoria and the Winter Garden.

But while he was starring in white vaudeville, a small fracas turned into a full-scale and prolonged race riot. Some whites were rioting on the streets, angry that the blacks migrating northward were competing for manual labor jobs and, as they saw it, threatening to flood New York with their numbers.

Harlem had been marketed to black people by real estate speculators who earlier had failed to entice whites to the uptown area of Manhattan. Harlem became a destination of choice for the Negroes fleeing the Jim Crow South. Whites attacked Negro citizens and looked for prominent blacks, such as Ernest Hogan, Bert Williams and George Walker, to batter and perhaps kill. One evening the mob spotted Hogan and Walker walking together. The two escaped after a harrowing chase. Some reports claim that Hogan was hurt badly. In any case, Hogan left town for a few months. It was about that time that Hogan married a young singer, Mattie Wilkes, whom he may have met through Walker when she was performing in the Williams & Walker show *The Policy Players* in 1899.

He returned in 1901 to play a record 40 weeks on the New York Roof Theatre. A year later, Hogan partnered with actor, dancer, writer and producer Billy McClain in a new show, *The Smart Set,* underwritten by white producer Gus Hill. *The Smart Set* toured for years. McClain soon left the show, and Hogan shepherded the show on the road as well as headlined. In 1904, S.H. Dudley, a vaudeville comedian and producer, took over the reins of the *Smart Set* tour.

In 1905, Will Dixon, a black music conductor, and Ernest Hogan assembled the Memphis Students, a collection of fine black acts, both musical and comedic. The ensemble played top vaudeville houses, including Proctor's 23rd Street Theatre and Hammerstein's Victoria, and then went on tour. It went to Europe as the Tennessee Students, an ensemble of 17 performers who sang and played instruments. Hogan was chief comedian, Ida Forsyne and Henry Williams danced, and Abbe Mitchell, a singer with a lovely trained voice, was the soubrette.

Musician Joe Jordon had come to New York, where he worked, off and on beginning in 1902, with Hogan on the score for *Rufus Rastus.* The librettist was William D. Hall, and Frank Williams was credited with lyrics. Hurtig & Seamon produced *Rufus Rastus,* which played on Broadway from 1905 into 1906 and then toured into 1907. It provided Ernest Hogan with his greatest success. He played a Negro actor trying to survive with a series of menial jobs as he looked for work on the stage. The script provided many comic opportunities that Hogan fully exploited. His character was desperate and subversive, certainly a first for white audiences—and for black comedians. *Rufus Rastus* brought Hogan to the peak of his career.

While the show was on tour in 1907, two young college boys, Flournoy Miller and Aubrey Lyles, avid fans of vaudeville and Ernest Hogan, approached Hogan while he was playing the Pekin Theatre in Chicago. The boys had written a sketch called *The Oyster Man.* With Hogan's support, Miller and Lyles expanded their sketch into the book for Hogan's next musical. With music by Will Vodery and lyrics by Henry Creamer and Lester Walton, *The Oyster Man* (aka *The Oysterman*) opened at the Fourteenth Street Theatre on 25 November 1907. Perhaps to increase revenue by playing larger theatres, the show played the subway circuit for a few weeks before heading on the road in late December. But Hogan was ailing. Second banana John Rucker took his place almost immediately. Hogan returned to the show for its Boston dates and collapsed. The producers closed the show.

Although Hogan was notable as a songwriter and a producer, his real importance is as a comedian. Hogan was a transitional figure in black entertainment. During his career, he had shifted away from the simpleminded buffoon, modeled on the white minstrel show's portrayal of blacks, toward a character that was more resourceful and assertive. The next two generations of black comedians, Bert Williams & George Walker and Flournoy Miller & Aubrey Lyles, established the semidependent relationship between two buddies, one sharp and the other dim, both believable. It was akin to the dynamic between Dutch comics Lew Fields and Joe Weber.

In 1908, the cream of the Negro entertainment world assembled in tribute to Ernest Hogan. Among those honoring him were Bob Cole, Bert Williams and his partner, George W. Walker. Within three years, Cole, Walker and Hogan were dead. Not only were they all-around theatrical talents, they were three of the leading comedians of their day. Hogan died of tuberculosis in a sanitarium in 1909.

It may be that, at the time, there was room for only one big Negro comic star in mainstream American show business. Bert Williams started his decade-long career with Florenz Ziegfeld in the *Follies of 1910.* Yet, had Hogan lived longer, there might have been two great Negro comedians helping to usher in a new era of top-notch vaudeville, revue and silent-films comedians. Had Bob Cole, George Walker and Ernest Hogan survived, black musical comedy might not have retreated from mainstream stages until 1921, when Miller & Lyles teamed with Noble Sissle & Eubie Blake to invigorate the art form and bring Broadway a great hit, *Shuffle Along* (1921), which prompted dozens of imitations.

Both Bert Williams and Ernest Hogan were well liked by other black performers, and their contemporaries were divided between them as to who was the greater artist. Surprisingly, music historians David A. Jasen and Gene Jones credit Hogan for combining pathos with comedy and having more bite than Bert Williams. In *Spreadin' Rhythm Around,* Jasen and Jones reported the view of some of Hogan's peers. Dancer Ida Forsyne claimed that "Bert Williams had just one style, but Ernest Hogan was great—he was really ingenious." Flournoy Miller deemed Hogan "the greatest of all colored showmen." For stride pianist Luckey Roberts, Ernest Hogan was "the greatest performer I ever saw."

The point is not who was better, Hogan or Williams. Rather than honoring one of them, and insulting him at the same time as though he were a single aberrant display of genius among black Americans of his day, the object is to recognize that dozens of fine black comedians reached an admirable level of artistry when only two generations earlier, most African Americans had been enslaved.

HOKUM

Corny, old-fashioned and familiar gags, devices and bits that might play in the sticks to rural audiences but were expected to flop with more sophisticated audiences were dismissed as hokum. Derived from *oakum,* fibrous pieces picked apart from old woven ropes used to caulk wooden ships, the term referred to ancient gags or pieces of business that were often reused.

LOU HOLTZ

b: 11 April 1893, San Francisco, CA—
d: 22 September 1980, Beverly Hills, CA

Lou Holtz was a vaudeville comedian who specialized in Jewish dialect routines. He became a headliner in the two-a-day, starred in a number of revues and survived into the era of presentation houses. After vaudeville was declared dead, he successfully took his act into nightclubs, but radio, movies and television failed to transmit his charm.

In his act, Holtz usually told stories about Sam Lapidus, a down-to-earth Jewish man. Another of Holtz's characters was called the Maharajah, whose ersatz Hindi doubletalk was rendered into English by Holtz, playing both parts, thus giving Lou two laughs for one joke. Big-city audiences, familiar with Jewish humor and intonation, made Holtz a star, but he was not that much of a draw west of the Hudson River or east of the Hillcrest Country Club.

Lou was discovered by Ma Janis, Elsie's mother, when he was playing San Francisco nightclubs in a

Lou Holtz

one-woman-and-two-men act called Boland, Holtz & Harris—Ms. Boland was Holtz's wife. Mrs. Bierbower, as Ma Janis was more formally known, was a shrewd judge of talent, and most other things as well. She renamed the act the Elsie Janis Trio and touted the act to Eddie Darling, the booker of the Palace Theatre at the time.

Rita Boland and Mr. Harris soon withdrew from the act, and Lou Holtz found his niche as a single, performing in blackface what later became known as stand-up comedy. When classic two-a-day began to slip, and managers of top houses like the Palace began to try employing masters of ceremonies to pep up their bills, Lou Holtz proved one of the best emcees in the business. By then he had scrubbed off the ebony greasepaint.

Holz' career in musicals began with *A World of Pleasure* (1915), a modest Shubert success at the Winter Garden that starred Stella Mayhew, Kitty Gordon and Sidney Greenstreet, but Holtz hit his stride in the 1920 and 1921 editions of *George White's Scandals.* (One of Holtz's quips to the mother of a young female hopeful was long remembered: "Do you want to be glorified by Ziegfeld or scandalized by George White?"

His next show was a revival of *A World of Pleasure* (1925) that promised more than it delivered, and he stepped into *Tell Me More* (1925), a Shubert book show that was deemed among Gershwin's lesser efforts but held forth for three months at the Winter Garden. Holtz brought one of his most familiar bits from vaudeville into this show. He sang a series of metered jokes to the tune of "O, Solo Mio," and reprised the chorus after each.

Manhattan Mary (1927–28) gave Lou his biggest hit on Broadway, a run of 264 performances during its eight months at the downtown Apollo Theatre. The star of the show was Ed Wynn, however, and Lou was in support along with Harland Dixon and George White (who produced and was co-librettist).

You Said It (1931), another book show, gave Lou Holtz the opportunity to render an Englishman through his Jewish dialect. Enough New Yorkers and out-of-towners were amused to keep the musical running for 192 performances. In 1934 Holtz starred on Broadway in *Calling All Stars*. His co-stars, Martha Raye, Phil Baker, Jack Whiting, Judy Canova, Ella Logan, Mitzi Mayfair and Gertrude Niesen, answered the call but customers did not, and the revue barely lasted a month.

His stage manner is captured in a Vitaphone short, *Idle Chatter* (1929), and he appeared in two more Vitaphone shorts, *When Do We Eat?* and *School for Romance* (1934). He repeated his stage role in *Manhattan Mary* (1930), which, pared down, became his only feature film, *Follow the Leader* (1930). The star of both the stage and screen versions was Ed Wynn.

Holtz also tried network radio. Like many other vaudevillians, he debuted on Rudy Vallee's *Fleischmann Hour,* and later he was a regular member of the cast when Paul Whiteman hosted *Kraft Music Hall* on NBC during the time between Bing Crosby's tenure and Al Jolson's. Unfortunately for Holtz, people were so nervous during the war with the Nazis that anyone who made Jews the center of jokes, as they were in Holtz's Sam Lapidus stories, was suspected of being anti-Semitic, even though Holtz was Jewish.

Although Holtz never told flat-out dirty jokes in vaudeville—no one did for long—he had always shaded some of his material and his delivery toward the blue. Producers and radio censors were always on alert when Holtz was on the air.

Lou returned to Broadway in *Priorities of 1942,* a solid hit, running 353 performances, despite a cheapjack Shubert production. The performers—Holtz, Phil Baker, Willie Howard, Hazel Scott, Paul Draper, Gene Sheldon and several standard acts—all brought their own material to the venture, so there were no sketches or production numbers and very little scenery. Given the mobilization for the USA's entry into the Second World War, the men in the show were all well above draft age.

When the producers tried to repeat the nickel-and-dime *Priorities of 1942* formula as *Star Time* (1944), Holtz joined Benny Fields and the dancing De Marcos, but the show eked out only three months on Broadway. While he was appearing in *Priorities of 1942,* Holtz told an interviewer that all his material, the work of a lifetime, was contained in a slim notebook. Even the best of material has to be changed. In 1951, he tried the stage again with *Lou Holtz' Merry-Go-Round,* but he failed to grab the brass ring and the ride quickly shut down.

Semiretired in the 1950s, Holtz made occasional forays into television, most notably on Ed Sullivan's *Toast of the Town* and several talk shows, but Myron Cohen had updated the Jewish monologist routine with more believable stories and an elegant style. Like his fellow Friars, Cantor, Jessel, Burns & Allen, Jack Benny and Milton Berle, Lou Holtz had entered vaudeville in its prime and had maneuvered his way through its decline.

Like Jessel, he did not manage to parlay his vaudeville popularity into a career in radio, motion pictures or television. He and Jessel spent their retirement at the Friars Club or Hillcrest Country Club in Los Angeles reminiscing or playing benefits while their vaudeville cohorts, Groucho Marx, Jack Benny, George Burns and Danny Kaye, were starring in television.

Lou continued in show business, performing at Catskill resorts that catered to Jews. He was also on call for many of the famous roasts held by the Friars when they raised money by saluting one of their own. Every roast is ribald, and anything goes as one comedian after another belittles the honoree. The Friars events gave Lou Holtz a chance to perform.

After his youthful marriage to a former partner, Rita Boland, Lou did not marry again or sire children until late in life. Unlike many vaudeville guys, he never wasted money gambling and was known as a careful man with a dollar. He invested wisely, became very rich and did not have to work. But no doubt, Lou Holtz would have liked to have been asked to work more often.

HONKY-TONKS

The differences between honky-tonks, box houses, free-and-easies, variety dives, concert saloons and melodeons were largely matters of size, configuration and geography. Although a low moral standard was common to all, regardless of how gussied up they were, some establishments were farther down the slide to disrepute.

Strictly defined, honky-tonks were a combination of saloon and dance hall and were primarily located in the West, but often the term honky-tonk was more liberally employed by *civilians* to gather in everything from dime museums to concert saloons and even theatres.

Melodeons emphasized entertainment and the premises closely resembled theatres, especially music-halls attached to the original barroom. Variety dives were at the other end of a descending scale. Honky-tonks were nearly indistinguishable from box houses—usually an establishment containing a bar, a dance hall with a stage.

The common ingredients for all of those establishments were liquor (of varying toxicity), gambling (as crooked as custom and lax law enforcement allowed), and hostesses who pushed drinks, usually danced and sang onstage and sometimes were available for private entertainment. Not all the hostesses were women. Some were boys impersonating females, a not uncommon practice. When they worked the boxes, the most the boys could offer without the chance of detection was a nineteenth-century lap dance, and only if the customer was very drunk.

It was supposed that these places fostered crime, and that assumption was from time to time proven given the laissez-faire posture of a police force beholden more to benefactors than to rules and regulations. The "tonks" and box houses were found in the older sections of cities, especially ports and transportation hubs. In Manhattan, they existed along the Bowery and Lower Broadway and eastward through Five Points to Corlear's Hook, where they prevailed for the better part of a century, beginning before the Civil War and ending after the First World War. Their heyday was ushered in by Civil War troops on leave.

Dance halls, box houses and melodeons sprang up like mushrooms in Seattle—a companion industry to logging on Skid Row—and along the Barbary Coast in San Francisco, a gateway to the Sierra Nevada, the land of Gold Rush fever. New Orleans boasted Storyville, a major attraction that made the Crescent City a favorite port of call until the First World War, when the navy put it permanently off-limits to sailors. Chicago and other major hubs around the USA provided similar establishments and diversions for travelers and indefinitely marooned transients.

It was not only metropolises that hosted concert saloons, box houses, tonks and the like. Any place where there were working men with money in their pockets and a family far away, as was often the case in Newport News, Virginia, Galveston, Texas, or Butte, Montana, was a haven for honky-tonks, and there were as many dancehall saloons as churches in the ranching and mining states, ranging from Texas to Colorado to Montana and westward to the Pacific Coast states.

HOOFER

In its narrowest definition, a hoofer is a buck dancer, although the term is often applied to clog and tap dancers as well. By the early twentieth century, all types of percussive dancers were called hoofers. This deceptively modest term conveyed a great deal of pride. Calling a dancer a hoofer was like calling an actor a trouper—one who had paid his dues. In its understated way, the term hoofer implied that the performer was regarded as both a professional and a skilled dancer. When a well-regarded dancer like Fred Astaire declared he was "only a hoofer," he was identifying with a solid tradition of workmanship, pride and skill and acknowledging the accomplishments of hoofers who danced before him and from whom he had learned.

HOOFERS CLUB

Located in Harlem on Seventh Avenue between 131st and 132nd streets and two doors away from the Lafayette Theatre, the Hoofers Club was the graduate school for black tap dancers. Whenever one of the tap dance greats played the Lafayette (or, years later, the Apollo Theatre), lesser lights would take a break from practicing downstairs in the Hoofers Club or from their daily ritual of wishing for work by touching the Tree of Hope outside on the Avenue. The dancers bought seats down front at the theatre; as soon as the dance act was over, they rushed down to the Hoofers Club to try to work out the new steps and variations they had just witnessed.

Managed, quite strictly, by Lonnie Hicks, a non-dancing, piano-playing fan of tap, the Hoofers Club occupied a few unadorned rooms beneath the street level. One could play pool, gamble, tell lies, get something to eat or drink or simply come in out of the cold. One room housed a lunch counter, another a few card tables; a third held a pool table and the last, an inner sanctum for which Lonnie charged no fee, featured a battered piano, a chair or two and a good floor that Lonnie replaced frequently. Here dancers showed off, challenged each other or simply sat, looked and learned.

Youngsters ringed the walls of the room, watching intently and keeping a respectful distance from the masters. Some of those masters, like King Rastus, willingly showed their steps. Others, like Bill Robinson and John Bubbles, were protective of their moves. No sooner did a dancer put together a new combination than a dozen others were putting variations of the combination into their own acts. The cardinal rule at the Hoofers Club was Thou Shalt Not Steal (Not So You Would Recognize It, Anyway). Even the top tappers would adapt other dancers' steps and change them into something that became their own. The trick was to make your steps and combinations too difficult to copy—and to demonstrate them only once!

James Barton, Hal Le Roy and the Condos Brothers were among the few white acts accepted as worthy competitors by black tappers. Women were not encouraged to attend sessions at the Hoofers Club. As Jeni LeGon, one of the few females to be invited, mused, there were hundreds of good female tappers, but few of them went into vaudeville as solo acts. Mostly they danced in revues to someone else's choreography.

The Hoofers Club endured for 30 years, between the First and Second World Wars.

HOOK

The hook, a long pole curved at one end and grasped at the other, was used in theatres that lacked a catwalk or fly floor. Supposedly fashioned after a shepherd's crook, and resembling tools used on ships and later adapted for various uses on land such as lighting gas lamps, it was devised by stagehands to reach up into the flies of a theatre to pull down tangled lines (ropes) or other paraphernalia that had stuck or entangled when flown into the flies.

The hook survived as a novelty element in amateur nights. Amateurs who incurred the displeasure of an audience and failed to take the hint to depart the stage were dragged off by the manager using the stagehand's hook. "Giving the hook" to amateurs, in small-time houses with crude audiences, became part of the fun. Some old-timers claimed to have seen the hook given to professional small-time acts that offended or bored an audience.

In *Show Biz: from Vaude to Video*, vaudevillian Joe Laurie Jr. and Abel Green, both historians, claimed that giving the hook was introduced as an amateur night device by H.C. Miner at his Miner's Bowery, a beer hall/theatre of the late 1870s and 1880s. According to burlesque chronicler Bernard Sobel, Tom Miner, son of H.C. Miner, claimed that he was the first to employ the hook. It was a Friday night in 1903, on the occasion of an amateur night at Miner's Bowery Theatre. A contestant persisted in a painful tenor solo despite being booed by an increasingly restive audience. Tom Miner ordered the stage manager, Charles Guthinger, to conceal himself behind the wings and use a nearby prop—a crook-handled cane discarded by a previous act—to pull the offending performer from the stage. To reach him, Miner and Guthinger lashed the cane to a pole and dragged the amateur offstage by the neck.

That version seems a bit fanciful, more geared, like many showbiz fables, to making a good story than reporting what happened accurately. An ordinary cane handle would not fit around anyone's neck, not even a sideshow thin man's. More likely, they simply used the pole itself to hook under the amateur's collar, belt, sleeve or cuff. It proved such a novelty that when the next amateur appeared and did not please, a lad in the galleries yelled, "Get the hook!" and both a legend and a novel bit of business were born. No doubt some theatre managers quickly adopted the hook and someone, possibly Tom Miner at a later date, had a pole fashioned with a shepherd's crook that would fit around a hapless amateur's neck.

Eddie Cantor claimed (probably facetiously) that when he started in show business he hopped around the stage while singing to avoid getting the hook, and thus developed his energetic song-and-dance style.

HOOTCHY-KOOTCHY OR KOOTCH (COOTCH)

Carnival shorthand for hootchy-kootchy dancing, which is what the yokels called the belly dancing that Little Egypt introduced to a shocked and slathering public at Chicago's Columbian Exhibition (World's Fair) of 1893. As a few jazz dancers and burlesque queens began to adopt variations of the *shimmy* and the *freeze*, flippant chroniclers in the popular press tagged all torso twisting as the *hootchy-kootch*.

BOB HOPE

b: (Leslie Townes Hope) 29 May 1903, Eltham, England—d: 27 July 2003, Toluka Lake, CA

He was the most American of performers. Everything about him, except his birthplace and his given name, bore the mark of all things American—his slang, his accent, his breezy but steely manner, his attire, even his looks. In time he became the only performer other than Will

Bob Hope

Rogers who truly was regarded as an American institution, even in the eyes of half a dozen U.S. presidents. Hope triumphed in all three mass media entertainment forms: network radio, talking pictures and television.

Hope's success and his embodiment of the American personality reflect many of the aspirations and ambitions of the USA during the twentieth century. His life ran parallel with the century. Born during its fourth year and living 100 years, he endured beyond its last. He did not spring onto the stage certain of his objective and fully developed. He was in his late teens before he settled on show business.

Born in the United Kingdom, he moved with his parents and six brothers to the USA in 1907 and was raised in Cleveland, Ohio. As he grew from childhood into a young man, he sold newspapers, was a butcher's assistant, quit high school, pool sharked, boxed (under the name Packy East) and taught dancing before deciding to go onstage.

His early acts were imitative: the first was a generic ballroom dance mixed-double act with Mildred Rosequist; his second, a throwback to an earlier era, a song-and-dance routine in blackface with Lefty Durbin. Gradually, the pair dropped blackface and emphasized the comedy. Bob was the straight man. He continued to play straight when he teamed up with George Byrne after Durbin's death from tuberculosis.

As any burlesque or vaudeville comedian discovered, playing straight was superb training for a comedian: he learned to get in sync with the audience, gauge his timing, build a routine and understand when an audience was getting the joke and when it was finished with it, so as to *feed* the next joke between the two points. When he thought he was ready, Bob went solo. After the usual scramble for work, Bob landed a job as a master of ceremonies at a Cleveland vaudeville theatre, the Stratford.

Just as he had learned timing as a feed in a double act, his extended gig at the Stratford gave him one-on-one experience with audiences, and he discovered how to spar with them. Ever ambitious, Hope next teamed with his girlfriend at the time, Louise Troxell, in an act similar in style to Burns & Allen and Block & Sully. Again, Bob was the feed.

Quickly he expanded the act, adding other comedy actors, and the act made it to New York—Proctor's at 86th Street—just as vaudeville was beginning to fade and talking pictures were emerging as the big act on the bill. While playing the Capitol Theatre in Manhattan, Bob found himself on the bill with Bing Crosby, already a rising star. They did an impromptu bit for the few nights they shared the bill, not realizing that a partnership was waiting in the wings.

Hope had his eye on Broadway, network radio and Hollywood movies. A Shubert musical of 1928, *Ups-a-Daisy,* provided Bob with a long run on Broadway, but his role as Screeves, the butler, was a relatively minor part, though he made the critics notice. Hope spent time, effort and money on publicists who could keep his name in the newspapers, and on good writers who could write routines tailored for big-city sophisticates as well as material for less urbane tastes. Hope also made himself available as an emcee for various charity functions. His unpaid work was a case of good conscience being in accord with good business sense.

Good works hyped by good publicity led to better work. In 1932, Bob captured more attention in a revue, *Ballyhoo of 1932,* which starred Willie & Eugene Howard. The show lasted 95 performances and Hope proved a laugh getter, which helped him win the second male lead in *Roberta* a year later. A middling book, hoary puns and dull lyrics by Otto Harbach were on the minus side, according to critics, but Jerome Kern's luscious music (his final work for Broadway) and 29-year-old Bob Hope were welcomed by critics and audiences, as were newcomers Lyda Roberti and George Murphy. The old guard turned out to greet the return of the beloved Fay Templeton, after a retirement, in the role that provided her swan song on the Great White.

Although 1932 was a low point in the Great Depression, it was a lucky year for Bob Hope. His career was clearly on the rise, and he met Dolores Reade, a nightclub singer who became his wife. Over the years they adopted four children, and their marriage lasted the rest of their lives, despite Bob's frequent travels.

Hope was less lucky with his next musical comedy. *Say When* (1934–35) was saluted by the critics, but audiences failed to show up to watch two song-and-dance men, Harry Richman and Bob Hope, woo a banker's daughters. The show closed after 76 performances. Hope would have much better luck in a song-and-dance pairing with another crooner in the future.

There were still vaudeville dates between shows. Sylvia Froos, the child singer, recalled being on a Proctor bill somewhere in New England with Bob Hope around 1935. He was doing basically a single, but Sylvia remembered a funny bit in his act where Bob waved a baton as though conducting a large orchestra, but only one saxophone player was onstage with him.

Bob returned to vaudeville until he joined the *Ziegfeld Follies of 1936.* John Murray Anderson staged it, George Gershwin and Vernon Duke wrote the songs, George Balanchine contributed a ballet, and the cast boasted four disparate female singers: Fanny Brice, Gertrude Niesen, Josephine Baker and Judy Canova. Hope was the chief male comedian, and he and Eve Arden dueted "I Can't Get Started with You." Bob Hope was now at his most sophisticated, the style he brought to his first feature film and his duet with Shirley Ross, "Thanks for the Memory," the seriocomic song forever associated with him.

Hope stayed with the *Follies* from 30 January 1936 until Fanny Brice's illness closed the show in mid-May. When the *Follies* reopened in September, Bob Hope was rehearsing for *Red, Hot and Blue.* Ethel Merman and Jimmy Durante costarred in the show with the able support of Grace & Paul Hartman. The much-anticipated Cole Porter show reunited many of the collaborators who had made the previous season's *Anything Goes* a hit, but the final product did not quite satisfy, although it recouped its investment—a good enough trick in the middle of the Depression.

Always looking for greener pastures, and still performing in *Red, Hot and Blue* (his final Broadway show), Bob Hope took on a radio series, *Rippling Rhythm Revue,* and made his feature film debut in *The Big Broadcast of 1938.* Earlier, between 1934 and 1936, Bob had already made eight short films that introduced him to moviemaking. The two-reelers were more important to Hope for the experience than for the final product.

The Big Broadcast of 1938, which began Hope's rise to movie stardom, was part of Paramount's new management's campaign to dump its expensive stable of older actors and comedians (Gloria Swanson, Marlene Dietrich, George Bancroft, Gary Cooper, Fredric March, W. C. Fields and Mae West) and take on a newer generation of less expensive stars-to-be. Other studios were doing the same thing—especially MGM, and except Universal. *Big Broadcast of 1938* was W. C. Fields' final film at Paramount and the first of four vehicles equally promoting Bob Hope and Martha Raye. When Martha's personal life hit a few bumpy patches, Paramount switched their bets to Bob. Dorothy Lamour was also working her way up the roster when Paramount put her into *The Big Broadcast of 1938.* Over the years, Dorothy and Bob costarred a dozen times.

It was radio and Hollywood that provided Bob Hope the means to becoming an American favorite. Hope's first three radio series had flopped in rapid succession, but his fourth try, the *Pepsodent Show,* proved a charm and kept Hope a radio favorite for more than a decade, until he was ready to invade television.

By 1938, when he made several feature films and began the *Pepsodent Show,* the enduring traits of the Bob Hope character emerged. Had not radio been pushing Bob toward comedy at the expense of singing and dancing, Hope might have been continued in films as an engaging song-and-dance man and light comedian perfect for musical comedies, rather like Eddie Albert and Jack Carson—and Bing Crosby.

Hope's radio series quickly set the pace for others and became the model for his own television shows. The weekly *Pepsodent Show* started off in high gear with Bob's machine-gun monologue: "Hello, this is Bob 'World's Fair' Hope, and I wanna tell ya. . . ." Topicality was the order of the day. For the remainder of the show, top-flight guest stars and a small repertory of character comedians, Jerry Colonna, Barbara Jo Allen (Vera Vague) and Skinny Ennis among them, joined Bob in a series of gags that punctuated a perfunctory plot. This mélange of rapid-fire monologue, a song or two and an exchange of quips, insults and self-deprecatory jokes seemed the very breath of American self-assurance and optimism despite the lingering Depression.

Interestingly, his dual stardom resulted in a divergence of character. On radio he was the brash, confident, clever, quick-thinking stand-up comedian who tamed his audience. In movies he played an average Joe, no brighter than most, who postured absurdly for the ladies (who always saw through his braggadocio) and behaved cravenly until the end of the movie when the plot demanded of him a foolhardy but lucky deed that won fair damsel and rang down the curtain. Leonard Maltin suggested that *The Cat and the Canary* (1939) was the movie in which Bob Hope's screen character gelled.

Hope made as many good movie comedies as any comedian or comedy team. No funnymen made more than a dozen top-flight, feature-length comedies—not Chaplin, not Keaton, not Laurel & Hardy, not W. C. Fields or The Marx Brothers. Among the candidates for Hope's golden dozen are the zaniest of the "Road" series—*Zanzibar* (1941), *Morocco* (1942) and *Rio* (1947)—with movie buddy Bing Crosby and the distracting object of their affections, Dorothy Lamour. A couple of his early features with Martha Raye and Burns & Allen remain fresh fun, as do several of Hope's spy spoofs: *The Cat and the Canary* (1939), *They Got Me Covered* (1943), *My Favorite Blonde* (1942) and *My Favorite Brunette* (1947). Also among Hope's better movies are *Louisiana Purchase* (1941), *The Paleface* (1948) and *Fancy Pants* (1950).

Through the 1940s, due to the ever mounting success of his motion pictures and his radio series, Bob Hope grew ever bigger as a star, reigning for the decade as a top box-office attraction along with Betty Grable, Bing Crosby and Abbott & Costello. By the early 1950s he solidified his position as an American institution, like Will Rogers before him and Johnny Carson to come.

Nowhere was he better than as the master of ceremonies for the Academy Awards. He combined just the right amount of irreverent joking with equal dollops of respect for Hollywood's annual celebration of itself. In his commentary and introductions, Bob's character reflected all the various petty feelings rampant in the hall. He gossiped to the members of the Academy along with a few million viewers, petulantly observed that he never won an Oscar and let it be known that he would sell his soul for the gold statuette. Bob Hope emceed or cohosted the annual Academy Awards presentations 17 times. No one was better at pacing the event and no one was funnier.

In triumph were the seeds of decline. His television appearances won huge ratings while his films became mechanical by the mid-1950s. He grew careless, relying on the teleprompter when earlier he would have memorized and honed his material to perfection. From the late 1950s onward, he seemed to show up for his films and for his television shows rather than invest himself in them. By 1960 Hope was turning increasingly to sex farces for the last of his more than fifty starring feature films. Perhaps it was too many irons in the fire—or in his golf bag. Hope seemed to stroll through his movies and TV shows as if he were on his way to the golf course, a charity event, a real estate acquisition, a testimonial dinner, a board meeting or a U.S. army base in Korea.

Hope made so many movies and hosted so many TV shows that his minor efforts swamped his best. Topicality cursed Hope's legacy. Bob's jokes were aimed at newsmakers, but a decade or two later the once famous butts of Bob's jokes had long been forgotten, together with the incidents that triggered the jokes.

Although many showbiz stars did their bit during various wars, there were a few famous performers who sacrificed their careers to entertain the troops in the Second World War, Korea and Vietnam: Joe E. Brown, Marlene Dietrich, Al Jolson, Martha Raye and Bob Hope were among them. Yet Hope's overseas tours for the troops turned into an enterprise. His work for the men and women in uniform yielded a book or two, an annual TV special every year and countless articles in the press. On the one hand, Bob Hope was generous in his gifts of money, talent and time to various causes. On the other hand, his good works were rewarded with enhanced reputation.

Bob Hope emerged in the 1920s, came of age in the 1930s, reached his pinnacle in the 1940s and consolidated his position in the 1950s. By 1960, he lost zest. The Second World War in the early 1940s required the nation to see itself as the bastion of truth, justice and righteous might. At the end of the decade, those who had endured the Great Depression and won the war were proud of their nation, its values and themselves. The good life was their expected reward, but they saw a new peril emerging—godless world communism. Their children, however, did not share their worldview.

A great schism divided the generations. Voices of disappointment, disillusion and dissent, underground for more than a half century, cracked through the margins of politics and the arts in the 1950s. By the early 1960s it seemed an entire generation was poised against the establishment.

Hope's wonderfully American comic character—by turns slick, transparent, brash, cowardly, sexually stirred, self-doubting, opportunistic, venal and good-hearted—confronted middle age after 1950, as did his generation, weary of economic depression and war. After decades at the top, Hope had every reason to believe his position in the entertainment pantheon was secure. It should have been, but his character—the overstimulated young man, hoping for a lucky break—did not age well. What was once fresh, brash and self-deprecating in Bob Hope had become stale, smug and nearly lewd. In one sense Hope remained constant; his character forever pursued women, but a youthful rascal on the make degrades with age into a paunchy, smirking letch.

It is in the quarter of a century of his prime that Bob Hope is to be measured. He became the most American of comedians and the most modern of his day. As a commentator, he was Will Rogers without the folksiness, because the USA was no longer folksy; its citizens had become urbane in aspiration. Like Will, Bob pricked politicians—regardless of party until he became a spokesman for the GOP. He deflated the pretentious and ridiculed the absurd. Hope was never a threat; he functioned more as a barometer and a safety valve.

(WILLIAM) DE WOLF HOPPER

b: 30 March 1858, New York, NY—
d: 23 September 1935, Kansas City, MO

If De Wolf Hopper is remembered today, it is for his recitation of "Casey at the Bat," or for his wives who bore similar first names: Ella, Ida, Edna, Nella and Hedda. His sixth and last wife, Lillian, seems to have broken the sound-alike jinx. In his day—and a very long day it was, for his career spanned 56 years—De Wolf Hopper was one of theatre's brightest stars.

His mother's line, the De Wolf family, descended from Colonial stock and was allied by marriage to several blue-blooded and blue-chip clans: Belmonts, Tiffanys, Lawrences and Aspinwalls. His father, a Quaker lawyer, expected his son to follow him into law. Instead, young William De Wolf Hopper escaped to the heady delights of an amateur theatre production at the 14th Street Theatre in Manhattan, an experience that convinced him he was made for the stage. For the theatre, he scrapped his given name because of its ordinariness and promoted his second name, De Wolf, to counter the Quaker plainness of Hopper.

The death of his father and the subsequent bequest to his son of $50,000 enabled young Hopper to organize his own theatrical touring company. Calling it the Criterion Comedy Club, De Wolf set forth and encountered failure. He retained his confidence and enough of his money to start once again. The result was strike two for his managerial career.

Accepting his immediate destiny as an actor for hire, Hopper played various minor roles until Edward (Ned) Harrigan, a leading producer of the time and Tony Hart's

De Wolf Hopper

onstage partner, gave Hopper his first role of note in 1882. *The Blackbird* was a melodrama rather than the usual music and comedy roughhouse that Harrigan's Theatre Comique audience demanded, so it failed.

Hopper had one of the finest speaking and singing voices ever heard in American theatre. Encouraged by others that grand opera might be his forte, Hopper began studying voice in earnest. But his splendid singing voice that effortlessly reached to the back of the largest of theatres was anchored to a very tall, leggy and loose-limbed physique that suggested comedy.

Naturally gifted for the opéra bouffe so popular at the time, Hopper found employment with the McCaull Opera Company in 1885. He became the company's chief comedian and a rising star within the first season and learned and performed more than a dozen lead roles in operetta over the next few years. For a reason now forgotten, sometime during the run of *Prince Methusalem,* Hopper departed from the text in the second act to recite "Casey at the Bat." It was a rousing hit and required encores. Thereafter, for the 50 years remaining of his career, Hopper was seldom able to appear in public without obliging with a recitation of his signature piece.

For the 1889–90 season, he organized the De Wolf Hopper Comic Opera Company to produce *Castles in the Air,* with his name placed above the title. Della Fox was the soubrette in this comedy about a debtor and his creditors, and she earned stardom with her performance. Hopper took no principal role but assigned himself the part of the judge who functioned as both a participant and an interlocutor.

Unlike the mighty Casey who struck out, Hopper, with two strikes against him as a manager, had learned his lessons well and hit one home run after another. *Castles in the Air* was followed by *Wang* (1891) and *Panjandrum* (1893). All three costarred Della Fox, and the first two were enormous hits whose successful New York seasons earned very profitable road trips and revivals. *Panjandrum* did well in New York but not on the road.

In 1893 came a financial panic, the Columbian Exposition in Chicago, and the rise of the Theatrical Syndicate or the Trust, an alliance of theatrical producers and theatre owners that would control the theatres and virtually end the era of actor-managers like Hopper.

Dr. Syntax (1894) was a marginal success while John Philip Sousa's *El Capitan* (1896) was a solid hit; both kept Hopper's company viable. *The Charlatan* (1898), modestly successful, was good enough to attract a London booking. *The Mystical Miss* (1899), though, seems to have been a failure as few references list it; perhaps it provided the hint to Hopper that he should quit management while he was ahead.

Will Hopper, as his friends knew him, accepted Weber & Fields' offer to join their company for their fifth season in 1900–01, and stayed for the sixth. Hopper assumed the sort of role that Peter Dailey had performed for the company before Pete left to head his own musical comedy company. For Weberfields, Hopper appeared in *Fiddle-Dee-Dee* (1900), *Quo Vass Iss?* (1900), *Hoity Toity* (1901) and *Twirly-Whirly* (1902).

In *Quo Vass Iss?,* which occurred in the reign of the Emperor Zero, Charlie Ross, justly proud of his voice, found himself outmatched by Hopper in both vocal range and physical size. The rest of the cast watched the two old pros battle each other onstage, raising and lowering their tones to disarm the other. Hopper was the clear winner, and a bit later in the season, Charlie Ross left Weber & Fields.

Mr. Pickwick (1903) was Hopper's next show after Weberfields, and since it was not a success he revived *Wang* to close out the season. *Happyland* (1905) was a happier affair, but *Pied Piper* in 1908 failed to lure audiences. Hopper kept his name before the public with mixed results in *A Matinee Idol* (1910), a revival of *H.M.S. Pinafore* (1911), a revival of *Patience* (1912), *The Beggar Student* (1913), *Hop o' My Thumb* (1913),

Lieber Augustin (1913) and more Gilbert & Sullivan revivals for 1915.

In 1917 he joined an all-star cast that included many of the other great stars of the day—Mrs. Fiske, George Arliss, George M. Cohan, Chauncey Olcott, Julia Arthur and James K. Hackett—in *Out There* (1917), a propaganda piece centered around Laurette Taylor as a valiant nurse to British soldiers. *Out There* toured the USA to incite enthusiasm for what would become the First World War, promoting enlistment in the armed forces and raising nearly $700,000 for the Red Cross.

But by the time he joined *The Passing Show of 1917,* Hopper was regarded as a star of yesteryear. *The Better 'Ole* (1918) gave him a nonmusical comedy role, and he was one of several to play the lead. A Hippodrome extravaganza, *Everything* (1918), ran 461 performances in that enormous theatre, however, and proved that Hopper in the right vehicle was still a great draw. *Snapshots of 1921,* a top-drawer vaudeville revue, continued his luck and costarred him with singer Nora Bayes, Lew Fields, comic Lulu McConnell and Gilda Gray (the shimmy queen). But a revival of *Erminie* (1921) and *Some Party* (1922) failed to sustain the momentum. By 1928, De Wolf Hopper was billed in support for the Shuberts' *White Lilacs.*

De Wolf Hopper's talents and successes were not limited to comic opera or burlesk; he played Shakespeare (Falstaff in the *Merry Wives of Windsor)* and Sheridan (David in *The Rivals*). There always seemed to be some venue in which he could profitably exercise his talents. In 1916 he was on the Keystone Comedy payroll, and several years earlier he filmed *Don Quixote, Casey at the Bat* and several other photoplays for the Fine Arts Company. These silent recordings cannot have been very satisfying without his rich voice, nor can radio or sound recordings have sufficed; though they captured tone and range, they deprived listeners of the sight of his movement and gesture.

Vaudeville was as appropriate a stage for him as comic opera, but after he achieved success in the latter, Hopper's vaudeville work became spotty, although as late as 1932 he was on hand as part of the opening bill at Radio City Music Hall. He never seemed to wholly retire, and he made occasional appearances into the 78th and final year of his life, 1935. He died the day following his last broadcast, in Missouri.

RUDY HORN

b: 5 June 1909, Cleveland, OH—d: 22 October 2005, Chicago, IL

Rudy's father, Henry Horn, owned the Green Mill, a Chicago nightclub that attracted stars as both patrons and performers, so Rudy caught the performing bug from people like Ray Bolger, whose eccentric dancing inspired him. When he was 12, Rudy ran away from home with a carnival. The authorities picked him up in New York and sent him home. Two years later Rudy left home again; this time he stayed on the road for a long time.

Rudy arrived in Manhattan in 1923. He worked as a soda jerk and auditioned every time he heard of a call for chorus boys. He danced in a unit called the Twelve Aristocrats, developed his comedy at the Nut Club in Greenwich Village and during the summertime he played in beer gardens at Asbury Park. Horn also won a slot in a Texas Guinan show at the 300 Club that opened in 1926 on 54th Street.

To play vaudeville or nightclubs, a performer needed an act. Rudy had become an eccentric dancer, extending his buck and tap dancing with acrobatics. By 1928 he had a stand-up comedy routine. Later he acted in comedy sketches and sang a bit. The trick was to be ready for any kind of work.

Although it was the twilight of vaudeville, Rudy Horn managed to get bookings on various circuits. A good way to showcase an act was playing Monday matinees at tryout houses like the Jamaica on Long Island or the Audubon on Broadway at 86th Street, which was a break-in house for the Loew's circuit. Although discouraged to attend break-in shows, managers and booking agents were invited to come to tryout matinees to spot new talent and to see established acts breaking in new material.

By the late 1920s, Horn had become a headliner on the small-time circuits like Loew's, Sun and Kemp time but took lesser spots on the big-time Orpheum circuit. In New York there was work at the Roseland Ballroom at 50th Street and Broadway and the Everglades. Horn was on a bill with Clayton, Jackson and Durante at the Silver Slipper on 48th Street at Broadway. In 1928 he was booked at the 5,000-seat Riviera Theatre back in his hometown of Chicago, where he enjoyed a long run.

Rudy watched some of the dance greats. There was James Barton. "I called him 'Mr. Barton,' you know what I mean? He was a great dancer and I was just a kid. He had a great drunk act. He sponsored a baseball team for kids." And there was John Bubbles, of Buck & Bubbles, who would become another lifelong friend. "I learned a lot from John—an excellent dancer. Later I worked with him in USO shows. We toured Europe together during the war [the Second World War] and after." Rudy also admired Hal Leroy ("he smoked himself to death") and the Berry Brothers ("a great act, the best in their style, but they didn't take care of themselves").

Work was in the hands of agents. The jobs got fewer and the pay lower as the Great Depression set in, started a recovery, then worsened and stayed bad for a long while. The houses that stuck with vaudeville were mostly small time, and the work was a short gig, a weekend here or there. "Hymie Goldstein, who had an office in the Palace Building, was an angel, the nicest man I ever met. He booked small clubs in New Jersey; he couldn't pay over $5 or $7 a night. Hymie would go where the acts hung out. He asked who wasn't working; they got the jobs.

"He booked Dean Martin, too. Dean and I shared a double room at the Bentmere Hotel—54th and Broadway. Nine bucks a week for two twin beds. Dean was a good guy. The women liked him, liked to go out with both of us because we were sharp dressers and good dancers. Dean's uncle was Leonard Barr—an eccentric dancer like me. Dean hit it big. Then he got lost; you know what I mean?

"Eddie Riley was another agent. Had an office in the Bond Building; booked Pat Rooney Jr. and Frank Sinatra. I was with Riley around 1933–35. Solly Shaw was another, he had an office at the Strand. Charles Rapp booked Grossinger's in the Catskills."

Rudy was with MCA for a while, under a contract that paid him $50 a week whether he was booked or not. Eddie Sly of Chicago was Horn's manager. However, Sammy Watkins, the orchestra leader at the Hollanden Hotel, tipped off Rudy that MCA was selling his act for $700 a week, so Rudy changed agents again. "They all took more than 10 percent! Out in Hollywood I booked through the Frederick Brothers, but mostly I played New York City, New Jersey, Pittsburgh, Detroit and Chicago. Up in Boston I did the Bradford Roof, Blinstrub's and the RKO Keith." In Milwaukee Rudy appeared with Sophie Tucker, and at the 1937 Cleveland Exposition, he was in the show along with Eleanor Holmes.

Another dear friend was Jackie Fields. "He booked me with Nutsy Fagan at the Nut Club in the Village, the Sunrise Club, at Grossinger's and Monticello in the Catskills. It wasn't good money, but if Jackie didn't book me, I wouldn't eat.

"I also worked burlesque, too: the Columbia Wheel, Izzy Mertz's and Minsky's. I performed in blackout sketches along with dancing and emceeing." When asked who had the best comedy act in burlesque, Rudy quickly replies, "Mike Sacks and Alice Kennedy," who were with Rudy Horn and others when they performed in 1937 for President Roosevelt at the White House.

Over the decades Rudy Horn's act changed to suit the venue and times. In vaudeville "you did 8 to 10 minutes. You weren't allowed to perform longer, and if you did they would fine you. Later, when I was an emcee in the clubs, I did about 35 to 40 minutes—stand-up comedy for nearly a half hour. ('Did you hear the bad news? My grandma died at the ripe old age of 97 and we were lucky we saved the baby!') I'd finish with my eccentric dancing, maybe the drunk act. I'd ask the audience for dance requests. They loved it. They'd call out 'Russian,' 'ballet,' 'acrobatic,' 'eccentric,' 'the Irish Jog,' 'the French Can-Can,' and I'd perform whatever they wanted. If I didn't know it, I'd improvise and make comedy out of it. Columnist Walter Winchell wrote that 'Rudy Horn shows the customers how comical an eccentric dancer can really be.'"

Vaudeville of sorts had a bit of a revival with the USO shows. Rudy Horn joined up. He was assigned, along with other vaudevillians, to big shows that played big bases as well as small shows designed for hospital wards or the front lines under fire. At the Battle of the Bulge, Rudy and the rest of the troupe had to double as nurses, doing their best to attend to thousands of wounded.

For Rudy Horn, the USO tours opened up new stages, and he stayed in Europe—Italy, especially, but Monaco, Tripoli and France as well—where he lived and worked for 18 years. Because he was a dancer and skilled in physical comedy, there was no language barrier between him and his audience. He revived his drunk act, and work was plentiful, as it was for many American acts. In the minds of many, Americans were the victorious saviors and American culture was the wave of the future. They embraced American jazz, dancing and movies.

When Horn visited the States occasionally to work in clubs as an emcee, his friends cautioned him to rebuild his career Stateside. "I was having too much fun, but because I stayed in Europe so long I missed out on the whole TV thing." When he returned home around 1970, Horn found the entertainment world vastly changed. Music was electronic and variety had disappeared. Among the last acts Rudy did was a marionette show with Ruth Hill. Television commercials brought Rudy back under the lights. Living past the turn of the twenty-first century, Rudy Horn was sought out by historians and appeared in several documentary films.

HARRY HOUDINI

b: (Erik Weisz/Ehrich Weiss), 24 March 1874, Budapest, Hungary—d: 31 October 1926, Montreal, Canada

Eva Tanguay may have been "vaudeville's greatest attraction," as she billed herself, and Al Jolson may have been "the world's greatest drawing card," as his contemporaries admitted, sometimes reluctantly, but no one was more famous than Houdini. No performer had a surer understanding of audiences or a cannier instinct for public relations.

If it had been a matter of only talent and skill, Harry Houdini would have been no better known or remembered than his equally brilliant and famous

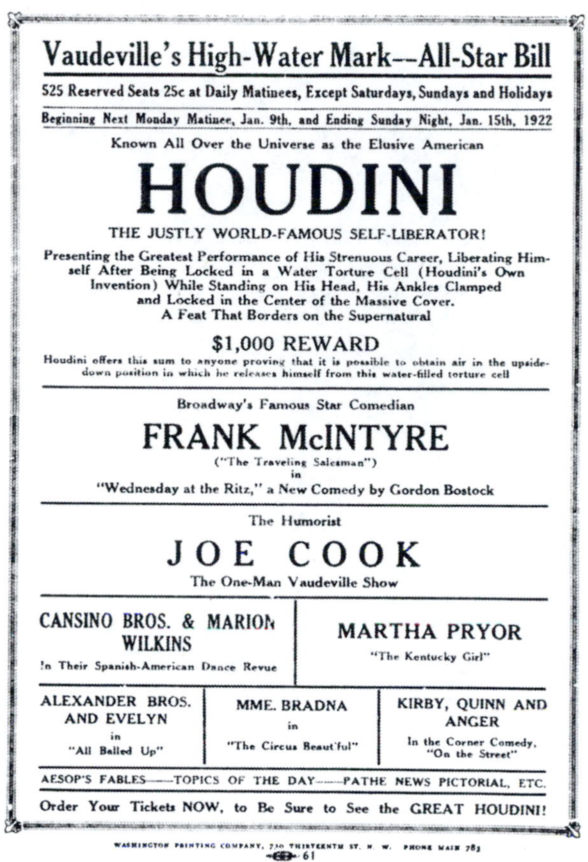

contemporaries, Thurston and Blackstone. Harry was not only as good as or better than other stage magicians of his time, he was also a peerless and untiring promoter who sold sensation, science and sex appeal. Houdini, "The Original Handcuff King and Jail Breaker," captured the press' attention and America's fancy by putting himself in supposedly death-defying situations from which he escaped. He refused the so-called occult trappings and insisted that what he did was not magical but was accomplished by the exercise of a rational mind upon technology.

American newspapers printed near naked photos of his compactly muscled physique as he enacted escape stunts to promote his stage appearances in each city. An ordinary man who appeared on a beach in nothing more than a breechcloth and a pair of handcuffs would have been arrested for indecency. Handsome Harry Houdini brought women into the audience for illusion acts.

When women bared a bit of their bodies onstage, even in leggings, it was to a chorus of tut-tuts. Bodybuilders like Sampson and Sandow, billed as strongmen, or acrobats and aerialists, whose lean musculature was encased in leotards and little more, did not raise as much ire or editorial comment. Perhaps the men who ran the dailies or the husbands and swains who accompanied fair ladies to the theatre did not wish to make too much of an issue in which they unfavorably compared.

When still an infant, Ehrich Weiss was brought by his mother and father to the USA. They settled in Appleton, Wisconsin and then Milwaukee, before moving back to their port of entry, New York City. As a schoolboy he excelled at swimming, track and other athletics, and throughout his life he held to his regimen of strengthening exercises and abstinence from drink and tobacco. He was a good student, and through his reading he developed an interest in stage magic that blossomed into his choice of career when he read *The Memoirs of Robert-Houdin, Ambassador, Author, and Conjuror, Written by Himself,* the celebrated nineteenth-century French illusionist.

Working in a men's tie factory to support himself and help his family, Ehrich taught himself the basics of card manipulation. When he felt ready to perform for a public, he billed himself as Harry Houdini, a tribute to the man who inspired him and provided a recognizable name to which Harry added a final *i.* His first bookings were in dime museums and men's smokers. From 1891 to 1893, Harry worked with a friend from the necktie factory, Jacob Hyman, as the Brothers Houdini. Theodore, Harry's brother, temporarily took Jacob's place, and the act was billed The Houdinis. Enduring all the mean venues that a novice act had to play, the Brothers Houdini worked up to an appearance at the Columbian Exposition (or World's Fair) in Chicago in 1893.

To the standard cards trick, Harry added his first important illusion, "Metamorphosis." Although it had been performed by others, Harry added the critical element of binding his hands together. A member of the audience was called onstage to tape Harry's hands behind his back, help Theo put Harry into a large sack and tie the end, then stuff the bag (and Harry) into a large wooden box that was then roped and padlocked. The box was then obscured from view by drawing a four-sided curtain around it. Alerting the audience that something astonishing was about to happen, Theo went behind the curtained area, clapped three times and Harry emerged. He then undid the box, opened the sack and revealed Theo tied exactly as Harry had been.

Also in 1893, Harry met and quickly married Wilhelmina Rahner, ever known as Bess. Theo took his own act on the road with a female assistant, and Bess took Theo's place with Harry. From 1893 to 1899, Harry and Bess played innumerable one-night stands in circuses, burlesque and medicine shows.

In 1895, Houdini was traveling the Great Plains states with a medicine show. Harry and Bess were doing a few tricks and playing in a popular melodrama of the day, *Kathleen Mavourneen.* The other cast members were Joe and Myra Keaton. The medicine show was in the town of Piqua, Kansas when a cyclone passed through town. Myra was giving birth back at the boardinghouse when the cyclone destroyed the medicine wagon, its stock of elixir, the tent and props. The baby was named Joseph Jr. The Houdinis and Keatons continued to travel together playing *Kathleen Mavourneen* and other small-cast "mellers," and when the baby was six months old he fell down a flight of stairs yet was unhurt. Houdini picked him up and said, "Joe, that was some buster your kid took." And baby Joseph Francis was Buster Keaton thereafter.

A few years later, desperate for work, Houdini even did a bogus medium act in vaudeville for a while. In each town, he ransacked the newspaper archives to learn about townsfolk so that he could provide spectators with messages from their dear departed. It was a dispiriting life for one as ambitious as Harry. Further, his father had died a few years earlier, and Harry had to send much of what he earned back to his mother to support her and the younger children. But Harry never stopped experimenting. He learned to free himself from handcuffs, straitjackets and other restraints.

Houdini was 25 in 1899 and a ten-year veteran of small-time show business when he was approached by Martin Beck, general manager of the Orpheum circuit's theatres and the man in charge of booking acts. Beck was intrigued by Harry's handcuff escape. After Houdini proved to Beck that he was able to escape from any handcuffs, Beck engaged him for a trial performance at the Orpheum Theatre in Omaha, Nebraska, but Beck told him to omit all the manipulations in his act and perform only the escape routine. It was excellent advice.

Once focused on escapes, Harry had police secure him with four or five handcuffs plus leg irons. The reports back to Beck from theatre managers were enthusiastic. When Houdini reached the Orpheum theatres in California, he was actively engaging the participation of local constabularies in his act. After the preparations of binding Houdini and setting him into an enclosure of sorts, nobody in the audience saw him again until the end of his act when he showed himself after freeing himself from the restraints. Will Rogers marveled that Houdini was the only performer who could hold an audience in its seats for 20 minutes to a half hour with nothing visibly happening onstage—just a box sitting onstage, supposedly with Houdini in it struggling to get out of chains and locks.

The Keith-Albee circuit booked him east of the Mississippi. In every jurisdiction where Harry played, the local police participated in Harry's manipulation of the local newspapers. Harry was stripped naked, bound and locked in jail cells. In minutes, Harry had freed

Harry Houdini

himself. The press dubbed him the champion jailbreaker, a claim that did more for Houdini's reputation than that of the local police departments. No one could buy publicity like that.

In 1900, Harry and Bess headed for Europe. He created a sensation wherever he played—England, Germany, the Netherlands and Russia. He instigated challenges and embarrassed challengers. He was news, news that followed him back to the USA. In Washington, D.C., he escaped from murderers' row in the federal penitentiary. He jumped shackled from high bridges into wide and deep rivers and freed himself underwater. His onstage tricks lived up to the promise of his publicity exploits. He escaped from manacles inside a large locked dairy can filled to the brim with water. He made a huge elephant disappear onstage. In 1910, he piloted an airplane and set a record for the first sustained flight in Australia.

He also made the first of a series of silent thrill movies. On celluloid, of course, Houdini could omit scenes and splice film. His first screen effort was a serial, *The Master Mystery* (1918). He followed that with five silent features: *The Grim Game* (1919), *Terror Island* (1920), *The Soul of Bronze* (1921), *The Man from Beyond* (1922) and *Haldane of the Secret Service* (1923).

When he toured Britain again in 1920, he was hailed as a movie star as well as the famous escape artist. During this visit Houdini became exposed to the revived interest in spiritualism. There was much debate about whether visits from the departed, materializations and other forms of interrealm communications were genuine or hokum. Some of Houdini's new friends, like Arthur Conan Doyle, the creator of Sherlock Holmes, were credulous. Houdini was not. He observed many séances yet held his tongue. He was making notes for future action.

By 1922, Houdini was ready to combat frauds that masqueraded as spiritualists and bilked grieving innocents of considerable amounts of money. He worked up a stage presentation to pair with the release of his film, *The Man from Beyond,* in which Harry projected photos of various so-called mediums and explained how they created their visual and aural effects. The publicity he received was nearly equal to that he had received for his escapes. However, for Harry Houdini, exposing phony mediums was a genuine crusade.

Houdini was by then 50 years old, a rich man for whom more accolades as an escape artist were superfluous. He began to be called as an expert debunker when claims were made for clairvoyance and contact with the netherworld. As a result of his exposés, he embarked on a series of lecture tours, playing prestigious venues like Symphony Hall in Boston. His act, when he chose to perform it over the next few years, was by then an evening-length event. He presented a number of illusions, enacted one of his escapes, and gave a demonstration and talk about fraudulent spiritualists. That more serious pursuit did not lessen his instinct for publicity or dull his cunning in securing it: in each city that he played, Houdini offered as much as $10,000 to anyone who could present a psychic manifestation that Harry was unable to figure out and duplicate. His engagements did turn-away business and had to be extended wherever he performed.

He was 52 and playing Montreal when a seemingly insignificant event turned perilous. Several McGill University students had come backstage on a Friday morning before the second-to-last show of the week. The purpose of the visit was so one of them could sketch Houdini. One of the others began questioning Houdini about miracles in the Bible. Then he asked if it was true that Houdini could take a punch in the gut without getting hurt. No sooner had Houdini replied that he could, the youth jabbed Harry four times in the stomach before Harry had time to tense his stomach and abdominal muscles. The other two lads jumped in and pulled the student away.

By the evening show, Harry was ill and sore and running a temperature. The next day, Saturday, his closing night, Bess called a doctor, who told Harry he needed an emergency appendectomy. Harry insisted on performing. He made it partway through his show but told his assistant to take over. His temperature was 104 degrees, and he collapsed at intermission and after the final curtain. He allowed himself to be taken to the hospital very early Sunday morning. Two days had elapsed since the beating. His appendix had ruptured and poison had spread throughout his system. Doctors operated Sunday and the following Friday. On Sunday, 31 October 1926, Houdini died. In addition to being Halloween, 31 October is also National Magic Day.

HOUSE

1. *House* was interchangeable with the theatre building, so a performer or newspaper reviewer would be as likely to speak of the "Keith house" in Boston as to call it a theater.
2. More specifically, *house* refers to the auditorium.
3. *House* also refers to the audience, as in "How is the house tonight?" If the manager was inquiring, he was asking about ticket sales and the number of customers, as in "Is it a full house?" If a performer was speaking, he was inquiring, "Is it a good house tonight (are they receptive)?" or making a judgment about the patrons' attitude: "What a bum house!"

"Playing two houses in one night" could have a different meaning for American vaudevillians than for British variety and music-hall performers. To the American it usually meant that he was *doubling,* or playing two different venues (e.g., an evening vaudeville bill and a midnight show at a cabaret) on the same night. To the British performer, it only meant playing to two different audiences at the same theatre on the same night.

HOUSE CURTAIN

See Front Traveler

HOUSE LIGHTS

House lights lit the auditorium in which the audience was seated. "House lights down" signaled the electrician to dim the house lights for the start of the show. "House at half" meant that the house lights were to be turned up (by dimmers, or if there were none, only half the lights would be turned on); this was done to accommodate those acts like prestidigitators and mentalists who called on members of the audience.

In smaller theatres there was no house manager to cue the electrician. The electrician, however, having attended the Monday morning rehearsal for incoming acts, had recorded the light cues and took care of them himself during the actual shows.

JOE HOWARD

b: 12 February 1867, New York, NY—
d: 19 May 1961, Chicago, IL

"I Wonder Who's Kissing Her Now?," "Hello, Ma Baby," and "Goodbye My Lady Love" are three of the more than 100 songs that Joe Howard wrote or cowrote, and it is for his songwriting that he is remembered. Joe Howard did a lot of things, however. As a performer, he sang in concert saloons, acted in a touring stock company, had a headlining vaudeville act, was host of a popular music program on network radio and played and sang his own compositions as a guest on television variety shows. Away from the public eye, he produced and wrote plays, composed music and lyrics for musical theatre and established the Joseph E. Howard Entertainment Company.

He did all of it all rather well. He had time. Running away from home, he started in show business when he was kid, and he lived to be 95. He worked full time well into his 70s and part time thereafter whenever a documentarian or a radio or television producer needed a touch of nostalgia.

Joe Howard

When he left home, he did not go far. The Bowery was well stocked with beer halls and free-and-easies where a kid could earn a few coins singing until the bartender or bouncer threw him out for being underage. The saloons were a good place to learn song craft, how to keep an audience's attention, what made them laugh and cry. Irving Berlin and others later attended the same school.

Joe played vaudeville with a number of partners, Ida Emerson, Mabel Barrison, Ethelyn Clark and Mabel McCane among them. They were also four of his nine wives. Joe, with and without a stage partner, had a reliable act, but he met with more than a few failures on Broadway. Perseverance and longevity were Joe Howard's strong suits.

Joe wrote music and lyrics for several Broadway musicals: *The District Leader,* a fast flop that came and went in a single week in 1906. Joe starred in it with Mabel Barrison and wrote the book, lyrics and music as well. (He revised the show and renamed it *Love and Politics* when he opened it in Chicago in 1911; he did not chance New York again with the show.) Joe tried again to cover all the bases when he wrote the words and music for *The Land of Nod* and starred in it with his wife Mabel Barrison, but the verdict was the same, although it took two weeks to flop this time. He was improving: *The Time, the Place and the Girl* opened four months later in 1907. This time he had help with the lyrics; Frank Adams and William M. Hough wrote the book. Joe wrote the music and did not perform; the show lasted four weeks. (That must have been encouragement enough for Joe, who revived it in 1942, when it ran for 13 performances.)

In 1908 Joe attempted the same across-the-board parlay with *The Flower of the Ranch* and failed. *The Girl Question* (1908) was an equally dismal failure. *The Prince of Tonight* (1909), created by the Howard, Adams and Hough combination, played St. Louis and Chicago. In it they introduced the song "I Wonder Who's Kissing Her Now." Joe Howard had purchased the tune from Harold Orlob but failed to credit him. When Howard recycled the song late that same year for *The Goddess of Liberty* (also Howard, Adams & Hough), Orlob stepped forward and demanded recognition.

It is a wonder the team could raise financing for each successive flop, but producing a show before 1910 was relatively inexpensive. *A Stubborn Cinderella* (ca. 1910) did not flop; it stayed on the boards for a modest total of 88 performances.

Joe was invited to appear on network radio, and this medium gave him his greatest success and only long run. Al Rinker, brother of singer Mildred Bailey and Bing Crosby's former partner in the Rhythm Boys singing trio, got the idea to re-create the era of *The Gay Nineties Revue* as a radio show. It began as a summer replacement in the late 1930s, but after a few seasons, CBS gave the show its own spot in the fall of 1944. It ran through 1944 with Joe Howard, then 73, as the host. He was reputed to be the oldest performer ever to host a big-time network radio show. Among the regulars were singers Aileen Stanley and Beatrice Kay.

When television was fishing about for program material to fill prime time, a successful radio show was a good chance if they could make it visually appealing. *The Gay Nineties Revue* (1948–49, ABC-TV) starred Joe Howard and Lulu Bates with Ray Bloch and His Orchestra. Joe was 81 and certainly in the running as the oldest person to host a television show. Joe guested on several other shows, including *Life Begins at Eighty,* a transfer from radio to television that started on NBC-TV early in 1950 and was seen on ABC-TV from late 1950 to 1952, again in 1955–56 and on Dumont in between (1952–55).

Joe Howard's songs continued to be revived occasionally, as in the 1980 musical *Tintypes;* and whenever *Showboat* was mounted, as late as in the 1990s, the audience heard the strains of "Hello Ma Baby," "Happy the Day," and "Goodbye My Lady Love," Joe Howard's interpolations in the Kern-Hammerstein score.

MAY HOWARD

b: (May Havill) ca. 1860, Toronto, Canada—d: ca. 1925

Although legend has attached itself to Billy "Beef Trust" Watson's Company for its corpulent cuties, it was May Howard who decreed that any and every girl in the May Howard Company must weigh between 150 and 200 pounds. In heft, at least, a May Howard show was the biggest in burlesque.

In the early days of burlesque, when it was primarily a female minstrel show with legs, one of its first queens was May Howard. An exceptional singer and noted for her shapely legs, May came to prominence in a Rentz-Santley show and quickly rose to the position of leading lady with several other burlesque companies, notably Bob Manchester's Night Owls, and finally headed her own outfit.

The May Howard Company was run by May's husband, Harry Morris, a Dutch comedian, and Thomas E. Miaco, and the company enjoyed great success until the mid-1890s. In 1897 she revived her troupe. By this time she had developed a flair for playing comedy, a skill that served her well, in her late 30s and 40s, as she became more stout. She brought her talents to the Casino Theatre in Manhattan, then under the management of George Lederer, and appeared in several farces. Early in the twentieth century, her husband, Harry Morris, went with Weber & Fields and May continued in farce, appearing as late as 1910 in *Tillie's Nightmare,* in support of Marie Dressler, the show's star.

In her heyday, she relished the role of the great star. Offstage, she was fun-loving and plainspoken, and she enjoyed nights of eating, drinking and gossiping with fellow burlesquers. As her star dimmed, parts grew smaller and her salary lessened. She grew litigious as she fought to protect her own rights. In the process, her battles blossomed into the larger issues of actors' rights in matters of employment.

WILLIE & EUGENE HOWARD

Willie Howard

b: (Wilhelm Levkowitz) 13 April 1886, Neustadt, Germany—d: 14 January 1949, Paramus, NJ

Eugene Howard

b: (Isidore Levkowitz) 7 July 1881, Neustadt, Germany—d: 1 August 1965, New York, NY

When the great stage comedians are discussed, among the first mentioned are Bert Lahr, Ed Wynn, Beatrice Lillie, Eddie Cantor, Bert Williams, Fanny Brice, Bobby Clark, W. C. Fields, Jimmy Durante and Victor Moore. Probably absent will be Leon Errol, Joe Cook, Ted Healy and Willie Howard. Of those comedians whom the public has forgotten, Willie Howard has a great claim to be the king of Broadway's comedians. His career on the Great White Way lasted from 1912 until 1948, and he starred in about two dozen different productions.

For much of his career, Willie partnered with his older brother, Eugene, one of the better straight men in comedy. Eugene acted dignified, and occasionally pompous or humorless as the role required. He balanced his plump physique with erect carriage and well-tailored suits, rather like a self-satisfied businessman. Willie slumped in contrast, his skinny body drooped, and in repose his bony face wore a hangdog expression. Only his dark, quick eyes and his wisecracks betrayed his alertness. Neither man, despite initial appearance, was fixed in a particular characterization. Eugene played the original heckler in "Comes the Revolution," in which Willie mounted a soap box, railed against capitalism and "de beeg boss-ez" of industry and promised that "comes the revolution, everyone will eat

Willie and Eugene Howard

strawberries and cream." When the heckler countered that he did not like strawberries and cream, the future commissar of the Lower East Side told him he would eat them and like it! By the time the sketch was committed to film, doubletalk comic Al Kelly had taken over as the heckler.

Another of their famous routines was a burlesk of a quartet from *Rigoletto.* Both Eugene and Willie had fine voices and were able to sing their roles straight; the laughs built as Willie's eyes strayed to the buxom soprano beside him. No exaggeration was necessary. The quartet stayed in character, never breaking stride or missing a note, as Willie's eyes registered the seismographic heaving of the soprano's bosom.

Much was made of Willie's dialect work. He essayed French, Scottish, Russian, Chinese and Spanish accents, but each was rendered through a persistent Yiddish. Willie's accents were as phony as Chico Marx's Italian, and that was why they were funny. Professor Pierre Ginsbairge (sometimes Ginsberg), purportedly French, was one character he played several times onstage and then brought to Al Christie's film studio, where he made five two-reel comedies in the mid-1930s, four of which were written by Billy K. Wells, who wrote the original sketch for the stage. The Professor Pierre Ginsbairge sketches for both stage and screen were short farces of mistaken identities and slamming-door races from one room to the next. The bogus professor usually delivered one monologue that provided a template for future nutty professors, like George Jessel's Professor Lafermacher and Sid Caesar's and Irwin Corey's professors; even Mel Brook's 2000 Year Old Man may owe a bit to Pierre Ginsbairge.

Willie's only other films were a couple of early Vitaphone talkies with Eugene, one of which was a spoof of opera, *Between the Acts at the Opera* (1926), and two full-length films. Willie's first movie without his brother was a feature, *Millions in the Air* (1935), that starred him with several Paramount contractees plus vaude vets Dave Chasen and Benny Baker. He waited until 1937 for his next call from a big studio. MGM stuffed *Broadway Melody of 1938* (1937) with as many Broadway big names as they could entice—Willie Howard, Sophie Tucker, Buddy Ebsen, Sid Silvers and Wilbur Mack, plus reliable Hollywood character comedians like Binnie Barnes, Billy Gilbert, Raymond Walburn, Robert Benchley and Charley Grapewin. Consequently there was not much for anyone to do. Even star Eleanor Powell was saddled with two leading men, dancer George Murphy and heartthrob hero Robert Taylor. No matter what anyone was able to do, 15-year-old Judy Garland stole the picture with a love song to MGM's top male star, Clark Gable, who was not even in the cast. Willie pushed a broom around and tried to get in a few lines before Sophie overpowered him.

The Levkowitz boys were born in Germany. The family emigrated around 1887 to the USA and settled in Harlem. Although Eugene was five years older than Willie, he may have been drawn into show business by his younger brother, but Gene, the better singer of the two, may have already been working in burlesque or vaudeville before they teamed. Willie was a class clown in school, and he tried to make it pay through street corner performances and amateur night shows at the local burlesque house, possibly Hurtig & Seaman's Theatre in Harlem.

In 1900, Willie gained employment as a song plugger (both Harry Von Tilzer and Witmark have been cited). Willie's job was to sit in the balcony of Proctor's 125th Street Theatre and join in his publisher's song after the act onstage had begun to sing it. At the turn of the twentieth century, spur-of-the-moment chiming in by a boy in the balcony became a popular device that gradually became a cliché.

Song plugging led Willie to his first truly professional job. Florenz Ziegfeld, not yet the impresario of the *Follies,* was promoting his first wife, Anna Held, and he hired Willie to sing from a box during a particular number sung by Ms. Held. Willie's engagement lasted one night only, and his Broadway debut was deferred more than ten years. It may be that, as was later reported, Willie's voice decided to change on the opening night of *The Little Duchess* (1901) during its tryout in Washington, D.C., or perhaps it simply made a good story.

Willie was 16 and Eugene was 21 when they played burlesque for the first time; they were hired, along with their friend Tom Dunne, and called themselves the Messenger Boys Trio. The company was Fred Irwin's Big Show, and the theatre was the Standard in St. Louis. Besides singing, they helped out in the sketches and however else they were needed. Getting a bit part in one of the skits, Willie decided he would play Jewish, but without the pointed beard or drab peddler's clothes.

As he waited in the wings for his cue, Irwin grabbed him. "Where's your beard?" he demanded. Willie explained he wanted to try something new—sounding Jewish, acting Jewish, but not wearing the costume that stage Jews had donned since Frank Bush set the mold. Fred Irwin would have no innovation. "Go back and put it on. If you don't wear a beard, the audience won't know you're a Jewish comedian."

Burlesque was tough, a boot camp for comedians just starting out. Some stagehands thought it good sport to try to discombobulate beginners like Willie and Eugene, misplacing their props and doing whatever came into their heads to destroy the young comedians' concentration and timing. Once the new guys proved themselves to the stagehands and to the veterans in the troupe, they were accepted, and the hanky-panky ceased. Willie won his stripes by making his stage entrance with a well-executed fall down a short flight of stairs. Skill and guts always prompted admiration.

Although burlesque, unlike vaudeville, paid the cost of transporting a performer's costumes and equipment, the company manager deducted for wigs, makeup and whatever else the company owned and the performers used. The Messenger Boys Trio contracted for $60 a week; they netted a lot less.

Willie & Eugene Howard formed a two-man song-and-patter team, billed as the Howard Brothers, for vaudeville, where salaries rose higher than in burlesque. Vaudeville acts paid for their own transport; if an act carried trunks filled with apparatus and costuming, the added costs ate into its salary. Willie and Eugene carried a change of clothes and some sheet music sides. They made the right decision; in a few years they were earning $250, then $450 a week in vaudeville.

The Shuberts hired Willie & Eugene, as they were then billed, for *The Passing Show of 1912*. The Howards joined a cast headed by Trixie Friganza, Charlotte Greenwood, Harry Fox and dance team Adelaide & Hughes. The show ran for four months at the Winter Garden. It became the first of a series of nearly annual

Willie (top) and Eugene Howard

revues that appeared on Broadway through 1924, with the single exception of 1920. Subsequent editions in 1932 and 1945 never reached Broadway. The Shuberts invited Willie and Eugene back for the 1915, 1920 and 1921 editions as well, all of which earned their keep at the huge Winter Garden Theatre.

The Whirl of the World (1914) was another Shubert revue masquerading as a book show, and Willie & Eugene kept the show on the boards for five months at the Winter Garden Theatre. After appearing in *The Passing Show of 1915,* the Howards joined Marilyn Miller, McIntyre & Heath and Walter C. Kelly in another Shubert production, *The Show of Wonders* (1916), which lasted six months at the Broadway Theatre.

When they were not working for the Shuberts, Willie & Eugene took dates in vaudeville. As the act grew progressively tighter and more polished, it was evident that Willie was the drawing card of the act. Gene Howard was a fine feed and a solid performer in his own right, but Willie had energy, sang well, was a superb comic sketch actor and did amusing impressions of other stars.

The Shuberts shared that view. They decided to produce *Sky High* (1925) as a vehicle for Willie Howard.

The script provided a fine role for Willie but there was nothing for Gene, so Gene began his decade-long pull-out from show business and started managing Willie's business affairs. The show and Willie's performance rewarded the Shuberts for their faith; the musical comedy ran more than six months. It was Howard's seventh show for the Shuberts.

Willie and Eugene accepted an offer from George White to switch to his annual revue series, the *Scandals*. *George White's Scandals of 1926* proved the most successful edition of that series thanks to Willie & Eugene, Ann Pennington and the chorus of dancers, Harry Richman, Frances Williams, and the songs by De Sylva, Brown & Henderson like "Birth of the Blues," "It All Depends on You," "(This Is) My Lucky Day," and Gershwin's "Rhapsody in Blue." George White re-signed Willie and Gene for his next two editions of the Scandals, 1928 and 1929. They were successes but that edition did not rival the year-long run that the 1926 entry had achieved.

Willie substituted for Bert Lahr in the Gershwin musical comedy *Girl Crazy* (1930), without Gene, but Ethel Merman, Ginger Rogers, Benny Goodman and other jazz greats were in the cast. The show ran most of the 1930–31 season.

Eugene was back in tandem with Willie for *George White's Scandals of 1931,* and they introduced the "Pay the Two Dollars!" sketch in this show. Ethel Merman, Everett Marshall and Rudy Vallee handled the songs, and Ray Bolger did the dancing. Audiences approved for six months. *Ballyhoo of 1932* barely made three months, but the Great Depression did not leave many people with enough money to buy theatre tickets. Willie and Gene were supported by Bob Hope, Lulu McConnell and Grace & Paul Hartman.

The Shuberts financed the *Ziegfeld Follies of 1934,* a posthumous edition, as Ziegfeld had died in 1932. Gene was in the show, but it was the antics of Fanny Brice and Willie that kept the show drawing customers for nearly six months despite the economy. *George White's Scandals of 1936* did not score as well despite the presence of Willie & Eugene, Bert Lahr and Rudy Vallee. Willie tried his hand at cowriting a farce, *Bet Your Life* (1937), but it breezed in and out of Manhattan in a week. *The Show Is On* (1937) came and went in two weeks.

Willie and Eugene shared the stage with The Three Stooges (Moe, Curley & Larry), Ella Logan, Ann Miller and Ben Blue in *George White's Scandals of 1939,* which ran four months and was the final edition in the *Scandals* series. It was also Eugene Howard's swan song as a performer. He was a year shy of 60. Gene Howard lived out his retirement from the stage well into his 80s.

From 1940 on, Willie was on his own, except when he employed Al Kelly as a stooge, but only once did he again appear in a hit show. *Crazy with the Heat* (1941) was not it, but he carried over his material from that show into *Priorities of 1942,* a packaged vaudeville show in which he headlined with Lou Holtz and Phil Baker. It was a hit and played 353 performances in ten months.

Although old-timers Willie Howard and Ethel Shutta and newcomers David Burns and Nanette Fabray did their best, not enough of *My Dear Public* (1943) were in attendance to keep the revue running more than five weeks.

Willie took Bobby Clark's place in the road show of Mike Todd's *Star and Garter,* a burlesque show passing as a revue or vice versa. It had been a huge hit on Broadway, keeping the Music Box Theatre tenanted for two seasons, and did good business on the road. The Shuberts tried to pump life into its ancient franchise *The Passing Show* with a 1945 edition, but it failed to reach Broadway even with Willie in the cast.

His last Broadway show was a revival of *Sally* (1948). It had been a big hit for Marilyn Miller and Leon Errol in 1920, but dancer Bambi Lynn and Willie Howard could not make a froth about refugee Russian nobles working as restaurant help seem interesting to postwar audiences. Willie Howard died, at age 63, just as the new network television was reaching out to the veterans of vaudeville to bring laughs to new audiences. Willie just missed that call.

GEOFF HOYLE

b: ca. 1950, England

Famous for his three-legged man in a topcoat, Geoff Hoyle was one of the original clowns of the Pickle Family Circus, along with founder Larry Pisoni and Bill Irwin. He has also performed with Cirque du Soleil and appeared on Broadway as Zazu in the original Broadway cast of *The Lion King,* a role for which the Drama Desk critics nominated him for outstanding featured performance in a musical.

Based in San Francisco, he has appeared in several films, starting with Robert Altman's *Popeye* (1980), and Geoff frequently tours in one-person shows, including *Theatre of Panic, Boomer!, Feast of Fools, The Convict's Return* and *Geni(us).*

ALBERTA HUNTER

b: 1 April 1895, Memphis, TN—
d: 17 October 1984, New York, NY

Had Alberta Hunter given her true age when she was hired as a practical nurse, her retirement would have come much sooner. The usual arbiter of a worker's value is not talent, energy, insight or the capacity for caring. It is the calendar. In 1977, when New York City's Goldwater Hospital retired Alberta Hunter, a practical nurse with 20 years of experience, she was 82 years old.

Casually dressed, a shopping bag in each hand (concealing her defensive weapons—knitting needles) and walking the streets of New York, Alberta seemed to be one of the thousands whose only rendezvous with fame could be through calamity, yet only three months after retirement, she was about to make one of the most endearing and legendary comebacks in show business history. Although no one at the hospital where she worked ever knew it, Nurse Hunter had been one of the famous Blues Queens of the 1920s and an international chanteuse of the 1930s. Her career began in gangster gin mills, circled the globe and spanned eras from the Edwardian to the nuclear. She was a star in vaudeville, continental cabarets and the USO, and her final and spectacular decade began with her singing engagement at the Cookery in Manhattan.

Born in Memphis in 1895, Alberta slipped away from home in 1911 to try her luck in Chicago. Her hope was to trade housecleaning work for show business. Still underage, she began singing at Dago Frank's for his clientele of white hookers and pimps. She preferred this to life at home, where her nickname was "Pig" and there was a stepfather who despised her, a mother who favored Alberta's older sister and a school principal who molested her.

Alberta spent about 15 years in Chicago, moving up to better clubs and learning about music, stagecraft and people. Her youthful voice was soprano, light and trilling, and she sang the popular songs of her day, adding the blues as she became aware of them. Despite working at Dago Frank's and at Hugh Hoskins', another small club with a black clientele, Alberta never smoked, drank, did dope or ran around with the fast crowd. She saved her money.

Alberta measured success by the amount of money she was able to send home. With the money came respect from her mother. Alberta was 18 when her mother and stepfather separated. Her mother moved to Chicago, where she shared an apartment with Alberta.

In 1914 Hunter made her move toward better clubs. She went to work at Elite Number One when its resident piano player was Tony Jackson. He proved to Alberta the importance of having a talented and simpatico accompanist.

She followed with a gig at the Panama Café, whose talent roster at the time included future stars Florence Mills, Cora Green, Mattie Hite and a young woman who would become as famous and enduring as Alberta—Bricktop. When the police closed the Panama Café after a murder in 1917, Alberta moved next door to the De Luxe Café, but a week later Bill Bottoms hired her to sing in his Dreamland Ballroom, Chicago's most important black club.

Hunter's last several years in Chicago were spent in reign as "the ragtime songbird deluxe" at Dreamland, where the King Oliver Band featured Sidney Bechet on clarinet, George "Pops" Foster on bass, Warren "Baby" Dodds on drums and Lil Hardin at the piano ("She could play anything in this world"). The integrated audience featured Sophie Tucker, Al Jolson and other white stars of the era. Although the salary was nominal, the tips amounted to several hundred dollars each night. Hunter worked Chicago's black vaudeville theatres as well, playing the Lyceum and the Monogram.

Like many ambitious entertainers, Hunter longed to try her professional luck in New York. The Chicago race riots in the summer of 1917 reinforced Alberta's intent, as did other matters. Alberta had already met Lottie Tyler, Bert Williams' niece, when Lottie was the backstage maid to actor Fay Bainter. Tyler invited Hunter to visit her in Harlem; Lottie and Alberta knew they were attracted to each other.

Hunter may have wanted only to stop gossip about her being a lesbian when, in 1919, she married Willard Saxby Townsend, a young waiter just home from the First World War in Europe, but he was in love with her. In later years Alberta admitted that "it's a shame the way I treated him. I only knew him a couple of days," said Alberta, not mentioning that he was a paying guest, renting a room in the apartment Alberta shared with her mother. Townsend petitioned for a divorce after two months. Alberta found it convenient not to respond to the court summons, so the decree was not granted until four years later, in 1923.

Shortly after she married Townsend, Hunter resumed her relationship with Lottie Tyler. Alberta realized there was quite a difference in their social standing when she first visited Lottie at Bert Williams' palatial home where Lottie lived with Bert and his wife. The Williams family's comings and goings were chronicled by Harlem society columnists. Although Alberta always had striven to be respectable, she now had the chance to learn the social graces. According to Hunter's biographers, Frank C. Taylor and Gerald Cook (who was also her longtime accompanist), Alberta and Lottie became longtime lovers and remained friends for many years, even through the long periods when Alberta's career and the independence they both cherished kept them apart.

Alberta returned to Chicago in 1920 to appear in a series of old revues and musical comedies that were revived for black audiences by Shelton Brooks, the songwriter and comedian. The last in this series,

Canary Cottage, traveled to the Dunbar Theatre in Philadelphia and the Lafayette in Harlem. After her theatre experience, Hunter opted for the better money (those tips) that Dreamland offered and stayed there through 1921. Under the guidance of a new special friend, Carrie Mae Ward, Alberta became a clotheshorse, and her new chic appearance helped to distinguish Hunter from other, less tastefully gowned and coifed café singers.

Alberta started recording blues for Black Swan in 1921 and moved a year later to Paramount, with whom she stayed throughout the 1920s. During these Paramount contract years she also cut a session with Louis Armstrong and the Red Onion Jazz Babies for the Gennett label using her sister's name, Josephine Beatty. Alberta composed some of her own songs, including "Downhearted Blues," which became Bessie Smith's first record and a very big hit. Sensing Alberta's naiveté, Lovie Austin, pit band leader at the Monogram Theatre and Bessie's childhood friend, scored "Downhearted Blues" for Alberta and showed her how to copyright. Hunter was forever grateful.

In those days before network radio, the best way to promote records was to tour vaudeville and introduce the songs in an act, so that meant going back to vaudeville. On Hunter's tour of the South in 1922, a young black boy was killed for sassing back to a white man; his body was tossed into the lobby of the theatre where Hunter was to have played.

Alberta crossed over to white vaudeville, playing the Keith-Albee-Orpheum circuit. Hunter made New York her home base in 1923 when she was tapped to replace Bessie Smith in the 1923 stage show *How Come?* She was determined to conquer black musical theatre when she tried out for the famously successful *Shuffle Along.* The show opened in 1921 with a book by the black comedy team of Flournoy Miller and Aubrey Lyles, and boasted music by Eubie Blake and lyrics by Noble Sissle. Late in life Alberta claimed that Noble Sissle rejected her because he was "dicty" (snobbish) and "color conscious."

For much of the time between 1922 and 1927, Hunter played vaudeville theatres between New York and Chicago, even playing the white Keith-Orpheum time but never again venturing South. There were also prestigious café engagements, both at home and in Europe.

Vaudeville was entering its decline late in 1927 when Alberta went to London to work British variety, including the Palladium. Jerome Kern and Oscar Hammerstein saw her there and cast her in their West End production of *Show Boat* (1928) with Edith Day, Paul Robeson and Cedric Hardwicke. Mabel Mercer, later the doyen of café singers, was in the chorus, and Alberta roomed in the same house as concert singer Marian Anderson. Their production ran a year.

By now Hunter had changed from a singer of blues into a polished performer of sophisticated songs. She learned the basics of several useful languages, including French and Yiddish, and profitably plied the international smart set's cabaret route as well as variety theatres in Britain and on the Continent. She did not return to the USA for good until the Second World War, although she came back for periodic tours of RKO presentation houses. Her London recordings from this period display a voice similar to that on the 1920s records, with clear enunciation yet a shade richer.

Hunter came home as the late 1930s segued into the Second World War years. She patched together a career in not-quite-dead vaudeville, on radio and onstage in *Mamba's Daughters,* Broadway's 1939 dramatic triumph for star Ethel Waters.

As the USA prepared for war, the government set up the United Service Organizations (USO). Among its many duties, the USO, like vaudeville of old, delivered entertainers to wherever an audience—in this case, servicemen in segregated units—could be found. Alberta joined the USO in 1944 and took the first Negro troupe overseas; she was put in charge because she was "tough," a stickler for regulations. Hunter received special notice from General Eisenhower. More USO tours followed, with treks to Burma, India, China and the South Pacific and continuing into the Korean Conflict until 1954, the year of her mother's death, when Hunter left singing for training as a practical nurse. She was 59 years old and had every reason to expect that her performing days were over.

The Alberta Hunter who returned to the world of music a quarter of a century later in 1977 had a flinty voice and a crackling delivery. She looked like a mischievous Nefretete and her no-nonsense, unsentimental attitude made her good copy for journalists and feature writers. Soon Alberta was on magazine covers and TV shows, playing the White House, composing a film score for Robert Altman and performing five nights of the week at the Cookery.

She continued this schedule almost to the end. Even at 89, Alberta Hunter had none of that halting, faltering manner of the aged. Her voice had settled into a low octave, and she deflected any wobbling in her tone with growls and bites, slapping the words along. Offstage Alberta Hunter seemed guarded and laconic; she wanted to be sure that everyone understood that she was not some sweet old lady who could be swindled. At times she could be demanding, but even then it was in a down-to-earth manner. Secretiveness was a lifetime trait, and not many people became true intimates. Her kindnesses were private and personal. When she gave she also got involved.

Alberta continued her lifetime habits of hard work and frugality, even in her last year when she used a wheelchair. Her pride did not surrender to age either, for she insisted on leaving her wheelchair at the edge in the wings and walking, sometimes with help, to center stage. Once she was there and her accompanist, Gerald Cook, began playing her music on the piano, she slipped away from her years for an hour of animated performance, fingers snapping, head tossing, winking, growling and singing with gusto, animated by the beat. Twice in her last year, she traveled to fulfill engagements in São Paulo in Brazil. She was back home in New York when she died peacefully in her sleep in her 90th year.

HURTIG & SEAMON

The collective name actually referred to the Hurtig brothers (Benjamin and Jules) and Harry Seamon. The Hurtigs began as merchants in Cincinnati but found their way into the circus, where they met juggler Harry Seamon. The three men formed a booking agency and a sheet music publishing business.

Hurtig & Seamon began with concert saloons in the 1870s and then turned to producing relatively inexpensive stage shows, such as the groundbreaking *In Dahomey* (1902–05), starring Williams & Walker on Broadway. They acquired a chain of theatres as well and were among the first white managements to introduce white and mixed-race audiences to great black performers, including Ernest Hogan (1860–1909), Bert Williams (1874–1922) and George W. Walker (1873–1911).

For a number of years extending well into the 1920s, they financed revues and musical comedies written and composed by and starring African Americans. At the same time, they were participating producers in the Columbia Amusement Corporation, sending a stream of burlesque shows out on the wheel.

WALTER HUSTON

b: (Walter Houghston) 6 April 1884, Toronto, Canada—d: 7 April 1950, Beverly Hills, CA

Family lore has it that a Salvation Army band was the first musical influence in baby Walter's life. Church was likely next, as the local preacher provided a target for Walter's early gift for comic mimicry. School was conspicuous for its lack of influence. Walter and his neighborhood chums preferred playing hooky and spending their days playing adventurous games in the woods or sitting in the balcony of Toronto's Shea Theatre watching—and later trying to imitate—the jugglers, ventriloquists, dancers and musicians on the vaudeville bill.

His first venture on the stage, however, left the eight-year-old frozen with stage fright. He did not try again until he was 14, when he sang and did some comedy in blackface for a minstrel show organized by the local Episcopal church. This time the audience stimulated Walter. He quit high school and plotted a stage career while he worked at jobs that failed to inspire.

When the chance came his way, Huston was 16. He and his close friend Archie Christie signed on with a traveling theatrical troupe; Walter played old men in a series of melodramas. In one of the "mellers," *In Convict's Stripes,* Huston hoisted atop his shoulders a five-year-old Lillian Gish, then making her stage debut. The troupe's engagements took Huston across the border into the USA and, while pay was a sometime thing, the experience was excellent grounding for a life in show business.

At tour's end near Rochester, New York, Walter and Archie, quite broke, rode the rails into New York City. By 1902, Walter, then 18, was working regularly as an actor in melodrama, on tour and in stock. At six feet tall, lean and with brown hair and a masculine mien, he looked right for leading man roles. Stage fright struck again in *Julius Caesar* during his Broadway debut at the Herald Square Theatre. Feeling disgraced, Walter fled the stage and played professional hockey for a season.

Huston worked his way back into the theatre, first as a stage manager, then as a touring actor. In 1904, while touring the South and West in an old chestnut, *The Sign of the Cross,* he met his future wife, Rhea. They were married a week later. Walter got into a tussle with the manager of his troupe and found himself out of work and broke. Again he bid adieu to the stage.

With some study and on-the-job training in the field, Walter worked as an engineer in various jobs over the ensuing five years of his marriage to Rhea. When they split, their son John, later to be a famous screenwriter and director, was three years old.

Walter was one of those souls who was a born storyteller and could amuse a roomful of guests. Their enthusiastic reception rekindled Houston's desire for the stage. By 1910, despite his youth (he was in his mid-20s) and leading-man looks, Walter had little luck finding work in the legitimate theatre. Finally accepting often-proffered advice, Huston turned to vaudeville. He hoped his storytelling would provide more regular work and better pay. Still married to Rhea, he met Bayonne Whipple, who became his second wife and vaudeville partner.

Bayonne urged Walter to write a skit for the two of them, one that employed a trick that Walter and his brother Alec had devised when they were kids: a sheet of rubber that when stretched seemed to animate the face painted on it. The act, called "Spooks," was lighthearted and made room within its length of 18 minutes for Walter to sing a comic song he wrote, "If You Haven't Got the Do-Re-Mi," while strutting the stage with top hat and cane.

As Whipple & Huston, they performed "Spooks" successfully for five years, until 1915. This sketch took them into big-time Keith and Orpheum circuits, and they secured good billing, solid bookings and a handsome salary. Although Walter became rather well known for singing "If You Haven't Got the Do-Re-Mi," Whipple & Huston were not headliners. They were a good number two act, popular with audiences, and they were grateful for their success, but five years in the same act was turning them stale. Traveling also brought the strain that afflicted many acts in vaudeville: a good salary was soon whittled down by traveling expenses, hotel bills and tips to stagehands and musicians who could make a performance a pleasure or a pain.

Walter devised another act for them, "Shoes" (later called "Boots"). Bayonne played the customer and Walter the sales clerk. Again he included a song-and-dance number for himself and usually performed another routine for an encore. The act earned them between $300 and $450 a week; with it they played the circuits for years and reached the Palace in New York.

While Walter wrote, Bayonne Whipple began dealing with managers and booking agents. Ever her husband's number one booster, Whipple approached Eddie Darling, in charge of booking the Palace and influential with the Keith-Albee management. She was intent on making Whipple & Huston a headline act. It was 1923 and jazz bands were popular. Offhandedly, Darling suggested they organize their act around a jazz band. In a month Huston had created a new act that included a jazz band; he called it "Time." But it was an expensive act, and they needed to break it in on the small time before they had a chance at getting booked on Keith-Albee time, especially the Palace. Small-time circuits like Loew's could not offer Whipple & Huston a salary sufficient to cover their costs.

Walter and Bayonne managed to sign with the Shuberts, who were making their second raid into vaudeville against Keith-Albee. Shubert paid them $1,500 a week, but ten weeks was all the fledgling circuit could offer them. When they completed their Shubert run they were at a turning point. Some sources claim that Albee, always anxious to blunt Shubert inroads into vaudeville, was willing to let Eddie Darling book them on Keith-Albee time at $1,250 a week. Other sources maintain that by working for the Shuberts their vaudeville careers were finished.

In either case, Walter Huston was nearly 40 years old. His wife was now as anxious and ambitious for him as he was tired of the precarious career of an aging song-and-dance man. An opportunity for change presented itself in the form of a script. *Mr. Pitt,* written by Zona Gale, was being produced by Brock Pemberton, who had approached William Carrington to invest in the production. Mr. Carrington agreed on the condition that his brother-in-law, Walter Huston, be given the lead.

Walter was not the only talented Huston of his generation. His sister Margaret became an opera singer of note and married a wealthy man and arts patron, William Carrington. Shortly after they married, William was crippled by a fall from a horse, and Margaret, who had enjoyed a far more successful career than her brother Walter, damaged her vocal cords by swallowing a fish bone. Her singing voice destroyed, Margaret Carrington turned to the study of voice production, devising a system of phonetics that made her the most sought after voice teacher for actors in early twentieth-century America. She accepted only a few students, without recompense, but those few students included John Barrymore (then turning from light comedies to Shakespeare), Lillian Gish, Alfred Lunt and Walter Huston.

Mr. Pitt ran three months and made Walter far more famous and respected than he was at any time in his 15 years in vaudeville. It also cost him his marriage. Bayonne Whipple, a vaudeville name when Walter Huston was unknown, had subordinated her career to his. She had fought for their act and for his talent. Now she was shut out by the process of the legitimate stage: Walter was in the hands of the director and his vocal coach. Offstage, she was a vaudevillian among people of the serious theatre. According to his biographers and his son, John, Walter seems to have felt he had outgrown his second wife.

Eugene O'Neill saw *Mr. Pitt* and decided he had found the man to portray the 75-year-old patriarch in his new play, *Desire Under the Elms.* Already a Pulitzer Prize winner, O'Neill had become a force on Broadway and remained so for 30 years. *Desire under the Elms* opened 11 November 1924, and controversy about the subject matter swirled around the production. Was it sexually obscene? It certainly was a success, running for eight months.

Walter had to wait two more plays for another success, but it came with the title role in *The Barker.* Familiar territory for Walter, the play was set in a carnival, and Huston made showy use of his sister's training by performing the long-winded spiels.

The 1926–27 season also hosted the debut of talking motion pictures. Walter tested and was devastated when he saw the results. He had made no adjustment for the new medium and played as he would onstage. The studio lost interest, and Walter realized that movies required a more intimate approach to the material. He retreated to vaudeville. This time, however, he was a headliner, famous for his Broadway credits.

George M. Cohan, wearing his producer's cap, came to Huston to offer Walter the lead role in Ring Lardner's play, *Elmer the Great.* It opened in 1928 with Walter as the braggart baseball hero from the sticks. Despite Lardner, Cohan and Huston, the play was not a success.

Offstage, Walter Huston wed his third and last wife, Nan Sunderland, with whom he had been involved since the waning days of his marriage to Bayonne Whipple. When he again got a chance to appear in films, Huston knew how to adapt his technique for the screen. He remained a successful character actor in films, making 48 of them from 1929 until his death in 1950. His most notable films include *The Virginian* (1930), *Rain* (1932), *Dodsworth* (1936), which won him the first of four Oscar nominations, and *The Treasure of the Sierra Madre* (1947), which was directed by his son, John, and won for Walter an Academy Award.

His later career on the stage had become secondary to the one on the screen, except for his performance in Sidney Howard's dramatization of Sinclair Lewis' *Dodsworth* in 1933 and his portrayal of Pieter Stuyvesant in *Knickerbocker Holiday* in 1938. The Kurt Weill–Maxwell Anderson musical provided Walter Huston with the song that followed him the rest of his career, "September Song." Equally memorable was his refusal of the role of Willie Loman in Arthur Miller's *Death of a Salesman.* He said he hated the script.

BETTY HUTTON

b: (Elizabeth June Thornburg) 26 February 1921, Battle Creek, MI

Her seasons in vaudeville were few. They came in the 1930s, during the dark days after the death of two-a-day. Twenty years later, Betty Hutton achieved her great success in vaudeville when, beginning the week of 12 April 1952, she topped the bill at the Palace. Earlier that season, Judy Garland had started a new, hopeful policy at the Palace that alternated with an attempt to revive old-time vaudeville. The old-style bill did not pay the mortgage. By giving over the second half of the show to a superstar—Garland, Hutton, Danny Kaye, Jerry Lewis, Liberace or Harry Belafonte—the grand old house of vaudeville pulled in the money, for a time at least.

Vaudeville revival bill at the Palace, April 1952, with Betty Hutton

Prior to opening at the Palace, Betty Hutton had been overseas entertaining the troops, so she had an act for her two-a-day show at the Palace. The first half of the bill offered the standard five acts. In the case of Betty's first engagement at the Palace, the show opened with a slapstick tumbling act, the Dassie Brothers (also known as Les Dassies), followed by a singing group, the Skylarks, and then with Borrah Minevitch's Harmonica Rascals. In the fourth and fifth spots were Andre, Andree & Bonnie, "The Dancing Mannequins," and humorist Herb Shriner.

Betty Hutton performed the second half of the bill, and for 50 minutes she sang, danced, clowned and evoked memories of old-time vaudeville stars like Eva Tanguay, whom she most resembled in style. Her act was staged by Charles O'Curran, dance director and husband. Every critic applauded Hutton's incomparable energy, and the bill held for four weeks.

Betty returned to the Palace 14 October 1953, again limiting herself to a four-week engagement. On the bill this time were Bil [*sic*] & Cora Baird and their Marionettes, the Chevalos, and a newcomer, comedian Dick Shawn. Audiences and the critics were so captivated by Shawn that Hutton insisted that the Palace management put his name up on the marquee alongside hers.

As Marian Spitzer explains in her memoir of the Palace Theatre, "Only two kinds of stars were receptive to the Palace lure—the ones who had spent not wisely, but too well, and the ones with an insatiable need for a live audience to play to." The old vaudeville stars who were still draws, like Jack Benny, Burns & Allen, Ed Wynn and Eddie Cantor, were old and occupied with their television shows, earning ten times what the Palace could afford. Like Garland, Betty Hutton had spent profligately and needed the money. Her movie career was over and she welcomed the healing power of a delighted audience.

Her father deserted the family when Betty was two. He committed suicide a few years later. Betty and her older sister Marion (1919–87) sang on the street to make money, and their mother turned the family flat into a "blind pig," a hole-in-the-wall that sold liquor illegally.

Both sisters entertained their mother's customers until the police closed their illegal operation and the family moved on to Detroit. Their mother worked in factories, and the girls sang on street corners. Neither girl had time for much schooling, nor was show business a good school in which to learn balance and perspective. When success came to Betty Hutton, neither she nor her mother knew how to manage it.

Lying about her age, Betty started work in her early teens as a band singer and hustling for vaudeville dates on the small time. In 1937, Vincent Lopez heard 16-year-old Betty and signed her. Marion was hired to sing with the Glenn Miller Orchestra. Betty made several short films as a dancer and singer, including two that featured the Vincent Lopez ensemble.

In 1940, Betty was hired for a Howard Dietz Broadway revue, *Two for the Show,* which featured Betty in an ensemble with Alfred Drake, Eve Arden, Richard Haydn, Keenan Wynn and Brenda Forbes. In October of that year, Betty opened in a featured role in *Panama Hattie,* a musical comedy that starred Ethel Merman, featured Arthur Treacher, James Dunn and Rags Ragland, and racked up 501 performances. After the show closed in January 1942, Paramount signed her for movies.

The Blonde Bombshell came crashing into the American public's consciousness with her first feature-length movie, *The Fleet's In* (1942), and two years later, in 1944, she first appeared in exhibitors' lists of the top ten movie stars of the day. For the following decade Betty Hutton was a happy-go-lucky perpetual motion machine and leather-lunged singer of novelty numbers in 16 films. She played the good-natured, excitable, daffy American girl next door whom the fellows treat like a sister or a pal until she turns 16 and wears her first prom dress. Sometimes the Hutton character was a roughhouse clown, other times a sensitive, guileless girl.

Betty Hutton was fortunate that she worked for Paramount Pictures. There was not a mentor at the studio to guide her in the ways of Hollywood, nor was the studio compassionate or forgiving, yet Paramount made many of the best movies in America, and most of Hutton's movies were well produced. Had she been stuck with Universal, Twentieth Century Fox or Republic Pictures, she would have made grade B programmers. An added bonus was that Paramount arranged for Hutton to tour presentation houses in a song-dance-comedy act to promote her movie musicals.

Several films gave Hutton the chance to show that she was more than a musical jumping jack or a tomboy growing moony-eyed with her first crush. *The Miracle of Morgan's Creek* (1944), a Preston Sturges film, stripped the Hutton screen persona down to the essential gal and let her act. As Texas Guinan in *The Incendiary Blonde* (1945), Betty was allowed to mature from a brash youngster into a woman. Another biopic, *The Perils of Pauline* (1947), gave her the chance to balance slapstick with sentiment. Judy Garland had been set for the lead in *Annie Get Your Gun* (1950), but she was too erratic at the time and Betty won out over other second choices: Judy Canova, Betty Garrett and Doris Day. Hutton delivered but MGM did not do justice to Irving Berlin's masterpiece stage musical, and Betty felt her coworkers resented her.

The Greatest Show on Earth (1952) offered Betty the prestige of top billing over other major stars and the chance to prove she was able to work the trapeze, but the film was dull, roles were underwritten and the production overblown with the usual Cecil B. DeMille stuffing. That same year, Betty played vaudeville singer Blossom Seeley to Ralph Meeker's Benny Fields in another biopic, *Somebody Loves Me.* It was intended as a grade A release, but it rendered bland the music of Blossom's and Benny's era.

Betty Hutton had been transformed from a happy, brassy soubrette into a glamorous movie star. The ambitions of her second husband, dance director Charles O'Curran, ensured the demise of Hutton's career. When Paramount failed to elevate Mr. O'Curran to the position of director of her future films, Betty walked out on her contract—and her career.

When her poorly conceived television series *Goldie* (later *The Betty Hutton Show*) lasted only a single season, 1959–60, there was nothing left of her career. By 1967, Betty Hutton had declared bankruptcy, been divorced four times, lost her mother to alcohol and become estranged from her three daughters. Still in her mid-40s, she had half her life yet to live. Alcohol and drug abuse accelerated her emotional decline. The ensuing decades were spent in humbling poverty, trying to figure out how it all went wrong and hoping to find a way to a measure of contentment. At one point, she was located in Rhode Island, cooking for Catholic priests in their rectory.

There were a few bright spots amid the storm as well. In 1965, she replaced Carol Burnett on Broadway in *Fade In, Fade Out,* a musical comedy, but by 1972 she was despondent again and attempted suicide. This led to a nervous breakdown.

In 1980, Hutton followed Dorothy Loudon and Alice Ghostley into the role of Miss Hannigan in the musical comedy *Annie* on Broadway. She also went to college, earned an advanced degree and taught acting for a while at Emerson College in New England.

Over the decades, her fans have been loyal, supportive and loving. Hutton retired to Palm Springs, California. Robert Osborne of Turner Classic Movies interviewed her in 2000. Betty Hutton, then 79, looked youthful and svelte, and sitting on the edge of her chair she bubbled with energy.

HYAMS & MCINTYRE

John Hyams

b: 6 July 1869, Syracuse, NY—
d: 9 December 1940, Hollywood, CA

Leila McIntyre

b: 20 December 1882, NY—d: 9 January 1953, Los Angeles, CA

John Hyams toured with minstrel shows, danced in Charles Hoyt's proto-musical comedies and appeared at the Casino Theatre in Manhattan in a George W. Lederer musical production, *The Belle of Bohemia* (1900), among other stage shows during the 1900s.

An important show for John was *The Sleeping Beauty and the Beast,* a Klaw-Erlanger extravaganza imported from the London stage and overhauled for American audiences. It ran most of the 1901–02 season at the Broadway Theatre, and it is in this show that various chroniclers claim that John Hyams and Leila McIntyre met and courted. This seems likely, as their daughter Leila Hyams was born in 1905, but there is no record of Ms. McIntyre in the opening night cast for the Broadway production, certainly not as Beauty, as has been reported. Leila may have been engaged as a replacement during the New York run or hired for the national tour.

John's next stage show was *Piff! Paff!! Pouf!!!,* a musical comedy that ran much of the 1904–05 season and returned John Hyams to the Casino Theatre. The star was Eddie Foy, and John had a good supporting role as Paffle, one of the suitors to a quartet of sisters.

Leila McIntyre did appear in a Klaw-Erlanger extravaganza, but it was *Mother Goose* (1903), not *The Sleeping Beauty and the Beast* (1901–02). *Mother Goose* kept the lights on at the New Amsterdam Theatre only from 2 December 1903 through February 1904. Leila fared worse in a straight play, *York State Folks;* it provided her with only four weeks' work in 1905.

Leila gave birth to her daughter on 1 May 1905, and Leila and John resumed work in vaudeville for the 1905–06 season. Their flirtation act played the better small time and occasionally in the big time. Leila McIntyre was a handsome young woman, and although John was a pleasant-looking chap, he was no matinee idol. Still, they made an engaging couple and they handled comedy and music with equal aplomb. Their onstage flirtation carried them through smart repartee and solo and double singing and dancing specialties.

In January 1914, Hyams & McIntyre played their first date at New York's Palace Theatre, then coming into its own, after a tenuous start, as a flagship of big-time vaudeville. Later that spring, both John and Leila were cast in a Shubert musical, *The Dancing Duchess,* but it closed on Broadway after little more than a week. Vaudeville proved a more reliable stage for the couple than Broadway musicals. Offering a few songs and a bit of dancing within the framework of a sketch act, Hyams & McIntyre remained a popular mixed-double act for a quarter of a century until vaudeville itself declined.

When major Hollywood studios committed to making sound features, many vaudevillians headed west, hoping to swim from the sinking ship of vaudeville to the sunny shores of movieland. John Hyams, Leila McIntyre and Leila Hyams were among the refugees. Both John and Leila made about three dozen films between 1927 and 1941. They found themselves cast in nine of the same movies, but not as a team. Generally, their roles were small and most were uncredited.

Their daughter, Leila Hyams (1905–77), was more successful during the decade or so that she acted in films. She made her debut in 1924 but did not pursue a movie career until 1927, after which she played ingénues in more than 50 features before retiring in 1935. She married Phil Berg, who was not in show business, and they remained married for half a century until her death in 1977.

HYPE

To aggressively sell a show or an act through ads and publicity; to engage in hyperbole, exaggerating the merits and notices of a show or an act.

HYPNOTIST

A stage hypnotist relied on volunteers seated in the theatre to convince audiences that the act was a legitimate exercise. Most audiences regarded hypnotism as a subset of magic or illusion acts, but in fact the legitimate hypnotist relied on his real ability to induce his subjects into a state of altered consciousness in which they were able to function physically, understood what was said to them, yet were susceptible to the commands of the hypnotist and were able to execute them.

To get a reaction from the audience, it was necessary to order the hypnotized subject to do something either dangerous or comic. Common sense dictated that the hypnotist try for laughs yet not truly embarrass or ridicule a customer and risk an audience's ire.

Some phony hypnotism acts employed plants in the audience whom the hypnotist selected to come up onstage and pretend to be placed under his power, but these acts had to be wary of legitimate audience members challenging them.

I

ILLUSIONIST

A term sometimes used as an alternative to *stage magician,* it more precisely refers to those acts that presented major illusions onstage such as escapes, levitations, quick-changes and the disappearance or materialization of people, large animals or good-sized items. Blackstone's "Vanishing Horse" was an illusion, and Siegfried and Roy do much the same thing with large cats.

Acts of illusion invariably needed a full stage with trapdoors, fly wires, major props, cabinets and machinery. They employed lots of flash, such as lighting, visual and aural effects. Occasionally these acts took up the entire second half of a bill, or even played an entire evening because the technical demands required a more elaborate setup than could be engineered between acts or during an intermission.

ILLUSTRATED SONG SLIDES

Early small-time vaudeville houses and nickelodeons found it advantageous to show illustrated song slides. A resident piano player pumped out the music as slides or silent moving pictures appeared on a blank white screen (or sheet) with the lyrics printed against painted, drawn or photographed backgrounds. The music publishers of Tin Pan Alley were happy to supply illustrated song slides free to the theatres because it was as effective a way to popularize their songs as sending salaried song pluggers into music stores.

The presentations also took place in small vaudeville houses, music stores and various other types of shops where a proprietor agreed to open up after hours for a split of the take. Many a haberdasher and dry goods merchant found they made more money after usual business hours showing illustrated song slides and half-reel and one-reel silent movies than they had earned during the long hours of their regular business day. Some such humble ventures grew into full-time nickelodeons and small small-time vaudeville houses.

The popularity of illustrated song slides ebbed in time, yet the concept survived. In the sound movie era, musical cartoons encouraged the audience to sing along by following the bouncing ball. Later, children's programming on television used the mutual reinforcement of pictures, music and words to teach and entertain.

IMHOF, CONN & CORINNE

Roger Imhof

b: 15 August 1875, Rock Island, IL—
d: 15 April 1958, Hollywood, CA

Marcel Corinne

d: 1977

During the golden age of two-a-day, one of the mostly highly regarded acts in vaudeville was "The Pest House," the most popular and longest running of several sketches that starred the portly pair Roger Imhof and Marcel Corinne. Everyone who saw and wrote about the act claimed it was hilarious. As a surefire comedy sketch, it ranked with Willie, West & McGinty's "Comedy Builders," yet very little has been written about the content of the act. It is supposed to have taken place in what was then commonly referred to as a lunatic asylum, and it ran about 30 minutes.

The act was known both as Imhof & Corinne and Imhof, Conn & Corinne. Corinne was sometimes spelled as Coreene, but next to nothing is known about her or Conn. Mr. Imhof was one of the first emcees in vaudeville, a relaxed commentator like Herman Timberg. Imhof's later career in Hollywood provides most of what little information remains in the record about him. Imhof was of the generation that came into show business around the early 1890s, when medicine shows, minstrel troupes, variety theatres, beer gardens and circuses provided the usual avenues into show business. Roger spent part of his early career as a clown with the Mills Orton Circus and then went into burlesque. He appeared in *Dainty Duchess* (ca. 1912) on the Columbia wheel.

In 1923, Roger Imhof (minus Ms. Corinne) appeared in the cast list for *Jack and Jill,* starring Lina Basquette, Clifton Webb and Brooke Johns. Joe Dimeglio, whose father and grandfather were in vaudeville, wrote in *Vaudeville U.S.A.* that Imhof, during the flush times of vaudeville, had invested in Chicago and Los Angeles real estate but lost much of his wealth in the stock market and during the ensuing Depression. Perhaps he was happy to retreat to Hollywood when big-time, two-a-day vaudeville was finished. He picked up a decent salary for small roles in more than 50 movies between his debut in 1932, when he was featured in several films with Will Rogers, and his retirement after playing Joe E. Brown's father in *Casanova in Burlesque* (1944).

Roger Imhof and Marcelle Coreene [sic]

IMPERSONATORS AND IMPRESSIONISTS

Impersonators are not the same as impressionists. One imitates; the other reveals. Impersonators endeavor to present an accurate portrayal of their subject, striving for a realistic re-creation of their subject's appearance, voice, manner and movement. The intent is to impersonate their subject so successfully that the audience forgets they are not seeing the real thing.

Impressionists do not offer a mirror image; they are selective, choosing one or two props, mannerisms, quirks and taglines to suggest the whole person. Impressionists possess a point of view that may or may not be sympathetic to their subject. They do not seek to fool the audience. Instead, they aim to persuade audiences to see the subject as the impressionist does, exaggerating certain traits, mannerisms, postures, movements and vocal patterns so as to suggest the inner as well as outer person.

Historically, there is another difference. Onstage, the impressionist always targets a specific person, whereas the impersonator may select a real person or portray a type (little girl, old man, immigrant). Early theatrical reviewers wrote of "impersonations" (or "delineations") of Negroes, Irish, Germans, Italians and Jews and applauded the impersonators for how closely they adhered to the prevailing stereotype (or how cleverly they deviated from it toward what the observer believed was a more authentic depiction).

In practice, impersonation most usually meant female and male impersonations in vaudeville and revue, whereas impressions became a staple of stand-up comics who used famous people's voices, postures and gestures to get laughs.

IN-AND-OUTERS

A mildly derisive term favored by acts who spent their entire careers in vaudeville. It refers to those performers who used vaudeville as a step toward careers in drama and the musical stage, yet returned to vaudeville between flops.

INDIE

Short for independent—a person, an operation or a business unallied with a syndicate or a larger corporate entity.

INFLUENZA PANDEMIC OF 1918

The deadliest in recorded history, the influenza outbreak of 1918 claimed more deaths in one year than the black plague of the mid-fourteenth century. No one knew how many people died worldwide; estimates varied between 20 and 40 million people. In the USA, the total number of deaths was reckoned at 675,000, all within the single year of 1918. The death tally in Europe and the USA was ten times higher than the number of people who had died in battle during the four years of the First World War. Among laypersons and the press, it was nicknamed *Spanish flu* and *la grippe.*

Characteristics of the influenza of 1918 differed from those of previous strains. It was highly contagious, spread rapidly and sometimes killed an infected person within a single day. Once its virulence was noted, officials closed places where the public gathered. In cities that were hardest hit, theatres were closed. Actors were put out of work. Performers had their bookings canceled, and managers were left with empty theatres and no revenue to offset mortgages.

Ticket sellers, stage crews, electricians, boardinghouse operators, songwriters, sketch writers, bookers, agents, producers, printers and every other profession that depended on show business for a substantial part of their income were severely hurt by the closing. Fortunately, theatres reopened, and show business regained much of its lost ground within two years. Some producers and theatre owners never recovered.

IN FOUR

A rarely used term, it refers to the full playing area of the stage. More commonly this is called playing *in full.*

IN FULL

Refers to playing on the full stage. When an act plays the full stage, it likely will be followed by a performer who works *in one*—in front of the house curtain. This arrangement allows the stagehands time to clear the *full* stage of the previous act and set it for a later one to follow.

IN ONE

The performing area downstage between the footlights and the first drop curtain (or front cloth) past the proscenium. Playing in this area allowed a wing space of a few feet, wide enough for the act to make its entrance in front of the first drop. The amount of space varied from theatre to theatre depending on whether the stage apron was cut straight across or bowed out over the orchestra pit, and how generously the entire stage was proportioned. Six feet was average for the space between the *foots* and the first drop, but the distance could range from four to eight feet. This allowed the stage crew to set up the next act behind the performers working in one. (*Also see* In Two *and* Full Stage)

INTERPRETIVE DANCE

Infrequently, serious dance appeared on a vaudeville programme. If it was not ballet, then it was deemed interpretive, the suggestion being that one must make of it what one could. Ruth St. Denis, as a solo dancer and later with her partner, Ted Shawn, and their large company, Denishawn, was one of the very few high-minded dance acts who successfully played vaudeville for decades. Although St. Denis and Shawn were classified as interpretive dancers, much of their vaudeville and concert work approached story dance, and the costumes and scenery provided the audience with clues—a temple to Isis, a Turkish bazaar—and an eyeful.

People writing about the arts tend to be writers or, at least, people who are most comfortable expressing their ideas and reactions in words. Usually they are sympathetic to literature, sometimes partisan. When discussing drama they are still close to their home ground. In theatre pieces, however, where narrative and dialogue are absent, as in concert dance, many critics are challenged.

In drama, words are the primary symbols; playwrights use dialogue to carry meaning and tell a story. The impulse for choreographed movement may be to tell a story, but it can also be ambiguous, inchoate, sensed but not analyzed, or just a single image or a particular sound. The dance may be totally free, as far as its creator knows, of any explicable meaning. Faced with dance that appeared non-narrative, abstract, unfamiliar or, indeed, interpretive, the tendency was to attribute any shortcoming to the artists rather than the reviewer. A *Variety* critic once reported of an interpretive dancer—whose vaudeville career must have been brief—that of his three dances, the first, second and third were over the heads of the audience.

The term *interpretive* had no fixed boundaries. Depending on who used it, it might include, along with Ruth St. Denis, Ted Shawn and the Denishawn company, the experiments of Loïe Fuller, a few Isadora Duncan knockoffs, dozens of Salomés shedding their seven veils and a hundred wriggling would-be Little Egypts and ecdysiasts.

It is likely that only a small percentage of any vaudeville audience applauded the artistic intentions of the interpretive dancer. More likely to find favor were colorful costumes or very small costumes. Female dancers were not the only ones to bare nearly all for art; Ted Shawn, possessed of a perfectly proportioned body, occasioned many flutters of the heart among the women in his audience when he portrayed one of his Greek, Aztec or Hindu gods wearing little more than a fig leaf or loincloth. The attendant charges of obscenity kept box offices busy and Denishawn booked. Some interpretive dance acts were solo presentations that would be slotted anywhere on a vaudeville bill, depending on the dancer's fame and following and how much room this individual needed on the stage. Acts like Denishawn were full-stage affairs requiring imposing scenery (for a vaude act) and employing a dozen or more dancers.

INTERSTATE TIME

Formally known as the Interstate Amusement Company, this circuit had vaudeville houses in cities from Texas headed north and east to Oklahoma, Arkansas, Kansas, Missouri, Kentucky, Georgia and Florida. Interstate booked out of Chicago, and for acts bridging the big time from one coast to the other, Interstate time offered play dates to break long jumps. Most of the Interstate theatres were named Majestic (Fort Worth, Dallas, Houston, Galveston, Beaumont and San Antonio in Texas; Little Rock and Hot Springs, Arkansas; Birmingham and Montgomery, Alabama; Jacksonville, Florida; Columbus, Georgia; and Charleston, South Carolina. Among others were the Lyric in Mobile, Alabama, and the Orpheums in Savannah, Georgia, and Key West, Florida. Its first general manger was E. F. Carruthers. He was followed by B. S. Muckenfuss, formerly affiliated with the St. Louis Cardinals baseball team. Muckenfuss later bought a controlling interest in Interstate.

Note: The list of the theatres attributed to this circuit is a composite of lists. It was culled from several sources, including *Julius Cahn's Official Theatrical Guide* (1910), *The [New York] Clipper Red Book and Date Book* (1910), Jack B. Shea's *The Official Vaudeville Guide* (1928) and Herbert Lloyd's *Vaudeville Trails thru the West* (1919).

Theatre affiliations with circuits, however, changed over time. A Proctor theatre later may have become a Keith-Albee house; a Pantages' or a Loew's theatre may have been a former Sullivan & Considine theatre; and independent circuits were often taken over by larger enterprises, like Keith-Albee. Theatres were bought and sold, and names were changed entirely or simply altered to reflect their new owners.

Some theatres were specifically designed as opera houses or vaudeville theatres, but generally theatres were able to accommodate several types of show. A theatre could host vaudeville for ten years and then change to exhibiting only motion pictures. A former burlesque house might be converted to vaudeville.

The following list of theatres is not a snapshot in time. It includes theatres that functioned at various times over a period of nearly 20 years; thus there will be duplications.

Fort Smith	Arkansas	Joie Theatre
Little Rock	Arkansas	MajesticTheatre
Pine Bluff	Arkansas	Pine Bluff Theatre
Pine Bluff	Arkansas	Sanger Theatre
Texarkana	Arkansas	Texarkana Theatre
Alexandria	Louisiana	Rapieds Theatre
Baton Rouge	Louisiana	Columbia Theatre
Monroe	Louisiana	Sanger Theatre
New Orleans	Louisiana	Orpheum Theatre
Shreveport	Louisiana	Strand Theatre
McAlester	Oklahoma	Busby Theatre
Oklahoma City	Oklahoma	Orpheum Theatre

Wichita, Kansas, 1923

Tulsa	Oklahoma	Orpheum Theatre
Amarillo	Texas	Fair Theatre
Austin	Texas	Majestic Theatre
Austin	Texas	Opera House
Dallas	Texas	Majestic Theatre
Fort Worth	Texas	Majestic Theatre
Galveston	Texas	Grand Opera House
Galveston	Texas	Mertini Theatre
Houston	Texas	Majestic Theatre
San Antonio	Texas	Majestic Theatre
Texarkana	Texas	Sanger Theatre
Waco	Texas	Auditorium Theatre
Wichita Falls	Texas	Majestic Theatre

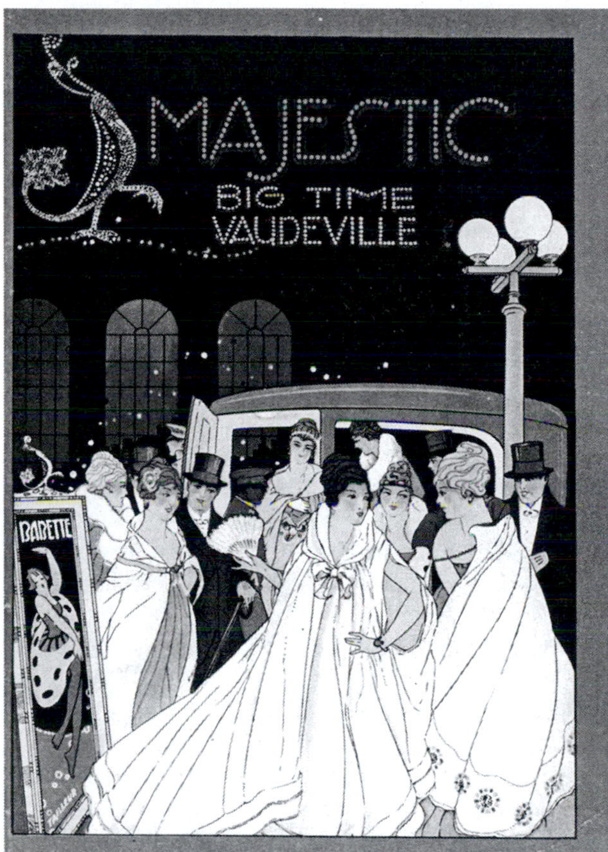

Majestic Theatre, Houston, Texas, 1918

IN THREE

Generally, acts played *in one*, *two*, or *full* stage—rarely in three. When an act played *in three* it used all of two (the front half of the stage), plus an additional three to six feet toward the back wall of the stage. The remaining few feet between a drop *in three* and the rear stage wall was enough to lower the farthest upstage drop and perhaps place a few props, furnishings or equipment against the drop if the act *in three* had to be followed by an act that required a full stage and provided the gear from the act *in three* could be cleared off the stage quickly.

INTRODUCTORY CARDS

There seems to have been no standard name for the cards propped on easels on either side of the stage to provide the audience with the name of the next act. How elaborately this was performed depended on the class of theatre. In smaller houses, a stagehand, an usher or even the manager might perform the task. In later vaudeville, some of the bigger houses hired young women, fetchingly costumed, to change the cards. In other big-time houses it was done mechanically. (*See "Annunciators"*)

IN TWO

If an act played *in two,* it performed within the front half of the stage. This space was defined in the area bounded by the footlights at the front of the stage apron, past the proscenium as far upstage as the middle set of drops and wings—about double the space an act played *in one.* This usually left another set of wings and drops, plus the area up to the back wall drops, to be readied by the stage crew for acts that required a full stage.

See In One *and* Full Stage

BILL IRWIN

b: 11 April 1950, Santa Monica, CA

In 1983, PBS telecast *The Regard of Flight.* Filmed while it was performed in front of a theatre audience, the prime-time broadcast introduced Bill Irwin and two colleagues, Doug Skinner and Michael O'Connor, to a national audience. All three, along with Nancy Harrington, collaborated on the script that presented Bill Irwin beset by antagonists, seen and unseen, as he performed.

Michael O'Connor, planted in the audience before the curtain rose, portrayed a fiercely academic critic who, instead of experiencing the show, took notes and interrupted the performance to demand explanations from Irwin. The clown, challenged to provide a rationale for what he intuits, was unable to parry O'Connor's barrage of questions and took flight. Not to be denied, the critic's pursuit became physical, and the pair chased around the stage like libertine and cuckold in a French farce.

The show's commentator and musical accompanist, Doug Skinner, provided counterpoint as pianist and droll monologist, yet was not above trying to introduce his ventriloquism act whenever the critic hounded Bill from the stage. Irwin's clown had to contend with unknown foes as well; whenever he got too close to the wings, a phantom power would drag him offstage (an action mimed wholly by Irwin).

The Regard of Flight was an actor's nightmare that took place on a stage bare except for the upstage center trunk, home to Bill's props and occasionally his refuge. A piano and lectern were set downstage right, the province of Mr. Skinner. A small, low trampoline immediately in front of the stage apron turned O'Connor's pursuit of Irwin into an Alice-through-the-looking-glass portal between stage and audience—or, perhaps, the spheres of imagination and material limits and rules. Irwin ran, jumped, fell, performed feats of illusion, juggled and danced, each with turn-on-a-dime dazzle as he veered from performance to flight. The sight gags, some venerable, provided fizz and accessibility to an intellectual script.

Following the broadcast, PBS viewers began asking who this unique new artist was. The San Francisco and New York performance communities already knew.

Bill Irwin. Photo credit Jim Moore

Irwin had been awarded Choreographer's Fellowships in 1981 and 1983 from the National Endowment for the Arts. In 1984 he received both a Guggenheim Fellowship and a five-year MacArthur genius grant—the first given to a stage performer. Many other honors have followed, including Tony, Obie, Drama Desk, Outer Critics Circle and Bessie awards.

Born in southern California and raised there and in Tulsa, Oklahoma, Bill is the oldest of Horace and Elizabeth Irwin's three children. At Oberlin College he studied theatre, joined Professor Herbert Blau's experimental performance group KRAKEN and was a featured guest with the Oberlin Dance Collective (the ODC showcased Bill's first original pieces). Bill met and worked with Michael O'Connor and Doug Skinner, spent a year as an exchange student in Belfast, Northern Ireland, and graduated from Ringling Bros. and Barnum & Bailey's Clown College. Settling in the Bay Area around San Francisco, he got work as a bike messenger until he successfully auditioned for the Pickle Family Circus (PFC) in 1974.

The reputation of the PFC grew in large measure from the fun conjured up by the three lead clowns: Larry Pisoni, a juggler, acrobat and clown, was a veteran of the San Francisco Mime Group; he adopted a less overtly political variant of their ethos when he founded the Pickle Family Jugglers, which evolved into the Pickle Family Circus. Bill Irwin was the next to join the PFC's clown corps, and Geoff Hoyle, an actor and mime, rounded out the celebrated threesome. Both Pisoni and Hoyle portrayed several comic characters, but Irwin was always Willie the Clown during the three years that the trio was together. Bill left the PFC in 1980 and moved to Manhattan. Before he left, he made his movie debut as Olive Oyl's rejected suitor, Ham Gravy, in Robert Altman's murky adaptation of *Popeye.*

Much has been made of Bill's career-long balancing act between art and entertainment. Never a question of integrity, and more than shuttling between experimental and commercial theatre, Bill's work is satisfying as art and as entertainment. Art in performance may offer profound ideas, fresh approaches and innovative construction, but if it is presented without talent, technique and the knack of engaging and charming an audience, it fails to entertain. On the other hand, professional entertainers have developed skills and an ability to connect with the audience, but if their material and delivery are trite, imitative and pitched to the lowest common denominator, their work fails to excite.

Offstage, Bill is a handsome man with a crinkly, friendly smile. Onstage Bill's clown is an innocent encountering each challenge, old or new, for the first time. Irwin's physical gifts are so extraordinary that his character seems more like a pen-and-ink cartoon figure than a clown of sinew, blood and bone. His legs wobble into jelly yet kick higher than a Rockette's. His torso inflates and collapses like a balloon as though powered by compressed air. His neck is a thing of wonder; in a turtlelike reflex it can sink into his chest below his shoulders or pop up six inches from his collarbone.

New York got to witness the fun when in 1981 Irwin and Skinner brought *Not Quite Solo Pieces* from San Francisco to the Dance Theatre Workshop in New York. Before they played New York the title was revised several times. "I did some things in San Francisco under the title *Not Quite Solo Pieces,* that then became *Not Quite* (and then *Still Not Quite*). When I did an evening in New York, I titled it *Not Quite/New York,* in the postmodern tradition of using /s (and also because I felt, with a mixture of insecurity and pride, that they were not quite New York in style). We had a wonderful cast—Michael Moschen, Tommy Sellars and Charlie Moulton."

The Regard of Flight made history the next year at Manhattan's American Place Theatre. It was remounted in 1983 for the Mark Taper Forum in Los Angeles and was revived in 1987 at the Vivian Beaumont Theatre at Lincoln Center.

The Courtroom, a brilliantly conceived 1985 piece, had Michael Moschen as the prosecutor literally juggling the evidence and Brenda Bufalino replicating the staccato of the court stenographer through her tap dancing. Bill Irwin was the defendant who eloquently and smoothly prepared his dance defense in private only to lose his composure in public, under pressure. Break-dancer Rory Mitchell and Bill's frequent collaborators Michael O'Connor and Doug Skinner also had major roles. A 50-minute piece, *The Courtroom* had a solid foundation in metaphor, but some observers felt it was not quite as much fun as expected; it was more to be admired.

As well as performing in theatre pieces of his own during the 1980s, Bill accepted acting roles in serious theatre, including Dario Fo's *Accidental Death of an Anarchist* in 1984 at the Belasco Theatre in New York. He played in Berthold Brecht's *A Man's a Man* and Chekhov's *The Seagull* in 1985, and *Three Cuckolds* in 1986—all three at La Jolla Playhouse in California.

According to some reviewers, *As Seen on TV,* prepared specifically for PBS' Live from Off Center series in 1987, was not managed as well as it could have been, for the production replaced Irwin's acrobatic comedy with camera tricks. PBS and Irwin were a better fit with Sesame Street, where Bill Irwin was a regular for years as Mr. Noodle in the Elmo segments. Bill has guested on a number of television variety shows and series, including *Northern Exposure, Saturday Night Live, The Tonight Show, Third Rock from the Sun, The Cosby Show and* the HBO special, *Bette Midler's Mondo Beyondo.* Hollywood also beckoned in the late 1980s. As much of Bill's theatre work was performed more for love than for money, television and movie work provided a reliable source of income. Bill and his wife, Martha Roth, adopted a son, Santos Patrick Morales Irwin, who was born in 1990.

From 1988 to 2006, Bill appeared in more than 20 movies. In none had he been more than featured, and none had ever given free rein to his talents. Sometimes producers hired Bill to perform his magic in a few scenes in spots where his comic routines gave their film a needed lift. In others, like *My Blue Heaven* (1990), *Stepping Out* (1991) and *How the Grinch Stole Christmas* (2000), he was well cast in decent roles that gave him opportunities. *Illuminata* (1998) and *The Laramie Project* (2002) were superior films that allowed Bill the chance to act.

In 1989, Irwin returned to the stage at the Seattle Repertory Theater City Center and to City Center in New York, where he developed *Largely New York.* Successful, it was booked next into Washington, D.C.'s Kennedy Center and then the St. James Theatre on Broadway, where it played four months in the spring of 1989 and received five Tony nominations as well as Drama Desk, Outer Critics Circle and New York Dance and Performance awards.

In 1992, *Mr. Fox: Ruminations on the Life of a Clown* also began life in workshop form at the Seattle Repertory Theatre. The Pew Charitable Trusts and Theatre Communications Group (TCG) funded a three-year collaboration between Seattle Rep and Irwin. The first result was Bill's adaptation and direction of the Molière classic *Scapin,* in which he played the title role. In 1997, the Roundabout Theatre engaged Bill to mount *Scapin* in New York. Bill stayed at Roundabout to direct Feydeau's *A Flea in Her Ear* in 1998. Between Seattle Rep and Roundabout, Bill danced in *Hip Hop Wonderland* in 1996.

His physical gifts have commanded the most attention, but some reviewers have observed that Irwin has a fine theatre voice, a well-modulated, rich baritone. Over the years, Bill has appeared in a variety of traditional productions—musicals, revues, straight contemporary drama and Shakespeare.

Fool Moon, probably Bill Irwin's most celebrated show since *The Regard of Flight,* had nearly as full a life. Developed with David Shiner, *Full Moon* won a special Tony Award when it played the Brooks Atkinson Theatre in New York in the 1998–99 season. It began life as part of the Serious Fun Festival of 1992 at Lincoln Center and then transferred to the Richard Rodgers Theatre for an eight-month run on Broadway. Thereafter it traveled to Los Angeles (1994), Vienna, Munich (1994), back to Broadway (1995), San Francisco (1998), back to Broadway again for the 1998–99 season, and closed in 1999 at the Kennedy Center in Washington, D.C. Mr. Irwin's collaborator and costar, David Shiner, a clown and comedian of distinction, shared fully in the applause and plaudits.

A limited-run production of *Waiting for Godot* in 1998 at Lincoln Center had a fine cast: Steve Martin and Robin Williams as the existential hoboes Estragon and Vladimir, F. Murray Abraham as the slavemaster Pozzo, and Bill Irwin as Lucky, the slave turned master. The role gave Irwin a single stunning monologue as well as the opportunity to exploit his physical inventiveness. The play could have run for months, but all the stars, including Mr. Irwin, had other commitments.

In 1991, at the Public Theater, Bill acted in a version of Samuel Beckett's *Texts for Nothing* developed by Joe Chaikin, founder of the legendary Open Theatre. A decade later, Irwin adapted, directed and performed *Texts* at the Classic Stage Company for the start of the 2000–01 season in New York. This time the conception and direction were his own, and he played Beckett's disenfranchised soul searching for his place in the world. A difficult feat, it was very well received by critics.

The 2003–04 season at Signature Theatre in Manhattan was devoted to the work of Bill Irwin. With him were cohorts Doug Skinner and Michael O'Connor. Another collaborator for the Signature season was Nancy Harrington, who, though sometimes overlooked by chroniclers, has been part of the creative team for many years, has the harried job of stage manager and doubles, as Bill puts it, as "outside eye."

The Signature season opened in September with *The Harlequin Studies,* Bill's take on the lewd and lazy scamp of the *commedia dell'arte*. Midseason, Bill revisited *The Regard of Flight* 21 years after its premier; the new updated work was titled *The Regard Evening.* Closing out Bill's 2003–04 season was *Mr. Fox: A Rumination,* an expanded version of the earlier workshop piece. It offered Irwin's take on George L. Fox, the famous and ill-fated white-faced clown of nineteenth-century America.

When Bill Irwin first surfaced in New York, critics hailed him as the second coming of Charlie Chaplin, Buster Keaton, Bobby Clark, Harpo Marx, Ray Bolger, Marcel Marceau and other clowns. Bill Irwin owes nothing to the masters except, perhaps, admiration. He is their peer and very much his own sweet self, a thoroughly original clown.

Each time Bill's clown character abandons himself to expressions of pure joy, an authority of one sort or another intrudes, demanding conformity to rules and a defense of his behavior. When Irwin begins to explain, extending himself across the divide, trying to put transcendent feelings into thoughts and words, the antagonist does not meet him halfway but drags Irwin into hostile territory and challenges him with more questions designed to deflate and coerce him.

Sometimes the antagonist is within—he questions why he should be intimidated by theory and why he clowns instead of doing something important or relevant. The clown and the intellectual are alter egos. They fight for control; each stands apart, ready to pounce on the other. It is sort of a two-man act in one body—between the artist and the didact. The didact commands Bill's intellect and speech. The artist possesses Bill's body and spirit.

Irwin returned to Broadway and to literary theatre in two Edward Albee dramas. *The Goat, or Who Is Sylvia?* (2002) was a new play; *Who's Afraid of Virginia Wolff* was a 2005 revival for which Bill was awarded a Best Actor Tony for his performance in the leading role of George.

MAY IRWIN

b: (Ada Campbell) 27 June 1862, Whitby, ON, Canada—d: 22 October 1938, New York, NY

If there is one thing for which May Irwin will be remembered, it is the first kiss that ever appeared in a movie. May Irwin and John C. Rice were not romantic stars when they smooched for posterity in 1896, but they set off the first outcry against immorality on the silver screen.

At the time, however, May was more famous for her theme song, "The Bully Song," written by a white Southern sportswriter, Charles E. Trevathan. Although listed as composer and lyricist, he required the services of a trained musician and arranger to transform a ditty into what audiences called "May Irwin's Bully Song."

In 1893, May Irwin, her costar Peter Dailey, and the cast of *The Country Sport* were returning by rail to Chicago, after a swing through the western and Pacific states, when she met Trevathan. Over the long ride, Trevathan, May, Pete and the other performers spent a few days sitting around in the parlor car telling stories and singing songs. Trevathan played guitar, and May became intrigued by a particular ditty. She advised him to put words to it. Days later, in Chicago, where *The Country Sport* was playing a return engagement, Trevathan handed her words to "The Bully Song." May persuaded the show's music director to convert Trevathan's tune into a musical arrangement.

After touring more months with Pete Dailey, May Irwin got a chance to get off the road. It had been eight years since she left Manhattan and Tony Pastor. May won the starring role in *The Widow Jones,* a comedy

May Irwin

with music, which opened 9 September 1895 in New York. Chief among the show's attractions was "The Bully Song." It was introduced not to New York audiences, but to those in Brockton, Massachusetts, who saw the show in its tryout tour. After New Bedford, the show moved on to the Boston Museum, a much-revered legitimate house, and then the company brought the show to Broadway. "The Bully Song" was a hit everywhere, and for the rest of her career May was never rid of it. It had become her signature song and encore.

Have yo' heard about dat bully dat's just come to town
He's round among de niggers a-laying' their bodies down
I'm looking for dat bully and he must be found
I'm a Tennessee nigger and I don't allow
No red-eyed river roustabout with me to raise a row
I'm looking for dat bully and I'll make him bow.

"The Bully Song" is a *coon song,* meant to get laughs, and many of the popular women singers of the day—Marie Dressler, Louise Dresser, Clarice Vance and Sophie Tucker—featured *coon songs* in their acts. No one was more successful singing them than May Irwin. She is often written of as the first *coon singer*. Never did she wear blackface as others did.

There was, however, far more to May Irwin than a notorious screen kiss and *coon singing*. Over the course of her nearly 50 years on the stage, May was crowned "The Funniest Stage Woman in America." Other bouquets of praise by delighted reviewers included "The Dean of Comediennes," "Madame Laughter," and "The Grand Old Lady of Comedy." President Woodrow Wilson told the press that he would like to appoint May Irwin "Secretary of Laughter."

May began her career as a child soloist in the church her family attended in Whitby, Ontario, a village 35 miles or so northwest of Toronto. May and her older sister Flora, then called by their christened names, Ada and Georgia, were asked to sing at church and community events. Young Ada was little more than ten when her father, Robert Campbell, died. When their mother, the former Jane Draper, realized that Robert had left his family without provision, mourning yielded to necessity. In 1875, desperate, Jane moved with her two girls to Buffalo, New York; she hoped that her daughters' singing could support the family.

Various accounts conflict on where May Irwin made her professional debut. The year was probably 1875, but how and where are in dispute. One source reports that the two sisters debuted in a small variety house in Rochester, New York; another holds that May began solo in a legitimate theatre show in Buffalo. What is generally conceded is that the booking was arranged through Daniel Shelby. The girls, if they were not at first a double act, soon were. They did well, and Shelby booked them into his Buffalo house, the Adelphi Theatre. According to researchers and authors Linda Martin and Kerry Segrave, Shelby claimed to have anointed the Irwin Sisters with the stage names May and Flora (Flora quickly became Flo). Other bookings followed with enough regularity to assure their mother that she had made a good move.

The premier presenter of variety of the day was Tony Pastor, who caught the Irwin Sisters act (in Detroit, some say) and engaged them for his self-named theatre, then at 585 Broadway. They remained with Pastor for seven years, singing and performing in comedy sketches. Pastor's shows included a lot of house acts, seen week after week for months on end, so the regulars constantly needed to find and learn new material, skits and songs or to improvise.

In 1878, May married Frederick W. Keller. They had two sons, and their marriage lasted until his death in 1886. May and Flo split up their act in 1883, when Augustine Daly prevailed upon May to join his stock company. Under Pastor's tutelage, she had learned comedy, timing and stage presence, and she entered the legitimate theatre as an assured, talented and experienced vaudevillian. Under Daly, she refined her skills and learned to balance individual performance within the ensemble. After three years of touring she accepted an offer of considerably more money to join the Howard Athenaeum company in Boston. By this time, producers and authors were shaping their productions to feature May Irwin's talents. The vehicles for her fun making were farces, many with interpolated songs.

She appeared under several managements, most notably Charles Frohman's, and by 1893, when she appeared in *The Country Sport,* she was billed second only to the great Pete Dailey, a Weberfields alumnus, hale fellow well met and master comedian.

The Widow Jones established May Irwin as a star of the New York stage. It was a scene from this show, the kissing scene, that Thomas Edison chose to photograph. The resultant uproar was urged on from pulpits and editorial pages, but May remained unscathed. She made one more movie, *Mrs. Black Is Back*—18 years later. Over the years, May had grown quite chubby. She was a butterball comedian, formidably corseted, exuding fun, singing in a strong, clear voice and at times doing a bit of fancy stepping, like a cakewalk. Many songs besides "May Irwin's Bully Song" were identified with her. Among those remembered more than a century later are "After the Ball," "May Irwin's Frog Song," and "A Hot Time in the Old Town."

Between the late 1890s and the First World War, May Irwin was at the height of her popularity. She acted in a dozen or more plays, none of which was of much interest beyond May's performance and as an example of the entertainment of the day. Most of the shows were under her own management; she was a very smart and sensible lady.

Before and after she retired from the stage in 1920, May invested wisely in stocks, bonds and real estate, based on recommendations by some of the most successful professionals of the day. She bought Manhattan real estate, including a full block on Lexington Avenue between East 53rd and 54th streets. It fetched $1 million when she sold it a few years before she died in 1938. She left several millions of dollars.

Her second husband, Kurt Eisenfeldt, survived her. They had wed in 1907; he was her manager and press agent, and they had two sons, Harry and Walter. According to contemporaries, May Irwin was respected by all and loved by those who knew her. Yet she could be a force to be feared. An ardent believer in protecting animals, she hounded one performer, a Mr. Galeman, out of vaudeville and out of the USA because he mercilessly beat the animals in his act.

On the other hand and far more frequently experienced, May Irwin was as natural, kind and unassuming offstage as she was on. Douglas Gilbert reported a story told him by Eddie Darling, the man who most often booked the Palace Theatre. For one week in 1920, Darling had booked Emma Calvé, one of the premier opera singers in the world. A couple of hours before the show was to begin, Calvé's manager phoned Darling to tell him that the singer had lost her voice, perhaps due to fright, and would not appear. Darling was frantic as he called around to various stars who he thought might be available. One of them was May Irwin, then nearly 70 and on the verge of retirement. Without any fuss, she told Darling she would arrive at the Palace in an hour or so.

Irwin went on, told the folks in the audience that she was there as a fill-in, told a few funny stories and sang her "The Bully Song." The audience loved her and she played the entire week—and refused Darling's offer of Emma Calvé's considerable salary. In May's mind, she was simply helping Eddie Darling, who was in a jam through no fault of his own.

May must have enjoyed herself because she agreed to appear in one of the occasional old-timers' bills Darling put together at the Palace. This time there were, besides Irwin, three other bona fide female star turns on the bill: Marie Dressler, Fritzi Scheff and Blanche Ring. Any one of them could rightfully expect the star dressing room. Darling was embarrassed. Dressler, who had fought long and hard for her preeminence, volunteered to surrender the star dressing room with its resting couch to May Irwin. May declined, saying that she did not need it; she would make up and dress at home before she came to the theatre. As to the couch, May said she preferred to stand in the wings and watch all the acts on the bill: "Maybe I can steal a few gags."

J

SAM T. JACK

b: ca. 1860—d: ca. 1925

One of Mike Leavitt's protégés, Sam T. Jack began his career in burlesque in 1881. He managed the number two company of a Rentz-Santley revue that played the western states out of Chicago. Soon he assisted George Lederer, Leavitt's top lieutenant.

Sam T. Jack had more ambition and nerve than most men who plugged along managing one burlesque company after another each season. The Sam T. Jack's Tenderloin Company pushed the limits as much as any burlesque outfit of the 1890s—and in more than one direction. While it is true that his shows were among the bawdiest of burlesque's, he also was the first white producer to recognize black talent.

In 1889, he put together what is likely the first show for white audiences that featured African American performers, all of whom appeared naturally, without blackface. This was a momentous event. *Sam T. Jack's Creole Show* (aka *The Creole Show*) first opened in Boston and then played several seasons at the Standard Theatre in Greeley Square, Manhattan. Included in the show was a chorus line of 16 young women, thus anticipating, as Marshall Stearns noted, a major feature of musical comedy, a form that historians trace to several of George Edwardes' productions, beginning with *In Town* (1892) and extending to *A Gaiety Girl* (1894), the first of which followed *The Creole Show* by five years and all of which originated in England, although musical comedy is usually considered an American theatrical form. Likewise, it is probably not an accident that Sam worked on Leavitt's shows with George Lederer, who later, when running the Casino Theatre in Manhattan, did much to advance the development of the American musical comedy form.

At the turn of the twentieth century, Jack acquired his own theatres, first in Chicago, then in New York City. New York was not as wide open as Chicago at the time, so Sam left his self-named theatre at Broadway and 29th Street in Manhattan and focused on his self-named theatre at Madison and State streets in Chicago. He sparked publicity for the Sam T. Jack Theatre by hiring Little Egypt, the woman who introduced belly dancing to the USA during the Chicago World's Fair of 1893.

Jack's Chicago house had an adjoining bar, through which all the girls in the show needed to pass, and nudity was unabashedly on display onstage, billed as tableaux vivant. Consequently, Sam and his theatre earned one of the wilder reputations in burlesque, and he and his operation were frequently the subjects of denunciation from the pulpits and on editorial pages. Shame was foreign to his nature; he proudly placed his photo in his ads and programmes.

He varied his managerial policy to suit the times. He organized touring shows that were applauded for showmanship but decried for smuttiness. Yet he was one of the earliest burlesque managers to organize a burlesque stock company for his theatre rather than play touring shows. His shows were dirtier than others, and stock, showmanship and smut made him a millionaire.

By 1905, Sam booked vaudeville acts to play between the two acts of his burlesque revues. According to Bernard Sobel, the Sam T. Jack Theatre in Chicago shared an alleyway with the Chicago Opera House. Sam made hush-hush arrangements with some of the vaudevillians who came each week to play on bills at the Opera House; they ducked out of the Opera House, ran down the alley and, under false names, provided the olio entertainment at Sam T. Jack's Theatre on the sly.

Upon his death, again according to Sobel, Sam left portions of his estate to his manager and to his second wife, with the provision that Mrs. Jack marry Sam's brother.

JOE JACKSON

b: (Josef Francis Jiranek) 1 January 1881, Vienna, Austria—d: 14 May 1942, New York, NY

Many decades after his death, Joe Jackson was still the name that sprang to mind when people thought of trick bicycling acts. Some cyclists demonstrated their skill on unicycles and large- and small-wheeled bicycles, even added some comedy, but Joe Jackson's tramp characterization made his act memorable.

Jackson performed on a full stage simply set with a street scene drop. When he entered the stage he spied a bicycle parked in front of a building. Joe treated the audience as his accomplice, shushing as he sneaked toward the bike and mounted it for a joyride. That was when the titters turned into belly laughs. Despite his efforts to remain furtive, the horn fell off—then the handlebars, the pedals and seat followed. The bicycle disintegrated while Jackson tried to keep it together and ride to his escape.

Joe Jackson

Other cyclists made a show of their expertise. Joe Jackson covered up his proficiency with gags, but to keep the bicycle moving and to stay balanced on it as it fell apart was its own demonstration of skill. Many people in the audience possibly were not aware of his athletic and inventive ability. They regarded him as a comedian. One theatre manager, in his weekly report to the booking office, judged Jackson "a funny act, but he can't ride a bicycle."

Indeed, Jackson was booked as a comedy act rather than as one of the *dumb acts* traditionally relegated to the opening or closing spots on a vaudeville bill. Joe had an inventive mind and, on his own, he constructed his trick bicycles and fabricated their various removable parts.

His sense of fun extended to practical jokes. Comedian Benny Rubin recalled an occasion when he was working the Loew's time, and Joe was one of the four other acts that alternated with the featured movie. The live performers played four shows a day, so there was little time to do anything but hang around the theatre between shows. Jackson was standing at the back of the house, chatting quietly with the theatre manager, when the manager realized that Joe was due onstage in ten minutes. Jackson was casual about it, telling the manager that he could be ready in five minutes. The manager nearly pushed Joe out the front door, urging him to run around to the backstage and put on his makeup and costume. Instead, while the manager watched in shock, Joe jumped in a taxi and sped off.

Astonished, the manager quickly collected himself, ran down the stage alley and grabbed the stage manager. He was about to tell him that Joe had left and to put on the following act when he saw Jackson. There he was, all made up and in costume, standing in the wing space with his trick bike, awaiting his entrance music. The manager stood and stared as Jackson went on and did the act perfectly.

The manager did not know that Joe had a son, Joe Jackson Jr., who, like his father, was a big man. The son, dressed in tramp clown makeup and tramp clothes, was a dead ringer for his dad and had inherited Joe Sr.'s talent as well as looks. Joe Jackson Sr. had sped off to the ball game; Joe Jackson Jr. was taking his place, and no one knew the difference. This subterfuge came in handy on more than a few occasions when Jackson had conflicts in his bookings or needed some time off.

The older Joe Jackson was born in Vienna and competed in cycling races on the Continent and in Britain. While in England, he made the switch to circus and developed his clowning act. The European circuses of the day were not the mammoth spectacles toward which their American counterparts were striving. Intimate comedy was possible, and, as in the case of Toto, Marceline and other largely silent clowns who worked both variety stages and circuses, the difference required only modest adjustments in presentation.

It is not certain when Joe Jackson came to the USA, but it was probably sometime around 1914, and the visit may have been prompted by the start of the First World War.

In any case, he had come to notice in both New York and Hollywood by 1915 through his vaudeville appearances. He opened 18 February 1915 in *Maid in America* at the Winter Garden. The show ran 108 performances with Nora Bayes, Yancsi (Jenny) Dolly of the Dolly Sisters, Harry Fox, Mlle. Dazie and Blossom Seeley in the cast. Later that year, Joe Jackson played the Palace.

Jackson spent much of the 1915–16 season on the Keystone lot in Hollywood, where he made a total of six short films. Mack Sennett had handed him and other Broadway comedians (De Wolf Hopper, Weber & Fields and William Collier, among them) fat weekly checks to make short comedies, but the Broadway comedians were hampered by stage technique. The homegrown Hollywood product—part stuntman and part circus clown like Mabel Normand, Roscoe Arbuckle, Ben Turpin, Fred Mace, Chester and Heine Conklin, Slim Summerville and Polly Moran—proved to be the better silent film comedians.

The first of Joe's Keystone comedies was *Fatty and the Broadway Stars* (1915). Directed by and starring Roscoe "Fatty" Arbuckle, it boasted cameo appearances by Weber & Fields, Sam Bernard, William Collier and Jackson.

On 17 January 1917, Jackson was back on Broadway, where he opened in *Dance and Grow Thin,* a floor show staged on the Century Theatre Roof (called the Century's Cocoanut Grove) in Ziegfeld's and Dillingham's *Midnight Revue.* Joe shared the stage with Leon Errol (who also staged the show), Gertrude Hoffman and Van & Schenck. He then returned to vaudeville.

When *Good Times,* one of the Hippodrome's patented extravaganzas, opened on 9 August 1920, Joe Jackson was in the cast that included the clown Marceline, opera singer Belle Story and the Hanneford Family. *Good Times* played for more than a year.

Most of Joe's career in the USA was spent in variety and vaudeville. After the cessation of European hostilities, he probably returned to variety stages and circus rings in Europe and Australia.

With war gathering once again in Europe, Joe returned to the USA and performed in *American Jubilee* at the New York World's Fair, 12 May to 2 October 1940. As he was about 60 years old, his son shared the appearances with him. In 1950, the name Joe Jackson was listed on a bill at the newly revived home of vaudeville, the Palace Theatre, but it was the son, not the father who had died eight years earlier.

TONY JACKSON

b: ca. 1880, New Orleans—d: April 21, 1921

Remembered only as the composer of "Pretty Baby," Tony Jackson was a singer and piano player for the Whitman Sisters' New Orleans Troubadours during their 1904 tour of black vaudeville. He toured again in 1910 with another of the Whitmans' annual shows that performed for mostly black audiences in Southern theatres.

Tony Jackson was playing honky-tonk piano in a bordello owned by Antonia Gonzales when, in 1917, the U.S. Navy shut down Storyville, New Orleans' red-light district. Storyville had provided work for many musicians and entertainers of every sort for decades. Madame Gonzales was as famous for singing opera and playing the cornet as she was for her hosting duties.

Jackson was a contemporary of other well-known "whorehouse professors," such as Jelly Roll Morton, Game Kid, Buddy Carter and Sammy Davis. Morton, not always generous in his estimate of others, said of Tony Jackson, "He was one of the greatest manipulators of the keys that I have ever seen in the history of the world," and "There was no [music] from any kind of opera or any kind of show or anything that was wrote on paper that Tony couldn't play."

During his many years in New Orleans Jackson wrote "Pretty Baby" and "I've Got Elgin Movements in My Hips with Twenty Years' Guarantee." The latter song had many knockoffs, including Cleo Gibson's "I've Got a Ford Engine Movement in My Hips, Ten Thousand Miles' Guarantee," in which precision Swiss works were replaced by mass-produced Detroit machinery.

The song "Pretty Baby" was inspired by a young male prostitute to whom Jackson was attracted. Generations of audiences, lulled by the song's gentle melody, have ignored the cynicism of lyrics like "Oh, I want a lovin' baby and it might as well be you" and its frank proposition to "let me rock you in my cradle of love."

After his tours with the Whitmans and the demise of Storyville, Tony made Chicago his base until 1920. He was a favorite entertainer at many black hot spots such as the Pekin and Elite No. 2, where he was the house pianist and accompanist to blues singers like Lucille Hegamin and Alberta Hunter.

He left Chicago to operate a horse farm in Kentucky. One day, perhaps still in Kentucky, he developed hiccups while drinking coffee—hiccups that lasted eight weeks and finally killed him in 1921, the same year that Mamie Smith's recording of "Crazy Blues" opened up the recording business to African American musicians. Tony Jackson, the extraordinary ragtime and early jazz pianist, never got the opportunity to record.

ELSIE JANIS

b: (Elsie Bierbower) 16 March 1889, Columbus, OH—d: 26 February 1956, Los Angeles, CA

Elsie Janis was a young lady, modest and natural, with charming wit and a sense of fun. Critics and audiences alike adored her, nearly as much for her gentility as for her considerable talent. Mothers prayed for a daughter like Elsie. Men loved her like an ideal sister. Janis was representative of vaudeville at its best, and only one or two vaudeville entertainers ever earned as much as little Elsie.

She first performed publicly at the improbable age of two. Her mother had arranged for Baby Elsie, as she was first billed, to sing at some church benefits. Their home situation was not pleasant, and Mrs. Bierbower divorced Mr. Bierbower. A good number of the most famous women stars of the early twentieth century rose from nearly identical circumstances, Lotta Crabtree, Mary Pickford and Lillian and Dorothy Gish among them. Absent a wage earner—a father who died, abandoned his family or abused them—the widow or divorced mother tried to support her girls.

ELSIE JANIS, the "sweetheart
of the A.E.F."

Elsie Janis

Invariably, circumstances sent them spiraling to the bottom of the social ladder, where they fell into the company of actors and performers. Like a lot of child actors, Elsie played a child in that indestructible perennial *East Lynne,* a staple of many melodrama troupes. Five at the time, she had to wait until she was seven for her first steady work in theatre, which she found with a stock company. Having outgrown Baby Elsie, she was billed as Little Elsie. When Elsie was ten, Ma Janis parlayed an acquaintance with the wife of President William McKinley into an invitation for Elsie to perform at the White House.

Encouraged by McKinley's warm reception, Ma Janis set about getting Elsie in vaudeville. She targeted Mike Shea, a rough but honest and committed vaudeville manager who owned theatres in and around Buffalo and Toronto. He accepted Ma's intriguing proposition for a week's engagement. If Elsie flopped, she worked without pay; if she made good, Shea was to pay them $125 for the week. Elsie was slotted in the second spot; only the opening and closing spots on the bill were more difficult for performers. By the evening of her first day, Elsie had been rescheduled to next-to-closing, the star spot. Shea provided a letter of recommendation.

Yet most of Little Elsie's work for the next few seasons was in stock melodrama. As well as acting, she performed her variety specialty in the olio during intermission. She sang, danced and did impressions of famous people, including President McKinley. Soon she had enough material to fashion a well-constructed vaudeville act. Quickly, she moved up the vaudeville ladder until she became a top act.

Part of Little Elsie's charm was in watching a young girl mimic the grown-up stars of the day—and not just women. She imitated Eddie Foy, George M. Cohan, Harry Lauder, Will Rogers and John Barrymore as well as Alla Nazimova and, later, Ethel Barrymore and Beatrice Lillie. It was not merely a mastering of the mechanics, duplicating the sound and rhythm of their speech or their idiosyncratic movements and expressions. According to those who saw her, Elsie, a fine actor, was able to capture the essence of those she impersonated.

Although her mother helped her at first, Janis wrote her own comedy material and occasionally wrote lyrics and even music for her act. She sang most pleasantly, but never would have become a headliner on that talent alone. Elsie was a superior dancer who could be graceful as a ballerina or eccentrically clownish; she could even turn an acrobatic trick or two. Most of all, it was a matter of personality. Everyone loved Elsie Janis and she seemed to love them.

Offstage and behind Elsie's success was Mrs. Bierbower, a hero in the stage mothers' hall of fame, as much for her loving nurture of Elsie as for her determination and business acumen. Ma Janis, as she called herself, or Ma, as she urged friends of any age to call her, was as affable, down-to-earth and fun loving as her daughter, but when it came to Elsie's career she showed her true mettle and negotiated deals like the Talleyrand of Tarrytown. Mrs. Bierbower did not bluff, shout or abuse the opposition when she demanded top billing, top salary and star dressing rooms; neither did she yield in her demands to the most powerful vaudeville managers or producers on Broadway.

Once, when she believed that the management of the Palace Theatre on Broadway had not lived up to Elsie's contract as negotiated, she pulled her daughter off the bill. In retaliation, Edward Albee ordered Elsie blackballed from the Palace, and a large notice to that effect was posted in the lobby of the Palace. Albee's decree backfired. The public assumed the fault was management's, and they protested. Albee retreated and sent Elsie and Ma a letter of apology in which he blamed the Palace's booker, Eddie Darling, who in fact had interceded with Albee on Elsie's behalf. Over the ensuing seasons, Elsie continued to play the Palace quite frequently, although some other acts that committed lesser offenses never played the Palace again.

Besides being Elsie's sole parent, Ma Janis was her agent, publicist, best friend and constant companion—nearly an alter ego. Frank Case of the Algonquin Hotel quipped that Elsie and mother were "the Jani." In a book of humorous pieces, *If I Know What I Mean*, Elsie wrote, "When it comes to mothers, I really know what I'm talking about. I've had experience. And if years of sticking at the job counts for anything, my maternal ancestor has more service stripes than a Spanish war veteran. She's never had any furlough, or even a day off. The Siamese twins were estranged as compared to Mother and myself."

By 1905, Broadway was calling for 16-year-old Elsie. Over the following decade, Elsie Janis appeared in musical comedies and revues. *When We Were Forty-One* (1905) was a musical farce that ran only two months despite the pairing of Elsie with Emma Carus. *The Vanderbilt Cup* (1906) played from mid-January to early May, a solid run for a musical comedy of that era. *The Hoyden* (1907) was the first of Elsie's shows for Charles Dillingham, one of the most respected and best liked producers on Broadway. Although the cast included Joseph Cawthorn and Mae Murray, it managed only 58 performances. That, however, did not discourage Mr. Dillingham, who produced Janis' next few shows. The musical *The Fair Co-Ed* (1909) achieved 136 performances. *The Slim Princess* (1911) made a respectable stand of about ten weeks with Elizabeth Brice, Joseph Cawthorn and Charles King joining Elsie in the cast. Later that year, Dillingham produced *A Star for a Night,* written by and starring Elsie Janis. (Elsie published it that same year in a novelized version.) Dillingham's faith and investment in *Lady of the Slipper* (1912) was rewarded by 232 performances, thanks in part to an outstanding cast of Montgomery & Stone, Peggy Wood, Vernon Castle and Elsie Janis.

In between Broadway shows, Elsie appeared in big-time vaudeville. As one of the top half dozen acts, she earned far more in vaudeville than on Broadway. In 1910, Elsie was drawing $2,500–$3,000 a week. Only two imports—Harry Lauder ($5,000) and Vesta Victoria ($3,000)—and two American acts—Eva Tanguay ($3,000) and Nora Bayes ($2,500)—were able to demand as much as or more than Little Elsie. Other stars, like Gertrude Hoffman, received $2,500 or $3,000 for their sketch or flash acts, but once they paid their assistants' salaries, they themselves netted less than the golden five.

As Gilbert Seldes observed in *The Seven Lively Arts*, Elsie was possessed of "abounding grace, a suppleness of body and of mind, and the measure of her skill is the exact degree in which her grace and simplicity are transformed into harshness or angularity or sophistication as she passes one after another of our stage personalities."

In 1914, Elsie went to London to star in *The Passing Show* for manager Alfred Butt. In the cast was Basil Hallam, a comedian of the silly-billy sort. He and Elsie became romantically involved, but his worry about entering the British armed forces probably began to grate on Elsie. She herself had no such misgiving; she became one of the first performers to volunteer to entertain the troops. In fact, she joined the war long before the USA did. Elsie was singing and telling funny stories to British and French lads on their way to the battle lines nearly as soon as hostilities began. When the troops arrived at the front, she soon joined them there.

Because the USA was still neutral, organizations like the YMCA and Salvation Army had not devised plans for sponsoring battlefield visits by entertainers. That Ma Janis was able to cajole, bully and arrange visits by Elsie and her to the troops on the front lines in France was testimony to Ma's resolve and her ability to cow military brass. What's a five-star general or two when you have handed E. F. Albee his head?

Elsie left the war zones occasionally to fulfill professional engagements. These included her one and only flop, *Miss Information,* a straight play that opened and closed on Broadway in October 1915. The best-remembered fact about the play was that Marion Davies made her debut playing a chorus girl. *The Century Girl* (1916) had everything. It was an extravagant revue coproduced by two friendly rivals, Dillingham and Florenz Ziegfeld, with music by Irving Berlin and Victor Herbert (but not one hit song), opulent settings by Joseph Urban, and a cast that included Marie Dressler, Sam Bernard, Leon Errol, Doyle & Dixon, Hazel Dawn, Frank Tinney and Van & Schenck as well as Elsie Janis. It scored 200 performances, but it is doubtful that either Charlie (as Elsie called him) Dillingham or Flo Ziegfeld recouped much of their backers' money because the production had cost a fortune.

The soldiers in the war zone greeted Elsie Janis as "The Sweetheart of the Doughboys." After the USA entered the fray, she became "The Sweetheart of the AEF" (American Expeditionary Forces). Elsie was a gal pal, not a pinup, although she was attractive. Indeed, another of her soubriquets was "A Regular Girl." When not entertaining the boys, the otherwise ladylike Elsie might be found on her knees, shooting craps with them. It was said with respect and affection that Elsie and Ma Janis saw more of the war than any general.

Other professional obligations during the First World War involved spending four months at the (Hobart) Bosworth Inc.'s New York studios (which released through Paramount), where she made films: *The Caprices of Kitty, Betty in Search of a Thrill, Nearly a Lady* and *'Twas Ever Thus,* all in 1915. She also fulfilled a couple of long-standing engagements in London. While there, she made the rounds of military hospital wards to visit the wounded.

One of Elsie's British bookings was *Hullo America* (1919), a revue in which she starred at London's Palace Theatre. Previously, she had met Maurice Chevalier in 1913 and admired his performance. When she appeared in *Hullo America,* she arranged for Chevalier to join the cast, thus providing him with his first appearance outside France for English-speaking audiences.

Back on the front, Elsie sang, danced, told her funny stories and regaled the troops with her impersonations. Always easygoing, Elsie performed from the back of pickup trucks, standing atop a shed or wherever she could find a flat surface so that as many as 5,000 soldiers could see her. She learned French to perform for the French troops, who assured her she spoke with faultless accent. Her performances usually ended in sing-alongs with the lads in uniform.

Elsie Janis

Elsie was featured in a documentary of sorts, *The Big Drive* (ca. 1919–20), about the doughboys on the front lines. It was made by Albert L. Rule and distributed by the First Division Forces. Nearly a decade after the fact, Vitaphone re-created the feel when they filmed Elsie giving a performance from the back of a truck in the 1926 short *Elsie Janis: Behind the Lines at the Front.*

After the Armistice, Elsie and her mother returned to New York on the SS *Rotterdam.* As it sailed into the harbor, it was met by a tugboat almost totally covered with a banner that read, "Welcome Home, Elsie Janis." She was as much of a hero to the American public as to her beloved doughboys, and she was feted all about town.

The recently formed Selznick Picture Corporation signed Elsie for a four-picture deal at $5,000 a week. She quickly accepted, as the 1919 Actors Equity strike had shut down Broadway theatres. Elsie had made only four films previously; thus the amount of money young Myron Selznick paid Elsie was a tribute to his faith in her ability to attract motion picture audiences who did not see much big-city vaudeville.

The first of Janis' movies for Selznick was *Everybody's Sweetheart,* and it was written by Elsie's dear friend Frances Marion, a Hollywood powerhouse. The title was changed before release in 1919 to capitalize on one of Elsie's nicknames: *A Regular Girl* turned Elsie into a young society woman who volunteered as a nurse in the First World War and returned home transformed.

Conspiring between them, Frances Marion and Elsie hired as many recently demobilized servicemen as they could in their movie. Both women were concerned that veterans who had put their lives in jeopardy and their careers on hold for four years were returning home to jobs that no longer existed. "Between us," admitted Elsie, "we put everything in the picture but the delousing station."

Critical of her suitability for movies, Elsie thought her movements were too quick for the motion picture camera. She laughed that she looked like a "Semitic jumping jack" on the screen, but she was well paid, found making movies was fun and, after shooting ended for the day, the set turned into a party with Elsie, the troops and crew singing songs from the war. Elsie also wrote and starred in *The Imp* for Selznick that same year. She did not appear onscreen again for 20 years, although she wrote material for several films.

When Elsie Janis returned to Broadway, she brought some doughboys with her. *Elsie Janis and Her Gang* (1919) played 55 performances and featured performers who had served in the military plus a few legitimate stage actors, like Eva LeGallienne, who had entertained the troops in wartime. The show went on tour. A production with the same title was revived in 1922 but, except for Elsie, this time the cast and songs were completely different. The new show ran for 56 performances on Broadway and then toured. Her next show was *Puzzles of 1925,* for which Elsie wrote lyrics and directed but did not appear.

Janis seemed to be winding down her career, or trying to change course. *If I Know What I Mean,* a collection of humorous pieces she had written, was published as a book in 1925. Elsie had worked ceaselessly on the stage for 30 of her more than 36 years, and the war had matured her. She had seen a lot of suffering, death and devastation. Also, her mother was ill, and Elsie stayed with her to the end. Of course, they were well-off, at least until the Great Depression, and could afford the best of medical and domestic care.

It was supposed that Mrs. Bierbower had been a shrewd investor, as there were few worldly matters she had not mastered. Even those who found her uncooperative and unyielding had to admit that she would have made an exceptional captain of industry. One of her investments was the purchase of an 11-acre historic property in the Hudson River Valley, just outside Tarrytown, New York, and one hour from Broadway. The large, sprawling Phillipsburg Manor had associations with George Washington and Washington Irving and was large and homey enough for the informal gatherings the Bierbowers liked to host. Along with Broadway stars, chorus girls and movie stars were some of society's 400 and visiting royalty, as well as people from less august walks of life: people who happened to interest Elsie and her mother. Those who did not have to do business with Ma Janis found her friendly, fun loving and democratic.

Because Elsie Janis sensibly strived to retain as much privacy as possible, it is not always possible to separate the men with whom she had romances from those on whom she had an unfulfilled crush. Among the men Elsie may have fancied and perhaps enjoyed were Owen Moore (who was married at the time to Mary Pickford), Doug Fairbanks Sr., Irving Berlin (who used to come to her Hudson River Valley estate to compose in quiet), Maurice Chevalier (whom she encouraged to try his luck in America) and Basil Hallam, an English music-hall comedian whom Elsie was engaged to wed. Everyone wondered how the couple found time alone given that Ma Bierbower went everywhere that Elsie went. Indeed, Elsie may have preferred it just that way. In her biography, she passed quite lightly over Hallam's death in the war.

By some reckonings, Elsie Janis had been a performer ever since she was two years old. Because she was one of the top acts in vaudeville during the 1910s and 1920s, the public and press maintained an interest in all things Elsie throughout her career. If the spotlight on and off the stage shone unrelentingly on Elsie, it had the benefit of keeping her in the public eye while intruding on her privacy. Elsie Janis spent most of her life, the latter half, away from the public eye, working on projects that were mostly unworthy of the talent she once had displayed as a star act. Perhaps Elsie, the grown-up, felt she earned her anonymity and regarded it as a blessing.

Mrs. Bierbower had also bought Elsie and herself a house in Beverly Hills. Upon the death of her mother in July 1930, Elsie spent more of her time at her West Coast home. True, vaudeville was hardly what it had been in Elsie's heyday, but Elsie could have continued to earn a decent living on the stage, in nightclubs or on network radio. The new talking pictures were perfect for her, yet, at 40, Elsie might have thought herself a bit old for starring roles in major movies, although Mae West was about to become a newly minted movie star at 40, and many female vaudeville stars of a certain age, such as Marie Dressler, Helen Broderick and Louise Dresser, met great success as older actors in Hollywood.

Instead, Elsie decided to write her autobiography, *So Far, So Good* (1932), and reestablish herself in Hollywood, this time behind the scenes as a scriptwriter and songwriter. She had always written her own highly successful vaudeville acts, as well as a couple of books and numerous magazine articles. Elsie began by fixing up a couple of scenarios for a few of the last silent films. She adapted Guy Bolton's play *Oh, Kay* for the screen in 1928, coscripted both *Close Harmony* (1929) and Cecil B. DeMille's *Madame Satan* (1930) and wrote one of the songs used in the latter film. When talkies appeared, Elsie easily adapted. She wrote songs for *The Trespasser* (1929), which starred Gloria Swanson, *Slightly Scarlet* (1930) and *The Sheik Steps Out* (1937). At Irving Berlin's request, she doctored his script for *Reaching for the Moon* (1930), and she provided additional dialogue for DeMille's remake of *The Squaw Man* (1931).

Her most prominent assignment was *Paramount on Parade* (1930), an all-star blockbuster revue designed to introduce the movie-going public to Paramount's roster of talking-picture stars. (Notably absent from the cast were The Four Marx Bros. and W. C. Fields.) Elsie helped convince Paramount to produce this film and, in addition to writing special material and some songs for it, she supervised its production. All Elsie's script work was completed before Ma's death. She was comfortable in Hollywood where she enjoyed the companionship of friends she had known since youth: screenwriters Frances Marion and Anita Loos, gossip columnist Hedda Hopper, director Edward Goulding, and film stars Mary Pickford, Marion Davies and Colleen Moore, among others.

In 1931, within months of her mother's death, Elsie Janis got married at her Tarrytown estate to Gilbert Wilson, then 26 and hoping for an acting career in lieu of heavy lifting. Elsie, 42, commented publicly, "My husband is much younger than I, but I thought as I had never had a husband or a child I might combine the two—sort of cut down on the schedule as it were." Her public reputation as a maiden had been a long-running, good-natured joke in which Elsie participated. (She once told the press, "I don't even keep my love letters; I burned both of them.") When asked to contribute, along with many celebrities, her own epitaph for a magazine article, Elsie offered, "Here lies Elsie Janis—still sleeping alone." The marriage did not last, but Elsie did not bother getting divorced until 1948, after Gilbert had returned from the Second World War.

Elsie's decision to take life easy had to compete with straightening out the Janis financial affairs, specifically her mother's estate, and the importuning of Leonard Sillman. Visiting Manhattan and walking through the Algonquin Hotel lobby one day in 1933, Elsie ran into Sillman, whom she had met on the West Coast. He was as determined as Elsie's mother, so Elsie did not really stand a chance against his pleas to direct his intimate West Coast revue, *Low and Behold,* for New York. Elsie watched a run-though and agreed; further, she pulled in the aged, retired and insolvent Charles Dillingham as nominal producer.

It was a blessing of sorts for him to have his name again connected with a show, no matter how modest, and with Janis and Dillingham on board, there was a better chance backers could be lured, although 1933 was not a good year to be asking for money. Soliciting backers took all winter, but the Sillman show, retitled *New Faces of 1934,* set a template for the new brand of intimate revues: no stars, minimal scenery and costumes and everyone working for scale—when they finally got it. *New Faces of 1934* also set the template for raising money: 136 backer's auditions.

New Faces of 1934 opened in early March and ran into the summer, and possibly made everyone a little bit of money. It made more than a little for Sillman. He had courted Elsie for her name value, and people connected with the show reported that little of what Elsie suggested made its way into Leonard's show.

Elsie returned to the stage in 1939 in a one-woman show, a mixture of drama and comedy that had a modest run at the Music Box. Back on the West Coast later that season, she joined *Frank Fay's Vaudeville* (aka *Frank Fay's Music Hall*), one of those revues in which former headliners like Fay, George Jessel and Lou Holtz tried to revive and repackage vaudeville. Only Olsen & Johnson and Ken Murray were greatly successful.

Elsie Janis' last performance was in a movie. She joined former film star Mae Clarke, comedian Billy Gilbert and current contractees Wendy Barrie and Patric Knowles in *Women in War* (1940), a quickie B picture about nurses and wounded servicemen that was rushed out too soon to ride war fever to box-office success.

There was a question about how well off Elsie found herself after the death of her mother. Elsie had been one of vaudeville's most highly paid performers, and supposedly Ma had socked it away for Elsie, yet the Great Depression had rendered many stock certificates as worthless as Confederate script. Perhaps Elsie was simply trying to deflect unwanted investment proposals when she told people she did not have money.

Whatever her financial situation, the wolf was not at her door—wolves were not allowed in Beverly Hills, where Elsie had a paid-in-full roof over her head. Perhaps there was not much cash in the bank, which may be why Elsie took various writing jobs that were beneath her talents and stature. Yet she had a housekeeper and chauffeur, longtime employees to whom she left the bulk of her estate. Elsie Janis died in 1956, a few weeks short of her 67th birthday, at her home in Beverly Hills with old friend Mary Pickford at her bedside. Elsie was interred beside Ma Janis at Forest Lawn.

JAZZ MUSIC

Few knew what constituted real jazz in the early years of vaudeville. The music was still in its adolescence and branching away from its foundations in gospel music, marching bands, blues and ragtime. It was called various names: black music (or more vulgar equivalents), as well as jass, jizz and jazz, among others.

Few could agree then or later on what distinguished jazz from its musical antecedents. Some insisted that improvisation, syncopation and a driving beat were essential characteristics of jazz, but those claims were countered by anomalies that lacked one or more essentials, yet still felt like jazz. The term itself was quite explicit as a sexual function, and raw feeling and energy may have been more fitting criteria than musical rules.

A vaudeville act performed for a set amount of time—8, 11, 15 or 22 minutes, or whatever the contract specified. Performers did not exceed their time onstage. They knew that to do so could result in cancellation. The tight time restrictions of vaudeville did not well suit blues and jazz ensembles that tended to play according to the spirit rather than a clock. The ersatz aggregations that were billed in vaudeville as "jazz" were usually combos that played ragtime or the bouncier products of Tin Pan Alley. Examples were acts such as Ted Lewis, "The Jazz King," Sophie Tucker, "Queen of Jazz & Her Seven Kings of Syncopation," and, later, Paul Whiteman, "King of Jazz."

Perhaps the first instance of a real African American jazz band accompanying a white vaudeville act was in 1914 when James Reese Europe and his 14 musicians traveled with Vernon & Irene Castle to accompany their dance act.

Many outfits, like the Original Dixieland Jass Band (ODJB), which made several series of successful sound recordings, were more at home performing in nightclubs and speakeasies, where they tricked out their performances with visual gags, much like a vaudeville act. A white group from New Orleans via Chicago, the ODJB played a brand of jazz that was arguably more ersatz than authentic, but its success, beginning in 1917, stirred a number of acts to promote themselves as jazz groups in an attempt to cash in on the novelty.

There were many jazz musicians in vaudeville, however. For some, vaudeville provided relatively steady work and pay. The style of music they were hired to perform frequently fell short of what they would like to have played, but they did, when permitted or encouraged, bring jazz sensibility to vaudeville performances—probably more often when providing music for percussive dancers than for singers. Over time, the energy and swing of jazz permeated vaudeville performances as ragtime had earlier.

The great majority of African American jazz musicians in vaudeville played in black vaudeville, both Toby time down south and the vaude-burlesque revues that were produced in Harlem for the more ad hoc circuit of theatres from Boston to Baltimore to Chicago.

The Whitman Sisters' shows that toured for the first four decades of the twentieth century were accompanied by bands that were distinguished by the presence at various times of Count Basie, Mary Lou Williams, Pine Top Smith, Lonnie Johnson and Tony Jackson. Ida Cox also hired blues and jazz musicians for her tours.

At the Monogram Theatre, the black vaudeville house in Chicago, Lovie Austin conducted a jazz-inspired ensemble from the pit, and African American vaudeville acts and revues starring Mamie Smith, Ethel Waters, Bessie Smith, Edith Wilson and Valaida Snow traveled with bands populated by black jazz musicians.

Blues, a close relative of jazz in the 1910s and 1920s, was a frequent visitor in black vaudeville. With the success of Mamie Smith's recordings, the first nonclassical sides ever cut by a black woman, several small and large companies jockeyed with each other in the rush to grab a share of the newly discovered market in *race records*. To advertise their product, the companies sent their singers, accompanied by a few blues and jazz players, to drum up interest in the recordings and sheet music with a series of personal appearances on vaudeville stages.

The closest thing to an early white jazz singer in vaudeville may have been Blossom Seeley, who started singing as a youngster on the Barbary Coast in the 1890s. Jazz did not simply travel up the Mississippi to Memphis, St. Louis and Chicago; it spread west and could be heard at the turn of the twentieth century in San Francisco.

At the end of vaudeville's reign, new and larger theatres were built to accommodate talking, singing and dancing motion pictures and live-on-stage acts. Single-person acts often looked Lilliputian on the large stages built for spectacular production numbers like the Fanchon & Marco prologues.

Although most of the big-name swing bands preferred and were more likely to play the big hotel ballrooms (where their fans could dance), some big bands, when they made promotional tours of the USA, brought their singers, tap dancers and novelty acts with them, especially if they were booked at the large vaudeville or presentation houses.

JELS

A corruption of *gels,* these are colored transparencies placed over sources of stage lighting to change the color of costumes and scenery and to alter the mood of a scene through the use of colored light beams. Originally made from gelatin, they were later made from synthetic materials. The word *jels* derives from their resemblance in colors to the jellies made from gelatin.

GEORGE JESSEL

b: 3 April 1898, Bronx, NY—d: 24 May 1981, Los Angeles, CA

It is odd that George Jessel, who seemed a typical vaudevillian, was always anxious to get out of vaudeville. Even as a tyke—if such a homey term can be applied to a short, cigar-chomping ten-year-old with adult appetites—he was anxious for a show that would keep him on Broadway, free of the boondocks. Over the course of a long career, Jessel sought work in revues, musical comedy and drama on Broadway, in the movies and on network radio and television. He had a few spectacular successes, but his defeats were far more numerous, and every time Jessel, young man or old, came a cropper, he headed back to vaudeville to replenish his coffers and salve his bruised psyche.

His failures in show business were not due to a lack of talent. He sang well and was a capable comic monologist. Jessel failed because his greatest performances were off rather than on the stage. He sought excitement in his private life, and he was always a bigger hit with showbiz insiders than with general audiences.

In most ways, George Jessel indeed was the typical vaudevillian. Show business attracted him not because he yearned to perform, not because of the riches it promised the lucky few who became headliners, but because show business offered an escape from the ordinary life with which most people had to make peace. Jessel claimed as an ancestor Sir George Jessel, Master of the Rolls of Great Britain and Solicitor General, one of a handful of English Jews, such as Disraeli and Lord Reading, to make their way into the empire's powerful elite. According to Jessel, his grandfather emigrated to the USA, reached California in time for the Gold Rush, joined a band of vigilantes that brought law and order to San Francisco (where it wasn't much wanted) and reached Chicago in time for the great fire to destroy records of his accomplishments, including the claim of being the uncrowned "King of the Auctioneers." Also according to Jessel, his father became a playwright and producer, touring with his creations and casts through the hinterlands until his career collapsed with the failure of a single play. Jessel senior became a traveling salesman, divorced his wife and married another woman, to whom Georgie was born, and then died ten years later, perhaps of boredom. Nurtured by ancestral tales, little Georgie Jessel was entranced by the siren song of destiny.

Anything was better than penury in the Bronx. The exalted station that should have been the legacy of Jessel's paternal line did not extend to George's inheritance. Georgie grew up in his maternal grandfather's tailor shop. He sang for customers and at his grandfather's lodge parties. His mother sold tickets in the box office of the Imperial Theatre on 116th Street. At Georgie's insistence, she wangled him a place in a singing trio of boys. All three proved to be destiny's darlings. Jack Weiner became a Hollywood agent, Walter Winchell became an influential newspaper columnist and the scourge of anyone who crossed him, and Georgie Jessel became a Broadway star. Prior to stardom, however, he got a job with one of Gus Edwards' much-imitated kiddie troupes. "School Boys and Girls" introduced 11-year-old Georgie to show business, booze and sex, all of which continued to preoccupy him until his final bow.

Young Master Jessel was a bold, small, dark, cigar-smoking youngster with a strong, low voice. He showed a flair for imitations and comedy, and Edwards put Jessel into another show, "Kid Kabaret" (1912), where he performed with Eddie Cantor, six years older. Temperamental opposites, Cantor and Jessel, despite frequent disagreements, remained friends for many decades. Jessel's growing conservatism and hawkishness was later at odds with Cantor's liberal politics. Both agreed on the need to support the fledgling state of Israel, and they proved two of its most effective fund-raisers.

When young Jessel hit his mid-teens, like all kid actors he outgrew cute roles, and work was hard to find. His first adult act partnered Jessel with a dancer, Lou Edwards, and after a season of touring the small time, with Jessel capitalizing on a Chaplin imitation, the pair made it to London on a fluke. Edwards was well received, but it took Jessel a while to accommodate his songs and humor to British audiences. The act broke up in England, and Jessel tried to get back to the USA. In addition to Jessel's being profligate (his lifelong state), the First World War was in play, and German U-boats threatened ship traffic on the Atlantic Ocean.

Back in the USA, it again took Jessel some time to find work. His pursuit of beautiful young women and elusive odds allowed little time for a career. He tried working as a monologist, but he did not have the right material until he developed his famous "phone call to Mama" routine. The telephone monologue was an approach followed 30 years later by Bob Newhart and Shelly Berman. Jessel called the local grocery store beneath her tenement flat in order to speak to his mother. He identified himself: "It's Georgie, Mama. . . . Yes, from the money every week." He added a few songs to his act and played the Keith big time. He had found his stage persona as a first-generation American who reveled in the modern world and success, yet could not disavow his Old World family. It was a situation familiar to a lot of young Americans. The essence of this conflict would be played out on the stage as *The Jazz Singer* (1925), which gave Jessel his greatest triumph and most heart-wrenching loss. But that was a few years into the future.

When George came into New York with his new act, managers and actors were just coming together after a successful strike for better working conditions. Both Ziegfeld and the Shuberts called. Jessel accepted a bid to join *The Shubert Gaieties* (1919), a revue that was reopening after the strike. George largely repeated his vaudeville act for the revue. His bravado won the early audiences, but his lovelorn state soon distracted him. He lost both show and fair lady. Fair lady was Florence Courtney of vaudeville's Courtney Sisters. He married Florence in 1919; they put their divorce on hold for nearly 20 years.

George Jessel had found his formula for living: work up a success, then fall in love, lose in love and have everything fall apart. Often gambling and money worries added to the explosiveness of the mixture.

Occasionally, George took control and produced his own vehicles, as he did with "Georgie Jessel's Troubles of 1919," a sketch he played in vaudeville and later turned into a full-length flash act for the Shuberts' new and hastily assembled vaudeville circuit that they fielded against Keith's. When the Shuberts quit vaudeville, Jessel teamed with Rufus LeMaire to produce a musical comedy, *Helen of Troy, New York* (1923). Jessel did not appear onstage, but Kalmar & Ruby wrote the music, lyrics and book and George S. Kaufman directed. In that same year, at the same time, Jessel appeared in *The Passing Show of 1923,* for which he no longer needed a prop phone, for Mama was sitting in a box seat where she could talk back for all to hear. When those shows closed, Jessel returned to the bosom of My Lady Vaudeville. By 1925, Jessel had ventured into nightclubs.

Jessel's golden year was 1925. *The Jazz Singer* catapulted Jessel to stardom. It was a short play that Jessel claims to have had a hand in expanding to an evening-length drama with music. He played the role of the tradition-bound rabbi's son who wanted to enter show business. The play established George Jessel as an actor and gave him some effective songs to sing. *The Jazz Singer* played 315 performances on Broadway at the Fulton Theatre and then racked up double that number on tour.

Though its plot spun around specifically Jewish American characters, its appeal proved far wider. The late 1910s and the early 1920s were times of disenchantment on the part of the young with the traditions and limitations of Old World culture and that witnessed a rise in secularism. African American families experienced the same widening gulf between generations, as did Italian Americans, Irish Americans and others. The lure of secular fame and fortune was in a tug-of-war with religious and patriarchal tradition. The surprise for old line producers and show business observers was that, instead of being limited in appeal to Jews, *The Jazz Singer* proved to have resonance for the young Italian and Irish men (and women) who rejected their parents' entreaties to give their lives to the church (as one member of each generation often did) or for the Negroes, like the Whitman Sisters, who spread their wings from gospel meetings to vaudeville, seldom with parental blessings.

When Warner Brothers bought the film rights to *The Jazz Singer,* Jessel expected to star and hoped it would be made as a sound motion picture. It was, but with Al Jolson in Jessel's role. There are many stories of how Jessel lost his role. Jolson was a bigger name nationwide while Jessel was essentially a New York performer. Jessel asked for too much money and too much input. Jessel complained that the ending of the play was changed for the film. (Instead of returning to his family and becoming a cantor, Warner Brothers had Jessel's character choosing the stage.) Whatever happened, Jessel began a long, slow fade. He appeared in a lifetime total of three dozen movies, silent and sound, that failed to engender the enthusiasm of many critics or audiences, but he was not a flop, either. His motion pictures made modest profits.

He produced a few shows on Broadway, appearing in a couple, and he made good money in vaudeville. In his next high-profile opportunity, early in 1930, George costarred with Fanny Brice and Hal Skelly in Billy Rose's *Corned Beef and Roses.* It opened in Philly to bad notices. It lacked the polish of a Ziegfeld, Dillingham or John Murray Anderson production. Rose's show was dirty and without the redeeming wit, style and fast pace expected of the naughty but chic revues of George White. Billy Rose, Fanny Brice's third husband, revamped his show, added James Barton as Brice's and Jessel's costar, and opened it in

New York as *Sweet and Low* just before the year-end holidays of 1930, but the show was not the success that Rose and Brice had hoped. Rose made a few changes and tried to milk more performances out of the show by sending it forth on the road as *Crazy Quilt.* Forty weeks later, *Crazy Quilt* (1931) had returned Billy and Fanny's investment and helped make up some of the big losses both had sustained in the stock market.

Jessel had left the show, preferring to stay in New York. He was back in vaudeville but this time doing a double act of sorts with Eddie Cantor at the Palace Theatre on Broadway. They headlined and emceed the show, which included the relatively new team of Burns & Allen. Having emcees in vaudeville was a new wrinkle; having two garnered good publicity and reviews. Cantor and Jessel stayed at the Palace for nine weeks, then went on tour with a packaged vaudeville unit. The Cantor-Jessel bill reverted to old-time practice and ended with an afterpiece that brought all the acts onstage in a production number.

George Jessel was faring rather well. So, of course, he had to jinx it. By his own admission, silent-screen star Norma Talmadge was the love of his life. If Norma Talmadge was the high point of his love life, his marriage to her ran parallel to his decline as a star performer. Through the 1930s and into the early 1940s, George continued to produce plays and revues, appeared in some shows, failed in radio, failed in television, wrote frankly and well and became better known as a well-paid after-dinner speaker and eulogist. Jessel's stories were witty and hit their mark. President Harry Truman acknowledged Jessel as the toastmaster of the United States, an offhand remark that became a title, one that Jessel took more seriously than perhaps it was intended.

Jessel's show business career was not over. Starting in 1943, George spent ten years with Daryl Zanuck's Twentieth Century Fox, profitably producing movies that lovingly displayed the charms and talents of Betty Grable, June Haver and Mitzi Gaynor. Of the 14 movies that Jessel produced, the most successful were those that told vaudeville's story, although through the lens of Technicolored sentimentality: *The Dolly Sisters* (1945), *I Wonder Who's Kissing Her Now?* (1947), *When My Baby Smiles at Me* (1948), *Oh, You Beautiful Doll* (1949), *Meet Me after the Show* (1951), *Golden Girl* (1951), *Wait Till the Sun Shines, Nellie* (1952) and *The I Don't Care Girl* (1953). George also wed his third wife, a teenaged Lois Andrews, with whom he had a daughter, his first child. Lois divorced him in 1943, after three years of marriage. From this point on, Jessel gave up the pursuit of love and romance, but not women. He acknowledged fathering two more children.

Other comedians took potshots at him for his May–December romances and dalliances. Jokes that started, "George couldn't be here tonight because . . ." finished with various tags along the lines of, "He couldn't get a baby sitter," "He had to pick up his wife after school," or "His wife is ill—she's teething." Later the jokes would be about his adoption of the persona of a super patriot. George Burns claimed that Jessel listed leeward when he walked, not because of age but for all the medals he pinned on his uniform. One of those medals was a Purple Heart awarded to the 70-year-old Jessel for jumping from a burning helicopter in Vietnam, where he was entertaining the troops.

Jessel bragged that he had been invited to the White House by every president from Coolidge to Reagan except Eisenhower and Gerald Ford. Intelligence and good stories, however, do not add up to punditry or political influence. Yet Jessel suggested that it was his introduction of Truman to a California rally largely composed of African Americans that swung that state to Truman in the election of 1948, thus causing the greatest upset to date in presidential politics.

During the Vietnam War, Jessel believed that his observations on the ground in Vietnam made him an authority. His hawkish posture was born of his loyalty to Richard Nixon and the servicemen and servicewomen fighting in Southeast Asia. He lashed out at liberals, peaceniks and hippies and promised, during his last years, to write a book, *The Crucifixion of Richard M. Nixon.* Fortunately, George never wrote it. Instead he authored *Elegy in Manhattan* (1961), a compilation of word sketches of many men and women he had met and known in his life. George's portraits were affectionate and compassionate, yet clear-eyed and spot-on.

Jessel also wrote two autobiographies. The first, *So Help Me,* was published in 1943 by Random House. In 1975, he made a few revisions to his 1943 autobiography, added several chapters to cover his declining years and called *The World I Lived In* a new book. Issued by Henry Regnery, the book listed John Austin as Jessel's coauthor.

George Jessel was an old, rather lonely man by the time *The World I Lived In* was published. By then, most of Jessel's cronies were dead and forgotten, and he knew his world was in the past tense. He spared himself in neither autobiography, recounting his failures, both professional and romantic, without apology, shame or guile. The jaunty tone of the first book, however, had soured in the second, while the name-dropping grew more insistent, as if to remind his dwindling audience and the author himself that his life had counted for something.

JIGGERS

Slang for tap dancers. Refers to *jigs,* Irish step dances.

BROOKE JOHNS

b: (William Brooke Johns) 24 December 1893, Washington, DC—d: 3 December 1987, Olney, MD

Many folks get trapped in their jobs. When custom, public taste or technology changes, they are unable to adapt. This was true of the vaudevillians who waited for the movie fad to blow over, the silent-picture players who thought sound tracks of dialogue ruined the art of silent pictures, and radio personalities who failed to understand that television required them to be visually interesting or attractive.

Brooke Johns was a success in everything he did, and he did many things, never allowing his past accomplishments to block his view of the future. In the course of his life, he seemed to flow with the seasons, moving naturally from one suitable endeavor to the next.

According to his friend and biographer, Buckey Grimm, Brooke and formal schooling were not a natural match. He bounced from one private school to the next and finally left high school without a diploma. At 18, he was a handsome, strapping lad of six feet, four inches. A football injury turned his attention to the stage. He had inherited a lovely singing voice from his mother, and his father had taught him to play banjo. While in prep school, Brooke played banjo in a small-time dance band.

Around 1916, he entered small-time vaudeville as a single, but banjo-strumming singers were as thick on the ground as sister acts, so his first dates in vaudeville were few and far between. However, he ran across Tempest & Sunshine, whose new sister act had a hole in it. At one point, they needed time offstage to change costumes, so they paid Brooke $20 a week for a song and a strum to cover their absence from the stage.

Brooke was not unaware of the impending war in the late 1910s. He volunteered for the naval reserves and was called to active duty. The brass decided he was of best use as an entertainer, and he was assigned to a navy show called *The Frolicking Tars.* Upon discharge, Brooke gathered a group of other recently demobilized sailors to form a 32-man glee club for touring.

When the tour ran its course, Brooke signed on with bandleader Meyer Davis to work in Florida. Producer Carl Carleton, summering in Miami, offered Brooke a part in a musical comedy, *Tangerine* (1921), that he was producing on Broadway for the Shubert organization. It starred the popular team of Frank Crummit and Julian Sanderson, ran the entire 1921–22 season at the Casino Theatre and was Brooke Johns' first Broadway show.

Johns left *Tangerine* before the end of its run to appear in a supper club called the Ted Lewis Room. This made him well known around Broadway, and he adapted his nightclub act for big-time vaudeville. He played the Palace the week of 6 November 1922 and was held over a second week. Ann Pennington, the dancing sensation of both the *Ziegfeld Follies* and *George White's Scandals,* performed that second week. As a gimmick, she danced to a player piano. There was some electrical trouble on the day the show was reviewed. The piano was out of synchronicity with her dancing. Brooke offered to accompany her instead, and she accepted. The pair went over big.

Following their joint triumph at the Palace, Pennington and Brooke Johns were pulled into the *Ziegfeld Follies of 1922* to fill a void left by Gallagher & Shean, who were having one of their spats, either with each other or with Ziegfeld. The show enjoyed an extended run and then went on tour. Either through choice or not, both Johns and Pennington left the *Ziegfeld Follies of 1922* before its run concluded and went into *Jack and Jill* (1923), a musical comedy directed by John Murray Anderson that ran only 12 weeks. Brooke and Ann were back with Ziegfeld for the *Ziegfeld Follies of 1923,* an edition not as well received as the previous year's edition by either the public or critics.

Brooke pulled together a jazz band and played the Palace again in 1923. He took his musical aggregation to London for dates at the Kit Kat Club with Sophie Tucker and at the Alhambra Theatre. When he returned to the USA in 1924, it was to appear with Ann Pennington, playing themselves, in Gloria Swanson's silent film *Manhandled* (1924). His only other venture in front of the motion picture camera did not challenge his acting skills, either; he played a musician in *That Old Gang of Mine* (1925), written and directed by vaudeville actor and sketch writer May Tully.

Following a tour on Keith time, Brooke Johns was engaged by Ziegfeld to support W.C. Fields and Ray Dooley in *The Comic Supplement* (1925), which opened and closed on the road. Johns went back to Keith time and then sailed to London for a variety theatre tour. Late in 1925, he married Hazel Mahaska Barnsley, the young daughter of family friends. They had six children.

From 1925 to 1934, Brooke Johns played vaudeville and then presentation houses as an emcee and singing banjoist. Realizing that the world of live performance—especially vaudeville—had been supplanted in large measure by movies and radio, Brooke decided to retire in 1934, just before his 40th birthday.

He became a restaurateur in Georgetown, a fashionable section of Washington, D.C., held several positions in appointive politics, hosted a weekly radio show starting in 1949, built a country club and golf course on part of his Maryland property and hosted a children's television show in the 1950s. Brooke Johns received many awards for service to the community, including the honorific title of goodwill ambassador for Maryland; he also received, 73 years after he left Georgetown Prep, his high school diploma.

JOHNSON & DEAN

Charley Johnson

b: (Charles Johnson) ca. 1865—d: 1955, Minneapolis, MN

Dora Dean

b: (Dora Babbige) ca. 1875—d: ca. 1945

Charley Johnson, whose mother had been born into slavery, entered minstrelsy in the 1870s. He is credited with reviving the chalk line walk, an earlier version of the cakewalk. The chalk line walk, a contest of skill among African Americans, was a holdover from slavery days. It was a high-stepping dance, with turns and reversals, performed while balancing a bucket of water on the head and following a line delineated by chalk. Johnson did away with the bucket of water but retained the required precision and high style. Some sources, such as Tom Fletcher, claim that Johnson devised the first cakewalk for the stage.

Dora Dean entered show business during the mid-1880s, traveling with touring black revues. In those days, even a chorus girl had to be able to carry a tune, dance up a storm and handle lines in the sketches. Those, like Dean, who sparkled in all three and were beautiful and shapely became featured performers; some eventually became stars.

Like many dancers of his era, Charley Johnson moved from the minstrel tradition into burlesque revue and then vaudeville. He developed a reputation as an early eccentric dancer; *grotesque dancing* was another nonpejorative and quite usual term of the day for acrobatic dancing.

Charlie Johnson and Dora Dean met in 1889 while both were engaged in *Sam T. Jack's Creole Show* (aka *The Creole Show*), an innovative show that combined elements of minstrelsy. It opened with the customary semicircle of song-and-dance men and musicians flanked by end men and centered on the interlocutor. Sam T. Jack, burlesque bred, retained the minstrel show opening but had a woman interlocutor and added female singers and dancers, among them Dora Dean, to the front semicircle. The end men remained male; one of them was Charley Johnson.

The true innovation was the elimination of blackface. All the African American and African Caribbean entertainers performed *neat.* There was, of course, the usual chorus of dancing girls, but, unlike most burlesque revues, *The Creole Show* included numbers where the men and women danced together. Dora partnered with Charley in the cakewalk number.

It does not overstate the case to note that self-esteem for black performers was at odds with the expectation that they had to "black up" and don costumes as cartoonish field hands, servants, tramps or aborigines. Charley Johnson was one of many star black performers who, having sampled dignity, persevered through talent and style and raised the bar onstage. "The pioneering team of Johnson & Dean was perhaps the first to break ground for class [dance] acts," claimed Marshall and Jean Stearns. "Johnson & Dean established the roles of the genteel Negro couple on the American stage—the courtly gentleman and the gracious lady."

Johnson & Dean married and became a popular dance act in big-time vaudeville in the 1900s and 1910s. Johnson made a handsome, impeccably tailored figure of a man, a dancer who strutted and performed legomania. Neither he nor Dora was a tap or clog dancer. Nor were they singers; they spoke-sang their songs in the act. Dora appeared splendidly gowned—some of her outfits cost $1,000. If Charley was handsome and dignified, Dora was beautiful and her personality lit up the theatre. In tribute to her beauty, George Walker and Bert Williams wrote the song "Dora Dean" (even while Aida Overton Walker, George's wife, was part of the Williams & Walker act):

Say, have you ever seen Miss Dora Dean?
She is the finest gal you've ever seen.
I'm a-goin' try and make this gal my queen
Next Sunday morning I'm goin' to marry
Miss Dora Dean.

Named to honor the much-feted Admiral Schley of the recently fought and concluded Spanish-American War, the Schley Theatre, located on West 34th Street between Sixth and Seventh avenues in Manhattan, opened in 1899 as a competitor to the established Koster & Bial's and was dedicated to the best in vaudeville. The Schley's first bill headlined Dave Montgomery & Fred Stone, a top comedy act, and Johnson & Dean were billed as an added star attraction.

Johnson & Dean introduced the Flicker Kinetoscope, a novelty spotlight backed by hand-cranked glass reflectors. The effect was like that of the black lights and mirrored balls of 1960s dance bars. Johnson & Dean wore dark clothes with white accents—Dora, a dark gown trimmed with white at the cuffs and hem, and Charley in dark formal Prince Albert attire with white gloves and spats. At some point in their dance, the light went dark except for the Kinetoscope that picked up the blurring whirl of white hands, feet and fabric.

The Johnson and Dean marriage was by all accounts given to storms. In 1895, Charley Johnson was one of the stars of the performance portion of Billy McClain's *Black America,* a groundbreaking exposition and extravaganza that occupied a large section of Ambrose Park in Brooklyn for most of that summer. Dora may have been part of the show. At some point, she wished to get off the road and settle down in one place, so 1895 may have been a time of trial separation. Later, Dora and a female partner went into partnership with a dress company.

Johnson & Dean played in the North and on the West Coast, but not the South. There is no evidence that they ever worked TOBA (Theatre Owners' Booking Association) theatres. They became a standard act in white vaudeville and thus had the opportunity to make at least one tour of Europe. From 1913 into 1914, they played in more than a dozen countries.

So successful were they in Europe that advance bookings took them into their second year, but the First World War broke up the tour, and Johnson & Dean returned home to Minneapolis. Then Charley and Dora broke up. Over the course of their joint career, stage dancing had, by leaps and taps, grown ever more sophisticated and complex. Cakewalking struts evoked minstrelsy. Clog and buck dancing had led to ever more precise percussive dance, and George Primrose, Ginger Wiggins and Bill Robinson were astounding audiences with tap dancing.

Johnson & Dean were occasionally talked into making appearances at old-timer events—Dora probably needed more persuasion than Charley. The last such event of record was in 1936 at Connie's Inn. Charley Johnson lived a long life, probably reaching 90. Dora is believed to have died ten or more years earlier.

JAY JOHNSON

b: (Jay Kent Johnson) 11 July ca. 1950, Lubbock, Texas

Although Jay Johnson had appeared on many television variety shows, it was his weekly appearance as a character with his puppet, Bob, in the television spoof of soap operas called *Soap* (1977–81, ABC-TV) that won him national recognition.

Jay's fascination with puppets began early, while he was in the third grade. In fact, he became far more interested in learning ventriloquism than the standard curriculum. By age ten, Jay had pulled together a ten-minute routine that he performed for local clubs and fraternal organizations in Abernathy, Texas, where the Johnsons lived. At $10 a performance, Jay figured that he had latched on to an agreeable life's work. The pay got better as he moved into his teens and the Johnsons relocated to Dallas. The big city gave him greater opportunities, including appearing in television commercials for Dallas businesses.

A drama scholarship tempted him, but Jay's dad convinced him that a business education was a wise pairing with his already developed talent. During Johnson's years at the University of North Texas, he continued to work in show business, appearing in industrial shows and at business banquets. His studies made him aware of issues in the corporate world. He graduated with a bachelor's degree in business with a minor in marketing. His business training continued to be of use throughout his career.

During college, summers were spent performing at theme parks, where he did ten shows a day. Despite the long hours, he managed time to meet his future wife, Sandy, a dancer.

After college, Jay moved to Los Angeles to be closer to show business opportunities. Although variety shows were no longer prevalent on prime time, daytime shows, hosted by Merv Griffith, Mike Douglas, Dinah Shore and John Davidson, were always looking for good variety acts that could enliven their talk show formats.

Even given his exposure to network bookers and ad agencies, it was still a surprise when the producers and writers of *Soap* engaged Jay Johnson as a regular in the series. Jay and his dummy were cast as Chuck Campbell and Bob. Theirs were no stranger for the times than the other roles in the series. There was a gay son, another who was a mobster trainee, a senile major and more than a few sexually stirred family members whose peccadilloes led to affairs of every stripe, illegitimate birth, gender confusion and murder.

Soap became a huge hit. Some stations were afraid to broadcast the show, although the same sexual subject matter was driving the afternoon soap operas they aired without qualm. The show's success and Jay's resulting popularity brought him three comedy specials and the opportunity to produce and perform various specials for both broadcast and cable networks.

Even during his busiest years on television, Jay Johnson continued to work before live audiences. He played the booming comedy clubs of the 1980s and went back to corporate shows and cruise ships in the 1990s.

In one spot during one of his later acts, Jay taught his puppet Bob how to be a ventriloquist by putting a piece of duct tape over Bob's mouth and forcing him to throw his voice to Jay's mouth. With this, Jay set up one of the more original tricks in ventriloquism. Jay spoke in Bob's voice and Bob spoke in Jay's voice. It took a few minutes for audiences to realize what had happened.

Throughout his act, Jay presented unusual examples of ventriloquism. In one spot, he used a white dry erase board to demonstrate his skill as a cartoonist. Suddenly the face drawn on the board came to life and talked to an amazed audience.

Jay Johnson also performed a one-man show he wrote called *The One and Only,* a carefully crafted deconstruction of ventriloquism and an examination of its history. Its first run began 13 May 2004 at the Atlantic Theatre Company, an Off-Broadway house in Manhattan. It featured several new characters, among which was a vulture named "Nethermore, the Bird of Death." This winged scavenger with an obsession for death took audiences on a journey through the dark beginnings of ventriloquism from the Oracle of Delphi to the witches of the middle ages. Despite its dark overtones, the show was both funny and a brilliant display of ventriloquism.

LONNIE JOHNSON

b: (Alonzo Johnson) 8 February 1899, New Orleans, LA—d: 16 June 1970, Toronto, Canada

One of the twentieth century's great blues guitarists and singers, Lonnie Johnson played in the Whitman Sisters' vaudeville bands off and on for nine years. He began his career when he was ten in New Orleans' notorious Storyville section. Later, he worked as a violinist with his brother, James "Steady Roll" Johnson, in their father's band. During the 1918 influenza outbreak, Lonnie was touring in England with a black revue. The epidemic killed ten of his siblings and his father. Only Lonnie, his mother and an older brother escaped.

Returning to the USA, Lonnie worked as a Mississippi River boat musician, including a stint with Fate Marable's band, 1920–22, and then he entered vaudeville, playing some dates as a single singing act. He joined comic dancers Glenn & Jenkins in an act that played both Toby time and Keith-Albee circuits during the 1922–24 seasons. In between vaudeville engagements Lonnie eked out a living with rent parties, nightclub gigs and playing in theatre pit bands.

In 1925 he began recording for OKeh Records, first with the Charlie Creath Jazz-O-Maniacs, then sessions with the Louis Armstrong Hot Five in 1925, Duke Ellington's Orchestra in 1928 and Louis Armstrong's Savoy Ballroom Five in 1929.

In 1929 he toured the South with Bessie Smith in her revue *Midnight Steppers.* From 1931 to 1932 he recorded for Columbia records, including a never-released session with Martha Raye. He was especially skilled as a guitarist and composer, and his singing voice was warm and lyrical, overlapping the baritone and tenor ranges.

Over the years, Johnson did whatever was needed to keep working: he headed his own trio at various times, worked solo or played in other blues, jazz and dance bands. Occasionally, he took jobs outside of show business to keep body and soul together. From the early 1930s to the mid-1950s, his career was a patchwork of one-nighters, bar gigs and recordings for Decca and Bluebird labels, 1937–40, and King Records, late 1940s. He went where the work was, and work took Lonnie all across the USA.

By the mid-1950s, most of Lonnie's income was earned outside show business. When the blues revival prompted record companies to round up the living masters they could find, Prestige/Bluesville Records rediscovered Lonnie working as a hotel janitor in 1960 and signed him up for a series of recordings. Although the largely white young folk music audience for the blues revival wanted the raw, country sounds of Reverend Gary Davis, Sonny Terry & Brownie McGhee and Big Mama Thornton, smoother, more jazz-oriented performers like Lonnie Johnson, Roosevelt Sykes and Victoria Spivey also rode the wave.

Lonnie Johnson began to get the respect that he deserved, and he played dates as varied as New York City's Town Hall, radio and television work, the Playboy Club, and the growing circuit of small clubs and festivals on both coasts that featured blues and folk music. Lonnie capped his comeback with a European tour and more recordings. In 1965 he settled in Toronto, where he owned and worked clubs until illness sidelined him. He died in 1970 after suffering a stroke.

Lonnie Johnson influenced a generation of blues guitarists and singers. Upon his death, Bob Groon wrote in *Blues World* magazine that "Lonnie Johnson was without a doubt a musical giant of the Twentieth Century: an exceptionally gifted guitarist, a sensitive, moving vocalist, and a composer of thoughtful, often highly original blues." He was also typical of talented black musicians who relied upon vaudeville for a significant portion of their income.

JOLLY CORKS

A group of friends, all performers from the variety stage and minstrelsy, decided to subvert New York City's *blue laws* that thwarted their weeklong conviviality by refusing them the pleasure of drink in a tavern on Sundays. In 1867, the friends banded together as the Jolly Corks. The original number of 13 to 16 members (the exact number has been disputed) included Charles Vivian (1842–80), W.L. Bowron, William Carleton, George F. McDonald, T.G. Riggs, William Shepard and George W. Thompson. The group met every Sunday evening and earned their name of Jolly Corks with repeated toasts, including at least one to absent members.

The group's purpose took a serious turn with the death of a member. The others pledged their assistance to his widow and her children, and later, in a formal annunciation of principles, the organization enlarged its purpose to the welfare of a wider citizenry. Serious purpose led to a more formal organization in 1868, and more performers joined the group.

There is considerable confusion as to how much of an active hand Charles Vivian, the impetus behind the Jolly Corks, had in the formation of the Jolly Cork's successor organization, the Benevolent and Protective Order of Elks (BPOE). While in England, Vivian had become a member of the Royal Antediluvian Order of Buffaloes in England. Buffaloes was suggested as the name for the American order, but an equally majestic animal, the elk, was also proposed. Supposedly a one-vote margin gave the honor to the elk.

Mike Leavitt, show business entrepreneur and chronicler, adamantly states that Charles Vivian never became an Elk; the BPOE claims otherwise. By 1900, BPOE membership was extended to *civilians* as well as show folk, and charters were issued to groups at other locations across the USA. By the turn of the twenty-first century, the Elks numbered well over one million members in more than 2,000 communities.

AL JOLSON

b: (Asa Yoelson) 26 May 1886(?), Srednike, Lithuania—d: 23 October 1950, San Francisco, CA

Al Jolson took an unabashed delight in his own cocky performance. He worked so hard and joyfully to please his audiences that they wholeheartedly joined him in his own admiration and enjoyment. On numerous occasions at the Winter Garden, Al would ask his audience, "These boys and gals, they've worked awful hard tonight. Why don't we let 'em go home and I'll finish the show alone?" The packed house would roar its approval, as he knew it would, and Jolie dismissed the dance line (whose only purpose was to give Al a breather at spots during the show) and sang as long as his public would have him. Whether it was midnight or two o'clock in the morning, when he finished, it was Al who paid, out of his own pocket, overtime to the stage crew. He could afford it. Jolson was one of the highest-paid entertainers of his day.

His fellow performers were more critical than his audience. To a person, they acknowledged (publicly, at least) Al's supremacy as *the* entertainer of their era, but the general consensus among his fellow entertainers and others who knew him intimately, such as his first three wives, was that Al's fatal flaw was coupling egocentricity with exhibitionism and petty pride. Show business is filled with ego-driven people, but most have the sense to mask their self-obsession with humor, public generosity, good fellowship or feigned humility.

Al Jolson could never admit to being wrong, and he was reluctant to give others credit for their

Al Jolson

achievements. Sometimes, he demanded and got co-credit as a songwriter from composers and lyricists because, as he maintained, it was he who interpreted the songs and made them famous.

Yet it is too easy to simply characterize Al Jolson as egotistical. A complicated man, he did not trumpet his acts of kindness. He handed out cash to the needy, left millions of dollars in his will to help youngsters get an education, gave financial help to his first partner, Joe Palmer, and wheeled him about to visit old vaudeville friends and haunts.

His birthdate is approximate; lacking birth records, there was only Al's word for when he was born, and admittedly he chose the 26th of May because he relished the idea of being born at the height of spring. The cherished baby of the family, Al lost his mother when he was about nine. He and his only brother, Harry, three years older, were raised along with their older sisters, Rose and Etta, by their father, Moses.

The family had emigrated from Lithuania to Washington, D.C., where Moses, sixth in his family line of cantors, became a rabbi as well. In turn, Moses Yoelson expected one of his sons, most likely Asa (later Al), to become the seventh cantor. Hirsch (later Harry) and Asa both wanted careers on the stage. From the time he was 13 until he was 15, Al slipped away from home to try to get into show business, as did Harry. Their father thrashed them each time they ran away. After one escapade, Al was caught by the Gerry Society and sent to a Roman Catholic school for wayward youth.

Harry had protected his younger brother against the racist youth gangs in their hometown and later led the way into theatrical careers for both of them. Yet Al was reported to have resented Harry, even though the older brother always admired Al's talent and admitted he was not in Al's class as an entertainer. On the other hand, Al actively helped his brother professionally.

About 14 years old when he began his professional career, Al based himself in New York City. His first performing jobs included plugging sheet music in music shops, singing in saloons, burlesque and circus, and as a singing waiter. Although he got work in burlesque with Al Reeves' Famous Big Company (whose stage personality had great influence on Al) and the Dainty Duchess show, more often his jobs were menial, like dishwashing.

As a promising boy soprano, Al attracted the attention of the Gerry Society, zealous in their efforts to protect children from a life on the wicked stage. Later, in his teens, the Gerry Society was no longer interested in Al and neither were producers—his voice was changing.

In 1903 he teamed up with his brother—they changed their family name to Joelson—in a two-man patter act, "The Hebrew and the Cadet." Al was the goyem straight man cadet to Harry's put-upon Jewish comic. They added songs to their act. A year later they teamed with an older singing comedian and impressionist, Joe Palmer, in a singing, dancing and patter act. Palmer was disabled and used a wheelchair, but he was a master of fast-patter songs. In their act with Palmer, the boys changed their names from Joelson to Jolson; it was also during this act that Al Jolson adopted blackface. They were essentially a number two act, a patchwork of joke-book wheezers and off-the-shelf songs. After a couple of years, conflicts between the brothers and disappointment with their reception led to breaking up the act.

Al worked his way across the country to San Francisco, where in 1906 he met his first wife, Henrietta Keller. He sang amid the aftermath of the famous earthquake and made his first real hit in show business. Henrietta quickly discovered what all Al's wives would learn: he was already married to his career. At last on his own as a performer, Al Jolson was not hemmed in by a script or having to relate to onstage partners. It did not annoy him that the city was noisily being rebuilt around him even as he was performing. For a couple of years, Jolson based himself in San Francisco, often working the Sullivan & Considine circuit.

He honed in on his audience, reacting to subtle shifts in mood, kidded with the folks who had paid to see him and pulled them into his performance. Their applause buoyed him and he gave them everything he had. Reviewers of the day described Jolson as a comedian, but he was more truly what we think of as a song-and-dance minstrel man.

Lew Dockstader, impresario and star of his own minstrel show, the last and most famous of its kind, witnessed Jolson in action and engaged him for his famous troupe. Dockstader was the star. Lew, however, yielded his own next-to-closing spot in the show when young Al proved to be the showstopper. Jolson was really past the point of being an ensemble player. It was time for him to become a big-time vaudeville headliner in New York, and as if on cue, Art Klein, an agent, approached Jolson. Klein's strategy took Al straight into Proctor's Fifth Avenue Theatre, where after a single performance he displaced Louise Dresser in the headliner's spot on the bill. Al toured two-a-day vaudeville throughout the Northeast. Hammerstein's new Victoria Theatre provided another triumph in Manhattan. Legend has it that Jolson commanded the Monday matinee audience of showbiz professionals with a few shrill whistles and the suggestion that they could resume their visiting and chatting after he finished his act. His chutzpah paid off because he could deliver the goods.

Jolson continued in vaudeville, playing Orpheum time out west and returning home to San Francisco.

While Al was enhancing his reputation in vaudeville, Art Klein was making one of the most important connections in Jolson's life. The Shubert Brothers had not been on the scene much longer than Al Jolson, but by 1911 they had quietly assembled the start of a theatrical empire. Jolson and the Shubert Brothers were fortunate in their timing and in finding each other. Jolson was unlikely to find any other producers who were as likely as the Shuberts to let him dominate a series of shows throughout the 1910s. In Jolson the Shuberts had gained a star who quickly became the mortgage payer on their Winter Garden theatre.

Breezy and informal with his audiences, Jolson courted them, alternating between a folksy friendliness and an imperious bravado. Sometimes intimate, he sauntered to the edge of the stage apron, loosened his tie and sat down, legs dangling into the orchestra pit, and charmed the spectators with song. On occasion he chose to drop down into the aisles and kibitz with people in the front rows. Other times, he assertively strutted and danced his way out on a runway, his feet a few inches above the heads of the audience seated in the orchestra.

Jolson's peak years were spent in a dozen musical comedies and revues, exclusively for the Shuberts, although he twice made a guest appearance in other shows. Working six days a week, giving eight performances in a week was not enough for Jolson. In addition to the Shubert revues and musicals at the Winter Garden, where Al reigned for 15 years, he frequently starred in Sunday night concerts. What few outside of those who worked with him realized was that Jolie was in agony before every show or concert and depressingly deflated after every performance.

La Belle Paree (1911) marked Jolie's first appearance in a Broadway show, one the Shuberts chose to open their new 1,600-seat Winter Garden. Opening night the show—really more of a three-part vaudeville revue than a cohesive book musical—ran so long that the critics and much of the audience left without seeing Jolson, who was spotted late into the evening. Pleased with his rendition of (the embarrassingly titled) "Paris Is a Paradise for Coons," the Shuberts added an earlier number for him, and Jolson was credited in large measure for the run of 104 performances.

Vera Violetta scored 112 performances during its New York run late in 1911. Gaby Deslys was the headliner, but it was Jolson who repeatedly earned encores. The Shuberts rushed both of them into another entertainment, *Whirl of Society,* that racked up 136 shows at the Winter Garden in 1912. This was the show where Jolson induced the producers to install a runway out over the audience. Adapted from burlesque, the runway let Jolson to flaunt his talent, much as the burlesque queens flaunted their charms.

In 1913 Jolson joined Gaby Deslys for a third time in a new show, *The Honeymoon Express,* which ran 156 performances. This farce with music also featured Ada Lewis and the great dance team of James Doyle & Harland Dixon and introduced youngsters Fanny Brice and Harry Fox. Deslys and Brice were replaced eventually by Grace LaRue and Ina Claire.

After each Jolson show completed its stand at the Winter Garden in New York, it went on the road, adding greatly to the Shubert coffers and Al's income. Jolson had perfected his act by 1913. His ego also hit its stride. It was opening night of *The Honeymoon Express* that Jolson first dismissed the rest of the cast and the show along with them. The evening was running late and Jolson turned to the audience and yelled, "Do you want to hear the rest of the story or do you want to hear me?" The audience voted for Al, and the rest of the cast got themselves offstage as best they could. On tour Al pulled the same trick while the star, Miss Gaby Deslys, was onstage. She left. Also while on tour, Doyle & Dixon, who preceded Jolson in the show, were so enthusiastically received that Jolson sniped at them as they left the stage, "Don't let that happen again."

The Shuberts were relying on formula to replicate success, but *Dancing Around* (1914), another Winter Garden revue/spectacle, had little to recommend it except Jolson and Doyle & Dixon, who had been slotted into the show so as not to spoil Jolson's entrances. Despite a lame plot, unmemorable songs and Jolson's sometimes arrogant attitude toward paying customers, it chalked up 145 performances.

Art Klein had taken Jolson as far as Jolson thought he could, so Art was let go. Jolson's new contract brought him 10% of the net and $1,000 a week from the Shuberts.

Robinson Crusoe, Jr., in 1916, was the closest Jolie got—or let himself get—to a true book show. The Shuberts billed Jolson, no doubt with his full consent, as "The World's Greatest Entertainer," and Al cavorted as the title character's man Friday. The show ran 139 performances. Two years later, in 1918, Jolson resumed his fling with exotic locales for 164 performances in *Sinbad.* Jolson sang most of the show's songs plus a few unrelated tunes he liked, including "Swanee." Kitty Doner was a featured player in both *Robinson Crusoe, Jr.* and *Sinbad,* and there were rumors of a casual romance between Kitty and Jolson.

Behind-the-scenes, matters were both bad and good. Al's marriage to Henrietta was ending, and there was also the beginning of trouble with Al's lung. A spot was discovered, and he was advised to lighten his workload. He did not. His career was in high gear, and he had asked Louis Epstein to be his new manager.

Al Jolson

Eppy was an old associate from the Dockstader days, and he remained Al's manager to the end. Al was even managing his brother Harry's career.

Who can say Jake Shubert was wrong to trust formulas? Next in line was *Bombo,* which won 218 performances and delighted audiences in 1921. The show was a melange of Jolson in blackface as usual, a disposable plot, extravaganza and lots of songs that suited the star: "California, Here I Come," "Toot-Toot-Tootsie," and "April Showers." By now Jolie was more than a star; he was an icon. *Bombo* opened in a newly built Shubert theatre that the owners gratefully named after Jolson. They were also paying Al $3,500 a week plus 25% of the gross.

Big Boy (1926) was his next musical, and Jolson, in blackface, treated the book as casually as it deserved, often jettisoning the plot to perform his act. Among Al's songs were "If You Knew Susie," but Jolie gave it to Cantor, whom he thought better suited to the song. *Big Boy* closed after six weeks (48 performances) when Jolson became ill.

Reviewers employed words like "electrifies," "thrills," and other words that could explain the current of excitement that ran through the audience and keyed them to rapt attention when Jolson burst onto the stage. Had he relied on chutzpah and energy alone, he would never had been acknowledged as "The World's Greatest Entertainer." He had great talent. Other white minstrel men were more amusing—Cantor, for instance, and others who could dance better, such as George Primrose, Harland Dixon and Eddie Leonard. But Jolson was a singular personality and a sophisticated singer.

Innately musical and blessed with a versatile tenor shading into light baritone, Al could produce musical sounds through head tones by filtering his voice through his facial mask or sending it rumbling forth from his chest. He was a master at marshalling his breath and expending to great effect; how else could he have managed such an even projection of sound and still fill in between the phrases when it struck his fancy? As he aged his voice darkened, deepened and grew a trifle leathery, but, in all, his voice was a remarkably robust and enviably sure instrument that served him well to the end of his days.

Al Jolson was at his zenith in the 1910s and the early 1920s, the years before, during and just after the First World War. The flappers, crooners and speakeasies that became symbols of the Roaring Twenties were signals of a shift in public taste. Jolson's heyday was the time that marked the passage of the USA from a still largely agrarian country, remote from the rest of the world, to a world power whose population numbered many immigrants. In performance Al Jolson melded Victorian sentimentality with Jazz Age brashness, and Old World intonation with New World syncopation. He was as American as blueberry blintzes, chop suey and macaroni and cheese.

Jolson began his habit of entertaining American servicemen during the First World War. Al married for a second and short time. Of more historic import is that Jolson performed a half dozen songs, at least, for the Vitaphone sight and sound recording process during the 1920s; these shorts represent his first foray into film. D. W. Griffith reportedly had tried to coax Jolson into a film, but Jolson had jilted the old movie master, who tried to sue. In Jolson's feature films on the big silver screen, it was apparent in the close-ups that Al was a decade or more older than most of the leading men in the movies, especially the new Broadway talent arriving daily to replace the silent veterans. Al was over 40, perhaps nearer 45, when he played *The Jazz Singer* for Warner Bothers in 1927.

The novelty of *The Jazz Singer,* a critical step on the path from silent film to synchronized sound track to all-talking—and all-singing and all-dancing—musical features, made moot the matter of Jolie's age, but subsequent features did not. *The Jazz Singer* was such a roaring success in terms of publicity and box-office returns that Jolson's stature in show business was enhanced by Jolie's mastery of a new and frightening medium, sound movies, and as a result each of his subsequent films had to be a Jolson vehicle—and this usually meant a role as a romantic leading man. Al was still trim and vigorous, but his expression and personality were beginning to toughen, and his hair, never luxuriant, was thinning and receding.

His second picture, *The Singing Fool* (Warner Brothers, 1928), capitalized on his first film success and provided Al with another maudlin story. Instead of being the aggrieved son, he played the grieving father. Smartly fitted with songs like "I'm Sitting on Top of the World" and "It All Depends on You," the formula produced an even greater success. The fact that by mid-1928 even the smaller cities had at least one movie house rigged for sound guaranteed that *The Singing Fool* garnered a wide audience. The film's ticket sales made it one of the biggest box-office smashes to date (along with *Birth of a Nation, Ben Hur* and *The Big Parade*) until *Gone with the Wind* came along a decade later.

After a cameo spot in 1929's *Sonny Boy,* Al made his third feature the same year, *Say It with Songs,* which pulled people into the theatres even though other musicals were starting to sag at the box office. All was not well, however, for Jolson or Warner Brothers. The word of mouth about *Say It with Songs,* although too slow to hurt ticket sales, was not favorable, and the film's profit fell below what the studio expected from a Jolson picture.

The escalating terms of Jolson's contract provided that he get $500,000 for his fourth feature, *Mammy* (1930). Those who came to see it got a better picture. Director Michael Curtis, a no-nonsense tough guy, did an admirable job. The movie offered the novelty of a Technicolor minstrel show sequence, but on the whole, unfortunately, the script relied on the old formula. The public turned its back and the flick was Jolson's first to lose money.

Big Boy (1930) was the first film to be adapted from one of Jolson's stage shows. It was a silly choice in that it was not as well known as his other shows. True, *Big Boy* sloughed off the melodramatic devices of Jolson's previous films, but as if to demonstrate how much Jolson and his producers were losing touch with audiences, Al played the entire film in blackface as Gus, a jockey (Big Boy was the horse). Box-office returns barely covered costs, and it was three years before Jolie made another film.

In a commendable effort toward relevance, Hollywood made *Hallelujah, I'm a Bum!,* released in 1933 through United Artists (UA). Most Hollywood movies in the dreary days of the Depression told their audiences that the best way to overcome the Great Depression was to cheer up, get happy, dance and sing their troubles away. *Hallelujah, I'm a Bum!* also focused on the Depression and people out of work, but less sanguinely. It did not quite have the courage to go all the way. There is a schizophrenic quality to the film despite excellent credits: story by Ben Hecht, screenplay by S. N. Behrman, lyrics and some rhymed dialogue by Larry Hart, music by Richard Rodgers. The production walked a slack wire between whimsical fantasy and social realism. Jolson was the unofficial tramp mayor of Central Park, and the message seemed to be that although the tramps had to be poor, they at least had the virtue denied capitalists (and the filmmakers) who were rich if ignoble.

French filmmakers and actors of the day might have pulled it off, likely even the German filmmakers, but it was too subtle a recipe for American cooks. As Jolson's sidekick, Harry Langdon was by style and temperament the best suited of the cast to the script, but the direction was not sympathetic and the production was earthbound. It was also a loud flop. Jolson and UA tore up their contract.

Two years earlier, in 1931, a musical, *The Wonder Bar,* had provided a Broadway comeback for Al Jolson with 86 performances (not bad for Depression box office). In 1934 the script also provided Jolson's film comeback vehicle at Warner Brothers. Jolie and Warner Brothers had made film history together with *The Jazz Singer,* so everyone was persuaded that the rematch could pay off in publicity and ticket sales. Busby Berkeley directed, and the result was provocative and sophisticated—almost a Paramount film. The stage show had featured Patsy Kelly and Arthur Treacher, but the film was a multistrand story about the patrons and performers of a continental nightclub peopled by Dolores Del Rio, Ricardo Cortez, Dick Powell, Kay Francis, Louise Fazenda, Ruth Donnelly, Guy Kibbee and Hugh Herbert—in short, an ensemble film, not a one-star vehicle. Hal Leroy and Eddie Foy Jr. were around only long enough to appear in the number "Goin' to Heaven on a Mule," which many film historians cite as the most insensitive and insulting portrayal of black people in musical films.

The Wonder Bar was enough of a success to lead to *Go into Your Dance,* a 1935 production that starred Jolson, in an unsympathetic role, with his third wife, Ruby Keeler, and a great cast of Glenda Farrell, Helen Morgan, Patsy Kelly and Barton MacLane. A year later, 1936, *The Singing Kid* failed to please. Jolson was at least 50 and looked it.

The modest revival of Jolson's movie popularity was fueled in part by his success in several network radio shows. *Presenting Al Jolson* lasted only four months of Friday nights on NBC during the 1932–33 season, but Jolson returned to that network in 1934 with *Kraft Music Hall* for a similarly short run. He was replaced with Bing Crosby. In 1935 NBC starred Jolson in the *Shell Chateau* and paid for big-name guest stars; the show was a success until Al left it to jump to CBS in 1936 for *The Lifebuoy Program.* Inferior to *Shell Chateau,* it still won good ratings, with Martha Raye sharing the songs and comedy until the show sagged in 1939.

Al did some of his best singing on radio in the 1930s when he broadened his repertoire to include contemporary ballads like "Isn't It a Lovely Day" and "Smoke Gets in Your Eyes." He tempered his vocal style a bit as he passed into the 1930s, 1940s and 1950s but never succumbed to the fashion of the moment.

In 1939, just as Jolson's radio career was waning, he had three movies in release: *Rose of Washington Square, Hollywood Cavalcade* and *Swanee River.* They were not Jolson vehicles, but they kept Al in front of a national audience. He again found work on the stage in the 1940 musical *Hold onto Your Hats,* in which Al costarred with his Lifebuoy buddy, Martha Raye. Jack Whiting, Bert Gordon and Gil Lamb were featured. The show ran 158 performances.

The Second World War ushered in the first of three codas for vaudeville (the other two were the Korean Conflict and live television). Movie stars were in demand, but there was not much they could add to a show. Jolson was heaven-sent for wartime. There was not a stage built that Jolson could not own, whether it was the size of Hammerstein's or as small as the back of transport truck. As soon as the Selective Service Draft was instituted and before Pearl Harbor was bombed, Jolson phoned Steve Early, FDR's press secretary, to volunteer his performing services at his own expense. Al Jolson was between 56 and 60 at the time. Shortly after Pearl Harbor, Jolson was touring Stateside air force bases with his pianist, Marty Fried, playing to 60,000 GIs in two weeks; Alaska and Trinidad were next.

Jolson learned he had to tell jokes—most of them quite raunchy—as much as he sang, and the boys loved him. As he was anxious to get overseas, the government sent him on a combined ENSA-USO (Entertainments National Service Association) tour with Merle Oberon, Frank McHugh, Allen Jenkins, Patricia Morrison and some musicians, but Al left the tour because he really wanted to perform solo (except for his new accompanist, composer Harry Akst).

Jolson was among the more dedicated performers playing for the troops. From Europe he headed into North Africa. He took a break when he caught malaria and returned to the States for his next to last radio series, a 13-week run in *The Colgate Show Starring Al Jolson* on CBS. Afterward, Jolson and Akst resumed the USO tour of North Africa. He was on a Purple Heart tour of hospitals when he met and began the long courtship of his fourth wife, Erle Galbraith; they married 23 March 1945.

In 1945 Al lost one of his lungs in an operation. Sidelined for a while, Jolson did not tour again until the Korean Conflict. Between the two wars, Jolson took over the Kraft Music Hall on radio for a few seasons in the late 1940s and returned to Hollywood. It was the start of the biopic era. Sudsy, sanitized and often lifeless films were made about Eddie Cantor, Blossom Seeley, Ruth Etting, Lillian Roth, Buster Keaton, Kalmar & Ruby, the Dolly Sisters and other showbiz veterans who came up through vaudeville. Warner Brothers proved the genre could be popular when it struck box-office gold with its release of *Yankee Doodle Dandy,* starring James Cagney as George M. Cohan. Jolie was among the next to get the treatment.

Columbia cut a deal with Jolson to film his story. Al wanted to play himself—he was at least 60—but Harry Cohn, who may have been the one showbiz veteran tougher than Jolie, would not have it. Larry Parks played the lead in *The Jolson Story* (1946), and it was such a success that they filmed a sequel, *Jolson Sings Again,* in 1949. It was Larry Parks onscreen, but Jolson dubbed in the singing for both flicks, and his career was revived again.

Jolson was still riding high when he volunteered for entertainment duty in the Korean Conflict. It is doubtful whether Al Jolson had ever been as content. His fourth marriage was peaceful and loving; Al and his young bride Erle had adopted two children. His new recordings topped the charts. He was in demand for radio, and the new medium of television wanted him. But Jolie decided to wait until television audiences grew larger and sponsors were willing to spend more money. The audiences he loved best, however, were the boys overseas.

Al Jolson had returned from a USO tour in 1950 when a heart attack felled him. Fellow vaudevillian (and his *Jazz Singer* rival) George Jessel delivered the eulogy in Hollywood (Eddie Cantor delivered another in New York), describing Al Jolson and his performance style—for the two seemed inseparable—as "a man vibrant and pulsating with youth, authority and courage who marched on the stage, head held high and with the look of a Roman emperor. He had a gaiety that was militant, uninhibited and unafraid."

The jealousies and rivalries were forgiven, and the brazen and aggressive posture toward the audience that Jolie pioneered became the pattern for rock and hip-hop performers (who too often lacked Jolie's charm and whose audiences too seldom expected it). What endures beyond the explorations of Al Jolson's personality is Al Jolson's voice and stage mystique.

"You ain't heard nothin' yet" was Jolson's response to applause. That promise that he would surpass himself was coupled with his confident expectation that the audience would give to him unqualified love and admiration in greater measure than they would grant to any other entertainer. This was the stuff that made Jolson's legend. Many fellow performers saw a contrary mix of egotism, talent, mean-spiritedness, generosity, insecurity and the intent to be the brightest star in the show business firmament. Jolson was loved by his audience; the best he got from his fellow performers was respect, yet it was a singular respect. When Jolson died they halted traffic in Times Square and turned the lights off over Broadway.

SISSIERETTA JONES

b: (Matilda Joyner) 1869, Portsmouth, VA—d: 1933, Providence, RI

A concert singer, Sissieretta Jones was African American, her race a bar to an extensive career in serious music during the late nineteenth and early twentieth centuries in the USA. Her voice, reputedly a glorious, clear instrument that spanned the contralto range into the dramatic soprano, led her into the serious study of music rather than a career in variety or musical comedy.

Her family moved to Providence, Rhode Island. Her father, Jeremiah, was a minister in the African Methodist Episcopal Church, and her mother, Henrietta (Beale), was a singer. Sissieretta married early, at 14, and the following year gave birth to a child who did not survive infancy. Her husband, David Richard Jones, worked in hotels while Sissieretta studied voice with Ada Baroness Lacombe at the Providence Academy of Music.

At 18, Sissieretta began vocal training with Louise Capianni, a member of the faculty at the New England Conservatory. Several biographic studies of Jones assert that she attended the New England Conservatory. In those days, very few students went to conservatories for degrees unless they intended to teach; most trained for performing careers as private pupils of faculty members.

Her father's church, the Pond Street AME Church, provided Sissieretta's first stage. Her mother may have been in the choir as well. Young Sissieretta became well known around Providence and was asked to sing at various events and functions. While she was performing at the Parnell Defense Fund in Boston in 1887, a concert manager arranged her New York City debut on 15 June 1888 in a Sunday concert at Wallack's Theatre, a playhouse in Union Square. This led to her engagement as a soloist with the famous Jubilee Singers of Fisk University, an all-black group that introduced Negro spirituals to a wider society of Americans. For six months Jones toured with the Jubilee Singers, including engagements in the West Indies and South America, which increased her prestige as a concert artist.

When she returned to Manhattan, there were concert managers satisfied that they could attract audiences with the novelty of a young African American woman who sang, beautifully, the music of Verdi, Gounod and Donizetti. From 1889 until 1896, Madame Jones, as she preferred to be called, toured Europe and South America, gave a concert at Carnegie Hall, participated in the Grand African Jubilee at Madison Square Garden and sang for two presidents in the White House (Benjamin Harrison and Grover Cleveland). Critics, in praise, compared her to a reigning diva of grand opera, the Italian-born Adelina Patti. Thereafter, perhaps intimidated by the spelling or pronunciation of Jones' first name, press agents called her "The Black Patti." The unwanted soubriquet was eagerly picked up by fans, reviewers and theatre managers eager to stimulate interest in Sissieretta as an attraction.

According to Ann Charters, a chronicler of the beat poets and a biographer of Bert Williams, Dick Jones arranged for his wife Sissieretta to undergo arsenic treatments in 1890 while in London to lighten her skin and relax her hair.

Although she earned as much as $2,000 for a week's performance at international expositions and on tour, individual concert bookings did not provide a steady stream of engagements, and no opera house would engage her to sing leading roles opposite Caucasian singers. A living still needed to be earned; her father had died and she had a mother and a husband to support.

In 1896, Jones was convinced by two white managers, Voelckel & Nolan, to become the centerpiece in a full evening's potpourri of popular entertainment. Part concert, part vaudeville turns and part minstrel show, it was called Black Patti's Troubadours to capitalize on her popular fame. The Troubadours' operation was a large show with an orchestra and a cast of 50, among whom were singer-dancer Aida Overton and comedy team Cole & Johnson. After disputes with Voelckel & Nolan, Overton, Bob Cole and Billy Johnson quit. Aida retired temporarily, and Cole & Johnson were replaced by the top black comedian of the day, Ernest Hogan. Sissieretta sang arias and spirituals, comedians cavorted and soubrettes danced—all in all, a three-hour package of variety. Until the Whitman Sisters shows of the early twentieth century, Jones' troupes were the best-known incubators of up-and-coming black talent.

Her husband, who was supposed to handle her personal affairs, did poorly; he preferred to drink and spend money. Sissie divorced him in 1898. She then entered into a common-law marriage with Rudolph Voelckel, her company manager. They remained together from 1900 until 1915, about the time her career began to sag.

Black Patti's Troubadours was her primary vehicle for the remainder of her career. Eventually the show was paired down to tab size and fit into vaudeville bills. In 1908, her show was renamed the Black Patti Musical Comedy Company and continued to tour vaudeville until 1915, when she ended her career with performances at two notable African American theatres, the Grand in Chicago and the Lafayette in Harlem.

Forty-six when she retired in 1916 to her hometown of Providence, she should have been well off financially after nearly three decades of performing. She was not, and she had her infirm mother to tend as well as children she took into her care. Her money ran out in the late 1920s. She sold three properties, keeping only the one she lived in, and then sold the bejeweled medals she had received from heads of state on her travels. But few had the means to bid high for her possessions as the Great Depression deepened. Local African American businessmen did what they could to help support Sissieretta Jones. Impoverished, she died at age 63 in 1933.

JOVEDAH

b: (Arthur Dowling) ca. 1870—d: ca. 1922, Chicago, IL

The mind reader with the farcical stage name of Prince Jovedah de Rajah was an African American who passed himself off as "The East Indian Psychic." He played the role onstage and off. In public, he always spoke with a pseudo-Indian accent and wore a turban and other garments that helped foster the illusion that he was a seer from mysterious Mother India. He traveled with his white Canadian-born wife, called Princess Olga, and assorted assistants.

All things *Oriental*, from belly dancers to magicians and so-called masters of the occult, had captured the American imagination. Because Jovedah posed as a Hindu, bookers were eager to engage him for white vaudeville and private events organized by the rich and credulous. Jovedah played the Keith and Orpheum circuits and the better small time.

Assistants passed through the audience handing out pencils and pads of paper while Jovedah stood onstage gazing into his crystal ball. What made his act superior to run-of-the-mill mentalists was that he often expanded his remarks beyond answering the specific questions people wrote on the papers they handed to his assistants. That required research.

Calling to Jovedah from their positions in the audience, his assistants read the questions submitted to them by audience members and conveyed the answer in a few terse words of code (or gestures). Sometimes, the assistants had the audience members whisper the question into their ears. If the question was a usual one, Jovedah divined the question as well as the answer. Questions that called for simple direct answers such as a date, number or place were easily coded; questions requiring more elaborate responses required prior research on a number of people who were expected to attend a specific performance. The local theatre manager was often a source of information, and he pointed out to the assistants where certain people were sitting in the audience.

A rival mind reader, Alexander, wrote a pamphlet in 1921 that exposed the codes used in their types of acts. Jovedah, after living in grandiose fashion for nearly 20 years, was in straightened circumstance when he died in 1922.

JUBA

b: (William Henry Lane) ca. 1825, Providence, RI—d: 1852, England

Although Lane's short career was restricted to saloons and minstrelsy, in the history of variety and vaudeville he is important as the forefather of tap dance. His biographer, Marian Hannah Winter, a dance historian, called William Henry Lane, or Master Juba as he was better known, "the most influential single performer of Nineteenth Century American dance."

Lane was born free, not enslaved, and moved, without family, as a youngster to the notorious Five Points District of Lower Manhattan, a center of poverty, crime, disease and violence. Five Points was home to freed slaves and equally impoverished Irish immigrants. While friction between blacks and whites was constant, there can be no doubt that in the matter of dancing they influenced each other. It was here that Lane began dancing in his early teens. Until he turned professional, he performed in clubs, dance halls and saloons, especially at Pete Williams', a dance hall on Orange Street.

An older black dancer known as Uncle Jim Lowe tutored Lane in Irish jigs, clogs, shuffles and step dancing. Lane combined those steps with African American dance movements remembered by former slaves and passed on to younger dancers. Lane created many variations on those combinations and called his style of dancing Juba after a competitive dance form found in the Caribbean and the American South. Unlike other dances among enslaved blacks that were social and romantic, the Juba called for a display of technique, endurance and personal inventiveness. It was called a *breakdown* and was the beginning of the challenge dance that survived more than another century and evolved into clog, buck and tap contests and resurfaced as break dancing contests.

His fans called William Henry Lane "Juba" or "Master Juba," and he was billed as "The Greatest Dancer in the World." By 1845 he had become the most famous exponent of the new American form of percussive dance. Most whites assumed that they were seeing authentic plantation dances as performed by former slaves, but even before the Civil War, African American dancers, free or enslaved, had begun to improvise and modify traditional dances with new influences.

As far as is known, Master Juba spent his entire professional career as a dancer in white minstrel companies. When Juba joined the Ethiopian Minstrels company, it was as a star. He received top billing over the four other established white performers in the troupe. The Georgian Champion Minstrels ballyhooed Juba as "The Wonder of the World, acknowledged to be the greatest dancer in the world." Another white dancer, Master John Diamond, a star of P. T. Barnum's traveling show, met Master Juba in a challenge dance at John Tryon's amphitheatre. It was deemed a draw, so two more breakdowns were arranged between the two rivals, one bout at the Chatham Theatre, the other at the Bowery Theatre. Juba was declared winner of both and awarded the title "King of All Dancers."

He was also a fine singer and a virtuoso on the tambourine, and critics remarked on the good cheer and sly humor that accompanied his dancing. He was perfect for minstrel troupes. Juba joined White's Serenaders in 1846; two years later, he went to London to join Pell's Ethiopian Serenaders, a five-man minstrel troupe playing at Vauxhall Gardens.

Earlier, during a trip to the USA, Charles Dickens had detailed a description of Juba's dance performance. It is an impressionistic account rather than analytical, though Dickens specifically noted shuffles, snapping of fingers, spinning on toes and heels and a twisting of legs, movements that seemed to prefigure legomania. From his days at Pete Williams' dance hall to his minstrel show tours, one of the highlights of his performance was an act in which he imitated the styles of other famous minstrel dancers, including Johnny Diamond.

After Lane, still a young man in his early 20s, arrived in London in 1848, the critics, perhaps primed by Dickens' effusive appreciation, took his dancing very seriously. He was treated as equal to an artist of the ballet. Lane stayed in London, married an English woman and started a dancing school, but he died at about 27 years of age, four years after arriving. He had danced strenuously, night after night, since the age of 13. In the early years he danced for his meals in unsanitary dives. In his later years he pushed himself toward excellence. He demanded more than his constitution could support.

JUGGLING

Manipulating props by tossing them into the air or against a resilient surface, then deftly retrieving them as they fall or are on the rebound, before they touch the ground or escape the performer's reach. A number of factors combine in an effective juggling act: speed, timing, surprise and the number and types of objects or props manipulated at the same time.

A juggler may choose to work with the usual props, such as balls and Kehoe clubs (Indian clubs), yet do unexpected things with them, such as seeming to drop one in error while tossing the others into the air, but retrieving all, or changing the trajectory of one or two of the objects while continuing to orbit the others. The audience appreciates the introduction of the sleight of hand.

Another juggler may manipulate disparate objects—differing in weight, size, texture and shape—such as a ball, a bunch of celery, a meat cleaver and a hoop. The more sophisticated audience comprehends the split-second mental and physical adjustments the juggler must make to accomplish the trick. Some jugglers choose large unwieldy props. Tiny Jimmy Savo juggled wagon wheels and dining room chairs.

Even if getting laughs is a goal, the juggler must top the laugh gotten by a supposed accident, a miss or a drop, by neatly accomplishing the trick on the second or third try. Juggling proved a particular boon to emerging comedians. It sharpened their focus and timing and fostered an ease in movement and gesture.

As is true for all specialty acts, a display of virtuosity usually is not enough to make a hit; a juggler needs to develop a characterization based on his own personality.

JUMPS

The distance (in space and time) between one vaudeville engagement and the next on the same route. Jumps could be relatively brief and made with ease, or they could take a day or two and involve difficult traveling conditions such as changing trains or switching from train to horse wagon.

If performers delivered a good act and did not challenge the rules or create problems for the managers, they were rewarded with a decent route that sequenced the bookings so that they traveled from one theatre and one town to the next with a minimum of difficulty. If the route was long, as was true when booked from

Chicago to Kansas City to Denver to Salt Lake City to San Francisco over the sparsely settled Great Plains and Rocky Mountains states, the booking office arranged some comparatively minor play dates on smaller, affiliated theatre circuits to break the jump.

However, an act that bucked management was punished with less money the next contract, a route of tank towns with longer jumps and less favorable billing. If an act had to travel two days to play a three-day date, they lost money.

K

HELEN KANE

b: (Helen Schroeder) 4 August 1903, Bronx, NY—d: 26 September 1966, Jackson Heights, NY

Helen Kane was a flash in the pan who left behind an iconic image of the Roaring 1920s. By the time Helen won her place in the American consciousness, however, the 1920s had ceased to roar and the Great Depression settled in for a decadelong residency. Helen was the "Boop-Boop-a-Doop Girl," a plump, five-foot-two-inch Kewpie doll with bobbed, curly, dark brown hair, large doelike eyes and a cupid's-bow mouth. She sang in a pouting baby voice punctuated with demure little squeaks and hiccoughs.

The 1920s were rife with icons from homegrown sheiks, vamps and hottentots to modern American flappers and collegiate roisters to bootleggers and celebrity gangsters. Although nationally recognized, these images were urban. Unlike airy or brittle flappers, Helen Kane's stage character was more representative of young working women everywhere, from little towns to big cities. Like many young American girls on the verge of womanhood, drawn to the new promise of equality and freedom, Helen's character was eager for love and sexual experience but realistic about her chances of getting hurt. So she dithered between shy yearning and aggressive pursuit.

She was born Helen Schroeder in the Bronx. The family was poor and without any connection to show business, but early on Helen was stagestruck and bent on a career. She was in her late teens when she landed a job with a touring tab show that eventually (1922) arrived in New York as *On the Balcony.* Helen was an onstage chorus girl and an offstage babysitter for the children of several of its stars, The Four Marx Brothers.

Vaudeville provided the most reliable source of work. She played the *subway circuit* of New York City boroughs while she continued to live with her parents in the Bronx. This arrangement changed when Helen married Joe Kane around 1923. Although they divorced in 1928, Helen kept his surname for the stage. She was able to spend much of her career in and around New York City, and, according to Marion Spitzer, Helen Kane was a favorite with Palace Theatre audiences in the mid- to late-1920s.

For a blessed few years, Helen Kane was all the rage, in demand to make records, guest on network radio shows and appear in the movies. She also starred in three Broadway shows. *A Night in Spain* opened 3 May 1927 and ran for a modest 174 performances at the Century Theatre. Phil Baker, Ted Healy, Aileen Stanley, Norma Terris and Sid Silvers were her cast mates. *Good Boy,* which debuted 5 September 1928, played 253 performances at the Hammerstein Theatre and featured Helen along with Eddie Buzzell, Dan Healy, Charles Butterworth, Sam Hearn and Borrah Minevitch. This show presented Helen with the opportunity to introduce "Don't Be Like That" as well as "I Wanna Be Loved by You," the Kalmar & Ruby song that became her theme song.

In 1929, Helen Kane was back at the Palace Theatre in Manhattan, on a bill with Clayton, Jackson & Durant and Jimmy Savo. This superb bill was playing on 18 November, the day the stock market thudded to the bottom following the crash a few weeks earlier. Despite the looming troubles, Helen's popularity continued to climb, and talking pictures were pulling folks into movie houses.

The movie studios were flirting with every Broadway star who could talk, sing and dance. Helen accepted Paramount's bid, and the studio sped her through six feature-length films in less than two years. Quickly, Paramount gave Helen a large role in *Nothing But the Truth* (1929), which starred Richard Dix and Wynne Gibson; Helen and Ned Sparks were featured as the comic leads. The studio then rushed Helen into *Sweetie* (1929), a routine coed programmer. Nancy Carroll was the star and Helen Kane and Jack Oakie were featured. The production provided Helen with a hit song, "He's So Unusual." *Pointed Heels,* still another Paramount release in 1929, toplined William Powell, Fay Wray and Phillips Holmes. Kane and Skeets Gallagher were added for laughs, and Helen introduced the clever little song "I Have to Have You."

Helen was among the new contractees who performed in *Paramount on Parade* (1930), a revue on film that served to introduce nearly the entire Paramount Studio's performing roster, old and new, to audiences for the talkies. In it, Helen had a turn as a schoolteacher, querying the class, "What Did Cleopatra Say?" After this one A movie, it was back to quickie programmers for Helen. Paramount scripts were not getting any better when *Dangerous Nan McGrew* (1930) partnered her with Victor Moore, Stuart Erwin and Frank Morgan. Helen sang "Aw! C'mon, Whatta Ya Got to Lose?"

In an effort to milk her vogue before it dried up, Paramount pushed Helen Kane into *Heads Up!* in 1930. Buddy Rogers starred, and Victor Moore was again featured with Helen. Despite remnants of a Rodgers & Hart score and interpolations by Vernon Duke and Yip Harburg, this adaptation of the stage musical to screen did not offer much in the way of memorable songs for Helen. She was finished in films except for a one-reel short, *A Lesson in Love* (1931).

Yet it is surprising how many of her song hits survived their era and remain recognizable. There was an undertone of naughtiness in some of her songs, such as "That's My Weakness Now," "I Have to Have You," "Do Something," and "Is There Anything Wrong in That?" Her little-girl voice got away with singing lyrics that would have unleashed a storm if Mae West had sung them. Other material was less suggestive yet still a plaint for love: "I Wanna Be Loved By You," "He's So Unusual," and "Don't Be Like That, whereas some songs, like "Aba Daba Honeymoon," were just cute novelties. All were well recorded. Often overlooked was Helen's clear enunciation and musicality. These skills made her a popular guest on network radio, good for a peppy tune and some funny cross talk with the host.

During her brief heyday, her phenomenal success led to Helen Kane dolls, other novelties and a host of amateur and professional imitators. Most prominent among the Helen Kane impersonators was Mae Questal, wife of Max Fleischer, the cartoonist of movie shorts fame. In 1930, Max and his brothers, Louis and Dave, wanted a girl friend for their cartoon character Bimbo the Dog. A staff animator drew the cartoon Betty Boop—too close in resemblance to Helen Kane, despite the long, droopy dog ears, to have been modeled on anyone else. Mae Questal provided the voice. The dog ears were quickly dropped and Betty Boop was made into a human. Evidently there was little objection to Betty's interspecies romance, but Bimbo the dog lost his star status and was relegated to a supporting role as the series soon focused on Betty Boop. The all-human Betty Boop was clearly a line drawing of Helen Kane.

Kane brought suit against Fleischer, but her case folded when the defense proved that an African American performer, Baby Esther, had "booped" earlier than Helen. The court's decision was the start of a long slide for Helen. Vaudeville was declining, Broadway shows were folding almost as soon as they opened and belt-tightening was the new fashion among millions of Americans who had lost their savings and were losing their jobs. Neither Paramount nor any other studio sought her for further feature films.

She wed Max Hoffman Jr. in 1932 and divorced him in 1933. Even more fleeting was Helen Kane's final Broadway show. *Shady Lady* opened 5 July 1933 at the Shubert Theatre and closed 30 performances later.

The big time was over for Helen Kane. Prospects dissolved for her. Club dates and occasional vaudeville weekends provided some work as the Depression deepened and the public's taste in music switched to the big band sounds of dance music and swing.

Other performers were in the same fix, including Dan Healy (3 November 1888–1 September 1969), her onetime stage partner who became Helen's third husband in 1939. Dan Healy's great glory was producing and emceeing the Cotton Club shows in Harlem during and just after Prohibition.

Both Dan and Helen tried to keep working decades after their careers had faded. Vaudeville historian Chet Dowling reports that Kane and Healy performed at parties in Manhattan hosted by show folk. For some years, Helen and Dan appeared annually at Jenny Grossinger's Catskill resort.

During her comeback attempts in nightclubs and on television, Helen Kane looked and sounded like the 20-year-old star she once was—plumper, but still the pretty round face and the brunette mop top framing large soulful eyes and a cupid's-bow mouth. In any assessment of Helen Kane, what gets slighted is that she was an exceptionally able light farceur. Instead of receiving her credit as a singing comedian, she was pegged as a mere novelty act from the 1920s.

Helen headlined the bill at the Palace, renamed RKO Palace, for the week of 17 August 1950. She also dubbed Debbie Reynolds' voice in the 1950 movie *Three Little Words,* while Debbie, onscreen, mouthed Kane's theme song, "I Wanna Be Loved by You." A decade after *Three Little Words,* "I Wanna Be Loved by You" enjoyed a bit of a comeback when Marilyn Monroe purred it in 1960's *Some Like It Hot.*

Helen and Dan Healy remained married until her death from cancer in 1966. It was the dawn of the 1920s revival craze of the late 1960s and 1970s. Had she lived, Helen might have enjoyed a resurgence in fame and the opportunity to work again.

KARA

b: (Michael Steiner) 31 January 1867, Nuremberg, Germany—d: 9 April 1939

Regarded as the first of the gentleman jugglers or salon jugglers, the slender, dapper, dark-haired and mustachioed Kara strolled onstage in tuxedo, top hat and overcoat, carrying an umbrella and a lit cigar. The scene was set as a gentlemen's club or a parlor, and pit musicians played waltz music throughout his act. Doffing his overcoat, he juggled his hat, cigar and umbrella, three objects of differing size, shape and weight, and at the finish, the umbrella ended up in his hand, the hat on his head and the cigar between his teeth.

His assistant, in the role of a waiter or servant, set a table with lit candelabra, carafes, wine goblets, covered dishes, plates, cutlery and food, all of which Kara juggled. No object onstage escaped his manipulation and balancing—not a chair, a table, pool cue, billiard ball, handkerchief or newspaper. His forte was in juggling ordinary yet disparate objects rather than traditional balls and clubs. At one point, he tossed a large coin from his toe into his eye, where it caught like a monocle.

His control was best when he tossed an uncooked egg high into the air and caught it unbroken on a plate. The trick was to lessen the impact by lowering the plate at the exact moment of contact, thus sparing the egg a collision. For laughs, Kara sometimes let the egg splat on his assistant's noggin before successfully executing the feat with a second egg.

Kara, Cinquevalli and Salerno were three contemporary master jugglers who performed in vaudeville during its prime as well as appeared in European music-hall and circus. There were many other skilled and amusing jugglers, but jugglers hold these three men supreme in the early twentieth century.

In 1872, when Michael Steiner was five, he moved with his family from Nuremberg to Munich, where he encountered his first juggler, a street performer. Inspired, he began practicing, using stones. He remained self-taught and was reported to have made his first public appearances at 16, as a ball juggler. According to his biographer, Hermann Sagemüller, whose research remains invaluable, young Michael Steiner was juggling some household objects at his parents' fish market when a local theatre owner spotted him and offered him an engagement. By 20, Michael was performing professionally under the name Carradini. He soon attracted the services of an agent, Franz Pospischil, who changed Michael's stage name to Kara and booked him in various venues across Europe, including the Folies Bergère in Paris.

Kara's first trip to the USA was late in 1900 as a member of the Robert Fulgaros Vaudeville Company. The troupe played American vaudeville dates into 1902, with a portion of their bookings in the big time Orpheum circuit. When he returned in 1906, he did a full season of 40 weeks between the upstart William Morris theatres and Pantages time.

Back in Europe, he was fully booked until the start of the First World War, at which time he was traversing France. He probably was carrying his German passport and was arrested and confined as a prisoner of war during the war's four-year duration until the Armistice of 1918. Meanwhile, his wife reportedly had disassociated herself from him but kept his bank accounts. Kara was 51 years old, out of practice and flat broke when he was released.

His colleague and friendly rival, Salerno, loaned Kara equipment to get back into shape and resume his career. Kara worked his way back into show business in Europe and made a last tour of American vaudeville in 1921. He continued to make a living as a juggler until he retired in 1927. Thereafter he performed for his own or friends' amusement. Kara died in 1939 as the Second World War began.

FRED KARNO'S SPEECHLESS COMEDIANS

b: (Frederick John Westcott) 26 March 1866, Exeter, Devon, England—d: 18 September 1941, Lilliput, Dorset, England

British music-hall was, as its name suggests, home to songs and stories in song. The usual turn featured a performer, man or woman, who sang some clever songs that showcased the singer's flair for characterization, and between numbers chatted with the audience, telling them a few funny stories. Some acts added dance steps, and others added a partner and earned their laughs through dialogue. Music-halls had grown out of the entertainment in taverns and inns where space was at a premium, yet there was always room at the bar for an amusing singer to entertain the men clustered around him.

Traditionally, music-hall entertainment had been more for the ear than the eye until Fred Karno arrived on the scene. He was the most successful of a number of physical comedians who made significant changes in music-hall fare. In his account *Stars Who Made the Hall,* author S. Theodore Felstead numbered Karno, Joe Boganny and His Lunatic Bakers, Joe Elvin, Lew Lake and the Six Brothers Luck as the "most memorable of this brigade—Karno easily the best of them all."

For one who became so famous and who is still recalled as the discoverer of Charlie Chaplin, Stan Laurel and a half dozen other star comedians, little is known about Karno's personal life. With little schooling to see him off, Fred bounced around and apprenticed in various trades without finding satisfaction. The one thing in his youth that seemed to engage him was gymnastics, which proved responsible for his becoming an acrobat in show business.

He was small but strong and agile and reputedly was good as a performer. Certainly he was athletic and able to perform the somersaults, rolls, jumps and feats of equilibrium that were required, but more important to his eventual success as an impresario was his native understanding of his audiences. He knew them because, like most successful artistes working the halls, he was one of them. Never an idle dreamer, Fred put away whatever he could spare through his performing years in the 1880s and 1890s. By 1897 he advertised "Fred Karno's Company of Speechless Comedians" in pantomime sketches that relied on acrobatic skill in physical comedy, quickly sketched characters and brisk pacing to get laughs. A couple of decades spent on the boards himself, he was a good judge of budding comedians. He bought them cheap, gave the best of them ample opportunity to shine and let them go when they got above themselves, as he saw it, with salary demands.

Karno always maintained that it was his sketches that won success, and that even exceptionally good comedians could be replaced by other promising comedians without his sketches losing laughs. Had Karno not believed that, the loss to movies from 1914 to the birth of the sound era of some of his most talented comedians might have destroyed him.

Silent films demanded movement to make audiences laugh. It was natural that Karno's troupes, rather than the singing and talking comedians like George Robey and Will Fyffe, would be the comedians sought first by silent moviemakers. Among the Karno alumni who found larger salaries and far more fame in silent comedies were Syd Chaplin, Charlie Chaplin, Stan Laurel, Eric Campbell, Billy Reeves and Billie Ritchie.

Among the pantomimes he devised were "Jail Birds," "Early Birds," and "Mumming Birds." The last of these was retitled "A Night in an English Music Hall" when it played American vaudeville.

In his public business, Fred Karno was a hard man, a determined bargainer with a tight hold on his purse, and an ambitious, clever and materialistic entrepreneur without airs. However, it was widely and credibly reported that in his private life he was more volatile. Karno visited repeated emotional cruelties upon his wife, such as flaunting his mistress. Worse, he beat his wife so severely as to leave scars.

When Karno produced his first music-hall sketches, he was confident enough to send as many as ten troupes to play the provincial halls from Aberdeen to Bristol as well as London. At the apex of his success dozens of Karno companies were on the road in Britain each season.

Karno branched out in show business to become a veritable supply house. He created Karno's Fun Factory—the House that Karno Built, on Bourne Street in southeast London. He scooped up costumes, scenery and props from various failed productions for pennies on the pound, and he maintained a talent roster of comedians, soubrettes, singers and dancers that other producers could book through him. It was a one-stop shop where a budding producer could buy or license a script, cast it and dress it—all they had to do was lease a theatre or get a booking in the halls or variety houses.

The advent of the First World War saw the first of several reversals for Mr. Karno. He was beginning to reach beyond his roots and experience. Karsino, his ambitious casino and hotel project, opened as opposing armies were maneuvering into place across Europe. A goodly portion of Britain's best was conscripted for the war that would consume much of Europe; precious few were left to squire their wives and sweethearts for a weekend of romance, dining, dancing and gambling on Tagg's Island in the Thames.

By 1918, Karno, then only in his early 50s, was losing touch with the changing realities of show business. Even though a half dozen of his brightest comedians left to make movies for Mack Sennett and Hal Roach, Fred expected to mount a revue, starring Charlie Chaplin at the London Opera House. He considered his offer to Chaplin of £1,000 ($5,000) a week generous and was astonished when Charlie politely declined, citing the schedule demands of his then current contract at £10,000 a week.

Karno had a hand in the development of other major comedians such as Max Miller, Will Hay and Chesney Allen & Bud Flanagan, but his touch and career were on the decline. Karno himself appeared in a few British films, including *Early Birds* (1923) and *The Bailiffs* (1932). But by the mid-1930s, his fortune had evaporated, and his career was finished.

When the Music Hall Benevolent Fund made known its intent to secure the old man's retirement with a share in a retail liquor shop in Dorset, Chaplin started the fund rolling with a £1,000 donation.

BEATRICE KAY

b: (Hannah Beatrice Kupper) 21 April 1907, New York, NY—d: 8 November 1986, Los Angeles, CA

In the 1940s, when songs like "Only a Bird in a Gilded Cage," "After the Ball," and "The Band Played On" were again heard, it was because the young and petite Beatrice Kay was singing them on radio and performing them in revues.

Beatrice Kay had put her best foot forward on a variety of stages before she reached her midteens. Somehow, at age six, she was transported from New York City to Louisville, Kentucky, where she made her stage debut as *Little Lord Fauntleroy* in Colonel McCauley's Stock Company. She also appeared, presumably back in New York, in a few silent photoplays and did an act in vaudeville billed as "The Miniature Mimic." Her act included vocal impressions of stars of the day and kidding some songs by doing them in various dialects.

Beatrice briefly used Honey Kay as her professional name when she was young, and it was as Honey that the 12-year-old was billed in *What's in a Name?* (1920), a John Murray Anderson revue that starred Herb Williams and Jim Corbett. She worked in vaudeville as well as stage productions throughout the 1920s; when vaudeville began to fade, and Beatrice was old enough, she brought her songs to nightclubs. Her goal, however, was musical comedy and operetta.

Beatrice took whatever decent work she could get, and she wished to develop as an actor. She got four months' work in a straight play, *Jarnegan* (1926), but, like most performers, Beatrice was finding work hard to get during the late 1920s. Vaudeville was in a slide, and the novelty of the talkies was pulling people away from live performance. The hard economic times ushered in by the stock market collapse in 1929 hurt all forms of show business except the least expensive: movies cost only 5 to 20 cents, and radio programs were free.

Back in the day when Off-Broadway encompassed about a dozen or so small playhouses, Beatrice Kay was one of the performers in *Provincetown Follies* (1935), a revue that ran two months at the Provincetown Playhouse in Greenwich Village. According to Beatrice, she developed laryngitis during this show; instead of withdrawing until she recovered, she persisted in singing. The result was permanent: her trademark whiskey alto.

Tell Me Pretty Maiden (1937) offered her another chance in a music-less comedy, but it lasted only 73 performances. She had better luck when she joined vaudeville veterans Joe E. Howard, Fritzi Scheff, Tom Patricola, Willie Solar and Noble Sissle & His Orchestra in *The Turn of the Century* (1939) at Billy Rose's Diamond Horseshoe, a huge nightspot in midtown Manhattan. For a year and a half the cast re-created the Gay 90s, two shows a night, every night of the week. Beatrice estimated that she sang "Ta-Ra-Ra-Boom-Dee-Ay" almost 1,200 times in the course of that show. It may have been arduous work, but it was work! Her next show, *Marching with Johnny* (1943), closed out of town and never reached New York.

Constant touring ended marriages. Beatrice Kay was no less desirous than most performers who had spent a long time on the road of working in one place and setting up a home. Making films and broadcasting on radio and television offered the chance. She guest starred on a number of radio variety shows, such as Kraft Music Hall when Bing Crosby was its weekly host.

Soon Beatrice Kay was a regular on *The Gay Nineties Revue* (1940–44, CBS). (Its host was septuagenarian Joe Howard, a legendary songwriter and vaudevillian who had performed since the 1870s. Aileen Stanley was also on the weekly bill, and the show was produced by Al Rinker, brother of singer Mildred Bailey and one of the original Rhythm Boys, along with Harry Barris and Bing Crosby.)

There was some criticism of Beatrice Kay's renditions. Joe Howard was proud of the sometimes joyous, sometimes sentimental songs he had written at the turn of the twentieth century, and he himself still sang them unabashedly. Although Kay never burlesqued the songs she sang, she did not always treat them with uncritical reverence. There was a hint that she understood the ripe sentimentality of some of the old standards.

Twentieth Century Fox called her for one of Betty Grable's period pictures, *Diamond Horseshoe* (1945, aka *Billy Rose's Diamond Horseshoe*); it was the kind of second-lead role intermittently filled in similar Grable flicks by June Havoc, Charlotte Greenwood and Carmen Miranda. After her Hollywood stint, Beatrice returned to weekly radio as the star of *Gaslights Gaieties* (1945, NBC).

During the 1950s, Beatrice was a frequent guest on variety shows but was never able to expand beyond either the producers' or the public's expectation to hear her belt Gay 90s tunes. She had better luck as a guest star on dramatic television series, usually detective shows or Westerns. Her one meaty dramatic role was in *Underworld U.S.A.* (1961). In the end, she reverted to type for work and by the 1970s was singing her Gay 90s songs at Santa Monica's Mayfair Music Hall.

DANNY KAYE

b: (David Daniel Kaminski) 18 January 1913, Brooklyn, NY—d: 3 March 1987, Los Angeles, CA

An undisciplined class clown, Dave Kaminski found himself without skills or a sense of direction and with little prospect for employment when he dropped out of high school in his sophomore year. It was a bad time to try to find oneself; the USA was being sucked into an economic depression that had already taken hold in Europe. He and a school pal, Lou Eisen, began to perform at local parties and clubs as a two-man song act.

Danny Kaye

They used material they copied from acts playing at their neighborhood vaudeville and burlesque houses.

A booker for the White Roe Lake House in the Catskills, part of the so-called borscht circuit, hired the boys as *tummlers* for that summer. Their job was to pep up proceedings morning, afternoon and night by leading games and outdoor activities, dancing with single women, putting on shows and doing everything necessary to keep guests from being bored or dissatisfied, especially when it rained.

Over the course of two summers, David Kaminski, following the lead of his older brothers, first shortened his name to Dave Kamin and then anglicized it to Danny Kaye. Unlike Lou Eisen and other entertainers, many of whom were teachers with summer vacations and who looked at the work as a lark, Danny Kaye decided he had found a profession. Most of the other tummlers and entertainers who worked summers in the Sour Cream Siennas did so for room, board and a small cash payment at the end of the season.

Danny's bonuses got larger each season as he proved an increasingly energetic and likable asset to the White Roe, which had newly built a casino for house dances and performances. Even an eventual increase of his year-end stipend to $1,000 could not tide him over a winter, so each autumn he took a new inconsequential civilian job for which he was temperamentally ill suited.

After the summer of 1933, Danny joined the ballroom dance team of Kathleen Young & Dave Mack, alumni of the White Roe Casino. As the Three Terpsichoreans, they secured vaudeville dates in upstate New York and the Midwest. This led to an improbable chance to tour Asia early in 1934. The booker did not want Danny, just Young & Mack, but Danny was fitted into the traveling vaudeville revue called *La Vie Paree* and proved a useful utility player. The 18-month tour covered Tokyo, Osaka, Shanghai, Hong Kong, Manila and the Malay States. By 1935, the imperialist ambitions of the Japanese military were a prelude to a Pacific front of the Second World War.

Twenty-two years old in 1935, Danny determined to make his living as an entertainer. In his last few seasons at White Roe, he had taken parts in various in-house productions of plays by Fredric Molnár, Robert E. Sherwood and Noël Coward. Danny had never seen a play, much less studied acting, yet he instinctively gave disciplined and effective performances. He had picked up a basic time step and demonstrated an ear for music that translated into a nasal but capable light baritone singing voice.

Yet he was neither a dancer nor the type of romantic crooner popular in those days. He was not even a comedian in the accepted sense. He got laughs by kidding with the audience, acting the fool, singing nonsense songs and engaging in comic patter routines with other White Roe performers. Consequently, while he definitely was an entertainer, exactly what kind was less clear. If a producer was looking for a dancer, a singer, a comedian or an actor, there were many others besides Danny Kaye who seemed more obvious candidates. He returned for a fifth season at White Roe.

For the summer of 1936, Danny Kaye took a professional step up by joining the entertainers as a master of ceremonies at the President Hotel, a more prestigious Catskill resort. This led to a wintertime booking at Billy Rose's Casa Mañana, where the headliners were such established vaudeville acts as Jimmy Durante and Pat Rooney Jr. At the President, Danny was the star act. At Billy Rose's, Danny played stooge to comedian and eccentric dancer Nick Long.

After the Casa Mañana engagement, Danny was at loose ends again. He got work as an extra in a couple of movies at Educational Pictures' studio in Astoria, Long Island. Educational was a budget studio that made short comedies for movie house bills. After one or two films as a bit player, Danny got a good opportunity in a supporting role opposite Imogene Coca and June Alyson in the two-reel short *Dime a Dance* (1937). Barry Sullivan, then unknown, was also cast. Danny starred in a two-reeler of his own, *Getting an Eyeful* (1938). He made several more shorts that year, including one in England.

Nick Long got them bookings as a double act several times during the 1936–37 season and generously permitted Danny to perform some of his own solo material. They went to England in 1938, and the Dorchester Hotel's Lounge in London was Danny's first engagement in the land that became his second home. Nick Long was held over. Danny Kaye flopped. The English had a long tradition of embracing eccentric comedians, but Danny's offbeat humor failed to strike a chord. While in London, however, Nick and Danny made a three-reel film starring Naughton Wayne.

Even before he had become successful in show business, Danny Kaye was described by associates and friends as moody and competitive. While he enjoyed performing at the drop of a hat, even offstage and among friends, his personality was quite unlike the silly madcap that so easily made friends with audiences. He was quite the ladies' man, always involved in one relationship or another, but the women were more involved than he. His one true and endearing love was show business, at least in those days.

After his ignominious failure in London, a scarcity of vaudeville and club dates in the USA and dead-end movie work at Educational Pictures, Danny auditioned for Max Liebman, who was directing an intimate revue, *The Sunday Night Varieties.* Liebman decided to bring his concept of the sophisticated revue from Camp Tamiment, a top Catskill resort, to winter audiences in Manhattan. The songwriter for the show and audition pianist was Sylvia Fine. A few years younger than Danny, she was from the same neighborhood in Brooklyn and remembered him—quite fondly. He did not recall her.

The Sunday Night Varieties (1937) closed as quickly as it had opened. Liebman, however, decided to hire Sylvia Fine to write next summer's show at Tamiment. Fortunately, Jules Munshin, the lead comedian at Tamiment, had decided to move on professionally, so Danny Kaye went back to the Catskills in 1938 for his tenth year. Future television star Imogene Coca and future Broadway leading man Alfred Drake were important members of the Liebman company, and future Broadway director and choreographer Jerome Robbins was the dance director.

Sylvia Fine had her eye on the man as well as the performer. She was as single-minded as Danny. She pursued him while he was pursuing stardom. She brought Danny intelligence and a clever talent and made herself professionally indispensable to him. Danny Kaye, in turn, performed her material as no one else could. In this way, Sylvia Fine cleared the stage of her rivals, dozens of young beauties more attractive than she but unessential to his career.

Each week of the ten-week season at Tamiment, Max Liebman and Sylvia Fine created a new revue. The performers had to learn the new material for the revue as well as perform their specialties in the weekly vaudeville show. Danny had mastered a variety of dialects: vaudeville versions of Russian, German, French and British. Sylvia also noted his facility with tongue twisters. Her own tastes in material were more intellectual and political, but she was happy to devise lighter, sillier material for Danny.

Undeterred by the previous season's failure, Liebman was determined to produce on Broadway. He talked the Shuberts into financing *The Straw Hat Revue,* a collection of the best numbers from the summerlong revues he had staged at Tamiment. It opened at the Ambassador Theatre on 29 September 1939, a few weeks after the crew packed up Tamiment, and ran for 75 performances. Being an inexpensively produced show with a small payroll, *The Straw Hat Revue* did not get tagged as a flop.

The next year, 1940, put Danny and Sylvia on top, at least among Manhattan's smart set. First, they were married, and then they launched professionally as a team when Danny, and Sylvia as his accompanist, were booked into La Martinique, one of the many supper clubs that were trying to be swank. Danny produced yawns for his first show but caught fire in his second. For an encore, Sylvia at the piano and Danny center stage dredged up an hour's worth of songs they had performed at Tamiment. For a finale, a frazzled but exuberant Danny led the patrons in a conga line that snaked through the tables in the club.

The critics, of course, had come to the late show, and in their morning columns they made Kaye the toast of Manhattan. His salary tripled over the course of a few weeks. Café society and showbiz professionals came down to the cellar club to see what all the buzz was about. The most consequential of those visitors was Moss Hart, then in his prime, a director and former writing partner of George S. Kaufman in several smash-hit comedies.

Four months at La Martinique were followed by a series of top nightclub engagements, during which Kaye introduced "Anatole of Paris," a patter song of Sylvia's that spoofed fashion designers, and he and Sylvia became friends with Kitty Carlisle, about to become Moss Hart's wife. All the while, Danny was waiting to see if Moss Hart, who had hinted that he was writing a part for Danny in his new Broadway show, would actually do it.

Kurt Weill composed the music for *Lady in the Dark,* Ira Gershwin wrote the lyrics, Moss wrote the book and directed, Sam Harris produced and Gertrude Lawrence starred. The show was a substantial success in a season of successes. Every night there was a battle for dominance between Danny Kaye and Gertrude Lawrence. Kaye's role was quite small, but his tongue-twisting song salute to "Tchaikovsky (and Other Russians)" was a showstopper. Lawrence, a top-flight star of London and Broadway stages for 20 years, demanded her own powerhouse number and got "The Saga of Jenny," which she sang immediately after Danny's big number. Both were born scene stealers, and both were hard nuts.

Danny was doubling, performing a midnight show back at La Martinique, where he shared top billing with Betty Hutton, who was also doubling after her show, *Panama Hattie.* The two of them created a highly energetic show. Danny and Betty attracted Hollywood's attention. Metro-Goldwyn-Mayer (MGM) offered Danny what it thought was a handsome salary for a newcomer, but he was making more doubling between Broadway and cabaret. Another consideration was that MGM might want Danny only for specialty spots or second leads as the leading man's best friend. The Ritz Brothers had to fight their way out of specialty numbers into features of their own. Jimmy Durante, Phil Silvers, Milton Berle and other Broadway comedy stars found themselves stranded in second leads. Danny said no to Louis B. Mayer's offer.

He also said no to Moss Hart. Producer Sam Harris had failed to pick up Danny's option, and Kaye left *Lady in the Dark* to star at five times the money in a new Cole Porter musical, *Let's Face It* (1941–43). Probably Danny also saw an opportunity to escape Gertrude Lawrence and to demonstrate that he could carry a show on his own. Although he did not begin as the star of *Let's Face It,* once the show proved a hit, Danny Kaye's name was placed on the theatre marquee.

Sam Goldwyn had been searching for a comedian to replace Eddie Cantor, who had starred in a series of Goldwyn films in the 1930s that began to have diminishing box-office draw. Sam wanted an all-around entertainer like Cantor, only younger and fresher. Goldwyn comedies were as much about music, color and décor as they were about comedy.

Danny Kaye played the same type of roles in movies as did Harold Lloyd and Eddie Cantor—seemingly milquetoast, nearly effeminate characters that had to rise to occasions of bravery. Harold was the Anglo-Saxon American boy, a clean-cut go-getter inspired by feats of derring-do. Eddie Cantor was a Jewish boy who overcame fear, neurosis and hypochondria to set matters right, and if he had to shave a corner for justice to triumph, so what?

Danny Kaye's movie character looked Anglo-Saxon enough (once the Goldwyn studios bleached his fire-red hair blond), and Danny's screen persona dreamed of future glory and getting the girl as did Harold Lloyd's character, but Danny's was rooted to his unhappy present by phobias and fear like Eddie Cantor's.

Kaye's first feature was adapted from Cantor's stage and movie hit *Whoopee!* and renamed *Up in Arms* (1944). His second feature, *Wonder Man* (1945), offered Danny the first of his double or twin roles. His third feature, *The Kid from Brooklyn* (1946), was based on *The Milky Way* (1936), one of Harold Lloyd's talking pictures. Like both Lloyd's and Cantor's, Danny's character lived an everyday, humdrum, even constricted life until, suddenly, at several junctures in the movie, Danny had something rather like an out-of-body experience and launched into one of Sylvia Fine's rapid-fire patter songs.

Those manic bursts of eccentricity set him apart from most other comedians (except Harry Ritz) until the advent of Sid Caesar. Certainly, Danny Kaye was unlike Bob Hope, Red Skelton and Abbott & Costello, the other top comedians during Danny's filmmaking career (mostly 1944–63), although, like Hope, Kaye was essentially a light comedy actor and a song-and-dance man who doubled as a sophisticated revue comedian with surprisingly outré material for a general audience.

Goldwyn provided Danny with a Technicolor showcase, decent scripts and splendid productions. *Up in Arms* and *Wonder Man* were hits. Between filming them, Kaye entertained the troops. Radio wanted Danny, and he signed to do a weekly radio show for CBS in 1945, but the show did not warrant a second year or Danny's continued interest.

Critics had some reservations about *The Kid from Brooklyn* (1946), but the public loved it and Danny promoted it on a long tour of presentation houses. Sylvia and Danny crossed paths occasionally, and a daughter, Dena, was born in December 1946. Danny loved traveling and performing live again, and he made a fortune on a salary plus percentage basis. He also made many female friends along the route.

Unconsciously, perhaps, he was changing his act. There was less of the smart cabaret material that Sylvia wrote and more seemingly off-the-cuff (but carefully rehearsed) presentation of Danny as a personality who chatted and kidded the audience. Perhaps it was a rebellious return to his borscht circuit tummler style before Sylvia Fine molded his act.

In Danny's packaged presentation house show were Tip, Tap and Toe, a trio of fine tappers, and Georgia Gibbs, a singer about to get lucky with a string of hit records. Danny did not behave in a comradely manner toward Gibbs and Tip, Tap and Toe. Danny Kaye loved performing but he did not mix much with show folk. He latched onto various types of people as long as he found them interesting. Unlike many performers who had little formal education, Danny was well-read and well-spoken

Sylvia stayed in Hollywood looking after Danny's interests as Goldwyn's staff prepared *The Secret Life of Walter Mitty* (1947). It became one of Kaye's most famous movies and was adapted (minus the whimsy) from James Thurber's fantasy story. Danny continued to tour and Sylvia continued to manage his career, but by 1947, their marriage was an understanding that permitted Danny freedom to travel and sometimes leave Sylvia behind. Rumors of homosexuality persisted about Danny Kaye throughout his career, but his documented romances were with women: Eve Arden and Gwen Verdon were among the better known.

A Song Is Born (1948) was a tepid movie at best, and it finished his contract with Goldwyn. He made one picture for Warner Brothers, *The Inspector General* (1949). It was good but did not sell. Some felt Danny's film career, too, was finished.

Danny Kaye played London's Palladium in 1948, and the recent years of touring American presentation houses paid off—audiences, critics, the royal family and the finest British actors adored Danny Kaye and made him an adopted Englishman. He returned the following year and then played Scotland. He could not put a step wrong with the English or the Scots.

In Hollywood, Kaye essayed another dual role in *On the Riviera* (1951). It met with a mixed response (some thought it too risqué) and did only middling business, but the middle-class family audience was lured back with the wholesome if bland *Hans Christian Andersen* (1952).

In 1952 and 1953, Danny was back on the road doing a series of live performances in a vaudeville package that began at the Curran Theatre in San Francisco and culminated with a booking at the newly revived Palace Theatre in Times Square. Judy Garland had brought to life the former flagship of vaudeville, and Betty Hutton created her own success following Judy. It was Danny's turn beginning 18 January 1953, and his success made it seem as if vaudeville was back in style. He remained at the Palace into April. Between film and vaudeville, Danny Kaye was more highly paid than Frank Sinatra or Martin & Lewis, both at the peak of their popularity.

His interests continued to widen. He began conducting symphony orchestras to raise money for the musicians' union. Then he became the United Nations' first celebrity ambassador for the United Nations Children's Fund (UNICEF), to which he brought international visibility and for which he raised millions of dollars.

Knock on Wood (1954) was a well-made suspense comedy to some and a bore to others. Unexpectedly, Kaye was asked to replace an ailing Donald O'Connor opposite Bing Crosby in *White Christmas* (1954); it fit the times and was a solid hit for Bing and Danny. *The Court Jester* (1956) was the kind of costume comedy that Bob Hope made, and the formula worked for Danny. Some feel it is his best movie, but it flopped at the box office. None of his remaining movies was a hit.

It was time for television. He made a smashing debut that was a ratings triumph, a documentary about his work for UNICEF filmed and edited by CBS. This was followed by two specials that failed; a third with Lucille Ball was good. The next season, 1962–63, Danny took on a weekly hourlong show for CBS. He was 50 years old, and that was an age when some funnymen lost their sense of fun. The show ran four years, but its ratings went from average to dismal.

There were still occasional triumphs in the closing years of Danny Kaye's career. On Broadway he starred in a musical about the biblical Noah, *Two By Two* (1970–71). He costarred in several TV specials and he gave a dramatic performance in *Skokie* (1981) that was highly praised.

Many people spoke of Kaye as aloof or cold; certainly joy had been ebbing out of him with each passing year. There were many views of Danny Kaye in his last years. Some found him selfish and impossible to deal with, others saw him as manic-depressive.

Those who remained friends to the end thought him lonely. His health failed in 1982, and his final five years were sad. Physical ailments piled up, and a heart operation went awry. He contracted hepatitis C from a blood transfusion. The hepatitis dogged him for two years and caused the heart attack that killed him.

STUBBY KAYE

b: (Bernard Katzin) 11 November 1918, New York, NY—d: 14 December 1997, New York, NY

Tall, rotund and bland-faced, Stubby Kaye was light on his feet and possessed a strong tenor-baritone and a sense of fun. Those qualities made him a valuable comedy actor for musical comedy.

He gave his first conspicuous performance on the Major Bowes Amateur Radio Hour in 1939, and he parlayed that into a brief vaudeville career before finding more regular work in USO shows during the Second World War. His big break came when he was cast as Nicely-Nicely, one of the Broadway muggs who populated *Guys and Dolls* (1950), Frank Loesser's musical adaptation of Damon Runyon's stories. His big number in the show was "Sit Down, You're Rockin' the Boat." He played the role in the London production and the film (1955).

He nearly equaled his triumph as Nicely-Nicely when he signed on to another Broadway musical adaptation, cartoonist Al Capp's *Li'l Abner* (1956). He played Marryin' Sam and scored a hit with his solo rendition of "Jubilation T. Cornpone." This too was filmed by Hollywood, but it did not achieve the movie success of *Guys and Dolls.*

The rest of Stubby's career was less spectacular. He continued to act on the Broadway stage: *Everybody Loves Opal* (1961), a short-lived revival of *Good News* (1974), *The Ritz* (1976), as a replacement for Jack Weston, and *Grind* (1985). He hosted a children's television game show, *Shenanigans* (1964), and had a supporting role in television's *Love and Marriage* (1959) and *My Sister Eileen* (1960), neither of which was renewed. For a couple of seasons, Stubby also appeared on the perennial *Pantomime Quiz.*

Kaye made about two dozen other films in addition to his two transfers from Broadway. The most notable among the rest were *Cat Ballou* (1965), *Sweet Charity* (1969) and *Who Killed Roger Rabbit?* (1988). Stubby lived for a time, after his Broadway successes, in both England and Ireland, as he was married to an English performer. He was ill much of his last years and died of lung cancer.

BUSTER KEATON

THE THREE KEATONS

Buster Keaton

b: Joseph Francis Keaton VI, 4 October 1895, Piqua, KS—d: 1 February 1966, Los Angeles, CA

Joe Keaton

b: (Joseph Hallie Keaton) 1867, Dogwalk, IN—d: 13 January 1946, Ventura County, CA

Myra Keaton

b: (Myra Edith Cutler) 13 March 1877, Modale, IA—d: 21 July 1955, Los Angeles, CA

There was never a time in his nearly seven-decade career when Buster Keaton was not a great comedian. From his stage debut a few months before his

Buster Keaton

third birthday to his last work, including a television appearance with Lucille Ball and the films *A Funny Thing Happened on the Way to the Forum* and *War Italian Style,* all within a year of his death from lung cancer, no one had to make allowances for Keaton's age, diminished physical capacity, or comedy sense.

Buster grew up in his family's act, and Joe & Myra Keaton were representative of thousands of acts, struggling each day against substantial odds to escape the mean grind of small-time vaudeville and graduate into the big time. The Keatons were atypical of small-time acts in that they had a son, Buster, who early on displayed comic genius and propelled the family into a headlining act. Until his arrival onstage at age three, his pop, Joe, and his mother, Myra, were mismatched and luckless entertainers who performed in medicine shows, a rung lower in show business than small, small-time vaudeville.

At first, it seemed that Buster had inherited his family's ill-favored destiny. There were a series of last-minute escapes from fires, train wrecks and falls. He was not quite a year old when the drawer of the costume trunk, which served as his cradle and was placed in the wing space, was shut accidentally by a stagehand while his mother and father were onstage. When Myra exited to change costumes in the wings she discovered baby Buster nearly smothered in their trunk.

His most famous misadventure provided his nickname. Harry Houdini, the escape artist, witnessed six-month-old Buster fall down a flight of stairs and land without crying. Admiringly, Houdini reportedly said, "That's some buster your kid took!" At the time, Harry Houdini, whose future fame would equal Buster's, traveled with Dr. Hill's California Concert Company along the trail that led from the Ozarks to the Oklahoma Indian Territories. The company included Houdini's wife, Bess, Joe, Myra and Buster Keaton, two Caughnawaga tribesmen and the bogus Doctor Hill. Theirs was a medicine show, and the Houdinis and Keatons sold Hill's fake elixirs and put on shows wherever they could rustle up enough townspeople and coax them into the tent. Melodramas and comedies were the usual entertainments, with Joe as the hero, Harry as the villain and Bessie and Myra the heroine and soubrette.

Dr. Hill's was neither the first nor the last of the medicine shows for Myra and Joe. They met in one. Myra's father, Frank Cutler, was a partner in the Cutler-Bryant Medicine Show. Joe joined the show and soon eloped with Myra. He had established a homestead in Oklahoma during the land rush but passed it on to his parents when he decided to become a performer. Myra played several musical instruments, including harmonium and cornet. Joe was an eccentric dancer and acrobat. His skills did not complement hers, nor hers his, and they performed as singles except when they shared the stage as actors in melodramas or comedies.

After the trunk incident, it was decided that Buster was to be left in the care of boardinghouse landladies while Myra and Joe performed at the theatres. Then occurred a trio of accidents, all supposedly in a single day before Buster turned three. He lost his right forefinger when he caught it in a clothes wringer. Next, he hit himself near his eye with a rock that ricocheted off his target—a peach hanging from a tree. Last, the roof of his boardinghouse bedroom was blown away and he was carried off by a cyclone that plunked him down in the middle of a street several blocks away. Myra and Joe decided it was safer to costume Buster and try to integrate him into the act, where he would be under their watch. Buster had crawled on to make his unofficial stage debut when he was nine months old, so there was no question that he wanted to become part of the act. When he did, it quickly became apparent that Buster was the star.

Myra and Joe performed a blackface melodrama. Between the acts, Myra played cornet and Joe then did a monologue. During the melodrama, Buster was restricted to a spot in the wing space where his parents could keep an eye on him, and he was cautioned to keep quiet and not move. For the olio, Buster was allowed onstage dressed in a miniature version of Joe's costume. Instead of standing still upstage as instructed, little Buster began to ape his father. The audiences loved it.

Joe decided it was time to play New York and try for the big time, or at least the better small time. The Keatons arrived in Manhattan in 1899 without any solid prospects until they finally wangled a date

Myra Keaton

Joe Keaton and Jingles

at Huber's, a dime museum that also offered small-time variety shows six times a day from 3:00 in the afternoon until 3:00 A.M. The billing matter was "The Man with the Table" and, a bit later, "The Man with the Table, a Wife and Three Kids." Long-legged Joe did his tumbling act—handsprings, dives, rolls, jumps—using a strong chair atop an oak table as his springboard and perch. His hitch-kick reached ten feet off the ground. While Joe caught his breath, Myra sang and performed instrumental solos.

When the Keatons had played the Great Plains states and surrounding territories, Buster's age was a charm, not yet a problem. The act, powered by the horseplay between Joe and Buster, proved a hit with small-time vaudeville audiences, but when they came into New York, they encountered problems with the Gerry Society. The Society for Prevention of Cruelty to Children (SPCC), as the society was formally known, was a personal crusade conducted by Elbridge T. Gerry.

Rather than ameliorate the conditions under which tens of thousands of orphaned boys and girls scrapped for survival in the slums of the city, stealing food, selling newspapers, flowers and sometimes themselves, Gerry focused on children on the stage, confident that performance was a greater moral threat to children than poverty, disease and criminality.

Such was Gerry's power in New York that Huber did not allow Buster to appear in his dime museum, so once again he was left in the care of a boardinghouse landlady. The situation was the same at their next engagement, the Atlantic Garden, a beer hall on the Bowery. The family nearly starved the winter of 1899–1900.

Then Joe got Myra and himself a week's work at Tony Pastor's Theatre. Pastor's led to five weeks playing Proctor's 23rd Street Theatre, his Pleasure Palace at 58th Street and Proctor's in Albany, New York, followed by a week each at the Old Howard Theatre and Austin & Stone's Museum—both in Boston, the Wonderland in Wilmington, Delaware, and Poli's Theatre in Hartford, Connecticut. Beer gardens in and around Manhattan and Brooklyn filled in between vaudeville bookings. The experience helped Joe to learn how vaudeville bookings worked in the East, and Joe got busy lining up their next season. It is worth noting that during their first vaudeville season Joe and Myra were seldom assisted by Buster, and the success they enjoyed was due to their own talents and appeal.

Bill Dockstader, the manager at the Wonderland in Wilmington, was willing to chance Buster in the act; the Gerry Society's reach grew feeble the farther it stretched from Broadway and the Bowery. Joe and Buster were dressed as stage Irishmen, with skullcap wigs that simulated a bald pate with curly hair around the edges leading into their chin whiskers. They wore baggy pants, short coats over white vests and spats over their slap shoes. Buster was five years old and about to become the star of the act.

Buster played the mischievous imp to his father's put-upon and often explosive character. There is an old expression in show business about swatting flies; it refers to upstaging. One performer is busy moving or otherwise distracting attention from the other performer whom the audience is supposed to be watching. Buster was doing it literally. While Joe attempted to sing a comic song or render a recitation, little Buster, dressed identically, would be stalking imaginary flies upstage and swatting them with a small broom, edging nearer to his dad until he "accidentally" thwacked Joe. From that point onward the violence escalated. Myra had sewn a suitcase handle onto the back of Buster's coat so that Joe could pick him up and tote him about like luggage or toss him into the wings, up against the backdrop, or, occasionally, into the audience. Joe got as good as he gave; one resounding whack from Buster with his broom regularly sent Joe headfirst over the edge of the stage so that he was hanging into the orchestra pit.

Theirs was one of the roughest roughhouse acts in vaudeville. When the SPCC brought the family into court and the judge ordered Buster to strip and show his bruises, Buster giggled when they could find no sign of abuse. Audiences unfamiliar with the act were aghast at the way Joe kicked and tossed his son about the stage. The only clue the audience got was when Buster counted five seconds before uttering an "Ouch!"

Even then, Buster's face was the picture of concentration. He never tried to be cute or to work the audience for sympathy; it probably never occurred to him or his parents. Instead, onstage he was watchful of Joe, engrossed in his business, and consequently he seldom smiled. It was not so much a stone face as a serious one. Both father and son were expert enough comedians to recognize that mock gravity added to the fun. Buster gave credit to Joe. Whenever Buster began to crack up onstage, Joe hissed at him, "Face!" and Buster froze it deadpan. What likely had been merely natural or accidental to Buster was adopted as style.

For a closing, Myra came on dressed in her finery to play a solo on a relatively new instrument, a saxophone. Borrowing a gag from burlesque, for their call at the end of their act, Joe hitch-kicked Myra's hat off her head while Buster yanked a cord that stripped Myra of her gown, leaving her standing in an Irish costume like Joe's and Buster's.

The act quickly became wanted by various bookers for the best of the small time and for the big time, but little Buster's growing fame attracted renewed attention from the Gerry Society. As long as they stayed west of the Hudson River, the Three Keatons were not bothered much by the SPCC. When they chanced the big cities of the East, Buster's so-called official age was hiked a few years, or he was represented as a "midget" to the authorities.

Buster had only a few days' formal schooling. Joe and Myra had a bit more, but both were barely literate. Had Buster had the entire public school course of 12 years, it is unlikely that he would have absorbed as much as he did in vaudeville. A bit of a loner and deeply curious, he lived backstage. He was fascinated by the machinery and by other people's acts and equipment. He learned to sing, dance, perform magic tricks and quick-change transformations, play musical instruments, hit targets with knives or by firing a shot, and juggle and tumble. He even learned to act. Like many of the great clowns, there was nothing in the way of performance that he could not do credibly. Yet his world of vaudeville was a place with few other children and was hardly typical of the *civilian* world most kids knew.

In time, Buster's younger siblings, Harry (1904–83), known as Jingles, and Louise (1906–81), were fitted with the same Irish outfits and made their appearances in the act, but they were little more than scenic dressing. They lacked Buster's interest and acrobatic and comic skills. Still, five identically dressed Keatons, "in graduated and assorted sizes, like the separated portions of a Chinese miracle box," as one journalist reported, made a fine photograph. Three underage Keatons onstage antagonized the Gerry Society, and until Buster turned 16 there were ongoing battles with the busybodies.

For one period in the early 1910s, when good vaudeville bookings were hard to get because of Gerry Society interference or because some vaudeville acts like the Keatons got caught in a squeeze between Proctor and Albee or Erlanger and Albee, Joe, Myra and Buster reverted to melodrama and hooked up with a traveling stock company for a few months. Improbably, Buster, "The Human Mop," actually played Little Lord Fauntleroy.

Over the years, the Keatons' vaudeville act varied. New tricks, more elaborate ones, were devised as Buster grew more capable and hardy, but the essentials of the act remained the same for the 17 years they played. Joe, however, never developed Buster's grace. Joe pushed and punished himself onstage; his scarred body and early aging were testimony. Instinctively, Buster knew how to relax his body into a fall—roll with the punches, as it were—but he was not immune to injury. His career from childhood to maturity was filled with accidents, but some of the things he did would have killed others.

When he was making his third feature film, *Our Hospitality* (1923), in Hollywood, he broke his neck and did not discover it until several years later, when x-rays for another injury revealed his mended neck. During his salad days in Hollywood, Buster would accommodate an actor or director friend by performing in disguise a stunt that not even professional stuntmen were willing to try. No other actor in Hollywood was as admired and beloved by stuntmen as Buster Keaton.

Joe weathered adversity better than success. Abstinent during tough times, he bellied up to the bar flushed with success. Myra stayed home with the kids and played cards with other actors. Joe got into fights and visited more than a few police stations as a result. Myra took it in stride, but fault lines were beginning to separate the family. Eventually, after Buster's movie career blossomed, Myra and Joe lived separately, though they remained in contact.

Joe was proud of his son—indeed, early on Joe advertised him as the star of the act—and the entire family was thankful for the comfort and security that headliner status afforded them, but as Buster grew into a young man with ever-increasing skills, energy and inventiveness, there grew a rivalry between him and Pop. Joe had become, at his worst, a drinker and a bit of a brawler, and his powers began to wane as he aged from 40 toward 50. Increasingly, the contest for supremacy between father and son played out onstage, and some of the hurt was no longer quite innocent. By Buster's late teens, his father was becoming a bit dangerous onstage. He hated aging, he was becoming a drunk and his resentment grew. Buster was not Joe's only target. Things had soured between Myra and Joe. Tired of the battle, Myra quit the act and the marriage. Buster went with her. Harry and Louise were in boarding school. Joe was left on his own. It was 1917.

Once it was known that the Three Keatons had split the act, Buster had a firm offer from the Shuberts to costar in their revue, *The Passing Show of 1917,* along with De Wolf Hopper, Irene Franklin and the Dolly Sisters. Buster was in New York to discuss the Shubert deal when a chance meeting with comedian Lou Anger changed his career and his life.

Lou Anger persuaded Buster to come to Joe Schenck's movie studio on the Lower East Side, the place where Roscoe Arbuckle made his two-reel comedies. Lou managed production for Schenck. Buster had been skeptical about the movies. He was cognizant of how fast a series of shorts ate up gags and how difficult it would be to maintain quality, but the technology intrigued him. Arbuckle was an accommodating host, and before the visit was over, Buster had grasped the basics of silent filmmaking and appeared in a scene in the movie Arbuckle was shooting that day.

Instead of signing his Shubert contract for $250 a week, Buster went to work for $40 a week at Arbuckle's and Schenck's Comique Film Corporation. In less than two years, Buster appeared in 14 two-reelers with Roscoe, and they became the best of friends. Schenck gave Buster his own film company in 1920, and Keaton made three dozen short comedies over the next three years. Most are as good as the best shorts made by his rivals and most remain classics. *Cops* (1922) is as good as any short ever made by any other silent film clown.

In 1920, on the recommendation of Doug Fairbanks, Buster Keaton starred in his first feature, *The Saphead,* for Metro Pictures. It was a drawing room comedy and Buster acquitted himself nicely. *The Three Ages* (1923), his next feature, made for his own outfit, the Keaton Film Company, was really three two-reelers stuck together—a prehistoric sequence followed by one in ancient Rome and another in the modern era, followed by an epilogue of sorts. Buster felt that if the feature bombed, he could recoup cost by cutting it up into three two-reelers. *Our Hospitality* followed the same year. Set in the South as a feud between two families, it alternated between quiet comedy and the thrills of an adventure movie. Buster's father, Joe, had a featured role, as he would have in *Sherlock Junior* and *The General,* but the role of antagonist had passed from his father to more physically imposing men like Joe Roberts and Ernest Torrence.

Sherlock Junior (1924) gave Buster the chance to experiment with film editing and processing. There was a surreal sequence that confounded film studies students for decades; Buster played a film projectionist who fell asleep and, in his dream, walked through the theatre onto the stage and entered into the film. The scenes changed without regard to his presence. As he sat on a garden bench, the scene shifted to the middle of a street filled with automobile traffic. No sooner had he jumped to safety than he found himself perched on the edge of a precipice. In quick succession he encountered lions, an island, snow and water. Elsewhere in the film and equally impressive were his split-second timing and neat execution of complicated physical stunts. It was a bravura turn.

Through the course of making his two-reelers, Buster had pulled together a loyal team of creators. Each film was a joint creation; everyone on the team was encouraged to make good suggestions. *The Navigator* (1924), however, was inspired by chance. Keaton heard of an ocean liner for sale on the cheap from a salvage company. The only thing to do was to fashion a story around it. Buster met and conquered machines large as an ocean liner and small as kitchen utensils. Keaton's character reverted to a variant of the clueless rich boy he had played in *The Saphead.* Through adversity he became a man and won the girl of his desires. *The Navigator* was extremely successful at the box office and remains one of his most popular features.

Schenck chose Keaton's next feature. *Seven Chances* (1925) was adapted from a stage farce about a man who had to marry within 24 hours to qualify for his inheritance. It took a lot of cinematic talent to make it screenworthy. The result was a lesser Keaton film redeemed by a stunning climactic chase. Scheck had hitherto allowed Keaton free rein in making his films, but moviemaking was becoming a large-scale industry, and small independent studios like Keaton's were getting absorbed into large corporations like MGM. Buster still had a few years of freedom left, but he was largely unaware that his creativity would be compromised by the economics of making sound pictures.

Buster was aware that his marriage to Natalie Talmadge was not all he wished. Natalie was the less talented sister of silent-screen stars Norma and Constance, and Norma was married to Joe Schenck, Buster's boss. Peg, the Talmadge girls' mother, was a determined matriarch who saw the Talmadge-Schenck clan as royals in the kingdom of Hollywood. Buster, who always preferred simple living, found himself with a wife who spent like a princess and required a palace for a home. He also had two children to support in Hollywood style. He was enmeshed in circumstances that required a constant flow of income and left him little unmortgaged ground on which to make his stand for independence.

Go West (1925) was a charming movie about a boy and his cow. Honest sentiment abounded, and Buster was called Friendless in the film. The cow, Brown Eyes, was his only companion, and he was bent on saving her from the slaughterhouse. *Go West* could have been a Chaplin movie. *Battling Butler* (1926) and *College* (1927) were Harold Lloyd films, and both rather ordinary, although *Battling Butler* ends with a ferocious boxing match that verges on cruelty. The movies must have appealed to contemporary audiences because both were among Keaton's biggest box-office successes.

Keaton made his masterpiece between filming *Battling Butler* and *College. The General* (1926) remains his most famous feature and appears on most lists of great movies, but it did not draw crowds into the theatres of its day. A Civil War story based on a true incident of a hijacked locomotive and train, the film was a perfect blend of comedy and adventure. It worked because it had the same air of historic authenticity that imbued *Our Hospitality.* When in the 1950s and 1960s interest revived in silent pictures in general and Keaton's in particular, *The General* and *The Navigator* were the usual films chosen for showing in film fests.

Keaton's last independent feature was *Steamboat Bill Jr.* (1928), an exciting adventure film with stunning effects and a storm that provided a thrilling denouement. It was one of his best features. Once again he was an inexperienced young man thrown into a situation that required him to call on inner strength and ingenuity he did not know he possessed.

His first film as an employee of MGM, to whom his contract was sold, was *The Cameraman* (1928), and it was nearly as good as his best. Toting about an old-style film camera, Buster played a young man trying to get hired to shoot newsreel footage. The story was thin; the two elements were his love interest and his filming escapades. But it was well told and filmed.

Spite Marriage (1929) was his only poor feature of his silent period. It was clumsy and pedestrian. Both *Spite Marriage* and *The Cameraman* did good business at the box office.

The accepted opinion has been that Buster's talkies were so inferior to the best of his silent features that they are not worth much discussion. Keaton provided one of the shining moments in MGM's *Hollywood Revue of 1929,* which served to introduce the singing and speaking voices of MGM's stable of stars. *Free and Easy* (1930) should have starred Joe E. Brown. *Doughboys* (1930) was a comedy about American soldiers fighting the First World War in Europe. Cliff Edwards supported Buster, and the result was a quite pleasant comedy.

Sidewalks of New York (1931), pictorially ugly, was worse than *Spite Marriage,* but *Parlor Bedroom and Bath* (1932) featured Buster in one of his longest and funniest single laugh-filled scenes, from the point that Buster and a young woman, both drenched with rain, enter a hotel until ten minutes on in the scene when Charlotte Greenwood, smartly suited to Keaton's style, endeavors to instruct Buster in the art of seduction. Truly abysmal were his three movies with Jimmy Durante. These two comedians played to neither's strength and ranked as one of the more inane and awkward casting combinations ever seen.

The blame for Buster Keaton's fall from creative grace was not MGM's alone. Buster was distracted by an unhappy marriage, and he lacked the energy or will to fight for the measure of independence that Chaplin and Lloyd preserved. He was also a drunk by the early 1930s. On the other hand, even if he had tried to fight for his artistic freedom, his films were not as popular and profitable as Lloyd's or Chaplin's, and thus he lacked their clout.

According to his friends, Buster could not drink. It took only a couple to make him woozy. But like his father, he drowned his disappointment in liquor. In several of his early 1930s features he was obviously drunk and his speech was slurred. He became unemployable in Hollywood and made a couple of second-rate films in Europe in the 1934–35 period.

Buster was divorced by Natalie Talmadge and lost custody of his sons. He was broke as well as drunk and made a couple of unfortunate subsequent short-lived marriages. But the worst of it was being committed several times in 1935 to mental wards in sanitariums. Through the tough times, Buster continued to support Myra and Joe, as well as Harry and Louise. He insisted that they get a good education.

Buster's road to recovery was a long one, but it began with a contract to make short, inexpensive two-reel comedies for Educational Films, the studio that specialized in comedians on the way up or the way down. Later in the 1930s and early 1940s, he made shorts for Columbia and helped create gags for

Red Skelton, The Marx Brothers and Abbott & Costello. With a few slips on the way, Buster again became a working actor.

Things had begun to change when Buster met Eleanor Norris, the young woman who became Buster's fourth and last wife. By the 1950s, he had his own weekly television series, was appearing in summer stock and was getting paid well for TV commercials. In 1953, Keaton, still physically fit despite his alcoholism, many injuries and long illnesses, performed at Cirque Medrano in Paris.

Back working in Hollywood movies, Buster was hired to liven up some below-par features and to appear in a few that were above average, such as *Limelight* (1952), in which he joined Chaplin for a fine music-hall comedy turn. In total, Keaton appeared in more than 60 shorts and features after his illness—a number roughly equal to those he had made in his prime.

In 1949, James Agee wrote an appreciation of the silent movie clowns that stimulated new interest in Chaplin, Lloyd, Langdon and Keaton. Shortly thereafter, actor James Mason, owner of Buster's former mansion, the one the Talmadges had urged him to purchase, discovered cans of films containing Buster's great silent comedies hidden away in the mansion's film vault. Gradually, the Keaton films were restored and revived by film societies. Accolades followed, and by 1960 Buster Keaton was the most celebrated of silent film comedians. Buster's artistic reputation was such that the revolutionary playwright Samuel Becket chose Keaton for a short piece of experimental filmmaking titled, simply, *Film* (1965).

Essentially shy and not susceptible to flattery, Buster was gladdened by the reception his old films were given, and he received many honors. Shortly before his death in 1966, and in poor health, Buster traveled with Eleanor to the Berlin Film Festival, where he was accorded a tribute that brought him to tears.

"It's all about the work" has long been a phrase uttered by actors. Popular stars claim the mantra, hoping it anoints them with serious purpose; also-rans employ it to defend their modest success. For Buster, it was always and genuinely about the work. He never gave a hoot for riches, and fame and success were useful only for the power they gave him to make movies the way he wanted.

FRANK KEENAN

b: 8 April 1858, Dubuque, IA—d: 24 February 1929, Los Angeles, CA

Some actors from the legitimate theater were smart enough to temper in public their snobbery about vaudeville, especially when the two-a-day paid them far more handsomely than did drama. Frank Keenan was not grateful to vaudeville, although it propped him up during the last decades of his career.

Frank Keenan

By that time, Frank Keenan was a "furniture actor," still capable of acquitting himself with an effective performance as long as he was sitting. But all bets were off when he chose to move. He supported himself by grabbing onto the backs of overstuffed chairs and couches or leaning against tables and sideboards. Usually, so smooth were his dialogue and gestures that few audiences guessed that he was intoxicated, until those occasions when arrogance overcame restraint and he visibly lurched. His grandson and his great-grandson called him "a monumental drunk," and theirs were voices of experience.

At six feet, three inches in height, Frank Keenan towered over most other men of his day, and he was handsome enough to be called a matinee idol. Well regarded as an actor of both classical and contemporary drama, he had been a Broadway star and a leading man in silent movies. For several seasons, beginning in 1902, he was the actor-manager of a repertory company, the Frank Keenan Players, that included future film stars William S. Hart, Lowell Sherman and Ford Sterling. No critic denied Frank Keenan's talent, but he was a target as well as a practitioner of theatrical snobbery. Throughout Frank's career, critics decried what they saw as his dalliance with "the flickers" and vaudeville.

Joe Laurie Jr. recalled *Man to Man* and *Vindication* as two of the popular dramatic sketches that Frank Keenan played in vaudeville for many seasons. It was in *Man to Man* that Frank Keenan was playing in 1912 when he chanced to be headlining a bill at the Orpheum Theatre in Winnipeg that also included a comedian 30 years his junior, Ed Wynn. Against Frank's wishes, Wynn courted his daughter, Hilda Keenan, who also acted in her father's dramatic sketch. Eventually Hilda and Ed married. Frank Keenan had attended Boston College, where he was taught by Jesuits, and he was intelligent and well informed, yet he had many of the prejudices that were all too common. Ed Wynn admired his father-in-law for his intelligence, talent, natural bearing and dignity. Keenan grew to respect Ed Wynn as a serious and industrious man.

Frank Keenan made more than 40 movies during 16 years in films. When he began in 1909, the films were one-reelers made on Long Island or near the New Jersey Palisades. He appeared in leading roles and in strong supporting parts. When he made his final motion picture, in Hollywood, silent films had reached their apogee and told their stories in multiple reels. Sound was just a year away for feature-length films, but Keenan's last movie was released in 1926.

He was married to his first wife, Catherine, for 44 years; she died of a heart attack in 1924 while in the wings watching Frank in performance. He wed twice again; neither marriage lasted.

Despite booze, Frank Keenan won great respect for his ability. As late as 1923, and back on Broadway instead of on a vaudeville stage or in a film role, Keenan earned excellent notices for his performance as an iron-willed patriarch in *Peter Weston* (1923). His last Main Stem appearance was in a revival of *Sherlock Holmes* (1928).

Clockwise from top center: Julie Mackey, Bernard Dyllyn, C. H. Unthan, De Laur & Derrimont, Mlle. Ottillie, Zamora, Carroll Johnson, Raymon Moore. Center: Bertoldi

KEENEY'S THEATRES

One of the smallest of small-time outfits, Keeney's Theatres were found on Third Avenue in Manhattan, in Binghamton in upstate New York and in New Britain, Connecticut.

KEITH-ALBEE CIRCUIT

The Keith circuit, and the Keith-Albee circuit that succeeded it, was no less a commercial concern than any other vaudeville circuit—Orpheum, Sullivan-Considine, Pantages or Loew's. In fact, Keith and Albee conducted business the way nations wage war. Like nations, the Keith-Albee empire wrapped itself in the banner of righteousness. They presented Benjamin Franklin Keith to the press and public as the savior who had rescued variety from immoral purveyors of smut, scrubbed it clean, reinvented it as polite vaudeville and made it fit and wholesome entertainment for the entire family.

There were several and successive principal powers in the Keith-Albee operation that spanned 45 years. B.F. Keith was a huckster who mostly worked circus sideshows and dime museums until, at age 37, he decided to settle in Boston and open a dime museum of his own. It had the usual street-level curio hall and a lecture hall above—a subterfuge that allowed Keith to circumvent regulations pertaining to theatres and his public to deceive themselves that they were patronizing an educational exhibit and demonstration. Keith also promoted the policy of continuous vaudeville, so that patrons could come in and leave as they wished. This made vaudeville an accommodating time killer but exhausted the performers.

The moral rectitude and allegiance to her faith of Mrs. Keith (the former Mary Catherine Branley) won the support of the Boston archdiocese of the Roman Catholic Church. The Boston archdiocese financed or arranged the financing of most of Keith's early expansion. Ma and Pa Keith were responsible for at least one innovation in vaudeville. Mrs. Keith insisted on a code of conduct that forbade performers using curse words or even expressions like *hully-gee, son of a gun,* or *slob* in their act and ordered the substitution of the word *trousers* for *pants.* Performers sneered that Keith time was the "Sunday school circuit."

Edward F. Albee joined the Keith operation soon after it started and became general manager by 1886. He convinced Keith to dress up his crummy little theatre and to open a second, fifth and tenth theatre, each larger and grander. Albee turned a mom-and-pop retail operation into a corporation and then into a monopolistic empire. Despite the boardroom rough stuff, Albee continued to genuflect at the Keith altar of propriety. Yet it was Albee who ordered the placement of a dozen full-length mirrors in a semicircle upstage when Annette Kellerman wore her skintight single-piece bathing suit in her act.

Albee hired as his right-hand man John J. Murdock, a onetime stage electrician who had assembled in Chicago the single greatest threat to Keith-Albee hegemony—the Western Managers' Vaudeville Association. It was assumed that Albee hired Murdock to deprive the opposing team of one of its ablest leaders, but Murdock proved invaluable to Albee. J.J. also feathered his own nest, and it was his maneuver, late in the vaudeville game, that benched Albee.

The spread of the Keith domain reached first to Providence, Rhode Island, and then to Philadelphia in 1899. To bring New York City under the Keith banner, Keith formed an uneasy partnership with F. F. Proctor, owner of several theatres in and around New York City. In 1906 they established the Keith-Proctor circuit, a short-lived alliance. But their two chains remained tethered through the United Booking Office in matters of common policy and organized booking.

Corporate wealth, largely invested and realized in real estate, was the business of the Keith-Albee empire. The power of controlling the industry—creating a united front with allies against competitors and dictating terms to performers—resided in the United Booking Office, which was dominated by Albee.

By 1915, the Keith circuit reached Savannah, Birmingham and New Orleans in the South, Ottawa and Toronto in Canada, Indianapolis and Grand Rapids in the Midwest and all major urban centers within that perimeter. Albee and Murdock built many theatres, but they leased or handled the booking for many more.

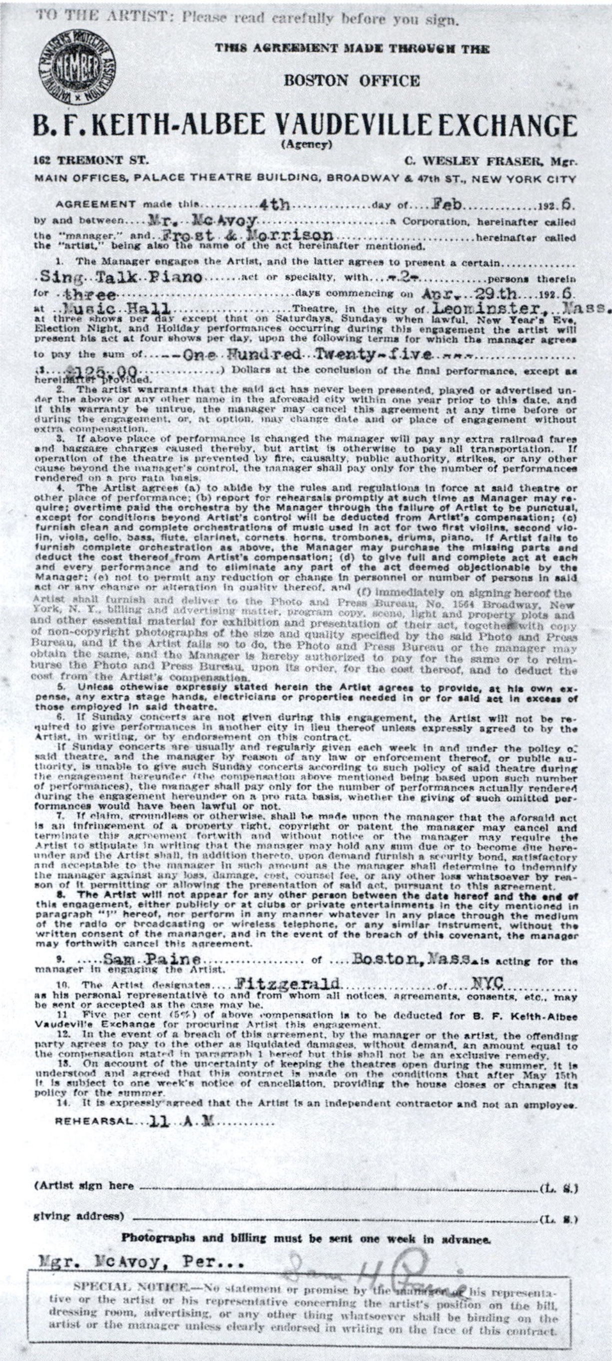

TO THE ARTIST: Please read carefully before you sign.

THIS AGREEMENT MADE THROUGH THE

BOSTON OFFICE

B. F. KEITH-ALBEE VAUDEVILLE EXCHANGE

(Agency)

162 TREMONT ST. C. WESLEY FRASER, Mgr.

MAIN OFFICES, PALACE THEATRE BUILDING, BROADWAY & 47th ST., NEW YORK CITY

AGREEMENT made this 4th day of Feb 1926 by and between Mr. McAvoy a Corporation, hereinafter called the "manager," and Frost & Morrison hereinafter called the "artist," being also the name of the act hereinafter mentioned.

1. The Manager engages the Artist, and the latter agrees to present a certain Sing Talk Piano act or specialty, with -2- persons therein for three days commencing on Apr. 29th 1926 at Music Hall Theatre, in the city of Leominster, Mass. at three shows per day except that on Saturdays, Sundays when lawful, New Year's Eve, Election Night, and Holiday performances occurring during this engagement the artist will present his act at four shows per day, upon the following terms for which the manager agrees to pay the sum of ---One Hundred Twenty-five--- ($125.00) Dollars at the conclusion of the final performance, except as hereinafter provided.

2. The artist warrants that the said act has never been presented, played or advertised under the above or any other name in the aforesaid city within one year prior to this date, and if this warranty be untrue, the manager may cancel this agreement at any time before or during the engagement, or, at option, may change date and or place of engagement without extra compensation.

3. If above place of performance is changed the manager will pay any extra railroad fares and baggage charges caused thereby, but artist is otherwise to pay all transportation. If operation of the theatre is prevented by fire, causalty, public authority, strikes, or any other cause beyond the manager's control, the manager shall pay only for the number of performances rendered on a pro rata basis.

4. The Artist agrees (a) to abide by the rules and regulations in force at said theatre or other place of performance; (b) report for rehearsals promptly at such time as Manager may require; overtime paid the orchestra by the Manager through the failure of Artist to be punctual, except for conditions beyond Artist's control will be deducted from Artist's compensation; (c) furnish clean and complete orchestrations of music used in act for two first violins, second violin, viola, cello, bass, flute, clarinet, cornets, horns, trombones, drums, piano. If Artist fails to furnish complete orchestration as above, the Manager may purchase the missing parts and deduct the cost thereof from Artist's compensation; (d) to give full and complete act at each and every performance and to eliminate any part of the act deemed objectionable by the Manager; (e) not to permit any reduction or change in personnel or number of persons in said act or any change or alteration in quality thereof, and (f) immediately on signing hereof the Artist shall furnish and deliver to the Photo and Press Bureau, No. 1564 Broadway, New York, N. Y., billing and advertising matter, program copy, scene, light and property plots and and other essential material for exhibition and presentation of their act, together with copy of non-copyright photographs of the size and quality specified by the said Photo and Press Bureau, and if the Artist fails so to do, the Photo and Press Bureau or the manager may obtain the same, and the Manager is hereby authorized to pay for the same or to reimburse the Photo and Press Bureau, upon its order, for the cost thereof, and to deduct the cost from the Artist's compensation.

5. Unless othewise expressly stated herein the Artist agrees to provide, at his own expense, any extra stage hands, electricians or properties needed in or for said act in excess of those employed in said theatre.

6. If Sunday concerts are not given during this engagement, the Artist will not be required to give performances in another city in lieu thereof unless expressly agreed to by the Artist, in writing, or by endorsement on this contract.

If Sunday concerts are usually and regularly given each week in and under the policy of said theatre, and the manager by reason of any law or enforcement thereof, or public authority, is unable to give such Sunday concerts according to such policy of said theatre during the engagement hereunder (the compensation above mentioned being based upon such number of performances), the manager shall pay only for the number of performances actually rendered during the engagement hereunder on a pro rata basis, whether the giving of such omitted performances would have been lawful or not.

7. If claim, groundless or otherwise, shall be made upon the manager that the aforsaid act is an infringement of a property right, copyright or patent the manager may cancel and terminate this agreement fortwith and without notice or the manager may require the Artist to stipulate in writing that the manager may hold any sum due or to become due hereunder and the Artist shall, in addition thereto, upon demand furnish a security bond, satisfactory and acceptable to the manager in such amount as the manager shall determine to indemnify the manager against any loss, damage, cost, counsel fee, or any other loss whatsoever by reason of it permitting or allowing the presentation of said act, pursuant to this agreement.

8. The Artist will not appear for any other person between the date hereof and the end of this engagement, either publicly or at clubs or private entertainments in the city mentioned in paragraph "1" hereof, nor perform in any manner whatever in any place through the medium of the radio or broadcasting or wireless telephone, or any similar instrument, without the written consent of the mananger, and in the event of the breach of this covenant, the manager may forthwith cancel this agreement.

9. Sam Paine of Boston, Mass. is acting for the manager in engaging the Artist.

10. The Artist designates Fitzgerald of NYC as his personal representative to and from whom all notices, agreements, consents, etc., may be sent or accepted as the case may be.

11 Five per cent (5%) of above compensation is to be deducted for B. F. Keith-Albee Vaudeville Exchange for procuring Artist this engagement.

12. In the event of a breach of this agreement, by the manager or the artist, the offending party agrees to pay to the other as liquidated damages, without demand, an amount equal to the compensation stated in paragraph 1 hereof but this shall not be an exclusive remedy.

13. On account of the uncertainty of keeping the theatres open during the summer, it is understood and agreed that this contract is made on the conditions that after May 15th it is subject to one week's notice of cancellation, providing the house closes or changes its policy for the summer.

14. It is expressly agreed that the Artist is an independent contractor and not an employee.

REHEARSAL 11 A.M.

(Artist sign here ______ (L. S.)

giving address) ______ (L. S.)

Photographs and billing must be sent one week in advance.

Mgr. McAvoy, Per... Sam H. Paine

SPECIAL NOTICE.—No statement or promise by the manager or his representative or the artist or his representative concerning the artist's position on the bill, dressing room, advertising, or any other thing whatsoever shall be binding on the artist or the manager unless clearly endorsed in writing on the face of this contract.

Contract from 1926 for Frost & Morrison at the Music Hall in Leominster, Massachusetts, for three days, three shows a day for $125.

Beyond the Mississippi River, however, the Western Managers' Vaudeville Association (WMVA) was the countervailing power to the United Booking Office. WMVA included a number of smaller circuits and was largely dominated by the Orpheum circuit. When the Orpheum circuit became a publicly held corporation,

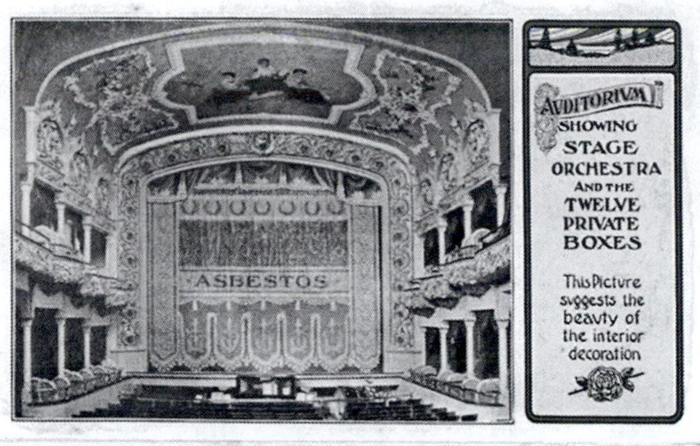

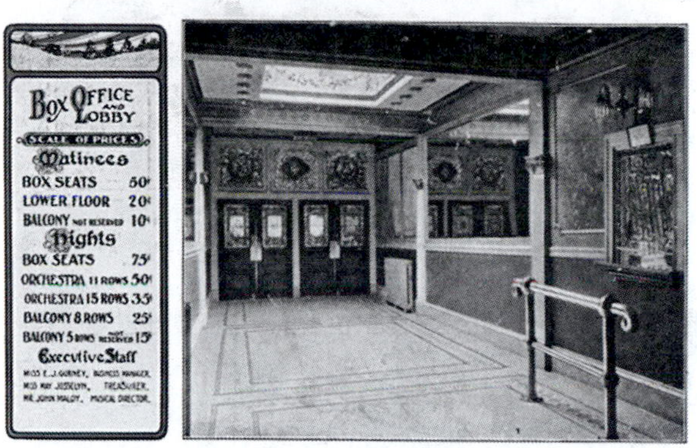

Folding postcard for Keith's Hathaway Theatre, Brockton, Massachusetts

Keith interests began acquiring its stock. In 1927, the two circuits merged—or the Orpheum was absorbed—into Keith-Albee-Orpheum (KAO). In 1928, Murdock sold his many shares of KAO stock to Joseph P. Kennedy, who merged KAO with his own small movie studio and with RCA to create RKO, a corporation looking to the future of radio and motion pictures. Albee had single-mindedly concentrated on vaudeville, the construction of theatres and the establishment of a monopoly, unlike virtually all his major rivals who had seen movie production, distribution and exhibition become a growing portion of their business.

The Keith-Albee circuit buried its corporate head in the sand by ignoring motion pictures. Even in their smaller theatres, Keith-Albee ignored motion pictures and refused to split their bills between live acts and films. In the heyday of vaudeville, however, the Keith-Albee circuit was predominant, a near monopoly.

Note: The list of theatres attributed to this circuit is a composite of lists. It was culled from several sources, including *Julius Cahn's Official Theatrical Guides* (1910), *The [New York] Clipper Red Book and Date Book* (1910), Jack B. Shea's *The Official Vaudeville Guide* (1928) and Herbert Lloyd's *Vaudeville Trails thru the West* (1919). Theatre historian Stan S. Spence sorted out the often tangled history of Keith-Albee theatres and added many names to the list of theatres owned or leased by Keith-Albee and booked by the United Booking Office.

Theatre affiliations with circuits, however, changed over time. A Proctor theatre later may have become a Keith-Albee house; a Pantages' or a Loew's theatre may have been a former Sullivan & Considine theatre; and independent circuits were often taken over by larger enterprises, like Keith-Albee. Theatres were bought and sold, and names were changed entirely or simply altered to reflect their new owners.

Some theatres were specifically designed as opera houses or vaudeville theatres, but generally theatres were able to accommodate several types of show. A theatre could host vaudeville for ten years and then change to exhibiting only motion pictures. A former burlesque house might be converted to vaudeville.

The following list of theatres is not a snapshot in time. It includes theatres that functioned at various times over a period of nearly 20 years, and thus there will be duplications.

Anniston	Alabama	Fox-Lyric Theatre
Birmingham	Alabama	Lyric Theatre
Birmingham	Alabama	Majestic Theatre
Mobile	Alabama	Grand Theatre
Mobile	Alabama	Lyric Theatre
Montgomery	Alabama	Grand Theatre
Bridgeport	Connecticut	Plaza Theatre
Bristol	Connecticut	Bristol Theatre
Hartford	Connecticut	B. F. Keith's Theatre
Hartford	Connecticut	Palace Theatre
Hartford	Connecticut	Shea's Theatre
Middletown	Connecticut	Grand Theatre
New Britain	Connecticut	Capitol Theatre
New Britain	Connecticut	Palace Theatre
New Britain	Connecticut	Russwin Lyceum Theatre
New Haven	Connecticut	B. F. Keith's Theatre
New London	Connecticut	Capitol Theatre
New London	Connecticut	Lyceum Theatre
Norwalk	Connecticut	Music Hall Theatre
Norwich	Connecticut	Auditorium Theatre
Norwich	Connecticut	Broadway Theatre

Billy Burke and the Avon Comedy Four, ca. 1917

Norwich	Connecticut	Davis Theatre
Norwich	Connecticut	Strand Theatre
Putnam	Connecticut	Bradley Theatre
Rockville	Connecticut	Palace Theatre
South Norwalk	Connecticut	Palace Theatre
Stamford	Connecticut	Alhambra
Watertown	Connecticut	Olympic Theatre
Willimantic	Connecticut	Capitol Theatre
Willimantic	Connecticut	Gem Theatre
Wilmington	Delaware	Aldine Theatre
Wilmington	Delaware	B.F. Keith's Theatre
Wilmington	Delaware	Dockstader's Theatre (1)
Wilmington	Delaware	Dockstader's Theatre (2)
Wilmington	Delaware	Garrick Theatre
Wilmington	Delaware	Queen Theatre
Washington	District of Columbia	B.F. Keith's Theatre
Washington	District of Columbia	Chase's Theatre
Washington	District of Columbia	Cosmos Theatre
Washington	District of Columbia	Earle Theatre
Daytona Beach	Florida	Vivian Theatre
Jacksonville	Florida	Arcade Theatre
Jacksonville	Florida	Bijou Theatre
Jacksonville	Florida	Jacksonsville Theatre
Jacksonville	Florida	Palace Theatre
Miami	Florida	Farifax Theatre
Orlando	Florida	Beacham Theatre
Palm Beach	Florida	B.F. Keith's Theatre
Pensacola	Florida	Saenger Theatre
Tampa	Florida	Victory Theatre West
Atlanta	Georgia	B.F. Keith's Georgia Theatre
Atlanta	Georgia	B.F. Keith's Lyric Theatre
Atlanta	Georgia	Bijou Theatre
Atlanta	Georgia	Forsythe Theatre
Atlanta	Georgia	Grand Theatre
Atlanta	Georgia	Lyric Theatre
Augusta	Georgia	B.F. Keith's Theatre
Augusta	Georgia	Grand Theatre
Augusta	Georgia	Imperial Theatre
Augusta	Georgia	Lyric Theatre
Augusta	Georgia	Wells Bijou Theatre
Macon	Georgia	Grand Theatre
Savannah	Georgia	Bijou Theatre
Savannah	Georgia	Savannah Theatre
Carbondale	Illinois	Irving Theatre
Chicago	Illinois	Star Theatre (1)
Chicago	Illinois	Star Theatre (2)
Danville	Illinois	Palace Theatre
Evansville	Indiana	Strand Theatre
Evansville	Indiana	Victory Theatre
Fort Wayne	Indiana	B.F. Keith's Theatre
Fort Wayne	Indiana	Palace Theatre
Hammond	Indiana	Parthenon Theatre
Huntington	Indiana	Huntington Theatre
Indianapolis	Indiana	B.F. Keith's Grand Opera House
Indianapolis	Indiana	B.F. Keith's Palace Theatre
Indianapolis	Indiana	B.F. Keith's Theatre
Indianapolis	Indiana	English Theatre
Indianapolis	Indiana	English's Opera House
Indianapolis	Indiana	Lyric Theatre
Indianapolis	Indiana	Majestic Theatre
Kokomo	Indiana	B.F. Keith's Strand Theatre
Kokomo	Indiana	Sipes Theatre
Lafayette	Indiana	B.F. Keith's Theatre
Lafayette	Indiana	Family Theatre
Logansport	Indiana	Colonial Theatre

Keith's and Bijou Theatres, Washington Street, Boston, Massachusetts

Muncie	Indiana	Wysor Grand Theatre
New Castle	Indiana	Princess Theatre
South Bend	Indiana	Indiana Theatre
Terre Haute	Indiana	B. F. Keith's Indiana Theatre
Terre Haute	Indiana	Indiana Theatre
Terre Haute	Indiana	Liberty Theatre
Lexington	Kentucky	Ben Ali Theatre
Louisville	Kentucky	Avenue Theatre
Louisville	Kentucky	B. F. Keith's Grand Opera House
Louisville	Kentucky	B. F. Keith's Metropolitan Theatre
Louisville	Kentucky	B. F. Keith's Strand Theatre
Louisville	Kentucky	B. F. Keith's Theatre
Louisville	Kentucky	Mary Anderson Theatre
Louisville	Kentucky	National Theatre
Louisville	Kentucky	Rialto Theatre
Paducah	Kentucky	Orpheum Theatre
Alexandria	Louisiana	Rapides Theatre
New Orleans	Louisiana	Palace Theatre
Augusta	Maine	Opera House
Bangor	Maine	Bijou Theatre
Bangor	Maine	Gaiety Theatre
Lewiston	Maine	Music Hall
Portland	Maine	B. F. Keith's Theatre
Portland	Maine	Portland Theatre (1)
Portland	Maine	Portland Theatre (2)
Rockland	Maine	Rockland Theatre
Baltimore	Maryland	B. F. Keith's Garden Theatre
Baltimore	Maryland	B. F. Keith's Maryland Theatre
Baltimore	Maryland	B. F. Keith's Theatre
Baltimore	Maryland	Hippodrome Theatre
Baltimore	Maryland	Kernan's Maryland Theatre
Allston	Massachusetts	Capitol Theatre
Amesbury	Massachusetts	Strand Theatre
Attleboro	Massachusetts	Bates Opera house
Boston	Massachusetts	B. F. Keith Memorial Theatre
Boston	Massachusetts	B. F. Keith's Bijou Dream Theatre
Boston	Massachusetts	B. F. Keith's Bijou Theatre
Boston	Massachusetts	B. F. Keith's Boston Theatre
Boston	Massachusetts	B. F. Keith's National Theatre
Boston	Massachusetts	B. F. Keith's New Theatre
Boston	Massachusetts	B. F. Keith's Theatre
Boston	Massachusetts	Bowdoin Square Theatre
Boston	Massachusetts	Gordon's Olympia Theatre
Boston	Massachusetts	Gordon's Scollay Square Theatre
Boston	Massachusetts	Gordon's Washington Street Olympia Theatre
Boston	Massachusetts	Keith's Orpheum Theatre
Boston	Massachusetts	Scollay Square Olympia Theatre
Boston	Massachusetts	Washington Street Theatre
Brockton	Massachusetts	B. F. Keith's Theatre
Brockton	Massachusetts	Brockton Theatre
Brockton	Massachusetts	Strand Theatre

Cambridge	Massachusetts	Gordon's Central Square Theatre
Cambridge	Massachusetts	Harvard Square Theatre
Clinton	Massachusetts	Philbin Theatre
Dorchester	Massachusetts	Codman Square Theatre
Dorchester	Massachusetts	Fields Corner Theatre
Dorchester	Massachusetts	Franklin Park Theatre
Dorchester	Massachusetts	Franklin Square Theatre
Dorchester	Massachusetts	Gordon's Strand Theatre
Dorchester	Massachusetts	Shawmut Theatre
Fall River	Massachusetts	Empire Theatre
Fall River	Massachusetts	Sheedy's Savoy Theatre
Fitchburg	Massachusetts	Cummings' Theatre
Fitchburg	Massachusetts	Lyric Theatre
Fitchburg	Massachusetts	Whitney Opera House
Gardner	Massachusetts	Bijou Theatre
Gloucester	Massachusetts	North Shore Theatre
Greenfield	Massachusetts	Victoria Theatre
Haverhill	Massachusetts	Colonial Theatre
Holyoke	Massachusetts	Victoria Theatre
Jamaica Plain	Massachusetts	Jamaica Theatre
Lawrence	Massachusetts	B. F. Keith's Theatre
Lawrence	Massachusetts	Colonial Theatre
Lawrence	Massachusetts	Empire Theatre
Lawrence	Massachusetts	Palace Theatre
Leominster	Massachusetts	Music Hall Theatre
Lowell	Massachusetts	B. F. Keith's Theatre
Lowell	Massachusetts	Hathaway's Theatre
Lowell	Massachusetts	Lowell Opera House
Lynn	Massachusetts	B. F. Keith's Theatre
Lynn	Massachusetts	Katz's Auditorium Theatre
Lynn	Massachusetts	Lynn Theatre
Lynn	Massachusetts	Olympia Theatre
Malden	Massachusetts	Granada Theatre
Malden	Massachusetts	Mystic Theatre
Medford	Massachusetts	Medford Theatre
New Bedford	Massachusetts	Gordon's Olympia Theatre
North Adams	Massachusetts	Empire Theatre
Northampton	Massachusetts	Calvin Theatre
Pittsfield	Massachusetts	Empire Theatre
Pittsfield	Massachusetts	Majestic Theatre
Pittsfield	Massachusetts	Palace Theatre
Quincy	Massachusetts	Quincy Theatre
Roxbury	Massachusetts	Dudley Theatre
Salem	Massachusetts	B. F. Keith's Theatre
Salem	Massachusetts	Federal Theatre
Somerville	Massachusetts	Union Theatre
South Boston	Massachusetts	Broadway Theatre

October 1910 program cover, Boston, Massachusetts

Southbridge	Massachusetts	Blanchard's Theatre
Waltham	Massachusetts	Waldorf Theatre
Webster	Massachusetts	Steinberg Theatre
Worcester	Massachusetts	B.F. Keith's Theatre
Worcester	Massachusetts	Park Theatre
Worcester	Massachusetts	Plaza Theatre
Battle Creek	Michigan	Bijou Theatre
Bay City	Michigan	Bijou Theatre
Detroit	Michigan	B.F. Keith's Temple Theatre
Detroit	Michigan	B.F. Keith's Uptown Theatre
Detroit	Michigan	Flint Theatre
Detroit	Michigan	Garden Theatre
Detroit	Michigan	Grand Riviera Theatre
Detroit	Michigan	La Salle Garden Theatre
Detroit	Michigan	La Salle Theatre
Detroit	Michigan	Masonic Temple Theatre
Detroit	Michigan	Palace Theatre
Detroit	Michigan	Temple Theatre
Escanaba	Michigan	Delft Theatre
Flint	Michigan	Majestic Theatre
Flint	Michigan	Palace Theatre
Gladstone	Michigan	Gladstone Theatre
Grand Rapids	Michigan	B.F. Keith's Theatre
Grand Rapids	Michigan	Columbia Theatre
Grand Rapids	Michigan	Empress Theatre
Grand Rapids	Michigan	Keith-Albee Regent Theatre
Grand Rapids	Michigan	Powers Theatre
Grand Rapids	Michigan	Ramona Park Theatre
Ionia	Michigan	Regent Theatre
Jackson	Michigan	Orpheum Theatre
Kalamazoo	Michigan	Majestic Theatre
Kalamazoo	Michigan	Regent Theatre
Lansing	Michigan	Bijou Theatre
Lansing	Michigan	Regent Theatre
Lansing	Michigan	Strand Theatre
Laurium	Michigan	Lyric Theatre
Marquette	Michigan	Marquette Opera House
Munising	Michigan	Delft Theatre
Muskegon	Michigan	Jefferson Theatre
Pontiac	Michigan	Oakland Theatre
Pontiac	Michigan	Regent Theatre
Saginaw	Michigan	Jeffers-Strand Theatre
Sault Sainte Marie	Michigan	Orpheum Theatre
Jackson	Mississippi	Century Theatre
Meridian	Mississippi	Grand Theatre
Concord	New Brunswick	Capitol Theatre
Manchester	New Brunswick	Palace Theatre
St. John	New Brunswick	B.F. Keith's Nickel Theatre
St. John	New Brunswick	B.F. Keith's Theatre
St. John	New Brunswick	Imperial Theatre
Claremont	New Hampshire	Magnet Theatre
Keene	New Hampshire	Latchis Theatre
Manchester	New Hampshire	B.F. Keith's New Theatre
Manchester	New Hampshire	B.F. Keith's Theatre
Portsmouth	New Hampshire	Leroy Theatre
Asbury Park	New Jersey	Reade's Main Street Theatre
Asbury Park	New Jersey	Reade's St. James Theatre
Atlantic City	New Jersey	B.F. Keith's Theatre
Atlantic City	New Jersey	Earle Theatre
Atlantic City	New Jersey	Globe Theatre (2)
Atlantic City	New Jersey	Savoy Theatre (1)
Atlantic City	New Jersey	Young's Million Dollar Pier (3)
Atlantic City	New Jersey	Young's Pier Music Hall (1)
Atlantic City	New Jersey	Young's Pier Theatre (2)
Camden	New Jersey	Broadway Theatre
Camden	New Jersey	Tower's Theatre
East Orange	New Jersey	Lyceum Theatre
Elizabeth	New Jersey	City Theatre
Elizabeth	New Jersey	Fabian's Ritz Theatre
Hackensack	New Jersey	Keith's Theatre
Hoboken	New Jersey	B.F. Keith's Empire Theatre
Jersey City	New Jersey	B.F. Keith's Jersey City Theatre
Jersey City	New Jersey	B.F. Keith's State Theatre
Jersey City	New Jersey	B.F. Keith's Theatre
Jersey City	New Jersey	Bijou Theatre
Jersey City	New Jersey	Keith & Proctor's Bijou Theatre
Jersey City	New Jersey	Keith & Proctor's Theatre
Jersey City	New Jersey	State Theatre
Kearney	New Jersey	Regent Theatre

Keith-Albee Circuit

Long Branch	New Jersey	B.F. Keith's Theatre
Long Branch	New Jersey	Reade's Broadway Theatre
Morristown	New Jersey	Lyon's Park Theatre
New Brunswick	New Jersey	Reade's State Theatre
Newark	New Jersey	F.F. Proctor's Family Theatre
Newark	New Jersey	F.F. Proctor's Palace Theatre
Newark	New Jersey	F.F. Proctor's Theatre
Newark	New Jersey	Odeon Theatre
Newark	New Jersey	State Theatre
Passaic	New Jersey	Montauk Theatre
Passaic	New Jersey	New Montauk Theatre
Passaic	New Jersey	Playhouse Theatre
Paterson	New Jersey	B.F. Keith's Theatre
Paterson	New Jersey	Empire Theatre
Paterson	New Jersey	Majestic Theatre
Paterson	New Jersey	Regent Theatre
Perth Amboy	New Jersey	Reade's Majestic Theatre
Plainfield	New Jersey	F.F. Proctor's Theatre
Plainfield	New Jersey	Reade's Oxford Theatre
Red Bank	New Jersey	Palace Theatre
Trenton	New Jersey	Capitol Theatre
Trenton	New Jersey	Taylor Theatre
Trenton	New Jersey	Trent Theatre
Union City/ Union Hill	New Jersey	B.F. Keith's Cameo Theatre
Union City/ Union Hill	New Jersey	B.F. Keith's State Theatre
Union City/ Union Hill	New Jersey	B.F. Keith's Theatre
Union City/ Union Hill	New Jersey	Capitol Theatre
Union City/ Union Hill	New Jersey	Hudson Theatre
Union City/ Union Hill	New Jersey	Lincoln Theatre
Union City/ Union Hill	New Jersey	Pastime Theatre
Albany	New York	B.F. Keith's Theatre
Albany	New York	F.F. Proctor's Grand Theatre
Albany	New York	F.F. Proctor's Theatre
Amsterdam	New York	Lyceum Theatre
Amsterdam	New York	Rialto Theatre
Auburn	New York	Jefferson Theatre
Binghamton	New York	Binghamton Theatre
Binghamton	New York	Stone Opera House
Binghamton	New York	Stone Theatre
Bronx	New York	B.F. Keith's Bronx Theatre
Bronx	New York	B.F. Keith's Chester Theatre
Bronx	New York	B.F. Keith's Fordham Theatre
Bronx	New York	B.F. Keith's Royal Theatre
Bronx	New York	B.S. Moss' Franklin Theatre
Bronx	New York	Percy G. Williams' Bronx Theatre
Brooklyn	New York	B.F. Keith's Boro-Park Theatre
Brooklyn	New York	B.F. Keith's Bushwick Theatre
Brooklyn	New York	B.F. Keith's De Kalb Theatre
Brooklyn	New York	B.F. Keith's Gotham Theatre
Brooklyn	New York	B.F. Keith's Greenpoint Theatre
Brooklyn	New York	B.F. Keith's Kenmore Theatre
Brooklyn	New York	B.F. Keith's Madison Theatre

Brooklyn	New York	B.F. Keith's Monroe Theatre	Brooklyn	New York	Percy G. Williams' Crescent Theatre
Brooklyn	New York	B.F. Keith's Montmartre Theatre	Brooklyn	New York	Percy G. Williams' Gotham Theatre
Brooklyn	New York	B.F. Keith's Novelty Theatre	Brooklyn	New York	Percy G. Williams' Greenpoint Theatre
Brooklyn	New York	B.F. Keith's Orpheum Theatre	Brooklyn	New York	Percy G. Williams' Novelty Theatre
Brooklyn	New York	B.F. Keith's Prospect Theatre	Brooklyn	New York	Percy G. Williams' Orpheum Theatre
Brooklyn	New York	B.F. Keith's Riviera Theatre	Brooklyn	New York	Star Theatre
Brooklyn	New York	B.S. Moss' Crescent Theatre	Brooklyn	New York	Tilyou Theatre
Brooklyn	New York	B.S. Moss' Flatbush Theatre	Buffalo	New York	Plaza Theatre
Brooklyn	New York	B.S. Moss' Madison Theatre	Buffalo	New York	Shea's Buffalo Theatre (1)
Brooklyn	New York	B.S. Moss' Prospect Theatre	Buffalo	New York	Shea's Buffalo Theatre (2)
Brooklyn	New York	B.S. Moss' Riviera Theatre	Buffalo	New York	Shea's Hippodrome Theatre
Brooklyn	New York	Brooklyn Academy Of Music	Cedarhurst	New York	E.F. Albee Theatre
Brooklyn	New York	Coney Island Theatre	Coney Island	New York	B.F. Keith's Brighton Beach Music Hall
Brooklyn	New York	E.F. Albee Theatre	Coney Island	New York	B.F. Keith's Central Theatre
Brooklyn	New York	Far Rockaway Theatre	Coney Island	New York	Henderson's Music Hall
Brooklyn	New York	Halsey Theatre	Çoney Island	New York	New Brighton Theatre
Brooklyn	New York	Henderson Theatre	Cortland	New York	Cortland Theatre
Brooklyn	New York	Keith's Prospect	Dunkirk	New York	Capitol Theatre
Brooklyn	New York	Madison Theatre	Elmira	New York	Majestic Theatre
Brooklyn	New York	Olympic Theatre	Far Rockaway	New York	B.F. Keith's Columbia Theatre
Brooklyn	New York	Percy G. Williams' Bushwick Theatre	Far Rockaway	New York	B.F. Keith's Tilyou Theatre
			Far Rockaway	New York	Morrison's Theatre
			Far Rockaway	New York	Strand Theatre
			Fitchburg	New York	Bijou Theatre
			Flushing	New York	B.F. Keith's Strand Theatre
			Flushing	New York	B.F. Keith's Theatre
			Glens Falls	New York	Empire Theatre
			Glens Falls	New York	Rialto Theatre
			Gloversville	New York	Glove Theatre

Keith-Albee Circuit

Harlem	New York	B.F. Keith's Harlem Theatre
Harlem	New York	F.F. Proctor's 125th Street
Harlem	New York	Keith & Proctor's Harlem Opera House
Harlem	New York	Percy G. Williams' Alhambra Theatre
Hornell	New York	Shattuck Theatre
Ithaca	New York	Star Theatre
Ithaca	New York	Strand Theatre
Jamestown	New York	Jamestown Opera House
Jamestown	New York	Shea's Theatre
Kingston	New York	Kingston Theatre
Kingston	New York	Orpheum Theatre
Kingston	New York	Reade's Kingston Theatre
Lockport	New York	Schine's Palace Theatre
Manhattan	New York	(Old) Winter Garden
Manhattan	New York	23rd Street
Manhattan	New York	Alhambra
Manhattan	New York	B.F. Keith's 81st Street Theatre
Manhattan	New York	B.F. Keith's Alhambra Theatre
Manhattan	New York	B.F. Keith's Bijou Dream Theatre
Manhattan	New York	B.F. Keith's Broadway Theatre
Manhattan	New York	B.F. Keith's East New York Theatre
Manhattan	New York	B.F. Keith's Family Theatre
Manhattan	New York	B.F. Keith's Jefferson Theatre
Manhattan	New York	B.F. Keith's New York Hippodrome Theatre
Manhattan	New York	B.F. Keith's Palace Theatre
Manhattan	New York	B.F. Keith's Regent Theatre
Manhattan	New York	B.F. Keith's Riverside Theatre
Manhattan	New York	B.F. Keith's State Theatre
Manhattan	New York	B.F. Keith's Theatre
Manhattan	New York	B.F. Keith's Tivoli Theatre
Manhattan	New York	B.F. Keith's Union Square Theatre
Manhattan	New York	B.F. Keith's Valentine Theatre
Manhattan	New York	B.F. Keith's Yorkville Theatre
Manhattan	New York	B.S. Moss' Broadway Theatre
Manhattan	New York	B.S. Moss' Coliseum Theatre
Manhattan	New York	B.S. Moss' Hamilton Theatre
Manhattan	New York	B.S. Moss' Jefferson Theatre
Manhattan	New York	B.S. Moss' Regent Theatre
Manhattan	New York	Brighton Theatre
Manhattan	New York	Broadway Theatre
Manhattan	New York	Capitol Theatre
Manhattan	New York	Chester Theatre
Manhattan	New York	Coliseum Theatre
Manhattan	New York	Colonial Theatre
Manhattan	New York	Columbia Theatre
Manhattan	New York	F.F. Proctor's 125th Street Theatre
Manhattan	New York	F.F. Proctor's 58th Street Theatre
Manhattan	New York	F.F. Proctor's 81st Street Theatre
Manhattan	New York	F.F. Proctor's 86th Street Theatre
Manhattan	New York	F.F. Proctor's Fifth Avenue Theatre
Manhattan	New York	F.F. Proctor's Pleasure Palace Theatre
Manhattan	New York	F.F. Proctor's Union Square Theatre
Manhattan	New York	Fordham
Manhattan	New York	Fox-Riverside Theatre
Manhattan	New York	Grand Theatre
Manhattan	New York	Hammerstein's Paradise Roof Garden Theatre
Manhattan	New York	Hammerstein's Victoria Theatre of Varieties
Manhattan	New York	Hampden's Theatre
Manhattan	New York	Hurtig & Seamon's Theatre
Manhattan	New York	Keith & Proctor's 23rd Street Theatre
Manhattan	New York	Keith & Proctor's Bijou Dream Theatre

Manhattan	New York	Keith & Proctor's Jefferson Theatre
Manhattan	New York	Percy G. Williams' Colonial Theatre
Manhattan	New York	Premier
Manhattan	New York	Regent Theatre
Manhattan	New York	Riverside
Manhattan	New York	Royal
Manhattan	New York	Willard Theatre
Mount Vernon	New York	F. F. Proctor's Theatre
Mount Vernon	New York	Keith-Albee Palace Theatre
Newburgh	New York	Academy of Music
Newburgh	New York	F. F. Proctor's Theatre
Niagara Falls	New York	Belleview Theatre
Niagara Falls	New York	Shea's Bellevue Theatre
Norwich	New York	Colonial Theatre
Olean	New York	F. F. Proctor's Family Theatre
Ossining	New York	Victoria Theatre
Plattsburgh	New York	Strand Theatre
Port Chester	New York	F. F. Proctor's Theatre
Port Chester	New York	Fehr's Opera House
Port Richmond	New York	Port Richmond Theatre
Poughkeepsie	New York	Avon Theatre
Poughkeepsie	New York	Bardavon Theatre
Poughkeepsie	New York	Collingwood Opera House
Richmond Hill	New York	B. F. Keith's Victoria Theatre
Rochester	New York	B. F. Keith's Park Theatre
Rochester	New York	B. F. Keith's Theatre
Rochester	New York	Cook's Opera House
Rochester	New York	Family Theatre
Rochester	New York	Keith's Grand Opera House
Rochester	New York	Temple Theatre
Rockaway Park	New York	B. F. Keith's Theatre
Saratoga Springs	New York	Congress Theatre
Schenectady	New York	Erie Theatre
Schenectady	New York	F. F. Proctor's Theatre
Schenectady	New York	Mohawk Theatre
Syracuse	New York	B. F. Keith's Theatre
Syracuse	New York	Crescent Theatre
Syracuse	New York	Grand Opera House
Syracuse	New York	Grand Theatre
Syracuse	New York	Temple Theatre
Troy	New York	B. F. Keith's Coliseum Theatre
Troy	New York	B. F. Keith's Theatre
Troy	New York	F. F. Proctor's Theatre
Utica	New York	Robbins' Gaiety Theatre
Utica	New York	Shubert Music Hall
Utica	New York	Shubert Theatre
Utica	New York	Wilmer & Vincent's Colonial Theatre
Utica	New York	Wilmer & Vincent's Orpheum Theatre
Watertown	New York	Avon Theatre
Watertown	New York	B. F. Keith's Crescent Theatre
White Hall	New York	White Hall Theatre
White Plains	New York	B. F. Keith's Dykeman Theatre
White Plains	New York	Lynn Theatre
White Plains	New York	State Theatre
Yonkers	New York	B. F. Keith's Yonkers Theatre
Yonkers	New York	F. F. Proctor's Theatre
Yonkers	New York	Orpheum Theatre
Yonkers	New York	Yonkers Theatre
Asheville	North Carolina	Plaza Theatre
Charlotte	North Carolina	Academy Theatre
Charlotte	North Carolina	Broadway Theatre
Charlotte	North Carolina	New Broadway Theatre
High Point	North Carolina	American Theatre
Raleigh	North Carolina	Raleigh Theatre
Raleigh	North Carolina	State Theatre
Raleigh	North Carolina	Strand Theatre
Winston-Salem	North Carolina	Elks' Auditorium
Sydney	Nova Scotia	Strand Theatre
Akron	Ohio	Colonial Theatre
Akron	Ohio	Keith-Albee Palace Theatre
Ashtabula	Ohio	Palace Theatre
Canton	Ohio	Lyceum Theatre
Cincinnati	Ohio	B. F. Keith's Columbia Theatre
Cincinnati	Ohio	B. F. Keith's Olympic Theatre
Cincinnati	Ohio	B. F. Keith's Theatre

Cincinnati	Ohio	B. F. Keith's Walnut Street Theatre
Cincinnati	Ohio	E. F. Albee Theatre
Cincinnati	Ohio	Keith-Albee Fountain Square Theatre
Cleveland	Ohio	B. F. Keith's 105th Street Theatre
Cleveland	Ohio	B. F. Keith's 17th Street Theatre
Cleveland	Ohio	B. F. Keith's Hippodrome Theatre
Cleveland	Ohio	B. F. Keith's Olympia Theatre
Cleveland	Ohio	B. F. Keith's Palace Theatre
Cleveland	Ohio	B. F. Keith's Pantheon Theatre
Cleveland	Ohio	B. F. Keith's Prospect Theatre
Cleveland	Ohio	B. F. Keith's Theatre
Cleveland	Ohio	Keith's Colonial Theatre
Cleveland	Ohio	Reade's Hippodrome Theatre
Columbus	Ohio	B. F. Keith's Palace Theatre
Columbus	Ohio	B. F. Keith's Theatre
Columbus	Ohio	Columbus Theatre
Dayton	Ohio	B. F. Keith's Colonial Theatre
Dayton	Ohio	B. F. Keith's Theatre (1)
Dayton	Ohio	B.F. Keith's Theatre (2)
Dayton	Ohio	Hurtig & Seamon's Lyric Theatre
East Liverpool	Ohio	American Theatre
Findlay	Ohio	Majestic Theatre
Lima	Ohio	Faurot Opera House
Lima	Ohio	Schine's Ohio Theatre
Lorain	Ohio	Opera House
Middletown	Ohio	Gordon Theatre
Portsmouth	Ohio	Laroy Theatre
Springfield	Ohio	Palace Theatre
Steubenville	Ohio	Capitol Theatre
Toledo	Ohio	B. F. Keith's Theatre
Toledo	Ohio	Hippodrome Theatre
Warren	Ohio	Robbins Theatre
Youngstown	Ohio	B. F. Keith's Palace Theatre
Youngstown	Ohio	B. F. Keith's Theatre
Youngstown	Ohio	Hippodrome Theatre
Zanesville	Ohio	Weller Theatre
Oklahoma City	Oklahoma	Metropolitan Theatre
Hamilton	Ontario	B. F. Keith's Theatre
Hamilton	Ontario	Dominion Theatre
Hamilton	Ontario	Lyric Theatre
Hamilton	Ontario	Temple Theatre
London	Ontario	Majestic Theatre
Ottawa	Ontario	B. F. Keith's Theatre
Ottawa	Ontario	Bennett's Theatre
Ottawa	Ontario	Dominion Theatre
Ottawa	Ontario	Franklin Theatre
Ottawa	Ontario	Shea's Hippodrome
Sault Sainte Marie	Ontario	Orpheum Theatre
Toronto	Ontario	B. F. Keith's Theatre
Toronto	Ontario	Shea's Hippodrome Theatre
Toronto	Ontario	Shea's Theatre
Windsor	Ontario	Capitol Theatre
Allentown	Pennsylvania	Colonial Theatre
Allentown	Pennsylvania	Wilmer & Vincent's Orpheum Theatre
Altoona	Pennsylvania	Lyric Theatre (1)
Altoona	Pennsylvania	Lyric Theatre (2)
Altoona	Pennsylvania	Mischler Theatre
Altoona	Pennsylvania	Mischler's Opera House
Altoona	Pennsylvania	Wilmer & Vincent's Orpheum Theatre
Beaver Falls	Pennsylvania	Regent Theatre
Bethlehem	Pennsylvania	Colonial Theatre
Bradford	Pennsylvania	Bradford Theatre
Bradford	Pennsylvania	Grand Theatre
Bradford	Pennsylvania	Shea's Bradford Theatre
Butler	Pennsylvania	Harris-Majestic Theatre
Butler	Pennsylvania	Majestic Theatre
Chester	Pennsylvania	Edgemont Theatre
East Liberty	Pennsylvania	Sheridan Square Theatre
Easton	Pennsylvania	E. F. Albee Opera House
Easton	Pennsylvania	State Theatre
Easton	Pennsylvania	Wilmer & Vincent's Orpheum Theatre
Erie	Pennsylvania	B. F. Keith's Theatre
Erie	Pennsylvania	Colonial Theatre
Erie	Pennsylvania	Columbia Theatre
Erie	Pennsylvania	Lyric Theatre
Erie	Pennsylvania	Perry Theatre
Germantown	Pennsylvania	Orpheum Theatre
Greensburg	Pennsylvania	Strand Theatre
Harrisburg	Pennsylvania	Wilmer & Vincent's Majestic Theatre
Harrisburg	Pennsylvania	Wilmer & Vincent's Orpheum Theatre
Hazleton	Pennsylvania	Feeley's Theatre

Indiana	Pennsylvania	Indiana Theatre
Johnstown	Pennsylvania	Majestic Theatre
Lancaster	Pennsylvania	Colonial Theatre
McKeesport	Pennsylvania	Harris' Hippodrome Theatre
McKeesport	Pennsylvania	White's Hippodrome Theatre
McKeesport	Pennsylvania	White's Opera House
Meadville	Pennsylvania	Park Theatre
Nanticoke	Pennsylvania	State Theatre
New Castle	Pennsylvania	Capitol Theatre
Norristown	Pennsylvania	Garrick Theatre
Philadelphia	Pennsylvania	B.F. Keith's Allegheny Theatre
Philadelphia	Pennsylvania	B.F. Keith's Bijou Theatre
Philadelphia	Pennsylvania	B.F. Keith's Chestnut Street Theatre
Philadelphia	Pennsylvania	B.F. Keith's Grand Theatre
Philadelphia	Pennsylvania	B.F. Keith's National Theatre
Philadelphia	Pennsylvania	B.F. Keith's Theatre
Philadelphia	Pennsylvania	B.S. Moss' Cross Keys Theatre
Philadelphia	Pennsylvania	Broadway Theatre
Philadelphia	Pennsylvania	Colonial Theatre
Philadelphia	Pennsylvania	Cross Keys Theatre
Philadelphia	Pennsylvania	Earle Theatre
Philadelphia	Pennsylvania	Grand Opera House
Philadelphia	Pennsylvania	Keith's New Theatre
Philadelphia	Pennsylvania	Keystone Theatre (1)
Philadelphia	Pennsylvania	Keystone Theatre (2)
Philadelphia	Pennsylvania	Nixon Theatre
Philadelphia	Pennsylvania	Nixon's Grand Theatre
Philadelphia	Pennsylvania	William Penn Theatre
Pittsburgh	Pennsylvania	Davis Theatre
Pittsburgh	Pennsylvania	Harris Theatre (1)
Pittsburgh	Pennsylvania	Harris Theatre (2)
Pittsburgh	Pennsylvania	Harry Davis' Grand Opera House
Pittsburgh	Pennsylvania	Keith's Alvin Theatre
Pittsburgh	Pennsylvania	New Davis Theatre
Pittsburgh	Pennsylvania	Sheridan Square
Pottsville	Pennsylvania	Hippodrome Theatre
Pottsville	Pennsylvania	Pottsville Theatre
Punxsutawney	Pennsylvania	Alpine Theatre
Reading	Pennsylvania	Hippodrome Theatre
Reading	Pennsylvania	Majestic Theatre
Reading	Pennsylvania	Rajah Theatre
Reading	Pennsylvania	Wilmer & Vincent's Orpheum Theatre
Shamokin	Pennsylvania	Capitol Theatre
Shennadoah	Pennsylvania	Strand Theatre
Tarentum	Pennsylvania	Harris Theatre
Washington	Pennsylvania	Harris State Theatre
Washington	Pennsylvania	State Theatre
Wilkes-Barre	Pennsylvania	Penn Theatre
Williamsport	Pennsylvania	Family Theatre
York	Pennsylvania	York Opera House
Montreal	Quebec	B.F. Keith's Theatre
Montreal	Quebec	Bennett's Theatre
Montreal	Quebec	Francaise Theatre
Montreal	Quebec	Imperial Theatre
Montreal	Quebec	Princess Theatre
Montreal	Quebec	St. Denis Theatre
Quebec City	Quebec	Auditorium Theatre
Newport	Rhode Island	Colonial Theatre
Pawtucket	Rhode Island	B.F. Keith's Bijou Theatre
Pawtucket	Rhode Island	B.F. Keith's Theatre
Pawtucket	Rhode Island	Scenic Theatre
Pawtucket	Rhode Island	State Theatre
Providence	Rhode Island	B.F. Keith's Empire Theatre
Providence	Rhode Island	B.F. Keith's Gaiety Museum
Providence	Rhode Island	B.F. Keith's New Columbus Theatre
Providence	Rhode Island	B.F. Keith's New Empire Theatre
Providence	Rhode Island	B.F. Keith's Theatre
Providence	Rhode Island	Bijou Theatre
Providence	Rhode Island	E.F. Albee Theatre (1)
Providence	Rhode Island	E.F. Albee Theatre (2)
Providence	Rhode Island	Keith's Gaiety Opera House
Woonsocket	Rhode Island	Bijou Theatre
Charleston	South Carolina	Academy Theatre
Charleston	South Carolina	Kearse Theatre
Charleston	South Carolina	Owen's Academy of Music
Charleston	South Carolina	Victoria Theatre
Charleston	South Carolina	Victory Theatre
Columbia	South Carolina	Columbia Theatre
Columbia	South Carolina	Pastime Theatre
Greenville	South Carolina	Grand Theatre
Spartanburg	South Carolina	Harris Theatre
Chattanooga	Tennessee	B.F. Keith's Theatre
Chattanooga	Tennessee	Bijou Theatre

Chattanooga	Tennessee	Chattanooga Theatre
Chattanooga	Tennessee	Orpheum Theatre
Chattanooga	Tennessee	Rialto Theatre
Knoxville	Tennessee	Bijou Theatre
Knoxville	Tennessee	Knoxville Theatre
Nashville	Tennessee	Nashville Theatre
Nashville	Tennessee	Princess Theatre
Brattleboro	Vermont	Latchis Theatre
Lynchburg	Virginia	Academy of Music
Lynchburg	Virginia	Trenton Theatre
Newport News	Virginia	Olympia (Olympic) Theatre
Norfolk	Virginia	Academy of Music
Norfolk	Virginia	Colonial Theatre
Norfolk	Virginia	Norfolk Theatre
Norfolk	Virginia	Norva Theatre
Norfolk	Virginia	Orpheum Theatre
Norfolk	Virginia	Wilmer & Vincent's Colonial Theatre
Norfolk	Virginia	Wilmer & Vincent's Majestic Theatre
Petersburg	Virginia	Century Theatre
Petersburg	Virginia	Keith's Vaudeville Academy Theatre
Portsmouth	Virginia	Wilmer & Vincent's Orpheum Theatre
Richmond	Virginia	B.F. Keith's National Theatre
Richmond	Virginia	B.F. Keith's Theatre
Richmond	Virginia	Bijou Theatre
Richmond	Virginia	Lyric Theatre
Richmond	Virginia	Murray Theatre
Richmond	Virginia	Wilmer & Vincent's Colonial Theatre
Roanoke	Virginia	Roanoke Theatre
Bluefield	West Virginia	Colonial Theatre
Charleston	West Virginia	Kearse Theatre
Charleston	West Virginia	Plaza Theatre
Clarksburg	West Virginia	Robinson Grand Theatre
Fairmont	West Virginia	Fairmont Theatre
Huntington	West Virginia	Keith-Albee Theatre
Parkersburg	West Virginia	Smoot Theatre
Rutland	West Virginia	Strand Theatre
Wheeling	West Virginia	Victoria Theatre

KEITH-ALBEE-ORPHEUM

In 1927, after a score of years of rivalry and increasing accommodation through joint booking arrangements between the two big-time circuits, the Keith-Albee and the Orpheum circuits merged into a single corporation, Keith-Albee-Orpheum. The event should have been momentous, two giants combining and consolidating their power and reach, but it occurred late in December 1927, ten weeks after the part-sound movie *The Jazz Singer* opened in New York City. By that time, any news that vaudeville could generate was relegated to the back pages; motion pictures that talked, sang and danced were the talk of the town.

The stronger of the two circuits was Keith-Albee, and as E. F. Albee held a substantial block of voting shares of the combined stock, he became president of the corporation. His lieutenant, J. J. Murdock, whose holdings were about half that of Albee's, was made vice president. It was Murdock who brought Joseph P. Kennedy into the deal.

Albee had assumed that Murdock was as loyal to him as Albee had been to B. F. Keith. Murdock had always made it seem that way, but J. J. was interested in getting into the movie business. He believed that Albee had failed to recognize the growing importance of motion pictures and the decline of vaudeville. Murdock looked to Kennedy to bring new energy and purpose into the Keith-Albee-Orpheum enterprise and to give Murdock a commanding role in the new order.

In less than a year, Keith-Albee-Orpheum was no more. It had been recast as Radio-Keith-Orpheum, and its business refocused by the participation of Radio Corporation of American (RCA), founded by David Sarnoff, who also headed the first and most developed radio network, National Broadcasting Company (NBC).

The new agenda included RCA's development of an improved system for sound motion pictures, the adaptation of the Keith-Orpheum operation to distribute and exhibit movies in their coast-to-coast network of theatres, and the utilization of Kennedy's FBO studios to produce talking pictures.

Albee's power, along with his name, had vanished from the new corporation, RKO, yet Murdock did not win the top executive slot and replace Albee. The era of showmen was over, and not just in vaudeville. Show business had become an industry, and financiers wielded the power in industry.

B.F. (BENJAMIN FRANKLIN) KEITH

b: 26 January 1846, Hillsboro, NH—
d: 26 March 1914, Palm Beach, FL

Given that the name Keith became the most prominent in vaudeville—known throughout the international world of variety—it is odd that B. F. Keith did not have more to do with his great success. His first wife and partner, Mary Catherine Branley, whom he wed in 1873, was a fervent Catholic, and it was her connections to the Boston diocese that produced the Roman Catholic Church's financing for Keith's early expansion—connections that soon-to-be right-hand man Albee nurtured.

Honoring the pledge she and her husband made in turn for diocesan support, Mary insisted that vaudeville performances be purged of profanity, double entendre and coarse slang—a prohibition, both celebrated and derided, that earned Keith theatres their reputation as the Sunday school circuit. It was Edward Franklin Albee who began taking control of the Keith operation soon after joining it, prodding Keith to forsake his penny-pinching and to reach for the gold ring instead of the brass. Under Albee's guidance, the Keith operation built a series of magnificent showplaces, epitomized two-a-day big time, presented the top acts in vaudeville, exercised wide influence and made both men multimillionaires.

Keith's partisans claimed, and Keith never denied, that he originated clean vaudeville, but instances of clean vaudeville bills had been in Boston at least as early as 1840, six years before Keith's birth, and Tony Pastor in New York had far greater claim to being the first manager to succeed with a long-term policy of presenting variety bills suitable for the entire family. If Keith had a particular skill, it was running his business like a small shopkeeper, staying in touch with his customers. It was a skill sharpened through his early years as a concessionaire in a sideshow, cajoling yokels into the tent, selling bogus elixirs and stale candy.

B. F. Keith

Indeed, the only major innovation that can be attributed to B.F. Keith is one that is unaccompanied by plaudits—the large-scale introduction of *continuous performance* into vaudeville on 6 July 1885. Upon becoming a theatre owner, he offered continuous vaudeville as a response to passersby who turned away from the box office when they were informed that the show had already begun. Soon his ads read: "Come when you please, stay as long you like," promising the public that they could watch the entire show no matter when they showed up. Considering that Keith gave his customers a short, one-hour show at the time, and the acts had to perform from 10 o'clock in the morning until 11 o'clock at night, his audiences witnessed tired performers giving dispirited performances for patrons, many of whom simply wished to kill some time before resuming shopping or moving on to their next appointments.

Yet, even continuous performance was not an original idea; it long had been the modus operandi of sideshows, where one brief nickel or dime show quickly followed another as customers from the concluding show were hustled out the back of the tent while new customers were herded in from the front.

At the time of Keith's boyhood on a farm in rural western Massachusetts, the arrival of circuses and carnivals was more of an event in small-town America than the minstrel show or the touring melodrama. Along with Wild West shows, circuses were the theatre of choice for men and boys. The lads thrilled to the derring-do of aerialists and ropewalkers; their fathers, if they could slip away from spouse and brood, gravitated toward the sideshow, where games of chance and promises of forbidden delights lured them into the tents.

The occasional appearance of a circus was not enough for young Master Keith. Like many boys of his day, he ran away from home to follow the tented shows; he did odd jobs for board. During his apprenticeship, Bennie Keith, as he was then known, worked for a variety of operations, including Bunnell's Museum in Lower Manhattan, P. T. Barnum's (where he learned the tricks of the promotional trade), as well as Batcheller & Doris' Circus and its successor, John B. Doris' Great Inter-Ocean Circus.

Married and on his own professionally, B. F. Keith, his wife and their son A. (Andrew) Paul Keith (1874–1918) came to Boston in 1882, and beginning with "Colonel" William Austin (who later opened the first nickelodeon in Boston), Keith and various partners opened or reopened, in quick succession, several dime museums. Keith and Austin's first big attraction was a diminutive infant of three months who weighed less than one and a half pounds. Indeed, she was their only attraction when they opened for business on 8 January 1883. Despite the lack of intense medical care that would today be considered mandatory, Baby Alice, as she was known, grew healthier and heavier. She survived and so ended her appeal as a so-called human freak.

Meanwhile, Keith and Austin had added other exhibits, but either the novelty or the partnership quickly wore thin because Austin took another partner and opened Austin & Stone's Museum elsewhere along Washington Street. Keith's second dime museum enterprise, this time with Andrew Cullen, came and went without more than a trace a month or so later. George H. Batcheller, Keith's onetime circus boss and John Doris' former partner, had come to Boston in the autumn of 1882 to find a way to generate income during the eight months a year that the touring circus laid off. Batcheller agreed to partner Keith in a more ambitious dime museum if Keith could come up with his half of the amount Batcheller estimated they needed as a financial stake. Keith turned to E. F. "Ned" Albee, who promptly bankrolled Keith's half interest. As it turned out, Batcheller's money was sufficient to open shop around April that same year, 1883.

Various names were attached to the Keith curio hall at 565–567 Washington Street: Gayety Museum, New York Dime Museum, Keith & Batcheller's Mammoth Museum and Gaiety Musee (neither the Gayety Museum nor the Gaiety Musee should be confused with the 1908 Gayety Theatre in Boston). Keith & Batcheller's occupied a street-level space, approximately 35 feet long, that narrowed from a 25-foot frontage to 15 feet wide in the rear. The space was carved out of the Adams House Annex. It was bordered on either side by the Boston Theatre and the Adams House hotel and restaurant.

The frontage of Keith & Batcheller's museum was bedecked with gaudily painted canvas banners depicting Bornean "savages," Siamese twins, African pygmies, sword swallowers and various so-called freaks such as the part man/part beast. The exhibits, some shams, failed to live up to the lurid promise of the *twelve-sheets*, and the appeal of the dime museums slackened as Keith headed into his first spring season. Bennie Keith again called on Ned Albee.

When Ned arrived, he was appalled at the shoddiness of the Keith-Batcheller operation. Neglected animals were crammed into filthy cages that exuded odors. Tawdry exhibits and advertisements discouraged the more fastidious. This time Albee agreed to stay in Boston, but Keith had to cede a fair amount of operational authority. The venerable Adams House hotel and restaurant and the conventional Washington Street shops that, at the time, were Keith & Batcheller's neighbors cannot have welcomed the sideshow storefront. Community pressure may have been more of a spur than any innate sensibilities possessed by Mr. and Mrs. B. F. Keith to clean up their enterprise and gradually adopt a policy that attested to their newfound virtue.

The block on Washington Street in Boston, from which Keith and Albee built their empire, had long hosted theatres. The Lion Theatre had been built there in 1836; it was renamed the Melodeon three years later. *Melodeon* was a frequently applied name for variety theatres as well as a common descriptive term for entertainment houses—akin to English music-halls—that served alcoholic beverages along with presenting variety performances. So the Melodeon (later known as Melodeon Varieties and New Melodeon) likely was the home of some of the earliest variety entertainments in Boston, further eroding Keith's reputation as the father of vaudeville. In 1878, the New Melodeon was enlarged and refurbished, with the auditorium moved to the second floor, and rechristened as the Gaiety Theatre.

The Gaiety was in operation next door to their dime museum and lecture hall when, in May 1883, Keith and Albee decided to enlarge their second-floor space into a proper theatre that seated 123. The Adams House owners leased Keith more space. Keith and Albee, in turn, cleaned up the vulgar signage and remodeled the curio hall as a box office and lobby, where customers waited to see the next show upstairs.

The second-floor lecture hall offered "educational and edifying" demonstrations. This stab at fake propriety had been a ploy since Colonial days to skirt local blue laws that discouraged common entertainments, either by banning them on Sundays or banning them every day. Keith's dime museum lectures and concerts included all manner of entertainments from pseudoscientific talks by Sam K. Hodgkin (who doubled as Keith's stage manager) about the resident thin man, bearded lady or dog-faced boy to musical offerings to song-and-dance routines by acts like Jerry & Helen Cohan (parents of baby boy George M. Cohan) and slapstick cross talk by a pair of 16-year-old boys, Joe Weber and Lew Fields, who later were to become producers and one of show business' bigger star attractions.

The third-floor attic housed lodging and eating quarters for the performers. Each person occupied an eight-by-ten-foot partitioned space in which to sleep and change into costumes. A large table occupied the center of the room and alternated as a communal table for makeup and dining. Ma Keith charged performers $6 per week, an amount that was one half to one third of what Keith paid the act.

Ned Albee, as he was known in his circus and carnival days, had begun as a roustabout and an outside ticket man (one who sold circus tickets at an inflated price outside the circus grounds). He proved a smart operator, so circuses hired him as a fixer, one who took care of problems. Through his good advice and industry, Albee rose in importance to the Keith-Batcheller operation, becoming Keith's fourth partner when, in a year's time, Batcheller departed Boston and Keith. Thus began the lucrative and legendary careers of Benjamin Franklin Keith and Edward Franklin Albee.

Theatre historian Stan S. Spence has made a long study of American theatres, including those owned, managed and booked by Keith and Albee. He confirmed that the first true Keith theatre (as distinguished from a dime museum lecture hall) was, indeed, the Bijou Theatre. Prior to Keith and Albee, George H. Tyler and Frederick Vokes had taken over the Gaiety Theatre, in December 1881. They gutted it, renovated it and renamed it the Bijou Theatre, and they opened for business 11 December 1882. They also leased part of the annex to the Adams House (hotel) for a first-floor lobby, and two stairways led to their second-floor auditorium. The Bijou's address was 545 Washington Street.

A great ballyhoo announced the Bijou's presence and attractions: fireproof construction and safety doors, electric lighting (the first theatre in the USA to have it) with a massive chandelier, a 40 foot dome, a 60-foot-high proscenium and seating for 1,000 patrons. A number of Gilbert & Sullivan operettas were performed at the Bijou.

Keith's and Albee's upstairs performance space prospered. In 1884, they added a 400-seat performance space within the ground-floor area that was a part of the Adams House Annex. Business increased, and Keith and Albee decided to expand further by acquiring, on 27 September 1886, the Bijou lease from Tyler and Vokes. It was at the Bijou Theatre, late in 1886, that Keith first launched continuous vaudeville.

Over the decades that it remained a Keith property, the Bijou was given several names: Keith's Bijou Theatre, Keith's Bijou Opera House, B.F. Keith's Bijou Dream Theatre and B.F. Keith's Bijou Theatre. After the Keith-Albee empire was taken over by Joe Kennedy and his associates, it became successively the RKO Bijou Theatre and the Intown Theatre and was again the Bijou Theatre when it closed 31 December 1943 and was razed in 1951.

Although the Bijou had hosted Gilbert & Sullivan productions under previous managements, neither Keith nor Albee seemed to appreciate the popularity of the comic operettas until the Hollis Street Theatre, four blocks south of Keith's, opened its doors in 1885 with a full-blown production of Gilbert & Sullivan's *The Mikado*.

W. S. Gilbert and Arthur Sullivan had failed to obtain copyright protection in the USA for their creations, so from the 1880s on, their shows were pirated regularly by American producers. Keith and Albee joined the ranks of the purloiners when they produced their own version of *The Mikado*—a stripped-down, one-hour show nearly devoid of the capable musicians, handsome sets and costumes expected by aficionados. Albee redid the entryway in a genteel Japanese motif. On the sidewalk, Ned Albee assumed his carny pitchman's persona and ballyhooed, "Why pay $1.50 when you can see our show for 25 cents?" Enough of the Boston public found a measure of appeal or logic in that slogan to turn Keith & Albee's nickel-and-dime *Mikado* into a paying proposition, and a season of *tabloid opera* ensued.

Four years earlier, Batcheller had left Boston because the dime museum had failed to yield the income he expected. The growing influence of Albee may have been a factor. Batcheller relocated to Providence, Rhode Island, to operate the Westminster Musee. Not to be outdone by a former partner, Keith, his wife and Albee made their move into Providence. They acquired the Providence Museum, renovated and expanded it and opened it 21 March 1887 as the Gaiety Museum. It alternated between comic opera and vaudeville. On 14 May 1888, they leased Loew's Opera House (W. H. Loew, not Marcus Loew), rechristened it the Gaiety Opera House and offered the same type of bills—vaudeville and comic opera; later they renamed it Keith's Gaiety Opera House. Committed fully to continuous vaudeville and eschewing light opera, they changed the name a third time—Keith Gaiety Theatre, then shortened it to Keith's Theatre.

Albee pushed for more expansion and turned to Philadelphia, where they acquired an existing commercial building on North Eighth Street, which they reconstructed into B.F. Keith's Bijou Theatre. When Albee discovered that the Union Square Theatre in Manhattan was for sale but on the brink of an agreement, Albee pushed Keith to a quick decision. They bought it, finished the season with the previously booked attractions, refurbished it throughout the summer (it had been renovated in 1888) and reopened it on 18 September 1893 as B.F. Keith's Union Square Theatre.

Back in Boston, Albee persuaded Keith in 1892 that the Bijou, as it existed, no longer was large enough for their business. They purchased the Bijou building, including the stores below it and the hotel annex above. The rear of the property backed up to Mason Street and the front was set on Washington Street between the Adams House to the south and the Boston Theatre on the north side. All of this they turned into a new theatre.

On 24 March 1894, two years after construction began, the local dignitaries of the day turned out for an inaugural reception at B.F. Keith's New Theatre, a lush medley of white marble, ornamental ironworks, gilt-framed mirrors, rose pink and Nile green brocaded wall surfaces, cherry-wood rails, carmine carpeting, brass and gold-finish fixtures, potted plants, murals galore, bric-a-brac, ersatz Louis XV furniture and an "electrolier" (electrically powered chandelier). Because of the hundreds of electric light fixtures, the preexisting available supply of electricity was inadequate for the theatre, so Keith and Albee installed their own generating system—three 100-kilowatt dynamos in the subbasement. This too was open for public inspection and approval.

Two days later, 26 March, the 3,000-seat house presented its first show to the general public. If Boston's leadership circle had been impressed with the new theatre, the hoi polloi were awed by its paradisiacal opulence and 115 uniformed attendants in evidence everywhere from ticket booths to lounges to boiler rooms. Perhaps nothing wowed them as much that summer as the cooled air from the ice chambers below that was forced up through vents under the orchestra seats.

For two months the bill of fare alternated between comic opera and continuous vaudeville, but by the summer, Keith's New Theatre adopted a straight vaudeville policy. To pull traffic from Boston's two major commercial thoroughfares, Washington and Tremont streets, which were parallel and little more than a block apart, Albee and Keith constructed two entrances. The main one was at 547 Washington Street, underneath the Bijou upstairs. A second entrance faced the Boston Common at 163 Tremont Street and led into a tunnel beneath the intervening Mason Street, creating an underground thoroughfare that funneled customers into Keith's New Theatre. The loading dock and stage entrance led to 40 Mason Street. With the opening of the new theatre, the old Bijou upstairs was renamed the Bijou Opera House.

After its initial summer season, B. F. Keith's New Theatre adopted a big-time policy of only two shows a day and reserved seating. Years later, when the Shuberts took over the lease, they named it the Shubert-Apollo Theatre and the Shubert-Lyric Theatre. After it became a motion picture house, it was renamed: the RKO Lyric Theatre and then, at various later times, the Normandie Theatre, the Art Movie Theatre, the Mirth Movie Theatre and the Laff Movie Theatre, by which name it was still known when it closed in 1951 and was torn down a year later.

In *Vaudeville: from the Honky-Tonks to the Palace,* author Joe Laurie Jr. mentioned Keith's Colonial Theatre and claimed that it opened in 1893. This reference has been repeated by others, including the respected John E. Dimeglio and Charles and Louise Samuels. These citations have caused some problems. Some folks have confused Keith's Colonial with the still-standing Colonial Theatre in Boston, a legit house that opened in 1903, a decade later. Further, a "Colonial Theatre" does not appear in the Keith records of its Boston theatres.

There are two possibilities for a Keith's Colonial. The close match in description suggests it was the same palatial edifice known as B. F. Keith's New Theatre, which has been recorded as opening in 1894, the year after the supposed opening of Keith's Colonial. Perhaps *Colonial* was the intended name and Keith's *New* Theatre was a bow to what all Boston must have called it during construction. The other possibility is that a Keith's Colonial never existed. The 1894 promotional material for Keith's New Theatre confirms that only six Keith houses were in operation at the time: two each in Boston and Providence and one each in Philadelphia and New York. Stan Spence cautions that there is no hard evidence as yet discovered that supports the existence of a Keith's Colonial in Boston.

Albee possessed vision and ambition, and he put a strong hand to the rudder. Increasingly over the next decade, Albee made decisions and Keith okayed them and took credit for them in newspaper stories and magazine articles. Their business expanded and prospered, but because they named and renamed their theatres, employing the same or similar names—Gaiety, Bijou, Keith's—for different theatres in different places, it has been difficult to sort out new enterprises from old. Sometimes there was simply a change of name. Other times, the building was expanded or replaced. To complicate matters further, the numbered street addresses may not have remained constant throughout the period.

Keith and Albee furthered each other's agenda, and the men remained fast and trusting partners. Keith wanted and got the glory. Albee wanted and took the power. Others they did business with were not as favored. On 12 May 1906, Keith and Albee took on a foremost competitor, F. F. Proctor, as a partner, forming the Keith & Proctor circuit. Proctor and Keith had a prickly relationship because both were acquiring theatres in New York City and Philadelphia, Keith did not trust Proctor, and Proctor had no respect for Keith. Albee had tried to make the partnership work, but it was dissolved 27 July 1911. However, Keith and Proctor continued to do business together when necessary to their financial interests, largely because Albee, as emissary, smoothed the way. By 1906, the story of Keith vaudeville had become Edward Franklin Albee's story, one of successful expansion and attempts at regulation and consolidation.

In later years, it became the Keith organization's mission to gild the history of its founder, obscuring his beginnings in sideshows and dime museums in the brighter light of comparative respectability afforded by *polite vaudeville*. Respectability had been a condition for the initial investment Keith received from the Roman Catholic Diocese in Boston and remained so for future diocesan financing; it also proved good business.

After Mary Keith died in 1910, B.F. Keith married Ethel Chase, the daughter (one expert who worked for the organization insists that she was Chase's niece) of P.B. Chase, then owner of Chase Theatre in Washington, D.C. Keith was not well; he was reported to be suffering from a nervous condition, a rather common euphemism of the day that covered a variety of incapacitating illnesses. In 1914, shortly after his second marriage, B.F. Keith died while yachting off the coast of Florida. His son, Paul, died four years later, a victim of the great influenza epidemic of 1918.

If there had been any question about who had been pulling the strings, the death of the Keith clan left the facts bare and apparent. Albee, long the puppeteer, was left in sole control in name as well as fact, and greater glory was ahead.

See E.F. Albee, Keith-Albee-Orpheum Circuit, Keith Vaudeville Exchange, National Vaudeville Artists, Inc., United Booking Office, Vaudeville Managers Association and Vaudeville Managers Protective Association

KEITH VAUDEVILLE EXCHANGE

Formally known as the B. F. Keith Vaudeville Exchange, this corporation was the successor to the United Booking Office (UBO). The change of name (to honor B. F. Keith after his death) was greater than any change in intent or policy. The Keith Vaudeville Exchange functioned, as the owners and managers saw it, as "a general board of trade for vaudeville theatres, artists and their representatives," in the words of Edward F. Albee. Like the UBO, the Keith Exchange maintained a streamlined and standardized process of booking, one that was to the owners' advantage. Performers did benefit from more coherent routes and, in the best of circumstances, knowing ahead of time how many weeks they would be booked in a season—but only if they were compliant employees. Those vaudevillians who tried to buck the UBO and the Keith Exchange likely found themselves stuck with long jumps between engagements and fewer bookings. Whether an act was submissive or regarded as a troublemaker, terms were dictated rather than negotiated.

HARRY KELLAR

b: (Heinrich Keller) 11 July 1849, Erie, PA—d: 10 March 1922, New York, NY

A daredevil youngster, Harry was a druggist's apprentice until, experimenting with soda and sulfuric acid, young Henry, as he then was called, caused an explosion and was fired. His solution to the problem was to hop a freight train. He ended up in Cleveland, where he got jobs clerking in a store and working in a newspaper printery.

He next headed to New York City, where he became one of the thousands of homeless newspaper boys, sleeping where he could until a minister took an interest in his welfare and brought him to Canandaigua in upstate New York to work as a farm boy. In a nearby town 15-year-old Harry saw a show performed by Isaiah Harris Hughes, billed as the "Fakir of Ava." Harry was enthralled. When Hughes advertised for an assistant, Harry's farming career ended.

In stage magic, as in many things, today's assistant becomes tomorrow's competition. Harry Keller failed at 16 when he first tried his own act, and he returned to the Fakir of Ava. Two years later Harry had developed enough as a performer to give a good show, but he had a hard time making a living. He needed money to invest in his act, and bookings were not easily obtained. One promoter ran off with the box office. He left Harry stranded, and Harry's props were attached for unpaid bills. Tiring of bad breaks and with his resolve dimmed, at age 20 he took a job as an assistant to the Davenport Brothers. At least the Davenports were a top-flight illusionist act that purported to be able to commune with spirits.

Besides learning a few tricks of the trade, Harry moved from being an assistant to an advance agent and then the business manager for the Davenport troupe. The haughty attitude of William Davenport prompted Harry to leave their show. William Melville Fay, Harry's senior in age and experience, also left the Davenport show, and the two men formed an act, the centerpiece of which was the Davenport Brothers' spirit cabinet act.

Fay & Keller began with some small-time engagements in Canada and the border states of the Dairy Belt and worked their way as far south as Mexico, Cuba, Panama, Ecuador, Peru, Chile, Uruguay, Argentina and Brazil. En route to Europe, the ship transporting Bill Fay and Harry Keller ran aground and sank off the coast of France. Bill and Harry lost their props, equipment, costumes, clothes and their savings—roughly $20,000 in gold coins and jewels packed in their trunks. The survivors were picked up out of the ocean and taken to England. Once there, Harry learned that he was broke; his banking house in the USA had gone belly up. William Fay, older and defeated, returned to the employ of the Davenport Brothers.

Harry Keller hocked what he had, salvaged some late deposits that had not been banked and rebuilt his act, calling it "The Royal Illusionists," and added a canary in a cage vanishing act to the cabinet séance. The new act played the Caribbean and western United States before embarking for a long tour that took Keller to Australia, Indonesia, China, India and on to the Middle East and to European settlements in Africa. While in Asia, Harry changed the spelling of his last name from Keller to Kellar so that people would not think he was trying to capitalize on the name of the far better known magician Robert Heller.

Harry Kellar was 29 years old when he reached London and Paris. When he arrived in New York he learned that Robert Heller had died unexpectedly. Despite altering the spelling of his own name, newspapers accused Harry of trading on Heller's name. Perhaps for that reason, Harry's dates in the USA failed to draw audiences, and he set sail for Brazil, Uruguay and then England, where he began his second world tour late in 1879, this time traveling from west to east.

To his featured illusions of the disappearing canary and the cabinet séance, Harry added several automatons—mechanical figures that performed as if taking instruction from Kellar. The automatons played musical instruments and drew sketches. Harry had appropriated both the automaton and canary disappearance acts from John Nevil Maskelyne in London, so Harry was careful when playing England not to use those illusions. The second world tour ended in September 1884, nearly five years after it had begun.

In Australia, Harry met Eva Medley; he married her in 1887, while as a star he was making his first extensive tour in the USA. After performing six months in Manhattan at the Comedy Theatre, Kellar played dates in the Midwest and on the West Coast. During his tour of the USA and then Mexico, a rivalry developed between Kellar and Alexander Herrmann, who was a half dozen years older than Harry and well established in America. The competition included dirty tricks and threatened to bankrupt both men. According to reports, Herrmann was the more deft, inventive and charming magician; Kellar was extraordinarily disciplined, attentive to detail and a master at large-scale illusions. The two rivals became friends before Herrmann retired.

Kellar was lean, and as he grew older, he sported a large mustache and made a dapper appearance onstage. Over the years, like all magic acts, he employed a number of assistants. To add variety to his evening-length show, he hired younger prestidigitators and illusionists, one of whom was William Ellsworth Robinson, who, calling himself Chung Ling Soo, later did a copycat act modeled on Ching Ling Foo.

Harry also added his wife, Eva, to the packaged show, and she performed a mentalist act. When not on the road, Harry and Eva Kellar resided in their Yonkers, New York, home.

By 1904, Harry Kellar was losing his sight and knew he had to make plans to retire. A younger stage magician, Howard Thurston, offered to buy Harry's act. In 1907 they joined forces in what was billed as Harry Kellar's farewell tour. Kellar had added a levitation illusion to his show.

Harry and Eva retired to a magnificent home in Los Angeles; unfortunately, Eva died within a few years. Kellar continued to experiment and create new illusions, and his home was open to old friends such as Harry Houdini and Ching Ling Foo, but he never performed on the stage again, except in 1917, when, at Houdini's urging, Kellar agreed to participate in a special show at the Hippodrome in Manhattan. It was staged by the Society of American Magicians for the benefit of families of American doughboys who had died in the First World War. He was 68 years old; for his part in the show he levitated a table and escaped from his spirit cabinet as of old. As Kellar's act concluded, Houdini and other fellow magicians brought onstage a sedan chair in which Kellar was seated. The huge Hippodrome orchestra played "Auld Lang Syne," and the 6,000-person audience rose in tribute as Kellar was borne offstage in a cascade of flowers to great applause.

ANNETTE KELLERMAN

b: 6 July 1887, Marrickville, New South Wales, Australia—d: 5 November 1975, Southport, Australia

If Harry Houdini had any rival who attracted the spotlight, it was a shapely young swimmer from Australia named Annette Kellerman. Other athletes had sought to cash in on the fame they won on the baseball diamond or the boxing ring. A World Series victory or a prize fight championship triumph was often good for a series of appearances in vaudeville theatres, but most sports figures' shelf life as vaudeville attractions usually dulled faster than the finish on a silver plate trophy cup. Among the male athletes, only James J. Corbett, the boxer turned monologist, was able to build a great vaudeville career.

Annette Kellerman was the only woman athlete to prosper in vaudeville season after season. She came to the entertainment business without silver cups, gold medals or Olympic laurel leaves. Annette had a father, however, who had an instinctive flair for publicity. He was not a Svengali exploiting his teenage daughter. Both he and his wife were musicians and had experience in show business. They had cared for their sickly daughter who had weak and deformed legs. The diagnosis at the

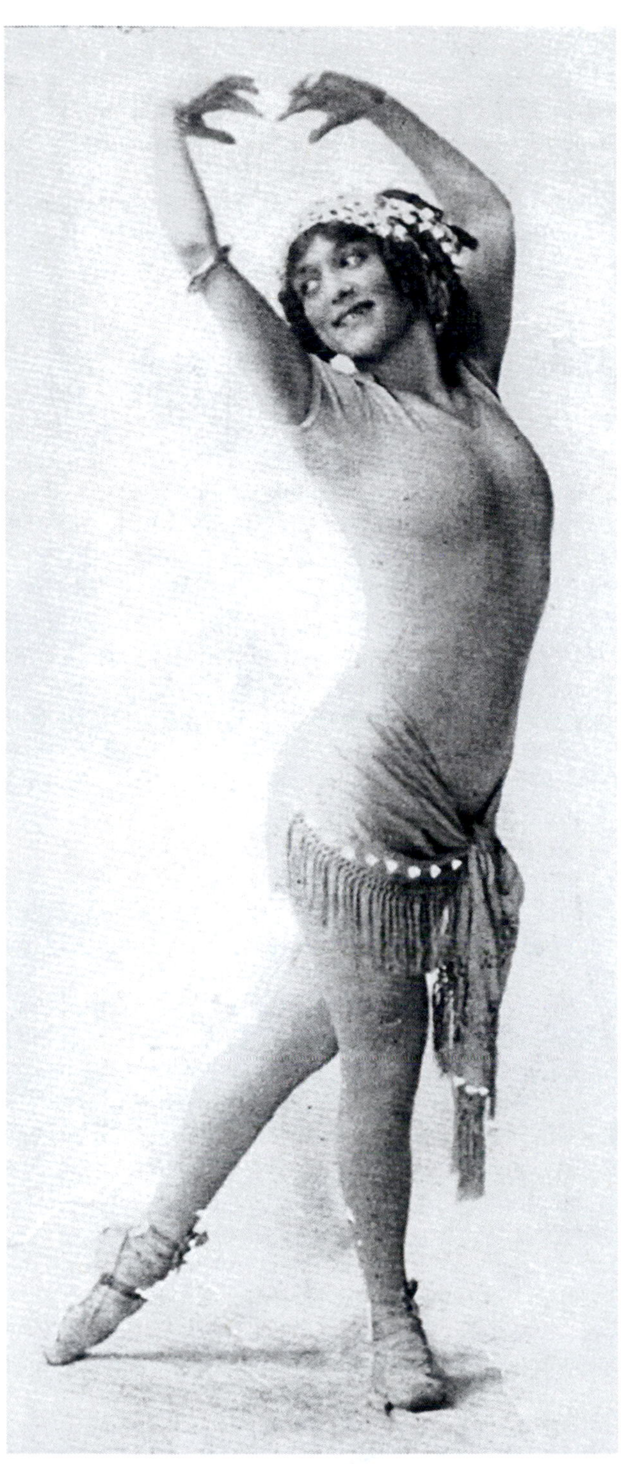

Annette Kellerman

time failed to name a cause, but it was later assumed by doctors that she had contracted polio.

Annette spent her baby years with iron leg braces that enabled her to totter about; the braces helped straighten her legs, and the local doctor recommended swimming. It was quickly apparent that Annette took to water; she learned to swim with minimal instruction. She felt more at ease in water than on land, and by her early teens she had developed into an accomplished swimmer.

She began training under former Olympic champion Freddie Lane and entered amateur competitions. In 1902, when she was 14, Annette won a few regional matches, including the New South Wales 100-yard swim in the women's division, and then set a world's record for completing a one-mile swim in 28 minutes. The trick was how to turn her amateur achievements into a professional career.

Annette's father became her manager, and they began a tour that took several years. They entered swimming events in eastern Australian cities, then traveled to Europe, where they tried to garner as much attention and publicity as they could. They were most successful in England, where Annette gave a well-publicized distance exhibition by swimming 15 miles down the Thames River from London. People crowded the route to cheer her.

Having demonstrated an ability to draw a crowd, music-hall entrepreneurs offered her contracts to swim onstage. That was not a matter casually arranged. A glass water tank had to be constructed that was large enough to permit Annette to dive into it, swim about gracefully and allow an audience to watch.

Newspapers were agreeably complicit in promoting Kellerman. For exclusive rights to photograph the event and to interview her, one newspaper underwrote the cost of an attempt to swim the English Channel. Annette and a half dozen male swimmers tried their best but failed to complete the crossing. Nevertheless, newspapers were sold. Annette tried twice again without success. News of her attempts flooded the French press, and she found willing audiences in Paris. Her defeat of an Austro-Hungarian champion in a long-distance swim of the Danube River helped stimulate box office in other large European cities that she toured in 1906.

Annette Kellerman and her father, determined to conquer America in 1907, established a beachhead at Revere, Massachusetts, a seashore and amusement park north of Boston. At the time, the accepted garb for women frolicking at the seashore was a three-piece outfit consisting of a headpiece like a large floppy shower cap to hold their pinned-up tresses, a pair of wide bloomers that reached well below the knees and a loose tunic with a skirt over the bloomers and sleeves at least to the elbows. They also wore rubberized slippers to keep feet dry.

Annette appeared on the beach in a form-fitting one-piece bathing suit. To ensure press coverage, Boston and New York City newspapers had been tipped off, and the local police were probably alerted that a transgression was to take place. The upshot was Annette's arrest. It had various ramifications. The injustice stirred the feminists. It is likely that this was the first time that a majority of men of that era agreed with feminists on a single issue of women's rights.

Of more immediate benefit to the Kellermans were offers from vaudeville managers, including Edward F. Albee, the power behind the Keith throne. It was Albee, despite Mr. and Mrs. Keith's puritanical insistence on banning anything that was sensuous, who put Kellerman onstage with a series of full-length mirrors arrayed in a semicircle in the background, ensuring that not one customer in his audience would miss an angle of Annette's diving technique. Her exhibition of fancy diving required a water tank, seven feet deep with a capacity of 25,000 gallons. After her success at Keith's New Theatre in Boston and Proctor's Fifth Avenue, her weekly vaudeville take was $2,000, and that was before her productions grew increasingly elaborate.

It was expensive to transport a glass tank to theatres (most of which did not have them). Major fairs and resort parks with aquatic facilities and hippodrome theatres, provided Kellerman with her best venues. In those she could give exhibitions of diving and various swimming strokes and present what essentially was becoming a flash act.

Annette's father was elderly, and management of her career was taken over in 1910 by James Sullivan, her press agent. They married. She attempted the legitimate stage once, in 1911, but the play, *Undine,* ran only four months. Vaudeville and fairs were better venues for her talents.

In 1912, a rumor, unsubstantiated by any press reportage, circulated that one of Kellerman's mermaids misjudged her dive into a seaside tank and broke her neck. Perhaps the management handled the matter with discretion and money. Kellerman remained a headliner in vaudeville.

The sensation that Annette Kellerman caused was reflected in her various billings: "The Australian Mermaid," "Divine Venus," "Queen of the Mermaids," and "Neptune's Daughter." Buried beneath the hoopla about Kellerman's alluring figure was a debate about morality, health and sensible fashion. What bluenoses saw as the corruption of virtue and depraved displays of near nudity, others, especially the younger generations, saw as attractive, sensible and far less immoral than the First World War being fought in Europe.

Annette framed the issue as one of healthful living. There was no doubt that severe corseting had caused damage to many women's organs. Instead of reducing and exercising, too many women laced themselves ever more tightly. Annette espoused exercise, moderation in eating and simpler clothing.

Annette's apogee in vaudeville was her performance at New York's Hippodrome Theatre, which was equipped with a 200-by-110-foot stage that opened to reveal a huge swimming tank below the stage floor. Annette's first production there was *The Big Show* (1916). Originally, prima ballerina Anna Pavlova was engaged to dance the "Sleeping Beauty" portion of the tripartite production. A Sunday performance by the ballerina resulted in an arrest (no dancing allowed on Sundays). Once that was quashed, Pavlova undertook a profitable tour of the USA.

"The Enchanted Waterfall" replaced Pavlova's portion of the show, and Annette Kellerman reigned over two hundred young female water sprites. They posed prettily, scampered about and dove into the pool, never to emerge. The water tank contained tunnel chambers at either end so that the young women exited into the air backstage, out of the audience's view. It was a magical effect. Annette capped the production number with a high dive over the onstage waterfall. The show ran 426 performances—an entire season.

Kellerman was back, as were Pavlova and Toto, at the Hipp the next season for *Cheer Up.* Annette's portion of the show was given a Luna Park, Coney Island, setting, complete with lagoon and attendant water nymphs, minarets, sparkling lights and stars against a night sky. Dancing girls and bathing beauties cavorted, music played and the Siren of the Sea gave a diving exhibition.

Annette Kellerman enjoyed a profitable career in silent movies. Her pictures were a blend of adventure, romance and exoticism. Many of them capitalized on her billing matter for their colorful titles, which suggest plot and setting: *The Bride of Lammermoor* (1909), *Jepthah's Daughter* (1909), *The Gift of Youth* (1909), *Entombed Alive* (1909), *Siren of the Sea* (1911), *The Mermaid* (1911), *Neptune's Daughter* (1914), *Daughter of the Gods* (1916), *Coney Island* (1917), *Queen of the Sea* (1918), *What Women Love* (1920) and *Venus of the South Seas* (1924).

Semiretired by 1925, Kellerman gave lectures and invested in a health food shop in Los Angeles. She frequently returned to Australia, where she performed for the motion picture camera every few years. She made five short films that demonstrated diving techniques and her versions of water ballet. The last was filmed in 1940–41.

The remainder of her life was quiet, at least until 1952, when MGM promoted a fictionalized biopic of Kellerman, *Million Dollar Mermaid,* a grand Technicolor splash starring Hollywood's greatest swimming star, Esther Williams. The press noted that, at 65, Annette Kellerman still swam daily, a discipline she continued into her 80s, but by the time the original Million Dollar Mermaid died in 1975 at age 88, most Americans and doubtless some British and even Australians were not quite sure what all the fuss was about. Annette Kellerman was inducted in 1974 into the International Swimming Hall of Fame.

AL KELLY

b: (Abraham Kalish) 18 December 1896—d: 7 September 1966, New York, NY

It has been the fantasy of many a comedian to meet his death with applause and laughter. For Al Kelly, a perennial second banana, that fantasy came true.

A member of the Friars Club and a frequent visitor at their Manhattan and Los Angeles locations, Al participated in many of the Friars' roasts. These events were primarily fund-raisers. To ensure a good draw, a full house, and a fat kitty, the Friars chose well-known honorees, guests of honor who got insulted by a dozen funny and foul-mouthed fellow comedians. Al was one of the comedians booked to roast the dean of nightclub monologists, Joe E. Lewis. Never was Al Kelly funnier. He had the crème of the comic crop falling off their chairs as he skewered Joe E. Lewis. Kelly returned to his seat on the dais, sat down and died during the applause.

Al Kelly, well loved, decent and generous, had never broken into the golden circle of comic greats. Yet at least a few of the star comedians who surrounded Al's dead body, sad as they felt for losing a dear friend, must have envied the way he died—at the top of his game and amid the rush of laughter and cheers.

He broke into vaudeville in a small-time act called the Nine Crazy Kids. Eventually, he went solo as a monologist but it was not until he bollixed up a joke that he did something that singled him out from the pack of stand-up comedians trying to break through into the big time. It was the 1930s, and Kelly was performing on the Borscht circuit in the Catskill Mountains district of midstate New York.

His fumbling of the joke proved funnier than his usual reading. It dribbled out in nonsense syllables and convulsed his audience. From that point on, Al Kelly was synonymous with double-talk. He claimed a difference with other comedians who employed it; Al maintained that they just spouted a lot of nonsense syllables whereas he, Kelly, inserted bogus words and phrases into otherwise sensible and well-phrased sentences. He claimed to have been hired to speak at several corporate functions—in the medical and technology fields—and to have been able to sustain the illusion of being expert in the science until well into his routine.

Mostly, however, he stooged for other comedians: chief among them, Lew Parker and Willie Howard. A short film, called *Comes the Revolution,* was made of Willie Howard's soap box socialist agitator act. Willie was able to attract only one listener as he spouted the party line. Al Kelly simply stood there, occasionally emitting a halfhearted cheer. When he had something more to say, it quickly degenerated into gibberish. Al and Willie appeared together in the short-lived *The Passing Show of 1945.* The show didn't even reach Broadway; it was the last time the Shuberts tried to revive the venerable revue series they had taken over in 1912.

Kelly came closer to being a full partner in an act when he and Joey Adams formed a team, but it was not a lasting arrangement. On television, Al Kelly was seldom hired to do more than a few minutes of his double-talk routine. During the late 1940s, the 1950s and the 1960s, Al appeared on TV variety shows such as Ed Sullivan's *Toast of the Town, The Steve Allen Show* and *The Dinah Shore Chevy Show,* but Ernie Kovacs made better use of Kelly's abilities. Al Kelly was a regular on Kovacs' series for the 1956 season.

Al was a thin, bony-faced man who looked like a Damon Runyon mugg. If his career was restricted by his success as a double-talk comedian, he had the satisfaction of knowing that his name was synonymous with the bit.

GENE KELLY

b: (Eugene Curran Kelly) 23 August 1912, Pittsburgh, PA—d: 2 February 1996, Los Angeles, CA

Fred Kelly

b: (Fredric Norbert Kelly) 29 June 1916, Pittsburgh, PA—d: 15 March 2000, Tucson, AZ

People were surprised to find out that Gene Kelly had a dancing brother, Fred, who danced with him in vaudeville and even made a movie with Gene. They were more surprised to learn there were Five Kellys—Joan, James, Gene, Louise and Fred, in that birth order—a vaudeville dance act.

Starting in 1921, when Fred, the youngest, was five, The Five Kellys played church socials, benefits, Elks halls and small-time vaudeville houses in and around their hometown of Pittsburgh. They got their first big break when, through some booking snafu, Eddie and the Younger Foys (as Eddie Foy and six of the then-grown Seven Little Foys were billed at the time) were unable to make their engagement at the Nixon Theatre, and the Five Kellys took their spot on the bill.

The Kellys became a reliable local act, and they worked rather regularly through the 1920s. Sometimes all five were booked; other times, it was Gene and Fred or Gene, Fred and Louise. The two oldest kids, Joan and James, were not as interested in dancing and sort of outgrew the act; they were young adults in a kid act.

Dancing was the energy of musical comedies that had toured the country since the 1910s, and movies that talked, sang, danced and showcased Ruby Keeler, Fred Astaire and Ginger Rogers, Hal Leroy, Bill Robinson and Shirley Temple made Americans tap happy. Mothers saw little Shirley on the big screen, her banana curls bouncing as she tapped, and thought that their children were capable of a 50-million-to-one shot.

The truth of the situation in the late 1920s was that dance jobs were declining, not increasing. Broadway shows were running fewer weeks than it had taken to rehearse the show. Vaudeville bills were cut by half because it was cheaper and more of an audience draw to play a feature-length motion picture than hire another four acts to flesh out the bills. Still, Americans were dance mad.

An operator came to Pittsburgh and opened a dancing school. It was a fancy operation, and he attracted a lot of students who paid up front for lessons. When he skipped town with all the prepaid tuition money in 1928, Mrs. Kelly, a former performer, stepped in and took over the operation. Harriet Kelly's reputation as a responsible and honest person saved the jobs of the dance teachers. Her husband, Jim Kelly, took over the books. They changed the name to the Gene Kelly Studio, as Gene was the oldest of the three Kellys who continued to dance. Fred Kelly was 12 and perhaps the youngest dance teacher in the nation. Gene and Louise were 16 and 14, and Gene was in charge.

According to Fred, who told the story to Rusty E. Frank when she compiled her history of great percussive dancers and put their stories into a narrative she called *Tap! The Greatest Tap Dance Stars and Their Stories, 1900–1955*, the Kelly Brothers' next big break came when the Cab Calloway Cotton Club show played Altoona, Pennsylvania, and the Nicholas Brothers abruptly left the unit for Hollywood to make a film. The Kelly Brothers were hired, loved working with a jazz band of Cab's caliber and were held over. Cab arranged for their names to appear on a marquee—the first time.

Fred and Gene made a couple of short films of their dancing in 1932: *The Kelly Brothers* and *The Cap and Gown Revue,* taught at the family dance school and took available dance gigs. Gene also attended college. Upon graduation with a major in economics, he found there were few jobs in that field to be had in the middle of the Great Depression. Gene decided to crack Broadway and auditioned for several shows in New York.

His first show was *Leave It to Me* (1938), starring Victor Moore, William Gaxton and Sophie Tucker. Gene's Broadway debut was overshadowed by Mary Martin's debut in the same show. Mary sang "My Heart Belongs to Daddy" and became a star.

Gene's Broadway career meant the end of The Kelly Brothers as an act. Fred continued to work solo, teach and choreograph. His best-known opportunity came to Fred while he was in the U.S. Army during the Second World War. Irving Berlin had devised *This Is the Army,* a goodwill morale builder that turned into a hit show because of Irving's songs and the earnest performances of the men in uniforms (not a few of whom were ringers of a sort—entertainers, like Gene Nelson, James ("Stump") Cross and Larry Weeks, who had joined or been drafted into the army).

Gene's second show on Broadway was *One for the Money* (1939), a low-budget revue written and staged by Nancy Hamilton, rather like Leonard Sillman's *New Faces,* a no-star-power revue in which Hamilton had appeared.

When *The Time of Your Life* was revived in 1940, Gene took over the one dancing role (originally performed by Paul Draper) in the Saroyan drama. The show went on tour and Gene with it; meanwhile, it continued to run on Broadway, and Fred Kelly took Gene's place and won the Donaldson Award for his performance. Back in New York, Gene choreographed a few floor shows at Billy Rose's Diamond Horseshoe, a theatre-nightclub-restaurant, and met Betsy Blair, a young dancer whom he married in 1941 (they divorced in 1957).

Pal Joey (1940–41) ran a year despite some critics' unease at seeing the selfish, scheming characters of John O'Hara's short stories set onstage without an upgrade in morals. John O'Hara adapted his stories into the libretto, Rodgers & Hart wrote some of their best music and lyrics, and director George Abbott proved once again why he was Mr. Broadway. Gene Kelly played the leading man, a cynical opportunist—a louse. *Pal Joey* was the making of Gene Kelly and his last role on Broadway.

David Selznick brought Gene to Hollywood but had nothing in the pipeline for him, so Selznick's father-in-law, Louis B. Mayer, signed Kelly for MGM. Gene's first picture was *For Me and My Gal* (1942) with Judy Garland. Six more films, including two battlefield dramas, followed in quick succession. The dramas established that Kelly could act. *Du Barry Was a Lady* (1943) and *Thousands Cheer* (1943) built up Gene's credits, and *Cover Girl* (1944), made on loan-out to Columbia, costarred Gene with the gorgeous dancer and pinup girl Rita Hayworth and proved that Gene had potential as a musical comedy matinee idol and was able to choreograph his own movies.

When Gene Kelly returned to MGM, he made it clear to the studio that he intended to have a creative voice in his movies, and five out of his next seven movies proved he could guide a film. (In the middle of that bunch of films, Kelly served a short tour of duty in the navy.) Gene chose Stanley Donen as his assistant, and the pair were responsible for the most enjoyable postwar musicals made in Hollywood: *Anchors Aweigh* (1945), *The Pirate* (1948), *Take Me Out to the Ball Game* (1949) and *On the Town* (1949). Gene teamed with a distracted Judy Garland and the challenging Nicholas Brothers for *The Pirate,* demonstrated that he could be acrobatic like Fairbanks and Flynn in *The Three Musketeers* and taught Frank Sinatra how to dance for *Anchors Aweigh, Take Me Out to the Ballgame* and *On the Town.*

On the Town was a vibrant creation by directors Kelly and Donen, composer Leonard Bernstein and lyricists Adolph Green and Betty Comden, who also adapted their Broadway libretto for the screen. Gene and Frank were joined by Vera-Ellen, Ann Miller, Betty Garrett and Jules Munshin in the leads of three couples who find each other during a weekend furlough.

MGM could deny golden boy Gene Kelly little if anything after *On the Town,* and he got the green light to do a Gershwin movie, *An American in Paris* (1951), an imaginative film that paired him with a great partner, Leslie Caron, and won seven Academy Awards, including those for best picture and (Gene's) choreography. For all of the plaudits it deserved and received, *An American in Paris* marked a turning point, depending on one's bias, toward greater artistry in Gene's moviemaking or degree of pretentiousness. *Singing in the Rain* (1952) was certainly a corrective, if one were needed.

Singin' in the Rain and *The Wizard of Oz* rank on most lists of top movie musicals. *Singin' in the Rain* (1952) was Gene's third masterpiece, but it would not be one without Comden & Green's book, the comedy of Jean Hagen and Millard Mitchell and, especially, Donald O'Connor's comedy, singing and dancing. It was Gene's last completely successful film.

Gene Kelly and brother Fred reunited on the silver screen in a tap dance number, "I Love to Go Swimmin' with Wimmen," for *Deep in My Heart* (1954), a fictionalization of the life of Sigmund Romberg. *It's Always Fair Weather* (1955) is *On the Town* without perfection and good cheer. *Brigadoon* (1954) was cramped by MGM into a soundstage when it needed the space of the outdoors in some scenes. *Invitation to the Dance* (1956) showcased some of the finest dancers of their day: Carol Haney, Tommy Rall, Tamara Toumanova and Igor Youskevitch, but it tried too hard to sell art to the masses and served neither the movies nor serious dance.

Kelly ended his 15-year run as movieland's top male dancer with *Les Girls* (1957). Ahead were many years of work in film and on television as a dancer, choreographer, actor and director.

There will always be debate as to whether Gene Kelly or Fred Astaire was the better dancer. Kelly described the difference: "Fred Astaire represented the aristocracy, I represented the proletariat." Fred was sophistication and grace. Gene was athletic and sexy. Neither was in the same class as the great tap dancers, and both knew it. Astaire's and Kelly's genius (abetted by Hermes Pan, Stanley Donen and Carol Haney) was in combining forms like tap, ballroom dance, ballet and jazz dancing into character exposition and storytelling and making it work brilliantly for the movies.

Gene was a capable actor, like Fred Astaire, and both were better than most dancers. Gene did not play comedy well; Fred did. Gene was able to seem good-humored and play the hearty fellow, but he had the sense to leave the job of getting laughs to Donald O'Connor, Betty Garrett, Oscar Levant, Jules Munshin and Kay Kendall.

The one area in which Gene Kelly was superior to all other male dancers in the movies was as a romantic lead. The women in the audience might fantasize about dressing up and going out to a cosmopolitan supper club escorted by Fred Astaire and spending the evening dancing and dining with him, but they hoped that Gene Kelly was around to take them home.

JOHN T. KELLY

b: 26 August 1852, Boston, MA— d: 5 January 1922, New York, NY

Kelly was the only principal performer to appear in all eight seasons of the Weberfields Music Hall. He had begun as a boy, clog dancing on street corners. He was only 12 when he showed up at Waite's Hall in South Boston to audition for the producer, M.B. Leavitt, whose company was about to embark on a six-month tour of a few eastern states and the Canadian Maritime Provinces. After nearly missing the ship leaving from Boston's Long Wharf, Johnny began his professional life at Eastport, Maine, in 1865.

Along the route, jig and clog dance contests were often held. As Leavitt related: "I had with my own minstrel and vaudeville company, traveling through the British Provinces, a mere youngster named John T. Kelly, who was marvelously clever at performances of this kind, and in whom I took a sort of paternal pride as being his discoverer. Kelly, although of immature years, won some championships at clog dancing for my show, the best of which, perhaps, was in St. John, N.B., where, as he himself now says in relating his early experience, he 'danced the other fellow off the stage.'"

Kelly then joined Jennie Kimball's company; he performed as a pantomime clown in whiteface— a popular device since the mid-nineteenth century in the USA and exemplified by George L. Fox, 1825–77. Kelly hit a few rough patches in his career and eventually was induced by his parents to leave the stage to apprentice to a tailor. A year later, at age 15, Kelly forsook his scissors and tape measure to join a singing act, The Mocking Bird Serenaders, and in Buffalo, 1870, he played his first vaudeville engagement and discovered the most compatible stage medium for his talents. Within a year he was a favorite at Tony Pastor's Theatre at 201 Bowery, New York, where Pastor first introduced a *polite vaudeville* policy to attract the patronage of women.

At Pastor's, John T. Kelly developed his character as an Irish comedian and teamed up with Thomas J. Ryan. Billed as "Kelly & Ryan, the Bards of Tara," and made up as miners, they were a knockabout song-and-dance act with a distinctly Irish air. Their partnership lasted from 1871 until 1885. Kelly teamed with new partners, first Dan Mason and then Gus Williams, both German dialect comedians. In 1891 Kelly and Williams costarred in *U and I,* offered as a musical comedy but really a series of vaudeville specialties held together by a dream sequence.

Joe Weber and Lew Fields engaged both John T. Kelly and Thomas. J. Ryan for the first season of the Weber & Fields Music Hall in 1896–97, but they were signed separately and they performed separately. Kelly and Ryan worked together in the show but never spoke to each other offstage. Whatever their disagreement or offense, it has faded from the record. When Kelly joined Weber & Fields he was 40, nearly a decade older than most of the other principals.

Typical of his era and profession, John T. enjoyed his liquor and gambling; nevertheless he seems to have served the company's purposes well. During the second season, in his first major role, he played opposite Sam Bernard in *The Geezer,* the burlesk of the then popular musical *The Geisha.* Dressed in kimonos, they played Chinese, but Sam spoke his version of Chinese in his German accent and John T. Kelly in his peat bog brogue. The burlesk was the funnier for it.

Among Kelly's greater contributions to the Weberfields Music Hall was suggesting his friend Julian Mitchell as stage director for the shows. Skeptical of Mitchell because of his deafness and knowing him only as a former Shakespearean actor, Joe and Lew nevertheless engaged him when he said he could bring the show in on time and would work for their price.

After the Weber & Fields partnership was dissolved, John T. Kelly returned to vaudeville as a sketch comedian. In 1906 he was seen in "Senator McFee," a one-act playlet that was cribbed from one of its various incarnations since it was first presented as "A Cup of Tea" when Kelly was young. The summer previous to Kelly's outing, his old playmates from Weberfields, Mabel Fenton and Charlie Ross, had revived the sketch with Joseph Cawthorne at Asbury Park.

Kelly had a brief run late in the 1911 season at Wallack's Theatre in *A Certain Party.* He returned to Weber & Fields for their 1912 Jubilee show that marked their brief reteaming. He was 60 years old. Thereafter his career ceased to make news. A decade later, on 5 January 1922, the press accorded Kelly his final notice.

J. W. KELLY

b: (John Walter Shields) September 1857, Philadelphia, PA—d: 26 June 1896, New York, NY

As a reporter for the *New York Mirror* stated at the height of Kelly's career: "Every comedian on the variety stage has a following of his own. That is, he is sure of a warm welcome of the people in every theatre he visits, even if the others think he is, in the expressive language of the gallery god, 'on the cheese.' This rule does not hold good in the case of J. W. Kelly, he is a universal favorite, and the whole audience joins enthusiastically in the applause when he appears."

Vaudeville singers and comedians depended on professional song and joke writers. Some performers, like John Walter Kelly, were able to write their own material. Better known as J. W. Kelly, "The Rolling Mill Man," he was a highly regarded storyteller. Kelly walked onstage carrying a chair, which he placed downstage center. He sat, settled back and invited the audience to suggest topics. Choosing one that struck his fancy, Kelly would spin it into a 30-minute monologue.

Kelly was not born to the stage. His parents, Michael and Ann Shields, laborer and housewife, were Irish immigrants who settled in Philadelphia around 1850, a time of strong anti-Catholic and anti-Irish sentiment. In 1844, before the Shields family arrived in Philadelphia, vicious riots had broken out, and thugs burned two Catholic churches and a nunnery. The state militia had to be mobilized to quell the riots. Fifteen people were killed and 50 wounded. By 1860, the anti-immigrant, anti-Catholic feeling had led to the formation of a nativist political movement called the American Party—more usually called the Know Nothings.

Details of the future J. W. Kelly's early life are few, but Chris Simmons, a specialist in nineteenth-century show business and popular Irish theatre, has documented much of what is known about Kelly's life and career. Kelly attended Philadelphia's

Girard College, a business-trade school, where he studied telegraphy and the Morse system of code. Graduating with honors, Kelly entered the workforce as a telegraphic key operator for the Western Union Company. In later years, when interviewed, Kelly preferred to talk about his days as a manual laborer and seldom referred to his college education.

Unsatisfied with his work, Kelly gave up his job and left his family to travel western Pennsylvania as an apprentice tinsmith. Eventually he ended up as a steelworker in the mills around Pittsburgh, Gary, Indiana and Chicago. The mills produced sheet metal and were known as rolling mills. He capitalized on the experience when he entered vaudeville as "Rolling Mill Kelly":

I've a first cousin named Dan Maloney,
An honest relation and friend,
Who always has made a good living,
And has often a dollar to lend.
He is well known by all of the neighbors—
For a short name we all call him Dan,
And there's no one in town more respected
Than Maloney, the rolling mill man.
CHORUS
You will find him at church every Sunday,
Himself and his wife, Mary Ann;
The one who takes up the collection,
Is Maloney, the rolling mill man.
—"Maloney, The Rolling Mill Man" (J.W. Kelly)

Kelly recalled: "I used to entertain my fellow workmen with funny remarks and they advised me to go and make a living on the stage. I took their advice." John got his professional start in show business with Hawkins Minstrels, a small-time outfit. Hawkins suggested John change his name from Shields to Kelly, and the two men paired in a Dutch dialect act.

The following season, Kelly went out on his own but flopped at Miner's Bowery Theatre in Manhattan. Kelly dropped the Dutch characterization to create an Irish American character, and he played the Midwest for several seasons. An undated newspaper clipping gives the best approximation of his act: "His turns were unusually long, sometimes lasting for three-quarters of an hour, he never wearied his audience nor failed to get justification for another encore had he chosen to take it. . . . He appeared as an undersized, middle-aged, Irish-American, decently and characteristically dressed in black, with spectacles over which he looked with a quizzically solemn expression, as he rolled out his aphorisms, not gags or stories, but odd bits of whimsical comment on the ways of men and classes, which were irresistibly amusing. He had a powerful bass voice and used the brogue of New York."

His talents were not limited to performance. Kelly managed the Park and Garden theatres and owned seven saloons in Chicago. He also discovered in himself a facility for songwriting—not only for himself but for other performers as well. Variety and vaudeville singers like Maggie Cline came to Kelly for special material. He obliged Maggie by giving her a trunk song that turned into her biggest success, "Throw Him Down, McCloskey." His most famous song of the period was "Slide, Kelly, Slide," inspired by America's new national pastime, baseball, and one of its stars, Michael "King" Kelly. The title "Slide, Kelly, Slide" was based on a chant taken up by King Kelly fans in 1887 during the ballplayer's tenure with the Boston Nationals. Kelly's song reigned until Jack Norworth and Harry Von Tilzer, both vaudevillians, wrote "Take Me Out to the Ball Game" in 1904, a song that remained baseball's anthem a century later.

J. W. Kelly wrote his songs and told his stories about the life he saw around him. The labor movement was trying to get a foothold, and labor challenged industry during the 1880s and 1890s in the USA.

This is the reason that we must have strikes,
When men with a principle see
That monopoly boastingly tramples their rights,
In a land that was made for the free.
—"Strike On The C, B & Q" (J.W. Kelly)

Kelly gained his renown as a monologist. To herald the start of his act, the pit band played a few bars of "The Wearing of the Green," and the short, bespectacled Kelly, dressed in a black frock coat and top hat, entered from the wings. Leaning forward over the footlights he addressed the audience confidentially:

> Now, it's aisy enough to get a drink with money, but to get a drink without money—now that's where ye show your superiority over your fellow-man. Don't go into a barroom with a sort of a hope I don't intrude air and say to the bar-tender: "It's a cold morning this morning," bekase the minute ye go in there with your sure thing weather tips, he's got your number. Do the way I do. Walk up boldly to the bar and say: "Gimme a little liquor out of that black bottle." Now, back of every bar there are two bottles containing liquor. They're both alike, only one's a little worse than the other. No matter which one he offers ye, don't touch it. Stand back with an injured air and say: "I asked for a little liquor out of that black bottle." Then ye take the bottle and pour out a nice moderate sized drink. About two fingers [Kelly extends his hand with the first and little finger separated.] Now, at the end of every bar there is a receptacle containing cloves and spices. Ye select a clove, and whilst ye stand there munching

> on your clove and feeling in your pocket for the money, which ye haven't got, ye look out the door and suddenly "Great heavens, there goes me car," and dash out the door. Always close the door after ye, bekase no sane bartender is going to throw a heavy beer mallet through a plate glass door. And be sure ye catch that car—no matter whether it's going uptown or downtown—that's your car.

In 1892, Kelly decided to try New York again. His success in Chicago and throughout the Midwest had proved his skill and the quality of his material. "Tony Pastor saw me in Chicago and wanted to engage me for a week or two. I told him if I went to New York I would stay a year, and so I did. I received a warm welcome, and the same act which had been hissed in 1880 was applauded in 1892." Kelly and his wife set up their household in Manhattan with their two children.

"Rolling Mill" Kelly became one of the highest-paid performers in variety. He enjoyed working for Tony Pastor and performed almost exclusively at Pastor's theatre or on tour with Pastor's variety troupes. Kelly's final public appearance was, fittingly, at Pastor's Theater for a Sunday benefit concert in 1896.

The cause of Kelly's death, according to the death certificate, was Bright's disease, a kidney ailment. He was 38 years of age. Tributes appeared in the New York newspapers. "He was a fellow of infinite jest and most exquisite fancy but his jests and his quaint fancies will never again amuse and entertain the public who were wont to hang upon his words and find relief from the work and worry of everyday life in listening to his delightful drolleries. J.W. Kelly is dead. This means that the American Stage has lost one of its brightest lights, whose place can never be filled."

PATSY KELLY

b: (Bridget Sarah Veronica Rose Kelly) 12 January 1910, Brooklyn, NY—
d: 24 September 1981, Los Angeles, CA

There were far more Patsy Kelly types among American women than there were glamour girls, but few of them showed up on the silver screen. Patsy was the kid next door, rather plain, a bit of a tomboy, a good scout who took kidding but not insults. She probably could have knocked down more than half the boys her age if they were silly enough to pick on her. Patsy Kelly was more than a type, though; she was a fine comedian, an able dancer and a decent actor.

The family was Irish, and Patsy was the youngest of their first-generation offspring. According to Patsy, her father was a boozer who beat her mother.

Patsy Kelly

Early on, Patsy knew that she would never be part of such a bad bargain. She was tomboyish and hung around at the fire station in the Williamsburg section of Brooklyn. To push her toward more feminine ambitions, Patsy's mother sent her to dancing school, where she learned tap.

Over the next few years she developed proficiency and began to teach beginners. She was 16 in 1926 when her brother brought her along to perform a dance duet as part of an audition for Frank Fay. A headliner, Fay was acknowledged as one of the wittier and more original comedians of his day. Fay hired Patsy to dance in his act; her brother accepted a job as Frank's chauffeur.

Once she was in Fay's act, her role changed. Fay realized that Patsy's street kid contrasted nicely with his suave manner. His barbs tended to be indirect, and he often used stooges off whom he bounced his insults. Patsy's ripostes were direct and plainspoken. Both were able to ad lib.

Although Fay, like any vaudevillian, had a structured act in which he sang as well as told stories, he allowed himself time to talk to the audience and extemporize. Patsy showed that she usually could keep pace with the master in their verbal give-and-take, but she could never truly top him. Patsy served as Fay's stooge for several seasons on Keith & Orpheum big time until Frank dismissed her. A few seasons constituted a long relationship—professional, married or in friendship—for Frank Fay. Patsy Kelly was rare among people who knew and worked for him. She refused to denigrate him, saying only that he was a master and that she owed him a debt for what he taught her.

Before they split forever, Patsy went with Frank Fay into the cast of a revue, *Harry Delmar's Revels* (1927), that also starred Bert Lahr and Winnie Lightner. By the time Patsy stopped working with Fay, vaudeville was on the ropes, but Patsy had found the revue format agreeable.

An old friend from tap school, Ruby Keeler, promoted Patsy to several Broadway producers. The result was that Kelly went from stooging for Fay to appearing in several Broadway shows: *Three Cheers* (1928), a musical comedy with Will Rogers and Dorothy Stone, *Earl Carroll's Sketch Book* (1929), a revue with Will Mahoney and William Demarest, *Earl Carroll's Vanities of 1930,* starring Jimmy Savo, Jack Benny, the Condos Brothers, Thelma White and Herb Williams, *The Wonder Bar* (1931), a musical with Al Jolson, *Earl Carroll's Vanities of 1932,* with Milton Berle, Helen Broderick, Harriet Hoctor and Max Wall, and *Flying Colors* (1932), a musical comedy starring Clifton Webb, Tamara Geva, Larry Adler, Charles Butterworth, Monette Moore, Imogene Coca and Buddy & Vilma Ebsen.

In 1932, Hal Roach offered to put Patsy in movies. The Roach Studio was home to the two-reel comedies of Laurel & Hardy, Charlie Chase and Our Gang, and Roach had paired light comedian Thelma Todd with ZaSu Pitts. Stan Laurel & Babe Hardy had come together in a nearly random pairing, and Roach hoped to strike gold a second time by creating the first female comedy team in Hollywood. Roach paid poorly compared to the major studios, and Thelma and ZaSu reserved the right to work in features elsewhere. The supporting comedians on the Roach lot were the best, but the filming schedule was often little more than a week or two, and the dialogue writing often was repetitious and usually lackluster. ZaSu Pitts quit the series after two years, and Patsy, a very different type of comedian, took her place until 1935, when Todd died. The Todd & Kelly two-reelers saw no improvement in quality, yet a good reputation has attached to them.

The decade of the 1930s was an opportune time for wisecracking gals. Working girls Glenda Farrell and Joan Blondell kept things snappy at Warner Brothers, society snipers Roz Russell and Eve Arden pepped up MGM and Paramount called in Patsy Kelly when a movie needed its sophisticated stars sassed by an uppity employee. Other studios called on Kelly as needed, and she was a popular featured player into the early 1940s.

Her career slipped with the Second World War. Between 1943 and 1960 she did not make a single film. She had grown dowdy, and her personal life wasn't a secret. Had she been discreet, she might have survived either her reputation for drinking or her lesbianism in Hollywood. She was not, and Hollywood studios closed the gates.

Patsy had long been a good friend and roistering buddy of Tallulah Bankhead. Patsy was broke when she moved into Tallulah's home. Tallu, fresh from a critical success as star of NBC's radio extravaganza *The Big Show,* became one of the rotating hosts of NBC's television comedy-variety show, *All Star Revue.* Responding to network and sponsor fears that Tallu was too sophisticated for the great unwashed masses that regularly watched TV, Tallulah suggested, for contrast, that Patsy Kelly and Phil Foster be engaged as an Alice and Ralph Kramden-like couple. Patsy got a season's paychecks out of the deal, because the network and sponsors were right. Bankhead was too hip for TV, and 1952–53 was her sole season as one of the *All Star Revue* hosts. Onstage, Kelly appeared in support of Tallulah in *Dear Charles* and was part of Tallulah's Las Vegas fling at a nightclub act. Gigs with Tallulah were most of Kelly's work in the 1950s.

Later she made a comeback of sorts. Her first work in Hollywood in 17 years was as the maid in the comedy *Please Don't Eat the Daisies* (1960). A few more features followed but nothing that grabbed the public until *Rosemary's Baby* (1968), in which Patsy played a dramatic role as a witch. A 1976 television series failed. "I didn't save a dime. I was just happy, living. How did I know my career was gonna go into a coma?"

The stage did more for her reputation. When her old friend Ruby Keeler was enticed back to the stage for a revival of *No, No, Nanette,* she pulled Patsy into the cast in the small role of a maid. In 1971 Patsy Kelly was awarded the Tony for the best performance by a featured female actor in a musical, and the production ran for over two years before going on national tour. In 1973, Patsy was nominated again for her supporting role in a revival of another musical, *Irene.* She did not win, but the 1960s–70s revival craze had made Patsy Kelly employable again.

WALTER C. KELLY, "THE VIRGINIA JUDGE"

b: 29 October 1873, Mineville, PA—
d: 6 January 1939, Philadelphia, PA

Walter was the older brother of the Pulitzer Prize–winning playwright George E. Kelly and John B.

Kelly, the Olympic oarsman, politician and father of actor Grace Kelly. Walter was also the family's black sheep. A machinist who gambled and drank, he refused to meet his father's expectations. At 20, shut out of the family home, Walter headed for Newport News, Virginia, to work at the Huntington Shipyards.

The Newport News of 1894 was a dirty, dreary settlement resembling a West Coast mining camp or a prairie cattle town rather than an Old Dominion city. Kelly spent his free time with sporting types like the politicians who kept one hand lightly on the lid of flagrant illegality and the other hand counting votes and selling favors to bar owners, madams, gamblers and fight promoters.

As a lark, Walter C. Kelly frequented the local police court, which dispensed assembly-line justice to the city's poor blacks who had run afoul of Jim Crow law. A budding raconteur, Walter fashioned Judge Brown's summary sentencing into anecdotes for his sporting colleagues:

"Jim, this is the third time you've been here for cutting folks. How old are you?"

"I'se jest twenty-fo', Jedge."

"Well, Jim, you will be just twenty-five when you get out."

Walter joined the armed forces for the Spanish-American War in 1898. When discharged, he returned to Newport News. With his back pay and gambling wins, Walter opened the Mecca Café and sublet the second floor as a gambling den. The protests of do-gooders and his laissez-faire relationship with his account books persuaded him it was time to move on. Early twentieth-century New York City had a lot to offer a young Irish American, especially one with Kelly's charm and storytelling skill. His new social circle included vaudevillians, the satraps of Tammany Hall and gamblers.

Kelly made his public debut as a storyteller at "Big Tim" Sullivan's political club at 207 Broadway in the Bowery in 1900. This led to theatre bookings, including Tony Pastor's Theatre at Tammany Hall. Kelly was next engaged by B. F. Keith for his Union Square Theatre and Keith's theatres in Providence, Rhode Island, New Bedford, Boston, Lowell, Massachusetts, and Portland, Maine. This was followed by F. F. Proctor's theatres in Albany and Schenectady, New York. Being a performer suited Kelly and his resolute bachelor style. The few hours preparing for the stage and performing his act left plenty of time to play the bon vivant and to travel from hotel to hotel.

In 1904, Percy Williams booked Marie Dressler, a major star, to play his circuit, and Marie chose newcomer Kelly to play opposite her in *Sweet Kitty Swellairs,* a burlesk sketch. When Dressler fell ill, Williams persuaded Kelly to fill the spot alone, telling his stories. Walter C. Kelly had joined the top ranks of his profession.

The next year Kelly settled on his billing as "The Virginia Judge" and for 25 years was a fixture in big-time vaudeville and a solid success in England, Egypt, South Africa and Australia. By 1921, Walter was pulling in $2,000 a week, working 48 weeks a year, playing all of Keith's theatres and a few dates on the Orpheum circuit. By 1927, according to his own suspect reckoning, Kelly was commanding $4,000 a week and playing every date he wished.

Most people found Kelly a hail-fellow-well-met and saluted his canny mimicry of white Southern gentlemen, Southern blacks and the Irish. Yet his act, though comically folksy, was essentially racist. His monologues featured befuddled and unlettered blacks standing guiltily before a sage, cracker-barrel judge. He played all the parts in his trials, accenting his summary justice with raps of his gavel.

> I want order in the court, and, Dan, get those dogs away from that stove. It smells like a tan yard in here. First case on the docket—Sadie Anderson. "Yes, sir, that's me." Thirty days in jail, Sadie. That's *me*. Rufus Johnson, you are charged with larceny of two chickens from the premises of Howard Brooks on Brierfield Road. What have you to say about it? "Well, Jedge, I never was near Mr. Brook's house and the Lord may strike me down dead if I stole those chickens." Well, Rufus, you stand aside for ten minutes, and, if the Lord don't strike you, I will give you thirty days. Next case: Henry Harper. Drunk again, eh, Henry? You have been arrested five times in the last six weeks. "Yes, Jedge, I would have been here that other week but I got arrested over in Phoebus and couldn't come."

Usually, Kelly was politician enough not to overtly exhibit his prejudice, but he customarily called African Americans "darkies." In 1909, he refused to work on a vaudeville bill with Bert Williams & George Walker at Hammerstein's Victoria; perhaps he was jealous that they were bigger stars than he and earning more money. When Kelly shared the bill with another famous black act, Avery & Hart, Kelly aimed to wound. Avery & Hart had just finished singing their big number, "I Care Not for the Stars that Shine," and were taking their curtain call when Kelly was heard in the wings singing "I Care Not for the Shines that Star."

Along with his major career in vaudeville, Walter Kelly sometimes took a flyer in musical revues, including the Shubert hit *Whirl of the World* (1914), *The Show of Wonders* (1916), another hit, and the short-lived *Great Day* (1929). He also added other sidelines. Kelly made a large number of phonograph recordings for Victor and appeared on radio for the fledgling networks.

Kelly returned to the stage in 1933 in Maxwell Anderson's Pulitzer Prize–winning drama *Both Your Houses* and Sinclair Lewis' *The Jayhawker,* a 1934 failure in which Kelly was second billed to Fred Stone. Kelly appeared in several films, including two 1935 Paramount programmers, *The Virginia Judge* and *McFadden's Flats.* His last Broadway venture was in *Lend Me Your Ears,* which closed in 8 days.

Times and taste had changed. Broadway lacked the gaiety of the pre-Depression era, and most of Kelly's cronies had gone to Hollywood in hopes of making enough money in movies to live out their lives on the golf course and to swap memories and tall tales over drinks in the clubhouse. For Kelly there were occasional film roles and lodge gigs to pay the bills until 8 December 1938, when he was hit by a car in Hollywood. Despite the millions of dollars he had earned, Walter died broke. His brothers John and Charles brought Walter's body back to Philadelphia and shared the funeral expenses.

Pert Kelton

PERT KELTON

b: 14 October 1907, Great Falls, MT—
d: 30 October 1968, Ridgewood, NJ

She debuted in the family act as a child of four or five. When she was eight or so, after a few years' seasoning, she contributed a Chaplin imitation to the family act. In 1915–17, at the height of his popularity, Chaplin impersonations became so ubiquitous in vaudeville that managers told bookers not to engage more.

When Pert was grown enough, she and her mother, Sue, did a sister act; part of the fun was a running argument with the bossy conductor of the pit orchestra, played by Pert's father, Ed. Pert was just a teenager, 17, when Charles Dillingham engaged her for a spot in his extravagant production of *Sunny* (1925–26). A vehicle for Marilyn Miller, it had a circus setting, and contributions by the top-notch cast were augmented by interpolations of specialty spots, including solos by Cliff Edwards as well as Pert Kelton.

Every few seasons between 1925 and 1967, Pert Kelton appeared on Broadway. Her best-known appearances came later in her career. The longest run of her Broadway career was *The Music Man* (1957–61), in which she played the mother of the female lead, Barbara Cook. Her next biggest success was in a Neil Simon comedy, *Come Blow Your Horn* (1961–62). Twice Pert was nominated for a Tony Award as a featured actress: in the musical *Greenwillow* (1960) and the straight comedy *Spofford* (1968).

Pert made two dozen feature films during the decade between 1928 and 1938. Audiences enjoyed Pert's tailored-for-movies, wisecracking, tart dame. Only a few of her films were considered A products at the time of their release: *The Bowery* (1933) with George Raft and Wallace Beery, *Annie Oakley* (1935) with Barbara Stanwyck, *Cain and Abel* (1936) with Clark Gable and an unbilled bit part in *You Can't Take It with You* (1938). Kelton's film career had come to a dead end; her smart-mouthed dame roles were taken over by a younger crop of wisecrackers.

Despite some radio work in the 1940s, Pert found few other opportunities in show business. The future looked brighter in 1951 when Pert was hired to play Jackie Gleason's wife, Alice Kramden, when Gleason was the host of *Cavalcade of Stars,* the struggling DuMont network's penny-ante answer to variety hours produced by NBC and CBS, two better established networks. Unfortunately, Pert was replaced by Audrey Meadows when *The Honeymooners* became a series. Few in the industry believed the official explanation that ill health forced Kelton to withdraw from the show. In 1951, Pert was blacklisted as a *pinko* during the Red Scare that had begun in the late 1940s and grew to a full fury in the early 1950s.

When she was again employable, it was on the stage. *The Music Man* provided a triumphal return to show business and the biggest hit of her career. She went to Hollywood for the film version of *The Music Man* (1962) and her final film role, a bravura turn as Michele Lee's mother in *The Comic* (1969) with Dick Van Dyke and Mickey Rooney. Pert Kelton died of a heart attack late in 1968, before *The Comic* was released.

JOSEPH P. (PATRICK) KENNEDY

b: 6 September 1888, Boston, MA— d: 18 November 1969, Hyannisport, MA

Unlike most showbiz entrepreneurs who spent some time in the trenches, learning the business, Joe Kennedy entered the entertainment industry at the top. Usually, he was introduced as a Wall Street wunderkind. When other voices whispered about his bootlegging past, his partisans countered that it had been very good bootleg, imported Scotch.

Kennedy entered vaudeville in 1928 only to dismantle it. His route was through Pathé Films, a slumping old-line movie studio into which he had been brought to make it profitable. Earlier, in 1926, he had acquired through stock purchases Robertson-Cole, an import-export business that included a small movie production studio and small-time operation that booked films, appropriately named Film Booking Office.

One of FBO's few profit centers had been Westerns. With one Western star, Fred Thomson, already under contract, Joe picked up Tom Mix after Fox discarded him. Mix still commanded an enormous salary, even though he had been in films since 1909 and was nearing 50. Tom Mix's six Western movies for FBO in 1928 failed to make expenses. Fred's highly respected screenwriter wife, Frances Marion, wrote Fred's scripts under the name Marion Jackson. Fred died unexpectedly in 1928.

The Kennedys: John, Joe, and Joe Jr.

Faced with the need for a bankable star in a profitable product, Kennedy produced a string of failures due to his lack of experience. Heedless of his dismal track record in films, Joe Kennedy offered advice to Gloria Swanson.

Many of the most popular screen actors—Mary Pickford, Douglas Fairbanks Sr., Charlie Chaplin, Lillian Gish, Buster Keaton, Harold Lloyd and others—had their own studios where they made their own films, which were released through United Artists, MGM or other studios. The profitability of the film industry had drawn Wall Street's notice in the 1920s. As the industry consolidated (a process that would greatly accelerate when sound technology required large investments by both studios and exhibitors), independent filmmakers were pressured to get under corporate tents. Financing was one spur. Distribution and publicity were two more. The conversion to sound pictures during the run-up to the Great Depression quickly added a fourth spur—access to sound equipment and laboratories.

Sound pictures were much more difficult technologically and very expensive compared to silents, and thus out of the reach of many independent producers. Only Chaplin could afford to continue as an independent, and he used sound gingerly. The larger studios had access to New York investors to finance laboratory facilities. The ownership of the major studios was in New York; the plants were in Los Angeles. The two halves of the operations distrusted each other. New York financiers compelled the independents to surrender their autonomy in return for continued access to the film public.

Joe Kennedy courted Gloria Swanson. She was at the height of her fame and producing her own movies. Production problems had bedeviled her last two films, and she was receptive to Kennedy's offer (through his FBO studio) to guide the production and finance of her latest film, *Queen Kelly,* an extravagance directed by Erich von Stroheim. All three principals should have realized that 1927 was too late to be filming a major silent film; the earliest it could be released was 1928, and then it would be eclipsed by talking pictures.

Perhaps Kennedy was more interested in learning about the income stream of Swanson's Paramount movies. Movie rental income is difficult to calculate. It is impossible to know how many tickets theatres have sold unless you have somebody planted in every box office. Like many top silent stars, much of the income from Swanson's movies came from the European market and remained in European banks. By studying Swanson's international grosses and nets, Kennedy got a crash MBA in international movie finance. He also added a glamorous film star to his list of romantic conquests.

For either personal or professional reasons, Kennedy pulled out of Swanson enterprises and

Queen Kelly was never finished. Swanson's career was damaged, although she had a fine speaking and singing voice suitable for sound. Von Stroheim was finished as a director. Joe Kennedy was off in New York firing Edward F. Albee from his position as head of the Keith-Albee-Orpheum (KAO) vaudeville circuit: "You're through, Ed. Get out." Unless someone actually overheard what transpired between Kennedy and Albee in the latter's second-floor office in the Keith Memorial Theatre in Boston, the actual command or dialogue is conjecture. But contemporaries attest to the quote's reliability, and some have cited Joe Kennedy himself as the source.

Preparatory to firing old Albee, who died soon after, Kennedy had acquired a large block of Keith-Albee-Orpheum stock by buying out Albee's lieutenant, J.J. Murdock. Once Albee was out of the way and Joe was in charge, Joe sold a major interest in KAO to David Sarnoff, founder and general manager of Radio Corporation of America (RCA) and president of the National Broadcasting Company (NBC).

RCA had bought 60% of Photophone, a sound-recorded-on-film alternative to Vitaphone (which recorded sound on a disk, separate from the filmed images). Pathé adopted Photophone. Yet for most studios (except Fox), Vitaphone was the sound technology of choice, despite its cumbersome technology. By buying a major interest in the Keith-Albee-Orpheum circuit, Sarnoff had about 1,200 theatres to exhibit his product.

Sarnoff and Kennedy converted vaudeville's most prestigious vaudeville circuit into a chain of theatres to show talking pictures—the Photophone kind, so they needed films to show in them. FBO became the scaffolding for a new studio, RKO Radio Pictures. Oddly, RKO did not become a hierarchical studio with a dynamic boss like Sarnoff or Kennedy. Sarnoff was pushing RCA into the recording business and, at NBC, Sarnoff was busy contending with upstart radio network CBS. Kennedy turned away from film toward politics.

Although President Franklin Roosevelt made Joe ambassador to England for services rendered, Joe rather botched the job and was considered soft on Nazis. It was left to three of his sons, John, Robert and Edward, to achieve in politics what Joe had accomplished in business. Joe Kennedy did not kill vaudeville. It was dying on its own. But he did help dig its grave.

KERNELL BROTHERS

b: ca. 1850

Comic Irish acts were as plentiful in vaudeville and variety in the 1880s as blackface. Among the more famous of the period were Harry and John Kernell, who formed a double comedy and song-and-dance act. By the 1870s, they performed at the best houses, including Tony Pastor's. Both brothers enjoyed esteem as a superior act and were well regarded in the profession, especially among those down on their luck. They were well known for being free with handouts.

For the 1889–90 season, Harry, the businessman of the pair, decided that he and his brother should go into management themselves. But Harry was a bit volatile, and in response John sometimes pulled away. Such was the case with the 1889–90 touring show. Harry renamed it Harry Kernell's Big Company, and he began the tour with an engagement at Tony Pastor's. In the troupe were Queenie Vassar, an English soubrette, and Emily Vivian. Queenie and Emily married Harry and John, respectively. Also aboard were Joe Weber and Lew Fields. When Joe and Lew took out their own troupe the next season, Harry Kernell accused them of pirating some of his performers and bookings. It was clear by 1890 that Harry's irascibility was caused by the advanced stages of syphilis, from which he died in 1893.

BILLY KERSANDS

b: 1842, Baton Rouge, LA—d: 29 June 1915, Artesia or Clovis, NM

Historically, the reputation of African American comedian Billy Kersands is between a rock and a hard place. He began entertaining in the South, probably before the Civil War, and remained a working entertainer for more than 60 years, most of them spent in minstrelsy. According to Tom Fletcher, the black performer whose memoir *100 Years of the Negro in Show Business* provided our only portrait of many of his fellow entertainers, Kersands' popularity with Southern black audiences was unsurpassed, and he demonstrated that a nineteenth-century black entertainer could become rich and famous.

He appeared before the British king and queen, Edward VII and Alexandria. (Billy even gave dance lessons to the King.) On the other hand, some of his contemporaries in black show business, both performers and reviewers, considered him a low comedian and a bit of an embarrassment. Despite his talents, he seems to have advanced little beyond the dim, lazy *coon* stereotype fostered by the cruder comedians of white minstrelsy.

Kersands' most notorious antic was stuffing two billiard balls in his wide mouth as he performed a monologue: "If God had made my mouth any bigger, he would have had to move my ears." None of his fellow comedians was ever recorded as faulting Billy as a fun maker.

Perhaps his imposing figure discouraged detractors. He was tall, weighed well over 200 pounds and carried it well. He dressed as a dandy and wore an oversized cravat with a large stickpin.

Generally forgotten in the obsession with his billiard ball trick is that he was an acrobat of uncommon skill who knew how to use his physical talents for both dancing and physical comedy. He has been credited with devising both the Virginia Essence, a forerunner of soft-shoe dancing, and the buck-and-wing combination. Such claims can never be substantiated, but is noteworthy than many dancers of his and the next generation point to Billy Kersands as the man they first saw doing the Essence or a buck-and-wing. Further evidence is that Billy was known to have performed the Essence in slow 4/4 time to Stephen Foster's melody "Swanee River," music and time still used for dancing the old soft shoe.

Billy Kersands was an all-around talent. He sang, danced, did acrobatics and was both a monologist and a clown. His versatility and his acceptance by both black and white audiences allowed him to stay abreast of change, and he played minstrelsy, musical comedy and vaudeville. When touring the segregated South in minstrel shows, white theatre managers—whose usual patrons were African American—met a demand from white people as well as black to see Billy Kersands. The house was divided in half from the orchestra seats up to the balcony; blacks and whites sat on opposite sides of a center aisle.

Billy began in Negro minstrel shows sometime around the Civil War; certainly he was performing by the start of the war because his skill as a dancer and acrobat had to have been developed as either a child or a young teenager. Perhaps he began as many black kids did, dancing and singing for pennies on street corners.

His first engagement in minstrelsy was in 1866 with a black-owned troupe, one of Charles Hick's first attempts to manage his own company. Later he traveled as chief comedian with Harvey Minstrels, the troupe that brought Billy to England for the first time.

When Richards & Pringle's Georgia Minstrels was formed, Billy was engaged not only as the lead comedian but also as the troupe's star, and his picture adorned the sheets that were plastered up in each town along the route as they traveled throughout the South and West. In 1882, Charles Hicks, then managing the white-owned Callender's Georgia Minstrels, hired Billy as a star comedian. Kersands worked out a number of bits with the other chief comic in the troupe, Bob Height, and no small amount of the company's success was due to the public's enjoyment of the team. In 1882, Billy's first year with the troupe, Callender's Georgia Minstrels played the prestigious Niblo's Gardens.

Like other black minstrel men and comedians, Kersands took out a minstrel company under his own name. This time it was he who hired Charles Hicks, who had proven to be a resilient and successful Negro entrepreneur. Hicks and Kersands lacked the capital and the managerial reputation and connections of white minstrel entrepreneurs like Callender and Haverly. The success of black managers like Kersands was not consistent. They seldom had sufficient financial reserves to weather a run of poor box-office returns or an unexpected calamity like a fire. When trouble struck, black managers and performers returned to white management. Billy must have prospered better than most black managers because he traveled in a private railway carriage that he purchased outright.

Minstrel shows did not vanish overnight. They edged into other forms. Billy starred in *The Blackville Twins,* produced by Richards & Pringle's Georgia Minstrels, and toured with it between 1889 and 1891. The show was illustrative of the developing bridge between minstrelsy and musical comedy because it was a full-length farce with musical interpolations. Billy Kersands played Dr. Cutum, which may be an indicator that the show was more nearly a burlesk than a true farce. Historically, it predated the same form soon to be employed by Weber & Fields.

Kersands toured with Rusko & Holland's Big Minstrel Festival in 1902; it was more truly a variety show than a traditional minstrelsy, and the all-black company included a magician as well as comedians, singers and dancers.

In 1904, Billy Kersands toured in *King Rastus,* which was promoted as a farcical vaudeville comedy. Few blacks lamented when *King Rastus* failed because, socially and artistically, the show was a major step backward. Its depiction of Negroes was as demeaning as had been common a generation earlier in some of the cruder white minstrel companies. In his compendium *A Century of Musicals in Black and White: An Encyclopedia of Musical Stage Works By, About or Involving African Americans*, Bernard L. Peterson Jr. provided a contemporary review that described numerous offenses in the show, including racist dialogue and a parade of flags, each one dignified except the rag whose symbols, a chicken and a watermelon, were supposed to represent the Negro nation.

Kersands tried to retire but could not. He did not need the money, just the activity. He and his longtime wife, Louise. put together a show, Billy & Louise Kersands' Minstrels, that was a collection of vaudeville acts. The show opened a bit like the traditional minstrel show as Professor James S. Lacey led the band and company through a series of instrumental pieces and songs. That was followed by comedian Kid Langford, then Billy, a trick cyclist named Arthur Maxwell, the Campbell Brothers' blackface comedy act and Alonzo Moore, a magician. The closing act was a comedy sketch with Billy and Louise. According to a local black newspaper, whites who attended were restricted to one side of the upper balcony. This changed as the number of whites who attended black theatres increased.

So successful was Billy that he and Louise traveled throughout the heartland of the USA in their private railway car, and they and their company were booked in Europe during much of the 1907–09 period, which included a command performance for Queen Victoria. When Billy returned to the USA in 1909, he decided to forego the burden of being a show manager. Kersands and Alonzo Moore joined Pringle's Georgia Minstrels. Billy had switched to R. M. Harvey's Minstrel Troupe by 1912.

He continued to work into his 70s, lastly with the Harrison Brothers' World's Greatest Minstrel Show. He began to tire easily and then, still on the road, died in New Mexico. Few who saw Billy in the last decade of his life, while he played white vaudeville like Loew's time or black vaudeville houses in the South, realized that the amiable, big comic dancer they were watching on the stage had bridged the era from pre–Civil War underground black entertainment to black and white minstrelsy to white vaudeville.

In their landmark book about American percussive dance, *Jazz Dance: The Story of American Vernacular Dance,* researchers and authors Marshall and Jean Stearns reported Kersands' defense of his work. Near the end of his life, Billy told Flournoy Miller, a comedian two generations Billy's junior, "Son, if they hate me, I'm still whipping them because I am making them laugh."

SLAWOMIR KIELBASINSKI

b: 26 July 1955, Warsaw, Poland

Trained since a child in Poland, Slawomir developed into a gymnast and dancer. From his early teens into his late 20s, he competed for his nation in trials throughout Europe, Asia and the USA. He won many awards, including a gold medal in sport acrobatics. When he returned to Poland, he was frank in his enthusiasm for many of the places he had visited, especially London and the USA.

The communist government of Poland, fearing his defection to the West, rescinded his passport. Until that action, Slawomir had not consciously considered the possibility. His passport was restored to him when he was chosen to represent Poland at the World Cup competitions in the USA. During the World Cup acrobatic competitions of the late 1970s, Kielbasinski won a silver medal and two bronze medals.

Slawomir also made the decision to defect to Canada. Initially, he trained circus performers in acrobatics and then became a featured performer with Cirque du Soleil and Cirque du Tonner. In early 1991, Slawak, as he is familiarly called, formed Human Design and has been performing that slow-motion and balancing acrobatic act ever since. Partnered by Misha Kalinin the act performs in Las Vegas and at various corporate functions and theatrical shows around the world. Their bodies are nearly nude and coated with makeup that gives them the appearance of statues. They leverage each other slowly into various difficult poses that demand great strength and muscular control.

HETTY KING

b: (Winifred Emms) 21 April 1883, Wimbledon, England—d: 29 September 1972, London, England

For some, the fashion of women wearing men's clothes started with Marlene Dietrich and her 1930s companions, Lili Damita, Mercedes d'Acosta and Jo Carstairs, who in public sometimes wore men's suits, tuxedos and sports gear. The fad for men's garb among American and British women predated the Hollywood set by at least two generations. In the 1890s, several well-known vaudeville and music-hall stars stimulated interest by performing in men's attire. Vesta Tilley, Ella Shields, Kitty Doner and Hetty King were among the more prominent.

Unlike the women who took principal boy roles in pantomime or burlesque, Tilley, Shields and King did not merely don a few items of male clothing, cinch their waists, plump their bosoms and encase their legs in tights to coyly demonstrate their femininity by flashing gams beneath token male attire. Tilley, Shields and King dressed as authentically male as possible and, without lurching into crude male stereotype, portrayed boys and men on the vaudeville stage.

Hetty King was the daughter of Will King (born William Emms), a one-man band of music-hall fame. When, at six years old, his daughter joined him onstage as part of his act, she was billed as Hetty King. In 1905, she began her male impersonations; like others in the same line, she inclined toward swells who brandished walking sticks and swanned down the Strand in top hats and Prince Albert coats.

The 1890s and 1900s witnessed the fullest expansion of British imperial power. With one quarter of the world under British dominion through annexations, protectorates and outright economic and military conquest (the popular South African War of 1899–1902, an example of the last), it was proudly observed that the

Hetty King

sun never set on the British Empire. The boulevardier was replaced in favor by the gallant soldier, and many women and men of the halls donned uniforms onstage and sang patriotic songs. Hetty joined the fervor with "Captain Reginald D'Arcy of the Guard" (1901). Perhaps the song was inspired by her real-life romance and marriage to Captain Alexander William Lamond of the York and Lancaster Regiment.

King made several tours of American vaudeville, beginning in 1907, returning in 1909 and perhaps again before the First World War made transatlantic travel too dangerous from 1914 to 1918.

When Hetty performed in Britain during the war, many of her numbers, like "All the Nice Girls Love a Sailor," "Follow the Tram-Lines" [trolley cars] and "I'm Afraid to Go Home in the Dark," continued to show the flag and gave more than a passing nod to the peril that threatened the small island seat of the Empire.

Other songs for which she was known were "Tell Her the Old, Old Story" ("get your girl all nervy, when her head's all topsy-turvy"), "Down by the Riverside" and "Piccadilly" ("the playground of the gay, where the traffic goes one-way"), all of which, along with "All the Nice Girls Love a Sailor," were closely associated with Hetty King for the duration of her career.

For more than 70 years, Hetty performed all over the English-speaking world. Even in her old age, she took a variety or concert party booking if it seemed right for her, and no excuses were made or needed for her age.

In 1970, historian David Robinson wrote and directed a three-reeler called *Hetty King: Performer.* Filmed at the Royal Hippodrome in Eastbourne, England, the documentary was narrated by Lindsay Anderson and featured Hetty in interview and performance. It was a lovely valentine remembrance of a grand performer.

MAC KING

b: (Paxson McCormick) 2 December 1959, Hopkinsville, KY

Exuding warmth and likability, Mac King is a magician who combines deftness with homespun country-style humor. Clad in his Appalachian Sunday best, he performs unique magic tricks, including vanishing his head in a paper bag and making an earthworm disappear in a straw. He also performs classic illusions that have rarely seen the light of day since the vaudeville era. Chief among these is catching goldfish from the air with a fishing pole.

Mac King began his career touring the country in comedy clubs. He resides in Las Vegas and performed his highly successful afternoon show, "The Mac King Comedy Magic Show," at Harrah's Casino and Hotel. He also created his own nationally syndicated cartoon strip, *Mac King's Magic in a Minute,* has appeared on several NBC-TV specials, including *The World's Greatest Magic* and has been named Magician of the Year by the Academy of Magical Arts.

KIRALFO BROTHERS

Gus (Gustave) Kiralfo

b: ca. 1865

Vincent Kiralfo

b: ca. 1870

Gus Kiralfo got his professional start as a song-and-dance man in the Great Wallace Show. Two years later he was traveling with Craig & Howard's Minstrels as a juggler. The spelling of his surname varied at first, and early bills sometimes listed him as Gus Grafula ("The World's Greatest Implement Juggler").

In the space of a few years he moved on to Hi Henry's Minstrel Show, which he joined up with in Memphis and stayed with for several seasons. He toured in shows, including *A Breezy Time, Gillhooley's Reception* and *Across the Desert.*

By 1902 he was playing vaudeville. He appeared at the Chicago Opera House in 1899, the week of 14 August. A date at the Boston Music Hall for the week of 12 May 1902 had him billed as Gus Kiralfo, "Unique Juggling Comique," and stuck in the closing spot. That same year Gus performed at Hashim's Grand Opera House in Philadelphia. Gus took his brother Vincent into the act, although he never gave him equal billing. Perhaps that was because Vincent was not always his partner. He was succeeded by Billy Retzel and there may have been others, so it was best to refer only to the Kiralfo Brothers.

As a single or a double act, Gus played medicine shows, minstrel shows, circus and vaudeville. The act was billed variously, including as the Kiralfo Brothers, "Unique Comedy Jugglers and Club Experts," Gus Kiralfo & Brother, "A Headline for Any Bill—An Act for Any Nation: Marvelous Comic Jugglers and Hat Dancers," the Kiralfo Brothers, "Axe Jugglers" and Gustave Kiralfo, "The World's Greatest Mystifier and Juggler."

It was well known that Gus never smoke or drank, and he took good care of his health. He was still around at age 80, attending juggling meets and, though not professionally active, he could still juggle. He enjoyed performing prestidigitation tricks and was considered a past master at chapeaugraphy, which he learned from Felician Trewey. Kiralfo spent his last years in San Antonio, Texas.

KNOCKABOUT COMEDY

Often confused with slapstick comedy. Knockabout (or knock-about) proceeded from acrobats who performed comedy acts, seeming to truly knock each other about the stage, getting laughs for their supposed inepti-tude (which required split-second timing and careful rehearsal). Carelessly, the term knockabout has been misapplied to all manner of physical comedy.

KNOCKOUT

To score a knockout was to stun the audience with the performance, wow them, render them helpless (with laughter, joy or admiration).

KOHL & CASTLE

ca. 1860–1940

Charles Edward Kohl and George W. Middleton began their association in 1882 as partners in a dime museum in Chicago, the West Side Museum, and followed that in 1883 with the Clark Street Museum, to which they added a performance hall for variety acts. In 1885, they leased the Olympic Theatre, and they hired Charles H. Castle Sr. to run the theatre. Within months, Castle persuaded Kohl and Middleton to scrap their legit drama policy that had not only failed to generate revenue but also sunk them into debt.

Castle began booking vaudeville and made the theatre very profitable; in turn, he was made a partner. Kohl and Middleton opened several more vaudeville houses, the Chicago Opera House and the Haymarket. Both George Middleton and George Castle Sr. were founding members of one of the first vaudeville theatre chains, the Mid West circuit.

C. E. Kohl was a dour man who had little love for show business and preferred his business office to the theatres he owned or leased. Minus a creative partner, he had little of the imagination or flair vital to success in show business, yet he was a shrewd dollars-and-cents man.

Castle, however, enjoyed show business. That he had nearly lost his shirt in his first venture, running the Adelphi Theatre in Toledo, Ohio, had not deterred him. He went on tour with Van Amberg's Circus in 1880. When the season was over, Castle settled in Chicago and opened the first variety and vaudeville agency. His talent for booking vaudeville prompted Kohl and Middleton to seek out Castle. With Castle on board, Kohl was certain that greater profits were in the future, so he bought out Middleton in 1900 and took on George Castle Sr. as secretary and treasurer for the new corporation of Kohl & Castle.

Castle handled the booking for all of the Kohl & Castle vaudeville theatres (and curio museums and performance halls), including the new Majestic Theatre, a magnificent house that Kohl and Castle built in Chicago. They also had theatres in Minneapolis and St. Paul.

George Castle Sr. booked his acts on the sidewalk outside the Olympic Theatre. He charged acts 5% to book them into the Kohl & Castle houses and recorded each act, date, price and theatre in a pocket memo book he always kept at hand. When George Castle Sr. retired, his son became Kohl's partner. A strict and humorless man, George Castle Jr. had little of his father's love for the business and none of his charm.

The Kohl & Castle circuit did not survive the takeover and amalgamation that marked the vaudeville business in the 1910s, but when Charles Kohl died in 1910, he left an estate of $7 million, extraordinary in show business at the time.

KOLB & DILL

Clarence William Kolb

b: 31 July 1874, Cleveland, OH— d: 25 November 1964, Los Angeles, CA

Max M. Dill

b: 15 September 1876, Cleveland, OH— d: 21 November 1949, San Francisco, CA

Clarence Kolb and Max Dill were boyhood friends in their hometown of Cleveland, Ohio, when they decided to go into show business. They spent a long apprenticeship in small-time show business. The earliest notice on record occurred when both men were about 25; Weber and Fields, the producers and stars of *Fiddle-Dee-Dee,* entrusted their own roles to Kolb & Dill for the Chicago run in 1901. For this to happen, Kolb & Dill must have been an experienced and respected act.

After years of working the Midwest, they headed west, playing both burlesque and vaudeville, and audiences and reviews noticed them by the time they had moved to San Francisco. There they could obtain bookings on Orpheum, Sullivan & Considine and Pantages time, plus a few smaller circuits. Like many of the better white and black West Coast acts, they found it profitable to take a small troupe to Australia, where they underwent a season's tour in 1904.

Their knockabout Dutch act became a favorite of San Franciscans. Clarence Kolb was the large, overbearing protagonist, and Max Dill played the pushed-around patsy. So closely modeled was their act on Weber & Fields' that they were routinely referred to as the West Coast version of Weber & Fields.

Neither Joe nor Lew seemed to mind. In 1911, Lew Fields fell ill and had to withdraw from his own production, *The Summer Widowers.* He contacted Kolb and hired Clarence to take over Field's role for its Boston run.

Clarence and Max got offers to film short comedies in Los Angeles, and they made five during the 1916–17 season. One of these was a silent version (minus all the songs, of course) of *A Peck of Pickles,* a musical comedy that they introduced in San Francisco and then toured around the West Coast.

A Peck of Pickles led to a switch in relations between Kolb & Dill and Weber & Fields. This time, Lew and Joe decided to follow Clarence and Max in the roles, and the Weberfields team tried to adapt it to their satisfaction. Weber was not really interested, but Fields was in one of his frequent periods of insolvency, so Joe agreed. The adaptation, retitled *Back Again,* did not work, and Joe refused to continue trying to produce and stage it.

Some vaudeville comedians found that silent films allowed them greater scope than the stage. Roscoe Arbuckle, Polly Moran, Charlie Chaplin, Ben Turpin, Buster Keaton, Stan Laurel and Harry Langdon were among the successful crossovers from vaudeville to the silent screen.

Other stage comedians, like Kolb & Dill, Joe Weber, Lew Fields, Joe Jackson, De Wolf Hopper and Eddie Foy either needed dialogue or were not young and athletic enough to take falls. Some silent-screen Western stars and comedians, especially those at Keystone, came from circuses and Wild West shows, and they began in films as stuntmen (and women). Unlike De Wolf Hopper and Eddie Foy, the previously anonymous refugees from the range and clown alley were more willing to risk life and limb or suffer pies in the face and being dunked in sewers.

In 1927, Kolb & Dill appeared in the W.C. Fields–Chester Conklin feature film, *Two Flaming Youths.* Paramount sold its film library to Universal, which, 80 years after the film's release, has failed to reissue it despite cameo appearances by stars like Weber & Fields, Clark & McCullough, the Duncan Sisters, Jack Pearl & Ben Bard, Moran & Mack, Stanley Rogers and Jay Brennan as Savoy & Brennan, Wallace Beery and, of course, Kolb & Dill, playing themselves.

Given his rough-and-tumble vaudeville act, it is a surprise that Clarence Kolb, after 1930, became one of the most reliable and sought-after character comedians in Hollywood. Looking at Kolb in films, dressed impeccably in business suits, with distinguished gray hair and trimmed mustache, he looks every inch and pound the successful, overbearing, gravel-voiced, fast-talking big shot without a scintilla of humor.

Between 1930 and 1956 (at which time he was 82) Clarence Kolb made five dozen feature films and capped his career as the jowly, scowly, growly businessman on the popular television series *My Little Margie* from 1952 to 1955. Max Dill was not as prominent. He seems to have appeared in small parts in some movies and then returned to the live stage in his hometown of San Francisco, where he retired. In 1947, Kolb and Dill reunited onstage to star in *The High Cost of Living.*

KOSTER & BIAL'S MUSIC HALLS

Neither John Koster nor Adam Bial intended to become a vaudeville power. They were brewers who wanted to sell their beer. To that end, they leased the former Bryant's Opera House on West 23rd Street at Sixth Avenue in Manhattan's Tenderloin. They fitted out the theatre as a melodeon, named it Koster & Bial's Music Hall, enlarged the bar, encouraged table service and prospered. Adam Bial cottoned to show business and managed the theatre end, while John Koster oversaw the bar and table service.

Koster & Bial's was not a classy operation. The emphasis was on drinking, and the only requirement for the entertainers was to keep the male clientele drinking. According to vaudeville witness and historian Douglas Gilbert, a stub from any other theatre was good for admission to Koster & Bial's because it was liquor sales that kept Koster & Bial's Music Hall thriving. The custom of honoring stubs from other theatres brought the youngbloods to Koster & Bial's after seeing shows elsewhere. Koster & Bial's became fashionable as a place to slum it up.

Bial, however, began to cater to his fashionable clientele's taste for naughty and clever acts instead of witless raunch, and the quality of performers vastly improved. He began to produce travesties of operas and classic plays, the types of burlesks that had proved popular elsewhere.

Koster & Bial program, Herald Square Music Hall, New York, 1899

Many accounts of Koster and Bial mention that they did away with the curtained stage and replaced it with a large, wide fan, but Gilbert gives the reason. Municipal law at the time forbade melodeons from employing the drop curtains and front travelers of true theatres. So Bial installed a huge fan behind the footlights. The fan was split in the middle and each section folded down toward different sides of the stage during an act or a scene. Between acts or a change in settings, both halves of the fan rose from either side of the stage and met in the middle, thereby signaling the end of a scene and allowing for a set change or a new number.

The only reason Oscar Hammerstein went into business with Koster & Bial was his perpetual need for money. In 1892, Hammerstein had built the Manhattan Opera House uptown between West 34th and West 35th streets, as the theatre district was moving farther up Broadway. Oscar intended his opera house as competition for the Metropolitan Opera House.

Oscar's great love was grand opera and, to a lesser degree, high-toned drama. On several occasions his love nearly bankrupted him. When the Manhattan Opera House failed, his only chance to survive was to find partners. Koster and Bial were Johnnies-on-the-spot. They understood better than Oscar that their alliance was a temporary one. There was no way to avert conflict over bookings. John and Adam were better businessmen, and Oscar was used to getting his own, sometimes disastrous way.

Their disagreements quickly surfaced and went public. On one infamous occasion, Oscar, sitting in a box, booed a singer onstage in his own theatre. Bial quickly bought out Oscar's remaining half interest (the reported total for Oscar's entire holdings was $1 million, which he reinvested in another albatross that he named the Olympia). Adam Bial retained both Koster & Bials' Music Hall at 23rd Street and Koster & Bial's New Music Hall at 34th Street.

John Koster died, and Adam Bial followed soon after. John Koster Jr. took over, but he was unable to keep the operations prosperous. The 23rd Street theatre remained viable under various managements into the 1920s, long after the deaths of Koster, Bial and Koster Jr. The 34th Street house was too large to be run effectively, and it closed in 1901.

KRIS KREMO

b: (Kristian-Gaston Kremo) 11 March 1951, Paris, France

Kris Kremo is the fourth generation of a European circus family. His great-grandfather, Josef Kremka

(1854–1917), began an acrobatic act while growing up in Bohemia. Josef's son, Karl Kremo (1882–1958), continued the tradition. Karl, in turn, had a son, Be'la Kremo (1911–79), who became a juggler. His act was built around the simple concept of juggling only three objects at a time—but with astounding virtuosity. Be'la then taught this act to his son, Kris Kremo.

The act begins with the tall and handsome Kris Kremo juggling a single ball, a large cigar, and a bowler hat at a very fast pace. The cigar is caught in his mouth; the brim of the hat lands and balances on the cigar. The ball is tossed high into the air. The hat flies from the cigar to the top of his head just as the ball is caught between his hat and his head. This routine is followed by the juggling of three balls to snappy music. Then three top hats are picked up and juggled and bounced off his head with musical accents from the drummer and horn section. Finally, Kris juggles three cigar boxes and ends by tossing a box into the air that he then catches between the two other boxes after completing a triple pirouette.

Because of his good looks and great showmanship, Kris took his father's act to another level with a style that has often been copied but seldom if ever equaled. He has appeared all over the world. In 1976 he began working for 11 straight years at the "Lido de Paris" show at the Stardust Hotel in Las Vegas.

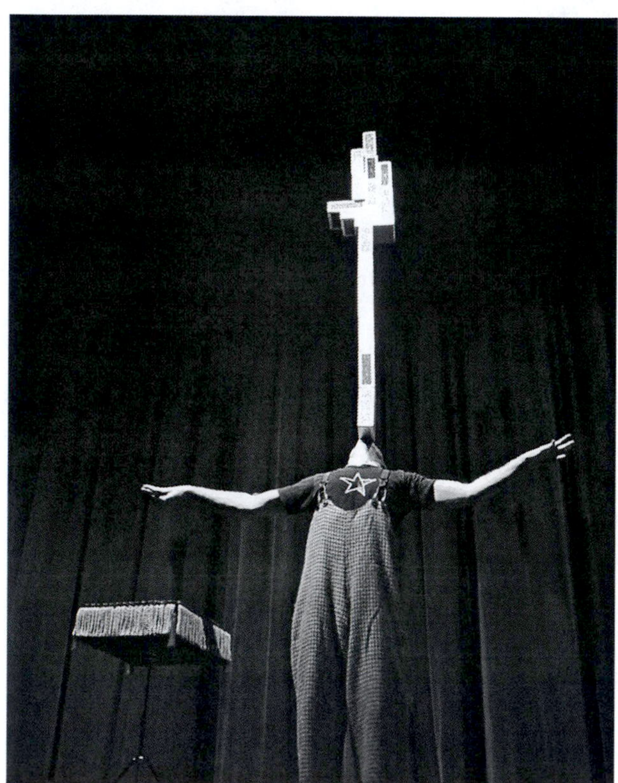

Adam Kuchler

ADAM KUCHLER

b: 2 October 1976, Milwaukee, WI

Adam grew up thinking that it was as normal to be a clown as it was to be a police officer or a doctor, and at the age of three, he made his clown debut in a talent show. He remembered hearing family stories about his uncle, Keith Crary, who, after graduating from the first class of Ringling Bros. and Barnum & Bailey's Clown College, spent six years touring with the Greatest Show on Earth. Later, Keith Crary daubed greasepaint on others and became an Emmy Award–winning makeup artist in Hollywood.

When Adam was ten years old, the Great Circus Parade returned to Milwaukee, and while watching it, Adam decided that he wanted to be a clown. He spent the next few years reading everything he could about circus, and practicing every skill he thought he might need to be a clown. Helping Adam along the way was "Mr. Bill" Machtel, a professional clown who had followed Keith Crary into Ringling Bros. In 1994, Adam sent a video audition to Circus Smirkus, the international youth circus based in Vermont. He was accepted and spent that summer and the next touring New England performing in their big-top show.

After the 1995 tour, Adam flew directly to Baraboo, Wisconsin, where he became a member of the 28th class of Clown College. He spent the next four years touring with Ringling's Blue Unit and opened the 128th edition with his cigar box act in the center ring. He then got to work alongside Pipo Sosman (son of the original Pipo Sosman), a classic European whiteface clown in the

Adam Kuchler

one-ring production *Barnum's Kaleidoscope,* where Adam got to "see the care he took with his costume and props. I went to work feeling like I was in one of the most beautiful shows in the world."

Kuchler then moved to Japan and spent the next year and a half working with another clown at the Kinoshita Circus, which has been traveling for over one hundred years. When Adam moved back to America, it was with the hope of beginning a solo career. In the fall of 2002, Adam ended up in New York, where he met Keith Nelson and Stephanie Monseu of the Bindlestiff Family Cirkus. After he performed several times in their Palace of Variety in Times Square (since demolished), Stephanie and Keith invited him along for their spring tour of *High Heels & Red Noses,* and Adam developed a hilarious "Hats and Bags" act, the capper of which is pushing himself, butt first, through a paper bag. He has also worked in Chicago with Jeff Jenkins and Julie Greenburg of the Midnight Circus, an outfit that combines circus and theatre. In Reno, Nevada, Adam performed at the International Jugglers' Association *Cascade of Stars* show.

In early 2005, Adam reunited with the Bindlestiffs and devised two new acts and partnered in a couple of turns with actor and clown Matthew Morgan of the clown trio Happy Hour. Later that year, Adam worked again with Midnight Circus; he added a tightwire routine to his juggling and comedy spots.